117115

The Book of Job

Commentary
New Translation
and Special Studies

Volume II in the **Moreshet** Series, Studies in
Jewish History, Literature and Thought

The Book of Job

Commentary
New Translation
and Special Studies

by Robert Gordis

AND THE BUSH WAS NOT CONSUMED
והסנה איננו אכל

THE JEWISH THEOLOGICAL SEMINARY OF AMERICA

NEW YORK CITY

5738—1978

Library of Congress Cataloging in Publication Data

Gordis, Robert,
    The book of Job: Commentary, New Translation, and Special Studies.
    (Moreshet series; v. 2)
    Text of Job in English and Hebrew on facing pages.
    Introduction, Commentary, Philological and Exegetical Studies.
    Bibliography and Indices.
    1. Bible. O.T. Job—Commentaries. I. Bible.
O.T. Job. Hebrew. 1978. II. Bible. O.T. Job.
English. Gordis. 1978. III. Title. IV. Series:
Moreshet (New York); v. 2.
BS1415.2.G62   223'.1'077   78–2305
ISBN 0-87334-003-5

TABLE OF CONTENTS

לזכר הקדושים
הי"ד

ארץ אל־תכסי דמי
ואל־יהי מקום לזעקתי

(איוב ט"ז י"ח)

Shall not the Judge of all the earth act justly?

(Genesis 18:25)

Und wenn der Mensch in seiner Qual verstummt,
Gab mir ein Gott, zu sagen was ich leide.

Though men in agony are struck dumb,
To me, God gave the power to tell my pain.

(Goethe, Torquato Tasso, ll. 3422–23)

אין בידנו לא משלות הרשעים ואף לא מיסורי הצדיקים
It is not given us to understand the well-being of the wicked
or the suffering of the righteous.

(Rabbi Yannai, Mishnah Abot 4:15)

Bring me the sunset in a cup,
Reckon the morning's flagons up
And say how many Dew,
Tell me how far the morning leaps —
Tell me what time the weaver sleeps
Who spun the breadths of blue!

Write me how many notes there be
In the new Robin's ecstasy
Among astonished boughs —
How many trips the Tortoise makes —
How many cups the Bee partakes,
The Debauchee of Dews!

Also, who laid the Rainbow's piers,
Also, who leads the docile spheres
By withes of supple blue?
Whose fingers string the stalactite —
Who counts the wampum of the night
To see that none is due?

Who built this little Alban House
And shut the windows down so close
My spirit cannot see?
Who'll let me out some gala day
With implements to fly away,
Passing Pomposity?   (Emily Dickinson)

PREFACE

The twentieth century has been marked by technological changes incredible in their number, extent, and rapidity. The rationalization of industry, the development of electronics and atomic energy, the rapid modes of communication and transportation, the new media of entertainment and information — all these developments have catapulted the human race into a state of permanent revolution affecting all aspects of human life, morality, religion, government, and international affairs. It is fair to say that the transformations of this century have been more far-reaching than the changes of the past five hundred years.

Unfortunately, these positive achievements of the human spirit have been dwarfed by the equally enlarged potential for evil that has been eagerly embraced by twentieth-century man. The wonders of science and technology have been overshadowed by the horrors they have unleashed: the Nazi Holocaust in Europe, the atomic bombs on Hiroshima and Nagasaki, the permanent competition for military supremacy that has sparked the exploration of outer space, the intercontinental ballistic missile race, and the experimentation with poison gas and bacterial warfare by the superpowers.

The evils confronting our age are not exhausted by this complex of potential disasters on the world arena. Virtually every country in the East or in the West, newly developing or highly industrialized, exhibits a widespread breakdown of moral standards in personal life, in commerce and industry, in education and government. The large-scale practice of violence, the acceptance of lying as an indispensable technique for success, and the callous suppression of the rights of the weak and the poor go hand in hand with the far-flung hypocrisy through which men express their loyalty to ideals that they trample under foot in practice.

The ubiquity of evil and its apparent triumph everywhere give particular urgency to the most agonizing riddle of human existence, the problem of evil, which is the crucial issue in biblical faith. But the tempo of change today is far too hectic and modern man is all too little disposed to take spiritual inventory of his situation. Our activistic, frenetic age is not an era of meditation.

Nevertheless, more and more sensitive men and women, whether rooted in some religious tradition or in none, have wrestled in the night with the demon of doubt and despair; for many the dawning of a new faith in life and its Giver has not yet come. In this far-flung quest, which takes on untold forms, many men, women, and young people have turned to the book of Job as a precious resource for grappling with the problem of evil. Never has this book, the most profound and — if such an epithet may be allowed — the most beautiful discussion of the theme, been more relevant than in our age, when man's suffering has exceeded his wildest nightmares, in this, the most brutal of centuries.

Together with most of my contemporaries, I have been deeply involved in the tragic events of these years. Yet long before the horrors of the twentieth century became fully manifest, I had been introduced, as a boy of fifteen, to the book of Job by a gifted scholar and teacher, Dr. Moshe Seidel, of blessed memory. From that day to this I have been held in thrall by "the grandest book ever written with pen," as Carlyle rightly described it. I have never been free from this preoccupation with *Job*, perpetually seeking to explore every nook and cranny of this Mount Everest of the human spirit, striving to understand its language and revelling in its beauty.

As I grew older, this concern with the details of the text was deepened by the desire to experience the depth of its emotion and to penetrate to the profundity of its thought. It was not enough to be interested in words and verses. What was the meaning of each speech, the standpoint of each speaker, and, by that token, the meaning and message of the book as a whole? This ultimate goal, I soon discovered, was inseparable from the exploration of the architectonic structure of the book. In other words, form and content in *Job*, as in any literary or artistic work of significance, are organically related to each other and mutually illuminating. Moreover, towering as *Job* is, it did not flower in a vacuum; it could not be understood apart from the environment of Israel, in which it arose, or in isolation from the wider Mid-Eastern culture-sphere that served both as background and challenge to the biblical world-view. My passionate interest in *Job*, therefore, broadened into a lifetime commitment to biblical and Oriental scholarship, in which Wisdom Literature has occupied a special place.

The results of my biblical research are embodied in some scores of papers, published in scholarly journals in the United States, Europe and Israel, and in several full-length studies of biblical books. Most of the papers are now assembled in two volumes, *Poets, Prophets and Sages — Essays in Biblical Interpretation* (Indiana University Press, 1971), and *The Word and The Book — Studies in Biblical Language and Literature* (Ktav Publishing House, 1976). The full-length studies include *Koheleth, The Man and His World — A Study of Ecclesiastes* (Third, Augmented Edition, Schocken, 1968) and *The Song of Songs and Lamentations* (Ktav Publishing House, 1974.) In each instance, the same basic pattern was followed: (1) an extensive Introduction dealing with all aspects of the book under discussion; (2) a Translation into modern, intelligible English, with brief introductory summaries before each section embodying my understanding of the book, its contents and structure; and (3) a detailed textual and philological Commentary on the Hebrew text, taking into account the history of the exegesis and presenting whatever new insights I had achieved.

In the case of *Job*, its greater length and incomparably more complex character made it impossible for me to encompass all three elements within a single volume, especially since my other heavy commitments made it clear that the completion of the work would require many years. Accordingly, I published a full-length treatment of Job containing the first two elements of the pattern under the title *The Book of God and Man — A Study of Job* (University of Chicago Press, 1965).

In this volume, the dual background of *Job*, both in Oriental Wisdom and in biblical thought, without which the book cannot be fully understood, is set forth. The complex questions concerning the authenticity and integrity of each section of Job, the Prose Tale, the three Cycles of the Dialogue, the Elihu chapters, and "the Speeches of the Lord" are discussed in detail, with special reference to their content and their contribution to the meaning of the book as a whole. The great variety of views on these issues obtaining among scholars, thinkers, and general readers is presented and analyzed, and my own approach to these questions is set forth. The study then turns to the place of *Job* in the history of biblical religion and traces its abiding contribution to religion on the basic question of evil in the world. Important elements in the style of *Job*, not previously recognized, provide valuable keys to the interpretation of the text and its structure. Such technical questions as the date of composition, the original language, and the canonicity of the book are then treated. The volume then offers a new and original translation of the book of Job into modern English.

This thumbnail summary of the contents of *The Book of God and Man* is included here, because the present Commentary, though an independent work, represents the completion of the earlier work, to which reference is frequently made and which the reader should consult as often as possible. The present work supplies the scholarly underpinning for my approach to *Job* through a detailed textual and philological Commentary.

The present work contains four sections: (a) a brief introduction presenting the methodological principles underlying the present work and indicating the principal areas in which it makes a new and hopefully significant contribution to the understanding of the book of Job; (b) a revised translation to accompany the Hebrew text of Job, with brief introductory summaries before each speech, setting forth its basic ideas and its relationship to the structure of the book as a whole; (c) a detailed textual and philological commentary on the entire text, taking into account the history of its interpretation and setting forth many new insights and approaches; (d) forty-two Special Notes consisting of studies in the content, structure and language of *Job*.

It should be kept in mind that the Translation and the Introductory Notes preceding each section and speech in the book, like the relevant Special Notes, constitute an integral part of the Commentary. They often contain material not repeated in the Commentary proper, or they embody the conclusion derived from the discussion in the exegetical notes. Hence, the Translation and the Introductory Notes should be consulted together with the verse-by-verse Commentary.

In view of the enormous complexity of the task and my career of active service in the community, I had almost given up hope of completing the Commentary, though I had been working on it for several years. The opportunity to achieve what originally seemed to be an all but impossible goal came about through the kindness and generosity of Temple University, where I served as Professor of Religion for seven years. Through the good offices of Dr. Marvin Wachman, now President of the University (then Vice-President for Academic Affairs), my good friend, Dean George W. Johnson, and my honored colleague, Dr. Gerard Sloyan, then Chairman of the Department of Religion, I was granted a study-leave by Temple University for the spring term of 1972. I am equally grateful to the Trustees of the John Simon Guggenheim Foundation, who awarded me a Fellowship in 1973. These extended periods of freedom from academic duties, together with the intensive use of summer vacations for several years, made it possible for me to carry out the arduous research required and to do the actual writing of this *Commentary on Job*.

As has been my privilege in the past, I have had, beyond my power to deserve, the invaluable assistance of my beloved and loyal friend, Dr. Abraham I. Shinedling, whose wide erudition and incredible penchant for accuracy were generously placed at my disposal in this work, as in all my earlier ones. He carefully read, cross-checked and, where necessary, corrected every line of the text, proofread the manuscript, and prepared the indices. In addition, he was a wise and faithful counsellor on many questions of substance and style. My debt to him is incalculable.

As authors and readers know to their cost, printing rates have increased astronomically during the recent past. Even with the transliteration of the hundreds of Arabic, Syriac and Greek words in the text, there remain thousands of Hebrew words and phrases, generally vocalized, scattered through the Commentary. The difficult problem of typesetting, added to the length of the manuscript, posed what seemed insurmountable obstacles to the early publication of the work.

Fortunately, relief and deliverance came from other quarters. The Joseph Meyerhoff Fund, which has made literally world-wide contributions to scholarship, education and culture, granted a most generous subvention toward the publication of this work. There are no words to express my profound gratitude to Mr. Joseph Meyerhoff, truly a prince in Israel, and to his dedicated advisor, the well-known scholar and educator, Doctor Louis L. Kaplan, for this gift of life to the work and its author.

The distinguished Chancellor of the Jewish Theological Seminary, Doctor Gerson D. Cohen, impelled by his boundless love for scholarship and, no doubt, by his friendship for the author, asked that the book be published under the auspices of the Seminary, where I have taught Bible to many generations of students. It was at his kind insistence that the Hebrew text of *Job* has been included in this volume. Of all available texts, only the edition of the British and Foreign Bible Society, edited by Professor Norman H. Snaith, prints *Job* as poetry. Warmest thanks are extended to the Trustees of the British and Foreign Bible Society, who graciously granted permission for the use of this text. Professor Snaith, who has himself enriched our understanding of the book of Job by his own publications in the field, utilized the beautiful illuminated Spanish manuscript, written in 1482 in Lisbon (British Museum Or. 2626-B), together with several others, as the basis for his edition. I am very thankful to Professor Snaith and to Mr. John Anderson of the Society for their good offices in this connection.

Chancellor Cohen's enthusiasm and deep interest in the work have been shared by my good friend, Mrs. Harriet Catlin, Director of Special Projects of the Seminary. She has been a tower of strength throughout a long and trying period. She supervised each step of the work produced by the Maurice Jacobs Press, Inc. in Philadelphia, now absorbed by Regency Typographic Services, Inc. who have completed the publication. To Mr. Arnold Fisher, Managing Director of the Maurice Jacobs Press, and to the dedicated and expert members of his staff, notably Dr. N. Joseph Kikuchi, Mr. David Skaraton, Mr. Meyer Weitzel, and Mr. Walter Hershey, my warm thanks are extended.

I want to thank also my secretaries and friends, Gertrude Lambert and Trudy Kramberg, who labored on the manuscript with exemplary devotion and skill beyond the line of duty.

The completed manuscript was placed in the hands of the original printers early in 1974. Three years were to elapse during which the Commentary recapitulated, on a lesser scale, to be sure, the trials and frustrations of the biblical hero. That the book has been published, and in so attractive a form, is due to all these friends and co-workers, to whom I shall always be thankful.

All through the years of research and writing my family made many a sacrifice for this enterprise, intangible but genuine. At all stages in the work, I had the benefit of the astringent yet warmhearted counsel of my sons, Enoch, Leon, and David, who demonstrate the truth of the Sage's words, "A wise son gladdens his father."

First and last, it is my dear wife, Fannie, my life's companion, whose love and understanding built our home and made it possible for me to engage in the research and writing of the present work, which was finally completed in 1973 on our forty-fifth wedding anniversary. I hope she will find it a not unworthy fiftieth wedding anniversary gift five years later! "All is yours and it is yours that I give back to you."

Through the goodness of God, many years of study and research in Job are culminating in the present Commentary. I should like to believe that in some measure I have contributed to a greater understanding and appreciation of this masterpiece of the ages. When it is read with empathy and insight, the book of Job emerges as a great architectonic unity, with each element organically related to the whole and contributing to the power, the wisdom, and the beauty of this, the greatest statement of God's ways with man and man's destiny on earth.

ROBERT GORDIS

New York City
  Tu Bishevat 5738
  January 23, 1978

INTRODUCTION — ON WRITING A COMMENTARY

Job is no easy book, and writing a commentary on it no easy task. In general, the difficult and elusive enterprise of penetrating into a culture and a world-view two or three millennia old, which is the basic task of biblical scholarship, is compounded in the case of the book of Job by many factors. Here the reader is confronted by a rich and often obscure vocabulary, a unique style, a complex structure, and profundity of thought, all of which make great demands, not only on the scholar's learning, but also on his insight. It should, therefore, prove useful to present, however briefly, the problems of methodology in biblical scholarship with particular reference to Job and the various techniques available to the interpreter in the writing of a commentary. Above all, in view of the extensive and constantly growing literature on Job, the reader may be interested in the presentation of the specific approach of the present work, both with regard to the detailed exegesis of the text, the larger issues of structure and meaning of the various sections, and the overall significance of the book as a whole.

Methodology of Biblical Research — Problems and Methods

No significant work in biblical research is possible today without the use of the comparative method, the full utilization of extra-biblical sources from the ancient Near East, Semitic, Hamitic and even further afield. As has been emphasized elsewhere, this comparative method has two elements. One I have called the "horizontal" aspect, reaching out in space from the biblical heartland to the surrounding peoples, cultures, and religions of the Middle East, in order to illumine Hebrew life and thought. The second is the "vertical" aspect, reaching out in time to later periods in the historical experience of the Jewish people, in order to utilize all the resources of post-biblical literature and language, apocryphal, mishnaic, talmudic, medieval, and modern, for the purpose of enhancing our understanding of the vocabulary, syntax, style, and content of biblical literature — and in turn to be illumined by it.

As is true of most manifestations of the modern spirit, the comparative method was not born yesterday — it actually goes back a full millennium. Judah ibn Koreish, who flourished in the tenth century, may be described as the father of the "horizontal aspect" of the comparative method, since he is the first known scholar to invoke Aramaic and Arabic for interpreting Hebrew words in his *Risalah*. His contemporary, the Gaon Saadia ben Joseph (882–942), in his *Al sabᶜina lafṣa* ("Seventy Words"), launched the "vertical aspect" of the comparative method by laying post-biblical Hebrew under contribution for the same purpose.

The value of both aspects needs no demonstration. But it should be pointed out that, other things being equal, the "vertical" method has one great advantage over the "horizontal." In the case of parallels from other cultures, the problem still remains of establishing the channels of communication and transmission by means of which these influences were brought to bear upon the Hebrew nation. For instance, how did a fifteenth-century North Canaanite literary usage reach a fifth- or third-century Wisdom writer in Jerusalem, as is alleged in some quarters? At the very least, the "horizontal aspect" raises the basic and perennial question of direct borrowing as against parallel development. Though all too often ignored, this is an essential step in the process of validating a theory of "borrowing." This observation is not intended to deny the tremendous contributions of the "horizontal" comparative method — only to indicate what it entails.

In the case of post-biblical Hebrew, it is, of course, important to make sure that the later usage is not merely a reminiscence of a biblical passage. When this is, however, established, there is no problem with regard to the relationship and the avenues of communication, since we are invoking successive stages in the organic life of the same culture, tradition, and language.

It is, therefore, all the more paradoxical that the horizontal method, which is concerned with bringing in parallels from other cultures, is far more widely practiced today than the vertical. Indeed, comparative material is so much in vogue that often it is permitted to take precedence, not only over post-biblical material, but even over intrinsic biblical evidence at hand when it points in another direction. Often the text is emended to conform to the extra-Hebrew parallel, even when the Hebrew usage supports the Masoretic text.

While this practice may be illustrated in virtually every book of the Bible, we shall cite only two instances in Job where the biblical evidence and Hebrew usage are ignored in favor of more distant considerations. The First Speech of The Lord out of the Whirlwind (38:1–40:2) advances the argument that the majesty of God's creation includes many creatures that are not intended for man's use and are not subject to man's control. In the Second Speech (40:6–41:26), God introduces two animals, *Behemot*, the hippopotamus, and *Leviathan*, the crocodile. They are not merely unbeautiful, but positively repulsive and even potentially dangerous to man. Yet even they are manifestations of the creative power of God, who finds joy in His creatures.

In the middle of the description of the crocodile (40:25–41:26), a passage occurs (41:1–4) which some modern commentators have radically emended, on the theory that the subject is not the natural animal described in the entire section, but a primordial beast familiar from Near Eastern mythology. A detailed analysis of this alleged identification is presented in Special Note 37, and the proposed emendations are discussed in the Commentary on the relevant verses. Here it suffices to note that these suggestions involve the assumption of multiple changes in the text and the creation of new *hapax legomena*. Moreover, the gratuitous assumption is made that the Masoretes "sabotaged gross pagan, mythological allusions in the text." Yet there is a perfectly clear reference to the gods being terrified by Leviathan in the Masoretic Text of the same chapter (verse 17), which is left unchanged.

Another instance in Job where the "vertical aspect" of the comparative method is ignored is afforded by the magnificent description of the horse poised for battle (39:19 ff.). In verse 25, stich b, "from afar he smells battle," is prosaically explained by a well-known contemporary scholar to mean that "the horse gives forth the scent of war, gives out a penetrating smell." The scholar insists that the noun *reah* "smell," cannot be used metaphorically and that the verb in the Hiphil is always intransitive. On the first point, he seems to be unaware of such rabbinic usages as *reah hagget* (*B. Git.* 86a a. e.), *reah pᵉsul* (*P. Git.* ix, 50b, etc.). On the second, he disregards the clearly transitive use of the Hiphil of the verb in Ex. 30:38; Lev. 26:31; Am. 5:21. Here both biblical and post-biblical evidence has been overlooked, with a grave loss for the interpretation of the passage.

There are other pitfalls threatening the biblical scholar. As a result of the triumph of the comparative method, the single most popular technique is the search for parallels, real or alleged, whether or not they are relevant or significant. This is compounded by the failure to recognize the unique character of some writers like Koheleth and Job. It is the very essence of Koheleth's style that he uses the available vocabulary for unconventional, personal purposes. Hence, the adducing of parallels may obscure rather than illumine the meaning of the original.

Another frequent hazard may be called the "pendulum syndrome," the tendency in scholarship to swing from one extreme position to the other, with the result that the errors of the first are "corrected" by contracting a new set, opposite and equal. The history of the modern study of the Prophets offers some striking illustrations of this peril, as I have indicated elsewhere. Until very recently, the Hebrew Prophets were pictured in modern biblical scholarship as strictly ethical teachers totally opposed to ritual in all its forms. This assumption necessitated deleting or distorting many passages, but this price was willingly paid. Came the discovery of material on non-Hebrew prophecy, notably in Mari, with abundant evidence of various categories of prophets associated with temples, such as the *apilu*, "answerers," the *assinnu* and the *muhhu*. As a result, a total reaction has set in during the past few decades. The Hebrew Prophets are now increasingly being described as cultic functionaries attached to the various sanctuaries in Israel and their oracles are interpreted as litanies accompanying sacrifices and other ritual acts.

The evidence would point to a conclusion less sensational than either extreme. The Prophets from Amos to Ezekiel represent a broad spectrum in their attitude toward temple, sacrifice, and cult. What the Prophets shared in common was the burning conviction that ritual could not be substituted for righteousness — that the value of the former was determined by the degree to which it enhanced the latter. They were neither ethical culturists nor ritual cultists; they were prophets of God.

To cite another instance, the great classical Prophets have generally been pictured as universalists, unconcerned with the ultimate fate of their own people because of their involvement with the Divine. Thus Eissfeldt declares of Amos: "Bei ihm ist Gott alles, Israel nichts" ("For him God is everything; Israel, nothing.") — a perfectly possible stance for a German theologian, but a rank impossibility for a Hebrew Prophet. Psychologically, it is inconceivable that a prophet who exposed himself to contumely and peril in order to warn his people against disaster would be unconcerned with their destiny. Theologically, the total destruction of Israel, who was the only bearer, however imperfect, of God's name, would necessarily mean the end of God's cause in a pagan world.

Here, too, the "pendulum syndrome" has recently come into play, perhaps under the influence of the contemporary drive toward "ethnicism." It is now being argued in some quarters that the prophets were completely particularists, entirely unconcerned with the well-being and destiny of other nations, and that the Bible envisaged no role for Israel in the context of world history.

The truth lies in neither oscillation of the pendulum. The prophets were neither exclusivists nor cosmopolitans; they were genuine *internationalists*. On the contrary, their loyalty to their people and their concern for humanity were in creative and fruitful tension with one another.

More directly germane to the study of Job is another instance of the operation of the "pendulum syndrome," in the field of textual criticism. With the rise of modern critical scholarship, a hypercritical attitude was adopted toward the Masoretic Text, so that wholesale emendations were proposed, often in a dialect of theological Hebrew that was wonderful to behold. Many scholars felt, as Samuel Johnson said in his *Notes on Shakespeare*, that "the allurements of emendation are scarcely resistible." Now the pendulum has swung to the other extreme and emendations are all too often ruled out of court under any and all circumstances. Now much of my own scholarly work has sought to demonstrate that the Masoretic Text was transmitted with exemplary fidelity through the ages, once a *textus receptus* was officially adopted. It is also true that our knowledge of ancient Hebrew is partial and that new light may dispel old obscurities. At the same time, one must be willfully blind to fail to recognize the existence of such phenomena as scribal errors in the text, the loss of letters, words, and even verses, as well as the misplacement of passages during the process of transmission. Deutographs like II Sam. 22 and Psalm 18, or Psalms 14 and 53, demonstrate the reality of scribal errors, including some radically divergent readings. The Third Cycle in Job (chapters 22–31), in the imperfect form in which it has reached us, is equally conclusive with regard to the loss of material and the accidental transposition of sections from their proper place. It cannot be too strongly emphasized that faith in the perfection of God's Word is not identical with faith in the infallibility of copyists!

Finally, humanistic scholarship is suffering from a strong "inferiority complex" vis-à-vis the natural sciences. It often strives to develop a mechanical, "objective" approach, in order to merit the term "scientific." *It needs to be recognized that exegesis is not a science, but an art, resting upon a complex of scientific disciplines.* An illuminating analogy is afforded by the practice of medicine. Though medicine is often described as a science, it is actually an art, utilizing many sciences, such as anatomy, pathology, pharmacology, and psychology, but requiring such intangible qualities in the practitioner as intuition, experience, and insight into the constitution of the patient. Similarly, the interpretation of a text requires not only a background of knowledge of phonology, morphology, syntax, linguistics, history, comparative religion, and literature, and many more, but also insight, creative imagination, and empathy with the material. This explains why two scholars of comparable competence will produce expositions varying widely in quality and pertinence. This inescapable, indeed, essential basis of subjectivity in all exegesis is the reason why literature, particularly the literature of religion, needs to be interpreted anew in every age in the light of new knowledge and new perspectives and concerns.

The distinguished Palestinian archaeologist, Paul W. Lapp, after a meticulous analysis of the problems involved and the techniques available in the writing of history, sets forth conclusions that are strikingly parallel to our own observations on the nature of exegesis:

"It seems to me that the ultimate source of history is the will of the historian to assert his particular faith in humanity and the will of people to accept the assertion. To be sure, he must have sources, he must employ considerable time and thought in order to understand and evaluate them, he must tax his reason to produce a convincing framework to present his views; in the end, he sets down statements based upon his own convictions about man and his world. In the end, he wills to be human, to present his own conception of humanity. If his conception convinces many, he is honored as a historian." (*Biblical Archaeology and History*, New York, 1969, pp. 33 f.)

What is true of history is at least equally true of literature. The interpretation both of events and of words is essentially a work of art, a construct of the creative imagination and the expression of a particular world-view. To be sure, the synthesis or the interpretation must conform to the objective data available. But the choice among various competing approaches, all of which may meet the test of external evidence, will depend on the degree to which each interpretation reveals a congruence of structure within the various elements of the work and the extent to which it succeeds in conveying a sense of its significance to the reader. In the deepest sense, the test of exegesis is esthetic.

These are some of the basic pitfalls and problems confronting the biblical scholar today that I have sought to keep in mind in the writing of this commentary.

Available Techniques in Commentary Writing

The interpretation of a biblical or classical text offers the writer a choice of several methods:

(1) The commentator may present his view of each passage, without any discussion of alternative views or the citation of other scholars. This method has the virtue of brevity. Thus Hölscher performed the feat of writing a commentary on Job in 99 pages, which includes an introduction and bibliography of 9 pages. To be sure, Hölscher's principal interest lay in the

Realien and in comparative material, rather than in the elucidation of the textual and exegetical problems of the book itself, or of the basic theme with which it is concerned.

Unfortunately, this approach has several drawbacks. Perhaps the lesser defect is that it is unfair to scholars who have toiled long and laboriously and whose only precarious immortality lies in not being ignored or, what is perhaps worse, having the fruits of their researches appropriated by others without reference to their source. The major defect is that the method is a disservice to students and readers, since it places them at the mercy of the commentator, giving them no opportunity to judge the evidence and to decide for themselves among varying views, and perhaps to arrive at new insights. In this method, the vital spark has gone out in biblical studies; the reader's task is simply to be the vessel receiving the author's ideas. This is especially disastrous in Job, where the difficulties are massive and manifold and where so many questions remain unsolved or, at least, subject to varying approaches.

(2) A second method open to the commentator is to write *Notes on the Text of Job,* as was done by Beer, Stevenson, and Guillaume and, of course, with great brilliance, by Ehrlich. Here the author discusses only those passages where he has something new to contribute. This is, of course, a far easier procedure than composing a full commentary. It avoids a good deal of drudgery, escapes the frustration of dealing with intractable texts, and makes for a shorter work.

But there are several disadvantages. Perhaps minor is the problem of deciding when a proposed interpretation is really "original," a question which can be answered only by a survey of the entire extent of exegetical literature. Second is the problem of determining whether a new restatement of earlier ideas, or a new approach to older views, may fairly be described as original. Moreover, studies of this kind tend to limit themselves to individual verses, ignoring larger issues of structure and the meaning of the book as a whole. Thus we have no idea of how Ehrlich conceived of such problems as the integrity of the book of Job, the authenticity of its various sections, and the basic thrust and meaning of the book as a whole. Finally, there is the principal defect of this method — the product is ancillary and not a fully independent work. The student can use it only as an adjunct to other, more comprehensive commentaries, since it deals with isolated passages.

By all odds, the most difficult and complicated procedure, and the one I have adopted, is the preparation of a full-dress original commentary on the book, which involves three stages.

The *first stage* entailed the following steps: (a) A first-hand, independent study of the vocabulary and the syntax of the text; (b) the utilization of Hebrew manuscript variants and the renderings in the Ancient Versions as a clue to possible variations in the original text; (c) the investigation of the larger issues of structure and meaning which are raised by a work as complex as Job; (d) the formulation of tentative conclusions on these various problems, major and minor, with a clear recognition of the differences in the degree of plausibility inherent in these conclusions.

It is only at this point that I proceeded to the *second stage:* (e) the reading of the major medieval and modern commentaries and studies on Job for the purpose of deriving additional insights and better interpretations, simultaneously testing my own tentative conclusions against them. These writers are cited by name whenever their views are of sufficient merit to deserve discussion and analysis, especially when their ideas commend themselves as correct. This is true even if I had arrived at these conclusions independently, so that these earlier scholars seem to be guilty of "plagiarism by anticipation."

In this connection, it should be indicated that the medieval Jewish commentators, who possessed a superb insight into the biblical text, though they lacked the advantages of the comparative material available to us and the improved methodology of the modern period, are still too often ignored, with great loss to biblical scholarship. (f) Finally, formulating the conclusions arrived at by my own independent research as enriched and corrected by the exegetical resources created by other scholars.

At this point, the *third stage*, the actual writing of the commentary, began. Obviously, the significant textual and exegetical material needed to be presented as succinctly as possible. However, I felt it important to preserve a sense of excitement by making the interpretation of the text a voyage of exploration shared in by author and readers, rather than a cut-and-dried summary statement of my own views. This psychological advantage aside, the presentation of a variety of views, together with an analysis of their strengths and weaknesses, enables the reader to develop his own critical faculties and to draw his own conclusions, even if they differ from those of the author.

The Structure of the Work.

The volume falls into three principal sections, its bulk being occupied by the verse-by-verse commentary. In spite of the august example of Driver-Gray in the *International Critical Commentary* and the obvious advantages of the method, I decided not to separate the substantive discussion from the textual and philological material. The reason inheres in an insightful statement of Buber: "As if a true message, a true saying, a true song, contained a What that could be separated from its How without damage, as if the spirit of speech were to be sought out anywhere other than in its linguistic form" (*Die Schrift und ihre Verdeutschung*, pp. 137 f.). Any significant discussion of the meaning must rest upon the form, and conversely the appreciation of form is dependent upon the meaning of the whole and its parts.

What has resulted is a rather large and detailed commentary. The effort has been made to set forth each problem inductively, whether it be specific or general, and thus to involve the reader in the exhilarating quest for understanding.

The Commentary is followed by a section containing 42 Special Notes. Many are no mere appendices dealing with minor or peripheral aspects, but are treatments in depth of fundamental questions. These include issues of style, structure and content that are mutually dependent and mutually illuminating in establishing the thrust and meaning of the book as a whole. The basic questions of the integrity and authenticity of the various sections of the book and their relationship to the entire work, as well as the intent of several extended passages in the text, are discussed. A genuine comprehension of Job also requires a grasp of the principles of biblical prosody, including several new and important insights. The poet's style is also marked by several rhetorical usages not previously recognized that are crucial for the understanding of the book. While many of these themes were treated in my earlier volume, the present work contains the product of additional intensive research. These Special Notes may be read, I believe, as an independent literary and linguistic study of the Book of Job. Their scope and contents are indicated in a special Table of Contents. In any event, whenever the Commentary makes reference to a given Special Note, the reader is strongly urged to consult the relevant material *before* studying the text and the Commentary.

As has been noted in the Preface, the book is enhanced by the inclusion of the beautiful Hebrew text edited by Professor Norman H. Snaith and published by the British and Foreign Bible Society.

The third section of the present work, which is printed on pages parallel with the Hebrew text, is the Translation. This new translation of Job into modern English is accompanied by brief, non-technical introductions designed to clarify the meaning and contents of each chapter and section in *Job* and make the text intelligible for the modern reader.

In a very basic sense, the translation is the capstone in the activity of the commentator, since it is the distillation of his work and embodies his conclusions. Ultimately, the goal of all research must be the enrichment of the life and thought of mankind. Hence, the results of scholarship must find their way into the mainstream of human culture, or scholarship is self-stultifying and ultimately meaningless.

Such a translation appeared in our study, *The Book of God and Man*, and was appreciatively received by many readers. The present version represents changes in several scores of passages, which are the result of additional research, and, hopefully, of a better understanding of the book, both in detail and as a whole. This translation into modern English has sought to capture the vigor of the original, including the cadences of the poet, though many of the effects of the Hebrew poem, including the assonances that occur in almost every verse in Job, are unavoidably lost.

A comment on the art of biblical translation is, perhaps, in order. I believe that modern translations of the Bible into so-called "simple" or "colloquial" English result in a distortion of the original. The Bible was not written in colloquial Hebrew; no ancient Hebrew on the street spoke like Isaiah, or Job, or the Psalms, or even like the books of Samuel or Kings. Whether or not we accept the view of Cassuto that a verse epic underlies the present prose narratives of the Torah and the Earlier Prophets, it is clear that they represent a very high level of literary art, combining loftiness and simplicity in extraordinary degree. Colloquial English may perhaps be an appropriate medium for New Testament *koine*; it is not adequate for the Hebrew Bible.

On the other hand, some translators, in their endeavor to transmit the feeling of the original Hebrew, have gone to the opposite extreme. They have consciously sacrificed the spirit of the language they were using and sought to create a Hebraic dialect in the vernacular.

Fortunately, it is not necessary to pay so high a price in order to do justice to the original. The first fundamental characteristic of biblical poetry is parallelism. The second consists of the various meter patterns, based not on syllables, either qualitative or quantitative, but on stressed words or thought-units. Hence the qualities of biblical poetry are communicable in translation to a large degree. It is possible to capture much, though obviously not all, of the vigor and beauty of the original without doing violence to the spirit of the language-medium employed. Fundamentally, the goal of a translator is to make himself invisible — his version should be a clear mirror through which the author speaks to his English readers with the same impact as does the original to its Hebrew readers.

A well-known biblical scholar has been quoted as saying that an honest scholar translating the Book of Job would leave his translation half blank. Unless this statement be regarded as hyperbole, it is patently mistaken. Far more than fifty percent of the text of Job is intelligible to the modern scholar and reader. To be sure, the mark of the honest scholar is that he is always conscious not only of the lacunae in the knowledge of the past available to scholarship in general, but also of the limitations in his own personal knowledge, however erudite he may be. What is at least equally important is that he never lose sight of the crucial and creative role that his own personality plays in his evaluation of the known data and in his understanding of the literature before him. He will, therefore, refrain from engaging in violent attacks upon rival views, or from claiming infallibility for his own conclusions. Above all, in presenting his views, he will always distinguish clearly between the various levels of certainty, that run the gamut from the barely conceivable at one end of the spectrum through different degrees of possibility to the probable, and finally to the virtually certain, the rarest category of all. Except for a very few instances, he may prefer to translate even highly difficult and probably corrupt passages on the basis of the best knowledge and insight available to him. If he indicates the tentative character of his interpretation, he cannot be faulted for lack of honesty.

It should be kept in mind that the Translation and the Introductory Notes preceding each section and speech in the book, like the relevant Special Notes, constitute an integral part of the Commentary. They often contain material not repeated in the Commentary proper, or they embody the conclusion derived from the discussion in the exegetical notes. Hence, the Translation and the Introductory Notes should be consulted together with the verse-by-verse Commentary.

The Approach to the Style, Structure, and Content of Job

The literature on Job is so voluminous that the student and the reader may be pardoned for wishing to know in what respects a new commentary on Job advances our understanding of the book, both with regard to the exegesis of specific passages and the larger issues of the meaning and structure of the book as a whole. For this reason, the two indices in this book list the new or unfamiliar interpretations proposed for individual verses, whether in the Book of Job or elsewhere in the Bible. As for our approach to the major questions of the architecture and content of Job, these are explicated in the forty-two studies presented as Special Notes following the Commentary, as well as in *The Book of God and Man — A Study of Job* (University of Chicago Press, 1965). It should be added that many of my textual and philological papers, published in various journals and *Festschriften*, that are cited in the present work, have now been assembled in my book, *The Word and The Book — Studies in Biblical Language and Literature* (Ktav Publishing House, New York, 1976).

Basically, the contribution of the present work may be subsumed under three principal headings:

A. *Lexicography and exegesis.* I may cite such instances as the explanation of *hapax legomena* not hitherto elucidated (e.g. 6:14; 10:23; 20:17; 21:24) and of homonyms not previously recognized (e.g. 20:25; 22:27; 27:10; 29:25). The MT is supported and its implications are often explained by reference to rare syntactic usages (e.g. 3:5; 11:6; 20:4; 27:7), phonetic phenomena (e.g. 8:4; 37:7), and the use of comparative material from Middle-East literary sources (e.g. 17:4; 39:25). Semantic usage resting ultimately upon the operation of human nature is illumined at times by psychological analysis and at others by parallel phenomena in other culture-areas, even as far removed as Elizabethan England (e.g. 6:7; 12:6; 21:4). Obviously, the testimony of the Versions critically evaluated and utilized proves helpful in many instances (e.g. 5:6). The Masoretic tradition of *tiqqunei sopherim* suggests an approach to some difficult passages in MT (e.g. 9:19, 35).

B. Of broader significance is the contribution to the understanding of *the style and rhetoric of Job.* In *The Book of God and Man*, chapter XIV is devoted to explicating the role of allusion in language and literature, to which the reader is referred for a discussion in depth. Briefly, speech, particularly poetry, uses words not only for denotation, to refer to concrete, definable objects, but also for connotation, to suggest the penumbra or aura that surrounds the denotation of words and goes beyond them. The connotative function of language, expressed by its implications rather than its explications, is especially significant in religious literature, which treats issues of ultimate and perennial concern, areas to which ordinary experience and expression cannot penetrate. Paul van Buren has reminded us in his *Edge of Language* that all religious discourse teeters on the edge of the known and seeks to express more than can possibly be said.

One important specific form of allusion is analogy. Analogy is particularly fundamental to Wisdom Literature, as is clear from the fact that the basic literary genre of *Hokmah* is the *mašal*, basically "resemblance, similitude," which includes proverb, fable, parable, and allegory. Closely related is the slightly less basic form, the *hīdāh*, "riddle." The Talmud describes the figure of Job himself as a *mašal*, a symbol or, if you will, a parable of man's condition in God's world.

This use of allusiveness and analogy is the key to the major problem in the overall interpretation of the book of Job. It is upon the meaning of the God Speeches that the significance of the book as a whole depends. The difficulties posed by this section are mirrored in the wide disparity of views discussed in detail in chapter X of *The Book of God and Man*. With all due respect for the scholars and critics who have labored on this fascinating book, I am unable to believe that the extraordinary genius who wrote Job could be guilty of the kind of lapses in logic attributed to him by many commentators. Some declare that the Speeches are designed to emphasize the power of God and that on that basis Job is overwhelmed. But Job has conceded this very point time and again during the Dialogue with the Friends. Others regard these Speeches as coldly contemptuous of man — this in a book which agonizes over human suffering as no other in world literature! Still other interpreters regard the God Speeches as emanating from another writer and hence totally irrelevant to the subject at issue, having been attached to the book in order to distract the reader from the painful problem of evil.

This atomization of the book is not limited to the God Speeches or even to the Elihu section. Also the authenticity of the three Cycles of the Dialogue between Job and the Friends has been denied by some critics, while others have transposed large sections from one speaker to another.

The net result of these procedures is to disregard the superb architectonic structure of the book and to convert it into a collection of *disiecta membra*. One important reason for the inadequacy of these various views is the fact that they operate with the explicit content of these Speeches rather than with the implications which the reader is expected to understand.

An important stylistic trait, valuable for the understanding of various passages that otherwise appear enigmatic, also derives from this predilection for implication rather than explicit utterance and the affinity of Wisdom writers for the the *hīdāh*. The poet will use the third person pronoun or suffix to introduce a new theme without explicitly identifying it. By our Western canons, this is a sudden intrusion of a new subject, but the ancient Hebrew reader derived a keen esthetic pleasure from the flash of recognition which came to him when grasping the intent of the text. Instances of this usage, which constitute the key to the exegesis of the particular passages, occur in 8:12 (*ōdenū*); 8:16 (*hūᵓ*); 13:28 (*wehūᵓ*); 24:2 (*hēm*; see the Comm.); 24:13 *hēmāh*); 24:5 (*hēn*); 41:2 (*tōhaltō*), though not all apparent examples represent the same degree of certainty. This use of allusion is also a staple element in the *payyetanic* style of medieval Hebrew poetry.

A major rhetorical usage to which I called attention several years ago has since been widely recognized as indispensable to the understanding of biblical and Oriental literature in general and Wisdom in particular. It also derives from the penchant of the ancient writers, to which, it may be added, our contemporary literature is returning, to enlist the active participation of the reader in grasping the intent of the text. I refer to the use of "virtual quotations" without a *verbum dicendi* or *cogitandi*, for which there is abundant and constantly growing evidence from Egyptian, Akkadian, biblical, and rabbinic literature. The recognition of this usage obviates the necessity for wholesale deletions, transpositions, and emendations in the text.

These "virtual quotations" in the biblical text fall into 11 categories, most of which are represented in Job. For details the reader is referred to the Commentary and to the treatment of the theme in a monograph, "Quotations in Biblical, Oriental and Rabbinic Literature," which first appeared in *Hebrew Union College Annual*, 1949, vol. 27, pp. 157–219 (reprinted in *Poets, Prophets and Sages*, Bloomington, Ind., 1971, pp. 104–60), and which is summarized and extended in *The Book of God and Man*, chapter XIII.

The types of "virtual quotations" represented in Job include: (a) Brief citations of folk Wisdom. These may take the form of proverbs or the point may be made by questions drawn from experience where the expected answer is in the negative. Whether these apothegms are quotations from extant literature or original formulations by the poet of fundamental truths cannot usually be determined. (b) Direct quotations of the speaker's thought. (c) The presentation of the previous attitude or outlook of the speaker. (d) The use of contrasting proverbs, where the author's view is embodied in the second member of the pair. (e) The rare use of indirect quotations without a *verbum dicendi*.

The most important use of "virtual quotations" in Job, indispensable to the understanding of the book, is (f) the citation of the arguments of opponents for the purpose of refutation. It is highly significant that this use of "virtual quotations" is to be met with in Job's speech at the end of the First Cycle (12:6 ff., 12; 13:14), at the conclusion of the Second Cycle (21:19a, 22, 28, 30a), and in the Third Cycle (chapter 24). It occurs in the polemical speeches of Elihu as well, who frequently cites Job explicitly or parodies his language. Finally, Job utilizes the same device in his closing response to the Lord (chapter 42:3a, 4a). The presence of the same literary usage in all three cycles of Job's Dialogue with the Friends, in the Elihu Speeches, and in Job's response to the Speech of the Lord Out of the Whirlwind does not *demonstrate* the unity of the book, but it certainly supports the view of the architectonic unity of the work.

Another stylistic trait uniquely characteristic of Job is a variation from the usual techniques employed in parallelism. It is well known that generally a poet will use different roots or vocables in parallel stichs. Unfortunately, this correct observation has been extended to make this an invariable rule. Hence where the Masoretic Text exhibits the same root in parallel or adjacent stichs, critics have proceeded to emend the text *ad libidinem* on the ground that the repetition must be due to a scribal error. What has not been noted is the *distribution* of the phenomenon. Thus while G. B. Gray finds only three such instances in the first 39 chapters of Isaiah, I have found more than 40 examples in the 39 poetic chapters of Job. Were these instances of scribal error, the distribution in different biblical books would be more nearly equal. It is clear that repetition of the same root or word in parallel or adjacent stichs is a stylistic characteristic of the author of Job. While his mastery of the Hebrew language and all its resources needs no demonstration, he, nevertheless, repeated words, whether for reasons of emphasis, or on subtler grounds that elude us today. At least one other biblical poet, the author of Lamentations, chapter 2, manifests a similar tendency. Other aspects of this usage, not previously recognized, but attested in Ugaritic as well, are discussed in R. Gordis, *The Song of Songs and Lamentations.* (Ktav, New York, 1974), pp. 121 f.

Finally, an important distinction is drawn in the Commentary between "myth" and "mythology," in Job. A reference to Mars in Virgil represents a different order of discourse from the use of "Mars" in Milton. For Virgil, it is myth, part of his religion; for Milton, it is mythology, a literary allusion, rich in connotation, to be sure, but not literally true. Job abounds in mythological references, considerable light on which has been shed by our increasing knowledge of Near Eastern literature and religion. There is, however, an important distinction between references to Leviathan in Job (3:8) or Rahab (26:12), or in Isaiah (27:1), both of whom were thoroughgoing monotheists on the one hand, and the striking parallels cited from Ugaritic and Akkadian literature on the other. The difference has all too often been ignored. For Hebrew writers of the level of Isaiah and Job, such references are literary ornaments, not cosmic truths.

In recent years it has been increasingly recognized that myths serve more than purely literary or aesthetic purposes. They are superb channels for conveying symbolic truths even for those who do not regard them as literally true. As in all poetry, their significance lies in their connotations rather than in their denotations, in what they imply rather than in what they explicate.

Nevertheless, it is important not to lose sight of the distinction between a myth, which is regarded as transmitting actual historical events, and mythology, which is believed to enshrine symbolic, trans-historical truth. Admittedly, it is not always easy or even possible to decide whether a given reference belongs to the one or to the other category. Nevertheless, the effort must be undertaken, if we wish to penetrate to the inner world of the writer or speaker in question. Thus, in the case of *Job*, our understanding of the poet's monotheistic faith depends, in large measure, on whether the poetic figures he uses are myth or mythology for him.

C. The third and most important area in the study of Job consists of the larger issues of *content and structure*, to which the bulk of *The Book of God and Man* is devoted. The conclusions set forth there are buttressed by the verse-by-verse exposition offered in the Commentary and the Special Studies here.

It is a reasonable assumption that the book represents the lifetime activity of a poet and is a complex literary work welded into a triumphant unity. The poet utilizes various literary genres, such as psalm compositions (chapter 5:19 ff.), parables (chapter 8:12 ff.), and "protestations of innocence" (chapter

31), which have their analogues elsewhere in biblical and extra-biblical literature. However, material of this kind is not to be regarded as lifted bodily
from extraneous sources; the poet is much too gifted to need to resort to
such devices. He has utilized the literary models current in his time to compose his own material, now thoroughly integrated into the body of his work.

The most striking instance of his use of extant material is the prose tale
which constitutes the Prologue and Epilogue of the book. Several stages in
the development of this widespread Oriental folk-tale, which was undoubtedly
not limited to Israel, may be reconstructed, and there may have been others
that have left no discernible traces behind. Even here, the poet has not in-
corporated the folk-tale bodily into his book. He has retold the tale with
exquisite artistry, as is clear from the striking alternation of the five scenes
between earth and heaven and the shifting between man-made and natural
disasters, in chapters 1 and 2. He has boldly eliminated references to Satan
in the Epilogue, which would have proved anticlimactic to his purpose.
Finally, he has linked the traditional folk tale to the poetic Dialogue by two
jointures (2:7–10 and 42:7–10), which serve to introduce the protagonists of
the debate at the beginning and to dismiss them at the end.

It is clear from the length of Job's speeches and their passion and elo-
quence, as well as from the explicit statement in the Dialogue (42:7, 8), that
the poet's sympathies lie with Job, and not with the Friends. Nevertheless,
the poet's genius is manifest in his treatment of the Friends. Their traditional
views on Divine justice are presented fully, fairly, and objectively by the
poet. Nowhere else is the traditional doctrine of retribution, with its major
and minor refinements, set forth as effectively as in Eliphaz's first speech
(chapters 4–5). In one sense, we are reminded of the high degree of insight
that Shakespeare shows into Shylock and his motivations ("Hath not a Jew
eyes?"), in spite of the fact that on the conscious level Shylock is the villain
of the play. In Job, however, the poet's relationship to the Friends goes
beyond empathy. He recognizes that their standpoint has large elements of
truth — retribution often does operate in the world. Its weakness is that it
claims fully to explain the existence of evil, and from this inadequate premise
it draws disastrous conclusions.

. The basic answer of the book is reserved for the God Speeches, but here
the implications are crucial. In the Speeches of the Lord out of the Whirlwind,
the natural world is described with great exultation as the handiwork of God.
At every turn, it exhibits the beauty in which God rejoices, and which even
man can recognize, however imperfectly. Not only is the natural order not
fully comprehensible to man; it is not under his control nor is it intended for
his use. For the author of Job, the universe is not man-centered. The first
implication is clear: if man cannot grasp the world, how can he pass judgment
upon its Creator?

There is a further and equally important implication. Paralleling the
natural order, which goes back to God the Creator, is the moral order, which
is equally an expression of the will of God, the arbiter of history. This basic
conviction of one Source for both nature and history which permeates the

thought of Deutero-Isaiah is transposed by the author of Job to the arena of man's individual life. God's law of righteousness operates in the life of each man; man's actions have inevitable consequences of good or ill. But the agonizing issue of the frequent lack of correspondence between right-doing and well-being on the one hand, and ill-doing and disaster on the other, remains all too palpable. Here the author of Job suggests not an answer, but an approach that makes it possible for man to live in the world. Though man does not fully grasp the natural order, since it contains much beyond his understanding, the sense of a cosmos, of a pattern in the natural order, is borne in upon him. The analogy with the moral order would not be lost upon the Hebrew reader — all explanations of evil, including those that appear true, are at best only partial. Though man can apprehend, he cannot fully comprehend either order, both of which emanate from God.

But the poet goes beyond the stance of *ignoramus*, "we do not know," beyond the residue of mystery, the irreducible core of evil that remains beyond man's ken. As Rabbi Jannai declared centuries later, "It is not given us to understand the well-being of the wicked or the suffering of the righteous." Here the literary form in which the Lord's response is couched is profoundly significant — we do not have a prosaic catalogue of what man does not know about the natural order, but a triumphant paean of joy to its beauty, calling upon us, *Gaudeamus*, "Let us rejoice." The beauty of the natural order in which man can rejoice suggests the existence of a pattern in the moral order, in which man may believe and be comforted. Both orders are expressions of the will of God, in which we may trust even when we do not fully understand.

In this connection, Job's two separate Responses to the Lord are entirely in place. In the First (40:3–5), Job is silenced by the overwhelming recognition of the mysterious natural order of nature which he cannot fathom. In the Second Speech of the Lord, God concedes that evil is not yet destroyed and ironically declares that if Job can succeed in destroying all the wicked, He Himself will make obeisance to Job (40:6–14). God then proceeds to describe with pride the beauty even of *Behemot*, the hippopotamus, and of *Leviathan*, the crocodile, creatures that are repulsive to man and even dangerous. Job, in his Second Response, now concedes his error in presuming to judge the ways of God who has created a world which is not anthropocentric, and he now "repents in dust and ashes" (42:1–6). Yet, be it noted, nowhere is it implied that Job's challenge to God's justice was mistaken or that his claim to basic integrity was false. On the contrary, in the jointure linking the poetry to the conclusion of the Prose Tale, Job is explicitly vindicated as "having spoken the truth" about Him, while the Friends are stigmatized as having been untrue to the God whom they were ostensibly defending (42:7, 10).

Contrary to widespread opinion, I believe that the Elihu chapters are essential to the architecture of the book. It would seem that, with the passing of the years, the poet developed another insight into the problem of suffering, to which he was also led by the influence of Deutero-Isaiah, whose impact is discernible throughout Job. The great Prophet of the Exile had expounded a doctrine of the suffering endured by the "Servant of the Lord." God has ordained that Israel be exposed to indignity and hatred far beyond the measure of its sins (Isa. 40:2). Hence Israel's suffering is not the sign or the consequence of Israel's transgression; its lowly estate in the present is the result of its role as God's messenger, the teacher of His law of righteousness, freedom, and justice (42:1–10; 44:1–5). This truth the nations are too blind as yet to comprehend and accept, but it will ultimately become clear to them as they attain to deeper insight and moral maturity (52:13–53:13).

This insight that Israel's degradation and misery are not the result of Israel's sin is applied by the author of Job to the problem of the suffering of the individual. The poet's fundamental response is to be found in the God Speeches, but a secondary answer is presented by Elihu. It should be noted that Elihu's position is distinct both from that of Job and from that of His Friends, and he therefore turns upon them both (chapter 32). The Friends have argued that Job's suffering is evidence that he is a sinner and that his suffering, therefore, is just. Job has denied both contentions. Elihu adopts an intermediate position. He contradicts the Friends' claim that Job's suffering demonstrated his sinfulness, but he also opposes Job's insistence that his suffering is unjustified. He argues that at times the righteous may suffer as part of a regimen of education. Suffering may serve as a Divine discipline, a prophylactic against the sins that threaten all men and to which the righteous are especially prone, notably *hybris*, the complacency and smugness of self-righteousness (chapter 33).

It thus becomes clear that Elihu's speeches do make a significant contribution to the discussion. Were that not the case, as is argued by many commentators, it is hard to see why the chapters were written and interpolated in the first place.

An analysis of Elihu's style, including vocabulary and morphology, indicates that it differs from that of the Dialogue, but only in degree, not in kind, that is to say, in the preference for one form as against another, or in the frequency of Aramaisms in the text. Both the similarities and the differences between the Friends' Dialogue and Elihu are real. They suggest the conclusion that the Elihu speeches emanate from the same author as the Dialogue, but from a later period in his life, perhaps from the very end of his career. They are, therefore, marked by stylistic changes which normally take place with the passing of time, including the greater obscurity and opacity of many passages.

Several illuminating parallels for this hypothesis are available from world literature, as well as from music. These analogies, ancient, medieval and modern, are presented in Special Note 28.

It would be fatuous to maintain that the approach to the style, structure and content of Job set forth in these pages has solved all the problems in the book and will command universal assent. Every reader and student creates a Job in his own image and finds in the book a voice for his own vision of life and its meaning. Yet it is hoped that the present work will persuade many of its readers that the views here presented possess cogency and correctness. The long and arduous labors involved in writing this Commentary will be amply rewarded if it will advance the understanding and appreciation of this masterpiece, which remains one of the supreme achievements of the human spirit.

The Structure of the Book of Job

THE PROLOGUE

    The Tale of the Righteous Job (1–2:10)

    The Jointure (2:11–13)

THE DIALOGUE

    Job's Lament (3)

    The First Cycle

        The Speech of Eliphaz (4–5)
        Job's Reply to Eliphaz (6–7)
        The Speech of Bildad (8)
        Job's Reply to Bildad (9–10)
        The Speech of Zophar (11)
        Job's Reply to Zophar (12–14)

    The Second Cycle

        The Speech of Eliphaz (15)
        Job's Reply to Eliphaz (16–17)
        The Speech of Bildad (18)
        Job's Reply to Bildad (19)
        The Speech of Zophar (20)
        Job's Reply to Zophar (21)

    The Third Cycle

        The Speech of Eliphaz (22)
        Job's Reply to Eliphaz (23–24)
        The Speech of Bildad (25; 26:5–14)
        Job's Reply to Bildad (26:1–4; 27:1–12)
        The Speech of Zophar (27:13–23)

    The Hymn to Wisdom (28)

    Job's Soliloquy

        In Remembrance of Happier Days (29)
        The Misery of the Present Condition (30)
        The Code of a Man of Honor (31)

    The Words of Elihu

        The First Speech (32–33)
        The Second Speech (34)
        The Third Speech (35)
        The Fourth Speech (36–37)

    The Lord Out of the Whirlwind

        The Lord's First Speech (38–40:2)
        Job's Response (40:3–5)
        The Lord's Second Speech (40:6–41:26)
        Job's Response (42:1–6)

THE EPILOGUE

    The Jointure (42:7–10)

    Job's Restoration (42:11–17)

The Book of Job

To present his ideas on the eternal problem of man's suffering in God's world, the poet utilizes a traditional tale as a framework. Several stages of this familiar story, which was well-known in the ancient Middle East, can — be reconstructed. See *BGM*, chap. VI, for details.

The first half of the tale, which describes Job's original prosperity and his succeeding trials, serves as the prologue (1:1–2:10). Then follows the elaborate poetic dialogue which is the heart of the book (3:1–42:6). The concluding part of the traditional narrative is used as an epilogue (42:11–17) to describe Job's eventual restoration to well-being.

The prologue and the epilogue are linked to the intervening dialogue by two brief passages (2:11–17 and 42:7–10) written by the poet, which connect the conventional prose tale with the profundities of the poetic debate.

THE PROLOGUE

The Tale of the Righteous Job (1–2:10)

The story of Job is told in five scenes, alternating between earth and heaven. In the land of Uz there lived a righteous and prosperous man named Job, surrounded by his large and united family. When the Lord in heaven boasts of Job's piety, Satan, the prosecuting angel in the heavenly court, cynically insists that Job has served God only because he has been well rewarded. Stung by this challenge, the Lord permits Satan to subject Job to a series of trials. The alternation in the character of these calamities is highly significant. The first and the third are man-made disasters; the second and the fourth are natural catastrophes. Thus it is subtly suggested that all events, whatever their immediate cause, have their origin in the will of God. Thus the stage is set for the debate on God's justice.

To argue, however, that the Lord is being exhibited as heartless, since He callously undertakes the wager which requires the destruction of Job's family, is to fail to penetrate to the spirit of the folk-tale, which is concerned not with God's responsibility, but with Job's reaction to his suffering. Neither the writer nor his earliest readers (or hearers) felt in the slightest that the Lord is guilty here of cruelty or injustice, particularly since He is pictured as a king who has unlimited power over His creatures. As for Job's children, they are, in accordance with the ancient outlook, regarded as the absolute property of their father.

2

Even this accumulation of mounting catastrophe on Job's head is unable to destroy his faith. He utters no word of complaint against his Maker, but silently accepts these blows as the will of God. But Satan is only slightly disconcerted by his apparent failure. He insists that if Job be struck in his own person, his piety will crumble. The Lord extends the wager to permit Satan to attack Job himself. The sufferer is stricken with a loathsome skin disease. He takes his place among the lepers on an ash-heap outside of the city which had been the scene of his former prosperity. Unable to witness his agony, Job's wife urges him to curse God and die. Job, however, sternly reminds her that he who has accepted God's blessings must be prepared to accept God's burdens, and he continues to remain silent in his affliction.

In a brief connecting passage the scene is set for the poetic Dialogue. Three of Job's friends, men of repute and position in their communities, Eliphaz the Temanite, Bildad the Shuhite, and Zophar the Naamathite, hear of the calamities that have befallen him. They come together from afar to comfort Job, but when they see the tragic change in him they are struck silent, and for seven days and nights no word is spoken.

Scene One — Earth

1   There lived a man in the land of Uz whose name was Job. And
2   that man was blameless and upright, fearing God and avoiding evil.
3   There were born to him seven sons and three daughters. His property
    was seven thousand sheep, three thousand camels, five hundred yoke of
    oxen, five hundred she-asses, and a very large household of slaves, so
4   that this man was the greatest among all the people of the East.
        His sons used to hold a feast in the house of each one in his turn, and
5   they would send and invite their three sisters to eat and drink with
    them. When the days of feasting had run their course, Job would send
    and sanctify them, rising early and offering burnt offerings according
    to the number of them all. For Job thought,
        "Perhaps my children have sinned by blaspheming God in their
    hearts."
    Thus Job was wont to do continually.

Scene Two — Heaven

6   Now one day, the sons of God came to stand in the presence of the
7   Lord, and Satan, too, came among them. And the Lord said to Satan,
        "Whence have you come?"
    And Satan answered the Lord and said,
        "From roaming the earth and walking to and fro on it."
8   Then the Lord said to Satan,
        "Have you noticed My servant Job?
        For there is no one on the earth like him:
        a man blameless and upright,
        fearing God and avoiding evil."
9   But Satan answered the Lord, saying,
10   "Is it for nothing that Job has feared God?
        Have You not safely hedged him in,
        and his house, and all he owns, on every side?
        You have blessed the work of his hands
        and his possessions have increased in the land.
11   But put forth Your hand and touch whatever he owns,
        and he will surely curse You to Your face!"
12 So the Lord said to Satan,
        "Behold, all he has is in your power.
        Only upon the man himself, do not lay your hand."
    So Satan went forth from the Lord's presence.

Scene Three — Earth

13 Now the day came when his sons and daughters were eating and
14 drinking wine in the home of their oldest brother. And a messenger
    came to Job, saying,
        "The oxen were plowing
        and the she-asses grazing nearby.

א א אִישׁ הָיָה בְאֶרֶץ־עוּץ אִיּוֹב שְׁמוֹ וְהָיָה ׀ הָאִישׁ הַהוּא תָּם וְיָשָׁר

2 וִירֵא אֱלֹהִים וְסָר מֵרָע: וַיִּוָּלְדוּ לוֹ שִׁבְעָה בָנִים וְשָׁלוֹשׁ בָּנוֹת:

3 וַיְהִי מִקְנֵהוּ שִׁבְעַת אַלְפֵי־צֹאן וּשְׁלֹשֶׁת אַלְפֵי גְמַלִּים וַחֲמֵשׁ
מֵאוֹת צֶמֶד־בָּקָר וַחֲמֵשׁ מֵאוֹת אֲתוֹנוֹת וַעֲבֻדָּה רַבָּה מְאֹד

4 וַיְהִי הָאִישׁ הַהוּא גָּדוֹל מִכָּל־בְּנֵי־קֶדֶם: וְהָלְכוּ בָנָיו וְעָשׂוּ
מִשְׁתֶּה בֵּית אִישׁ יוֹמוֹ וְשָׁלְחוּ וְקָרְאוּ לִשְׁלֹשֶׁת אַחְיֹתֵיהֶם לֶאֱכֹל

ה וְלִשְׁתּוֹת עִמָּהֶם: וַיְהִי כִּי הִקִּיפוּ יְמֵי הַמִּשְׁתֶּה וַיִּשְׁלַח אִיּוֹב
וַיְקַדְּשֵׁם וְהִשְׁכִּים בַּבֹּקֶר וְהֶעֱלָה עֹלוֹת מִסְפַּר כֻּלָּם כִּי אָמַר
אִיּוֹב אוּלַי חָטְאוּ בָנַי וּבֵרְכוּ אֱלֹהִים בִּלְבָבָם כָּכָה יַעֲשֶׂה אִיּוֹב

6 כָּל־הַיָּמִים: וַיְהִי הַיּוֹם וַיָּבֹאוּ בְּנֵי הָאֱלֹהִים לְהִתְיַצֵּב

7 עַל־יְהוָה וַיָּבוֹא גַם־הַשָּׂטָן בְּתוֹכָם: וַיֹּאמֶר יְהוָה אֶל־הַשָּׂטָן
מֵאַיִן תָּבֹא וַיַּעַן הַשָּׂטָן אֶת־יְהוָה וַיֹּאמַר מִשּׁוּט בָּאָרֶץ

8 וּמֵהִתְהַלֵּךְ בָּהּ: וַיֹּאמֶר יְהוָה אֶל־הַשָּׂטָן הֲשַׂמְתָּ לִבְּךָ עַל־
עַבְדִּי אִיּוֹב כִּי אֵין כָּמֹהוּ בָּאָרֶץ אִישׁ תָּם וְיָשָׁר יְרֵא אֱלֹהִים

9 וְסָר מֵרָע: וַיַּעַן הַשָּׂטָן אֶת־יְהוָה וַיֹּאמַר הַחִנָּם יָרֵא אִיּוֹב

י אֱלֹהִים: הֲלֹא־אַתָּ שַׂכְתָּ בַעֲדוֹ וּבְעַד־בֵּיתוֹ וּבְעַד כָּל־
אֲשֶׁר־לוֹ מִסָּבִיב מַעֲשֵׂה יָדָיו בֵּרַכְתָּ וּמִקְנֵהוּ פָּרַץ בָּאָרֶץ:

11 וְאוּלָם שְׁלַח־נָא יָדְךָ וְגַע בְּכָל־אֲשֶׁר־לוֹ אִם־לֹא עַל־פָּנֶיךָ

12 יְבָרְכֶךָּ: וַיֹּאמֶר יְהוָה אֶל־הַשָּׂטָן הִנֵּה כָל־אֲשֶׁר־לוֹ בְּיָדֶךָ

13 רַק אֵלָיו אַל־תִּשְׁלַח יָדֶךָ וַיֵּצֵא הַשָּׂטָן מֵעִם פְּנֵי יְהוָה: וַיְהִי
הַיּוֹם וּבָנָיו וּבְנֹתָיו אֹכְלִים וְשֹׁתִים יַיִן בְּבֵית אֲחִיהֶם הַבְּכוֹר:

14 וּמַלְאָךְ בָּא אֶל־אִיּוֹב וַיֹּאמַר הַבָּקָר הָיוּ חֹרְשׁוֹת וְהָאֲתֹנוֹת

טו רֹעוֹת עַל־יְדֵיהֶם: וַתִּפֹּל שְׁבָא וַתִּקָּחֵם וְאֶת־הַנְּעָרִים הִכּוּ

---

v. 10. אתה ק׳

15   Then the Sabeans fell upon them and took them captive.
          The slave boys they put to the sword;
          and I alone have escaped to tell you."
16   While he was still speaking, another came and said,
          "A great fire fell from heaven
          and burned the sheep and the slaves and consumed them;
          and I alone have escaped to tell you."
17   While he was still speaking, another came and said,
          "The Chaldeans formed three companies
          and swooped down upon the camels and took them captive.
          The slaves they put to the sword;
          and I alone have escaped to tell you."
18   While he was speaking, another came and said,
          "Your sons and daughters were eating and drinking
          in the home of their oldest brother.
19   Suddenly, a mighty wind came across the desert,
          and it struck the four corners of the house.
          It fell upon the young people, and they died.
          and I alone have escaped to tell you."

20   Then Job arose and rent his robe and shaved his head, and fell upon
21   the earth and worshipped. And he said,
          "Naked I came from my mother's womb,
          naked shall I return.
          The Lord gives, and the Lord takes.
          Blessed be the name of the Lord."
22   Yet in all this, Job did not sin or impute anything unseemly to God.

Scene Four — Heaven

2   Again there was a day when the sons of God came to stand in the
      Lord's presence, and Satan also came among them to stand in the Lord's
2   presence. And the Lord said to Satan,
          "Whence have you come?"
      And Satan answered the Lord, saying,
          "From roaming the earth and walking to and fro on it."
3   Then the Lord said to Satan,
          "Have you noticed My servant Job?
          For there is no one like him on the earth,
          a man blameless and upright,
          fearing God and avoiding evil.
          He still holds fast to his integrity.
          Yet you incited Me against him
          to destroy him without cause."
4   Then Satan answered the Lord, saying,
          "Skin for skin!
          All a man has
          he will give for his life!
5   But put forth Your hand
          and touch his own flesh and bones
          and he will surely curse You to Your face."
6   Then the Lord said to Satan,
          "He is in your power,
          but preserve his life."

16 לְפִי־חֶרֶב וָאִמָּלְטָה רַק־אֲנִי לְבַדִּי לְהַגִּיד לָךְ: עוֹד ׀ זֶה
מְדַבֵּר וְזֶה בָּא וַיֹּאמַר אֵשׁ אֱלֹהִים נָפְלָה מִן־הַשָּׁמַיִם וַתִּבְעַר
בַּצֹּאן וּבַנְּעָרִים וַתֹּאכְלֵם וָאִמָּלְטָה רַק־אֲנִי לְבַדִּי לְהַגִּיד

17 לָךְ: עוֹד ׀ זֶה מְדַבֵּר וְזֶה בָּא וַיֹּאמַר כַּשְׂדִּים שָׂמוּ ׀ שְׁלֹשָׁה
רָאשִׁים וַיִּפְשְׁטוּ עַל־הַגְּמַלִּים וַיִּקָּחוּם וְאֶת־הַנְּעָרִים הִכּוּ

18 לְפִי־חֶרֶב וָאִמָּלְטָה רַק־אֲנִי לְבַדִּי לְהַגִּיד לָךְ: עַד זֶה
מְדַבֵּר וְזֶה בָּא וַיֹּאמַר בָּנֶיךָ וּבְנוֹתֶיךָ אֹכְלִים וְשֹׁתִים יַיִן בְּבֵית

19 אֲחִיהֶם הַבְּכוֹר: וְהִנֵּה רוּחַ גְּדוֹלָה בָּאָה ׀ מֵעֵבֶר הַמִּדְבָּר וַיִּגַּע
בְּאַרְבַּע פִּנּוֹת הַבַּיִת וַיִּפֹּל עַל־הַנְּעָרִים וַיָּמוּתוּ וָאִמָּלְטָה

כ רַק־אֲנִי לְבַדִּי לְהַגִּיד לָךְ: וַיָּקָם אִיּוֹב וַיִּקְרַע אֶת־מְעִלוֹ וַיָּגָז

21 אֶת־רֹאשׁוֹ וַיִּפֹּל אַרְצָה וַיִּשְׁתָּחוּ: וַיֹּאמֶר עָרֹם יָצָתִי מִבֶּטֶן
אִמִּי וְעָרֹם אָשׁוּב שָׁמָּה יְהוָה נָתַן וַיהוָה לָקָח יְהִי שֵׁם יְהוָה

22 מְבֹרָךְ: בְּכָל־זֹאת לֹא־חָטָא אִיּוֹב וְלֹא־נָתַן תִּפְלָה
לֵאלֹהִים:

ב א וַיְהִי הַיּוֹם וַיָּבֹאוּ בְּנֵי הָאֱלֹהִים לְהִתְיַצֵּב עַל־יְהוָה וַיָּבוֹא גַם־

2 הַשָּׂטָן בְּתֹכָם לְהִתְיַצֵּב עַל־יְהוָה: וַיֹּאמֶר יְהוָה אֶל־הַשָּׂטָן
אֵי מִזֶּה תָּבֹא וַיַּעַן הַשָּׂטָן אֶת־יְהוָה וַיֹּאמַר מִשֻּׁט בָּאָרֶץ

3 וּמֵהִתְהַלֵּךְ בָּהּ: וַיֹּאמֶר יְהוָה אֶל־הַשָּׂטָן הֲשַׂמְתָּ לִבְּךָ עַל־
עַבְדִּי אִיּוֹב כִּי אֵין כָּמֹהוּ בָּאָרֶץ אִישׁ תָּם וְיָשָׁר יְרֵא אֱלֹהִים

4 וְסָר מֵרָע וְעֹדֶנּוּ מַחֲזִיק בְּתֻמָּתוֹ וַתְּסִיתֵנִי בוֹ לְבַלְּעוֹ חִנָּם: וַיַּעַן
הַשָּׂטָן אֶת־יְהוָה וַיֹּאמַר עוֹר בְּעַד־עוֹר וְכֹל אֲשֶׁר לָאִישׁ יִתֵּן

ה בְּעַד נַפְשׁוֹ: אוּלָם שְׁלַח־נָא יָדְךָ וְגַע אֶל־עַצְמוֹ וְאֶל־בְּשָׂרוֹ

6 אִם־לֹא אֶל־פָּנֶיךָ יְבָרֲכֶךָּ: וַיֹּאמֶר יְהוָה אֶל־הַשָּׂטָן הִנּוֹ

Scene Five — Earth

7   So Satan went forth from the presence of God and he struck Job
with loathsome sores from the sole of his foot to the crown of his head,
8   so that he took a potsherd with which to scrape himself as he sat in the
9   midst of the ash-heap. Then his wife said to him,
> "Are you still holding fast to your piety?
> Curse God and die."
10   Then he said to her,
> "You talk like an impious, foolish woman.
> Shall we accept good from God
> and not accept evil?"
Yet even in all this, Job committed no sin with his lips.

11   Then Job's three friends heard of all the trouble that had come upon
him. And they came, each from his place — Eliphaz the Temanite,
Bildad the Shuhite, and Zophar the Naamathite — having arranged
12   together to come to condole with him and comfort him. Now when they
caught sight of him from afar, they could not recognize him. So they
raised their voices and wept and rent their robes and threw dust over
13   their heads toward the heavens. They sat with him on the ground for
seven days and for seven nights, no one saying a word, for they saw
that his agony was very great.

7 בְּיָדֶ֔ךָ אַ֖ךְ אֶת־נַפְשׁ֣וֹ שְׁמֹ֑ר׃ וַיֵּצֵא֙ הַשָּׂטָ֔ן מֵאֵ֖ת פְּנֵ֣י יְהוָ֑ה וַיַּ֤ךְ

8 אֶת־אִיּוֹב֙ בִּשְׁחִ֣ין רָ֔ע מִכַּ֥ף רַגְל֖וֹ .עַ֣ד קָדְקֳד֑וֹ׃ וַיִּֽקַּֽח־ל֣וֹ חֶ֔רֶשׂ

9 לְהִתְגָּרֵ֖ד בּ֑וֹ וְה֖וּא יֹשֵׁ֥ב בְּתוֹךְ־הָאֵֽפֶר׃ וַתֹּ֤אמֶר לוֹ֙ אִשְׁתּ֔וֹ עֹדְךָ֖

י מַחֲזִ֣יק בְּתֻמָּתֶ֑ךָ בָּרֵ֥ךְ אֱלֹהִ֖ים וָמֻֽת׃ וַיֹּ֣אמֶר אֵלֶ֗יהָ כְּדַבֵּ֞ר אַחַ֤ת
הַנְּבָלוֹת֙ תְּדַבֵּ֔רִי גַּ֣ם אֶת־הַטּ֗וֹב נְקַבֵּל֙ מֵאֵ֣ת הָֽאֱלֹהִ֔ים וְאֶת־
הָרָ֖ע לֹ֣א נְקַבֵּ֑ל בְּכָל־זֹ֛את לֹא־חָטָ֥א אִיּ֖וֹב בִּשְׂפָתָֽיו׃

11 וַֽיִּשְׁמְע֞וּ שְׁלֹ֣שֶׁת ׀ רֵעֵ֣י אִיּ֗וֹב אֵ֣ת כָּל־הָרָעָ֣ה הַזֹּאת֮ הַבָּ֣אָה עָלָיו֒
וַיָּבֹ֙אוּ֙ אִ֣ישׁ מִמְּקֹמ֔וֹ אֱלִיפַ֤ז הַתֵּֽימָנִי֙ וּבִלְדַּ֣ד הַשּׁוּחִ֔י וְצוֹפַ֖ר

12 הַנַּֽעֲמָתִ֑י וַיִּוָּעֲד֣וּ יַחְדָּ֔ו לָב֥וֹא לָנֽוּד־ל֖וֹ וּֽלְנַחֲמֽוֹ׃ וַיִּשְׂא֨וּ אֶת־
עֵֽינֵיהֶ֤ם מֵֽרָחוֹק֙ וְלֹ֣א הִכִּירֻ֔הוּ וַיִּשְׂא֥וּ קוֹלָ֖ם וַיִּבְכּ֑וּ וַֽיִּקְרְעוּ֙ אִ֣ישׁ

13 מְעִל֔וֹ וַיִּזְרְק֥וּ עָפָ֛ר עַל־רָאשֵׁיהֶ֖ם הַשָּׁמָֽיְמָה׃ וַיֵּשְׁב֤וּ אִתּוֹ֙
לָאָ֔רֶץ שִׁבְעַ֥ת יָמִ֖ים וְשִׁבְעַ֣ת לֵיל֑וֹת וְאֵֽין־דֹּבֵ֤ר אֵלָיו֙ דָּבָ֔ר כִּ֣י
רָא֔וּ כִּֽי־גָדַ֥ל הַכְּאֵ֖ב מְאֹֽד׃

CHAPTER I

On the metrics of chaps. 1–2, see Special Note 6.

1:1 הָיָה אִישׁ. The classical formula for introducing a narrative is וַיְהִי אִישׁ. Cf. I Sam. 1:1 and the openings of Jos., Jud., Ezek., Ruth, Est. However, our formula occurs exactly in Est. 2:5 אִישׁ אֶחָד הָיָה בְּשׁוּשַׁן הַבִּירָה. There are no objective grounds for assuming that the formula in our passage is discontinuous, while the other represents a continuing narrative (ag. TS, P.). Nor, on the other hand, is our formula a late expression (ag. Dh.), since it is met with in Nathan's parable (II Sam. 12:1). Its use here, as in the latter instance, may be intended to suggest that what we have here is a tale and not actual history.

עוּץ is identified by some scholars with Hauran in northern Mesopotamia (cf. Uz as the son of Nahor, Gen. 22:21), or with a district in Arabia (Del.). It seems preferable to equate it with Edom or a district in that country, since it is parallel with Edom in Lam. 4:21 and Uz is the son of an Edomite chieftain, Dishan (Gen. 36:28), and most of the personal names in the book have an Edomite provenance (see the Comm. on 2:11).

For an important distinction, not hitherto recognized, between the origin of the name "Job" and that of the names of the Friends, and its bearing on the structure of the Prose Tale, see the Comm. on 2:11.

Like the patriarchs in Genesis, Job is depicted as a semi-nomad living in a district on the edge of the desert (v. 19) east of Palestine, in an area near a town (2:8).

אִיּוֹב. The name is common in the second millennium B.C.E. It occurs as A-ja-ab in Tel-el-Amarna Letter no. 256 (14th cent. B.C.E.), in the Mari document as Ha-a-ia-bu-um, as A-ia-bi in the Alalakh Tablets and perhaps in the Egyptian Execration texts (2000 B.C.E.) as ʾybn. Albright suggested that its original form and meaning were ʾayya-ʾabun, "Where is my father," which occurs in an Egyptian list of Palestinian chiefs, and for which analogues are available (*JAOS*, vol. 74, 1954, pp. 225 f., 232). In the last century, Ewald suggested a derivation from the Arabic ʾAwab, "he who turns to God." Meyer identifies Job with Jobab, a name which occurs also in the genealogy of Esau (Gen. 36:33) and is used for our protagonist in the apocryphal Testament of Job.

The most probable view is that *Iyyob* is a Hebrew folk etymology of a previously existing Semitic name, a passive participial noun from the verb ʾāyab, "to hate," hence, "the hated, persecuted one." The philological evidence for this passive use can scarcely be described as "slight" (BDB), in view of yillōd, "born" (Ex. 1:22; II Sam. 5:14; 12:14), and šikkōr, "drunken" (I Sam. 25:36, and often), which are passive in meaning (ag. Dh.) rather than gibbōr, "brave, strong," lit. "one who magnifies himself." Another striking instance of folk etymology is afforded by the name Moses, which is authentically

Egyptian (MESU = "son, child"); cf. *Rameses*, "son of Ra," *Tutmose*, "son of Tut." In the case of Moses, the theophoric element has been dropped, as is frequent in biblical names, such as Jacob, Joseph, etc. By giving the name the form of an active participle (Mōšeh), the theme, "the one drawer forth, the savior" is suggested. The interpretation in Ex. 2:10, "for from the water have I drawn him forth," represents a second folk etymology. If the name actually bore this meaning, it would need to be revocalized as a participle passive *māšūi*, "the one drawn forth."

Increasingly, contemporary research in folklore and literary history attributes a high measure of credibility to the nucleus of fact underlying such epics as the *Iliad* and the *Song of Roland*. Such legendary figures as King Arthur, Robin Hood, and Dr. Faustus are no longer dismissed as figments of the imagination. These trends strengthen the likelihood that there originally was a historical figure named Job who became the nucleus of a folk-tradition which was later utilized by the poet.

תָּם not "perfect, free from sin," a claim Job does not even put forth for himself (cf. 9:20 f.; 13:26; 14:16; 14:4), but "whole, free from double-dealing, morally innocent, sincere," like Horace's *integer vitae*. It is thus virtually equivalent to the rabbinic phrase תוכו כברו "lit. his 'within' was like his 'without,'" i.e., his inner character was like his outside demeanor" (*B. Yoma* 72b).

1:2 The use of "seven" and "three" in the narrative, adding up to "ten," and of multiples of these numbers, is characteristic of Semitic life and thought.

1:3 עֲבֻדָּה, which occurs also in Gen. 26:14 parallel to "cattle," is not to be taken as "work animals" (ag. Ehr.), but as a broken plural of ᶜ*ebhedh*, hence "slaves, collectively viewed, i.e., a household of slaves." Cf. זָכוּר (Ex. 23:12; 34:23; Deut. 16:16; 20:13), which is to be rendered "males," not "male" (ag. BDB) as a broken plural of זָכָר; פְּקוּדָה "officialdom" (Isa. 60:17; cf. parallel). Probably גְּבוּרָה "brave men" (Isa. 3:15) and מְלוּכָה in זֶרַע הַמְּלוּכָה (II Ki. 25:25; Jer. 41:1; Ezek. 17:13; Dan. 1:3), "offspring of kings, children of royalty," are also broken plurals of *gibbōr* and *melekh* respectively.

גָדוֹל = "rich" (cf. I Sam. 25:2).

קדם "east." In the Egyptian letter of *Sinuhe* (2nd millennium B.C.E.), it refers to the region east of Byblos. In Gen. 29:1 the term is applied to the Arameans; in Isa. 11:14, to Israel's eastern neighbors.

1:4 The verse pictures not only the rich, generous scale of living of Job's children, but, more significantly, the unity and the affection binding brothers and sisters alike. The sisters are obviously unmarried, or their husbands would have been included. They are therefore still young, another indication that Job, both in the prose and in the poetry, is conceived of not as an aged "patriarch," but as being in the midst of his vigorous years (cf., e.g., 15:10; 19:17). This is entirely in keeping with the passion of his challenge to God throughout the Dialogue.

והלכו בניו ועשו משתה "go and make a feast," the auxiliary verb initiating an activity; cf. BDB, s.v. *hālakh*, 5b, p. 233. The idiom means "furnish a feast" (Gen. 19:3; Est. 1:3, 5, 9).

לשלשת, the feminine numeral need not be corrected to לשלש; cf. Gen. 7:13. Particularly in the plural, masculine forms of the verb are frequent, while in mishnaic Hebrew the feminine forms of the plural verb have completely disappeared.

בית איש יומו lit. "each man on his day." This can hardly mean on every day of the year (so LXX, Da., Du.), as v. 5 makes clear, or "the week of celebration at sheep-shearing" (Jud. 14:12, 17) (so Bu., Di., D-G).

יומו "his day" may possibly mean "his birthday" (cf. Job 3:1, and see יום מלכנו Hos. 7:5, which may mean "birthday" or "coronation day"). The word is more probably to be taken to mean "on his appointed day, his turn," the precise character of which the narrative with fine economy leaves unclear because it is of no real importance. Nor is the phrase to be construed as meaning "a week of celebration" with each brother acting as host for one day (so Ra., Ibn E.), since it is clear from our verse that each banquet was in a different home, at a different time, with separate invitations extended to the brothers and the sisters. So understood, there is no need to assume a breviloquence (ag. D-G). This view of the passage (see the Comm. on v. 5) obviates any implied criticism of Job's sons as inveterate revelers devoting themselves exclusively to extended feasting and riotous living, as some commentators aver.

1:5 הקיפו, the Hiphil of נקף (a metaplastic form of קוף, whence תְּקוּפָה "circuit, season"), is intransitive like the Qal in Isa. 29:1. סְפוּ שָׁנָה עַל־שָׁנָה חַגִּים יִנְקֹפוּ "add year to year, let the feasts run their round"; i.e., "when the festival cycle is complete"; cf. תְּקוּפַת הַשָּׁנָה Ex. 34:22; תְּקוּפַת הַיָּמִים. I Sam. 1:20. In Ugaritic, the verb is also used in connection with the passing of a year, *šbʿ šnt tmt tmn nqpt*, "Seven years were ended, eight had passed" (text 52, lines 67, 68 in C. H. Gordon, *Ugaritic Textbook*, Part II, p. 175). The vocable *nqpt* is construed by Gordon as a noun meaning "year" (*idem*, Glossary, no. 1700, p. 447).

A semantic parallel is afforded by the rabbinic חזר "go round," whence מַחֲזוֹר "cycle of time" and later "prayerbook for the festivals of the year"; cf. E. Ben Yehuda, *Thesaurus*, vol. 6, pp. 2905b, s.v.

On the basis of the Hebrew and Ugaritic usage, our passage describes not a year-end festival (ag. TS), but the course of a year during which each brother would sponsor a banquet. The reference to sending for the sisters also suggests that these occasions were separated from one another in time and space. The opening clause is, therefore, to be rendered, "When the days of feasting had completed their cycle, i.e., had run their course."

וַיִּשְׁלַח "he sent," used to initiate an action expressed by the finite verb following; cf. Gen. 27:45; II Ki. 11:4, and see BDB, s.v. lc, p. 1018a.

ויקדשם not "he invited them" (T, Ra., Ehr.), which is out of place after the banqueting. Moreover, if that were the meaning, the succeeding clause, "perhaps my children have sinned by blaspheming God in their hearts," would more naturally have been in the second person, "perhaps you have sinned," addressed to the children who would be present. Nor can it be that Job invited them to a sacred banquet at his home (Jacob, *ZATW*, 1912, p. 278), in view of the lack of any reference to such a meal. The most natural meaning is that once a year, at the end of the series of feasts given by his sons, Job would conduct a ritual of expiation for his children. Hence the verb is to be rendered "he sanctified, purified them" from any possible sin. This is generally taken to mean "through ritual washings" (Gen. 35:2; Ex. 19:10, 14). On the other hand, no specific ritual may be intended by the author, especially since Job is not an Israelite and therefore not bound by biblical ritual ordinances.

והשכים may exhibit an epexegetical Vav, "he sanctified them by rising in the morning and offering burnt offerings."

Job shows his good sense in not foisting his presence on his children during their merrymaking, nor by compelling their attendance at his home thereafter. He reveals his moral sensitivity in recognizing the possibility of some offence having been committed during the banqueting. Significantly, he is not concerned about some major, overt sin on their part — only that they might have been guilty of blasphemy in thought (בלבבם "in their hearts, minds"), such as loose speech or the arrogance induced by their happy estate.

ברכו, a self-evident euphemism for "curse" (cf. 1:11; 2:5, 9; I Ki. 21:10, 13; on Ps. 10:3 cf. Gordis, "Ps. 9:10, An Exegetical Study," in *JQR*, 1957, vol. 48, pp. 112 f.). It is generally assumed that the root *brk* was substituted for *qll* "curse" by later scribes. However, the same psychological process postulated for a scribe may well have operated for the author. The text may therefore be original.

יעשה a classic use of the imperfect, "was wont to do."

כל הימים does not mean "all the days of the feasting" (ag. Du., D-G.) but "always, continually," a usage attested in all periods of biblical Hebrew (cf. Gen. 43:9; 44:32; Deut. 4:40; II Chr. 7:16; 10:7; 12:15; 21:7; see BDB, s.v. יום, sec. 7f, p. 400b).

1:6 ויהי היום = "it happened." Cf. II Ki. 4:8. The Targum and the Midrash refer the two sessions of the heavenly court in the Prologue to Rosh Hashanah and Yom Kippur, when the fates of men are written and sealed.

בני האלהים lit. members of the *genus* ᵓ*elohim*, "divine beings," cf. *ben* ᵓ*adam, ben baqar, benei hanebhiyim*, etc. The term, which occurs outside our narrative in Gen. 6:2, is identical in meaning with *bar* ᵓ*elohin* (Dan. 3:25), *benei* ᶜ*elyon* (Ps. 82:6), and *benei* ᵓ*elim* (Ps. 29:1; 89:7), with analogues in Ugaritic, *bn ilm*, "sons of El" (cf. H. L. Ginsberg, *Kithbei Ugarit*, Jerusalem, 5696 = 1936, p. 126; C. H. Gordon, *UT*, p. 51), and in Arslan Tash, *bn* ᵓ*elm*. However, the pagan mythological background which is still palpable in Gen. 6:2 has quite disappeared here and in Ps. 29:1 (where Dahood's rendering, "O Gods," is to be rejected as an example of the genetic fallacy). In biblical Hebrew, these phrases refer to the angels or divine beings who serve as God's courtiers in heaven. Similarly, no polytheism inheres in the rabbinic phrase פמליא של מעלה "the family of God on high" (*B. Berakhot* 17a), which has precisely the same meaning. While "the sons of God" are obviously personified here, like "the messengers" (in Ps. 104:4) who do His bidding (Zech. 6:4), they are identified elsewhere with the forces of nature. In Ps. 104:4, the messengers are the wind and fire. In Job 38:7, they are equated with the heavenly bodies (cf. Rashi on our passage: "The heavenly hosts who are close enough to the Divine presence to be members of His household are therefore called his sons").

The phrase להתיצב על ה' is interpreted by some midrashically, "to stand against God, to quarrel with Him" (so Rashi, who compares Isa. 3:13). The basic meaning of the verb in our passage is obviously "to stand in the presence of God, as courtiers before a monarch" (cf. Zech. 6:5; Job 2:1). On the other nuance, which does inhere in the verb, see the Comm. on 2:1.

השטן "the adversary, opponent, enemy." The noun refers either to a personal or a national foe (Nu. 22:22; I Sam. 29:4). In later biblical and postbiblical thought it becomes "the adversary *par excellence*, the superhuman opponent," as in Zech. 3:1, 2, and in both instances here. In these latter passages it occurs with the article and is still a common noun. Here he is merely one of "the sons of God," singled out as the prosecutor, who cynically denies that men are capable of disinterested righteousness. In Goethe's words, he is *der Geist der stets verneint*, "the spirit who always negates." In I Chr. 21:1, *Satan* has become a proper noun, "Satan," without an article. On the bearing of the usage here for the dating of the Book of Job, see *BGM*, pp. 216 f.

That the verb *sātan*, which occurs in Zech. 3:1, Ps. 38:21, 109:4, is derived from the noun (so Gerber, BDB) is doubtful, in view of the verb *sātam*, "hate" (Gen. 27:4; 49:23; 50:1; Ps. 55:4; Job 16:9; 30:21). The relationship between *sātan* and *sātam* was recognized in antiquity, as is clear from the proper name *Mastema* which occurs in the Apocrypha and Pseudepigrapha for a fallen angel. "Mastema," derived from Hos. 9:7, 8, is described as "the chief of the spirits" in Jubilees (10:1–14), the source of evil and disease in the Book of Noah (l. 155), and is explicitly identified with Satan in the *Zadokite Fragment* (16:5). See L. Ginzberg, *Legends*, vol. I, p. 173; vol. V, p. 196, n. 74; J. D. Eisenstein, *Oṣar Midrašim* (New York, 1915), p. 400; A. M. Haberman, *Megillot Midbar Yehudah* (Tel Aviv, 1959), p. 88.

The existence of the two related roots — *sātan* and *sātam* — militates against the proposal that "Satan" was originally read with a Shin, from the root *šūt*, "go to and fro," suggested long ago by Luzzatto and independently by TS (*op. cit.*, pp. 38 ff.).

It cannot be stressed too strongly that in all periods of Jewish thought, biblical and rabbinic, "the Satan" or "Satan" is not co-equal with God, but is subservient to Him. There is no Hebrew equivalent for the phrase "the kingdom of Satan."

1:7 On the meter of all the speeches in the Prose Tale, see Special Note 6.

Satan's answer is in 2:2 meter, a short staccato rhythm which expresses his impudence before his Master, as well as his desire, clearly expressed by his laconic answer in 2:2, to volunteer as little information as possible. Hence both verbs, *šūṭ*, "wander about without a set purpose" (cf. Jer. 49:3), and *hithhallekh*, "to walk to and fro" (cf. Jos. 18:4; Zech. 1:10 f.), are evasive in intent. They are not to be given the nuance, suggested by some commentators, of "investigate, survey."

The Lord's question need not imply that Satan is "the vagabond among the heavenly beings" (Du.), or that, unlike the other angels, he has no special domain. As Satan's master, the Lord begins the conversation, which it would not be seemly for an inferior being to initiate (cf. Gen. 3:9; 4:9; Ex. 4:21 in similar confrontations).

1:8 Satan can be expected to have noticed Job among all other human beings because of his exemplary life. Hence, *ki* = "for" (so RV), not "that" (D-G).

1:9 יָרֵא is not the participle with the force of a present tense, "Does Job fear God for nothing?", for the word order would then have been החנם איוב ירא אלהים. The verb is in the perfect tense, "Is it for nothing that Job has feared God?" Satan will not concede more than he must; Job has been God-fearing only up to the moment that Satan had last seen him and not an instant longer! (D-G). It may be noted that we have a Jewish Satan here, who answers a question by a question!

1:10 אַתְּ, the defectiva spelling, occurs in late as well as in earlier texts (as in I Sam. 24:19; Ps. 6:4; Ecc. 7:22; Neh. 9:6).

שַׂכְתָּ from *sūkh*, "hedge in," an ע״י root closely related to the ע״ע root *sākhakh*. In their orthography and vocalization the various forms of the Hebrew noun for "hedge" (Isa. 5:5, מְשׂוּכָה; Prov. 15:19, מְשֻׂכַת; Mic. 7:4, מְסוּכָה) reflect the Masoretic uncertainty as to which root underlies it. In our passage the "hedging in" is obviously a protection for man, not an obstacle on his path, as is the case in Job 3:23; 38:4; and Hos. 2:8.

1:11 אִם־לֹא = הֲלֹא, "indeed, surely" (cf. 17:2, and see Ges.-K. 149a). On אִם as an emphatic, like Arabic *inna*, cf. the Comm. on Job 6:13; 8:4; 14:5; 17:13; and Yel., p. 13.

עַל־פָּנֶיךָ = "to your face," i.e., "directly, impudently, without hesitation" (so most comm., rather than "immediately" as Rashi, whose view Ehrlich seeks to buttress by a reference to Deut. 7:10).

1:12 Satan obviously is forbidden to kill Job, for that would make the test impossible.

1:13 P omits יי both here and in v. 18; LXX omits it in v. 18 only. MT, which contains the word in both instances, is to be preferred here: a) on the principle of *difficilior lectio*, the common phrase being אכל ושתה as in I Sam. 30:16; I Ki. 11:25; Isa. 21:5; 22:13; Jer. 22:15; Ecc. 2:24; b) P exhibits the common practice of "levelling" and may have wished to avoid the inference that Job's children had been guilty of carousing to excess. On the significance of the LXX reading, see the Comm. on v. 18.

1:14 The impact of the narrative is heightened by its compression. The calamity is not described in the narrative. We are informed of the disaster exactly as Job hears it, in the impassioned words of each breathless survivor.

חרשות is fem. pl. with *baqar* (as in Gen. 33:13), where it is more appropriate, unless we are to assume here that cows rather than bulls were used for plowing.

1:15 שְׁבָא, the South Arabian people (Gen. 10:21), whose territory was located some twelve hundred miles south of Jerusalem, now familiar from the Sabean inscriptions. Elsewhere in the Bible, Sheba is mentioned for its trade and incense, gold, and precious stones (I Ki. 10:1 ff.; Isa. 60:4; Jer. 6:20; Ezek. 27:22; Joel 4:8; Ps. 72:10, 15). Our passage is the only reference to the Sabeans as raiders or bandits. On the problem raised by this apparent contradiction in our sources, see D-G, vol. I, pp. 16 f. Both Sheba and Kasdim here reflect an early period, before Sheba became a rich trading center and Kasdim the nucleus of the Babylonian empire. The well-known conservatism of folktales preserves the names unchanged into a later period, when both ethnic groups had attained to wealth and power, as virtually all other biblical references attest. In Gen. 22:21 Kesed is listed among the sons of Nahor along with Uz and Buz. Isa. 23:13 speaks of the Kasdim as עַם לֹא הָיָה, "the people that (once) had not been," but the text is difficult. This conception of Sheba and Kasdim as marauders is additional testimony to the antiquity of the Job tale in its oldest stage.

נפל Qal = "attack," used absolutely here, occurs with Beth (Jos. 11:7), with ʿ*al* (Jer. 48:32), and with ʾ*el* (Jer. 46:15). לקח = "take captive, seize," used of nonhuman objects (Nu. 21:25; Deut. 3:14; Jos. 11:19; I Sam. 2:16; 5:1; II Sam. 8:8), including animals like the hippopotamus (Job 40:24).

נְעָרִים = "slave boys," not Job's children. וָאִמָּלְטָה, the cohortative ending emphasizes the energy and the will involved in the messenger making good his escape (Ehr.).

1:16 אֵשׁ אלהים = "a great fire, i.e., lightning." On the use of the various divine names to express the superlative degree, cf. Gen. 10:9, גִּבּוֹר צַיִד לִפְנֵי ה'; Isa. 13:6, כְּשֹׁד מִשַּׁדַּי; and such formations as מַאְפֵּלְיָה (Jer. 2:31); שַׁלְהֶבֶתְיָה (Cant. 8:6); and possibly מֶרְחַבְיָה (Ps. 118:5).

In passages such as Nu. 11:1, 3; I Ki. 18:38, אֵשׁ ה' carries a stronger consciousness of the Divine origin of the fire, but the difference is only one of degree.

1:17 כשדים without the definite article like פלשתים (D-G) or = "some

Chaldeans" (Ehr). On the marauding character of the Chaldeans in our narrative, see the Comm. on v. 15. The reference is not to the builders of the army and the empire of Nebuchadnezzar, but to roving bands who were probably their nomadic ancestors in an earlier age.

ראשים "companies" (Jud. 7:20; 9:34; and I Sam. 11:11 with the verb *sūm*.

ויפשטו "swoop down upon" construed with ᶜal (Jud. 9:33) and with ᵓel (Jud. 20:37; I Sam. 27:8; 30:1), the prepositions being generally interchangeable in biblical Hebrew. The suggested derivation from the meaning "strip off, make a dash from a sheltered place" (BDB) is less likely than from the meaning common in rabbinic Hebrew, "stretch out, spread out," as, for example, *M. Shab.* 1:1, פשט העני את ידו "if the poor man stretches out his hand" (also *M. Men.* 1:2 and often). On the other hand, there is no need to assume (with TS) that our verb represents an ellipsis for ויפשטו ידיהם בגדוד "they stretched out their hands in a troop," on the basis of the rabbinic phrase occurring in *B. Ber.* 3b.

It was long maintained that the camel was not domesticated in the second millennium B.C.E., but this position is no longer tenable in view of recent research. See the exhaustive bibliography *apud* Terrien, *Job, Poet of Existence*, pp. 56 f., n. 3.

1:18 עַד should be vocalized as עֹד, as in vv. 16, 17, in spite of the authenticated use of the conjunction עַד "while" (Jud. 3:26; I Sam. 14:19; Jonah 4:2) (ag. Yel.). It is significant that LXX, which preserves יַיִן in v. 13, omits it here. Its omission here is supported by metric considerations (see Special Note 6); on the other hand, its occurrence in the prose passage in v. 13 is original (see above). The process of leveling led the Hebrew scribe to add it in our passage here, and led P to omit it in v. 13, as well as here.

1:19 רוח גדולה, "a mighty wind," is expressed in Gen. 1:2 by רוח אלהים. On the use of the Divine name for superlatives, see the Comm. on v. 16. נערים here = "children," unlike vv. 15, 16, 17, where it means "servants." The servants may, however, be included in the term here as well.

1:20 וַיָּגָז אֶת־רֹאשׁוֹ has been rendered "tore his hair" (Ra., Yel., who compares Targum on Jer. 7:29) (תלש for גזז). See also Ezra 9:3. However, such uncontrolled paroxysms of grief would not be in keeping with the stoic quality of Job's bearing under adversity in the Prose Tale. Moreover, the references to the mourning rite of rending the garments (II Sam. 3:31; 13:19; Joel 2:13, which may be referred to in Ps. 35:15 and Ecc. 3:7; see *KMW ad loc.*) suggest that we have here the widespread mourning custom of shaving the head to make it bald (Isa. 15:2; 22:12; Jer. 7:29; 16:6; Mic. 1:16; Ezek. 9:3). This making of a tonsure the Torah sought to prohibit (Lev. 21:5; Deut. 14:1), probably because it was a pagan rite, but, as the biblical references indicate, with relatively little success. Bending to the ground and worshipping constituted additional mourning rites through which the mourner expressed his submission to the Divine power and his acceptance of its fiat.

Ugaritic has revealed that the common biblical verb *hištaḥavah*, long regarded as the Hithpael of *šḥw*, is to be derived from the root *ḥwy* in the Shaphel conjugation, corresponding to the tenth conjugation in Arabic. Cf. Gordon, *UT*, p. 395.

1:21 יָצָתִי is a defectiva spelling for יָצָאתִי, perhaps representing an assimilation of the *tertiae Aleph* root to *tertiae Yod*, a process completed in mishnaic Hebrew. שָׁמָּה is referred by Rashi to the earth whence man came or to his mother, now in the land of the dead. Similarly, Ben Sira applies the biblical description of Eve (Gen. 3:20) to the earth, from which man emerges and to which he returns:

עסק גדול חלק אל   ועול כבד על בני אדם

מיום צאתו מרחם אמו   עד יום בואו אל אם כל חי

A great concern has God assigned,
a heavy burden, to the sons of men,
from the day man comes forth from his mother's womb,
until he returns to the Mother of all the living. (40:1)

So, too, Ps. 139:15 refers to the womb of mother earth. There is no need, however, to press for any such identification here. Compared to the concrete evidence of life on earth, the shadowy existence of Sheol after death, which is a basic concept of biblical thought, is virtually on a par with the non-existence of the period before birth.

This use of שמה as a euphemism for the period after life, hence the grave, finds a parallel not only in the Egyptian idiom "they are there" (Hö.) and in the Greek *ekei* (Euripides, *Medea*, 1.1065), but in biblical usage as well. Cf. Ecc. 3:17, "for there is a proper time for everything and every deed — over there!" (See *KMW*, pp. 224 f., and Job 3:19.)

The use of the Divine name JHVH by Job, a non-Israelite, is entirely comprehensible in a Hebrew ritual formula. We may note its occurrence in another common phrase יַד ה' עָשְׂתָה זֹּאת cited in Job 12:9 from Isa. 41:20. These instances offer additional evidence of the Hebrew origin of the book, all the more impressive because they are unconscious and unreflective.

The formula used in northern Arabia when a death has taken place, "The Lord has taken him" (Kraeling, p. 184), may be reminiscent of our passage.

1:22 תִּפְלָה has been unnecessarily emended to עוֹלָה, נְבָלָה or תְּפִלָּה (= "protest," Ehr.). The meaning is clear from the noun תָּפֵל "tasteless, unseasoned food" (Job 6:8), "unsatisfactory prophecies" (Lam. 2:14). Our noun means "emptiness, worthlessness" (Jer. 23:13), "unseemliness, wrong" (Job 24:14). It may be related to the Arabic *tifl*, "spittle" (TS).

Nāthan like *yāhabh*, lit. "give, attribute," as in *nāthan kābhōd* (I Sam. 6:5), *nāthan ʿōz* (Ps. 68:35; Ps. 29:1 ff.). It is here used in a negative connotation, hence "charge, impute." The closing clause is to be rendered, "He did not impute anything wrong to God."

Chapter 2

2:1 LXX omits the second לְהִתְיַצֵּב עַל־ה׳, "to stand in the Lord's presence" (so D-G, Ehr., Hö., TS, NAB, and many moderns). However, the deletion would deprive the passage of a very special nuance. When used the first time, the phrase means "to stand in God's presence, like courtiers" (as in 1:6). The second time, the phrase bears the connotation of the insolence and rebelliousness of the Satan vis-à-vis his Master (so Yel). For the first of these two distinct connotations of the verb *hithyaṣṣēbh* see Zech. 6:5; for the second see Nu. 16:27; Deut. 7:24; Ps. 2:2. The repetition of the same phrase with a different implication each time gives an ironic overtone to the verse. For another striking instance of the repetition of a phrase with different connotations, cf. וַיֵּלְכוּ שְׁנֵיהֶם יַחְדָּו, occurring in the narrative of the sacrifice of Isaac (Gen. 22:6, 8). The first time, the clause indicates that Abraham and Isaac walked off separately, leaving the slaves behind. The second time, after Isaac has inquired as to the animal for the sacrifice and Abraham has given his son the evasive but nonetheless clear indication of who the sacrifice is to be, the clause means, "they walked off together, of one mind." On the first connotation of *yahdāv*, "separately," cf. Ezek. 4:3. On the second, "of one mind," cf. Am. 3:3.

2:2 In accordance with the immemorial practice of subordinates vis-à-vis their superiors, whether in the army or in other areas, the Satan offers the Lord as little information as possible. He makes no reference to Job or to the effect that his trials have had upon him.

2:3 The Lord obviously is not in need of Satan's help in learning what has taken place, since He is all-knowing. The Vav consecutive with the imperfect in וַתְּסִיתֵנִי cannot mean "although" (D-G ag. RSV, NAB). It is best rendered, "But, yet you have incited Me" (cf. Gen. 32:3, "I have seen God face to face וַתִּנָּצֵל and yet my soul is delivered"; Deut. 4:33 וַיֶּחִי "and yet live"; 5:23; Jud. 1:35, etc.; see Driver, *HT*, sec. 74b).
    ותסיתני, "incite, lead astray" (cf. Deut. 13:7; Jos. 15:18, etc.), is a bold anthropomorphism (so Ibn E.). It is in keeping with the image of the Lord in the unsophisticated folktale. The verb is never used in a favorable sense (ag. TS, P.). In Job 36:16; II Chr. 18:31, etc., the Hiphil of the verb *sūth* does not mean "incite, induce," but "withdraw, remove, save," and is virtually synonymous with the Hiphil of *sūr*. It may well be an entirely distinct root. In these two latter instances it is therefore followed by the particle Mem, whereas in its basic meaning it takes the acc. of pers. and is governed by a Bet. To declare that the Lord "gives Satan credit for instigating the experience" (P.) is to overlook the Lord's obvious displeasure at Job's unmerited suffering. In view of the inherently negative character of ותסיתני, חנם does not modify the verb, "You would incite Me without reason" (so Hö.), but rather לבלעו, "to destroy him without reason."

לְבַלְּעוֹ, "to destroy," cf. Isa. 3:12. The Talmud (*B. Hagigah* 5a) makes the moving comment, "When Rabbi Johanan reached this verse he wept, saying, 'When it is possible to incite a master against his servant, is there any hope for his servant's restoration?'"

2:4 עוֹר בְּעַד עוֹר. The cryptic and enigmatic character of the phrase bears all the earmarks of a folk-saying which has been stripped down to its essentials by dint of repetition. It is noteworthy that the entire verse is in 3‖3 meter, which testifies to its proverbial character.

Among the various explanations offered for the opening phrase are: 1) One part of the body for another, i.e., a man will interpose his arm to save his head (so Tar., Ra., Ibn E., Del., D-G, Ehr.). However, ᶜor does not mean "a part of the body." 2) One layer of skin for another (so Bu.). There is no evidence, however, for this differentiation in the noun ᶜor. In Arabic two distinct nouns are used for the outer and the inner layer of skin. 3) "One skin (lies) upon (or about) another" (Sch., Merx). 4) TS renders: "skin before skin" (i.e., "there are layers of skin protecting his soul"), but his interpretation, q.v., is far too involved. 5) Both the usage of the noun and the context suggest that it is best to interpret "a man will give anyone else's skin on behalf of, i.e., to save his own skin" (so Ros., Hupf., Da., Du., Thilo, Hö.). In addition to several Arabic proverbs cited by Thilo, Hö. cites the parallel *rāᵓs birāᵓs*, "one head (of cattle) for another" (R. Dozy, *Supplément*, vol. I, p. 494), and the German saying *Wurst wider* (or *um*) *Wurst*, "tit for tat," lit., "sausage for sausage." The phrase may have originated in the barter practices of the nomadic Bedouins. This interpretation is most appropriate to Job's situation, his children having been lost while he is still alive. It also does justice to the meaning of ᶜor, "skin," and beᶜad, "in exchange for." Ter. perceptively notes that a distinction is here being introduced between the early Semitic and Hebraic conception of collective personality and that of individual destiny.

The Vav of וְכֹל is epexegetical, "namely, all a man has, etc." It is therefore unnecessary to read . . . עוֹר בְּעַד עוֹרוֹ, כֹּל (ag. D-G).

There is no need to assume that LXX and P read לְאִישׁ instead of MT לָאִישׁ (ag. D-G, TS). While the indefinite noun may be used for a general statement, as in Cant. 8:7, the definite article is excellent classical Hebrew; cf. Gen. 9:6; I Sam. 9:9.

2:5 אֶל־עַצְמוֹ וְאֶל־בְּשָׂרוֹ = "his own flesh and blood, i.e., his own person." Cf. Gen. 2:23; 29:14. For the closing clause see the Comm. on 1:11.

2:6 The condition the Lord interposes is, of course, entirely reasonable and indeed necessary. Were Satan permitted to slay Job, it would be impossible to assay the effects of the trial upon him.

2:7 שְׁחִין (cf. Ex. 9:9f.; Deut. 28:27; and Arabic *sahuna*, "to be hot, inflamed") is a malignant ulcer identified by some scholars with elephantiasis because of various references in the book to the swelling of the skin, its blackening (30:30), the growth of maggots on the skin, its cracking and fluid emissions (7:5), as well as such psychological symptoms as onsets of terror (3:25; 6:4) and nightmares (7:4, 14). Most probably the author had no specific disease in mind — he seeks to give a picture of Job physically afflicted, loathsome in appearance, and isolated from the warmth of human fellowship.

The K. עַד and the Q. וְעַד are both equally satisfactory. This is one more indication that the Qere is not a "correction" of the Kethib, as was demonstrated long ago in *BTM*. Whether the variations arose through dittography or haplography cannot be determined.

2:8 לְהִתְגָּרֵד, "to scrape oneself," a root common in rabbinic Hebrew (cf. *M. Shab.* 8:6; *B. Shab.* 81a).

Job sits on the ash-heap outside the city, not as a sign of mourning (Ibn E.), but rather because of the contagious character of his disease and his loathsome appearance. (Note the ordinance for the leper's isolation in Lev. 13 passim, esp. vv. 45 f.) Del. cites Wetzstein's vivid description of the dung-heap in Hauran towns and villages, *mezbele* (cf. rabbinic Hebrew *zebhel*, "dung, manure," *M. Shab.* 4:1; 8:5, and often): "The dung . . . is carried in baskets in a dry state to that place outside the village and is there generally burnt, the ashes remaining. . . . Often the *mezbele* attains a height far greater than that of the place itself. . . . There lies the outcast, who, smitten by loathsome disease, is no longer admitted to the dwellings of men."

2:9 On the role of Job's wife, see *BGM*, pp. 10 f., 71 f., 223). She was greatly sinned against by St. Augustine, who called her *adiutrix diaboli*, "the helpmeet of the devil," as well as by St. John Chrysostom and T. K. Cheyne, who insists that one of Job's trials was that his wife was *not* taken! Her laconic plea to Job is expanded in the Septuagint into a moving rhetorical address in the Greek tradition. She is pictured far more sympathetically in the Testament of Job and in rabbinic literature (*BGM*, p. 226). Ter. cleverly describes her advice to Job as "a theological method for practicing euthanasia!" On בָּרֵךְ, a euphemism for "curse," cf. the Comm. on 1:11.

2:10 There is no need to emend the imperfect תְּדַבְּרִי in MT to the perfect דִּבַּרְתְּ, in spite of LXX and P, which translate the verb in the past (ag. D-G). The force of the imperfect in MT is not "will you speak?" (so Du., D-G), but "are you speaking, do you talk?" It is noteworthy that Job does not call his wife a *nebhālāh*, but only that she speaks like one. His oblique mode of chastisement, like his effort to win her over to his own faith in God, testifies to his recognition that her bitter words came out of her love and concern for him (so Ter.).

The noun *nābhāl* is rendered by KJV as "fool," as in the famous passage in Ps. 14:1: "The fool says in his heart, 'There is no God.' " However, the root, both in the concrete as well as in the abstract *nebhālāh*, refers not to intellectual weakness but to moral obtuseness and blindness to religious truth, as in our context. It signifies desecration (Jos. 7:15), immorality (Gen. 34:7; Deut. 22:21; II Sam. 13:12), and churlishness of manner coupled with penuriousness (I Sam. 25:25). The latter idea is evident, also, in Isa. 32:5, where the *nābhāl* is equated with the "miser." It is moral rather than intellectual folly which is basic to the root. The equation of stupidity and sin is, of course, a basic insight of Wisdom literature.

Merx, Sieg., Yel. and many moderns vocalize אֵת גַּם as גַּם אַתְּ and attach the two words to the opening clause: "Like an impious woman you, too, speak." Hebrew usage, however, would dictate that the particle אֵת be repeated before הַטּוֹב parallel to וְאֶת־הָרָע. If this vocalization were to be adopted, we would need to assume the haplography תְּדַבְּרִי גַּם אַתְּ אֶת־הַטּוֹב וְגוֹ'. MT is preferable, not only because it avoids the necessity of assuming an error in the text, but because "you, too" would be irrelevant here, since no one else has spoken thus far. גַּם is emphatic. "Shall we indeed accept the good?" (so BDB, s.v. *gam* II, p. 169a).

The root *kibbel* occurs only in late biblical books in the meaning "receive, take" (Est. 4:4; 9:27; Ezra 8:30; I Chr. 12:19; 21:11; II Chr. 29:16, 22), and is very common in Aramaic. It has therefore been usually described as a late Aramaism. Note, however, its occurrence in Pr. 19:20 and its use in a special technical sense in Ex. 26:25; 36:12. Finally, W. F. Albright discovered our root in a Canaanite proverb in the Tel-el Amarna Letters of the 14th cent. B.C.E. (*BASOR*, no. 89, 1943, pp. 29 ff.). On the dangers of undue dogmatism in dating a word as "late," see our observations in the *Louis Ginzberg Jubilee Volume* (Eng. vol., New York, 1945), pp. 74 f., and the instances there adduced. It is also necessary to avoid lumping all Aramaisms together. On the four distinct categories of Aramaisms in biblical Hebrew, see *BGM*, pp. 161–63.

בִּשְׂפָתָיו is pressed by the Talmud (*B. Baba Batra* 16a) to mean "Job did not sin with his lips, but in his heart he did" (so Ra.). Ibn E. sees in the phrase a hint that Job had not thus far sinned with his lips, but would do so in the future. Actually, as Ehr. correctly insists, neither implication is here intended. Cf. Ps. 39:2, "I guard my way from sinning with my tongue." Purity of speech reflects the integrity of one's spirit.

With this verse, the poet's version of the folktale draws to a close, and the jointure written by the poet begins (so also Hö.). On the implications for the composition of the book and the Higher Critical issues involved, as well as on the Alt-Macdonald theory of two independent prose tales, which we find unacceptable, cf. *BGM*, pp. 72–75 and notes.

2:11   For the news to reach the Friends in their several countries and for them to arrange for a meeting suggest that Job's suffering has extended over a considerable period of time.

On the Near Eastern provenance of the names of the Friends and their places or origin, see *BGM*, pp. 66 f. The names of the Friends are all drawn from the Pentateuch, primarily from the genealogy of Esau in Genesis,

chap. 36. Eliphaz occurs there as the oldest son of Esau (36:4), and Teman
is the son of Eliphaz (36:11), in addition to being the well-known district in
Arabia. Zophar is the LXX reading for the Masoretic *ṣephō* in Gen. 36:11.
It contains the same consonants as *Zippor*, the father of Balak, king of Moab
(Nu. 22:2). *Naᶜamāh* is the name of a female descendant of Cain (Gen.
4:21) and of an Ammonite princess married to King Solomon (I Ki. 14:21).
Šuaḥ is the name of a son of Abraham by his concubine, Keturah (Gen.
25:2 = I Chr. 1:32). *Bildad* does not occur outside of *Job*, but its two elements
have analogues in the biblical text. The first element occurs in such non-
Hebrew names as Bilhah (Gen. 30:4), Bilᶜam (Nu. 22:5) and Bilhan, a
descendant of Esau (Gen. 36:27). The second element enters into the names
of Eldad and Medad, the mysterious figures who break into prophecy in the
wilderness (Nu. 11:26 f.). The first element of the name *bil* is the Akkadian
pronunciation of the name of the familiar Semitic deity. The second element
dad from the basic Semitic root *dwd* "to love" may be the name, or an epithet,
for a local god worshipped in Trans-Jordan; it occurs in Mesha Inscription,
line 12, as *dwdh*. The root occurs as a proper name in Tel-el-Amarna Letters
44 and 45, in Palmyrene and Aramaic, and in Hebrew as *dōdō* (Jud. 10:1,
David and *Dodawyahu* (II Chr. 20:37).

In this regard, the name *Job* is totally different. While it has early Oriental analogues (see the Comm. on 1:1) and is referred to in Ezekiel, chap. 14
together with Noah and Dan'el, it does not occur in early Hebrew literature.
This observation lends support to the view, though it obviously does not
prove it, that the poet utilized an ancient Oriental folk tradition about Job,
in which the Friends played no part, as a framework for the poetry. He then
created the three Friends to serve as protagonists in the Dialogue, adding a
jointure in the Prologue (2:11–13) and in the Epilogue (42:7–10), to link
the prose and the poetry. In giving names to these characters, the poet turned
to the classical Hebrew sources with which he was familiar for names appropriate to non-Hebrew characters.

This distinction between Job and the names of his Friends militates
against the theory of A. Alt (*ZAW*, vol. 14, 1937, pp. 265–68, adopted in
varying form by MacDonald and E. Kraeling, *The Book of the Ways of God*,
New York, 1938, p. 169) that there were two folktales originally and that the
Friends, like Job's wife, urged him to blaspheme against God. The economy
of the narrative opposes the assumption that both Job's wife and the Friends
would represent the same standpoint. For other decisive objections to the
Alt-Macdonald theory, see *BGM*, pp. 72 f. and notes.

Eliphaz is mentioned first as the oldest and, as it turns out, the most
urbane of the Friends. וַיִּוָּעֲדוּ "they arranged to meet" before coming to Job,
instead of arriving separately. Their joint appearance would have a greater
effect on their suffering friend and at the same time would minimize the
unpleasantness involved in seeing him so degraded and deformed.

הַבָּאָה with its penultimate accent is the perfect, not the participle (ag.
LXX). The particle *ha* is relative, as in Gen. 21:3, הַנּוֹלַד־לוֹ. Hence our verb
is to be rendered "that had come upon him."

נוּד lit. "to shake the head in sympathy," hence to offer consolation (Isa. 51:19; Jer. 15:5; Nah. 3:7; Jer. 16:5; 22:10).

2:12 מֵרָחוֹק "from afar off," since the dung-heap was often higher than the village (cf. the Comm. above on v. 8).

הַשָּׁמַיְמָה is omitted by LXX, a procedure accepted by most commentators (e.g., Hö.), who find the noun unnecessary, if not meaningless. The clause is then taken to describe the usual mourning act of putting dust on one's head (I Sam. 4:12; II Sam. 13:19, and elsewhere; so D-G). However, this rite is never expressed by the root זרק, and the deletion of the noun השמימה cannot be accounted for easily (so D-G). TS (1926) brilliantly suggested that הַשָּׁמַיְמָה is to be read מַשְׁמִים, "desolate." In the third version of his commentary, TS reads הַשָּׁמֵם, which is grammatically more defensible in view of the plural subject. He cites Ezek. 3:15 וָאֵשֵׁב שָׁם שִׁבְעַת יָמִים מַשְׁמִים; Ezra 9:3, וָאֵשְׁבָה מְשׁוֹמֵם; and Micah 6:13 הַשְׁמֵם עַל חַטֹּאתֶךָ. However, in all these passages it is the mourner himself who is being described by the term, and the same consideration militates against deleting השמימה, since putting dust on one's head is the act of the mourner, and not of his comforters.

In an unpublished paper, the late Barnett A. Elzas suggested what we believe to be the correct interpretation of our passage, without recourse to emendation. When the visitors see Job in his affliction, they throw dust over their heads heavenwards, as an apotropaic rite, in order to ward off the evil from themselves. Almost the identical practice has survived in ultra-Orthodox Jewish circles. At a funeral, the participants tear some grass from the plot after the burial and throw it backwards over their shoulders, reciting the enigmatic passage in Ps. 72:16 וְיָצִיצוּ מֵעִיר כְּעֵשֶׂב הָאָרֶץ, "And may men blossom forth from the city like the grass of the field" (RSV). The ritual is interpreted as a reference to immortality. The original apotropaic character of the practice has obviously been forgotten. Traditional Judaism, like all religion, possesses other apotropaic rites of a similar kind which have been reinterpreted, such as the breaking of a glass at the conclusion of a wedding, or the pouring out of wine at the Seder table when the ten plagues are mentioned (see Gordis, *Judaism for the Modern Age*, New York, 1955, pp. 135 f.). Apotropaic rites of this character are, of course, universal. Thus Dean Leslie F. Harris, of the Memorial University in Newfoundland, reports that when he was a youngster and would go berry-picking, "my grandmother would give me a bun of fresh bread. When you heard fairies talking, you had to throw it over your left shoulder." The fairies who were feared were euphemistically called "the good people" (*New York Times*, Dec. 22, 1968, sec. 1, p. 18).

2:13 The conduct of the Friends in Job's presence became ritualized in the laws of mourning in rabbinic Judaism. Many of these customs, however, were already observed in the biblical period. Such are the rending of the garments (Gen. 37:29, 34; Joel 2:13, etc.; see also *KMW* on Ecc. 3:7) and the seven-day mourning period (*shibhᶜah*), when the mourners sit on the ground (Lam. 2:10) and do not go outdoors. We believe this to be the significance of Mic. 1:11, *lo yāṣᵊʾāh yōšebhet ṣaᶜanān*, "the inhabitants of Zaᶜanan do not come forth." Another ritual derived from our passage is the practice that visitors remain silent until the mourner speaks first (*B. Moed Katan* 28b).

כְּאֵב not merely physical suffering (ag. D-G), but also spiritual pain (Isa. 17:11; 65:15; Jer. 15:18). Hence, "anguish, agony."

With regard to the origin and the character of the Prose Tale, there are substantial considerations against the view that the prose and the poetry are two distinct and independent compositions, each unknown to the author of the other and joined together by an editor, or that originally there was an altogether different Prose Tale now lost, or that there were originally two independent prose tales joined into one.

Perhaps the most widely held view is that the poet took an old folk-tale and attached it in its original form to his poetical work. In recent years, the conclusion is frequently added that the Prose Tale is a very old composition, going back to the First Temple period. We find this last view untenable as well.

On literary grounds, the narrative is no naive folk-tale, but a work of superior literary art. The architectonic structure of the story (see Intr. Note to the Prologue), the energy and the economy of the narrative, the subtle delineation of character and the touches of irony in the dialogue between God and Satan represent a high level of sophistication.

On linguistic grounds, it is true that the vocabulary and the style are reminiscent of the finest examples of the Golden Age of biblical Hebrew, thus testifying both to the author's familiarity with Israel's traditional literature and to his ability to imitate the style of *Genesis* and *Samuel* (cf. *ᶜabhūdāh*, 1:3, *qᵉsīṭāh*, 42:11, *zāqēn uśᵉbhaᶜ yāmīm*, 42:17). Nevertheless, several tell-tale signs of late biblical Hebrew make it clear that the provenience of the Prose Tale is to be sought in the post-exilic period. Cf. the Aramaism *qibbēl* (2:10), on which see *BGM*, p. 345, n. 32, and some other examples of late Hebrew usage to which attention has been called by A. Hurvitz ("The Date of the Prose Tale of Job Linguistically Reconsidered," *HTR*, vol. 67, 1974, pp. 17–34), such as *hithyaṣṣēbh ᶜal* (1:6; 2:1) as against the earlier *liphᵉnei, hithpallēl ᶜal* (42:8) as against the classical *bᵉᶜad* (but see Comm.), and *ʾaḥᵃrei zōth* (42:16).

The post-exilic author of the Prose Tale is archaizing, another striking instance of which may be found in the book of Ruth. Here too we have a narrative that recalls the style of *Judges* and *Samuel*, with only a few marks of the author's later period. See our study, "Love, Marriage and Business in the Book of Ruth — A Study in Hebrew Customary Law," reprinted in *WB*, pp. 84–108.

Our view on the origin and character of the Prose Tale and its relationship to the poetry may be set forth briefly as follows. The poet, concerned with the problem of human suffering, needed a frmework for his work. He found it in the traditional tale of a sufferer named Job, who maintains his faith and integrity, and is triumphantly restored to his former estate. The poet proceeds to retell the story, keeping the main features of the well-known tale intact, even when various discrepancies between the Prose Tale and his poetic Dialogue are involved. He then effects the transition from the prose Prologue to the poetic Dialogue, and from the Dialogue to the prose Epilogue by means of two brief jointures (2:11–13 and 42:7–10 respectively), which serve as a superb background for his great poetic achievement (see *BGM*, pp. 65–75, 163 f.).

THE DIALOGUE

Job's Lament (3)

Job breaks the silence with a lament on his cruel fate. His words are addressed neither to his friends, of whose presence he is only dimly aware, nor to God, whom he does not yet directly charge with his calamities.

Job curses the day of his birth, which marked his entrance into the land of the living. How much better it would have been if he had never been conceived or, failing that, had died in his mother's womb, or had perished at the moment of birth. Even to be an untimely birth and thus be deprived of a proper burial would have been preferable to his present lot.

Were he dead he would be in Sheol, the land of shadows, where kings and princes fare no better than slaves, and where the oppressor and his victim are equally at rest. Why is life given to men who suffer and would rejoice if death came? So he, too, wishes to escape from his life which is an unending succession of terrors.

3   Afterwards, Job began to speak and cursed the day of his birth. Job
2   spoke, saying,
3   Perish the day when I was born,
               and the night that said:
               "A man-child is conceived."
4   That day — may it be darkness!
               Let God not seek it from above
               and no light shine upon it.
5   Let blackness and gloom reclaim it;
               may clouds rest upon it
               and the demons of the day terrify it.
6   That night — may deep darkness capture it!
               Let it not be counted in the days of the year
               or enter in the number of months.
7   May that night be lonely as a crag
               and no joyful sounds penetrate it.
8   Let them curse it who rouse the Sea,
               those skilled in stirring up Leviathan.
9   Let the stars of its dawn be dark;
               may it hope for light, but have none,
               nor see the eyelids of the morning,
10   because it did not shut the doors of my mother's womb
               and thus hide misery from my eyes.

11   Why did I not die in the womb?
               Or perish as I came forth from it?
12   Why were there knees to receive me?
               And why breasts for me to suck?
13   For then I should have lain down and been quiet,
               I should have slept and been at peace,
14   with kings and counselors of the earth
               who rebuild ruined cities for themselves;
15   or with princes rich in gold
               who fill their houses with silver.

16   Or even if I had been an aborted birth,
               like the stillborn infants who never see the light.

17   There the wicked cease their raging:
               There their victims are at rest.
18   All the prisoners are at ease,
               they hear the taskmaster's shouts no more.
19   There the small and the great are equal
               and the slave is free from his master.

ג א אַחֲרֵי־כֵן פָּתַח אִיּוֹב אֶת־פִּיהוּ וַיְקַלֵּל אֶת־יוֹמוֹ:

2 וַיַּעַן אִיּוֹב וַיֹּאמַר:

3 וְהַלַּיְלָה אָמַר הֹרָה גָבֶר: יֹאבַד יוֹם אִוָּלֶד בּוֹ

4 אַל־יִדְרְשֵׁהוּ אֱלוֹהַּ מִמָּעַל הַיּוֹם הַהוּא יְהִי חֹשֶׁךְ

ה וְאַל־תּוֹפַע עָלָיו נְהָרָה: יִגְאָלֻהוּ חֹשֶׁךְ וְצַלְמָוֶת

תִּשְׁכָּן־עָלָיו עֲנָנָה יְבַעֲתֻהוּ כִּמְרִירֵי יוֹם:

6 הַלַּיְלָה הַהוּא יִקָּחֵהוּ אֹפֶל אַל־יִחַדְּ בִּימֵי שָׁנָה

7 בְּמִסְפַּר יְרָחִים אַל־יָבֹא: הִנֵּה הַלַּיְלָה הַהוּא יְהִי גַלְמוּד

8 אַל־תָּבֹא רְנָנָה בוֹ: יִקְּבֻהוּ אֹרְרֵי־יוֹם

9 הָעֲתִידִים עֹרֵר לִוְיָתָן: יֶחְשְׁכוּ כּוֹכְבֵי נִשְׁפּוֹ

יְקַו־לְאוֹר וָאַיִן וְאַל־יִרְאֶה בְּעַפְעַפֵּי־שָׁחַר:

י כִּי לֹא סָגַר דַּלְתֵי בִטְנִי וַיַּסְתֵּר עָמָל מֵעֵינָי:

11 לָמָּה לֹא מֵרֶחֶם אָמוּת מִבֶּטֶן יָצָאתִי וְאֶגְוָע:

12 מַדּוּעַ קִדְּמוּנִי בִרְכָּיִם וּמַה־שָּׁדַיִם כִּי אִינָק:

13 כִּי־עַתָּה שָׁכַבְתִּי וְאֶשְׁקוֹט יָשַׁנְתִּי אָז ׀ יָנוּחַ לִי:

14 עִם־מְלָכִים וְיֹעֲצֵי אָרֶץ הַבֹּנִים חֳרָבוֹת לָמוֹ:

טו אוֹ עִם־שָׂרִים זָהָב לָהֶם הַמְמַלְאִים בָּתֵּיהֶם כָּסֶף:

16 אוֹ כְנֵפֶל טָמוּן לֹא אֶהְיֶה כְּעֹלְלִים לֹא־רָאוּ אוֹר:

17 שָׁם רְשָׁעִים חָדְלוּ רֹגֶז וְשָׁם יָנוּחוּ יְגִיעֵי כֹחַ:

18 יַחַד אֲסִירִים שַׁאֲנָנוּ לֹא שָׁמְעוּ קוֹל נֹגֵשׂ:

19 קָטֹן וְגָדוֹל שָׁם הוּא וְעֶבֶד חָפְשִׁי מֵאֲדֹנָיו:

20   Why is light given to the sufferer
          and life to embittered souls
21   who long for death — but it comes not —
          and dig for it more than for buried treasure,
22   who would exult in great joy
          and be happy to find a grave?
23   Why is life given to the man whose way is hidden,
          whom God has fenced in?

24   Indeed, my sighing comes like my daily bread,
          my groans are poured out like water.
25   For the fear I had has come upon me,
          and what I dreaded has overtaken me.
26   I have no ease, no peace, no rest.
          What has come is agony.

‏כ לָמָּה יִתֵּן לְעָמֵל אֹור וְחַיִּים לְמָרֵי נָפֶשׁ:‏

‏21 הַמְחַכִּים לַמָּוֶת וְאֵינֶנּוּ וַיַּחְפְּרֻהוּ מִמַּטְמֹונִים:‏

‏22 הַשְּׂמֵחִים אֱלֵי־גִיל יָשִׂישׂוּ כִּי יִמְצְאוּ־קָבֶר:‏

‏23 לְגֶבֶר אֲשֶׁר־דַּרְכֹּו נִסְתָּרָה וַיָּסֶךְ אֱלֹוהַּ בַּעֲדֹו:‏

‏24 כִּי־לִפְנֵי לַחְמִי אַנְחָתִי תָבֹא וַיִּתְּכוּ כַמַּיִם שַׁאֲגֹתָי:‏

‏כה כִּי פַחַד פָּחַדְתִּי וַיֶּאֱתָיֵנִי וַאֲשֶׁר יָגֹרְתִּי יָבֹא לִי:‏

‏26 לֹא שָׁלַוְתִּי ׀ וְלֹא שָׁקַטְתִּי וְלֹא־נָחְתִּי וַיָּבֹא רֹגֶז:‏

Chapter 3

On the metric structure of chap. 3, see Special Note 7.

3:1 יוֹמוֹ clearly "the day of his birth"' (so most, ag. Ehr.). Cf. יוֹם מַלְכֵּנוּ (Hos. 7:5), either "the king's birthday" or "the king's coronation anniversary."

3:2 וַיַּעַן not "answer," Arab. ʿana (tertiae ya), but "break into speech, intone, chant" (Arab. ghana (tertiae ya), "sing"), hence "begin to speak." The verb can therefore occur at the beginning of a chant or of an address, as, e.g., Ex. 15:21; Deut. 26:5 (cf. Ra., Ibn E.), and not as a response to another speaker.

3:3 The sinewy character of biblical poetry is nowhere clearer than in this opening stich, which is stripped bare of the definite article or the relative pronoun. For this reason one would also have expected *laylah* without the article. The use of the article may have been induced by *hayyom* in the next verse.

LXX: *hodou arsen*, "behold a male," does not presuppose a reading הִנֵּה זָכָר. The demonstrative in the Greek may represent the mishnaic Hebrew הֲרֵי = "here is." For another instance of postbiblical Hebrew, attested to by LXX, cf. Amos 9:6 וַאֲגֻדָּתוֹ, which it renders *epangelian*, "promise," treating the noun as the Aramaized mishnaic form וַאֲגָדָתוֹ. The noun גֶּבֶר, which need not be emended to זָכָר, means a male child, with the connotation of health and vigor.

הֹרָה not a Hiphil = "my father taught my mother to become pregnant" (Ra.), or a Pual, though it resembles it externally, since there is no Piel of the root *hārāh*. The form is the Qal passive of הָרָה; cf. יֻלַּד (Gen. 4:26 and often).

The sequence of ילד and הרה has troubled some commentators, as though the verse were a physiological report rather than a line of poetry. The poet needs two terms which he uses as synonyms to express his entrance into the world, so that it is irrelevant whether Job laments his birth or his conception (ag. D-G). Ibn. E. noted, too, the use of *hārāh* in a prose context as equivalent to *yālad* (I Chr. 4:17).

וְלַיְלָה אָמַר, not "the night in which one announced" (Ra., Ibn E.), but "the night that said." Though not entirely parallel, the personification of "day" and "night" in Ps. 19:3; Job 32:7 is to be noted.

3:4 הַיּוֹם הַהוּא "that day, i.e. each year when the day comes round" (Ra.) In a poetic context there is no need to argue about the logical inconsistency of Job's first demanding that the day be destroyed (vv. 2, 3) and then (v. 4) calling for it to be consigned to darkness, the primordial condition of the world before creation, a theme carried on in 5a. נְהָרָה is a Hebraized form of the Aramaic noun נְהוֹרָא, the determinative Aleph becoming a He, and the gender therefore becoming fem. The process of femininizing masculine Aramaic nouns is widespread in modern Hebrew, which has borrowed liberally from talmudic Aramaic.

3:5 יִגְאָלֻהוּ not "pollute it," as in Isa. 63:2; Mal. 1:7 (Ra., Ibn E.), but "redeem it, by restoring it to its original condition of darkness before creation" (Gen. 1:2). Underlying the usage is the Hebrew institution of the Jubilee and the practice of the restoration of land to its original owner by payment (Lev., chap. 25; Ruth, chap. 4). עֲנָנָה, a collective noun, the force of which is not transmitted by the English "clouds," but by the German *Gewölke*. צַלְמָוֶת "deep darkness" (Arab. *ẓalmatun* "darkness"; Akk. *salāmu*; Eth. *salama*, "be black, dark," originally צַלְמוּת. The familiar Masoretic vocalization is a folk etymology, "the shadow of death." It is much older than the Masorah, and probably was part of the living language. This is attested by the LXX *skia thanatou*.

כִּמְרִירֵי יוֹם is emended by many moderns to כַּמְרִירֵי, and rendered "blacknesses of the day," based on the Syriac cognate *kamar*, "to be black." Not only does this procedure create a *hapax legomenon* in Hebrew, but it eliminates a clear mythological reference, of which there are many in Job. P. renders *meriri* as "eclipse," on the basis of Am. 8:10, *yōm mar*, "bitter day," but there is no evidence for interpreting this latter passage as an eclipse, either, in view of the parallel *ᵓebhel yāḥīd*, "mourning for an only son."

The key to the passage, as noted long ago by Ra. and Ibn E., is to be found in Deut. 32:24, קֶטֶב מְרִירִי. Note the reference to *Rešeph*, the North Semitic storm-god immediately preceding, and cf. *benei rešeph*, Job 5:7; *rešeph ‖ debher* (in Hab. 3:5) and *ketebh ‖ debher* (Ps. 91:6). Hence the passage in Deut. is to be rendered "the destruction of demons," and our stich, "may the demons of the day terrify it." The phrase is cited in Ben Sira 41:4 and in the Qumran Thanksgiving Hymns (5:34). The etymology of *meriri* is unclear. It may be derived from the common Semitic root *mārar*, "to be bitter." Hence "a bitter, hostile spirit"; cf. Arab. *mara IV*, "to be hostile." We prefer to derive it from the Arab. *mara*, "pass, pass by." Hence "the passing, flitting being," a reference to demons in flight. This root probably inheres also in Job 13:26 מְרֹרוֹת = "past actions" (so Ehr., and see the Comm. *ad loc.*).

What impelled the emendation to *kamerirei*, in spite of the Masoretic word in Deut. 32:24, was the problem of the prefixed Kaph. It is to be construed as the "asseverative Kaph," correctly recognized by the medieval Jewish commentators (*Kaph haᵓamitut*) and unaccountably disregarded by the moderns. It is now validated by the Ugaritic texts (cf. Gordis, "The Asseverative Kaph in Hebrew and Ugaritic," *JAOS*, vol. 63, 1943, pp. 176 ff.), and such biblical passages as Nu. 11:1 כְּמִתְאֹנְנִים; Hos. 4:4 כִּמְרִיבֵי כֹהֵן (read כִּמְרִיבֵי כֹהֵן); Ps. 119:9 כְּדָבָרֶךָ; 122:3 כְּעִיר; Lam. 1:20 כַּמָּוֶת; Neh. 7:2 כְּאִישׁ אֱמֶת, etc. This Kaph occurs frequently in the predicate nominative, but is not limited to this syntactic usage, as is clear from Isa. 10:3 Kethib כַּאבִיר; Ps. 119:9; Ecc. 10:5, and our passage, where the noun is the subject of the verb: "May the demons of the day affright it."

3:6 יָחַדְּ on the basis of the Masoretic vocalization, the root would be חדה (cf. Ex. 18:9), and would mean "let it not rejoice."

On the other hand, stichs b and c recall Gen. 49:6, so that it is generally revocalized as יֵחַד from the root יחד "be reckoned, counted." The Masoretic vocalization, however, is not to be dismissed out of hand. Our passage (6b and c, together with 7a and b) exhibits chiastic parallelism, 6b being parallel to 7b ("isolation") and 6c being parallel to 7a ("joylessness"). יָחַדְּ is an instance of *talḥin*, where two meanings are simultaneously intended by the writer, one primary ("be reckoned"), the other secondary ("rejoice"). On the psychological mechanism involved and for a substantial number of additional illustrations of this rhetorical figure, cf. *Gordis* in *Sepher Moshe Seidel* (Jerusalem, 5722 = 1962, pp. 255–61), and see, e.g., Lam. 2:13 גָּדוֹל כַּיָּם שִׁבְרֵךְ "Your break" (secondary meaning, "breaker, wave") "is great as the sea." For another possible instance of *talḥin*, see the note on 3:22. For another example of chiasmus, see the Comm. on v. 10. Our verse is a tristich, because the opening stich, 6a ("night"), is the complement to 4a ("day"), and is not part of the parallelistic structure of vv. 6 and 7.

3:7 גַּלְמוּד a highly picturesque word occurring in Isa. 49:21; Job 15:34; 30:3; Arab. *jalmud* "rock, stone." Hence "lonely as a crag" and parallel to 6b.

3:8 The traditional interpretation of אֹרְרֵי יוֹם "those who curse the day (of their birth)" (Ra., Ibn E.) is appropriate to the context in and of itself and is maintained by Dh. among the moderns.

It has, however, been increasingly surrendered by modern commentators on the basis of the Ugaritic evidence for the primordial god *Yam* whom Baʿal vanquishes, as Marduk conquers and dismembers *Tiamat* in order to create the world in Babylonian mythology (note the parallelism of *Tehom* and *Yam* and their personification in Job 28:14). Our text is therefore emended to אֹרְרֵי יָם. That the reference in stich b to Leviathan, the monster of the deep, supports the mythological interpretation was pointed out long ago by Gunkel. On this basis, P. renders "Let the sea-cursers damn it, those skilled to stir Leviathan." He seeks to support this translation by calling attention to the fact that in the Ugaritic myth there is a reference to incantations pronounced by the god, Koshar, which rendered the Sea's weapons ineffective.

On the other hand, there are several objections to this view. Aside from the fact that there is no reference to cursing even in the Ugaritic myth, there are two more fundamental difficulties. In Semitic cosmogony the Sea, personified as a monster (Akkadian *tiamat*; Hebrew *yām*, *nāḥāš*, *livyathān*, *tehōm*; Ugaritic *ym*, *thm*), symbolizes the primordial chaos that the god must conquer in order to create the world. It follows that those who curse the Sea, or render his weapons ineffective, are allies of the positive forces in the cosmos and are not advocates of chaos! On the other hand, stich b, which is a call to "stir up Leviathan," calls upon the dragon to rise up and destroy the world or plunge it into darkness in an eclipse. Thus the proposed text and interpretation of stich a would mean that the two stichs, far from being parallel, would contradict each other, in addition to the fact that stich a would be entirely inappropriate to the context. There is no need to invoke the Arabic root ᶜaʾra *mediae ya* II or VI "abuse, revile" or the Akkadian root *aru, awāru* "revile" (Wilson, in *JSS*, 1962, p. 181; G. R. Driver, *VT Supp.* III, p. 12). Nor is TS's involved rendering of stich b, "the heroes whom Leviathan awoke to curse the light," acceptable, both because of the word-order and because there is no real evidence in Isa. 14:9 of a practice of rousing heroes to curse God.

The solution lies, we believe, in emending stich a to read עֹרְרֵי יָם and render the verse: "Let them curse it who rouse the Sea, those skilled in stirring up Leviathan." For the predilection of the author of Job for the same word or root in two parallel stichs, cf. Job 8:3; 11:7; 12:23; 38:22, and see Special Note 4. The verse thus receives a clear and appropriate meaning. Job invokes the creatures of chaos to emerge and destroy his "day."

Leviathan is the name of the great Sea Dragon (cf. Isa. 27:1) used figuratively of Egypt as an all-engulfing power (Ps. 74:14; cf. v. 13). With the total triumph of the monotheistic principle in Judaism, Leviathan is used to refer to the crocodile (Job 40:25) and the whale, who now is a peaceful plaything of God, the Lord of Creation (Ps. 104:26). In postbiblical Jewish thought, the Leviathan will be served up as food at the heavenly banquet of the righteous in the world to come (*B. Baba Batra* 75a). The primordial battle against the monster is transposed in rabbinic Aggada to the Messianic Age, when the angel Gabriel will drag him onto the dry land and God will destroy him (Ginzberg, *Legends*, V, p. 43; VII, pp. 285 ff.).

It is easy to account for the two minor changes in the text we postulate. When the mythological reference to *Yam* was no longer recognized, let alone understood, יָם was vocalized as יוֹם, particularly in view of vv. 1, 2 and the proximity to *laylāh* in v. 7. עֹרְרֵי was now written with an Aleph, either through a scribal or aural error or probably because it seemed appropriate in the context after יקבהו "curse."

3:9 נֶשֶׁף lit. "the breeze, blowing time." It is used to refer both to the evening twilight (II Ki. 7:5, 7; Isa. 5:11; 59:10; Pr. 7:9; Job 24:15) and to the morning light, as in Ps. 119:147; Job 7:4 (Ibn E., and BDB), as well as in our verse, which describes the dawn that does not come. The stars grow dim at daybreak, but no sunlight appears. עַפְעַפֵּי שָׁחַר "the eyelids of the dawn," a superb metaphor for the morning sky, streaked with patches of light and shadow at sunrise. One recalls Homer's famous figure, "rosy-fingered dawn."

3:10 The subject of סגר may be impersonal (so Ra., Ehr.): hence = "the doors were shut." However, in view of the curse pronounced upon the day of his birth, we prefer to regard "the day" as the subject of the verb. Job expresses three wishes, in a descending order of preference: that (a) his mother had not conceived him (v. 10), (b) or that he had perished in the womb (v. 11a; see below), or (c) that he had died at birth (11b, 12). The same three periods, but in an ascending order, are to be found in Hos. 9:11 f., which is the key to the understanding of our passage and on which see the Comm. on 3:11 below.

The entire passage (vv. 10–16) exhibits a chiastic structure: a, b ‖ b′, a′. Like vv. 7, 8, the chiasmus deals with the two last alternatives that Job has mentioned and their consequences: a (v. 11a) and a′ (v. 16) death in the womb, b (v. 11b) and b′ (vv. 13–15) death immediately after birth.

עמל, a term common in Wisdom literature, though not restricted to it, much favored by Ecc. and Job. In Ecc. it generally bears its basic meaning, "labor, toil" (Ecc. 1:3; 2:11; 3:9; 4:4, 6, 8; 8:15, 17; 9:9; 10:15), and, more rarely, the derived meaning "the result of labor, hence wealth" (Ecc. 2:10, 19; 5:18). For a discussion of the important semantic principle that a word can be used to signify both an act or a quality and its consequence, see *KMW*, 1968 edition, Supplementary Note D, "On the Meaning of ᶜ*Amal in Koheleth*," pp. 418–20. In Job, on the other hand, the root is frequently used as a generic term for "evil," derived from its original meaning "toil, labor." It is noteworthy that the Friends use the term to refer to "doing evil" (Job 4:8; 15:35), while Job himself uses it in the meaning of "suffering evil, trouble, misery" (3:10; 7:3; 11:16). In the crucially important passage 5:6, 7, ᶜ*āmāl* carries both meanings of "sin" and "trouble." In 16:2 it is virtually synonymous with *šāwᵓ*, "falseness, worthlessness" or *hebhel* "emptiness, meaninglessness."

When the chiastic structure is recognized, the transposition of v. 16 after 11 is seen to be unnecessary, especially when the force of מֵרֶחֶם in v. 11 is correctly understood. See below.

3:11 מֵרֶחֶם not "coming from the womb, i.e. at birth," but "while in the womb." This rendering, attested by LXX, does not presuppose an emendation to בְּרֶחֶם. On the "Mem of condition," hitherto unrecognized, cf. Gordis in *Sepher Tur-Sinai*, Jerusalem, 1960, p. 167. The usage occurs in both biblical and post biblical Hebrew. Cf. Hos. 9:11, אֶפְרַיִם כָּעוֹף יִתְעוֹפֵף כְּבוֹדָם מִלֵּדָה וּמִבֶּטֶן וּמֵהֵרָיוֹן. "Ephraim — his glory will fly away, at the time of birth, nay more, in the womb, indeed, at the time of conception." The next verse exhibits this Mem of condition once more: "If they should raise their children, I shall bereave them while they are in the condition of adulthood (מֵאָדָם)." For rabbinic Hebrew, cf. *M. Abot* 4:9: כל המקיים את התורה מעוני סופו לקיימה מעושר "He who fulfills the Torah in a state of poverty is destined to fulfill it in a state of wealth"; *B. Shab.* עוֹמְדוֹת מֵעוֹמֶד נוֹפְלוֹת מְיוֹשֵׁב: "The standing ears of grain she would glean in a standing position, those that had fallen from a sitting position." Our precise word and usage occur in Ps. 22:11, עָלֶיךָ הָשְׁלַכְתִּי מֵרֶחֶם מִבֶּטֶן אִמִּי אֵלִי אָתָּה "Upon You have I been cast while I was in the womb; in my mother's stomach, you have been my God."

וָאֶגְוַע, with Sheva, represents a weakened pronunciation of the Vav consecutive = lit. "and I would have perished." Cf. v. 13 below (וְאֶשְׁקוֹט); Isa. 43:28 (וַאֲתַנָּה); 48:3 (וָאַשְׁמִיעֵם); 51:2; 57:17, and see Ges.-K., sec. 107, n. 2, for other instances.

3:12 מַדּוּעַ קִדְּמוּנִי בִרְכַּיִם = "Why were there knees to receive me?" Receiving a newborn infant upon one's knees symbolized the recognition of parenthood (Gen. 30:3; 50:23; Ecclus. 15:2), similar to a woman's taking the baby to her bosom (Ruth 4:16). In these three instances, to be sure, the parent-child relationship is symbolic, but it is obviously patterned on what was the customary procedure at the birth of a child.

מה = "why"; cf. Ex. 14:15; 17:2; II Kings 6:33; Ps. 42:6; Lam. 3:39; and cf. BDB, s.v. 553b.

3:13 וָאֶשְׁקוֹט with Sheva, another instance of the weakened form of the Vav consecutive. See the Comm. on 3:11.

יָנוּחַ לִי impersonal; cf. Isa. 23:12.

3:14 חֲרָבוֹת, "ruins," has sustained a plethora of emendations: הֵיכָלוֹת (Be.); אַרְמוֹנוֹת (Ol., Dil.); קְבָרוֹת (Cheyne). Ew., Bu., Du. create a *hapax legomenon*, הֲרָמוֹת, on the basis of the Arabic *hiram*, "pyramids." Daiches calls attention to מחרב, "fortress, city," in South Arabian inscriptions (*JQR*, 1908, pp. 607 ff.). Hö. suggests that perhaps the Egyptian Jews call the pyramids "ruins," for Rameses the Second already used Gizeh as a quarry for stones. The most acceptable view is already to be found in Rashi, who interprets the word as "ruined cities" for "it is the practice of those seeking to perpetuate their names to build cities that have been destroyed" (Isa. 58:12; 61:4; so T, P). Mid-Eastern archeology has demonstrated that this practice was widespread. Mesopotamian kings frequently boasted of the restoration of ancient sites. The exploits of Hellenistic and Roman rulers in rebuilding older cities, generally giving them new names, as in the case of Samaria-Sebaste, need no documentation.

3:15 The conjunction אוֹ "or" is omitted by many as an error from v. 16. Actually, some conjunction or other connective is required. The retention of אוֹ in the text suggests that there was a hierarchy even in Sheol, an aspect of the older biblical conception of the hereafter which has often been overlooked. That such distinctions existed is clear from Isa. 14:18, 19. The existence of such differentiations in rank or in character in the early biblical concept of Sheol may well have served as the basis for the later idea of judgment after death, in Pharisaic Judaism and Christianity. Like the belief in Satan, the doctrine of retribution in another world is therefore not an altogether uncongenial borrowing or a total innovation. These differences in Sheol do not vitiate the essential equality of all men in death.

3:16 On the chiastic structure of the entire passage, which obviates the need to transpose this verse after v. 11 (ag. P.), see n. on v. 10 above. לֹא is omitted by Bu. It should be revocalized לֻא "if, if only" (so Gr., Yel.); cf. II Sam. 18:12 לֹא K.; לֻו Q.; and 19:7.

עוֹלֵל = "child" (I Sam. 15:3; 22:19; II Ki. 8:12; Hos. 14:1, and often), here used of a stillborn infant. Particularly in view of its unknown etymology (cf. BDB, 760b), Rashi's delightful comment deserves to be quoted: תינוקות כולם שחוק ולכלוך, "Children, who are all mischief and dirt." He cites Job 16:15 and Jud. 19:25.

TS renders לֹא אהיה "I should be nothing!" and cites Job 6:21. In the latter passage Kittel (*BH* 4) reads לֹא as Kethib and לוֹ as Qere, a variation which Norzi *ad loc.* regards as a Madinchae reading, the Maᵓarbae reading being לוֹ with no K.-Q. Even if the reading with לֹא be accepted there, the word order here militates against this rendering. On the meaning of 6:21, see the Comm. *ad loc.*

3:17   The superb rhythm of this verse in the Hebrew original has its parallel in the justly famous rhythmic rendering of AV, which is a perfect trochee: "There the wicked cease from troubling and there the weary are at rest." רְשָׁעִים is emended to רֵעֵשִׁים by Be., who renders it "lords," and by Ehr., who translates it as "proletarians." That the emendation is unnecessary will become clear below. רֹגֶז, being a noun, cannot be transitive (so D-G). It means "strong agitation, raging"; cf. Hab. 3:2 and Job 3:26; 14:1; 37:2; and Deut. 28:65, לֵב רַגָּז, "an agitated heart." יְגִיעֵי כֹחַ, not "the weary" but "lit. those exhausted by violence, hence victims of oppression." Cf. Ecc. 4:1, וּמִיַּד עֹשְׁקֵיהֶם כֹּחַ, "power in the hands of their oppressors," and see *KMW ad loc.* The two stichs are therefore in direct contrast to one another and describe the two extremes in society, the malefactors and those who suffer at their hands. Vv. 17 and 18 are thus in chiastic structure, 17a and 18b referring to the oppressors, and 17b and 18a to their victims.

שָׁם "there," an oblique reference to another world. Cf. 1:21, and especially Ecc. 3:19, and see *KMW ad loc.* for classical parallels.

3:18   יַחַד is frequently used as a poetic synonym for *kol*, particularly in parallelism; cf. Deut. 33:5; Ps. 33:15; Job 38:7. Stich b = not "heedless of the slave driver's shout" (so P.), which would suggest that the shouts are still continuing, but "they hear the taskmaster's shouts no more."

3:19   קָטֹן וְגָדוֹל שָׁם הוּא cannot mean "The great and the small are there" (D-G), which would require שָׁם הֵם. Besides, the context wishes to emphasize the basic equality of the various social strata, not their location, as Gr. recognized by his emendation שָׁוֶה הוּא "are equal." It is a graphically easier emendation to read קָטֹן גָּדוֹל שָׁם הוּא, "the small is great over there," but this rendering suggests a transposition of roles rather than the basic equality of all, which is the theme of the passage. Actually, no emendation of MT is required. שָׁם הוּא = lit. "are the same, alike." Cf. Ps. 102:28, וְאַתָּה הוּא וּשְׁנוֹתֶיךָ לֹא יִתָּמּוּ, "But You are the same and Your years have no end." Cf. Arabic *huᵓ huᵓ* "the same." Ehr. correctly points out that the word order in Hebrew and English is reversed, as in 2:7, מִכַּף רַגְלוֹ וְעַד קָדְקֳדוֹ, which is expressed in English: "from head to foot." Classical Hebrew prefers to place קָטֹן before גָּדוֹל (Deut. 1:22; I Sam. 5:9; 30:2; etc.) So, too, כֶּסֶף וְזָהָב, "gold and silver."

3:20   LXX, P יִתֵּן is impersonal, hence virtually a passive (so T, V). Job is not yet voicing a charge against God (ag. Ra.) but complaining against life itself. On עָמֵל, "the sufferer," see note on 3:10.

3:21 LXX, S, V, rendering "like treasures," may have read כְּמַטְמוֹנִים, the Kaph and the Mem being similar in the old script. Or they may have interpreted freely, because חפר means not merely "dig," but also "search, desire" (11:18; 39:29). On the semantics involved, note the contemporary American slang usage "dig it" = "desire it." P. cites W. M. Thomson (*The Land The People*, 1913 ed., p. 112), who considers this the most vivid comparison within the whole compass of human action.

3:22 Because of the parallelism with קֶבֶר, גִּיל is commonly emended to גַּל and rendered "burial heap." (So 1 Kenn. ms., Gr., Be., Du., P., etc.) The idiom in MT is, however, clearly attested in Hos. 9:1 in the meaning "rejoice greatly." This evidence is, of course, eliminated by those who emend the latter passage as well. Sound method would dictate that caution be employed, particularly when an idiom would seem to be in question. Moreover, the parallel in our passage suggests that we have here another instance of *talḥin*, with גִיל carrying the primary meaning of "exultation" and suggesting the secondary meaning of "burial heap." On this subtle poetic figure, see note 10 on 3:6 and the references there.

3:23 The Lamed is governed by the verb יתן in v. 20: "Why is life given to the man?" In vv. 20–22 Job has lamented the lot of suffering mankind in general. In v. 23 he turns to his own tragic lot, using the third person as a bridge between the previous passage and the succeeding verses, which are in the first person. וַיָּסֶךְ אֱלוֹהַּ בַּעֲדוֹ, "whom God has fenced in," the first indication that God is the cause of his misery. On the idiom, cf. Hos. 2:8 and the similar use of the synonym *gādar* in Job 19:8; Lam. 3:7. It is obviously not being used here in the favorable sense of "protection," which occurs in Job 1:9.

3:24 לִפְנֵי, originally "before," as is clear from the parallelism with כַּמַּיִם, has the meaning of "as, like"; cf. Job 4:19 לִפְנֵי עָשׁ; I Sam. 1:16 לִפְנֵי בַּת־בְּלִיַּעַל. On the semantics, cf. the Latin preposition *prō*, "before, instead of, as." For the sense of the passage, cf. Ps. 102:10. Job's sighs and groans are as regular as his bread and water. נתך, "pour out," is used intransitively here in the Qal; cf. Jer. 42:18; 44:6; Dan. 9:11, 27; II Chr. 12:7; 34:25, as well as in the Niphal (Ex. 9:33; Jer. 42:18, etc.).

3:25 There is no reason for interpreting stich a as a virtual hypothetical condition (D-G). The fear to which Job refers is the natural sense of insecurity felt by any sensitive human being with regard both to his actions and to his fate. These two aspects of anxiety regarding the human condition are expressed in Hillel's apothegm, אל תאמן בעצמך עד יום מותך, "Do not believe in yourself until the day of your death" (*M. Abot* 2:5), and in the Greek utterance, "Count no man fortunate until the day of his death." For Job's ethical sensitivity, cf. 1:5 and n.

3:26   The 2:2:2 rhythm of this verse gives the chapter a sense of agitation reflecting Job's innermost mood. On רֹגֶז see n. on 3:17 above. The Midrash (*Ex. Rabbah*, chap. 26) gives the verse a specifically Jewish historical interpretation, embodying the experience of Israel, the Job people: לא שלותי מבבל ולא שקטתי ממדי ולא נחתי מיון ויבא רגז מאדום "I had no ease from Babylonia, no peace from Media, no rest from Gréece, and agony — from Edom (i.e. Rome)."

The First Cycle

The Speech of Eliphaz (4–5)

Eliphaz, the oldest and most urbane of the Friends, is the first to answer. He begins by asking for permission to speak. He reminds his afflicted friend how often he himself has consoled sufferers in the past by recalling the great truth of religion — that the righteous are never destroyed, but that the wicked are sure to be punished either in their own persons or through their children.

Eliphaz then describes a revelation from on high that has brought him new insight: all men are imperfect in the eyes of God; therefore, even the suffering of the righteous has its justification. In view of these two great truths it is foolish for Job to lose patience and surrender his faith in the divine government of the world.

After picturing the punishment which ultimately overtakes sinners, Eliphaz delivers himself of a third doctrine: neither God nor His universe can fairly be charged with the creation of sin and suffering, because evil is a human invention. Since man is the source of sin, he must be prepared to suffer.

Rather than speak of man's limitations, however, Eliphaz prefers to extol God's great wisdom. He makes a fleeting reference to a fourth basic idea: suffering serves at times to discipline and instruct the righteous, and thus guards them against evildoing.

Eliphaz concludes with a triumphant hymn of praise to God, the savior of the just. He describes the various calamities to which man is exposed, from which God saves the righteous. Since Job has always been upright, he may expect to attain harmony with the world of nature and with man and to end his life at a ripe old age in serenity and peace.

In the proud consciousness that he has effectively presented the basic doctrines taught by religion — as is indeed the case — Eliphaz calls upon Job to recognize and accept the truth he has proclaimed.

4   Eliphaz the Temanite then answered, and said,

2   If one tried a word with you, would you be offended?
        Yet who can refrain from speaking?

3   Behold, you have encouraged many
        and strengthened weak hands.

4   Your words have upheld the stumbling,
        and the weak-kneed you have strengthened.

5   But now that it has come to you, you cannot bear it;
        it touches you, and you are dismayed.

6   Indeed, your fear of God should be your confidence
        and your hope — the uprightness of your ways!

7   Think now, what innocent man was ever destroyed;
        where were the upright cut off?

8   Whenever I have seen those who plow iniquity
        and sow trouble — they reap it!

9   By the breath of God they are destroyed,
        and by the blast of His wrath they are consumed.

10   The lion roars, the fierce beast cries —
        but the teeth of the whelps are shattered.

11   The mighty lion wanders about without prey,
        and the young of the lioness are scattered.

12   Now to me a word came stealthily,
        and my ear caught an echo of it

13   amid thoughts and visions of the night,
        when deep sleep falls upon men.

14   Terror came upon me, and trembling,
        and all my limbs it frightened.

15   A wind passed before my face;
        a storm made my skin bristle.

16   It stood still,
        but I could not tell its appearance;
     a form stood before my eyes;
        silence — then I heard a voice:

17   "Can a human being be righteous before God?
        Can a mortal be pure before his Maker?

18   Even in His servants God puts no trust;
        Even His angels He charges with folly.

19   How much more so those who dwell in clay houses;
        whose foundation is in the dust,
        who are crushed like a bird's nest!

20   Between morning and evening they are crushed:
        While they pay no heed, they are destroyed forever.

21   Indeed, their tent cord is plucked up within them;
        they die, having gained no wisdom."

5   Call out — who is there to answer you?
        For to whom rather than to the Holy One can you turn?

2   Anger surely kills the fool,
        and impatience slays the simpleton.

3   I myself have seen a fool striking root,
        but I declared folly's dwelling to be cursed.

ד א וַיַּעַן אֱלִיפַז הַתֵּימָנִי וַיֹּאמַר׃

2 הֲנִסָּה דָבָר אֵלֶיךָ תִּלְאֶה וַעְצֹר בְּמִלִּין מִי יוּכָל׃

3 הִנֵּה יִסַּרְתָּ רַבִּים וְיָדַיִם רָפוֹת תְּחַזֵּק׃

4 כּוֹשֵׁל יְקִימוּן מִלֶּיךָ וּבִרְכַּיִם כֹּרְעוֹת תְּאַמֵּץ׃

5 כִּי עַתָּה ׀ תָּבוֹא אֵלֶיךָ וַתֵּלֶא תִּגַּע עָדֶיךָ וַתִּבָּהֵל׃

6 הֲלֹא יִרְאָתְךָ כִּסְלָתֶךָ תִּקְוָתְךָ וְתֹם דְּרָכֶיךָ׃

7 זְכָר־נָא מִי הוּא נָקִי אָבָד וְאֵיפֹה יְשָׁרִים נִכְחָדוּ׃

8 כַּאֲשֶׁר רָאִיתִי חֹרְשֵׁי אָוֶן וְזֹרְעֵי עָמָל יִקְצְרֻהוּ׃

9 מִנִּשְׁמַת אֱלוֹהַ יֹאבֵדוּ וּמֵרוּחַ אַפּוֹ יִכְלוּ׃

י שַׁאֲגַת אַרְיֵה וְקוֹל שָׁחַל וְשִׁנֵּי כְפִירִים נִתָּעוּ׃

11 לַיִשׁ אֹבֵד מִבְּלִי־טָרֶף וּבְנֵי לָבִיא יִתְפָּרָדוּ׃

12 וְאֵלַי דָּבָר יְגֻנָּב וַתִּקַּח אָזְנִי שֵׁמֶץ מֶנְהוּ׃

13 בִּשְׂעִפִּים מֵחֶזְיֹנוֹת לָיְלָה בִּנְפֹל תַּרְדֵּמָה עַל־אֲנָשִׁים׃

14 פַּחַד קְרָאַנִי וּרְעָדָה וְרֹב עַצְמוֹתַי הִפְחִיד׃

טו וְרוּחַ עַל־פָּנַי יַחֲלֹף תְּסַמֵּר שַׂעֲרַת בְּשָׂרִי׃

16 יַעֲמֹד ׀ וְלֹא־אַכִּיר מַרְאֵהוּ תְּמוּנָה לְנֶגֶד עֵינָי דְּמָמָה וָקוֹל אֶשְׁמָע׃

17 הַאֱנוֹשׁ מֵאֱלוֹהַ יִצְדָּק אִם מֵעֹשֵׂהוּ יִטְהַר־גָּבֶר׃

18 הֵן בַּעֲבָדָיו לֹא יַאֲמִין וּבְמַלְאָכָיו יָשִׂים תָּהֳלָה׃

19 אַף ׀ שֹׁכְנֵי בָתֵּי־חֹמֶר אֲשֶׁר־בֶּעָפָר יְסוֹדָם יְדַכְּאוּם לִפְנֵי־עָשׁ׃

כ מִבֹּקֶר לָעֶרֶב יֻכַּתּוּ מִבְּלִי מֵשִׂים לָנֶצַח יֹאבֵדוּ׃

21 הֲלֹא־נִסַּע יִתְרָם בָּם יָמוּתוּ וְלֹא בְחָכְמָה׃

ה א קְרָא־נָא הֲיֵשׁ עוֹנֶךָ וְאֶל־מִי מִקְּדֹשִׁים תִּפְנֶה׃

2 כִּי־לֶאֱוִיל יַהֲרָג־כָּעַשׂ וּפֹתֶה תָּמִית קִנְאָה׃

3 אֲנִי־רָאִיתִי אֱוִיל מַשְׁרִישׁ וָאֶקּוֹב נָוֵהוּ פִתְאֹם׃

4   His sons will be far from safety;
          they will be crushed in the judgment gate
          with none to deliver them.

5   His harvest the hungry will devour;
          his substance the starving will carry away,
          and the famished will drag off his wealth.

6   Indeed, misfortune does not come forth from the ground,
          nor does evil sprout from the earth.

7   It is man who gives birth to evil,
          as surely as the sparks fly upward.

8   As for me, I would seek after God
          and to God entrust my cause,

9   who does great things without end,
          wonders without number.

10   He gives rain to the earth
          and sends water upon the open places.

11   He sets the lowly on high,
          and the afflicted are raised to safety.

12   He confounds the plans of the crafty,
          so that their hands achieve no success.

13   He traps the wise in their own cunning,
          and the schemes of the perverse come to a speedy end.

14   In daylight they encounter darkness
          and at noon they grope as in the night.

15   But from their sharp tongue and heavy hand
          He saves the needy,

16   so that the poor have hope,
          and injustice shuts her mouth.

17   Behold, happy is the man whom God reproves;
          hence do not despise the chastisement of the Almighty.

18   For He wounds, but binds up;
          He strikes, but His hands bring healing.

19   From six troubles He will save you,
          and in seven, no evil will touch you.

20   In hunger He will redeem you from death,
          and in battle, from the power of the sword.

21   When the tongue of fire moves about, you will be hidden;
          nor need you fear the onrushing flood.

22   At the ravage of famine you will laugh,
          and the beasts of the earth you will not fear.

23   For with the stones in the field you will be leagued,
          and the beasts of the field will be at peace with you.

24   You will know that your tent is at peace;
          when you visit your home, you will find no one missing.

25   You will know that your children are many
          and your offspring like the grass of the earth.

26   You will come to your grave in ripe old age,
          like a shock of grain to the threshing floor in its season.

27   Behold, this we have searched out — it is true —
          We have heard it; now you take it to heart.

4 יִרְחֲקוּ בָנָיו מִיֶּשַׁע   וְיִדַּכְּאוּ בַשַּׁעַר וְאֵין מַצִּיל:

ה אֲשֶׁר קְצִירוֹ ׀ רָעֵב יֹאכֵל   וְאֶל־מִצִּנִּים יִקָּחֵהוּ

6 וְשָׁאַף צַמִּים חֵילָם: כִּי ׀ לֹא־יֵצֵא מֵעָפָר אָוֶן

7 וּמֵאֲדָמָה לֹא־יִצְמַח עָמָל: כִּי־אָדָם לְעָמָל יוּלָּד

8 וּבְנֵי־רֶשֶׁף יַגְבִּיהוּ עוּף: אוּלָם אֲנִי אֶדְרֹשׁ אֶל־אֵל

9 וְאֶל־אֱלֹהִים אָשִׂים דִּבְרָתִי: עֹשֶׂה גְדֹלוֹת וְאֵין חֵקֶר

י נִפְלָאוֹת עַד־אֵין מִסְפָּר: הַנֹּתֵן מָטָר עַל־פְּנֵי־אָרֶץ

11 וְשֹׁלֵחַ מַיִם עַל־פְּנֵי חוּצוֹת: לָשׂוּם שְׁפָלִים לְמָרוֹם

12 וְקֹדְרִים שָׂגְבוּ יֶשַׁע: מֵפֵר מַחְשְׁבוֹת עֲרוּמִים

13 וְלֹא־תַעֲשֶׂינָה יְדֵיהֶם תֻּשִׁיָּה: לֹכֵד חֲכָמִים בְּעָרְמָם

14 וַעֲצַת נִפְתָּלִים נִמְהָרָה: יוֹמָם יְפַגְּשׁוּ־חֹשֶׁךְ

טו וְכַלַּיְלָה יְמַשְׁשׁוּ בַצָּהֳרָיִם: וַיֹּשַׁע מֵחֶרֶב מִפִּיהֶם

16 וּמִיַּד חָזָק אֶבְיוֹן: וַתְּהִי לַדַּל תִּקְוָה

17 וְעֹלָתָה קָפְצָה פִּיהָ:   הִנֵּה אַשְׁרֵי אֱנוֹשׁ יוֹכִחֶנּוּ אֱלוֹהַּ

18 וּמוּסַר שַׁדַּי אַל־תִּמְאָס: כִּי הוּא יַכְאִיב וְיֶחְבָּשׁ

19 יִמְחַץ וְיָדָו תִּרְפֶּינָה: בְּשֵׁשׁ צָרוֹת יַצִּילֶךָ

כ וּבְשֶׁבַע ׀ לֹא־יִגַּע בְּךָ רָע: בְּרָעָב פָּדְךָ מִמָּוֶת

21 וּבְמִלְחָמָה מִידֵי חָרֶב: בְּשׁוֹט לָשׁוֹן תֵּחָבֵא

22 וְלֹא־תִירָא מִשֹּׁד כִּי יָבוֹא: לְשֹׁד וּלְכָפָן תִּשְׂחָק

23 וּמֵחַיַּת הָאָרֶץ אַל־תִּירָא: כִּי עִם־אַבְנֵי הַשָּׂדֶה בְרִיתֶךָ

24 וְחַיַּת הַשָּׂדֶה הָשְׁלְמָה־לָךְ:   וְיָדַעְתָּ כִּי־שָׁלוֹם אָהֳלֶךָ

כה וּפָקַדְתָּ נָוְךָ וְלֹא תֶחֱטָא: וְיָדַעְתָּ כִּי־רַב זַרְעֶךָ

26 וְצֶאֱצָאֶיךָ כְּעֵשֶׂב הָאָרֶץ: תָּבוֹא בְכֶלַח אֱלֵי־קָבֶר

27 כַּעֲלוֹת גָּדִישׁ בְּעִתּוֹ:   הִנֵּה־זֹאת חֲקַרְנוּהָ כֶּן־הִיא

שְׁמָעֶנָּה וְאַתָּה דַּע־לָךְ:

CHAPTER 4

4:2 Eliphaz is not only the oldest, but also the most urbane of the Friends. He begins by requesting permission to speak. Similarly, he opens with a question in 15:2 and 22:2, as do Bildad in 8:2; 18:2; and Zophar in 11:2.

Stich a is best rendered not, "Because one trial has come to you, are you wearied?" (Ra.), but lit., "If one tried a word with you, would you be unable (to bear it)?" (so most). The only appropriate meaning for the Hebrew *lāʾāh* is "be unable" (cf. Ex. 7:18; Pr. 26:15). The meaning generally adduced in the Lexica and the Commentators, "to be weary," is actually nonexistent in biblical Hebrew. (See below.) Nor is there any evidence for this latter meaning in the Arabic cognate verb *laʾay*, which means "to be slow" (Frey), or in the noun, which means "difficulty" (Lane). On the other hand, the Tibbonides, in translating the medieval Jewish philosophic works, correctly render the Arabic root *ʿajaza*, "be unable," by *lāʾāh*. This meaning for *lāʾāh* is particularly clear when it is used with a complementary infinitive, as in Gen. 19:11, וַיִּלְאוּ לִמְצֹא הַפָּתַח, "they were unable to find the entrance." So also Ex. 7:18; Isa. 1:14; Jer. 6:11; 15:6; 20:9. In our verse and in v. 5, the complementary infinitive is to be understood, hence the meaning is "be unable to bear it"; cf. the parallel use of *yākhōl*, "be able," in Isa. 1:13 and Jer. 20:9.

The same meaning in an absolute sense, "be helpless," occurs in Isa. 16:12 כִּי־נִלְאָה מוֹאָב = "Moab is left helpless." Job 16:7 הֶלְאָנִי = "He has left me helpless," and in Isa. 7:13, where the Hiphil is used declaratively: "Is it not enough that you consider men helpless, that you consider God also unable to help?" Ps. 68:10 נַחֲלָתְךָ וְנִלְאָה is extremely difficult, and none of the proposed interpretations is satisfactory. Perhaps the second noun may be regarded as an elision of נהלאה and treated as a denominative from הָלְאָה "further," hence "distant." The stich would then be rendered: "Your inheritance (i.e., what is near to You) and what is distant — You have fashioned them both." Ezek. 24:12 is surely corrupt (see the Comm.). In Mic. 6:3, מָה הֶלְאֵיתִיךָ, the precise force of the verb is unclear; it may be rendered: "How have I left you helpless?", which is as satisfactory as the usual reading, "How have I wearied you?"

Our verse is a conditional sentence, with the perfect in the protasis and the imperfect in the apodosis; cf. 7:20; 23:10.

4:3 יִסַּרְתָּ is generally rendered "instructed" (so D-G and P.), but this meaning is inappropriate in the context and is not borne out by the parallelism. It is, therefore, emended to עָזַרְתָּ (D-G) or יִסַּדְתָּ (Per., Ehr., TS). MT is, however, validated by Hos. 7:15, where the same sequence of verbs occurs: יִסַּרְתִּי חִזַּקְתִּי (so Yel.). The verb here is a metaplastic form for אסר, "bind, strengthen" (cf. the contamination of אסף and יסף in תֵּאָסְפוּן (Ex. 5:7). For the semantics, note that the meanings "bind," "tighten," and "strengthen" are often expressed by the same root; cf. Arabic *ḥazaqa*, "bind, tie fast";

Hebrew חָזָק, "strong"; אַמִּיץ (II Sam. 15:12), mishnaic Hebrew הַמְאַמֵּץ "close the eyes" (*M. Shab.* 23:5), and the Latin *stringere*, "bind," whence Eng. "*strong.*"

4:5 כִּי עַתָּה not "because, i.e., the reason for Eliphaz's speaking," but rather, "But now," and it requires no emendation (ag. Per.).

וַתֵּלֶא "You cannot bear it"; cf. 4:2.

4:6 הֲלֹא is a petrified interrogative, best rendered nearly always as "indeed." יִרְאָה, an ellipsis for יִרְאַת אֱלֹהִים (cf. Gen. 20:11; II Sam. 23:3; Neh. 5:15) or יִרְאַת ה' (Isa. 11:3; Pr. 1:29). The term is the closest approximation in biblical Hebrew to "religion, piety."

The root כסל has the original meaning "fat"; cf. כֶּסֶל (Lev. 3:4; 10:15; Job 15:27). It then develops the secondary connotation of "fool" in כְּסִיל, a semantic relationship exhibited also by טָפַשׁ "grow fat" (Ps. 119:70) and mishnaic Hebrew טִפֵּשׁ "fool," probably because the fool is one whose heart, the seat of understanding, is overlaid by fat; cf. Isa. 6:10, הַשְׁמֵן לֵב הָעָם הַזֶּה. Moreover, the fool, unlike the wise man, is one who trusts everyone too easily. (Cf. Pr. 14:16, חָכָם יָרֵא וְסָר מֵרָע וּכְסִיל מִתְעַבֵּר וּבוֹטֵחַ, which is to be rendered: "A wise man is cautious and avoids trouble, but the fool pushes on and falls." (On בטח see the Comm. on Job 11:18.) Hence, the tertiary meaning "trust, confidence" develops in כֶּסֶל (Ps. 78:7; Pr. 3:26; Job 8:14; 31:24) and כִּסְלָה "trust, confidence" in our passage (so, partially, BDB, s.v.; Yel.).

4:7 נִכְחָדוּ, "cut off" (Ex. 9:15).

4:8 Lit., "When I have seen those who plow iniquity and sow trouble, they reap it." The poetic caesura (after ʾāven) does not coincide here with the logical caesura (after ʿāmāl). It is also possible to place the logical caesura after raʾithi. "As I have seen, those who plow iniquity . . . reap it." For other instances of such a divergence, see Nu. 23:7 and Lam. 1:7, f, g, and the Comm. *ad loc*. Both nouns, ʾāven and ʿāmāl, have the generic meaning of "evil," from which comes the second meaning of "wrongdoing, sin" (Hos. 8:7; 10:13; Ps. 10:14). On the important semantic principle involved, see the Comm. on 3:10 and the reference there.

4:9 נִשְׁמַת "blast, breath," so Ra.: נשימת. For the figure of plowing, sowing and reaping, see Hos. 8:7; 10:13; Pr. 22:8, a usage that has entered into all languages.

4:10 The richness of the Hebrew vocabulary, which has reached us only in part, is attested by the five terms used here for "lion," the precise distinctions of which are largely lost to us today. Only *kephīr*, "young lion," and *lābhīʾ*, "lioness," possess specific meanings. The verse is an instance of zeugma, since the verb in stich b, however interpreted, is inapplicable to the nouns in stich a, to which it serves as a predicate. The lion as a powerful beast of prey is a highly appropriate metaphor for a successful malefactor (cf. Ps. 17:12; 22:14, 22). However, in Ps. 34:11 כְּפִירִים is to be rendered "heretics," equivalent in meaning to late Hebrew כופרים "deniers (sc. of God)," the form being a participial formation like פָּרִיץ lit., "breacher," עָרִיץ, "terrifier," נָבִיא lit., "announcer," קָצִיר "reaper." On the morphology cf. Barth, *Nominalbildung*, pp. 182–85.

נִתָּעוּ has been interpreted a) as a denominative verb from מַלְתָּעוֹת "teeth," used privatively, hence "the teeth of the whelps are removed" (Ibn Janah); b) as an error for נִתָּצוּ "are destroyed" (cf. Ps. 58:7, D-G); or c) as an Aramaism with the Ayin equivalent to the Hebrew Ṣade, as in צאן, עאן, etc. The absence of a cognate in Aramaic does not completely rule out this view (ag. D-G). Since Aramaisms are frequent in Job, there is the possibility of the existence in Hebrew both of the Hebrew (נתץ) and the "Aramaic" forms (נתע); cf. פתר and פשר "interpret, explain."

4:11   On the parallel use of the two verbs in both stichs, cf. Ps. 92:10, אבד "wander about," and cf. Deut. 26:5 אֲרַמִּי אֹבֵד. "The pack of lions must scatter in the search for food."

4:12   On Revelation in Wisdom, see Special Note 8.

יְגֻנַּב "came stealthily, i.e., in private." Eliphaz is one of the seven Gentile prophets listed in *B. Bat.* 15b. On the basis of the verb used, Rashi infers that while Hebrew prophets received God's word publicly, non-Hebrew seers could only expect a less direct form of communication!

4:12 ff.   שֵׁמֶץ lit., "a particle, fraction," rather than "whisper" (BDB); cf. Job 26:14 and Ben Sira 10:10, שמץ מחלה, and 18:36, שמץ תענוג. The noun may be derived from the Arabic *šamiṣa* "speak rapidly, indistinctly" (BDB). On the unusual but authentic equivalence of Hebrew Šin and Arabic Šin, particularly when in proximity to a guttural, see J. Barth, *Etymologische Studien*, pp. 48 ff. (so Yei.). Cf. Hebrew חָשַׁשׁ and Arabic *ḥašašun*. See below on 4:19 on עָשׁ.

מֶנְהוּ the older and archaic form of מִמֶּנּוּ; cf. מִנְהֶם (11:20).

4:13   By a semantic process not clear to us today, the same biblical noun סָעִיף (שְׂעִיף) means both "branch" (I Ki. 10:21; Isa. 17:6) and "thought" (here and Job 20:2). The same noun סַרְעַפָּה (שְׂרְעַף), with epenthetic *Reš*, also occurs in the two meanings of "branch" (Ezek. 31:6) and "thought" (Ps. 94:19; 139:23).

The Mem of מֵחֶזְיֹנוֹת is deleted by Ehr. and Yel., but since both nouns are in apposition, one would expect the repetition of the preposition. Perhaps the word should be read with Beth. MT may, however, be preserved and rendered, "with thoughts arising out of visions of the night" (D-G).

תַּרְדֵּמָה, "heavy sleep," is often associated with a contact with the Divine, as in Abraham's covenant (Gen. 15:12), or in a prophetic vision (Isa. 29:10; Job 33:15); cf. also Gen. 2:21; Ps. 76:7; Dan. 8:18; 10:9. In Jonah 1:5, 6, the author may be employing the same word with ironic intent in order to underscore the fact that here was a prophet who fell asleep, not in order to establish contact with God, but to escape it. A. J. Heschel (*The Prophets*, p. 336) interprets the word as "ecstasy," a meaning which is particularly appropriate in Isa. 29:10.

4:14 קְרָאַנִי correctly rendered by T, ערעני lit., "chanced to come upon me," the *tertiae Aleph* root being equivalent to *tertiae Yod*. The verb *qārā⁾* is used of the encounter of God with the Gentile prophet Balaam (Nu. 23:3). Cf. above on 4:12.

רֹב "the multitude, i.e., all," cf. the rabbinic saying רובו ככולו. On the basis of the Kethib in Job 33:19 Ehr. emends the noun to וְרִיב and renders "and pain frightened my bones," but the change is unnecessary. In the former passage, Elihu is describing illness as an instrument of Divine communication. Here Eliphaz pictures his terror before the Divine, but there is no reference to pain.

4:15 רוח not "spirit" but "breath, wind."

The verb סמר "bristle" is used in the Qal (Ps. 119:120). Hence the Piel used here must be transitive (ag. D-G, P.). Ra., Ibn Ezra recognize this transitive meaning of תְּסַמֵּר and render "the wind (stich a) causes the hair of my flesh to bristle." This requires the assumption that רוּחַ is masculine in stich a and feminine in stich b. In addition, שַׂעֲרַת, if derived from שֵׂעָר, "hair," is a *nomen unitatis* and therefore cannot mean "the entire hair of the body" (Ehr.), but "one strand of hair." Ehr. emends the stich to read תְּסַמֵּר שַׂעֲרָה אֶת רֹאשִׁי, but the emendation which inserts את in a poetic passage is dubious. שַׂעֲרַת should be construed as the older form of the absolute, with Tav; cf. Ges.-K., sec. 80, 2b, note 2. This older, absolute form exists in II Ki. 9:17; Isa. 33:6; Jer. 8:9 (חָכְמַת), בָּרְקַת (Ezek. 28:13). The noun is the subject of the verb תְּסַמֵּר and parallel to רוּחַ: "a storm made my skin bristle."

On the storm as the vehicle for Divine revelation, we need refer not merely to the theophany on Sinai (Ex. 19:16), but also to Job 38:1; 40:6. On the orthography with Sin, cf. 9:17.

4:16 MT יַעֲמֹד "It (i.e., the undescribed and undescribable form) stood still," is superior to LXX, Sym., and Aquila's reading אֶעֱמֹד. This latter reading may be due to a phonetic confusion of prefixed Yod and Aleph (cf. Isa. 51:19, יְנַחֲמֵךְ = מִי אֲנַחֲמֵךְ; Ben Sira 4:17 יבחנו = אבחננו). On the other hand, dogmatic considerations may have influenced the change, the desire to avoid any approximation of an image of God.

מַרְאֶה "appearance" and תְּמוּנָה "form" are both used of the appearance of God to Moses (Nu. 12:8), which is uniquely different from His communication with lesser prophets.

In stich c דְּמָמָה וָקוֹל is not equivalent to קוֹל דְּמָמָה in I Ki. 19:12 (ag. Ibn Ezra, D-G), though the older phrase may well have been familiar to the poet. We have here two stages in the revelation, silence followed by a voice.

The pausal vocalization with *Qameṣ* links וָקוֹל to דְּמָמָה, while the accentuation joins it to אֶשְׁמָע. The latter is preferable: "Silence — then I heard a voice."

4:17 This verse introduces the contents of the Divine message received by Eliphaz. מֵאֱלוֹהַּ means not "more than God" (as in 32:2; KJV), but "in the presence of, before his God." Cf. Nu. 32:22: וִהְיִיתֶם נְקִיִּם מֵה' וּמִיִּשְׂרָאֵל.

4:18 תָּהֳלָה has been emended to הַתָּלָה "error" (Beer), תִּפְלָה "error, folly" (Hu., Me., Sieg., D-G), or revocalized as תְּהִלָּה "praise" with לֹא understood from stich a (Ehr.). Others invoke the Ethiopic *tahala*, "wander about."

The vocalization in MT suggests the root *halal*, from which the noun is derived, particularly common in Ecc. with a constellation of meanings, "revelry, madness, folly." Particularly apposite to our context where the meaning "folly" is required is the usage in Ecc. 2:2; 7:7, 25; 10:13. See *KMW* on 1:17 and the other passages.

יָשִׂים ב' = "charge with, impute to." Cf. I Sam. 22:15.

4:19 A powerful *a fortiori* argument. If the heavenly beings are impure in His sight, how much the more so, human beings!

בָּתֵּי חֹמֶר "clay houses," refers not to actual dwellings, but to the human body; cf. Wisdom of Solomon 9:15, "a tent of earth." On clay as the material from which man is fashioned, see Job 10:9; 33:6. Stichs b and c describe the nature and the ultimate decay of the human frame respectively, paralleling Gen. 3:19, which characterizes the dust as both the source and the destination of man.

In stich e, the form of the verb is difficult, and the usual meaning of "moth" is inappropriate in our context (ag. P.), since this noun is invariably used in the Bible to describe the insect that wreaks destruction, not the victim himself (cf. Isa. 50:9; 51:8; Hos. 5:12; Job 23:28). Hence BDB emends to עַכָּבִישׁ "spider," while Herz (*ZATW*, 1900, p. 160; TS) emends the entire stich to יְדֻכְּאוּ לִפְנֵי עֹשָׂם, "They will be crushed before their Maker." The emendation is, however, unnecessary. The third person plural of the verb in MT is to be taken as impersonal, and therefore equivalent to a passive; hence lit., "They will destroy them, i.e., they will be destroyed." On this usage, cf. Gen. 29:3, וְגָלֲלוּ; the Comm. on 6:2; 18:18; 34:20, and Ges.-K., sec. 144, 3b.

For עָשׁ cf. the Arabic cognate *ʿušnu*, "bird's nest," Akk. *ašašu*, a meaning which occurs again in Job 27:18 (note the parallel with סֻכָּה). The simile stresses the fragility of human existence (Ges., Del., Yel.). On the Hebrew *šin* for Arabic *šin*, see the Comm. above on 4:12. There is no need, therefore, to revocalize MT as עָשׂ with Sin (ag. Ehr.).

4:20 Man's life is compared to a day, from dawn to dusk. מִבְּלִי מֵשִׂים is an ellipsis for מֵשִׂים לֵב "pay heed, attention," as in Isa. 41:20; Job 23:6 (Ibn E. and D-G). The form, a Hiphil of שִׂים is an erroneous *Rückbildung* from such forms as יָשִׂים that seem like the Hiphil of a *Mediae Vav* verb instead of the Qal of a *Mediae Yod* verb.

The emendation proposed by Herz (*ZATW*, 1900, p. 160), בְּלִי שֵׁם "without a name," has been revived by Dahood, who reads מִבְּלִי[ם] שֵׁם (with enclitic Mem). However, the emendation is unnecessary and disrupts the parallelism (see below). In vv. 19, 20, Eliphaz is describing the brevity of life, not the absence of fame.

The phrase in stich b: a) "while they (the victims) pay no heed, are unaware," or b) "with no one else paying heed, they perish." Now vv. 20 and 21 are in alternate parallelism: a ‖ b; a¹ ‖ b¹, so that 20b and 21b are to be interpreted similarly. Since it is more natural to render 21b as "without any wisdom (on the part of the victims)," it is preferable to render 20b as "while they (the victims) are unaware." Cf. also Job 36:12: וַיִּגְוְעוּ בִּבְלִי דַעַת.

4:21 יִתְרָם. The older meaning, "excellence, pride" (T, V, P, Ra.), is inferior to the image available in the rendering "tent-cord" (cf. Ps. 11:2; Job 30:11; so D-G, P.). For the familiar Oriental figure of life as a tent, cf. Isa. 38:12; Wisdom of Solomon 9:15, "tent of earth"; and the *Rubaiyat*, *passim*. נִסַּע, Niphal of נסע = "be plucked up," occurs in both Isaianic passages cited above. בָּם lit., "within them," would mean "by themselves, *per se*, by virtue of their own nature"; cf. Ps. 90:10 יְמֵי שְׁנוֹתֵינוּ בָהֶם "the days of our years are of themselves seventy years," and the related use of לָהֶם in Ecc. 3:18. (See *KMW ad loc.*) וְלֹא בְחָכְמָה see the Comm. on v. 20 above. Lit., "without any wisdom, having learnt nothing during their brief pilgrimage in life."

As is frequent in Semitic literature generally and in Wisdom in particular, the conclusion is left unstated, but clearly implied — since all men are imperfect, all men suffer rightfully. On this implication, left to be inferred, which is basic to the rhetoric of allusion and analogy, see *BGM*, chap. XIV.

CHAPTER 5

5:1 Stich b is generally rendered, "To which of the holy ones can you turn?" The reference is taken to refer to angels (as in Job 15:15; Zech. 14:5; Ps. 89:7; Dan. 4:10, 14; Ben Sira 42:17), for whose intercession Job can only wait in vain (D-G, Duhm, P.). The verse is then excised as an interpolation of a later idea (so Duhm) or it is defended as a polemic against the Mesopotamian idea of a personal God to whom a man could appeal as against the assembly of the great gods (P.), in which case it is equally irrelevant.

The key to the passage lies, we believe, in recognizing מְקְדָשִׁים as an epithet for "God" (so Ehr., who compares Prov. 9:10 דעת קדושים ‖ 'יראת ה, to which we may add Hos. 12:1 קדושים ‖ אל). Ehr.'s interpretation of our passage, however, is very involved: "To whom can you turn in order to bring your complaints against God?" We believe a better interpretation is possible. Eliphaz, who began by reminding Job that righteousness triumphs and that he should therefore trust in his own piety for restoration (4:6–11), again warns Job against impatient anger in the face of temporary injustice

(5:2-5), and informs Job that his only recourse is to turn to God, for there is no other arbiter of man's destiny. Stich b is therefore to be rendered, "To whom rather than to the Holy One can you turn?" מִקְּדֹשִׁים is a contraction of מֵאֶל קְדֹשִׁים, a syntactic construction identical with that of Est. 6:6: לְמִי יַחְפֹּץ הַמֶּלֶךְ לַעֲשׂוֹת יְקָר יוֹתֵר מִמֶּנִּי, "To whom would the king wish to do honor more than to me?" (מֵאֲלֵי or מֶלִי = מִמֶּנִּי).

5:2 כִּי is the emphatic particle "surely" (so Yel.; cf. Isa. 15:1; 28:1; Ps. 128:2; Job 28:2) which is used not only at the beginning of a poem or a section (Isa. 15:1; Ps. 128:2; Job 28:1), but also within a clause (cf. Gen. 18:20; Ps. 128:2, "you will surely eat the fruit of your labor"; cf. Deut. 28:33). On the similar use of the proclitic Kaph as an asseverative in Hebrew and Ugaritic, cf. Gordis, in *JAOS*, vol. 63, 1943, pp. 35-43.

כַּעַשׂ (and כַּעַס), the basic meaning of which is "vexation" (cf. 6:2), here has its common meaning of "anger." קִנְאָה = lit. "jealousy," here has the connotation of "impatience."

אֱוִיל and פֹּתֶה (cf. Hos. 7:11), two terms for "fool," are taken by many commentators as equivalent here to "sinner," a usage common in Wisdom literature (cf. the next verse). However, at this point Eliphaz is not describing the disaster which overtakes the sinner, but is warning Job against letting his impatience at the delay in Divine retribution lead him into senseless anger. The two terms are therefore best rendered "fool." The word order, which places the object "fool" and "simpleton" at the beginning, is emphatic: "it is the fool whom vexation kills" (D-G; cf. Pr. 12:16). The proverbial character of the utterance is clear from the parallelism. As is nearly always the case with apothegms, it cannot be determined whether the verse is original with the author or is a quotation from conventional Wisdom literature.

5:3 Once again Eliphaz invokes his own observation of life (cf. 4:8). Here אֱוִיל, "fool," is the sinner who ostensibly is well entrenched (3a), but whose children will bear his punishment (vv. 4, 5). The traditional doctrine of family retribution (Ex. 20:5), already hinted at in 4:10b, 11, is here made explicit. Cf. *BGM*, chap. XI, for a detailed discussion of the theme of group retribution.

מַשְׁרִישׁ a Hiphil = "taking root," the Piel being privative, "be uprooted" (cf. Job 31:12 and often).

וָאֶקּוֹב, Qal, from qabab (cf. יִדְּמוּ, Ex. 15:16, from dāmam), the Aramaic form of the geminate, with the doubling of the first consonant. The literal meaning, "I cursed," is obviously inappropriate. On the basis of LXX, ebrothe; P ואבדא, = "was eaten away, perished," most moderns emend to the grammatically impossible וְרָקָב (Me., Be., Sieg., Hö.), or to וַיִּרְקַב (Du., Ehr.) = "it rotted away," or to וַיֻּקַּב (P.) = "his abode was suddenly accursed." The parallelism with the first pers. of the verb (רָאִיתִי) suggests that MT is to be preferred. We believe that וָאֶקּוֹב is to be given a declarative sense. Generally, the declarative is expressed by the Piel (וְטִהֲרוֹ, Lev. 13:6; וְטִמְּאוֹ, Lev. 13:8) and the Hiphil וְהִצְדִּיקוּ וְהִרְשִׁיעוּ, Deut. 25:1, etc. (cf. the second conj. in Arabic, kabbara, "call Allah great"; sallama, "provide salām for someone"; and see C. Brockelmann, *Grundriss der semitischen Sprachen*, vol. I, pp. 509, 522, for other examples). D. R. Hillers (in "Delocutive Verbs in Biblical Hebrew," in *JBL*, vol. 86, 1967, pp. 320–24) argues in favor of the term "delocutive" rather than "declarative," and is critical of the fact that usually "the function is sought in the conjugation at the grammatical level rather than in the peculiar use of particular words on the lexical level" (p. 322). In any event, it is clear that the declarative (or delocutive) use occurs also in the Qal, as, e.g., וְלֹא תֶחְטָא (Job 5:24) "you will not find it missing" (Job 5:25), וַיַּעְקְשֵׁנִי, "it would prove me perverse" (Job 9:20). Hence וָאֶקּוֹב = "I declared cursed." The stich would therefore be rendered, "I declared his dwelling place cursed, doomed to sudden destruction."

On the other hand, the theme of suddenness is neither evident nor appropriate in the context. The parallelism with אֱוִיל suggests that the noun is to be vocalized פִּתְאֹם, exactly as in Pr. 3:25, where פַּחַד פִּתְאֹם is parallel to שֹׁאַת רְשָׁעִים (see the commentaries and *BII ad loc.*). The second *Vav* of נָוֵהוּ is possibly to be read as the article, הַפִּתְאֹם, or, preferably, is to be deleted. The phrase נְוֵה פְּתָאִים may be rendered "the dwelling of fools" or "the dwelling of folly," both satisfactory in the context. On פְּתָאִים as an abstract noun, cf. Pr. 9:6, where it is parallel to בִינָה, "understanding," and the frequent use of the plural form in abstractions, like *zekūnīm*, "old age"; *bethūlīm*, "virginity"; *neūrīm*, "youth"; cf. also בְּטֵלִים, "reasons for idleness" (*M. Aboth* 4:10 and cf. the commentators *ad loc.*). There is no real difference in meaning between the abstract sense "the dwelling of folly" and the concrete, "the dwelling of fools," as is clear from נְוֵה צֶדֶק, Jer. 31:22; נְוֵה צַדִּיק, Pr. 24:15; and נְוֵה צַדִּיקִים, Pr. 3:33. The rendering "fools" has the additional advantage of supplying a plural referent for the suffix חֵילָם and for קְצִרוֹ, if it be adopted for קְצִירוֹ in v. 5.

5:4 יֵשַׁע, "safety, help" in the gates, where the judges sat in judgment (Job 31:21; Deut. 25:7; Ps. 127:5; Pr. 22:22). וְיִדַּכְּאוּ is generally taken as a Hithpael with assimilated *Tav* = וְיִתְדַּכְּאוּ. It may be an instance of the archaic Hebrew Hippaᶜel conjugation proposed by Yel. (cf. *Debir*, vol. 1, p. 30). In any event, the reflexive develops a passive meaning, as in the Aramaic Ithpeᶜel and in later Hebrew (cf. וְיִשְׁתַּכְּחוּ, Ecc. 8:10 and *KMW ad loc.*).

5:5 אֲשֶׁר קְצִירוֹ is read by LXX and P as קְצָרוּ (sc. בָּנָיו) = "What his sons have reaped" (so Me., Bi., Bu., Dil., D-G, Ehr., TS). While the Masoretic text *per se* is satisfactory (so also P.), the plural verb of the emendation is favored by the suffix of חֵילָם and of אֵלָם (on which see below), and it would also refer back to פְּתָאִם in v. 3; see the Comm. *ad loc.*

On the other hand, stich b in MT is impossible to interpret satisfactorily. מִצִּנִּים, is generally taken to be equivalent to מִצְּנִינִים, "thorns" (cf. Jos. 23:13) and hence rendered "from among thorns" (Ibn Janah) or given the *ad hoc* meaning "a basket of thorns" (Ibn E.). Ehr. reads מְזָוִנים "granaries" (cf. Ps. 144:13). D-G accept the emendation of Bu. וַאֲלֻמָּתָם עָנִי יִקָּחֵהוּ "their sheaf a poor man will take," but this is graphically distant from MT, as is Be.'s reading וְאוֹנָם צָנִים יָקָחֵהוּ. TS has proposed a brilliant emendation requiring no consonantal change at all: וְאֵלָם צָנִים יָקָחֶה, interpreted as follows אוּל = "strength" (cf. Ps. 73:4), here = "substance, wealth," a semantic development well authenticated for כֹּחַ (see Pr. 10:10; Job 6:22), חַיִל (Gen. 34:29; Nu. 31:9), אוֹן (Hos. 12:9; Job 20:10); cf. *KMW*, Supplementary Note D, pp. 418–21. צָנִים is a *kâtîl* substantive from the root *ṣnm*, "be shriveled up," cf. צְנוּמוֹת (Gen. 41:23), פת צנומה (*B. Ber.* 39a), medieval צנמון, "drought, dearth," etc.; פניו צנומות, "his face is dried up," in Abraham ben Hasdai's *Ben Hammelekh Vehanazir*, and see Ben Jehuda, *Thesaurus*, s.v., p. 5452–b. The two rare words ואלם צנם led to an erroneous word division as ואל מצנים. Render the stich: "Their substance the starving will seize."

צַמִּים has been interpreted as (1) "wild men or tribes, i.e., those who wear their hair long," from צַמָּה "veil" (Cant. 6:7), so T.; Ibn Melekh. (2) "young women with veils" (*apud* Ibn Ezra). (3) More generally, it is revocalized as צְמֵאִים (Sym., P, Ibn E., Ew., Ehr., Hö., Me., Del.). (4) It is also read as צָמִים "fasters," from the root *ṣûm* "to fast," "avoid food" (cf. Isa. 58:3), but this is not equivalent to "be hungry." We suggest that צַמִּים is a *Kattil* form parallel to the *katil* form. Cf. the morphologic variants צַדִּיק and שָׁמִיר; פַּטִּישׁ, "hammer" and בְּרִיחַ, "bolt"; אָסִיר and אַסִּיר "prisoner," and Barth, *NB*, pp. 186, 197. For examples of this form in geminates, cf. such nouns as יָשִׁישׁ "aged," mishnaic עָצִיץ "earthen vessel." The basic meaning of the root *ṣâmam* is "constrict, contract, famished," which recalls Shakespeare's "lean and hungry look." In postbiblical Hebrew, the Pilpel form of the root became common (cf. *ṣimṣēm*, "contract, constrict" and the important Kabbalistic term *ṣimṣūm*, "the contraction of the Divine"). צַמִּים occurs in Job 18:9 in the meaning of "trap, lit. that which closes in upon its victim." (Cf. מַלְכֹּדֶת and עֲצוּמָיו, Ps. 10:10, on which cf. Gordis, "Ps. 9–10, A Textual and Exegetical Study," in *JQR*, vol. 48, 1957, pp. 117 f.) Here צַמִּים means "one contracted through lack of food; hence, lean." וְשָׁאַף means either "pant for" (cf. Job 7:2) or, better, "snatch away, drag off."

It is now clear that the three stichs are in perfect parallelism. The poet uses his extraordinarily rich vocabulary in order to find two synonyms for רָעֵב : צָנִים and צַמִּים.

The presence of a third stich in the verse is entirely in consonance with the principle of a longer meter-pattern at the conclusion of a poem or of a section. On this usage, cf. *PPS*, pp. 70–71. Hö.'s deletion of stich b and Ehr.'s doubts with regard to stich c are therefore both unjustified.

5:6 The two nouns אָוֶן and עָמָל, which frequently occur in parallelism (cf. Nu. 23:21; Ps. 7:15; 10:7; 55:11; 90:10; Isa. 10:1), are all-inclusive terms meaning "trouble, evil." However, in spite of the classic rendering of the next verse, "Man is born to trouble" (AV, P.), this cannot be the meaning of our passage, for this is precisely Job's complaint — it can hardly be his comfort. Hence, Sieg., Be., Wel. omit both verses as irrelevant, a procedure which is both arbitrary and unnecessary. We have already noted the semantic principle that *the same word will be used in Hebrew to express both a quality or act, and the consequences of that quality or act.* Hence the two terms mean both "evil-doing" and "evil consequences, punishment, suffering." The nouns meaning "sin" also denote "suffering, punishment" (cf. חֵטְא Isa. 53:12, not "sin," Lam. 3:39; חַטָּאת Zech. 14:19; Lam. 4:6; Jer. 2:3; עָוֹן II Ki. 7:9; Isa. 53:6, 11; Lam. 4:6). Cf. the Comm. on 3:10 and *KMW*, pp. 418–20, for the specific meanings of ʿāmāl in particular.

Eliphaz is emphasizing the idea that not God or "nature" (אֲדָמָה, עָפָר) is the source for evil in the world, but man. This is a basic doctrine of biblical and postbiblical religion, which sees man as created in the Divine image (cf. Gen. 1:27 and Ben Azzai's emphasis on Gen. 5:1 as the fundamental principle of the Torah, *Sifra* on *Kedoshim*, Lev. 19:18). Man is, therefore, free to choose between good and evil (cf. Deut. 12:26 ff.; 30:19) and is thus the source of evil in the world. The uniquely paradoxical statement in Isa. 45:7 is a polemic against Zoroastrian dualism. Man's reason is the source of his freedom of will, and hence the basis of his moral responsibility. In 12:16b Job objects and insists that God is the source of the evil in man's nature.

5:7   On the untenability of the familiar rendering "Man is born for trouble" see note on 5:6 above and cf. Hö. Read with Bu. and Hö. יוֹלִד in the Hiphil. The Lamed of לְעָמָל is a direct accusative (cf. Lev. 19:18; II Sam. 3:30; and often). "It is man who gives birth to evil." The Vav linking the two stichs together is the *Vav adaequationis*, frequent in Proverbs for making a comparison (cf. Pr. 25:25; 26:14). Possibly MT = "man is born (to produce) evil."

רֶשֶׁף is the Phoenician god רֶשֶׁף חֵץ who appears with lightning bolts (cf. Ps. 76:4; 78:48; Hab. 3:5) and was equated in the Hellenistic period with Apollo. In the Ugaritic pantheon he is identified with the Mesopotamian deity Nergal, the god of pestilence (cf. Deut. 32:24, and see Ps. 91:6b and Hab. 3:5). In our passage, "the sons of Resheph" is appropriate in either meaning, referring either to the sparks of lightning or to the shafts of the pestilence.

5:8   אֲנִי is emphatic: "But were I in your place, I would seek the Lord." Eliphaz thus returns to the theme of 5:1 — that the only right course for Job is repentance and return to God. The alliteration in the verse is striking. Hence the substitution of *Šaddai* for ʾelohim in stich b is uncalled for. Not only are ʾel and ʾelohim different vocables, but the poet is not averse to using the same word in parallel stichs; cf. 8:3; 41:16, etc.

The rarity of ʾelohim in the Dialogue (but cf. 28:23; 34:9 and see the Comm. on 11:6) is an argument for its authenticity.

5:9   חקר literally "searching out — the end"; cf. Ps. 145:3; Pr. 25:3, etc. The theme is a commonplace of biblical hymnology. The repetition of the verse by Job in 9:10 is ironic, a fact which has not generally been noted (see the Comm. *ad loc.*).

5:10   Rainfall, particularly in the Orient, is the greatest of wonders (cf. Jer. 10:13–16). Note the phrase מַשִּׁיב הָרוּחַ וּמוֹרִיד הַגֶּשֶׁם, "He causes the wind to blow and the rain to fall," which is introduced into the *Amidah* of the Jewish liturgy immediately after the miracle of the resurrection of the dead is mentioned. The phrase is called גבורות גשמים, "the power of rains" (*M. Ber.* 5:2).

5:11   The effort to relate this verse to the preceding because of the infinitive with Lamed, "in order to set the lowly on high," is farfetched and unconvincing. לָשׂוּם is the infinitive consecutive which occurs both in the construct (cf. Isa. 44:14 לִכְרָת; Ps. 104:21 וּלְבַקֵּשׁ; Job 28:25 לַעֲשׂוֹת), as well as in the absolute (Isa. 37:19; Jer. 14:5; Hab. 2:15; Est. 8:8, and see Ges.-K., sec. 113, 4a). In this usage, the infinitive takes on the same tense as the finite verb preceding it in the passage. Hence לָשׂוּם = the participle הַשָּׂם. The translation of the verb by the participle in LXX and V is, therefore, not due to a variant reading (ag. D-G), but is a correct rendition of the infinitive consecutive used here.

קֹדְרִים "lit. blackened ones" (cf. Arabic *kadura*, "be dirty"; Aram. "be dark") is not a figure of mourning here, as in Jer. 8:21; Ps. 35:14, etc., but means "afflicted, miserable, poverty-stricken" (cf. חֲשֻׁכִים "dark ones, obscure men," Prov. 22:29; from Arab. *ḥalaka* "black, black ones, poor"; Ps. 10:8; 10:14). שגב "be raised up" (cf. Deut. 2:36; Ps. 20:2). יֶשַׁע is an adv. acc., literally "exalted with respect to safety."

5:12   While עֲרוּמִים has no negative connotation in Pr. 1:4; 8:5, 12 ("prudence"), in usage it has generally been polarized as "cunning, crafty" (cf. Gen. 3:1 and often).

תּוּשִׁיָּה, a term characteristic of Wisdom literature (and limited to it except for Isa. 28:29; Mic. 6:9), is obscure in etymology. It is perhaps best derived from יֵשׁ "substance," or the Akkadian *issu usatu*, "prop, support" (cf. אָשְׁיוֹתֶיהָ, Jer. 50:15.) Its usage in the Bible indicates that it possesses two meanings that are related to each other, in accordance with the semantic principle already adduced (see the Comm. on 5:6 and 5:7 above): (a) effective wisdom; (b) its result, i.e., success (cf. the similar usage of הִשְׂכִּיל "be wise," and "succeed"; see BDB s.v. and D-G, vol. 2, pp. 30 f. for a full discussion). At times the theme of "wisdom" predominates so that it is virtually a synonym for חָכְמָה (Isa. 28:29; Pr. 3:21; 8:14; Job 11:6; 12:6; 26:3). At other times, the emphasis is upon "success," as in our passage and 6:13; Pr. 2:7, which has led some critics to emend it unnecessarily to תְּשׁוּעָה "salvation."

5:13   בְּעָרְמָם is treated as the infinitive construct of a verb in the Qal by Yel., Ehr., but it occurs elsewhere only in the Hiphil (I Sam. 23:22; Pr. 15:5; 19:25). On the other hand, BDB postulates a noun עֹרֶם, which is, otherwise, nonexistent. We believe that in biblical Hebrew feminine nouns might in exceptional cases have the suffix added to their stem, since the *He* ending was not sounded. See Special Note 9. Hence בְּעָרְמָה + suff. = בְּעָרְמָם.

נִמְהָרָה, apparently derived from מָהַר, "speed, hasten," is interpreted as "is precipitate, carried headlong to a speedy end." The other uses of the root in the Niphal are not helpful here, being applied to human beings and with no single meaning appropriate to them all: in Isa. 32:5 "disturbed"; in Isa. 35:4 "hasty"; in Hab. 1:6 "impetuous." Perhaps the substantive is a denominative from מֹהַר "gift" (cf. Akk. *mâru* "send"), with the meaning "sold out, is betrayed" (cf. the similar use of מָכַר "sell," Deut. 32:30; Jud. 2:14; 3:8; Ps. 44:13, which has this derived meaning, as well as נכר (Hos. 3:2, on which see Gordis, "Hosea's Marriage and Message," in *PPS*, p. 251, note 37).

5:14 יְפַגְּשׁוּ the Piel, used only here, may have been induced by the Piel (יְמַשְׁשׁוּ) in stich b, a type of phonetic assimilation not without analogy; cf. מוֹבָא in II Sam. 3:25 Qere; Ezek. 43:11, because of מוֹצָא.

5:15 Stich a has been variously emended: (1) מֵחֶרֶב to מָחֳרָב (Ew.), "devastated," but this root is never used of human beings; (2) to מִפִּיהֶם יָתוֹם (Bu.); (3) to מִפִּי הָם, which TS renders: "from the hand of the oppressor" on the basis of Est. 9:24; (4) to מֵחֶרֶב פִּיפִיּוֹת (Ehr.); and to פְּתָאִים (P.). None of these emendations commend themselves. P, T, V, do not reproduce the Mem of מִפִּיהֶם, but this does not represent a variant textual reading (ag. D-G). מֵחֶרֶב מִפִּיהֶם is a hendiadys, lit. "from the sword, from their mouth, i.e., from their sharp tongue" (cf. Ps. 59:8; 64:4). On this rhetorical figure, see Gordis, in *Sepher Moshe Seidel* (Jerusalem, 1962), pp. 260 ff., and cf. Isa. 53:8, מֵעֹצֶר וּמִמִּשְׁפָּט לֻקָּח, "he has been seized because of the suppression of justice." The hendiadys is here used asyndetonically. Our verse is an example of complementary (or climactic) parallelism, a, b, ‖ b, c (cf. Ps. 29:1; 94:1; and *PPS*, pp. 74 f.). See also the Comm. below on לְשֹׁד וּלְכָפָן (5:22).

5:16 The three verses 16–18 are clearly based, as Yel. pointed out, on other biblical passages: 16b = Ps. 107:42; 17a = Ps. 94:12; 17b = Pr. 3:11; 18a = Hos. 6:1; 18b = Deut. 32:34. Obviously, it is Job who has borrowed from older writers, a fact which points to a later, post-exilic date rather than to the earlier pre-exilic period for its composition.

    This verse is the only adumbration in the Friends' Dialogue of the theme of suffering as a divine discipline (cf. Ps. 94:12; Pr. 3:11), which is the basic contribution of Elihu to the discussion in our book. Similarly, the theme of the mystery of the world as being beyond human comprehension, which is the essence of the God Speeches, is also referred to in the Dialogue, but only briefly by Zophar in one short passage (11:7–9). This observation supports our thesis of the unity of authorship of the book — ideas that germinated early in the poet's career were fully developed later. These two elements of the conventional theodicy which the poet accepted as valid, he reserved for full treatment not by the Friends, to whom he is not sympathetic, but by the two closing speakers, Elihu and the Lord. Though the Friends are not his authentic spokesmen, he does not completely eliminate these two ideas from their speeches.

While the idea finds expression in conventional Wisdom (Pr. 3:11 and here), it is entirely comprehensible that its role would be limited, since the upper-class orientation of Wisdom writers made the theme of undeserved suffering largely superfluous for their pupils and their readers. It was the poor for whom the idea would hold far greater appeal, as, e.g., the Psalmist (94:12), whose complaints against legalized injustice (vv. 20, 21) demonstrate his affiliation with the lower groups in society.

5:17   הִנֵּה is an instance of anacrusis (cf. Ps. 1:1a, 4a), introducing a new and striking idea and therefore is not to be deleted (ag. Hö). מוּסָר, "chastisement, instruction," develops the specific theme of "inflicting pain" (cf. Deut. 8:5; Pr. 19:18; 29:17) and the common rabbinic יסורים, "suffering."

The theological outlook embodied in this semantic development is made explicitly clear in the talmudic dictum: אם רואה אדם שיסוריו באין עליו יפשפש במעשיו, "If a man sees suffering coming upon him, let him scrutiinze his actions" (*B. Ber.* 5a).

5:18   תִּרְפֶּינָה. The *tertiae Aleph* root *rāphāʾ* has coalesced here with the *tertiae Yod*, a process which came to completion in rabbinic Hebrew, where the former conjugation disappears almost completely (cf. מצינו for מצאנו etc.).

5:19   The use of ascending numeration (X, X + 1) is a characteristic of biblical and Semitic poetry in general. It occurs in two forms: (a) where the numbers are used as equivalent to "several" and no effort is made to spell out the exact number of items (Am. 1:3 ff., 6, 9, 11, 13; 2:1, 4, 6; Mic. 5:4; Ecc. 11:2; B. S. 25:7, etc.; and (b) where the list of items following the numbers is identical with the higher figure (Pr. 6:16 ff.; 30:5 ff., 18 ff., 21 ff., 24 ff., 29 ff.).

Our passage, which apparently falls into the latter type, presents several problems (a): the text would seem to indicate nine disasters: (1) רעב (2) מלחמה (3) שוט לשון (4) שוד (5) שד (6) כפן (7) חית הארץ (8) אבני השדה (9) חית השדה and (b) several of them appear repetitious: רעב and כפן, שוד and שד, חית הארץ and חית השדה. Both these problems can be solved by deleting v. 22 (so Be., Du., Bu., Hö.). However, the conjunction כִּי in v. 23 makes it clear that v. 22 is essential to the context. Moreover, there are two additional problems which have not generally been noted (but see D-G); (c) the calamities listed are all mass disasters, not merely individual troubles. The usual interpretation of לָשׁוֹן in v. 21 as "slander, the evil tongue" (cf. Jer. 18:18), is therefore not appropriate. (d) Two major calamities — fire and flood — seem to be missing from this extensive list of calamities.

In essence, MT needs no emendation or deletion, when these last two difficulties are taken into account. The nine calamities are reduced to seven, when it is recognized that (a) חית השדה and חית הארץ are identical, (b) while רעב and כפן, the precise nuances of which are no longer clear to us, refer to different types of starvation, due to different causes, such as drought or insects (cf. Ehr.); (c) לְשֵׁד וּלְכָפָן is a hendiadys = "the devastation of drought"; (d) שׁוֹט לָשׁוֹן is an elliptical expression for שׁוֹט לְשׁוֹן אֵשׁ (so Ehr.); and (e) שׁוֹד in v. 21 means "flood." Note the plene spelling from the root שׁוּד and see the Comm. on 5:21. Hence the seven mass disasters are famine, war, fire, flood, drought, rocks, and wild beasts.

5:20 פָּדְךָ is the perfect of prophetic certitude (D-G); cf. גָּלָה (Isa. 5:13), נִדְמוּ (Hos. 4:6).

5:21 בְּשׁוֹט is best taken, not as the noun "scourge," but as the infinitive construct of the verb šūṭ which occurs as שׁוּט in Job 1:7, 22; but cf. môṭ, "die," which is both inf. abs. (Gen. 2:17 and often) and inf. constr. (Lev. 16:1); môṭ "totter" (Ps. 38:17; 46:3). On the meaning of this verse see Note on 5:19 above.

　　לָשׁוֹן is generally interpreted as "evil tongue, slander." It is better regarded as equal to לְשׁוֹן אֵשׁ (cf. Isa. 5:24), exactly as לָשׁוֹן in Jos. 15:2 is an ellipsis for לְשׁוֹן הַיָּם (Ehr.). Referring stich a to a fire is preferable to interpreting it as a flood (ag. Barth, ZATW, vol. 33, p. 306, and vol. 34, p. 69; G. R. Driver, in JBL, 1936, vol. 55, p. 110). In stich b, שׁוֹד, written plene, from the root "šūd," is a metaplastic form for šdy, "pour, flow," common in Aramaic and occurring also in Arabic. The root šūd is well attested in Syriac in the meaning "pour, rush in with force" (Payne-Smith, Thesaurus Syriacus, pp. 4088–89). It is to be recognized in Ps. 91:6 (yasūd ‖ yahalōkh) and in Isa. 13:6; Joel 1:15, כְּשֹׁד מִשַּׁדַּי, "as a mighty storm." The root šdy is to be read in several biblical passages, notably II Sam. 1:21 (reading שְׁדִי = "outpouring") and Jer. 18:14; and see Gordis, "The Root ŠDY-ŠD in Biblical Hebrew," J. Th. S. (1940), pp. 34–41.

　　On the impact of torrents on the Mid-Eastern terrain, see J. A. Montgomery, Arabia and the Bible (Philadelphia, 1934), p. 85. On the reasons for not deleting this verse, see the Comm. on 5:19. The catalogue of calamities now includes both fire and water.

5:22 The precise difference between רָעָב and כָּפָן is not clear. The latter may mean "hunger due to bad crops"; BDB renders it "dearth." That the two terms are regarded as referring to two distinct calamities is evident from the enumeration "seven" in v. 19; see the Comm. above. Similarly, the Mishnah (Abot 5:8) lists seven punishments that may be visited upon a community, three of which are different varieties of famine: (1) rāʿābh šel baṣṣōret, "famine due to drought"; (2) rāʿābh šel mehūmāh, "famine due to disturbance (caused by armies)"; and (3) rāʿābh šel kelāyāh, "famine of total annihilation."

5:23 The stones of the field are a hazard both for planting (cf. Isa. 5:2; II Ki. 3:19, 35) and for walking (cf. Ps. 91:12). The ancient variant אַדְנֵי הַשָּׂדֶה "mountain-men" (cf. Mid. Koh. R. on 6:11; Sifra on Lev. 11:27; and see Rashi *ad loc.*) and the proposed emendation בְּנֵי, "sons, i.e., spirits of the field" (Be., *ZATW*, vol. 35 (1915), pp. 67 f.), are not necessary. Neither is the change of הַשָּׂדֶה in stich b to הָאֲדָמָה (ag. Dr.) or הָאָרֶץ, in order to avoid the repetition of the same vocable in both stichs, in view of the well-attested usage by the poet to use the same root in parallel stichs (cf. 5:8; 7:8; 8:3; 11:18 and see Special Note 4).

הָשְׁלְמָה the Hophal need not be emended to the Qal שָׁלְמָה. As the passive of the Hiphil "make peace" (Jos. 10:1, 4; Deut. 20:12 a. e.), the Hophal means "are caused, i.e., persuaded, to make peace with you."

5:24 וּפָקַדְתָּ in stich b exhibits an example of *talḥin*, the root carrying, in addition to its primary meaning "visit," the secondary meaning "miss" (cf. I Sam. 20:18). On *talḥin* cf. Gordis in *Sepher Tur Sinai* (Jerusalem, 1962), pp. 149 ff. תֶחֱטָא here bears its primary sense "miss the mark" (cf. Jud. 20:16). The Qal is here used declaratively, "find nothing missing." On this use of the Qal, see the Comm. on וְאָקוֹב, 5:3 above.

5:26 כֶּלַח, which occurs again in 30:2, is best rendered "ripe old age" (Ra., Ibn E., Ki.), which must be pronounced an *ad hoc* interpretation. BDB adduces the Arabic *kalaḥa*, "look hard, stern," which is still remote from our context. The various emendations proposed: בְּחֵילְךָ "in your strength" (Be.), בְּלֵחֲךָ "in your moisture" (Me.), בְּקֶלַח "in your stalk harvest," i.e. = "children" (TS), do not commend themselves.

גָּדִישׁ = "harvest heap," a highly apposite figure for the burial pile as well (cf. Job 21:32).

5:27 For שְׁמָעֶנָּה read שְׁמַעֲנָה, "we have heard it" (LXX, Sym., Ehr., D-G) which is supported both by the parallelism and by the adversative clause introduced by וְאַתָּה, "but now *you* take it to heart." The two verbs refer to the two sources of wisdom: חקר = "search out" on the basis of one's own observation, שמע = "hear, learn by tradition from the past." לְךָ = "for thy good" or it may be merely an ethical dative.

Job's Reply to Eliphaz (6–7)

Job seems not to have heard Eliphaz's elaborate argumentation. Weighted down with his own misery, he indulges in a painful reverie. Life is a burden that he cannot bear. He wishes to die and end his agony. Perhaps he has been unrestrained in his grief, but it is only the measure of his agony. If all were well with him he would have no cause for complaint, any more than an animal at a well-filled trough.

The truth is that he has heard Eliphaz all too well, but has found his words tasteless and meaningless. In the face of these finespun explanations Job knows only that he has not violated the commands of God. Bitterly he calls upon God to reward him — by a speedy death — for he can bear his torture no longer.

Job then turns in fury upon his friends, who have proved unreliable when he needed them most. In a powerful figure he compares them to a desert stream which the footsore and thirsty traveler struggles to reach, only to find it frozen over in the winter and dried up in the summer.

In repeating the threadbare argument that justice always prevails, Eliphaz has implied that Job is sinful. Pathetically Job protests his innocence and asks for sympathy. He paints a moving picture of his physical pain and mental anguish, which are all the more difficult to bear because life is fleeting, with little time or hope for improvement.

Job's only relief lies in speaking out against the injustice he suffers at the hands of the God whom he has served and obeyed all his life. In a bitter parody of the Eighth Psalm he asks why man is worthy of God's jealous and vengeful attention. Granted that he has sinned, why does God torment him? Why not kill him at once and thus end his agony?

Job raises two fundamental issues here that are never even remotely approached by the Friends, who can only restate the conventional theology of the day. The first is the question: Why is man important to God and why are his sins and weaknesses the subject of divine concern? The answer of biblical religion is implicit in its view of the nature of man. The concept that man is created in the image of God is expressed in the opening chapter of Genesis, and its major implications are spelled out in the Eighth Psalm, which Job parodies. It follows that man and God are intimately and indissolubly linked together, for man's deeds have a direct bearing upon God's purposes in the world. Stated less theologically, man is endowed with extraordinary capacities which place upon him extraordinary responsibilities.

The second problem posed by Job is equally searching: Why should a man, even a sinner, be made to suffer, seeing that he is not master of his destiny? As is characteristic of biblical thought, Job does not operate in syllogistic form. Nevertheless, he is raising here the problem of God's omnipotence and man's responsibility. The dilemma of free will versus determinism was never resolved in the Hebraic tradition and remains a challenge to our own day. In approaching the issue, Rabbinic Judaism seized hold of both horns of the dilemma, as in Rabbi Akiba's classic formulation, "All is foreseen, yet free will is given to man." A millennium and a half later, Samuel Johnson declared with equal succinctness, "As for free-will, all philosophy is against it and all experience is for it." In spite of all the logical difficulties involved, the Judeo-Christian world view, with few exceptions, has continued to hold fast to man's freedom as the indispensable foundation for man's moral responsibility.

To rearrange the material in these chapters in accordance with Western canons of logic and relevance, as some scholars have proposed, is to violate the passion and sweep of the poetry. Job's basic theme is his unbearable agony, to which he reverts time and again when challenging God's justice, or pleading for his death, when berating his friends for their lack of sympathy or demanding to know why he is the object of God's baleful concern. It is emotion, not logic, that constitutes the underlying unity in Job's moving outburst.

6   Then Job replied, saying,
2   If indeed my anguish were weighed
              and all my calamity placed in the scales,
3   they would be heavier than the sand of the sea —
              therefore I may have spoken rashly.
4   For the arrows of the Almighty are in me;
              my spirit drinks in their poison;
              God's terrors are arrayed against me.
5   Does the wild ass bray when he has grass,
              or the ox low over his fodder?
6   Can tasteless food be eaten without salt,
              or is there any savor in the juice of mallows?
7   I refuse to touch my food;
              I loathe it as if it were diseased.

8   O, that I might have my petition
              and God would grant my hope —
9   that it would please God to crush me,
              to loose His hand and cut me off!
10   For this would still be my consolation
              as I trembled in pitiless agony —
              that I never have denied the words of the Holy One.

11   What is my strength, that I should be quiet,
              and what my end, that I should be patient?
12   Is my strength the strength of stones,
              is my flesh made of bronze?
13   Indeed, there is no help for me,
              and effective aid has been cut off from me.

14   He who pleads for kindness from his fellow man
              has forsaken the reverence due the Almighty.
15   My brothers betray me like a desert stream,
              like freshets that pass away,
16   that grow dark with ice,
              when the snow is heaped upon them.
17   But in the time of heat, they disappear,
               when it is hot, they vanish from their place.
18   Their paths wind away,
              they go up into nothingness and disappear.
19   The caravans of Tema looked to them;
              the travelers of Sheba hoped for them.
20   They are disappointed because they counted on them;
              When they reach them, they are put to shame.
21   Now you have become like that stream;
              you see my disaster and are seized with fear.
22   Have I ever said, "Give something on my behalf,
              and from your wealth offer a bribe for me;
23   deliver me from the enemy's hand
              and ransom me from the hand of the oppressors"?

ו א וַיַּעַן אִיּוֹב וַיֹּאמַר׃

2 לוּ שָׁקוֹל יִשָּׁקֵל כַּעְשִׂי וְהַוָּתִי בְּמֹאזְנַיִם יִשְׂאוּ־יָחַד׃

3 כִּי־עַתָּה מֵחוֹל יַמִּים יִכְבָּד עַל־כֵּן דְּבָרַי לָעוּ׃

4 כִּי חִצֵּי שַׁדַּי עִמָּדִי אֲשֶׁר חֲמָתָם שֹׁתָה רוּחִי

5 הֲיִנְהַק־פֶּרֶא עֲלֵי־דֶשֶׁא בְּעוֹתֵי אֱלוֹהַּ יַעַרְכוּנִי׃

6 אִם־יֵאָכֵל תָּפֵל מִבְּלִי־מֶלַח הֲיֵאָכֵל־שׁוֹר עַל־בְּלִילוֹ׃

7 מֵאֲנָה לִנְגּוֹעַ נַפְשִׁי אִם־יֶשׁ־טַעַם בְּרִיר חַלָּמוּת׃

8 מִי־יִתֵּן תָּבוֹא שֶׁאֱלָתִי הֵמָּה כִּדְוֵי לַחְמִי׃

9 וְיֹאֵל אֱלוֹהַּ וִידַכְּאֵנִי וְתִקְוָתִי יִתֵּן אֱלוֹהַּ׃

י יַתֵּר יָדוֹ וִיבַצְּעֵנִי וּתְהִי־עוֹד ׀ נֶחָמָתִי

וַאֲסַלְּדָה בְחִילָה לֹא יַחְמוֹל כִּי־לֹא כִחַדְתִּי אִמְרֵי קָדוֹשׁ׃

11 מַה־כֹּחִי כִּי־אֲיַחֵל וּמַה־קִּצִּי כִּי־אַאֲרִיךְ נַפְשִׁי׃

12 אִם־כֹּחַ אֲבָנִים כֹּחִי אִם־בְּשָׂרִי נָחוּשׁ׃

13 הַאִם אֵין עֶזְרָתִי בִי וְתֻשִׁיָּה נִדְּחָה מִמֶּנִּי׃

14 לַמָּס מֵרֵעֵהוּ חָסֶד וְיִרְאַת שַׁדַּי יַעֲזוֹב׃

טו אַחַי בָּגְדוּ כְמוֹ־נָחַל כַּאֲפִיק נְחָלִים יַעֲבֹרוּ׃

16 הַקֹּדְרִים מִנִּי־קָרַח עָלֵימוֹ יִתְעַלֶּם־שָׁלֶג׃

17 בְּעֵת יְזֹרְבוּ נִצְמָתוּ בְּחֻמּוֹ נִדְעֲכוּ מִמְּקוֹמָם׃

18 יִלָּפְתוּ אָרְחוֹת דַּרְכָּם יַעֲלוּ בַתֹּהוּ וְיֹאבֵדוּ׃

19 הִבִּיטוּ אָרְחוֹת תֵּמָא הֲלִיכֹת שְׁבָא קִוּוּ־לָמוֹ׃

כ בֹּשׁוּ כִּי־בָטָח בָּאוּ עָדֶיהָ וַיֶּחְפָּרוּ׃

21 כִּי־עַתָּה הֱיִיתֶם לוֹ תִּרְאוּ חֲתַת וַתִּירָאוּ׃

22 הֲכִי־אָמַרְתִּי הָבוּ לִי וּמִכֹּחֲכֶם שִׁחֲדוּ בַעֲדִי׃

23 וּמַלְּטוּנִי מִיַּד־צָר וּמִיַּד עָרִיצִים תִּפְדּוּנִי׃

24	Teach me, and I shall be silent,
	and where I have erred, make me understand.
25	How forceful are true words!
	But what can your argument demonstrate?
26	Do you regard empty words as proof
	but a despairing man's speeches as mere wind?
27	You would cast lots even over an orphan
	and drive a bargain over your friend.
28	And now, pray, give me heed,
	you may turn away, if I should lie.
29	Please stay, there is no wrong in me,
	stay with me, my integrity is still intact.
30	Is there any wrong upon my tongue?
	Cannot my taste discern falsehood?
7	A term of hard service awaits man upon earth;
	his life is like a hireling's days.
2	Like a slave, he yearns for the shadow;
	like a hireling, he waits for his wage.
3	Indeed, I have been allotted months of emptiness,
	and nights of misery have been meted out to me.
4	When I lie down, I ask, "When shall I arise?"
	but the night is long, and I say,
	"I have had my fill of tossing till daybreak."
5	My flesh is clothed in worms and clods of dirt;
	my skin hardens and then breaks out again.
6	My days are swifter than the weaver's shuttle;
	they end in the absence of hope.
7	Remember that my life is but a breath —
	my eye will never again see good.
8	The eye of the beholder will see me no more;
	while your eyes are upon me, I am gone.
9	As a cloud fades and disappears,
	so he who goes down to Sheol rises no more.
10	He will not return to his home,
	and his place will know him no longer.
11	Therefore I will not restrain my speech;
	I will speak out in the agony of my spirit;
	I will complain in the bitterness of my soul.
12	Am I the Sea, or the Dragon,
	that You place a guard about me?
13	When I think, "My couch will comfort me,
	my bed will share the burden of my complaint,"
14	then You terrify me with dreams
	and frighten me with visions,

24 הוֹרוּנִי וַאֲנִי אַחֲרִישׁ   וּמַה־שָּׁגִיתִי הָבִינוּ לִי:

כה מַה־נִּמְרְצוּ אִמְרֵי־יֹשֶׁר   וּמַה־יּוֹכִיחַ הוֹכֵחַ מִכֶּם:

26 הַלְהוֹכַח מִלִּים תַּחְשֹׁבוּ   וּלְרוּחַ אִמְרֵי נֹאָשׁ:

27 אַף־עַל־יָתוֹם תַּפִּילוּ   וְתִכְרוּ עַל־רֵיעֲכֶם:

28 וְעַתָּה הוֹאִילוּ פְנוּ־בִי   וְעַל־פְּנֵיכֶם אִם־אֲכַזֵּב:

29 שֻׁבוּ־נָא אַל־תְּהִי עַוְלָה   וְשֻׁבִי עוֹד צִדְקִי־בָהּ:

ל הֲיֵשׁ־בִּלְשׁוֹנִי עַוְלָה   אִם־חִכִּי לֹא־יָבִין הַוּוֹת:

ז א הֲלֹא־צָבָא לֶאֱנוֹשׁ עַל־אָרֶץ   וְכִימֵי שָׂכִיר יָמָיו:

2 כְּעֶבֶד יִשְׁאַף־צֵל   וּכְשָׂכִיר יְקַוֶּה פָעֳלוֹ:

3 כֵּן הָנְחַלְתִּי לִי יַרְחֵי־שָׁוְא   וְלֵילוֹת עָמָל מִנּוּ־לִי:

4 אִם־שָׁכַבְתִּי וְאָמַרְתִּי   מָתַי אָקוּם וּמִדַּד־עָרֶב

ה וְשָׂבַעְתִּי נְדֻדִים עֲדֵי־נָשֶׁף: לָבַשׁ בְּשָׂרִי רִמָּה וְגִישׁ עָפָר

6 עוֹרִי רָגַע וַיִּמָּאֵס: יָמַי קַלּוּ מִנִּי־אָרֶג

7 וַיִּכְלוּ בְּאֶפֶס תִּקְוָה: זְכֹר כִּי־רוּחַ חַיָּי

8 לֹא־תָשׁוּב עֵינִי לִרְאוֹת טוֹב: לֹא־תְשׁוּרֵנִי עֵין רֹאִי

9 עֵינֶיךָ בִּי וְאֵינֶנִּי: כָּלָה עָנָן וַיֵּלַךְ

י כֵּן יוֹרֵד שְׁאוֹל לֹא יַעֲלֶה: לֹא־יָשׁוּב עוֹד לְבֵיתוֹ

11 וְלֹא־יַכִּירֶנּוּ עוֹד מְקֹמוֹ:   גַּם־אֲנִי לֹא אֶחֱשָׂךְ פִּי

אֲדַבְּרָה בְּצַר רוּחִי   אָשִׂיחָה בְּמַר נַפְשִׁי:

12 הֲיָם־אָנִי אִם־תַּנִּין   כִּי־תָשִׂים עָלַי מִשְׁמָר:

13 כִּי־אָמַרְתִּי תְּנַחֲמֵנִי עַרְשִׂי   יִשָּׂא בְשִׂיחִי מִשְׁכָּבִי:

14 וְחִתַּתַּנִי בַחֲלֹמוֹת   וּמֵחֶזְיֹנוֹת תְּבַעֲתַנִּי:

15   so that I prefer strangling —
            death rather than this existence.
16   I loathe my life; I shall not live forever.
            Let me alone, for my days are but a breath.

17   What is man that You exalt him
            and You give him Your attention,
18   that You visit him each morning,
            and You test him every moment?
19   How long till You turn aside from me
            and release me for an instant?
20   If I have sinned, how have I harmed You,
            O Guardian of man?
        Why have You made me Your target
            and I have become a burden to You?
21   Why not carry off my sin,
            and remove my transgression,
        so that in the dust I can lie,
            and when You seek me, I shall be no more.

טו וַתִּבְחַר מַחֲנָק נַפְשִׁי   מָוֶת מֵעַצְמוֹתָי׃

16 מָאַסְתִּי לֹא־לְעֹלָם אֶחְיֶה   חֲדַל מִמֶּנִּי כִּי־הֶבֶל יָמָי׃

17 מָה־אֱנוֹשׁ כִּי תְגַדְּלֶנּוּ   וְכִי־תָשִׁית אֵלָיו לִבֶּךָ׃

18 וַתִּפְקְדֶנּוּ לִבְקָרִים   לִרְגָעִים תִּבְחָנֶנּוּ׃

19 כַּמָּה לֹא־תִשְׁעֶה מִמֶּנִּי   לֹא־תַרְפֵּנִי עַד־בִּלְעִי רֻקִּי׃

כ חָטָאתִי מָה אֶפְעַל לָךְ נֹצֵר הָאָדָם לָמָה שַׂמְתַּנִי לְמִפְגָּע לָךְ

21 וָאֶהְיֶה עָלַי לְמַשָּׂא׃   וּמֶה לֹא־תִשָּׂא פִשְׁעִי וְתַעֲבִיר אֶת־עֲוֹנִי
כִּי־עַתָּה לֶעָפָר אֶשְׁכָּב   וְשִׁחֲרְתַּנִי וְאֵינֶנִּי׃

CHAPTER 6

6:2 כַּעַשׂ an aberrant spelling or dialectic variant for כַּעַס (used only in Job 5:2; 10:17; 17:7). Job's כַּעַשׂ is not being weighed against his הַוָּה (ag. D-G, Gers.), but, as v. 2 makes clear, both are being placed in the scales together as against the sands of the sea. כַּעַשׂ represents his mental anguish; הַוָּה the physical disaster that has come upon him. The poetic caesura comes after כַּעֲשׂי, but not the logical pause, a usage already encountered in 4:8. יִשָּׂאוּ is impersonal, sc. הַנֹּשְׂאִים = "men raised them up," i.e., "they are raised up together." The Qere is a *mediae Vav* root (cf. Arab. "fall"), and cf. הֱוֵה אָרֶץ (Job 37:6), hence, "calamity, ruin" (Isa. 47:11; Ezek. 7:26). The Kethib הַיָּה, a *tertiae Yod*, does not occur elsewhere, and may be a scribal error. However, the commingling of both roots is well-attested, as in the verbs היה and הוה, "to be" (cf. Gen. 27:29; Isa. 16:4; Ecc. 2:12; Neh. 6:6, and frequently in rabbinic Hebrew). The precise meaning "fall" may occur in Ex. 9:3, יַד ה' הוֹיָה בְּמִקְנְךָ, and perhaps in Ezek. 37:1; 40:1, הָיְתָה עָלַי יַד ה' (cf. וַתִּפֹּל עָלַי שָׁם יַד אֲדֹנָי, Ezek. 8:1; 11:5).

6:3 The etymology of לָעוּ is doubtful. Cognates that have been adduced include (a) *laᶜa* (Arab. "lick up"; cf. Ob. 1:16, "swallow"; Pr. 23:2, לוֹעַ, "throat"); (b) *laghiya*, "make a mistake"; and (c) *lagha*, "to speak much or rashly" (BDB). Hence stich b is rendered, "therefore I may have spoken rashly," or "my words are confused" (Rashi) or "are vehement" (P.), or "are broken" (JPSV).

6:4 יַעַרְכוּנִי is read or emended by LXX to יַעַכְרוּנִי, a reading adopted by Bu., Du., D-G, P., and rendered "destroy me." Ehr. reads: יְכִירוּנִי "know me." However, MT "set out, arrayed against me," is entirely satisfactory. For the elliptical use (without מִלְחָמָה), cf. Jud. 20:22; II Sam. 10:9 f.; Job 33:5. The actual textual basis for LXX may be an assumed root, related to כרה, "dig" (Jer. 19:20, 22; Ps. 7:16), or the enigmatic כאר "bore" (Ps. 22:17).

Introductory Note on 6:5 — 6:6

The rhetorical questions posed in these verses are derived from common experience and call for the answer, "Obviously not"! This usage is characteristic of Wisdom style, but is not limited to it (cf. Am. 3:3–6; Jer. 13:23). For a similar instance in Oriental Wisdom, cf. the *Instruction of King Amenemhet*, *ANET*, p. 419a:

> "Have women ever marshalled the battle array,
>   Have contentious people been bred within the house,
>   Has the water which cuts the soil ever been opened
>   So that men were frustrated at work?"

The intent of the questions is left to the reader to grasp, entirely in conformity with the large extent to which ancient writers (and not only they) utilized allusion and analogy, depending upon their readers to participate actively in the process of communication. (Cf. *BGM*, chap. 14, for a full discussion of this fundamental aspect of Job.)

Having explicitly indicated (vv. 2–4) the depths of his suffering, Job now obliquely expresses the idea that his lament is not without cause, by asking whether a well-fed animal is likely to emit sounds of dissatisfaction. As for Eliphaz's view, Job stigmatizes it as meaningless, by asking whether tasteless food can be expected to please the palate (v. 6).

6:5 פֶּרֶא "wild ass or zebra" (So Köhler, Hö.). נהק, cf. *nahaqa*, Arab., "bray (of an ass)." בְּלִיל lit. "mixture" = "fodder" (Isa. 34:24; Job 24:6).

6:6 תָּפֵל "insipid, tasteless" (cf. 1:27; Lam. 2:14 ‖ שָׁוְא).
The general intent of stich b is clear, but the specific meaning of רִיר חַלָּמוּת is not. Hence the various interpretations proposed constitute a riot of gastronomic failures. LXX renders freely "empty words," or perhaps reading דִּבְרֵי חֲלָמוֹת (see Ibn E.). רִיר lit. "spittle" (cf. I Sam. 21:14), hence "juice, liquid." חַלָּמוּת has been rendered (a) "egg" by synecdoche for "yolk" (Ra., AV); (b) the "slime of cheese," called *ḥalwa* in Arab. (cf. A. S. Yahuda, in *JQR*, vol. 15, p. 704); (c) *halum*, "the slime of purslane" (D-G); and (d) "the juice of mallows" (JPSV).

6:7 Stich a, though the object is unexpressed, is clear, "my soul refuses to touch it." Stich b, הֵמָּה כִּדְוֵי לַחְמִי, lit. "they are like the sickness of my flesh (or meat)" (so P.), is interpreted variously: (a) דְּוֵי לַחְמִי is assumed to be the equivalent of לֶחֶם דְּוָי, "diseased food" (cf. עֶרֶשׂ דְּוָי, Ps. 41:4); (b) "They, (i.e. my sufferings) are like disease in my meat" (Dil., BDB); (c) "They (i.e. my sufferings) are putrid like my flesh" (P.). These views are unsatisfactory for several reasons: (1) there is no antecedent for the masc. pl. pronoun; (2) there is no parallelism between the two stichs; (3) the proposed renderings of the two final words are not borne out by the text.

The clue to the passage lies in the rendering of LXX *bromon*, "odor," as the equivalent for הֵמָּה, and in the citation of the verse by Elihu in 33:20: וְזִהֲמַתּוּ חַיָּתוֹ לָחֶם וְנַפְשׁוֹ מַאֲכַל תַּאֲוָה. Hence read here וְזִהֲמָה כִּדְוֵי לַחְמִי (so also Dh.), "it, i.e. my soul, loathes it like diseased food." Even better, revocalize כִּדְוֵי as an absolute, reading וְזִהֲמָה כִּדְוַי לַחְמִי, "it loathes my food like a sickness" (cf. Ps. 41:4). The verse now exhibits complementary parallelism: verb (a), subject (b) ‖ verb (a'), object (c); cf. *PPS*, pp. 74–76 and Special Note 1, sec. 3. It is noteworthy that Shakespeare uses precisely this figure, which cannot be a reminiscence of our passage, since this text did not exist for him: "but like a sickness did I loathe this food" (*Midsummer Night's Dream*, II, Scene 1, line 177).

6:8 The proposed change of שְׁאֵלָתִי to תַּאֲוָתִי, "my desire," on the basis of

LXX (Dil., Ehr.), would eliminate a striking instance of the bitter irony which characterizes the entire passage; see the Comm. on vv. 9:10.

6:9 וְיֹאֵל = "let it please God to crush me" (cf. Jud. 19:6; I Sam. 12:22; II Sam. 7:29, an instance of ironic courtesy. יַתֵּר יָדוֹ = "let loose his hand" (cf. Ps. 105:20; 146:7). בָּצַע "cut off" (cf. Isa. 38:12; Am. 9:1; Job 27:8, and frequently in mishnaic Hebrew, as in בוצע לחם, "cut off bread." Hence, the participle, בּוֹצֵעַ = "man of violence, evildoer" (Ps. 10:3), the verb בָּצַע in the Qal "do evil" (Job 27:8), and the noun בֶּצַע "portion, something cut off," hence "unjust gain, plunder" (Jud. 5:19; Mi. 4:13), "profit" (Gen. 37:26; Mal. 3:14; Job 22:3).

6:10 For the general sense see the Trans. The comfort which Job anticipates in bitter irony is his consciousness of never having denied the word of the Holy One. וַאֲסַלְּדָה is a *hapax legomenon* in the Bible. The meaning "exult, revel, rejoice" (Del., Dil., Bu., Du., P.) is an *ad hoc* interpretation without any genuine evidence. The Arabic root cited, *salada* (with a Sad), is phonetically incompatible with our root (with a Samekh), and the Arabic meanings "be hard, strong, enduring (and, stamp, press upon the ground)" are remote from "exult." The root occurs in rabbinic Hebrew, as in היד סולדת "The hand rebounds, recoils from burning in boiling water" (*B. Shab.* 40b); נפשו סולדת לאחוריה (*Pesik. Beshallah* 103a), "his soul recoils"; לובן ביצה סולד (*B. Git.* 57a), "the white of the egg shrinks because of the heat." The basic meaning would therefore be "recoil, leap back," and in our context "tremble, leap in pain" (Del., Hi., Bu.).

בְּחִילָה לֹא יַחְמֹל. The usual form is masc., חִיל "pain of childbirth." The phrase means "in a pain that has no pity, i.e., unrelenting agony."

קָדוֹשׁ The Holy One (cf. קְדֹשִׁים 5:1). The more particularistic form קְדֹשׁ יִשְׂרָאֵל, characteristic of the Prophets (Isa. 1:4; 5:19, 24; 41:14, 16, 20, etc.), is universalized here by the omission of the name of the nation. This is particularly appropriate for a Wisdom book dealing with a non-Hebrew character, but the difference in usage does not betoken a cleavage between particularism and universalism, as is clear from the use in the Prophets of קָדוֹשׁ in Isa. 6:3; 40:25; Hos. 11:9; Hab. 3:3; and קְדֹשִׁים in Hos. 12:1; cf. Pr. 9:10; 30:3; and Job 5:1. The recognition of the organic relationship between universalism and particularism, all too often lacking, is basic to the understanding of biblical religion and of Judaism generally.

The deletion by Hö. of the closing stich because קָדוֹשׁ does not occur elsewhere in Job (but cf. the Comm. on 5:1), and P.'s doubts as to its authenticity are gratuitous. The context requires that the source and nature of Job's "comfort" be indicated.

The root כחד generally means "hide, efface." TS accordingly renders "conceal." However, the Syriac Paᶜel of the root "put to shame" and the Ethiopic "deny, apostasize" justify the generally accepted meaning "deny." Perhaps the same semantic development from "hide" to "deny" underlies the root כפר, Arab. *kafara*, "cover over"; biblical Hebrew "cover over, propitiate," and the mishnaic Hebrew כּוֹפֵר, "heretic, denier of God." For this latter meaning, which we believe occurs in כְּפִירִים (Ps. 34:11), see the Comm. on 4:10.

6:11 אַאֲרִיךְ נַפְשִׁי, not "extend my life" (Ehr.) or "bolster my spirit" (P.), but "be patient"; cf. Nu. 21:4: וַתִּקְצַר נֶפֶשׁ הָעָם, "the people became impatient." אֲיַחֵל, generally rendered, "that I should wait," is satisfactory in the context. On the nuance "be silent" that we have proposed for the root, see the Comm. on 32:11, 16.

6:12 נָחוּשׁ. The form occurs only here, and the particle with He, הַאָם, in v. 13, nowhere else, except for the difficult passage in Nu. 17:28. Moving the He from הַאָם to the preceding word to read נְחוּשָׁה (Job 20:24; 28:2; 40:18) removes the exceptional forms in v. 12 and solves the difficulties of the following verse as well (so most moderns).

6:13 The only proper rendering of MT is "Is there not any help for me?" (so AV), as a question containing a negative which therefore expects an affirmative answer. This is manifestly out of place here. Hi., Bu., therefore, render "If I have no help within me . . .," with the assumption of an aposiopesis. P. ignores the negative אֵין and renders "Have I any help within me?" As Yel. has pointed out, the solution lies in recognizing ʾim as an emphatic particle, occurring frequently in Job (8:4; 14:5; 17:2), like the Arab. ʾanna, "indeed," hence: "Indeed, there is no help for me." On תּוּשִׁיָּה, "effective aid," which is not to be emended to תְּשׁוּעָה, see the Comm. on 5:12.

6:14 This famous crux has elicited a great variety of interpretations, the only point of agreement being the recognition that some general statement is being made. The implications, however, for its exegesis have not been recognized. The root of the difficulty lies in the opening word לַמָּס. The stich has been rendered: (1) "to the one melting (from מסס) i.e., the despairing one, mercy is due from his friend" (D-G; similarly TS). (2) "He who melts away from his friend (i.e., deserts him), commits infamy (ḥesed) disgrace" (Lev. 20:17; Pr. 14:34) (Ibn E.). (3) "He who removes mercy from his friend" (so P. כלא; V. *qui tollit*) etc., which, it is assumed, represents הַמֹּנֵעַ or הַמָּשׁ. (4) Ewald cleverly suggests that two stichs fell out, which he proceeds to supply:

> "Kindness is due to the despairing one from his friend,
>> And compassion from a brother to the afflicted of God,
> That he succumb not to the pain of his heart,
>> And forsake not the fear of God."

While the Masoretic text here is uncertain, Ewald's procedure is much too bold. (5) Hö. solves the problem by deleting the verse completely. Yel. adduces the Arabic root *lamasa* VIII, "to seek, desire something," and regards לָמָס as a *nomen agentis* like גַּנָּב, טַבָּח, etc. He then reads לַלָּמָס and renders "O you, the man who seeks mercy from his friend and thus forsakes the fear of God," which he regards as a prelude to vv. 15–20. However, this interpretation seems to us overly involved, and Yel. himself is uncertain of the meaning.

We prefer to utilize the Arabic cognate differently, treating לָמָס either as a *nomen agentis* or reading it as a participle לֹמֵס, and to render the verse, "He who seeks mercy from his friend forsakes the reverence due to Shaddai." As is characteristic of Wisdom literature, Job is utilizing a conventional apothegm for his own special purposes. He is declaring that he who trusts in man's goodness manifests a lack of faith in God, a theme frequent in traditional religion (Isa. 2:22; Ps. 118:8; 146:3). The truth of this doctrine Job has discovered through his own bitter experience with his Friends, as the entire chapter and in particular the following passage makes clear.

The verse may also be rendered as a conditional sentence: "If anyone seeks mercy from his friend, he forsakes the reverence due God." For the use of the participle in the protasis of a condition, see Gen. 4:15; Nu. 35:38; Jos. 2:11; Pr. 17:14; Job 41:18, and cf. Gordis, "A Note on Conditional Sentences in Hebrew" (*JBL*, vol. 49, 1930, pp. 200 ff.). On the introduction of the apodosis by Vav, cf. Pr. 23:24; Job 19:18; II Sam. 7:14; Ges.-K., sec. 159, 2-g, and see Dr., *IIT*. The identical use, both of the participle in a conditional sentence and of the Vav for the apodosis, is to be found in I Sam. 2:12 (וּבָא. . . וְבָח).

While Arabic Sin generally corresponds to Hebrew Šin, the equivalence Arabic Sin = Hebrew Samekh (Sin) is attested by Arabic ꜥarisa, Hebrew ארש, ארס, "betroth," Arabic sarida, "arrange," שְׂדֵרָה, I Ki. 6:9; סְדָרִים (Job 10:22) and common in mishnaic Hebrew סֵדֶר (by metathesis), vulgar Arabic ḥasaka II (with Sin), "keep back, save for time of need" (Dozy, *Supplément* I, p. 286) = Hebrew חשׂך; cf. Job 38:23, originally with a Samekh (Barth, *ES*, pp. 56 f.).

The root meaning of the Arabic *lamasa* I is "touch"; IV, "seek eagerly." On the semantic development, cf. פגע, "touch, implore," and as we shall point out, נגע — ענג as well (Isa. 57:4; Job 22:26; 27:10) (cf. the Comm. *ad loc.*). The root occurs again only in Job 9:23, on which see the Comm.

6:15   We have here the highly appropriate simile of the *wady*, "the stream of the desert," which is filled with water during the rainy season. Often it is useless in the winter because it freezes over, and unavailable in the summer because it dries up in the heat. Thus the figure expresses the high hopes of weary travelers and the deep disappointment that overtakes them. Jeremiah similarly accuses God of being like an unreliable stream (15:18). יַעֲבֹרוּ does not refer back to the Friends, nor does it mean "they overflow" (P.), since the picture is not of an overabundant stream, but on the contrary, of one drying up in the heat. The verb modifies נְחָלִים; hence "like the bed of streams that pass away" (cf. Job 11:16; 30:15). אָפִיק "channel," perhaps from the root אפק, "be strong" (cf. Job 12:12); here, "the riverbed which confines the waters."

6:16 The assonance in stich a of the Koph and the Reš (which, incidentally, are the consonants of the word *qor*, "cold") is very striking, as is the use of the liquid Lamed in stich b. הַקֹּדְרִים (cf. the Comm. on 5:11) apparently means "grow dark, turbid" (D-G). עָלֵימוֹ contains the archaic and poetic ending of the third person plur. (Pr. 32:23; Job 21:17; 30:2, etc.), which is used at times for the sing. as well (Job 20:23; 22:2; 27:23). The poetic form מִנִי occurs 19 times in Job and 13 times elsewhere. עָלֵימוֹ יִתְעַלֶּם־שָׁלֶג can hardly mean "upon them the snow hides itself, or, disappears" (AV, RV, RSV, D-G and most), since the snow is obviously very much in evidence. יִתְעַלֶּם is best regarded as a phonetic variant for יִתְעָרֵם "is heaped up," the change being induced by the proximity of the Lameds both before and after the word (Yel.). Rhotacism is, of course, a well-known phonetic phenomenon. The reverse process, "lamdacism," to coin a term, also exists (cf. אַלְמְנוֹתָיו for אַרְמְנוֹתָיו, "palaces" (Isa. 13:12; Ezek. 19:7), Hebrew שלח; Arabic *saraha*. For other cognate examples, cf. Barth, *ES*, pp. 40–43. The same process may be involved in the word הִרְהִיבֻנִי (Cant. 6:5), which may mean "have inflamed me" = הִלְהִיבֻנִי. The change is not a scribal error, as is generally assumed. That is clear from such forms as *eclachat* for *ecrachat; floter* for *froter; graine* for *glaine* in Judeo-French. (See R. Levy, *Trésor de la Langue des Juifs Français du Moyen Age*, Austin, Texas, 1964.)

6:17 יְזֹרְבוּ Pual of זרב ‖ צרב (cf. עלף ‖ עלז; זעק ‖ צעק; cf. Ezek. 21:3; Pr. 16:27) = lit. "when they are heated up." נִצְמָתוּ "are exterminated" (cf. Ps. 88:17; Job 23:17; Lam. 3:63). In בְּחֻמּוֹ the suffix is impersonal (cf. the subject in יֵחַם לוֹ I Ki. 1:1). Hence, "when it is hot." דעך = "be extinguished" (cf. Job 18:6; 21:7; Pr. 13:9).

6:18 The verse refers not to the caravans that are not mentioned until the following verse (ag. D-G, TS, P.), but to the streams (Del., Bu.). It gives a poetic yet accurate description of the evaporation of water into the atmosphere. לפת = "turn, wind" (so in Arab., Aram., and Syr.), a metathetic form from the Hebrew פתל. There is no need to revocalize אָרְחֹות, "paths," as אֹרְחֹות "caravans." On the reduplication of the nouns in אָרְחֹות דַּרְכָּם, cf. דֶּרֶךְ אֲרֹחֹתֶיךָ (Isa. 3:12); מְעוֹן בֵּיתֶךָ (Ps. 26:8), and the Comm. on 36:33; 37:6.

6:19 Here אָרְחֹות = "caravans," either by metonymy from אֹרַח "way, path," or to be revocalized as אֹרְחֹות (cf. Gen. 37:25; Isa. 21:13). לָמוֹ from stich b is understood in stich a — "had looked to them," or the verse is an instance of complementary parallelism. (Cf. the Comm. on 6:7 and references.) קִוּוּ is a pluperfect, "had hoped for them" (cf. חָמַק עָבָר, Cant. 5:6). הֲלִיכֹות generally = "goings" (Ps. 68:25; Pr. 31:27; Nah. 2:6; Hab. 3:6). Here, "bands." On שְׁבָא, cf. the Comm. on 1:15. תֵּימָא, a son of Ishmael (Gen. 25:15) is an Arab tribe or people *not* identical with תֵּימָן in spite of LXX, *thaiman* (cf. Isa. 21:14; Jer. 25:23).

6:20 בּוֹשׁוּ and וַיֶּחְפָּרוּ, lit. "be ashamed," is the biblical equivalent of our

modern "be disappointed" (Jer. 2:36; 12:3; Isa. 1:29, and often). בָּטַח is
to be read as a plural בָּטָחוּ; on the other hand, the change of עָדֶיהָ to עֲדֵיהֶם
is not absolutely essential. Perhaps read עָדֵיהוּ. The plural suffix in לָמוֹ
(v. 19) refers to the נְחָלִים in v. 15b; the singular suffix in עָדֶיהָ and in לוֹ
(v. 21) refers to נַחַל in v. 15a, in a chiastic structure.

6:21   כִּי עַתָּה הֱיִיתֶם לוֹ. For the *Maᶜarbae* reading, לוֹ, the *Madinchae* register
a Kethib לֹא and a Qere לוֹ. The stich has been read and emended variously:
(1) reading לֹא "for now you are nothing" (T., AV, TS). (2) "For now you
are His" (i.e., God's) (Ki., JPSV). (3) Reading: כֵּן אַתֶּם הֱיִיתֶם לִי "so are you
become for me" (D-G, P.). (4) "You have come to me without pity" (LXX —
a rendering which is equated with לְאַכְזָר, but for which there is no textual
warrant.
　　MT is preferable to these emended texts, if we recognize the meaning
of the idiom . . . הָיָה ל "to become"; cf. גַּם הוּא יִהְיֶה לְעָם, "he too will become
a people" (Gen. 48:19); יְהִי לְתַנִּין (Ex. 7:9), "let it become a serpent"; and
see BDB s.v. היה, II, d, p. 226a). Hence, the stich is to be rendered "now
you have become it, i.e., the stream." Biblical style generally prefers a
metaphor, where we would use a simile, "now you have become like it."
Cf. the Comm. on 8:9. The paronomasia in stich b תראו . . . ותיראו, is striking.

6:22   הֲכִי = הַאִם, "the sign of the question" (ag. TS). לִי = "on my account." כֹּחַ = "strength" and "a product of strength, i.e. wealth, substance."
For the semantic principle, see the Comm. on 3:10 and *KMW*, 3rd edition,
pp. 418 ff.

6:25   For מרץ the cognates would seem to be Arab. *mariṭa*, Aram. *mᵉraᶜ*
"be ill," from which the meaning "grievous" is inferred in I Ki. 2:8; Mic. 2:10,
though not quite satisfactorily. This meaning is obviously inappropriate
here and in Job 16:3. The suggestion to emend or equate our verb with נִמְלְצוּ
"be sweet" on the basis of Ps. 119:103 (T, Du.) is too weak for Job to use
in our bitter passage and also inapplicable to 16:3. The root is best treated
as an instance of the frequent semantic phenomenon of *addad*, "words of
opposing meaning," on which cf. Th. Noeldeke, "Wörter mit Gegensinn," in
Neue Beiträge zur semitischen Sprachwissenschaft (Strassburg, 1904), pp. 67–
108; Gordis in *AJSL*, 1938, vol. 55, pp. 270-273; *idem*, "Studies in Hebrew
Roots of Contrasted Meanings," in *JQR*, 1936, vol. 27, pp. 33-58. To cite
only one instance, the Hebrew אָבָה "be willing," is cognate to Arab., Eth.,
ʾabay, "refuse." On *ḥadal-ḥālad*, see the Comm. on Job 10:20; 14:6. We may,
therefore, postulate for the Arab. *m-r-ṣ*, and Aram. *m-r-ᶜ* "be ill," the opposite
meaning "be strong, vigorous." This meaning, proposed by Ibn E., is required in the context in both Job passages (see Trans.), and is appropriate
in Kings and Micah.
　　הוֹכֵחַ here and הוֹכַח in v. 26 are both instances of the Hiphil infinitive
used as a noun = "reproof, argument, demonstration." While Hebrew generally uses the feminine form of the Hiphil infinitive as a noun (cf. הַצְלָחָה

"success"; הַבְדָּלָה "separation"), the masculine occurs as well; cf. Job 25:2, הַמְשֵׁל "dominion." In mishnaic Hebrew, the Pataḥ is often thinned to a Seghol; cf. הֶסְכֵּם "agreement," הֶעְלֵם "disappearance," הֶבְדֵּל "difference," and see M. H. Segal, *Diqduq Leshon Hamishnah*, pp. 79–80.

Hence, stich b is to be rendered "what can an argument from you demonstrate?"

6:26 Stich a is not to be rendered "do you think to reprove me with words?" (D-G, P.). Both stichs exhibit the same construction of a double factitive object after חשב (cf. Gen. 50:20, אֱלֹהִים חֲשָׁבָהּ לְטֹבָה). הוֹכַח a contraction for הוֹכֵחַ (cf. v. 25 above), probably induced by the guttural, like אָרַח = אֹרַח (Job 31:32). The verse is to be rendered "Do you regard (your) empty words as proof, but as mere wind, a despairing man's speeches?" The verse exhibits alternate structure, c, b, a ‖ c', b'.

6:27 תַּפִּילוּ is an ellipsis for תַּפִּילוּ גּוֹרָלוֹת "cast lots" (cf. I Sam. 14:42). עַל־יָתוֹם has been emended to עֲלֵי תָם "over the innocent" (Gr., Bi., Du.), and to עָלַי תָּוִים "you cast markers, lots, over me" (TS). וְתִכְרוּ has been rendered "dig a pit" (cf. Jer. 18:20; Ps. 7:16) (so Ra., Ibn E., Yel., JPSV). The parallelism, however, favors the rendering "to buy, make merchandise, drive a bargain" (cf. Deut. 2:6; Job 40:30). The emendation to תָּכֹרוּ "make war," from the root כרר (Schult., Me., Bi., Be.), is unnecessary.

It should be noted that since there is no logical progression in the thought presented in the Dialogue, Job may react to ideas that have not yet been articulated. Thus Job has not yet been explicitly accused of heinous crimes. This charge will be made later by Bildad (8:4 ff.), Zophar (11:3–6), and Eliphaz (15:5 f.). However, the idea that Job is guilty of sin is implicit in Eliphaz's defense of God's justice (4:7 ff.; 5:7 f.). Job now bitterly accuses the friends not merely of callousness and indifference towards him, but of being capable of robbing the defenseless and selling a friend into slavery for the sake of gain.

6:28 פנה, which generally governs the prep. אֶל (cf. Nu. 12:10), and also occurs with Beth in Ecc. 2:11, = "turn to, observe, pay heed." וְעַל פְּנֵיכֶם אִם־אֲכַזֵּב is generally rendered "for I would not lie to your face" (RSV, JPSV, D-G, P.), or "(and see) whether I would lie to your face" (TS). Not only is this idea banal, but the word order should have been וְאִם אֲכַזֵּב עַל פְּנֵיכֶם. The inversion makes it clear that the first two words are emphatic. We suggest the reading וְאַל פְּנֵיכֶם אִם אֲכַזֵּב. On the use of a noun after אַל, cf. II Sam. 1:21 אַל טַל וְאַל מָטָר אַל־דָּמִי; (Isa. 62:6; Ps. 83:1). Lit. "but not your faces, etc." The two stichs are now in contrast with one another: "And now, pray, give me heed, but turn away your face, if I should lie."

6:29 שֻׁבוּ not "return, turn" (so most), but "stop, stay." On this meaning of the root *šūb*, "stop, stay," cf. Nu. 10:36 שׁוּבָה "stay, dwell" (note וּבְנֻחֹה); Isa. 30:15 (בְּשׁוּבָה); שׁוּבִי (Cant. 7:1); and see Gordis, "Some Hitherto Un-

recognized Meanings of The Root *Shub*," in *JBL*, vol. 52, 1933, pp. 153–162.
אַל־תְּהִי עַוְלָה, not "let there be no iniquity done me by you," but, as the
parallelism indicates, "there is no wrong in me." On לֹא = אַל used in poetry
for emphasis, cf. BDB, s.v. אַל a, c, and Driver, *HT*, sec. 56–58; and see
Job 5:22; Ps. 41:3; 50:3; 121:3; Pr. 3:25. בָּה is generally emended to בִּי
(Hi. Bu., Be., JPSV). However, the fem. suf. may here be used in a neutral
sense, and the stich would mean "lit., my integrity is still in itself, i.e., it
is intact." The usage may be illustrated by בָּהֶם (Ps. 90:10); see the Comm.
on 4:21. The emended text would mean "my integrity is still with me,"
the sense not being very different.

6:30 The difficulties encountered in this verse have been due to the failure
to recognize the correct nuance of יָבִין. Hence לֹא is deleted by Yel., while P.
renders הַוּוֹת on the basis of the Ugaritic *hwt* "words," which destroys the
parallelism. הַוּוֹת, the basic meaning of which is "ruin, destruction" (cf. 6:2),
here has the meaning of "deceit, falsehood"; cf. Mic. 7:3; Ps. 5:10 (opp. to
נְכוֹנָה "truth," Deut. 13:15; 17:4; Job 42:7, 8; Ps. 52:4). The verb יָבִין here has
its basic meaning "discriminate, distinguish, tell apart," as in the prep. בֵּין
"between" and the Arabic *baˀna med. ya*, "be separated, distinct." Hence,
stich b is to be rendered "cannot my taste discern falsehood?" This overlooked nuance of the root *bin* occurs in Ezra 8:15, וָאָבִינָה בָעָם וּבַכֹּהֲנִים, not
"I viewed the people and the priests" (so JPSV), which is meaningless, but
"I distinguished among the people and the priests" (note the prep. Beth).
Ezra was separating those of authentic lineage from those whose family
background was more dubious. The same nuance may also inhere in Pr.
14:15: פֶּתִי יַאֲמִין לְכָל־דָּבָר וְעָרוּם יָבִין לַאֲשֻׁרוֹ "The fool believes everything but
the wise man distinguishes his steps" (= "looks where he is going," RSV).

CHAPTER 7

7:1 הֲלֹא is generally rendered as an interrogative, *nonne*, "is not?", introducing a question. Actually it is a petrified emphatic vocable and should
be translated virtually always as "indeed, surely." Similarly, in rabbinic
Hebrew the negative particle לֹא, without the interrogative He, becomes an
emphatic "indeed," and may often be omitted in translation. It has not
been noted that this emphatic use of לֹא occurs in biblical Hebrew as well
(cf. Hos. 10:4; 11:5, on which see Gordis, "Studies in the Relationships of
Biblical and Rabbinic Hebrew," in *Louis Ginzberg Jubilee Volumes*) (New
York, 1941), English volume, pp. 182 ff.; Comm. on Job 11:11 and 37:24.
צָבָא, the original meaning of which is "wage war," develops the connotation of "hard service" (cf. Job 14:1; Isa. 40:2; Dan. 10:1).

7:2 כְּעֶבֶד יִשְׁאַף צֵל is rendered by some (D-G, JPSV, P.) as a subordinate
clause, "like a slave that gasps for the shadow," thus establishing a comparison with v. 3 כֵּן, "thus I am allotted empty months." The comparison,
however, is meaningless — the slave looking forward to the end of his toil

does not resemble Job, who has been given months of misery! Our v. is to be interpreted as containing two main clauses and should be attached to v. 1, with which it stands in alternate parallelism: 1a and 2a — comparing man to a slave at hard service; 1b and 2b to a dayworker.

שָׁאַף lit. "inhale, pant" (Isa. 42:14; Ecc. 1:5), whence "long for" (Ps. 119:31 and see the Comm. on 5:5, and now in modern Hebrew "aspire." פֹּעַל here = "lit. the result of labor, wage" (cf. Jer. 22:13 and the fem. noun פְּעֻלָּה, Lev. 19:13; Isa. 40:10; 49:4).

7:3 כֵּן not "thus" (see the Comm. on 7:2), but = אָכֵן, an emphatic "indeed, surely." הָנְחַלְתִּי a Hophal, "I am made to inherit," is a pathetic word" (Da.). שָׁוְא is here used in its most general sense, "emptiness, vanity," from which it develops a constellation of more specific meanings, "lying, worthlessness, uselessness, vanity" (cf. BDB s.v.). מִנּוּ may be construed as an impersonal use of the 3rd pers. plural, the subj. being הַמְמַנִּים (cf. יְדַכְּאוּם, Job 4:19; וְגָלְלוּ, Gen. 29:8), a usage very frequent in rabbinic Hebrew. On the other hand, it is preferable to regard the form as a phonetic variant of the Puʿal מֻנּוּ. For the sharpening of the ū vowel to ĭ, cf. הַמַּבְדְּלוֹת = הַמַּבְדִּלוֹת; בִּסְרוֹ = בֻּסְרוֹ from בֹּסֶר (Job 15:33), and many other instances adduced by S. Pinsker, *Maboᵓ Laniqqud Ilaᵓašuri Vehababhli* (Vienna, 1863), p. 153; R-O, Introd., p. 19.

יְרָחֵי = months. Rabbi Akiba deduced from this word that Job's affliction lasted one year (*M. Eduy.* 2:10), while the Testament of Job (5:19) assigns seven years of suffering to him. Interpreting יְרָחֵי as "moons, i.e. nights" (suggested by my student, now Rabbi, Shalom Schwartz) would give an excellent parallel to לֵילוֹת. The usage, however, here as in 29:2, makes the noun mean "a period of time."

7:4 For many commentators (e.g., Du.), following LXX, this verse recalls the passage (Deut. 28:67) in which the misery of the night is parallel to the misery of the day. Hence, Du. and Hö. emend our verse to read:

מָתַי יוֹם וְאָקוּם   אִם שָׁכַבְתִּי וְאָמַרְתִּי
וְשָׂבַעְתִּי נְדוּדִים עֲדֵי נָשֶׁף   וְאִם קַמְתִּי מָתַי עֶרֶב

Not only is this radically emended text rhythmically inferior, but it is prosaic and exegetically impossible, since נְדוּדִים in stich b, lit. "the fleeing of sleep," can refer only to tossings at night; cf. Gen. 31:40; Est. 6:1. This procedure if one more illustration of the unfortunate practice, popular in biblical studies, os mechanically adducing parallels, both biblical and extrabiblical. Deuteronomy spells out the future misery of the sinful people both by day and by night. Our poet is a sufficiently original writer to treat his theme in his own way. He describes Job's agony in the night when his physical pain becomes particularly unbearable. Both stichs in our verse are thus parallel in meaning.

וּמִדַּד need not be emended to וּמְדֵי (ag. D-G). The root means "stretch, extend," cf. I Ki. 17:21 וַיִּתְמֹדֵד, Arabic *madda*, Akk. *madâdu*, whence the

Hebrew and Aramaic מִדָּה "measure." The form מְדַד may be regarded as a
phonetic variant of מָדַד (cf. the Comm. on מִנּוּ in v. 3 above). Hence "the
night is extended, is long." Both the Vav in וְשָׂבַעְתִּי and the parallelism with
אָמַרְתִּי suggest that the closing stich is a virtual quotation, with the *verbum
dicendi* to be understood: "The night was extended *and I said*, I have had
my fill of tossings." On this use of quotations varying in the use or the
absence of a *verbum dicendi*, cf. *PPS*, pp. 120–24. נֶשֶׁף = lit. "blowing
time," is used both of "daybreak, morning" (Ps. 119:147; I Sam. 30:17) (?),
and of "twilight, evening" (Job 3:9; 24:15; Pr. 7:9, and often).

7:5 The agonizing physical symptoms described here may include sup-
purating boils, fever, speech impediment, difficulty in breathing, sleeplessness,
night terror, and delirium. Whether the poet had a specific disease like
elephantiasis or lepra tuberculosis in mind (so Hö.), or was describing a
variety of phenomena, cannot be determined.

   גִּישׁ Kethib, גּוּשׁ Qere, "clod, lump of earth." רָגַע (Eth. *ragaᶜa*), congeal,
is the equivalent of קָפָא, "freeze" (Ex. 15:8; Job 10:10). וַיִּמָּאֵס, from the
root מאס, is a metaplastic form for מסס "melt"; cf. Ps. 58:8 and שׁאף "crush"
(Am. 2:7; 8:4; Ps. 56:2, 3; 57:4) by the side of שׁוּף (Gen. 3:15).

7:6 אֶרֶג, "loom, weaver's shuttle" (cf. Jud. 16:14), is the basis of a superb
rhetorical figure in stich b, a *talḥin*, where one word conveys two levels of
meaning simultaneously, one primary, the other secondary (cf. the Comm.
on 3:6, 10, and the references there). The noun תִּקְוָה, "hope," carries in addition the meaning of "thread" (Jos. 2:18); so Ibn E., Yel. The thread of
life runs out in the weaver's shuttle, thus ending hope as well.

7:7 זְכֹר is addressed to God, not to the friends. רוּחַ "wind, breath," here
underscores the brevity of life. As has been correctly noted, Job here negates
the later doctrine of the resurrection of the dead (Ra.), which became basic
to Pharisaic Judaism and Christianity. The earlier Hebrew concept of the
shadowy existence of the dead in Sheol did not offer the comfort of fellowship
with God; cf. Ps. 6:8; 8:6, 11–13; Isa. 38:18 (D-G).

7:8 רֹאִי The ultimate accent rules out the possibility of regarding the
noun as an abstract, "vision, seeing," like חֳלִי, דְּפִי (ag. R-O). It is to be
construed as the participle with first pers. sing. suf., "He who beholds me."
The second pers. suf. in עֵינֶיךָ is not a reference to God (ag. D-G, JPSV), but
is an impersonal suffix, as is וְשִׁחַרְתַּנִי in 7:21 (cf. Pr. 19:25; 23:5; 30:28),
and the old petrified form בֹּאֲכָה, "when you come, i.e. on the road" (Gen.
10:19, 30; 13:10; 25:18; I Ki. 18:46, and see Ges.-K., sec. 144, 3-c). The
repetition of the word in both stichs (עין) is a characteristic of Job's style,
often overlooked by commentators; cf. 8:3; 10:5; 11:7.

7:9 The correlative כֵּן in כאשר . . . כן is often omitted in poetry (cf. Isa.
54:9; 55:9; Hos. 11:2; and see BDB, p. 486-b, 2-d).

7:10 Stich b occurs in Ps. 103:16b. It is a commonplace of folk wisdom which may well have been part of ordinary speech.

7:11 גַּם is correlative (BDB, s.v. 109b), "I on my part will show no regard for Him by restraining my speech" (cf. Jer. 4:2; Hos. 4:6; Ps. 52:7; 71:22). שִׂיחַ, basically "talk, musing," tends to be polarized as "complaint" (Ps. 55:3, 18; 64:2; Job 7:13; 9:27; 10:1; a.e.).

7:12 יָם is the god of the sea in Canaanite mythology identified with the primordial monster (תַּנִּין, נָחָשׁ, רַהַב, לִוְיָתָן), in Isa. 27:1; 51:9; Ps. 74:13; 104:26; cf. Special Note 37). מִשְׁמָר, the guard placed upon the sea is the sand which limits the domain of the waves (cf. Jer. 5:22; Ps. 104:9; Job 38:10 f.). Ehr. finds a *talḥin* here since the Arabic root *samara* means "be awake, sleepless," for which we may compare לֵיל שִׁמֻּרִים, "night of watching, vigil" (Ex. 12:42). On the semantics, compare the German *wachen*, "guard, be awake," and the English "wake" = "watch."

7:13 כִּי introduces the protasis of a condition, the apodosis of which is to be found in v. 14. . . . . נָשָׂא בְ = "share the burden" (cf. Nu. 11:17).

7:14 The Mem of וּמֵחֶזְיֹנוֹת is rendered as "by" by LXX, P, T, V, which may represent the easier reading בְּחֶזְיֹנוֹת, but Saadia's similar rendering makes it plausible to assume that the Vss. are rendering *ad sensum*. Mem and Beth are, however, both graphically and phonetically close, and the original reading with Beth is quite possible.

7:15 מֵחֲנָק, in spite of the Pataḥ, is to be construed as an absolute (cf. מִשְׁפָּט, Lev. 24:22; מִקְסַם-חָלָק, Ezek. 12:24, etc.). נַפְשִׁי = "my soul, I," and is to be understood as the subject of the verb. מֵעַצְמֹותַי, is generally emended to מֵעַצְבֹותַי, "rather than my pains" (Me., Dil., Sieg., Bu., Du., D-G, P.), on the basis of Job 9:28; Ps. 147:3. MT, however, means not "death from my bones" (ag. P.), but "death rather than my bones, my frame, my present being." MT is retained by TS, who vocalizes מֵעַצְמֹותַי, "my being," and renders "my being (chooses) death." The creation of this *hapax legomenon* is unnecessary. On עֶצֶם in the plural as representing the entire person, a usage characteristic of Wisdom literature, cf. Pr. 3:8; 14:30; 15:30; 16:24, and see BDB, p. 782, s.v. 1d.

7:16 מָאַסְתִּי, which has no object, has been taken as a metaplastic form of מסס (cf. 7:5 above; Ps. 58:8; so Rosenmüller, Hö.). Most commentators render the verb "I despise" and supply an object to be understood, "my life" (R-O, D-G; cf. 9:21). Deleting the verb or attaching it to v. 15 is ruled out by metric considerations, since our verse exhibits a 4:4 pattern. It is possible that the verb is to be given a reflexive meaning, "I loathe myself" (cf. וַיְגַלַּח, Gen. 41:14; יְמַלֵּט, Am. 3:15). הֶבֶל This popular word in Wisdom literature literally means "breath, vapor." In this verse it underscores the brevity rather than the meaninglessness of life. Failure adequately to recognize this distinct aspect of its meaning had led to radical misunderstandings and deletions in Ecc. 11:10 and elsewhere (cf. *KMW ad loc.*)

7:17 For irony this passage is unsurpassed in world literature. In the Eighth Psalm the poet glories in God's continual concern and love for man, whom He has made little lower than the angels. Job here bitterly parodies the Psalm, vv. 8:5, 6. Here כִּי תְגַדְּלֶנּוּ, "You exalt him," instead of the Psalmist's כִּי תִזְכְּרֶנּוּ, "You remember him." "The unending care of God has here been distorted into a maddening espionage" (Peake). שִׁית לֵב = "pay heed, attention" (cf. Ex. 7:23; Job 1:8), the heart being the seat of intellect in biblical psychology (cf. Hos. 7:1).

7:18 וַתִּפְקְדֶנּוּ because of the Vav consecutive, with Pataḥ, the verb must express a fact, not a possibility, as in Ps. 50:16 (so D-G). Hence, "that you visit him," not "you should visit him" (JPSV).
לִרְגָעִים = "each moment." פקד = "visit for the purpose of testing and punishing" (cf. the classic phrase "visit the sins of the fathers on the children" (Ex. 20:5).

7:19 כַּמָּה, originally "how much, how many" (Gen. 47:8; Job 13:23, a. e.), is used temporally = a) "how often" (Ps. 78:40; Job 21:17); b) "for how long" (Ps. 35:17); and here, literally, "for how long will you not turn aside?" The emendations עַד מָה and לָמָה, allegedly based upon the Vss., are therefore unnecessary. עַד בִּלְעִי רֻקִּי = "until I swallow my spittle," an idiomatic phrase for "an instant," like the Arabic *ablicni riki*, "let me swallow my spittle," i.e., "wait a moment." Basing himself on our passage, Dobsevage solved the crux in Nu. 4:20, וְלֹא יָבֹאוּ לִרְאוֹת כְּבַלַּע אֶת־הַקֹּדֶשׁ וָמֵתוּ as an ellipsis of our idiom, rendering "and they" (i.e.), "the Kehathites (a branch of the priestly family), will not come to look upon the Holy, even for an instant, lest they die."

7:20 חָטָאתִי מָה אֶפְעַל לָךְ is best construed as a condition, "If I have sinned, what have I done to you?" On the use of the perfect and the imperfect in a conditional sentence, cf. Job 23:10. Job argues that even if he had sinned, what harm has God sustained? Elihu will make the same point to draw an altogether different conclusion — to underscore God's transcendence and independence of man (cf. 35:6, אִם־חָטָאתָ מַה תִּפְעַל בּוֹ). נֹצֵר הָאָדָם is another striking example of irony. The root נצר, applied to God in a favorable sense in Ex. 34:7; Isa. 27:3; Pr. 22:12; 24:12, is a synonym for שמר (Ps. 34:21; 77:10; 116:6; 121:3, 5).
מִפְגָּע = "target, lit., object of hostile contact, attack"; cf. מַפְגִּיעַ (Job 36:32).
וָאֶהְיֶה עָלַי לְמַשָּׂא. MT can be rendered "so that I am a burden to myself" (RSV, JPSV). Militating against this rendering is (a) the parallelism (לָךְ) and (b) the well-attested rabbinic tradition of *tiqqunei Sopherim*, "corrections

of the Scribes" (*Tanhuma, Midrash Beshallah*, sec. 16; the *Masorah Magna* on *Num.*, beginning; and *Masorah* on Ps. 106). A lesser number of instances is cited in the *Mekhilta* on Ex. 15:7, and *Sifre* on Nu. 10:35, *Minhat Shai* on Zech. 2:12). These *tiqqunei Sopherim* are discussed, *inter alia*, in C. D. Ginsburg, *Introduction to a Masoretico-Critical Edition of the Hebrew Bible* (New York, 1966 reprint), pp. 347–63; E. Levita, *Masoreth Hamasoreth*; and S. Lieberman, *Hellenism in Jewish Palestine* (New York, 1950), pp. 28–37.

According to this ancient rabbinic tradition, minor textual changes were introduced in some biblical passages, כינה הכתוב lit., the vs. changed its reading, to avoid attributing to God any unseemly or negative aspect that would impugn His majesty. Later ages found it difficult to make peace with the idea that the sacred text had actually been modified. Hence, some rabbinic sources reinterpreted the tradition to mean that the original authors had themselves modified their mode of expression to avoid giving offense! As between the two views, the latter theory is to be rejected as manifestly apologetic. On the other hand, the idea that the text was actually changed could not have been invented in later rabbinic times. The persistence of the tradition of changes in the text testifies to its authenticity and antiquity.

It is obvious that the exact number of these tendentious changes was not known; hence the variation in the lists given in the various sources. It is, therefore, a fair inference that other instances of this type of change occurred. For some additional suggested examples, cf. the Comm. on Job 9:19, 35, and our discussion on Hos. 5:14 in the *Louis Ginzberg Jubilee Volumes* (English Volume, New York), pp. 195–98.

Hence read in our passage וָאֶהְיֶה עָלֶיךָ לְמַשָּׂא, with LXX, and a few Hebrew manuscripts (Me., Del., Gr., Du., etc.). The passage וְהָיִיתָ עָלַי לְמַשָּׂא (II Sam. 15:33), far from supporting the unchanged Hebrew text, militates against it, since in the Samuel passage the verb and the preposition refer to two different persons exactly as in our verse when the *Tiqqun Sopherim* is recognized and accepted.

7:21 וּמֶה = "why" (cf. Ex. 14:51; II Ki. 6:33; Ps. 42:6; Job 15:12, and the Latin *quid* = "why." The idiom נשא פשע (עון) means (a) "incur sin" (Ex. 28:43); (b) "bear punishment" (Gen. 4:13; Lev. 5:1); and (c) "take away guilt, forgive" (Gen. 50:1; Ex. 32:2; Hos. 14:3). It is the last meaning which is required here, as the parallelism with stich b makes clear.

The bitter irony of this passage is evident here as well — Job asks God to forgive him — the proof of which will be his early death. For the same mood and plea, cf. 6:9 and the Comm. *ad loc.* וְשִׁחַרְתַּנִי, "when you seek me." If the second person is understood as being addressed to God, it would mean that God would seek him in love (so D-G), but the transition from bitter sarcasm to a pathetic plea for love seems too rapid and extreme a change even for Job. It is better to construe the second person as impersonal, "if you, i.e., anyone, should look for me" (cf. the Comm. on עֵינֶיךָ בִּי in 7:9).

אֶשְׁכָּב need not be emended to אָשׁוּב, with LXX. The Lamedh means "near, at"; cf. Gen. 49:13; Jud. 5:17; Pr. 8:3.

The Speech of Bildad (8)

With none of the courtliness characteristic of Eliphaz, Bildad leaps into the fray. He has been driven into a fury by Job's denial of God's justice. Bildad has not the slightest doubt that the law of retribution prevails. Since Job's children have been killed, they must surely have sinned. If, on the other hand, Job makes his peace with God, he will again attain to prosperity and well-being. To be sure, the process of retribution needs more than the life-span of a single generation to become manifest. Bildad therefore calls upon the wisdom of the ancients to bear witness to the truth of his position. As surely as effect follows cause in the natural world, suffering is the result of sin in the life of man.

Bildad now dramatizes his faith in God's justice through the use of a well-known technique in Wisdom literature. In the name of the sages of the past, whom he has invoked, he presents a parable, which has been generally misunderstood. It is a parable not of one plant, but of two. One is apparently verdant and fresh, but doomed to shrivel quickly. The other preserves its moisture even under the hot sun, making its way through stony ground and, if need be, taking root in a new soil. The first plant symbolizes the evildoer, whose prosperity finally ends in destruction (vv. 11–15); the second represents the just man who survives adversity and ultimately attains to renewal and well-being (vv. 16–19). In accordance with Semitic usage, which relies upon the insight of the reader, the two plants are not identified, nor is there a transitional phrase between the two descriptive passages. For the modern reader, it is best to add the phrase, "Here is one plant" before v. 12, and the words "And here is the other plant" before v. 16.

Only at the conclusion of his speech does Bildad reveal what the reader is expected to recognize at the beginning — that the two plants being described symbolize the short-lived prosperity of the wicked and the ultimate triumph of the righteous. For a discussion of the problems, both general and specific, posed by this difficult passage, see Special Note 10 on vv. 12 ff and the Commentary on 8:16.

85

8 Then Bildad the Shuhite answered, saying,
2   How long will you mouth such notions
             and the words of your mouth be a mighty wind?
3   Does God pervert justice?
             Does the Almighty pervert the right?
4   Your children must surely have sinned against Him,
             and so He has dispatched them for their transgression.
5   If you will seek God
             and make supplication to the Almighty
6   if you are pure and upright,
             He will surely watch over you
             and safeguard your righteous dwelling.
7   And though your past may have been lowly,
             your future will be greatly exalted.
8   For inquire, I pray you, of an earlier generation,
             and heed the insight of their fathers —
9   (for we ourselves are mere yesterdays and know nothing;
             our days, only a shadow upon earth) —
10   Indeed, they will teach and inform you
             and out of their understanding utter these words:

11   "Can papyrus grow where there is no marsh?
             Can reeds flourish without water?
12   Here is one plant:
             while yet in flower — not ready to be cut down —
             before any other plant, it withers.
13   Such is the fate of all who forget God;
             the hope of the godless must perish.
14   His self-confidence is mere gossamer thread,
             his trust, but a spider's web;
15   If one leans upon it, it will not stand;
             if one grasps it, it will not endure.
16   And here is the other plant:
             it is fresh even under the hot sun
             as its shoots spread beyond its garden.
17   Even over a stone heap the roots are entwined
             as it cuts through a bed of rocks.
18   If its place should destroy it
             and deny it, saying, 'I have never seen you,'
19   behold, it goes on its way,
             and from the earth elsewhere it will sprout again.
20   Indeed, God will not spurn the blameless man,
             nor will He uphold the evildoers."

21   God will yet fill your mouth with laughter
             and your lips with shouts of joy.
22   Your enemies will be clothed with shame,
             and the tent of the wicked will be no more.

ח א   וַיַּעַן בִּלְדַּד הַשּׁוּחִי וַיֹּאמַר׃

2   עַד־אָן תְּמַלֶּל־אֵלֶּה   וְרוּחַ כַּבִּיר אִמְרֵי־פִיךָ׃

3   הַאֵל יְעַוֵּת מִשְׁפָּט   וְאִם־שַׁדַּי יְעַוֵּת־צֶדֶק׃

4   אִם־בָּנֶיךָ חָטְאוּ־לוֹ   וַיְשַׁלְּחֵם בְּיַד־פִּשְׁעָם׃

5   אִם־אַתָּה תְּשַׁחֵר אֶל־אֵל   וְאֶל־שַׁדַּי תִּתְחַנָּן׃

6   אִם־זַךְ וְיָשָׁר אָתָּה   כִּי־עַתָּה יָעִיר עָלֶיךָ

7   וְשִׁלַּם נְוַת צִדְקֶךָ׃   וְהָיָה רֵאשִׁיתְךָ מִצְעָר

8   וְאַחֲרִיתְךָ יִשְׂגֶּה מְאֹד׃   כִּי־שְׁאַל־נָא לְדֹר רִישׁוֹן

9   וְכוֹנֵן לְחֵקֶר אֲבוֹתָם׃   כִּי־תְמוֹל אֲנַחְנוּ וְלֹא נֵדָע

י   כִּי צֵל יָמֵינוּ עֲלֵי־אָרֶץ׃   הֲלֹא־הֵם יוֹרוּךָ יֹאמְרוּ לָךְ

11   וּמִלִּבָּם יוֹצִאוּ מִלִּים׃   הֲיִגְאֶה־גֹּמֶא בְּלֹא בִצָּה

12   יִשְׂגֶּה־אָחוּ בְלִי־מָיִם׃   עֹדֶנּוּ בְאִבּוֹ לֹא יִקָּטֵף

13   וְלִפְנֵי כָל־חָצִיר יִיבָשׁ׃   כֵּן אָרְחוֹת כָּל־שֹׁכְחֵי אֵל

14   וְתִקְוַת חָנֵף תֹּאבֵד׃   אֲשֶׁר יָקוֹט כִּסְלוֹ

טו   וּבֵית עַכָּבִישׁ מִבְטַחוֹ׃   יִשָּׁעֵן עַל־בֵּיתוֹ וְלֹא יַעֲמֹד

16   יַחֲזִיק בּוֹ וְלֹא יָקוּם׃   רָטֹב הוּא לִפְנֵי־שָׁמֶשׁ

17   וְעַל־גַּנָּתוֹ יֹנַקְתּוֹ תֵצֵא׃   עַל־גַּל שָׁרָשָׁיו יְסֻבָּכוּ

18   בֵּית אֲבָנִים יֶחֱזֶה׃   אִם־יְבַלְּעֶנּוּ מִמְּקֹמוֹ

19   וְכִחֶשׁ בּוֹ לֹא רְאִיתִיךָ׃   הֶן־הוּא מְשׂוֹשׂ דַּרְכּוֹ

כ   וּמֵעָפָר אַחֵר יִצְמָחוּ׃   הֶן־אֵל לֹא יִמְאַס־תָּם

21   וְלֹא־יַחֲזִיק בְּיַד־מְרֵעִים׃   עַד־יְמַלֵּה שְׂחוֹק פִּיךָ

22   וּשְׂפָתֶיךָ תְרוּעָה׃   שֹׂנְאֶיךָ יִלְבְּשׁוּ־בֹשֶׁת

וְאֹהֶל רְשָׁעִים אֵינֶנּוּ׃

Chapter 8

8:2 תְּמַלֵּל is an Aramaism, belonging to the "first category," an example of a Northwest-Semitic word indigenous to both Aramaic and Hebrew, but frequent in Aramaic and rare (or poetic) in Hebrew (cf. Gen. 21:7). It can therefore not be invoked for a late date. On the four categories of Aramaisms in biblical Hebrew, see *BGM*, pp. 161 ff.

אֵלֶּה, "these things, such notions," carries overtones of scorn (cf. Job 12:8) (Yel.).

8:3 The repetition of the same root in both stichs to which exception has been taken (Bu., D-G, Hö.) is a characteristic trait of our poet (cf. the Comm. on 7:8). That LXX used two distinct words in translating is due to its desire to avoid monotony for non-Semitic readers, who would find parallelism itself unfamiliar and repetitious.

Introductory Note on 8:4–6, Repetition and Variety

It has been generally assumed that אִם must have the same meaning "if" in all three verses 4–6 (D-G). What is overlooked is that the repetition of the same word in each verse endows the passage with power, while a variety of meanings gives it greater interest. Failure to recognize the ambivalent character involved in the repetition of a vocable is responsible for a host of deletions, transpositions, and the assumption of missing material in Job, chap. 31 (cf. Du., Hö., TS, Yel.). On the three distinct uses of *ʾim* in chap. 31, see *BGM*, p. 352, n. 47, and this Comm. *ad loc.* Similarly, in Gen. 44:16, מַה occurs three times in two distinct senses, "what" and "how."

In 8:4, אִם cannot mean "if," for there is nothing hypothetical about the destruction of Job's sons, and therefore, in Bildad's view, no doubt whatsoever about their sinfulness. The vocable here means "indeed"; cf. Arabic *ʾinna* and see 6:13; 14:5; 17:2, 13 (as noted by Yel.). On the other hand, in vv. 5 and 6, אִם means "if," the protasis of a condition completed in 6 b and c and verse 7.

8:4 אִם־בָּנֶיךָ חָטְאוּ־לוֹ is generally rendered conditionally: "If your sons sinned against Him." D-G explained the use of "if" as due to Bildad's desire to spare Job's feelings. This is hardly likely in view of the strong language Bildad employs in v. 2b. The particle *ʾim* is here used for emphasis, "indeed"; cf. the Comm. on 6:13; 14:5; 17:2, 13, 16. Bildad has no doubts about God's justice: "Indeed your sons have sinned and He has sent them away for their sins." On בְּיַד as a phonetic variant for בְּעַד, already extant in the *Tel-el-Amarna Letters*, cf. Gordis, "A Note on Yad," *JBL*, vol. 62, 1943, pp. 341–44. *Beyad* equivalent to *beʿad*, "on behalf of," Latin *pro*, occurs in עֵץ יוֹסֵף אֲשֶׁר בְּיַד אֶפְרַיִם, "the tree of Joseph which stands for Ephraim" (Ezek. 37:19); אוֹרֶה אֶתְכֶם בְּיַד אֵל, "I shall teach you *in loco Dei*, on behalf of God" (Job

27:11; also in Job 37:7, verbs of shutting being governed in biblical Hebrew by בְּעַד). In Isa. 10:5b וּמַטֶּה־הוּא בְיָדָם זַעְמִי. is to be rendered "He is the staff for My wrath," בְיָדָם being the equivalent of בְּעַד plus the enclitic Mem. On the effectiveness of the repetition of the particle in varied senses, see Special Note 9 above.

8:5 Though שׁחר generally governs the direct accusative, it is not necessary to delete אֶל in stich a; the verb may be used variously, like דרשׁ (Job 5:8; so Be., D-G).

8:6 יָעִיר not "will arouse himself" (D-G, P.), nor need it be emended to יֵצֹר, which, incidentally, governs a direct object (ag. TS.). עור and its Arabic cognate *samara* mean a) "be awake" and b) "watch." (Cf. the Comm. on 7:12.) The same semantic development exists in the German "*wachen*" and English "*watch.*" Hence Deut. 32:11–a "like an eagle he guards his nest," a thoroughly appropriate meaning for the verb in our verse.

וְשִׁלַּם has been interpreted as (a) "give peace" (Ibn E.), i.e., (b) "reward," (i.e.), (c) "restore, renew" (Bi., Del., Dil., D-G, P.), (d) "keep whole, safeguard" (Ra., Del.), the last of which we believe to be preferable. נְוַת צִדְקֶךָ = lit. "the dwelling of your righteousness = your righteous dwelling," in accordance with the predilection of Hebrew for nouns against adjectives; cf. the Comm. on 5:3 and such passages as Deut. 26:15; Isa. 63:18; Ps. 5:8; 51:13; 15:1; 119:7, 62, 106, 123, 160 and 164.

8:7 To balance the extended protasis in vv. 5 and 6a, as well as for reasons of sense, it is best to regard this verse, as well as 6b, as constituting the apodosis.

אַחֲרִית = "future" (cf. Jer. 29:11; Pr. 14:20; 23:18, 24). רֵאשִׁית therefore has the connotation of "the past" (cf. Isa. 46:10, where it is parallel to קֶדֶם), and cf. the frequent use in Deutero-Isaiah of רִאשֹׁנוֹת, "the former things, i.e., past events" (Isa. 41:22; 43:9, 18; 46:9; 48:3; cf. the Comm. on 8:8 and see BDB, s.v., p. 911–b). The masc. gender of the verb with a fem. subj., though irregular, is common (cf. Ex. 12:49; Pr. 2:10; 12:25; 29:5, and Ges.-K., sec. 145-u).

8:8 Bildad here presents an argument which the Wisdom teachers and the ancients generally regarded as irrefutable — he appeals to the teaching of the past! דֹר רִישׁוֹן is not "the first generation" (Ra.), but "an earlier generation," and אֲבוֹתָם refers to "their fathers." This is the direct antithesis of Ecc. 1:11, where "the later generations" are linked with "those who come at the very end." (Cf. *KMW ad loc.* and note also Deut. 9:20, 21.) Hence the emendation of אֲבוֹתָם to אָבוֹת or to אֲבוֹתֵינוּ (Yel.), or the rendering of אָבוֹת "as spirits of the dead" is totally unnecessary.

On the phonetic spelling of רִישׁוֹן, the usual orthography of the Samaritan Pentateuch, cf. also רָאִישׁוֹן (Job 15:7); רָאִישֹׁנָה (Jos. 21:10, Kethib).

כּוֹנֵן may be taken (a) either as an ellipsis for כּוֹנֵן לִבְּךָ, "set your heart, give heed," like שִׂים לֵב and שִׁית לֵב (cf. the Comm. on 4:20). (הֵכִין לֵב in Ps. 10:17; Job 11:13, has a different meaning, "direct one's heart, i.e. one's will"); or (b) as equal to a reflexive, "prepare yourself" (cf. וַיְגַלַּח Gen. 41:19 and the Comm. on 7:15). The change to בּוֹנֵן, "understand" (Du., Ehr., Hö.), is not only unnecessary, but without linguistic warrant; the Polel *bīn* occurs only once, in Deut. 32:10, where it has an altogether different meaning, "move among"; cf. Gordis in *Sepher Tur Sinai* (Jerusalem) 5720 = 1960, p. 153.

8:9 This verse offers a justification for relying upon the wisdom of past generations — the individual is short-lived with a correspondingly limited span of experience. The proposed changes to מִתְמוֹל (so Tar.) and כְּצֵל (P; so D-G, Hö) are gratuitous examples of "leveling" based upon biblical passages elsewhere. Our poet is more original, preferring a vigorous metaphor to a weaker simile — "we are mere yesterdays" and "our days are only a shadow." Cf. such usages as Ps. 92:9 וְאַתָּה מָרוֹם; Job 5:24 שָׁלוֹם אָהֳלֶךָ; Ps. 120:7 אֲנִי שָׁלוֹם, and see the Comm. on 6:21.

8:10 In biblical psychology, and particularly in Wisdom literature, the heart, which is the seat of desire and will, is preeminently the seat of the intellect. Hence מִלִּבָּם = "out of their understanding" (cf. Pr. 6:32; 7:7; 8:5; 15:32; 19:8 and often; Job 12:24; Ecc. 7:3, 7; 10:2). The passage that follows, vv. 11–20, constitutes the solemn teaching on Divine justice as enunciated by the wisdom of earlier generations.

8:11 גֹּמֶא "papyrus" (Ex. 2:3; Isa. 18:2; 35:7), and אָחוּ "reed" (Gen. 41:2, 18; Hos. 13:15), are Egyptian loan words. They do not, however, prove the Egyptian origin of our poet any more than of Hosea and Isaiah. The poet's use of the words is entirely in keeping with his deep familiarity with Egyptian fauna, evident in the description of Behemoth and Leviathan (40:15 ff.; 40:25 ff.), and is entirely congruent with our view of the book as the work of a Hebrew author who had visited Egypt. (Cf. *BGM*, passim, especially chap. 15.) בִּצָּה, "marsh, swamp," occurs in Ezek. 47:11; Job 40:21; the masculine בֹּץ, in Jer. 38:22.

We have here a characteristic usage of Wisdom literature, employed effectively by the Prophets (cf. Am. 3:3, 6), the presentation of a truth through a rhetorical question which must be answered in the negative on the basis of experience (cf. the Comm. on 6:5, 6, and the basic discussion in *BGM*, pp. 205 f.). Here the ordinary observation of the workings of nature is raised to the level of a universal insight — man's action and God's retribution operate in the moral sphere as surely as cause and effect in the world of nature. This principle is then graphically presented through an extended parable which has been generally misunderstood (vv. 12–19). (See Special Note 8.)

On "the Parable of the Two Plants," see Special Note 10.

8:12 In keeping with the predilection of Wisdom literature for the *māšāl* "parable" and the *ḥîdāh* "riddle," the theme of the plant that withers prematurely is introduced without its being identified. The reader is expected to discover it by his own creative participation in the process of communication; in fact, his esthetic pleasure derives in large measure from this recognition on his part. On the parallel lack of identification of the second plant, see the Comm. on v. 16. The recognition of the role of allusion and analogy in Wisdom literature is fundamental for an understanding of our section. (See *BGM*, chap. 15, and especially pp. 200 ff.)

בְּאִבּוֹ "in its freshness, green state" (cf. Cant. 6:11), from Akk. *inbu*, "fruit," Aram. אִנְבָּא (Dan. 4:9, 11, 18; Targum on Gen. 3:6), or = אָבִיב "springtime."

לֹא יִקָּטֵף, a circumstantial clause = "not yet cut" (P) or, better, "not ready to be cut down." The Vav introduces a conclusion (cf. Ges.-K., sec. 143).

8:13 For אָרְחוֹת, "paths," read with almost all commentators אַחֲרִית, following LXX (cf. Jer. 29:11; Pr. 23:18), "future, fate." The same scribal metathesis occurs in Pr. 1:19.

8:14 יָקוֹט has been rendered a) "brief, short-lived" (so Ra. R-O, Del.); b) "is cut down," either from Arab. *qatta*, "pare, cut down," or related to Hebrew קצץ; c) "despise" (V.), on the basis of Ps. 95:10, which is itself unclear. Most commentators recognize that the parallelism requires a noun here and not a verb. Saadia's rendering *hablul samsi*, "sun cords, gossamer threads" (cf. Ger. *Sommerfäden* and the parallelism), has suggested the emendation of יָקוֹט to קוּרִים, "threads" (cf. Isa. 59:5, 6). (So Be., Du., Dh., Hö.). Somewhat closer graphically would be קַוִּים or קֻוִּים (cf. the Tar. קוּיָא for Isa. 59:5) and קוּאָה "spinner" (*B. Shab.* 113a). This latter reading may indeed be the original text in Isa. 59:5, 6, as D-G suggests, since there is no etymology for קוּר. This noun may be identical with the common Hebrew word קַו "line, thread." (Cf. Akk. *ku*, "cord"; Arab. *kuwwa*, "strand of rope.")

כִּסְלוֹ "trust" (cf. the Comm. on 4:6).

8:15 The subject of the verse is generally taken to be the sinner, so that the parable would be abandoned in this verse. For this reason Hö deletes it completely. The parable may, however, be maintained if the verse is taken to refer to the spider's house, with vv. 14 and 15 containing a chiasmus (14a and 15b referring to "the gossamer thread"; and 14b and 15a, to "the spider's web"). Note the repetition of בית in 14b and 15a. The subject of the verbs in v. 15 is impersonal. Render the passage:

> "His self-confidence is a mere gossamer,
> His trust, but a spider's house;
> If one leans upon it, it does not stand,
> If one grasps it, it does not endure."

In his first speech, Bildad, being eager to win Job back to repentance, is still conciliatory. He therefore gives only a brief description of the sinner's destruction and emphasizes at greater length that the righteous can hope to survive his misfortune and attain to well-being. In his second speech, Chapter 18, Bildad has lost hope in the possibility of Job's repentance. He compensates for the brevity of his description of the sinner by devoting his entire discourse to this theme.

8:16 For the intent of this and the succeeding verses, see Special Note 10.

It is true that the change from the parable of the evildoer to that of the righteous seems abrupt by our literary standards. Hence, TS declares that "an express mention of the righteous person is required." Virtually all modern scholars (except Yel. and TS) have ignored the correct insight into the passage by Saadiah, who prefixes *as-saliḥ*, "the righteous," to this verse, which is an explanatory phrase and not a variant reading. Actually, the use of the 3rd person pronoun here to introduce a change of subject without explicit identification seems to be a hitherto unrecognized stylistic trait of the poet; cf. 13:28 (וְהוּא); 24:2 (see the Comm.); 24:5 (הֵן); 24:13 (הֵמָּה); and the Comm. *ad loc.* It should be noted that the plant depicting the sinner is introduced with equal abruptness in v. 12. On the role of allusiveness in Wisdom literature and particularly in Job, cf. *BGM*, chap. XIV, and Special Note 37.

רָטֹב "moist, fresh." לִפְנֵי שָׁמֶשׁ "even under the hot sun" (LXX, P., Gers.), not "before the sun rises" (T., Ra., Ibn E., Ki.). וְעַל־גַּנָּתוֹ either "over his garden" or "beyond his garden."

8:17 גַּל means not "spring, well" (Gers., Me., Che., who cite Cant. 4:12 and Jos. 15:9; Jud. 1:15), but "a heap of stones," as the parallelism makes clear. TS argues that a heap of stones is no shelter for a plant. This, however, is not the intent of the passage — the heap of stones represents the difficult environment in which the plant must maintain itself — a metaphor of the temporary suffering of the righteous.

יְחֱזֶה, "he sees," is obviously impossible, in spite of the efforts (Menahem ben Saruq, Ra., Ibn E., Jonah Abulwalid Ibn Janah) to make sense in the context. LXX read *zesetai* = יִחְיֶה "will live" (Sieg., Gr., Du.). This latter reading may itself be an error for יִרְוֶה "will flourish" (cf. Ps. 76:9), an error which occurs in Hos. 14:8, where MT יְחַיּוּ דָגָן is to be read as יִרְווּ כַּגָּן, "they will flourish like a garden." Most moderns emend יְחֱזֶה to a) יֹאחֵז (= יֹאחֵז "he grasps") (Bu., Hö., D-G); on the orthography, cf. II Sam. 20:9; b) or to יָחֹז, a geminate root from Arab. *ḥazza* "cut, incise, pierce" (Ew., Dil.); or c) יָחוּר "go round" (Be.), a common mishnaic verb. We prefer to interpret יְחֱזֶה in MT as = יֶחֱצֶה "cleave, pierce, divide" (cf. Isa. 30:28, and the common noun "arrow," חֵץ).

בֵּית אֲבָנִים "house of rocks, bed of rocks," may contain the Syriacism *beit*, "among," which occurs in Ezek. 41:9; Pr. 8:2. The plant has no fertile soil in which to grow, but on the other hand it is hardy enough to make its way even through rocks.

8:18 The suf. of יְבַלְּעֶנּוּ in MT is either "God" or is impersonal (sc. המבלע). Hence "if he is destroyed from his place," but then we have no subject for the verb in stich b. It is far better to delete the first Mem of מִמְּקוֹמוֹ as a dittography and make the noun the subject: "If his place should destroy him and deny him, etc." On the personification of "place," cf. the identical context in Job 7:10 and Ps. 103:16. For stich b cf. Deut. 33:9.

8:19 The crux מְשׂוֹשׂ has been explained as "a touch of irony" (D-G) and the stich is generally rendered, "this is the joy of his way" (D-G, P., who declares that "admittedly it makes little sense"; similarly Hö.). On the basis of LXX *katastrophe*, the Hebrew word has been emended to מְשׁוֹאַת "destruction" (Job 30:3; 38:2) or מְסוֹס "melting" (Be., Hi.), but LXX may be rendering *ad sensum*. Ehr. reads יָבוֹשׁ מַדְרְכּוֹ. TS cleverly assumes an erroneous translation, "joy," for "something like an Aramaic original חדות meaning renewal," but this is hardly convincing.

We propose that משוש be regarded as the Polel participle (with prefixed Mem elided) of מוש (= מְמוֹשֵׁשׁ), the common Hebrew root meaning "depart, move" (cf. Arab. *ma³sa Mediae ya*, "walk with elegant, proud gait"). On the use of the Hiphil of מוש, in this meaning "depart," cf. Ex. 33:11; Isa. 46:7; Jer. 17:8; Nah. 3:1; a. e. Revocalizing מְשׂוֹשׂ as מוֹשֵׁשׁ gives a clear and unforced meaning to the stich: "thus he departs on his way." On the equivalence of the Polel and the Hiphil, cf. מְשִׁיבַת, Ps. 19:8 and יְשׁוֹבֵב, Ps. 23:3; יְעוֹדֵד, Ps. 149:6 and אֲעִידֵךְ Lam. 2:13.

The proposed derivation and meaning for משוש is the key to another crux containing the same word, וּמְשׂוֹשׂ אֶת רְצִין (Isa. 8:6), where the usual rendering "and he rejoices with Rezin" is difficult, both from the standpoint of syntax and sense. Revocalize as מֹשֵׂשׂ and render: "He goes with Rezin, i.e., he makes an alliance with Rezin," and the context is entirely clear. On this meaning "walk with" = "enter into fellowship with," cf. the frequent use of הלך (Mal. 2:6; Mic. 6:8; Pr. 13:20) and התהלך (Gen. 5:22; 24:6, 9). The same meaning for משוש may occur also in Isa. 32:14, where it is parallel to מִרְעֶה "pasturage." Whether Ex. 10:21 may be brought under the same rubric is doubtful.

וּמֵעָפָר אַחֵר יִצְמָחוּ not "and from the dust, another will spring forth" (so D-G, P.), but "and from some other dust, it will sprout again." On transplanting as a means of renewal, cf. the beautiful passage in Job 14:6–10, which may indeed constitute Job's rejection of the idea here advanced by Bildad that man can be restored after suffering disaster.

יִצְמָחוּ, in the plural, is either (a) an extreme case of a singular noun and a plural verb (cf. Isa. 16:4; Job 19:19) (D-G) or (b) an error for יִצְמָח or (c) a singular verb with the old indicative ending with a small u (so P.).

יַחֲזִיק בְּיַד. "grasp the hand" equals "strengthen, support, uphold" (cf. Isa. 43:6; 51:18).

8:21   For עַד read עֹד; cf. the Comm. on 1:18. יְמַלֶּה a *tertiae yod* for the classic and more common *tertiae aleph* verb. (Cf. Ges.-K., sec. 75, Note 6, and Ezek. 28:16.) This assimilation of *tertiae aleph* to *tertiae yod* verbs is a usage increasingly common in later Hebrew, under the influence of Aramaic. In mishnaic Hebrew the *tertiae aleph* verbs completely disappear. For the theme of this verse, cf. Ps. 126:2.

Bildad has not been expounding the doctrine of retribution in the abstract — he has Job in mind. Hence the 2nd pers. in MT is preferable to LXX, which changes the suffixes in vv. 21–22 to the 3rd pers. out of a mistaken sense of logical coherence.

Job's Reply to Bildad (9–10)

Job now launches a vigorous attack upon the moral government of the world. He recognizes that God is mighty and man too feeble to argue with Him. Eliphaz has painted a graphic picture of God's power. Job proceeds to demonstrate that he can do as well. But his paean of praise stresses the negative and destructive aspects of God's might and thus becomes a searing attack upon God's irresponsible and unjust power. Although Job's mouth can be perverted against him, he is resolved to call God to justice, for might does not make right.

He now reaches the apex of his bitterness. The world is given over to unrighteous men, while God mocks the suffering of the innocent. No wonder Job's suffering is without limit. He relapses into a pathetic realization that since God and he are not coequal in power, he cannot prove himself upright.

Job pictures his personal misery by comparing his brief days on earth to a swift messenger, to a skiff of reeds, and to a vulture sweeping down upon its prey. Through these similes Job does more than underscore the brevity of human existence. He passes judgment on life as fleeting, fragile, and cruel.

Job now appeals from the God of power to the God of justice, who must exist somewhere in the universe. If only there were an arbiter, a higher power who could judge equally between Job and the God of might, he could speak out freely without fear. For all its bitterness, his outcry contains the seed of a faith that grows deeper as the debate continues and passions grow stronger.

Job next turns to entreaty and asks why his Maker torments him. Does God get any pleasure out of mistreating him? Is God's vision limited, that He judges Job wrongly? Or is God short-lived, that He hastens to ferret out Job's sin? The answers to the second and third questions are self-evident. It is the first which Job discusses at length.

Surely, no one knows Job better than his Maker, for every step in the process of his creation, from his conception to his birth, has been an expression of the divine will. It now appears that the marvels involved in God's creation of Job are only a mask for the pleasure He derives from afflicting him. It is clear that God's decision to punish Job bears no relationship to his innocence or guilt. From his boundless suffering Job cries out once more for the peace of death.

95

9   Then Job answered and said,
2   I surely know that it is so,
          when you say, "How can a man be just before God?"
3   If one wished to contend with Him,
          He would not answer once in a thousand.
4   However wise and stouthearted one might be,
          who has ever argued with God and emerged unscathed?
5   He removes mountains and they know it not,
          overturning them in His wrath.
6   He shakes the earth from its place
          and its pillars tremble.
7   He commands the sun, and it does not rise,
          and He seals up the stars.
8   He alone stretches out the heavens
          and treads upon the back of the Sea.

9   He covers up the Bear and Orion,
          the Pleiades and the constellations of the South.
10   Yes, He does great things beyond understanding,
          and wonders without number.
11   Lo, He passes by me, and I do not see Him,
          He moves on, and I do not perceive Him.
12   Behold, when He robs, who can make Him return it?
          Who can say to Him, "What are You doing?"
13   God will not restrain His wrath,
          beneath which Rahab's helpers were brought low.

14   Can I then answer Him,
          choosing my words with Him?
15   For even if I am right, I cannot respond,
          but must make supplication to my opponent.
16   If I called Him, would He answer me?
          I cannot believe that He would hear my voice.
17   For He crushes me for a trifle,
          and increases my wounds without cause.
18   He does not let me catch my breath,
          but fills me with bitterness.
19   If it be a matter of power, He is strongest,
          But if of justice, who will arraign Him?
20   Though I am in the right, my mouth would condemn me;
          though I am blameless, it would prove me perverse.
21   I am blameless —
          I am beside myself — I loathe my life.
22   It is all one — I say —
          the blameless and the wicked He destroys alike.
23   When disaster brings sudden death
          He mocks the plea of the innocent.
24   The land is given over to the hand of the evildoer
          who is able to bribe the judges.
          If not He, who then is guilty?

ט

וַיַּעַן אִיּוֹב וַיֹּאמַר:	**א**
אָמְנָם יָדַעְתִּי כִי־כֵן　　וּמַה־יִּצְדַּק אֱנוֹשׁ עִם־אֵל:	2
אִם־יַחְפֹּץ לָרִיב עִמּוֹ　　לֹא־יַעֲנֶנּוּ אַחַת מִנִּי־אָלֶף:	3
חֲכַם לֵבָב וְאַמִּיץ כֹּחַ　　מִי־הִקְשָׁה אֵלָיו וַיִּשְׁלָם:	4
הַמַּעְתִּיק הָרִים וְלֹא יָדָעוּ　　אֲשֶׁר הֲפָכָם בְּאַפּוֹ:	5
הַמַּרְגִּיז אֶרֶץ מִמְּקוֹמָהּ　　וְעַמּוּדֶיהָ יִתְפַלָּצוּן:	6
הָאֹמֵר לַחֶרֶס וְלֹא יִזְרָח　　וּבְעַד כּוֹכָבִים יַחְתֹּם:	7
נֹטֶה שָׁמַיִם לְבַדּוֹ　　וְדוֹרֵךְ עַל־בָּמֳתֵי יָם:	8
עֹשֶׂה־עָשׁ כְּסִיל וְכִימָה　　וְחַדְרֵי תֵמָן:	9
עֹשֶׂה גְדֹלוֹת עַד־אֵין חֵקֶר　　וְנִפְלָאוֹת עַד־אֵין מִסְפָּר:	**י**
הֵן יַעֲבֹר עָלַי וְלֹא אֶרְאֶה　　וְיַחֲלֹף וְלֹא־אָבִין לוֹ:	11
הֵן יַחְתֹּף מִי יְשִׁיבֶנּוּ　　מִי־יֹאמַר אֵלָיו מַה־תַּעֲשֶׂה:	12
אֱלוֹהַּ לֹא־יָשִׁיב אַפּוֹ　　תַּחְתָּו שָׁחֲחוּ עֹזְרֵי רָהַב:	13
אַף כִּי־אָנֹכִי אֶעֱנֶנּוּ　　אֶבְחֲרָה דְבָרַי עִמּוֹ:	14
אֲשֶׁר אִם־צָדַקְתִּי לֹא אֶעֱנֶה　　לִמְשֹׁפְטִי אֶתְחַנָּן:	**טו**
אִם־קָרָאתִי וַיַּעֲנֵנִי　　לֹא־אַאֲמִין כִּי־יַאֲזִין קוֹלִי:	16
אֲשֶׁר־בִּשְׂעָרָה יְשׁוּפֵנִי　　וְהִרְבָּה פְצָעַי חִנָּם:	17
לֹא־יִתְּנֵנִי הָשֵׁב רוּחִי　　כִּי יַשְׂבִּעַנִי מַמְּרֹרִים:	18
אִם־לְכֹחַ אַמִּיץ הִנֵּה　　וְאִם־לְמִשְׁפָּט מִי יוֹעִידֵנִי:	19
אִם־אֶצְדָּק פִּי יַרְשִׁיעֵנִי　　תָּם־אָנִי וַיַּעְקְשֵׁנִי:	**כ**
תָּם־אָנִי לֹא־אֵדַע נַפְשִׁי　　אֶמְאַס חַיָּי:	21
אַחַת הִיא עַל־כֵּן אָמַרְתִּי　　תָּם וְרָשָׁע הוּא מְכַלֶּה:	22
אִם־שׁוֹט יָמִית פִּתְאֹם　　לְמַסַּת נְקִיִּם יִלְעָג:	23
אֶרֶץ נִתְּנָה בְיַד־רָשָׁע　　פְּנֵי־שֹׁפְטֶיהָ יְכַסֶּה	24

ט׳ **v. 13.** תחתיו ק׳

25   My days are swifter than a runner;
           they have fled without seeing any joy.
26   They speed by like skiffs of reed,
           like a vulture swooping upon its prey.
27   If I say, "I shall forget my complaint,
           set aside my sadness, and be of good cheer,"
28   then I am frightened by all my pains,
           and I realize You will not set me free.
29   I shall surely be condemned —
           why then labor in vain?
30   Were I to wash myself in nitre
           and cleanse my hands with lye,
31   You would plunge me into the pit
           and would make my clothes loathsome to me.

32   For God is not a man like me, whom I could answer
           when we came to trial together.
33   If only there were an arbiter between us
           who would lay his hand upon us both,
34   who would remove God's rod from me
           so that my dread of Him would not terrify me.
35   Then I would speak, and not fear Him,
           for He is far from just to me!

10   I loathe my life —
           I will give free rein to my complaint;
           I will speak out in the bitterness of my soul.
2   I say to God: Do not condemn me.
           Let me know why You contend against me.
3   Does it do You good to practice oppression,
           to despise the work of Your hands
           and show favor to the plans of the wicked?
4   Have you eyes of flesh;
           do You see as does a mere man?
5   Are Your days short like those of a mortal,
           or Your years brief as those of a man,
6   that you search after my iniquity
           and ferret out my sin?
7   Though You know that I am not guilty,
           no one can deliver me from Your hand.
8   Your hands fashioned and made me
           altogether — yet now You destroy me!

9   Remember that of clay You made me
           and to the dust You will return me.
10   It was You who poured me out like milk,
           and like cheese You curdled me.
11   You clothed me in skin and flesh
           and knitted me together with bones and sinews.
12   In Your love You granted me life;
           Your command kept me alive.
13   Yet all this You have buried in Your heart;
           I know that this is in Your mind.

כה אִם־לֹא אֵפוֹא מִי־הוּא: וְיָמַי קַלּוּ מִנִּי־רָץ

26 בָּרְחוּ לֹא־רָאוּ טוֹבָה: חָלְפוּ עִם־אֳנִיּוֹת אֵבֶה

27 אִם־אָמְרִי אֶשְׁכְּחָה שִׂיחִי: אֶעֶזְבָה פָנַי וְאַבְלִיגָה

28 יָגֹרְתִּי כָל־עַצְּבֹתָי: יָדַעְתִּי כִּי־לֹא תְנַקֵּנִי

29 אָנֹכִי אֶרְשָׁע   לָמָּה־זֶּה הֶבֶל אִיגָע:

ל אִם־הִתְרָחַצְתִּי בְמוֹ־שָׁלֶג

31 אָז בַּשַּׁחַת תִּטְבְּלֵנִי   וַהֲזִכּוֹתִי בְּבֹר כַּפָּי:

32 כִּי־לֹא־אִישׁ כָּמוֹנִי אֶעֱנֶנּוּ   וְתִעֲבוּנִי שַׂלְמוֹתָי:

33 לֹא יֵשׁ־בֵּינֵינוּ מוֹכִיחַ   נָבוֹא יַחְדָּו בַּמִּשְׁפָּט:

34 יָסֵר מֵעָלַי שִׁבְטוֹ   יָשֵׁת יָדוֹ עַל־שְׁנֵינוּ:

לה אֲדַבְּרָה וְלֹא אִירָאֶנּוּ   וְאֹמְתוֹ אַל־תְּבַעֲתַנִּי:

כִּי לֹא־כֵן אָנֹכִי עִמָּדִי:

י א נָקְטָה נַפְשִׁי בְּחַיָּי   אֶעֶזְבָה עָלַי שִׂיחִי

2 אֹדַבְּרָה בְּמַר נַפְשִׁי: אֹמַר אֶל־אֱלוֹהַּ אַל־תַּרְשִׁיעֵנִי

3 הוֹדִיעֵנִי עַל מַה־תְּרִיבֵנִי: הֲטוֹב לְךָ כִּי־תַעֲשֹׁק

כִּי־תִמְאַס יְגִיעַ כַּפֶּיךָ   וְעַל־עֲצַת רְשָׁעִים הוֹפָעְתָּ:

4 הַעֵינֵי בָשָׂר לָךְ   אִם־כִּרְאוֹת אֱנוֹשׁ תִּרְאֶה:

ה הֲכִימֵי אֱנוֹשׁ יָמֶיךָ   אִם־שְׁנוֹתֶיךָ כִּימֵי גָבֶר:

6 כִּי־תְבַקֵּשׁ לַעֲוֹנִי   וּלְחַטָּאתִי תִדְרוֹשׁ:

7 עַל־דַּעְתְּךָ כִּי־לֹא אֶרְשָׁע   וְאֵין מִיָּדְךָ מַצִּיל:

8 יָדֶיךָ עִצְּבוּנִי וַיַּעֲשׂוּנִי   יַחַד סָבִיב וַתְּבַלְּעֵנִי:

9 זְכָר־נָא כִּי־כַחֹמֶר עֲשִׂיתָנִי   וְאֶל־עָפָר תְּשִׁיבֵנִי:

י הֲלֹא כֶחָלָב תַּתִּיכֵנִי   וְכַגְּבִנָּה תַּקְפִּיאֵנִי:

11 עוֹר וּבָשָׂר תַּלְבִּישֵׁנִי   וּבַעֲצָמוֹת וְגִידִים תְּשֹׂכְכֵנִי:

12 חַיִּים וָחֶסֶד עָשִׂיתָ עִמָּדִי   וּפְקֻדָּתְךָ שָׁמְרָה רוּחִי:

13 וְאֵלֶּה צָפַנְתָּ בִלְבָבֶךָ   יָדַעְתִּי כִּי־זֹאת עִמָּךְ:

ט׳ v. 30. במי ק׳ v. 34. ט׳ רבתי v. 35. ט׳ אין כאן פסקא

14   If I sin, you never overlook it,
         You do not let me escape my guilt.
15   If I sin, woe betide me,
         yet if I am righteous, I cannot raise my head,
         being filled with shame and sated with misery.
16   For You take pride in hunting me like a lion,
         time and again You show Your wonders against me.
17   You constantly send new witnesses against me
         and increase Your hostility toward me;
         wave after wave of foes assails me.

18   Why did You take me out of the womb?
         Would I had died and no eye had seen me!
19   Would I were as though I had never lived
         and had been carried from the womb to the grave.
20   Indeed, few are the days of my life;
         turn away from me so that I may be happy just a little
21   before I go — never to return —
         to a land of darkness and gloom,
22   a land whose light is darkness,
         deep gloom and disorder,
         even when it shines it is darkness.

וּמֵעֲוֹנִי לֹא תְנַקֵּנִי:	14 אִם־חָטָאתִי וּשְׁמַרְתָּנִי
וְצָדַקְתִּי לֹא־אֶשָּׂא רֹאשִׁי	ט אִם־רָשַׁעְתִּי אַלְלַי לִי
וְיִגְאֶה כַּשַּׁחַל תְּצוּדֵנִי	16 שְׂבַע קָלוֹן וּרְאֵה עָנְיִי:
תְּחַדֵּשׁ עֵדֶיךָ ׀ נֶגְדִּי	17 וְתָשֹׁב תִּתְפַּלָּא־בִי:
חֲלִיפוֹת וְצָבָא עִמִּי:	וְתֶרֶב כַּעַשְׂךָ עִמָּדִי
אֶגְוַע וְעַיִן לֹא־תִרְאֵנִי:	18 וְלָמָּה מֵרֶחֶם הֹצֵאתָנִי
מִבֶּטֶן לַקֶּבֶר אוּבָל:	19 כַּאֲשֶׁר לֹא־הָיִיתִי אֶהְיֶה
יָשִׁית מִמֶּנִּי וְאַבְלִיגָה מְּעָט:	כ הֲלֹא־מְעַט יָמַי יֶחְדָּל
אֶל־אֶרֶץ חֹשֶׁךְ וְצַלְמָוֶת:	21 בְּטֶרֶם אֵלֵךְ וְלֹא אָשׁוּב
צַלְמָוֶת וְלֹא סְדָרִים	22 אֶרֶץ עֵפָתָה ׀ כְּמוֹ אֹפֶל
	וַתֹּפַע כְּמוֹ־אֹפֶל:

י׳ v. 20. וחדל ק׳ ibid. ושית ק׳

CHAPTER 9

9:2 אָמְנָם "indeed" is used ironically (D-G). Stich b is a quotation of the Friends' view expounded by Eliphaz in 4:17 and by Bildad in 8:3 but on radically different grounds, "Man cannot be just with God, not because man is wicked, but because God overpowers him, so that the adversaries are unequal." עִם אֵל carries a double connotation: (a) "in the estimation of God" (cf. I Sam. 2:26; II Sam. 6:22); and (b) "in a contest with God" (cf. Ps. 94:16). The particle Mem is similarly used in a double sense in 4:17. See the Comm. *ad loc.*

9:3 The problem here is to identify the suffixes and the subjects of the verbs. Stich a has been interpreted as (a) "If God wished to argue . . . . . man could not answer" (so Hö., P.); and (b) "If a man wished to argue" (so TS, D-G), which is preferable. Similarly, stich b has been rendered: "Man could not answer God" (so D-G, TS, P.). We prefer "God would not answer man" (so Hö., Ehr., and R-O).

9:4 חֲכַם־לֵבָב וְאַמִּיץ כֹּחַ "wise of heart and mighty in strength" in stich a is not a *casus pendens* taken up by the suffix in אֵלָיו and therefore a description of God (ag. D-G), but a compound modifier of מִי, with concessive force, descriptive of man: "However wise and mighty a man might be, who could ever, etc." (Ehr. and TS). הִקְשָׁה is generally taken as an ellipsis for הִקְשָׁה לִבּוֹ "hardened his heart," for which Ex. 13:15 is cited (Ra., Ibn E., D-G). In view of the forensic character of the passage (cf. ריב "argue," Isa. 3:13, and ענה "respond"), it is better to interpret the verb in the mishnaic sense of "argue, dispute, raise a question." Cf. חריף ומקשה (*B. Hor.* 3a), מדלית מקשה (T on Job 6:6, "there is none to disprove it," and often). וַיִּשְׁלָם "emerged whole, unscathed," a nuance of the verb present in Job 5:25.

9:5 On the theme of 9:5–10, see Special Note 11 on "The Destructive Power of God." הַמַּעְתִּיק not "makes old" (LXX), but "removes" (cf. Gen. 12:8; 26:22; and Job 32:16, where it is used figuratively).

וְלֹא יָדָעוּ is interpreted as: (a) "and men know it not" (TS) or "before one knows it" (Ra.), i.e., "suddenly, without warning"; or (b) it is emended to וְלֹא יָדַע "without God's knowing it, i.e., effortlessly" (D-G). However, the personification of the forces of nature whom God terrorizes (cf. "in His wrath," v. 5, and "He commands the sun," v. 7) suggests that the mountains are personified here too. Hence, "they do not know it, i.e., the mountains are unaware of the doom descending upon them."

אֲשֶׁר הֲפָכָם "who overturns them" is parallel to the participle in stich a. For the use of a finite verb parallel to the participle, cf. Ps. 84:5: אַשְׁרֵי יוֹשְׁבֵי בֵיתֶךָ עוֹד יְהַלְלוּךָ סֶּלָה. This familiar verse, which has not been generally understood correctly, is to be rendered: "Happy are they who dwell in Your house,

who are still praising You, i.e., are still among the living." On the relationship
of the two themes of being alive and praising God, cf. Isa. 38:18; Jonah 2:5;
Ps. 146:17 f. For metric reasons the relative before אֲשֶׁר is omitted in the
Psalms passage and is inserted here.

9:6 A poetic description of an earthquake. In the biblical cosmogony, the
earth was pictured as resting upon pillars (cf. Job 38:6; I Sam. 2:8; Ps. 105:5)
surrounded by waters welling up from the subterranean depths, with the
sky overhead and Sheol beneath.

9:7 אמר, in its original sense still present in Arabic, "command," a nuance
strongly felt in the Creation narrative in Genesis, chap. 1. חרס occurs only
once more, and with epenthetic He (Jud. 14:18), where it has been emended
to הַחִדְרָה by Stade. Its authenticity, however, is supported by its occurrence
as a place-name (Jud. 1:35; 8:13; and perhaps in Isa. 19:18, where MT
עִיר הַהֶרֶס "city of destruction" is either a tendentious change by a scribe
or a pun by the author on עִיר הַחֶרֶס "city of the sun, Heliopolis"; but see
LXX *ad loc.*). Cf. *B. Men.* 110a for the noun. Verbs of closing and sealing
like סגר, גדר, חתם, and שׁוך govern the preposition בְּעַד; cf. BDB s.v. 1, b,
p. 126.

9:8 There is no need to read נָטָה in the perfect, with TS, who nevertheless
is correct in recognizing here a reference to the creation. The element of
terror and violence becomes clear when the Semitic myth of creation is recalled. Thus in *'Enuma elish* IV 11. 137, 8, Marduk "splits her (Tiamat)
like a shellfish; half of it he set up and called it sky" (*ANET*, p. 67b).

לְבַדּוֹ need not mean "for his wine-press," as TS cleverly interprets it,
for which there is no evidence in our sources. The poet is emphasizing the
monotheistic theme "God alone, without any aids, vanquished the primordial
chaos." The poet here is virtually quoting Deutero-Isaiah 44:24: נֹטֶה שָׁמַיִם
לְבַדִּי (cf. also Isa. 49:21; 63:3).
בָּמֳתֵי־יָם. The traditional rendering, "the high places of the sea," has
been generally abandoned, as the mythological background of the phrase has
been recognized. In Ugaritic במת means "the back of an animal or god."
Here it is used of a defeated foe. Cf. F. M. Cross, and D. N. Freedman in
JBL, 1948, vol. 67, pp. 196, 210; also TS in *JPES*, 1934, vol. 2, pp. 3–16;
Lašon Vasepher, vol. 3, pp. 235 ff.
Originally Yam is the god of the Sea, who appears under a variety of
names: *Leviathan, Tehōm, Rahab, Tannin, Nāḥāš,* and symbolizes the chaos
before Creation (cf. the Comm. on 3:8; 9:13; 28:14). Yam is demythologized
early and then becomes a) the sea waters and b) the bed or channel of the
sea (cf. Isa. 11:9). The same constellation of meanings develops with *Tehōm*.
The other names retain their mythological character more consistently.
The vocalization of בָּמֳתֵי (Isa. 14:14; Am. 4:13) instead of בָּמוֹתֵי, which
occurs only as the Qere in Deut. 32:13, is inexplicable. See the involved and
unsatisfactory attempt to explain the form in D-G II, p. 56. It may perhaps

be the result of a contamination of בָּמָה "high place" (Akk. *bamâte*; Moabite
במת) and במת Ugaritic "back."

9:9 The diphthong *ai* was originally written without a Yod; cf. דבלתן
(Mesha inscription 1. 30) and דִּבְלָתַיְמָה (Nu. 33:46, 47; דִּבְלָתַיִם Jer. 48:22),
דֹתָיְנָה and דֹתָן (Gen. 37:17). For a fuller discussion of this orthography, cf.
BTM, p. 100.

עָשׁ spelled עַיִשׁ in 38:32, where "her children" are referred to, would
seem to be a reference to the Bear and the three stars of his tail. Some, like
LXX, identify it with the Pleiades. כְּסִיל, cf. Job 38:31, where "his chains"
are mentioned (occurring in the plural in Isa. 13:10), is called "the fool,"
a mythological giant bound by chains, hence probably Orion.

כִּימָה either the Pleiades or Sirius. חַדְרֵי תֵימָן "the chambers of the South"
seems to refer to some southern constellation. The emendation תֹמָן = תְּאוֹמִים
"twins, the Gemini," is unnecessary. In Am. 5:8, where עָשׁ does not occur,
the passage is cosmological, with no negative connotations, which our context would require.

It may be suggested that עָשָׂה used here is not the familiar root "make,"
but the Hebrew cognate to the Arabic *ghaŝawa* (*tertiae Vav*), "cover, conceal," recognized by Eitan and Yel., who cite Job 23:9; Pr. 12:23; 13:16;
Isa. 32:6 and the folk-etymology for *Esau* in Gen. 25:26. We may add the
paronomasia in Ob. 1:6: אֵיךְ נֶחְפְּשׂוּ עֵשָׂו נִבְעוּ מַצְפֻּנָיו "How has Esau (i.e. the
covered one) been uncovered — his secrets revealed!" Cf. Jer. 49:10. An
equally striking *double entendre* occurs in our passage between the conventional sense of עשׂה עשׁ and the poet's usage: "He covers up the Bear, Orion
and the Pleiades." For the idea of hiding the stars, note 7b וּבְעַד כּוֹכָבִים יַחְתֹּם.

TS, who recognizes the need of a negative characterization here, interprets the phrase conventionally, but explains that God had created the
stars by crushing rebellious giants and turning them into heavenly bodies.
However, on this view the essential feature of the destruction of the giants
is totally absent in the verse.

9:10 The virtual identity of this verse with 5:9 has, of course, been noted.
What has not been observed is the ironic tone it bears here — after the
destructive praise of God has been hymned by Job, "Yes, indeed, God does
great things beyond understanding."

9:11 Ehr.'s attractive suggestion to read וְלֹא אֶרְאֶהוּ יַחֲלֹף is not absolutely
necessary, since the suffix may be understood from stich b. On לֹי as a dir.
acc., cf. Job 14:26. The verse is not irrelevant (ag. TS) — God is not only
violent (vv. 5–10) and wrathful (v. 13), but also elusive (v. 11). Nevertheless,
Job insists upon confronting Him (v. 14). Job restates the themes of God's
physical superiority and his inability to challenge Him (vv. 15–18), and then
summarizes the idea v. 19. Rearranging the chapter to meet our Western
canons of relevance and logical organization is gratuitous and does violence

to the spirit of biblical and Oriental poetry, with its rapidly shifting emotions and attitudes.

9:12 For יַחְתֹּף, the Aramaic cognate חתף, "break into pieces," and the Arab. *ḥatafa*, "kill," are not really appropriate, in view of stich b, "who can make Him return it?" Most moderns, therefore, emend to יַחְטֹף "seize, rob," but the change is unnecessary, in view of the spelling with Tav, חֶתֶף "prey" (Pr. 23:28; B. S. 50:4) and the gloss in B. S. 15:17 וישיתהו ביד חותפו "he has placed him in the hand of his despoiler." On the phonetic interchange of Tav and Tet, note e.g. the Arab. *qatala* (with *ta*) and the Hebrew and Aram. קטל with Tet; Arab. *turfaᵗun* (with *ta*) and Hebrew טֶרֶף (food); and see J. Barth, *ES*, pp. 35 ff.

9:13 The older view of the passage, "If God does not turn away His anger, even the proud helpers stoop beneath Him" (AV), is inappropriate. It has therefore been proposed to interpret, "Even a god cannot turn back His (i.e. God's) anger." (TS, Kissane, P.) This view is effectively refuted by several considerations: (1) There is no warrant for assigning to אֱלוֹהַּ the meaning of "a god." The noun occurs 37 times in Job, always in the meaning of "God." With regard to the one difficult passage adduced for this new meaning (12:6), see the Comm. *ad loc.* The other biblical passages for which this meaning is proposed either do not contain the noun (II Kings 17:31; see Qere) or are manifestly unclear and corrupt (II Chr. 32:15; Dan. 11:37). (2) Even more decisive, if possible, is the fact that the idiom הֵשִׁיב אַף always means "to withdraw *one's own* anger," the suffix always referring back to the same subject (cf. Pr. 24:18; Ps. 85:4; 78:38; see also Isa. 66:15; Jer. 18:20; Ps. 106:23). A third and better rendering, "God will not turn back His anger; beneath Him bowed the helpers of Rahab," has the disadvantage of making the two stichs unrelated to each other. We suggest that stich b is best construed as a subordinate clause modifying אַפּוֹ, and hence render:

> "God will not restrain His wrath,
>   beneath which Rahab's helpers crouched."

Rahab is the sea monster whom God at creation crushed in the war against chaos (cf. Isa. 51:9; Ps. 89:11; Job 26:12). Rahab has helpers, like Tiamat in the Babylonian myth. These may be identical with "the heads of Leviathan" referred to in Ps. 74:13. On the figure of God's wrath frightening the sea monster and his cohorts, cf. the creative theme in Ps. 104:7, which has been largely demythologized: מִן־גַּעֲרָתְךָ יְנוּסוּן, "before Your loud rebuke they (sc., the waters) flee." The root meaning of Rahab may be "be excited, agitated" (so P.) or, more probably, "be arrogant, boisterous." Cf. Targumic Aramaic רהב "be arrogant," Akk. *raᵓabu* "to storm at, in anger," and Isa. 3:5, as well as the use of "Rahab" as an epithet for Egypt (Isa. 30:7, "Arrogant Do-Nothing"; Ps. 87:4). שָׁחֲחוּ, "bowed down," with the clear connotation of being humbled (Isa. 2:11, 17; Hab. 3:6; Ps. 107:29).

9:14 Stich a is generally taken to mean "how much more so (i.e. how much less) am I able to answer Him" (so Ra., D-G, etc.). It is better to treat אַף as an emphatic interrogative particle: "Can I indeed answer Him?" Cf. Gen. 3:1, אַף כִּי־אָמַר אֱלֹהִים, "Did God really say, etc.?"; Gen. 18:13, 23; Am. 2:11. It is particularly characteristic of Job's style; cf. Job 19:4; 34:17; 40:8. The existence of this usage in the Dialogue, in the Elihu Speeches, and in the God Speeches is another indication of the unity of authorship of the book.

9:15 The antecedent of the first clause in v. 15 is אָנֹכִי in v. 14, hence "lit. I, who even if I am right, etc." (cf. Hos. 14:4: אֲשֶׁר בְּךָ יְרֻחַם יָתוֹם.)

לֹא אֶעֱנֶה "I cannot respond," a forensic term. The MT לִמְשֹׁפְטִי has been emended to לְמִשְׁפָּטִי "for my right" (Hi., Bu.) and to לְמוֹ שֹׁפְטִי "to my judge" (Gr.). But MT is to be preferred on the principle of *difficilior lectio*. The Polel, though rare in Hebrew with strong verbs, occurs in עוֹיֵן I Sam. 18:9; מְלוֹשֶׁן Ps. 101:5 (Kethib) in the context of "attack" (Ges.-K., sec. 55b, c), or in a conative sense, "one intending to judge me."

9:16 The verse has been treated as a conditional sentence: "If I called Him and He answered me, I would not believe that He heard my voice" (D-G, P.). The parallelism is preserved and a better meaning emerges if the verse is taken as a question, with the Vav moved, to read "אִם קְרָאתִי יַעֲנֵנִי," "If I called Him, would He answer me? I cannot believe that He would hear my voice" (so Yel., R-O, TS).

9:17 בִּשְׂעָרָה is generally rendered "with a tempest" (cf. Nah. 1:3; Job 4:15 and the Comm. *ad loc.*; so LXX, D-G, P.). The parallelism with חִנָּם suggests, however, that שְׂעָרָה is to be understood as the *nomen unitatis* of שֵׂעָר "hair," and hence it would have the meaning of "a strand of hair" (I Sam. 14:45; II Sam. 14:11; I Ki. 1:52; Ps. 40:13; 69:5), with the meaning here "for a mere hair, i.e., for a trifle," parallel to חִנָּם. The talmudic utterance, הקב״ה מדקדק עם הצדיקים כחוט השערה "The Holy One, blessed be He, deals with the righteous with great exactitude," lit. "to a strand of hair (i.e., is very severe with them)," is based on this view of the passage, which T introduces here in his rendering דעד חוטי בינתא. Hi. also interpreted the noun as "hair," rendering stich a, "who drags me by the hair." שׁוּף = "crush" (cf. Gen. 3:15; T on Deut. 9:21 [for כתת], and the metaplastic form שאף, Ps. 56:2; 57:4; Am. 2:7; 8:4).

9:18 הָשֵׁב רוּחִי "to bring back my breath, catch my breath."

מַמְרֹרִים need not be emended to מִמְּרֹרִים (ag. D-G) on the basis of Ps. 104:13, where the verb governs a Mem, or emended to בַּמְּרֹרִים on the basis of Lam. 3:15, where it governs a Beth. The double accusative of person and substance after *sābhaᶜ* is far more common (cf. Ps. 81:17; 91:16; 105:40; 132:15; 147:14). For the morphology of the noun with prefixed Mem, cf. מַחְסוֹר, מַשְׁקוֹף, מַלְקוֹחַ, מַלְקוֹת, etc. On the *dageš forte dirimens* cf. Ges.-K., sec. 20, 2b.

9:19 כֹּחַ cannot mean "legal authority" (ag. P.), as the verse establishes a contrast between physical power in stich a and justice in stich b. כֹּחַ here carries a clear connotation of violence and unjust power; cf. Ecc. 4:1, וּמִיַּד עֹשְׁקֵיהֶם כֹּחַ. Stich a in MT is to be rendered "If it is to be the strength of a mighty one, here (He is)." It is preferable to construe אַמִּיץ הִנֵּה as the predicate and perhaps vocalize הִנֵּהוּ (cf. Jer. 18:3; Kethib) by haplography, rendering "if it be a matter of power, He is stronger"; so Du., Ehr., Be., TS, P. In stich b most commentators emend מִי יוֹעִידֵנִי, "who will summon me," to מִי יוֹעִידֶנּוּ "who will summon Him"; so LXX. R-O has plausibly suggested that MT may be a *Tiqqun Sopherim,* "a correction of the scribes," intended to avoid an offensive reference to the Deity. The varying numbers of *Tiqqunei Sopherim* given in rabbinic sources are obviously incomplete, with other such examples not having been preserved in the traditional rubrics. For other possible instances, see the Comm. on 7:20 and 9:34. On Hos. 4:15 cf. Gordis in the *Louis Ginzberg Jubilee Volumes* (New York, 1945), English volume, pp. 195–98.

On the *Tiqqunei Sopherim* in the Masorah, cf. C. D. Ginsburg, *Introduction to The Massoretico-Critical Edition of the Hebrew Bible* (London, 1897; New York, 1966), pp. 347–63, especially p. 360; F. Buhl, *Canon and Text of the O. T.* (Edinburgh, 1892), p. 103; P. Kahle, *Der masoretische Text des A. T.* (Leipzig, 1902), pp. 76 ff.; B. J. Roberts, *The Old Testament Text and Versions* (Cardiff, 1951), pp. 34 f.

9:20 יַרְשִׁיעֵנִי is a declarative use of the Hiphil. Cf. Deut. 25:7, which suggests strongly that וַיַּעְקְשֵׁנִי is also declarative, "prove me perverse." The latter form has therefore been interpreted as a shorter form of the Hiphil = וַיַּעְקִישֵׁנִי or revocalized as a Piel וַיְעַקְּשֵׁנִי. However, as we have noted, the Qal is used declaratively as well. Cf. the Comm. on וְאָקוֹב, 5:3, and תֶּחֱטָא, 5:24. No change in MT is therefore called for.

9:21 The 3:3 meter predominant in this section is violently disturbed here by the staccato 2:2:2 rhythm in this verse, by the 4:4 meter in v. 22, and by the extremely rare 2:3 rhythm in v. 29, all expressions of Job's deep emotional agitation. תָּם, as generally, not "perfect," but "a man of wholeness, integrity, upright, blameless."

לֹא אֵדַע נַפְשִׁי has been interpreted: (a) "I would not know myself, i.e., my innocence, if I were in a suit with God" (TS); and (b) "I care not for myself," on the basis of yadaᶜ "know, love" (Deut. 33:9, to which Am. 3:2 may be added) (D-G, P.). However, the obviously idiomatic phrase apparently occurs in Cant. 6:12: לֹא יָדַעְתִּי נַפְשִׁי שָׂמַתְנִי מַרְכְּבוֹת עַמִּי־נָדִיב. On the difficulties of this crux and the abortive efforts made to solve them, see SS, p. 92. Both passages suggest that the phrase "not to know, or recognize, oneself" can well mean "to be moved beyond the normal emotional state." In Cant. it would mean "I am beside myself with joy"; here, "I am beside myself with misery." Pr. 19:2 is unclear and cannot shed any light on our problem.

9:22 This verse is probably the strongest indictment of God to be found in the book. It is noteworthy that it is not softened in the text by emendations or pious glosses, a situation similar to that of Ecc. 3:18, 22. This observation renders highly dubious the still widely held view that heterodox works like Job and Ecclesiastes were subjected to extensive interpolation in order to make them palatable to conventional religious believers, an assumption which has made a shambles of countless passages in Wisdom literature. Cf. *KMW*, passim; *BGM*, pp. 81 ff., 185 ff.; and the Comm. on chaps. 12 and 21. LXX completely blunts the impact of this challenge to Divine justice by omitting stich a completely and rendering stich c "wrath slays the great and the mighty man."

Stich a, "it is all one," may mean "whether one lives or dies" (so D-G), or preferably it is "one measure, one fate for the righteous and the wicked" (so T, Del., TS). This theme (מקרה אחד) is frequently expounded by Koheleth (Ecc. 3:18 ff.; 9:2 ff.); (מקום אחד) Ecc. 6:6.

9:23 שׁוֹט ("lit. lash, scourge") is a symbol of destruction. לְמַסַּת is derived from מסס "melt" and is interpreted as "calamity" (JPSV), or "despair" (Ew., Dil., Bu.) or it is derived from נסה "test," hence "trials" (Ibn E., Hi., Dil., D-G). Both the forms and the meanings assigned to the noun are highly questionable. On the basis of Arabic *lamasa* VIII, "seek, plead for," which occurs also in 6:14 (see the Comm.), Yel. suggests reading לְלְמָסַת "plea," one Lamed having been lost through haplography, when the rare root was not recognized. Stich b = "He mocks at the plea of the innocent."

9:24 Stich b is generally rendered "He, i.e., God, covers the face of the judges," but the impersonal use of the Niphal in stich a (which P. therefore tacitly vocalizes as נִתְּנָה) militates against it. Similarly, the idea of God's covering the face of judges by a bribe, so that they cannot see justice, is more appropriate for a human agent rather than for God (so also Ibn E.). It is therefore better to treat stich b as a subordinate clause modifying "wicked" in stich a, and render "the land is given over to the hand of the evildoer, who is able to bribe the judges." For כִּסָּה פָנִים cf. כִּפֶּר פָּנִים (Gen. 32:21), "cover the face, pacify," and כְּסוּת עֵינַיִם (Gen. 20:16), "a covering of the eyes, pacification gift." For the omission of the relative ʾašer in poetry, cf. 3:3 and 9:13b (and the Comm.).

Stich c is rendered: (a) "If this is not so, then who will refute me?" (Ibn E., TS); (b) "If not then, who is it?" (D-G); and (c) "If this is not so, then who is He?" (P.). Here, too, it is preferable to regard our passage as a virtual *Tiqqun Sopherim* for אִם־לֹא הוּא מִי־אָפוֹ, "If not He, then who is it (that is guilty)?" This is actually the reading proposed by a Masoretic *Sebir*, an attractive reading against which the Masorah warns the scribe as being non-Masoretic; see Kit., *BH* ad loc. See the Comm. on 9:35. אֵפוֹ is an enclitic particle, spelled thus in Job 17:15; 19:6, 23, but elsewhere אֵפוֹא (Gen. 27:33; Ex. 33:16), similar in usage to the Aramaic פוֹן (T on Gen. 26:10; Nu. 11:29).

9:25 In this verse and in the following we have three magnificent similes, whose full significance needs to be savored. Job compares his life to a runner, a skiff, and a vulture. Each is not only swifter than the preceding, but suggests an additional nuance — the runner represents speed, the papyrus skiff adds the idea of fragility, the vulture — the theme of cruelty. Life is brief, precarious, cruel.

9:26 אֵבֶה (Arab. ʾaba, Akk. abu) = "reed, papyrus." Cf. Isa. 18:2, כְּלֵי־גֹמֶא, and Pliny *papyraceae naves*, "boats of papyrus."

יָטוּשׂ "swoop, fly" is a *hapax legomenon* in the Bible that occurs in mishnaic Hebrew, as in עוֹף טס "a flying bird" (*J. Taan.* iv, 69–b). This root has experienced a rebirth in modern Hebrew. From this root come the nouns מָטוֹס "airplane," טִיסָה "flight," טַיָּס "pilot," and שְׂדֵה מָטוֹס "airport."

9:27 Since a finite verb is required after the conjunction אִם, אָמְרִי must be emended to אָמַרְתִּי. On the verse cf. 7:13. While פָּנִים "face" is generally neutral, it develops a negative connotation "sad countenance, sadness" here, and in I Sam. 1:18, even without a qualifying adjective, as in Gen. 40:7. וְאַבְלִיגָה "be of good cheer"; cf. the Arab. *balaja* "to have a cheerful countenance." Mohammed was described as ʾablaju alwajihi, "cheerful of countenance" (Schultens, D-G).

9:28 יָגֹרְתִּי governs an adverbial accusative, "in all my pains." The perfect tense יָדַעְתִּי represents Job's total conviction, "I know you will not set me free," from נָקִי a legal term, "innocent" (Ex. 23:7).

9:29 אָנֹכִי אֶרְשָׁע, in the imperfect, hence, not "I am already guilty" but "I shall surely be condemned" (so D-G), hence, "Why labor in vain to justify myself?" The changes of mood are characteristic of Job. His sense of the hopelessness of his efforts to vindicate himself (vv. 26–32) is transformed with lightning speed into a wish for an arbiter to judge between him and his adversary (vv. 33–34), and concludes with an unflinching reaffirmation of his innocence (v. 35).

9:30 שֶׁלֶג may mean "snow" in accordance with the folk-belief, based on its white appearance, that it could whiten whatever it was rubbed on (cf. Isa. 1:18; Ps. 51:9). The Arab. fable of *Lokman* No. 13 describes the black man rubbing his body with snow to become white (so Hö.). It nevertheless seems preferable, on the basis of the parallelism and the fact that snow is not a cleanser in reality, to render שֶׁלֶג as "nitre"; cf. mishnaic אשלג (*M. Shab.* 9:5; *M. Nid.* 9:6). Hence the Kethib בְּמוֹ "in" with the archaic enclitic *mō* is preferable to the Qere בְּמֵי "in the water of." בֹּר, generally taken as "cleanness" (Hi., Yel.), is better rendered "lye" as in Isa. 1:25 (כַּבֹּר = כְּבֹר, "as with lye"). Cf. בֹּרִית, Jer. 2:22; Mal. 3:2. This vegetable alkali was in use in Babylonia as long ago as 2000 B.C.E. (cf. Thureau-Dangin, *Revue* d'*Assyriologie*, 1910, p. 111). There may be a *talḥin* intended here with בֹּר "lye" suggesting the homonym "pit"; cf. v. 31 (so Yel.).

9:31 The emendation of בַּשַּׁחַת to בַּסָּחוֹת or בַּשְׁחָה (Be., Du., Ehr.) because of LXX *en rupo*, "in mud," is totally unnecessary, particularly in view of the *talḥin* with v. 30. A pit was naturally conceived of as consisting of mud and water (cf. Gen. 37:24 for the exception). In view of the cosmogony which pictured the abyss of water beneath the earth, the same term was applied to the area where Sheol was to be found (Job 17:14; 33:28; Ps. 16:10; 49:10). Here the term is used for a natural pit (Ezek. 19:4, 9; Ps. 35:8; 94:13; a. e.).

In stich b the emendation of the noun שַׂלְמוֹתָי to מְשַׁלְּמָי (P. A. de Lagarde) or שֹׁלְמָי (Du.) rendered "my friends," has been aptly described by Bu. as "ein schlechter Einfall." The clause has been interpreted to mean that Job would be unfit to wear the clean garments given a prisoner once he is acquitted. The evidence for this practice, adduced from Zech. 3:3–5, is exceedingly doubtful. The stich has also been rendered, "my clothes make me an abomination to others" (Ew.) or, better, "my clothes abhor me, i.e., want no contact with me," a poetic description of the wet garments hanging loosely around his frame, after he has been dipped in the mud and filth of the pit.

However, it is evident that the suggested interpretation of stich b suffers from several drawbacks: (a) the parallelism is faulty; (b) wet clothes cling more closely to the body and cannot, therefore, be said to "abhor" or "refuse to touch me."

We suggest a change of one letter, a Tav for a Vav, reading וְתִעַבְתַּנִי: "You would make my clothes loathsome for me (because they are drenched in filth)." For the idea, cf. Lam. 4:14: "They wandered blind through the streets, so defiled with blood that none could touch their garments" (RSV).

תָּעַב in the Piel means "abominate, make abominable" (Deut. 7:26; Isa. 49:7). It is here used causatively, exactly as Hiphil forms of verbs normally used in this conjugation are causative in meaning; cf. the Comm. on 11:3; 20:2. The pronominal suffix here designates an indirect object, "for me"; cf. הֲצוֹם צַמְתֻּנִי אָנִי: "Have you been fasting *for* Me?" (Zech. 7:5); גְּדֵלַנִי כְאָב "He grew up *with* me as with a father" (Job 31:18); and the Comm. *ad loc.*, for other instances of this looser governance of suffixes. In our v., which is the apodosis of the condition introduced in v. 30, the verbs are used in the imperfect (תִּטְבְּלֵנִי) and in the perfect with Vav (וְתִעַבְתַּנִי); cf. the identical tense structure in the condition in 7:13, 14 וַחֲתַתַּנִי and תְּבַעֲתַנִי. שַׂלְמוֹתָי is the direct object of the verb.

9:32 לֹא־אִישׁ "he is not a man like me, whom I could answer." Cf. Gen. 29:7, לֹא־עֵת. Stich b is a circumstantial clause, "when we came to trial together."

9:33 This is the first of three passages in which Job's attitude toward God unfolds. Here he expresses a wish that some impartial judge would intervene between him and the God who has oppressed him so mercilessly. This hope represents the first level of faith to which Job attains; the second is enunciated in 16:19, when he sees God as his witness; in 19:25 he beholds Him as his vindicator and redeemer. For the implication of these three important passages, see Special Note 15.

While לֹא יֵשׁ has been defended on the basis of the Aramaic לָא אִית and Arab. *lais*, "there is not," LXX and S, like most moderns, vocalize the first word as לוּ, "would that," thus introducing a protasis with v. 35 as the apodosis. מוֹכִיחַ = "judge, arbiter" (cf. Isa. 2:4). The jussive forms יָשֵׁת and יָסֵר (v. 34), originally voluntative in force, have been weakened here to express a potentiality or eventuality, so that they become virtually subjunctive: יָשֵׁת = *qui ponat*, "who would place" (cf. וְיָבֶן Jer. 9:11; שִׁילֵךְ Ecc. 5:14. See Ges.-K., sec. 109, for a discussion of this usage, as well as of the use of the jussive as equivalent to a simple imperfect). In some cases, the jussive form may have been used for rhythmic considerations, as in Job 23:9, 11; Lam. 3:50; in others, because of a desire to add emphasis (e.g. Ps. 11:6; 18:12). This latter motive may have played a part in our passage, as well as in 11:14, which is likewise a conditional sentence; and in 6:29, where Job vigorously protests his innocence. See the Comm. *ad loc.*

The majuscule *Teth* of שְׁבַטוֹ in MT can be explained only as a *lapsus calami* by a scribe whose codex was later adopted as the archetype with all its features meticulously transcribed thereafter. Cf. *BTM*, Prolegomenon, p. XI.

9:35 Stich b has been rendered: (a) "for not so am I with myself, i.e., I know nothing that can make me afraid" (D-G); (b) "in my own soul I am not as you think" (Ibn E.); (c) "for I do not think myself unjust with Him" (LXX). This rendering suggests the reading עִמָּדוֹ for עִמָּדִי (so P.); but there is no such Hebrew word! We prefer to regard this stich as another *tiqqun sopherim* in this chapter (cf. Comm. on 9:19 and 9:24). Hence, read with Ehr. כִּי־לֹא־כֵן הוּא עִמָּדִי "for He is not honorable, just, with me" (cf. Gen. 42:11). The LXX rendering supports the meaning "just" for כֵּן.

The existence of three *tiqqunei sopherim* in this chapter (vv. 19, 24, 35) is entirely plausible, in view of the vigorous denunciation of God in this passage. It is noteworthy that in two of the three suggested instances, vv. 19 and 35, the change is a modification of a pronoun, and in v. 24 a shift of words. The "official" *tiqqunei sopherim* given in the sources, all designed to avoid imputing anything unseemly to God, fall into three categories: (a) avoidance of the juxtaposition of "curse" with God (I Sam. 3:13; I Ki. 21:13; Job 1:5; 2:9); (b) changes in the pronoun (Nu. 11:15 בְּרָעָתִי instead of בְּרָעָתֶךָ; Jer. 2:11 כְּבוֹדוֹ instead of כְּבוֹדִי; Ezek. 8:17 אַפָּם instead of אַפִּי; Hab. 1:12 נָמוּת instead of יָמוּת; Zech. 2:12 עֵינוֹ instead of עֵינִי); and (c) a change of the word order (Gen. 18:22 וַאַבְרָהָם עוֹדֶנּוּ עֹמֵד לִפְנֵי ה' instead of וה' עוֹדֶנּוּ עֹמֵד לִפְנֵי אַבְרָהָם). The proposed instances in our chapter belong to the predominant group b in two instances, and to category c in one.

CHAPTER 10

10:1 נָקְטָה is a contracted form of the Niphal קוּט "despise," instead of נָקֹטָה (Ezek. 6:9; 21:43; 36:31). For an analogy, cf. נָסַבָּה (Ezek. 41:7) as a contraction of נָסַבָּה (D-G). עזב, the opposite of מנע, cf. Job 20:13, "let loose, give free rein." עָלַי need not be emended to עָלָיו (so Me., Be., Du., on the basis of LXX) or to עֵלִי (Ehr.). It is the pathetic use of the pronoun who is the subject, as in Ps. 42:6; Neh. 5:7 (cf. BDB, p. 753b).

The deletion of stich c (Hö.) in order to reduce the verse to two stichs ignores the natural tendency of a poet to vary his meter pattern, especially in a long poem, as was clear even before the discovery of Ugaritic poetry.

10:3 In order to heighten the pathos, man is described here not merely as מַעֲשֵׂה יָדֶיךָ "the work of God's hands" (Job 14:15; 34:19), but as יְגִיעַ כַּפֶּיךָ "the product of toil by Thy hands." Since Job is the symbol of Everyman, he constantly moves from his own particular situation to the human condition in general. Failure to recognize this fact has led to extreme transpositions and deletions. A case in point is afforded by the closing stich of our verse, which is omitted as irrelevant by Ehr., Hö. Similarly, we may note that the bulk of Eliphaz's first speech, which is designed to comfort Job, is directed not to the suffering of the righteous, which is the real gravamen of Job's complaint, but to the prosperity of the wicked (4:8–5:5), perhaps because it is easier to explain! הוֹפָעְתָּ "shine" (Job 3:4; 10:22; Ps. 52; 94:1).

10:5 Note the repetition of the same words in both stichs (יְמֵי), a characteristic practice of the poet. See Special Note 4.

10:6 On the Lamed after בקש cf. Pr. 18:1. It may, however, not be the simple *nota accusativa*, but may carry a special nuance, "seek after that which is not available or non-existent."

10:7 עַל דַּעְתְּךָ כִּי־לֹא אֶרְשָׁע lit., "in spite of your knowing that I am not guilty" (cf. Isa. 53:9; BDB, 754b). In order to bring stich b into parallelism with stich a, the former is emended to וְאֵין בְּיָדִי פָּשַׁע (Be., Dil.) or to וְאֵין בְּיָדִי מָעַל (Du.). Ehr., on the contrary, seeks to bring stich a into parallelism with stich b, by changing אֶרְשָׁע into אִוָּשֵׁעַ. Both procedures are unnecessary. Vv. 7 and 8 exhibit alternate structure, 7a being parallel to 8a (God knows Job's nature) and 7b to 8b (nevertheless God is intent on destroying him) (so also R-O).

10:8 עצב "fashion, shape" (cf. Arab. *ghadaba*), whence עֶצֶב "vessel" (Jer. 22:28), the common עֲצַבִּים "idols" (Isa. 10:11 a. e.) and the denominative verb in Jer. 44:19. The verb occurs in mishnaic Hebrew in the meaning of "manipulating, molding the shape" (*M. Shab.* 22:6): אין מעצבין את הקטן בשבת, "an infant's body is not to be shaped on the Sabbath."

אַחַר תְּשׁוּב יַחַד סָבִיב וַתְּבַלְּעֵנִי in stich b is emended to אַחַר סַבּוֹת (Hö.), or אַחַר תְּשׁוּב (Be., Dil., P.) or אַחַר תְּסוֹב on the basis of LXX, "after these turnings" (reading אַחַר סוֹבב?). Whether LXX had an illegible text or attempted to make sense of a passage it did not understand, the change in MT is totally unnecessary. The two words continue the description of God's creating man "altogether, on all sides." Here the logical caesura (after סָבִיב) does not coincide with the poetic caesura (after וַיַּעֲשׂוּנִי), another instance of an exceptional usage, noted above in the Comm. on 4:8. בלע = "swallow, destroy" (Job 8:18; II Sam. 20:19–20; Isa. 25:7, 8).

10:9   On the theme of "Job and the Sexual Process," see Special Note 12.

כַּחֹמֶר is better read as בַּחֹמֶר (so Ehr., Hö.), "out of clay," a figure frequently used to describe God's creation of man (Job 4:19; 33:6; Isa. 45:9; 64:7). On the Beth of material, cf. Ex. 38:8; it is closely related to the Beth of means and of price.

Stich b is generally taken interrogatively, "will you turn me into dust?" (D-G, Bu., Hö., P., etc.). In spite of this broad consensus, we believe it to be in error on several grounds: (1) The intrusion of a question in the middle of the description is stylistically difficult, especially in the absence of any formal sign of the question; (2) Job can hardly protest his being returned to dust, since this is obviously the lot of all men; (3) the proposed view operates with Western canons of relevance rather than with the Oriental principle of association. Stich a, having focused attention on man's having been created from clay, suggests his return to dust, the two ideas being closely linked in the familiar classic formulation, "dust thou art and to dust wilt thou return" (Gen. 3:19; cf. Ecc. 12:7). The stich is to be interpreted declaratively and the verse rendered: "Remember that of clay You made me, and to the dust You will return me."

10:10   While חָלָב "milk" is common, גְּבִינָה "curd, cheese" is a *hapax legomenon* in biblical Hebrew, though well attested in mishnaic Hebrew, Arabic, and Ethiopic. Hö. aptly quotes a Pehlevi physician Borzoe, who describes the liquid semen mixing with the dampness in the uterus, becoming thick like the water of cheese and then even thicker, like buttermilk.

10:11   תְּשֹׂכְכֵנִי "You will knit, weave me together"; cf. תְּסֻכֵּנִי (Ps. 139:13), and מַסֶּכֶת "web" (Jud. 16:15) and frequently in mishnaic Hebrew (*M. Ohol.* 8:4; *M. Kel.* 21:1), whence the meaning "treatise" (cf. Lat. *textus*).

10:12   Both because of the unusual juxtaposition of חַיִּים וָחֶסֶד and the use of the verb עָשִׂיתָ, the opening phrase has generally been emended to חֵן וָחֶסֶד (Be., D-G) or to חַיִּים וָחֶלֶד (Hö.), or חַיִּים is deleted entirely (Ehr.). Actually, the use of the verb with חַיִּים is thoroughly explicable as an instance of *zeugma*, where וָחֶסֶד עָשִׂיתָ עִמָּדִי serves as the bridge to חַיִּים; cf. the Comm. on 4:10 for another instance of *zeugma*.

חַיִּים וָחֶסֶד is best interpreted as a *hendiadys*, lit., "a life of free grace, i.e., You have granted me a life out of your freely bestowed love." Job's life was a gift flowing out of God's love to him, beyond his power to demand.

וּפְקֻדָּתְךָ is generally rendered "gracious visitation" (BDB, P.), though the term is always used elsewhere negatively (Hos. 9:7; Isa. 10:3; Jer. 8:12 a. e.). It is better rendered "command," used concretely of "men under command" in II Ki. 11:18; Isa. 60:17; Ezek. 44:11; II Chr. 24:11, etc. It is the Divine will that has kept Job alive.

10:13 The Vav is to be taken adversatively, "but yet." אֵלֶּה and זֹאת are generally taken to be parallel and to refer to the theme of the following vvs.: "In spite of your apparent kindness, this was always in your mind — my punishment." This interpretation suggests that the Divine love that Job has extolled so enthusiastically in vv. 9–12 was not real but hypocritical. This idea is, however, inappropriate in this paean to God's concern for man. צפן "hide, store away" (Job 17:4; 21:19; Hos. 13:12) suggests that God's love, which was genuine, has now been stored away. Stich b is parallel in meaning and also refers to God's previous love which, Job knows, God actually felt for him.

The verse lit., "But these things (the marks of your concern) you have hidden in your heart; I know that it (your love) was within you."

10:14 The usual rendering of וּשְׁמַרְתָּנִי, "you watch," is inept, since God watches him even if Job does not sin. To meet this difficulty, the verb has been rendered "you would mark me," but there is no warrant for this meaning, aside from the fact that it still suffers from the same illogicality. Ehr. calls attention to the use of שמר as "bear a grudge," parallel to נטר (Jer. 3:5), which occurs with the dir. obj. in Lev. 19:18. Stich a is therefore to be rendered: "If I sin, You keep it in mind, You never overlook it," an excellent parallel to stich b.

10:15 The deletion of stich c on metric or other grounds (Du.) is uncalled for. רְאֵה need not be emended to רְוֵה, in view of Ps. 91:16, אַשְׂבִּיעֵהוּ וְאַרְאֵהוּ ‖, and Isa. 53:11, יִשְׂבָּע ‖ יִרְאֶה. On the relationship of *mediae Aleph* and *mediae Vav* roots, cf. גָּאָה (Pr. 8:13) and גֵּוָה (Jer. 13:17; Pr. 8:13; Job 22:29; 33:17; Dan. 4:34). רְאֵה is the construct of רָאֶה; cf. Isa. 58:11, גַּן רָוֶה, and such adjectives as קָשֶׁה, כָּלֶה.

10:16 וְיִגְאֶה has been emended to: (a) וְאֶגְאֶה "when I am proud, You hunt me" (S, D-G) or, better, to: (b) וְתִגְאֶה, "You are proud to hunt me." For graphic considerations as well as on grounds of meaning and syntax, it is best to read וְגֵאֶה, "proudly You hunt me like a lion," with the adjective modifying the subject of the clause, exactly as in Job 9:4 and Ps. 107:5. The simile in stich a is generally taken to mean that God is compared to a lion, as in Hos. 5:14; 13:7, but in those passages there is no talk of hunting. Here God takes pride in revealing His prowess as a hunter of big game; the lion is the hunted, not the hunter (so Ehr.) This view is supported by the parallelism with תִּתְפַּלָּא, "You show Yourself wonderful." The coordinate use of the verbs in stich b is equivalent to a complementary infinitive; cf., e.g., the use of הוֹאִיל in Deut. 1:5; Hos. 5:11; Job 6:9, 28, as against Gen. 18:27; Ex. 2:21. שׁוּב here = "do repetitively." Cf. Lam. 3:3; Ecc. 1:7; 4:1, 7; 9:11, and see BDB s.v. sec. 8, p. 998–a and Ges.-K., sec. 120, d-g.

There is bitter irony in the use of the verb "You show yourself wonderful."

10:17 עֵדֶיךָ Ehr. vocalizes as עֲדֶיךָ, which he renders "attack, onslaught," on the basis of the Arabic ʿadday. While this proposal is far superior to the suggested emendation נִגְעֵי (Bi.) or the complicated series of assumptions underlying TS' emendation, MT may be preserved in its normal meaning of "witnesses." In the traditional religious theodicy, suffering is regarded as the sign of sin, so that each blow of fate is a witness testifying against the victim. Cf. Job 16:8, where Job protests vigorously that his shriveled form and leanness now serve as witnesses against him.

There is no need to emend חֲלִיפוֹת וְצָבָא עִמִּי. The phrase is a *hendiadys*, "lit. changes of the military guard are upon me," i.e., one blow succeeds another.

10:18 LXX to the contrary notwithstanding, לֹא need not be supplied (ag. Ehr.) or understood (ag. R-O) before אֶגְוַע, which means "would I had died" (cf. the verbs in v. 19).

10:20 Stich a is rendered by LXX: "The life of my time," which is an inner Greek error for "the time of my life," on the basis of which virtually all commentators read יְמֵי חֶלְדִי. The Hebrew noun חֶלֶד "lifetime, world" (Job 11:17; Ps. 17:14; 39:6; 49:2; 89:48) has the Arab. cognate huld, "perpetual duration." However, it is not necessary to transpose the letters of the noun in our passage. The noun חֶלֶד occurs in metathesis as חֶדֶל (in Isa. 38:11; in Ps. 39:5, render: "How long shall I survive?") Hence our passage, reading the Kethib, requires no emendation except for the deletion of one Yod: הֲלֹא־מְעַט יְמֵי חֶדְלִי שִׁית מִמֶּנִּי וְאַבְלִיגָה מְּעָט. The brevity of life is underscored by the same word at the beginning and at the end of the verse.

10:22 This powerful description of Sheol is in apposition with the closing stich of v. 21. וַתֹּפַע in stich c, from the root יפע, means "it shines, gives light"; cf. הוֹפִיעַ (Job 3:4; 10:3, a. e.). This suggests that the noun עֵיפָתָה in stich a, which apparently occurs also in Am. 4:13, means not "darkness" but "light," its root being עוף, a metathetic form of יעף (cf. נוק, ינק; שׁוע, ישׁע; בוש, יבש). The existence of a meaning "be dark" for the root עוף (BDB 734 a) is highly doubtful, Isa. 8:22, 23 being very obscure. If this latter meaning be allowed, the root would be an instance of ʾaḍdad, "words of like and opposite meaning" on which cf. Th. Noeldeke, "Wörter mit Gegensinn," in *Beitraege zur semitischen Sprachwissenschaft*," and Gordis, "Studies in Hebrew Roots of Contrasted Meanings," in *JQR*, 1936, vol. 27, pp. 33–58. It is noteworthy that this theme of "light-darkness" occurs as an instance of ʾaḏdad in אוֹר "light," meaning also "twilight, evening"; cf. *M. Pes.* 1:1: אור לארבעה עשר, "on the evening of the 14th day of Nisan," and the discussion in the Talmud on the meaning (*ibid.* 2a).

TS renders stich a: "The land of Ephatha demons within darkness" (apparently reading בְּמוֹ for כְּמוֹ), on the basis of an incantation text from *Arslan Tash* (see his study in *JNES*, vol. 6, 1947, pp. 18–29; in *Halashon Ve-hasepher*, vol. 1, pp. 53–65; and his Commentary, *ad loc.*). There is, however, no clear evidence that the incantation refers to night demons. Even if this be granted, the word might well be a euphemism; cf. the Greek *Eumenides*, lit. "the well-intentioned ones," for "the Furies." Our verse, however, is best rendered:

> "A land whose light is blackness,
>   gloom and disorder,
>   where the light is as darkness."

Milton, in *Paradise Lost*, intuitively grasped the sense of our passage: "The light in that region is no light, but rather darkness visible."

The Speech of Zophar (11)

Zophar, who is probably the youngest of the Friends and surely the least urbane, now joins the debate. Far less restrained than Bildad, he plunges at once into an attack upon Job. In spite of his tactlessness, Zophar is by no means negligible as a thinker.

He declares that Job's insistence upon his uprightness is both false and arrogant. Far from punishing Job unjustly, God has reduced the extent of his penalty, for every man is guilty of secret sins known only to God. This is not astonishing in a mysterious universe that is beyond man's power to grasp. God's wisdom and power are limitless. This truth Job ignores when he presumes to challenge God's justice and, by that token, to pass judgment upon his Maker. Almost equally great are man's sinfulness and folly, the full dimensions of which are known only to God. If Job wishes to be restored to peace and weil-being, he should repent his sins and thus become worthy of God's forgiveness and favor.

11   Zophar the Naamathite answered, saying,
2   Shall a multitude of words go unanswered,
                 and a man full of talk appear in the right?
3   Your rantings force men to silence;
                 you mock the truth, with no one to shut you up,
4   as you say, "My doctrine is pure,
                 and I am pure in Your eyes."
5   But O, if only God would speak
                 and open His lips to you,
6   and tell you the secrets of wisdom —
                 for there are mysteries in understanding.
             Then you would know that God is exacting
                 less from you than your guilt demands.

7   Can you penetrate the essence of God?
                 Can you discover the nature of the Almighty?
8   It is higher than heaven — what can you do?
                 and deeper than Sheol — what can you know?
9   It is longer than the earth in measure,
                 and wider than the sea.

10   If God seizes hold and imprisons and arraigns,
                 who can hinder Him?
11   For He is well acquainted with worthless men;
                 He sees their sin, though He pretends not to notice.
12   But a stupid man will get understanding,
                 as soon as a wild ass's colt is born a man.

13   If you direct your heart aright
                 and spread out your hands to Him —
14   if there be iniquity in your hand, put it away;
                 let no wickedness dwell in your tent —
15   you will be able to lift your face free from blemish;
                 you will be firmly set, with nothing to fear;
16   all your misery you will forget,
                 recalling it only as waters that have passed away.
17   Brighter than the noonday will be your world;
                 its darkness will shine like the morning.
18   You will lie down, knowing there is hope;
                 you will make your couch and lie down in safety.
19   You will lie down, and none will make you afraid —
                 indeed, many will entreat your favor.
20   But the eyes of the wicked will fail with longing,
                 all escape will be cut off from them
                 and their hope will turn into despair.

יא א וַיַּעַן צֹפַר הַנַּעֲמָתִי וַיֹּאמַר:

2 הֲרֹב דְּבָרִים לֹא יֵעָנֶה   וְאִם־אִישׁ שְׂפָתַיִם יִצְדָּק:

3 בַּדֶּיךָ מְתִים יַחֲרִישׁוּ   וַתִּלְעַג וְאֵין מַכְלִם:

4 וַתֹּאמֶר זַךְ לִקְחִי   וּבַר הָיִיתִי בְעֵינֶיךָ:

ה וְאוּלָם מִי־יִתֵּן אֱלוֹהַ דַּבֵּר   וְיִפְתַּח שְׂפָתָיו עִמָּךְ:

6 וְיַגֶּד־לְךָ ׀ תַּעֲלֻמוֹת חָכְמָה   כִּי־כִפְלַיִם לְתוּשִׁיָּה

7 וְדַע ׀ כִּי־יַשֶּׁה לְךָ אֱלוֹהַ מֵעֲוֺנֶךָ:   הַחֵקֶר אֱלוֹהַ תִּמְצָא

8 אִם עַד־תַּכְלִית שַׁדַּי תִּמְצָא: גׇּבְהֵי שָׁמַיִם מַה־תִּפְעָל

9 עֲמֻקָּה מִשְּׁאוֹל מַה־תֵּדָע: אֲרֻכָּה מֵאֶרֶץ מִדָּה

י וּרְחָבָה מִנִּי־יָם: אִם־יַחֲלֹף וְיַסְגִּיר

11 וְיַקְהִיל וּמִי יְשִׁיבֶנּוּ:   כִּי־הוּא יָדַע מְתֵי־שָׁוְא

12 וַיַּרְא־אָוֶן וְלֹא יִתְבּוֹנָן: וְאִישׁ נָבוּב יִלָּבֵב

13 וְעַיִר פֶּרֶא אָדָם יִוָּלֵד: אִם־אַתָּה הֲכִינוֹתָ לִבֶּךָ

14 וּפָרַשְׂתָּ אֵלָיו כַּפֶּךָ:   אִם־אָוֶן בְּיָדְךָ הַרְחִיקֵהוּ

טו וְאַל־תַּשְׁכֵּן בְּאֹהָלֶיךָ עַוְלָה: כִּי־אָז ׀ תִּשָּׂא פָנֶיךָ מִמּוּם

16 וְהָיִיתָ מֻצָק וְלֹא תִירָא: כִּי־אַתָּה עָמָל תִּשְׁכָּח

17 כְּמַיִם עָבְרוּ תִזְכֹּר: וּמִצָּהֳרַיִם יָקוּם חָלֶד

18 תָּעֻפָה כַּבֹּקֶר תִּהְיֶה: וּבָטַחְתָּ כִּי־יֵשׁ תִּקְוָה

19 וְחָפַרְתָּ לָבֶטַח תִּשְׁכָּב: וְרָבַצְתָּ וְאֵין מַחֲרִיד

כ וְחִלּוּ פָנֶיךָ רַבִּים: וְעֵינֵי רְשָׁעִים תִּכְלֶינָה

וּמָנוֹס אָבַד מִנְהֶם   וְתִקְוָתָם מַפַּח־נָפֶשׁ:

11:2 הַרֹב דְּבָרִים need not be vocalized as הֲרַב (LXX, V). The abstract "multitude of words" (cf. Ecc. 5:2) is parallel to the concrete אִישׁ שְׂפָתַיִם, "man of lips, empty babbler." For this stylistic usage, which makes for greater variety and interest in parallelism, cf., e.g., Isa. 13:11; 14:4; Ps. 26:4; Pr. 10:18; 11:2; 12:27; 17:4. Another instance occurs in our own chapter, in v. 11.

11:3 בַּדֶּיךָ, from the root בדד, a metaplastic root for בדא "invent, lie" (I Ki. 12:33), means "idle talk, ranting," as in the Phoenician *Inscription of Eshmunazzar*, line 6, בדנם, and the Syriac בדיא. The noun occurs in Isa. 16:6; Jer. 48:30, in the meaning of "boastings," and in Isa. 44:25; Jer. 50:36, in the meaning of "praters, boasters." The Hiphil יַחֲרִישׁוּ is transitive, "make silent, compel to be still."

מַכְלִים in its usual sense, "put to shame" (I Sam. 30:24; 25:7, 15), is interpreted "there is none to put you to shame" or "rebuke you," for which Ruth 2:15 is adduced. However, the parallelism, as well as the context, militates against this interpretation and suggests that the stich means "there is none to silence you." In Nu. 12:14 תִכָּלֵם is parallel to תִּסָּגֵר and has the meaning "shut up, close up." This sense is admirably suited to the crux, Jud. 18:7, שֹׁקֵט וּבֹטֵחַ וְאֵין מַכְלִים דָּבָר בָּאָרֶץ which is to be rendered "they were at ease and secure, with no one shutting anything up in the land." Both these meanings for כלם inhere in כלא: (a) "close up, restrain," as in כָּלֻא וְלֹא אֵצֵא, "I am shut up and I cannot come forth" (Ps. 88:9); and (b) "to silence," as in אֲדֹנִי מֹשֶׁה כְּלָאֵם, "my lord Moses, shut them up" (Nu. 11:28); note the English slang "shut up" = "be silent." The form תִכָּלֵם in Nu. 12:14 is to be explained as תִכָּלֵא + enclitic Mem. Similarly, מַכְלִים in Jud. 18:7 and in our passage is מַכְלִיא + enclitic Mem. In all three cases, the *Lamed Aleph* root has been assimilated to *Lamed Yod* orthographically (Ges.-K., sec. 74, n. 4) or morphologically (Ges.-K., sec. 75, n. 6), a process carried much further in mishnaic Hebrew under the influence of Aramaic (cf. Segal, *Diqduq Lešon Hamišnah*, Tel-Aviv, 1930, par. 273–75). In our root, the *tertiae Yod* occurs as a by-form of the *tertiae Aleph* in יִכְלֶה = יִכְלָא (Gen. 23:6); כָּלוּ = כָּלְאוּ (I Sam. 6:10), in the meaning, "shut off, deny" and "shut in" respectively. The *tertiae Aleph* form in lieu of the *tertiae Yod* occurs in לְכַלֵּא (Dan. 9:24).

Another instance of the enclitic Mem added to a *tertiae Yod* verb occurs in Job 29:25, ינחם; see the Comm. *ad loc.* It is interesting that P, which translates our stich with a doublet, renders our verb דכלא. For the use of the Hiphil, cf. Jud. 18:7 cited above.

11:4 וַתֹּאמֶר. The Vav consecutive suggests that this verse is linked to the preceding, "as you say, 'my teaching is pure.' " לֶקַח "doctrine, teaching," a characteristic term of Wisdom literature (Pr. 1:5; 7:21; 4:2; 16:21, 23; and also Deut. 32:2; Isa. 29:24 (both Wisdom contexts). Those who emend לִקְחִי to לָקְחִי, for which, incidentally, the LXX "my works" is no proof, overlook the fact that the adjective would need to be emended to the fem., besides being inappropriate.

In stich b, either בְּעֵינֶיךָ is emended to בְּעֵינָיו (Be., Me., Hö.), or הָיִיתִי is changed to הָיִיתָ (Ehr., TS, P.). In either case, the direct quotation is limited to stich a. MT is to be preferred, because it continues the quotation for the entire verse, "I am pure in Your (i.e. God's) eyes." Job has clearly insisted that God knows that he is innocent (cf. 10:7), to which Zophar now responds by recalling the mysterious character of the world in general and of man's actions in particular, so that Job has no right to take his innocence for granted.

11:5 מִי־יִתֵּן אֱלוֹהַּ דַּבֵּר "O, would that God would speak!" The usual word order would be מִי יִתֵּן דַּבֵּר אֱלוֹהַּ (cf. Ex. 16:3) or מִי יִתֵּן יְדַבֵּר אֱלוֹהַּ (cf. Job 6:8; 14:13). The reversal of this order, which moves אֱלוֹהַּ forward, may be dictated by Zophar's desire to contrast God with Job.

11:6 כִּי־כִפְלַיִם לְתוּשִׁיָּה has been interpreted from כִּפְלַיִם "double" (Isa. 40:2) to mean "manifold" or "two sides" (BDB, R-O, P.). TS emends it to כָּפַל יָם, "He hath folded the sea." Hö. emends the word to כִּפְלָאִים and then renders the clause "which are like wonders for the understanding." The key to the passage, we believe, lies in recognizing the parallelism of stich a and b (note the nouns in Isa. 28:29; Pr. 3:21; 8:14) and revocalizing the word as a *defectiva* spelling of כִּי כִפְלָאִים, with the Kaph of כִּפְלָאִים retained as the asseverative Kaph; cf. the Comm. on 3:5. Stich b is then to be rendered "for there are mysteries to wisdom," a perfect parallel to "mysteries in understanding." On this meaning of the root פלא, "mysterious, hidden," cf. Jud. 13:8; Ps. 131:1; Pr. 30:18; and B.S. 3:21

פלאות ממך אל תדרוש
ומכוסה ממך אל תחקור

"What is too mysterious for you do not seek; what is hidden do not search." Stich c is deleted by Be., Bu., Hö., because it breaks the metric pattern. This is never in itself a sufficient cause, particularly here where it is essential to the sense. The verb יַשֶּׁה has been interpreted (a) from the root נָשָׁה "forget" (Ibn E., D-G, BDB, P.), hence "He forgets some of your iniquity," or (b) from נשה "demand payment" (cf. Deut. 24:10) (Ra., Ehr.), "He demands of you less than your iniquity" — God is actually punishing Job less than he deserves. My former student, Rabbi Michael Kurz, suggested reading יַשֶּׁה לְךָ אֱלֹהִים עֲוֹנֶךָ "God demands payment only for your sins." However, Zophar's emphasis on the unknown suggests the partitive use of the preposition Mem. Stich c has also been emended to יִשְׁאָלְךָ אֱלוֹהַּ מֵעֲוֹנֶךָ and rendered "God will interrogate you about your sin" (Ehr. TS, Dh.), but the emendation is unnecessary. Besides, the verb שאל never governs the Mem *rei*.

11:7 חֵקֶר "lit. depth, innermost nature, i.e., essence." It is parallel to תַּכְלִית "end, furthest limit." Once again the poet uses the same root in both stichs, a stylistic trait already encountered in 5:8, 23; 7:8; 8:3; 10:5, 20; 11:18. There is no need to try to give the verb different meanings in both stichs (ag. Ehr.). See Special Note 4.

11:8 Stich a is generally rendered, "the heights of Heavens — what can you do?" However, the parallelism with עֲמֻקָה, אֲרֻכָּה and רְחָבָה suggests that the correct reading is גְּבֹהָה מִשָּׁמַיִם (so Jerome, V, Be., Bu., Ehr.). It is possible here to reconstruct the evolution of MT from the original reading, גבה משמים. The feminine adjective was written *defectiva*, because the early scribes avoided writing two-vowel letters consecutively. This practice is still registered in MT; cf. II Sam. 5:2; I Ki. 21:11, and other passages discussed in *BTM*, pp. 95 f. When word-separation was introduced, the Mem was erroneously attached to the first word, which was read as גְּבֹהִם שָׁמַיִם "the heavens are high" (so LXX). This assumed plural adjective was then written with the apocopated plural גבהי שמים; cf. Isa. 5:1 שִׁירַת דּוֹדִי; Cant. 7:9 לְדוֹדִי (דּוֹדִים); *idem* 8:2 רִמּוֹנִים = רִמֹּנִי. In the absence of the Mem, it was then vocalized as גָּבְהֵי, our present Masoretic reading. For an instance of the reverse process, where the Mem was supplied because the text was mistakenly regarded as containing an apocopated plural, cf. Cant. 4:15 מַעְיַן גַּנִּים, to be read גַּנִּי; see *SS ad loc.* The four fem. adjectives represent the "four dimensions," height, depth, length, and breadth, and refer to the limits of God's nature, which are beyond man's comprehension.

11:9 מִדָּה "her measure" (with Mappiq He) is another instance of the suffix being added to the stem of fem. nouns. Cf. Jer. 13:25; Ps. 10:9; 27:5; Pr. 7:8; and Job 5:13, on which see the Comm.

11:10 יַחֲלֹף "he passes by" is obviously inappropriate, nor can it legitimately be given the meaning of "overlook" (P.), especially since the other verbs indicate acts of commission. Hence, read with LXX and virtually all moderns יַחְתֹּף or יַחְתּוֹף (cf. 9:12 and see below). The error may have been induced by the scribe's recalling the proximity of both verbs in 9:11b, 12a. Be. deletes the entire verse on alleged metric grounds, but if it is eliminated, v. 11 hangs in the air. Actually, we have here another instance where the logical *caesura* (after וְיַקְהִיל) does not coincide with the poetic *caesura* (after וְיַסְגִּיר), a usage already encountered in 4:8; 10:8, as well as in Gen. 49:9; Nu. 23:23. The verse is in 3:3 meter, אִם receiving an accent for metric reasons, particularly since both verbs in the stich are rather long. Cf. *PPS*, p. 67.

יַסְגִּיר "imprison," used in Lev., chaps. 13 and 14, of the leper, and cf. מַסְגֵּר "dungeon" (Isa. 24:22; 42:7; Ps. 142:8).

יַקְהִיל is generally rendered "summon an assembly for judgment." We prefer to relate the root to qaʾla (Arab.), "speak out." On the relationship of *mediae He* and *mediae Vav*, cf. Aramaic and Hebrew רהט, רוץ; בהת, בוש, and the name of the Patriarch, אַבְרָהָם, which is morphologically parallel to אַבְרָם. The verb יַקְהִיל would therefore mean "speak" as in קֹהֶלֶת "speaker." In our passage it would have the special nuance "speak out against." Cf. Ezek. 16:40; 23:46; and Neh. 5:7: וָאֶתֵּן עֲלֵיהֶם קְהִלָּה גְדוֹלָה, "I set forth a powerful accusation against them" (F. Zimmermann). In all these passages the meaning "arraign" seems more appropriate than "condemn" (P.). The verse details three steps in the judicial process — arrest, incarceration, and arraignment. יְשִׁיבֶנּוּ is "hold him back, hinder, restrain Him."

11:11 For the parallelism between the concrete and the abstract (מְתֵי שָׁוְא and אָוֶן), see the Comm. on 11:2.

וְלֹא יִתְבּוֹנָן has been rendered: (a) interrogatively, "Will he not consider"? (JPSV, P.); (b) "He does not need to observe closely" (Ibn E.); (c) The clause is also construed as a passive in the Polal: "He himself is unobserved"; and (d) the clause is emended to וְלוֹ יִתְבּוֹנָן "He gives heed to it" (Hö.). We prefer to interpret the clause: "He acts as though he did not understand, he pretends to take no notice" (so Ra.). Zophar is conceding that at times it seems as though God is unaware of injustice in the world. On this use of the Hithpael, "play a role," cf. the familiar התנבא (I Sam. 18:10 and often, and see Ges.-K., sec. 54, 3).

11:12 The verse is obviously a proverb — the two stichs being linked by the *Vav adaequationis*; cf. 5:7. נָבוּב = "hollow, empty, stupid"; cf. Ex. 27:8. Curiously, in medieval Hebrew poetry the word occurs in the opposite meaning of "wise, understanding." This is probably based on the rendering of T in our passage וּבַר נַשׁ מְפַלְפַּל, who may have interpreted the root in the sense of "penetrating" (cf. *Šir HaYiḥḥud for Tuesday*). This meaning is not appropriate in our passage. The context also requires that יִלָּבֵב be taken not privatively, "is deprived of understanding," but positively, "will acquire sense." עַיִר "male ass" and פֶּרֶא "wild ass" are in apposition with each other, the second noun delimiting the first, as is the case with the common phrase, נַעֲרָה בְתוּלָה. The fanciful explanations which base themselves on Ugaritic are therefore unnecessary. The juxtaposition of עַיִר and פֶּרֶא is undoubtedly a reminiscence of Gen. 16:12. By introducing them in a totally different meaning, the poet affords the reader the esthetic delight of recognition. This type of poetic conceit is familiar to all readers of medieval Hebrew poetry, which utilizes the Bible as its source.

The verse has been interpreted in radically opposing fashions: (a) "Even a hollow man can achieve understanding, and a wild ass's colt is born a man" (so Ra., Ibn E., Hi., Del., Dil., Du., Volz). This would mean that even Job may become wise or can be "tamed" like a wild ass. However, Zophar's general hostility and intransigence against Job, as well as the remote comparison of the wild ass's becoming a man, militates against this view. It is better rendered "a hollow man is as likely to get understanding as a colt is to become a man." No wisdom or insight can be expected from Job. The succeeding passage, in which Zophar urges Job to repent and keep far from sin in order to be restored, does not invalidate this negative interpretation of the verse, which is supported by other considerations as well; see the Comm. on vv. 13–14.

The utilization of older familiar texts in a new and unfamiliar form is a basic rhetorical device of medieval Hebrew literature. It is becoming clear, however, that this device is much older. We have called attention to a related usage in the Qumran scrolls previously known only from medieval literature (cf. Gordis, "Naʿalam and other Observations on the Ain Feshkah Scrolls," *JNES*, vol. 9, 1950, pp. 44–47). In our passage, the poet uses the phrase פֶּרֶא אָדָם (Gen. 16:12) in a manner radically different from the original, the two words being separated in sense here. Another illustration of this usage occurs in 9:19, where the common phrase כֹּחַ אַמִּיץ (Isa. 40:26; Job 9:4; Nah. 2:2; Ps. 24:5) is again utilized altogether differently by the poet, who separates the words; cf. the Comm. *ad loc.*

11:13 The use of אַתָּה is emphatic — "If even you will direct your heart aright" (D-G). הֵכִין לֵב "direct one's heart, order aright" (Ps. 78:8; II Chr. 12:14, a. e.) may govern אֵלָיו, which is understood from stich b.

11:14 Structurally the verse is a parenthesis, interrupting the conditional sentence (vv. 13–15) and incidentally betraying Zophar's passionate conviction that Job is indeed a sinner. תַּשְׁכֵּן, the Hiphil, "do not let dwell," is stronger than the Qal read by S, V. תִּשְׁכֹּן. אֹהָלֶיךָ cannot be a plural, but is best construed as a *plene* spelling of the singular (so all Vss.).

11:15 כִּי אָז (6:2; 8:6) "for then," like כִּי עַתָּה, is the introduction to the *apodosis*; cf. BDB, s.v. p. 23 a. The idiom נשא פנים, "lift the face," carries a large variety of meanings in biblical Hebrew: (a) "grant a request"; (b) "show consideration for"; (c) "be gracious to"; (d) "show partiality to." None of these meanings is appropriate here. Neither is the rendering "possess the sign of a good conscience" (ag. BDB). It here means "to be cheerful, happy, self-confident," and is the opposite of נָפְלוּ פָנֶיךָ (Gen. 4:6), "Your face has fallen, you are sad." מִמּוּם means either: (a) "away from blemish"; cf. Nu. 15:24; or, better, (b) "without, free from blemish." Cf. Job 21:9 בָּתֵּיהֶם שָׁלוֹם מִפָּחַד. On the basis of T, which read סנן מחבולא, "purified from evil," Me., Wr. read מֻצָק "purified." Zophar is, however, describing not Job's moral state, but his well-being after he will have made peace with God. Hence, MT מֻצָק (lit. "firmly set") is correct. The root יצק means "cast metal" (Ex. 25:18; 26:37, a. e., and see כִּרְאִי מוּצָק, Job 37:18).

11:16 כִּי אַתָּה has been emended to כִּי עַתָּה (R-O, Ehr., Hö.), but the use of כִּי אָז in v. 15 militates against the change. Waters are a common biblical metaphor for troubles (cf. Jonah 2:6; Ps. 124:4, and often). If Job will remember his misery at all, it will be like waters that have passed away.

11:17 חֶלֶד, lit. "duration, world, hence, a man's life," occurs in Ps. 17:14;

39:6; 49:2; 89:48 and in *metathesis* as חֶדֶל in Isa. 38:11 and Job 10:20, on which see the Comm.

תָּעֻפָה in MT with a penultimate accent can be construed only as a verb from the root עוּף "be dark." The stich would then be interpreted as a condition: "though it be dark, it will be as the morning" (so D-G). It is preferable, however, to interpret the word as a noun (so S, Ew., T, Ra. and most moderns), treating the form as similar to תַּנּוּר, "stove," though with a shift in accent, or preferably, revocalizing it as תְּעֵפָה "darkness," like תְּרוּמָה, תְּנוּפָה, תְּלוּנָה, etc. The feminine noun is the subject of the verb in stich b.

11:18 וּבָטַחְתָּ is best taken here in the original concrete meaning of the root, "lie down, fall down," for which cf. Arab. *bataḥa* I, "throw to the ground" VII, "be thrown to the ground, lie down, lie extended on the ground." This meaning of the root was noted by the Karaite grammarian, David ben Abraham Alfasi, and the medieval Solomon ibn Parhon, *Mahberet*, s.v., who interpreted Jer. 12:5; Ps. 22:10; Job 40:2 along these lines. (Cf. S. L. Skoss, in *Jewish Studies in Memory of G. A. Kohut*, New York, 1935, pp. 549–53.) Though not hitherto noted, this meaning is particularly appropriate in our passage, as is clear from the parallel with תִּשְׁכָּב in stich b and וְרָבַצְתָּ in 19a. The usual Hebrew meaning "trust" is derived, as is generally the case, from the original, more concrete meaning. The verse exhibits a paronomasia in the use of the root in both stichs.

וְחָפַרְתָּ has generally been rendered "search out carefully before lying down" or emended to וְחֻפַּרְתָּ, to which the meaning "be protected" has been assigned (Ehr., Dh., Hö.). The verb is used in its common meaning "dig." The figure is that of an animal digging a resting-place for itself and then lying down in security. For this metaphor, see the Comm. on 40:24.

11:19 חלה פני פלוני "entreat, appease, beg for the favor of, lit., sweeten the face of," cf. Aram. חֲלִי, Arab. *ḥalaᵓ*, *tertiae ya*, whence *ḥalwah*, "candy, sweet" in modern Arabic. Cf. Ps. 45:13; Pr. 19:6. The entire phrase in stich a occurs in Isa. 17:2; Zeph. 3:13. The verb is applied to human beings in Ps. 23:2.

11:20 מִנְהֶם, the fuller archaic form of the preposition with suf., which occurs only here in poetry. Cf. מִנְהוּ (Job 4:12).

מַפַּח־נָפֶשׁ "lit., breathing out," not "expiration, death," but "despair." Cf. Job 31:39, וְנֶפֶשׁ בְּעָלֶיהָ הִפָּחְתִּי, which obviously means not "I killed their owners," but "I brought despair to them"; see the Comm. *ad loc.*

Job's Reply to Zophar (12–14)

Job's closing speech in the first cycle is his most extensive rejoinder. These chapters have been widely misunderstood and consequently have been subjected to a plethora of emendations and deletions. The key to their meaning and power lies in recognizing the use of quotations. At times Job cites — and inevitably distorts — the words of the Friends in order to refute them. Or he quotes maxims drawn from Wisdom literature in order to buttress his own position. This is indicated in the translation by quotation marks and brief introductory phrases.

The speech begins with a sarcastic reference to the Friends' claim that they possess superior wisdom and a more intimate knowledge of God. Were he in their place, Job, too, would find it easy to bear the calamities of the unfortunate! He parodies the speeches of the Friends, who have sought to avoid any straightforward discussion of God's justice by extolling the wonders of nature. Job then refers to the Friends' claim to greater wisdom because of their greater age by citing a traditional apothegm. This argument he undermines obliquely by citing another proverb which declares that all wisdom and might are with God.

Job now proceeds to describe God's power in a speech which differs significantly from the hymns previously intoned by the Friends. While they have praised God's creative goodness, Job pictures God's power negatively, as manifested in the destruction of the order of nature, in the overthrow of the upper classes in society, and in the changing destinies of nations.

Job then insists that the Friends' defense of God is worthless, because God wants no partiality or false pleading on His behalf. At least God knows that Job is no flatterer and speaks the truth in his heart. Finding neither compassion nor truth in the Friends, Job flees from God to God, seeking refuge from His wrath in His mercy. He asks God that his sins be clearly set forth and his torment be brought to an end.

What is man — short-lived, impure, and frail! All Job asks is a brief respite from his misery before he dies and disappears forever. An aging tree, Job muses, may come back to life through transplanting. If man only possessed the same power of self-renewal! Job toys longingly with the idea of man's immortality, but then sorrowfully rejects it. He finds it impossible to accept this new idea of life after death, a belief which was beginning to penetrate many circles. Job concludes that death is universal and final. After a man is gone he cannot share the joys and sorrows of his children, for with death all knowledge and sentience end.

Thus Job rejects even the vicarious immortality of children, the lesser joy of participating in their experiences which take place beyond a man's own life-span.

12   Then Job answered, saying,
2   No doubt you are the people that count,
           and with you all wisdom will die!
3   Yet I have a mind as well as you;
           I am not inferior to you.
           Who does not know such things as these?
4   I am a mockery to God's friend
           who calls to Him and is answered —
           a mockery to the perfect saint!
5   The unfortunate deserve only contempt
           in the opinion of the safe and secure —
           a beating is proper for those who stumble!
6   You admit, "The tents of robbers are at peace,
           the dwellings of those who provoke God,
           all those who have deceived Him."
7   "But," you say, "ask the cattle to teach you,
           and the fowl of the sky to tell you,
8   or speak to the earth that it instruct you,
           and let the fish of the sea declare to you."
9   Who does not know in all this,
           that the hand of the Lord has made it,
10   in whose hand is the life of every living thing
           and the breath of all humankind!
11   Surely the ear tests words,
           as the palate tastes food!
12   You say, "With the aged is wisdom,
           in length of days is understanding."
13   But I say, "With God is wisdom and strength,
           His are counsel and understanding."

14   Behold, He destroys and it cannot be rebuilt,
           He imprisons a man and he is not released.
15   He shuts up the waters and they dry up,
           or He sends them forth and they overwhelm the earth.
16   With Him are strength and sound counsel;
           The misled and the misleaders — all are His.
17   He drives counselors mad,
           and of judges He makes fools.
18   He opens the belt of kings
           and removes the girdle from their loins.
19   He drives priests into madness
           and temple votaries into confusion.
20   He deprives counselors of speech
           and removes the discernment of the elders.
21   He pours contempt on princes,
           and looses the girdle of the strong.
22   He reveals deep secrets from the darkness,
           and brings the blackest gloom to light.
23   He makes nations great, and then destroys them.
           He expands nations, and forsakes them.
24   He removes understanding from the people's leaders
           and leads them in a pathless waste astray.

יב א וַיַּעַן אִיּוֹב וַיֹּאמַר׃

2 אָמְנָם כִּי אַתֶּם־עָם   וְעִמָּכֶם תָּמוּת חָכְמָה׃

3 גַּם־לִי לֵבָב ׀ כְּמוֹכֶם   לֹא־נֹפֵל אָנֹכִי מִכֶּם

4 וְאֶת־מִי־אֵין כְּמוֹ־אֵלֶּה   שְׂחֹק לְרֵעֵהוּ ׀ אֶהְיֶה
קֹרֵא לֶאֱלוֹהַּ וַיַּעֲנֵהוּ   שְׂחוֹק צַדִּיק תָּמִים׃

5 לַפִּיד בּוּז לְעַשְׁתּוּת שַׁאֲנָן   נָכוֹן לְמוֹעֲדֵי רָגֶל׃

6 יִשְׁלָיוּ אֹהָלִים ׀ לְשֹׁדְדִים   וּבַטֻּחוֹת לְמַרְגִּיזֵי אֵל

7 לַאֲשֶׁר הֵבִיא אֱלוֹהַּ בְּיָדוֹ׃   וְאוּלָם שְׁאַל־נָא בְהֵמוֹת וְתֹרֶךָּ

8 וְעוֹף הַשָּׁמַיִם וְיַגֶּד־לָךְ׃   אוֹ שִׂיחַ לָאָרֶץ וְתֹרֶךָּ

9 וִיסַפְּרוּ לְךָ דְּגֵי הַיָּם׃   מִי לֹא־יָדַע בְּכָל־אֵלֶּה

10 כִּי יַד־יְהוָה עָשְׂתָה זֹּאת׃   אֲשֶׁר בְּיָדוֹ נֶפֶשׁ כָּל־חָי

11 וְרוּחַ כָּל־בְּשַׂר־אִישׁ׃   הֲלֹא־אֹזֶן מִלִּין תִּבְחָן

12 וְחֵךְ אֹכֶל יִטְעַם־לוֹ׃   בִּישִׁישִׁים חָכְמָה

13 וְאֹרֶךְ יָמִים תְּבוּנָה׃   עִמּוֹ חָכְמָה וּגְבוּרָה

14 לוֹ עֵצָה וּתְבוּנָה׃   הֵן יַהֲרוֹס וְלֹא יִבָּנֶה

טו יִסְגֹּר עַל־אִישׁ וְלֹא יִפָּתֵחַ׃   הֵן יַעְצֹר בַּמַּיִם וְיִבָשׁוּ

16 וְיִשַׁלְּחֵם וְיַהַפְכוּ אָרֶץ׃   עִמּוֹ עֹז וְתוּשִׁיָּה

17 לוֹ שֹׁגֵג וּמַשְׁגֶּה׃   מוֹלִיךְ יוֹעֲצִים שׁוֹלָל

18 וְשֹׁפְטִים יְהוֹלֵל׃   מוּסַר מְלָכִים פִּתֵּחַ

19 וַיֶּאְסֹר אֵזוֹר בְּמָתְנֵיהֶם׃   מוֹלִיךְ כֹּהֲנִים שׁוֹלָל

כ וְאֵתָנִים יְסַלֵּף׃   מֵסִיר שָׂפָה לְנֶאֱמָנִים

21 וְטַעַם זְקֵנִים יִקָּח׃   שׁוֹפֵךְ בּוּז עַל־נְדִיבִים

22 וּמִזִּיחַ אֲפִיקִים רִפָּה׃   מְגַלֶּה עֲמֻקוֹת מִנִּי־חֹשֶׁךְ

23 וַיֹּצֵא לָאוֹר צַלְמָוֶת׃   מַשְׂגִּיא לַגּוֹיִם וַיְאַבְּדֵם

24 שֹׁטֵחַ לַגּוֹיִם וַיַּנְחֵם׃   מֵסִיר לֵב רָאשֵׁי עַם־הָאָרֶץ

25   They grope in the dark without light,
             and He makes them stagger like a drunkard.

13   Behold, all this my eye has seen;
             my ear has heard and understood it.
2   What you know, I know too;
             I am not inferior to you.
3   But I wish to speak to the Almighty;
             I desire to argue my case with God.
4   But you are plasterers of lies;
             worthless physicians are you all.
5   If only you would keep silent,
             this would count as a mark of your wisdom.
6   And now hear my argument;
             listen to the pleadings of my lips.
7   Is it for the sake of God that you speak falsehood,
             on His behalf that you utter lies?
8   Will you show partiality toward Him;
             is it for God that you are arguing?
9   Will it be well with you when He searches you out?
             Can you deceive Him as one deceives a man?
10   Will He declare you in the right,
             if you show partiality to one side?
11   Will not His terror affright you
             and His awe fall upon you?
12   Your arguments are maxims of ashes;
             Your rejoinders, rejoinders of clay.

13   Be silent before me and I shall speak,
             and let there befall me what may.
14   You ask why I place my flesh in my teeth
             and take my life in my hand?
15   Yes, He may slay me; I shall not be quiet,
             but I will justify my ways to His face!
16   Indeed, He will surely be my salvation,
             for it is no flatterer coming before Him.
17   Listen attentively to my words,
             and let my declaration be in your ears.

18   Now, if I could present my case
             I know that I would be vindicated.
19   But if God says, "Who dares to argue with Me?"
             then I must perish in silence.
20   Spare me two things only
             and I shall not need to hide from Your face:
21   remove Your hand from me,
             and let not the dread of You terrify me;
22   Then You may call and I shall respond,
             or I shall speak, and You answer me.
23   How many are my iniquities and sins?
             Let me know my transgression and my sin.
24   Why do You hide Your face
             and consider me Your enemy?

כה וַיַּתְעֵם בְּתֹהוּ לֹא־דָרֶךְ: יְמַשְׁשׁוּ־חֹשֶׁךְ וְלֹא־אוֹר
וַיַּתְעֵם כַּשִּׁכּוֹר:

יג א הֶן־כֹּל רָאֲתָה עֵינִי שָׁמְעָה אָזְנִי וַתָּבֶן לָהּ:

2 כְּדַעְתְּכֶם יָדַעְתִּי גַם־אָנִי לֹא־נֹפֵל אָנֹכִי מִכֶּם:

3 אוּלָם אֲנִי אֶל־שַׁדַּי אֲדַבֵּר וְהוֹכֵחַ אֶל־אֵל אֶחְפָּץ:

4 וְאוּלָם אַתֶּם טֹפְלֵי־שָׁקֶר רֹפְאֵי אֱלִל כֻּלְּכֶם:

5 מִי־יִתֵּן הַחֲרֵשׁ תַּחֲרִישׁוּן וּתְהִי לָכֶם לְחָכְמָה:

6 שִׁמְעוּ־נָא תוֹכַחְתִּי וְרִבוֹת שְׂפָתַי הַקְשִׁיבוּ:

7 הַלְאֵל תְּדַבְּרוּ עַוְלָה וְלוֹ תְּדַבְּרוּ רְמִיָּה:

8 הֲפָנָיו תִּשָּׂאוּן אִם־לָאֵל תְּרִיבוּן:

9 הֲטוֹב כִּי־יַחְקֹר אֶתְכֶם אִם־כְּהָתֵל בֶּאֱנוֹשׁ תְּהָתֵלּוּ בוֹ:

י הוֹכֵחַ יוֹכִיחַ אֶתְכֶם אִם־בַּסֵּתֶר פָּנִים תִּשָּׂאוּן:

11 הֲלֹא שְׂאֵתוֹ תְּבַעֵת אֶתְכֶם וּפַחְדּוֹ יִפֹּל עֲלֵיכֶם:

12 זִכְרֹנֵיכֶם מִשְׁלֵי־אֵפֶר לְגַבֵּי־חֹמֶר גַּבֵּיכֶם:

13 הַחֲרִישׁוּ מִמֶּנִּי וַאֲדַבְּרָה־אָנִי וְיַעֲבֹר עָלַי מָה:

14 עַל־מֶה ׀ אֶשָּׂא בְשָׂרִי בְשִׁנָּי וְנַפְשִׁי אָשִׂים בְּכַפִּי:

טו הֵן יִקְטְלֵנִי לֹא אֲיַחֵל אַךְ־דְּרָכַי אֶל־פָּנָיו אוֹכִיחַ:

16 גַּם־הוּא־לִי לִישׁוּעָה כִּי־לֹא לְפָנָיו חָנֵף יָבוֹא:

17 שִׁמְעוּ שָׁמוֹעַ מִלָּתִי וְאַחֲוָתִי בְּאָזְנֵיכֶם:

18 הִנֵּה־נָא עָרַכְתִּי מִשְׁפָּט יָדַעְתִּי כִּי־אֲנִי אֶצְדָּק:

19 מִי־הוּא יָרִיב עִמָּדִי כִּי־עַתָּה אַחֲרִישׁ וְאֶגְוָע:

כ אַךְ־שְׁתַּיִם אַל־תַּעַשׂ עִמָּדִי אָז מִפָּנֶיךָ לֹא אֶסָּתֵר:

21 כַּפְּךָ מֵעָלַי הַרְחַק וְאֵמָתְךָ אַל־תְּבַעֲתַנִּי:

22 וּקְרָא וְאָנֹכִי אֶעֱנֶה אוֹ־אֲדַבֵּר וַהֲשִׁיבֵנִי:

23 כַּמָּה לִי עֲוֹנוֹת וְחַטָּאוֹת פִּשְׁעִי וְחַטָּאתִי הֹדִיעֵנִי:

24 לָמָּה־פָנֶיךָ תַסְתִּיר וְתַחְשְׁבֵנִי לְאוֹיֵב לָךְ:

י"ב v. 25. אין כאן פסקא   י"ג v. 15. לו ק׳

25   Will You harass a driven leaf
          and pursue dry chaff,
26   that You charge my past actions against me
          and make me inherit the sins of my youth?
27   You put my feet in the stocks;
          You stand guard over all my paths,
          and put your brand on my feet.

28   Wasting away like a wine-skin,
          like a garment devoured by the moth —
14   Man, who is born of woman,
          is few in days and sated with turmoil.
2   Like a flower he comes forth, and withers;
          he flees like a shadow, and does not endure.
3   Is it upon such a one that You open Your eyes
          and summon to judgment with You?
4   Men say, "Who can distinguish the pure from the impure?
          No one!"
       But You, God, can and should!
5   For indeed, man's days are determined,
          the number of months is fixed by You;
          You have set the limits he cannot pass.
6   Turn away from him — let him alone —
          until he complete, like a hireling, his day.
7   For there is hope for a tree —
          if it be cut down, it can sprout again
          and its shoots will not fail.
8   If its roots grow old in the earth
          and its stump dies in the ground,
9   at the mere scent of water it will bud anew
          and put forth branches like a young plant.

10   But man grows faint and dies;
          and breathes his last, and where is he?
11   As water vanishes from a lake,
          and a river is parched and dries up,
12   So man lies down and rises not again;
          till the heavens are no more he will not awake,
          nor will he be roused from his sleep.

13   O, if You would hide me in Sheol,
          conceal me until Your wrath is spent;
          set a fixed time for me, and then remember me!
14   If a man die, can he live again?
          all the days of my service I would wait,
          till my hour of release should come.
15   You would call and I would answer You,
          for You would be longing for the work of Your hands.
16   For then You would number my steps;
          You would not keep watch over my sin.
17   You would seal up my transgression in a bag,
          and You would cover over my iniquity.

כה הָעָלֶה נִדָּף תַּעֲרוֹץ   וְאֶת־קַשׁ יָבֵשׁ תִּרְדֹּף׃

26 כִּי־תִכְתֹּב עָלַי מְרֹרוֹת   וְתוֹרִישֵׁנִי עֲוֺנוֹת נְעוּרָי׃

27 וְתָשֵׂם בַּסַּד ׀ רַגְלַי   וְתִשְׁמוֹר כָּל־אָרְחֹתָי

28 עַל־שָׁרְשֵׁי רַגְלַי תִּתְחַקֶּה׃   וְהוּא כְּרָקָב יִבְלֶה

כְּבֶגֶד אֲכָלוֹ עָשׁ׃

יד

א אָדָם יְלוּד אִשָּׁה   קְצַר יָמִים וּשְׂבַע־רֹגֶז׃

2 כְּצִיץ יָצָא וַיִּמָּל   וַיִּבְרַח כַּצֵּל וְלֹא יַעֲמוֹד׃

3 אַף־עַל־זֶה פָּקַחְתָּ עֵינֶךָ   וְאֹתִי תָבִיא בְמִשְׁפָּט עִמָּךְ׃

4 מִי־יִתֵּן טָהוֹר מִטָּמֵא   לֹא אֶחָד׃

ה אִם־חֲרוּצִים ׀ יָמָיו   מִסְפַּר־חֳדָשָׁיו אִתָּךְ

6 חֻקּוֹ עָשִׂיתָ וְלֹא יַעֲבֹר׃   שְׁעֵה מֵעָלָיו וְיֶחְדָּל

7 עַד־יִרְצֶה כְּשָׂכִיר יוֹמוֹ׃   כִּי יֵשׁ לָעֵץ תִּקְוָה

8 אִם־יִכָּרֵת וְעוֹד יַחֲלִיף   וְיֹנַקְתּוֹ לֹא תֶחְדָּל׃

9 אִם־יַזְקִין בָּאָרֶץ שָׁרְשׁוֹ   וּבֶעָפָר יָמוּת גִּזְעוֹ׃

י מֵרֵיחַ מַיִם יַפְרִחַ   וְעָשָׂה קָצִיר כְּמוֹ־נָטַע׃

11 וְגֶבֶר יָמוּת וַיֶּחֱלָשׁ   וַיִּגְוַע אָדָם וְאַיּוֹ׃

12 אָזְלוּ־מַיִם מִנִּי־יָם   וְנָהָר יֶחֱרַב וְיָבֵשׁ׃

13 וְאִישׁ שָׁכַב וְלֹא־יָקוּם   עַד־בִּלְתִּי שָׁמַיִם לֹא יָקִיצוּ

וְלֹא־יֵעֹרוּ מִשְּׁנָתָם׃   מִי יִתֵּן ׀ בִּשְׁאוֹל תַּצְפִּנֵנִי

תַּסְתִּירֵנִי עַד־שׁוּב אַפֶּךָ   תָּשִׁית לִי חֹק וְתִזְכְּרֵנִי׃

14 אִם־יָמוּת גֶּבֶר הֲיִחְיֶה   כָּל־יְמֵי צְבָאִי אֲיַחֵל

טו עַד־בּוֹא חֲלִיפָתִי׃   תִּקְרָא וְאָנֹכִי אֶעֱנֶךָּ

16 לְמַעֲשֵׂה יָדֶיךָ תִכְסֹף׃   כִּי־עַתָּה צְעָדַי תִּסְפּוֹר

17 לֹא תִשְׁמֹר עַל־חַטָּאתִי׃   חָתַם בִּצְרוֹר פִּשְׁעִי

י״ד v. 5. חקיו ק׳   י״ג v. 28. אין כאן פסקא

18 But as a mountain falls and crumbles
    and a rock is moved from its place,
19 as waters wear away stones
    and a torrent washes away the earth's soil,
    so You destroy man's hope.
20 You overpower him forever and he departs;
    You change his visage, and send him off.
21 His sons may grow great, but he will never know it,
    or they may be humbled, but he will be unaware of it.
22 Indeed, his flesh is pained within him
    and his spirit is in mourning.

18 וַתִּטְפֹּל עַל־עֲוֺנִי׃   וְאוּלָם הַר־נוֹפֵל יִבּוֹל

19 וְצוּר יֶעְתַּק מִמְּקֹמוֹ׃   אֲבָנִים ׀ שָׁחֲקוּ מַיִם

תִּשְׁטֹף־סְפִיחֶיהָ עֲפַר־אָרֶץ   וְתִקְוַת אֱנוֹשׁ הֶאֱבַדְתָּ׃

כ תִּתְקְפֵהוּ לָנֶצַח וַיַּהֲלֹךְ   מְשַׁנֶּה פָנָיו וַתְּשַׁלְּחֵהוּ׃

21 יִכְבְּדוּ בָנָיו וְלֹא יֵדָע   וְיִצְעֲרוּ וְלֹא־יָבִין לָמוֹ׃

22 אַךְ־בְּשָׂרוֹ עָלָיו יִכְאָב   וְנַפְשׁוֹ עָלָיו תֶּאֱבָל׃

CHAPTER 12

On the structure and content of Job's Third Response, see Special Note 13.

12:2 The assonance of the *m* sound in the verse suggests the bitter ironic murmur of Job's rejoinder. The changes of עָם to הַיֹּדְעִים (Klos., D-G), עֲרוּמִים (Be.), or נָבוֹן (Bi.) are all unnecessary. עָם is obviously idiomatic, in the sense of "the people who count." P. appositely cites "the gentry" in English.

12:3 לֵבָב "heart, seat of understanding." Stich c literally "with whom are ideas such as these not to be found?"

12:4 This verse and the two following are deleted as irrelevant, only because they have not been properly understood. It is generally rendered (Bu., Dil., D-G, and so essentially P.):

> "I am as one who is a laughing-stock to his neighbor,
>   I who called upon God and was answered;
>   The just, the perfect man is a laughing-stock."

The various emendations proposed (as, e.g., לְרֵעִי, Ehr.) are unnecessary.

לְרֵעֵהוּ is "His friend, i.e., God's friend." Stichs b and c, which are parallel, are ironic epithets applied to the Friends, each of whom is confident of his own rectitude and intimate relationship to God. שְׂחֹק, "laughing-stock" (Jer. 20:7; Hab. 1:10; Lam. 3:14), is in the construct in both cases. The bitter irony of the verse, which climaxes the tone of v. 2, is clear from this rendering:

> "A mockery to God's friend am I
>   Who (unlike me invariably) calls upon God and is answered,
>   A mockery of the perfect saint."

12:5 The interpretation of לַפִּיד as "torch" is today merely a curiosum.

פִּיד "calamity" is limited to Job (30:24; 31:29) and Pr. (24:12). Stich a = "For the one suffering calamity, there is only contempt." לְעַשְׁתּוּת שַׁאֲנָן "according to the opinion of the secure," from עשת, Aram., "think," the root occurring in biblical Hebrew elsewhere only in Jonah 1:5 and Ps. 148:4.

נָכוֹן either (a) "this is proper" or (b) in view of the parallelism, a noun from נכה "strike," hence "a beating" (Ew., Bu., Du.) — cf. רָצוֹן, חָזוֹן, from *tertiae Yod* verbs. Though the verb נכה is generally used in the Hiphil and Hophal and rarely in the Piel (Nu. 22:6) and Pual (Ex. 9:31, 32), note the adjective נָכֶה (Isa. 66:2; II Sam. 4:4; 9:3) which is derived from the Qal.

מוֹעֲדֵי רָגֶל lit. "stumbling of foot" (Ps. 26:1; 37:31).

12:6 אֹהָלִים לְשֹׁדְדִים and אֶל לְמַרְגִּיזֵי וּבַטָּחוֹת are late forms of the construct, with Lamed. Cf. the Comm. on 11:6 and see Ps. 123:4; 122:5.

It is not necessary to supply a noun meaning "dwelling places" before בַּטָּחוֹת. On בטח, "lie down, recline," cf. the Comm. on 11:17 and such nouns as מַרְבֵּץ, מִשְׁכָּן. Hence, בַּטָּחוֹת means "reclining or dwelling-place."

Stich c is a famous crux which has been explained as: (a) the idolator, "who makes his God with his hand" (Ra.); (b) the idolator "who brings his God in his hand"; (c) "who holds God in his power" (D-G); (d) "who sees his God in his strength"; (e) "who makes might his God" (Buttenwieser, Moffat), "God's terror-spreaders, whom God brings up for him" (TS). The stich has been emended to לַאֲשֶׁר הֵנִיף בֵּאלוֹהַּ יָדוֹ (Sieg.), לַאֲשֶׁר הֵבִיא בֵּאלוֹהַּ יָדוֹ, "who raised his hand against God" (Be.), or לֵאמֹר הֲכִי אֱלוֹהַּ בְּיָדִי, "who says, 'Is not God in my hand?'" (Du.), כַּאֲשֶׁר הֵבִיא אֱלוֹהַּ בְּיָדָם "as when God gives everything into their hand" (Ehr.).

The totally unconvincing character of these interpretations and emendations has, predictably enough, served to suggest deleting the clause, or the verse, or the entire section, as a gloss, leaving unexplained how and why these inexplicable words were interpolated into the text.

Probably the best interpretation is "who has God in his power" (D-G, P.). However, our stich cannot be equated with the common biblical phrase: יֵשׁ לְאֵל יָדִי lit., "it is within the power of my hand" (Gen. 31:29; Deut. 28:32; Mic. 2:1; B. S. 14:11). Not only is the verb הֵבִיא superfluous and inappropriate in this sense, but the prepositions and the suffixes are totally different.

Our phrase is obviously idiomatic. We suggest that it has its exact analogue in Elizabethan English, where we find a well-attested idiom "to bear someone in hand," in the meaning of "to deceive, delude." We may cite the following examples from Shakespeare:

> "To bear a gentleman in hand
> and then stand upon security."
> (*King Henry IV*, Part Two, I, 2, 1.34)
> "How you were borne in hand
> how crossed . . ."
> (*Macbeth*, III, i, 1.181)
> "That so his sickness, age and impotence
> was falsely borne in hand."
> (*Hamlet*, II, i, 11.66 f.)

Not only is the English idiom identical with the Hebrew phrase in question, but its meaning, "to deceive," is highly appropriate to the context.

12:7 The singular suffixes demonstrate that vv. 7 and 8 are Job's ironic restatement of the Friends' injunction addressed to him and not vice versa. Job is not saying that these ideas are familiar even to the beasts and the birds and are therefore *a fortiori* very well known to him (D-G). He is implying that praising God as the Creator, however justified in itself, is an attempt to deflect the discussion from its true theme — the problem of man's suffering and God's justice. Cf. the similar contention in 9:19.

12:8 שִׂיחַ is the imperative "speak, converse with." לָאָרֶץ is an elliptical phrase for metrical reasons for לְרֶמֶשׂ הָאָרֶץ, "the creeping things on earth" who are mentioned along with the beasts, the birds, and the fish. TS interprets ארץ on the basis of the Arabic ʾaraḍ as "little insect, ant."

12:9 בְּכָל־אֵלֶּה "with regard to all these."
יַד־ה' עָשְׂתָה זֹּאת. This solitary use of JHVH in the body of the Dialogue (אֲדֹנָי occurs in 28:28) is the unconscious usage of a Hebrew poet who includes a reminiscence of a phrase from Deutero-Isaiah (41:20; cf. also 66:2). This use incidentally supports the view that Job is later than the Exilic prophet, who plays a decisive role in his thinking, on which cf. *BGM*, chap. 11, esp. pp. 144 ff.; chap. 15, esp. pp. 216 f.

12:10 וְרוּחַ כָּל־בְּשַׂר־אִישׁ apparently "the spirit of all human flesh," unless MT contains a conflate of two readings: (a) רוּחַ כָּל בָּשָׂר; (b) רוּחַ כָּל אִישׁ.

12:11 Job's distaste for the Friends' irrelevant argument is expressed by his citing a conventional proverb here. In 6:6 he made the same point by a rhetorical question. לוֹ is the ethical dative; cf. 5:27; 13:1.

12:12 For this verse none of the commonly suggested procedures commend themselves, neither its deletion nor its rendering as an interrogative nor the radical insertion of the negative *lō*. Actually, MT is authentic and textually accurate. Vv. 12 and 13 are an instance of contrasting quotations (as only Hi., Bu. have recognized), the second constituting the refutation of the first. For this usage, particularly widespread in Wisdom literature, cf. Ecc. 4:5, 6, and *KMW ad loc.*, and Pr. 26:3, 4, where there is no polemic intent, and see *PPS*, pp. 138 ff. for instances in extra-biblical and Oriental literature as well. Job cannot directly deny the universal view of the ancients that Wisdom was with the aged. Note the youthful Elihu's elaborate apology for intervening among his elders in 32:7-9. Job can therefore rebut the argument of the Friends concerning the wisdom of the aged only obliquely, by saying that God is superior to the aged by possessing additional qualities, not merely wisdom but also strength, not only understanding but counsel as well. It cannot be determined, nor is it important, whether the poet as a Wisdom writer is citing previously extant *mesālīm* or is composing them himself. The same question remains open in Ecclesiastes (cf. *KMW*, passim).

12:13 There is no need to emend עֵצָה to עָצְמָה. The verse clearly recalls Isa. 11:2, רוּחַ חָכְמָה וּבִינָה רוּחַ עֵצָה וּגְבוּרָה. Here the theme of Wisdom is expressed by the same three terms as in our passage (except that בִּינָה is replaced by תְּבוּנָה), and the idea of "strength" by one term.

12:14 יַהֲרוֹס may refer either to cities (Peake) or figuratively to persons (Jer. 1:10) (so D-G). Both LXX and P replace the negative by the interrogative מִי, which would apparently indicate a variant Hebrew text in their *Vorlage*, not superior to MT.

12:15 The negative character of Job's praise is clear, when this verse describing the disaster wrought both by drought and by flood is contrasted with Eliphaz's glorification of the rain (5:9 ff.).

12:16 תּוּשִׁיָה "effective counsel, sound wisdom" will at times emphasize the element of wisdom and at others its efficacious character; cf. the Comm. on 5:12. Here the former theme seems somewhat more prominent, so that עֹז וְתוּשִׁיָה is equivalent to חָכְמָה וּגְבוּרָה in v. 12.

שֹׁגֵג וּמַשְׁגֶּה is a *merismus*, lit. "the one in error and the one causing error," equivalent to "all human beings"; cf. "small and great" in 3:19. The bitter spirit actuating Job is obvious in the particular principle of division he has adopted here. The nature of men is determined by God, who makes them all either dupes or cheats. Job is rebutting Eliphaz's view in 5:6, 7.

שֹׁגֵג is a metaplastic form of שׁגה. For the use of two conjugations of the same root in *merismus*, cf. the Arabic ʾassaʾmiʿu wamusaʾmiʿu = "the one who hears and the one who causes to hear." aʾššaʾhidu wamušaʾhidu = "he who testifies and he who causes to testify" (Gesenius, *Thesaurus*, 136, 2a). Other instances of *merismus* are עָצוּר וְעָזוּב, "the imprisoned and the free," which is a characteristic Hebrew usage (Deut. 32:37; I Ki. 14:10; 21:37; II Ki. 9:8; 14:36), and עֵר וְעֹנֶה (Mal. 2:12), etc.

12:17 שׁוֹלָל "stripped," whence שָׁלָל "booty." The concrete use means "stripped of clothes, naked" (as, e.g., Mic. 1:8 ‖ עָרוֹם), and the derived meaning, "stripped of sense, mad" (Ps. 76:6). Either meaning is appropriate here as a parallel to יְהוֹלֵל, "drive mad" (Ecc. 2:2 and passim).

12:18 מוּסַר, as has been generally recognized, is to be vocalized (with T, V) as מוֹסֵר "bonds" (cf. Ps. 2:3; Job 39:5), and stich a has been rendered "the bonds imposed by kings" (Ibn Janah, D-G). However, the parallelism suggests that it is the garb of the kings themselves which is described. מוֹסֵר is better understood here as "the belt, the symbol of authority," parallel to אֵזוֹר, which never means "loin cloth," but always "girdle" (II Ki. 1:8; Isa. 5:27; 11:5; Jer. 13:1). There is no need to emend אֵזוֹר to אָסוּר. וַיֶּאְסֹר is an erroneous *plene* spelling for וַיַּסָּר Cf. יָאֵהִיל = יָהֵל (Job 25:5; cf. Comm.). The opposite process, the omission of an Aleph, occurs in Ex. 14:25, which is to be read וַיֶּאְסֹר אֵת אֹפַן מַרְכְּבֹתָיו instead of וַיַּסַר (so LXX, S), and is to be rendered, "He bound up (i.e. slowed) the wheels of his chariots." אֵזוֹר בְּמָתְנֵיהֶם "the girdle which is upon their loins," the relative אֲשֶׁר being understood. Hence there is no need to read מִמָּתְנֵיהֶם.

The verse describes the breakdown of royal power, which is pictured as a sign of the destructive power of God. See Special Notes 9 and 11.

12:19 אֵיתָנִים basically means "constant, unfailing"; cf. Arabic *watana*. It is an elative form, the opposite of אַכְזָב "unreliable, undependable," often applied to a stream (Am. 5:24; Ps. 74:15; cf. also Ex. 14:27). The meaning "permanent, enduring" is then applied to a nation (Jer. 5:15), an abode (Nu. 24:21; Jer. 49:14 = 50:44), a bow (Gen. 49:14), pain (Job 33:19), and mountains (Mic. 6:2, where Wel. reads הַאֲזִינוּ). In our passage, too, the noun is generally rendered "firmly rooted, established men."

However, the parallelism with "priests" in our verse suggests a technical meaning. The term here may mean "one given over to Temple services, votary," from the root יתן (Phoenician "give") with prosthetic Aleph, as, e. g., אַכְזָר, אֶשְׁנָב, אֶזְרוֹעַ (cf. Ges.-K., sec. 19, 4). It is similar to the late Hebrew term נְתִינִים used only in Ezra, Nehemiah, and Chronicles (I Chr. 9:2; Ezra 2:43, 58, 70; Neh. 7:46, 60, 73; cf. also Nu. 3:9, 8; 16:9). In these passages the Levites are described as "given to the service of God." In our context, this class would seem to occupy a higher social level than the *Nethinim*, who are distinguished from the Priests and the Levites in I Chr. 9:2. יְסַלֵּף = "confuse, in the performance of their precise ritual tasks."

12:20 It is tempting to regard נֶאֱמָנִים as a *nomen agentis* from נָאַם "speak" (cf. Jer. 23:31) with suffix Nun (cf. רַחֲמָן, סָלְחָן in rabbinic Hebrew). However, in view of the rarity and the specific oracular meaning of the verb, it is preferable to render "counselor" derived from "trusted one." שָׂפָה לְנֶאֱמָנִים is a late form of the construct; cf. the Comm. on 12:6.

12:21 מְזִיחַ like מֵזַח (Ps. 109:19), "girdle," is an Egyptian loan-word *mdḥ*. "Loosening the girdle" (v. 18 above) means weakening the power and authority of its wearer.

אֲפִיקִים need not be emended to אַמִּיצִים (Bu.), אַבִּירִים (Du.), or תַּקִּיפִים (Be.). For the meaning "strong, mighty" cf. Akk. *epequ*, "be strong," whence probably the Hebrew verb הִתְאַפֵּק "control oneself, be master over oneself" (Gen. 43:31; 45:1, etc.) This root would seem to be unrelated to אָפִיק, "channel," as P. has pointed out. When the upper-class orientation of wisdom is kept in mind, the verse is entirely appropriate to the context.

12:22 Those who delete this verse refer to God's control of darkness and see in it a reference to some cosmic myth. This leaves unexplained why it was interpolated here. In the context the verse would refer not to "the conspiracies of men in general," but rather to the plans of the wise counselors which God puts to naught. (Cf. Isa. 29:15 for the theme.)

12:23 God exalts nations at first, only to destroy them in the end. מַשְׂגִּיא, "make great"; cf. the Qal in Job 8:11. The parallelism suggests that וַיְנַחֵם, must carry a negative meaning. It has been interpreted as "lead them away," but נָחָה always means "guide, lead" in a favorable sense. Hence, the verb is to be revocalized, with most moderns, as וַיַּנִּחֵם, an instance of Hiphil B of נוח; cf. BDB, s.v., p. 628b, 629b. The identical error in vocalization occurs in I Sam. 22:4 (reading with the Versions and most moderns, וַיַּנְחֵם "he left them behind." In our passage the special nuance is "leave, abandon, forsake." Cf. Jer. 14:9 אַל־תַּנִּחֵנוּ; Ps. 119:121 בַּל־תַּנִּיחֵנִי. Cf. also Gen. 42:33; Ezek. 16:39; Ecc. 10:4.

The use of גּוֹיִם in both stichs is another instance of a stylistic trait characteristic of the poet, whose mastery of the Hebrew vocabulary needs no demonstration. See Special Note 4.

12:24 LXX omits עַם. It is possible that MT is a conflate of two readings: (a) רָאשֵׁי הָאָרֶץ; and (b) רָאשֵׁי עַם. Cf. the Comm. on 12:10 above. On conflates as an early Masoretic device for preserving variants, cf. the Prolegomenon to *BTM*, pp. 40 ff.

12:25 Note the use of the same verb in vv. 24b, 25b. The change to וַיִּתְעוּ (D-G) is not necessary.

CHAPTER 13

13:1 Vv. 1–2 serve as the conclusion to the section introduced by 12:2, 3. אלה was understood, not read by LXX, S, V. Rhythmic considerations militate against introducing the vocable here, vv. 1–4 being in 4:4 meter.

13:3 The assonance of Aleph is striking but not mechanically maintained; cf. 5:8. הוֹכֵחַ here = "argue"; in 13:15 and 19:15 it is used declaratively, "declare right, justify," the meaning which is required also in 13:10. See the Comm. *ad loc.*

13:4 טֹפְלֵי־שֶׁקֶר "plasterers of lies," an idiom occurring in Ps. 119:69; cf. the Hebrew noun with Tav תָּפֵל "plaster, whitewash" (Ezek. 13:10, 11, 15; 22:28; Aram. טפילא "mortar." TS renders: "putting on red paint" (to make one look healthy), on the basis of Aram. סיקרא "red paint," and Isa. 3:16. which he interprets similarly. רֹפְאֵי אֱלִיל "lit. physicians of worthlessness, of no value." Cf. רֹעִי הָאֱלִיל "worthless shepherd," Zech. 11:17 and Jer. 14:14. The assumed relationship of the noun with the negative particle אַל is probably a folk etymology.

13:5 The plea to the Friends is a restatement of a common proverb; cf. Pr. 17:28.

13:6 רִבוֹת "pleadings, accusations," like תּוֹכַחְתִּי "argument," is a forensic term; cf. Isa. 3:13; Hos. 2:4.

13:7 The word order is emphatic: "Is it for God that you speak falsehood?"

Introductory Note: The Literary Form of 13:7–11

This section exhibits some well-defined literary characteristics. It should be noted that the whole passage consists of questions hurled at the Friends. V. 10 constitutes only an apparent exception — see the Comm.

The poet used a varied meter: vv. 6, 7 are in 3:3; v. 8 in 2:2; v. 9 in 4:4 (giving two beats to כִּי יַחְקֹר). Hence no words need to be added to v. 13; see the Comm.

13:8 The idiom in stich a means "show partiality, particularly in judgment"; cf. Deut. 10:17; Pr. 18:5; 33:21, etc. There is no need to emend stich a to read הֲפְנֵי שַׁדַּי תִּשָּׂאוּן and to add שֶׁקֶר to stich b for rhythmic reasons.

13:9 הֲטוֹב = "will it be well with you?" הָתֵל "mock, deceive." Here the Hiphil of תלל as in Gen. 31:7; Ex. 1:25 (cf. Arabic *talla*, "act coquettishly"), with retained He, the original form of the Hiphil. The verb need not be assimilated (and emended) to the secondary root הָתֵל (I Ki. 18:27; Job 17:2; Isa. 30:10). Secondary root formations are particularly common in mishnaic Hebrew, as, e.g., תרם, "bring the heave offering," from the noun תרומה. The pausal form תְּהָתֵלּוּ (with Şere) is exceptional.

13:10 The verse is generally rendered declaratively: "He will surely reprove you." The entire passage, however, gains in meaning and force if instead it is construed interrogatively, with the interrogative He either understood or supplied as an instance of haplography: הַהוֹכֵחַ = "Will He declare you right?" For this declarative use of הוכיח, cf. 13:15; 19:5; and, with a slightly different nuance, Gen. 24:14, 44, "declare right, appropriate."

In stich b, בַּסֵּתֶר in its usual meaning of "in secret" is meaningless, since there has been nothing clandestine about the Friends' defense of God to which Job objects. TS recognizes the difficulty and therefore interprets בַּסֵּתֶר = "as a mask," rendering the stich, "or would you put a veil on your face?", which he interprets to mean "can you hide from Him behind a veil?" We regard בַּסֵּתֶר as an aberrant orthography for סֵטֶר (Aram. סְטַר), "side." For the interchange of Tav and Tet, cf. תפל, טפל; Heb.-Aram. קְטַל; Arabic *katala*, טִלְטֵל, Arab. *taltala*. It has not been noticed that the spelling with Tav occurs in I Sam. 25:20, בְּסֵתֶר הָהָר, which is synonymous with בְּצֵלַע הָהָר (II Sam. 16:13) and מִצַּד הָהָר (I Sam. 23:26, Tar. מסטר טורא). While סֵתֶר "side" is used literally in the passage in Samuel, it is used figuratively in our passage to refer to "one side in a controversy." Cf. the medieval Jewish term סטרא אחרא "the other side," as an epithet for Satan. Hence, render our verse: "Will He justify you if you show favor to one side?"

Job is once again appealing to the God of justice, who, he fervently believes, will vindicate him against the God of violence who has been persecuting him. Cf. the basic passages in which he expresses his faith: 7:23 ff.; 16:19; 19:24 ff.

13:11 שְׂאֵת is usually rendered "majesty, excellence" (Gen. 49:3; Ps. 62:5). It is, however, better interpreted as "terror," parallel to פַּחַד; cf. Job 31:23; 41:17. If it is related to שׁוֹאָה (Ps. 35:8; Pr. 3:25), as P. suggests, it may require revocalization, in all three passages, to שְׂאֵתוֹ here and in 41:17 and to מִשּׂוֹאָתוֹ in Job 31:23; cf. the Comm. *ad loc.*

13:12 זִכְרֹנֵיכֶם, not "memories" or "maxims," but "arguments from history" (cf. Est. 6:1). This recourse to the past has been a basic element in the position of the Friends, who invoke the testimony of the ancients (8:8 ff.) and their own superior age (15:10). Since there is no logical progression of thought in the speeches of the Friends, Job may at any point take into account ideas expressed later in the Dialogue.

מִשְׁלֵי־אֵפֶר are "maxims of clay" lacking substance or sustaining power.

גַּבֵּיכֶם has been rendered (a) "defenses, ramparts," for which 15:26 is compared, where, however, it refers to the back of a shield; or, better, (b) on the basis of the mishnaic Hebrew and Aramaic root, גבב "pile up, collect," as "heaps of words." Cf. *M. Shev.* 9:6 המגבב ביבש; *Tos. Zeb.* 1:1; *B. Yoma* 76a עד מתי אתה מגבב דברים ומביא עלינו, "How long will you heap up words against us?" While this interpretation is satisfactory, we prefer to relate the noun (so Dh.) to the Aram. גוב, Syriac *gawab*, "respond," whence the modern Hebrew verb הֵגִיב "react." Hence our word = "your rejoinders, responses." Geminate and *mediae Vav* roots are closely related.

The Lamed is the emphatic Lamed common in Arabic and occurring in Hebrew as well; cf. Ecc. 9:4: כִּי לְכֶלֶב חַי (cf. *KMW ad loc.*; Ps. 89:19 כִּי לה׳ מָגִנֵּנוּ; Isa. 32:1 וּלְשָׂרִים; Isa. 60:19 וּלְנֹגַהּ (so Yel).

13:13 Because of the difficulties of the next verse, many moderns add עַל־מֶה from it to our verse, reading וְיַעֲבֹר עָלַי מָה עַל־מָה, and rendering "let there pass over me anything whatsoever," on the basis of the Arab. *mahma* (Bi., Du., Kl., Hö.). The change is required neither here nor, as indicated below, in v. 14. For stich b, "let there come what may," cf. II Sam. 18:22 וִיהִי מָה; I Sam. 19:3.

13:14 The verse contains two obvious idioms, of which only the second occurs elsewhere (Jud. 12:3; I Sam. 19:5; 28:21; Ps. 119:109), where it invariably means "Why should I endanger my life?" One would therefore most naturally assign the same sense to stich a, but this is felt to be highly inappropriate for Job: "Why should I put my life in peril?" Several alternate procedures have therefore been suggested: (a) the idiom is taken to mean "Why should I try to save my life (by submitting to God)?" (Ew., Dil., Del.). This rendering Herz (*OLZ*, 1913, p. 343; *JThS*, vol. 15, p. 263) tried to support by suggesting an alleged Egyptian parallel for the idiom meaning "to take extra care of one's life." However, the biblical usage for the idiom in stich b is clearly opposed to this rendering; (b) עַל־מֶה is either attached to v. 13 or deleted as a dittography of עָלַי מָה (Me., Dil., Bu., D-G, Ehr., P.). However, in this truncated form the verse is virtually meaningless, since it simply asserts that Job is imperiling his life. We suggest that the verse is best taken as an instance of the relatively rare usage of indirect quotations in biblical and Oriental literature, on which see *BGM*, pp. 188 f., 355 f., and cf. Job 19:28; 35:2 f.; Hos. 7:2a; 12:5c, d; Ps. 32:6 f.; 69:5; and the *Hammurabi Code*, sec. 96 (*ANET*, pp. 169–70; Qoran, Sura 16, vv. 58–59). So interpreted, the passage (vv. 14, 15) receives a relevant and unforced meaning: "You ask, Why do I endanger my life (by speaking)?, and I answer, Though He slay me, I must justify my ways to His face."

13:15 This verse has become famous as an affirmation of unshakable faith in the face of adversity: "Yea, though He slay me, yet will I trust in Him" (AV). Most moderns have correctly recognized the inappropriateness of this rendering in our context, and prefer the Kethib לא to the Qere לו, on which this traditional interpretation has been based. Hence they render: "Indeed, He may slay me, I have no hope." Ehr. emends לֹא אֲיַחֵל to לֹא אָחִיל "I shall not tremble," but the adversative conjunction אַךְ indicates that a contrast with the preceding is required.

We have suggested that the root יחל "hope, wait" develops the special nuance of "be silent." Cf. the Comm. on 6:11 and esp. on 32:11, 16 for the semantic process involved. This meaning suits our context admirably:

> Indeed, though He kill me, I shall not be silent,
> But shall justify my ways to His face.

The Qere is not "an ingenious emendation of the Masoretes." It cannot be too strongly stressed that modifying the text was definitely not a Masoretic purpose or activity (*BTM*, passim). Far more heterodox passages in our book and elsewhere were left unmodified by the Masoretes, whose self-imposed task was the *preservation of the received text*. The Kethib-Qere are both variations in the text preserved by the Masoretes. In our case both variations are attested in an interesting passage in the Mishnah, *Sotah* 5:5: בו ביום דרש ר׳ יהושע בן הורקנוס לא עבד איוב את הקב״ה אלא מאהבה שנא׳ הן יקטלני לו איחל ועדיין הדבר שקול לו אני מצפה או איני מצפה ת״ל עד אגוע לא אסיר תומתי ממני מלמד שמאהבה עשה א״ר יהושע מי יגלה עפר מעיניך רבן יוחנן בן זכאי שהיית דורש כל ימיך שלא עבד איוב את המקום אלא מיראה שנאמר איש תם וישר ירא אלהים וסר מרע הלוא יהושע תלמיד תלמידך למד שמאהבה עשה, "On that day R. Joshua b. Hyrcanus expounded: Job served God from love, for it is written, Though He slay me, yet will I trust in Him (Job 13:15). Still the matter is undecided — do I trust in Him (לו) or I do not trust (לא). Another verse teaches that he served from love (Job 27:5), Until I depart I shall not allow my integrity to be taken from me. Said R. Joshua, "Who will remove the dust from your eyes, O Rabban Johanan b. Zakkai, for all your days you expounded that Job served the Lord only from fear, as it is said, Perfect and upright, fearing God and eschewing evil (Job 1:1). But now Joshua (b. Hyrcanus), your pupil's pupil, teaches that he served from love" (cf. *BTM*, p. 51, Note 27).

אוֹכִיחַ a declarative use of the Hiphil, "to declare right, justify." (Cf. the Comm. on 13:10.)

13:16 גַּם is emphatic, "surely, indeed." (Cf. Ex. 4:9; Nu. 22:33; Hos. 9:12; Job 2:10; and cf. BDB, s.v. #2, p. 169–a.) Together with the pronoun הוא

the phrase emphasizes that God will be Job's salvation, because he is no servile flatterer coming before Him. In this statement there is both irony and insight. Job feels that his probity deserves at least some reward, even if it be only a speedy and merciful death (cf. the passage 6:7–10 and see the Comm. *ad locum*). There is also the basic theme that Job's honesty is itself the deepest faith in God; that his onslaught on the God of violence is an act of loyalty to the God of righteousness. In addition to the significant passage 42:7, 8 (see the Comm.), we may cite a striking talmudic statement highly apposite in this connection. יודעין הן הנביאים שאלוהיהן אמיתי ואין מחניפין לו (*J. Ber.* 7:3), "The Prophets know that their God is a God of truth who cannot be flattered."

13:17 אַחֲוָה "declaration," an Aramaism from the root חוה (15:17; 32:6; 36:2).

13:18 ערך משפט "set forth, present a case"; cf. 23:4. If the verse is taken declaratively, "Behold I have set forth my case; I know I shall be vindicated," it would contradict Job's persistent cry that he cannot get a fair hearing (cf. 9:2 f., 19 f., 33 ff., etc.). It is better to interpret the v. as a conditional sentence: "If I could present my case, I know·I would be vindicated." For a condition contrary to fact with a perfect tense in the protasis and apodosis, cf. Jud. 8:19; 13:23; Jer. 20:9; Pr. 24:10; 26:15; 27:12; and cf. Dr., *HT*, sec. 154.

13:19 The difficulties of the verse disappear if we recognize that stich b is the apodosis of a conditional sentence and that stich a, the protasis, is a virtual quotation. Hence, the verse is to be rendered: "But if God says, 'Who is this who dares to contend with Me?' (i.e., if God refuses to let me present my case), then I can only die in silence (lit. be silent and die)."

13:20 The two "things" that Job wishes to be spared are referred to in the two stichs of v. 21, the removal of "the hand" and of "the terror," though they are logically one. Similarly, in Isa. 49:15, the plural אֵלֶּה refers to the two preceding stichs, both of which refer to the single instance of a mother and her young (אשה and מרחם = womb, woman). Cf. Gordis, in the *Ginzberg Jubilee Volume* (New York, 1945) (English Section), pp. 184–87.

13:21 כַּפְּךָ equals "your hand, might," used not positively as in Ex. 33:22, but negatively as in Ex. 9:3; Jer. 15:17; Ruth 1:13. The verse is cited by Elihu, who uses the Aram. form אַכְפִּי = "pressure, power." See the Comm. on 33:7.

13:22 It is a matter of indifference to Job whether he or his Divine adversary initiates the legal procedures, so long as God is willing to come to court. הֲשִׁיבֵנִי may be an ellipsis for הֲשִׁיבֵנִי דָבָר (D-G), but in mishnaic Hebrew השיב (like the Aram. התיב) is used as "refute, respond," without the noun, as in our book (20:2; 33:5, 32).

13:23 Job does not pretend to be free from all guilt (see the Comm. on 9:20); he contends only that his weaknesses do not justify his agonized suffering. The poet once again does not hesitate to use the same root in parallel stichs.

13:25 ערץ is used both intransitively, "fear" (Jos. 1:9), or transitively, "frighten," as in Isa. 2:19, 21, and our passage. The use of אֶת with an indeterminate noun is rare (Ges.-K., sec. 117, 1, 8; 2), but examples may be found (Ex. 21:28; I Sam. 26:20). Hence there is no need to emend it to וְאִם (ag. Be., Bu., D-G).

13:26 כתב על "charge with," like the mishnaic זקף על, is a commercial term (Ehr.). מְרֹרוֹת in the meaning of "bitter things" (D-G, P.) is manifestly inappropriate. TS suggests מרתא, an Aram. form meaning "inheritance." The suggestion of Ehr. to derive the noun from the Arab. *marra*, "pass by," hence, "past action," is far superior. We have suggested that the same Semitic root may be the origin of מְרִירִי, "flying, passing demon"; see the Comm. on 3:5.

13:27 סָד "stock, pillory made of wood" occurs in the Syriac סדאה and Aram. (*B. Pes.* 28a). Stich c is extremely difficult. שָׁרְשֵׁי רַגְלַי, literally, "the roots of my feet," is generally interpreted to mean "footprints," and תִּתְחַקֶּה as "mark out for yourself," from חקה, a metaplastic form for חקק, "inscribe," hence "set limits," but the Hithpael remains inexplicable. A more natural rendering of the verb would be "You mark yourself, i.e., you place your brand on my feet, hence, you make me your slave," which would be an excellent parallel to stich a. See the Translation.

13:28 כְּרָקָב = "like a wineskin" (so LXX, P); cf. Aram. רוקבא (T for חֵמֶת, Gen. 21:14, 15, 19). The third person pronoun וְהוּא is changed to וַאֲנִי (LXX, Ehr., JPSV, etc.), but it is hard to understand how a simple, clear text would have been changed to our present problematical one. The verse is accordingly deleted (Hö.) or moved after 14:2a or 2b, or 3. Two other procedures recommend themselves: (1) to regard the v. as the conclusion of the question raised in v. 25, with vv. 26, 27 as a rather long parenthesis; or, better, (2) to treat our verse as modifying or describing אָדָם in 14:1. The introduction of a new subject through the third person pronoun הוא has its analogue in רָטֹב הוּא (8:16), הֵן פְּרָאִים (24:5), and chap. 24, *passim*. Cf. the Comm. *ad loc.* and see *BGM*, chap. 14, for a discussion of the esthetic satisfaction an ancient reader derived from recognizing and identifying a theme not made explicit by the poet.

CHAPTER 14

14:1 On the possible relationship of 13:28 to our v., see the Comm. *ad loc.*
The clauses in 1a, 1b, and 2a can be construed either as coordinate or subordinate, with every conceivable combination among them: (1) "Man is

born . . . and is few of days; (2) Man, who is born . . ., is few in days; (3) Man, who is born . . . and is few in days . . ., comes forth."

רֹגֶז = "turmoil" (cf. 3:17, 26), of which man is both the cause and the victim.

14:2 יָצָא need not be emended to יָצִיץ or יִצְמָח, since it means "flourish, grow" (cf. I Ki. 5:13; Isa. 11:1; Ps. 104:14). וַיִּמָּל is either a Niphal from מול ‖ מלל "cut off" (Ps. 58:8; Ps. 116:10, 11), or, better, a Qal from מלל "languish, wither" (18:16; 24:24; Ps. 37:2; 90:6).

14:3 וְאֹתִי is read as וְאִתּוֹ by G, S, V, Me., Dil., Wr., D-G, etc. It is favored by the parallelism and perhaps is to be preferred. MT may, however, be maintained; Job frequently oscillates between his own tragic lot and that of all men (cf., e.g., 3:22 followed by vv. 23–26).

14:4 This linguistically easy verse is extremely difficult to interpret in context. It has been rendered (1) "Who can bring forth a pure being from a filthy drop? No one!" (Ra., Ibn E., Ehr.); (2) "Would that a clean thing could come from an unclean! Not one can" (D-G). On either view the verse is entirely irrelevant for Job's position and it is, therefore, excised as a gloss by most moderns (Be., Bi., Che., Bu., Hö.). However, its incomprehensibility on the surface militates against the idea that it is an interpolation.

The verse is both meaningful and relevant, if, in accordance with a well-established proclivity of the poet, the verse is understood as a restatement by Job, in the form of a virtual quotation, of the idea expressed by Eliphaz that all men are sinful and hence deserve some measure of punishment (4:17 ff.; 15:13 ff.). The passage is to be rendered simply: "Who can tell a pure man apart from an impure one? No one!" לֹא אֶחָד is the late biblical rendering for "no one"; cf. Ps. 139:16; Mal. 2:15. This popular view of man's universal sinfulness Eliphaz had originally presented as a direct revelation from on high (4:17 ff.). Since the argument that all men are morally imperfect is basically unanswerable, Job counters it in oblique fashion (v. 5) by taking the words literally and replying, "You, God, should have no difficulty in telling the pure man apart from the impure, since You created men and know their nature and limitations." For another instance of an oblique response by Job to an unanswerable argument of the Friends, cf. 21:22–26. For an example of a literalistic answer to a contention of the Friends, cf. 21:28–29 and see the Comm. *ad loc.*

Vv. 4 and 5 and their implications are, therefore, to be rendered:

Men say, "Who can tell the pure and the impure apart?"
No one!

I reply, *"You can, and should, distinguish between them!*
For indeed man's days are determined,
The number of his months is fixed by You.
You have set the limits he cannot pass."

14:5 Whether or not this verse is brought into relation with the preceding (see the Comm. above), it describes the brevity of human life as ordained by God. Dil., D-G take אִם as introducing the protasis of which v. 6 is the apodosis, but the meaning "if" is inappropriate and the particle does not mean "since." אִם is best interpreted as the emphatic "indeed."

The Kethib may be a singular ("his limit") or more probably a defective spelling of the plural suffix, "his limits"; see *BTM*, pp. 86–92.

14:6 On the basis of 7:16; 10:20, most moderns read וַחֲדָל "cease from him, and let him alone." MT וְיֶחְדָּל is rendered "that he may cease (to complain or to suffer)." However, I Sam. 2:5 וּרְעֵבִים חָדֵלּוּ "the hungry cease (being hungry)" does not offer a genuine parallel, and the slight emendation is to be preferred.

For יִרְצֶה, the rendering "enjoy," applied to a hireling's day, is scarcely appropriate, as P. has correctly noted. Actually the meaning of the root seems to be entirely distinct from "desire, favor." It occurs in the Qal in Lev. 26:34 אָז תִּרְצֶה הָאָרֶץ אֶת־שַׁבְּתֹתֶיהָ (cf. also Lev. 26:43; II Chr. 36:21) and in the Hiphil in Lev. 26:34 וְהִרְצָת, as well as in mishnaic Hebrew, *B. Shab.* 22a: אסור להרצות מעותיו כנגד נר חנוכה "One is forbidden to count one's money by the light of the Chanukah lamp." (See Rashi *ad locum* למנות). In all languages, counting and recounting are expressed by the same root; cf. Hebrew סָפַר, סִפֵּר; German *zählen, erzählen*; English *tell* (as in *bank teller*); French, *compter, raconter*. We suggest that both meanings inhere in the root רצה. Hence the root רצה = 1) "count, complete," which alone satisfies the passages in Leviticus and Chronicles that declare that the earth will count out the sabbatical years that the nation had failed to observe while living in the land; and 2) "set forth words, discourse, speak," common in mishnaic Hebrew (*A.Z.* 36b; *Hag.* 14b and often, and in the modern Hebrew noun הַרְצָאָה "discourse, lecture"). This latter meaning may occur in biblical Hebrew as well, e.g. יְרְצוּ ‖ יְבָרְכוּ בְּפִיו (Ps. 62:5); וְאַחֲרֵיהֶם בְּפִיהֶם יִרְצוּ (Ps. 49:14). This meaning for *rāṣāh* is also preferable in these passages: "When you see a thief, you converse with him" (Ps. 50:18); "He speaks like a father with his son" (Pr. 3:12). Hence render stich b "until he complete, like a hireling, his day."

14:7 יַחֲלִיף not "will be exchanged for another" (Ibn E.), but "will grow," the idea of "again" being understood from the context; cf. Isa. 9:9, where נַחֲלִיף is parallel to נִבְנֶה, and the theme of "again" is implicit. Cf. Ps. 90:6 יָצִיץ וְחָלָף contrasted with יְמוֹלֵל וְיָבֵשׁ and the Aramaic חלפתא, "a species of willow."

14:8 יַזְקִין an inchoative use of the Hiphil, "begin to grow old," like הַמְתִּיק "grow sweet" (Job 20:12); הַאֲמִיץ "become brave" (Ps. 27:14); הֶעֱשִׁיר "grow rich" (Ps. 49:17); יַפְרִחַ "begin to bud again" (in v. 9).

14:9 מֵרֵיחַ מַיִם a hyperbole, "from the mere scent, i.e. the proximity, of water" (so Ehr.). He compares such rabbinic usages as רֵיח הגט (*B. Git.* 86a) and רֵיח פסול "an approximation to unchastity," etc. See also בַּהֲרִיחוֹ "when it smells fire" (Jud. 16:9) and Comm. on 39:25. The revocalization יִפְרַח is unnecessary (see the Comm. on v. 18 above) and weakens the assonance. קָצִיר here = "branches" (Isa. 27:11; Ps. 80:11 f.; Job 18:16; 29:19).

14:10 וְגֶבֶר Vav adversative, "but man, etc." וַיֶּחֱלָש need not be emended to וַיַּחֲלֹף (Wr., Gr., Bu., D-G), or to וְיִשְׁלַח (TS) on the basis of the *ad hoc* rendering of LXX. Nor is Ex. 17:16, וַיַּחֲלֹש יְהוֹשֻׁעַ אֶת־עֲמָלֵק relevant here. The stich exhibits an instance of *hysteron proteron*: "but man dies and grows faint, i.e., man grows faint and dies." (Cf. נַעֲשֶׂה וְנִשְׁמַע, Ex. 24:7, "We shall do and we shall obey"; קִיְּמוּ וְקִבְּלוּ (Est. 9:27), and probably Isa. 64:4 אַתָּה קָצַפְתָּ וַנֶּחֱטָא. On this rhetorical figure, see Gordis, in *Sepher Seidel*, pp. 262 f.

The interrogative וְאַיּוֹ "and where is he?" is preferable to the proposed declarative וְאֵינֶנּוּ "and he is no more." It is possible that the Vss. read this latter form, but more probably they translated more prosaically *ad sensum*.

14:11 This verse and the following are united, as is common in proverbial literature, by the *Vav adaequationis*: "As the waters vanish . . ., so man dies" (Ra.). Our verse is a quotation from Isa. 19:5, differing only in the use of the early Aramaism אָזְלוּ instead of נִשְׁתּוּ. These minor variations in citations and in poetic refrains are a characteristic of biblical style. (Cf. Ps. 49:13, 21; Job 28:12, 20.)

Our passage illustrates admirably the creative use to which the author of Job puts his Hebrew literary heritage. Isaiah gives a description of the physical drying-up of the Nile River. Here the disappearance of water, the symbol of life, is used as a metaphor for the final extinction of man. Omitting the verse (Bi., Bu., Du.) impoverishes the pathos of the poet's description of man's irrevocable death.

14:12 וְאִישׁ "so man sleeps." The use of אִישׁ rather than אָדָם may carry the nuance of "man, the mighty being"; cf. Ps. 49:3 גַּם בְּנֵי־אָדָם גַּם בְּנֵי אִישׁ.

עַד בִּלְתִּי שָׁמַיִם is read by A, Sym., Th., as עַד בְּלוֹת שָׁמַיִם, "until the heavens rot away," in support of which Ps. 102:27; Isa. 51:6 are cited (Geiger). MT is, however, more powerful — "Until the heavens be no more," for which cf. Ps. 72:7, עַד בְּלִי יָרֵחַ, "until there be no moon"; cf. also מִכַּת בִּלְתִּי סָרָה (Isa. 14:6); עַד בְּלִי דָי (Mal. 3:10); so D-G. We find incomprehensible Hö's statement that the verse is a dogmatic orthodox insertion designed to assert that "only when the heavens crumble will the resurrection take place." In general, the assumption of widespread glosses by pious annotators has wrought havoc with our understanding of Koheleth and Job, which are robbed of much of their depth, power, and subtlety. Fortunately, this tendency is receding as a deeper insight into the Wisdom writers is growing.

14:13 Job wishes that it were possible for him to have a temporary sojourn in Sheol until God's anger is abated.

14:14 The idea of life after death penetrated Judaism during the Second Temple period. Unlike Koheleth, who dismisses this doctrine with a shrug of the shoulders (cf. Ecc. 3:17–22, especially v. 21; see *KMW ad loc.*), Job's warmer and more emotional nature passionately wishes he could accept this comforting idea, but sadly he finds that he cannot believe it. The relationship of the denial of life after death to the social background of Wisdom is analyzed in *PPS*, pp. 175–80. For the pathetic interrogative הֲיִחְיֶה, "Will he live again?" LXX reads *zesetai*, "He will live!" and thus effectively disposes of the theological heresy.

On צָבָא, "time of service," and חֲלִיפָה, "change of the guard," cf. the Comm. on 10:17. Hence the term means "release for the soldier who has completed his tour of duty."

14:15 Job permits his fancy to indulge itself in the pleasant prospect of his being recalled to life by a God who would love His creatures and yearn for them. On תִּכְסֹף "lit., grow pale with longing," cf. Gen. 31:30; Ps. 17:12; 84:3.

Introductory Note on 14:16–17

The two verses 14:16–17 may be understood in two diametrically opposite senses: (A) as a description of God's actual hostility to Job in the present (*ki ʿattāh*), "but now"; cf. 7:21 (so Ew., Dil., Del., Du.); or (B) as a continuation of Job's imagined future bliss at the hands of a loving God, if a renewal of life were possible (Umbreit, Hi., Me., Bu.) with *ki ʿattāh* = "for then" — cf. 3:13.

If A is adopted, the negative in לֹא תִשְׁמֹר appears inappropriate and the verb is accordingly emended to לֹא תַעֲבֹר, "You do not overlook my sin." The emendation is unnecessary, if *lōʾ* be recognized as the negative emphatic derived from the original interrogative הֲלֹא, which is common in rabbinic Hebrew and occurs in biblical Hebrew as well; cf. Isa. 7:25; Job 37:24; Hos. 10:9; 11:5 and see Gordis in *LGJV*, English sec., pp. 181 ff.). Hence 16b would be understood as "you surely watch my sin." In v. 17, חָתַם "sealed up" and וַתִּטְפֹּל "You have plastered over" are then taken to imply that the sins are kept intact for the future day of reckoning; cf. Hos. 13:12: צָרוּר עֲוֹן אֶפְרָיִם צְפוּנָה חַטָּאתוֹ.

On the basis of B, God would count Job's steps to make sure he does not fall, and v. 16b offers no problem. On this view the Paʿul form חָתֻם, which is the participle passive referring to the present, offers a problem, on which see the Comm. V. 17 would be understood to mean that Job's sins will be covered up and plastered over. On this meaning for the verb, cf. Isa. 8:16, צוֹר תְּעוּדָה חֲתוֹם תּוֹרָה בְּלִמֻּדָי, "hide the testimony, seal up the teaching among my disciples."

Neither approach is free from problems. The determining factor, we believe, in favor of B, is that of context. On this view, (a) vv. 16 and 17 continue the favorable picture in v. 15; (b) the verb חָתַם in 17a, which suggests the permanent sealing of Job's sins, has its parallel in the Isaiah passage, not in Hosea; (c) most decisively, וְאוּלָם in v. 18, which introduces the picture of man's dissolution, is adversative, "but, however." This conjunction makes it clear that the previous passage described Job's fantasies regarding a happier fate. View B is accordingly adopted. For details see the Trans. and the Comm.

14:16 כִּי־עַתָּה = "for then" (cf. 3:13). S inserts the negative, "you would not count my steps." However, counting or watching someone's steps is not necessarily a negative attitude (see 31:4; 34:21), but may be one of supervision and protection, like a father counting his child's early steps, out of solicitude lest he fall. In stich b, it has been proposed to render "step" on the basis of the Arabic *ḥatwa* "step" and the parallelism with stich a (Eitan), but the Hebrew root is much too frequent to bear so radically divergent a meaning here alone.

14:17 חָתֻם, a participle passive, may possibly be rendered "it would be sealed," but the *defectiva* spelling in MT and the syntax suggest that it be revocalized as חָתֹם, an infinitive abs. consec., as in הוֹכֵחַ (Job 15:3); הָרֹה (15:35); וְנָתוֹן (Est. 2:3) and often. The infinitive would here be equivalent to the imperfect tense, rendering unnecessary even the slight emendation to תַּחְתֹּם by haplography from the Tav of חַטָּאתִי.

14:18 וְאוּלָם — a world of tragedy inheres in this "but." How far from the happiness man hopes for is the bleak reality of existence, a lifetime of suffering climaxed by death, from which there is no escape or return.

The connotation of the three metaphors that the poet employs in vv. 18, 19 should be noted. The mountain which crumbles into rock, the rock that disintegrates into dust, and finally the dust of the earth, all three vividly suggest the stages in the dissolution of man's life and hope, a process both irresistible and irreversible.

For another instance of the poet's superb use of three figures (in this case similes rather than metaphors), and the rich overtones of meaning they convey, cf. the Comm. on 9:25, 26.

Stich a: "The mighty mountain crumbles, being washed away by torrents." MT = lit. "the mountain, falling, crumbles away." נבל = "rot, fall away." My former student, Rabbi Shamma Friedman, suggested that stich a may contain a conflate: (a) וְאוּלָם הַר נֹפֵל and (b) וְאוּלָם הַר יִבּוֹל.

צוּר "rock" recalls its Aram. cognate טוּרָא "hill," but note the parallelism and אֲבָנִים in v. 19.

14:19 The word order in stich a is emphatic: "even stone the water wears away." סָפִיחַ "aftergrowth" (Lev. 25:5; II Ki. 19:29 = Isa. 37:30) is obviously inappropriate here. Read (with Gr., Bu., Be.) סְחִיפָה "torrent, downpour" (cf. Pr. 28:3 מָטָר סֹחֵף and *M. Keth.* 1:6 שדך נסתחפה "your field has been swept away," as well as נִסְחַף, Jer. 46:15). Stich c is introduced by the *Vav adaequationis* (cf. 5:7) to indicate the comparison.

14:20 תקף "seize, take hold" (Ibn Janah), for which we may adduce יְתְקְפוֹ "attack (Ecc. 4:12) and mishnaic Hebrew תוקף טליתו של חבירו "he seizes his friend's garment" (*B. Yeb.* 54a and often). In view of the Vav with וַיַּהֲלֹךְ, the verb is better rendered "overpower" (cf. תַּקִּיף Ecc. 6:10, so Ra., Ibn E.).

The Arab. cognate *halaka*, "die, perish," suggests the nuance of the Hebrew verb intended here.

מְשַׁנֶּה the participle is syntactically awkward, which leads most moderns to read תְּשַׁנֶּה. "Change his face" refers to death, probably to *rigor mortis* (Ibn E.).

14:21 The verbs יִכְבְּדוּ and וְיִצְעֲרוּ may be given either a quantitative meaning, "grow many" and "become few" respectively (cf. Jer. 30:19) or a qualitative sense, "attain to glory" and "become low" (cf. Mic. 5:1). The second view is preferable, since it is the dead man's inability to share in the joys and sorrows of his offspring, rather than his mere lack of knowledge of the number of his descendants, that Job finds so deeply tragic. Koheleth, too, finds man's inability to know the future course of events his major source of frustration (cf., e.g., Ecc. 3:11; 8:17); but it is man's general intellectual limitations that he regrets, not the emotional void that Job feels as a loving father cut off from the life of his children.

14:22 This difficult verse has been rendered variously: (1) "While his flesh is upon him, i.e., while he is still alive" (D-G, TS). On this view, which is against the accents, וְנַפְשׁוֹ עָלָיו "while his soul is in him" in stich b, if parallel in meaning, is highly irregular, as we should have expected וְנַפְשׁוֹ בוֹ (cf. Job 27:3 כִּי־כָל־עוֹד נִשְׁמָתִי בִי (2) "In death, man still feels his own pain (but not that of his children)" (Ra., Ehr.). For the idea that the dead still feel pain, cf. *B. Ber.* 18:b קשה רימה למת כמחט בבשר החי "The worm is as difficult for the dead body as a needle in living flesh." In the ensuing discussion in the Talmud (*ibid.*), the effort is made to resolve the contradiction between v. 21 and v. 22. The conclusion is reached: בצערא דידהו קא ידעי בצערא דאחריני לא ידעי "their own pain the dead know, but the pain of others they do not know." (3) "In death man is still subject to pain" (so P.). On this view, however, stich b is not in parallelism with stich a. Moreover, one would expect, in view of the frequent preoccupation of Wisdom with man's inability to know the future, which is basic to Koheleth (cf. 3:11, 22; 6:12; 8:17; 9:1, and *KMW*, passim), that the theme of v. 21 would not be dismissed in a single verse, and the speech would end with another idea.

Moreover, there is no evidence in Wisdom literature or in the Bible as a whole for the belief that men feel physical pain after death. The passages adduced by P., Isa. 66:24 and Job 18:13, describe only the physical destruction of the sinners. Judith 16:17 expresses the later Pharisaic view of judgment and punishment after death for the wicked. This outlook is far removed from the classical concept of death in the Bible as a shadowy type of semi-existence. On the reasons for the retention of this view by Wisdom literature to the end, cf. "The Social Background of Wisdom Literature" in *PPS*, esp. 175–80.

The key to the passage lies in recognizing that בשר and נפש represent the biblical mode of expressing "the person, total personality." Cf. Ps. 63:2 נפש ‖ בשר; Job 12:10 נפש ‖ רוח ‖ בשר and often. עליו is the "pathetic" על (cf. Jer. 8:18; Jonah 2:8; Ps. 42:6, 7; 43:6, 7; Lam. 3:20; BDB, s.v. על 1 b, d). The force of the preposition can be felt, but it is difficult to render: "within him, for him, as far as he is concerned, etc." אך is the emphatic "surely, indeed." For this asseverative use of the particle, cf. Gen. 26:9; 29:14; 44:28; I Sam. 16:6; Jer. 5:4; Ps. 58:12; Job 16:7; 18:21. Vv. 21 and 22 are closely linked. When a man is dead, he cannot participate in the joys and sorrows of those dearest to him (v. 21). This thought continues to harass him during his lifetime (v. 22). At this enforced estrangement caused by death, his being is pained and in mourning.

The Second Cycle

The Speech of Eliphaz (15)

Eliphaz's pomposity — or his lofty seriousness — comes to the surface again. His patience is wearing thin in the face of Job's obstinacy and folly and his refusal to learn from those who are older and wiser than he. He reminds Job again that all men are imperfect and therefore have no cause to complain about their suffering. Eliphaz pictures in detail the destiny of the wicked man: his prosperity is temporary, and his life is doomed to end in exile and suffering.

However, a new note is added here. Eliphaz emphasizes that even while the sinner is ostensibly at peace he lives in constant trepidation, never knowing when the sword of doom will descend upon him. Thus, in effect, he is being punished during the time of his prosperity. The ultimate punishment of the wicked is the annihilation of his offspring.

15   Eliphaz the Temanite answered, saying,

2   Should a wise man answer empty opinions
               and fill his stomach with wind?

3   Should he argue in useless talk,
               in words that do no good?

4   You are undermining the sense of reverence
               and diminishing communion with God.

5   It is your guilt that teaches your mouth
               and makes you choose crafty speech.

6   Your mouth condemns you, not I;
               your own lips testify against you.

7   Were you born the first among men,
               and brought forth before the hills?

8   Did you eavesdrop in the council of God
               and garner all wisdom for yourself?

9   What do you know that we do not;
               what do you understand that is beyond us?

10   Both the graybeard and the aged are among us,
               older in years than your father.

11   Are God's consolations too slight for you,
               or the words gently spoken to you?

12   Why does your passion inflame you,
               why do your eyes flash with ire,

13   that you let loose your anger against God,
               and let such words issue from your mouth?

14   What is man that he should be pure,
               and can one born of woman be righteous?

15   Behold, God puts no trust even in His holy ones;
               the heavens themselves are not pure in His sight.

16   How much less one who is abominable and corrupt,
               a man who drinks in iniquity like water!

17   I will tell you — listen to me;
               what I have seen I will declare,

18   What wise men have told,
               and their fathers did not deny —

19   to whom alone the land was given,
               with no stranger passing among them —

20   All his days, the wicked is atremble
               throughout the number of years stored up for the oppressor.

21   The sound of terror is always in his ears;
               even while at peace he fears the despoiler coming upon him.

22   He does not hope to escape from the darkness,
               but can look forward only to the sword.

23   He wanders about for bread, asking, "Where is it?"
               knowing that the day of darkness awaits him.

24   Anguish and agony terrify him;
               they seize him like a king ready for the attack,

25   because he stretched out his hand against God
               and played the hero against the Almighty —

26   running against Him stubbornly
               with the thick bosses of his shields,

טו ‏א וַיַּעַן אֱלִיפַז הַתֵּימָנִי וַיֹּאמַר:

2 הֶחָכָם יַעֲנֶה דַעַת־רוּחַ   וִימַלֵּא קָדִים בִּטְנוֹ:

3 הוֹכֵחַ בְּדָבָר לֹא יִסְכּוֹן   וּמִלִּים לֹא־יוֹעִיל בָּם:

4 אַף־אַתָּה תָּפֵר יִרְאָה   וְתִגְרַע שִׂיחָה לִפְנֵי־אֵל:

ה כִּי יְאַלֵּף עֲוֹנְךָ פִּיךָ   וְתִבְחַר לְשׁוֹן עֲרוּמִים:

6 יַרְשִׁיעֲךָ פִיךָ וְלֹא־אָנִי   וּשְׂפָתֶיךָ יַעֲנוּ־בָךְ:

7 הֲרִאישׁוֹן אָדָם תִּוָּלֵד   וְלִפְנֵי גְבָעוֹת חוֹלָלְתָּ:

8 הַבְסוֹד אֱלוֹהַּ תִּשְׁמָע   וְתִגְרַע אֵלֶיךָ חָכְמָה:

9 מַה־יָּדַעְתָּ וְלֹא נֵדָע   תָּבִין וְלֹא־עִמָּנוּ הוּא:

י גַּם־שָׂב גַּם־יָשִׁישׁ בָּנוּ   כַּבִּיר מֵאָבִיךָ יָמִים:

11 הַמְעַט מִמְּךָ תַּנְחוּמוֹת אֵל   וְדָבָר לָאַט עִמָּךְ:

12 מַה־יִּקָּחֲךָ לִבֶּךָ   וּמַה־יִּרְזְמוּן עֵינֶיךָ:

13 כִּי־תָשִׁיב אֶל־אֵל רוּחֶךָ   וְהֹצֵאתָ מִפִּיךָ מִלִּין:

14 מָה־אֱנוֹשׁ כִּי־יִזְכֶּה   וְכִי־יִצְדַּק יְלוּד אִשָּׁה:

טו הֵן בִּקְדֹשׁוֹ לֹא יַאֲמִין   וְשָׁמַיִם לֹא־זַכּוּ בְעֵינָיו:

16 אַף כִּי־נִתְעָב וְנֶאֱלָח   אִישׁ־שֹׁתֶה כַמַּיִם עַוְלָה:

17 אֲחַוְךָ שְׁמַע־לִי   וְזֶה־חָזִיתִי וַאֲסַפֵּרָה:

18 אֲשֶׁר־חֲכָמִים יַגִּידוּ   וְלֹא כִחֲדוּ מֵאֲבוֹתָם:

19 לָהֶם לְבַדָּם נִתְּנָה הָאָרֶץ   וְלֹא־עָבַר זָר בְּתוֹכָם:

כ כָּל־יְמֵי רָשָׁע הוּא מִתְחוֹלֵל   וּמִסְפַּר שָׁנִים נִצְפְּנוּ לֶעָרִיץ:

21 קוֹל־פְּחָדִים בְּאָזְנָיו   בַּשָּׁלוֹם שׁוֹדֵד יְבוֹאֶנּוּ:

22 לֹא־יַאֲמִין שׁוּב מִנִּי־חֹשֶׁךְ   וְצָפוּ הוּא אֱלֵי־חָרֶב:

23 נֹדֵד הוּא לַלֶּחֶם אַיֵּה   יָדַע כִּי־נָכוֹן בְּיָדוֹ יוֹם־חֹשֶׁךְ:

24 יְבַעֲתֻהוּ צַר וּמְצוּקָה   תִּתְקְפֵהוּ כְּמֶלֶךְ עָתִיד לַכִּידוֹר:

כה כִּי־נָטָה אֶל־אֵל יָדוֹ   וְאֶל־שַׁדַּי יִתְגַּבָּר:

26 יָרוּץ אֵלָיו בְּצַוָּאר   בַּעֲבִי גַּבֵּי מָגִנָּיו:

---

27   his face covered with fat,
          and thick flesh gathered upon his loins.

28   He will live in devastated cities
          in houses no one inhabits,
          that are destined to be heaps of ruins.

29   He will not stay rich; his substance will not endure,
          nor will his wealth remain long upon the earth.

30   He will not escape from the darkness;
          his shoots will shrivel up in the hot wind,
          and his branch in the breath of God's mouth.

31   Let no man deluding himself believe in emptiness,
          for emptiness will be his reward!

32   Before his time he will be cut off,
          and his frond will not be green.

33   His green grapes will be stripped like the vine
          and his bloom will shed like the olive tree.

34   For the assembly of the godless is left desolate,
          and fire devours the tents of the corrupt,

35   who conceive evil and beget sin,
          and whose womb prepares deceit.

וַיַּעַשׂ פִּימָה עֲלֵי־כָסֶל׃ 27 כִּי־כִסָּה פָנָיו בְּחֶלְבּוֹ

בָּתִּים לֹא־יֵשְׁבוּ לָמוֹ 28 וַיִּשְׁכּוֹן ׀ עָרִים נִכְחָדוֹת

לֹא־יֶעְשַׁר וְלֹא־יָקוּם חֵילוֹ 29 אֲשֶׁר הִתְעַתְּדוּ לְגַלִּים׃

לֹא־יָסוּר ׀ מִנִּי־חֹשֶׁךְ ל וְלֹא־יִטֶּה לָאָרֶץ מִנְלָם׃

וְיָסוּר בְּרוּחַ פִּיו׃ יֹנַקְתּוֹ תְּיַבֵּשׁ שַׁלְהֶבֶת

כִּי־שָׁוְא תִּהְיֶה תְמוּרָתוֹ׃ 31 אַל־יַאֲמֵן בַּשָּׁו נִתְעָה

וְכִפָּתוֹ לֹא רַעֲנָנָה׃ 32 בְּלֹא־יוֹמוֹ תִּמָּלֵא

וְיַשְׁלֵךְ כַּזַּיִת נִצָּתוֹ׃ 33 יַחְמֹס כַּגֶּפֶן בִּסְרוֹ

וְאֵשׁ אָכְלָה אָהֳלֵי־שֹׁחַד׃ 34 כִּי־עֲדַת חָנֵף גַּלְמוּד

וּבִטְנָם תָּכִין מִרְמָה׃ לה הָרֹה עָמָל וְיָלֹד אָוֶן

Chapter 15

15:2 דַּעַת רוּחַ either (a) as an adv. acc. "with windy knowledge" (JPSV, D-G) (b) or as a direct acc. "answer empty opinions." דַּעַת is common in mishnaic Hebrew in the meaning of "opinion, view"; cf. also דֵּעַ (Job 32:6,10). On the acc. after the verb, cf. Job 32:12; 40:2. The stich is better rendered "should a wise man answer empty opinions?" קָדִים = "east wind," a reference to the empty words of the opponent, with which the wise man would fill his stomach if he opened his mouth to reply.

15:3 הוֹכֵחַ is an inf. abs. consec. Hence, it is equivalent to the imperf. used in v. 2, "should he reprove, argue?" יִסְכּוֹן = "to be useful, profit," a usage limited to Job 22:2; 34:9; 35:3. Stich b is "profitless talk" governed by the Bet in stich a.

15:4 אַף is emphatic, "indeed"; cf. Job 14:3 and BDB, s.v.
יראה = "fear of God," the biblical term most nearly equivalent to our "faith, religion" (cf. 4:10). גרע = "reduce, subtract" (Deut. 4:2; Ecc. 3:14). שִׂיחָה "conversation, communion with God."

15:5 כִּי is the asseverative "indeed." עֲוֺנְךָ is the subject of the clause, as the parallelism with stich b indicates: "It is your sinfulness that teaches your mouth, so that you choose crafty speech."
עֲרוּמִים is generally rendered "crafty men"; it may be an abstract noun, "craftiness," like עֲשׁוּקִים, זְקוּנִים, נְעוּרִים (Ecc. 4:1).

15:6 The v. is either deleted (Bi., Bu., TS, Ball), or transposed and placed before v. 13 (Du., Hö.). Both procedures are unnecessary. V. 5 has said that Job's sins cause him to speak as he has; hence his words testify to his sins. Both verbs are to be understood in the present, "condemns" and "testifies."

15:7 For the *plene* spelling of רִאישׁוֹן, the regular orthography in the Samaritan Pentateuch, cf. רִאישׁוֹנָה (Jos. 21:10) and רִישׁוֹן (Job 8:8). הֲרִאישׁוֹן אָדָם is to be understood not as "as the first to be a man" with אָדָם construed as an acc. of product (D-G), but as a construct, "the first of humankind," hence "the first man, Adam." The reference is clearly to the concept of primordial Adam, who is the apogee of wisdom and perfection, an idea to be found in such biblical passages as Ezek. 28:12 ff.; Ps. 82:6–7, which underlies the Paradise narrative in Genesis, chaps. 2–3 (cf. esp. 3:18). It is far more extensively and explicitly developed in apocryphal and rabbinic literature (*ādām kadmōn*). Cf. Gordis, "The Significance of the Paradise Myth," in *AJSL*, vol. 52 (1936), pages 86–94; and "The Knowledge of Good and Evil in the Old Testament and the Qumran Scrolls," in *JBL*, 1957, vol. 76, pp. 123–38, the latter reprinted in *PPS*, chap. 7.

The reference to creation is clear in stich b, which occurs identically in Pr. 8:25 in describing the birth of Wisdom at the creation of the world. Stich b may well carry the overtone "Are you Wisdom personified?" (Bu.).

Since Job has presumed to criticize God, Eliphaz sarcastically asks whether he claims to be as wise as Adam before the Fall.

15:8 The Beth in בְּסוֹד suggests "listening in, eavesdropping"; cf. Gen. 27:5. וְתִגְרַע lit. "reduce, appropriate for yourself." סוֹד אֱלוֹהַ "the council of God"; cf. Jer. 23:18 and the synonymous use of עֲדַת אֵל (Ps. 82:1). The verse may be an allusion to primal Adam, who derived his supernal wisdom by overhearing the council of God.

15:10 Here Eliphaz delivers himself of what is the decisive argument in the ancient world — Wisdom is synonymous with age. Hence, Elihu, as a younger man, is constrained to deliver a long apology for daring to intrude on a discussion of his elders and his betters (chap. 32).

15:11 תַּנְחֻמוֹת אֵל "God's consolations" refers to the doctrines of the ultimate reward to the righteous and retribution for the evil-doers, beliefs supported by the ancillary idea of the imperfection of all men. Eliphaz calls it "the consolations of God" not merely because this is the truth *par excellence*, but because it has come to him by Divine inspiration (4:16 ff.). Now he obligingly repeats his insight for Job's benefit (15:14–16; cf. also 25:4). Note the strictly legal sense that Job imparts to the phrase in 9:2.

לָאַט is difficult. It is generally rendered "act gently" (cf. II Sam. 18:5) and hence, "speak gently" here. The subject may be God or it may be impersonal, "words spoken gently to you," an allusion to Eliphaz's first speech which, he feels, has been tactful and considerate of Job's feelings. That לָאַט is the adverb = לְאַט "in gentleness" (D-G) is doubtful, since a verb is obviously required here. However, the occurrence of אַט without a Lamed (I Ki. 21:27) makes it difficult to decide what the verb is.

15:12 Job's anger and impatience against which Eliphaz has warned him before (5:2) have led him into attacking God.

The heart and the eyes are sources of desire and passion and, therefore, in the rabbinic phrase, "the middle-men of transgression" (סרסורי עבירה); cf. Nu. 15:39: וְלֹא תָתוּרוּ אַחֲרֵי לְבַבְכֶם וְאַחֲרֵי עֵינֵיכֶם.

לקח "inflame"; cf. אֵשׁ מִתְלַקַּחַת "self-kindling flame" (Ex. 9:24; Ezek. 1:4). יִרְזְמוּן has been (a) emended to יִרוּמוּן "grow haughty," as in Ps. 6:7; 30:13; (b) interpreted as "grow weak, dwindle" (TS, P.); and (c) treated as a metathesis of רמז "wink, flash." The last meaning suggests the connotation here of "flash with anger," the most appropriate of all in our context.

15:13 רוּחֶךָ "anger" (cf. Jud. 8:3). מִלִּין = "mere words, empty words."

15:14 Stich a is to be rendered, not "how can man be innocent?", but "what is man that he should be pure?" Stich b, which has its own subject, is not a subordinate clause, but a coordinate clause parallel to stich a.

וְכִי is best taken as the sign of a question, a common usage in mishnaic Hebrew, and parallel to the biblical אִם (cf., e.g., *B. Giṭ.* 19a, וכי מפני שאנו עומדים, "And because we are standing?"). Hence, render the v.:

> What is man that he should be pure?
> Can one born of woman be righteous?

15:15 Eliphaz repeats briefly the substance of God's revelation to him (4:17–21), which Job has spurned. God does not trust His angels, nor even the heavens, the very essence of purity (*laṭōhar*, Ex. 24:10).

15:16 אַף כִּי "how much more so," an *a fortiori* argument. In 4:19, the argument is general: "All men are frail and imperfect." Here it is personal: "Job is a deliberate sinner." נֶאֱלָח "loathsome"; cf. Ps. 14:3; Arab. "to grow sour (of milk)." The root is apparently a metathesis of חלא; cf. Ezek. 24:6 חֶלְאָתָהּ.

אִישׁ = "man" generically (cf. 14:10, 11). The later biblical writers were not always exact in distinguishing between אדם and איש, as does the Psalmist in 49:3. Cf. Ecc. 7:28, where אָדָם is contrasted with אִשָּׁה, and אִישׁ would have been expected; but cf. *KMW ad loc.* for the semantic principle involved.

On the other hand, אִישׁ may be used here specifically with the nuance "a prominent, powerful man," a reference to the important position Job occupied in society. Thus the crimes that he is charged with by Eliphaz in 22:5–9 are the sins of a powerful malefactor. The synonym גֶּבֶר (Job 38:3) underscores the element of strength and courage; "gird up your loins like a man."

15:17 וְזֶה is not the demonstrative pronoun, but the relative (Ex. 15:13); cf. the old Aram. זִי, later Aram. דִי "that which, what."

15:18 MT is usually rendered: "what wise men declare, without hiding it from their fathers" (D-G). Ehr., who attaches the first Mem of מֵאֲבוֹתָם to כִּחֲדוּ, construes the pronoun as the acc. of person, for which he cites the use of מנע (Nu. 24:11; Job 31:16) and interprets contrariwise "which their ancestors did not hide from them, i.e. the sages." It is, however, hardly likely either that the sages teach wisdom to their fathers or that the fathers teach wisdom to the sages. Eliphaz, who has previously cited the truths that have come to him by revelation, now invokes two other sources of enlightenment — the testimony of the sages and the wisdom of the ancients. This view is supported by the parallel use of the two verbs הִגִּידוּ, לֹא כִחֵדוּ in Isa. 3:9; hence the sages told and the ancestors did not deny.

In מֵאֲבוֹתָם, the first Mem is not to be deleted; it is best regarded as an enclitic Mem belonging to the previous word or it is to be joined to it and read כִּחֲדוּם, which then would mean "they did not hide these things." "Their fathers" refers to the ancestors of the sages, who thus add the virtue of antiquity to that of wisdom. (Cf. Ecc. 1:11 for a reference to successive generations of the past.) Eliphaz's nonmediated revelation, the rich wisdom of the sages and the accumulated experience of the ancients — how can Job dare to rebel against this triply attested truth!

15:19 The verse has been interpreted as an allusion to a pure community of believers or to Eliphaz's home country, or to the purity of his tribal descent. Some have seen in it a reference to the time before Palestine was under foreign rule. However, such indications of specific national events or conditions, which have indeed been read into the text by some older commentators (cf., e.g., Rashi on 3:26; 5:10), are out of the question for our poet, who sets his stage on a broadly human basis, with no hint of particularism. Actually, none of these ideas are remotely hinted at in the text.

There is no justification for deleting the verse (Hö., P.). The verse is a subordinate clause (אֲשֶׁר understood) modifying מֵאֲבוֹתָם in v. 18.

The verse describes "their fathers" as remote ancestors who lived long ago, at a time when men were few on the earth, unlike its present crowded condition. The earlier the period of the ancestors, the greater their wisdom.

15:20 מִתְחוֹלֵל = "he trembles," from חוּל. Stich b is not the independent clause, "Few years are in store for the oppressor" (P.), for nowhere does the conventional theory argue that the lifetime of evildoers is brief, only that their prosperity is short-lived. Moreover, D-G correctly point out that "a few years" would be expressed by שְׁנֵי מִסְפָּר (cf. Nu. 9:20; Job 16:22), not מִסְפַּר שָׁנִים. Stich b is a clause of condition, "during the number of days that are stored up for the oppressor." Cf. BDB, s.v. Vav, 1–k, p. 253a (bottom) and b, and see Jud. 2:21 (וַיָּמֹת); 13:9; I Sam. 18:23; I Ki. 19:19; Ps. 72:12, etc.; Job 29:12; and Dr., *HT*, sec. 156–60.

15:21 Stich b cannot mean that while the sinner is at peace, the despoiler will overtake him (RSV), since the following verse still describes him as anticipating the blow. The parallelism also supports the rendering "when he is at peace he *fears* that the despoiler will reach him." On this use of indirect quotations, see *BGM*, pp. 179–81, and the Comm. on 13:14.

15:22 The sinner does not believe that he will return, i.e., escape from darkness. צָפוּי "he is expecting, looking toward." The Kethib צפו is not an error (ag. D-G) but the older form of the Qal participle passive of *Lamed Yod* verbs, to be read צָפוּ, while the Qere registers the later form. For this category of Kethib-Qere cf. *BTM*, list 20, p. 105, and see I Sam. 25:18; II Ki. 23:4; Isa. 3:16, as well as Job 41:25, הֶעָשׂוּ, which has no Qere variation. We interpret similarly Hos. 2:11, וְכֶסֶף הִרְבֵּיתִי לָהּ וְזָהָב עָשׂוּ לַבָּעַל, "and silver I increased for her and gold (which was) fashioned for the Baal." On this form of the participle, cf. Ges.-K., sec. 75, 76, Note I, and J. Barth, *NB*, par. 123a.

15:23 לַלֶּחֶם אַיֵּה has been emended to לְלֶחֶם אַיָּה and the stich then rendered "He wanders as food for vultures" (Bu.), on the basis of LXX. However, the introduction of a brief interrogative quotation into a declarative text is a thoroughly idiomatic biblical usage; cf. וְאַתָּ ה׳ עַד מָתָי (Ps. 6:4); שׁוּבָה ה׳ עַד מָתָי (Ps. 90:13). Even more apposite is *Lachish Letter* No. 4, 1. 8; ועבדך אדני שלח שמה איהו "Your servant, my Lord, sent thither (asking) 'Where is he?' "

Because of the difficulties encountered with כִּי־נָכוֹן בְּיָדוֹ and for metric reasons, Du., D-G, and others emend the words to כִּי־נָכוֹן כִּידוֹ and add יוֹם חֹשֶׁךְ to the following verse, which in turn requires the revocalization of two verbs there. Actually, neither the emendation nor the transposition of the text is necessary. בְּיָדוֹ is another instance of the phonetic spelling of בַּעֲדוֹ; cf. the Comm. on 8:4; 37:7 and ref. there. Hence, stich b is to be rendered: "He knows that the day of darkness is ready for him," the theme expressed in v. 22b.

Our verse is in 4:4 meter, the same pattern carried through in v. 24.

15:24 There are no metric considerations for revocalizing the opening verb as a singular. The present MT is a perfect 4:4 rhythm, the opening verb יְבַעֲתֻהוּ receiving two beats because of its length. תִּתְקְפֵהוּ "you seize him," or "you overpower him"; cf. the Comm. on 14:20. כִּידוֹר is a *hapax legomenon*, for which a rather doubtful Arabic etymology *kadara* VII, "dart, rush down," has been adduced. "Hence, like a king ready for the attack."

15:25 Vv. 25–28 are omitted by Sieg., Be., Bu., but quite unnecessarily. To a reader familiar with Hebrew tradition the passage suggests the traditional picture of Goliath, with his gargantuan size, his frame overlaid with fat and weighted down by armor, and his blasphemy against the God of Israel (I Sam., chap. 17). Fatness is a particularly felicitous example of symbolism, since in addition to suggesting physical grossness, it is a frequent metaphor for religious insensitivity; cf. Deut. 32:15; Isa. 6:10; Jer. 5:28; Ps. 73:3; 119:70, and the Biblical כְּסִיל rabbinic טִפֵּשׁ "fool," both derived from roots implying "thickness."

יִתְגַּבָּר the Hithpael in its meaning to "play the role of," hence, "play the hero" (cf. התהולל, התנכר, התנבא).

15:26 בְּצַוָּאר has been rendered "with a stubborn neck" (cf. Ps. 75:6). TS interprets the noun to mean "the neck of a shield, hauberk," for which he compares the medieval Hebrew use of בית צואר, or צואר של בגד, "the neck of a garment" (Maimonides, *Comm. on the Mishnah, Kelim* 22:17). This meaning would be appropriate if it were better attested. We prefer to render the noun as "with a thick neck," for which see the next verse and the American colloquial idiom, "red neck, bull neck," to stigmatize a large, fleshy, pugnacious individual. Stich b is lit. "with the thickness of the layers of his shields."

15:27 פִּימָה = פְּאִימָה with the Aleph elided (cf. Arab. *faʾama* II, IV "widen," *ufʾima* "become full of fat.")

15:28 The verse does not describe the sinner's *crime* in dwelling in cities laid under the ban and therefore forbidden (so Dil., Bu., D-G) (Deut. 13:17; Jos. 6:26), but the sinner's *punishment* — "You will be compelled to live in ruins uninhabited by men and destined to remain heaps of rubble." Hence, בָּתִּים לֹא יֵשְׁבוּ לָמוֹ is not "that they should not inhabit," but "that men do not inhabit." לָמוֹ an ethical dative, lit. "for themselves"; cf. Gen. 21:16; 22:5. הִתְעַתָּדוּ from the root עתד "be ready, prepared" (cf. Job 3:8; 15:24; Est. 3:14, and mishnaic Hebrew עתיד "the future, i.e., the prepared, destined era." Hence, render our phrase, "which are prepared, i.e., destined for heaps of ruin."

15:29 לֹא יֶעְשַׁר not "he will not become rich," a destiny which, Eliphaz cannot deny, does come to the wicked and which would be expressed by the Hiphil יַעֲשִׁיר (cf. Pr. 23:4), but, "he will not remain rich," as is also clear from the parallelism. D-G's problem with the verse is thus obviated. וְלֹא יָקוּם חֵילוֹ = "his wealth will not endure."

מִנְלָם is a *hapax legomenon*. It has been translated (a) "he will not cast a shadow on the earth" (LXX); (b) rendered, "he will not send his roots into the earth" (V), but the underlying reading of the Versions is unclear. S read or interpreted the word as "words" (מללא). Modern emendations include שִׁבֲּלִים "ears of grain" (Dil.) and מְלִלִים as in Deut. 23:26 (Hö). The best interpretation still remains that of Saadia, "wealth, acquisition," for which he adduces the Arab. *nīl*, for which see the Arabic version of Gen. 49:3. D-G points out that if it be derived from a *mediae Yod* root, the noun should be vocalized מְנָלָם like מְקֹמָם. However, this observation would apply only if it were a cognate; if it is a borrowing, it is idle to speculate about its precise form.

15:30 לֹא יָסוּר = "he will not turn aside, escape." יֹנַקְתוֹ = "a shoot coming up from the root" (cf. Isa. 53:2). שַׁלְהֶבֶת, usually "flame," would here seem to refer to "a hot wind"; cf. the Palestinian Arab. *šalhuba* and the rabbinic use of a denominative verb *šilhebh*, "burn, glow," e.g., *Mid. Koh. Rab.* 1:5 הוא משלהב "when the sun wants to go forth, it is burning hot." In stich c, וְיָסוּר, the usual rendering of the verb, "he will turn aside," is obviously much too weak for the context. The stich has therefore been variously emended and interpreted: (1) "His flower will fall away" (reading פִּרְחוֹ for בְּרוּחַ and interpreting ויסור as equal to וְיִשּׁוֹר from נשר "fall away" (so LXX); and (2) "His fruit will be carried away by the wind (of God's mouth)," emending the stich to וְיִסּוֹעַר בְּרוּחַ פְּרִיו (Be., Bu., Du., and D-G). We suggest that יָסוּר is a noun meaning "branch, i.e., a part separating itself from the trunk" and like חֹטֶר, גֶּזַע, עָנָף, בֶּן (Gen. 49:23; Ps. 80:16?) is a metaphor for "off-spring"; cf. the common Semitic usage which occurs in Job 18:16.

This noun, derived from סור ‖ יסר "move aside, separate," occurs, we believe, in at least two other passages, both in Jeremiah. In Jer. 2:21, it occurs as סור (cf. בּוּל ‖ יְבוּל; see the Comm. on Job 40:20; יָקוּם from קוּם). For another instance of the elision of the Yod, cf. שָׂרוֹן from *יִשְׂרוֹן "plain." The phrase סוּרֵי הַגֶּפֶן נָכְרִיָּה = "lit., alien branches of the vine," is contrasted with זֶרַע אֱמֶת "faithful seed." In Jer. 17:13, both forms of the noun occur, with the Yod in the Kethib יְסוּרַי and with the Yod elided in the Qere וְסוּרַי. Stichs c and d of this v. are therefore to be rendered "My offspring will be inscribed for the ground, or, death" (Ugaritic ʾard) "for they have forsaken the fountain of life." In both Jeremiah passages, the contrast is striking. In our passage, the ínterpretation gives an excellent parallelism with a *parono-masia*: לֹא־יָסוּר in stich a, "he will not escape" and וְיָסוּר in stich c, "and his branch, offspring." The noun should probably be revocalized with a suffix as וִיסוּרוֹ.

15:31 It cannot be denied that the v. seems inappropriate here, in a series of figures drawn from plant life. TS makes a valiant effort to bring the v. in line by vocalizing תְּמוּרָתוֹ as תְּמוֹרָתוֹ (*sic*), "his palm tree," but it does not really remove the difficulty.

The defectiva spelling שָׁ in the Kethib occurs in the Qumran Isa. I Scroll at 5:18; 59:4. יַאֲמֵן may refer to the wicked or be an impersonal. Since נִתְעָה is vocalized as in the perfect tense, stich a may be rendered: "Let no man believe in vanity, having been misled." On the other hand, the verb may be revocalized as a masc. participle נִתְעֶה and then be the subject. The Niphal in נִתְעָה may here carry its older reflexive sense, "deluding himself." Hence, render stich a: "let no man, deluding himself, believe in emptiness." שָׁוְא "emptiness, vanity," like עָמָל and אָוֶן, means both sin and its punishment. תְּמוּרָה = "exchange, price" (cf. Job 28:17), hence "recompense, gain."

15:32   בְּלֹא יוֹמוֹ "before his time";. cf. בְּלֹא עִתֶּךָ, Ecc. 7:17; Lev. 15:25, and the *Elephantine Ahikar Fragment* (ed. Cowley), l. 122, לא ביומיך "not on your day." LXX adds the noun *tome* "harvest" in stich a, on the basis of which Me., Bi., Du., add גִּזְעוֹ and Be., Bu., add תְּמוּרָתוֹ at the beginning of the verse. To be sure, S read מועיתא, which occurs for תְּמוּרָתוֹ in v. 31, and as an equivalent for נִצָּה (v. 33b), for גֶּזַע (14:8) and צֶמַח (Ps. 65:10). However, the 3:3 meter pattern in the v. militates against the addition of another vocable in stich a. The Vss. have merely supplied a subject on the basis of their understanding of the context.

תִּמָּלֵא need not be emended to תִמָּלֵל "will wither." The *tertiae Aleph* form is a metaplastic form for the geminate, which has arisen as a result of dissimilation; cf. בָּזְאוּ Isa. 18:2, parallel to בזז, and מאס parallel to מסס (cf. the Comm. on 7:5, 16). כִּפָּה = "broad-leaf frond" (cf. Lev. 23:40)-רַעֲנָנָה, accented on the penultimate, is the verb, not the adjective.

15:33 יַחְמֹס a denominative from חָמָס "robbery, violence," hence "he will strip, remove violently." The verb is used impersonally and is, therefore, equal to a passive: "One will strip, i.e., his green grapes will be stripped." The verse contains a breviloquence in its two similes: כַּגֶּפֶן and כַּזַּיִת = "as one normally strips the vine and the olive, in due season." The sinner (v. 32) and his offspring (v. 33), however, will die before their time. בִּסְרוֹ from בֹּסֶר

"unripe fruit," with an *ǐ* vowel sharpened from *ū* בְּסְרוֹ (cf. the Comm. on וּמְדַד 7:4). נִצָּה "blossom."

15:34 אֹהֶל "tent" recalls the Arab. *ʾahl* "family." גַּלְמוּד "desolate, lonely" (cf. the Comm. on 3:7).

15:35 הָרֹה and יָלֹד are both inf. consecutive; cf. 15:3. Both verbs are used synonymously, as in 3:3. While עָמָל and אָוֶן may refer both to sin and its punishment, as in 5:5, 6 (see the Comm. *ad loc.*), the reference here to "conceiving" and "begetting" suggests that Eliphaz is referring not to the penalty that overtakes the sinners, but to their activity in plotting evil, as in 4:8 and Ps. 7:14. Moreover, מִרְמָה "deceit" can hardly bear the meaning of "disappointment" (ag. P.). The verse is best regarded as describing the tents of the corrupt, "who conceive evil and beget sin and whose womb prepares deceit."

Job's Reply to Eliphaz (16–17)

Job has heard the Friends reiterate the conventional doctrine that justice prevails and that suffering is the result of sin. They have not hesitated to brand Job a sinner, mitigating their attack only slightly by urging him to repent of his iniquities. Yes, Job muses, if their positions were reversed, he, too, could offer his Friends easy but meaningless words of comfort. But how remote their platitudes are from the harsh reality of his situation! What Job wishes is not the Friends' sympathy for his plight, but their identification with his cause, their sharing his indignation at the injustice perpetrated against him.

Job describes his alienation from all who once loved and respected him. God is his adversary on the battlefield of life. Yet in spite of his agony, Job reaffirms his righteousness; beneath his rebellion he has an unconquerable faith that there must be justice somewhere in the world. This faith he expresses, not in impersonal terms, but with characteristic Hebraic concreteness in relation to his condition.

At this point, Job reaches a second, higher, level of faith. In 9:32, he had expressed his hope that there might be an arbiter between him and the Gof of violence. Here (16:19) Job voices his conviction that there actually is not merely an impartial judge, but a witness who will testify on his behalf. His deepest conviction is yet to be attained in his later vision of a redeemer, a blood avenger and kinsman arising to vindicate him (19:25).

Although Job sees his witness and his redeemer in his mind's eye, he does not expect immediate vindication. Hence, in our passage, he calls upon the earth not to cover up his blood. In chapter 19, he prays that his words be inscribed on a monument for future generations (19:25). In calling upon the earth not to hide his blood, Job is speaking not only out of bitterness at his undeserved misery, but also out of faith in the God of righteousness, a faith as passionate as his protest against the God of might.

In his response, Job, too, adds a new dimension to the discussion. As he thinks of his brief and miserable existence, he turns to God and not to his friends for understanding. Job is certain that his unjust suffering will arouse universal pity among good men, but will not deflect them from virtue. Thus he introduces the revolutionary idea that the righteous life is to be lived for its own sake, and not for the desire of reward. Once again his misery breaks in upon him. He sees all his hopes, which once gave light to his existence, going down to the grave with him.

16 Job answered, saying,

2   I have heard many such things;
           worthless comforters are you all!

3   Is there no end to words of wind,
           and what compels you to answer?

4   I, too, would speak as you do,
           were you in my place,
       Either I would string words together toward you
           or shake my head silently at your plight.

5   I would either encourage you with my speech,
           or sympathy would restrain my lips.

6   But now if I speak, my pain is not assuaged,
           and if I forbear, what relief have I?

7   Now He has left me helpless;
           He has laid waste my whole company.

8   He has shriveled me up —
           this has been the testimony against me!
       My leanness has risen up against me —
           this has been the evidence against me!

9   In His wrath He has torn me apart, for He hates me;
           He has gnashed his teeth at me;
           my foe sharpens his eyes against me.

10   Men gape at me with open mouths;
           in contempt they strike my cheeks;
           they mass together against me.

11   God hands me over to the evildoer,
           and through the hands of the wicked He wrings me out.

12   I was at ease, and He smashed me;
           He seized me by the neck, and crushed me;
           He set me up as His target.

13   His archers surround me,
           He pierces my kidneys without mercy,
           He pours out my gall to the ground.

14   He cracks me with breach upon breach;
           He rushes upon me like a warrior.

15   I have sewn sackcloth upon my skin,
           I have buried my dignity in the dust.

16   My face is red with weeping,
           and on my eyelids is deepest gloom,

17   though there is no violence in my hands
           and my prayer is pure.

18   O earth, cover not my blood;
           let my cry have no resting-place.

19   Behold, even now, my witness is in heaven,
           and he who vouches for me is on high.

20   Alas! Are my intercessors my friends?
           it is to God that my eye pours out its tears,

21   that He judge between a man and God,
           as between one man and his fellow.

22   For only a few years are yet to come
           and I go the way I shall not return.

טז א

וַיַּעַן אִיּוֹב וַיֹּאמַר׃

2 שָׁמַעְתִּי כְאֵלֶּה רַבּוֹת מְנַחֲמֵי עָמָל כֻּלְּכֶם׃

3 הֲקֵץ לְדִבְרֵי־רוּחַ אוֹ מַה־יַּמְרִיצְךָ כִּי תַעֲנֶה׃

4 גַּם ׀ אָנֹכִי כָּכֶם אֲדַבֵּרָה לוּ יֵשׁ נַפְשְׁכֶם תַּחַת נַפְשִׁי אַחְבִּירָה עֲלֵיכֶם בְּמִלִּים וְאָנִיעָה עֲלֵיכֶם בְּמוֹ רֹאשִׁי׃

ה אֲאַמִּצְכֶם בְּמוֹ־פִי וְנִיד שְׂפָתַי יַחְשֹׂךְ׃

6 אִם־אֲדַבְּרָה לֹא־יֵחָשֵׂךְ כְּאֵבִי וְאַחְדְּלָה מַה־מִּנִּי יַהֲלֹךְ׃

7 אַךְ־עַתָּה הֶלְאָנִי הֲשִׁמּוֹתָ כָּל־עֲדָתִי׃

8 וַתִּקְמְטֵנִי לְעֵד הָיָה וַיָּקָם בִּי כַחֲשִׁי בְּפָנַי יַעֲנֶה׃

9 אַפּוֹ טָרַף ׀ וַיִּשְׂטְמֵנִי חָרַק עָלַי בְּשִׁנָּיו צָרִי ׀ יִלְטוֹשׁ עֵינָיו לִי׃

י פָּעֲרוּ עָלַי ׀ בְּפִיהֶם בְּחֶרְפָּה הִכּוּ לְחָיָי יַחַד עָלַי יִתְמַלָּאוּן׃

11 יַסְגִּירֵנִי אֵל אֶל עֲוִיל וְעַל־יְדֵי רְשָׁעִים יִרְטֵנִי׃

12 שָׁלֵו הָיִיתִי ׀ וַיְפַרְפְּרֵנִי וְאָחַז בְּעָרְפִּי וַיְפַצְפְּצֵנִי וַיְקִימֵנִי לוֹ לְמַטָּרָה׃

13 יָסֹבּוּ עָלַי ׀ רַבָּיו יְפַלַּח כִּלְיוֹתַי וְלֹא יַחְמֹל יִשְׁפֹּךְ לָאָרֶץ מְרֵרָתִי׃

14 יִפְרְצֵנִי פֶרֶץ עַל־פְּנֵי־פָרֶץ יָרֻץ עָלַי כְּגִבּוֹר׃

טו שַׂק תָּפַרְתִּי עֲלֵי גִלְדִּי וְעֹלַלְתִּי בֶעָפָר קַרְנִי׃

16 פָּנַי חֳמַרְמְרָה מִנִּי־בֶכִי וְעַל עַפְעַפַּי צַלְמָוֶת׃

17 עַל לֹא־חָמָס בְּכַפָּי וּתְפִלָּתִי זַכָּה׃

18 אֶרֶץ אַל־תְּכַסִּי דָמִי וְאַל־יְהִי מָקוֹם לְזַעֲקָתִי׃

19 גַּם־עַתָּה הִנֵּה־בַשָּׁמַיִם עֵדִי וְשָׂהֲדִי בַּמְּרוֹמִים׃

כ מְלִיצַי רֵעָי אֶל־אֱלוֹהַּ דָּלְפָה עֵינִי׃

21 וְיוֹכַח לְגֶבֶר עִם־אֱלוֹהַּ וּבֶן־אָדָם לְרֵעֵהוּ׃

22 כִּי־שְׁנוֹת מִסְפָּר יֶאֱתָיוּ וְאֹרַח לֹא־אָשׁוּב אֶהֱלֹךְ׃

17 My spirit is broken,
  my days are burnt out;
   only the grave awaits me.
2 Indeed, there are mockers all about me,
  and my eye must abide their provocations.
3 God, pray take my pledge with You;
  Who else would accept a surety from my hands?
4 Since You have closed their minds to understanding,
  You will win no glory from them.
5 As men say,
  "He invites his friends to share his bounty,
   while the eyes of his own children grow faint with hunger!"
6 God has set me up as a byword among people;
  I am one in whose face men spit.
7 My eye has grown dim from grief,
  and all my limbs are like a shadow.
8 Upright men will be horrified at this,
  and the innocent will rise up against the godless.
9 But the just will hold fast to his way,
  and he who has clean hands will increase his strength.

10 But as for you all, come back now;
  not one wise man can I find among you.
11 My days have outlasted my hopes;
  cut off are the desires of my heart,
12 that could turn night into day
  and darkness into blessed light.
13 Indeed, I have marked out my home in Sheol
  and spread out my couch in the darkness.
14 To the pit I call, "You are my father,"
  and to the worm, "my mother," "my sister."
15 Where then is my hope?
  my hope, who can see it?
16 To the chambers of Sheol it descends;
  together we shall go down to the dust.

יז

א   רוּחִי חֻבָּלָה יָמַי נִזְעָכוּ   קְבָרִים לִי׃

2   אִם־לֹא הֲתֻלִים עִמָּדִי   וּבְהַמְּרוֹתָם תָּלַן עֵינִי׃

3   שִׂימָה־נָּא עָרְבֵנִי עִמָּךְ   מִי־הוּא לְיָדִי יִתָּקֵעַ׃

4   כִּי־לִבָּם צָפַנְתָּ מִּשָּׂכֶל   עַל־כֵּן לֹא תְרֹמֵם׃

ה   לְחֵלֶק יַגִּיד רֵעִים   וְעֵינֵי בָנָיו תִּכְלֶנָה׃

6   וְהִצִּיגַנִי לִמְשֹׁל עַמִּים   וְתֹפֶת לְפָנִים אֶהְיֶה׃

7   וַתֵּכַהּ מִכַּעַשׂ עֵינִי   וִיצֻרַי כַּצֵּל כֻּלָּם׃

8   יָשֹׁמּוּ יְשָׁרִים עַל־זֹאת   וְנָקִי עַל־חָנֵף יִתְעֹרָר׃

9   וְיֹאחֵז צַדִּיק דַּרְכּוֹ   וּטְהָר־יָדַיִם יֹסִיף אֹמֶץ׃

י   וְאוּלָם כֻּלָּם תָּשֻׁבוּ וּבֹאוּ נָא   וְלֹא־אֶמְצָא בָכֶם חָכָם׃

11   יָמַי עָבְרוּ זִמֹּתַי נִתְּקוּ   מוֹרָשֵׁי לְבָבִי׃

12   לַיְלָה לְיוֹם יָשִׂימוּ   אוֹר קָרוֹב מִפְּנֵי־חֹשֶׁךְ׃

13   אִם־אֲקַוֶּה שְׁאוֹל בֵּיתִי   בַּחֹשֶׁךְ רִפַּדְתִּי יְצוּעָי׃

14   לַשַּׁחַת קָרָאתִי אָבִי אָתָּה   אִמִּי וַאֲחֹתִי לָרִמָּה׃

טו   וְאַיֵּה אֵפוֹ תִקְוָתִי   וְתִקְוָתִי מִי יְשׁוּרֶנָּה׃

16   בַּדֵּי שְׁאֹל תֵּרַדְנָה   אִם־יַחַד עַל־עָפָר נָחַת׃

CHAPTER 16

16:2 עָמָל is synonymous with and parallel to אָוֶן (cf. 15:35). Hence מְנַחֲמֵי עָמָל is not "comforters causing anguish, galling comforters," but "worthless comforters" (cf. Isa. 59:4; Job 4:8, etc.), a usage similar to that of רֹפְאֵי אֱלִיל, רֹעִי אֱלִיל (cf. Jer. 14:14; Zech. 11:17; Job 13:4). עמל is well defined by A. Hakham as having "the three-fold meaning" of הבל צער ורשע, "emptiness, pain and evil-doing."

16:3 Stich a has been generally rendered, "Is there an end to words of wind?" But a question couched in this form without a negative normally anticipates the answer "No," which is not in harmony with the context or the parallelism. We have here an instance of a rhetorical use of the interrogative, where an affirmative answer is expected, though the negative which is usual in such cases is omitted. Cf. *inter alia* הֲבֵן יַקִּיר לִי אֶפְרַיִם (Jer. 31:19), "Is not Ephraim my beloved son?"; הֲזֹאת יָדָעְתָּ "Don't you know?" (Job 20:4); הֲנִגְלֹה נִגְלֵיתִי, "Was I not revealed?" (I Sam. 2:27). On this usage and its psychological basis, see Gordis, "A Rhetorical Use of Interrogative Sentences in Biblical Hebrew," in *AJSL*, 1933, vol. 49, pp. 212–17. Our stich is therefore to be rendered "Is there no end to words of wind?"

אוֹ = ו "and" (as in Lev. 26:41; Nu. 15:6). The equivalence may have been due to the dual meaning of Vav as "and" and "or."

מרץ "force, compel." (Cf. the Comm. on 6:25.)

16:4 לוּ here means not "would that" (D-G), but "if"; cf. Gen. 50:15; Jud. 13:23; Ecc. 6:3, a particle which occurs in mishnaic Hebrew as אלו. It introduces the protasis of a condition, the apodosis of which is to be found in 4a, b, 5.

אַחְבִּירָה has been interpreted: (a) = אַכְבִּירָה hence, "increase words"; (b) from the Arab. *habara*, "beautify, adorn"; hence, "I could be brilliant in words against you" (Koehler-Baumgartner); (c) "make noise" from an original Ugaritic root *ḥbr* taken to mean "make a sound, noise," hence, "harangue" (J. J. Finkelstein, in *JBL*, vol. 75, 1956, pp. 328–31); or d) "I could speak to you with mere noise" (O. Laurentz, *CBQ*, vol. 23, 1961, pp. 293 f.). However, the common biblical root חבר "unite, join," which is richly attested, is entirely adequate for the meaning "I would join words together," particularly in view of the later Hebrew usage of the root in the sense of "compose, indite."

The passage is generally understood to mean that if the role of Job and that of the Friends were reversed, he would be equally hostile and unsympathetic toward them. But if this were his meaning, he could scarcely complain at the treatment they are now meting out to him! Ehrlich has correctly noted that Job is not suggesting here that the Friends are hostile, but that they are trying to comfort him either by long speeches or by expressing silent sympathy (cf. Eliphaz's opening words: 4:2–6). Both procedures, it may be noted, were actually employed by the Friends (2:13; 4:2 ff.). Hence, the preposition עֲלֵיכֶם is not to be taken as "against you," but = אֲלֵיכֶם "towards you, in your direction." The interchange of עַל and אֶל, both in biblical and extrabiblical sources, is very common. (Cf. BDB, pp. 41-a and 7:57-a, and out of untold examples, cf. Isa. 53:1; 62:10; Ezek. 29:14, etc.) Hence the Vavs in vv. 4c and 5b are to be understood adversatively, "or."

נִיד "shaking the head" was a silent mode of expressing sympathy (cf. Job 2:11, 13). The failure to recognize the intent of this passage has made the interpretation of v. 5b virtually impossible. See below. The preposition in בְּמוֹ רֹאשִׁי is the Beth of means, which is an alternative to the direct object used in יָנִיעוּ רֹאשׁ (Ps. 22:8), and note פָּעֲרוּ עָלַי בְּפִיהֶם (Job 16:10) as against וּפָעֲרָה פִיהָ (Isa. 5:14). In the first instance of each pair, the noun is regarded as the means of the action. The same usage of the Beth of means occurs in Am. 2:7 הַשֹּׁאֲפִים עַל־עֲפַר אֶרֶץ בְּרֹאשׁ דַּלִּים, which has been emended unnecessarily and is to be rendered: "Who crush to (אֶל = עַל) the dust of the earth (by means of) the heads of the poor." נַפְשְׁכֶם = "your person, you."

16:5 Stich b is generally rendered "the movement of my lips would reduce, sc., the pain," the object to be supplied from 6a in the next v. This is a highly dubious procedure. נִיד is an ellipsis for נִיד רֹאשׁ "shaking of the head, sympathy"; cf. the verb נוד (Job 2:11; 42:11). The sympathy may be either genuine, as in 2:11; 42:11, or derisive, as in Isa. 32:22; Ps. 22:8, etc. The stich is to be rendered: "or my sympathy would hold my lips in check (from saying the wrong things), keep me silent." (Cf. חוֹשֵׂךְ שְׂפָתָיו מַשְׂכִּיל, Pr. 10:19; 17:27.) Vv. 4 and 5 are in alternate parallelism, 4b and 5a dealing with sympathy expressed in speech, and 4c and 5b with silence, the Vav in each case (וְנִיד, וְאָנִיעָה) being adversative. See the Translation of the entire passage.

16:6 Job now turns from imagining a reversal of roles with his Friends, that he has been contemplating, to the tragic realities of his present position, and finds that neither speech nor silence brings him any relief. The change of mood and theme, without any external mark of transition which seems to us abrupt, is characteristic of Job (cf., e.g., 8:16; 19:22, 27c). Ehr. regards this verse, too, as describing Job's hypothetical position were the roles reversed. But in that event the references should have been in the second person, "If I spoke, your pain would not have departed from you."

לֹא יֵחָשֵׂךְ כְּאֵבִי "My pain is not diminished, assuaged." מַה־מִּנִּי יַהֲלֹךְ, lit., "What part of my suffering will depart from me?"

16:7 The change from 2nd to 3rd person is frequent and virtually normal in biblical Hebrew. Emending הֶלְאָנִי to הֶלְאַתְנִי (Bu., D-G.) is no solution, since the 3rd person reappears in v. 9. הֶלְאַנִי = "make me helpless, unable to do anything," from the basic meaning of the root "be unable" (Gen. 19:11; Ex. 7:18; Isa. 1:14; Jer. 20:9; Job 4:2, 5; see the Comm.). עֲדָתִי does not refer to Job's three adversaries, whose alienation from him could hardly be described as their "destruction," but must refer to the circle of his intimates,

particularly his family, whose death has destroyed his power to act. On עדה
as "family, intimates," cf. 15:34, where it is parallel to אהל. Here, as in
19:13–18, the poet is not concerned with harmonizing the details of the
poetry and the prose narrative. On this feature of biblical and Semitic composition, see *BGM*, pp. 73, 326, n. 42.

The difficulties that scholars have found with the stichometry of vv. 7
and 8, on the basis of which the text has been emended, are not decisive.
On the two-beat meter in these vv. see the Comm. on the next v.

16:8 Because of its importance and even more because of its length, וַתִּקְמְטֵנִי
receives two beats (cf. *PPS*, p. 67), so that the v. exhibits a perfect 2:2 ‖ 2:2
(or a 4:4) meter, like the preceding v. (2:2). While the 3-beat stich predominates in this chapter, it is varied here not merely to avoid monotony,
but also to express Job's heightened emotion, as in 17:1.

For וַתִּקְמְטֵנִי, cf. Arab. *qamaṭa*, "seize, compress," Aram. קמט, "seize"
(T on Pr. 4:4; 5:22), Syriac "press." The root develops two meanings:
(a) "seize," as in Job 22:16; and (b) "draw together, become wrinkled," as in
Syriac אתקמט, rabbinic Hebrew קמטים "wrinkles," אלו שמקמטים עצמם, "students who wrinkle themselves," *B. Ḥag.* 14a. In our passage, render lit., "You
have shriveled me up." The parallelism favors rendering כַּחֲשִׁי not as "my
rebellion" (Nah. 3:1), but "my leanness" (Ps. 109:24; T on Gen. 41:27;
Ecc. 12:5). וַיָּקָם בִּי, "rise against me," and בְּפָנַי יַעֲנֶה, "testify against me,"
are forensic terms.

Job complains that God has punished him and that his physical condition
now serves to condemn him, on the basis of the conventional theory that
suffering is invariably the result and therefore the proof of wickedness.

16:9 The subject of וַיִּשְׂטְמֵנִי must be God, and therefore בְּאַפּוֹ = אַפּוֹ, "in
his wrath He tore me apart."

Stich a may be an instance of *hysteron proteron* and is therefore = "He
hates me and in His anger tears me apart." On this rhetorical usage, see
Gordis, in *Sepher Moshe Seidel* (Jerusalem, 1962), pp. 253–66, and the Comm.
on 14:10. On the Beth of means in בְּשִׁנָּיו, cf. the Comm. on 16:4.

Both because of the vigor of the epithets in stichs b and c and their
physical character, some commentators have referred them to human enemies,
revocalizing צָרִי as צָרַי (so S), but the number of changes in the suffixes
militates against it, nor is this procedure necessary. Job has described God's
enmity elsewhere in very strong terms (cf. 7:20 and vv. 12–14 below). On
the other hand, there is no need to omit the references to Job's human foes
(vv. 10–11). Like the Psalmist (e.g., Ps. 22:2–8), Job complains of his human
foes, who are conceived of as the emissaries of God (cf. v. 11a and v. 13,
"His archers"), so that no clear line of demarcation is to be expected, or
indeed is possible between his divine and his human foes. This is particularly
true in view of the basic biblical concept of "fluid personality." This is the
key to the identification of God with the Prophet, and here to that of God

with the enemy. The passage 9–12 is in chiastic arrangement: vv. 9 and 12 describing God, and vv. 10 and 11, Job's human foes.

16:10 For stich a, "opening the mouth in hatred or contempt," cf. Ps. 22:14. On בְּפִיהֶם *the Beth of means*, cf. the Comm. on 16:4 and the direct accus. use in Isa. 5:14. יִתְמַלָּאוּן is a denominative verb "to gather" from מָלֵא "assemblage, gathering"; cf. Gen. 48:19; Isa. 31:4, and Arab. *malaʾa*.

16:11 עֲוִילִים = "children" in 19:18; 21:11; here it is a variant for עַוָּלִים "evil-doers" (Ges., Ew.). יִרְטֵנִי is often explained on the basis of Nu. 22:32 יָרַט הַדֶּרֶךְ (which is itself incomprehensible) and rendered "He degrades me" or "He tosses me" (= יִירְטֵנִי). The verb is far better rendered on the basis of the mishnaic root רטה, "wring out" (so Rashi); cf. *Tos. Toh.* 5:16 הרוטה פשתנו "He who wrings out his flax"; רטיה "compress," *Mid. Cant. Rab.* 4:5. *Mid. Ex. Rab.*, sec. 21, correctly interprets our passage, but sees a reference to Satan in it, "He has wrung me out through Satan," הרוטה אותי בידו.

16:12 פִּרְפֵּר, the Pilpel of פרר, is here equivalent to the Polel פּוֹרֵר (Isa. 24:19; Ps. 74:13). It has the meaning "smash, break into bits," and is apparently distinct from the mishnaic homonym = "flutter, writhe." פִּצְפֵּץ, the Pilpel of פצץ, is equivalent to the Polel פּוֹצֵץ (Jer. 23:29; Lam. 3:12; Job 7:20b, "crush").

16:13 רַבָּיו "His archers" (cf. Gen. 49:23; Jer. 50:29), rather than "His arrows" (T, *ad loc.*). מְרֵרָתִי "gall" is vocalized with Holem in 20:25.

16:14 פֶּרֶץ עַל־פְּנֵי־פָרֶץ "breach upon breach" (cf. שֶׁבֶר עַל־שֶׁבֶר Jer. 4:20; הֹוָה עַל־הֹוָה Ezek. 7:26; and *shibishu ana pan shibitan* "seven times upon seven," in the *Tel el Amarna Letters*, 4, 189, cited by Friedrich Delitzsch. After the wall is breached at many points (14a), the besieger rushes in for the attack (14b).

16:15 The sackcloth may serve as a sign of Job's misery and mourning (II Ki. 16:30) or it may mean that the sackcloth never leaves his body (Ehr.). גֶּלֶד "skin" or "the scab that forms on a wound"; whence the mishnaic denominative root הגליד "harden," *M. Ohol.* 8:5; *M. Miqvaot* 9:2; *B. Keth.* 76b. וְעֹלַלְתִּי from the Aram. עלל "enter, thrust" — Arab. *ghalla* "thrust," whence the Hebrew עוֹל "yoke." Stich b: "I have thrust, buried my glory in the dust."

16:16 חֲמַרְמְרָה, the Kethib to be revocalized with Qameṣ, represents the older third person fem. plur. of the perfect still extant in Arab. *qatala* and Aram. *qetala*, but occurring only rarely in biblical Hebrew. In thirteen passages, including ours, the Qere reads the later form with Vav, a variation, not a correction, of the Kethib. In eight other passages there is no variation in MT, e.g. בָּנוֹת צָעֲדָה (Gen. 49:22). On this form, see *BTM*, list 18, pp. 104 f., and notes. In our passage, פָּנַי is fem., as in mishnaic Hebrew; cf. the common idiom בְּסֵבֶר פָּנִים יָפוֹת, "with a pleasant demeanor" (*M. Abot* 1:15); פָּנִים חֲדָשׁוֹת "a new face" (*B. Keth.* 7b). Hence the fem. plur. of the verb.

The verb חֳמַרְמָר occurs with two other subjects, with מֵעַי in Lam. 1:20 and with עֵינַי in Lam. 2:11. Two etymologies have been proposed; from *ḥamara* (undotted ḥa) "to dye red"; or *ḥamara* (dotted ḥa) "ferment, boil up." It is not impossible that both Arabic roots represent a secondary differentiation, since the two meanings are not too far apart. In our passage the verb may be rendered either "grow red" or "be puffed up, swollen." G. R. Driver's suggestion (*Festschrift Alfred Bertholet*, p. 137) that our verb is to be separated from the other two passages and rendered "twisted" would seem to be unnecessary.

Stich b refers either to the darkness of approaching death or to the loss of sight, due to weeping (D-G).

16:17 Stich a is almost surely a reminiscence of Isa. 53:9 עַל לֹא־חָמָס עָשָׂה (like Arabic *ᶜalay*, "notwithstanding = in spite of"; cf. Job 10:7; 34:6). Hence, stich a, "though there is no violence in my hands." In stich b the usual rendering "my prayer" for וּתְפִלָּתִי זַכָּה has been felt to be an inappropriate parallel to stich a, which is concerned with deeds vis-à-vis man, not with words vis-à-vis God. The emendations proposed, נְתִיבָתִי "my way" (Du.) or הִתְהַלַּכְתִּי (*sic*) "my walking" (Be.), are unappealing. On the basis of the root פלל "intervene, interpose," hence "arbitrate, judge" (cf. BDB, p. 813), it may be possible to render וּתְפִלָּתִי as "my judgment, i.e., the judgment issued upon me" (an objective genitive.) The stich would mean: "I have been adjudged free from guilt." On the other hand, the usual rendering may mean that Job has been upright in his relationship both with man and with God, which is the goal of Wisdom teaching. Cf. Pr. 3:4, "and find favor and grace in the eyes of God and man." וּתְפִלָּתִי may represent speech in generalized form; cf. Rashi, "I have never cursed my friends or wished them ill" (TS), so that the v. would represent Job's avowal of integrity, both in deed and in word.

16:18 The blood must be covered up, lest it continue to pollute the earth and bring a curse upon its inhabitants (Gen. 4:10; Ezek. 24:6–9), for blood demands vengeance if unjustly shed (Isa. 26:21). On the widespread blood taboo which served as the primitive basis for the exalted ethical prohibition of murder, cf. J. G. Frazer, *Folklore of the Old Testament* (London, 1918); Th. Gaster, *Myth, Legend and Custom in the Old Testament* (New York, 1969), pp. 69–72.

מָקוֹם "a place where it can be absorbed." TS renders the noun "stop, end, the place where one stands."

16:19 Job's second affirmation of faith. He sees God not merely as an impartial arbiter, but as a witness taking his part in his controversy with the unjust God of might who has afflicted him. The third and highest level of faith is reached in 19:25. On these important passages, see Special Note 15.

שְׁהֲדִי with *Sin* (cf. Gen. 31:47), an Aramaism chosen to serve as a synonym for the Hebrew עֵד. For other cases of Aramaisms being utilized to expand the vocabulary and give a parallel to Hebrew, cf. מִלִּין and דָּבָר (15:3); שַׂגִּיא and רַב (37:23); עֲרוֹד and פֶּרֶא (39:5) (D-G).

16:20   It is generally recognized that MT has suffered some errors. Stich a is both difficult to understand and shorter than stich b, a phenomenon which we believe to be highly dubious, except at the end of a section or poem (cf. *PPS*, pp. 67, 70 f.). LXX reads *aphikoito mou he deesis pros kurion*, which Be. renders: תְּפִלָּתִי תִגַּע אֶל אֱלוֹהַּ. This is, however, graphically far too distant to be related to MT. It is probably to be regarded as the effort to supply an appropriate stich for the v., especially since the original was incomprehensible to the translators.

In stich a, both words have been subjected to varied interpretations. רֵעָי, most naturally rendered "my friends," may have the meaning "my thoughts"; cf. Ps. 139:2. מְלִיצַי has been rendered: (a) "my interpreters" (on the basis of Gen. 42:23, *CIS*, I, 44, 88); (b) "intercessors" (as in Job 33:23); or (c) "my mockers" on the basis of לוץ (cf. Ps. 119: 51, etc.). The stich has, therefore, been understood variously: (a) "are my friends my intercessors?" (T); or (b) "my friends are my scorners" (D-G); or (c) "my inward thoughts are my intercessors" (Ehr., JPSV); (d) Theodore Gaster (VT, 1954) suggests: "my friends seek to divert me," citing Arabic *laʾṣa*; but the evidence is tenuous. The first view requires the assumption of a question. As for the second, there is actually no warrant for the meaning of "scorners" for the noun מְלִיצַי either in biblical or in postbiblical Hebrew. It is obviously distinct from the verb. The third interpretation — that his unspoken thoughts would intercede on his behalf — is too subtle and sophisticated a modern concept for Job in his bitter position.

P., following Ter., makes the attractive suggestion to read: מֵלִיץ רֵעִי אֶל אֱלוֹהַּ אֵלָיו דָּלְפָה עֵינִי which he interprets to mean: "Interpreter of my thoughts to God, toward whom my eyes drip." The reference would be to the unidentified "umpire" discussed in Special Note 15.

We propose a simpler change which would require only the assumption that by haplography אל was omitted once out of three pairs of identical letters. We would read: מְלִיצַי רֵעֵי אֵל אֶל אֱלוֹהַּ דָּלְפָה עֵינִי "My intercessors are God's friends, but to God does my eye drip." This reading restores an acceptable meter pattern (3:3) and avoids the necessity of assuming a question. For the ironic epithet "God's friends" applied to his adversaries, cf. **12:4** and the Comm. *ad loc.*

On the other hand, the meter of MT may be defended as containing an anacrusis, with the first two nouns being in the vocative and, therefore, outside the rhythm pattern. The v. may then be rendered: "Oh, my intercessors, my friends! It is to God that my eye weeps." The bitter irony is obvious.

As an instance of anacrusis, cf. Ps. 1:1; for an example where the presence of anacrusis leads to the total abandonment of the parallelistic structure, exactly as is proposed in our instance, cf. Ps. 1:4. For the vocative use of רֵעִי by Job, cf. 19:21.

דָּלְפָה "drip"; cf. Ecc. 10:18 and Ps. 119:28, hence "weep." For the up-surge of bitterness that follows after the mystic vision, cf. 19:25–27a, b, which is succeeded by vv. 27c, 28, 29.

16:21 The Vav introduces the conclusion of the plea implicit in 20b; "so that He might judge a man in controversy with God as fairly as He would judge between one man in a suit with his fellow." וְיוֹכַח "judge, decide"; cf. Isa. 2:4. On the preposition עִם in legal controversy, cf. Isa. 3:14; and on Lamed, cf. Ezek. 34:17. While אֵל is most often parallel to שַׁדַּי, it is parallel to אֱלֹהִים in 5:8, and occurs in parallel stichs in 12:6 and in adjoining stichs in 27:8, 9.

וּבֶן־אָדָם, "son of man, i.e. man," is, of course, a hallmark of Ezekiel's style. It occurs elsewhere in Job only in 25:6. However, five mss. read וּבֵין אָדָם and the defectiva spelling for the *ai* diphthong is amply attested: cf. דֹּתָינָה and דֹּתָן (Gen. 37:17), קַרְתָּן (Jos. 21:32) by the side of קִרְיָתַיִם; the Moabite orthography of דבלתן = דִּבְלָתָיְמָה (Jer. 48:22), and the usual spelling of יְרוּשָׁלַיִם without *Yod*; and see *BTM*, list 12, "The diphthong *Ai*," and the Comm. on 9:9. It is, therefore, better to regard וּבֵן = וּבֵין "between." On the parallel use of בֵּין and Lamed with verbs of judging, cf. Isa. 2:4.

16:22 יֶאֱתָיוּ = "are yet to come." For the masc. plur. verb after a fem. plur. subj., cf. Hos. 14:1; Cant. 6:9, etc.

CHAPTER 17

17:1 The metric change to a staccato two-accented tristich reflects Job's tremendous anguish (cf. 16:7, 8). נִזְעָכוּ, like the cognate נִדְעָכוּ (Job 6:17), = "be extinguished, burnt out." קְבָרִים לִי = literally "graves are before me, i.e., the grave awaits me." There is no need to dispose of the final Mem, either by the emendation קֶבֶר מִלִּי "the grave is before me," or to treat the Mem as the enclitic. קְבָרִים is a pl. of extension = "graveyard, cemetery" (cf. Ges.-K., sec. 124c), like קְבָרֹת in 21:32; II Ki. 22:20 = II Chron. 34:28; II Chron. 16:14 (D-G) and the plural יְצוּעִים (Ps. 63:7; Job 17:13), as against the sing. in Gen. 49:4; Ps. 132:3. The pl. suffix *ōth* as against *īm* does not affect the use, since both pl. endings become virtually interchangeable with masc. nouns. Cf. מִשְׁכָּנִים (Ps. 46:5) and מִשְׁכָּנוֹת (Ps. 132:5); זִכְרֹנִים (Job 13:12) and זִכְרֹנוֹת (Est. 6:1, etc.). The *oth* ending for masc. nouns is particularly characteristic of mishnaic Hebrew.

17:2 הֲלֹא = אִם לֹא = "indeed." הַתֻלִים here is not the abstract noun "mock-ery," like עֲשׁוּקִים in Ecc. 4:1 (D-G), but the Qātūl participle with middle force = "mockers." Cf. זָכוּר "mindful" (Ps. 103:14); אָחוּז "grasping" (Cant. 3:8); בָּטוּחַ "trusting" (Ps. 112:7). Nor need the noun be emended to הֲתֻלִּים

or הַתּוֹלִים. The Qātūl form corresponds to Qātōl, as in Syriac, which has both forms. For the latter form, cf. בָּחוֹן (Jer. 6:23); בְּגוֹדָה (Jer. 3:7, 10); and its frequent use in the Mishnah, as טָחוֹן "grinder"; לָקוֹחַ "buyer"; דָּרוֹכוֹת "treaders" (cf. Barth, *NB*, sec. 27).

וּבְהַמְרוֹתָם the Hiphil of מרה "to anger, provoke," which is used elsewhere with the preposition עִם (Deut. 9:7, 24; 31:27). On the use of the noun "eye" with the verb, cf. Isa. 3:8.

תָּלַן is an aberrant vocalization for תָּלֶן = תָּלִין "dwells" (cf. Isa. 1:21, צֶדֶק יָלִין בָּהּ). The eye is constantly exposed to their provocation and therefore yields to tears.

17:3 It has been generally recognized that עָרְבֵנִי is to be read as a noun עָרְבֹנִי (not עָרְבֵנִי), thus supplying an object to the verb שִׂימָה. Hence, stich a: "Set my pledge with you, i.e., accept my pledge." In stich b, however, the force of the Niphal has not been noted, and the use of the Qal תקע כף "strike the hand in pledge," as in Pr. 6:1; 11:15; 17:18; 22:26, etc., has been indiscriminatingly cited, the stich being rendered "and who will make a pledge?" (so P.). However, this meaning is entirely inappropriate. Since the Qal has the meaning = "strike the hand, *give* a pledge," the Niphal נתקע כף ל' means "permit the hand to be struck, i.e., *accept* a pledge." This is a clear instance of the *Niphal tolerativum*; cf. הַדְרֵשׁ "permit to be sought" (Ezek. 14:3; 20:3, 31, etc.); הַמָּצֵא "permit oneself to be found" (Isa. 65:1); הַוָּסֵר "let oneself be instructed" (Jer. 6:8; 31:18). It is Job who is offering a pledge for his integrity and it is God whom he asks to accept the pledge from His hand. Both stichs constitute a plea for God's trust in Job's uprighteousness.

17:4 תְרוֹמֵם lacks an object. It has therefore been emended to תְרוֹמְמֵם or תְרִימֵם "You will therefore not exalt them" (Me., Dil., D-G). However, on this view, the verse which accuses the Friends of lacking in sense is itself defective in logic — "Because you have deprived their minds of reason, you will not exalt them." MT is to be retained; the verb is to be revocalized as a Polal תְרוֹמֵם "You will not be exalted." On the Polal of the verb, cf. Neh. 9:5, where it likewise refers to God: וּמְרוֹמָם עַל כָּל בְּרָכָה וּתְהִלָּה. That the Friends have not been doing well in defending God has been Job's constant contention (cf. 13:7–12, and the Comm. *ad loc.*). Rashi's intuitive insight leads him to interpret "Your glory will not be exalted by them."

17:5 This difficult verse has been regarded by some as a marginal gloss, but since the meaning of the verse is obscure, one cannot see what purpose the gloss would have served. Others dismiss the verse as hopelessly corrupt, which the clear idiomatic Hebrew would seem to negate. It has been rendered:

(1) "He that for a reward (or for prey) denounces his friends — the eyes of his children shall fail," i.e., the Friends betraying Job deserve to have their children punished (D-G, Du., P.). Aside from the doubtful use of חֵלֶק in this meaning, Job has been objecting to the conventional idea that children should be punished for the sins of the fathers (cf. 21:19, 30, and the Comm.

ad loc.), a theory which both Eliphaz and Bildad have presented in their theodicy (4:10, 11; 18:19, 21, etc.). (b) חֵלֶק has been taken as "flattery," hence "he that speaks flattery to his friend" (AV) or "he who denounces his friend for the sake of flattery." The meaning assigned to the noun is dubious. (c) חֵלֶק has been rendered "share of the property" and therefore "he who informs against his friend, in order to get a share of the property" (RSV). However, the idea that the Friends expect to enrich themselves at Job's expense is nowhere even remotely indicated. (d) "At the sound of flattery, lit. smooth words (Pr. 7:21), a man announces 'These are true friends!' (and so he entrusts his wealth to them so that) his children's eyes fail with longing" (TS), a view which adds considerable baggage to the verse!

The brevity and idiomatic character of the verse suggest that what we have here is a familiar saying (so Bu., D-G, Du., Ehr., Peake, Hö.):

"He invites friends to a feast,
While his own children's eyes fail with longing (for food)."

This folk saying would seem originally to refer to those who seek to put on a pretense of wealth while they are actually poor. Here it is used metaphorically and effectively — Job's friends are dispensing wisdom to him when their own stock of this commodity is very slender. This view of the verse comports excellently with v. 4 above.

לְחֵלֶק may be rendered "to a share of the feast" (Bu.) or emended to לְחַלֵּק "to share his table" (cf. T למפלג, so Hö.). In either case, the usage remains unattested, as is the meaning assigned to יַגִּיד, but it is quite comprehensible. On the clipped character of popular phrases, see the Comm. on Job 2:4.

17:6 וְהִצִּיגֵנִי has been emended to וַתַּצִּיגֵנִי (Me., Sieg., Be., Du., D-G) = "You, i.e., God, have set me up" or וְהִצִּיגֻנִי "they have set me up" (Bu.). The third pers. sing. of the verb in MT would refer either to one of the Friends or preferably to God. It may perhaps be regarded as Job's bitter comment on the folk saying he has quoted: "Yet this fool dares to make me a byword among the people." On the practice of Wisdom writers, to cite a proverb and to append a comment, either in support or in ironic agreement, cf. *PPS*, pp. 135–38, and *BGM*, pp. 169 ff., especially p. 175, and note such passages as Ecc. 4:9–12; 5:9 f.; 7:9–18; 8:2–4, and see *KMW ad loc.*).

לִמְשֹׁל is vocalized in MT with a Holem and can therefore be construed only as an infinitive, "lit., he has set me up for the pronouncing of a byword of the nations." The word should obviously be vocalized as לִמְשֵׁל "a proverb, byword" (as in Deut. 28:37; I Ki. 9:7; Ps. 44:15, a. e.).

תֹּפֶת is derived from תּוּף "spit" (cf. נֹפֶת from נוּף, בֹּשֶׁת from בּוֹשׁ), and see *B. Keth.* 61b תוף שדאי "eject the spittle." Eth. *tafa* and Arab. *tuffa* "fie, shame" may be related to our word.

לְפָנִים is to be revocalized or understood as לַפָּנִים. Stich b is to be rendered "I have become spittle in the face," a breviloquence for "I have become one in whose face men spit" (cf. 30:10; Deut. 25:9). For the construction, cf.

Isa. 53:3 וּכְמַסְתֵּר פָּנִים מִמֶּנּוּ. "as one from whom there is a hiding of face" = "one from whom men hide their faces" (D-G). The attractive emendation מוֹפֵת לִפְנֵיהֶם, "a horrible example for them" (cf. Ps. 71:7) (so Perles and Be., Bu., D-G), is therefore not necessary. The older traditional rendering of תֹּפֶת as "Gehenna" (T) or "drum" (Ra.) are manifestly inappropriate in the context.

17:7 Stich a: "My eye has grown dim" — the familiar idiom symbolizing the loss of bodily vigor (Gen. 27:1; Deut. 34:7). יְצֻרַי = "my created parts, i.e., limbs, organs."

17:8 On the theme of 17:8–9, virtue and its reward, see Special Note 14. יָשֹׁמּוּ = "be astounded" (cf. 18:20; I Ki. 9:8; Jer. 19:8, a. e.). עַל־זֹאת "at the spectacle of Job's misery."

17:9 יֹּאחֵז = "will hold fast, cleave." יֹסִיף אֹמֶץ = "increase in strength, i.e., become more determined to follow his chosen path."

17:10 כֻּלָּם is probably a scribal error for כֻּלְּכֶם (so 5 mss.), induced by וְאֻלָם. The usage שִׁמְעוּ עַמִּים כֻּלָּם (I Ki. 22:28; Mic. 1:2) is not apposite. There the interposed noun breaks the need for complete agreement in person and permits the use of the basic third person form (as in Isa. 22:16; 54:1, 11; Mal. 3:9). תָּשֻׁבוּ = "return, i.e., try once again to justify your position."

17:11 According to the Masoretic accentuation, the verse is a tristich, lit. "my days are past, my thoughts are severed, desires of my heart." However, one would expect a verb in stich c. LXX correctly treated the verse as a distich, but was unable to do justice to the text. It renders: "My days have passed on the run, broken are the joints of my heart." Following LXX, the caesura is to be placed after זִמֹּתַי, thus restoring a 3:3 rhythm. זִמֹּתַי, which generally carries a negative connotation, "evil thoughts" (Isa. 32:7; Hos. 6:9; Job 31:11; Lev. 18:17), is here used neutrally, "my thoughts, plans, hopes." Similarly, מְזִמָּה, which generally means "evil plan, plot," is a synonym for wisdom in Pr. 1:4; 2:11; 3:21; 5:2, etc., and is used of God's plan in Job 42:2. עָבְרוּ = "pass on the road, hence, outstrip"; cf. Gen. 32:17; I Sam. 25:19; II Sam. 15:22; 16:11; Pr. 4:15.

מוֹרָשֵׁי לְבָבִי = מְאֹרָשֵׁי, cf. Akk. *êrištu* "desire" (Del., Dil., Du.), not "inheritances of my heart" but "desires of my heart"; cf. תַּאֲוַת לִבּוֹ ‖ אֲרֶשֶׁת שְׂפָתָיו (Ps. 21:3).

The verse is now to be rendered: "My days have passed (i.e. outstripped) my hopes (i.e., my life has lasted longer than my hopes); the desires of my heart are cut off." An analogy for the meaning we have proposed for stich a is to be found in Gen. 47:9 — "Few and evil have been the days of my life and they did not reach the days of the years of my fathers' life during the days of their sojourning."

17:12   This verse is generally taken to refer to the Friends who are charged with turning truth topsy-turvy: "they turn night into day." However, the analogy generally offered, Isa. 5:20: "Woe to those who call evil good and good evil, turn darkness into light and light into darkness," is an inadequate parallel, since both stichs in our verse speak of night (or darkness) turning into day (or light), which is a very weak charge indeed. Stich b has been rendered: "The light is short because of the darkness" (JPSV), which gives קָרוֹב a strange meaning and the verse a peculiar sense. Equally meaningless is the rendering; "The light, say they, is near unto darkness" (D-G). As they recognize, the radical change from stich a is difficult. In addition, מִפְּנֵי does not mean "into." Moreover, if the Friends are being denounced, the second person in direct address would have been far more appropriate, as in v. 10.

We believe that this verse exhibits a characteristic syntactic feature of the poet's style — the use of an entire verse as a subordinate clause, modifying a noun in the preceding verse without the use of the conjunction אֲשֶׁר. (Cf. the Comm. on 15:19.)

קָרוֹב is to be understood as "excellent, praiseworthy." Cf. M. Seidel in *Debir* (Berlin, 1923, vol. 1, pp. 3 ff.), who suggests that the root קרב has the meaning "praise, glorify" in וְקָרוֹב שִׁמְךָ (Ps. 75:2); קָרוֹב אַתָּה (Ps. 119:151). We have interpreted וְקָרוֹב לִשְׁמֹעַ (Ecc. 4:17) as "it is better to understand" (see *KMW ad loc.*). מִפְּנֵי is not prepositional; the idiom is שִׂים מִן "make something out of," as Ehr. brilliantly points out, citing כִּי שַׂמְתָּ מֵעִיר לַגָּל "for you have made out of the city a heap" (Isa. 25:2). Hence, our stich b means: "lit., they make blessed light out of the face of the darkness," i.e., "they make light out of darkness." The entire verse describes מוֹרָשֵׁי לְבָבִי in v. 11: "the desires of my heart, that could make night into day, excellent light out of darkness." Job has been deprived of the comfort that could be derived from thought and hope.

17:13   אִם is generally rendered "if," introducing the protasis of a condition extending over vv. 13, 14, and with 15 as the apodosis. However, there is nothing conditional about his imminent or ultimate death, and the particle does not mean "since." It is, therefore, better understood here, as often in Job, as the emphatic "indeed," like the Arab. *°inna* (cf. 6:13; 8:4; 14:5; 17:2, 16). אֲקַוֶּה not "await, hope for" but, as is clear from the parallelism, "I mark out," a denominative from קַו "line," תִּקְוָה "thread" (Jos. 2:17; Job 7:6) (so Yel.). On the theme, cf. Ps. 16:5; Am. 7:17. רפד "spread out, bed down" (cf. Job 41:22). רְפִידָתוֹ (Cant. 3:10) is a phonetic variant for רבד (Pr. 7:16). חֹשֶׁךְ, an obvious epithet for the grave. Stich a is to be rendered: "Indeed, I have marked out my home in Sheol."

17:14   שַׁחַת, from שׁוּחַ "sink down," a reference to Sheol as a pit in the earth. On the figure of speech employed by the poet, cf. Jer. 2:27; Pr. 7:4. The 4:3 rhythm of MT is a perfectly acceptable form of the *Qinah* rhythm; cf. 5:3; 9:10; 17:10; 18:2; 19:23; 23:23; 29:25; 30:16, 20; 33:1; 36:12; 37:2; 38:4, which are cited by D-G, who nevertheless delete אַתָּה to restore the 3:3 rhythm, quite unnecessarily. An even more radical procedure is adopted by Du., Be., who read לַשַּׁחַת קָרָאתִי אָבִי אַחֹתִי לָרִמָּה. We have pointed out (*Lešonenu*, 5732, vol. 36, pp. 71 f.) that the juxtaposition of אָבִי וַאֲחֹתִי in MT is validated by the Semitic usage noted by A. Loewenstamm (*Lešonenu*, 5730, vol. 34, p. 146), in which a vassal-king addresses his superior as both "father" and "brother," the former indicating the addressee's higher position, the latter their equivalent status as kings. This usage is also the key to the biblical name *Ahab*, which means "father-brother," both being epithets for God. On the various unsatisfactory efforts to interpret the name, see the Lexica. Job here calls the worm both "mother" and "sister" — "mother" because the worm has power over him, and "sister" because they are equally encased in the earth.

17:15 There is no real basis for changing תִּקְוָתִי to טוֹבָתִי in stich b following LXX, or to תַּאֲוָתִי. The author of Job, who had an unequalled command of the Hebrew vocabulary, could indulge his penchant for using the same root in both stichs, as has been repeatedly noted. (Cf. the Comm. on 8:3.) It is not unlikely that the paronomasia with אֲקַוֶּה in v. 13 influenced the repeated choice of תִּקְוָה here.

17:16 For stich a, LXX renders: הַעְמָּדִי שְׁאוֹל תֵּרַדְנָה which many moderns accept because they construe ʾim in stich b as interrogative (Du., D-G). Not only would the question be rather inept, but it would give a weak close to Job's speech; ʾim, as in v. 13 and frequently, is the emphatic particle "indeed."

בַּד "part, section," from בדד "to separate," occurs in various connotations: (a) "part of a tree, hence rod" (Exodus, chaps. 25 and 27 passim); (b) בַּדֵּי עוֹרוֹ "sections of flesh, i.e. organs" (Job 18:13); and (c) here "sections of the house, hence, chambers."

M. J. Dahood interprets בַּד as a contraction of *beyade* (*sic*), "in the hands of" (correctly, בְּיָדֵי). For the form, Ugaritic *b-d*, Tel-el-Amarna *ba-di-u* (contracted from *ba-yadi-hu*), and מִיַּד שְׁאוֹל, "out of the hand of Sheol" (Ps. 49:16), may be adduced. (Cf. Dahood, "Northwest Semitic Philology and Job," in J. L. McKenzie, *The Bible in Current Catholic Thought*, 1962, pp. 62 ff.) We have called attention to the opposite process, *beyad* as a phonetic equivalent of *beʿad* "for, on behalf of," which is well-attested in biblical Hebrew (cf. Gordis, "A Note on Yad," in *JBL*, vol. 62, 1943, pp. 341–44.) In our verse, however, the assumption of such a contraction is unnecessary, particularly since the verb "go down" suggests a destination. תֵּרַדְנָה is not a plural (Ehr.), but the fem. sing. subject with the *Nun energeticus* ending; cf. Ex. 1:10 כִּי־תִקְרֶאנָה; Jud. 5:26 תִּשְׁלַחְנָה; Isa. 27:11; 28:3; Ob. 1:13; Pr. 1:20; 8:3; נָחַת, as virtually all moderns have recognized, is to be revocalized as the Qal imperf. of נחת "go down," נֵחָת; i.e., "I and my hopes will descend." This "Aramaism" may well belong to the first category of "Aramaisms," part of the common North-West Semitic vocabulary, rather than a borrowing, since it occurs in Jer. 21:13; Ps. 38:3; Pr. 17:10; Job 21:13. On the four categories of "Aramaisms" in biblical Hebrew, see *BGM*, p. 162 and notes, and *KMW*, chap. VII and notes. On the utilization of Aramaic for poetic synonyms in parallelism, cf. the Comm. on 16:19.

The Speech of Bildad (18)

Job's misery evokes not one friendly word from Bildad. He feels keenly that he and his friends have been insulted. In spite of Job's unbridled attacks upon the justice of God, the laws of the universe remain unshaken, and retribution will ultimately overtake the evildoer. Bildad proceeds to describe the punishment of the sinner: his person, his family, his very name, all will be destroyed.

18   Bildad the Shuhite answered, saying,
2   How long will you go hunting for words?
             Acquire understanding and then we can speak.
3   Why are we accounted as cattle,
             considered stupid in your sight?
4   O you who tear yourself to shreds in your anger,
             shall the earth be forsaken on your account,
             or the rock be removed from its place?

5   In due course the light of the wicked is put out
             and the flame of his fire ceases to glow.
6   The light grows dark in his tent,
             and his lamp above him is put out.
7   His strong steps grow narrow,
             and his own schemes hurl him down.
8   For he is cast into a net as he walks,
             and he must tread over a snare;
9   A trap seizes him by the heels,
             a noose closes in upon him;
10   a rope is hidden for him in the ground,
             a trap upon his path.
11   Terrors frighten him on every side
             and pursue him in his tracks.
12   His child will go hungry;
             and disaster awaits his wife.
13   Each part of his body is consumed;
             Death's first-born devours his limbs.
14   He is torn from his tent where he felt secure,
             and is marched off to the King of Terrors.
15   A flood of fire is ensconced in his tent,
             brimstone is scattered on his dwelling.
16   His roots dry up below
             and his branches wither above.
17   His memory perishes from the earth,
             and he has no name abroad.
18   He is thrust from light into darkness
             and is driven out of the world.
19   He has neither kith nor kin among his people
             and no survivor in his dwelling.
20   At his day of calamity earlier ages are appalled,
             and horror seizes later generations.
21   Surely such are the dwellings of the evildoer,
             and this the place of him who knows not God.

יח א וַיַּעַן בִּלְדַּד הַשֻּׁחִי וַיֹּאמַר:

2 עַד־אָנָה | תְּשִׂימוּן קִנְצֵי לְמִלִּין   תָּבִינוּ וְאַחַר נְדַבֵּר:

3 מַדּוּעַ נֶחְשַׁבְנוּ כַבְּהֵמָה   נִטְמִינוּ בְּעֵינֵיכֶם:

4 טֹרֵף נַפְשׁוֹ בְּאַפּוֹ   הַלְמַעַנְךָ תֵּעָזַב אָרֶץ

5 וְיֶעְתַּק־צוּר מִמְּקֹמוֹ:   גַּם אוֹר רְשָׁעִים יִדְעָךְ

6 וְלֹא־יִגַּהּ שְׁבִיב אִשּׁוֹ:   אוֹר חָשַׁךְ בְּאָהֳלוֹ

7 וְנֵרוֹ עָלָיו יִדְעָךְ:   יֵצְרוּ צַעֲדֵי אוֹנוֹ

8 וְתַשְׁלִיכֵהוּ עֲצָתוֹ:   כִּי־שֻׁלַּח בְּרֶשֶׁת בְּרַגְלָיו

9 וְעַל־שְׂבָכָה יִתְהַלָּךְ:   יֹאחֵז בְּעָקֵב פָּח

10 יַחֲזֵק עָלָיו צַמִּים: טָמוּן בָּאָרֶץ חַבְלוֹ

11 וּמַלְכֻּדְתּוֹ עֲלֵי נָתִיב: סָבִיב בִּעֲתֻהוּ בַלָּהוֹת

12 וֶהֱפִיצֻהוּ לְרַגְלָיו: יְהִי־רָעֵב אֹנוֹ

13 וְאֵיד נָכוֹן לְצַלְעוֹ:   יֹאכַל בַּדֵּי עוֹרוֹ

14 יֹאכַל בַּדָּיו בְּכוֹר מָוֶת: יִנָּתֵק מֵאָהֳלוֹ מִבְטַחוֹ

טו וְתַצְעִדֵהוּ לְמֶלֶךְ בַּלָּהוֹת: תִּשְׁכּוֹן בְּאָהֳלוֹ מִבְּלִי־לוֹ

16 יִזֹרֶה עַל־נָוֵהוּ גָפְרִית: מִתַּחַת שָׁרָשָׁיו יִבָשׁוּ

17 וּמִמַּעַל יִמַּל קְצִירוֹ:   זִכְרוֹ־אָבַד מִנִּי־אָרֶץ

18 וְלֹא־שֵׁם לוֹ עַל־פְּנֵי־חוּץ: יֶהְדְּפֻהוּ מֵאוֹר אֶל־חֹשֶׁךְ

19 וּמִתֵּבֵל יְנִדֻּהוּ:   לֹא נִין לוֹ וְלֹא־נֶכֶד בְּעַמּוֹ

כ וְאֵין שָׂרִיד בִּמְגוּרָיו: עַל־יוֹמוֹ נָשַׁמּוּ אַחֲרֹנִים

21 וְקַדְמֹנִים אָחֲזוּ שָׂעַר: אַךְ־אֵלֶּה מִשְׁכְּנוֹת עַוָּל

וְזֶה מְקוֹם לֹא־יָדַע אֵל:

CHAPTER 18

18:2 The use of the 2nd pers. pl. תְּשִׂימוּן, תָּבִינוּ, and בְּעֵינֵיכֶם in direct address is strange, since Bildad is apparently addressing Job alone. Transferring these verses to Job or treating them as Bildad's summation of Job's position (so TS) does not solve the problem. Not only is the use of עַד־אָנָה characteristic of Bildad's style (cf. 8:2), but, more important, the verbs נֶחְשַׁבְנוּ and נִטְמִינוּ, which refer to the speaker, are also in the plural. On the other hand, emending all the plurals to the singular (so LXX) requires three changes which are not easy, in view of the *Nun Energeticus* ending of תְּשִׂימוּן and the pl. suffix of בְּעֵינֵיכֶם. There are some grounds for assuming that the pl. was used at times in direct address even to one person; cf. Cant. 5:1 שְׁתוּ וְשִׁכְרוּ דוֹדִים, and see the evidence from Arabic poetry in Gordis, *Song of Songs ad loc.*, as well as the later use in both the Hebrew and Arabic of the pl. in the greeting שָׁלוֹם עֲלֵיכֶם, *sala³m ᶜaleikum*, "Peace be upon you."

The Paseq after עַד־אָנָה may represent an effort by the Masorah to suggest the reading "How long — put an end to words!" treating קִנְצֵי as a dissimilation of קִצֵּי "end" (so Ra., Ges., Joseph Kimḥi). Hö. renders: "How long — put a fetter on your words!" But the abrupt pause after עַד־אָנָה contradicts its use everywhere else (e.g., Ex. 16:28; Nu. 14:11; Jos. 18:3; Jer. 47:6; Hab. 1:2; Ps. 13:2, 3; 62:4; Job 8:2; 19:2). The Arab. *qanṣa*, "take, ensnare, capture," has suggested the rendering of stich a as "How long will you set a trap of words?" Stich b, however, suggests that Job is being accused here not of cunning, but of a lack of understanding. Hence we render stich a "How long will you set a snare for words?" קִנְצֵי לְמִלִּין is a late form of the construct; cf. מְשַׁחֲרֵי לַטָּרֶף (Job 24:5); כִּסְאוֹת לְמִשְׁפָּט; הַבּוּ לַגֵאוֹנִים (Ps. 123:4); כִּסְאוֹת לְבֵית דָּוִד (Ps. 122:5); also Ps. 122:4, where we suggest vocalizing עֵדוּת as עֵדוֹת לְיִשְׂרָאֵל "the communities of Israel," parallel to שִׁבְטֵי יָהּ.

18:3 נִטְמִינוּ a *hapax legomenon* from the *tertiae Yod* root טמי, a metaplastic form for טמם, which occurs in Aramaic and in rabbinic Hebrew in the meaning of "stop up" (Targum Onkelos on Gen. 26:15 סְתֻמוּם — טמינון). Hence, the verb here means "considered stupid." (Cf. the rabbinic phrase טמטום הלב) Both the reading of LXX, "we are compared" (= נִדְמִינוּ), and that of Jerome, "we are polluted" (= נִטְמֵאנוּ), are inferior to MT.

18:4 Stich a is in the vocative, modifying the suffix of לְמַעֲנָךְ: "O, you who tear yourself to shreds in your anger." For the third person, cf. II Ki. 9:31 הֲשָׁלוֹם זִמְרִי הֹרֵג אֲדֹנָיו.

Job, like "the impassioned fool" in 5:2, has failed to display the patience which the true believer manifests in waiting for the process of Divine retribution to work itself out. Job's anger, not God's (cf. 16:9), is destroying him. In attacking the moral order, Job is demanding the overthrow of the natural order — for both are the manifestations of God. Therein lies the heart of the biblical faith — the God of nature and of human history is one, and the universe is therefore indestructible (cf. Isa. 45:18; Ps. 93:1–2). This faith in the identity of the God of nature and of history on a level incomparably deeper than Bildad's simplistic understanding will be reaffirmed in the God speeches at the end of the book.

18:5 גַּם "also" carries a connotation of reassurance, virtually "in due course," as in the phrase "this too will pass." Light is the obvious symbol of life, as darkness is of death. Note once again the poet's use of the same root in 5a and 6a.

שָׁבִיב "flame" occurs elsewhere only in Aramaic (Dan. 3:22; 7:9) and in modern Hebrew in the meaning of "spark."

18:7 צַעֲדֵי אוֹנוֹ "lit. the steps of his strength," a characteristic Hebraism for "his strong steps" (cf. הֵיכַל הַקֹּדֶשׁ = "holy temple"; Ps. 5:8; 79:1; 138:2, etc.). "Narrowing one's steps" means "to be in trouble" (cf. Pr. 4:12), the opposite of "broadening one's steps" (Ps. 18:37). For MT תַּשְׁלִיכֵהוּ "it will cast him down," LXX read by metathesis תַכְשִׁילֵהוּ "It will cause him to stumble." The assonance with שֶׁלַּח in v. 8, as well as the principle of *difficilior lectio*, supports MT.

18:8 Most moderns drop one Beth in stich a, reading either שֶׁלַּח בְּרֶשֶׁת רַגְלוֹ on the alleged basis of Septuagint, S (so Hö.), or שֶׁלַּח רֶשֶׁת בְּרַגְלוֹ. On either view there would be a lack of agreement between the masc. verb and the alleged fem. subject. More important, the parallelism suggests that the evil-doer is the subject. Hence, MT is to be preferred: "He is sent, i.e., cast, into a trap by his feet, i.e., as he walks."

The six synonyms for "trap" in vv. 8–10 shed light on one aspect of ancient Hebrew life, of which we otherwise know little (cf. Hö. *ad loc.*).

שְׂבָכָה is a network of branches covering the pit (cf. II Sam. 18:9 and 22:13).

18:9 On צַמִּים, a geminate from the root צמם "shrivel up, close up," hence "trap"; cf. the Comm. on 5:5.

18:11 בַּלָּהוֹת "terrors," probably a metathesis from בהל. וַהֲפִיצֻהוּ has been variously emended to הֶאִיצֻהוּ "rush him off"; הֵצִיקֻהוּ "they oppress him" (Hö.); הִפְלִיצֻהוּ "cause him to tremble" (TS). However, the root פוץ is obviously related to פצץ "crush," a meaning present in Pr. 25:18, where מֵפִיץ = מַפֵּץ "club, hammer" (cf. Nah. 2:2). Hence, MT can mean "crush him." However, even the usual meaning of the root פוץ is also satisfactory, "cause him to scatter, i.e. pursue, chase him" (RSV). לְרַגְלָיו "in his tracks" (cf. 13:27).

18:12 The various interpretations of this verse have been generally unsatisfactory. Thus, stich a: "His trouble shall be ravenous" (JPSV). Stich b: "Accident waits for his fall" (D-G). Hence, the text is regarded as uncertain (Hö.) and is drastically emended (Be.).

The parallelism demonstrates that T (לאתתיה) and Ra. understood the verse correctly. צֵלָע "rib" is by synecdoche a synonym for "woman, wife," on the basis of the familiar tale of woman's creation from Adam's rib (Gen. 2:21–22). The term occurs in this meaning in rabbinic Hebrew. Among the possible legal formulae of betrothal, the Talmud asks צלעתי מהו "if a man says to a woman, 'you are my rib,' is the marriage formula valid?" (*B. Kid.* 6a). We may also note the English slang term "rib" for woman. אֹנוֹ is "offspring"; lit., "product of man's strength, hence offspring." Cf. Gen. 49:3: כֹּחִי וְרֵאשִׁית אוֹנִי.

The verse now receives a simple and unforced meaning, "His offspring will go hungry and calamity awaits his wife." The suffering of a man's family was tantamount to his own punishment in biblical theology. Job takes vigorous exception to this doctrine in his refutation (chap. 21:19 f., 31).

18:13   This verse has been subjected to a plethora of emendations. Actually, it is an excellent example of complementary parallelism: a, b ‖ a', b', c, with a ballast added to b, עורו, to create a 3:3 meter. (Cf. Ps. 94:1, and see *PPS*, pp. 74 f.)

בַּד represents three homonyms in biblical Hebrew: (1) the root בדא, בדה "to lie, boast" (Isa. 12:6; 44:25; Job 11:3); (2) = בַּד "linen" (Ex. 28:42, a. e.); and (3) the root בדד "separate." The last-named meaning inheres in our passage. On the basic meaning of the noun, "section, part," and its specific connotation, see the Comm. on Job 17:16. The meaning "part of the body, limb" (Job 41:4 and probably Ex. 22:26 לְבַדָּה = לְבַדֹּה ‖ לְעֹרוֹ) is appropriate here.

בְּכוֹר מָוֶת "the first-born of death, i.e., the oldest son of the god Mot." In Babylonian mythology the plague is described as "a branch of Erech-Kigal, goddess of the nether-world." In Arabic, fever is described as *bint el manija*, "the daughter of fate." The god Mot, now familiar to us from Ugaritic, is personified in Isa. 28:15; Ps. 49:15; Job 28:22. It is part of biblical mythology (not myth!). A myth is a narrative about the gods and their actions, which is believed to be true; mythology is the utilization of myth for literary and artistic purposes by those who do not regard them as true. Thus, Mars in Virgil is myth; in Milton, mythology. On this crucial distinction, see Intr. and Special Note 37.

18:14   מֵאָהֳלוֹ מִבְטַחוֹ is a case of apposition, lit., "his tent, his security," virtually a hendiadys "the tent of his security" (cf. the Comm. on 5:15). וְתַצְעִידֵהוּ lit., "and it will make him march, i.e., he will be marched off." The impersonal may be expressed in biblical Hebrew, not only by the masc. sing. and by the masc. plural, but also by the fem. sing.; cf. וַתֵּצֶר לְדָוִד (I Sam. 30:6); תִּפָּקֵד (Isa. 29:6); תִּמָּשֵׁךְ (Ezek. 12:15); נֶעְכָּרֶת (Pr. 15:6); and see Ges.-K., sec. 144, 2. For another view of this passage, see M. Sarna in *JBL*, vol. 82, 1963, pp. 317 f.

מֶלֶךְ בַּלָּהוֹת, "the king of terrors, i.e., of the nether-world," may or may not be identical with Mot.

18:15 Stich a has been rendered: "There shall dwell in his tent those who are not his, i.e., his tent will be inhabited by strangers" (JPSV). TS refers stich a to his wife, "She will dwell in his tent without means, (or, better) without him." However, on the basis of the parallelism, we would expect not that strangers or his widow would inhabit his tent, but that his dwelling would be destroyed. Hö. has, therefore, proposed changing מִבְּלִי־לוֹ to לִילִית, the female night-demon mentioned in Isa. 34:14 and frequently in postbiblical literature. However, the parallelism with "brimstone" in stich b suggests that stich a carries a reference to fire. Actually, it is a witness to a very ancient mythological conception of "the flood of fire" which would destroy the world. It was familiar to Hellenistic Jewish writers (Philo, *Vita Mosis* 2, 36; Josephus, *Antiquities* 1, 2, 3), and is frequently referred to in rabbinic literature (*Mekhilta Yithro*, beginning p. 188; *Mekhilta de Rabbi Simon Bar Yohai*, p. 127; *B. Sanh.* 108b; *B. Zebahim* 116a; *Tosefta Taanit* 2:13, where the reading is מבול של אש ושל גפרית). The entire concept has been studied by Louis Ginzberg in his paper *Mabbul šel Eš* (*HaGoren*, vol. 8, pp. 35–51); cf. *idem, Legends of the Jews*, vol. 5, p. 149, Note 53; and S. Lieberman, *Tosefta Kipheshutah* (New York, 1962, Taanit, p. 1897, line 87), who cites additional early sources for the idea.

Our passage should therefore be emended slightly to read תִּשְׁכּוֹן בְּאָהֳלוֹ מַבּוּל and rendered "a flood of fire shall dwell in his tent." The biblical word מַבּוּל occurs elsewhere only in connection with the flood in Noah's day (Genesis, chaps. 6 ff., and Ps. 29:10), and so the word was understood only to refer to water, rather than to fire — thus helping to create and perpetuate the error in our text. The etymology of מַבּוּל is unknown, as is its gender. The older derivation was from יבל (Ges. *Thesaurus*); the more recent interpretation, "heavenly store of water jars" (Begrich, in *Zeitschrift fuer Semitistik*, vol. 6, pp. 135–53; Albright, in *JBL*, vol. 58, p. 98); both are doubtful. The derivation from Akk. *nabâlu*, "destroy" (Del.), is morphologically the soundest in view of the Dagesh in the Beth. Dahood (*Biblica*, vol. 38, 1957, pp. 312 ff.) correctly notes the meaning that is required in this stich. But there is no need to create a new *hapax legomenon mabhal*, "fire," on the basis of alleged Akk. and Ugaritic cognates, in view of the existence of מַבּוּל, well-attested in all stages of Hebrew, and of the concept of "the flood of fire." For a parallel to the use of "flood" without "fire," cf. the Comm. on 5:21, where "tongue" = "tongue of fire."

18:16 The verse contains a characteristic Semitic figure of total destruction of the person, occurring frequently on sarcophagi as a curse against desecration; cf. the Phoenician inscription of Eshmunazzar of Sidon, lines 11:12: אל יכן לם שרש למט ופר למעל and Hos. 9:16; Am. 2:9; Isa. 37:3.

יִמַּל better "wither" than "cut off" (cf. the parallelism and 14:2).

18:17 Destruction of the evil-doer will include the obliteration of his memory and of his offspring (v. 19).

18:18 יַנְדֻּ֫הוּ, as vocalized in MT, is either derived from נדד or is a defectiva spelling for יְנִידֻהוּ from נוד. In either case = "cause to wander."

18:19 נִין וָנֶ֫כֶד is an assonance, keeping the idiom intact in Gen. 21:23; Isa. 14:22, here broken up for the purpose of parallelism.

18:20 יוֹם "the day of calamity" (cf. I Sam. 26:10; Jer. 50:27; Ps. 37:13). אַחֲרֹנִים and קַדְמֹנִים is a merismus representing the totality of the human race. The terms may be construed geographically "men of the west" and "men of the east" (cf. Joel 2:20; Deut. 11:24; 34:2; Ezek. 47:18; Zech. 14:8). It is preferable to give the nouns a temporal meaning, namely, "later and earlier generations." Cf. Ecc. 1:11; Isa. 41:4; Ps. 48:14; and the frequent use in Deutero-Isaiah of the fem. רִאשֹׁנוֹת to refer to past events (Isa. 41:22; 42:9; 48:3). Bildad appeals to history to testify to the inevitable punishment of the wicked, as Eliphaz has done (15:18 ff.).

In describing terror, Hebrew may speak either of "terror seizing the person" (Ex. 15:14) or the person "taking hold of terror" (Job 21:6, and here: "earlier generations seize terror"; cf. Ezek. 27:35; 32:10).

18:21 מְקוֹם is construct to the entire phrase following; cf. Lam. 1:14, בִּידֵי לֹא־אוּכַל קוּם. "Knowing God" is the basic prophetic concept of obedience to the moral law; cf. Isa. 11:9; Hos. 4:1, where the catalogue of moral infractions is summarized in the closing stich by the phrase וְאֵין דַּעַת אֱלֹהִים בָּאָרֶץ.

Job's Reply to Bildad (19)

In this, his briefest utterance, Job touches both the depths of despair and the heights of faith. Bitterly he arraigns his friends, who have scorned him and ignored his misery. God's enmity has its counterpart in his estrangement from his kinsfolk and in the contempt of slaves and young upstarts. He pleads without hope for his friends' mercy.

In a passionate outburst, Job demands that his words be permanently engraved on a monument so that he may ultimately find vindication. In an ecstatic vision he is carried to the pinnacle of faith. In his unshakable assurance that there must be justice in the world, he sees the God of righteousness rising to his defense. God is not merely an arbiter waiting to judge him fairly, or even a witness ready to testify on his behalf, but a Redeemer who will fight his cause, even at the end of time. His faith reaches a new pinnacle in another respect as well. Earlier he had seen his witness in the heavens; now he sees his vindicator on the earth.

In this moment of mystical exaltation, Job feels his ultimate reconciliation with God engraved on his very flesh. He yearns to hold fast to the ecstatic experience, but it flees. The vision of the future fades as quickly as it has come, and there remains only the agony of the present. In wrath Job turns upon his friends and warns them of the dire punishment that awaits them for their cruelty toward him. Thus he ends as he began, bitterly upbraiding his hostile and uncomprehending Friends.

19 Then Job answered, saying,
2 How long will you torment me
   and crush me with your words?
3 It is now ten times that you have insulted me
   and have not been ashamed to abuse me.
4 Have I indeed erred,
   does my error adhere to me?
5 If, indeed, you wish to quarrel with me
   and justify the humiliation I have suffered,
6 know then that God has subverted my cause
   and surrounded me with His siegeworks.
7 Behold, I cry "Violence!" but I am not answered;
   I call out, but there is no justice.

8 He has fenced in my way so that I cannot pass,
   He has set darkness upon my paths.
9 My glory He has stripped from me,
   and removed the crown of my head.
10 He has broken me down on every side, and I perish;
   my hope He has uprooted like a tree.

11 He has kindled His wrath against me,
   and treats me as His foe.
12 His troops come forth all together;
   they have paved their road against me
   and have encamped around my tent.

13 My brethren are distant from me,
   and my friends are wholly estranged.
14 My kinsfolk and intimates no longer know me;
   the guests in my own house have forgotten me.
15 My maidservants count me a stranger —
   an alien have I become in their sight.
16 I call to my servant, but he does not answer.
   In words I must plead with him.
17 I am repulsive to my wife
   and loathsome to my own children.
18 Even my youngsters despise me;
   when I rise, they talk against me.
19 All my intimate friends abhor me,
   and those I loved have turned against me.
20 My bones cling to my skin and my flesh,
   and I have escaped only with the skin of my teeth.

21 Have pity on me, O my friends, have pity,
   For the hand of God has struck me.
22 Why do you persecute me like God
   and are not satisfied with my flesh?

23 O that my words were now written;
   O that they were inscribed on a monument,
24 that with an iron pen and lead
   they were hewn in the rock for ever!

יט א   וַיַּעַן אִיֹּוב וַיֹּאמַר׃

2   עַד־אָנָה תֹּוגְיוּן נַפְשִׁי   וּתְדַכְּאוּנַנִי בְמִלִּים׃

3   זֶה עֶשֶׂר פְּעָמִים תַּכְלִימוּנִי   לֹא־תֵבֹשׁוּ תַּהְכְּרוּ־לִי׃

4   וְאַף־אָמְנָם שָׁגִיתִי   אִתִּי תָּלִין מְשׁוּגָתִי׃

ה   אִם־אָמְנָם עָלַי תַּגְדִּילוּ   וְתֹוכִיחוּ עָלַי חֶרְפָּתִי׃

6   דְּעוּ־אֵפֹו כִּי־אֱלֹוהַּ עִוְּתָנִי   וּמְצוּדֹו עָלַי הִקִּיף׃

7   הֵן אֶצְעַק חָמָס וְלֹא אֵעָנֶה   אֲשַׁוַּע וְאֵין מִשְׁפָּט׃

8   אָרְחִי גָדַר וְלֹא אֶעֱבֹור   וְעַל נְתִיבֹותַי חֹשֶׁךְ יָשִׂים׃

9   כְּבֹודִי מֵעָלַי הִפְשִׁיט   וַיָּסַר עֲטֶרֶת רֹאשִׁי׃

י   יִתְּצֵנִי סָבִיב וָאֵלַךְ   וַיַּסַּע כָּעֵץ תִּקְוָתִי׃

11   וַיַּחַר עָלַי אַפֹּו   וַיַּחְשְׁבֵנִי לֹו כְצָרָיו׃

12   יַחַד ׀ יָבֹאוּ גְדוּדָיו   וַיָּסֹלּוּ עָלַי דַּרְכָּם

13   וַיַּחֲנוּ סָבִיב לְאָהֳלִי׃   אַחַי מֵעָלַי הִרְחִיק

14   וְיֹדְעַי אַךְ־זָרוּ מִמֶּנִּי׃   חָדְלוּ קְרֹובָי

טו   וּמְיֻדָּעַי שְׁכֵחוּנִי׃   גָּרֵי בֵיתִי וְאַמְהֹתַי לְזָר תַּחְשְׁבֻנִי

16   נָכְרִי הָיִיתִי בְעֵינֵיהֶם׃   לְעַבְדִּי קָרָאתִי וְלֹא יַעֲנֶה

17   רוּחִי זָרָה לְאִשְׁתִּי   בְּמֹו־פִי אֶתְחַנֶּן־לֹו׃

18   וְחַנֹּתִי לִבְנֵי בִטְנִי׃   גַּם־עֲוִילִים מָאֲסוּ בִי

19   אָקוּמָה וַיְדַבְּרוּ־בִי׃   תִּעֲבוּנִי כָּל־מְתֵי סֹודִי

כ   וְזֶה־אָהַבְתִּי נֶהְפְּכוּ־בִי׃   בְּעֹורִי וּבִבְשָׂרִי דָּבְקָה עַצְמִי

21   וָאֶתְמַלְּטָה בְּעֹור שִׁנָּי׃   חָנֻּנִי חָנֻּנִי אַתֶּם רֵעָי

22   כִּי יַד־אֱלֹוהַּ נָגְעָה בִּי׃   לָמָּה תִּרְדְּפֻנִי כְמֹו־אֵל

23   וּמִבְּשָׂרִי לֹא תִשְׂבָּעוּ׃   מִי־יִתֵּן אֵפֹו וְיִכָּתְבוּן מִלָּי

24   מִי־יִתֵּן בַּסֵּפֶר וְיֻחָקוּ׃   בְּעֵט־בַּרְזֶל וְעֹפָרֶת

25   For I know that my Redeemer lives,
          though He be the last to arise upon earth!
26   Deep in my skin this has been marked,
          and in my very flesh do I see God.
27   I myself behold Him,
          with my own eyes I see Him, not with another's —
          my heart is consumed with longing within me!

28   When you say, "How shall we persecute him,
          since the root of the matter must be found in him?"
29   I answer, "Be afraid of the sword,
          for yours are crimes deserving the sword,
          and you will learn that there is a judgment."

כה לָעַד בַּצּוּר יֵחָצְבוּן׃   וַאֲנִי יָדַעְתִּי גֹּאֲלִי חָי

26 וְאַחֲרוֹן עַל־עָפָר יָקוּם׃   וְאַחַר עוֹרִי נִקְּפוּ־זֹאת

27 וּמִבְּשָׂרִי אֶחֱזֶה אֱלוֹהַּ׃   אֲשֶׁר אֲנִי ׀ אֶחֱזֶה־לִּי

עֵינַי רָאוּ וְלֹא־זָר׃   כָּלוּ כִלְיֹתַי בְּחֵקִי׃

28 כִּי תֹאמְרוּ מַה־נִּרְדָּף־לוֹ   וְשֹׁרֶשׁ דָּבָר נִמְצָא־בִי׃

29 גּוּרוּ לָכֶם ׀ מִפְּנֵי־חֶרֶב   כִּי־חֵמָה עֲוֹנוֹת חָרֶב

לְמַעַן תֵּדְעוּן שַׁדִּין׃

CHAPTER 19

19:2   Both verbs contain the imperfect with *Nun energeticus* (cf. Hos. 5:15; Pr. 1:28). Yel., who calls attention to the assonance of *Nun* in the verse, suggests that the original text may have read בְּמִלִּין with a Nun.

תּוֹגְיוּן the Hiphil of יגה "cause to suffer" (Isa. 51:23; Lam. 1:5, 12; 3:32).

19:3   תַּהְכְּרוּ is a *hapax*, except possibly for Isa. 3:7. A variety of interpretations have been proposed on the basis of Semitic cognates: (1) "be impudent toward me" (not "harden your hearts at me," D-G), on the basis of an Arab. root *hakara*, which Joseph Kimhi explained as תעיזו פניכם לי and for which Isa. 3:9 הַכָּרַת פניהם is adduced. (2) *hakara* "wonder" (Ki., Schultens, Del.); (3) *ḥakara* "wrong, detract from" (Ew., Del.). (4) The parallelism with תַּכְלִימוּנִי suggests the meaning "insult, despise," for which the Arab. *ḥaqara* may be noted, in spite of the assumed equivalence of Arabic qa and Heb. Kaph (Eitan, Yel.).

19:4   The verse may be taken as a condition, with stich a as the protasis, "and even indeed if I have erred," and stich b as the ironic apodosis, "the error has lodged with me!" Job would be asserting that the evil of his error has not infected anyone else. On the other hand, Ehr. emends אַף to הַאַף and takes stich a interrogatively and parallel to stich b:

> "Have I indeed sinned?
> Has my offense lodged with me?"

This proposed emendation is, however, not called for. Thus Gen. 3:1 אַף־כִּי אָמַר אֱלֹהִים, "Did God really say?" corresponds exactly to כִּי וְאַף אָמְנָם being the asseverative. On the use of הַאַף, cf. Gen. 18:13, 23, 24; Am. 2:1; Job 34:17; 40:8, and BDB, p. 65a.

The latter interpretation is favored not merely by the parallelism but also by the use of the verb תָּלִין "dwell, abide" (cf. Job 17:2; Isa. 1:21). In this verse, Job denies that he has been guilty of error. In the two succeeding verses he argues that if some imperfection adheres to him, it is due to the sufferings he has undergone at God's hand.

19:5   This verse is the protasis of which v. 6 is the apodosis. תַּגְדִּילוּ is usually rendered "you magnify yourself against me." The idiom occurs frequently (Jer. 48:26, 42; Ezek. 35:13; Zeph. 2:10; Ps. 35:26; 38:17; 55:13). However, the parallelism in most of these passages and the Arab. cognate *jadala* III, "to quarrel"; IV, "quarrel with one another"; *jidaᵓl* "dispute," suggest a more appropriate meaning here and in most of the other passages: "If you wish to quarrel with me." וְתוֹכִיחוּ is declarative, "declare right, justify." Cf. the Comm. on 13:15.

19:6 עִוְּתָנִי = "has perverted my cause"; cf. Lam. 3:36. מְצוּדוֹ is not the noun מָצוֹד "net, trap" (Ecc. 7:26), but, as the verb הִקִּיף, "surrounded," indicates, מְצוּדָה "fortress, stronghold," with the pronominal suffix added to the stem. On this morphological usage, not hitherto recognized, which would remove some nonexistent nouns from the lexica, see the Comm. on 5:13; 11:9. Here the noun means "breastworks, siegeworks," a reference to the temporary wall that besiegers built around a city they were attacking. The metaphor is clearly that of military action (cf. v. 12), not a hunting trip (as in 18:8–10).

19:10 וָאֵלַךְ has the connotation of the Arab. *halaka*, "perish" (cf. Job 15:20).

19:11 The assonance of the Heth and the ā vowel in vv. 11 and 12a is particularly striking; hence וַיַּחַר in the Hiphil, "he heats up his anger"; כְצָרָיו the plural is distributive, "as one of his foes"; cf. the Comm. on לְנַעֲרוֹתֶיךָ (Job 40:29); בְּעָרֵי גִלְעָד (Jud. 12:7); בֶּן־אֲתֹנוֹת (Zech. 9:9); and Ges.-K., sec. 124, 1, note 2 (p. 387).

19:12 Stich b refers most naturally to the paving of roads for the passage of chariots and horses. The troops gather — roads are made ready for their march and siege is laid to Job's tent. God's troops may refer to the plagues or other calamities that He has inflicted on him.

19:13 Job now turns from the external miseries he has suffered at God's hands to the anguish he has sustained within the circle of his home. He describes his alienation in a crescendo of agony, first from his friends (vv. 13, 14), then from his slaves (vv. 15, 16), and, finally, from his wife and children (vv. 17, 18).

הִרְחִיק, if taken transitively, would mean "He, i.e., God has removed" (D-G). The parallelism suggests, however, that it is best taken intransitively and read as a plural (so LXX, S): הִרְחִיקוּ "are distant" (cf. Gen. 44:4), the Vav having been lost by haplography. יֹדְעַי = "my friends, they who know me," or "relations" (cf. מוֹדָע Ruth 2:1, Qere; Pr. 7:4). LXX read or interpreted the verb in stich b as אַכְזָרוּ "were cruel," but the preposition *min* requires a substantive. אַךְ is the emphatic particle (Deut. 16:15; 28:29; Isa. 16:7; 19:11), and the stich is to be rendered "my friends are wholly alien to me."

19:14 The 2:2 meter in this verse and the 5:3 meter (!!) of v. 15 are anomalous in a chapter where the 3:3 pattern prevails with great consistency, as virtually all moderns have recognized. Fortunately, the remedy is at hand — גָּרֵי בֵיתִי is to be added to v. 13 and the caesura placed after וּמְיֻדָּעַי, so that both vvs. 14 and 15 now exhibit a 3:3 pattern.

The Vav of וְאַמְהֹתַי is best deleted as a virtual dittography from the Yod in בֵיתִי. חָדְלוּ קְרוֹבָי "my relatives ceased (being near)." (Cf. I Sam. 2:5 וּרְעֵבִים חָדֵלּוּ "those hungry ceased (being hungry)." וּמְיֻדָּעַי could be either "kinsmen" (cf. Ruth 2:1 Kethib; מוֹדַע Ruth 2:1 Qere; Pr. 7:4); or "friend" (II Kings 10:11; Ps. 31:12; 55:14; 88:19.)

19:15 גָּרֵי בֵיתִי is "friends lodging in my house." (Cf. מִשְׁכֶנְתָּה וּמִגָּרַת בֵּיתָהּ, Ex. 3:22.)

תַּחְשְׁבֻנִי is a violent contraction of the third pers. fem. plur. תַּחְשְׁבֻנָה with suffix.

19:16 Stich b may be taken either as co-ordinate: "I must supplicate him with my mouth," or subordinate: "Even though I supplicate him." The word order is emphatic: "In words I must supplicate him." In the West Indies and in other parts of the world, the master never calls his servant by words; he merely claps his hands to summon him. Job must demean himself to speak, indeed to plead with his slave — but even this is unavailing.

19:17 רוּחִי has been rendered: (a) "breath" (JPSV); (b) "sighing" (cf. Lam. 3:56–TS). It is best taken as "my passion, desire"; cf. וּשְׁאָר רוּחַ לוֹ (Mal. 2:15, and see Ehr. *ad loc.*). This nuance may be derived from the rapid and intense breathing during sexual excitation. זָרָה "is abhorrent," from זוּר "be strange," Arab. *dha'ra*, not "abhors" (D-G), which is transitive and not appropriate here.

וְחַנּוֹתִי is generally taken as "and I supplicate her for children," a Qal from חנן. It is better understood as cognate to Arab. *hanna*, "emit an evil odor," hence "I am loathsome to my children" (cf. הִבְאַשְׁתֶּם אֶת־רֵיחֵנוּ, Ex. 5:21). The death of Job's children in the Prologue is no objection to this interpretation, since the poet does not trouble to harmonize every detail of the prose tale with the poetry. Note the difference between Job's complaint here about his wife (v. 17a) and her deep sympathy for him in 2:9. This lack of concern with apparent "contradictions" is a characteristic of Semitic literary composition important for an understanding of Job, and reflected elsewhere in the Balaam pericope (Numbers, chaps. 22–24), and the David narratives in Samuel (I Sam. 16:22; 17:55), as well as in Arabic literature. (Cf. *BGM*, p. 73 and p. 326, note 42.)

בְּנֵי בִטְנִי need not be understood as "children of my tribe" on the basis of the Arabic cognate (Robertson-Smith, TS), but "children of my womb," a breviloquence for "the children I have engendered." On the inexact use of בֶּטֶן, cf. the Comm. on 1:21 and 3:10.

19:18 עֲוִילִים is a diminutive from Arabic *gha'la* "suck," עָלוֹת "suckling cows" (I Sam. 6:7; Isa. 40:11; 49:15), or from the Arabic *'a'la* "feed, sustain"; hence "youngster, child"; cf. Rabbi Levi's statement in *Midrash Ber. Rabba*, chap. 31 בערביא צווחין ליניקא עוילא, "In Arabia they call a child *'avila*." The Mem is best deleted as a dittography from מָאֲסוּ (Wetz., Del., Yel.), and the noun vocalized as עֲוִילַי "my children," thus bringing it into harmony with all the other nouns in vv. 13–16. The LXX reading *eis ton aiona* "to all eternity"(= עוֹלָם, or even עֹלָם) demonstrates that defective orthography was in existence, in some Hebrew mss. at least, as late as the Greek version of Job.

19:19   וְזֶה is the archaic conjunction (Old Aram. זי, late Aram. די) = אֲשֶׁר; cf. Jud. 20:16; Job 15:17, not the demonstrative pronoun with the relative omitted (D-G). Hence the plural verb is in place.

19:20   In stich a, "my bones cleave to my skin and my flesh" constitutes a vivid description of emaciation and illness (Ps. 102:6; Lam. 4:8). עוֹר is the outer skin; בָּשָׂר, the inner layer of flesh (cf. Job 10:11).

Stich b is a famous crux — three possible bases for the root have been suggested: (a) from the meaning "escape," AV renders: "I am escaped only with the skin of my teeth." This rendering has become an English idiom. This is taken to mean that all his flesh has wasted away, except his gums (Ra., Gers.). (b) from the root מלט "to tear out the hair," for which the Arab. and Ethiopic *malaṭa* is a cognate and Hebrew מרט a parallel form. Sym. renders *exetillon*, hence "I am bald at my lips" (J. D. Michaelis) or "at my cheeks" (Ibn Masnut), or "I am left bald with the skin of my teeth" (Be.). (c) from a root מלט "cleave," whence מֶלֶט "mortar, cement" (Jer. 43:9) and the Syriac *melaṭa*. Hence, "I cleave to the skin of my teeth, i.e. my cheeks are emaciated." The parallelism with דָּבְקָה would favor this interpretation, but the first pers. is difficult and the etymology of the root uncertain.

Out of the welter of emendations proposed, the best is בְּעוֹרִי דָבְקָה עַצְמִי וָאֶתְמַלְּטָה בִּשְׂרִי בְּשִׁנָּי "My bones cleave to my skin and I am escaped, with my flesh in my teeth" (Bi., Bu.), since it is graphically closest to MT (D-G), and is, at least, not un-Hebraic. However, it cannot be pronounced superior to MT. The repetition of the same word עוֹר in both stichs is characteristic of Job's style and cannot be invoked to delete the noun. See Special Note 4. Moreover, the omission of the noun would destroy the *Qinah* rhythm (4:3) which is highly appropriate for Job's outcry and continues in the entire section. See Special Note 16 for a discussion of the meter of the entire section.

There is no valid reason for surrendering MT, which may be understood — either according to the first or the last interpretation — to mean "I escaped with nothing left," or "and I was cleaving to the skin of my teeth."

19:21   אַתֶּם רֵעָי. The pronoun is emphatic, "you who are my friends."

19:22   The unrestrained vigor of Job's onslaught may be too strong for some Western tastes, but not for Job in his agony. Hence stich a: "Why do you persecute me like God?" need not be emended to כְּאַיָּל "like a stag" (Reiske). Similarly, stich b is not to be given a figurative meaning, "slander," on the analogy of the Aram. idiom אכל קרצי פ׳ lit., "to eat the figs, i.e. slander" (Dan. 3:8; 6:25), Akk. *karṣe akâlu* and the Syriac *ʾakelquarsa*, "the Slanderer," an epithet for the Devil. The stich is to be taken literally: "And you are not satisfied with my flesh."

19:23 On the theme of 19:23–29, Job's vision of his Vindicator, see Special Note 16.

In view of Job's desire for *ultimate* vindication, בַּסֵּפֶר must refer to durable material and can scarcely mean "book" or "scroll," particularly in view of the instruments mentioned in 24a. TS seeks to meet the problem by regarding this verse as a quotation of a suggestion advanced by the Friends which Job rejects, but the alleged idea is highly involved and the refutation by no means clear. בַּסֵּפֶר has accordingly been interpreted: (a) "in writing" (Israel Friedlander, in *JQR*, 1903, pp. 101 f.); (b) "in bronze" (cf. Akk. *sipparu*, Arabic *sufr*, *sifr*, "bronze, copper"). In this connection, Pope calls attention to the Copper Scroll found in *Qumran*; (c) or, best, "inscription, monument" (cf. Isa. 30:8 סֵפֶר ‖ לוּחַ; *Aḥiram Inscription* l. 2), which is supported by the reference to בַּצּוּר "on a rock" (v. 24), the material on which the text is to be inscribed.

וְיֻחָקוּ the Hophal of חקק "inscribe, engrave" (Isa. 10:1; 49:16; Ezek. 4:1; 23:14). We have here the Aramaizing form of the geminate, in which the first consonant rather than the second is compensated for by a *Dageš* (cf. יִדְּמוּ Ex. 15:16; וַיַּכְּתוּ Deut. 1:44); hence, the Koph does not receive a *Dageš*. However, since the Heth is a guttural, it is "virtually" duplicated, and it, too, receives no *Dageš*. Because the verb is in pause, the original Pataḥ becomes a Qameṣ.

19:24 In stich a, D-G and Bu. emend to read בְּעֹפֶרֶת and then interpret vv. 23b and 24 as representing three types of writing: (a) סֵפֶר "scroll"; (b) עֹפֶרֶת "lead tablet"; and (c) צוּר "stone." Not only is the change unnecessary, but Jer. 17:1 is highly instructive for our passage: חַטַּאת יְהוּדָה כְּתוּבָה בְּעֵט בַּרְזֶל בְּצִפֹּרֶן שָׁמִיר חֲרוּשָׁה עַל־לוּחַ לִבָּם וּלְקַרְנוֹת מִזְבְּחוֹתֵיכֶם. The Jeremiah passage describes the writing instruments by two terms: an iron stylus (עט ברזל) and a diamond point (צפרן שמיר), and the material upon which the writing is done by one, a tablet (לוח) emblazoned on the altars. Similarly, in our passage, two terms are used to describe the instruments, עט ברזל and עפרת, and one, the material upon which the writing is done (צור). Ra. explains that the lead was poured into the chiseled-out letters, but there is no evidence for this practice in antiquity, and the text should then have read differently (Hö.). Dh. suggests that in the mixture of lead and iron, the lead served to color and mark the letters to be inscribed by the hewer. Hö. renders עֹפֶרֶת as "magnesite," citing Bertholet, Haupt, and Jensen. In view of our ignorance regarding the technology involved, it is best to retain the more familiar term "lead" and refer it to an alloy used in making the stylus.

19:25 The older Jewish and Christian exegetes saw in this verse and the following an affirmation of faith in bodily resurrection. This view has been rightly surrendered by modern scholars. Nevertheless, the passage is of crucial importance, marking the crescendo of faith to which Job attains. On his three levels of faith and their implications, see Special Notes 15 and 16.

Since Job has demanded that his words be inscribed on a permanent memorial, the most natural view of this verse is to interpret it as expressing his assurance of future vindication, for he knows that his Redeemer is now alive.

It is noteworthy that the formula וַאֲנִי יָדַעְתִּי, "I surely know," occurs in two radically different passages in Oriental literature which have come to light.

In a Ugaritic liturgical text which has described the death of the god Aliyn Baʿal, the worshipper triumphantly announces the rebirth of his god:

> And I know that the powerful Baal lives;
> Existent is the prince, Lord of the earth.
>
> (ANET, p. 140)

The idea of a dying god coming to life is obviously appropriate to the Canaanite worshipper. For the Hebrew poet the notion is totally impossible, since his God is not a nature deity whose life fluctuates with the seasons, but a God who rules over nature and stands above it. Job is contrasting his own brief and tragic life, during which he has found no vindication, with the eternal God, by whom he will ultimately be justified.

In the Babylonian poem, *I will praise the Lord of Wisdom*, the so-called "Babylonian Job," the poet first describes the hatred of his foes and then proclaims his faith

> My ill-wisher heard it and his countenance shone (with joy)
> They brought the good news to the woman
>   who was my ill-wisher and her spirit was delighted.
> But I know the day when my tears will come to an end,
> When among the protecting deities their divinity will show mercy.
>
> (Tablet II, ll. 52–55; ANET, pp. 435 f.)

Here we have another instance of the sudden change of mood from despair to confidence which is particularly striking in the Job passage. Unlike the Babylonian poet, however, Job looks forward to his moral vindication, not to his physical restoration. Moreover, the Babylonian poet does not invoke his god as do Job and the Ugaritic worshipper.

The biblical poet thus shares points of similarity and of difference with the Ugaritic and Babylonian writers. What all three passages have in common is the triumphant affirmation: "I know." Whether the usage existed as a fixed liturgical formula or is simply coincidental cannot be determined. In any event, in view of the vast temporal and geographical disparities, there is no likelihood of direct borrowing by the Hebrew poet. At most, we have here another element common to the ancient Oriental culture-sphere.

A human *gōʾēl* is a kinsman; hence an active defender of one's interests, redeeming one from bondage (Lev. 25:48, 49), repurchasing a field (Lev. 25:26, 33; Ruth 4:4, 6) and marrying a childless widow (Ruth 3:4, 6, 13) which, incidentally, is not a case of a levirate marriage. (Cf. Gordis, "Love and Business in the Book of Ruth," in *Jacob Myers Festschrift*.) The *gōʾēl* is, above all, the blood avenger (Nu. 35:19; Deut. 19:6, 12: Jos. 20:3; II Sam. 14:11).

God as the *gō^ʾēl* is the redeemer from Egyptian bondage (Ex. 6:8) and from the Babylonian Exile (Isa. 43:14; 44:22, 23, etc.). In personal relations, He is the avenger of wrong (Ps. 119:154; Pr. 23:11).

In view of the uncompromising monotheism of the Book of Job, there is no basis for postulating a third, intermediate being either as a kinsman in our passage, or as an arbiter (9:33), or as a witness (16:1). See Special Note 15. It is God to whom Job appeals and whom he sees rising to vindicate him even in the distant future. At the other extreme is Ibn E.'s view that the *gō^ʾēl* is a human figure who will vindicate Job. This approach is equally unacceptable in view of 16:19 ("in the heavens") and the clear implications of the v. that Job's redeemer may not emerge until the end of time. Ra. has correctly understood the passage: לאחר שיכלו כל שוכני עפר הוא אחרון יעמוד "After all the dwellers in the dust will have completed their life's course, He will arise at the last."

Stich b is best taken as a concessive clause of condition: "Though He be the last to stand on the dust." The emphatic position of וְאַחֲרוֹן is unmistakable. עַל־עָפָר "lit., upon the dust, i.e., upon the earth"; cf. Job 41:25.

19:26 As has often been noted, the verse cannot refer to Job seeing God after his body decays (AV, JPSV, D-G). Nor, coming after the vision of God, can the passage refer to his present sufferings. It is best interpreted as meaning that he sees the vision of God vividly in his own person, unmediated by any other being or tradition. וְאַחַר עוֹרִי "from behind my skin" (cf. אַחַר הַדֶּלֶת וְהַמְּזוּזָה Isa. 57:8), hence, "deep in my skin" is parallel to מִבְּשָׂרִי "out of my flesh."

עוֹר and בָּשָׂר, like עֶצֶם and בָּשָׂר, represent the person (Job 2:5) or, figuratively, the *alter ego* (Gen. 2:23; 29:14; II Sam. 19:13, 14); cf. the use of עוֹר in Job 2:4.

נִקְּפוּ is difficult whether derived from נקף I "strike off" (Ibn E., Wr.) whence "after my skin which they have struck off" (BDB), or "if my skin be crushed" (Hö.), or from נקף II "go around." The latter root in the Hiphil (Lev. 18:27 has the meaning "round off," which suggests for our passage "mark off." נִקְּפוּ may be construed with difficulty as a third pers. masc. plur. used impersonally, "they mark this off, i.e., this is marked off," or it is to be emended to the Niphal נִקְּפָה. אֶחֱזֶה אֱלוֹהַּ "I see God," uses the poetic verb חזה in reference to God (Ex. 24:11; Ps. 11:7; 17:15). The more prosaic and palpable root ראה was generally vocalized by the Masorah as a Niphal on theological grounds (Ex. 23:15; 34:23; Deut. 16:16, and see BDB, p. 908a bottom. Ex. 24:10 is an exception).

19:27 The use of the pronoun אֲנִי and the entire stich b make it clear that Job is stressing the fact that he himself is experiencing the mystic vision. Hence, it need not be regarded as a perfect or prophetic certitude referring to the future (D-G). לִי is an ethical dative, which heightens the emphasis on the immediacy of the experience for Job. Unlike the Friends, he is not citing the teaching of tradition or the testimony of the ancients, but his own existential experience. But this moment flees as rapidly as it came, and Job is left with a passionate but helpless longing for the lost ecstasy.

וְעֵינַי רָאוּ וְלֹא־זָר can hardly be construed as referring to the future, "my eyes shall see (no stranger)" even if a Yod be added to read יִרְאוּ (Bu.) and the Vav of וְלֹא be deleted. The stich means "my eyes see Him, and not a stranger's, i.e., no other person's eyes." Cf. יְהַלֶּלְךָ זָר וְלֹא פִיךָ (Pr. 27:2; B.S. 40:29).

The verb כָּלָה "complete, be at an end, be spent" is used with various bodily organs to mean "fail with longing"; cf. כָּלָה שְׁאֵרִי וּבְשָׂרִי (Ps. 73:26); כָּלוּ עֵינַי (Ps. 69:4; 119:82, 123); כָּלְתָה נַפְשִׁי (Ps. 84:3). The reins (or kidneys) were the seat of the emotions in Hebrew psychology (cf. Ps. 16:7; Pr. 23:16).

On the swift alternation of mood, see Special Note 16. The profound dejection that follows the exaltation of the mystic experience has been described frequently in literature (see the quotation from Rabbi A. I. Kuk in *BGM*, p. 89). Far from being "a rather limp conclusion to what precedes" (P.), it marks the sad aftermath to Job's ecstatic vision and is eminently appropriate to the context.

19:28 If מַה is rendered "how" (cf. מַה־נִּצְטַדָּק Gen. 44:16; Nu. 23:8; I Sam. 10:27), stich b is a circumstantial clause, "seeing that the root of the matter is in him, i.e., Job." If מַה is rendered "why" (cf. מַה־תִּצְעַק אֵלָי Ex. 14:15; 17:2; II Ki. 6:33; Ps. 42:6), stich b is the answer: "If you say, 'Why do we persecute him?', the root of the matter is found in him." We prefer the first interpretation. On either view בִּי is to be changed to בּוֹ with LXX, Th., T, V, and about one hundred manuscripts. Job declares that the Friends are convinced that at the very least Job must have been guilty of some sins to have received such heavy punishment.

19:29 The difficulties of vv. 28 and 29 lead P. to describe them as "a jumble of verbiage." Actually, matters are not so hopeless. Job responds to the Friends' explanation of their hostility in v. 28 by warning them of condign punishment for their offense against him. גּוּרוּ = "fear." Stich b has been rendered (a) "For God's anger is aroused against sins of the sword"; (b) "For wrath brings punishment of the sword"; (c) "For wrath will destroy iniquity (or the sinners)" supposed to be the meaning of כִּי חֵמָה עֲוֹנִים תָּבוֹא! (Hö.) All these interpretations are at best irrelevant, and at worst meaningless. If חֵמָה is read as הֵמָּה (Ges., Dil., Bu.) the stich receives an entirely appropriate meaning, "For these (acts on your part) are sins worthy of the sword." On this interpretation of עֲוֹנוֹת חֶרֶב, cf. חֵטְא־מָוֶת "sin worthy of death" (Deut. 22:26); עָוֹן פְּלִילִי (Job 31:11); עָוֹן פְּלִילִים (Job 31:28), "sins worthy of judgment."

Stich c contains a Kethib-Qere variation. The Qere שַׁדּוּן has proved intractable, all the Vss. and the commentators utilizing the Kethib שדין. The latter has been interpreted: (a) as an error for שַׁדַּי "that you may know the Almighty" (Reuss, Wr., Dil., Be.), but "knowing God" is used only in a favorable sense (cf. Hos. 2:22). Its universal meaning is the worship of God through obedience to His law (Jud. 2:10; I Sam. 2:12; 3:7; 5:4; 8:2; Ps. 79:6; Job 18:21). (b) It has been vocalized as שַׁדָּיָן "that there is a Judge" (V, T), or, (c) best, שֶׁדִּין "that there is judgment" (A., Sym., Th., S, Ibn E., D-G). Du. reads שָׁם דִּין. While the particle would be expected in prose, the breviloquence may be explained as due to the exigencies of meter. The relative שׁ may be vocalized with a Segol, which is the more usual form, or with a Pataḥ (Gen. 6:3; Jud. 5:7; Cant. 1:7). The last two interpretations are far superior to the suggestion to read *shaddayan*, which has been proposed as a variant of the divine name Shaddai, though there is no evidence of the word as a divine name, even in Ugaritic (L. R. Fisher in *VT*, vol. 11, 1961, pp. 342 f., adopted by P.). Like interpretation a above, it would be unsatisfactory in the context, even if the alleged meaning and etymology were allowed.

The contradiction between Job's threatening the Friends with God's judgment here and his constant denial of the existence of justice is merely a logical difficulty. Psychologically, Job is incapable of abandoning his conviction that right must triumph in the world. He has just demonstrated his affirmation of faith in his ultimate vindication (19:25; cf. 16:19). A similar logical contradiction that is psychologically credible is Job's warning to the Friends that they will be punished for their false and unworthy defense of God's cause (see the Comm. on 13:7–11), at the same time that he protests his unjust treatment at the hand of God (13:15).

The Speech of Zophar (20)

The accepted doctrine has already been set forth fully and Zophar has nothing new to add. His sensitive nature, however, has been aggrieved by Job's onslaught, which demands an answer. Zophar proceeds to describe the short-lived prosperity of the wicked and the inevitable doom that comes both upon the sinner and his progeny.

20 Zophar the Naamathite then answered, saying,
2   Indeed, my thoughts force me to answer
                because of the feelings within me.
3   I hear words of censure which insult me,
                and my spirit of understanding impels me to reply.
4   Don't you know this, that from eternity,
                ever since man was placed upon the earth,
5   the exultation of the wicked is short-lived,
                the joy of the godless but for a moment?
6   If his greatness rises up to heaven
                and his head touches the clouds,
7   at the height of his triumph, he is destroyed forever.
                Those who have seen him will ask, "Where is he?"
8   Like a dream he will fly off and will not be found;
                he will flee like a vision of the night.
9   The eye which saw him will see him no more,
                nor will his place behold him again.
10   His sons will try to appease the poor,
                and his offspring will return his ill-gotten gains.
11   While youthful vigor still fills his bones
                it will lie down with him in the dust.

12   If wickedness grows sweet in his mouth
                and he hides it under his tongue,
13   if he loves it and does not let it go
                and saves it in his mouth,
14   his food in his stomach is turned
                into the gall of asps within him.
15   The wealth he has swallowed he must spew forth;
                from his stomach God will drive it out.
16   He will suck the poison of asps;
                the tongue of the viper will kill him.
17   He will never see the rivers of oil,
                the streams of honey and milk.
18   He will disgorge his wealth and not swallow it;
                he will spew forth his gain and not chew it down.
19   For he has oppressed and tortured the poor
                and seized houses which he did not build.

20   Because he knew no rest within him,
                he will not save himself for all his wealth.
21   No remnant is left of all he has eaten;
                indeed, his prosperity will not endure.
22   When all his needs seem filled he will find himself in straits;
                every embittered sufferer will attack him.
23   To fill his belly to the full
                God will send His wrath against him
                and rain down upon him in His anger.
24   If he flees from an iron weapon,
                a bronze arrow will pierce him.

כ‎

א‎ וַיַּעַן צֹפַר הַנַּעֲמָתִי וַיֹּאמַר:

2 לָכֵן שְׂעִפַּי יְשִׁיבוּנִי   וּבַעֲבוּר חוּשִׁי בִי:

3 מוּסַר כְּלִמָּתִי אֶשְׁמָע   וְרוּחַ מִבִּינָתִי יַעֲנֵנִי:

4 הֲזֹאת יָדַעְתָּ מִנִּי־עַד   מִנִּי שִׂים אָדָם עֲלֵי־אָרֶץ:

ה‎ כִּי רִנְנַת רְשָׁעִים מִקָּרוֹב   וְשִׂמְחַת חָנֵף עֲדֵי־רָגַע:

6 אִם־יַעֲלֶה לַשָּׁמַיִם שִׂיאוֹ   וְרֹאשׁוֹ לָעָב יַגִּיעַ:

7 כְּגֶלֲלוֹ לָנֶצַח יֹאבֵד   רֹאָיו יֹאמְרוּ אַיּוֹ:

8 כַּחֲלוֹם יָעוּף וְלֹא יִמְצָאֻהוּ   וְיֻדַּד כְּחֶזְיוֹן לָיְלָה:

9 עַיִן שְׁזָפַתּוּ וְלֹא תוֹסִיף   וְלֹא־עוֹד תְּשׁוּרֶנּוּ מְקוֹמוֹ:

י‎ בָּנָיו יְרַצּוּ דַלִּים   וְיָדָיו תָּשֵׁבְנָה אוֹנוֹ:

11 עַצְמוֹתָיו מָלְאוּ עֲלוּמוֹ   וְעִמּוֹ עַל־עָפָר תִּשְׁכָּב:

12 אִם־תַּמְתִּיק בְּפִיו רָעָה   יַכְחִידֶנָּה תַּחַת לְשׁוֹנוֹ:

13 יַחְמֹל עָלֶיהָ וְלֹא יַעַזְבֶנָּה   וְיִמְנָעֶנָּה בְּתוֹךְ חִכּוֹ:

14 לַחְמוֹ בְּמֵעָיו נֶהְפָּךְ   מְרוֹרַת פְּתָנִים בְּקִרְבּוֹ:

טו‎ חַיִל בָּלַע וַיְקִאֶנּוּ   מִבִּטְנוֹ יוֹרִשֶׁנּוּ אֵל:

16 רֹאשׁ־פְּתָנִים יִינָק   תַּהַרְגֵהוּ לְשׁוֹן אֶפְעֶה:

17 אַל־יֵרֶא בִפְלַגּוֹת   נַהֲרֵי נַחֲלֵי דְּבַשׁ וְחֶמְאָה:

18 מֵשִׁיב יָגָע וְלֹא יִבְלָע   כְּחֵיל תְּמוּרָתוֹ וְלֹא יַעֲלֹס:

19 כִּי־רִצַּץ עָזַב דַּלִּים   בַּיִת גָּזַל וְלֹא יִבְנֵהוּ:

כ‎ כִּי ׀ לֹא־יָדַע שָׁלֵו בְּבִטְנוֹ   בַּחֲמוּדוֹ לֹא יְמַלֵּט:

21 אֵין־שָׂרִיד לְאָכְלוֹ   עַל־כֵּן לֹא־יָחִיל טוּבוֹ:

22 בִּמְלֹאות שִׂפְקוֹ יֵצֶר לוֹ   כָּל־יַד עָמֵל תְּבוֹאֶנּוּ:

23 יְהִי ׀ לְמַלֵּא בִטְנוֹ   יְשַׁלַּח־בּוֹ חֲרוֹן אַפּוֹ   יַמְטֵר עָלֵימוֹ בִּלְחוּמוֹ:

24 וְיִמְטֵר עָלֵימוֹ בִּלְחוּמוֹ:   יִבְרַח מִנֶּשֶׁק בַּרְזֶל

25   It is drawn forth and comes out of his body,
         and its glitter as it passes casts terror upon him.
26   Total darkness waits for his treasures;
         a fire not blown will devour him
         and consume what is left in his tent.
27   The heavens will reveal his sin
         and the earth will rise up against him.
28   A flood will wash away his house,
         torrents in the day of his wrath.
29   This is the sinner's portion from God,
         and the evildoer's inheritance from God.

כה תַּחְלְפֵהוּ קֶשֶׁת נְחוּשָׁה: שָׁלַף וַיֵּצֵא מִגֵּוָה
וּבָרָק מִמְּרֹרָתוֹ יַהֲלֹךְ עָלָיו אֵמִים:
26 כָּל־חֹשֶׁךְ טָמוּן לִצְפוּנָיו תְּאָכְלֵהוּ אֵשׁ לֹא־נֻפָּח
27 יָרַע שָׂרִיד בְּאָהֳלוֹ: יְגַלּוּ שָׁמַיִם עֲוֹנוֹ
28 וְאֶרֶץ מִתְקוֹמָמָה לוֹ: יִגֶל יְבוּל בֵּיתוֹ
29 נִגָּרוֹת בְּיוֹם אַפּוֹ: זֶה ׀ חֵלֶק־אָדָם רָשָׁע ׀ מֵאֱלֹהִים
וְנַחֲלַת אִמְרוֹ מֵאֵל:

CHAPTER 20

20:2 The various rearrangements of the stichs in vv. 2, 3 are unnecessary, since the four stichs are in chiastic structure: 2a ‖ 3b (Zophar's thoughts) and 2b ‖ 3a (his sensitivity). שְׂעִפַּי "my thoughts" (cf. the Comm. on 4:13).

יְשִׁיבוּנִי, like יַעֲנֵנִי in 3b, is causative Hiphil, "compels me to answer." הֵשִׁיב, originally with an expressed object, דָּבָר "word," as, e.g., I Sam. 17:30; Job 35:4 = "answer"; it is used without an object in later biblical Hebrew, in Job 13:22; 33:5, 32 (in the Elihu speeches); and in II Chr. 10:16; and is usual in mishnaic Hebrew. חוּשִׁי "my feeling, pain," common in mishnaic Hebrew. The form in Ecc. 2:25 cannot be adduced here (see *KMW ad loc.*). For our meaning here cf. *B. Erub.* 54a: חש בראשו "If one has a pain in the head."

20:3 In מוּסַר כְּלִמָּתִי the second noun is an appositional genitive, lit. "reproof which is my shame, i.e., censure which shames me."

יַעֲנֵנִי is the Hiphil, "which makes me answer."

20:4 A question expecting an affirmative answer normally has a negative inserted: "Is not, etc.?" Since this is obviously what is expected here, most commentators emend הֲזֹאת to הֲלֹא. There is, however, no evidence from LXX for this proposed reading. The translator, then as now, can transmit the intent of the Hebrew only by inserting a negative in the question. However, we have called attention to the existence of this usage in biblical Hebrew and ventured to suggest a psychological explanation, viz., that where the speaker's certitude is overwhelming, he dispenses with the negative. (Cf., *inter alia*, I Sam. 2:27; Jer. 31:19, etc.) On this biblical use and explanation of the psychological mechanism involved, see Gordis, "A Rhetorical Use of Interrogative Sentences in Biblical Hebrew," in *AJSL*, vol. 49, 1933, pp. 212–17.

Job obviously does not know the truth from the time man was created, because he has not been alive all this time! Syntactically, vv. 4 and 5 are an instance of what we have called "anticipation," where part of a subordinate clause is lifted out of its position and made the object of the verb in the main clause preceding. Thus, וַיַּרְא אֱלֹהִים אֶת־הָאוֹר כִּי־טוֹב = וַיַּרְא אֱלֹהִים כִּי הָאוֹר טוֹב "God saw that the light was good" (Gen. 1:4; see Ehr. *ad loc.*). MT כִּי יָדַעְתִּי כִּי אַחֲרֵי מוֹתִי הַשְׁחֵת תַּשְׁחִתוּן = כִּי יָדַעְתִּי אַחֲרֵי מוֹתִי כִּי הַשְׁחֵת תַּשְׁחִתוּן "I know that after my death you will act corruptly" (Deut 31:29). For another unrecognized instance, see Gordis, "A Note on Josh. 22:24," in *AJSL*, vol. 48, 1931, pp. 287 f. Hence: "Don't you know that from old, etc." The logical caesura (after יָדַעְתָּ) does not coincide here with the poetic caesura (after עַד). Cf. the Comm. on 4:8 for another instance.

שִׂים is best construed as the infinitive "from (the time of) the placing of man upon the earth," rather than as the participle passive of the Qal (Yel.), though the latter view is possible.

20:5 TS refers מְקָרוֹב to the future, citing Ezek. 7:8, so that it is virtually equivalent to בְּקָרוֹב. However, this interpretation necessitates a circumlocution: "The exaltation of the wicked *lasts* for a short time." Besides, the use of the two prepositions מִן and עַד in the two stichs favors the idea that Zophar is covering the entire extent of time from the past to the future.

רְשָׁעִים is probably to be read in the sing., with the final Mem being deleted as a dittography, though sing. and plural occur in parallels (cf. 17:8), נָקִי and יְשָׁרִים. מְקָרוֹב "from near" is generally used spatially, here temporally; hence "recent" (Deut. 32:17). "The joy of the wicked began only a little while ago, and will last only a little longer."

20:6 שִׂיאוֹ from נשא "his greatness, exalted position," a *hapax legomenon*; cf. the related nouns שׂוֹא (Ps. 89:10); שְׂאֵת (Gen. 49:3; Ps. 62:5; Job 13:11; 31:23, but see the Comm.).

20:7 כְּגֶלְלוֹ has been rendered (a) "like his dung" (Ra., Ibn E., Gers., JPSV, P.); (b) "when he begins to roll down," from גלל "roll"; for the assumed meaning of the verse, Est. 6:13 is cited. The verb is best interpreted as (c) "at the time of his greatness" (so LXX); cf. the Arab. verb *jalla*, "be great, powerful, sublime"; the noun *jaᵓlal*, "greatness, exaltation" (Ew., Yel.). This may well be the meaning in Gen. 43:18 לְהִתְגּוֹלֵל עָלֵינוּ "to show himself great against us."

20:8 The wicked will be destroyed, leaving no trace (8:9). יִמְצָאֻהוּ is the third pers. plur., used impersonally and equal to the passive, "they will not find him, i.e., he will not be found." יֻדַּד may possibly be the Hophal of נדד, but the other alleged instances (cf. Job 18:18; II Sam. 23:6) are doubtful. The form is probably a phonetic variant of the Qal יִדַּד, which Hayyug apparently read. The interchange of ū and ī occurs in Job 7:4 and elsewhere (cf. the Comm. *ad loc.*). Yel. interprets the form as the imperfect passive of the Qal on Arabic analogy, but no passive is really required (cf. Gen. 31:40; Nah. 3:7; Ps. 55:8, a. e.)

20:9 שׁוּף properly "glimpse, look upon," occurs elsewhere only in Cant. 1:6, whence the modern Hebrew use of the word for "sunburn." מָקוֹם is fem. here and in Job 28:6; cf. the Comm. *ad loc.*

20:10 The evil-doer's sons will need to make restitution of his ill-gotten gains. יְרַצּוּ is the causative use of the Piel with conative force: "They will try to win favor, appease." (Cf. *M. Abot* 4:18 אל תרצה את חבירך בשעת כעסו "Do not try to appease your friend in the hour of his anger"; הקב״ה מרצה אותו "The Lord appeased him," *Mid. Ex. Rab.*, sec. 45). In stich b יָדָיו cannot mean "his own hands," since stich a refers to the next generation. The emendation יְלָדָיו is impossible since the verb is fem. plur. MT יָדָיו here has the special meaning of "offspring," the hand being a limb of the body. Thus the proverb cited in *B. Erub.* 70a יורש כרעיה דאבוהו "an heir is the knee of his father." This meaning also inheres, we believe, in II Sam. 18:18: "Now Absalom in his lifetime had taken and reared up for himself the pillar, which is in the king's dale; for he said: 'I have no son to keep my name in remembrance'; and he called the pillar after his own name; and it is called (יד אבשלום) Absalom's monument unto this day"; and in Isa. 56:5: וְנָתַתִּי לָהֶם בְּבֵיתִי וּבְחוֹמֹתַי יָד וָשֵׁם טוֹב מִבָּנִים וּבָנוֹת "I shall give them, i.e. (the eunuchs) who observe the Sabbath within My house and My walls, offspring and a name better than (physical) sons and daughters." The two stichs are now in perfect parallelism with each other.

אוֹנוֹ "his wealth, lit. his strength," as in Hos. 12:9.

20:11   The Kethib is עֲלוּמָו, a defective spelling of the plural suffix (cf. *BTM*, p. 90). The noun is a plural abstract with the verb in the fem. sing. (cf. Ps. 103:5; Job 27:20).

20:12   אִם introduces the protasis of a condition extending over vv. 12 and 13; the apodosis is in vv. 14 and 15. תַּמְתִּיק is an inchoative use of the Hiphil, "begins to grow sweet." (Cf. the Comm. on 14:18; Ps. 49:17; Dan. 10:11.) יַכְחִידֶנָּה, a Hiphil, "he conceals it in order to preserve." The Piel of the root in Isa. 3:9; Jer. 50:2; Job 15:18; 27:11, carries the nuance of "conceal in speech," hence "deny" and "disown" in Job 6:10. The passage gives a vivid picture of the love the sinner has for his evil-doing, which is like a sweetmeat that one keeps in one's mouth as long as possible, to savor its taste, but it turns to poison in his system. For the figure, cf. Cant. 4:11: "Honey and milk are under your tongue."

20:13   וְיִמְנָעֶנָּה lit., "He withholds (from others) i.e., saves it for himself." Similarly, חָשַׂךְ "withhold, refrain" (Gen. 22:12; Pr. 21:26; cf. the Comm. on Job 16:5) develops the sense of "save, preserve" (Job 21:30).

20:14   The apodosis of the condition. נֶהְפָּךְ "lit. is changed (into gall)." מְרוֹרָה with Holem is a phonetic variant for מְרֵרָה with Ṣere (Job 16:13).

20:15   Stich a: "The wealth that he has swallowed he must spew forth." The Hiphil of ירש is common in the meaning "dispossess" with an accusative of pers. (Deut. 9:3; Jos. 14:12, and often); here with an *accus. rei*, "will cast, drive it out."

20:16   פֶּתֶן, Ugaritic *btn* "asp" (Deut. 32:33; Ps. 91:13). אֶפְעֶה "viper" (Isa. 30:6; 59:5), perhaps from פעה "groan" (Isa. 42:14; cf. also Ex. 1:15), hence "a whistling creature" (Ges.). The word was originally applied to a mythological monster like *tannīn* and *nāḥāš*; cf. Ugaritic בתן ברח and בתן עקלתן and the Hebrew parallel: נָחָשׁ בָּרִחַ .... נָחָשׁ עֲקַלָּתוֹן (Isa. 27:1), and see Special Note 37.

20:17   אַל is emphatic, "surely not, never." The usual rendering, "He will surely not see the channels of rivers of streams of honey and milk" is obviously unsatisfactory. There is no real caesura in the verse and three synonyms for "streams" are too many! Most moderns therefore follow Klostermann and insert יִצְהָר or שֶׁמֶן after בְּפַלְגּוֹת, for which there is no warrant. In addition, the meter pattern which would emerge (3:4) differs from the entire section which is 3:3, and is intrinsically suspect; cf. *PPS*, pp. 66 f., 70 f., and Special Note 1, sec. 16. The solution to these problems lies in recognizing in נַהֲרֵי a noun from the root נהר "shine," common in Aramaic, but occurring in Hebrew as well, which is used figuratively elsewhere in biblical Hebrew (Isa. 60:3; Ps. 34:6). That it originally had a concrete physical meaning is clear not only from general considerations of semantics, but from the Aram. נהורא "light" (cf. נְהָרָה Job 3:4) and Arab. *nuratum* "liniment." The noun we are postulating would mean "the shining substance," exactly like יִצְהָר, which is related to צהל "shine" II (cf. Ps. 104:15) לְהַצְהִיל פָּנִים מִשָּׁמֶן, "to make the face shine with oil." Other instances of descriptive epithets doing duty as nouns, particularly in parallelism, are נֹזְלִים "flowing substance, hence water" (Ex. 15:8); נָמֵס "the melting substance, hence wax" (Ps. 22:15). Our noun is to be vocalized as an absolute נַהֲרֵי like אַשְׁרֵי, construct אַשְׁרֵי (see Ehr. on Gen. 30:13); כִּילַי, "knave" (Isa. 32:5, 7); אָחֳלַי (constr. אָחֳלֵי) (II Ki. 5:3; Ps. 119:5); אֲלָלַי, and such proper names as אָחְלָי (I Chr. 2:31; 11:41), שָׁרַי, חַגַּי, etc. TS recognizes that a noun meaning "oil" is required, and he emends to בְּפַלְגֵּי תַנְהֵר וְנַחֲלֵי, because of an Arab. cognate *tanwir*, "oil used for illumination." There is no reason, however, why the Hebrew noun should be morphologically identical with the Arabic, especially since it requires emending the text.

With the caesura after נַהֲרֵי "oil," the verse now exhibits a 3:3 meter in perfect parallelism:

> "He will surely not see the channels of oil,
> The streams of honey and milk."

The curdled milk here referred to is a popular beverage in the Orient, and increasingly so in the Occident, in various sophisticated forms.

A striking parallel to the use of oil and honey, including the same sequence, occurs in Ugaritic:

> The heavens rained oil
> and the creeks ran with honey:
> (Gordon, *UT*, p. 49, III, 2021)

20:18 מֵשִׁיב "gives back, i.e., vomits." For the important semantic principle in Hebrew that the same term is used to express both a quality or an act, and the consequences of that quality or act, see *KMW*, Supplementary Note D, pp. 418 f., and see the Comm. on 20:15. Hence יְגַע from the root יגע "labor," means "the product of toil, hence wealth." It need not be emended to גִּיעַ (ag. D-G); cf. such variations as נְטִיעַ (Ps. 144:11) and נֶטַע (Job 14:9).

Stich b is generally rendered as "as his wealth increases he does not enjoy it," עלס being regarded as a related form to עלץ, עלז "rejoice" (cf.

Ps. 7:18; Job 39:13). This idea is both anticlimactic after stich a and completely lacking in parallelism. 50 Hebrew mss. read בְּחֵיל which is to be revocalized בֵּחֵל "he loathes" (so also TS); cf. Zech. 11:8 וְגַם נַפְשָׁם בָּחֲלָה בִי and the Syriac cognate *behel* "be nauseated." יַעֲלֶס is rendered correctly as "swallows" by LXX, S. MT is a scribal metathesis for יִלְעֹס "chew" (so Yel.). The word is common in mishnaic Hebrew, e.g., *M. Pes.* 2:7 ולא ילעוס אדם חטין "a man should not chew wheat." Stich b now exhibits perfect parallelism with stich a: "He will spew forth his gain and not chew it down."

20:19 The order of the verbs in stich a seems to be anticlimactic, indeed largely impossible: "He has crushed and forsaken the poor." Hence, עָזַב has been emended to זְרוֹעַ (cf. 22:9), "He has broken the arm of the poor" (Be.) or changed to עֶצֶב "painful toil" (Du., Hoff., D-G). Ehr. has emended the verb to עֹזֵב a new *hapax legomenon*, to which he assigns the meaning of "hut," citing the mishnaic מעזיבה (*M. Baba Metzia* 10:2), which means "the pavement of the ceiling, serving as the floor of an upper-story." The passage is best understood as an instance of *hysteron proteron*, where the order of two sequential acts is reversed because the more important obtrudes upon the consciousness of the speaker or writer. For this usage, cf. נַעֲשֶׂה וְנִשְׁמָע lit., "We shall do and we shall obey" (Ex. 24:7); קִיְּמוּ וְקִבְּלוּ "they perpetuated and accepted" (Est. 9:27), where the chronological order is, of course, reversed. For this usage, cf. Gordis, in *Sefer Moshe Seidel*, pp. 262 f. Hence, MT is to be rendered here "He has forsaken, indeed crushed, the poor."

In stich b וְלֹא יִבְנֵהוּ is generally rendered "and he does not build it up," but this can hardly in itself have the sense of "which he does not enjoy" (Ew., Me., Dil., Bu., D-G). It is better taken as a subordinate clause, "a house that he did not build." In Deut. 6:10 the promise is held out to the invading Israelites that they will possess cities they had not built (cf. Jos. 24:13).

20:20 The verse is best taken as describing not his predatory tactics (so P.), but the punishment which is the burden of the entire section, vv. 18–29. Stich a, introduced by כִּי, presents the cause of the punishment described in stich b (T). The sequence of cause and effect here is the reverse of the sequence of effect and cause in vv. 18–19. שָׁלֵו "quiet, i.e. contentment" need not be emended to שַׁלְוָה or a segolate form שֶׁלֶו (the occurrence of which in Ps. 30:7 is highly doubtful, since the suffix there is probably added to the stem of the common fem. noun שַׁלְוָה). On the form of the noun, cf. גֶּדֶר by the side of גָּדֵר and חֵף "nakedness" (Jer. 2:25). Because the greed of the wicked knows no rest, the calamity will come upon him. Stich b may be rendered: "of his wealth he will save nothing." The emphatic word order suggests instead: "in spite of all his wealth he will not save himself." On the reflexive use of the Piel, cf. וַיְגַלַּח Gen. 41:14; Amos 2:15 יְמַלֵּט.

20:21 Stich a describes either his greed: "Nothing is left that he did not devour" (JPSV, P., D-G) or his destruction: "No remnant is left of all that he has eaten." Ehr. objects to referring שָׂרִיד to objects, since the noun is used only of persons, and renders: "No one survives his greed, lit., his eating." עַל כֵּן may be the emphatic "indeed" (cf. Isa. 13:13; 21:3; Ps. 119:126), paralleling the usage of לָכֵן (Jer. 5:2). יָחִיל = "be strong, endure"; cf. Ps. 10:5; 20:22.

20:22 שִׂפְקוֹ "his sufficiency," as in I Ki. 20:10; Isa. 2:6; Job 36:18. The verb הִסְפִּיק is common in mishnaic Hebrew in the meaning "be enough, suffice."

יֵצֶר לוֹ is impersonal, "It will be narrow for him, i.e., he will be in straits."

עָמֵל lit., "sufferer, miserable one," refers to those he has wronged, who will now take vengeance upon him (cf. 20:10). The reading "misery" (P.) requires revocalizing the noun as עָמָל, but the reference to "hand" militates against it.

כָּל־יַד is equivalent to יַד כָּל, "the hand of every sufferer." M. Seidel interpreted the phrase like the German *allerhand*, "every kind."

20:23 The difficult stich a is dismissed by D-G as a gloss or a fragment. It is obviously a breviloquence due to metric causes. It may possibly mean: "It shall come to pass when his stomach has its fill" (Rabbi David Gordis), or "It will happen, in order to fill his belly to the full (with God's wrath)." עָלֵימוֹ contains the masc. sing. suf. "upon him," as in Phoenician and sporadically in Hebrew (Isa. 44:16; 53:8; Ps. 11:7; Job 22:2; 27:23); cf. Ges.-K., sec. 103, 2, Note 2.

בִּלְחוּמוֹ has been rendered: (a) "upon his flesh" (Arab. *laḥm*) or "his bowels" (cf. Zeph. 1:17) דָּמָם ‖ וּלְחָמָם כַּגְּלָלִים (Ibn E., Hi., Del., BDB). (b) Reading בְּלַחְמוֹ "upon his bread" (Dil., Bu.). (c) "With his weapons of war" (Yel.). The emendation may be avoided by the assumption that the noun is a broken plural used collectively, like עֲבֻדָּה (Gen. 26:14; Job 1:3); פְּקֻדָּה "officers" (Isa. 60:17); גְּבוּרָה "heroes" (Isa. 3:25), with the suffix added to the stem of the feminine noun, hence = בִּלְחוּמָתוֹ. (d) On the basis of the parallelism with חֲרוֹן אַפּוֹ. בִּלְחוּמוֹ is best rendered "his heat, anger." The form with Vav may represent a morphological variant for the segolate בְּלַחְמוֹ "heat"; cf. 28:5, a form familiar from Qumran, e.g., להוב for להב in *Thanksgiving Psalms*, col. 2, l. 26; col. 3, l. 30 (*Megillat Hahodayot*, ed. J. Licht, Jerusalem, 5717 = 1957, p. 9), and see Y. Kutscher; *Halašon Vehareqaᶜ Halešoni šel Megillat Yešayahu* (Jerusalem, 5719 = 1959, pp. 50–52). This variant of a segolate may also occur in MT נְחוּמָי "my compassion" (Hos. 11:8), which is not to be emended to רַחֲמַי (ag. Wel.), but is a phonetic and vocalic variant for it.

Ra. intuitively recognized the meaning appropriate to the context in his interpretation: "In the wrath of his warfare." Dahood (*Biblica*, vol. 38, 1957, pp. 314 ff.) makes the suggestion to emend (*sic*) וְיַמְטֵר עָלָיו מַבֵּל חַמּוֹ which he renders, "He shall rain on him the fire of his wrath." Aside from the new noun *mabbel* being proposed, *ḥammo* cannot be a noun.

20:24 The verse is a conditional sentence. If he flees the sword at close range, the arrow will reach him at a distance. נֶשֶׁק "weapon, armament," here qualified by בַּרְזֶל, refers to the sword. The threat of escaping one peril only to fall into another is a familiar figure (Isa. 24:18; Am. 5:19). קֶשֶׁת "bow," a synecdoche for "arrow." תַּחְלְפֵהוּ has been interpreted: (a) on the basis of Arab. *ḥalafa*, "succeed, follow," to mean "the arrow will follow him"; (b) on the basis of the usual meaning of the root in Hebrew, "the arrow will pass through him"; (c) "the arrow will pierce him." The latter meaning, which is the most vivid, does not require emendation to תִּפָּלְהֵהוּ; cf. מָחֲצָה וְחָלְפָה רַקָּתוֹ, "she struck and pierced his temple" (Jud. 5:26). That this is not a scribal error is clear from the late Hebrew noun חלף "piercing instrument, hence, knife."

20:25 שָׁלַף = "he draws forth" is an impersonal = "it is drawn forth," a description of the arrow in its passage. גֵּוָה, as a contraction of גַּאֲוָה "pride" (Jer. 13:17; Job 22:29; 33:17; ʂ e the Comm. *ad loc.*), is manifestly impossible here. Read with virtually all moderns מִגֵּוָה "from his body."

Placing the caesura after יַהֲלֹךְ leaves עָלָיו אֵמִים for stich c, which is then rendered by most commentators "terrors are upon him." Not only is this too short, but the word order should have been אֵמִים עָלָיו. Thus Du. inserts a verb יַהְפְכוּ in the stich. On metric grounds also it is better to follow the accentuation of those Hebrew manuscripts that place the pause after מִמְּרֹרָתוֹ, and read the last three words together. The verse then exhibits a 3:3:3 meter, with the long word מִמְּרֹרָתוֹ receiving two stresses (cf. Special Note 1, sec. 6). The same metric pattern is in v. 26.

בָּרָק "flashing, glitter," which is applied to the sword (Deut. 32:4; Ezek. 21:15, 20, 33), and to the spear (Nah. 3:3; Hab. 3:11), refers here to the arrow's glistening point. וּבָרָק מִמְּרֹרָתוֹ is generally interpreted as "the gleaming point coming out (or, will come out) from his gall." The difficulties, both intrinsic and in relation to the rest of the verse, are obvious.

On the basis of the Arabic root *marra*, "pass," which occurs in Job 13:26 (cf. the Comm. *ad loc.*), we suggest interpreting the noun as "passage," and interpret the phrase "lit., the lightning of its passage" or "the glitter of its passage." It may be better, though not absolutely necessary, to delete the first Mem of מִמְּרֹרָתוֹ as a dittography and vocalize וּבְרַק as a construct. What is required here is a verb with a transitive meaning, with ברק as the subject and אֵמִים as the object. This was recognized by Saadia, who rendered *ad sensum* "will hurl terrors upon him." We suggest vocalizing יַהֲלֹךְ as a Piel יְהַלֵּךְ or as a Hiphil יַהֲלֵךְ (on the analogy of a strong verb), and giving it a causative meaning, equivalent to the Hiphil "cause to walk" (Lev. 26:13; Ezek. 36:12). Hence יַהֲלֵךְ עָלָיו אֵמִים "makes terror stalk upon him." The Haphel of the verb occurs in biblical Aramaic in Dan. 4:34 (מַהְלְכִין) though in an intransitive sense, corresponding to the Pael.

Another suggestion — יהלך may perhaps be emended to יַשְׁלַךְ. In any event, the passage is to be rendered: "The lightning of its passage will hurl terrors upon him." (Cf. Ex. 23:27.)

20:26 לִצְפוּנָיו from צפן "hide, treasure up," either "his treasured ones, i.e., loved ones" (so apparently Ps. 83:4), or, better, "his hidden things, i.e. his treasures" (cf. Ps. 17:14).

תְאָכְלֵהוּ. The unusual vocalization (cf. also תְּרָצְחוּ, Ps. 62:4) may represent a variation of the Piel = תְּאַכְּלֵהוּ (*Qameṣ* + *Raphe* = *Pataḥ* + *Dageš*). It is noteworthy that both instances occur with a guttural. Yel. postulates the existence of an archaic variant form of the Qal, like the Ethiopic *yeqatel*.

אֵשׁ לֹא נֻפָּח = "a fire not blown (by human agency), i.e., a conflagration from God." Cf. Job 34:20, "removed by no (human) hand"; Lam. 4:6, "Sodom overturned in an instant, with no (human) hands falling upon it." אֵשׁ usually fem., is masc. in Jer. 48:45; Ps. 104:4; and is both masc. and fem. in our passage and in Jer. 20:9.

Stich c is rendered: (a) "His remnant will fare ill in his tent," the verb being construed as the Qal of רעע (so JPSV, P.), but this is much too weak at this point; (b) "will break, smash" (Gers.), which will require revocalizing to יָרֹעַ from רעע. The stich is best interpreted "the fire will devour, feed upon his remnant," from רעה "graze"; cf. רֹעֶה אֵפֶר "feeds on ashes" (Isa. 44:20; Pr. 15:14); וְרָעוּ אֶת־אֶרֶץ אַשּׁוּר, "devastate" (Mic. 5:5; Ps. 80:14).

20:27 As against Job's call to the earth to avenge his suffering, and to the heavens to testify to his probity (16:18, 19), Zophar declares that the heavens will reveal Job's sin and the earth will rise up against him. מִתְקוֹמָמָה with a Qameṣ under the first Mem is anomalous; being active in sense, it should have been vocalized with a Ṣere or a vocal Shewa.

20:28 יְבוּל is used elsewhere only of "produce" (Deut. 11:17; 32:22; Ps. 67:7). It is here explained as (a) "the produce of the house, hence possessions," or (b) "the members of his family" (Ra.). (c) LXX renders, perhaps *ad sensum*: "Let destruction drag his house to an end." (d) Dh. makes the attractive suggestion to render יְבוּל as "flood," and Yel. similarly compares יוּבַל (Jer. 17:5) יִבְלֵי מַיִם (Isa. 30:25; 44:4) and the Arab. *wabala* "to rain strongly."

יִגֶל either "will drive into exile," or, revocalizing as יָגֹל from גלל, "will roll away," with "flood" as the subject of the verb (cf. Job 14:19).

נִגָּרוֹת, the Niphal of גרר, "pour, flow, run" (cf. II Sam. 14:14; Mic. 1:4). The fem. plur. would mean "the flowing substance," hence "torrents." Cf. the Comm. on 20:17 for this substantive use of an adjective.

D-G reverses vv. 27 and 28 on the ground that, after v. 27, a return to the judgment is not satisfactory, but this exercise in Western logic is not binding on an Oriental poet. V. 27 describes the judgment upon the sinner himself, v. 28 upon his offspring ("his house"), the ultimate calamity for a Semite.

20:29 אִמְרוֹ is generally interpreted as "His word, promise," and stich b is then rendered: "The heritage appointed him by God," which is far-fetched. The parallelism here, as well as the almost identical verse in 27:13 זֶה חֵלֶק־אָדָם

רָשָׁע עִם־אֵל וְנַחֲלַת עָרִיצִים מִשַּׁדַּי יִקָּחוּ suggests that אִמְרוֹ must refer to the sinner. It has been suggested that the noun is the Arabic *ᵓamrun* "man" (Eitan, Yel.). In that event, רָשָׁע would be understood from stich a. Or the noun may be the common Arabic noun *ᵓamīr*, "prince, ruler," here negatively polarized like נָדִיב "prince," which in Job 21:28 means "wealthy evil-doer" (see the Comm. *ad loc.*). Either procedure offers a basis for rendering stich b as "the inheritance of the evil-doer from God." The Vav in אִמְרוֹ is the petrified suffix of the original nominative case; cf. Nu. 23:18; 24:3; Ps. 104:11, 20, and elsewhere.

מֵאֱלֹהִים may perhaps be deleted as a dittography from מֵאֵל (so also P.), and the meter would be 3:3. The verse would then be an excellent example of complementary or climactic parallelism, as in Ps. 29:1; 94:1, and cf. *PPS*, pp. 74 ff.

Job's Reply to Zophar (21)

In contrast to Zophar's mythical picture of the misery of the sinner and his offspring, Job pictures the actual ease and contentment of the malefactor, the well-being of his family, and, finally, his quick and easy death.

In this, Job's closing speech in the second cycle, he follows the practice he employed at the end of the first cycle (chapter 12), by quoting and then demolishing the arguments of the Friends. Job cites five of the arguments that have been advanced and refutes them in turn:

(1) "The lamp of the wicked is extinguished" (18:6). Bildad has contended that the wicked are invariably destroyed. Job asks ironically how often it really happens.

(2) "The sinner's descendants are punished." Since it was he who sinned, why is he himself not punished?

(3) "God is too exalted to be taught or judged by man." Job counters this contention, not directly but obliquely. He contrasts the happy lot of the wicked with the misery of the righteous. This inevitably raises questions about the extent of the divine wisdom.

(4) "Where is the house of the prosperous sinner? It is sure to be utterly destroyed!" Far from it; any passer-by can point out the mansion standing in all its glory!

(5) "God spares the wicked only until the day of doom." "Why the delay?" Job asks. "Why not immediate punishment for his evildoing?"

Job adds one finishing touch to his portrait of the prosperous sinner. There is a final indignity: even in death there is no moment of truth. The evildoer is given an elaborate funeral and is borne to his grave in pomp and honor.

21 Then Job answered, saying,
2   Listen carefully to my words,
               and this will count as your consolation.
3   Bear with me, that I may speak,
               and after I have spoken, you may mock me.
4   As for me, is my complaint to a mere man?
               Why, therefore, should I not be impatient?
5   Look at me and you will be horrified,
               and put your hand to your mouth.

6   When I think of it, I am appalled,
               and a shudder takes hold of my flesh —
7   why do the wicked live on,
               reach old age, and grow hale and hearty?
8   Their children are well set before them,
               their offspring, before their very eyes.
9   Their houses are safe from fear,
               and no rod of God comes upon them.
10   Their bull genders and does not fail;
               their cow calves, and does not lose her young.
11   They send forth their youngsters like a flock,
               and their children go dancing.
12   They sing to the timbrel and harp
               and make merry to the sound of the pipe.
13   They spend their days in well-being
               and in peace they go down to Sheol.
14   Yet they say to God, "Depart from us.
               We do not wish to know Your ways.
15   What is the Almighty that we should serve Him?
               And what shall we gain if we pray to Him?
16   Indeed, our prosperity is not in His hands!" —
               Far be from me the counsel of the wicked!

17   How often do the sinners' lamps go out
               and calamity come upon them
               as He metes out punishment in His anger,
18   that they become like stubble before the wind,
               like chaff which the storm has swept away?
19   You say,
            "God saves His punishment for his children" —
               Let Him recompense *him*, that *he* may know it!
20   Let his own eyes see his downfall,
               and he himself drink of the Almighty's wrath.
21   For what concern has he for his house afterwards,
               after the number of his months is cut off?

22   You ask,
            "Shall anyone teach God knowledge,
               seeing that He judges on high?"
23   Yet one man dies in the fullness of strength,
               wholly at ease and secure,
24   his vital organs full of milk,
               and the marrow of his bones moist;

כא

א　וַיַּעַן אִיּוֹב וַיֹּאמַר׃

2　שִׁמְעוּ שָׁמוֹעַ מִלָּתִי　וּתְהִי־זֹאת תַּנְחוּמֹתֵיכֶם׃

3　שָׂאוּנִי וְאָנֹכִי אֲדַבֵּר　וְאַחַר דַּבְּרִי תַלְעִיג׃

4　הֶאָנֹכִי לְאָדָם שִׂיחִי　וְאִם־מַדּוּעַ לֹא־תִקְצַר רוּחִי׃

ה　פְּנוּ־אֵלַי וְהָשַׁמּוּ　וְשִׂימוּ יָד עַל־פֶּה׃

6　וְאִם־זָכַרְתִּי וְנִבְהָלְתִּי　וְאָחַז בְּשָׂרִי פַּלָּצוּת׃

7　מַדּוּעַ רְשָׁעִים יִחְיוּ　עָתְקוּ גַּם־גָּבְרוּ חָיִל׃

8　זַרְעָם נָכוֹן לִפְנֵיהֶם עִמָּם　וְצֶאֱצָאֵיהֶם לְעֵינֵיהֶם׃

9　בָּתֵּיהֶם שָׁלוֹם מִפָּחַד　וְלֹא שֵׁבֶט אֱלוֹהַּ עֲלֵיהֶם׃

י　שׁוֹרוֹ עִבַּר וְלֹא יַגְעִל　תְּפַלֵּט פָּרָתוֹ וְלֹא תְשַׁכֵּל׃

11　יְשַׁלְּחוּ כַצֹּאן עֲוִילֵיהֶם　וְיַלְדֵיהֶם יְרַקֵּדוּן׃

12　יִשְׂאוּ כְּתֹף וְכִנּוֹר　וְיִשְׂמְחוּ לְקוֹל עוּגָב׃

13　יְבַלּוּ בַטּוֹב יְמֵיהֶם　וּבְרֶגַע שְׁאוֹל יֵחָתּוּ׃

14　וַיֹּאמְרוּ לָאֵל סוּר מִמֶּנּוּ　וְדַעַת דְּרָכֶיךָ לֹא חָפָצְנוּ׃

טו　מַה־שַּׁדַּי כִּי־נַעַבְדֶנּוּ　וּמַה־נּוֹעִיל כִּי נִפְגַּע־בּוֹ׃

16　הֵן לֹא בְיָדָם טוּבָם　עֲצַת רְשָׁעִים רָחֲקָה מֶנִּי׃

17　כַּמָּה ׀ נֵר־רְשָׁעִים יִדְעָךְ　וְיָבֹא עָלֵימוֹ אֵידָם

18　חֲבָלִים יְחַלֵּק בְּאַפּוֹ׃　יִהְיוּ כְּתֶבֶן לִפְנֵי־רוּחַ

19　וּכְמֹץ גְּנָבַתּוּ סוּפָה׃　אֱלוֹהַּ יִצְפֹּן־לְבָנָיו אוֹנוֹ

כ　יְשַׁלֵּם אֵלָיו וְיֵדָע׃　יִרְאוּ עֵינוֹ כִּידוֹ

21　וּמְחַמַּת שַׁדַּי יִשְׁתֶּה׃　כִּי מַה־חֶפְצוֹ בְּבֵיתוֹ אַחֲרָיו

22　וּמִסְפַּר חֳדָשָׁיו חֻצָּצוּ׃　הַלְאֵל יְלַמֶּד־דָּעַת

23　וְהוּא רָמִים יִשְׁפּוֹט׃　זֶה יָמוּת בְּעֶצֶם תֻּמּוֹ

24　כֻּלּוֹ שַׁלְאֲנַן וְשָׁלֵיו׃　עֲטִינָיו מָלְאוּ חָלָב

כ״א v. 12. בס״א בתף　כ״א v. 13. יכלו ק׳　v. 20. עיניו ק׳

25 and another dies in bitterness of soul,
        never having tasted of joy.
26 Alike they lie down in the dust,
        and the worm covers them both.

27 Behold, I know your thoughts
        and the schemes you plot against me.
28 If you say,
    "Where is the house of the nobleman,
        and where is the dwelling of the wicked?"
29 Why not ask the passers-by —
        you cannot deny their evidence!

30 You declare,
    "The sinner is being saved for the day of calamity;
        on the day of wrath, he will be led to his doom."
31 But who will denounce his way to his face,
        and for what he has done — who will requite *him?*
32 But, in fact, he is borne in pomp to the grave,
        and men keep watch over his tomb.
33 The clods of the valley are sweet to him;
        all men follow his bier,
        and before him marches an innumerable host.
34 How then do you comfort me with empty words,
        while your answers are nothing but falsehood?

כה וּמֹחַ עַצְמוֹתָיו יְשֻׁקֶּה׃   וְזֶה יָמוּת בְּנֶפֶשׁ מָרָה

26 וְלֹא־אָכַל בְּטוֹבָה׃   יַחַד עַל־עָפָר יִשְׁכָּבוּ

27 וְרִמָּה תְּכַסֶּה עֲלֵיהֶם׃   הֵן יָדַעְתִּי מַחְשְׁבוֹתֵיכֶם

28 וּמְזִמּוֹת עָלַי תַּחְמֹסוּ׃   כִּי תֹאמְרוּ אַיֵּה בֵית־נָדִיב

29 וְאַיֵּה אֹהֶל ׀ מִשְׁכְּנוֹת רְשָׁעִים׃   הֲלֹא שְׁאֶלְתֶּם עוֹבְרֵי דָרֶךְ

ל וְאֹתֹתָם לֹא תְנַכֵּרוּ׃   כִּי לְיוֹם אֵיד יֵחָשֶׂךְ רָע

31 לְיוֹם עֲבָרוֹת יוּבָלוּ׃   מִי־יַגִּיד עַל־פָּנָיו דַּרְכּוֹ

32 וְהוּא־עָשָׂה מִי יְשַׁלֶּם־לוֹ׃   וְהוּא לִקְבָרוֹת יוּבָל

33 וְעַל־גָּדִישׁ יִשְׁקוֹד׃   מָתְקוּ־לוֹ רִגְבֵי נָחַל

וְאַחֲרָיו כָּל־אָדָם יִמְשׁוֹךְ   וּלְפָנָיו אֵין מִסְפָּר׃

34 וְאֵיךְ תְּנַחֲמוּנִי הָבֶל   וּתְשׁוּבֹתֵיכֶם נִשְׁאַר־מָעַל׃

CHAPTER 21

21:3 The singular תַּלְעִיג is generally revocalized as the plural (Ol., Me., Bi., Be., Du.), but the singular may be addressed to Zophar in particular; note the sing. in 16:3 between the plural in 16:1 and 16:4 (Bu., D-G).

21:4 Since Job's argument is with God, he has a right to receive a more understanding response than from mere men. Hence, his impatience and anger are justified. וְאִם־מַדּוּעַ represents a telescoped condition, "If it is so, i.e., that I am not speaking to a mere mortal, why should I not be impatient?" TS cites the *Aḥiqar Text* in the Elephantine Documents (Cowley, p. 81), "Do not withhold your son from the rod; if so (הן), you cannot keep him from wickedness." Another analogue from a different culture-sphere may be quoted from Shakespeare, *Antony and Cleopatra*, IV, 2, lines 26 f.:

> "Haply you shall not see me more; or if,
> a mangled shadow."

"Or if" = "or if you do."

In our passage, as in the Shakespeare passage, the contraction was dictated by metric necessity. Render in our context as "why, if this is so, should I not be impatient?"

21:5 הָשַׁמּוּ with a Pataḥ; cf. הֵסַבּוּ (I Sam. 5:9, 10). The usual vocalization of the imperative of geminate verbs is with a Ṣere; the Pataḥ may have been induced by the pause. The Hiphil expresses a condition and is intransitive; cf. Ezek. 3:15. The root occurs in the Qal, Niphal and Hiphil, with the same meaning, "be astonished."

Placing one's hand on the mouth is an obvious sign of silence. Thus, Juvenal, *Satires*, I, 160: *digito compesce labellum*, "restrain your little lip with your finger." The Roman god of silence, Harpocrates, was pictured with his finger on his mouth (Hö.).

21:6 In stich b, פַּלָּצוּת "trembling" is the object of the verb; it is the subject in Isa. 21:4; Ezek. 7:18; Ps. 55:6.

21:7 The basic meaning of the root עתק is evidently "move, proceed, advance," from which a whole constellation of meanings has developed: (1) "move forward (tent)" (Gen. 12:8; 26:22); (2) "remove (mountains) (Job 9:5); (3) "remove words," hence (a) "become silent" (Job 32:16); (b) "transcribe, copy" (Pr. 25:1); and (c) in medieval Hebrew, "translate"; (4) "grow old and weak" (Ps. 6:8). Here the verb means (5) "advance in years" or (6) "grow great, exalted," for which cf. II Sam. 2:3; Ps. 75:6.

In direct contradiction to the Friends' and Zophar's last speech in particular, Job pictures the well-being and long life of the sinner (v. 7), the security of his offspring (vv. 8–9), the fecundity of his animals (v. 10), the happy proximity of his descendants (vv. 11, 12, 13a), and, finally, his quick and painless death (v. 13b).

21:8 עִמָּם, lacking in the Septuagint, is deleted as redundant after לִפְנֵיהֶם by most moderns, a procedure which improves the meter. On the other hand, the vocable may possibly be joined to stich b and vocalized עַמָּם "their kinsfolk." The interpretation of עִמָּם as "in their lifetime" and לִפְנֵיהֶם "close by, in their presence" (Ehr., TS) is ingenious, but not convincing. At the very least, a Vav would have been required with לִפְנֵיהֶם. The presence of both prepositions in the text is best explained as a conflate reading of נָכוֹן לִפְנֵיהֶם and נָכוֹן עִמָּם (cf. Ps. 89:22).

21:9 שָׁלוֹם, the use of a substantive where we would use an adjective, is characteristic of biblical Hebrew, and is one of the sources of the vigor of biblical style. (Cf. אֲנִי שָׁלוֹם Ps. 120:7; Gen. 43:7; II Sam. 20:9; Pr. 3:17, and Ges.-K., sec. 141, note 1.)

21:10 עִבַּר "impregnate" is frequent in mishnaic Hebrew, and is probably distinct from the common root עבר "pass" (ag., BDB). יַגְעִל, from the root געל "abhor, loathe," a Hiphil here, has a factitive meaning: "The bull does not allow (the cow) to reject (the semen) as loathsome" (Ra., Del., Dil.), or "does not reject as loathsome" (Hö.). תְּפַלֵּט "deliver, give birth" (cf. Mic. 6:14 and the related וְהִמְלִיטָה Isa. 66:7). תְּשַׁכֵּל = "bear dead offspring" (Gen. 31:38). The evil-doer's animals will not fail both to become pregnant and to bear living offspring. Both calamities are referred to in Ex. 23:26: מְשַׁכֵּלָה וַעֲקָרָה.

21:12 יִשְׂאוּ sc. קוֹל "they will raise their voices, i.e., sing." The reading כְּתֹף (with a Kaph) found in many manuscripts and printed editions is manifestly inferior to the text cited on the margin of some mss., בְּתֹף. All the Vss. and some mss. read with Beth, which is either that of means or accompaniment. Hence, "they sing with the sound of the timbrel and the harp."

21:13 Both the Kethib יְבַלּוּ "they wear out, spend their days" and the Qere יְכַלּוּ "they end their days," are acceptable readings — proof once again that the Qere is not a correction of the Kethib. For the favorable use of בלה, cf. וּמַעֲשֵׂה יְדֵיהֶם יְבַלּוּ בְחִירָי "The work of their hands my chosen ones will fully enjoy" (Isa. 65:22; ag. TS). In modern Hebrew, the verb is usual in the meaning of "spending time," and the noun בילוי means "amusement, entertainment."

וּבְרֶגַע has been interpreted either as "peacefully" (LXX, Hupf., Be., Bu., Du.), on the basis of the Arab. *raja*ᶜ*a* "return to rest," e.g., in Isa. 34:14; Jer. 31:2; 50:34; or "in a moment, quickly" (Ra., and P.). The word is best understood as a *talḥin*, with both meanings present simultaneously in the consciousness of the poet and his reader: "Peacefully — in a moment."

Cf. the Comm. on 7:6 and see Gordis, in *Sepher Tur-Sinai* (pp. 255–62), for a discussion of this rhetorical figure. It is obviously impossible to convey both meanings by a single term in another language.

יֵחַתּוּ not "they are broken," from חתת, but = יֵחַתּוּ, an Aramaism "they go down," from נחת (cf. the Comm. on 17:16).

21:14, 15 The sinner impudently denies any value to serving and praying to God or walking in His ways. פגע = "lit. meet, encounter," hence "pray (to God)" (Jer. 7:16; 27:18; 36:25) or "pray (to man)" (Gen. 23:8; Ruth 1:16).

21:16 Stich a, translated as "Behold, their prosperity is not in their hands (but in God's)," is a pious position manifestly inappropriate to Job, and therefore the verse is frequently deleted (Hö., P.). Stich b is then dropped as an intrusion from 22:18. This procedure, however, is purely arbitrary, as are the omission of לֹא (Gr., Me., Be.) and the rendering of stich a as "Behold, their prosperity is in their own hands." The same meaning may be derived by interpreting הֵן לֹא = הֲלֹא, "Is not, indeed." Particularly at this point, however, after the long description of the prosperity of the wicked and their impudent disavowal of God's ways, the stich is not in place and stich b bears no relationship to it. TS regards stich a as a quotation by Job of what the Friends are saying; "*You say* that their good is not for them" (treating בְּיָדָם as = to בַּעֲדָם). He then reads מֶנּוּ "from Him." This would require the assumption of two series of quotations, first the words of the wicked (vv. 14, 15) and immediately thereafter the words of the Friends (v. 16). Moreover, interpreting stich b as "The counsel of the wicked is far from God" is highly unnatural, and the entire procedure very complicated.

We propose emending stich a (so also Yel.) to read (or בְּיָדוֹ) הֵן לֹא בְּיָדָיו טוּבֵנוּ "Indeed, our prosperity is not in His hands" — an excellent conclusion of the speech of the wicked in vv. 14 and 15.

מֶנִּי is an archaic and rare form for מִמֶּנִּי "from me." רָחֲקָה is a precative perf., and the entire phrase is to be interpreted as an apotropaic utterance by Job. After citing the impious sentiments of the sinners (vv. 14, 15, 16a), Job adds the prayer, "The counsel of the wicked be far from me!" This meaning is equally appropriate in 22:18b. For this usage, cf. modern Hebrew להבדיל "may this be separate from that," and Aramaic רחמנא ליצלן "may the merciful One save us" used after an unpleasant idea has been stated.

The confusion of final Mem with *Yod Vav*, and final Mem with *Nun Vav*, was induced by their graphic similarity. (Cf. Jos. 5:1, Kethib עברנו Qere עָבְרָם; Jer. 31:14, MT אֵינֶנּוּ for אֵינָם; Ps. 12:8 תִּצְּרֶנּוּ ‖ תִּשְׁמְרֵם, etc.

21:17 On the use of quotations in argument, see Special Note 17.

כַּמָּה usually quantitative, "how much"? (cf. Zech. 7:3), is used temporally (a) "how long?" כַּמָּה תִרְאֶה (Ps. 35:17; Job 7:19) (b) "how often?" (Ps. 78:40 and here). Here, of course, it is an ironic expression of the idea "how seldom."

The variation in word order in stich c (object, verb) from stich b (verb, subject) and the absence of a Vav suggests that the two stichs are not coordinate and that stich c is a clause of condition, "as He apportions punishment in His anger." חֲבָלִים cannot mean "cord, measured portion," here, because of the verb יְחַלֵּק "divide, assign." It is to be understood as "pains, sorrows." Though usually referring to birth pangs (Hos. 13:13), it is applied figuratively to the stress of exile (Isa. 26:17) and the sufferings of nations (Isa. 13:8).

21:18 This verse is governed by כַּמָּה in v. 17 and continues the description of the deserved but all-too-rare destruction of the wicked, which the Friends are proclaiming with such assurance.

21:19 Stich a is not interrogative (Hö.), but is Job's citation of the basic doctrine of traditional religion, reaffirmed again and again by the Friends, that the children are punished for the sins of their fathers. יִצְפֹּן "will store up, save." אָוֶן "trouble, sorrow" (Gen. 35:18; Pr. 22:8; Job 4:8, 15, 35), hence, "suffering, punishment." The masc. sing. suffixes in 20b and 21 are emphatic, "To *him*."

21:20 The *hapax legomenon* כִּיד need not be emended to פִּיד (BDB, Hö.); cf. the Arab. cognate *kaid* "warfare" (Schultens) and *kaʾada* (*mediae Aleph*) "be in an evil state" (BDB). The general sense required in the passage is clear.

21:21 The other biblical uses of the root חצץ (in Pr. 30:37; חָצָץ "gravel," Lam. 3:16) are not helpful here. Our root is probably a cognate of Arab. *haṣṣa*, "cut off" and related to the root קצץ "cut off" (Deut. 25:12) and, in rabbinic Hebrew, "decide, stipulate" (*B.B. Metzia* 61b). The stich, which is a subordinate clause of condition, is to be rendered either" (a) "when the number of his days has been apportioned, determined" (cf. גזר "decide," Job 22:28 and in rabbinic Hebrew) or (b) "cut off, finished." (Cf. בצע "cut," Isa. 10:12; Zech. 4:9.)

21:22 The verse is not to be deleted as an interpolation (D-G, P.). Ehr. interprets stich a: "Will any man teach knowledge on God's behalf, i.e., can anyone explain the facts of life?", but the language does not support this interpretation. The straightforward rendering of the verse, "Can anyone teach God knowledge?", is entirely appropriate if the verse is recognized as Job's citation of the Friends' contention (Eliphaz 4:17; 15:8–14; Zophar 11:5–9) that man cannot presume to criticize and by that token to instruct God, who transcends man's limited gaze (so also Hi.). D-G objects to this view on the ground that Job does not refute this argument. But obviously Job cannot deny the vastly superior knowledge of God, so that a direct rebuttal is out of the question. Instead, Job offers an oblique response in vv. 22–26 by calling upon men to observe the injustice of life manifest in the unmerited fate both of the righteous and the sinners. This ironic and oblique mode of argumentation is also favored by Koheleth; cf. Ecc. 4:9–12; 7:1–14; 8:2–4; and see *KMW ad loc.*, especially pp. 103 ff.

הַלְאֵל with the Lamed of the accusative is emphatic; יְלַמֶּד is impersonal: "Can anyone teach *God* understanding?"

Stich b may be interpreted in one of two ways: either as a circumstantial clause, "seeing that God judges the highest?"; or as a parallel to stich a: "Can he, i.e., man, judge the All-High?" This rendering has the advantage of giving a better parallelism to the verse. For *rāmīm* as an epithet of God, compare the biblical, perhaps originally Canaanite, use of עֶלְיוֹן (Nu. 24:16; Deut. 32:8; II Sam. 22:14; Isa. 14:14; Lam. 3:35, 38; frequently in Ps. 91:1, 9; 92:2, and often), as well as the very common title גָּבוֹהַּ, "The All-High" in rabbinic literature—probably a development from the usage in Ps. 138:6. Note also the use of רָם וְנִשָּׂא in Isa. 57:15. The plural רָמִים here would be analogous to similar epithets for God, like קְדוֹשִׁים (cf. Hos. 12:1; Pr. 9:10; the Comm. on Job 5:17). Dahood (*Biblica*, vol. 38, 1957, pp. 312 f.) eliminates the plural by construing the final Mem as the enclitic, which, though invoked too liberally in contemporary scholarship, is well authenticated in Ugaritic and biblical Hebrew (cf. e.g. Isa. 10:1b, 5b).

21:23 In stich b note the assonance of Lamed, which may have induced its insertion in שַׁלְאֲנָן. For the infixed Lamed, cf. זַלְעָפָה (Ps. 119:53 a. e.) by the side of זַעַף (Isa. 30:30 a. e.).

21:24 עֲטִינָיו is a *hapax legomenon* for which a variety of interpretations, largely guesses, have been proposed: (a) "intestines, viscera" (LXX, V); (b) "pails" on the basis of an Arabic cognate meaning "watering-place of camels" (Ibn Janah, Ibn E., JPSV); (c) "breasts, teats" (T), but this is physiologically inappropriate to a male. Based on this rendering of T, עֲטִינִים has been appropriated in modern Hebrew for the teats of animals; (d) an emendation to עֲטָמָיו, an assumed Aramaism for "bones," but this would create a *hapax legomenon* in Hebrew: (e) "solid part, flank, haunches" (P.), on the basis of the Syriac ʿatma, talmudic אטמא (B. *Hul.* 42b and often). These emendations, however, also require changing חָלָב "milk" to חֵלֶב "fat" (Hö., Yel.), but the parallelism with יְשֻׁקֶּה "is moistened" favors "milk" in stich a.

To emend a *hapax legomenon* and create another instead is methodologically unsound, especially when the original root is amply attested by cognates. We may compare the Arabic ʿatana "moisten, cause to drip" and the mishnaic verb עטן "pack olives in a vat," as, e.g., *P. Moed Qatan* II, 81a: העוטן הזית השלישי עוטנו בתוך ביתו "he who packs olives in his house"; ביתו עד שילקה "the third crop of olives (which are hard) he packs in the house until they begin to rot"; also *M. Men.* 8:4; *T. Toh.* 10:4 and the noun מעטן "a vessel for crushing olives" (M. *Toh.* 9:1 a. e.). Directly germane to our text is a passage in *P. Moed Qatan* II, 81a, beginning: מתניתין בעטינין מה דתני רבי חייה בגרגרים "Our Mishnah deals with packed olives; Rabbi Hiyya's statement with loose berries." TS, who also cites this talmudic passage, translates עֲטִינִין as "oil pressed for olives." He then emends stich a in our v. to read עָטִין יִמָּלֵא וְחָלָב "with oil he is filled and with milk." Aside from the changes required, and the unnatural word order that results, this rendering of עֲטִינָיו as "oil" is difficult because of the plural and the contrast with גרגרים in the talmudic passage.

Actually no change is needed. On the basis of the mishnaic usage, our passage receives a clear meaning, though it must be confessed not in harmony with our conventional aesthetic standards. The noun עֲטִינִים means "olives," particularly "dripping olives"; here a designation for the male genitals. The "milk" is the seminal fluid, with which the testes are filled. This fluid has already been compared by the poet to milk in 10:10: "You who poured me out like milk," as has been generally recognized (cf. the Comm. *ad loc.*). Because of the fluid they contain and their size and shape the testes are designated by the term "olives," which is thus considerably older than its occurrence in rabbinic Hebrew. In all cultures, the genitals are described by various metaphors which may or may not be euphemisms (cf. ביצים "eggs" in colloquial Hebrew and "nuts, balls" in English slang). For another instance of a usage in biblical Hebrew that does not conform to our practice, cf. TS's demonstration that the noun תַּחְרָא means "anus" (Ex. 28:32; 39:23) in his *Lašon Vasefer*, Jerusalem, 5711 = 1951, Kerekh-Hasefer, pp. 219–23.

Job declares that the sinner retains his sexual potency all his life. On the other hand, in describing the usual weaknesses of old age, Koheleth refers to the sexual organ growing heavy like a grasshopper and useless (Ecc. 12:5; cf. *KMW ad loc.*).

מֹחַ "marrow" common in mishnaic Hebrew, Aramaic, and Arabic; מֵחִים "fatlings"; cf. Isa. 5:17; 66:15. יְשֻׁקֶה "will be watered, i.e., be moist." Health is expressed by the moisture of the bones (Pr. 3:8) and of the body in general (Deut. 34:7).

21:27 תַּחְמֹסוּ a denominative verb from חָמָס "do me wrong, plot against me." None of the alternate suggestions are superior: (1) תִּכְמֹסוּ "plot secretly" on the basis of the difficult כָּמֻס (Deut. 32:34); (2) תַּעֲמֹסוּ "load up" (Gr.); (3) תַּחְפֹּשׂוּ "dig" (Du.); (4) תַּחְרְשׁוּ "plot" (Be.); (5) תהמסו on the basis of the Syriac *hemas* "think" (Jacob, in *ZATW*, 1912, p. 286; Hö., TS). But the creation of a *hapax legomenon* is especially dubious when other alternatives are available.

21:28 נָדִיב is used of (a) "a man of princely rank" (Pr. 19:6; 25:7; Job 34:18), and (b) "a man of noble character" (Pr. 17:36; Isa. 32:5). If this latter meaning be assigned to the noun here, the two stichs are in contrast with one another. Job would then be citing the view of the Friends that there is a radically different destiny awaiting the righteous and the sinners. Now the Friends have frequently declared that the house of the evil-doers is destroyed (Eliphaz 15:34; Bildad 6:22; 18:15 f.; Zophar 20:9, 26 ff.). However, at no point have they described the tents of the righteous as permanent.

Moreover, the righteous and the wicked are both included in a moving passage in Babylonian Wisdom literature, which is similar in form to our

verse, but its intent is quite the opposite of what our passage requires. In
"The Pessimistic Dialogue of a Master and His Slave," we read:

> "Go up on the ancient mounds and walk around them,
> See the skulls of more recent and of ancient men,
> Which is the evil-doer and which the benefactor?" (*ANET*, pp. 47 f.)

In other words, one fate overtakes them both (cf. Ecc. 2:14; 9:1–3). This
cannot be the standpoint of the Friends.

It is, therefore, preferable to interpret the two stichs as parallel in meaning. נָדִיב must accordingly be interpreted as "a man of princely rank," with
overtones of "the powerful and the oppressors," as Ibn Ezra recognized:
בעל ממון ואינו צדיק "a rich man who is unrighteous." For an instance of this
semantic polarization, cf. the Comm. on 20:29 (אָמְרוֹ). Hence render: If you
say, "Where is the house of the aristocrat and where is the dwelling of the
wicked?" If, says Job, you claim that the tents of the wicked are of brief
duration, you have only to ask any passerby! (v. 29).

The combination of synonyms in a construct relationship אֹהֶל מִשְׁכְּנוֹת
in stich b is common; cf. דֶּרֶךְ אָרְחֹתֶיךָ (Isa. 3:12); וּמִבְצַר מִשְׂגַּב חוֹמֹתֶיךָ (Isa.
25:12); מְעוֹן בֵּיתֶךָ (Ps. 26:8); גֶּשֶׁם מְטָרוֹת (Job 37:6). Nevertheless, stich b
may be overlong, since the entire section (vv. 27, 29, 30) is in a 4:3 meter,
while the verse is in 3:4 or 4:4. It may be regarded as a conflate of two readings, מִשְׁכְּנוֹת רְשָׁעִים and אֹהֶל רְשָׁעִים.

21:29   The Friends have asked rhetorically "Where are the dwellings of the
evil-doers?" Job takes them at their word and answers their question by a
question: "Haven't you asked the passers-by, who will point out the dwellings
of the wicked standing firm and secure? Their testimony cannot be denied."
For a similar ironic rejoinder, cf. Jonah 4:11. אוֹת "sign, testimony." The
root תְּנַכֵּרוּ is an *addad*, a word of like and opposite meaning; hence (a) "recognize" and (b) "mistake, deny." Both meanings have been invoked for our
passage: a) "Do you not recognize?"; and b) better, as a denominative from
נָכְרִי, "You cannot treat it as alien, deny, falsify." (Cf. Deut. 32:27, פֶּן־יְנַכְּרוּ
צָרֵימוֹ "lest their foes deny the truth"; and Jer. 19:4.) So TS.

21:30   The failure to recognize the quotation here has led commentators to
regard this verse as "stultifying and impossible for Job's argument" (D-G)
and therefore to propose emendations, such as reading twice בְּיוֹם for לְיוֹם
and יוּצָלוּ for יוּבָלוּ, joining 29b and 30 together, and rendering:

> "Do you not find this tale strange,
>   that the wicked is spared in the day of disaster,
>   they are saved from the day of wrath?"

The final stich, 30b, receives an even more far-fetched interpretation: "In
the day when God's angers are brought into the world" (Hö., P.).

Actually, Job is here citing the conventional view that the wicked are
spared for a greater ultimate punishment, and hence their present prosperity.

כִּי is the emphatic particle, used at the opening of a statement (cf. Isa. 15:1; Job 28:1, etc.). The verse means "The evil-doer is spared for the day of calamity and will be led forth in the day of God's wrath." (So Ra.). Cf. 38:23: "The instruments which I have saved up for the day of trouble." The plural יוּבָלוּ may refer to the plural רְשָׁעִים in v. 28b, as the sing. in stich a carries on the sing. in 28a. D-G points out that where a class of persons is referred to, the Hebrew poet often alternates between singular and plural. LXX read the plural here. It is therefore not absolutely necessary to re-vocalize the final verb as a singular.

21:31 This verse is now a direct rebuttal. יַגִּיד "tell" carries the nuance of "denounce"; cf. Jer. 20:10; Est. 6:2.

עַל פָּנָיו "to his face" means "at once." (Cf. the Comm. on 2:5.)

21:32 Instead of being "carried off in the day of wrath," the sinner will be "carried in pomp to his final resting place." The Wisdom writers were particularly exercised by the fact that after a lifetime of ill-gotten prosperity, there is no moment of truth for the evil-doers even at the very end. Their true character is not revealed even then, but high-flown obsequies of praise are offered before they are taken to their graves. (Cf. Ecc. 8:10 and *KMW ad loc.*) The plural קְבָרוֹת suggests the elaborate character of their sepulchre. (Cf. II Chr. 21:20; 24:25; 35:24.) On גָּדִישׁ as "funeral mound, grave," cf. Arab. *jadath* and the Comm. on 5:26. יִשְׁקוֹד "watch, stand guard," is used impersonally. Ehr. and Yel. emend to יִשְׁקוֹט "he rests."

21:33 Stich a apparently describes the choice land in which he is buried. רֶגֶב "clod of earth" (Job 38:38). Cf. the proper noun חֶבֶל אַרְגֹּב (Deut. 3:4, 13, 14; I Ki. 4:13), a district in Bashan. נַחַל "valley," used for the burial of Moses (Deut. 34:6). It is not necessary, and indeed no improvement, to render the noun here as "dust," on the basis of Christian Palestinian Aramaic (Jacob, in *ZDMG*, vol. 55, p. 41).

יִמְשׁוֹךְ, generally transitive, is probably intransitive in Jud. 4:6; 20:37; Job 24:22; see the Comm. *ad loc.*). Here it has the meaning "proceed, march." Or it may be taken as a reflexive intransitive, "is drawn."

The two closing stichs are not to be interpreted, with some commentators, to mean that the death of the evil-doer is no different from that of all men before and after his time (Ibn E.), because this idea is not appropriate in the context here nor a sufficiently powerful presentation of Job's standpoint. The stichs are much better understood as describing the large number of participants in the funeral procession walking before and after his bier. Cf. the Arab. proverb in Burkhardt, "The bier of a stranger — no man before it or behind it," and see Koheleth's bitter reference to the elaborate procession at the malefactor's funeral (Ecc. 8:10 and *KMW ad loc.*).

21:34 Stich b is a *casus pendens* without a pronominal referent; hence, lit. "your answers — falsehood remains (of them)." Cf. such instances as I Sam.

20:23; I Ki. 6:12; Isa. 66:18; Jer. 44:16; Hos. 8:13; Dan. 1:20; on Ps. 9:7, cf. Gordis, "Ps. 9–10," in *JQR*, vol. 48, 1957, pp. 110 ff.

מַעַל "betrayal of the truth, i.e., falsehood." Cf. Arabic *maᶜala* "fraud." There is no need to emend to עָמָל (Ehr., Yel.). The connotations of the root *māᶜal* are noteworthy. It is a priestly term occurring in the Priestly Code, Ezek. and Chronicles (e.g., Lev. 5:15; Ezek. 14:13; II Chr. 36:14) in the meaning of "violation of a sacred object" and, by extension, treachery by a woman against her husband (Nu. 5:12, 27) and by Israel against God (Deut. 32:51; Ezra 10:2, etc.). Here, Job declares the Friends' answers to be an act of faithlessness against the truth and by that token against God. He thus anticipates God's final judgment on the Friends: "For you have not spoken the truth about Me as has my servant Job" (42:7, 12).

The Third Cycle

Introductory Note

Unlike the first two cycles, which have reached us intact, the third cycle has suffered obvious dislocation and loss of material. Thus, only the opening speeches of Eliphaz (chapter 22) and of Job (chapters 23–24) are in order. Yet even here in chapter 24 we are confronted by major difficulties with regard to the interpretation of the text and its relevance to the argument.

Fortunately, much of the third cycle can be restored, especially when the stylistic traits of the book are taken into account. Chapter 25 is much too short for Bildad. Most of Chapter 26, on the other hand, which is assigned to Job in our received text, is inappropriate to his position, but highly congenial to Bildad's. Similarly, the latter part of chapter 27, which is also attributed to Job, stands in direct antithesis to all he has maintained.

Chapter 28 is a "Hymn to Wisdom," differing radically in its lyrical form from the dialogic structure of the debate. It is, however, significant that it has found its way into the book. It reflects in brief compass the basic outlook of the poet, which is elaborated upon in the God speeches that constitute the climax of the book. Chapter 28 is therefore best regarded as an independent poem by the author of Job or by a member of his school.

By allocating the appropriate portions of chapters 26 and 27 to Bildad and Zophar, respectively, and by recognizing the independent character of the "Hymn to Wisdom" (chapter 28), we gain an additional advantage. We are able to reduce the dimensions of Job's reply, which is much too long, occupying six chapters in the received text (chapters 26–31).

While the evidence of injury sustained by the text is clear, all proposed restorations, of which there have been many, our own included, are necessarily tentative and uncertain. The reconstruction proposed here requires a minimal change of order in the Masoretic text. For details, the reader is referred to *BGM*, chapter VIII, Special Note 20, and the Commentary below.

The Speech of Eliphaz (22)

Job's continued recalcitrance has stripped even Eliphaz of his urbanity. Finding his theory of Divine justice contradicted by the facts, Eliphaz proceeds to the time-honored device of adjusting the facts to the theory. Accordingly, he invents a long catalogue of crimes committed by Job, of which we have previously heard nothing. Eliphaz is able to explain these alleged actions of Job on the ground that he expected to be safe from punishment because God is so far away from man.

Nevertheless, all is not lost. Job has only to repent sincerely of his sins and he will be restored to God's favor. Not only will he become prosperous himself, but he will be able to intercede for other sinners through his virtue. Thus, to the familiar biblical doctrine of "vertical responsibility" (in time), which is expressed in the idea of God's visiting the sins of the fathers upon the children, Eliphaz adds the concept of "horizontal responsibility" (in space). This idea underlies the narrative in Genesis which tells how the patriarch Abraham pleaded with God to spare the sinful city of Sodom because of the merit of ten righteous men who might be living in it (Gen. 18:20–33).

There is exquisite irony in the fact that Eliphaz's confident assurance that the righteous can intercede for sinners is fulfilled to the letter in a dramatic and totally unexpected way — after the Dialogue is completed, it is Job who is called upon to plead for Eliphaz and his Friends (42:7–10).

At all events, Eliphaz, the oldest and the wisest of the Friends, who began with words of comfort, is able to close on a note of hope.

22   Eliphaz the Temanite answered, saying,
2   Is it God whom a man benefits
            when he is wisely in harmony with Him?
3   Is it a favor to the Almighty if you are righteous,
            or His gain if you keep your ways blameless?

4   Is it because of your piety that He reproves you
            and enters into judgment with you?
5   In fact, your wickedness is immense,
            there is no end to your iniquities.
6   For you have taken pledges even from your kinsmen without reason,
            and stripped the naked of their clothing.
7   No water have you given to the weary,
            and from the hungry you have withheld bread.
8   For you believe,
      "The man of violence owns the land,
            and he who is powerful lives upon it."
9   Widows you have sent away empty-handed,
            and the arms of the fatherless are crushed.
10   Therefore snares are round about you,
            and sudden terror dismays you.

11   Since you cannot see through darkness
            or when a flood of waters covers you,
12   you thought,
      "Indeed, God is in the lofty heavens,
            and see the host of stars, how high they are!"
13   So you said,
      "What does God know?
            Can He judge through the thick cloud?
14   Clouds cover Him, so that He cannot see
            as He strolls about the circuit of heaven."

15   Will you keep to the old ways
            which wicked men have trodden,
16   who were cut off before their time,
            whose foundation a river has washed away,
17   who said to God, "Turn away from us,
            for what can the Almighty do for us?"
18   Yet it was He who filled their houses with good things —
            far be from me the counsel of the wicked!
19   The righteous will see this and be glad,
            the innocent will laugh them to scorn,
20   saying, "Indeed, our enemies are cut off,
            and their wealth is consumed by the fire."

21   Put yourself in harmony with Him and make peace,
            and thus you will attain to well-being.
22   Accept instruction from His mouth
            and place His words in your heart.
23   If you return to the Almighty, you will be rebuilt;
            if you remove iniquity from your tent,

כב א וַיַּעַן אֱלִיפַז הַתֵּמָנִי וַיֹּאמַר:

2 הַלְאֵל יִסְכָּן־גָּבֶר כִּי־יִסְכֹּן עָלֵימוֹ מַשְׂכִּיל:

3 הַחֵפֶץ לְשַׁדַּי כִּי תִצְדָּק וְאִם־בֶּצַע כִּי־תַתֵּם דְּרָכֶיךָ:

4 הֲמִיִּרְאָתְךָ יֹכִיחֶךָ יָבוֹא עִמְּךָ בַּמִּשְׁפָּט:

ה הֲלֹא רָעָתְךָ רַבָּה וְאֵין־קֵץ לַעֲוֺנֹתֶיךָ:

6 כִּי־תַחְבֹּל אַחֶיךָ חִנָּם וּבִגְדֵי עֲרוּמִּים תַּפְשִׁיט:

7 לֹא־מַיִם עָיֵף תַּשְׁקֶה וּמֵרָעֵב תִּמְנַע־לָחֶם:

8 וְאִישׁ זְרוֹעַ לוֹ הָאָרֶץ וּנְשׂוּא פָנִים יֵשֶׁב בָּהּ:

9 אַלְמָנוֹת שִׁלַּחְתָּ רֵיקָם וּזְרֹעוֹת יְתֹמִים יְדֻכָּא:

י עַל־כֵּן סְבִיבוֹתֶיךָ פַחִים וִיבַהֶלְךָ פַּחַד פִּתְאֹם:

11 אוֹ־חֹשֶׁךְ לֹא־תִרְאֶה וְשִׁפְעַת־מַיִם תְּכַסֶּךָּ:

12 הֲלֹא־אֱלוֹהַּ גֹּבַהּ שָׁמָיִם וּרְאֵה רֹאשׁ כּוֹכָבִים כִּי־רָמּוּ:

13 וְאָמַרְתָּ מַה־יָּדַע אֵל הַבְעַד עֲרָפֶל יִשְׁפּוֹט:

14 עָבִים סֵתֶר־לוֹ וְלֹא יִרְאֶה וְחוּג שָׁמַיִם יִתְהַלָּךְ:

טו הַאֹרַח עוֹלָם תִּשְׁמוֹר אֲשֶׁר דָּרְכוּ מְתֵי־אָוֶן:

16 אֲשֶׁר־קֻמְּטוּ וְלֹא־עֵת נָהָר יוּצַק יְסוֹדָם:

17 הָאֹמְרִים לָאֵל סוּר מִמֶּנּוּ וּמַה־יִּפְעַל שַׁדַּי לָמוֹ:

18 וְהוּא מִלֵּא בָתֵּיהֶם טוֹב וַעֲצַת רְשָׁעִים רָחֲקָה מֶנִּי:

19 יִרְאוּ צַדִּיקִים וְיִשְׂמָחוּ וְנָקִי יִלְעַג־לָמוֹ:

כ אִם־לֹא נִכְחַד קִימָנוּ וְיִתְרָם אָכְלָה אֵשׁ:

21 הַסְכֶּן־נָא עִמּוֹ וּשְׁלָם בָּהֶם תְּבוֹאַתְךָ טוֹבָה:

22 קַח־נָא מִפִּיו תּוֹרָה וְשִׂים אֲמָרָיו בִּלְבָבֶךָ:

23 אִם־תָּשׁוּב עַד־שַׁדַּי תִּבָּנֶה תַּרְחִיק עַוְלָה מֵאָהֳלֶךָ:

כ״ב v. 15. חצי הספר בפסוקים

24   you can safely place your gold in the dust,
           and the gold of Ophir mid the rocks of the valley,
25   because God will be your true gold,
           and your real treasure of silver.
26   Then you will be able to plead with the Almighty
           and lift your face to God.
27   When you pray to Him, He will hear you,
           and you will pay your vows in thanksgiving.
28   When you issue a decree it will be fulfilled for you,
           and light will shine upon your ways.
29   When men are brought low you will say, "Rise up,"
           and he who has been humbled will be saved.
30   Even the guilty will escape punishment,
           escaping through the purity of your hands.

24 וְשִׁית־עַל־עָפָר בָּצֶר   וּבְצוּר נְחָלִים אוֹפִיר:

כה וְהָיָה שַׁדַּי בְּצָרֶיךָ   וְכֶסֶף תּוֹעָפוֹת לָךְ:

26 כִּי־אָז עַל־שַׁדַּי תִּתְעַנָּג   וְתִשָּׂא אֶל־אֱלוֹהַּ פָּנֶיךָ:

27 תַּעְתִּיר אֵלָיו וְיִשְׁמָעֶךָ   וּנְדָרֶיךָ תְשַׁלֵּם:

28 וְתִגְזַר־אֹמֶר וְיָקָם לָךְ   וְעַל־דְּרָכֶיךָ נָגַהּ אוֹר:

29 כִּי־הִשְׁפִּילוּ וַתֹּאמֶר גֵּוָה   וְשַׁח עֵינַיִם יוֹשִׁעַ:

ל יְמַלֵּט אִי־נָקִי   וְנִמְלַט בְּבֹר כַּפֶּיךָ:

CHAPTER 22

22:2 The intent of the verse is clear — a righteous man really confers no benefit on God by his goodness. The specific meaning of the words, however, offers difficulties. The root סכן has a large number of homonyms in Hebrew. Thus BDB and KB list three distinct roots: (I) "to be of use or service" (Job 15:3; 34:9). Under this rubric are listed (a) סֹכֵן "caretaker, steward" (Isa. 22:15; *Tel-el-Amarna, sakanu*; Phoenician סכן "prefect," (b) "be used or accustomed" (Nu. 22:20), and (c) "be familiar, know intimately" (Ps. 139:3 and our passage), (d) "supply, store," whence מִסְכְּנוֹת (Ex. 1:11). (II) "endanger" (Ecc. 10:9 and frequently in mishnaic Hebrew). (III) "be poor," whence מִסְכֵּן (Ecc. 4:13; 9:15, 16), probably an Akkadian loan-word, which has entered not only most Semitic languages but also Indo-European tongues, French *mesquin*; Spanish *mesquino*. It is clear that the plethora of meanings given under the first root are not easily derived from the same source, and may represent several distinct roots. Moreover, several biblical passages, including 22:21, cannot be interpreted satisfactorily by any of these meanings. (Cf. the Comm. there and Gordis, in *LGJV*, pp. 184–87.)

In our passage, the meaning "be useful, benefit, profit" is generally given to the verb in both stichs. Stich a is rendered "Can a man bring a benefit to God?" Stich b has been taken either as a subordinate clause: (a) "when a sage, i.e., a righteous man, does good to himself" or (b) "when a man does good to his fellow-man" (Ehr.). Or stich b is taken as coordinate and parallel to stich a, "Can even a sage benefit Him?" (P.) or as an answer to stich a: "Indeed, the sage benefits himself" (most).

The key to our passage lies in an explicit citation by Elihu in 34:9: כִּי־אָמַר לֹא יִסְכָּן־גָּבֶר בִּרְצֹתוֹ עִם־אֱלֹהִים "For Job has said, it does a man no good, when he is in favor with God, i.e. when he acts acceptably toward Him." It is therefore clear that stich b in our passage must express an idea similar to 34:9b. Similarly, 22:21 הַסְכֶּן־נָא עִמּוֹ וּשְׁלָם must express the idea "be in harmony with Him and at peace." This meaning "agree with" probably inheres also in Ps. 139:3 וְכָל־דְּרָכַי הִסְכַּנְתָּה "You have approved all my ways." We suggest, therefore, an independent homonym for our root, הַסְכֵּן being a metaplastic form for הַסְכֵּם "agree," common in mishnaic Hebrew. For the two roots, cf. שָׂטַן "hate, act as adversary" (Gen. 27:41; Ps. 55:4) and שָׂטַם (Hos. 9:7, 8), which becomes a name for Satan, *Mastema*, in Apocryphal literature (Jubilees 17:18; see Ginzberg, *Legends*, vol. VII, Index, s.v.). עָלֵימוֹ is the sing. masc. suffix = עָלָיו; cf. the Comm. on 20:2; Isa. 44:5, etc. In 22:21, the verb governs the preposition עִם. Here it governs the preposition עַל = אֶל "to Him, with Him." In Ps. 139:3, it governs the accusative.

מַשְׂכִּיל lit. "sage, wise man," is synonymous in Wisdom literature with the righteous (cf. Ps. 14:2 = 53:2; Dan. 11:33, 35; 12:3, 10). Here the noun may be the subject of the verb: "When a wise man puts himself in harmony with Him," or it may be used adverbially with גָּבֶר in stich a as the subject: "When a man puts himself wisely in harmony with Him." As is so often the case, the poet uses the same root in both stichs, but here for the purpose of a paronomasia. For similar instances cf. שׁוּב (Jer. 4:1; 8:4) and בצר in Job 22:24. The position of הַלְאֵל, as in 21:22, at the beginning is emphatic. Our verse now receives a clear and unforced meaning:

> "Is it God whom man benefits
> When he wisely puts himself in harmony with Him?"

22:3 חֵפֶץ, as the parallel בֶּצַע "profit, gain" indicates, here has the nuance "special benefit, favor." That God "desires" man's piety and integrity is of course a commonplace of biblical religion. תַּתֵּם a Hiphil, for תָּתֵם (cf. וַיַּסֵּב for וַיָּסֵב, Ex. 13:18). The doubling of the first consonant in geminate verbs is the Aramaic mode. As Max L. Margolis pointed out, Aramaic phonetics and morphology are imbedded in the structure of biblical Hebrew and are no evidence for a "late" date.

22:4 A bitterly ironic taunt against Job: "Is it because of your reverence that God is reproving you?" יִרְאָה = יִרְאַת ה׳ = "religion," both faith in God and obedience to His will (cf. 4:6; 15:4).

22:5 No more sweeping charge against Job has been lodged by any of the Friends, including the impolitic Zophar.

22:6 תַּחְבֹּל "take a pledge" (Ex. 22:25; Pr. 20:16; 27:13). Job has not only taken a pledge of objects which the poor borrower desperately needed (Deut. 24:6; Ezek. 18:12), like clothing (cf. Deut. 24:17; Am. 2:8), but he has compounded his heartless action by taking pledges from his kinsmen (אַחֶיךָ) who had a claim upon his help. Worst of all, he has done it חִנָּם "for nothing," actually giving nothing real or substantial in return for his pledge. In view of this triple crescendo of malfeasance, it is not necessary to revocalize אַחֶיךָ in the singular אָחִיךָ (so T, some mss., and Ehr.), which would mean "your fellow-man" (cf. Lev. 19:17). Stich b literally "the garment of the naked you have stripped." For the prolepsis here, anticipating the conclusion of the act in its operation, cf. וְכִי יָמוּת מֵת עָלָיו, Nu. 6:9; Deut. 17:6; Ezek. 18:32, as well as Isa. 47:2.

22:7 לֹא is emphatic, as in לֹא־מוֹת תְּמֻתוּן "you will surely not die" (Gen. 3:4). Here: "No water have you given to the thirsty." עָיֵף "faint," used specifically of thirst (Isa. 29:8; Pr. 25:25), and of "dry land" (Isa. 32:2; Ps. 63:2).

22:8 Many commentators delete the verse as a gloss or move it elsewhere (Sieg., Bu., Peake, D-G). In order to bring the verse into context, some commentators regard it as an oblique reference to Job, virtually in apposition to the 2nd pers. of the previous verse — "You, who are a mighty man who owns the earth, a privileged inhabitant of it" (D-G, P.).

However, the verse bears all the earmarks of an independent folk-utterance. This is clear from the parallelism, the general terms in which it is couched, and its striking paraphrase as an aphorism in rabbinic literature: לא ניתנה קרקע אלא לבעלי זרוע "land should be owned only by men of power" (*B. Sanh.* 58b). The verse is entirely appropriate as a quotation of the thought that Eliphaz attributes to Job:

> "For you thought (or think)
> The man of violence owns the land, etc."

Virtual quotations, without an explicit *verbum dicendi* or *cogitandi*, are used, both in biblical literature generally and in Wisdom in particular, to express the *present* thought of the subject (Gen. 26:7; Ps. 8:4 f.; 10:4; 59:8; Job 7:4; 15:21; 22:12–14, etc.), or his *former* position (Job 31:1–4, 13, 15; 27:5–12). On this subject, see the basic discussion in *PPS*, pp. 120–29; *BGM*, chap. XIII; and the Comm. on vv. 11–12 below. It is highly interesting that the Fragmentary Targum found in Qumran Cave 11 understood the passage correctly, prefixing its translation of the verse, which has not survived, by the introductory formula ואמרת "and you say."

Thus, an insight into biblical and Semitic style, first recognized and documented in the twentieth century, was known and utilized by an ancient translator two millennia ago, surely a remarkable confirmation of the usage.

נשׂוּא פָנִים "A man held in repute, eminent, important" (II Ki. 5:1; Isa. 3:3; 9:14), "to whom others show partiality, deference" (Lev. 19:15; Deut. 10:17; Mal. 2:9).

Eliphaz argues that Job has not hesitated to oppress the poor and the weak, because he believed, to cite Napoleon's epigram, that "God is on the side of the heaviest battalions."

22:9 רֵיקָם "empty-handed," Job has sent the widows away without any gift when they solicited charity and without any payment of their due when they sued in the courts. יְדֻכָּא "lit., are crushed," as the *difficilior lectio*, is more likely to be the original than תְּדֻכֶּא which LXX, S, V, T may have chosen for smoothness in translation.

22:11 On the subject of God's distance from man and the consequent failure of retribution, see Special Note 18.

This verse has been interpreted as a description of Job's punishment, his being exposed to darkness and inundation by a flood, both symbolic of trouble (Dil., Da., P.). But for this meaning, v. 11 is too weak, especially after v. 10. Even more decisive is the use of the entire stich b in Job 38:34, to refer to "the waters in the heavens." Finally, the reference to darkness and clouds, through which Job cannot see (vv. 13–14), strengthens our view that Eliphaz is presenting here the basis for Job's lack of fear of retribution. For the parallelism of darkness and clouds, cf. Ps. 18:12.

שִׁפְעַת "multitude," used of men (II Ki. 9:17), of camels (Isa. 60:6), of horses (Ezek. 26:10), and here (as well as in 38:4) of waters in the heavens.

22:12 גֹּבַהּ שָׁמָיִם adv. accus., "in the heights of the heavens." רֹאשׁ כּוֹכָבִים either (a) "the central star" (Bu.); (b) "the highest of the stars" (P.); or, better, (c) "the troop of stars." The noun רֹאשׁ, which is applied to an armed band (Job 1:17), is highly appropriate in view of the frequent biblical references to the stars as the "host of heaven" (I Ki. 22:19; Ps. 103:21, and often), since they served as the instruments for God's purposes.

כִּי־רָמוּ, the Dagesh in the Mem referred to by the Masorah is the *dagesh forte affectuosum*, in order to stress a consonant in pause (cf. Job 29:21; Ex. 27:19, and see Ges.-K., sec. 20, 2, 2c). The verse is in 4:4 meter and need not be reduced to 3:3 by deleting רֹאשׁ (Bu., D-G). Thus, vv. 13 and 14 are in 4:3 meter, vv. 15 and 16 in 3:3, vv. 17 and 18 in 4:4, and v. 27 in 3:2 meter. For this variation in meter, cf. the Song of the Sea (Exodus, chap. 15), the usage validated in Egyptian, Akkadian, and Ugaritic verse as well, and see *PPS*, p. 69.

22:13 Note the presence here of a *verbum dicendi* and its absence in vv. 11, 12. On this use of both methods, in the same passage, attested in biblical and Oriental literature, see *PPS*, pp. 116–20, and such instances as Jer. 2:25; 3:5; 4:7; 6:9; 12:6 f.; Job 21:19, 22, 28, 30, and the Sumerian epic, "Gilgamesh and the Land of the Living," lines 16–22 (S. N. Kramer, in *Journal of Cuneiform Studies*, vol. 1, 1947, pp. 3–46.) See Special Note 17.

22:14 חוּג "circle, circuit," from the root "draw around, make a circle," is applied to the earth (Isa. 40:12), to the deep (Pr. 8:27), and here to the heavens. The entire cosmos was conceived of as consisting of several circular layers, the heavens above the earth and the sea and Sheol beneath it. Stich b is a subordinate clause of condition: "As He strolls about the circuit of heaven." Not only is God far away, but He saunters about in His heavenly realm, unconcerned with men far below.

22:15 הָאֹרַח עוֹלָם "the ancient paths," which stich b particularizes as "those trodden by evil-doers." In Jer. 6:16, the same description is applied to the "good way" (נְתִיבוֹת עוֹלָם). Both paths of conduct open to man go back to the very beginning of his existence (Gen. 4:7; Deut. 11:26; 30:19; Ps. 1; Jer. 17:5–10). On the other hand, the phrase has also been revocalized as הָאֹרַח עֲוָלִים "the path of sinners" (Z. P. Chajes, Hö., TS), on the basis of the parallelism. The stich has been interpreted as "the paths of darkness" on the basis of Ugaritic *glm*, "grow dark" (Dahood, P.; though the root is not given in Gordon, *Ugaritic Textbook*, Glossary).

תִּשְׁמוֹר either (a) "observe" (I Sam. 1:12; Jer. 8:17; Am. 11:4) or (b) "cleave to," especially frequent in connection with a road (II Sam. 22:20; Ps. 18:22; Pr. 2:20).

22:16 קֻמְּטוּ "cut off," as in Arab. and mishnaic Hebrew (*M. Sheviit* 2:4): מזהמין את הנטיעות וקומטין אותן "They smear plants with rancid oil and cut

them off." The root is probably distinct from the one in Job 16:8, וַתִּקְמְטֵנִי
(cf. the Comm. *ad loc.*).

לֹא עֵת = "not at the (proper) time," an accusative of time; cf. Gen.
14:15. On the noun, cf. לָמָּה תָמוּת בְּלֹא עִתֶּךָ (Ecc. 7:18; Lev. 15:25; Job 15:32).
In stich b, treating יְסוֹדָם as the subject: "Their foundation is poured as a
river" produces a far-fetched figure. Render: "A river is poured upon, hence,
washes away, their foundations" (so Ra., Dh., Hö.). The poet may have had
the tradition of Noah's flood in mind here.

22:17 Vv. 17 and 18 are deleted on the grounds (a) that they disturb the
connection between v. 16 and v. 19; and (b) that they are a repetition of
21:14–16 (Bu., Dh., Hö., D-G). The imposition of Western categories of logic
upon Oriental literary structure is a methodologically dubious procedure, in
view of the Oriental principle of association rather than relevance (cf. Gordis,
"On Methodology in Biblical Exegesis," in *JQR*, vol. 61, 1970, pp. 114 f.).
In fact, if relevance be the test, v. 19 should also be deleted, since vv. 16 and
20 both describe the destruction of the wicked. As for the relationship of our
passage to chap. 21, it should be noted that of the six stichs in 21:14–16,
only the first and the last re-occur in chap. 22, and the four intermediate
stichs of the earlier chapter are replaced by two different stichs here. In
stich b לָמוֹ should be corrected to לָנוּ (LXX, P), as in Ps. 64:6; 80:7. The
confusion of Mem and Nun is common, the opposite occurring in v. 20 below
(see the Comm.).

22:18 Stich a is Eliphaz's comment on the real source of the evil-doers'
well-being. Stich b is a ritual formula of separation from their sinful sentiments (see the Comm. on 21:16).

22:19 If a specific event like the Flood were being described in v. 16, one
would have expected the perfect רָאוּ, "the righteous saw it." It is more
probable that Eliphaz is generalizing about the doom of evil-doers and therefore the imperfect tense is in place, either in a frequentative sense, "they
see it," or simply "they will see it."

22:20 The verse is a "virtual quotation" of what the righteous say when
the sinners receive their just deserts. Hence a *verbum dicendi*, "saying," is
understood. אִם־לֹא = הֲלֹא "indeed." The suffix in קִימָנוּ is manifestly incorrect;
it should be in the 3rd pers. plur., as the parallelism makes clear. For another
instance of נו = ם, cf. Ps. 12:8. The noun cannot mean "enemies, opponents,"
nor need it be emended to קָמֵינוּ (Ol.). The noun קִים or קִימָה is a *hapax legomenon*
which it is hazardous to emend. The proposed יְקוּם (plus suffix) (Me., Bu.,
P., Ehr.) occurs only in Gen. 7:4, 23; Deut. 11:6, where it has the meaning
of "living creatures," which is inappropriate here. The rabbinic קִיּוּם (Hö.)
means "preservation," and is also unsatisfactory. The emendation קִנְיָנָם
(Perles) is preferable, but not necessary. The root קוּם "stand, endure" is
semantically parallel to "substance" from Latin *stare*, i.e., "that which stands,

endures." Hence, the word means "wealth, possessions." קִימָם may be a
fem. noun קִימָה with the suffix added to the stem, like יְתְרָם (from יְתְרָה) in
the adjoining stich. Cf. the Comm. on 5:13; 11:9; 19:5.

יִתְרָם "their abundance, wealth"; cf. יִתְרָה (Isa. 15:7), יִתְרַת (Jer. 48:36),
the late biblical noun יִתְרוֹן "profit" (Ecc. 1:3 a. e.), and the proper noun
יִתְרוֹ (Ex. 4:18; Jud. 8:20, and often).

22:21   On הַסְכֶּן cf. the Comm. on 22:2a. Stich a: "agree with Him and be
at peace (with Him)." The plural בָּהֶם refers to these two verbs, though
they are synonymous in meaning. For other illustrations where biblical
Hebrew uses a plural pronoun to refer to a single act or object, if it is expressed by two distinct terms, cf. Isa. 49:15; Ezek. 18:26; 33:18; Zech. 2:6 f.;
and see Gordis, in *Louis Ginzberg Jubilee Volume*, English Section, pp. 184 ff.,
and the Comm. on Job 13:20 f. Stich b: "Through them good will come to
you." The second Tav in the verbal form is anomalous (cf. Deut. 33:16
תְּבוֹאתָה); it may be the result of a psychological confusion of the verb with
the noun תְּבוּאָתְךָ "your produce, income." The verb is obviously required here.

22:22   תּוֹרָה occurs only here in Job. It obviously refers not to ritual law,
but to moral and religious guidance. This is its usual meaning in the Prophets
(cf., e.g., Isa. 1:10; 2:3; 5:24; 8:16; 42:21; 51:7; Jer. 9:12; 16:11; Hos. 4:6;
8:1; Am. 2:4), and its exclusive meaning in Wisdom (cf. e.g., Pr. 4:2; 13:14;
21:4, 7, 9, etc.). It is particularly appropriate for Eliphaz, since he has already
twice given Job the benefit of his revelation (4:12 ff.; 15:11).

22:23   For the Hebrew תִּבָּנֶה Septuagint renders *tapeinoses* "you will humble
yourself." This has been invoked as a basis for reading תֵּעָנֶה (Ew., Del.,
D-G, Ehr.) or תִּכָּנַע (Me., Sieg., Gr., Hö.). However, if either emendation is
adopted, the word order would need to be totally different, as it rightly is
in LXX, and a Vav would need to be added to the verb: "If you turn and
humble yourself before the Lord." The MT is to be preferred: "You will
be rebuilt." The verb suggests the theme of the granting of offspring; cf.
אוּלַי אִבָּנֶה מִמֶּנָּה; (Gen. 16:2; 30:2), which is the only meaning the Niphal
has with a personal subject. Stich b can be construed in two ways: (a) Either
אִם and תִּבָּנֶה are understood: "If you remove iniquity from your tent (you
will be rebuilt)." The two succeeding verses are then independent conclusions; or (b) it is preferable to regard v. 23a as containing an independent
and complete condition, while stich b represents the protasis of a new condition of which the apodosis is to be found in vv. 24 and 25: "If you will return
to the Almighty, you will be rebuilt. If you remove iniquity from your tent,
you can place your gold on the ground, etc." On the Vav introducing the
apodosis, cf. Ex. 12:44; I Sam. 25:27; II Sam. 14:10; and see BDB, s.v.
Vav. 5, p. 254b.

22:24   בֶּצֶר is rendered "fortress," like מִבְצָר by Ra. Generally it is understood as "precious ore, gold" (and also in v. 25), primarily on the basis of

the parallelism with אוֹפִיר. This meaning is generally derived from the Arab. cognate *baṭara* "break off, cut off."

The verse has been interpreted as a call to Job to regard gold as of no value: "Cast off gold to the ground and Ophir in the rock of the valleys." However, for this idea the verb שִׁית "place" is inappropriate; cf. the diametrically opposite use of its synonym שים in Job 31:24. Hö. changes עַל־עָפָר to לֶעָפָר and בְּצוּר to כְּצוּר (the latter change on the basis of LXX, V, T), and renders: "Consider as dust the gold and Ophir like the rock of the valleys." He then proceeds to delete vv. 24 and 25 as inappropriate in the context. However, Job has not been accused by the Friends at any point of greed and love of gold, so that this injunction to him would be gratuitous. Here, as at the end of his first speech (5:19–25), Eliphaz holds out to Job the promise of security when he has made his peace with God — Job will be able to leave his gold unguarded. עַל־עָפָר = "on the earth" (cf. Job 19:25; 41:25). Ophir is the traditional home of fine gold, probably in southern or southeastern Arabia. See the biblical encyclopedias on the various theories as to its location.

22:25 וְהָיָה שַׁדַּי בְּצָרֶיךָ is rendered "The Almighty will be your helper against your enemies" (LXX, V), obviously construing בְּצָרֶיךָ as "against your foes" (so Ra.). However, as he recognizes, the idiom would normally mean: "God will be among your foes" (cf. Jud. 11:35). The stich is therefore generally rendered: "Shaddai will be your gold," a rather strange figure, which is perhaps supported by stich b. On the other hand, it would be entirely natural (cf. Ps. 18:3; 48:4; 94:22) to speak of God as a "fortress" (בֶּצֶר, a parallel form to מִבְצָר). Cf. the place name בֶּצֶר (Deut. 4:43; Jos. 20:8; I Chr. 6:63); בֶּצֶר "enclosure" (Mic. 2:12). It is tempting to see in the choice of this rare noun instead of מִבְצָר a *talḥin*, with both meanings, "gold" and "fortress," present simultaneously in the consciousness of the poet. A *talḥin* which is morphologically an exact parallel to ours occurs in Lam. 2:13, where שֶׁבֶר "break" is chosen by the poet because it recalls מִשְׁבָּר "wave." On *talḥin*, see Gordis, in *Sepher Moshe Seidel*, pp. 255–63, and the Comm. on 3:6; 12:6, *inter alia*.

תּוֹעָפוֹת for which Arab. *yafaʿa* "ascend," *yafiʿun* "hill" has been adduced, is generally rendered "eminence, height," a meaning satisfactory in Ps. 95:4, less so in Nu. 23:22, and highly dubious in our passage. It has been rendered here: "heaps, bars of silver" (BDB), or "most exalted, finest of silver." Hö. renders the phrase "shining silver" on the basis of B. S. 45:11, where the description of the High Priest Aaron contains the phrase ויאזרהו בתועפות ראם, which he understands to mean, "He girded him with horns, i.e., the rays of the wild ox." However, this latter passage seems merely to be a reminiscence of Nu. 23:22 and its meaning may well not have been clear even to Ben Sira himself. Yel. renders "silver from dark recesses" on the theory that יעף is a metaplastic form for the roots יפע and עוף in Job 10:22. See the Comm.

22:26 The verb תִּתְעַנָּג is generally rendered "You will take delight, rejoice," a meaning which it possesses in Isa. 55:2; 58:14; 66:11; Ps. 37:11. However, it cannot have this meaning in Isa. 57:4; Ps. 37:4; Job 27:10; and in our passage, as is clear from the parallelism and the context (see the next verse). In all these passages its appropriate sense is "implore, importune," a meaning related to the Arab. cognate by metathesis, *naja^ca* VIII "seek a favor or present" and *ghanaja* I, V, "play the coquette, use amorous gestures, feign coyness." (Cf. Lane, *Arabic Lexicon*, vol. I, Part 6, p. 2299; Dozy, *Supplément aux Dictionnaires Arabes*, vol. 2, p. 228b.) This latter meaning was recognized by Saadia, who rendered the Hebrew verb here by the root *dalla* "be coquettish" (whence the proper name "Delilah" in Jud., chap. 16). So too Ehr.: "like a spoiled child, you can put every desire before him." (Also Yel.) On the semantics of these two meanings "be impudent" (Arab. *ghanaja*) and "demand, importune" (Hebrew ענג), cf. Lat. *peto* "beg, demand" and *petulans* "forward, pert, impudent." On the other hand, the meanings "touch" (Hebrew *nāga^c*) and "implore" (Hebrew *^canag*) may also be semantically related, perhaps because the suppliant sought to touch the garment of his superior, as in the encounter of Saul and Samuel (I Samuel, chap. 15; esp. v. 26). Cf. פגע "meet" (Ex. 5:20), "touch" (Jos. 16:7; 19:21, 22; etc.), and "entreat" (Jer. 36:25; Ruth 1:16), and the root למס (cf. the Comm. on 6:14; 9:23). When Job makes his peace with God, he will be able to importune God with the assurance that he will be answered, like a favored child by an indulgent parent (cf. v. 27).

Stich b וְתִשָּׂא אֶל־אֱלוֹהַּ פָּנֶיךָ "you will be able to lift your face to God with confidence" (LXX, with cheerfulness) (as in II Sam. 2:22; Job 11:15). The phrase here carries the additional nuance of "lifting one's face to God in prayer" (so Ra.). Cf. Ezra 9:6 בֹּשְׁתִּי וְנִכְלַמְתִּי לְהָרִים אֱלֹהַי פָּנַי אֵלֶיךָ כִּי עֲוֹנֹתֵינוּ רָבוּ "I am ashamed, O my God, to lift my face to You because our sins are many."

22:27 Job's prayers will be answered (stich a) and he will therefore be able to pay his vows of thanksgiving. (Cf. Jonah 2:10; Nah. 2:1; Ps. 65:2; 116:14.)

22:28 Eliphaz here introduces the idea of "horizontal" collective responsibility, which is basic to biblical theology and receives elaborate development in postbiblical Judaism. For this important subject, cf. *BGM*, pp. 94 f., 138 ff., and Gordis, "Corporate Responsibility in Job," in *JNES*, vol. 4, 1945, pp. 54 f. Eliphaz assures Job that when he is again reconciled with God, his righteousness will not only bring him well-being, but will also make it possible for him to set aside God's decree of punishment against evil-doers. Cf. *B. Mo^ced Qatan* 16b: אמר הקב״ה אני מושל באדם ומי מושל בי. צדיק שאני גוזר גזירה והוא מבטלה "Said the Holy One, Blessed be He, 'I rule over man, and who rules over Me?' The saint, for I issue a decree and he sets it aside." Similarly, the Talmud applies our passage to the rabbinic wonder-worker, Honi Ha-me^caggel: "You decree below and the Holy One, blessed be He, fulfills your command above" (*B. Taan.* 23a). The 4th-century Babylonian sage, Abaye, declared, "The world could not endure with less than the thirty-six saints who greet the Divine Presence daily" (*ibid.*). The tradition of the thirty-six humble saints upon whom the preservation of the world depends sustained extensive development in the posttalmudic period and finds poignant expression in André Schwarz-Bart's novel *The Last of the Just*, which deals with the Nazi Holocaust.

Stich b: "When you issue a decree, it will be fulfilled for you." On the use of the verb, cf. Isa. 14:24; Jer. 44:29.

22:29 הִשְׁפִּילוּ is best interpreted not as a transitive (P.), but as a stative describing a condition, "if men are brought low"; cf. הַמַּשְׁפִּילִי "is low" (Ps. 113:6); הַמַּגְבִּיהִי "is high" (*ibid.*; Job 5:7; 39:27; Ob. 1:4). Ehr. makes the attractive suggestion to revocalize the verb as הִשְׁפִּילוֹ, "when God brings someone low," but the change is not necessary.

וַתֹּאמֶר גֵּוָה "lit., you will say, 'pride'." גֵּוָה is a contraction for גַּאֲוָה; cf. Jer. 13:17; Job 33:17; Dan. 4:34 וְדִי מַהְלְכִין בְּגֵוָה יָכִל לְהַשְׁפָּלָה; it is here used as an exclamation: "Go in pride, rise upward!"

שַׁח עֵינַיִם = "low of eyes, humble" opposed to גְּבַהּ עֵינַיִם "lofty-eyed, arrogant" (Isa. 5:15; Ps. 101:5). יוֹשִׁעַ = "He will save," may be revocalized as a Niphal יִוָּשַׁע "will be saved," or understood as an impersonal, equivalent to a passive.

22:30 אִי־נָקִי is definitely not to be emended to אִישׁ נָקִי (D-G) or אֶת נָקִי (Parhon, Reiske, Hö.) and then translated "innocent" (LXX). On the contrary, MT is to be rendered: "The one not innocent, i.e., guilty." אִי is the ordinary negative in Ethiopic, occurring also in Phoenician (*CIS*, I, 3, 5). It is exceedingly common in rabbinic (and modern) Hebrew, as in the common phrase אִי אפשר "not possible." In addition to our passage, this negative particle may occur in another biblical passage. In I Sam. 4:21, the proper name אִי כָבוֹד is given a folk-etymology that underlies the explanation in the text, "Glory has departed from Israel." The name was probably understood as אִי "no" + כָּבוֹד "glory." It is less likely that אִי was taken to mean "alas"; that occurs in Ecc. 4:10; 10:16, and in mishnaic Hebrew אִי חָכָם "alas, the wise" (*B. Taan.* 7a a. e.).

יְמַלֵּט in the Piel may be transitive: "God will deliver the guilty" or, better, may be given a reflexive, passive sense: "He will be saved by the purity of your hands." For this reflexive-passive use of the Piel, cf. וַיְגַלַּח (Gen. 41:14), יְמַלֵּט (Am. 2:15), וָאֲפַלְּטָה (Job 23:7).

Job's Reply to Eliphaz (23–24)

Job does not dignify Eliphaz's accusations with a direct denial. Instead, he tells of his efforts to find God, hoping to be vindicated through this confrontation. Even in his extremity Job still believes that if he could meet his divine Adversary, God would recognize his essential uprightness. Job has therefore sought Him everywhere, but God has eluded him. Nevertheless, Job stoutly reaffirms his innocence in the face of the terror and darkness that envelop him (chapter 23).

Chapter 24 is extremely difficult, both with regard to the interpretation of individual verses and to the appropriateness of the chapter as a whole to Job's outlook. Some scholars have deleted the text in whole or in part as unauthentic, or have assigned some sections to Zophar's third speech. Since the meaning of many verses is highly obscure, these procedures are methodologically questionable. It would seem sounder to try to relate the chapter to the context in which it is actually found.

Basically, the chapter seems to be a complaint about the injustice of the world. It thus belongs to a literary genre amply attested in Babylonian and Egyptian Wisdom literature. The chapter contains a series of descriptions alternating between the criminal oppressors and their hapless victims. As is frequent in Wisdom literature, the subject of each section is not explicitly identified by the poet. The reader is expected to recognize the specific theme from the context.

The complaint opens with a lament by Job that God's saints do not see the promised hour of retribution coming upon the sinners. Then follow two themes in alternation: descriptions of the acts of evildoers (vv. 2–4), the suffering of the weak (vv. 5–8), the robbery perpetrated by the rich (v. 9), the misery of the poor (vv. 10–12), and, finally, the crimes of the malefactors (vv. 13–17).

Next comes a passage that contends that for all their superficial success the wicked are ultimately destroyed (vv. 18–24). This comfortable doctrine is obviously not Job's own position. It is better to regard it as a quotation by him of the conventional belief of the Friends. This stylistic usage of citation and refutation has been characteristic of Job in both earlier cycles (chapters 12 and 21). The conventional view of retribution in this chapter must therefore have been rebutted by Job in a passage that originally followed in the text but was lost when the third cycle became disarrayed. After this lacuna comes the closing verse of the chapter, in which Job challenges the Friends to disprove the truth of his contentions (v. 25).

23 Job answered, saying,
2   Though my complaint still remains defiant today,
            God's hand upon me is heavier than my groaning.
3   O that I knew where to find Him,
            that I could come to His dwelling!
4   I would lay my case before Him,
            and my mouth would not lack for arguments.
5   I would learn what He would answer me
            and understand what He would say to me.
6   Would He contend with me merely through His great power?
            No, He would surely pay heed to me,
7   for it would be an upright man arguing with Him,
            and I would be acquitted by my Judge for all time.

8   But I go to the east and He is not there;
            to the west, and do not perceive Him;
9   to the north, where He is concealed, and I do not behold Him;
            He is hidden in the south, and I cannot see Him.

10   He surely knows the way that I have taken;
            if He tested me, I would emerge pure as gold.
11   In His footsteps I have followed;
            His way I have kept without swerving.
12   From His commandments I have not departed;
            in my bosom I have treasured the words of His mouth.

13   But He is determined, and who can turn Him back?
            Whatever He desires, that He does.
14   He will surely carry out what He has decreed for me —
            and He has many more such cases!

15   Therefore am I terrified at His presence;
            when I consider, I am in dread of Him.
16   For God has made my heart grow faint,
            the Almighty has terrified me.
17   Indeed, I am destroyed by darkness,
            and before my face is all-encompassing gloom.

24 Since the times of judgment are not hidden from the Almighty,
            why do those who love Him never see the days of retribution?
2   The wicked remove the ancient landmarks;
            they steal flocks and pasture them as their own.
3   They drive off the ass of the fatherless
            and take the widow's ox in pledge.
4   They force the needy off the road,
            so that the poor of the earth all cower in hiding.

5   The oppressed, as wild asses in the desert,
            go forth to their toil;
        they seek food in the wilderness,
            bread for their young.
6   They reap in a field not their own
            and toil late in the vineyard of the wicked.

כג א וַיַּ֥עַן אִיּ֗וֹב וַיֹּאמַֽר:

2 גַּם־הַ֭יּוֹם מְרִ֣י שִׂחִ֑י   יָ֝דִ֗י כָּבְדָ֥ה עַל־אַנְחָתִֽי:

3 מִֽי־יִתֵּ֣ן יָ֭דַעְתִּי וְאֶמְצָאֵ֑הוּ   אָ֝ב֗וֹא עַד־תְּכוּנָתֽוֹ:

4 אֶעֶרְכָ֣ה לְפָנָ֣יו מִשְׁפָּ֑ט   וּ֝פִ֗י אֲמַלֵּ֥א תוֹכָחֽוֹת:

5 אֵ֭דְעָה מִלִּ֣ים יַעֲנֵ֑נִי   וְ֝אָבִ֗ינָה מַה־יֹּ֥אמַר לִֽי:

6 הַבְּרָב־כֹּ֭חַ יָרִ֣יב עִמָּדִ֑י   לֹ֥א אַך־ה֝֗וּא יָשִׂ֥ם בִּֽי:

7 שָׁ֗ם יָ֭שָׁר נוֹכָ֣ח עִמּ֑וֹ   וַאֲפַלְּטָ֥ה לָ֝נֶ֗צַח מִשֹּׁפְטִֽי:

8 הֵ֤ן קֶ֣דֶם אֶהֱלֹ֣ךְ וְאֵינֶ֑נּוּ   וְ֝אָח֗וֹר וְֽלֹא־אָבִ֥ין לֽוֹ:

9 שְׂמֹ֣אול בַּעֲשֹׂת֣וֹ וְלֹא־אָ֑חַז   יַעְטֹ֥ף יָ֝מִ֗ין וְלֹ֣א אֶרְאֶֽה:

י כִּֽי־יָ֭דַע דֶּ֣רֶךְ עִמָּדִ֑י   בְּ֝חָנַ֗נִי כַּזָּהָ֥ב אֵצֵֽא:

11 בַּ֭אֲשֻׁרוֹ אָחֲזָ֣ה רַגְלִ֑י   דַּרְכּ֖וֹ שָׁמַ֣רְתִּי וְלֹא־אָֽט:

12 מִצְוַ֣ת שְׂ֭פָתָיו וְלֹ֣א אָמִ֑ישׁ   מֵ֝חֻקִּ֗י צָפַ֥נְתִּי אִמְרֵי־פִֽיו:

13 וְה֣וּא בְ֭אֶחָד וּמִ֣י יְשִׁיבֶ֑נּוּ   וְנַפְשׁ֖וֹ אִוְּתָ֣ה וַיָּֽעַשׂ:

14 כִּ֭י יַשְׁלִ֣ים חֻקִּ֑י   וְכָהֵ֖נָּה רַבּ֣וֹת עִמּֽוֹ:

טו עַל־כֵּ֭ן מִפָּנָ֣יו אֶבָּהֵ֑ל   אֶ֝תְבּוֹנֵ֗ן וְאֶפְחַ֥ד מִמֶּֽנּוּ:

16 וְ֭אֵל הֵרַ֣ךְ לִבִּ֑י   וְ֝שַׁדַּ֗י הִבְהִילָֽנִי:

17 כִּֽי־לֹ֣א נִ֭צְמַתִּי מִפְּנֵי־חֹ֑שֶׁךְ   וּ֝מִפָּנַ֗י כִּסָּה־אֹֽפֶל:

כד א מַדּ֗וּעַ מִ֭שַּׁדַּי לֹא־נִצְפְּנ֣וּ עִתִּ֑ים   וְ֝יֹדְעָ֗ו לֹא־חָ֥זוּ יָמָֽיו:

2 גְּבֻל֥וֹת יַשִּׂ֑יגוּ   עֵ֥דֶר גָּ֝זְל֗וּ וַיִּרְעֽוּ:

3 חֲמ֣וֹר יְתוֹמִ֣ים יִנְהָ֑גוּ   יַ֝חְבְּל֗וּ שׁ֣וֹר אַלְמָנָֽה:

4 יַטּ֣וּ אֶבְיוֹנִ֣ים מִדָּ֑רֶךְ   יַ֥חַד חֻ֝בְּא֗וּ עֲנִיֵּי־אָֽרֶץ:

5 הֵ֤ן פְּרָאִ֨ים ׀ בַּֽמִּדְבָּ֗ר   יָצְא֣וּ בְּ֭פָעֳלָם מְשַׁחֲרֵ֣י לַטָּ֑רֶף   עֲרָבָ֥ה ל֥וֹ לֶ֝֗חֶם לַנְּעָרִֽים:

6 בַּ֭שָּׂדֶה בְּלִיל֣וֹ יִקְצ֑וֹרוּ

כ״ג v. 17. אין כאן פסקא   כ״ד v. 1. וידעיו ק׳

v. 4. עניי ק׳   v. 6. יקצורו ק׳

7   At night they lie naked without clothes —
          with no covering in the cold,
8   drenched by the mountain rains
          lacking shelter, clinging to the rocks.

9   The wicked snatch the orphaned child from the breast
          and take the poor man's babe in pledge.

10   The oppressed go about naked, without clothes,
          and are hungry as they carry the sheaves.
11   Mid rows of olive trees they press out oil,
          they tread the wine vats — but remain thirsty.
12   The dying groan in terror
          and the wounded cry out for help —
          yet in all this God sees nothing wrong!

13   The evildoers rebel against the light;
          they refuse to know its ways
          and do not stay in its paths.
14   At nightfall the murderer arises,
          he kills the poor and the needy,
          and in the night he is a thief.
15   The eye of the adulterer also waits for dusk,
          saying, "No eye will see me,"
          as he places a disguise on his face.
16   In the dark they dig through houses,
          which they marked for themselves by day.
17   They never see the light,
          for to them every morning is like darkness
          and daybreak, like the terrors of deepest gloom.

18   You say to me,
       "They perish swiftly, like water,
          their estate is cursed in the land,
          no treader of vineyards will turn their way.
19   As drought and heat carry off snow-water,
          So does Sheol those who have sinned.
20   Even his mother's womb forgets him;
          the worm finds him sweet to the taste
       and he is remembered no longer —
          thus wickedness is broken as a tree.
21   Because he crushes the barren woman
          so that she cannot give birth,
          and he ill-treats the widow,
22   The mighty man may continue in his strength,
          he may survive, but has no faith in life.
23   God may let him feel safe and secure,
          but His eyes are on man's ways.

עָר֤וֹם יִֽלִּ֨ינוּ֙ מִבְּלִ֣י לְב֔וּשׁ   וְכֶ֖רֶם רָשָׁ֣ע יְלַקֵּֽשׁוּ׃ 7

מִזֶּ֖רֶם הָרִ֣ים יִרְטָ֑בוּ   וְאֵ֥ין כְּס֖וּת בַּקָּרָֽה׃ 8

יִגְזְל֣וּ מִשֹּׁ֣ד יָת֑וֹם   וּֽמִבְּלִ֣י מַחְסֶ֔ה חִבְּקוּ־צֽוּר׃ 9

עָר֤וֹם הִלְּכוּ֙ בְּלִ֣י לְב֔וּשׁ   וְעַל־עָנֵ֥י יַחְבֹּֽלוּ׃ י

בֵּין־שׁוּרֹתָ֥ם יַצְהִ֑ירוּ   וּֽרְעֵבִ֗ים נָשְׂא֥וּ עֹֽמֶר׃ 11

מֵעִ֤יר מְתִ֨ים ׀ יִנְאָ֗קוּ   יְקַבִּ֣ים דָּרְכ֣וּ וַיִּצְמָֽאוּ׃ 12

וֶֽאֱל֗וֹהַּ לֹא־יָשִׂ֥ים תִּפְלָֽה׃   וְנֶֽפֶשׁ־חֲלָלִ֨ים תְּשַׁוֵּ֗עַ

לֹֽא־הִכִּ֥ירוּ דְרָכָ֑יו   הֵ֤מָּה ׀ הָיוּ֙ בְּמֹֽרְדֵ֣י א֔וֹר 13

לָא֗וֹר יָ֮ק֤וּם רוֹצֵ֗חַ   וְלֹ֥א יָֽשְׁב֗וּ בִּנְתִֽיבֹתָֽיו׃ 14

וּבַלַּ֗יְלָה יְהִ֥י כַגַּנָּֽב׃   יִקְטָל־עָנִ֥י וְאֶבְי֑וֹן

לֵאמֹ֣ר לֹֽא־תְשׁוּרֵ֣נִי עָ֑יִן   וְעֵ֤ין נֹאֵ֨ף ׀ שָֽׁמְרָ֬ה נֶ֗שֶׁף טו

חָ֬תַר בַּחֹ֥שֶׁךְ בָּתִּ֑ים   וְסֵ֖תֶר פָּנִ֣ים יָשִֽׂים׃ 16

לֹא־יָֽדְע֥וּ אֽוֹר׃   יוֹמָ֖ם חִתְּמוּ־לָֽמוֹ

כִּֽי־יַכִּ֥יר בַּלְה֣וֹת צַלְמָֽוֶת׃   כִּ֤י יַחְדָּ֨ו ׀ בֹּ֣קֶר לָ֭מוֹ צַלְמָ֑וֶת 17

תְּקֻלַּ֣ל חֶלְקָתָ֣ם בָּאָ֑רֶץ   קַל־ה֤וּא ׀ עַל־פְּנֵי־מַ֗יִם 18

צִיָּ֤ה גַם־חֹ֨ם יִגְזְל֣וּ מֵֽימֵי־שֶׁ֑לֶג   לֹֽא־יִפְנֶ֗ה דֶּ֣רֶךְ כְּרָמִֽים׃ 19

יִשְׁכָּחֵ֨הוּ רֶ֗חֶם ׀ מְתָ֨קוֹ   שְׁא֣וֹל חָטָֽאוּ׃ כ

וַתִּשָּׁבֵ֥ר כָּעֵ֣ץ עַוְלָֽה׃   רִמָּ֗ה ע֤וֹד לֹֽא־יִזָּכֵ֗ר

וְ֝אַלְמָנָ֗ה לֹ֣א יְיֵטִֽיב׃   רֹעֶ֣ה עֲ֭קָרָה לֹ֣א תֵלֵ֑ד 21

יָ֝ק֗וּם וְֽלֹא־יַאֲמִ֥ין בַּֽחַיִּֽין׃   וּמָשַׁ֣ךְ אַבִּירִ֣ים בְּכֹח֑וֹ 22

וְ֝עֵינֵ֗יהוּ עַל־דַּרְכֵיהֶֽם׃   יִתֶּן־ל֣וֹ לָ֭בֶטַח וְיִשָּׁעֵ֑ן 23

24   Wait just a little and they are no more.
           They are brought low, fading like grass
           and are cut off like a head of grain."

       .   .   .   .
       .   .   .   .
       .   .   .   .
       .   .   .   .

25   If this is not so, who will prove that I lie,
           and show that my words are worthless?

וְהֻמְּכוּ כַּכֹּל יִקָּפְצוּן   24 רוֹמוּ מְּעַט ׀ וְאֵינֶנּוּ

וְאִם־לֹא אֵפוֹ מִי יַכְזִיבֵנִי   כה וּכְרֹאשׁ שִׁבֹּלֶת יִמָּלוּ׃

וְיָשֵׂם לְאַל מִלָּתִי׃

CHAPTER 23

23:2 גַּם הַיּוֹם, generally understood as "also, even to-day," is better rendered as "though today," thus linking the two stichs in a logical sequence. גַּם = "yet, but" (cf. Jer. 6:15; Ezek. 20:23; Ps. 95:9; 129:2; Ecc. 3:13; 4:8, 16, etc.). מְרִי, a substantive, "rebelliousness, defiance" (Nu. 17:25; Ezek. 2:8), a characteristic Hebrew use of a noun where we would use an adjective; cf. Isa. 30:9 עַם מְרִי "a rebellious people."

יָדִי is to be read יָדוֹ "God's hand" (LXX, P., Ew., Me., Dil., Du., D-G, Hö.). עַל here = "more than." (Cf. Gen. 48:22; Ex. 16:5; and BDB s.v. 2, p. 755a.) Job concedes that he has been defiant, but insists that God's oppressive hand (cf. 13:21; 19:21; Ps. 32:4) has been far worse.

23:3 The verse is virtually the protasis of a condition, the apodosis of which is in vv. 4–8. תְּכוּנָתוֹ, "lit., established place" (cf. אָכִין מוֹשָׁבִי 29:7; הֵכִין כִּסְאוֹ Ps. 103:19). יָדַעְתִּי וְאֶמְצָאֵהוּ, two finite verbs with a Vav, is one of the characteristic biblical modes of expressing the complementary infinitive, "I knew how to find him." Cf. חִמַּדְתִּי וְיָשַׁבְתִּי (Cant. 2:3).

23:4 תּוֹכָחוֹת not "reproof" but "argument." Cf. the use of the root throughout the book in a forensic sense, as in 6:25, 26; 13:15; 23:7, etc.

23:5 If God would meet him in judgment, Job would learn the content of God's complaints against him.

23:6 Though stich a is couched interrogatively, it logically continues to spell out the consequences of such an encounter. "Would God then be arguing with me merely by the exercise of superior power. as He has been doing until now?" (9:4, 19; 13:21). Stich b: "No, He would surely pay heed to me." שִׂים is an ellipsis for שִׂים לֵב. Cf. מִבְּלִי מֵשִׂים (Job 4:20); the synonymous שִׁית מִמֶּנִּי (10:20); וְיָשִׂימוּ וְיַשְׂכִּילוּ (Isa. 41:20). אַךְ is the emphatic particle (Deut. 16:15; Job 13:20; 19:13).

23:7 Another continuation of the conditional sentence, setting forth the reason why Job wishes the confrontation — his innocence (stich a) and the inevitable consequence of his vindication (stich b). For these two themes in the same sequence, cf. 13:16b and 13:18b. Cf. also 6:10.

שָׁם not "there" (Arab. *thamma*), but "then" (Arab. *thumma*); cf. כְּרָמֶיהָ מִשָּׁם "her vineyards from of yore, lit. from then" (Hos. 2:17); 6:7; Isa. 65:20 (directed to the future); Ps. 14:5; 36:13; 66:6; and see *PPS*, p. 250, note 33.

נוֹכָח, a reciprocal use of the Niphal, "engage one another in discussion"; cf. Isa. 1:18. וַאֲפַלְּטָה the Piel need not be revocalized as a Qal, since it is intransitive; cf. the Comm. on 22:30. מִשֹּׁפְטִי is emended to the plural מִשֹּׁפְטַי "from my judges" (Ehr.), but MT, which refers it to God, is entirely satisfactory.

23:8, 9   The proposed deletion of these two verses (Bu., Sieg., Du., D-G, Hö.) represents another illegitimate application of Western standards of logical relevance to Oriental composition, which is based upon the association of ideas. Having concluded the long condition (vv. 3–7), Job reverts to the theme with which he began in v. 3 — the impossibility of finding his Divine opponent and Judge.

The omission of v. 9 (but not v. 10) by LXX is no evidence of the absence of these verses in the original Hebrew text, since the two verses are linked together (see below). LXX probably omitted v. 9 because it found the text incomprehensible. The two verses contain all the four directions — east, west (cf. אָחוֹר Isa. 9:11; הַיָּם הָאַחֲרוֹן Deut. 11:24; 34:2; Joel 2:20), north, שְׂמֹאל "left hand" (Gen. 14:15; Jos. 19:27; Arab. *simal* "north wind"), and south (יָמִין I Sam. 23:19, 24; Ezek. 16:46; Ps. 89:13). The designation of the directions is based upon the Semite's facing east (Ra., Ibn E., Yel., P.). Cf. also the "four dimensions" of God's wisdom in Zophar's description, 11:8, 9.

23:9   בַּעֲשֹׂתוֹ has been emended because of the failure to recognize it as the Hebrew cognate of the Arabic *ghaša* (*ṭertiae Wa*) "cover," which occurs in Isa. 32:6; Pr. 12:23; 13:6; and in the proper name "Esau," "lit., the covered one," who is described as being like "a hairy coat" (Gen. 25:25); so Eitan, Yel.

It may be added that this meaning is the key to one of the most striking instances of paronomasia in the O. T. In Ob. 1:6 אֵיךְ נֶחְפְּשׂוּ עֵשָׂו נִבְעוּ מַצְפֻּנָיו "How has Esau (the covered one) been uncovered, his hidden treasures sought out!" The verb נֶחְפְּשׂוּ is in the plural because עֵשָׂו resembles a plural noun with masculine suffixes.

בַּעֲשֹׂתוֹ is a perfect parallel to יַעֲטֹף "covers himself" (Ps. 65:14; 73:6). The parallelism militates against rendering יַעֲטֹף as "he turns" (Ibn Janah, Du., Be., Bu., D-G), in spite of the Arab. and Syrian cognates, that carry this meaning.

In stich a the verb אֶהֱלֹךְ from 8a is understood, as it is in 8b. Render: "When I go to the north where He is hidden, I cannot see Him; when He is concealed in the south I do not behold Him."

The north was the hidden seat of the gods in Northwest Semitic mythology, as the etymology of the noun צָפוֹן "the hidden," indicates. Cf. יַרְכְּתֵי צָפוֹן II Ki. 19:23 = Isa. 37:24, a phrase then applied to Jerusalem as the seat of God (Ps. 48:3), in spite of its location in the south.

אָחֹז the pausal form for אַחַז = אֶחֱזֶה (cf. v. 11 אָט and וְתַחַז, Mic. 4:11).

23:10   כִּי is either the asseverative, "surely He knows," or perhaps "but He knows," i.e., "there is no need for Him to search for me as I search unavailingly for Him."

דֶּרֶךְ עִמָּדִי "The path that is with me, my usual path" (Ew., Bu., D-G). On the basis of P וקימי, Gr., Be. read דַּרְכִּי וְעָמְדִי, which D-G rightly rejects as inferior. Stich b is a hypothetical conditional sentence, with the perfect in the protasis and the imperfect in the apodosis: "If He tested me, I would emerge pure as gold." (Cf. 7:20 and see Ges.-K., Sec. 159, 3, Note, b; Dr., *HT*, Sec. 154.)

23:11 בַּאֲשֻׁרוֹ "in His steps, i.e., Job has followed God's path." אָט, the pausal form for אַטֶּה, the Hiphil of נטה "turn," here intransitive; cf. Isa. 30:11.

23:12 Stich a is a *casus pendens* without a pronominal link like מִמֶּנָּה which is omitted for metric reasons (cf. Ps. 9:7 for another instance). On the Vav cf. Dr., *HT*, Sec. 124. Render: "The command of his lips — I did not swerve from it."

Stich b in MT can mean only (a) "more than my own law, i.e., inclination, I treasured up the words of His mouth," or (b) "more than my daily portion (Gen. 47:22; Pr. 30:8; 31:15), I treasured up the words of His mouth." (So Ra.)

On the basis of LXX, most moderns read בְּחֵקִי and render: "In my bosom I kept the words of His mouth" (cf. Ps. 119:11 בְּלִבִּי צָפַנְתִּי אִמְרָתֶךָ), which is favored by the parallelism. TS objects that the heart and not the lap could be regarded as the hiding place for knowledge and conscience. However, his own emendation creates an unacceptable *hapax legomenon* מְחֻקּוֹ. A less extensive emendation which would also explain the LXX reading, and does justice to the parallelism, would be כְּחֻקִּי "as my law, I kept the word of His mouth." The scribal and oral confusion of Kaph and Mem is common; cf. אליך Kethib; אֱלֹהִים Qere (I Ki. 1:47); בְּרוּם = בָּרוּךְ כְּבוֹד ה׳; כְּבוֹד ה׳ מִמְּקוֹמוֹ (Ezek. 3:12), etc.

23:13 The unusual phrase וְהוּא בְאֶחָד has been emended to וְהוּא בְאַחַת "He is set on one idea." Another suggestion has been to read וְהוּא בָּחַר "He has chosen" (Be., Bu., Du., Hö., D-G), as a parallel to אִוְּתָהּ in stich b, for which Ps. 132:13 is cited. However, the latter passage deals with an act of choice, an idea totally irrelevant here. Obviously, the phrase in MT is idiomatic. It is best rendered "He is one, i.e., unchangeable, fixed, determined." The Beth is the *Beth essentiae* (cf. Ex. 6:3; 18:4; Isa. 40:10; Ps. 35:2; 118:7; and see Ges.-K., sec. 119, 3, 1).

23:14 כִּי is not to be emended to כֵּן or כֹּה (Bu.); it is obviously not the reason for the preceding (D-G). It is best taken asseveratively, "surely." יַשְׁלִים = "complete, fulfill."

חֻקִּי "my limit"; cf. 14:5. Stich b is best understood not as "many more troubles are with Him" (Ehr.), for Job has had enough misery, past and present, without anticipating future woes. The stich is better taken to mean "many other instances of similar treatment meted out to other men are with Him." Job is Everyman, and his suffering is paradigmatic for all men.

23:17 Stich a has been rendered, "my heart is faint because I was not destroyed by the darkness," a rendering which is interpreted to mean that

Job would have preferred to be dead rather than in agony, but the connection is forced. Another interpretation is "I am not undone because of the darkness," which is taken to mean that Job is overwhelmed not by his troubles but by his estrangement from God, but on this view the essence of his complaint is totally lacking in the text. Hence, most moderns delete לֹא (Bi., Bu., Be., Du., Yel., Hö., D-G). However, the negative was already present in LXX, and in any event it is difficult to see how a relatively clear text could have been distorted by the addition of a negative. P. accepts the re-vocalization לֻא "Would that I were destroyed in the darkness," but the introductory כִּי, whether rendered "because" or "indeed," links the verse to the description of his present agony in v. 16, rather than introduces a new theme of his wish for death, which would, incidentally, be much too briefly treated.

We have called attention to the use of לֹא as an emphatic, both in biblical and postbiblical Hebrew. It develops this meaning from its use as an interrogative, expecting an affirmative answer: לֹא = הֲלֹא "Is it not, indeed." Thus in Hos. 11:5 לֹא יָשׁוּב אֶל־אֶרֶץ מִצְרַיִם וְאַשּׁוּר הוּא מַלְכּוֹ the parallelism makes it clear that stich a is an affirmation; cf. also II Sam. 23:5; Hos. 10:9; Isa. 7:25, and the Comm. on Job 31:24. This use is frequent in rabbinic Hebrew. Thus *Abot de Rabbi Nathan* 6:2, in the Vilna Edition, reads: אמר מי חקק אבן זו אמרו לֹא המים שתדיר נופלין עליה כל יום where Vs. A (ed. Schechter) reads without a negative אמרו לוֹ המים "They said to him. The water, which perpetually falls upon it every day.' " (Cf. also *Mid. Tanḥuma, Zav*, ed. Buber, vol. 3, p. 12. The passage is discussed in Gordis, "The Relationship of Biblical and Rabbinic Hebrew," in *Louis Ginzberg Jubilee Volumes*, English vol., pp. 181 ff.)

In stich b the Mem of מִפָּנַי is deleted by Bi., Bu., Du., TS, Yel., but MT can mean "before my face."

The parallelism is now clear and unforced:

> "Indeed, I am destroyed by the darkness,
> and before my face deep gloom covers all."

CHAPTER 24

24:1 On the structure and meaning of chap. 24, see Special Note 19.

עִתִּים = "times of judgment, doom" (cf. וִיהִי עִתָּם לְעוֹלָם "may their doom be forever," Ps. 81:16; Ezek. 21:30, 34; Ecc. 9:12; Dan. 8:17; 11:13, 35, 40).

Stich a has generally been rendered: "Why have the times (of judgment) not been laid up by the Almighty?", which is interpreted to mean "Why did not God appoint times for punishing the wicked?" (D-G, P.). However, נִצְפְּנוּ does not mean "appoint, set"; its meaning is "conceal, hide" (Ex. 2:2; Jos. 2:4; Jer. 16:7) and "store up" (Ps. 119:11; Pr. 10:14; Job 10:13; 15:20). Even more important, Job has just objected to the conventional idea that God "stores up" the time of judgment for the future, citing this conventional argument of the Friends and using the same verb in 21:19. He is hardly likely to ask what he has just rejected! LXX omits לֹא in an effort to make sense of the passage (so also Mi., Me., Du.), while other deletions and emendations are plentiful.

The verse exhibits a special syntactic construction (so R-O): stich a contains a subordinate clause of condition, with מַדּוּעַ governing stich b: "Why, since the times of judgment are not hidden from Shaddai, do His Friends not see His day (of judgment)?" An exact syntactic parallel occurs in Isa. 5:4 מַדּוּעַ קִוִּיתִי לַעֲשׂוֹת עֲנָבִים וַיַּעַשׂ בְּאֻשִׁים where מַדּוּעַ governs stich b, with stich a as a subordinate clause of condition. The passage is correctly rendered in RSV: "When I look for it to yield grapes, why did it yield wild grapes?"

Job is reiterating his question why good men do not experience the actuality of the promised Day of Judgment, which is obviously not hidden from God — a point he has raised more than once (21:19 f., 30 f.; see the Comm.).

חָזוּ "see, experience" (Job 15:17; 27:12), like its synonym לִרְאוֹת (Ps. 34:13; Ecc. 2:1; 9:9, and *passim*).

יֹדְעָו "those who know and love Him, hence the righteous," a usage probably derived from prophetic and psalm literature; cf. 18:21 and I Sam. 2:12; Jer. 2:8; Hos. 4:1; Ps. 9:11; Dan. 11:32.

24:2 The verse introduces Sec. A (vv. 2–4), which describes the oppression of the poor by the evil-doers. The verse is metrically defective, with stich b longer than stich a, a condition which we regard as questionable (cf. *PPS*, 67 ff.). LXX, P, V, Targum, Saadia, all supply varying subjects, which make it clear that their renderings are explanations designed to make the text intelligible, not reproductions of a Hebrew original. Modern commentators supply רְשָׁעִים (Me., Dil., Du., Hö., D-G, P.). Bu. suggests הֵמָּה, which may more easily have fallen out after יְמָיו. This is not only graphically preferable, but accords with the poet's use of a pronoun to introduce a new subject (cf. Special Note 19 above). This insertion would create a 3:3 meter.

יַשִּׂיגוּ a variant spelling for יַסִּיגוּ, as in II Sam. 1:22. The Masorah lists 18 examples of the spelling with Sin for Samekh (*Masorah Magna* on Hos. 2:8; *Ochlah Ve Ochlah*, list 191).

The removal of landmarks is a cardinal sin in biblical law and religion (Deut. 19:14; 27:17; Pr. 23:10), and throughout the ancient Near East.

24:3 יַחְבְּלוּ "they take in pledge" (Job 22:6). Taking the necessities from the poor as security was regarded as reprehensible (Am. 2:8; Ezek. 18:16). A garment taken in pledge had to be returned at nightfall (Ex. 22:25 f.; Deut. 24:10 ff.); while it was forbidden to take millstones, used for grinding flour (Deut. 24:6), or a widow's garment (Deut. 24:17), at least in theory. In the *Hammurabi Code*, Sec. 241, taking an ox as security was punishable by a fine of two-thirds of a mina of silver. Yel.'s interpretation of יַחְבְּלוּ as a denominative verb from חֶבֶל "cord," hence, "lead by a rope," is clever but unconvincing and not really necessary.

24:4 Stich a can mean either that they rob the poor of their rights (cf. Am. 5:12), or, better, that they force the poor off the highways by violence or the threat of violence (cf. Jud. 5:6). The Kethib עֲנָוֵי "humble" and the Qere עֲנִיֵי "poor" are interchangeable in meaning, exactly as in Am. 8:4; the reverse Kethib-Qere occurs in Ps. 9:13. The term refers to the economically depressed elements in society, from whose rank came the pietistic groups referred to in the Psalms, as well as the Hasideans of the Maccabean age and the Ebionites in a still later period.

24:5 This v. introduces Sec. B (vv. 5–8), that describes the privations of the destitute. The effort to refer this section to the activity of the wicked (Ra., Yel.) leads to far-fetched interpretations of many of the verses. The disjunctive accent on לַטָּרֶף creates an impossible meter-pattern (3:2 ‖ 2:4). In addition, it requires a forced interpretation of עֲרָבָה לוֹ לֶחֶם לַנְּעָרִים "the wilderness (must yield) food for their children."

הֵן is generally rendered "behold." In order to introduce the new subject, the oppressed, V properly supplies *alii*, "the others," which is an interpretation and not a variant reading. Bu. changes הֵן to הֵם or הֵמָּה. In view of the Aramaisms in the chapter (cf. יִקְטָל, v. 14; בַּחַיִּין, v. 22) and in Job generally, the emendation is not necessary; הֵן is the masc. plur. pronoun; cf. Gen. 30:26, 37; Ruth 1:13. On the poet's practice of using a third person pronoun in order to introduce a new subject, cf. the Comm. on 8:16 (הוּא); 13:28 (וְהוּא); and 22:13 (הֲמָה); cf. also 41:1.

Placing the pause at עֲרָבָה improves the parallelism, avoids a far-fetched interpretation for stich b, and gives an excellent 3:2 ‖ 3:2 meter. The only textual change required is the deletion of לוֹ as a dittography from the next word. Incidentally, this approach replaces one alleged tristich in this chapter by two distichs. On the construct with Lamed, cf. יֹשְׁבֵי לָבֶטַח (Ex. 38:11), כִּסְאוֹת לְבֵית־דָּוִד (Ps. 122:5). עֲרָבָה is an accusative of place "in the wilderness"; cf. Gen. 38:11; I Sam. 17:15; Isa. 3:6; Hos. 12:5; Mic. 6:10; Job 22:12 (גֹּבַהּ שָׁמַיִם), and cf. Ges.-K., sec. 118, 2, b.

The verse is to be scanned and rendered as follows:

> "They (i.e., the oppressed), like wild asses in the desert,
>   go forth to their toil,
> They seek food in the wilderness,
>   bread for their young."

24:6 בְּלִילוֹ is referred by some commentators to "the mixture of straw and barley," hence "fodder, inferior food." However, not only was it apparently restricted to animals, but the mixture can scarcely be said to be "reaped." Emendations include יְבוּלוֹ (R-O), בַּלַּיִל (Du., Be., D-G, Hö.), בְּלִיַּעַל (Larcher, P.). T renders "not their own," taking the vocable as a compound בְּלִי לוֹ "a land not theirs," for which cf. בְּלִימָה (Job 26:7); בְּאֶרֶץ לֹא לָהֶם (Gen. 15:13); מִשְׁכָּנוֹת לֹא־לוֹ (Hab. 1:6). The sing. suff., which is felt to be difficult in view of the plural verb, may be explicable on the assumption that בְּלִי לוֹ

has become a petrified form = "not his, alien." We may compare the common adverb יַחְדָּו, originally "his unitedness, with him," with its origin being forgotten and applied without regard to number, gender or person (BDB, p. 403a) in the meaning "together"; cf. e.g. Ps. 34:4.

In יקצירו Kethib, יְקְצוֹרוּ Qere, the Kethib is a scribal error of a Yod for a Vav; the Qere is, of course, the correct form.

יְלַקֵּשׁוּ. The basic meaning of the root is "be late," as in Arabic. In rabbinic Hebrew it is used in the meaning (a) "retard," as, e.g., והלקשתי אתכם "Did I ever retard you?" (*Mid. Num. Rabbah*, Sec. 23); (b) "do a thing late," as, e.g., מה הפועל לכשיפליג ממלאכתו קימעא וילקישנה בסוף "as a laborer who waits for the time when he may rest awhile from his task and finally does it when it is late" (*Mid. Lev. Rabb.*, sec. 30). In the Gezer calendar, the month of לקש follows that of זרע, hence, "late planting." In biblical Hebrew מַלְקוֹשׁ is the late rain." The verb in our passage has therefore been rendered as the privative Piel, "they take the late ripe fruits, gleaning the poorest remnants of the crop" (D-G). The parallelism suggests, however, that it is not for themselves but for their employers that the poor are gathering the produce. Hence, the verb is best interpreted as "they work late," on the basis of the rabbinic usage adduced above.

רָשָׁע need not be emended to עָשִׁיר. The terms are used almost synonymously in Isa. 53:9; and the equivalence of "the poor" and "the righteous" is commonplace in the Psalms and the Bible generally.

24:7 In view of the poet's proclivity for using the same forms in close proximity, there is no justification for regarding stich a as a variant of v. 10a and deleting (D-G) or emending it (Du.).

24:9 The passage now reverts to the actions of the wicked (Section C, v. 9). מִשֹּׁד is an aberrant vocalization for מִשַּׁד "from the breast" (cf. Isa. 60:16; 66:11). The form has an analogue in the rare Arabic *thud* by the side of the more common *thady*. Stich b, when rendered "they take a pledge from the poor," is not parallel to stich a. Moreover, the verb always governs an accusative of person (Pr. 20:16; 27:13; Job 22:6). Hence it is preferable to vocalize עֻל "they take the poor man's babe in pledge" (cf. Isa. 49:15; 65:20 "suckling child.").

24:10 Section D (vv. 10–12) now takes up the description of the exploited, starving poor. עָרוֹם is an accus. of condition, hence in the sing., as in Arab. The poor farmhands are forbidden by their masters to eat of the sheaves they carry, in violation of such ordinances as Deut. 25:4, which forbids muzzling an animal while threshing, and Deut. 23:25 f., which permits a visitor to a vineyard or a field to eat of its produce. This law was interpreted in the Talmud to refer to an agricultural worker (*B. Baba Metzia* 87b; *P. Maᶜaserot* 2:4).

24:11 שֻׁרֹתָם is not restricted in meaning to "walls" (ag. D-G) and therefore requires no emendation. The noun is common in mishnaic and modern Hebrew in the meaning of "row" and is applied to rows of vines in *M. Kil.* 4:5; *P. Ber.* iv, 7d: שורות שורות בכרם. In our passage the noun means "rows of olive trees." The final Mem refers either to the rich landowners or may be the enclitic; there is no need to create a dual form שׁוּרֹתַיִם (Be., Bu., Ch., D-G). יַצְהִירוּ a denominative from יִצְהָר "oil," hence "they press oil" (Ra.). A less likely view derives the verb from צָהֳרַיִם "midday"; hence, "they must work in the midday heat" (Parhon, as well as V, T, P), a meaning which occurs with a somewhat different nuance in B. S. 43:3, בהצהירו "when (the sun) is at midday."

Stich b is parallel in sense to 10b, and וַיִּצְמָאוּ is understood in stich a. The workers are not allowed to partake of the oil or wine that they are preparing.

24:12 The tristich in this verse may be due to the fact that it marks the end of a section, the description of the misery of the poor. On this change of meter at the conclusion of a section, cf. *PPS*, pp. 68–71. מֵעִיר "in the city" would be appropriate if the poet developed a theme of oppression in the city as a counterpart to his extensive picture of the oppression of the poor in the country, but this is not the case. The noun has, therefore, been emended to מֵעֲבֹדָתָם "from their labor" (Steuernagel, Hö.), but this is graphically very distant. The noun עִיר means "terror, fright," as in Jer. 15:8 עִיר וּבֶהָלוֹת (so TS). מְתִים "men, people" (Job 11:3) is best vocalized מֵתִים (so P) in parallelism with חֲלָלִים and the stich rendered: "in terror the dying groan"; for the prolepsis, cf. בְּמוֹת הַמֵּת (Ezek. 18:32). נֶפֶשׁ "throat," rather than "soul, person" (cf. Jonah 2:6; Ps. 69:2). חֲלָלִים lit. "pierced, fatally wounded" (Jer. 51:52; Ezek. 26:15; Ps. 69:27; Lam. 2:12).

Stich c has been rendered "God pays no heed to the folly," לֵב being understood after the verb, as in Isa. 41:20; Job 4:20; 23:6. This interpretation is entirely possible. However, the verb שִׂים also carries the connotation "attribute, impute, regard" (like נתן, יהב); cf. אַל־יָשֵׂם הַמֶּלֶךְ בְּעַבְדּוֹ דָבָר (I Sam. 22:15); וּבְמַלְאָכָיו יָשִׂים תָּהֳלָה (Job 4:18). תִּפְלָה "unworthiness," as in 1:22, "Job did not attribute anything unseemly to God." Hence, stich c is better rendered: "God attributes nothing wrong (to this spectacle of human misery)" — a genuine Joban touch.

24:13 On the pronoun הֵמָּה introducing a new subject, cf. the Comm. on 24:5. "Rebels against the light" is a striking phrase denoting the propensity of the evil-doers for the darkness of night, but also connoting their hostility to God's light of righteousness.

On the Beth, cf. וְאַתְּ הָיִית בְּעֹכְרָי (Jud. 11:35), "lit., You were among my troublers" or it may be understood as the *Beth essentiae*: "They were rebels against the light" (cf. the Comm. on 23:13). יָשְׁבוּ is not to be emended to יָשֻׁבוּ (Ehr.); cf. מְשׁוֹבֵב נְתִיבוֹת לָשָׁבֶת (Isa. 58:12) for the juxtaposition of "road" and "dwelling."

24:14 לָאוֹר "at nightfall"; cf. Aramaic אורתא "evening" and *M. Pes.* 1:1 אור לארבעה עשר, "on the evening of the 14th of Nisan." The murderer does not rise until nightfall.

The last stich can hardly mean "at night he becomes *like* a thief" (P.). It has therefore been emended to יְהַלֵּךְ גַּנָּב "he walks as a thief" (Wr., Dil., Bu., D-G, Hö.) or to יְהָךְ גַּנָּב, the Aram. impf. of הלך in Ezra 5:5; 6:5; 7:13 (Perles, Margolis). The changes become unnecessary if the prefix is here recognized as the asseverative Kaph, as in כְּמִתְאֹנְנִים (Nu. 11:1) כְּאִישׁ אֱמֶת (Neh. 7:2); and see the Comm. on 3:5. The asseverative Kaph is probably related to the emphatic use of the particle *ki*. While it is most common in the predicate nominative, as in our passage, it is not limited to it (cf. Isa. 10:3 Kethib). On the asseverative Kaph, see Gordis, in *JAOS*, vol. 63, 1943, pp. 173–78. Hence, stich c: "At night he is a thief."

24:15 שָׁמְרָה "wait for"; cf. Ps. 130:6. סֵתֶר "cover, mask," used by the adulterer going out at night.

24:16 Stich a refers to the thief digging a tunnel in order to enter a house (Ex. 22:1). Stich b is generally rendered: "by day they shut themselves up" (Ra.), thus linking it to stich c, but there is no connection with stich a. Since the Piel of חתם occurs nowhere else, it may carry a special connotation here, "place a seal, a mark." The two stichs may then be rendered:

> "In the dark they dig through houses,
>   Which they had marked by day"

(so Ra., AV). לֹא־יָדְעוּ אוֹר = "they refuse to know the light" (Ehr.). Stich c is to be joined to v. 17. See below.

24:17 In stich a, either noun may be the subject and the other the pred. nominative. It is simpler to follow the word-order and render: "For the criminal the morning is darkest night, i.e., he sleeps by day, since he 'works' by night." The other interpretation would be "darkness is as morning to them," which is a less natural idea. יַחְדָּו is equivalent to כֹּל (Isa. 45:16; Ps. 14:3), and is best linked to בֹּקֶר, "every morning." On its use with a noun, cf. Isa. 10:8; Job 3:18; and with a sing. noun used collectively, Zech. 10:4.

Stich b is difficult. The *pis aller* is to render: "He knows, i.e., he is familiar with, the terrors of darkness." However, it is tempting to recognize in כִּי יַכִּיר a contracted idiom for "daybreak" parallel to בֹּקֶר (Gersonides, Ehr.). The idiom would have its origin in such usages as Ruth 3:14 בְּטֶרֶם יַכִּיר אִישׁ אֶת־רֵעֵהוּ "before one man could recognize his neighbor," and *M. Ber.* 1:2, where "morning" is defined as משיכיר בין תכלת ללבן "when men can recognize the difference between purple and white." Hence the impersonal כִּי יַכִּיר would mean "recognizing time, daybreak." Another instance of an idiom for "morning" is the biblical and postbiblical use of משכים, "lit., rising time" (Hos. 6:4; 13:3; Damascus Scroll, ed. Schechter, p. 10; *Seder Olam*,

ed. Marx, p. 31; and *M. Bik.* 3:2: למשכים היה הממונה אומר "and in the morning the official says, etc."; see Gordis, in *Sepher Tur Sinai*, p. 158). For another
instance of a contracted idiom, cf. the Comm. on 7:19.

The two stichs are now in perfect parallelism. Stich 16c is to be joined
to 17, which supplies the reason:

> "They never see the light,
> for to them every morning is (as) darkness,
> and daybreak, (like) the terrors of deepest gloom."

Note once again the repetition of the same noun in both stichs. The fluctuation in number is normal in view of the collective character of the evil-doers
being described.

24:18 On this difficult and highly ambiguous section, vv. 18–24, see Special
Note 19. It is best interpreted as describing the destruction of the evil-doers
and hence is a quotation by Job of the standpoint of the Friends.

Stich a has been rendered optatively: "Let him be swift upon the waters,
i.e., the wicked will flee when doom descends" (LXX, S, T). However, the
optative would have required the jussive forms יְהִי and יִפֶן (D-G). Hence,
it is better rendered: "You say to me, in case of danger, he moves along
swiftly by water." However, locomotion by water was scarcely the most
rapid mode, especially in ancient Israel. We suggest that עַל־פְּנֵי, like לִפְנֵי
(1 Sam. 1:16; Job 3:23; 4:19; see Comm.), be given the meaning "like"
(cf. Latin *pro*). קַל has the connotation, "pass away swiftly" (cf. Job 9:25;
7:6), hence: "He perishes swiftly, like water." The unsubstantial character
of water is expressed in פַּחַז כַּמַּיִם אַל תּוֹתַר "unstable as water, you shall not
have preeminence" (Gen. 49:4; RSV); the same figure is at the basis of
Job 11:16.

The difficult stich b has a paronomasia (with קַל) to recommend it.
Render: "Their estate is cursed in the land." If it means that his land hold-
ings are not fertile, the obscure closing stich may express the same idea.
This can be derived with difficulty from a literal translation: "He does not
turn to the way of vineyards." It is better to read, modifying only the vowels
of two words: לֹא יִפְנֶה דֶּרֶךְ כַּרְמָם "No (grape) treader will turn to their
vineyards" (Bi., Du., D-G). The awkwardness of the suggested Hebrew is
perhaps reduced if we revocalize only one word דֶּרֶךְ, and render "No treader
of vineyards will turn their way (because there will be no grapes to tread)."
For the phrase דֶּרֶךְ כְּרָמִים, cf. דֶּרֶךְ עֲנָבִים (Am. 9:13); יְקָבִים דָּרְכוּ (Job 24:11);
and דְּרָכִים גִּתּוֹת (Neh. 13:15).

24:19 This verse, like the preceding, is extremely difficult. It has almost
surely suffered some injury, and the Vss. offer no help. The emendations
proposed lack plausibility and sometimes even meaning. Thus Hö. reads:
צִיָּה וָחֹם יִגְזְלוּם וּמֵי שֶׁלֶג שְׁאוֹל יַנְחִיתוּ which he renders: "May drought and heat
despoil them, and snow-water lower them into the land of the dead." MT
has been generally understood as a description of the sinner's activity: "In

the desert during the heat, they steal snow-water, they have sinned grievously, i.e., unto death"; cf. הֵיטֵב חָרָה־לִי עַד־מָוֶת (Jonah 4:9), or חֵטְא מָוֶת "a sin worthy of death" (Deut. 22:26). It has also been understood as a description of the punishment of the sinners. The desert and the sun's heat destroy snow-water, so Sheol will devour the evil-doers (cf. Ps. 49:15). In view of the context, which seems to deal with the alleged destruction of the evil-doers, the latter interpretation is perhaps preferable, but see v. 22.

24:20 Here, too, MT, difficult as it is, is superior to the various proposed emendations, such as: יִשְׁכָּחֵהוּ רְחֹב מְקֹמוֹ רָמֹה עוֹד לֹא יִזָּכֵר (Bu., Be., D-G, Du., Hö.). This is taken to mean: "The square of his native place forgets him, and his name is remembered no more."

The verse in MT would seem to mean: "Even his mother's womb forgets the evil-doer (contrast Isa. 49:15); the worm finds him sweet (as it devours him); he is no longer remembered and evil is destroyed like a tree."

24:21 This verse supplies the reason for v. 20. Even his mother's womb will forget him, because he injured another woman — an instance of *lex talionis* on which see the Comm. on chap. 31. רֹעֶה need not be interpreted as "de-pasture, strip" (D-G). The Lamed He verb is a by-form of the geminate; cf. חקק ‖ חקה (Job 13:27); רנה (Job 39:23) ‖ רנן; שסה ‖ שסס (Hos. 13:15) (Ps. 89:42); סלה (Job 28:16, 19) ‖ סלל, etc. Hence, the verb is equivalent to רעע "smash, crush." The root occurs in וְרָעוּ (Mic. 5:5); יְרֹעוּךְ קָדְקֹד (Jer. 2:16).

לֹא תֵלֵד "so that she cannot give birth." The rendering: "He keeps com-pany with a barren woman" (cf. Pr. 28:3), so that there is no danger of her conceiving (Marshall), is based on the Midrash that relates the chapter to the sins of the generation of the Flood.

24:22 The verse has been interpreted in several radically diverse fashions, generally on the basis of emended texts: (a) "God draws the mighty away to destruction" (D-G, Bi., Be., Du., R-O); (b) "the wicked lures the mighty with his powers" (P); and (c) "God seizes the mighty despite his power" (Dh., Hö.).

Particularly in the light of vv. 23, 24, the verse seems to suggest that the wicked may indeed survive for a time, but even during the time of his ostensible power he is in dread of the doom which finally overtakes him, because God's eyes are upon him. This idea has been propounded by Eliphaz (15:20–22):

> "All his days, the wicked is atremble
> throughout the few years stored up for the oppressor.
> The sound of terror is always in his ears;
> even while at peace he fears the despoiler coming upon him.
> He does not hope to escape from the darkness,
> but can look forward only to the sword."

וּמָשַׁךְ = "draw out, prolong, continue" is transitive in Ps. 36:10; 85:6; 109:12, which would yield the sense: "God prolongs the life of the powerful." However, since the sinner is the subject of the other verbs in the verse, it is preferable to interpret the verb intransitively, "continue, endure" parallel to יָקוּם (cf. the Comm. on 15:29). The Qal is here used like the Niphal (Ezek. 12:25, 28; *B. Horay.* 12a נמשכה מלכותם, "their reign endured.") The Mem of אַבִּירִים may be the enclitic or a virtual dittography because of its proximity to Beth; in either case the meaning is the singular. Stich b = "He (the wicked) may survive" (but he does not have confidence in his life). The idiom is used exactly as in Deut. 28:66. בַּחַיִּין an Aramaism (Dan. 12:13), of which Job contains many, e.g., יְקָר, נְחַת, קְטַל, אַחְוָה, כָּפַן and cf. D-G 1, pp. xlvi ff.

Another view of this difficult verse may be proposed. The original meaning of the Hebrew root *māšak* is "seize, take hold," the meaning which its Arabic cognate *masaka* has (cf. BDB, Koehler-Baumgartner, s.v. and Tur Sinai, *Halashon Vehasepher*, vol. 1, pp. 383 ff.). This meaning occurs in several biblical passages, e.g. Ex. 12:21; Am. 9:13; Ecc. 2:3 (see *KMW*, p. 200) and lies at the basis of the noun *mesekh* in Job 28:18 (see Comm. *ad loc.*). On the basis of this meaning, the verse may be rendered: "He (i.e. God) seizes the mighty one despite all his power; when He (i.e. God) confronts him, he has no faith in his life." The Vav in stich b introduces the apodosis in a conditional sentence.

It is true that the subject of v. 21 is the malefactor, while v. 22 in this interpretation would introduce a new subject. This is characteristic of the poet's style and, in any event, the change in subject, which would appear to us to be abrupt, would need to take place in v. 23.

On this view of the passage, vv. 22 and 23 are in alternate parallelism: 22a ‖ 23a and 22b ‖ 23b.

24:23 Stich a is a breviloquence for יִתֶּן לוֹ לָשֶׁבֶת לָבֶטַח dictated by metrical exigencies: "He may let him dwell in security." וְיִשָּׁעֵן lit., "lean, rely, trust" (cf. Isa. 10:20; 31:1; 50:10; Pr. 3:5).

24:24 רֹמּוּ is not derived from the common root רוּם "be raised, exalted," hence "they are exalted for a while" (so most). It is the imperative of a homonym "wait" occurring in Isa. 30:18: לָכֵן יְחַכֶּה ה' לַחֲנַנְכֶם וְלָכֵן יָרוּם לְרַחֶמְכֶם where it is parallel to חכה (R-O). T correctly translates אוריכו כזעיר פון "wait a little time then"; it did not read דֹמּוּ (Wilhelm Bacher, A. S. Yahuda, P. Churgin, *Targum Kethubim*, p. 104).

כַּכֹּל rendered like "all men" is banal and has therefore been emended on the basis of LXX (*moloche*) to כַּמַּלּוּחַ "as mallows" (Cf. 30:4.) The change is, however, graphically distant from the Hebrew, and it is clear that LXX rendered *ad sensum*, and correctly, as the parallelism indicates. Ehr. suggests that the word is an error for a substantive cognate with the Arab. *ᵓaklil* "the umbel of a plant." The assumption is unnecessary. We may adduce the Arab. noun *kaᵓlun* "forage, herbage" and render כֹל here as "grass."

It may be added that the word may occur also in II Sam. 17:3: וְאָשִׁיבָה

272 The Book of Job

כָּל־הָעָם אֵלֶיךָ כְּשׁוּב הַכֹּל הָאִישׁ אֲשֶׁר אַתָּה מְבַקֵּשׁ. On the ground that the MT has suffered corruption, most commentators adopt the LXX rendering, *hon tropon epistrephei he nymphe pros ton andra autes*, which is taken to represent כְּשׁוּב כַּלָּה אֶל אִישָׁהּ "as a bride returns to her husband." Aside from the rather strange simile underlying this reading, it is noteworthy that כַּלָּה never occurs in juxtaposition with אִישׁ, always with חָתָן (Isa. 62:5; Jer. 7:34; 16:9; 25:10; 33:11; Joel 2:16). LXX would therefore seem to be an interpretation due to unfamiliarity with this rare noun, rather than an original reading. MT in Sam. may be rendered: "I shall bring back all the people to you as surely as the grass returns (in the spring); is it not the one man you are seeking? Let all the people have peace."

In any event, the proposed meaning "grass" for כֹּל in our passage seems certain.

וְהֻמְּכוּ is the "Aramaic" form of the geminate with the *Dageš* in the first radical; cf. the Comm. on Job 22:3. The verb means "are brought low" (Ps. 106:43; Ecc. 10:18). יִקָּפְצוּן "shut, close" (Deut. 15:7) "shrivel up" (Job 5:16).

24:25   After Job has cited the Friends' optimistic description of the male-factors' temporary prosperity and ultimate destruction (vv. 18–24), there must have followed a rebuttal by Job, as is the case in chaps. 12 and 21, where he quotes his opponents and refutes them. However, in chap. 24, only one verse, 25, of Job's refutation has survived, due to the radical injury and dislocation suffered by most of the Third Cycle (chaps. 23–28, 31). See Special Notes 19 and 20. אַל is used here substantively, "nothingness, worth-lessness." It need not be emended to לְאַיִן (Isa. 40:23).

The Speech of Bildad (25; 26:5–14)

The reasons for adding 26:5–14 to Bildad's speech are explained in the Special Note and the Commentary. Even with this addition, Bildad's reply remains fragmentary. Unable to refute Job's picture of injustice rampant everywhere in the life of man, Bildad takes refuge in an eloquent description of the glory and power of God. His dominion keeps peace in heaven among the warring elements of nature and penetrates even to the land of the dead. How then can man hope to maintain the claim to perfection in the presence of God?

God's greatness is revealed in the recurrent wonders of the natural order. Above all, He made His power manifest in creating earth and sky, with light and darkness meeting at the horizon, each a miracle and a mystery. The act of creation required conquering the primordial monsters of chaos. Yet all that men know of God's might is a mere echo of His limitless power.

25 Bildad the Shuhite answered, saying,
2   Awesome dominion is with Him;
                He makes peace in His high heaven.
3   Is there any number to His armies?
                Upon whom does His light not shine?
4   How then can man be just before God
                and how can one born of a woman be clean?
5   Behold, He commands the moon and it does not shine,
                and the stars are not clean in His sight.
6   How much more so man, who is a maggot,
                the son of man, who is a worm!

·   ·   ·   ·   ·   ·   ·   ·   ·   ·   ·   ·   ·   ·   ·   ·   ·   ·
·   ·   ·   ·   ·   ·   ·   ·   ·   ·   ·   ·   ·   ·   ·   ·   ·   ·

26 The shades tremble below,
                the waters and their inhabitants.
6   Sheol is naked before God,
                and Abaddon has no covering.
7   He stretches out the north over empty space
                and suspends the earth over nothingness.
8   He binds up the waters in His thick clouds,
                yet the cloud is not split by their weight.
9   He hides the sight of His throne,
                and spreads His cloud upon it.
10   He has marked out the limit of the waters
                at the boundary of light and darkness.
11   The pillars of heaven tremble
                and are astounded at His rebuke.
12   By His might He stilled the sea;
                by His understanding He smote Rahab.
13   His breath stretched out the heavens,
                His hand pierced the straight Serpent.
14   Lo, these are only the outskirts of His ways.
                How small an echo can we hear!
                The full thunder of His power, who can understand?

כה א   וַיַּעַן בִּלְדַּד הַשֻּׁחִי וַיֹּאמַר:

2   הַמְשֵׁל וָפַחַד עִמּוֹ   עֹשֶׂה שָׁלוֹם בִּמְרוֹמָיו:

3   הֲיֵשׁ מִסְפָּר לִגְדוּדָיו   וְעַל־מִי לֹא־יָקוּם אוֹרֵהוּ:

4   וּמַה־יִּצְדַּק אֱנוֹשׁ עִם־אֵל   וּמַה־יִּזְכֶּה יְלוּד אִשָּׁה:

ה   הֵן עַד־יָרֵחַ וְלֹא יַאֲהִיל   וְכוֹכָבִים לֹא־זַכּוּ בְעֵינָיו:

6   אַף כִּי־אֱנוֹשׁ רִמָּה   וּבֶן־אָדָם תּוֹלֵעָה:

כו ה   הָרְפָאִים יְחוֹלָלוּ   מִתַּחַת מַיִם וְשֹׁכְנֵיהֶם:

6   עָרוֹם שְׁאוֹל נֶגְדּוֹ   וְאֵין כְּסוּת לָאֲבַדּוֹן:

7   נֹטֶה צָפוֹן עַל־תֹּהוּ   תֹּלֶה אֶרֶץ עַל־בְּלִימָה:

8   צֹרֵר־מַיִם בְּעָבָיו   וְלֹא־נִבְקַע עָנָן תַּחְתָּם:

9   מְאַחֵז פְּנֵי־כִסֵּה   פַּרְשֵׁז עָלָיו עֲנָנוֹ:

י   חֹק־חָג עַל־פְּנֵי־מָיִם   עַד־תַּכְלִית אוֹר עִם־חֹשֶׁךְ:

11   עַמּוּדֵי שָׁמַיִם יְרוֹפָפוּ   וְיִתְמְהוּ מִגַּעֲרָתוֹ:

12   בְּכֹחוֹ רָגַע הַיָּם   וּבִתְבוּנָתוֹ מָחַץ רָהַב:

13   בְּרוּחוֹ שָׁמַיִם שִׁפְרָה   חֹלְלָה יָדוֹ נָחָשׁ בָּרִחַ:

14   הֶן־אֵלֶּה | קְצוֹת דְּרָכָו   וּמַה־שֵּׁמֶץ דָּבָר נִשְׁמַע־בּוֹ
     וְרַעַם גְּבוּרֹתָו מִי יִתְבּוֹנָן:

Chapter 25

Bildad's Third Speech (25:1–6; 26:5–14)

On the structure and content of the Third Cycle, see Special Note 20.

Even when both sections are combined (25:1–6; 26:5–14), Bildad's speech consists only of 15 verses, shorter than any other in the Dialogue. Clearly, some portions of his speech have been lost, more probably at the beginning or in the middle, since 26:14 is an effective conclusion.

The extant material falls into two distinct sections, which are linked to 25:2–6. Bildad's final response describes God's greatness under four aspects: (a) His boundless sway over the heavenly bodies (25:3–6); (b) His rule of the subterranean regions (26:5–6); (c) the wonders of the natural order, hence the use of participles (26:7–9); and (d) God's might as revealed in creation, hence the perfect tense (26:10–13). The first three aspects are encompassed by the rabbinic terms מעשה מרכבה, "the work of the Chariot" (Ezek., chap. 1), the fourth by מעשה בראשית, "the work of creation."

25:2 The abruptness of the beginning of Bildad's speech and the absence of a personal challenge, such as he has addressed to Job in his two earlier rejoinders (8:2–8; 18:2–4), make it not unlikely that a *lacuna* occurred at the opening of his words here.

הַמְשֵׁל, "dominion," is the Hiphil infinitive absolute, serving as a noun. For this nominal use of the masculine form of the infinitive, cf. הַשְׁמֵד (Isa. 14:23); הַפְצֵר (I Sam. 15:23); הוֹכֵחַ (Job 6:25; and cf. the Comm. *ad loc.*). It becomes frequent in mishnaic Hebrew, as, e.g., הפקר, הבדל, where it is frequently vocalized with a Segol, perhaps to differentiate the noun from the infinitive. הַמְשֵׁל וָפַחַד may be a hendiadys (cf. 10:17) = "dominion of fear, awe-inspiring rule." שָׁלוֹם need not be emended to שִׁלּוּם "retribution" (TS); God's cosmic power is capable of imposing peace among the warring elements in heaven (cf. Isa. 24:21 ff.), that were originally independent forces which He subjugated at creation (cf. 26:12a).

25:3 אוֹרֵהוּ with the archaic suffix ending (cf. וְעֵינֵיהוּ, 24:23). God's legions are innumerable and His light penetrates everywhere. Stich b: "Upon whom does His light not shine?" (cf. Isa. 60:1). Hence no human failing can escape His searching judgment (v. 4). The reading אוֹרְבוֹ, "His ambush" (LXX followed by Du., Be.), is an attempt to make the stich obviously parallel to stich a, but the epithet is scarcely appropriate in Bildad's mouth for God.

25:4 עִם־אֵל. In 9:2 the phrase means "in confrontation with God"; here, "in God's presence."

25:5 עַד־יָרֵחַ וְלֹא יַאֲהִיל has been rendered "even the moon has no brightness," but עַד in this meaning remains strange. No more satisfactory is the rendering "as far as the moon is concerned." TS, following Ra., renders the vocable as a verb, emending to יָעַד. The change is not required. עַד may be a contracted form of the verb יָעַד "He orders." Aphaeresis (the loss of an opening consonant in pronunciation) undoubtedly characterized spoken Hebrew. It has left apparent traces in the biblical text; cf. הַיּוֹם רַד for יָרַד (Jud. 19:11); תַּתָּה for נָתַתָּ (II Sam. 22:41; Ps. 18:41); קַח (Ezek. 17:5) and קָחָם (Hos. 11:3) from לקח. (On this phenomenon, cf. Koenig, *Lehrgebäude*, p. 300; Ges.-K., sec. 20, 3a.) Aphaeresis may also explain clipped forms in the medieval Hebrew *piyyut* which have generally been explained as artificial creations, like גָּשׁ for נִגַּשׁ, צָג for יָצַג, etc.

יַאֲהִיל represents an extreme plene spelling for יָהֵל, familiar in the Qumran Scrolls and occasionally encountered in MT, e.g. וְקָאם (Hos. 10:14), דָּאג (Neh. 13:26 Kethib) and וַיֵּאֹסֹר (Job 12:18; see the Comm. *ad loc.*). The use of a Yod for a Ṣere, common in later postbiblical orthography, is noteworthy. Cf. the Comm. on 41:4 (וְחִין).

25:6   For the theme, cf. Ps. 22:7; Isa. 41:14. For the omission of the relative *ʾašer*, "man who is a worm, etc.," cf. *Lachish Letter* 2, 3 מי עבדך כלב "who is your servant that is merely a dog that my lord has remembered him?"

CHAPTER 26

26:5   הָרְפָאִים "shades of the dead" (Isa. 14:9; 26:14; Ps. 88:11; Pr. 2:18; 9:18) carries the same meaning in Phoenician (*Tabnith Inscription* in Cooke, *NSI* 4, line 8). However, the rendering "giants" (LXX, V, Th., Sym., S, T) preserves the memory of the ancient myths that have come to light in Ugaritic texts (1 *Aqhat*, 20:36-37, etc.; *Danʾel* 1024:15; 1046:8). The term also represents an ethnic group (Deut. 2:10 f.; I Chr. 20:4), for which extrabiblical evidence is accumulating. The link between the two meanings may reside in the belief that the *rpʾm* were a powerful people who fought with the gods and, being conquered, were exiled to the land of the dead. (Cf. J. Gray in *PEQ*, vol. 84, 1949, pp. 127–39; A. Caquot, in *Syria*, vol. 37, 1900, pp. 75–93; B. Margulis, in *JBL*, 1970, vol. 89, pp. 299–302.)

יְחוֹלָלוּ "tremble" (cf. 15:20). The rhythm in MT (2:3) is suspicious, in view of the longer stich b (cf. *PPS*, pp. 66 f.). Dh., following Hö., accordingly reads: הָרְפָאִים יְחוֹלְלוּ מִתַּחַת יֵחַתּוּ מַיִם וְשֹׁכְנֵיהֶם; interpreting the inserted verb in stich b from חתת = "be shattered." A less drastic procedure is to place the poetic caesura after מִתַּחַת (so Ehr., D-G), reading הָרְפָאִים יְחוֹלְלוּ מִתָּחַת ‖ מַיִם וְשֹׁכְנֵיהֶם; and creating a 3 ‖ 2 meter (or a 3:3 meter, if וְשֹׁכְנֵיהֶם receives two beats because of its length). Render: "The shades tremble below, the waters and they who dwell in them." For the divergence between the metric and the logical caesura, see the Comm. on 4:8; 10:8. The shades dwell below the waters and the fish who inhabit them (Gen. 1:20; Ps. 8:9). P. points out that the nether world was a watery abyss (II Sam. 22:5 מִשְׁבְּרֵי־מָוֶת; Jonah 2:4; Ps. 88:7, 8). Note also *Šelaḥ*, the river leading to Sheol; cf. the Comm. on Job 33:18; 36:12.

The verse is an instance of formal (or synthetic) parallelism; in which there is actually no repetition of thought, as in Gen. 21:7; Ps. 2:6 (cf. *PPS*, pp. 75 f.).

The parallelism in the figure is identical with that in 24:7, and may perhaps be an echo of it.

On the underworld as being under God's rule, cf. Pr. 15:11: "Sheol and Abaddon are open before the Lord, how much more the hearts of men!" אֲבַדּוֹן "the land of destruction"; cf. T. The term occurs only in Wisdom literature (Ps. 88:12; Pr. 15:11; 27:20; Job 28:22; 31:12). It is probable that שְׁאוֹל and אֲבַדּוֹן were originally the proper names of gods of the nether world, like the Greek *Hades*. Thus the proper name מְתוּשָׁאֵל (Gen. 4:18) may mean "the man of Sheol," as מְתוּשֶׁלַח (Gen. 5:21) means "the man of *Šelaḥ*, the subterranean river." In Rev. 9:11, *Abaddon* is the name of "the angel of the bottomless pit."

Since the term *Abaddon* is apparently later than Sheol, it may carry the meaning of "the land of destruction for the evil-doers," as against the older idea of Sheol as the undifferentiated domicile of all the dead. A distinction within Sheol between the honored and the dishonorable dead seems clear in Isa. 14:18 f. and Ezek. 32:17–32. Etymologies are notoriously hazardous, and a plethora of suggestions for *Sheol* has been suggested (see BDB, p. 982; KB, p. 934a; and the biblical encyclopedias). Its origin has been sought in Arabic "harm, hell" (Littmann, Köhler), in Egyptian (Albright, Baumgartner), but these are very doubtful. If it is derived from the Hebrew verb *šā'al* "ask, inquire," Sheol may mean "the place of inquiry," not as a reference to necromancy (Jastrow, in *AJSL*, vol. 14, p. 170; *JBL*, 1900, vol. 19, pp. 88 ff.), but "the place of God's inquiry" (cf. Alfred Jeremias, *Das Leben nach dem Tode*, p. 109: "the place of decision"; Ivan Engnell, *A Rigid Scrutiny*, Nashville, Tenn., 1969). This meaning for *Sheol* would suggest an indigenous Hebraic origin for the ideas of the resurrection and the judgment of the dead, which developed later in rabbinic Judaism and Christianity. This would not, of course, rule out the presence of foreign influence in addition.

26:7   צָפוֹן is not to be equated with or emended to סְפוּן "ceiling" (Yel., TS) on the basis of Saadia's rendering "sky." Zaphon, "the north" lit. "the hidden place" was the original dwelling place of the gods. Cf. Isa. 14:13:

> "You said in your heart, I will ascend to heaven;
>   above the stars of God I will set my throne on high;
>   I will sit on the mount of assembly in the far north."

In Northwest Semitic mythology, Mount Zaphon is the dwelling place of the underworld god, Hadad or Baal. The term is then applied to Jerusalem as the shrine of God, in spite of its location in southern Palestine; cf. Ps. 48:3:

> "Beautiful in elevation, joy of all the earth,
>   Mount Zion in the far north, city of the great king."

In accordance with the well-attested tendency of monotheistic religion to degrade pagan deities to the level of evil spirits, "the north" becomes the dwelling of dangerous beings and demons (cf. *Midrash Yalkut Shimeoni*, sec. 913).

בְּלִימָה "without anything, nothing." The earth is suspended in space, even though it rests upon pillars. Hö., who cites parallels from Lucretius, *De rerum natura*, II, lines 602 f., and Ovid, *Fasti*, VI, lines 269 f., correctly calls our passage a noteworthy speculation on cosmogony. On this form of a compound noun, generally rare in Hebrew, cf. בְּלִילוֹ (24:6 and the Comm.).

26:8 A description of the miracle of the clouds not splitting under the weight of their water.

26:9 The Piel of אחז occurs only here. It has the meaning "cover"; cf. I Ki. 6:10; Neh. 7:3 "shut the gates"; II Chr. 9:18, and the cognates, Akk. *uḫuzu*, Arab. *aḥada* "cover over with gold," as well as the rabbinic Heb. אֲחִיזַת עֵינַיִם "delude the eyes by an optical illusion" (*M. Sanh.* 7:11; *B. Sanh.* 65b).

כִּסֵּה is an aberrant spelling for כִּסֵּא "the throne of God," particularly appropriate in connection with צָפוֹן "the dwelling place of God." There is no need to vocalize with a suffix כִּסְאוֹ or כִּסְאֹה (D-G). The throne of God needs no particularizing; cf. Ps. 2:7 אֲסַפְּרָה אֶל חֹק "I shall proclaim the decree of God."

פַּרְשֵׁז with Šin in the Masorah, though Baer reads with a Sin on the basis of mss. This anomalous form has been explained as (a) a dissimulation of a quadriliteral פַּרְשֵׁשׁ; (b) a combination of פרשׂ and פרז; or (c) as an error, the final consonant to be deleted, and the word read פָּרַשׂ. The form is either the inf. consecutive or the participle with a preformative Mem elided before a labial; cf. מָאֵן (Ex. 7:27); מַהֵר (Zeph. 1:14; Isa. 8:13). Whatever the explanation of the form, the meaning "spreads" is clear from the context.

MT is superior to the suggested reading כְּסֶה (Ps. 81:4; כֶּסֶא Pr. 3:20) adopted by Bu., Ehr., Hö., P., which does not mean "moon" but "the day of the full moon" in Phoenician and Syriac, as well as in the two biblical passages cited (TS).

26:10 In stich a, MT has a noun followed by a verb, "a limit He has circled"; cf. מְחוּגָה "circle, compass" (Isa. 44:13) and the related root עוג in *M. Taan.* 3:8 עג עוגה "He drew a circle." However, on the basis of Pr. 8:27 בְּחֻקוֹ חוּג עַל־פְּנֵי תְהוֹם, "When he decreed a circle on the deep," many moderns revocalize our passage to read a verb followed by a noun חַק חָג (or חָקַק). However, the gain is slight and the change is unnecessary. In stich b "the boundary of light and darkness" is the horizon. Hö. rightly calls this a remarkable scientific concept (*eine merkwürdige naturwissenschaftliche Vorstellung*).

26:11 "The pillars of heaven" are the great mountains that sustain the sky; cf. Akk. *išid šami*, "the foundations of heaven."

גַּעֲרָתוֹ "His rebuke" is the thunderclap; cf. II Sam. 22:16; Isa. 50:2; Ps. 18:16; 104:7.

26:12 The root רָגַע occurs in two diametrically opposite senses, which suggests that it is not a case of homonyms, but an instance of ʾaḍdad, a word of like and opposite meaning. In any event, both meanings have been invoked here: (a) "disturb, stir up," as in Isa. 51:15 רֹגַע הַיָּם וַיֶּהֱמוּ גַּלָּיו; (b) "quiet," as in Isa. 34:14; Jer. 31:1; 47:6; 50:34. The obvious mythological character of the passage strongly favors the second view. Thus in the Babylonian epic *Enuma Elish*, Marduk is described as conquering Tiamat!

> He released his arrow, it tore her belly
> It cut through her insides splitting the heart
> Having thus subdued her, he extinguished her life.
> He cast down the carcass to stand upon it.

> (*The Myth of Creation*, Tablet IV, ll. 101–104, in *ANET*, p. 67).

God quiets the sea (or Yam the sea monster) by smiting the sea dragon, Rahab, on which see the Comm. on 9:13. Similarly, in the Ugaritic version of Baal's battle with Yam. The verb הִשְׁבִּית also has the two meanings "quiet, put an end to" (Hos. 2:13) and "destroy" (II Ki. 23:5, 11; Am. 8:4).

תְּבוּנָה "understanding," like בִּינָה (Job 28:12, 20), a synonym for Hokmah, the practical wisdom required to subdue a foe, hence rendered "strategy" by Ehr. Marduk is described as "the wisest of the gods" (*Enuma Elish*, IV, l. 93) who uses craft to defeat Tiamat (ll. 95–100).

26:13 שִׁפְרָה, from the root שפר, "be beautiful" (Ps. 16:6), is a common Aramaic root; cf. Dan. 6:2. The MT form can only be a noun "fairness, cleanness." Hence: "By His wind, the sky becomes fairness," but a verb in stich a would be preferable (D-G). Thus T "The face of the heavens has been cleared." It is best to delete the Beth of בְּרוּחוֹ as a dittography (so Ibn E., Dh., Hö.) and to vocalize שִׁפְּרָה with a dageš as a Piel. However, the stich is not to be rendered "sweeps clean" (Dh., Hö.). Stich b, that describes God's piercing the primordial serpent at creation, makes it clear that stich a, which is parallel to it, describes not a recurrent natural phenomenon, such as the clearing of the sky after a storm, but God's original creative act. Hence, S. Daiches (*ZA*, 1911, p. 3) and, more recently, J. Jacobowitz (*Hadoar*, November 11, 1947) cite the noun שפרור Kethib, שַׁפְרִיר Qere in Jer. 43:10 "tent" (Kimhi; cf. T. אפדניה), which, like our verb is a cognate of the Akkadian root šuparruru "spread out (a canopy)." Render stich a: "His breath spread out the heavens," and cf. Isa. 40:22 and Deut. 33:33b (reading וּמִתַּחַת זְרֹעֹת עוֹלָם "the outstretching of the everlasting arms"; see Gordis, in *JThS*, vol. 67, 1948, pp. 69–72; vol. 68, 1949, pp. 407 f.).

In the Akkadian creation myth, the slaying of the primordial monster and the use of its corpse constitute the prelude to the creation of heaven and earth:

"Lord trod on the legs of Tiamat
>with his unsparing mace he crushed her skull.
When the arteries of her blood he had severed
>the North Wind bore it to places undisclosed . . .
Then the Lord paused to view her dead body
>that he might divide the monster into artful works.
He split her like a shellfish into two parts:
>half of her he set up and sealed it as sky,
pulled down the bar and posted guards.
He bade them to allow not her waters to escape."

(*Enuma Elish*, Tablet IV, ll. 129–132; 135–139; *ANET*, p. 67b.)

This theme occurs as a mythological reference in Isa. 51:9, "You are the cleaver of Rahab, the piercer of the Dragon."

In Isa. 27:1, נָחָשׁ בָּרִחַ is coupled with נָחָשׁ עֲקַלָּתוֹן as mythological epithets for Egypt and Assyria. Both terms occur in Ugaritic (Baal epic II):

"You will surely smite *ltn btn brḥ* (= לותן פתן ברח)
You will destroy *btn ᶜqltn*, the ruler with seven heads."

For this final reference, cf. Ps. 74:13 f. Ugaritic *btn* = Heb. פֶּתֶן "serpent."

בָּרִחַ is generally interpreted "fleeing, or flying serpent." C. H. Gordon (*Orientalia*, vol. 22, 1953, p. 243) suggests the meaning "evil." However, the juxtaposition with עֲקַלָּתוֹן, "crooked," suggests that בָּרִחַ means "straight," perhaps "shaped like a spear" (Akk. *buruhu*) or "shaped like a bar" (Heb. בְּרִיחַ, Ex. 26:26 ff.; Deut. 3:5; Am. 1:5; Nah. 3:13, etc.). TS renders similarly: "The stretching dragon." The specific myth concerning these two monsters has not been recovered, but the contrast seems clear.

26:14 שֵׁמֶץ "fraction," better, "echo"; cf. the Comm. on 4:12. The implication from Bildad's elaborate description of God as creator and governor of the world is superbly expounded in the Midrash (*Gen. Rabba* 7:2): א״ר הונא על סודו של רעם אי אתה יכול לעמוד על סדרו של עולם על אחת כמה וכמה "Rabbi Huna said: the secret of the thunderbolt you cannot fathom; the order of the universe even less!" The Kethib גבורתו, "His power," in the sing., is preferred by the Vss. (LXX, Sym., P, T, V). However, the Qere גְּבוּרֹתָיו, "His mighty acts," in the plural (Deut. 3:24; Isa. 63:15 a. e.), is equally satisfactory.

Note the use of a tristich at the end of Bildad's speech which has previously utilized distichs only. This observation strengthens the view that the verse constitutes the end of Bildad's address. On this technique for concluding on a powerful note, cf. *PPS*, pp. 71 f.

Job's Reply to Bildad (*26:1–4; 27:1–12*)

As indicated in the introductory note to the Third Cycle, two sections of Job's reply are to be found in parts of our present chapters 26 and 27. The remainder of his speech is missing and can no longer be recovered. When our present text emerged, Job was credited with an address extending over six chapters (chapters 26–31). The editors sought to break up this very long speech by adding a special introductory formula at the beginning of chapters 27 and 29, "Job again took up his discourse, saying. . . ." Thus the editors recognized that there was something exceptional in the condition of the text before them.

To revert to the content, Job realizes that he can expect no help from his friends, who are unable or unwilling to understand him. He takes a passionate oath, insisting that he will never concede that he is guilty and, by that token, deserving of the agony he has suffered. Knowing that he has never blasphemed, he restates the faith in God's justice that actuated him during the earlier and happier period of his life when he had no reason to doubt the triumph of the right. The extant portion of his speech ends with a call to the Friends to desist from their empty talk.

26   Job answered, saying,
  2   How have you helped the powerless
              and saved the arm wanting in strength?
  3   What have you advised him who has no wisdom?
              What sound counsel have you given the inexperienced?
  4   With whose help have you uttered your words,
              and whose breath has come forth from you?

27   (Job again took up his discourse, saying,)
  2   As God lives, who has robbed me of my right,
              and by the Almighty, who has embittered my soul —
  3   as long as the breath of life is in me
              and God's spirit is in my nostrils,
  4   my lips will speak no falsehood
              and my tongue utter no deceit.
  5   Heaven forbid that I declare you in the right;
              until I die I will not be stripped of my integrity.
  6   My righteousness I have held fast, and never let it go;
              my heart harbored no blasphemy all my days.
  7   For I said,
              "Let my enemy be in the wrong
              and my opponent be the evildoer,
  8   for what hope has the evildoer when he is cut off,
              when God calls for his life?
  9   Will God hear his cry
              when trouble comes upon him?
 10   Is he free to implore the Almighty —
              can he call upon God at any time?"
 11   Let *me* teach you, speaking on God's behalf;
              what He has in mind, *I* shall not deny.

       . . . .
       . . . .
       . . . .
       . . . .

 12   Indeed, you have all seen this —
              Why then do you spew forth emptiness?

כו א　　　וַיַּעַן אִיּוֹב וַיֹּאמַר:

2　מֶה־עָזַרְתָּ לְלֹא־כֹחַ　　הוֹשַׁעְתָּ זְרוֹעַ לֹא־עֹז:

3　מַה־יָּעַצְתָּ לְלֹא חׇכְמָה　　וְתֻשִׁיָּה לָרֹב הוֹדָעְתָּ:

4　אֶת־מִי הִגַּדְתָּ מִלִּין　　וְנִשְׁמַת־מִי יָצְאָה מִמֶּךָּ:

כז א　　וַיֹּסֶף אִיּוֹב שְׂאֵת מְשָׁלוֹ וַיֹּאמַר:

2　חַי־אֵל הֵסִיר מִשְׁפָּטִי　　וְשַׁדַּי הֵמַר נַפְשִׁי:

3　כִּי־כָל־עוֹד נִשְׁמָתִי בִי　　וְרוּחַ אֱלוֹהַּ בְּאַפִּי:

4　אִם־תְּדַבֵּרְנָה שְׂפָתַי עַוְלָה　　וּלְשׁוֹנִי אִם־יֶהְגֶּה רְמִיָּה:

5　חָלִילָה לִּי אִם־אַצְדִּיק אֶתְכֶם

עַד־אֶגְוָע　　לֹא־אָסִיר תֻּמָּתִי מִמֶּנִּי:

6　בְּצִדְקָתִי הֶחֱזַקְתִּי וְלֹא אַרְפֶּהָ　　לֹא־יֶחֱרַף לְבָבִי מִיָּמָי:

7　יְהִי כְרָשָׁע אֹיְבִי　　וּמִתְקוֹמְמִי כְעַוָּל:

8　כִּי מַה־תִּקְוַת חָנֵף כִּי יִבְצָע　　כִּי יֵשֶׁל אֱלוֹהַּ נַפְשׁוֹ:

9　הַצַעֲקָתוֹ יִשְׁמַע ׀ אֵל　　כִּי־תָבוֹא עָלָיו צָרָה:

י　אִם־עַל־שַׁדַּי יִתְעַנָּג　　יִקְרָא אֱלוֹהַּ בְּכָל־עֵת:

11　אוֹרֶה אֶתְכֶם בְּיַד־אֵל　　אֲשֶׁר עִם־שַׁדַּי לֹא אֲכַחֵד:

12　הֵן־אַתֶּם כֻּלְּכֶם חֲזִיתֶם　　וְלָמָּה־זֶּה הֶבֶל תֶּהְבָּלוּ:

Job's Third Response

CHAPTER 26

26:2 Because the three opening vv. are in the sing., some scholars assume that they are addressed to Job and once belonged to the Friends, probably to Bildad (Du., Hö.). The vv. must then be interpreted as Bildad's sarcastic challenge to Job as to how he has helped God whom he has accused of lacking wisdom and power. It is obvious that this interpretation is more than "a little labored" (D-G). Actually, the original assumption is questionable. At times, Job uses the sing. in addressing the Friends, perhaps because he is singling out one, particularly at the beginning of his response; cf. 16:3b; 21:3b. In any event, the theme of vv. 2-4, a denial that any help has been forthcoming, is appropriate only when addressed to the Friends, whose original and doubtless sincere purpose was to comfort and sustain Job in his affliction (2:11; especially 4:2 ff.). Hence the verses must emanate from Job.

מַה־עָזַרְתָּ "How have you helped?, lit. how much help have you given?" (cf. Nu. 24:5). לֹא־כֹחַ, and לֹא־עֹז "the weak," like לֹא חָכְמָה "the unwise," are abstracts used for the concrete, "a man lacking in strength (or wisdom)."

26:3 תֻשִׁיָּה effective, practical counsel," a characteristic Wisdom term; cf. the Comm. on 11:6. לָרֹב generally rendered "abundantly" has been emended to לְבַעַר (*sic*) "to the dolt" (Gr.) or לָרַךְ "to the tender" (Be.) because of the parallelism. We believe the vocable in MT is to be vocalized לָרַב (or לָרְבֶה with the He having been lost through haplography), which means "youth"; cf. the mishnaic use הרובין שומרים שם "the youths watch there" (*M. Tamid* 1:1); יקבלו הרובין את תשובתן "let the youngsters receive their answer" (*B. Hul.* 20a); שכן בבבל קורין לינוקא רביא "in Babylonia they call a child *rabhya*" (*B. Suk.* 5b). If our noun be regarded as an Aramaism, the word may be vocalized לְרָב; cf. רָבְיָא (T on Lam. 1:5). The word may also occur in Gen. 21:20 וַיְהִי רֹבֶה קַשָּׁת "and the young man was a bowman." (Note נַעַר in the v. and the *nomen agentis* קַשָּׁת.) In the ancient world, the idea of "youth" is related to lack of experience and wisdom, almost as a self-evident truth. Cf. Arab. *fatay*, "young man" and its Heb. cognate פֶּתִי "fool"; and note Pr. 1:4 לִפְתָאִים ‖ to לְנַעַר. For the theme, cf. Isa. 28:9.

26:4 אֶת־מִי lit. "with whom, i.e., with whose participation have you spoken?"; cf. 12:3. Stich b: "whose breath speaks through you?" Job ironically asks what divine source do they credit with their utterances, as Eliphaz has been doing consistently (4:12 ff.; 15:11).

It is quite likely that part of Job's address at this point was lost. He continues in 27:2.

CHAPTER 27

27:1 After the massive dislocation suffered by the Third Cycle, the special caption was added by an editor who was conscious of the inordinately long speech assigned to Job (chaps. 26–31). *Māšāl*, the basic literary form of Wisdom literature, lit. "comparison," includes the proverb, the parable, the fable, and the allegory. It is also applied to song and poetic discourse; cf. Nu. 23:7; Ps. 49:5. On *māšāl* see *BGM*, pp. 199–202. Our approach diverges in some respects from that of O. Eissfeldt, *Der Māšāl im A. T.* (Giessen, 1913); cf. also G. Rinaldi in *Biblica*, vol. 40, 1959, pp. 267–89.

27:2 הֵסִיר מִשְׁפָּטִי "who has robbed me of my right"; cf. וּמֵאֱלֹהַי מִשְׁפָּטִי יַעֲבוֹר (Isa. 40:27). חַי אֵל "as God lives," the formula of an oath concluded in v. 4. There is deep irony in Job's swearing that he has lived uprightly by the God who has dealt unjustly with him. The passage is a decisive refutation of the view that Job has been appealing to an unnamed third party to judge between him and God (Terrien, P.; cf. the Comm. on 9:33; 16:19; 19:25). For Job the God to whom he is appealing is identical with the God who has wronged him. The rabbinic comment here is thoroughly justified: אמר רבי יהושע מאהבה עבד איוב את המקום אין אדם נודר בחיי המלך אלא אם כן אוהבו "Rabbi Joshua said: 'Job served God out of love, for no man swears by the life of the king unless he loves him'" (*Tos. Sotah*, chap. 6, beginning).

In oaths invoking God, the word is vocalized with a Pataḥ חַי; in oaths by the life of a king or other human being, it is always pointed with a Ṣere חֵי, the change probably being induced by a sense of reverence.

27:3 For the idiom, cf. כִּי־כָל־עוֹד נַפְשִׁי בִּי (II Sam. 1:9), lit. "while my breath is yet in me." D-G finds a grammatical difficulty in כָּל before the adverb עוֹד. The usage is to be explained by the fact that עוֹד is originally a noun. Hence, כָּל עוֹד = lit. "all the existence." The idiom כָּל עוֹד as "so long as" has entered modern Hebrew from these verses and under the influence of the Israeli national anthem, "Hatiqvah," which begins with the words, "so long as within the heart."

The v. may possibly be understood as a parenthesis: "for I still have my strength" (Dr.). It is better taken to mean "as long as I live, I shall speak truthfully and act righteously" (cf. especially 27:6b).

רוּחַ אֱלוֹהַ may be understood as "God's spirit" or "the breath of life coming from God." The subtle distinctions between the two terms drawn by modern theologians did not exist for the ancient Hebrews.

27:4 אִם in oaths originally introduced a self-imposed curse: "May I be punished if," which was then followed by the opposite of the affirmation. Hence stich a in translation: "that my lips would speak no falsehood." יֶהְגֶּה "murmur, muse," here "utter"; cf. Ps. 35:28. לָשׁוֹן, usually fem., is masc. in Lam. 4:4.

27:5 The caesura belongs after אֶתְכֶם and the meter is 4:4. אַצְדִּיק is declarative, "pronounce you in the right"; אָסִיר is either causative, "lit. I will not let men strip me of my integrity," or declarative, "I will not say that my integrity has been taken from me" (so Ra.).

27:6 יֶחֱרַף occurs in the Qal elsewhere, though only in the participle (Ps. 69:10); hence it need not be emended to the Piel יְחָרֵף (Bu.). D-G claims that the verb must have an object expressed; however, in our passage, it does not mean "reproach," but carries a secondary, specialized meaning "blaspheme" (as in Ps. 74:10 יְחָרֶף צָר) with the object, God, being understood. The usage is common in rabbinic Heb., e.g. מחרפת ומגדפת "Rome blasphemes and reviles" (*Mid. Lev. Rab.*, sec. 7). The change to יֵחְפַּר, "my heart is not ashamed" (Du., Dh., Hö.), destroys the parallelism and is totally unnecessary. מִיָּמָי "lit. from the days of my birth"; cf. I Sam. 25:28; I Ki. 6:8; Job 38:12.

27:7 On the theme of Job's former faith described in 27:7–10, see Special Note 21.

כְּרָשָׁע and כְּעַוָּל contain the asseverative Kaph (see Gordis, "The Asseverative Kaph in Hebrew and Ugaritic," in *JAOS*, vol. 63, 1943, pp. 176–78). Hence render:

> "Let my enemy indeed be the sinner
>   and my opponent be the evil-doer."

In the days of his innocence and firm faith in God's justice, Job would curse his foes only through the wish that they would be in the wrong so that they would inevitably be punished.

27:8 The verb יִבְצַע is transitive in the Piel (Isa. 10:12; Lam. 2:17; Job 6:9). Here in the Qal, the verb may be interpreted transitively as well: "When God cuts him off." It is, however, better to treat it as intransitive: "When he is cut off," as in Joel 2:8 וּבְעַד הַשֶּׁלַח יִפֹּלוּ לֹא יִבְצָעוּ "they, i.e. the locusts, fall by the sword, but are not cut off, i.e. they keep on coming, no matter how many are killed." The verb used transitively in the Piel refers to the cutting off of man's life in Isa. 38:12. From this basic meaning "break, cut" the other connotations of the root are derived: (a) "break bread" (*B. Ber.* 46a; *B. Ḥul.* 7b); (b) בֶּצַע "a portion cut off, hence bribe" (Gen. 37:26; Ex. 18:21; cf. the English slang term "cut" = "share, bribe"); (c) "gain, profit," Gen. 37:26; (d) בֹּצֵעַ "practitioner of violence, violent man" (Ps. 10:3); (e) "split the difference, compromise" in mishnaic Heb. אסור לבצוע (*B. Sanh.* 6b).

יֵשֶׁל in stich b has been dealt with variously: (a) reading יִשַּׁל (Ra., Ibn E.) from נשל "cast off," but the verb is intransitive in Deut. 28:40; (b) reading יָשֹׁל from שלל "carry off as booty" (Dil.) or "carry off sheaves" (Ruth 2:16); (c) reading כִּי יִשָּׂא לֶאֱלוֹהַּ נַפְשׁוֹ "when he raises his soul, i.e. yearns for God" (Perles, Ehr., Hö.) (cf. Deut. 24:15; Ps. 24:4; 25:1; 86:4); (d) treat יֵשֶׁל as a defectiva spelling for יִשְׁאַל: "when God asks for his soul" (Wel., Wr., Sieg., Bu., Du., Be.); (e) derive the verb from שלה "draw forth"; cf. *B. Baba Kamma* הַשּׁוֹלֶה דגים מן הים "he who draws forth fish from the sea"; cf. Syriac šelaʾ, occurring in the Pešita for משה in Ex. 2:10; Ps. 18:7. Either of the last two interpretations, which requires no modification of the text, is appropriate to the context.

27:10 The v. has generally been rendered: "Will he be able to rejoice in God whenever he calls upon God?" One would, however, have expected a Vav to introduce the subordinate clause postulated for stich b. Actually, the two vv. are in perfect parallelism. Stich a is to be rendered: "Will he be able to importune the Almighty?" On the meaning "plead with, importune," see the Comm. on 22:27. בְּכָל עֵת = "at any time" is emphatic, as Ehr. recognizes, though his explanation of its meaning is complicated. The meaning is: "Is God accessible to him at all times and not merely at specially propitious hours?" Cf. the synonyms עֵת מְצֹא (Ps. 32:6); בְּהִמָּצְאוֹ (Isa. 55:6); עֵת רָצוֹן (Isa. 49:8; Ps. 69:14).

This v. marks the conclusion of Job's earlier views that he has been recalling.

27:11 Stich a is rendered: "I shall teach you about God's power" (יָד = strength) and יוֹרֶנּוּ בְּדֶרֶךְ יִבְחָר (Ps. 25:12) is invoked for the use of the Bet after the verb (D-G, Hö.). But this sentiment is hardly appropriate for Job, who has insisted throughout that not God's power, but His justice, is the issue. Because of its inappropriateness, this v. (together with vv. 8–10) is often transposed to Zophar (D-G, Hö.). However, the plural אֶתְכֶם here, as in v. 12, demonstrates that it is the Friends who are being addressed, and the words must, therefore, emanate from Job.

TS refers the v. to Job's past activity: "I was wont to teach you about God" — a reference to what he has just presented as his previous standpoint. But would Job *now* call these ideas that he has abandoned "the truth that is with God"?

We believe the solution lies elsewhere. עִם־שַׁדַּי = "lit. what is with God, i.e. what God has in mind"; cf. Job 12:3 וְאֶת־מִי־אֵין כְּמוֹ אֵלֶּה: "with whom are these ideas not to be found?" בְּיַד־אֵל is parallel to these words, בְּיַד being a phonetic equivalent to בְּעַד, "*pro Deo*, on behalf of God, in God's stead." On this phonetic equivalence, cf. בְּיַד פִּשְׁעָם (the Comm. on 8:4); אֲשֶׁר בְּיַד אֶפְרַיִם (Ezek. 37:19), etc., and see Gordis, "A Note on Yad," in *JBL*, vol. 62, 1943, pp. 341 ff.

Eliphaz in particular has presumed to be the oracle of God. Job insists, on the contrary, that he will reveal what is really in God's mind. It is highly unfortunate that the succeeding passage, which contained Job's presentation of what he believes is in God's mind, has been lost in the dislocation of the Third Cycle.

27:12 The plural makes it certain that the Friends are being addressed.

Job avers that they really know the facts of life, but persist in setting forth conventional lies about the government of the world. This v. may well have served as the conclusion of Job's response to Bildad.

The Speech of Zophar (27:13–23)

Only a small fragment of Zophar's speech has survived. It presents the conventional doctrine in straightforward, simplistic form — the wicked will be punished by God. If the evildoer has children, they will die by the sword or famine. If he amasses wealth, it is only for the sake of the righteous who will inherit it. Terrors will overwhelm him, and he will be swept away and forgotten.

27 13 This is the sinner's portion from God,
    the heritage which oppressors receive from the Almighty —
14 If his children be multiplied, it is for the sword,
    and his offspring will lack for bread.
15 Those who survive him will be buried by the plague,
    and his widows will not mourn.
16 If he heaps up silver like dust,
    and stores up clothing like clay,
17 he may store it up, but the just will wear it,
    and his silver, the innocent will divide.
18 The house he builds is as frail as a nest,
    like a booth set up by a watchman.
19 He goes to bed rich, but not for long —
    when he opens his eyes, he is rich no more.
20 Terrors overwhelm him like a flood;
    in the night a whirlwind carries him off.
21 The east wind lifts him up and he is gone,
    and whirls him out of his place.
22 It hurls itself upon him without pity
    as he tries to flee from its power.
23 Men will clap their hands at him in horror,
    and whistle over him in his former place.

. . . .
. . . .

זֶה ׀ חֵלֶק־אָדָם רָשָׁע ׀ עִם־אֵל וְנַחֲלַת עָרִיצִים מִשַּׁדַּי יִקָּחוּ: 13 כז

אִם־יִרְבּוּ בָנָיו לְמוֹ־חָרֶב וְצֶאֱצָאָיו לֹא יִשְׂבְּעוּ־לָחֶם: 14

שְׂרִידָו בַּמָּוֶת יִקָּבֵרוּ וְאַלְמְנֹתָיו לֹא תִבְכֶּינָה: טו

אִם־יִצְבֹּר כֶּעָפָר כָּסֶף וְכַחֹמֶר יָכִין מַלְבּוּשׁ: 16

יָכִין וְצַדִּיק יִלְבָּשׁ וְכֶסֶף נָקִי יַחֲלֹק: 17

בָּנָה כָעָשׁ בֵּיתוֹ וּכְסֻכָּה עָשָׂה נֹצֵר: 18

עָשִׁיר יִשְׁכַּב וְלֹא יֵאָסֵף עֵינָיו פָּקַח וְאֵינֶנּוּ: 19

תַּשִּׂיגֵהוּ כַמַּיִם בַּלָּהוֹת לַיְלָה גְּנָבַתּוּ סוּפָה: כ

יִשָּׂאֵהוּ קָדִים וְיֵלַךְ וִישָׂעֲרֵהוּ מִמְּקֹמוֹ: 21

וְיַשְׁלֵךְ עָלָיו וְלֹא יַחְמֹל מִיָּדוֹ בָּרוֹחַ יִבְרָח: 22

יִשְׂפֹּק עָלֵימוֹ כַפֵּימוֹ וְיִשְׁרֹק עָלָיו מִמְּקֹמוֹ: 23

Zophar's Third Speech

27:13 On Zophar's final speech, which has survived only in fragmentary form, see Special Note 22.

The opening of Zophar's address, including the characteristic assault on Job (11:2 f.; 20:2 ff.), is missing. Probably the end is also lacking, unless we transpose v. 13 to the end, like 20:29, to which it bears an obvious resemblance. There is no reason for deleting this v. (Hö.); note the thematic repetition in Eliphaz (4:17 f.; 15:13; and see 25:4).

עִם־אֵל = "with God, i.e., in God's mind" or "stored up with Him" (Deut. 32:34; cf. 11b above and note the parallelism here). The emendation to מֵאֵל on the basis of 20:29 (Altschüller, in *ZATW*, 1886, p. 212; Ehr.) is not needed.

The Mem of עָרִיצִים may be deleted as a dittography from מִשַּׁדַּי or understood as an enclitic, but the use of the plural after the sing. in stich a is normal in referring to the evil-doers as a class (cf. Isa. 5:23; Job 16:11; 24:16–20, 24 for such fluctuations in number).

The v. is in 4:4 meter, like v. 4 above; deletions *metri causa* in both cases are gratuitous.

27:14 לְמוֹ־חָרֶב is a breviloquence: "It is for the sword." Cf. בִּפְרֹחַ רְשָׁעִים כְּמוֹ עֵשֶׂב (Ps. 92:8, where the last two words also constitute the apodosis, as the Masorah may have understood it, in placing a Paseq before them: "When the wicked blossom — they are like grass"). Hence our stich a: "if his children increase — it is for the sword." If he does beget offspring, war, hunger, and the plague will destroy them (14a, 14b, 15a).

27:15 שְׂרִידָיו "lit. his remnant, his survivors." בַּמָּוֶת יִקָּבֵרוּ, not "will be buried in death," but "will be buried by the plague," the Beth being instrumental; cf. Ex. 5:3; Isa. 28:3; and see BDB, s.v., p. 89 b. On מָוֶת as the plague, cf. Jer. 15:2; הַרְגֵי מָוֶת 18:21; 43:11; Tel el Amarna *Mutu*, "disease"; Syriac *mautana*, and the medieval phrase, "the Black Death." The Northwest Semitic god Mot known from Ugaritic and Philo of Byblos is here personified.

The plural וְאַלְמְנֹתָיו is one of the few biblical references to polygamy, the practice of which was restricted to the wealthy classes, for economic as well as for biological reasons. LXX, troubled by the polygamous reference, renders "no one will pity their widows." On this basis, the suffix is emended to the plural (Bi., Bu., Du., Be., Ehr., D-G). However, MT is to be preferred on the principle of *difficilior lectio*. The upper-class provenance of Wisdom literature makes this reference to polygamy entirely appropriate.

D-G objects to MT since the death of the wicked man is not referred to until v. 19. However, stich b is to be understood in connection with stich a to mean that his widows will not weep for their children that have prematurely died. The devastation wrought by the plague will be so widespread and commonplace that even mothers will not lament the death of their offspring. Cf. the powerful description of a plague in Am. 6:9–10, bringing in its wake mothers' cruelty toward their offspring (Deut. 28:56 f.; Lam. 4:10). The tragedy of the death of children is here compounded by the absence of the proper mourning rites; cf. Jer. 22:10, 18, 19.

27:16 This v. and the succeeding one are in chiastic structure.

27:17 יַחֲלֹק in the Qal, "the innocent will divide"; cf. I Sam. 30:24; Pr. 17:2.

27:18 כָּעָשׁ rendered "like a moth" (P, Hö.) is inappropriate, particularly in view of the parallelism (וּכְסֻכָּה), which militates also against the emendation כְּעַכָּבִישׁ "like a spider" (Me., Hi., Bu., Du., D-G). The noun is to be rendered here, as in 4:14, "like a bird's nest"; cf. Arab. ᶜuš̌un (Schultens, Ehr., Yel.). Nor need the word be revocalized with a Sin (D-G), since instances of the Hebrew Šin = Arab. Šin are not uncommon, e.g., Hebrew שקק, תשוקה, Arab. šawaqa, "desire"; Hebrew מְשֻׁגָּע, Arab. mušjaᶜun, "insane," etc. Cf. J. Barth, *ES*, pp. 46–50.

27:19 Stich a, with the accusative of status at the beginning, is emphatic; cf. עָרֹם יָצָתִי (1:21). לֹא יֵאָסֵף has been rendered "he will not be gathered for burial," on the basis of Ezek. 29:5, but the reference to his burial is premature at this point, since stich b and the succeeding vv. 20–21 describe him as still being alive and suffering terrors. The clause is better understood: "He goes to bed rich, but he will not continue (to be rich)." The form of the verb is an aberrant vocalization and orthography for וְלֹא יֹסִיף = וְלֹא יֹאסֵף; cf. לֹא תֹאסִפוּן לָתֵת תֶּבֶן "you shall not continue to give straw" (Ex. 5:2); וַיֹּאסֶף (I Sam. 18:20).

In stich b, the verb may be impersonal: "When one opens one's eyes, the wicked is no longer there, i.e., he is dead" (Ew., Dil., Du., Del., Dr.). However, the reference to his going to sleep in stich a suggests that the subject of פָּקַח is "the evil-doer." If the latter interpretation is accepted, and the verse be understood to refer to his death, the naive mode of expression (when he wakes up he is dead!) may be supported by וַיַּשְׁכִּימוּ בַבֹּקֶר וְהִנֵּה כֻלָּם פְּגָרִים מֵתִים: "When they rose up early in the morning, behold they were all dead corpses" (II Ki. 19:35 = Isa. 33:36). However, the parallelism indicates that both stichs refer to his sudden loss of wealth. Hence וְאֵינֶנּוּ = "he is not, sc. rich any more." See the Trans.

27:20 תַּשִּׂיגֵהוּ for the fem. sing. with a plural verb, cf. Isa. 34:13; Ps. 37:31; Job 27:20; and see Ges.-K., sec. 145, 4. Stich a in MT is satisfactory per se, since "waters" frequently suggest considerable destructive force (II Sam. 5:20; Isa. 28:17; Am. 5:24; Hos. 5:10). Hence render "terrors overtake him like floodwaters." However, לַיְלָה in stich b suggests the possibility of reading בַּיּוֹם (Me., Gr.) or יוֹמָם (Wr., B. Stade, Bu., Hö., Ehr., P.) for מַיִם: "Terrors overtake him by day; by night a whirlwind carries him off."

27:21 וִישָׂעֲרֵהוּ "will carry him off in a storm," a variant orthography for the spelling with Samekh; cf. Hos. 13:3; Job 38:1; 40:6 by the side of Nah. 1:3; Job 9:17; see the Comm. *ad loc.* LXX omits vv. 21–23, perhaps because it interprets v. 20 as marking the evil-doer's death (but see the Comm. above).

27:22 The subject of stich a is not God, who has not been mentioned, but קָדִים, the sirocco wind. יַשְׁלֵךְ in the Hiphil need not be revocalized as יְשֻׁלַךְ; it is a reflexive, "hurls itself." וְלֹא יַחְמוֹל is a clause of condition, adverbial in force, "without pity"; cf. the exact idiom and usage in 6:10.

Stich b may be taken as coordinate with stich a and rendered: (a) "He flees from its power"; or (b) לֹא from stich a being understood, "he cannot flee from its power." It is better taken as a subordinate clause: "as he tries to flee from its power." The use of the infinitive absolute carries the connotation of his unremitting attempts to escape.

27:23: The subject of the verbs in both stichs is impersonal = "Men will clap their hands" and "men will whistle upon him." The suffixes in עָלֵימוֹ and כַּפֵּימוֹ are both the sing. (cf. the Comm. on 22:19b; Isa. 44:15; Ps. 11:7; the Mem being used as the sing. suffix regularly in Phoenician and sporadically in Hebrew). Thus the difficulties D-G encounters with the suffixes (II, p. 188 f.) are nonexistent, and the proposed emendations of the verbs to the plural are unnecessary. מִמְּקֹמוֹ lit. "from his former place" is best understood as "in his former place." On the use of Mem = "on the side of, in," cf. such forms as מִמַּעַל, מִתַּחַת and מִקֶּדֶם (Gen. 2:8), מֵרָחוֹק "afar off" (Isa. 23:7); and see BDB, s.v. 1, c, p. 578b.

Clapping the hands was a mark of grief or horror, either genuine (Nu. 24:10; Nah. 3:19) or feigned (Lam. 2:15). Booing or whistling was a sign of astonishment at disaster and contempt for the victims (Jer. 49:17; Ezek. 27:36; Zeph. 2:15; Lam. 2:15).

The Hymn to Wisdom (28)

The "Hymn to Wisdom" is clearly an independent lyrical poem with a characteristic refrain, "Wisdom, where may she be found?" (vv. 12 and 20). Unlike the preceding dialogue, it is not argumentative and reveals no echo of a passionate debate. Moreover, the presence of the Hymn at this point in the book would weaken tremendously the impact of the God speeches and, in fact, make them anticlimactic. For it expresses virtually the same fundamental theme, though set forth more briefly — the world is a mystery to man, who will never be able to penetrate the great supernal Wisdom by which God has created and governs the universe.

There are strong grounds for believing that this poem was written by the author of Job. In addition to the basic harmony of outlook already mentioned, the vocabulary and style of the Hymn have many affinities with those of the God speeches. Moreover, both sections reveal the same wide knowledge of the science and technology of the day. This poem is therefore best regarded as an early effort by the poet to treat the theme which he later elaborated in the God speeches.

While the beautiful "Hymn to Wisdom" is not an integral part of the book of Job, it is a highly welcome product of the poet's pen. In view of the vast dislocations sustained by the third cycle of the dialogue, it is easy to understand how this poem found its way into the text at this point.

The poem obviously does not belong here since it anticipates the theme of the God speeches. Nor can it be placed after them at the end of the book where it would be superfluous. It was probably preserved with the other writings of the poet by his early readers and admirers and included by a copyist with the book of Job. That a great theme should have occupied the poet for a lifetime is not astonishing. In its present position after the conclusion of the third cycle, the "Hymn to Wisdom" is well described as "a musical interlude" between the debate and Job's final soliloquy.

The "Hymn to Wisdom" differs in emphasis from the God speeches. The Hymn stresses the mystery of the universe and the inaccessibility of the Divine Wisdom which served God as the pattern of creation. The God speeches go further with the added insight that the cosmos is miracle as well as mystery and should evoke joy and awe as well as humility from man.

The "Hymn to Wisdom" describes how men mine the earth and face unknown hazards in their search for precious stones in volcanic areas far from human habitation. Yet no such search will avail to find the supernal Wisdom, nor can it be purchased with all the treasures of the world. Even the deep sea does not know its place. Only God, who created the universe, knows the transcendental Wisdom. As for man, the only wisdom that is accessible to him consists of religion and morality, reverence for the Lord and avoidance of evil.

28 Surely there is a mine for silver
        and a place where gold is refined.
2   Iron is taken from the earth
        and ore is poured out as copper.
3   Men put an end to darkness,
        and to the furthest ends they penetrate.
    The lava, dark and pitch-black,
4   cleaves a channel from the crater
    never trodden by human foot,
        bereft even of wandering men.
5   It is a land from which heat pours forth,
        while its lower regions are convulsed by fire,

6   a place whose stones are sapphires
        and whose dust is gold.
7   The path to it no bird of prey knows,
        and the falcon's eye has never seen it.
8   The proud beasts have not trodden it,
        nor has the lion passed over it.
9   Man puts his hand to the flinty rock
        and overturns mountains by the roots.
10 He hews out channels in the rocks,
        and his eye sees every precious thing.
11 He binds up the flow of rivers,
        and what is hidden he brings to light.

12 But Wisdom, where may she be found,
        and where is the place of Understanding?
13 Man does not know her place,
        nor is she found in the land of the living.
14 The Deep says, "Not in me,"
        the Sea says, "Nor with me."
15 She cannot be acquired for gold,
        and silver cannot be weighed as her price.
16 She cannot be valued in the gold of Ophir,
        in precious onyx or sapphire.
17 Gold and glass cannot equal her,
        nor objects of fine gold be exchanged for her.
18 Coral and crystal cannot be mentioned,
        for the price of Wisdom is above pearls.
19 The topaz of Ethiopia does not compare,
        nor can she be valued in pure gold.

20 But Wisdom, whence does she come,
        and where is the place of Understanding?
21 For she is hidden from the eyes of all living things,
        concealed even from the birds of the air.
22 Abaddon and Death say,
        "We have heard only her echo."

23 But God understood her way
        and He knew her place,
24 when he looked to the ends of the earth
        and saw everything under the heaven.

וּמָקוֹם לַזָּהָב יָזֹקּוּ׃	**כח** א כִּי יֵשׁ לַכֶּסֶף מוֹצָא
וְאֶבֶן יָצוּק נְחוּשָׁה׃	2 בַּרְזֶל מֵעָפָר יֻקָּח
וּלְכָל־תַּכְלִית הוּא חוֹקֵר	3 קֵץ ׀ שָׂם לַחֹשֶׁךְ
פָּרַץ נַחַל ׀ מֵעִם־גָּר	4 אֶבֶן אֹפֶל וְצַלְמָוֶת׃
הַדַּלּוּ מֵאֱנוֹשׁ נָעוּ׃	הַנִּשְׁכָּחִים מִנִּי־רָגֶל
וְתַחְתֶּיהָ נֶהְפַּךְ כְּמוֹ־אֵשׁ׃	ה אֶרֶץ מִמֶּנָּה יֵצֵא־לָחֶם
וְעַפְרֹת זָהָב לוֹ׃	6 מְקוֹם־סַפִּיר אֲבָנֶיהָ
וְלֹא שְׁזָפַתּוּ עֵין אַיָּה׃	7 נָתִיב לֹא־יְדָעוֹ עָיִט
לֹא־עָדָה עָלָיו שָׁחַל׃	8 לֹא־הִדְרִיכֻהוּ בְנֵי־שָׁחַץ
הָפַךְ מִשֹּׁרֶשׁ הָרִים׃	9 בַּחַלָּמִישׁ שָׁלַח יָדוֹ
וְכָל־יְקָר רָאֲתָה עֵינוֹ׃	י בַּצּוּרוֹת יְאֹרִים בִּקֵּעַ
וְתַעֲלֻמָהּ יֹצִא אוֹר׃ פ	11 מִבְּכִי נְהָרוֹת חִבֵּשׁ
וְאֵי זֶה מְקוֹם בִּינָה׃	12 וְהַחָכְמָה מֵאַיִן תִּמָּצֵא
וְלֹא תִמָּצֵא בְּאֶרֶץ הַחַיִּים׃	13 לֹא־יָדַע אֱנוֹשׁ עֶרְכָּהּ
וְיָם אָמַר אֵין עִמָּדִי׃	14 תְּהוֹם אָמַר לֹא בִי־הִיא
וְלֹא יִשָּׁקֵל כֶּסֶף מְחִירָהּ׃	טו לֹא־יֻתַּן סְגוֹר תַּחְתֶּיהָ
בְּשֹׁהַם יָקָר וְסַפִּיר׃	16 לֹא־תְסֻלֶּה בְּכֶתֶם אוֹפִיר
וּתְמוּרָתָהּ כְּלִי־פָז׃	17 לֹא־יַעַרְכֶנָּה זָהָב וּזְכוֹכִית
וּמֶשֶׁךְ חָכְמָה מִפְּנִינִים׃	18 רָאמוֹת וְגָבִישׁ לֹא יִזָּכֵר
בְּכֶתֶם טָהוֹר לֹא תְסֻלֶּה׃ פ	19 לֹא־יַעַרְכֶנָּה פִּטְדַת־כּוּשׁ
וְאֵי זֶה מְקוֹם בִּינָה׃	כ וְהַחָכְמָה מֵאַיִן תָּבוֹא
וּמֵעוֹף הַשָּׁמַיִם נִסְתָּרָה׃	21 וְנֶעֶלְמָה מֵעֵינֵי כָל־חָי
בְּאָזְנֵינוּ שָׁמַעְנוּ שִׁמְעָהּ׃	22 אֲבַדּוֹן וָמָוֶת אָמְרוּ
וְהוּא יָדַע אֶת־מְקוֹמָהּ׃	23 אֱלֹהִים הֵבִין דַּרְכָּהּ
תַּחַת כָּל־הַשָּׁמַיִם יִרְאֶה׃	24 כִּי־הוּא לִקְצוֹת־הָאָרֶץ יַבִּיט

25   When He gave the wind its due weight
          and meted out the waters by measure,
26   when He made a law for the rain
          and a way for the thunderbolt,
27   then He saw Wisdom, and described her;
          He marked her and searched her out.
28   But to man He said,
          "To be in awe of the Lord — that is wisdom,
          and to avoid evil — that is understanding."

כה לַעֲשׂוֹת לָרוּחַ מִשְׁקָל   וּמַיִם תִּכֵּן בְּמִדָּה׃

26 בַּעֲשֹׂתוֹ לַמָּטָר חֹק   וְדֶרֶךְ לַחֲזִיז קֹלוֹת׃

27 אָז רָאָה וַיְסַפְּרָהּ   הֱכִינָהּ וְגַם־חֲקָרָהּ׃

28 וַיֹּאמֶר ׀ לָאָדָם   הֵן יִרְאַת אֲדֹנָי הִיא חָכְמָה

וְסוּר מֵרָע בִּינָה׃

CHAPTER 28

On Chap. 28, "The Hymn to Wisdom," see Special Note 23

Introductory Note on 28:2–11 — Mining for Precious Metals and Stones

Ra. and Ibn E. refer this passage to God, who penetrates to the mysteries of nature. Since vv. 1–2 obviously referred to human activity, TS, who accepts this view, is forced to assume a lacuna after v. 2. Aside from this difficulty, what relevance would God's search have upon the inaccessibility of wisdom to *man*? The most natural view of vv. 3–11 is to see in the passage a description of mining operations in remote areas, probably in volcanic regions. Both the technology and the terminology of the ancients are unfamiliar to us, complicating the understanding of this passage.

28:1 כִּי is the asseverative particle (Nu. 23:23; I Sam. 20:26; Isa. 32:13; Jer. 22:22; 31:19; Am. 3:7; and see BDB, s.v., p. 472b). It is also familiar in Akkadian (Holma in *ZA*, vol. 28, p. 102) and in Ugaritic (*UT*, Glossary, No. 1184, 1220). It also occurs at the beginning of poems in Hebrew (cf. Isa. 15:1; on Jos. 22:34, see Gordis, in *AJSL*, vol. 48, 1931, pp. 287 f.). It is, therefore, unnecessary to assume with Du. that the refrain in vv. 12, 20 originally stood before v. 1 as well.

מוֹצָא "source," of water in II Ki. 2:21, here of silver, hence "a mine." Stich b, lit. "a place where they refine gold," with Lamed of the accusative.

The two stichs are in complementary parallelism, the first dealing with mining silver (and gold), the second with refining gold (and silver).

28:2 After the gold and silver the poet describes iron and copper. Stich b is generally rendered: "From the stone, copper is poured out," with the Mem of stich a understood in stich b. Yel. treats יָצוּק as the Qal imperfect, used impersonally, of צוק (like אָגוּר, Deut. 32:27, from גור). He renders: "From the stone one pours out copper." However, the rock itself was regarded as becoming metal; cf. Deut. 8:9; אֶרֶץ אֲשֶׁר אֲבָנֶיהָ בַרְזֶל וּמֵהֲרָרֶיהָ תַּחְצֹב נְחֹשֶׁת "A land whose rocks (i.e., ore) are iron and from whose hills you may hew out copper." High-content iron ore has been found in the plateaux of Trans-Jordan, and copper was mined in Edom. Solomon's refineries at Ezion-Gebher have been graphically described by Nelson Glueck. It is, therefore, better to render stich b: "lit. the rock is poured out as copper." אֶבֶן, generally fem., is masc. in I Ki. 10:9, and see the Comm. on 28:3, 4 below.

28:3 By digging an opening in the earth, the miner brings light into dark areas. The v. may refer to lamps used by miners that are mentioned by Diodorus Siculus (1st century B.C.E.) in his description of gold-mining in Nubia (P.).

תַּכְלִית = "end"; cf. 26:9.

The pronoun הוּא introduces a subject which the reader must recognize.

On this important stylistic trait of the poet, cf. the Comm. on 8:16; 13:28; 24:5, 13; 41:1. The deletion of הוּא (Be., Du.) and, contrarywise, the insertion of אָדָם (Bu.) or אֱנוֹשׁ (Bi.) are both unnecessary.

Stich c is difficult, lacking a verb and impossible to relate to the preceding stichs. Hence Hö. suggests that a stich is missing after stich b. Yel. makes the excellent proposal to attach stich c to v. 4, thus supplying a subject for פָּרַץ and, incidentally, eliminating the only tristich in the poem, by converting vv. 2–4 into 3 distichs.

אֶבֶן אֹפֶל וְצַלְמָוֶת "the rock of darkness and gloom" represents the lava, being the subject of 4a, with אֶבֶן again masc.

28:4 גָּר has sustained many emendations: (a) גִּר "limestone," on the basis of LXX, *konia*, "dust" (so Field, Dil.); (b) מֵעַם נֵר "from the light" (J. Ley, Peake); (c) מֵעַם־גָּר אוֹר "from a people living in the light" (Bi., Bu.); (d) מֵעַם גֵּר "by a foreign people" (Ehr.); (e) פָּרַץ נְחָלִם עַם־גָּר "a foreign people opening shafts" (Gr., P.). None of these emendations are convincing, and many are unhebraic. A preferable approach is to render גָּר as "crater" on the basis of Arabic *jawraṭun*, "deep hole" (Yel.) and מֵעַם = "from within" (cf. Gen. 48:12; Ruth 4:10), hence "from within the crater."

The usual interpretation of v. 4 is to see in it a description of the remote uninhabited region where the mining operations are carried on. 4a is then rendered "one cleaves a channel away from the sojourner (or, from a human dweller)" (AV, JPSV). Stich b is reasonably clear: "forgotten by (human) foot." Stich c is again extremely difficult. It has been viewed as a description of the miners being suspended on a shaft: "They are lifted up above men and swinging" (Hö.). The parallelism with stich b suggests that it is better rendered "They are lifted up, i.e. separated from wandering men."

דַּלּוּ from דלל "hang, dangle." The verb is not a *hapax legomenon* (D-G); it occurs in Isa. 38:14, דַּלּוּ עֵינַי לַמָּרוֹם, "my eyes are lifted up high," as well as in the noun דַּלָּה, "threads of the warp hanging from the loom" (Isa. 38:12) and "hair hanging from the head" (Cant. 7:6). Moreover, the geminate root is related to the *tertiae Yod* root "draw up water" דָּלָה used in the Qal (Ex. 2:6, 16, 19); in the Piel דִּלִּיתָנִי "raise up" (Ps. 30:2); and in the nouns דְּלִי "bucket" (Isa. 40:15) and דָּלִית "branch" (Jer. 11:16; Ezek. 17:6, 7). The verb may refer to the swinging shaft of the miners (so most). In their position, however, stichs b and c are better taken as describing the land, more specifically the crater which is far from human habitation. דַּלּוּ "lifted up" may be interpreted as "removed"; cf. late Hebrew נסתלק "he was lifted up, removed (from earth), died." אֲשֶׁר is understood before נָעוּ, which means "wander far"; cf. Gen. 4:12, 14; Am. 8:12; Lam. 4:14, 15.

On the basis of these meanings and by linking 3c to v. 4, the following rendering emerges:

> "The lava dark and pitch-black,
>   cleaves a channel from the crater,
> forgotten by men's foot,
>   bereft even of men who have wandered far."

28:5 The verse has been generally understood (D-G, P.) as contrasting the surface of the earth, which produces food (Ps. 104:14), with its bowels, which are convulsed by fire. On the nature of this fire see below. However, אֶרֶץ and תַּחְתֶּיהָ are scarcely adequate contrasts. As TS has also recognized, the parallelism suggests that stich a like b must refer to heat. His emendation יֶאֱצַל חוֹם "heat emanates" is, however, unnecessary. לֶחֶם itself has the meaning of "heat"; cf. the Comm. on 20:23 בִּלְחוּמוֹ which is a morphological variant of the segolate לֶחֶם, familiar from the Qumran Scrolls.

תַּחְתֶּיהָ "her bottom side" is not an acc. dependent upon the impersonal passive נֶהְפַּךְ (Hi., D-G), but the subject of the verb, meaning "its lower regions." The word in later Hebrew becomes a noun, used for "buttocks," like the English *bottom*.

כְּמוֹ אֵשׁ is generally treated as a contraction and rendered "as if by fire"; however, it is not a comparison with fire, but its actual presence, which is required here. Hence read with V בְּמוֹ אֵשׁ "by fire" (so Hö.). The fire may refer to an ancient prehistoric technique still in use in the Middle Ages for dislodging hard rocks by kindling wood in a shaft (M. Lohr, in *OLZ*, 1916, pp. 178 f.; Hö.), or the verse may be describing the natural heat of the volcano as evidenced by the burning lava pouring forth; cf. v. 4.

28:6 The Masorah links מְקוֹם to סַפִּיר both by vocalizing it as a construct and by placing a Maqqeph between them. However, the usual rendering, "a place of sapphires are its stones," is difficult. It is best to interpret מְקוֹם as in construct relationship to the entire clause with the relative conjunction אֲשֶׁר understood, "a place — the rocks of which are sapphire." מְקוֹם occurs in construct to a clause introduced by אֲשֶׁר no less than 15 times (e.g., Gen. 39:20; 40:3; Lev. 4:24, 33; 7:2; Ezek. 6:13), and in other clauses (Ps. 104:8; Job 18:21; Ecc. 1:17; 11:3) with *še*. In this clause, מְקוֹם is feminine (Job 20:9; II Sam. 17:12, Kethib; cf. *BTM ad loc.*). For the idea and the structure in a prose context, cf. אֶרֶץ אֲשֶׁר אֲבָנֶיהָ בַרְזֶל, "a land whose rocks are iron" (Deut. 8:9). סַפִּיר is not our sapphire, which was first used in Roman days, but lapis lazuli.

In stich b, לוֹ refers not to סַפִּיר but to מְקוֹם, which is here masculine. For another instance of a noun used in both genders within one verse, cf. Gen. 32:9. Render stich b: "lit., that has gold dust." This is a reference to the sparkling particles of iron pyrites in the lapis lazuli referred to by ancient writers (Theophrastus, *de Lapide*, chap. 4; Pliny, *Historia Naturalis* 37:38 f.).

28:7 עַיִט a generic term for "bird of prey" (Gen. 15:11; Isa. 18:6; a. e.); cf. Arabic *ᶜayyata* II "shriek." אַיָּה is "falcon" (Lev. 11:14; Deut. 14:13), possibly derived from the cry אוֹי "howl." The path to these remote areas not even the birds of prey know. The comment that these verses are ridiculous (Du.) is itself ridiculous. As Ehr. pointed out, certain birds of prey were believed to have preternaturally keen vision; cf. *B. Hul.* 63b, where our verse is cited and the אַיָּה is equated with the רָאָה (Deut. 14:13) and explained

שְׂרוּאָה בְיוֹתֵר "because it sees very well." Ehr. also calls attention to the German idiom *Adlerblick, Adlerauge*, "eagle's gaze"; cf. English *eagle eye*.

28:8 בְּנֵי שָׁחַץ is generally rendered "proud beasts"; cf. 41:26. The word is used in the Talmud in two meanings: a) "arrogant, vainglorious" (*Pesikta Rabbati*, par. 40a) שהיה שחץ "Simon the High Priest was vainglorious"; and b) "abomination, disgrace" אנשי ירושלים אנשי שחץ היו "the men of Jerusalem were disgraceful in conduct" (*B. Shab.* 62b). The Talmud includes the term, together with שַׁחַל, among the six names for "lion" (*B. Sanh.* 95a).

שַׁחַל always "lion" in biblical Hebrew (4:10 f.; Hos. 5:14; 13:7; Pr. 26:13). S. Mowinckel (followed by P.) suggests that there are Semitic cognates meaning "lion" in one language and "serpent" in another, e.g., Hebrew *naḥaš* "snake," Akkadian *nêšu* "lion"; Hebrew *ʾaryeh*, Eth. *ʾarwe* "serpent." He believes that our term was originally mythopoetic in origin. He cites Mesopotamian *mušruššu* on the Ishtar temple at Babylon, the serpent griffin at the Marduk temple at Nippur, and the blending of leonine and serpentine features in the figures flanking the caduceus on Gudea's vase. Hence שַׁחַל may have originally been "serpent-dragon."

הִדְרִיכוּהוּ, usually rendered "tread" (Isa. 11:15; 48:17; Hab. 3:19; Pr. 4:11), has been rendered here as "reach" as in Jud. 23:43 (Yel.).

עָדָה "pass"; cf. Arab. *ʿadaw*, Aram. עֲדִי "pass, go by," and Ps. 32:9, עֶדְיוֹ "his flight."

28:9 The unspecified subject here, as in vv. 3, 9, 10, is "man."

28:10 Vv. 10a and 11a are not parallel (ag. Du., D-G), but describe opposing processes which are both needed in mining. At times the miner needs to hew out a channel in order to wash away some rocks that impede his work (10a). At others, he needs to dam up a flow of water in order to get to his objective (11a). In both cases his goal is to bring to light buried treasure (10b, 11b).

The unusual plural of צוּרוֹת instead of the normal *im* ending (Nu. 23:9; Jos. 5:2; Ps. 78:15, etc.) anticipates the mishnaic tendency to use *ōth* for the plural of masculine nouns; cf. מִשְׁמָרוֹת, פִּדְיוֹנוֹת, זִכְרוֹנוֹת, etc. The noun is not to be derived from the root בצר and rendered "treasures" (ag. Yel., TS). Note also the Aramaism יְקָר.

28:11 The older interpretation of stich a was "he binds the streams from weeping, i.e. from trickling" (AV, JPSV). This view has been generally surrendered in the light of the Ugaritic parallel (Gordon, *Ugaritic Manual*, Rome, 1955, p. 249): *ʿm mbk nhrm qrb ʾapq thmtm* "toward the spring of the rivers, amid the channels of the two deeps." Here מבך is parallel to אפק (Heb. אָפִיק). Long before this welcome parallel from Ugaritic appeared, ancient versions and the medieval commentators recognized that מִבְּכִי was best construed as a noun: LXX and V: "He has laid bare the depths of the rivers," probably interpreting חִבֵּשׁ as = חִפֵּשׂ, which Be., Ehr., Bi. actually

accept as the reading in our text. Ra. and Ibn E. related מִבְּכִי to נִבְכֵי־יָם
(Job 38:16), and the latter rendered our word as "course" (מרוץ). The word
in MT is to be vocalized as מִבְּכֵי or מַבְּכֵי (so already J.G. Wetzstein, Del.,
Hoff., Be., Bu.) and render: "He binds up the springs of the rivers."

In stich b, וְתַעֲלֻמָה occurs with *Mappiq* in some Masoretic traditions,
but if correct it is only for euphony (לתפארת הקריאה). אוֹר is the acc. of motion:
"The hidden things he brings to light." This stich is an excellent conclusion
to the first strophe: "All hidden material things man can bring to light, but
not Wisdom, the light of the world."

28:12   The introductory Vav is adversative, "but Wisdom, etc." בִּינָה a
synonym, only slightly less technical, of חָכְמָה (Isa. 11:2; Pr. 9:10), like
תבונה (Pr. 3:13; 8:1; Job 12:12; 26:12; cf. the Comm. *ad loc.*).

The variation in the refrain (תִּמָּצֵא here and תָבוֹא v. 20) is characteristic
of Hebrew poetry; cf. Ps. 49:13, 21. LXX and some Hebrew mss. level the
readings. The change may also have been induced by the poet's wish to have
the verse stand in contrast to v. 1: יֵשׁ מוֹצָא and מֵאַיִן תִּמָּצֵא.

28:13   On the basis of LXX, עֶרְכָּהּ is emended to דַּרְכָּהּ (Dil., Hi., Bu.,
D-G, Ehr.), but the change is not necessary. עֵרֶךְ "order, row, disposition"
here means "place"; cf. מַעֲרָכָה "row" (Ex. 39:37), "battle line" (I Sam. 4:2;
12:16, and often), עֵרֶךְ (Ex. 40:23), מַעֲרֶכֶת "row (of shew-bread)" (Lev.
24:7). A homily on the Torah which is equated with Hokmah in rabbinic
thought offers a striking analogy to this entire section (*B. Shab.* 87a).

28:14   תְּהוֹם like יָם is personified here. It is masculine also in Jonah 2:6;
Ps. 42:8. Both nouns refer to the bed of the sea; cf. Isa. 11:9 כַּמַּיִם לַיָּם מְכַסִּים
"as waters cover the sea, i.e. the sea bed." What the sea denies is that it
possesses Wisdom (Ehr.).

28:15   An object may be inaccessible, either because it is difficult to find or
because it is costly in price, so that the one idea suggests the other to the
poet by association. Those who delete vv. 15–19 cannot legitimately invoke
the testimony of LXX, which omits v. 14 as well as vv. 15–16 while preserving vv. 17–19. The deletion also destroys the strophic structure of the
poem. See Special Note 24.

סְגוּר cf. זָהָב סָגוּר, "fine gold, bullion" (I Ki. 6:20, 21; 7:49, 50; 10:21,
etc.). The noun is of unknown etymology, perhaps "shut up, prized" (D-G).
It has its cognate in Akk. *ḫurâsu sagru*, which may possibly be a borrowing
from the Hebrew.

28:16   לֹא תְסֻלֶּה "it cannot be weighed"; cf. the *tertiae Aleph* form סלא,
"lift up in the scale, weigh" (Lam. 4:2), and the geminate root סלל (Isa.
62:10; Ps. 68:5; Pr. 4:8; 15:19; and the Comm. on 5:2).

שֹׁהַם "onyx," found in the land of Havilah (Gen. 2:11 f.), used for engraving, in the breastplate of the high priest (Ex. 25:7; 28:9, 20). The identity

of the stones mentioned in this passage is uncertain. See the discussion in
D-G and TS.

28:17 זְכוּכִית (from זכך "clear," like Aram. זוּגִית from זגג) is "a transparent
substance, hence glass." In ancient times glass was an expensive and precious
material. It is referred to in Egyptian sources from the 20th Dynasty on-
wards as "gold of *k-t-n*, i.e. Nubia" (S. Yeivin, *Lešonenu*, vol. 6, p. 47; TS),
and it is mentioned, together with gold, as used in expensive flagons in Aristophanes, *Acharnians*, ll. 73 f. (*The Eleven Comedies of Aristophanes*, Liveright,
New York, 1930, p. 91). וּתְמוּרָתָהּ = "her exchange, equivalent" (Lev. 27:10,
13; Ruth 4:7). כְּלִי is probably to be read, with Th., Sym., T, V and some
mss., as a plural כְּלֵי.

Recently, experts examining the jewelry of Egyptian king Tutankhamen
have found that many stones reported earlier to be costly lapis lazuli and
turquoise are, in fact, pieces of colored glass. It is true that some Egyptian
texts suggest that glass was considered to be inferior to natural gem stones.
Nevertheless, no signs have been reported that there was any dishonesty in
the use of glass or that glass inlay stones had been exchanged for gems after
the fact. Indeed, the glass inlays were put in as painstakingly as precious
stones with each separate piece carefully cut and shaped, and then cemented
into position (*New York Times*, July 21, 1976). It is, therefore, clear that glass
was highly esteemed, at least on the level of semi-precious stones.

28:18 רָאמוֹת "coral" (Ezek. 27:16). גָּבִישׁ "crystal"; cf. אֶלְגָּבִישׁ "hail" (Ezek.
13:11, 13; 38:22). Both meanings inhere also in the Greek *krystallos*. לֹא יִזָּכֵר
"cannot be remembered" or "mentioned," in relationship with Wisdom.

מֶשֶׁךְ has been interpreted (a) "drawing up, like pearls from the sea"
(Dil.); (b) "thing drawn along, extending far, hence, fame" (Ki., AV, D-G).
However, as TS has demonstrated (*Lašon Vasepher*, vol. 1, pp. 383–97),
the basic meaning of the root is "grasp, seize, take hold"; cf. Ex. 12:21;
Ecc. 2:3; and *KMW ad loc.* Hence the noun means "grasping, acquiring,
taking possession," and therefore "price." For the meaning of the stich,
cf. Pr. 31:2, "her price is far beyond rubies." In talmudic law, *mešikhah*
becomes a technical term for pulling an object as a mode of establishing
legal ownership.

מִפְּנִינִים "more than pearls," rather than "rubies." While Lam. 4:7 אָדְמוּ
עֶצֶם מִפְּנִינִים seems to suggest that the gem was red in color (cf. Cant. 5:10),
the meaning "pearls" as against "rubies" is vigorously defended by Del.,
Dil., Dr. The former meaning is the significance it bears in modern Hebrew
as well.

28:19 פִּטְדַת־כּוּשׁ "topaz of Ethiopia"; cf. Ex. 28:17. We have already pointed
out that the poet does not hesitate to repeat a verb or noun even in the same
verse. There is, therefore, no reason for deleting 19a as a doublet of 17a,
and 19b as a doublet of 16a (Du.).

28:20 On the slight change in the refrain, see the Comm. on v. 12 above.

28:21 וְנֶעֶלְמָה the Vav is unexpressed in LXX, P, V, and is deleted by D-G. unnecessarily. It introduces a subordinate clause of condition, "for it is hidden."

28:22 The land of the dead, called Sheol and Abaddon (cf. the Comm. on 26:6), is here personified. Wisdom has been sought in the earth (v. 13), the sea (v. 14), the heavens (v. 21), and in the pit (v. 22). No living creature knows the supernal Wisdom. Only the dead may have some inkling of her. The universal interest in a man's "last words" derives from this widespread feeling that on the threshold of death a deeper wisdom is granted to men than they enjoy during their ordinary lifetime.

28:23 It is God alone who understands Wisdom in all its fullness, because He was able to search everywhere and find her (v. 24) and to use her in order to create the world by her pattern (vv. 25–27). That there was therefore no earth or heaven before He found her and created them both and that therefore Wisdom would not have been sought there (vv. 13, 21) is a logical difficulty only formally. "Heaven" and "earth" are a merismus equivalent to "everywhere and everything." TS treats the entire section (vv. 23–28) as the words of Sheol and Abaddon.

28:24 On the relevance of this verse, which Bu. and Hö. delete and Du. transfers after v. 11, see the Comm. on v. 23.

28:25 לַעֲשׂוֹת need not be emended to בַּעֲשֹׂתוֹ (Bu., Ehr.) or to הָעֹשֶׂה (Du.) on the basis of S, V, who render "who made." The Versions treated the form in MT as equivalent to a participle. This view is entirely possible, the verb being then construed as an infinitive construct consecutive, taking on the finite tense of the previous verbs יַבִּיט and יִרְאֶה; cf. the Comm. on 5:11, and see Ps. 104:21b. Hence, the verb is to be translated generally "when He made." It is also possible, though less likely, on the basis of the observation in the Comm. on v. 23, to construe the Lamed as expressing purpose, "God looked everywhere for Wisdom, *in order to* give the wind its proper weight," or result, "so that He gave." מִשְׁקָל "the proper weight"; cf. מִדָּה in stich b and חֹק in v. 26. תִּכֵּן "measured out"; cf. Isa. 40:12; Ps. 75:4, and the noun in Ex. 5:8, 18.

28:26 חֹק "limit." חֲזִיז קֹלוֹת occurs in Job 38:25 and Ben Sira 40:13; in Zech. 10:1 as חֲזִיזִים. It seems to mean "the rolling of thunder" (JPSV) or "the flash of lightning" (BDB), from חזז parallel to חצץ "cleave, cut" (cf. the Comm. on 21:21); hence perhaps the "fork of lightning" (D-G). The Talmud understood the phrase as meaning "clouds" (*B. Taan.* 9b), hence "thundershowers" (P.). In mishnaic Hebrew and Aramaic it carries the meaning of "shining clouds"; cf. T on Cant. 2:6.

28:27 וַיְסַפְּרָה cannot mean "He declared Wisdom to man," for it is precisely the unavailability of Wisdom to man that is the theme of the poem. The verb has, therefore, been rendered: (a) "He recounted Wisdom's attributes in general" (D-G), but it is not clear to whom, unless it be to the heavenly court, with whom, according to rabbinic legend, God consulted before creating the world and man (*B. Sanh.* 38b; *Mid. Genesis Rabbah*, chaps. 8, 17, 19; *Pesikta Rabbati* 14, etc.). This entourage is presupposed in Gen. 1:26 and explicitly referred to in Job 1:6; Ps. 82:1, etc. However, the absence of any reference to it makes this less plausible in our context.

The Piel in MT has been emended to the Qal וַיִּסְפְּרָה (Be.) and given the meaning "He counted, described her." Actually, the Piel is used in the same sense as the Qal in Ps. 22:18 and perhaps in Job 38:37 (but see the Comm. *ad loc.*). This meaning seems the most appropriate as a parallel to חֲקָרָה. The same root is used with regard to Wisdom in לִתְבוּנָתוֹ אֵין מִסְפָּר (Ps. 147:5), where it is equivalent to Isa. 40:28 אֵין חֵקֶר לִתְבוּנָתוֹ, the passages using the same two roots that are parallel in our verse.

רָאָה is emended to בְּרָאָה to bring it into closer parallelism with הֱכִינָה (Yel.). Others emend הֱכִינָה to הֱבִינָה on the basis of five mss. in order to create a parallel in the opposite direction (Hö.). Neither change is required, as MT is satisfactory. The verb הֱכִינָה may carry the connotation of "arrange, set in order" (II Chr. 29:19; 35:20) or "delimit, mark, measure out" (cf. תִּכֵּן in v. 25). The verbs would then be in chiastic structure, "saw" and "searched" being parallel to each other, as are "described" and "arranged," a, b ‖ b', a'.

28:28

For a discussion of the meaning of the v. and its integral relationship to the basic theme of the chap., see Special Note 24.

Job's Soliloquy

Introductory Note

The debate has ended. Job's friends, who had come to comfort him, are now estranged from him. They have spoken in the name of established religious doctrine, and he has responded from his own bitter immediate experience; no one has been able to bridge the abyss. The confrontation ended, the Friends fade from Job's consciousness. He began with a lament on his tragic fate (chapter 3); he now concludes with a soliloquy which describes first his former well-being and honor (chapter 29) and then his present agony and degradation (chapter 30). The climax of Job's soliloquy is reached in his great protestation of integrity, in which he sets forth the code of behavior from which he has not swerved. His closing words are a plea for God to answer, so that he may confront Him honorably and be vindicated (chapter 31).

In Remembrance of Happier Days **(29)**

Job paints an unforgettable picture of his former glories when God's favor shone upon him. He describes the respect in which he was universally held by young and old. This honor he had earned by his sense of responsibility toward the weak and the defenseless and by the noble dignity of his dealings with his fellow men.

29 Job again took up his discourse, saying,
2   O, that I were as in the months of old,
           as in the days when God watched over me,
3   when He had His lamp shining
           and by His light I walked through darkness,
4   as I was in my days of vigor
           when God was an intimate in my tent,
5   when the Almighty was still with me
           and my children were all about me,
6   when my steps were washed in milk
           and the rock poured out streams of oil for me.

7   When I went out to the city gate
           and set up my seat in the square,
8   the young men saw me and became quiet
           and the aged stood up in silence,
9   the princes refrained from talking
           and laid their hands to their mouths,
10   the voices of the nobles were hushed
           and their tongues clove to their palates.

11   Every ear that heard me called me blessed,
           and every eye that saw me encouraged me,
12   because I delivered the poor man crying out,
           and the fatherless who had none to help him.

13   The beggar's blessing came upon me,
           and I brought a song to the widow's heart.
14   I put on righteousness and it clothed me;
           justice was my robe and my turban.
15   Eyes to the blind was I
           and feet to the lame.
16   A father to the poor was I,
           and I took up the cause of the stranger.
17   I broke the fangs of the evildoer
           and snatched the prey from his teeth;
18   and I thought, "I shall die in my nest,
           and shall multiply my days as the phoenix,
19   with my roots open to the water,
           and the dew all night on my branches,
20   my glory fresh within me,
           and my bow ever new in my hand."

כט א   וַיֹּסֶף אִיּוֹב שְׂאֵת מְשָׁלוֹ וַיֹּאמַר׃

2   מִי־יִתְּנֵנִי כְיַרְחֵי־קֶדֶם   כִּימֵי אֱלוֹהַּ יִשְׁמְרֵנִי׃

3   בְּהִלּוֹ נֵרוֹ עֲלֵי רֹאשִׁי   לְאוֹרוֹ אֵלֶךְ חֹשֶׁךְ׃

4   כַּאֲשֶׁר הָיִיתִי בִּימֵי חָרְפִּי   בְּסוֹד אֱלוֹהַּ עֲלֵי אָהֳלִי׃

5   בְּעוֹד שַׁדַּי עִמָּדִי   סְבִיבוֹתַי נְעָרָי׃

6   בִּרְחֹץ הֲלִיכַי בְּחֵמָה   וְצוּר יָצוּק עִמָּדִי פַּלְגֵי־שָׁמֶן׃

7   בְּצֵאתִי שַׁעַר עֲלֵי־קָרֶת   בָּרְחוֹב אָכִין מוֹשָׁבִי׃

8   רָאוּנִי נְעָרִים וְנֶחְבָּאוּ   וִישִׁישִׁים קָמוּ עָמָדוּ׃

9   שָׂרִים עָצְרוּ בְמִלִּים   וְכַף יָשִׂימוּ לְפִיהֶם׃

י   קוֹל־נְגִידִים נֶחְבָּאוּ   וּלְשׁוֹנָם לְחִכָּם דָּבֵקָה׃

11   כִּי אֹזֶן שָׁמְעָה וַתְּאַשְּׁרֵנִי   וְעַיִן רָאֲתָה וַתְּעִידֵנִי׃

12   כִּי־אֲמַלֵּט עָנִי מְשַׁוֵּעַ   וְיָתוֹם וְלֹא־עֹזֵר לוֹ׃

13   בִּרְכַּת אֹבֵד עָלַי תָּבֹא   וְלֵב אַלְמָנָה אַרְנִן׃

14   צֶדֶק לָבַשְׁתִּי וַיִּלְבָּשֵׁנִי   כִּמְעִיל וְצָנִיף מִשְׁפָּטִי׃

טו   עֵינַיִם הָיִיתִי לַעִוֵּר   וְרַגְלַיִם לַפִּסֵּחַ אָנִי׃

16   אָב אָנֹכִי לָאֶבְיוֹנִים   וְרִב לֹא־יָדַעְתִּי אֶחְקְרֵהוּ׃

17   וָאֲשַׁבְּרָה מְתַלְּעוֹת עַוָּל   וּמִשִּׁנָּיו אַשְׁלִיךְ טָרֶף׃

18   וָאֹמַר עִם־קִנִּי אֶגְוָע   וְכַחוֹל אַרְבֶּה יָמִים׃

19   שָׁרְשִׁי פָתוּחַ אֱלֵי־מָיִם   וְטַל יָלִין בִּקְצִירִי׃

כ   כְּבוֹדִי חָדָשׁ עִמָּדִי   וְקַשְׁתִּי בְּיָדִי תַחֲלִיף׃

21   Men listened to me and waited
            and kept silent for my counsel.
22   Once I had spoken they did not speak again
            when my word dropped upon them.
23   They waited for me as for the rain,
            opening their mouths as for the spring freshets.
24   When I smiled on them, they could scarcely believe it;
            they did nothing to cause me displeasure.
25   I chose the way for them
            like the leader of a camel train,
        I sat at their head in ease
            like a king with his troops.

וְיִדְּמוּ לְמוֹ עֲצָתִי: לִי־שָׁמְעוּ וְיִחֵלּוּ 21

וְעָלֵימוֹ תִּטֹּף מִלָּתִי: אַחֲרֵי דְבָרִי לֹא יִשְׁנוּ 22

וּפִיהֶם פָּעֲרוּ לְמַלְקוֹשׁ:   וְיִחֲלוּ כַמָּטָר לִי 23

וְאוֹר פָּנַי לֹא יַפִּילוּן: אֶשְׂחַק אֲלֵהֶם לֹא יַאֲמִינוּ 24

וְאֶשְׁכּוֹן כְּמֶלֶךְ בַּגְּדוּד   אֶבְחַר דַּרְכָּם וְאֵשֵׁב רֹאשׁ כה

כַּאֲשֶׁר אֲבֵלִים יְנַחֵם:

כ״ט v. 25. אין כאן פסקא

CHAPTER 29

29:1 On the structure and content of chap. 29, see Special Note 25.

The heading, as in 27:1, testifies to the recognition by the editor that Job's address is far longer than usual. On *māsāl*, see the Comm. there.

29:2 כְּבִיַרְחֵי קֶדֶם = כִּירַרְחֵי קֶדֶם "as in the months of the past," the two prepositions, as usual, being coalesced into one; cf. כְּבַאֵשׁ = כִּבְאֵשׁ (Ps. 118:11).

29:3 בְּהִלּוֹ, not the Qal, but the Hiphil of the root הלל = בַּהֲהִלּוֹ, with elision of the He; cf. לַשְׁמִיד (Isa. 23:11) and often. The Hiphil of the root. which is intransitive in Job 31:26, is best construed as transitive in Isa. 13:10; Job 41:10, and here, in view of the suffix. Hence: "When He caused His lamp to shine" rather than "When it, namely His lamp, shone upon my head." On the causative use of the Hiphil for verbs normally used intransitively in that conjugation, cf. the Comm. on 20:2, 3.

29:4 חָרְפִּי has been interpreted from חֹרֶף "autumn" (Gen. 8:22; Am. 3:15; Ps. 74:17). Hence, "the days of my ripeness," but the term, which includes the winter, is hardly appropriate in a favorable sense. Moreover, contrary to the general impression, Job is not a patriarch advanced in years, but a man in the prime of life, probably in his early forties. Cf. the Comm. on 19:17. Marriage in the East taking place early, Job would have grown children at the end of his fourth decade. Other interpretations of the noun are (a) "the early period" on the basis of the Aramaic חרפי ואפלי "early and late clouds" (*B. Taan.* 3b); and (b) "earlier and later crops" (*B. Nid.* 65b) and note אֲפִילֹת "late crops" (Ex. 9:32; so Ra.). A third interpretation renders the term "vigor, peak of power" on the basis of the Arab. *harfun*, "mountain peak" (Ehr.). While the etymology of our word remains obscure, either of the two last cited interpretations may serve in our context.

On the basis of LXX, "when he made a visitation" (cf. LXX on סַכֹּתָה, Lam. 3:44), Sym., "he carefully considered," and P, "when he was a shield," בְּסוֹד has been emended to בְּסוֹךְ "when he covered." TS defends MT by citing Akk. *sadâdu* and interprets "God keeps sheep." The variety of renderings in the Vss. suggests that they are paraphrasing the text *ad sensum*. The word in MT occurs as a noun meaning (a) "circle of friends, intimates" (Gen. 49:5; Jer. 6:11; 23:18, 22; Job 15:8; 19:19) and (b) "intimacy" (Ps. 25:14; Pr. 3:32). In our passage, we have not the noun, but the infinitive construct of the Qal of the verb, which occurs elsewhere only in related *primae Yod* form, נוֹסְדוּ (Ps. 2:2), הִוָּסְדָם (Ps. 31:4), "they gather in conclave." Hence stich b is to be rendered: "when God was an intimate in my tent." See the following stich.

29:5 The parallelism here sheds a significant light on Job's broken heart.

The sign of God's nearness to him is the presence of his children that constitute God's blessing par excellence (cf. Ps. 127:3; Gen. 15:2, and *passim*).

נְעָרַי "my children," not "my servants"; for the idea, cf. 8:4; 13:26;
19:13; for the term, cf. 1:19; II Sam. 18:29.

29:6 הֲלִיכַי "my steps," a *hapax legomenon*. בְּחֶמָה = בְּחֶמְאָה, written defectiva, is "curdled milk," modern *lebben*.

Stich b literally "the rock is poured for me as streams of oil"; not mere
water flowed for Job from the rock, but oil. Cf. Deut. 32:13, 24. On the hyperbole of the rock itself turning into another substance, cf. the Comm. on 28:2,
and Deut. 8:9. Milk and oil, together with honey, were the symbols of blessing
and fruitfulness; cf. the Comm. on 20:17.

In MT stich b is longer than stich a. For this reason וְצוּר is omitted by
Du., Be., and the remainder of the text is then emended to provide an impossible reading (D-G), or עִמָּדִי is deleted as a dittography from v. 5 (D-G).
However, some reference to Job in the first person is needed; it occurs in all
the other seven stichs (vv. 2–6). The unusual metric pattern in this verse
(3:4 or 3:5), with the closing stich longer than the opening, is in place here
at the end of the section describing God's favor. On this technique at the
end of a poem or section, cf. *PPS*, pp. 70 ff., and see the Comm. on 28:28.

29:7 קֶרֶת the Phoenician word for city used poetically in Heb. (Pr. 8:3;
9:3, 14; 11:11), usually קִרְיָה (Isa. 1:21; 29:1, a. e.).

Stich a need not mean "when I left the gate (of my house to go) to the
city" (so D-G). It is an idiomatic mode of saying, "when I went out to the
gate at the city, i.e., the city gate"; cf. Gen. 19:1; Am. 5:12 f.; Pr. 14:19;
etc. (so Ibn E.). The "gate" or open space where the judges sat was outside
of the city and by that token near it. Cf. II Sam. 21:12, "the open place
(רְחֹב) of Beth Shean"; I Sam. 31:12 "חֹמַת, the wall of Beth Shean"; and
Neh. 8:1, "the open place before the watergate."

Stich b implies that Job had a permanently fixed place in the square
among the elders.

29:8 עָמָדוּ, generally rendered "remained standing," is better understood as
"remained silent"; cf. Zech. 3:5 וּמַלְאַךְ ה' עֹמֵד and the Comm. on 30:20
and 32:16.

29:10 נֶחְבָּאוּ is in the plural by attraction to נְגִידִים; cf. 15:20b; 21:21b; 38:21b;
Isa. 60:5 (D-G). On the ground that "hidden" is a strange figure for "voice,"
it has been suggested that נֶחְבָּאוּ was erroneously inserted from 8a and is
to be emended to נֶאֱלָם (Sieg., Bu.) or נִכְלָא (Du.). The emendations are uncalled for. חבא, "hide, withdraw," develops the connotation of "be quiet,
silent"; cf. לָמָּה נַחְבֵּאתָ לִבְרֹחַ "Why did you run away in silence and deceive
me, for if (reading וְלֹא for וְלֹא) you had told me, I would have sent you away
with songs, the timbrel and the harp" (Gen. 31:27). Guillaume cites the Arab.
ḫabi'a = "the fire died out," but he applies the meaning "silent" only to

v. 10 and not to v. 8, calling it an example of *jinas*, the rhetorical use of the same word in different meanings. Hence render stich a: "the voice of princes became hidden, i.e. silent."

29:11 כִּי = "for" (D-G) or the asseverative, "indeed." Stich a: "Indeed, when the ear heard me, it called me blessed." On the verb, cf. Gen. 30:13; Mal. 3:12, 15; Ps. 72:17; Pr. 30:28; Cant. 6:9.

וַתְּעִידֵנִי is generally rendered "attested me." Not only does the parallelism militate against this rendering, but the evidence adduced for this meaning (I Ki. 21:10, 13) is faulty since the verb in these passages means "to testify *against*" (Naboth) and is usually construed with Beth (Ps. 50:7; 81:9; Neh. 13:21). In Lam. 2:13 מָה־אֲעִידֵךְ does not mean, "how shall I testify for you?", but as the chiastic parallelism (with וַאֲנַחֲמֵךְ) makes clear: "how shall I strengthen you?" This meaning of the Hiphil of עוד occurs in B. S. 4:11 חכמות למדה בניה ותעיד לכל מבינים בה "wisdom strengthens all who understand her" (cf. Lévi *ad loc.*). The Hiphil of עוד corresponds to the Polel יְעוֹדֵד (Ps. 146:9), as יְשׁוֹבֵב (Ps. 23:3) corresponds to מְשִׁיבַת (Ps. 19:8); cf. *CTL*, pp. 15 f. Hence stich b is to be rendered: "every eye that saw me gave me strength, encouraged me, i.e. wished me well (when I engaged in defending the weak and the oppressed)." The meaning of the verse is very similar to Isa. 41:6.

29:12 כִּי is to be rendered "because" or "when," thus linking this section to v. 11. See Special Note 25 above.

עָנִי מְשַׁוֵּעַ "the poor man crying out." LXX: "from the hands of the powerful" and a few mss. read מִשּׁוֹעַ from the "prince," but the change is not needed. וְלֹא עֹזֵר לוֹ, a subordinate clause "the orphan with none to help him." For the entire v., cf. Ps. 72:12.

29:13 אֹבֵד may be "the perishing, dying" (Nu. 17:27; Jonah 1:6, 14; Ecc. 7:15) or "wanderer, beggar" (Deut. 26:5 and the Comm. on Job 4:11).

עָלַי either (a) "to me" or (b) "upon me, i.e. the blessing descended upon me."

29:14 מִשְׁפָּטִי a subjective genitive, = "the justice I practiced" is more forceful than מִשְׁפָּט (LXX, V, Du., Be.).

29:16 Stich b: וְרִב לֹא־יָדַעְתִּי "the case of one I did not know, i.e. the cause of a stranger" (cf. 18:21). TS argues that the parallelism is inadequate and makes the attractive suggestion to read וְרַב, which he renders "a helpless one, whom I did not know, I searched out," citing 4:3; 26:3 for this proposed meaning of רַב, but see the Comm. on 26:2. Besides, the verb חקר is appropriate for investigating a case (cf. Pr. 18:17; 25:2), and MT is entirely satisfactory.

29:17   The noun in stich a occurs in Joel 1:6; Pr. 30:14 and as a metathesis מַלְתְּעוֹת in Ps. 58:7.

29:18   In this difficult verse, the Vss. offer a plethora of conflate double renderings, *ad hoc* translations, free paraphrases, and probably some variant readings. LXX renders: "My age shall grow old as the stem of a palm tree; I shall live a long time." This may go back to a text אֶזְקַן "I shall grow old" instead of קִנִּי and a reading נַחַל "palm" (cf. Arab. *naḥl* "palm"). This meaning probably existed in Hebrew as well as in Nu. 24:6 and B.S. 50:12, which the Greek renders "the stem of the palm tree." However, it is impossible to retrovert the rendering of LXX into a Hebrew text which is graphically at all similar to MT or even remotely as poetic. P renders: "I shall save the poor and like a reed (קנינא) I shall end and like the sand of the sea I shall increase my days." V renders: "In my nest I shall die and like the palm increase my days." T translates עם תוקפי בשרכפי אתנגיד "with my strength in my nest (cf. Palestinian Targum on Deut. 32:11; Ps. 84:4), I shall perish (cf. Tar. on Gen. 25:8 וַיִּגְוַע) and like the sand I shall increase my days." As is not uncommon with T, we have a conflate of two renderings for MT, one literal and one periphrastic. It is clear that a variety of combinations of MT with presumed readings from the Vss. may be created, but no alternative text is as attractive as MT.

In stich a עִם־קִנִּי "with my nest" has been emended (a) on the basis of P to כְּקָנֶה "like a reed," that was presumed to live long (Me., Bi.), or (b) מִזֹּקֶן "because of old age" (Ehr.), or (c) בִּזְקָנִי (P.), but the comparison is very remote (D-G). MT is incomparably superior — Job hopes to die "in his nest," i.e. with his family around him, not as an outcast from his loved ones.

Stich b is interpreted "I shall multiply my days like the sand" (D-G, P.). On this view, וְכַחוֹל is an adjectival phrase modifying יָמִים. Were that the meaning, the more natural word order would have been וְאַרְבֶּה כַּחוֹל יָמִים or וְכַחוֹל יָמִים אַרְבֶּה. Others emend וְכַחוֹל to וְכַנַחַל "like a palm tree" (Be.) on the basis of LXX and S.

It is far preferable to render וְכַחוֹל as "and like the phoenix" (Hi., Ew., Be., Bu., Peake, JPSV, NAB). This interpretation was already advanced in the Talmud (*B. Sanh.* 108b). It presupposes a folk-belief current long before the talmudic period in an immortal or long-lived bird. For a detailed study of the myth in classical and post-classical traditions, cf. R. van den Brock, *The Myth of the Phoenix* (Leiden, 1972). Both Hesiod (Frag. 50) and Herodotus (II, 73) refer to this belief as current in Egypt. The Hellenistic Jewish tragedian, Ezekiel (2nd century B.C.E.), speaks of the bird's bright plumage. In *Mid. Gen. Rabba*, chap 18, it is said, all the animals in the Garden of Eden ate the forbidden fruit offered by Eve, except one bird whose name was Ḥol (חוץ מעוף אחד ושמו חול). The bird lives 1,000 years, then a fire burns its nest and only a small piece, the size of an egg, remains, out of which the bird is reborn. In *B. Sanh.* 108b the אוורשנא was blessed by Noah with immortality, because it alone did not torment him with demands for food in the Ark. Del. claims to find a cognate *allōe* for חול in a Coptic-Arabic

glossary. D-G.'s argument against this interpretation, on the ground that
Job throughout denies immortality (14:1–12), is irrelevant. Job is here using
a mythological reference as a hyperbole to express his early hopes for long
life, not his present pessimistic views with regard to immortality and resurrection. Hence the v. requires no emendation and receives a clear, straightforward meaning:

> "I thought, within my nest I shall die
> and like the phoenix multiply my days."

The vocalization חוֹל in the tradition of the Masoretes of Nehardea
may have arisen in order to differentiate our noun from the common word
for "sand." It may, however, simply represent a phonetic variant; cf. חֻר
(Isa. 11:8) and חוֹר (Cant. 5:4). The Aram. cognate חָלָּא (T) would tend to
substantiate the form with Holem.

It is noteworthy that Job's expectations during the period of his well-
being — that he would be surrounded by his family and would live to a ripe
old age — are precisely the features that he discovers in the lives of the
wealthy malefactors (cf. 21:7 ff., especially vv. 11–12).

29:19 The four clauses in these two verses are circumstantial, describing
the conditions under which Job hoped to spend his long life. Both in v. 19a,
the participle פָּתוּחַ, and in v. 20a, the adjective חָדָשׁ, pass over into the
imperfect verbs יָלִין and תַּחֲלִיף. On the construction, cf. Driver, *HT*, sec. 117.
קָצִיר = "branch"; cf. 14:10.

29:20 תַּחֲלִיף "show freshness," applied in 14:7 to a tree and here to a bow
as being pliable, not hard and useless. The bow is used figuratively for the
"manly vigor" of an individual (Gen. 49:24; I Sam. 2:4; Ps. 37:16). Cf. the
verb with כֹּחַ in Isa. 40:31; 41:1.

29:21 וְיִחֵלּוּ, with a *dageš forte euphonicum*, is the Piel of יחל "wait, hope
for" (cf. Mic. 5:6), with the clear nuance "remain silent"; note the parallel
יִדְּמוּ, and see the Comm. on 32:10.

29:22 דְּבָרִי is perhaps to be vocalized דַּבְּרִי, "my speaking"; cf. 21:3b (Me.,
Dil., Bi., Bu., Du., D-G); or דְּבָרַי "my words"; note the parallel לֹא יִשְׁנוּ מִלָּתִי.
"they did not repeat after me, i.e. mine was the last and decisive word."
תִּטֹּף = "drops like the refreshing rain"; cf. Deut. 32:2.

29:23 In stich b, the comparative Kaph from stich a is to be understood:
לְמַלְקוֹשׁ = כְּלַמַלְקוֹשׁ "as for the latter rain." For an instance of the contraction of a dual preposition, cf. 29:2 above.

29:24 Baer, following 90 mss., reads וְלֹא יַאֲמִינוּ. In either case, the words
constitute the conclusion of a condition.
The verse has been interpreted to mean: "I laughed at them when they

did not believe, i.e. but their despondency never beclouded my cheerfulness"
(Dr.). It is better to interpret stich a to mean: "When I smiled on them,
they could not believe it" (Ra., Ibn E.). In the ancient Orient, dignity required severity of demeanor. Cf. the advice given in *B. Keth.* 103b: זרוק מרה
בתלמידים "cast bile among the students, i.e. be austere with them"; *M. Abot*
3:13 שחוק וקלות ראש מרגילין את האדם לערוה "laughter and levity accustom
a man to unchastity." When Job, at rare intervals, displayed a smiling
demeanor, the men around him could not believe it.

Stich b, lit. "they would not let fall the light of my face" would seem
to combine two clauses of the Priestly Blessing (Nu., chap. 6, v. 24 — "May
God cause His countenance to shine upon you" and v. 25, "May God lift
up His countenance upon you." Such a telescoping of the familiar benediction
may actually inhere in Ps. 4:7 נְסָה־עָלֵינוּ אוֹר פָּנֶיךָ ה'. On this view, the stich
would mean "They never let fall (any part of) the light of my countenance,
i.e. my favor" (P.). This rendering of MT, though strained, is superior to
the various emendations proposed.

Yel. has suggested that יַפִּילוּן is a defectiva spelling of יַאֲפִילוּן "darken,"
with the elision of the Aleph. Hence, "they did not darken the light of my
face, i.e. they did nothing to provoke my displeasure." On the elision of the
Aleph, cf. וַתְּאַזְּרֵנִי = וַתַּזְּרֵנִי (1I Sam. 22:40); מַאֲכֹלֶת = מַכֹּלֶת (I Ki. 5:25);
יָהֵל = יַאֲהֵל (Isa. 13:20); מָאֳסֶרֶת = מַאַסֶרֶת (Ezek. 20:37); בְּחֵמָה = בְּחֶמְאָה (Job
29:5); and see Ges.-K. 23, 2. This defectiva orthography also occurs in Job
1:26; 5:18; 32:18, unless these *Lamed Aleph* verbs are being assimilated to
Lamed Yod.

29:25 The closing stich is often deleted (Bi., D-G, NEB), since the usual
rendering "as one who comforts mourners" is meaningless. The stich is
emended to בַּאֲשֶׁר אֲבִילֵם יָנְחוּ = "wherever I bring them they are guided"
(P. after Herz).

We propose another solution utilizing in part a suggestion of Dr. Isaac
Nahmani, a student of Yel., and another by Ehr. אֲבֵלִים is to be understood
as a cognate or borrowing from the Arabic ʾiblun "camels" (collective), ʾabala
"be skilled in the management of camels," II "acquire camels, etc." (so Yel.).
יְנַחֵם, to be vocalized as יַנְחֶה, with the final Mem as the enclitic, "he leads,"
familiar in Ugaritic, both with nouns and verbs, and extensively noted in
Hebrew as well. Another instance of a *tertiae Yod* verb (a byform of a *tertiae
Aleph*) with enclitic Mem occurs in Job 11:3 מַכְלִים = ם + מַכְלִיא (see the
Comm. *ad loc.*). The verb *naḥah* "lead, guide" is frequently used in connection
with caravans in the wilderness (Ex. 13:17; 15:13; Ps. 77:21), often in juxtaposition with *derekh* (Ex. 13:21; Neh. 9:19). In כַּאֲשֶׁר, the Kaph, like that in
stich c, is comparative, "like." For a pronominal clause being introduced
by כַּאֲשֶׁר, cf. כַּאֲשֶׁר נֹשֶׁה בּוֹ "like him against whom there is a creditor" (Isa.
24:2); כַּאֲשֶׁר שְׁבוּעָה יָרֵא "like one who fears an oath" (Ecc. 9:1); cf. also לַאֲשֶׁר
(Gen. 43:16), and see BDB, p. 82a.

The verse contains two similes, that of a king and the leader of a camel-
train, to express Job's erstwhile role as a leader among his contemporaries.

In the past, he would decide their route like the leader of a caravan and he would sit at their head in dignity like a king with his troops. The four stichs are in chiastic parallelism: a, b, ‖ b′, a′. Other instances of chiasmus are to be found in Hos. 2:21 f.; Pr. 23:15 f.; Job 20:2; Ecc. 11:3 f. See *PPS*, pp. 80–82. For an extended instance of chiasmus, see Job, chap. 8, and Special Note 10. The modern prejudice against "mixed metaphors" or double similes was not felt in the past, either by biblical authors or even by Western writers like Shakespeare, Blake, and Arnold (cf. *BGM*, pp. 202 f.). Note such instances as Ps. 23 (v. 1 f. "shepherd"; v. 4 "host"); Ps. 48:7 "a woman in travail"; v. 8 "the east wind" (reading כְּרוּחַ with Ehr.). The meter is 2:3 ‖ 2:3 with the principal caesura after I, וָאֶשְׁכּוֹן. The v. is to be scanned:

אבחר דרכם   ואשב ראש ואשכון

כמלך בגדוד   כאשר אבלים ינחם

On this phenomenon of a longer stich after a shorter one at the end of a section in order to give it greater force, cf. the comm. on 29:6, and cf. *PPS*, pp. 70 ff. The v. exhibits chiastic structure (a, b ‖ b, a). A literal rendering following the sequence of stichs in the Hebrew would read:

      (a) "I chose the way for them,
      (b) I sat at their head and was ensconced,
      (b) like a king with his troops,
      (a) like one leading a camel train."

It is also possible to scan the verse slightly differently. The Masorah places the caesura after רֹאשׁ, which has the pausal accent *ᶜōleh veyōrēḏ*. The meter pattern would then be 2:2 ‖ 3:3. The sense of the verse is not affected.

For purposes of easier comprehension, the translation above joins the first and the fourth stichs and the second and the third. It is not necessary to revocalize וָאֶשְׁכּוֹן as וְאֶשְׁכּוֹן; cf. Isa. 43:28; 51:2; 57:17; Job 3:11 וָאֶגְוַע and 3:13 וָאֶשְׁקוֹט.

The Misery of the Present Condition (30)

Job's situation has been catastrophically changed: now he is confronted by the contempt of the dregs of society. The misery of his alienation is compounded by the physical agony that his body is suffering. Despised by men and attacked by God, Job is left in loneliness and despair.

30 But now they deride me,
        men younger than I,
        whose fathers I disdained
        to set with the dogs of my flock.
2   For I thought,
        "What can I gain from the strength of their hands,
        from men whose vigor is spent?
3   Gaunt through want and hunger,
        they flee to the parched desert,
        wander away to a land dismal and desolate.
4   They pluck saltwort by the bushes
        and broom-roots for firewood.
5   From all human fellowship they are cut off,
        and men shout after them as after a thief.
6   They must dwell in the gullies of the torrents,
        in the caves of the earth, among rocks,
7   groaning among the bushes,
        huddling together under the nettles,
8   men low-born and nameless
        lower than the ground."
9   But now I have become the subject of their mockery;
        I am a byword among them.
10 They abhor me and keep aloof from me
        and hold back no spittle from my face.
11 Because God has loosed my cord and humbled me,
        they have cast off all restraint before me.
12 On my right the young rabble rises,
        sending me sprawling
        and casting up against me their destructive ways.
13 They hedge my path with thorns;
        they promote my calamity
        with no one to restrain them.
14 Like a wide torrent they rush in,
        like a storm they roll on.
15 Terrors are turned loose upon me,
        my lofty rank is driven off like a wind,
        my high position passing like a cloud.
16 And now my soul pours itself out,
        as days of affliction have taken hold of me.
17 At night He stabs my bones within me
        and my veins know no rest.
18 With great power He grasps my garment,
        He holds me tight by the collar of my tunic.
19 He has hurled me into the mire
        and I have become dust and ashes.

20 If I cry out to You, You do not answer me;
        if I remain silent, You pay me no heed.
21 You have turned cruel toward me,
        with all Your might You hate me.
22 You lift me up and make me ride the wind;
        You toss me about in the roaring storm.

ל　א　וְעַתָּה ׀ שָׂחֲקוּ עָלַי　　　צְעִירִים מִמֶּנִּי לְיָמִים

אֲשֶׁר־מָאַסְתִּי אֲבוֹתָם　　　לָשִׁית עִם־כַּלְבֵי צֹאנִי׃

2　גַּם־כֹּחַ יְדֵיהֶם לָמָּה לִּי　　　עָלֵימוֹ אָבַד כָּלַח׃

3　בְּחֶסֶר וּבְכָפָן גַּלְמוּד　　　הַעֹרְקִים צִיָּה

4　אֶמֶשׁ שׁוֹאָה וּמְשֹׁאָה׃　　　הַקֹּטְפִים מַלּוּחַ עֲלֵי־שִׂיחַ

5　וְשֹׁרֶשׁ רְתָמִים לַחְמָם׃　　　מִן־גֵּו יְגֹרָשׁוּ

6　יְרִיעוּ עָלֵימוֹ כַּגַּנָּב׃　　　בַּעֲרוּץ נְחָלִים לִשְׁכֹּן

7　חֹרֵי עָפָר וְכֵפִים׃　　　בֵּין־שִׂיחִים יִנְהָקוּ

8　תַּחַת חָרוּל יְסֻפָּחוּ׃　　　בְּנֵי־נָבָל גַּם־בְּנֵי בְלִי־שֵׁם

9　נִכְּאוּ מִן־הָאָרֶץ׃　　　וְעַתָּה נְגִינָתָם הָיִיתִי

י　וָאֱהִי לָהֶם לְמִלָּה׃　　　תִּעֲבוּנִי רָחֲקוּ מֶנִּי

11　וּמִפָּנַי לֹא־חָשְׂכוּ רֹק׃　　　כִּי־יִתְרוֹ פִּתַּח וַיְעַנֵּנִי

12　וְרֶסֶן מִפָּנַי שִׁלֵּחוּ　　　עַל־יָמִין פִּרְחַח יָקוּמוּ

　　　רַגְלַי שִׁלֵּחוּ　　　וַיָּסֹלּוּ עָלַי אָרְחוֹת אֵידָם׃

13　נָתְסוּ נְתִיבָתִי　　　לְהַוָּתִי יֹעִילוּ

14　לֹא עֹזֵר לָמוֹ׃　　　כְּפֶרֶץ רָחָב יֶאֱתָיוּ

טו　תַּחַת שֹׁאָה הִתְגַּלְגָּלוּ׃　　　הָהְפַּךְ עָלַי בַּלָּהוֹת

　　　תִּרְדֹּף כָּרוּחַ נְדִבָתִי　　　וּכְעָב עָבְרָה יְשֻׁעָתִי׃

16　וְעַתָּה עָלַי תִּשְׁתַּפֵּךְ נַפְשִׁי　　　יֹאחֲזוּנִי יְמֵי־עֹנִי׃

17　לַיְלָה עֲצָמַי נִקַּר מֵעָלָי　　　וְעֹרְקַי לֹא יִשְׁכָּבוּן׃

18　בְּרָב־כֹּחַ יִתְחַפֵּשׂ לְבוּשִׁי　　　כְּפִי כֻתָּנְתִּי יַאַזְרֵנִי׃

19　הֹרָנִי לַחֹמֶר　　　וָאֶתְמַשֵּׁל כֶּעָפָר וָאֵפֶר׃

כ　אֲשַׁוַּע אֵלֶיךָ וְלֹא תַעֲנֵנִי　　　עָמַדְתִּי וַתִּתְבֹּנֶן בִּי׃

21　תֵּהָפֵךְ לְאַכְזָר לִי　　　בְּעֹצֶם יָדְךָ תִשְׂטְמֵנִי׃

22　תִּשָּׂאֵנִי אֶל־רוּחַ תַּרְכִּיבֵנִי　　　וּתְמֹגְגֵנִי תְּשֻׁוָּה׃

---

23   Yes, I know that You will bring me down to Death —
           to the meeting-place of all the living.
24   Yet I always believed,
      "Surely, if a man pleads, one must extend one's hand,
           when he cries out under the affliction of God."
25   Did I not weep for him whose fate was harsh;
           was I not grieved for the poor?

26   Because I hoped for good and evil came;
           I waited for light, but there was darkness,
27   my heart is in turmoil and knows no rest;
           days of affliction come to meet me.
28   I walk about blackened, but not by the sun;
           I rise up and cry out in a loud voice.
29   A brother have I become to jackals,
           a companion to ostriches.
30   My skin has turned black upon me
           and my bones burn with the heat.
31   My lyre is turned to mourning
           and my flute to the sound of lamentation.

23 כִּי־יָדַעְתִּי מָוֶת תְּשִׁיבֵנִי   וּבֵית מוֹעֵד לְכָל־חָי:

24 אַךְ לֹא־בְעִי יִשְׁלַח־יָד   אִם־בְּפִידוֹ לָהֶן שׁוּעַ:

כה אִם־לֹא בָכִיתִי לִקְשֵׁה־יוֹם   עָגְמָה נַפְשִׁי לָאֶבְיוֹן:

26 כִּי טוֹב קִוִּיתִי וַיָּבֹא רָע   וַאֲיַחֲלָה לְאוֹר וַיָּבֹא אֹפֶל:

27 מֵעַי רֻתְּחוּ וְלֹא־דָמּוּ   קִדְּמֻנִי יְמֵי־עֹנִי:

28 קֹדֵר הִלַּכְתִּי בְּלֹא חַמָּה   קַמְתִּי בַקָּהָל אֲשַׁוֵּעַ:

29 אָח הָיִיתִי לְתַנִּים   וְרֵעַ לִבְנוֹת יַעֲנָה:

ל עוֹרִי שָׁחַר מֵעָלָי   וְעַצְמִי־חָרָה מִנִּי־חֹרֶב:

31 וַיְהִי לְאֵבֶל כִּנֹּרִי   וְעֻגָבִי לְקוֹל בֹּכִים:

CHAPTER 30

30:1   On the structure and content of chap. 30, see Special Note 26.

There is probably nowhere in literature a more powerful expression of scorn than in this verse. It consists of 4 stichs of 3 beats each. There is no objective ground for arguing that צְעִירִים מִמֶּנִּי לְיָמִים is "prosaic" or needlessly "circumstantial," in view of the great stress the ancient world laid upon age as worthy of respect in itself; cf. Job 12:12; 15:10, 18; 32:6 ff. D-G, who inexplicably regards the verse as "unoriginal," concedes that all the emendations and deletions proposed are inferior to MT.

The dog was regarded as filthy and vicious (Ex. 22:31; I Ki. 14:11), and the word was used as an insult (I Sam. 17:43) or as a term of self-abasement (I Sam. 24:14; Isa. 56:10, 11, and the Tel el Amarna and the Lachish Letters).

30:2   לָמָּה לִּי "What good is it to me?"; cf. Gen. 25:32; 27:46. In all these cases the idiom clearly bears the stamp of the experiential present. Hence stich a cannot properly be referred to the past, "what *was* the strength of their hands to me?" The verse is therefore best regarded as a virtual quotation, a statement of Job's thoughts in the past. For this usage, especially frequent in Job's final speech, cf. the Comm. on 27:7 ff. and 31:2 f. and passim. Render: "For I thought, 'What good is the strength of their hands to me?'" The suffix may refer either to the young men or preferably to their fathers, whose physical weakness is the reason that Job did not employ them as shepherds; see stich b.

עָלֵימוֹ. On the "pathetic" עַל, denoting the subject upon whom an experience has made an impact, cf. Ps. 42:5, 6; 131:2; Dan. 2:1; 10:8; and see BDB s.v. עַל, 1, d, p. 753 b. For an instance in Job, cf. 14:22.

כֶּלַח occurs elsewhere only in 5:26; see the Comm. The Arabic cognate suggests the meaning "strength, firmness," which is appropriate to the context.

Stich b is best regarded as a subordinate clause with the relative understood: "(men), for whom strength is spent."

30:3   For the Aramaic כָּפָן cf. 5:22. גַּלְמוּד (cf. the Comm. on 3:7; 15:34) has the Arabic cognate *jalmadᵘⁿ* "rock" and the adjective *jalmadatᵘⁿ* "stony." Hence it is to be rendered "lowly as a crag" in 3:7 and "desolate" in 15:34. Here it would carry the connotation, "stiff, bare, gaunt like a rock."

הָעֹרְקִים may be equated with the Syriac and Arabic cognate "gnaw," hence "who gnaw the dry land" (D-G, P.), though the figure of gnawing the desert is somewhat too bold. More plausibly, the root may be the Aramaic עֲרַק "flee"; hence, "they flee to the parched land." See below.

אֶמֶשׁ, like its Arabic cognate *ᵓams*, strictly means "yesterday" or "last night" (Gen. 19:34; 31:29, 42), and not "darkness, night" in an absolute sense, which is the *ad hoc* meaning generally assigned to it (T, Ra., Ki., Ges., Del., Hi.). The proposed emendations to אֶרֶץ (Ol., Sieg.), or אָם (Hoffmann), or אֵם "mother," being a reference to Mother Earth! (Klos., Bu.), are unconvincing. We suggest a less extreme change, to revocalize and understand the word as יָמִישׁוּ or יָמוּשׁוּ "they move, wander off," from the root מושׁ (cf. Ex. 33:11; Nu. 14:44; Jud. 6:18; Isa. 46:11; and the Comm. on 8:19). The consonantal change may be unnecessary; the orthography with Aleph may represent a phonetic weakening of the third person prefix Yod; cf. מִי אֲנַחֲמֶךְ ‖ מִי יָנוּד לָךְ (Isa. 51:19); הַאֶזְכֶּה = הַיִזְכֶּה (Mic. 6:11) and the Akkadian Qal preformative *i*, as well as the spelling of יֵשׁ with Aleph (II Sam. 14:19; Mic. 6:1; Pr. 18:24; cf. Ges.-K., sec. 19, 6 n.; sec. 24, 1, b, n.; sec. 47, 2 n.). It would not be absolutely necessary to revocalize as a plural יָמוּשׁוּ in view of גַּלְמוּד in stich a, and the use of either the singular or the plural in referring to a class of men; cf. the Comm. on 24:6.

שׁוֹאָה וּמְשֹׁאָה a powerful alliterative phrase for "desolation" (Zeph. 1:15), used in Job 38:27, refers to a desolate land, a desert. If הָעֹרְקִים is rendered "flee," stichs b and c now exhibit perfect parallelism, "who flee to a parched desert, wander away to a land of desolation." For the idea of the destitute scouring the wilderness for food, cf. the Comm. on 24:5. The nouns are in the acc. of motion, indicating destination.

30:4 מַלּוּחַ (from "salt") is identified with "salt-wort," which has thick, sour-tasting leaves. The term describes inferior food. According to rabbinic legend, it was eaten by the generation of the wilderness that was occupied with the building of the Temple (*B. Kid.* 66a), as well as by believers in the advent of the Messiah (*Pesikta Rabbati*, sec. 15).

עֲלֵי־שִׂיחַ "by the bushes"; cf. Nu. 24:6. Saadia's rendering: "and the leaves of bushes" (so also V) does not necessarily represent a reading with a Vav. He may have understood the phrase asyndetonically: "who plucks salt wort, the leaves of bushes," and supplied the conjunction for his readers. רֹתֶם "juniper, broom," is the largest shrub in the desert, with very bitter roots, that yields the best charcoal (cf. Ps. 120:4).

לַחְמָם either (a) "as their bread" (Av., Dil., Del., Du.), or, better, (b) "to heat up, for warmth" (Ges.); cf. Isa. 47:14. The form is an example of the uncontracted Qal infinitive of a geminate verb, the Patah under the Lamed due to the proximity of the guttural.

30:5 גֵּו (Aramaic גּוּ "midst," Syriac *gawa* "interior"; also talmudic Hebrew מִגּוֹ, a logical category with regard to evidence, literally "from its own midst") here means "community," similar to its use in Syriac for "church," and in Phoenician for "corporation" (Cooke, *NSI*, p. 33, line 2). Stich a: "They are driven from the community" may refer either to the specific group from which they are expelled or to the larger fellowship of mankind. Stich b: "They are driven off, with a hue and cry after them," כְּעַל גַּנָּב = כַּגַּנָּב "as after a thief."

30:6 בַּעֲרוּץ is pointed with a Holem in some mss. and printed editions; either "in the most feared of valleys" or, better, from Arabic ʿ*ird* "gully" (so Wetz., Hö., D-G, P.). לִשְׁכֹּן is the Lamed of result: "so that they must dwell." וּכְפִים an Aramaism (cf. Jer. 4:29), the third noun governed by the Beth in stich a.

30:7 נהק = "bray" has cognates in Aram., Arab. and Ugaritic. There is no basis for referring the root to the cry of lust (Peake, D-G). In 6:5, its only other use in Hebrew, it is a sign of the animal's hunger. Similarly, יְסֻפָּחוּ in the Pual, "they are joined, attached," used elsewhere in the Qal, Niphal, Piel and Hithpael, never has a sexual connotation in Hebrew (I Sam. 2:36; 26:19; Isa. 14:1) or in postbiblical Hebrew. חָרוּל is a plant growing in the wasteland (Zeph. 2:9; Pr. 24:31), generally rendered "nettles."

30:8 On נָבָל, see the Comm. on 2:10. The noun is an example of ᵓaddad, "words of like and opposite meaning," the Arab. *nabala* meaning "be noble, distinguished," whence probably the proper name, Nabal (I Sam. 25:25), which David subjects to a bitter paranomasia (v. 26). In Hebrew, on the other hand, the basic meaning of the common noun is "lacking in ethical and religious insight" (Deut. 32:6; Ps. 14:1; 74:18) and therefore, "ignoble, disgraceful" (II Sam. 3:33; Jer. 17:11). Because of its upper-class provenance, Wisdom literature gives the term the additional nuance of "lowly born"; cf. Pr. 30:22, "the earth cannot bear . . . a slave becoming a king or one lowly born (*nābhāl*) being filled with food." We may compare the English "ignoble, knave" with the German cognate *Knabe*, "boy, servant," etc. In our verse, נָבָל is identical with בְּלִי־שֵׁם "nameless, lowly born." The epithet may describe the sons — "men without a name" — or it may refer to their fathers, "sons of those without a name."

נִכְּאוּ. The root נכה "strike, smite" is, of course, very frequent in Hebrew, particularly in the Hiphil הִכָּה. The *tertiae Aleph* form נכא occurs only here in addition to the adjectival form נְכָאִים (Isa. 16:7) and רוּחַ נְכֵאָה (Pr. 15:13; 17:22; 18:14). Our passage is generally rendered: "they are smitten out of the land," a rather strange figure. Guil. adduces an Arab. root *nakaᵓ*, "put to flight." However, we suggest that the root is not a metaplastic form of נכה, but that its meaning is "brought low, depressed," a sense highly appropriate to the passages in Isaiah and Proverbs, where it has the meaning of "sad" (parallel to לֵב שָׂמֵחַ). The same meaning may inhere in נֵכִים "lowly men whom I know not" (Ps. 35:15). In our passage it would have a concrete meaning "low in station"; cf. שְׁפָלִים (Job 5:11; Ezek. 21:31). Hence stich b: "they are lower than the ground" (so Ibn E.), a perfect parallel to stich a.

The description of Job's unworthy enemies, taking the form of a "virtual quotation" of Job's earlier thoughts (vv. 2–8), ends here. On this view, וְעַתָּה is particularly apt with its adversative connotation "but now, etc."

30:9 נְגִינָתָם "their taunt song, mockery" (Ps. 69:13; Lam. 3:14), parallel to מִלָּה. שָׂחֹק is used in the sense of "byword" only here.

30:11 The Kethib is יִתְרוֹ, "his cord" (LXX, V); the Qere יִתְרִי "my cord"

(P, T). The noun is used of a "bow string" (Jud. 16:7, 8, 9; Ps. 11:2) and of a "tent cord" (Job 4:21; see the Comm.). The latter may have been used as a cord for tying the girdle (so also Hö.), the loosening of which is a sign of weakness (cf. Job 12:18), as "girding one's loins" (Ex. 12:11) is a symbol of energy and strength. The Qere would then mean "God has weakened me and tormented me." The verbs in stich a need not be emended to the plural וַיְעַנְּנִי, פִּתְּחוּ (Bi., D-G), in order to make them parallel to stich b. God's weakening of Job (stich a) created the basis for the hostile action of his enemies (stich b). The Kethib יִתְרוֹ (unless emended to יִתְרָם, as by Bi.) refers to God's loosening the cord, i.e. the restraint that had held Him in check — a rather unlikely anthropomorphism.

רֶסֶן "halter (Isa. 30:28; Ps. 32:9), here "restraint." Stich b: "and they, therefore, cast off all restraint before me." The stich is emended to דִּגְלִי מִפָּנַי שָׁלֵחוּ (Bi., Du., D-G) and taken to mean, "my banner before me, my foes cast down." Have these scholars confused שלח with הִשְׁלִיךְ?

30:12 עַל־יָמִין is generally rendered "on the right," i.e., the side which is strongest and could normally be most effectively defended. Perhaps it should be emended to יְמִינִי. Ehr. treats יָמִין as an Aramaism for יָמִים = "old age, the aged"; cf. 32:8. However, though Elihu might call the Friends or even Job old, Job would not so describe himself, especially since he was in the prime of life. See the Comm. on 19:17 and 29:20. פִּרְחַח in MT is a quadriliteral created by reduplicating the third radical. The term recalls the mishnaic usage: בקש להתנמנם פרחי כהונה מכין לפניו באצבע "If the high priest was about to doze off, the young priests would snap their forefingers before him" (*M. Yoma* 1:7; cf. also *M. Middot* 1:8). The noun, from the root פרח "bud, bloom" is related to אֶפְרֹחַ "young bird" (Deut. 22:6; Ps. 84:9; Job 39:32). It is semantically interesting that the Arab. *farḫun* means both "young bird" and "base man," and this negative connotation inheres in our term here. We may also cite the English slang term "bird," which carries a contemptuous overtone. If the noun in our passage is a collective, the plural verb, which is in harmony with stichs b and c, would be in order. Render "young rabble."

רַגְלַי שִׁלֵּחוּ is generally rendered "they send my feet, i.e. hurl me from place to place" (D-G). Ehr. reads רֶגֶל יְשַׁלֵּחוּ "they send their feet against me, i.e., they rush at me" (Ew., Dil.,) or "they kick me" (Ehr.). The stich is often omitted as an inexact dittography of רֶסֶן מִפָּנַי שָׁלֵחוּ in v. 11 (Me., Wr., Bi., Du., Be., D-G). However, the stich can be understood simply on the basis of its literal meaning. "They send my feet" means they "spread my feet, send me sprawling."

Stich c is borrowed from military operations: "they build up against me their roads of destruction"; for the figure, cf. 19:12; also 16:13 f.

30:13 נָסְתוּ is generally treated as cognate to נָתְצוּ "they have crushed," which is the reading of five mss.; cf. such forms as עָלַז, עָלַס, עָלַץ. However, the Arab. noun *natsun* means "thorns." Hence our verb may be a denominative, "they have placed thorns in my path"; cf. Hos. 2:8, הִנְנִי־שָׂךְ אֶת־דַּרְכֵּךְ בַּסִּירִים (Yel.).

Stich c "there is none to prevent them"; cf. the Arab. ʿazara "prevent, turn away from" (Ehr., Yel.). The root עזר would thus be an instance of ʾaḍdad, a word of like and opposite meaning, bearing the significance of both "help" and "hinder." The cognate obviates the need to emend to עצר (Dil., Du., Be., Gr., D-G). In this instance, English affords a parallel in the idiom "without let or hindrance," where the first noun, which usually means "permit," here means "obstruct."

30:14 Stich a may be rendered either (a) "and through a wide breach they come," or, better, (b) "like a wide torrent they come"; cf. כְּפֶרֶץ מַיִם (II Sam. 5:20 = I Chron. 14:11; Isa. 30:13).

תַּחַת שֹׁאָה הִתְגַּלְגָּלוּ has been rendered "under the crash of falling masonry" (Dr., Du., Bu.), but the noun is used elsewhere only of the crash of a storm (e.g., Ezek. 38:9). Hence render "like a storm they roll on."

תַּחַת = "in place of, instead of," develops the connotation of "like"; cf. the semantics of Latin *pro* and Hebrew לִפְנֵי, both of which develop the connotations of "instead of" and "like." Cf. the Comm. on 3:24; 4:19.

30:15 הׇהְפַּךְ "turned over, turned loose." On a sing. passive verb preceding a plur. subj., cf. Ges.-K., sec. 121; for the Hophal, cf. Ex. 10:8; 27:7. The use of the masc. with a fem. subj. is even more common. In MT, the subj. of תִּרְדֹּף must be בַּלָּהוֹת, with נְדִבָתִי as the object, but the phrase is not apt. On the basis of LXX, "my hope is gone like the wind," Bu., Gr., Du., Be., D-G emend to תִּנְדָּף. However, Reš and Nun are phonetically interchangeable both in Hebrew and in Arabic (Guillaume); we may cf. בְּאַלְמְנוֹתָיו = בְּאַרְמְנוֹתָיו (Isa. 13:21; Ezek. 19:7); עָכַן, עֲכׇרְתָּנוּ (Jos. 7:25, etc.), and note the assonance of רדף — נדף in Job 13:25. Hence, no consonantal emendation is required; read תֵּרֵדֵף and render "is driven off," with נְדִבָתִי as the subject.

נְדִבָתִי = "my station as a נָדִיב, my princely position." יִשְׁעָתִי either "my welfare, prosperity," or "my power (to win in the courts; cf. 31:21 and contrast Pr. 22:22; Job 5:4), my high position." The latter meaning, which is highly appropriate in view of the parallelism, may be achieved more directly by rendering יִשְׁעָתִי as "the station of a שׁוֹעַ, nobleman" (Job 34:19). נָדִיב and שׁוֹעַ are parallel in Isa. 32:5. *Primae Yod* and *mediae Vav* roots (ישע and שוע respectively) are frequently interchanged; cf. טוב, יטב; נוק, ינק and the nouns תְּשׁוּעָה and יְשׁוּעָה.

30:16 As the introductory word indicates, Job now turns from the description of men's actions to the real source of his misery — the hostility of God. נַפְשִׁי "soul," as often, represents the human person in biblical language.

תִּשְׁתַּפֵּךְ. with pathetic עָלַי, "pours itself out," has the connotation either of (a) in weakness, hence wasting away (cf. Lam. 2:12; 4:1), or (b) in grief; cf. I Sam. 1:15, where the Qal means "pour out the heart in prayer or in grief."

Stich b is best taken as a subordinate clause of condition, since the two stichs are not parallel in meaning: "As days of affliction have taken hold of me."

30:17 נִקַּר "He stabs, pierces" need not be emended to נִקְּרוּ. "my bones are pierced upon me" (Dh., Hö.), since God is accused of being the final cause of Job's misery in vv. 18, 19. For וְעֹרְקַי many renderings have been proposed: (a) "my gnawing pains," on the basis of Arabic and Syriac cognates; (b) "my sinews" (Ki., Ibn E., for which he claims an Arab. cognate, AV, RV); (c) "my veins," on the basis of the T on Ezek. 27:19 ערקין דברזל and Arab. ʿirq "veins and sinews" (TS); (d) "my fleshless bones," on the basis of Arab. ʿaraqa (Ehr.). A specific bodily organ is preferable, as a parallel to עֲצָמַי.

30:18 This difficult verse is left untranslated by D-G. יִתְחַפֵּשׂ means "is disguised" (I Sam. 28:8; I Ki. 20:38; 22:30) and here must carry the connotation of "is disfigured, becomes unsightly," by virtue of Job's becoming emaciated and his clothes hanging badly (?). כְּפִי is generally rendered "like the mouth, i.e. the collar," but the garments of the ancient Hebrews had no tight-fitting collars! Because of these difficulties, and the LXX rendering: "my disease has taken hold of my garment," the verse has been emended to בְּרָב־כֹּחַ יִתְפֹּשׂ לְבוּשִׁי בְּפִי כֻּתָּנְתִּי יֹאחֲזֵנִי (Hö., P.). Of the three changes proposed, only one is essential. The change of the first verb is not necessary, if it be recognized that חפשׂ is a phonetic variant for חבשׁ, which means "bind" (Ex. 29:9; Ezek. 16:10), "press down" (Job 40:13), and "bind up, restrain" (Job 28:13). The Hithpael form in MT is a conflate of the second person תְּחַפֵּשׂ and the third person יְחַפֵּשׂ, which arose because the passage fluctuates between the third person (vv. 17, 19) and the second person (vv. 20–24). Hence "with great power, He grasps my garment." כְּפִי is better read בְּפִי "by the collar of my tunic." יַאַזְרֵנִי "He girds me" here carries the connotation of "He holds me tight." On the suggested consonantal interchange, cf. כפשׂ (Lam. 3:16) and כבשׂ. See *SSL*, *ad loc*.

30:19 Stich a is too short, but the proposed additions and emendations are not persuasive. הֹרַנִי from יָרָה = "he hath hurled me, cast me down," used elsewhere of shooting arrows (e.g., I Sam. 20:36). וָאֶתְמַשֵּׁל = "I have become like," a late Heb. use of the Hithpael as a passive, like the Niphal; cf. Isa. 14:10; Ps. 28:1. The poetic (not logical) caesura may be placed after וָאֶתְמַשֵּׁל; the resulting *Qinah* (3:2) meter is entirely appropriate here.

30:20 As is clear from the parallelism, each stich in the verse contains a condition. עָמַדְתִּי not "I stand in prayer," nor is it to be emended to עָמַדְתָּ, "You stand." Render "if I remain silent"; cf. the Comm. on 29:8 and 32:16 (so also Ehr.). In stich b, V *et non respicis me* does not go back to a reading וְלֹא תִתְבֹּנֵן בִּי, but is a proper interpretation of MT, לֹא being understood from stich a; cf. 30:25b. Whether Job cries out or remains silent, God remains unresponsive; cf. 16:6.

30:21 LXX read the final verb as "you scourged me," evidently reading it as a denominative from שׁוֹט "whip," hence תְּשֹׂטְטֵנִי; this may be the original though not attested elsewhere.

30:22 Stich a: "Upon the wind you make me ride." תְּמֹגְגֵנִי = "dissolve me, toss me about." The Qere תּוּשִׁיָּה "effective counsel" (cf. 5:12) is clearly inappropriate. The Kethib תשוה is an aberrant orthography, תְּשֻׁוָה = תְּשָׁאָה "noise of the storm"; cf. 36:29; in 39:7, it refers to the "noise of the city." Cf. also שָׁאָה in v. 14 above. The noun is an acc. of place: "In the storm, You toss me."

30:23 תְּשִׁיבֵנִי literally, "bring me back to the realm of nonexistence." Cf. the Comm. on 1:21. "The meeting house of all the living" is a superb description of the land of the dead. The nouns are in the accusative of motion.

30:24 That this verse, one of the most difficult in the book, has sustained damage is beyond question. A valiant effort to interpret MT is made by Hö.: "Yet in response to the plea (of a sufferer) He did not extend His hand (and slay him, taking him out of his misery), when in his calamity for them (death and Sheol, v. 23) he issues a cry (שׁוּעַ as a noun)!" The plethora of emendations, many graphically distant or unhebraic, may be studied in D-G, who finally accepts: אַךְ לֹא טֶבַע יִשְׁלַח יָד וּבְפִידוֹ לֹא יְשַׁוֵּעַ which he renders "But will not one sinking stretch out a hand (for help) and in his calamity will he not cry out?" (Dil., Bu., Du., Hö.). Be. objects that שָׁלַח יָד, unlike פָּרַשׂ יָד, does not mean "stretch out a hand seeking for help." He proposes instead: אַךְ לֹא בְעָנִי אֶשְׁלַח יָד אִם בְּפִידוֹ לֹא נוֹשָׁע "Did I not stretch out my hand to help the one in affliction; was he not saved in his calamity?" P. renders this same emended text of stich a better: "One does not turn one's hand against the needy, when in his distress he cries for help." He apparently deletes לָהֶן. TS renders stich a as a quotation: "'Only let him not stretch out his hand against the ruin!' when he thus cried out over them in his calamity."

We would make another suggestion which requires revocalizing one word in stich a and making two slight graphic changes in stich b, a Vav to an Aleph and a final Nun to a Yod. Our proposed reading is: אַךְ לֹא בָּעֵי יִשְׁלַח יָד אִם בְּפִיד אֱלוֹהַ יְשַׁוֵּעַ "If a man pleads, one must extend one's hand, if under the calamity of God he cries out." On לֹא as לְא cf. Jud. 21:22; I Sam. 13:13; 20:4; Job 9:33; and the Comm. *ad loc.* אַךְ is the emphatic "surely"; cf. Gen. 26:9; I Sam. 16:6; Job 19:13; and BDB s.v. בעי retains its Yod in Isa. 21:12: אִם תִּבְעָיוּן בְּעָיוּ. On the idiom שלח יד = "to extend help," cf. שְׁלַח יָדֶיךָ מִמָּרוֹם (Ps. 144:7).

The v. is a statement of Job's earlier thinking. Hence a phrase like "for I believed" is to be understood. On this use of virtual quotations, cf. the Comm. on 26:7; 30:2; chap. 31, passim; and *PPS*, pp. 126–29.

30:25 אִם־לֹא = "did I not" (6:12), a usage which reappears in chap. 31,

on which see the Comm. The v. is transposed to that chap. on the ground
that it is inappropriate here, but see our Translation.

לִקְשֵׁה־יוֹם "literally, hard of day, i.e. unfortunate"; cf. LXX on I Sam. 1:15
עָגְמָה קְשַׁת יוֹם. "be grieved," a common noun in mishnaic Heb.

30:26   כִּי "because" is anticipatory, giving the reason for v. 27. On this
usage, cf. Gen. 3:14, 17 (Ehr.).

30:27   רֻתְּחוּ "boiling," because of great distress; cf. Lam. 1:20; 2:1. וְלֹא דָמּוּ
"are not quiet" or "do not cease, i.e. unceasingly"; cf. Ps. 35:15.

30:28   קֹדֵר, "lit. blackened," has been referred either to dark attire (D-G),
the unkempt skin of the mourner (Ew.), the dark color of sackcloth worn
in mourning (Del.), or the black skin of the leper (Del.). The phrase בְּלֹא חַמָּה
has been regarded as "unsatisfactory" and "ambiguous" (D-G), and has
been subjected to a series of unnecessary emendations: בְּלֹא נֶחָמָה, "without
comfort" (Bi., Du.); בְּלֹא חֶדְוָה, "without joy" (Voigt); בְּלֹא חֶמְדָּה, "without
desire" (Be.). Actually, the text is vouched for by LXX, whose reading
aneu phimou, "without a muzzle, restraint," is an inner Greek error for *aneu
thymou*, "without anger" = בְּלֹא חֵמָה; so also P, V, though this meaning is
obviously inappropriate. חַמָּה "sun" (Isa. 24:28; 30:28; Cant. 6:10). The
phrase בְּלֹא חַמָּה = "without the sun, i.e. not due to the sun" (cf. 8:11 for
the syntactic use). Others render "not before the sun, i.e. in dark places"
(TS). The phrase makes it clear that the body and not the attire is referred
to. Unlike the swarthy maiden in the Song of Songs (Cant. 1:5, 6, 7), Job's
face has become black, not by virtue of the sun's rays, but through illness
and misery; cf. Jer. 8:22; 14:2; Ps. 35:14; 38:7; Job 5:11; and see v. 30
(Hi., Du., Dil., Bu.).

בַקָּהָל is generally rendered "in the community." One need not, however, invoke the Prologue to see that Job is far from being in the midst of
the populace; his loneliness is clearly indicated in the very next verse. Hence
the noun is to be treated as an Aramaism with *mediae He* corresponding to
the Heb. *mediae Vav*; cf. בהת בוש, רהט ;רוץ אברהם, אַבְרָם. Hence בַקָּהָל =
בְּקוֹל "with a loud voice." Cf. וָאֶתֵּן עֲלֵיהֶם קְהִלָּה גְדוֹלָה (Neh. 5:7), which
Zimmermann has plausibly rendered "I set up a great hue and cry against
them."

30:29   תַּנִּים "jackals." The jackal has a doleful, mourning sound and the
ostrich (בְּנוֹת יַעֲנָה) a hissing moan; cf. Mic. 1:8 for the same similes in
parallelism. Both creatures live in desolate regions far from human habitation. They, therefore, serve as an excellent simile for Job, who wails in vain
and is an outcast among men. It has been argued on biological grounds that
both creatures named here are species of bat (Felix in Ha., p. 233).

30:30   מֵעָלַי an idiomatic use for עָלַי; cf. v. 17. עַצְמִי a collective noun, "my bones, my frame." מִנִּי־חֹרֶב "by the heat," of fever, obviously not the sun; see the Comm. on v. 28 above.

30:31 בֹּכִים, "weepers," may be an abstract noun "weeping" parallel to אֵבֶל; cf. עֲשֻׁקִים "oppression" (Am. 9:7; Ecc. 4:1; Job 35:9).

The Code of a Man of Honor (31)

Job brings his soliloquy to a close, presenting the ideals of conduct by which he has lived. In a series of oaths, he calls down punishment upon himself if he has violated any of the standards of integrity that he has professed, and in a series of indignant questions he categorically denies his guilt. Job lists fourteen possible transgressions from which he has kept himself free. These are not gross crimes, punishable by law, which are totally beyond the realm of possibility for him, but subtler sins that often prove a temptation to the respectable and respected citizen. It is noteworthy that this "Code of a Man of Honor" is almost exclusively ethical, the only ritual element being the avoidance of the worship of the moon and the stars.

Job has adhered to the principles of personal morality in his attitude toward women, who are too weak to defend themselves. His actions have been marked by fair dealing even toward the slave, and by consideration for the poor, the widow, and the orphan, because he has been conscious of the equality of all human beings. Verse 15 contains the most striking affirmation in the Bible — unsurpassed anywhere else — of the equality of all human beings, which is rooted in their common origin as the handiwork of God.

He has also been sensitive to the deeper and less obvious forms of unethical behavior to which even good men are liable. He has been free from the arrogance that comes with wealth. He has never rejoiced in the discomfiture of his foes. He has not feared the tyranny of the mob, nor has he been ashamed to confess his errors in public. The outer integrity of his actions has been a reflection of the inner probity of his spirit.

Conscious of his fundamental rectitude, Job calls upon God to appear and answer him. Having nothing to hide, Job is confident that in a free and fair confrontation he would be vindicated.

31 I set a ban upon my eyes,
           how then could I look lustfully upon a maid?
2   For I thought,
           "If I sinned,
               what would be my portion from God above
               and my lot from the Almighty on high?
3   Surely calamity waits for the unrighteous
           and disaster for the workers of iniquity!
4   God will certainly see my ways
           and count all my steps!"

5   Have I walked with falsehood,
           has my foot ever hastened to deceit?
6   Let Him weigh me in a just balance
           and God will know my integrity!
7   If my step has turned aside from the right path
           and my heart has strayed after my eyes,
           if ever a spot has cleaved to my hands —
8   let me sow and another eat,
           and may my crops be rooted out.

9   If my heart has been enticed by a woman,
           and I have lain in wait at my neighbor's door,
10   may my wife grind for a stranger,
           and let others crouch upon her.
11   For I thought,
           "That is a heinous crime,
               worthy of the judges' punishment.
12   indeed, a fire burning to Abaddon,
           that will consume all my increase to the roots."

13   Have I despised the cause of my manservant,
           or of my maidservant, when they contended with me?
14   For I always remembered,
           "What shall I do when God rises up,
               and when He examines me, how shall I answer Him?
15   Did not He make him in the womb, as He made me,
           and fashion us both alike in the womb?"

16   Have I withheld what the poor desired,
           or caused the eyes of the widow to fail,
17   eating my morsel alone
           while the orphan ate none of it?
18   Indeed, from the period of my youth
           he grew up with me as with a father,
       and throughout all my life
           I was a support to the widow.

19   When I saw a beggar without clothes
           or a poor man without a garment,
20   did not his loins bless me,
           and was he not warmed with the fleece of my sheep?

21   If I have raised my hand against the fatherless
           because I saw my help in the gate,
22   let my shoulder blade fall from my shoulder
           and my arm be broken from its socket.

א	בְּרִית כָּרַתִּי לְעֵינָי	וּמָה אֶתְבּוֹנֵן עַל־בְּתוּלָה:
2	וּמֶה וּ חֵלֶק אֱלוֹהַ מִמָּעַל	וְנַחֲלַת שַׁדַּי מִמְּרֹמִים:
3	הֲלֹא־אֵיד לְעַוָּל	וְנֵכֶר לְפֹעֲלֵי אָוֶן:
4	הֲלֹא־הוּא יִרְאֶה דְרָכָי	וְכָל־צְעָדַי יִסְפּוֹר:
ה	אִם־הָלַכְתִּי עִם־שָׁוְא	וַתַּחַשׁ עַל־מִרְמָה רַגְלִי:
6	יִשְׁקְלֵנִי בְמֹאזְנֵי־צֶדֶק	וְיֵדַע אֱלוֹהַּ תֻּמָּתִי:
7	אִם תִּטֶּה אַשֻּׁרִי מִנֵּי הַדֶּרֶךְ	וְאַחַר עֵינַי הָלַךְ לִבִּי
8	וּבְכַפַּי דָּבַק מְאוּם:	אֶזְרְעָה וְאַחֵר יֹאכֵל
9	וְצֶאֱצָאַי יְשֹׁרָשׁוּ:	אִם־נִפְתָּה לִבִּי עַל־אִשָּׁה
י	וְעַל־פֶּתַח רֵעִי אָרָבְתִּי:	תִּטְחַן לְאַחֵר אִשְׁתִּי
11	וְעָלֶיהָ יִכְרְעוּן אֲחֵרִין:	כִּי־הוּא זִמָּה
12	וְהִיא עָוֹן פְּלִילִים:	כִּי אֵשׁ הִיא עַד־אֲבַדּוֹן תֹּאכֵל
13	וּבְכָל־תְּבוּאָתִי תְשָׁרֵשׁ:	אִם־אֶמְאַס מִשְׁפַּט עַבְדִּי וַאֲמָתִי
14	בְּרִבָם עִמָּדִי:	וּמָה אֶעֱשֶׂה כִּי־יָקוּם אֵל
טו	וְכִי־יִפְקֹד מָה אֲשִׁיבֶנּוּ:	הֲלֹא־בַבֶּטֶן עֹשֵׂנִי עָשָׂהוּ
16	וַיְכֻנֶנּוּ בָּרֶחֶם אֶחָד:	אִם־אֶמְנַע מֵחֵפֶץ דַּלִּים
17	וְעֵינֵי אַלְמָנָה אֲכַלֶּה:	וְאֹכַל פִּתִּי לְבַדִּי
18	וְלֹא־אָכַל יָתוֹם מִמֶּנָּה:	כִּי מִנְּעוּרַי גְּדֵלַנִי כְאָב
19	וּמִבֶּטֶן אִמִּי אַנְחֶנָּה:	אִם־אֶרְאֶה אוֹבֵד מִבְּלִי לְבוּשׁ
כ	וְאֵין כְּסוּת לָאֶבְיוֹן:	אִם־לֹא בֵרֲכוּנִי חֲלָצָו
21	וּמִגֵּז כְּבָשַׂי יִתְחַמָּם:	אִם־הֲנִיפוֹתִי עַל־יָתוֹם יָדִי
22	כִּי־אֶרְאֶה בַשַּׁעַר עֶזְרָתִי:	כְּתֵפִי מִשִּׁכְמָה תִפּוֹל

---

v. 11. היא ק׳ והוא ק׳ ibid. ‏v. 20. חלציו ק׳

23   For I always feared a calamity coming from God,
          and I could not have borne His destroying me.

24   Have I ever put my trust in gold
          or called fine gold my security?
25   Have I rejoiced because my wealth was great
          or because my hands had acquired riches?

26   Have I looked up at the sun in its brightness
          or at the full moon in its movements,
27   so that my heart was secretly enticed
          and I kissed my hand in worship?
28   This, too, would be an offense worthy of judges' punishment,
          for I should have been false to God above.

29   Have I rejoiced at my enemy's ruin
          or exulted when evil overtook him?
30   Never did I permit my mouth to sin
          by asking for his life in a curse.

31   Did my kinsmen ever say,
          "If only we had our foe's flesh,
          we could never gorge ourselves enough!"
32   No stranger ever lodged in the street;
          my doors were always open to the wayfarer.

33   Have I ever concealed my transgressions like Adam,
          hiding my sin in my bosom,
34   because I stood in fear of the crowd
          and the contempt of the masses terrified me —
          so that I kept silence and did not go out of doors?

38   If ever my land has cried out against me
          and its furrows have wept together,
39   because I ate its yield without payment
          and brought its owners to despair,
40   let thorns grow instead of wheat
          and foul weeds instead of barley.

35   O, that I had someone to hear me!
          Behold, this is my desire:
      that the Almighty answer me,
          and my opponent write out his indictment.
36   Upon my shoulder I would carry it,
          and like a crown bind it upon me.
37   An account of my steps I would give Him;
          like a prince would I approach Him.

      The words of Job are ended.

23 וְאֵזְרֹעִי מִקָּנֶה תִשָּׁבֵר: כִּי פַחַד אֵלַי אֵיד אֵל

24 וּמִשְׂאֵתוֹ לֹא אוּכָל: אִם־שַׂמְתִּי זָהָב כִּסְלִי

כה וְלִכֶתֶם אָמַרְתִּי מִבְטַחִי: אִם־אֶשְׂמַח כִּי־רַב חֵילִי

26 וְכִי־כַבִּיר מָצְאָה יָדִי: אִם־אֶרְאֶה אוֹר כִּי יָהֵל

27 וַיֵּרַח יָקָר הֹלֵךְ:   וַיִּפְתְּ בַּסֵּתֶר לִבִּי

28 וַתִּשַּׁק יָדִי לְפִי: גַּם־הוּא עָוֹן פְּלִילִי

29 כִּי־כִחַשְׁתִּי לָאֵל מִמָּעַל: אִם־אֶשְׂמַח בְּפִיד מְשַׂנְאִי

ל וְהִתְעֹרַרְתִּי כִּי־מְצָאוֹ רָע: וְלֹא־נָתַתִּי לַחֲטֹא חִכִּי

31 לִשְׁאֹל בְּאָלָה נַפְשׁוֹ:   אִם־לֹא אָמְרוּ מְתֵי אָהֳלִי

32 מִי־יִתֵּן מִבְּשָׂרוֹ לֹא נִשְׂבָּע: בַּחוּץ לֹא־יָלִין גֵּר

33 דְּלָתַי לָאֹרַח אֶפְתָּח: אִם־כִּסִּיתִי כְאָדָם פְּשָׁעָי

34 לִטְמֹן בְּחֻבִּי עֲוֹנִי: כִּי אֶעֱרוֹץ ׀ הָמוֹן רַבָּה

וּבוּז־מִשְׁפָּחוֹת יְחִתֵּנִי   וְאָדֹם לֹא־אֵצֵא פָתַח:

38   אִם־עָלַי אַדְמָתִי תִזְעָק

39 וְיַחַד תְּלָמֶיהָ יִבְכָּיוּן: אִם־כֹּחָהּ אָכַלְתִּי בְלִי־כֶסֶף

מ וְנֶפֶשׁ בְּעָלֶיהָ הִפָּחְתִּי: תַּחַת חִטָּה ׀ יֵצֵא חוֹחַ

וְתַחַת־שְׂעֹרָה בָאְשָׁה

לה מִי יִתֶּן־לִי ׀ שֹׁמֵעַ לִי   הֵן־תָּוִי שַׁדַּי יַעֲנֵנִי

36 וְסֵפֶר כָּתַב אִישׁ רִיבִי: אִם־לֹא עַל־שִׁכְמִי אֶשָּׂאֶנּוּ

37 אֲעַנְּדֶנּוּ עֲטָרוֹת לִי: מִסְפַּר צְעָדַי אַגִּידֶנּוּ

כְּמוֹ־נָגִיד אֲקָרֲבֶנּוּ:

תַּמּוּ דִבְרֵי אִיּוֹב:

CHAPTER 31

31:1 On the content and literary form of this chapter, see Special Note 27.

Stich a: "I imposed a covenant upon my eyes." The Lamed indicates not a treaty among equals, expressed by עִם (e.g., Gen. 26:28; Ex. 24:8), but a covenant imposed by a superior upon an inferior (e.g., I Ki. 20:34) or a conqueror on the vanquished (cf. Ex. 23:32; 34:12, 15); cf. BDB, p. 503b, bottom.

Stich b is the conclusion:·"So how could I look closely at a maiden?" The rhetorical use of מַה approximates the negative, like the Arab. *mah* (מַה לָּנוּ חֵלֶק) (I Ki. 12:16) as against אֵין לָנוּ (II Sam. 20:1); מַה־תָּעִירוּ (Cant. 8:4); אִם תָּעִירוּ (Cant. 3:5).

TS, following Kaminka, attaches this v. to chap. 30 as a sign of mourning rather than as a mark of piety, on the ground that glancing at a woman was not regarded as sinful in rabbinic tradition. However, the verb used here, אֶתְבּוֹנֵן, means "look intently, carefully," not "glance momentarily"; cf. Ps. 107:43; 119:95; Job 11:11; 30:20; 37:14. Our passage is virtually cited in בבתולה אל תתבונן (B. S. 9:5).

Job asserts his adherence to a standard of personal purity and pious conduct (*Middat ḥasidut*) beyond the letter of the law, which does not forbid a man's looking upon an unmarried woman (cf. the notes of S. Buber on *Mayyan Gannim*, ed. Buber, Berlin, 1889, p. 99). Cf. *Abot de Rabbi Nathan*, Chap. 2, and Ra., *ad loc.*; "This was the measure of my piety (מדת חסידותי) that I did not look even upon an unmarried girl, lest she marry later and I find myself drawn after her." Note the basic rabbinic principle קדש עצמך אף במה שמותר לך "Keep yourself holy (by self-restraint) even in what is legally permitted to you" (*B. Yeb.* 20a). Similarly, rabbinic legend declares that Abraham was long unaware of Sarah's beauty (*B. Baba Batra* 16a). The entire thrust of ancient rabbinic thought and legal enactment was to minimize contact between the sexes; cf. L. M. Epstein, *Sex Laws and Customs in Judaism* (New York, 1948). Nevertheless, rabbinic Judaism does not go as far as Mt. 5:28, which equates "looking lustfully" upon a woman with adultery.

Asceticism is a genuine strand in the Bible and in postbiblical Judaism, gaining strength in the medieval era. Nevertheless, it is not dominant. Note the stress upon feminine beauty in the lives of the Patriarchs and other biblical worthies, the presence of the Song of Songs in the canon, as well as the elaborate poetic description of Sarah's beauty in the *Genesis Apocryphon* from Qumran. Note, too, the rabbinic blessing to be pronounced at the sight of a beautiful woman, שככה לו בעולמו "Blessed is God, who has such in His world" (*B. Ber.* 58b), and Rabbi Akiba's lament upon seeing an attractive woman, דהai שופרא בלי ארעא "Alas, that such beauty the earth must devour" (*B. Abodah Zarah* 20a).

Emending בְּתוּלָה to נְבָלָה (P.) is totally unwarranted. Similarly, removing the verse from Job's Code of Honor or placing it before v. 9 and thus merging the theme with that v. is ruled out on structural grounds, since it would destroy the double heptad structure of 14 possible offenses. See Special Note 27. Actually, the sharp distinction in Semitic and biblical law and thought between the status of a virgin and that of a married woman rules out the combining of these two themes on substantive grounds as well.

31:2 On the structure of vv. 2–4 as "virtual quotations" setting forth Job's former conviction that man is answerable to God for his actions, see Special Note 27. His standpoint is presented by a question (v. 2) followed by an affirmation (v. 3). For the Western reader, it. is necessary to add a phrase, "for I thought."

חֵלֶק "share, here, penalty" (Job 20:29; 27:23).

31:3 נֵכֶר "disaster, calamity," a meaning required by the context here and in נָכְרוֹ (Ob. 1:12). The noun is of uncertain etymology. It may be related to the root *nkr*, "buy, sell." On וָאֶכְּרֶהָ in Hos. 3:2, cf. *PPS*, pp. 239, 251.

31:5 While the sin here seems general in character, like the opening statement in the Egyptian *Protestation of Guiltlessness*: "I have not committed evil against men" (*ANET*, p. 340), the reference to scales in v. 6 suggests, on the principle of *lex talionis* which pervades the chap., that Job refers here to cheating in business, probably giving false weight and measure. Note the use of the same terms as here in describing the merchant: כְּנַעַן בְּיָדוֹ מֹאזְנֵי מִרְמָה לַעֲשֹׁק אָהֵב "Canaan (the trader) has deceitful scales in his hand; he loves to rob" (Hos. 12:8).

אִם here cannot be the protasis of an oath, "if I walked with falsehood," since v. 6 cannot be the logical apodosis — God weighs a man in just scales whether or not he has sinned! Moreover, if Job *has* sinned, how can God know his rectitude (stich b)? Hence אִם is clearly the interrogative particle usually expecting a negative answer, like Latin *num*. It is used either alone as in Jud. 5:8; I Ki. 1:27; Isa. 29:16; Jer. 48:27; Am. 3:6; Job 6:12, or in a disjunctive interrogative הֲ . . . אִם; see BDB, p. 60b.

וַתַּחַשׁ Qal from חוּשׁ "hasten" with two Patahs instead of a Qames because of the guttural; cf. וַתַּעַט (I Sam. 15:19).

31:6 Construing v. 5 as a condition leaves v. 6 uncompleted and requires interpreting it as a parenthesis (D-G). The entire procedure is unnecessary. Job calls to God, "let Him weigh me in a fair balance" (Ezek. 45:10), not in false scales מֹאזְנֵי מִרְמָה (Hos. 12:8; Am. 8:5; Pr. 11:1), "and He will discover my integrity." Till now no such just evaluation of Job by God has been forthcoming. On the scales of judgment, cf. Dan. 5:27, and see Special Note 27.

31:7 The v. refers to coveting and taking the property of others, not land, which is treated in vv. 38–40, but movable objects that can "cleave to the hand." The v. is the protasis of the condition which is completed in v. 8.

הַדֶּרֶךְ, "the road par excellence, the right road." For stich b, cf. *J. Ber.* I, 3c
ליבא ועינא סרסורי דחטאה "the heart and the eyes are the agents of sin; the
eye sees and the heart covets"; cf. Nu. 15:39 and *Midrash Numbers Rabba*,
chap. 10. In stich c, the hand seizes what the eye covets. מְאוּם, vocalized
with quiescent Aleph in the Masorah, is designed to represent מוּם "blemish,
spot" (Dan. 1:4). On the other hand, the orthography with Aleph suggests
מְאוּמָה = "anything," which is actually the Kethib reading of the Orientals
and some of the Versions, S and T. This meaning is also acceptable in the
context (cf. Deut. 13:18; I Sam. 12:5) and is preferred by Ehr., TS.

31:8   Job calls down retribution upon himself in accordance with the *lex
talionis* — if he enjoyed what belonged to others, may others now reap what
he has sown.

        צֶאֱצָאַי from יצא "sprout forth"; cf. Job 38:27. The noun is generally
used metaphorically of children; here it is literal, "produce, crops of the
earth"; cf. Isa. 34:1; 42:5. There is no need to insert כָּל before the noun
(Be.) or שָׂדַי after it (D-G) on rhythmic grounds. The two long words in
stich b receive three beats between them; see *PPS*, pp. 65 ff., and cf. such
instances as Isa. 51:7; Ps. 2:3, 5, 6b. See Special Note 1, sec. 6.

31:9   The same legal-moral principle of retribution is invoked here in connection with the sin of adultery.

        Stich b, "if I lay in wait at my neighbor's door"; cf. Pr. 7:6 ff. The
noun פֶּתַח may have a sexual connotation as in rabbinic Heb. פתח פתוח מצאתי
(*B. Ket.* 9b), used of a husband's charge of the lack of virginity in his wife.
The opposite complaint is voiced by the lover in Cant. 4:12 גַּל נָעוּל . . . גַּן נָעוּל
מַעְיָן חָתוּם "A closed garden is my sister, my bride, a closed spring, a fountain
sealed." The noun פֶּתַח rather than דֶּלֶת, etc., may have been chosen for this
double meaning, thus creating a *talḥin*.

31:10   Stich a, "May my wife grind for another, i.e. serve as a slavewoman";
cf. Ex. 11:5; Isa. 47:2. However, the verb "grind" may carry a sexual connotation (so T, V, Ra., Ibn E.); cf. Greek *mullein*, Latin *molere*, rabbinic
Heb. אדוני זקן טוחן ולא פולט "My husband is old, he grinds but does not
eject" (*Mid. Gen. Rabbah*, sec. 48, end, where our passage is cited as evidence
for this meaning). Our verb is explained by R. Johanan: אין טחינה אלא לשון
עבירה "Rabbi Johanan said 'grinding' means 'sexual transgression' " (*B. Sotah*
10a). This interpretation would afford us another excellent instance of *lex
talionis*. The verb need not be revocalized as a Niphal תִּטָּחֵן (Hö.), if it be
recognized as a *talḥin* carrying both meanings, "grind" and "be sexually
used"; cf. note on v. 7 above. The parallelism supports this interpretation
of stich a.

        אַחֲרִין is an Aramaism: the Nun ending may have been induced by the
proximity of יִכְרָעוּן. Note also the use of אחר in both stichs.

        That the wife should suffer for the adultery of her husband, which was
actually a sin committed against her (!), is entirely comprehensible in terms

of the ancient doctrine of corporate responsibility and family solidarity, according to which husband and wife constitute one organism (Gen. 2:23 f.). The doctrine has both "horizontal," or spatial, as well as "vertical" or temporal aspects, both of which meet in the case of Achan (Joshua, chap. 7). For this important theme, see *BGM*, chap. 11, especially pp. 138 ff.

31:11 This v. and the succeeding one give the grounds for Job's avoidance of adultery, paralleling similar passages with other offenses (vv. 2–4 and vv. 14–15). Hence, deleting the v. (Hö.) is uncalled for.

In stich a, the Kethib is הוא, the Qere היא; the Kethib is using the masc. pronoun "for this act," while the Qere is a fem. pronoun agreeing in gender with the predicate nominative זִמָּה. In stich b, the Kethib is היא, agreeing in gender with the preceding noun זִמָּה, the Qere הוא is in agreement with the masc. pred. nom. עָוֺן. This agreement with the predicate nominative characteristic of the Qere has its parallel in Virgil's famous line in his *Aeneid*, *hoc opus, hic labor est* (VI, 129). זִמָּה "heinous crime," often used of sexual offenses (Lev. 18:17; 20:14; Jud. 20:6). עָוֺן פְּלִילִים "a sin (punishable by) the judges." פָּלִיל = "judge" (Deut. 32:31; see also Ex. 21:22). In v. 28 below, פְּלִילִי is either an adjective "judicial, calling for judgment," or an apocopated plural for פְּלִילִים; cf. שִׁירַת דּוֹדִי = דּוֹדִים (Isa. 5:1); עַמִּי = עַמִּים (Ps. 144:2); רִמֹּנִי = רִמֹּנִים (Cant. 8:2). For the vocalization of עָוֺן as an absolute in our v., one would expect the construct עֲוֺן. On the other hand, the absolute form עָוֺן may be preserved if we treat פְּלִילִים as the adjective פְּלִילִי + the enclitic Mem. In any event, the phrase should be read identically both in v. 11 and in v. 28.

31:12 כִּי is the emphatic, "indeed." Adultery is compared to a fire because of the strength of the sexual passion (cf. Cant. 8:6) and its destructive potential (Pr. 6:23–29; B. S. 9:8). תְּשָׁרֵשׁ "uproot" need not be emended to תִּשְׂרֹף "will burn" (Du., Bu., TS), being entirely appropriate to תְּבוּאָתִי which is here used metaphorically like צֶאֱצָאִים and זֶרַע to refer to "offspring," not to crops (D-G). The Beth is the Beth of means which Heb. frequently utilizes in order to express the object of an action; cf. the Comm. on 16:4.

31:13 Here, as in v. 5, אִם does not introduce a condition, but a question, with vv. 14, 15 (וּמָה . . . הֲלֹא) describing Job's earlier rationale for ethical conduct. Cf. Special Note 29 on Chap. 31. The verse with the caesura after עַבְדִּי (against the accents) is an excellent example of *enjambement*, like 29:14. בְּרִבָם עִמָּדִי is understood at the end of stich a and אִם־אֶמְאַס is understood at the beginning of stich b. בְּרִבָם is in the plural, by attraction to the two nouns immediately preceding it.

31:14 יָקוּם, which LXX renders "take vengeance" (= יִקֹּם) (so Be., Ehr.), is inferior to MT, since the figure is that of a lawsuit, not the imposition of punishment, as is clear from the forensic terms employed. אֲשִׁיבֶנּוּ = "shall I respond"; cf. the Comm. on 20:2. So, too, קוּם = "stand up in a lawsuit either as a plaintiff or as a judge passing sentence" (cf. Mic. 6:1; Ps. 74:22; 76:10; 82:8; 94:16) or an accusing witness (cf. Deut. 19:15, 16; Mic. 6:1; Ps. 27:12; 35:11). That there was not always a clear line of demarcation between these functions is clear from some of these passages and Deut. 17:7. פקד "visit in order to cross-examine," parallel to בחן (Ps. 17:3; Job 7:18).

31:15 As vocalized in MT, stich a would mean, lit., "in the womb my Maker made him," and stich b in MT would mean "and One fashioned him in the womb" (T, V, Ra., Ibn E., D-G). The v. would then simply be affirming God's creation of the slave but not the equality of all men. As Ehr. well observes, animals are also the handiwork of God. At best the passage would suggest the kind treatment of inferiors; cf. also Pr. 17:5; 22:2. An incomparably better sense emerges from a slight revocalization, reading: הֲלֹא בְבֶטֶן עָשַׂנִי עָשָׂהוּ וַיְכוּנֶנּוּ בְּרֶחֶם אֶחָד "Did He not make him in the belly in which He made me, and did He not fashion us (both) in the same womb?" (so LXX, P). The Masoretic accents link ברחם and אחד hence "in one womb," thus diverging from the vocalization (Minhat Shai), and agreeing with LXX, P (so Geiger, Del., Ehr.).

וַיְכוּנֶנּוּ is a contraction of וַיְכוֹנְנֶנּוּ; cf. וַתְּמוּגֵנּוּ for וַתְּמוֹגְגֵנוּ (Isa. 46:6) and תַּחְשְׁבֵנִי for תַּחְשְׁבָה plus נִי (Job 19:15). The phrases "in the womb" in stich a, and "in one womb" in stich b, are hyperbolic equivalents to "similar"; cf. the similar use חֲלוֹם פַּרְעֹה אֶחָד הוּא (Gen. 41:26) and the frequent usage in mishnaic Heb., e.g. אֶחָד אֲנָשִׁים וְאֶחָד נָשִׁים "men and women alike, etc." (*M. Temurah* 1:1).

The v. is a ringing affirmation of Job's conviction that all men, the lowest and the highest alike, are equal in rights because they have been created by God in the identical manner. It is on the same high ethical level as Malachi's exhortation (2:10), "Have we not one Father, has not one God created us all?", but without any ethnic limitation.

Hö. deletes the entire v. on the ground that the masc. suffix does not refer to the maidservant, overlooking the grammatical principle of masculine preference. Is it possible that in publishing his commentary in Germany in 1937 in the heyday of Nazism this statement of human solidarity was not palatable and that its deletion represents a tribute which virtue paid to vice?

31:16 מנע "deprive, deny" occurs with the Mem of person and the acc. of object in Job 22:7 and with the reverse construction, the acc. of person and the Mem of object, in Nu. 24:11 and in our v. חֵפֶץ equals "desire, or desired object." אֲכַלֶּה "cause to fail, with unsatisfied longing."

31:17 Job shared his food with the needy, not only on festive public occasions, but in private and every day when his fare was more modest.

31:18 Because of its alleged difficulties, this v. has been emended to כִּי מִנְּעוּרַי גִּדְּלַנִי כְאָב וּמִבֶּטֶן אִמִּי נָחַנִי (Merx, Bi., Du., Volz, Ehr., D-G) or יַנְחֵנִי (Hö.), and it is explained as referring to God: "For from my youth He brought

me up like a father and from my mother's womb He led me." D-G admits
that this is very abrupt and suggests placing v. 14 between vv. 17 and 18,
which does not help matters at all. Bi., Hö. delete the v. completely. A more
satisfactory sense is achieved by reading (Gr., Bu., Dh.): מִנְּעוּרַי אֲגַדְּלֶנּוּ כְּאָב
וּמִבֶּטֶן אִמּוֹ אַנְחֶנּוּ "from my youth I raised him (i.e. the orphan) as a father
and from his mother's womb I guided him." Militating strongly against this
approach, however, is the destruction of the obvious parallelism between
מִנְּעוּרַי and מִבֶּטֶן אִמִּי present in MT, which leads TS to read מִנְּעוּרָיו (in his
Comm., not his translation).

Actually, when properly understood, MT is satisfactory. מִנְּעוּרַי and מִבֶּטֶן
אִמִּי are both hyperbolic, like our common Eng. usage in "all my life I have
loved Shakespeare" which obviously does not refer to one's infancy. Note,
too, the same hyperbole in Jer. 1:5, "before you came forth from the womb
I sanctified you," and in v. 15 above "in one womb." The suffix in גְּדָלַנִי,
be it noted an intransitive verb in the Qal, is indirect: "he grew up with me."
Cf. the suffixes with the intransitive verb בוא "come toward" as, e.g., Ps.
35:8; 36:12; Pr. 10:24; 11:27; Job 20:22; 22:21 (see the Comm.); Ecc. 5:9
(cf. *KMW ad loc.*; צַמְתֻּנִי "you fasted for Me" (Zech. 7:5); יַעַרְכוּנִי "they are
ranged against Me" (Job 6:4); זְהַמַתּוּ "polluted for him" (33:20); אַגִּידֶנּוּ "I
will tell to him" (31:37). See also the discussion in the Comm. on 9:31.

כְּאָב = "as with a father," a contraction of two prepositions; cf. כְּאֵשׁ =
כְּבָאֵשׁ (Ps. 118:12); כְּבִירַרְחֵי = כְּיַרְחֵי (Job 29:2).

Stich b: "and from my mother's womb I guided, i.e. supported her,
i.e. the widow" (Ibn E.). See the parallelism in Isa. 51:18. As this latter
passage makes clear, leading and sustaining one's parent was an obligation
of a child. Job acted with filial loyalty toward the widow. The authenticity of
MT is buttressed by the chiastic structure of the passage, 16b referring to
the widow, 17 to the orphan, 18a to the orphan and 18b to the widow.

31:19 אִם can be construed here either as the interrogative particle = *num*
expecting a negative answer, "did I see?", or as introducing the protasis of a
condition, the apodosis of which is in v. 20, couched in interrogative form.

31:20 אִם־לֹא בֵרְכוּנִי חֲלָצָיו "did not his loins bless me, etc.?" This is far
preferable to deleting לֹא and then treating the v. as the continuation of the
condition begun in v. 19, with the conclusion unstated (ag. D-G). In stich b
לֹא is understood from stich a, "was he not warmed?" גֵּז "shearing, fleece"
(Deut. 18:4). Or stich b may be treated as a subordinate clause of condition,
"as he warmed himself by the fleece of my sheep" (TS). Bu. praises the
poetic figure in stich a in which the wayfarer's loins are endowed with speech.
Ehr. counters by the contention that the phrase means only that the loins
have cause to bless Job. Both are right!

31:21 Here the offense is the corruption of justice "in the gate." The orphan
symbolizes the weak classes in society who have no influence with the judges.
It is emended to עֲלֵי תָם "against the innocent" (Gr., Dr., Be., Hö.) because

the orphan has already been mentioned in v. 17, but there the offense is totally different.

31:22 A clear instance of an oath with *lex talionis* — the arm that practiced violence is to be stricken. Though מִשְׁכְמָה and מִקָּנֶה are noted as *Raphe* by the Masorah, the nouns obviously contain the suffix and thus a virtual Mappiq (so Minhat Shai). This is clear from the vocalization מִקָּנֶה plus the fem. suff. (Ex. 25:31; 37:17). שֶׁכֶם here "socket" generally "shoulder." קָנֶה "shoulder joint," generally "reed, shaft, beam."

31:23 Stich a, lit. "for a terror to me was the calamity coming from God." עָלַי = אֵלַי "unto me, upon me"; cf. Jer. 2:19 וְלֹא פַחְדָּתִי אֵלַיִךְ "the fear of Me was not upon you." In stich b, MT can only mean "because of His majesty, I could not (do so)" (D-G). Both the parallelism and the construction are improved, if מִשְׂאֵתוֹ is revocalized as מְשֹׁאָתוֹ "His ruin, destruction." The noun, from the root שאה "devastate," occurs in a variety of forms: שׁוֹאָה (Isa. 10:3; 47:11; Pr. 3:25), שְׁאִיָּה (Isa. 24:12), שֵׁאת (Lam. 3:47) and מַשּׁוֹאוֹת (Ps. 73:18; 74:3) (emended to מְשׁוֹאוֹת by Hupf., Wr., Nowack, BDB) and שׁוֹאָה וּמְשׁוֹאָה (Zeph. 1:15; Job 30:3; 38:27). Hence לֹא אוּכָל not "I could do no evil," but "I could not endure," governing מְשֹׁאָתוֹ as a direct object; cf. Isa. 1:13; Jer. 20:9; Ps. 10:5; lit. "his devastation I could not have borne." The suff. in מְשֹׁאָתוֹ, like the *nomen regens* in פַחַד אֵל, is a subjective genitive, "the devastation coming from Him."

31:24 Job here repudiates the idolatry of wealth, which takes on two forms, trusting in one's possessions so as to feel free to act oppressively (v. 24) and rejoicing in the possession of gold, like a miser (v. 25). In both vv. *ʾim* is the interrogative part. *num*, "Have I etc." On the parallelism of the nouns here, cf. 8:14.

31:25 כַּבִּיר, occurring only in Isaiah and Job, "mighty, much," used of a strong wind (Job 8:2), of great age (15:10), and of great wealth, here.

31:26 In this instance, *ʾim* may be interpreted either as introducing a conditional oath with v. 28 as the apodosis or as the interrogative particle *num*, "Have I, etc." The second view is preferable, since v. 28 is not a completely logical conclusion — even if Job had not been guilty of pagan worship, it would still be a serious offense! On this logical consideration, cf. the Comm. on v. 5 above.

The worship of the moon and the stars is the only non-ethical transgression mentioned, but one of fundamental importance and so worthy of inclusion. The worship of the sun and the moon was central to pagan religion and exerted a powerful appeal in Israel as well, being widespread in the 7th century (II Ki. 21:3; 23:4, 5; Ezek. 8:16). Obeisance toward the heavenly bodies was a basic ritual among the Essenes (Josephus, *Bellum*, II, 8, 2–13) and the Therapeutai (Philo, *de vita contemplativa* 27). Its popularity is attested in

the description of the festival of *Simhat Beth Hasho'ebah*, "the Festival of
the Drawing of Water," during Succot in the Second Temple period. אבותינו
שהיו במקום הזה אחוריהם אל ההיכל ופניהם קדמה והמה משתחוים קדמה לשמש ואנו
ליה ועלינו עינינו "Our ancestors who were in this place would stand with their
backs to the sanctuary and their faces eastward while they bowed eastward
toward the sun, but we — we are for God and to Him are our eyes turned"
(*M. Suk.* 5:4).

אוֹר in parallelism with "moon" is "the sun"; cf. 37:21; Hab. 3:4.

Stich b has generally been rendered "moving along as a glorious one"
(D-G) or "moving along as a jewel" (Bu.) on the basis of the Aramaic יְקָר
"glory" (Est. 1:4; 6:6). However, these renderings are far-fetched and syntactically awkward. The key to the passage lies in noting that the same
parallelism occurs in the apocalyptic vision in Zech. 14:6: לֹא־יִהְיֶה אוֹר יְקָרוֹת
יִקְפָּאוּן (כתיב) וְקִפָּאוֹן (קרי). Here the Kethib יִקְפָּאוּן, which supplies a verb
in stich b, is obviously superior to the Qere וְקִפָּאוֹן, which leaves the v. with
one long stich impossible to interpret. The caesura is to be placed after אוֹר
in Zechariah and suggests that both in Zechariah and in our passage יְקָר
has the meaning "rare, precious" (cf. I Sam. 3:1; Isa. 13:12; Pr. 3:15), and
is an epithet for the full moon (cf. Ibn E.), when lunar worship reached its
climax. Cf. the biblical כְּסָא (Pr. 3:20) and כֶּסֶה (Ps. 81:4) "full moon." The
full moon is described as הֹלֵךְ either "moving, changing its position in the
sky," or "departing, as it begins to diminish." A lit. rendering of the v. is:

> "Did I look at the sun as it was shining
> Or the rare moon as it was moving?"

The passage in Zechariah is to be rendered:

> "It shall come to pass on that day
> There will be no sun,
> The rare one (i.e. the moon) will be congealed."

The plural may refer to the phases of the moon.

31:27 וַיִּפְתְּ used in the Qal here and in Deut. 11:16 and in the Niphal in
v. 9 above and Jer. 20:7. No revocalization is called for.

In stich b, the hand is described as kissing the mouth rather than the
reverse because the hand is more noticeable in the act of throwing a kiss
in the direction of the heavenly bodies. Kissing of idols is mentioned in I Ki.
19:18; Isa. 13:4; Hos. 13:2. Throwing kisses to objects of worship is widespread; cf. S. Langdon, in *JRAS* (1919), pp. 531–55, for many illustrations
in Semitic literature.

TS reads with a Sin וַתִּשַּׂק = וַתִּסַּק from סלק "rise," the common Aramaic
verb that occurs in Heb. in Ps. 139:8; he renders "my hand was lifted up
to my mouth" as a sign of reverence.

31:28 On פְּלִילִי see the Comm. on v. 11. כִחַשְׁתִּי "for I should have denied
God above." The verb is followed by Beth in Isa. 59:13; Jer. 5:12; Hos. 8:2;

Job 8:18; it is used absolutely in Pr. 30:9 and is followed by a Lamed here in our passage.

31:29 Job maintains that he has been free from *Schadenfreude*, gloating over the troubles of others. The Wisdom teachers warned against this deeply rooted human weakness (Pr. 17:5; 24:17 f.) as vigorously as they did against the taking of vengeance on one's enemies (Ps. 7:5; Pr. 20:22; 24:29) except in the exquisite, sublimated form of giving one's foe food and drink (Pr. 25:21 f.) and helping him in his trouble (Ex. 23:4 f.). ʾim is again the interrogative part. *num*, "have I rejoiced?" If it is rendered "if," no conclusion to the condition exists. וְהִתְעֹרַרְתִּי "I arose, stirred myself" is inferior to the rendering of T, ויבבית = וְהִתְרֹעַעְתִּי "I shouted for joy, rejoiced"; cf. Ps. 60:10; 65:14.

31:30 Though the declarative structure is not characteristic of the chap. as a whole, it does occur in v. 32. It is, therefore, unnecessary to revocalize וְלֹא as וְלָא and treat it as equivalent to אִם (cf. Gen. 50:15; Jud. 13:23) in order to give the v. an interrogative structure. It may not be accidental that both declarative statements, which, incidentally, are negative in content, occur toward the end of the chapter, after the extensive use of ʾim. The poet may have wished to vary his style in order to avoid monotony.

Stich b, lit. "to ask for his life in a curse" through an incantation; cf. וְלֹא שָׁאַלְתָּ נֶפֶשׁ אֹיְבֶיךָ (I Ki. 3:11).

31:31 Stich a is rendered by LXX: "And if my handmaids have often said, 'Who would give us of his flesh to satisfy us,' " i.e. his servants never complained of lack of food. This rendering presupposes the reading אַמְהֹתַי for מְתֵי אָהֳלִי and deleting the negative particles in both stichs. Substantively this complaint can hardly be placed on the level with the other infractions of morality in the chapter, and the singling out of the maidservants would also be strange.

MT has generally been rendered "If the men of my tent said not, 'Who can find one that has not been satisfied with his meat?' " (D-G, P.). This interpretation suffers from several major drawbacks: (a) the phrase מִי יִתֵּן is denied its usual idiomatic meaning, "would that"; (b) it is necessary to supply an object which is by no means self-evident, "who can find *one*"; (c) it requires the assumption of a Niphal for the verb שבע which occurs nowhere else; (d) it gives a far-fetched meaning to מִבְּשָׂרוֹ לֹא נִשְׂבָּע; contrast the clear sense in 19:22.

All these difficulties disappear if we delete לֹא as a dittography from v. 30 or 32, or, possibly, treat MT as a conflate of אִם and לֹא (originally vocalized as לָא and therefore equivalent to לוֹ (see the Comm. on v. 30). With the negative omitted by either procedure, the v. now receives a simple and unforced meaning; lit. "Did my kinsmen ever say, 'If only we had his flesh, we would never be satisfied'?" Job is averring that not only he, but also his kinsmen, were free from virulent hatred of their enemies. In view of the strong sense of collective responsibility, the sinfulness of Job's kinsmen would also be a blot upon Job's integrity.

TS revocalizes לֹא in stich b as לוֹ and renders, "if only we could satisfy ourselves with his flesh," referring it to sexual abuse. P. follows this interpretation on the basis of a fragmentary and unclear Ugaritic text, in disregard of the clear use of the idiom in 19:22. The Hebrew terms for homosexual practices are found in Gen. 19:7, 8; Jud. 19:22; Lev. 20:13; Nu. 31:17. In addition, the phrase would be much too brief, abrupt and cryptic for so heinous an offense.

31:32 אֹרַח is a contraction of אֹרֵחַ, "wayfarer," induced by the guttural; cf. הַנֹּטֵעַ = הַנֹּטֵעַ (Ps. 94:9); לְרוֹקַע = לְרֹקַע (Ps. 136:6).

31:33 Vv. 33 and 34 are not a repudiation of hypocrisy (D-G), but a denial that he has ever been led to conceal his sins (33a) or failed to speak out against evil (34c) because he feared the hostility or the scorn of the mob.

אִם, once again the interrogative particle *num*, "have I concealed, etc.?"

כְּאָדָם is generally rendered "like ordinary men" (Ibn E., Ew., Dil., Du.) or it is emended to בָּאָדָם "among men" (Du., Be.) or to מֵאָדָם "from men" (Gr., Bu., D-G) or to וָאֶדֹּם "and I remained silent" (Ehr.). It is inexplicable why references to Adam outside of Genesis are generally eliminated by modern interpreters. Is it conceivable that the Adam motif which played so far-reaching and fundamental a role in postbiblical thought should have left few or no traces elsewhere in the Hebrew Bible? Thus Ps. 82:7 אָכֵן כְּאָדָם תְּמוּתוּן should be rendered "You will surely die like Adam," and Hos. 6:7 וְהֵמָּה כְּאָדָם עָבְרוּ בְרִית "and they, like Adam, have transgressed the covenant" (cf. *PPS*, p. 211, note 16). Our passage is to be rendered, "Have I, like Adam, concealed my transgressions?"

בְּחֻבִּי not "in a hiding place" (Ra., Ibn E., TS, P.), which would require revocalization to בַּחֲבִי, but "my bosom," an Aramaism; cf. T to Pr. 5:20 and the Palestinian Targum for Ex. 4:6 (Hebrew חֵיק); חובו של אילן "the bosom of the tree" (*B. Baba Kamma* 81a).

31:34 For the theme, see the Comm. on v. 33. ערץ "fear" (Deut. 1:29; 7:31; Jos. 1:9 and here). It is transitive "frighten" in 13:25.

הָמוֹן "multitude" is fem. here and in Ecc. 5:9 (reading וּמִי אֹהֵב בֶּהָמוֹן לֹא תְבוֹאֵהוּ, lit. "if one loves a multitude of money, it will not come to him"; see *KMW ad loc.*). TS reads הֲמוֹן רַבָּה (as a construct) and renders "the hum, noisy talk of the city" on the basis of I Ki. 1:41; Job 39:7; Ruth 1:19, but it is preferable to render: "because I feared the great multitude."

Stich c: "so that I remained silent and did not go out of doors." TS revocalizes the stich as וְאָדָם לֹא אֹצֵא פָתַח, "but I brought no man out to the door (for sexual attack)" as in the incidents narrated in Gen. 19:5, 6; Jud. 19:22. This clever interpretation has two major difficulties: (a) the essential idea of sexual molestation is lacking; and (b) the "families" might hate him for failing to turn over the victims, but hardly despise him (בוז).

The existence of a tristich here and in v. 35 has disturbed many commentators, who have either deleted or transposed the material. These varied procedures prove unsatisfactory upon examination (see D-G I, p. 271). Moreover, the idea that a poet can use only one meter-pattern in a composition is a preconceived notion which is not only indefensible per se, but contradicted by the evidence of Egyptian, Akkadian, and Ugaritic poetry; cf. *PPS*, p. 69. Particularly toward the end of a long poem like our chap. the desire to avoid monotony by varying the rhythm either in the number of stichs (vv. 34, 35) or in the meter (v. 35) would be especially strong. On this motive as playing a part in varying the style, see the Comm. on v. 30 above.

31:38 On the clear grounds for placing vv. 38–40b after v. 34, see Special Note 27.

The particle ʾim here introduces a conditional oath completed by the apodosis in 40a, b. יַחַד like יַחְדָּו = "altogether, all," parallel to כָּל (Isa. 45:16; Ps. 33:15; see BDB, s.v., p. 403a, b).

The earth cries out against any offense committed upon it, be it murder (Gen. 4:10), or undeserved suffering (Job 16:18), or the unjust expropriation of land, as here, the classic case of which is that of Naboth (I Kings, chap. 21).

31:39 כֹּחַ "strength, yield" (Gen. 4:12). הִפָּחְתִּי, literally "blow out," has been interpreted (a) in a concrete sense, "caused to expire" (most moderns, D-G, II, p. 236), and (b) in an abstract sense, "I caused to grieve," by the ancient Vss. (LXX, P, V). The latter view is supported by Jer. 15:9, where נָפְחָה נַפְשִׁי means "mental anguish" (cf. בּוֹשָׁה וְחָפְרָה). In Job 11:20, מַפַּח נָפֶשׁ is best interpreted, not as physical death, but as despair of the spirit; see the Comm. *ad loc.* This latter meaning, too, exists in Aram. (T on I Sam. 2:33 and Deut. 28:65) and is common in rabbinic Hebrew in the phrase מפח נפש (Mid., *Tanhuma Shemini*, chap. 11); בפחי נפש (B. *Shab.* 127a; B. *Abodah Zarah* 2b) in the meaning "despair, disappointment." This is its regular significance in modern Hebrew. Hence, render our passage: "I brought its (rightful) owners to despair." בְּעָלֶיהָ refers to human owners, surely not, as Hö. correctly points out, the Baᶜalim, the protecting spirits of agriculture (ag. Pedersen, *Israel*, I, 375 f., and Sigmund Mowinckel, *Psalmenstudien*, Christiania, 1921–1924, II, p. 95; *The Psalms in Israel's Worship*, New York, 1902).

31:40a, b. Again an illustration of *lex talionis*. חוֹחַ "thorns." בָאְשָׁה "evils plants"; cf. בְּאֻשִׁים, Isa. 5:4, or "stinking weeds," from באש "befoul." Thus Saadia equates it with זוֹנִין "darnel, rye-grass" (*M. Kilayim* 1:1). The more general meaning seems more appropriate here.

31:35 In the concluding section, Job reiterates his constant demand for a fair hearing from God. There is no need to omit either the first לִי (with LXX, S, and some mss.) or the second (D-G). A repetition of the pronoun emphasizes his plea; cf. כַּרְמִי שֶׁלִּי לֹא נָטָרְתִּי "but *my* vineyard I did not guard" (Cant. 1:6).

תָּוִי is treated by many moderns as referring to Tav, the final letter of the alphabet, which was in the shape of an X in the old Heb. script (Bi., Hoff.). There is, however, no evidence for the use of the names of the letters of the alphabet in this early period or for the addition of a suffix to any name in any period of the language. A better rendering is "mark, signature" (cf. Ezek. 9:4, 8). Hence: "Here is my signature; let Shaddai answer me" (Ibn E., D-G, JPSV, P.). However, several considerations militate against this interpretation: (a) the parallelism (see below); (b) the word order, which on this view should have been יַעֲנֵנִי שַׁדַּי as, e.g., יִשְׁמָעֵנִי אֱלֹהָי Mic. 7:7; and (c) the absence of an indication anywhere of a written document by Job, whether a protestation of his innocence (Du., Dil.) which really requires no answer, or an indictment of God (Ew., Bu., Du.; see D-G I, pp. 274 f.). It is, therefore, preferable to render: "This is my desire — that Shaddai answer me" (V *desideratio mea*, T רגוני "my desire"; AV). תָּוִי need not be emended to תַּאֲוָתִי (ag. Be.). It is best treated as a defective spelling without Aleph (so Ibn E., Yel.); cf. בְּחֻמָּה 29:6 and the Comm. *ad loc.* תָּוִי (= תַּאֲוִי = תַּאֲוָתִי) would be an instance of a suffix added to the stem of a fem. noun; cf. the Comm. on 5:13; 20:3; and see Special Note 9.

סֵפֶר = "scroll" as a writ of divorce (Deut. 25:1), or a bill of sale (Jer. 32:10), or an indictment, here. P. suggests that it may have been a document of acquittal. Stich c with כָּתַב in the perfect can mean only "the scroll which my accuser has written" (D-G, Yel.), treating the noun as the object of כָּתַב, but it articulates poorly with the preceding stichs, which express Job's desire for the future. Nor does it link up well with the following to constitute a *casus pendens*, "as for the scroll my opponent has written, I will carry it on my shoulder" (LXX, Hi., Bu.). The suggestion has therefore been made to assume that a stich was lost before stich c. It is far simpler to emend כתב to יִכְתֹּב, which is the rendering of S and V, though they may be translating *ad sensum* rather than offering a textual reading. The form of the verb is hardly likely to be a precative perfect. Render the v.: "O that I had someone to hear me! Behold, this is my desire — that Shaddai answer me and my opponent write out his indictment."

The v. is in 4:4:4 meter. אִישׁ רִיבִי is an opponent in a lawsuit (Isa. 41:11); not the three friends collectively viewed (Del., Cheyne), but God (cf. 9:3, 14 f., 32; 10:2, etc.).

31:36 The pronominal suffixes of this v. refer to the bill of indictment which Job, far from hiding in shame, would carry with pride, conscious of his rectitude. הֲלֹא = אִם־לֹא "indeed." ענד "bind"; cf. Pr. 6:21. עֲטָרוֹת may refer to the several tiers of the crown (D-G) or be revocalized as a singular (Be., Bu.).

31:37 The paronomasia אַגִּידֶנּוּ ... נָגִיד is striking. The pronominal suffixes of this v. refer to the Almighty. Job will disclose to God all his steps and approach Him with dignity like a prince. אֲגִידֶנּוּ "I shall tell to Him," a verb with an indirect suffix. Cf. the Comm. on 31:18 for this usage.

Because of the Piel אֲקָרְבֶנּוּ, stich b is often rendered "like a prince I will bring it near" (Ges., Me., Bu., D-G). Not only is the simile unclear in itself, but the parallelism with stich a and the structure of the entire passage, on which see below, make it clear that it must refer to Shaddai and not to the indictment. The verb has also been rendered "I would let my adversary come near" (Du.). It is better to treat the Piel as intransitive, "approach, come near," which is apparently its force in Ezek. 36:8 כִּי קֵרְבוּ לָבוֹא and is attested for the Hiphil as well וּפַרְעֹה הִקְרִיב (Ex. 14:10; cf. also Gen. 12:11).

Vv. 35–37 now exhibit a clear chiastic structure a, b ‖ b′ a′: 35a and b referring to God, 35c to the indictment, while 36a refers to the indictment, and 37 to God.

31:40c   תַּמּוּ דִּבְרֵי אִיּוֹב is an editorial addition like עַד־הֵנָּה דִּבְרֵי יִרְמְיָהוּ (Jer. 51:64); כָּלּוּ תְפִלּוֹת דָּוִד בֶּן־יִשָׁי (Ps. 72:20). It already existed in the text before LXX, which rendered it freely "and Job ceased speaking" and attached it to chap. 32. Nevertheless, the words have an undeniable resonance at the conclusion of Job's impassioned utterance.

The Words of Elihu

Introductory Note

Silence has descended upon the little group huddled in the ashes. Now a new loud voice is heard: it is Elihu ben Barakhel, a young brash bystander, probably one of several witnesses to the debate. He has been following the arguments with growing impatience. He is angry not only with Job for impugning God's justice, but also with the Friends for defending His cause so inadequately.

In essence, Elihu occupies a middle ground between Job and the Friends. The Friends, as protagonists of the conventional theology, have argued that God is just and that suffering is therefore the consequence and the sign of sin. Job, from his own experience, has denied both propositions, insisting that since he is suffering without being a sinner, God is unjust. Elihu rejects both the Friends' argument that suffering is always the result of sin and Job's contention that God is unjust. He offers a new and significant insight which bears all the earmarks of being the product of the poet's experience during a lifetime: suffering sometimes comes even to upright men as a discipline, as a warning to prevent them from slipping into sin. For there are some weaknesses to which decent, respectable men are particularly prone, notably the sins of complacency and pride.

In the course of his speeches, Elihu restates some of the ideas that have already been expressed. Though they are of more limited scope and validity, they are not insignificant as representing some small aspect of man's experience and his understanding of it. It is, however, Elihu's emphasis upon suffering as a moral discipline in the life of man that constitutes his basic contribution to the discussion.

The First Speech (32–33)

In the ancient Orient, where age is synonymous with wisdom, the young were not expected to participate in the deliberations of their elders, let alone interrupt their discussion. Being younger than Job and the Friends, Elihu is acutely conscious of his breach of etiquette in speaking out. He therefore offers a truculent apology for joining in the discussion. He insists that the spirit within a man, and not mere age, should determine his right to speak. He has waited as long as he could for the Friends to answer Job properly, but he finds that they have not done justice to God's cause. Therefore, unable to contain himself any longer, he will speak out without fear or favor.

Job has charged God with injustice, wanton power, and a lack of concern for His creatures. What Job has failed to note is that God speaks to man in many ways. One mode of divine communication is through visions and dreams in the night. When these do not avail to restrain a man from falling into sin, God warns him through the medium of physical pain and illness. A man may be brought to the very threshold of death, when his virtues prove his salvation. As he is restored to well-being and health, man recognizes that he was indeed sinful and that the discipline of pain has chastened his spirit and saved him from perdition.

32   So these three men ceased answering Job because he still considered
2   himself to be right. Then Elihu, the son of Barakhel the Buzite, of the
family of Ram, became angry. He was angry with Job for considering
3   himself more righteous than God. He was also angry with his three
friends because they had found no answer and thus had placed God in
4   the wrong. First Elihu waited with Job for them to speak, for they
5   were older than he. Now, when Elihu saw that these three men had no
answer, he became very angry.
6   Elihu, the son of Barakhel the Buzite, spoke out, saying,
I am young, and you are old,
therefore I was afraid, and dared not
voice my opinion in your presence.

7   I thought,
"Age should speak,
and the years should teach wisdom,"
8   but it is the spirit in a man,
and the breath of the Almighty that gives understanding.
9   Not always are old men wise;
or do the aged understand the truth.
10   Therefore I say, "Listen to me,
let me also declare my opinion."
11   Behold, I waited for your words;
I listened for your wise thoughts
while you searched for words.
12   I paid attention to you,
and lo, there was no one to refute Job —
no one among you to answer his words.
13   Beware lest you say, "We have attained wisdom,
but only God can rebut him, not man!"
14   And I thought,
"If Job had directed his words to me
I would not have answered him with speeches like yours;
15   Now they are beaten, they answer no more,
they have not a word to say.
16   And shall I be quiet, for they have ceased speaking,
and are silent, answering no more?"
17   Now I, too, will give my views;
I also will declare my opinion.
18   For I am full of words;
the spirit within me presses upon me.
19·   Behold, my bosom is like wine which has no vent,
like new wineskins, ready to burst.
20   Let me speak and find relief;
let me open my lips and answer.
21   I will show no partiality to anyone
or flatter any man,
22   For if I were skilled in flattery,
my Maker would speedily carry me off.

לב א וַֽיִּשְׁבְּתוּ שְׁלֹשֶׁת הָאֲנָשִׁים הָאֵלֶּה מֵעֲנוֹת אֶת־אִיּוֹב כִּי הוּא

2 צַדִּיק בְּעֵינָֽיו:　　　וַיִּחַר אַף ׀ אֱלִיהוּא בֶן־בַּרַכְאֵל הַבּוּזִי
מִמִּשְׁפַּחַת רָם בְּאִיּוֹב חָרָה אַפּוֹ עַל־צַדְּקוֹ נַפְשׁוֹ מֵאֱלֹהִֽים:

3 וּבִשְׁלֹשֶׁת רֵעָיו חָרָה אַפּוֹ עַל אֲשֶׁר לֹא־מָצְאוּ מַעֲנֶה וַיַּרְשִׁיעוּ

4 אֶת־אִיּֽוֹב: וֶאֱלִיהוּ חִכָּה אֶת־אִיּוֹב בִּדְבָרִים כִּי זְקֵנִים־הֵמָּה

5 מִמֶּנּוּ לְיָמִֽים: וַיַּרְא אֱלִיהוּא כִּי אֵין מַעֲנֶה בְּפִי שְׁלֹשֶׁת הָאֲנָשִׁים
וַיִּחַר אַפּֽוֹ:

6 וַיַּעַן ׀ אֱלִיהוּא בֶן־בַּרַכְאֵל הַבּוּזִי וַיֹּאמַר
צָעִיר אֲנִי לְיָמִים וְאַתֶּם יְשִׁישִׁים　　עַל־כֵּן זָחַלְתִּי וָאִירָא ׀

7 מֵחַוֺּת דֵּעִי אֶתְכֶֽם:　　　אָמַרְתִּי יָמִים יְדַבֵּרוּ

8 וְרֹב שָׁנִים יֹדִיעוּ חָכְמָֽה:　　　אָכֵן רֽוּחַ־הִיא בֶאֱנוֹשׁ

9 וְנִשְׁמַת שַׁדַּי תְּבִינֵֽם:　　　לֹא־רַבִּים יֶחְכָּמוּ

י וּזְקֵנִים יָבִינוּ מִשְׁפָּֽט:　　　לָכֵן אָמַרְתִּי שִׁמְעָה־לִּי

11 אֲחַוֶּה דֵּעִי אַף־אָֽנִי:　　　הֵן הוֹחַלְתִּי ׀ לְדִבְרֵיכֶם
אָזִין עַד־תְּבוּנֹֽתֵיכֶם　　　עַד־תַּחְקְרוּן מִלִּֽין:

12 וְעָֽדֵיכֶם אֶתְבּוֹנָֽן　　　וְהִנֵּה אֵין לְאִיּוֹב מוֹכִיחַ

13 עוֹנֶה אֲמָרָיו מִכֶּֽם:　　　פֶּן־תֹּאמְרוּ מָצָאנוּ חָכְמָה

14 אֵל יִדְּפֶנּוּ לֹא־אִֽישׁ:　　　וְלֹא־עָרַךְ אֵלַי מִלִּין

טו וּֽבְאִמְרֵיכֶם לֹא אֲשִׁיבֶֽנּוּ:　　　חַתּוּ לֹא־עָנוּ עוֹד

16 הֶעְתִּיקוּ מֵהֶם מִלִּֽים:　　　וְהוֹחַלְתִּי כִּי־לֹא יְדַבֵּרוּ

17 כִּי עָמְדוּ לֹא־עָנוּ עֽוֹד:　　　אַעֲנֶה אַף־אֲנִי חֶלְקִי

18 אֲחַוֶּה דֵּעִי אַף־אָֽנִי:　　　כִּי מָלֵתִי מִלִּים

19 הֱצִיקַתְנִי רוּחַ בִּטְנִֽי:　　　הִנֵּה־בִטְנִי כְּיַיִן לֹא־יִפָּתֵחַ

כ כְּאֹבוֹת חֲדָשִׁים יִבָּקֵֽעַ:　　　אֲדַבְּרָה וְיִרְוַח־לִי

21 אֶפְתַּח שְׂפָתַי וְאֶעֱנֶֽה:　　　אַל־נָא אֶשָּׂא פְנֵי־אִישׁ

22 וְאֶל־אָדָם לֹא אֲכַנֶּֽה:　　　כִּי לֹא יָדַעְתִּי אֲכַנֶּה
כִּמְעַט יִשָּׂאֵנִי עֹשֵֽׂנִי:

33   But now, hear my speech, O Job,
             and listen to all my words.
 2   Behold, I open my mouth;
             the tongue in my mouth now speaks.
 3   My heart proclaims words of wisdom,
             my lips declare the truth.
 4   It is the spirit of God that has made me,
             and the breath of the Almighty that gives me life.
 5   If you can, answer me;
             prepare for the contest, take your stand.
 6   Behold, I am equal with you before God;
             I, too, have been molded from clay.
 7   Surely, no dread of *me* will terrify you;
             my pressure will not be heavy upon you.

 8   Now you have spoken in my hearing
             and I have heard the sound of your words:
 9   "I am clean, without transgression;
             pure am I, without guilt.
10   Yet God invents complaints against me,
             for He counts me as His enemy.
11   He puts my feet in the stocks,
             and watches all my paths."

12   Behold, in this you are wrong — I shall answer you
             when you declare, "God is stronger than man."
13   Why do you argue against Him, saying,
             "And therefore He answers none of man's words"?
14   For God speaks once
             And then again — if only man noticed!
15   In a dream, in a vision of the night
             when deep sleep falls upon men
             while they slumber upon their beds,
16   He opens the ears of men,
             and as a warning, He terrifies them,
17   to turn man aside from secret misdeeds
             and to separate him from pride.
18   Thus He saves him from the Pit
             and his soul from crossing the river of Death.

19   Or a man may be chastened by pain upon his bed,
             by a perpetual strife in his bones,
20   so that he loathes his bread,
             and his appetite abhors the daintiest food.
21   His flesh wastes away so that it cannot be seen,
             and his bones protrude and cannot be looked upon.
22   He himself draws near to the Pit
             and his life approaches the emissaries of Death.
23   But if there be one spokesman for him,
             one advocate among a thousand
             to vouch for a man's uprightness,

לג א וְאוּלָם שְׁמַע־נָא אִיּוֹב מִלָּי וְכָל־דְּבָרַי הַאֲזִינָה:

2 הִנֵּה־נָא פָּתַחְתִּי פִי דִּבְּרָה לְשׁוֹנִי בְחִכִּי:

3 יָשֶׁר־לִבִּי אֲמָרַי וְדַעַת שְׂפָתַי בָּרוּר מִלֵּלוּ:

4 רוּחַ־אֵל עָשָׂתְנִי וְנִשְׁמַת שַׁדַּי תְּחַיֵּנִי:

ה אִם־תּוּכַל הֲשִׁיבֵנִי עֶרְכָה לְפָנַי הִתְיַצָּבָה:

6 הֵן־אֲנִי כְפִיךָ לָאֵל מֵחֹמֶר קֹרַצְתִּי גַם־אָנִי:

7 הִנֵּה אֵמָתִי לֹא תְבַעֲתֶךָּ וְאַכְפִּי עָלֶיךָ לֹא־יִכְבָּד:

8 אַךְ אָמַרְתָּ בְאָזְנָי וְקוֹל מִלִּין אֶשְׁמָע:

9 זַךְ אֲנִי בְּלִי־פָשַׁע חַף אָנֹכִי

י וְלֹא עָוֹן לִי: הֵן תְּנוּאוֹת עָלַי יִמְצָא

11 יַחְשְׁבֵנִי לְאוֹיֵב לוֹ: יָשֵׂם בַּסַּד רַגְלָי

12 יִשְׁמֹר כָּל־אָרְחֹתָי: הֶן־זֹאת לֹא־צָדַקְתָּ אֶעֱנֶךָּ

13 כִּי־יִרְבֶּה אֱלוֹהַּ מֵאֱנוֹשׁ: מַדּוּעַ אֵלָיו רִיבוֹתָ

14 כִּי כָל־דְּבָרָיו לֹא יַעֲנֶה: כִּי־בְאַחַת יְדַבֶּר־אֵל

טו וּבִשְׁתַּיִם לֹא יְשׁוּרֶנָּה: בַּחֲלוֹם חֶזְיוֹן לַיְלָה בִּנְפֹל תַּרְדֵּמָה עַל־אֲנָשִׁים בִּתְנוּמוֹת עֲלֵי מִשְׁכָּב:

16 אָז יִגְלֶה אֹזֶן אֲנָשִׁים וּבְמֹסָרָם יַחְתֹּם:

17 לְהָסִיר אָדָם מַעֲשֶׂה וְגֵוָה מִגֶּבֶר יְכַסֶּה:

18 יַחְשֹׂךְ נַפְשׁוֹ מִנִּי־שָׁחַת וְחַיָּתוֹ מֵעֲבֹר בַּשָּׁלַח:

19 וְהוּכַח בְּמַכְאוֹב עַל־מִשְׁכָּבוֹ וְרִיב עֲצָמָיו אֵתָן:

כ וְזִהֲמַתּוּ חַיָּתוֹ לָחֶם וְנַפְשׁוֹ מַאֲכַל תַּאֲוָה:

21 יִכֶל בְּשָׂרוֹ מֵרֹאִי וְשֻׁפּוּ עַצְמֹתָיו לֹא רֻאּוּ:

22 וַתִּקְרַב לַשַּׁחַת נַפְשׁוֹ וְחַיָּתוֹ לַמְמִתִים:

23 אִם־יֵשׁ עָלָיו מַלְאָךְ מֵלִיץ אֶחָד מִנִּי־אָלֶף

24   God is gracious to him, and He commands,
            "Free him from descending to the Pit;
            I have found a ransom for him."

25   Then his flesh becomes fresh as in youth;
            he returns to the days of his vigor.
26   He then prays to God, and finds favor,
            and joyfully enters His presence.
        He recounts to men His goodness,

27   and proclaims to men, saying,
            "I sinned and perverted the right,
            but it was not to my advantage.
28   He has redeemed me from going down to the Pit,
            so that I might see the light of life."

29   Behold, all these things does God do,
            twice — yes, three times — with a man,
        to bring him back from the Pit,
            that he may bask in the light of life.

31   Give heed, O Job, listen to me.
            Be silent and let me speak.
32   Then if you have anything to say, answer me;
            speak out, for I'd love to see you right.
33   But if not, you listen to me;
            be silent, let me teach you wisdom.

24 לְהַגִּיד לְאָדָם יָשְׁרוֹ: וַיְחֻנֶּנּוּ וַיֹּאמֶר
פְּדָעֵהוּ מֵרֶדֶת שַׁחַת מָצָאתִי כֹפֶר:
כה רֻטֲפַשׁ בְּשָׂרוֹ מִנֹּעַר יָשׁוּב לִימֵי עֲלוּמָיו:
26 יֶעְתַּר אֶל־אֱלוֹהַּ ׀ וַיִּרְצֵהוּ וַיַּרְא פָּנָיו בִּתְרוּעָה
27 וַיָּשֵׁב לֶאֱנוֹשׁ צִדְקָתוֹ: יָשֹׁר ׀ עַל־אֲנָשִׁים וַיֹּאמֶר
חָטָאתִי וְיָשָׁר הֶעֱוֵיתִי וְלֹא־שָׁוָה לִי:
28 פָּדָה נַפְשִׁי מֵעֲבֹר בַּשָּׁחַת וְחַיָּתוֹ בָּאוֹר תִּרְאֶה:
29 הֶן־כָּל־אֵלֶּה יִפְעַל־אֵל פַּעֲמַיִם שָׁלוֹשׁ עִם־גָּבֶר:
ל לְהָשִׁיב נַפְשׁוֹ מִנִּי־שָׁחַת לְאוֹר בְּאוֹר הַחַיִּים:
31 הַקְשֵׁב אִיּוֹב שְׁמַע־לִי הַחֲרֵשׁ וְאָנֹכִי אֲדַבֵּר:
32 אִם־יֵשׁ־מִלִּין הֲשִׁיבֵנִי דַּבֵּר כִּי־חָפַצְתִּי צַדְּקֶךָּ:
33 אִם־אַיִן אַתָּה שְׁמַע־לִי הַחֲרֵשׁ וַאֲאַלֶּפְךָ חָכְמָה:

---

v. 28. נפשו ק׳ ibid. וחיתו ק׳

CHAPTER 32

On the authenticity and content of the Elihu chapters (32–37), see Special Note 28. On Elihu's apology (chap. 32), see Special Note 29.

32:1 The final clause in MT, "for he was still righteous in his own eyes." For בְּעֵינָיו LXX and P (also one Heb. ms.) read בְּעֵינֵיהֶם, interpreting the clause "for he had become righteous in their eyes." However, such a rendering would require reading הָיָה for הוּא. Moreover, there is nothing to suggest that the Friends had conceded the truth of Job's position. Elihu's citation of the Friends' standpoint in 13b, "God can refute him, not a man," describes them as helpless before Job's onslaught, not as convinced.

32:2 אֱלִיהוּא, with final Aleph (I Sam. 1:1; I Chr. 12:2), or without it (I Chr. 26:7; 27:18) is identical with אֱלִיָּהוּ. The difference in vocalization may be intended to distinguish it from the name of the Prophet Elijah (R-O). TS calls it an artificial differentiation. For בַּרַכְאֵל cf. יְבֶרֶכְיָהוּ (Isa. 8:2); בֶּרֶכְיָה (I Chr. 3:20; 9:16; 15:23, etc.); and *Ba-rik-ilu*, the name of several members of the Jewish banking family of the Murashu in the reign of Artaxerxes I. בּוּז is the brother of עוּץ and a nephew of Abraham (Gen. 22:21). רָם is an ancestor of David (Ruth 4:19; I Chr. 2:9, 25).

On the symbolic significance of this solitary Hebrew name with the patronymic and the family pedigree, see Special Note 28 and *BGM*, 115 f. The elaborate genealogy may also have been intended to indicate that though Elihu lacked the attribute of age, he did possess the virtue of status and therefore had some right to speak.

The final clause, lit. "because of his considering himself more righteous than God." The declarative use of צדק in the Piel (Jer. 3:11; Ezek. 16:51, 52; Job 33:32) is a later use than the Hiphil (Ex. 23:7; Deut. 25:1; I Ki. 8:32, etc.).

32:3 וַיַּרְשִׁיעוּ אֶת־אִיּוֹב has been interpreted in two ways: (a) "they could not prove Job in the wrong" by supplying לֹא from לֹא־מָצְאוּ (D-G), but this point has already been made in v. 2; (b) "and yet they have condemned Job" (D-G, TS). However, it is psychologically unlikely that Elihu would become so greatly exercised over Job's unjustified condemnation, as is clear from v. 1. On the other hand, if v. 2 condemns Job and v. 3 attacks the Friends for putting God in the wrong, we have a logical and meaningful structure. This interpretation inheres in the reading preserved by the Masorah, according to which our passage is one of the *tiqqunei Sopherim*, "the corrections of the scribes," introduced into the text to avoid an offensive reference to God. Thus the original reading was וַיַּרְשִׁיעוּ אֶת־אֱלֹהִים, "and they put God in the wrong." The tradition of *tiqqunei Sopherim*, which declares that the scribes have actually changed the biblical text, runs counter to the boundless reverence of the Masoretes for the received text and hence bears the stamp of authenticity. For a discussion of this phenomenon, cf. *BTM* (new augmented edition, New York, 1971, Intr., pp. XXI ff., and the Comm. on 9:35). The original text וַיַּרְשִׁיעוּ אֶת־הָאֱלֹהִים is therefore to be adopted and rendered "and they put God in the wrong" (Ra., but not Ibn E.; Minhat Shai *ad loc.*).

32:4 The opening clause has been emended to וְאֵלִיהוּ חִכָּה לְרֵעֵי אִיוֹב "he waited for the Friends of Job" (Hi.) or חִכָּה לְהָשִׁיב אֶת אִיוֹב "he waited to respond to Job" (Du.), but there is no warrant for either. Most critics delete אֶת־אִיוֹב and read בְּדַבְּרָם "he waited as they spoke" (Wr., Hö., TS, P.). A far less drastic procedure is available, requiring only the revocalization בְּדַבְּרָם and interpreting אֶת as = "with." Ehr., who so reads the text, renders בְּדַבְּרָם as "while they were speaking." However, the context suggests that the clause is better understood as "and Elihu waited with Job for their speaking, i.e. for them to speak." The verb חִכָּה governs a Lamed 9 times (Isa. 8:17; Job 3:21, etc.), and occurs with a direct object once, in Hos. 6:9, וּכְחַכֵּי אִישׁ גְּדוּדִים, "as bandits lie in wait for a man." On this view, the verb would govern a Beth here; a parallel usage occurs: נַפְשִׁי יָצְאָה בְדַבְּרוֹ "my soul passed out, i.e. yearned for his speaking" (Cant. 5:6).

Job had delivered himself of a very long address ending with chap. 31, anticipating a response from the Friends, as had been the case at each earlier occasion. Elihu, too, a silent but impatient bystander, had waited for the Friends' rejoinder, but they now remained silent (32:1) and offered no response (v. 5).

32:6 זָחַלְתִּי is the Hebrew cognate (or old Aramaic) for the Aram. דחל "fear" (cf. זי, די; זקן, דקן). In spite of the relatively late date of the composition of Job, the vocable may be the old Aram. form with Zayin for the later Daled, which occurs in the 9th century inscription of Zakir, King of Hamath אל תזחל. Hö., who denies the possibility, overlooks the use of the relative זו (later Aramaic די), which occurs both in early and late biblical texts (Ex. 15:13, 16; Isa. 42:24; 43:21; Ps. 9:16; 10:2; 17:9; 32:8; 68:29; 142:4; 143:8), as well as the use of *zeh* as a relative in Job 15:17; 19:19 a. e.)

32:7, 8 When the Hebrew writer wishes to express an earlier idea which is then abandoned in favor of another, he may, as has been noted above, have recourse to several devices; (a) the use of "virtual quotations" (as, e.g., Job 27:8 ff.); or (b) the use of contrasting apothegms (e.g., Job 12:12, 13); see the Comm. *ad loc.* and *BGM*, pp. 182 ff. A more explicit technique is obviously also available: the earlier idea is expressed by אָמַרְתִּי "I thought," which is followed by אָכֵן, "but indeed," that introduces the new idea which replaces the old; cf. Isa. 49:4; Zeph. 3:7; Ps. 31:23; 82:7; cf. also Isa. 53:4; Jer. 3:20; 8:8.

32:8 רוּחַ without the article, "the spirit" par excellence, i.e. "the spirit of God" (cf. אִישׁ אֲשֶׁר־רוּחַ בּוֹ, Nu. 27:18), as is clear from the parallelism. The Hiphil is used causatively, "which causes them to understand."

32:9 רַבִּים "great, many (in days), old"; cf. Gen. 25:23. P. appositely calls attention to the use of רַבִּים for "the elders" in the Qumranite *Manual of Discipline*.

32:10 The singular imperative is changed to the plural so that it is addressed to the Friends (Be., Hi., Bu., D-G), but there is no evidence that LXX, S, V, and Saadia, who render the verb in the plural, had this reading in their mss. A translator naturally seeks to make his version as smooth as possible. The singular imperative may well be correct, since it is Job and not the Friends whom Elihu constantly addresses; cf. 33:1 etc.

32:11 הוֹחַלְתִּי is generally rendered "I waited for your words," which is entirely satisfactory. However, cf. the Comm. on v. 16, where it is suggested that the root יחל "wait" develops the added connotation "be silent." Hence our stich here might also be interpreted, "I was silent at your words."

אָזִין a defectiva spelling for אַאֲזִין; cf. יֶהֱל = יָהֵל (Isa. 13:20); הַסוּרִים = הָאֲסוּרִים Ecc. 4:14, where the long vowel Qameṣ as in our passage compensates for the loss of the Aleph and its short Hateph vowel. Cf. also מֵזִין for מַאֲזִין (Pr. 17:4) and מִלֵּתִי in v. 18. The verb is followed by the preposition עַד in Nu. 23:18, evidently a poetic usage.

תְּבוּנָה "understanding" generally refers to the faculty of comprehension (Ex. 31:3; Job 12:13) or the act (Ps. 78:72; 136:8; Job 26:12). It also indicates the object or the content of wisdom; cf. Pr. 5:1; 19:8. In this last sense, the plural occurs in Ps. 49:4 and here. Hence render the noun here "wise thoughts."

Stich c, "while you searched for words" (D-G) or "until you came to the end of your words." The verb is a denominative of חֵקֶר, "search out, hence limit, end"; cf. Isa. 40:28; Ps. 145:3; Job 5:9; 9:10; 34:24; 36:26.

32:13 פֶּן "lest" is apparently a breviloquence for "beware lest"; cf. Deut. 29:17; Isa. 36:18; Jer. 31:46; Job 36:18.

Stich a מָצָאנוּ חָכְמָה has been rendered variously: (a) "we have formed a wise plan" (TS); (b) "we have found in Job wisdom; only God can overcome him" (Dr., Ehr.); (c) "we have discovered the truth that only God can refute him" (my former student, Rabbi Samuel Dresner). We believe it best to render: "We have attained wisdom, but only God can refute him, not man."

יִדְּפֶנּוּ from נדף "drive" (Ps. 68:3; Job 13:25) is here used in the abstract "rebut, refute." The root is probably related to הדף (Jer. 18:18, etc.). There is no proof that our verb is itself derived from הדף with a Dageš for the loss or assimilation of the He (Ha.).

TS relates the root נדף to נוף "chide, reprove," also "place under a ban" in rabbinic Heb. and Aram. The emendation of יִדְּפֶנּוּ to יַלְפֵנוּ, "God teaches us" (Dh., Hö.), creates a parallel with stich a, to be sure, but makes the v. irrelevant. Elihu is describing the Friends not as confident in their own wisdom, but as insisting that Job's obstinacy and refusal to listen to reason can be overcome only by God. This excuse Elihu denies (cf. 33:5, 6), feeling certain that he can do better than they.

The asyndeton, "God can refute him, not a man," is common in poetry and adds to the vigor of the expression.

32:14–16 By combining a reading from LXX "like these" and one from S, "I shall arrange," Hö. creates a Heb. text לֹא אֶעֱרֹךְ כָּאֵלֶּה מִלִּין "I shall not set forth words like these." This striking reading would be in parallelism with stich b, but the changes are not required. If לֹא be revocalized as לֻא "if," a conditional sentence emerges: "If Job had addressed me, I would not have answered him as have you." (So also Yel.) The v. may well be a virtual quotation, a presentation of Elihu's thoughts, continuing into vv. 15 and 16. See the Trans. This statement of Elihu's thoughts explains the change from second to third person and the repetition of the theme already expressed (vv. 3, 5, 11, 12), that the Friends have proved unsuccessful in their debate and have therefore lapsed into silence. It therefore obviates the necessity for deleting these vv.

32:15 חַתּוּ "they are shattered," here "beaten in an argument." הֶעְתִּיקוּ in the Hiphil is intransitive, "are removed," like the Qal (Gen. 12:8; 28:22; Job 18:4).

32:16 וְהוֹחַלְתִּי with the Vav consec. followed by the perfect is used to introduce a question; cf. וְהִשְׁבַּתֶּם "will you stop them?" (Ex. 5:5); וּבִקַּשְׁתֶּם "will you seek?" (Nu. 16:10; and cf. I Sam. 25:11; Isa. 66:9, and *HT*, p. 141.) Hence the v. is interpreted: "Am I to wait because they speak not?" (Ew., Hi., Del., Dil., Du., D-G, P.). Ehr. correctly objects to this interpretation, not only because waiting has already been indicated in v. 11, but on the logical ground that the silence of the Friends is a reason for Elihu to speak, not to remain silent. וְהוֹחַלְתִּי has therefore been emended to וַהֲחִלּוֹתִי "and I began" (Ehr.) or to וְהוֹאַלְתִּי "I desired" (TS). However, both these verbs normally are followed by a complementary infinitive which is lacking here.

As has been indicated on v. 11 above, we suggest that the root יחל "wait" has developed the nuance of "wait silently," which is explicit in Lam. 3:26, טוֹב וְיָחִיל וְדוּמָם, which is to be read טוֹב וְיָחִילוּ דוּמָם, "it is good to wait silently for the salvation of the Lord." Cf. also Job 29:21, where יחל is ‖ to דמם. The root may, therefore, mean "be silent." The reverse semantic development occurs with דמם from "be silent," to "wait" and "hope"; cf. Jos. 10:13 ‖ to עמד; I Sam. 14:9; Ps. 37:7; 62:6 ‖ to תִּקְוָתִי.

This nuance for יחל is highly appropriate in several passages: (1) here, "Should I be silent because they no longer speak?" (2) In Job 6:11, where it is parallel to אַאֲרִיךְ נַפְשִׁי "be patient," so that stich a means "what is my strength that I should remain silent?" (3) In 14:14 stich b means "all the days of my service I would be silent, i.e. uncomplaining." (4) In the famous passage 13:15, לֹא אֲיַחֵל would no longer need an emendation and the parallelism would be substantially improved:

"Indeed, He may kill me; I will not be silent,
　　but I will justify my ways to His face."

32:17　אַעֲנֶה with Pataḥ is not to be construed as a Hiphil, "I will make my part answer" (D-G), which is far-fetched, but rather as a retroversion by analogy from the second or third person of the Qal with Pataḥ, תַּעֲנֶה, yielding אַעֲנֶה, "I will answer." In the Babylonian *supra-linear* vocalization, the same sign marks the Pataḥ and the Segol.

32:18　Eliphaz had pictured his prophetic vision in serene, majestic lines (4:12 ff.). The youthful, impetuous Elihu describes his compulsion to speak in terms of bursting wine bags, or wine-jars (see the Comm. on v. 19). Similarly, Jeremiah had spoken of the pent-up fire in his bones (Jer. 20:7; cf. also 6:11). There is no need to insert a word here such as כִּי (Ley) or אֲנִי or אָנֹכִי (Be., Du.) to create a 3:3 meter. Exceptionally, a short word like כִּי receives an accent for metrical reasons; cf. Ps. 27:5; Job 34:2 and see Special Note 1, sec. 6 and *PPS*, p. 67.

32:19　לֹא־יִפָּתֵחַ "which has no opening."
　　　Hö. objects to stich b as a bad simile, by a *Stubengelehrter* (a scholastic pendant), who is presumably ignorant of the fact that new skins hold wine better than old (Mt. 9:17; Mk. 2:22; Lk. 5:37 f.). Hence stich b has been rendered: "like skins (filled with) new (wine); it is ready to burst" (D-G), but this leaves much to be supplied. There are two better approaches available: (a) to carry לֹא over to stich b (cf. Pr. 3:3; Job 32:9, 12) and render "like new wine skins that are not opened"; or (b) render יִבָּקֵעַ "that are ready to burst (because they are filled to the brim)."
　　　The masc. singular verb יִבָּקֵעַ is explicable in several ways: (a) בֶּטֶן, the subject, though generally fem., may be masc. here; (b) as the masc. sing. form is basic and need not agree with its subject, cf. 22:9 וּזְרֹעוֹת יְתֹמִים יְדֻכָּא; (c) with a passive verb the logical subject becomes a grammatical object; cf. Gen. 27:42 וַיֻּגַּד לְרִבְקָה אֶת־דִּבְרֵי עֵשָׂו; cf. Ges.-K., sec. 121. In any event, the verb therefore need not be emended to תְּבָּקֵעַ (Du.). On the subordinate clause of condition, cf. 8:12 עֹדֶנּוּ בְאִבּוֹ לֹא יִקָּטֵף "while yet in flower, not ready to be cut," and cf. *HT*, sec. 37 ff. For אֹבוֹת "wine skins" Guillaume (*PEQ*, 1961, pp. 147–50) suggests the meaning "wine jar" on the basis of the Arab. waʾb, "a wide vessel." He points to Jer. 13:12–14 as containing a play on אָבוֹת. While the poor used wine skins (Mt. 9:17), the rich had wine-jars.

32:20　For וְיִרְוַח־לִי "lit. that there may be space for me, i.e. that I may find relief," cf. Est. 4:14; the noun רְוָחָה "space, relief" occurs in Ex. 8:11, but not in Lam. 3:56, where it means "sighing" (ag. D-G).

32:21　אַל is the emphatic neg. "I will surely show no partiality to any man."

כִּנָּה "give an epithet"; cf. Arab. *kunya* "epithet, additional name." The root means "give a title of honor" (Isa. 44:5; 45:4; B. S. 36:17; 44:23; 47:6). Here the verb is used pejoratively, "give an undeserved title of honor" hence "flatter, show undue deference." The verb here governs אֶל. In rabbinic Heb. the verb means "modify or disguise an expression" as in כינה הכתוב "the Bible modifies the expression" (*Sifre, Nu.* 84). Hence Ehr. interprets our passage to mean "I shall call things by their right name," but this does not do justice to the first two words of the stich, which clearly mean "show partiality."

32:22 In stich a כִּי לֹא יָדַעְתִּי אֲכַנֶּה is equivalent to a complementary infinitive; for the use of the imperfect, see יַגְדִיל תּוֹרָה וְיַאְדִיר (Isa. 42:21; cf. also 47:1; Hos. 1:6; Job 19:3; Lam. 4:14; and see *HT*, p. 206).

Stich b contains a striking assonance. The verb is here used virtually in its basic sense "carry off"; cf. 30:22. The profound influence of Deutero-Isaiah on Job, both in language and thought, is reflected in our v., which echoes אֲכַנְּךָ וְלֹא יְדַעְתָּנִי (Isa. 45:4). Vocalizing לא as לֻא = לוּ (so also Yel.) creates an excellent conditional sentence; cf. Isa. 1:9 כִּמְעַט ... (כִּי לוּלֵי). Hence our v. means: "If I did know how to flatter, my Maker would quickly carry me off." For כִּמְעַט cf. Ps. 2:12; 81:15; 94:17.

CHAPTER 33

33:1 As has been noted, Job is addressed by name because Elihu speaks both to Job and to the Friends. There is, however, a psychological cause as well. Feeling insecure, he seeks to hold Job's attention by calling him by name. It is no evidence of another writer (D-G); note the characteristic use of וְאוּלָם which occurs as many times in Job as in the rest of the O. T.

33:2 The v. is not "empty of meaning" (D-G). Together with v. 3, it constitutes the proem designed to evoke the reader's or the listener's attention by commending the quality of the message he is about to receive; cf. Deut. 32:1 f.; Ps. 46:2; 49:2–5.

33:3 Stich a in MT can only be interpreted: "the purity of my heart (is reflected) in my words," which is far-fetched and awkward. In addition, there is a verb lacking in stich a. Finally MT offers a metric pattern in which the second stich is longer than the first (3:4), which is highly doubtful; cf. *PPS*, pp. 66 ff. Most scholars, therefore, read אִמְרֵי דַעַת (cf. Pr. 19:27) and emend יֹשֶׁר in various ways in order to create a verb: יָשִׁיק "overflows" (Du.), רָחַשׁ "is astir" (Be.), יָשׁוּר "repeats" (?) (Dh.), יֶשֶׁר "be strong, confirm" (Hö.), all of which are either graphically distant or semantically doubtful. We suggest revocalizing the word as יָשִׁיר or יָשׁוּר, verbs *mediae Yod* and *mediae Vav* being interchangeable; cf. שִׁיח, שׁוּחַ; שִׁים, שׁוּם, etc. The root שׁוּר = "sing" occurs in I Ki. 18:6, while conversely in Am. 8:3 שִׁירוֹת הֵיכָל is not to be emended to שָׁרוֹת "singers" but interpreted as = שׁוּרוֹת "the walls of the palace will wail." Our root occurs again in this very chap. in v. 27, possibly in v. 14; like עֲנֵה it means "chant, declaim." Cf. the Comm. on 3:1. By revocalizing the first word, reading יָשָׁר לְבִּי אִמְרֵי דַעַת, and placing the caesura after דַעַת, the verse exhibits excellent parallelism and a 4:3 meter.

33:4 Ehr. relates the v. to the preceding. Elihu will speak the truth (v. 3) because he is conscious that he was created by God (v. 4). However, self-praise is a characteristic convention of biblical (cf. Ps. 45:2; 49:4) as well as of medieval Heb. and Arab. poetry. Probably the verse expresses the idea that Elihu is not a superior being, but a creature fashioned by God just like Job (Ra.). Hence he calls upon Job to answer (v. 5) without the fear of being at a disadvantage. Omitting the v. (Bu., Be., Du.) or transposing it after v. 6 (Peake) are both unnecessary procedures.

33:5 עֶרְכָה, is not used in a military sense, "order yourself for battle" (D-G). It is a forensic term, "set forth your words, or your case," used here without an object. Similarly, הִתְיַצָּבָה "stand up at the trial" (Isa. 3:13; Ps. 82:1).

    In stich a, הֲשִׁיבֵנִי, being a longer word, receives two beats *metri causa*, hence the v. is in 3:3 meter.

33:6 כְּפִיךָ has been interpreted: (a) "with regard to power" on the basis of Gen. 31:29, or "as you asked" (Ra., R-O); (b) TS interprets it as "your equal" on the basis of the Arab. *kafī* "equal" and renders "I am God's, as are you"; (c) Ball, Ehr. emend לֹא אֵל "not God." The MT may be interpreted "in your proportion, i.e., as you are vis-à-vis God"; cf. אִישׁ כְּפִי אָכְלוֹ (Ex. 16:21); כְּפִי אֲשֶׁר אֵינְכֶם שֹׁמְרִים "in proportion as you do not keep My ways" (Mal. 2:9). Hence stich a "lit. I am in your proportion, i.e. like you, before God."

    קרץ "nip, pinch," as in Akk. and Ethiopic. It is used of the baker's nipping off dough in rabbinic Heb.: קוֹרֵץ עָלָיו אֶת הָעִיסָה (*M. Kelim* 15:6) or cutting off grapes in a lump. The root is used of creation in Babylonian mythology, *ṭi-ṭa iktariṣ* "he nipped off the clay" (*Gilgamesh Epic*, Tablet I, col. 2, l. 34: *ANET*, p. 74a).

33:7 An almost verbatim quotation and rebuttal of 13:21, except that for כַּפְּךָ Elihu substitutes אַכְפִּי. Emending it to כַּפִּי (Hi., Wr., Sieg., Be., Bu., Du.) is ruled out by the masc. verb. The root, which occurs in Aram. and Syr., appears as a verb in כִּי־אָכַף עָלָיו פִּיהוּ "for his mouth, i.e. his appetite, presses upon, compels him (to work)" (Pr. 16:26). The noun in the fem., אַכְפָּה "pressure, weight," occurs in B. S. 46:5:

כי קרא אל אל עליון כאכפה לו אויבים מסביב

"For he called to God the all highest,
When there was pressure from foes all about."

In rabbinic Heb. the noun occurs in the phrase מאי אכפה ליה "What burden is it for him, i.e. why does it concern him?" (*P. Sotah* V, 20b) and in the more common איכפת with the older *t* ending (*B. Taan.* 25a; *B. B. Metz.* 40a). Note also rabbinic אוּכָּף "saddle," in Arab. *ikaf* "pack saddle, weight."

33:8 אַךְ rendered "yet, nevertheless, indeed" by virtually all commentators is satisfactory. Hence the attractive suggestion to revocalize the particle as אֵיךְ "how" is not necessary. This change is, however, required in Jonah 2:5.

33:9 Vv. 9–11 are a citation from Job, in part a direct quotation (v. 11 = 13:27a, b), in part a restatement of Job's argument. As is common in debate, he distorts his opponents' position. To be sure, Job has declared תָּם אָנִי (9:20, 21), but he meant not that he was pure and without sin (cf. the Comm. *ad loc.*), but that he possessed integrity, had been wholeheartedly loyal to God. Job has made frequent references to his errors and transgressions (7:21; 10:5, 6; 13:26; 19:4 f.). But he has insisted that he is fundamentally upright and therefore does not deserve the calamitous doom that has come upon him. זַךְ "pure," used of distilled oil (Ex. 27:20,) has been applied to Job by Bildad (8:6) and Zophar (11:6). Job himself has used it only of the purity of his prayer (16:17). חף "clean," the verb being used in rabbinic Heb. of cleaning the scalp ערב שבת היה והלל חפף את ראשו, "it was the afternoon before the Sabbath and Hillel was cleaning his head" (*M. Shab.* 33:1).

33:10 תְּנוּאוֹת, from the root נוא "hinder, restrain, frustrate" (Nu. 30:6; Ps-33:10), occurs in Nu. 14:34, "you shall know My opposition." It has, therefore, been interpreted here as "frustration" (D-G). On the other hand, the noun is generally brought into connection with the similarly sounding *Lamed Yod* root אנה, "to cause without reason" as, e.g., לֹא יְאֻנֶּה לַצַּדִּיק כָּל־אָוֶן, "no evil will come without cause to the righteous" (Pr. 12:21); Ex. 21:13; מִתְאַנֶּה הוּא לִי, "he is inventing a pretext against me" (II Ki. 5:7), whence תֹּאֲנָה, "excuse, pretext" (Jud. 14:4), which is the reading adopted here in the plural תוֹאֲנוֹת by Wr., Bu., Du., Be., D-G, Hö., TS. This latter meaning, however, may well inhere in the Masoretic reading, which would be an aural metathesis, and not a merely scribal error.

Stich b is a virtually exact quotation of 13:24.

33:11 An exact quotation of Job 13:27 a, b; cf. the Comm. there.

33:12 Stich a "lit. in this regard, wherein you are not right, I shall answer you." Modern critics find a difficulty in this stich because Elihu does not answer Job's contention. LXX renders "Yet how do you say I am righteous and He has not answered me?" Various emendations have, therefore, been proposed, as, e.g., הנה אם אצעק לא ענה (Du.) or היך תאמר צדקתי ולא אֶעֱנֶה, but both require violent changes to the text (D-G), while the tendency of LXX to paraphrase is well known. Actually, Elihu's total address constitutes his answer to Job.

Stich b has been interpreted variously: (a) "because God is greater than man" (D-G), but this is no answer to Job. In fact, this has been the burden of Job's complaint. (b) "God acts too severely against men" (Ehr.), but the verb can hardly sustain this meaning. (c) to interpret the passage as an unrecorded *tiqqun Sopherim* for כִּי יִרְבֶּה אֱנוֹשׁ מֵאֱלוֹהַ "that man is greater than God" (R-O), but this idea has never been advanced by Job.

A better procedure is to refer זאת to Job's contention cited by Elihu in 12b and 13b. To make the virtual quotation clear, we need only to add a *verbum dicendi* "when you say, 'God is stronger than man.'" Elihu refers to Job's argument that God uses His superior force against man (9:19 ff.; 16:9 ff.; 19:6 ff.). V. 13 is in alternate parallelism with v. 12, both stichs being parallel and the two stichs b containing the conclusion of the citation. See the Comm. on the next v. and the Trans. The source for Job's view is 9:2–4.

33:13   Stich b (unlike 12b) has been generally recognized as a quotation of Job's view (D-G). The emendation of דְּבָרָיו to דְּבָרָי is unnecessary; the suffix goes back to אֱנוֹשׁ "man's words." Elihu cites Job as arguing that "God is mightier than man" (12b) and therefore "He does not deign to answer any of his words" (13b). This charge is almost identical with Koheleth's observation: "A man cannot contend with One mightier than he" (Ecc. 6:10); see *KMW ad loc.* This view seems more appropriate here than the rendering of TS, "Man cannot answer all God's arguments." On the ambiguities produced by the 3rd person prefixes and suffixes, cf. the Comm. on 9:3.

33:14   In stich b, וּבִשְׁתַּיִם is virtually an ordinal, "and in a second." שׁוּר "see," common in Job (cf. 35:12).
     The two numbers are generally explained as the two means of communication which God employs, the nocturnal vision and the onslaught of illness. However, illness is not described until v. 19, while vv. 15–17 are clearly concerned with the nocturnal vision. It is, therefore, better to render בְּאַחַת and וּבִשְׁתַּיִם as "the first time, once" and "the second time, again." God sends His messages through visions again and again before taking more drastic steps. Compare the three calls to the young Samuel in the sanctuary (I Sam. 3:4 ff.). Ascending numeration may be used to refer to a specific number of instances (as, e.g., Pr. 30:15, 18, 21, 24; see the Comm. on 5:19), or in the more general sense of "several," required here. Cf. Am. 1:3, 8, 9, 11, etc. For the suggested meanings "once" and "twice," cf. אַחַת דִּבֶּר אֱלֹהִים שְׁתַּיִם זוּ שָׁמָעְתִּי "Once God has spoken, twice have I heard this" (Ps. 62:12, RSV).
     Stich b is either a subordinate clause of concession, "though man does not regard, notice it" (D-G, TS), or a subordinate clause of condition, "if man does not notice it," i.e. the first mode of God's speaking. It may be better to vocalize לא as לֻא and render, "if only man would perceive it!" — an expression of God's hope that His message would find a response. Cf. לוּ עַמִּי שֹׁמֵעַ לִי (Ps. 81:14).

33:16   Stich b has been rendered (a) "He seals their fetters" (cf. Ps. 2:2);

(b) "He seals their instruction"; (c) or it is emended to וּבְמוֹרָאִים יְחִתֵּם "He frightens them with terrors" (Du., Be., Hö.) or וּבְמַרְאִים "He frightens them with visions" (D-G, P.) on the basis of LXX "in visions of terror." It is sufficient to revocalize as וּבְמוּסָרָם יְחִתֵּם "and with a warning administered to them, He frightens them." The suffix in וּבְמוּסָרָם is an objective genitive; cf. חֲמָסִי עָלֶיךָ "the violence done to me is your fault" (Gen. 16:5). D-G (II, p. 243) asks whether מוּסָר means "discipline in the sense of suffering" (Dil., Ehr.) or "disciplinary instructional warning" (Bu., Del.). The noun carries both meanings, like the mishnaic Heb. יסורים "suffering," which is viewed as a divine warning. Cf. the famous rabbinic utterance: אם רואה אדם יסורין באין עליו יפשפש במעשיו "If a man sees suffering coming upon him, let him scrutinize his actions" (*B. Ber.* 5a). Elihu is the chief biblical source for this fundamental doctrine of postbiblical religion.

33:17   In this difficult v., stich a has been all but universally emended to לְהָסִיר אָדָם מִמַּעֲשֵׂהוּ "to rescue man from his (evil) deeds" (D-G). However, the suffix on the noun is not expressed by LXX and T, and may have been supplied in translations by S, V. מִמַּעֲשֶׂה, which is indeterminate, is supported by the undetermined noun וְגֵוָה in stich b. The context makes it clear that evil action is meant, as in פָּעֳלָם (36:9), which is unqualified, but its negative connotation there too is clear from the parallelism. Hence the emendations מֵעַוְלָה (Bi., Du., P.) or מֵעֹשֶׁק or מִפֶּשַׁע (Be.) cannot legitimately be based on LXX *adikia* "unrighteousness," which translates *ad sensum* (Bu.).

The singling out of גֵוָה "pride" (Jer. 13:17; Dan. 4:34; cf. Job 22:29) in stich b as a surrogate for generic "evil" is significant. It is *hybris*, the arrogance to which men, particularly good men, are prone, and which is attenuated by trouble. It is the man who has never suffered who remains insufferable. In the words of a Hasidic teacher, "Better a sinner who knows that he is a sinner than a saint who knows that he is a saint." Ra. grasps the intent of the entire passage superbly by rendering מַעֲשֶׂה in stich a as שהיה בדעתו לעשות "the deeds which he intended to do.".

In stich b, וְגֵוָה is a defectiva spelling of וְגַאֲוָה (cf. Jer. 13:17; Job 22:29; Dan. 4:34). Render "and to hide, i.e. separate pride from man." This is equivalent to "separate man from pride," exactly as "they turn aside the way of the humble" (Am. 2:7) is an alternative to "they turn aside the needy from the way" (Job 24:4). The various emendations for the verb, such as יְכַלֶּה "He destroys" (Dil., Du., Be.) or יְכַסֵּחַ "prune away" (Bi., Bu., Du.) are in no sense better than MT.

33:18   חַיָּתוֹ "his soul" lit. "the living one" (Ps. 78:50; 143:3; and vv. 22–28 below). בַּשֶּׁלַח formerly rendered "by means of a sword" (cf. Joel 2:1; Neh. 4:11) was emended by Hö. to בִּשְׁאוֹלָה "into the grave." However, שֶׁלַח is a subterranean canal which the dead must cross to reach Sheol, like the Akk. *Hubor*, Greek *Styx* (cf. Dhorme, *JPES*, 1920, p. 45; M. Tsevat in *VT* 1954, vol. 4, pp. 41 ff.). Apparently, the same noun appears in "the pool of Shelaḥ" (Neh. 3:15), the more familiar form being *Shiloaḥ* (Isa. 8:6). The patriarchal name "Methuselah," "the man, or subject, of Shelaḥ" (Gen. 5:21 ff.), is equivalent to "Methushael, the man, or subject, of Sheol" (Gen. 4:18), like the epithet *mt-rfᵓ* "the man of the shade," applied to Danᵓel in Ugaritic (so also TS).

33:19 Stich b may be coordinate to stich a: "But the strife of his bones is enduring" or subordinate, modifying stich a: "lit. with the enduring strife of his bones." The Kethib וְרִיב "quarrel" gives excellent sense. The Qere וְרוֹב is supported by 4:14, but see the Comm. *ad loc.* It obviously cannot mean "most" here. In view of the frequent interchange of *mediae Yod* and *mediae Vav* roots, the two forms may well represent morphological variants, for which the Kethib-Qere apparatus offers many examples; cf. *BTM*, pp. 117 ff. Dh. renders "trembling" on the basis of Akk. *râbu*; TS "mental anguish." Hö. reads וְדוּב, an Aramaism (?) for Hebrew זוּב, "flow." The parallelism supports MT in the more general sense, "strife, pain."

33:20 For this v., which is basic to the textual criticism and exegesis of 6:7, cf. the Comm. *ad loc.* וְזִהֲמַתּוּ has the Arab. cognate *zahima* "befoul," also in Syriac and rabbinic Heb. מזוהם "rendered foul." The Piel is factitive, "make foul," and declarative, "consider foul." Hence = "abhor." The form need not be emended to וְזִהֲמָה, nor need the suffix be regarded as the rare anticipatory suffix as, e.g., Ex. 2:2; I Sam. 20:14, referring to the object לֶחֶם. It is the indirect object, virtually an ethical dative: "lit. and his soul loathes food for itself." On pronominal suffixes as indirect objects, cf. the Comm. on 31:18.

33:21 מֵרֹאִי the privative Mem "lit. from appearance, so that he has no appearance"; cf. I Sam. 16:12. G. R. Driver has rendered "without moisture" on the basis of an Arab. cognate (*Analecta Louvain*, series 20, p. 351).

For the root שפה here, we have an embarrassment of etymological riches. It is generally connected with Arab. *safa* (*tertiae Ya*) "raise, carry off dust," whence הַר נִשְׁפֶּה (Isa. 13:2); שְׁפָיִים "wind-swept mountain" (Isa. 41:18; 49:9, a. e.), and is rendered here "become bare, thin." Hö. cites Arab. *safa* IV "become thin." The Aram. שפי means "crush, grind"; cf. Heb. שׁוּף (Gen. 3:15) and שׁאף (Am. 2:7; 8:4; Ps. 56:2 and T *ad loc.*; Ps. 57:4).

The Kethib can only be construed as שְׁפִי, a noun, "the bareness (or the crushing) of his bones cannot be looked upon." The verbal form in the Qere וְשֻׁפּוּ is preferable: "his bones are bare (or crushed), so that they cannot be looked upon." רֻאוּ is not a Pual (D-G), but the Qal perfect passive; cf. Isa. 9:5 יֻלַּד and the Comm. on הֹרָה 3:2. It may have been chosen in preference to the usual Niphal because of the vocalic assonance with וְשֻׁפּוּ. Note the creation even of a "non-form" in the Qere of II Sam. 3:25 מוֹבָאֶךָ because of the proximity of מוֹצָאֶךָ.

33:22 לַמְמִתִים has been emended to לְמוֹ מֵתִים "to the dead" or לִמְקוֹם מֵתִים on the basis of LXX "in Hades" (Hoff., Perles, Du., Be., Hö.) or to מְמִתִים

"to Death" on the basis of Jer. 16:4; Ezek. 28:8 (Ehr., TS). The meter requires no change, the v. being in a 3:3 pattern and the last word receiving two beats because of its length; cf. *PPS*, p. 67. The MT preserves a reference, not to be eliminated, to the ancient mythological belief in special beings connected with death, that is elaborated upon in postbiblical literature in such phrases as "the angel of the Lord and of Satan" (*Testament of Asher* 6:4). The most common form is, of course, the Angel of Death (*M. Gen. Rabba*, sec. 9, and very often), also מַלְאֲכֵי חַבָּלָה "Angels of Destruction" (*B. Ket.* 104a). The Book of Job preserves a few tantalizing echoes of these beliefs in "The River of Death" (v. 18 above), "the First Born of Mot" (18:13); and "the King of Terrors" (18:14).

33:23 While the Masoretic accentuation links מַלְאָךְ מֵלִיץ, the meter pattern (3:3:3) divides the two nouns between stichs a and b. For other instances of such erroneous stich divisions, cf. Nu. 23:7; Cant. 3:9 (and see *SS ad loc.*). מַלְאָךְ "messenger" is man's representative or spokesman before the Heavenly Court (cf. Ecc. 5:5, "the Temple emissary"). מֵלִיץ from its original meaning of "interpreter" (Gen. 42:23) develops the connotation of "intermediary, advocate" (as in Isa. 43:27 and Job 16:20). T correctly translates it as פרקליט "defense attorney," the Greek *paraclete*. The Angel as man's defender (or prosecutor) is a well-known belief in postbiblical thought (cf. I Enoch 9:3 ff.; 15:2; II Enoch 7:5; Jubilees 30:20; Testament of Levi 3:5; Testament of Dan 6; Testament of Asher 6). The idea becomes fundamental in the rabbinic concept of the High Holy Days as the period when each man is judged by the court on high. (Cf. S. Y. Agnon, *The Days of Awe*, for a comprehensive and poetic collection of the sources.) The later Heb. phrase מֵלִיץ יֹשֶׁר "defender" is based on our v.

אֶחָד מִנִּי־אָלֶף, a hyperbolic phrase = "however rare, difficult to find"; cf. Ecc. 7:27, "one man in a thousand."

Stich c has generally been rendered "to tell to man what is right for him" (D-G, Hö.), but the v. is concerned not with man's moral rehabilitation, but with his physical restoration. If in the heavenly assizes one advocate arises and finds a merit for him, he will be saved from death (v. 24) and become healthy and vigorous once more (v. 25). Hence render: "lit. to proclaim for man his uprightness, i.e. to vouch for his righteousness" (so also P.). לְאָדָם "concerning man"; cf. אָמְרִי־לִי אָחִי הוּא "say about me, 'he is my brother'" (Gen. 20:13). V. 23 is the protasis of a condition and v. 24 the apodosis.

TS offers a surprisingly modern psychological interpretation: "if there is within him, that is in his conscience, one interpreter to tell him what is right."

33:24 The subject of the verb is not the angelic advocate who does not possess the authority to redeem man, but God. The v. is the apodosis of the condition introduced in v. 23: "Then God is gracious to him and says, etc." פְּדָעֵהוּ is generally rendered as פְּדֵהוּ "redeem him." This fails to explain how the familiar Heb. root became the anomalous form in MT. The occurrence of our form in *J. Kid.* I, 61d is an obvious reminiscence of our passage and cannot be invoked as an independent witness, nor is the possible mishnaic orthography with an Aleph פדאהו helpful here. Guillaume makes the clever but unconvincing suggestion that the letter Pe is the Arabic conjunction *fa* and that the rest of the word is the imperative of the Arab. *wadaᶜa*, which he renders "and let him off." Another emendation is פְּרָעֵהוּ "let loose" as in Ex. 32:25; Pr. 1:25; 8:33; 13:18; 15:32 (Ew., Dil., Bi., D-G, Hö.). Generally the term is used in a negative sense, but cf. Pr. 4:15, where the two parallel verbs, though generally used pejoratively, are neutral in meaning: פְּרָעֵהוּ אַל־תַּעֲבָר־בּוֹ שְׂטֵה מֵעָלָיו וַעֲבֹר "Turn loose from him, do not pass near him; turn away from him and pass over." TS, who adopts the same reading, interprets "paid ransom for him" from the rabbinic פרע "pay," which would also be a good parallel to stich c. The rendering "let him loose, free him from going down to the Pit," is completely appropriate as God's command to the angel deputized for this purpose.

כֹּפֶר, originally "redemption money" (Ex. 30:12), is "ransom for a life" (Ps. 49:8; Job 36:13).

33:25 This v. describes his physical rehabilitation, v. 26 the restoration of his close relationship with God, and v. 27 his public avowal of his own unworthiness and God's goodness. Hö. regards v. 25 as the conclusion of the divine fiat rather than as the description of the happy result.

As the context makes clear, רֻטֲפַשׁ must mean "grow fresh." The quadriliteral has been explained (a) as a combination of רטב and טפש "grow fat" (Hakham); (b) as an expansion of רטב plus Sin like פַּרְשֵׁז (פרש plus *Zayin?*) in Job 26:9. The phenomenon may be illustrated in Arab. *ḥalbasa* from *ḥalaba* "deceive with soft words" and Syriac *kulbasa* "basket" from *kelubh* (Guillaume); or (c) טָפַשׁ "grow fat" (Akk. *tapâsu*), which is used metaphorically in Ps. 119:70, with prefixed Reš (cf. infixed Reš in שַׂרְבִיט). It is probably best to explain it (d) as a metathesis for טְרְפַשׁ "grow fat," on the basis of talmudic טרפשׁא "fatty membrane" (D-G, Hö.).

מִנֹּעַר = either "more than in youth" or "by reason of renewed youth." It need not be emended to כִּנֹּעַר "as in youth" (LXX).

33:26 The erstwhile sinner now prays to God and finds favor. רצה is a ritual term used of acceptable sacrifices (Lev. 7:18; Deut. 33:11; Mic. 6:7) and then of God's favor (Ps. 30:8; Ecc. 9:7). The sufferer now sees God's face with sounds of joy (Ps. 27:6; Job 8:21). Cf. Eliphaz's similar conditional promise to Job of restoration to God's favor (22:17). While the phrase in stich b is used elsewhere of visiting the Temple at festivals (Ex. 23:16; 34:20 a. e.), and is undoubtedly derived from this usage, there is no cultic emphasis here — it symbolizes being alive through the favor of God (cf. Jonah 2:5; Ps. 11:7; 84:5).

Stich c has been interpreted: (a) "as God requites man according to his righteousness," or it may be rendered (b) "as He (God) restores to man His blessing upon him, lit. the reward of his righteousness"; cf. Ps. 24:5, where

צְדָקָה is parallel to בְּרָכָה. However, either interpretation of stich c is awkward after stichs a and b, which describe man's state of well-being as already attained. In addition, אֱנוֹשׁ carries here a collective connotation "mankind" rather than that of a single individual; cf. אָדָם in v. 23.

Stich c would find a more natural meaning if it were linked to 27a, "He recounts to men God's goodness." Hence וַיָּשֶׁב has been emended to וַיְבַשֵּׂר "he announces" (Du., Be., D-G, P.) or וַיְסַפֵּר "he tells" (Hö.). However, both emendations are graphically remote. Fortunately they may be dispensed with.

The Latin verb *reddere* "give back" and its English derivative "render" develop the meaning "give something as due or expected" without the idea of "return" (Cassels, *New Latin Dictionary*, p. 505b). Thus Cicero's phrase *honorem reddere*, "give honor," or Horace's *peccatis veniam reddere*, "give forgiveness for sins," is very similar to our passage. The Hebrew הֵשִׁיב has the identical connotation as in the idiom הֵשִׁיב מִנְחָה "pay tribute" (II Ki. 17:3; Ps. 72:10; cf. also II Ki. 3:4; Ezek. 27:15; II Chr. 27:5). Verbs of "giving" similarly mean "ascribe"; cf. יהב (Ps. 29:1); נתן (I Sam. 6:3; Job 36:3). Hence stich c means "he proclaims before men His goodness." On צְדָקָה in the nuance of "goodness," cf. Mal. 3:20; Ps. 35:6; Pr. 21:21, etc. and the later meaning in postbiblical Hebrew of "charity." For the theme of a man's public proclamation of God's goodness after restoration, cf. Ps. 22:31; 35:18; 40:10 f.

Linking stich c to 27a, to which it is parallel, creates 3 distichs instead of two tristichs in vv. 26 and 27.

33:27 On the reasons for linking 26c to 27a, see the Comm. above. יָשֹׁר is not to be derived from the root "to see" (V, Ibn E., Ibn Janah), nor need it be emended to יָשִׁיר (D-G). The *mediae Vav* is a metaplastic form of the *mediae Yod* form of the verb; cf. the Comm. on v. 3. Hence the stich is to be rendered: "He sings out to men." Cf. Pr. 25:20 and the Ugaritic usage adduced by Dahood. *yšr ʿl bʿl* "he sings out before Baal" (NWSPJ, pp. 29 f.).

וְיָשָׁר הֶעֱוֵיתִי "I perverted the right" (cf. Isa. 59:8; Jer. 3:21; Mic. 3:9). וְלֹא־שָׁוָה לִי has been rendered variously: (a) it has been emended to the Piel שִׁוָּה (Du., Hö.) from the root שׁוה = "be smooth, equal," and reading וְלֹא שִׁוָּה לִי כַּעֲוֹנִי "He did not requite me fully according to my sin" (LXX, Du., Hö., Jer. Bible); or (b) reading אֵל לֹא שִׁוָּה לִי "God did not treat me equal (to my sins)" (Bu.). The proposed readings are graphically distant and questionable both in style and meaning. It is simpler to vocalize the verb as a Piel, and render "He did not give me like for like" (TS).

The exact usage, however, of the verb in the Qal with *Lamed* may be explained in terms of the use of the root in the meaning "to be worth" in Esther: וְלַמֶּלֶךְ אֵין שֹׁוֶה לְהַנִּיחָם "it is not worthwhile for the king, i.e., it is not to the king's advantage to let them be" (Est. 3:8); and in וְכָל־זֶה אֵינֶנּוּ שֹׁוֶה לִי "All this is not worthwhile for me" (5:13 and cf. also 7:4). This meaning is common in rabbinic Hebrew, as e.g., שוה לי המות משתתחתני "death is more worthwhile to me than to be married to this man." (*Abot de Rabbi Nathan*, chap. 16). Guillaume compares the Arabic *wala yaswa li* "It is worth-

less to me." Stich c is, therefore, to be rendered "it was not worthwhile for
me, i.e., it did not prove to my advantage." The traditional rendering in
RSV "and it profited me not" is thus much more justifiable than D-G
recognizes.

33:28   The Kethib, in the first person (נַפְשִׁי, חָיָתִי), which makes the v. the
continuation of the former sinner's proclamation, is superior to the Qere,
which reads the third person suff., rendered by T.

33:29   פַּעֲמַיִם שָׁלֹשׁ "twice, thrice," i.e. "several times," is an instance of
ascending numeration. For this usage frequent in Wisdom literature, cf.
the Comm. on 5:19 and 33:14. On the omission of the Vav, cf. Isa. 17:6.

33:30   לְאוֹר is the Niphal infinitive with the elision of the He; cf. Ex. 10:3;
Ezek. 26:15; Pr. 24:17; Lam. 2:11. Render: "To be illumined by the light
of life."

33:32   Stich b is ironic: "I would want to justify you, i.e., declare you in
the right." Elihu insists that he is not arguing for the sake of victory — he
wants the truth to prevail — but he is quite certain that Job has nothing
to say and so he will undertake to teach wisdom to the sinner. The omission
of vv. 31b–33 in LXX (so also Du., Hö., D-G) met the taste of Greek readers
for whom Hebrew parallelism was basically redundant, but not that of
Oriental readers, who find repetition, like the heaping up of epithets, entirely
congenial to their taste. Nor is this passage to be regarded as the beginning
of a new discourse (Du.), for which, incidentally, no proper place is available.
It is characteristic of Elihu's impetuous nature that he calls upon Job to
speak and then gives him no opportunity to do so, even if Job were so
minded. Instead, after catching his breath, Elihu plunges into the fray once
again (chap. 34).

The Second Speech (34)

Citing a proverb which Job himself had quoted, Elihu declares that Job has denied the justice of God only to bolster his own pretensions to innocence. In fact, Job has been guilty of false accusations against God, whose creation of the world is evidence of His love for the world, not His hostility. Actually, God is beholden to no one, and has no need to play favorites. He shows no partiality to rulers or rich men. If He so wills it, He can destroy them in a moment. To be sure, at times He may delay their punishment, but there are good reasons for the postponement. It may be because the misrule of tyrants itself constitutes a penalty upon sinners, since tyrants are instruments of God's justice at work in the lives of men and nations. Or He may be hoping for their genuine repentance.

Elihu calls upon Job to submit to God and ask for His guidance. For how can Job expect that God's actions will be governed by a man's wishes? Charging God with injustice, as Job has done, means, in effect, trying to take His place as judge in the world. Job has demanded that God present the indictment against him. This plea Elihu emphatically endorses. He wants Job to be tested because of his many sins, such as his agreement with evil-doers, his heaping up of iniquity, and his rebellion against God.

34 Then Elihu said,

2   Hear my words, you wise men;
        give ear to me, O men of knowledge.

3   For the ear tests words
        as the palate tastes its food.

4   Let us seek the right together,
        let us decide among ourselves what is good.

5   For Job has said, "I am innocent,
        but God has taken away my right.

6   Though I am in the right, I am counted a liar;
        my wound has no cure, though I am without fault."

7   Where is there a man like Job,
        who laps up blasphemy like water,

8   who is in league with evildoers
        and consorts with wicked men?

9   For he has said, "It does a man no good
        to be in favor with God."

10   Therefore, men of understanding, hear me —
        far be it from God to do evil
        and from the Almighty to do wrong.

11   For according to a man's deeds, God requites him,
        and according to his ways, He ordains his destiny.

12   In truth, God will not act wickedly;
        the Almighty will not pervert justice.

13   Who entrusted the earth to Him,
        and gave Him charge over the whole world?

14   If He should withdraw His spirit
        and gather his breath to Himself,

15   all living things would perish
        and man would return to the dust.

16   Therefore, understand and hear this:
        listen to what I say.

17   Can one who hates justice rule —
        will you condemn God who is both just and strong —

18   who says, even to a king, "You are a knave,"
        and to a nobleman, "You are a villain";

19   who shows no partiality to princes,
        nor favors the rich man over the poor,
        for they are all the work of His hands?

20   In a moment they die — at midnight —
        the rulers are shaken up and pass away,
        and the mighty are removed by no human hand.

21   For God's eyes are on a man's ways
        and He sees all his steps.

22   There is no gloom or deep darkness
        where evildoers may hide.

23   For it is not for man to appoint the hour
        when men are to appear before God in judgment.

24   He crushes mighty men without number
        and sets up others in their stead.

25   Indeed, He destroys their works,
        He overturns them in the night, and they are crushed.

לד

א   וַיַּעַן אֱלִיהוּא וַיֹּאמַר:

2   שִׁמְעוּ חֲכָמִים מִלָּי   וְיֹדְעִים הַאֲזִינוּ לִי:

3   כִּי־אֹזֶן מִלִּין תִּבְחָן   וְחֵךְ יִטְעַם לֶאֱכֹל:

4   מִשְׁפָּט נִבְחֲרָה־לָּנוּ   נֵדְעָה בֵינֵינוּ מַה־טּוֹב:

5   כִּי־אָמַר אִיּוֹב צָדַקְתִּי   וְאֵל הֵסִיר מִשְׁפָּטִי:

6   עַל־מִשְׁפָּטִי אֲכַזֵּב   אָנוּשׁ חִצִּי בְלִי־פָשַׁע:

7   מִי־גֶבֶר כְּאִיּוֹב   יִשְׁתֶּה־לַּעַג כַּמָּיִם:

8   וְאָרַח לְחֶבְרָה עִם־פֹּעֲלֵי אָוֶן   וְלָלֶכֶת עִם־אַנְשֵׁי־רֶשַׁע:

9   כִּי־אָמַר לֹא יִסְכָּן־גָּבֶר   בִּרְצֹתוֹ עִם־אֱלֹהִים:

י   לָכֵן ׀ אַנְשֵׁי לֵבָב שִׁמְעוּ לִי   חָלִלָה לָאֵל מֵרֶשַׁע

11   וְשַׁדַּי מֵעָוֶל: כִּי פֹעַל אָדָם יְשַׁלֶּם־לוֹ

12   וּכְאֹרַח אִישׁ יַמְצִאֶנּוּ:   אַף־אָמְנָם אֵל לֹא־יַרְשִׁיעַ

13   וְשַׁדַּי לֹא־יְעַוֵּת מִשְׁפָּט: מִי־פָקַד עָלָיו אָרְצָה

14   וּמִי שָׂם תֵּבֵל כֻּלָּהּ:   אִם־יָשִׂים אֵלָיו לִבּוֹ

טו   רוּחוֹ וְנִשְׁמָתוֹ אֵלָיו יֶאֱסֹף: יִגְוַע כָּל־בָּשָׂר יָחַד

16   וְאָדָם עַל־עָפָר יָשׁוּב: וְאִם־בִּינָה שִׁמְעָה־זֹּאת

17   הַאֲזִינָה לְקוֹל מִלָּי: הַאַף שׂוֹנֵא מִשְׁפָּט יַחֲבוֹשׁ

18   וְאִם־צַדִּיק כַּבִּיר תַּרְשִׁיעַ:   הַאֲמֹר לְמֶלֶךְ בְּלִיָּעַל

19   רָשָׁע אֶל־נְדִיבִים: אֲשֶׁר לֹא־נָשָׂא ׀ פְּנֵי שָׂרִים

     וְלֹא נִכַּר־שׁוֹעַ לִפְנֵי־דָל   כִּי־מַעֲשֵׂה יָדָיו כֻּלָּם:

כ   רֶגַע ׀ יָמֻתוּ וַחֲצוֹת לָיְלָה   יְגֹעֲשׁוּ עָם וְיַעֲבֹרוּ

21   וְיָסִירוּ אַבִּיר לֹא בְיָד: כִּי־עֵינָיו עַל־דַּרְכֵי־אִישׁ

22   וְכָל־צְעָדָיו יִרְאֶה: אֵין־חֹשֶׁךְ וְאֵין צַלְמָוֶת

23   לְהִסָּתֶר שָׁם פֹּעֲלֵי אָוֶן: כִּי לֹא עַל־אִישׁ יָשִׂים עוֹד

24   לַהֲלֹךְ אֶל־אֵל בַּמִּשְׁפָּט: יָרֹעַ כַּבִּירִים לֹא־חֵקֶר

כה   וַיַּעֲמֵד אֲחֵרִים תַּחְתָּם: לָכֵן יַכִּיר מַעְבָּדֵיהֶם

26   In return for their wickedness, He strikes them down
            in the sight of all men,
27   because they turned aside from Him
            and had no regard for His ways,
28   thus bringing to Him the cry of the poor
            and causing Him to hear the cry of the afflicted.
29   When He grants peace, who can stir up strife;
            but when He hides His face, who can see Him?
30   When both over a nation and over all its members
            He allows a godless man to rule,
            it is because of the sins of the people.

31   Indeed, you should say this to God,
            "I have borne my just punishment; I will offend no more.
32   What I do not see, You teach me.
            If I have done wrong, I will do it no more."
33   Is it by your leave that God should make retribution,
            depending on whether *you* reject or approve — not I?
            What you really know, declare.
34   Men of understanding will say to me,
            and the wise man who hears me will declare,
35   "Job speaks without knowledge;
            his words are without insight.
36   Would that Job were tried to the end
            because of his confidence in evildoers,
37   for he adds constantly to his sins,
            he increases impiety among us
            as he multiplies his words against God."

26 וְהָפַךְ לַיְלָה וְיִדַּכָּאוּ׃   תַּחַת־רְשָׁעִים סְפָקָם

27 בִּמְקוֹם רֹאִים׃   אֲשֶׁר עַל־כֵּן סָרוּ מֵאַחֲרָיו

28 וְכָל־דְּרָכָיו לֹא הִשְׂכִּילוּ׃   לְהָבִיא עָלָיו צַעֲקַת־דָּל

29 וְצַעֲקַת עֲנִיִּים יִשְׁמָע׃   וְהוּא יַשְׁקִט ׀ וּמִי יַרְשִׁעַ

    וְיַסְתֵּר פָּנִים וּמִי יְשׁוּרֶנּוּ   וְעַל־גּוֹי וְעַל־אָדָם יָחַד׃

ל מִמְּלֹךְ אָדָם חָנֵף   מִמֹּקְשֵׁי עָם׃

31 כִּי אֶל־אֵל הֶאָמַר נָשָׂאתִי   לֹא אֶחְבֹּל׃

32 בִּלְעֲדֵי אֶחֱזֶה אַתָּה הֹרֵנִי   אִם־עָוֶל פָּעַלְתִּי לֹא אֹסִיף׃

33 הֲמֵעִמְּךָ יְשַׁלְמֶנָּה ׀ כִּי־מָאַסְתָּ   כִּי־אַתָּה תִבְחַר וְלֹא־אָנִי

34 וּמַה־יָדַעְתָּ דַבֵּר׃   אַנְשֵׁי לֵבָב יֹאמְרוּ לִי

לה וְגֶבֶר חָכָם שֹׁמֵעַ לִי׃   אִיּוֹב לֹא־בְדַעַת יְדַבֵּר

36 וּדְבָרָיו לֹא בְהַשְׂכֵּיל׃   אָבִי יִבָּחֵן אִיּוֹב עַד־נֶצַח

    עַל־תְּשֻׁבֹת בְּאַנְשֵׁי־אָוֶן׃

37 כִּי יֹסִיף עַל־חַטָּאתוֹ פֶשַׁע בֵּינֵינוּ יִסְפּוֹק

    וְיֶרֶב אֲמָרָיו לָאֵל׃

CHAPTER 34

34:2 By the epithet "wise," Elihu is addressing either the Friends or more probably the wise in general. יֹדְעִים "lit. the knowers, men of knowledge," used absolutely in Ecc. 9:11.

34:3 A proverbial quotation used in Job 12:11, which would suggest the reading here וְחֵךְ יִטְעַם לוֹ אֹכֶל (D-G, Ehr.). But this is not absolutely required since quotations in biblical literature are rarely exact.

34:4 נִבְחֲרָה generally rendered "let us choose." The parallelism, however, suggests the possibility that the root here is equivalent to בחן; cf. בְּחַרְתִּיךָ = בְּכוּר עֹנִי בְּחַנְתִּיךָ (Isa. 48:10) and כֶּסֶף נִבְחָר (Pr. 10:20) and the colloquial Palestinian Arabic *baḥḥar* "to look" (TS). This interpretation is, however, not required. Hence either "let us choose" or "let us test."

34:5 Stich b is a citation of 27:2.

34:6 עַל מִשְׁפָּטִי has been rendered: (a) "because I demand my justice" (Ibn E.), or, better (b) "in spite of my being in the right"; cf. עַל־דַּעְתְּךָ "though You know" (10:7); עַל לֹא־חָמָס "though there is no iniquity" (16:17).
אֲכַזֵּב is difficult. It has been rendered: (a) "am I to lie against my right?" (Dil., Del.); (b) "concerning my judgment, I declare it a lie" (Ra.); (c) It has been emended to יְכַזֵּב and the stich rendered: "concerning my judgment, He lies" on the basis of LXX (Hö., P.); (d) it has been emended to אֶכְאָב "I am in pain" (Ehr.), thus creating a parallel with stich b. However, the usage in Pr. 30:6 פֶּן־יוֹכִיחַ בְּךָ וְנִכְזָבְתָּ, "lest He reprove you and you are proved a liar," is precisely what our context requires. Cf. also Ps. 116:11: אֲנִי אָמַרְתִּי בְחָפְזִי כָּל־הָאָדָם כֹּזֵב "I said in my impatience, 'every man is a liar.'" While the *verbum dicendi* is expressed in the Psalm passage, we have a virtual indirect quotation here, i.e. without a *verbum dicendi*. On indirect quotations, cf. *BGM*, pp. 188 f., and the Comm. on 13:14. Render: "In spite of my right, they say that I lie, i.e. I am held to be a liar" (so Ibn E.).
אָנוּשׁ "weak, sick, incurable" (Jer. 15:18; 17:4; Mic. 1:9). חִצִּי need not be emended to מַחֲצִי "my blow" (Ibn E. tacitly, Yel., Hö.). The phrase is a transferred epithet: "My arrow is incurable, i.e. it produces incurable illness"; cf. כָּל־הַדְּבָרִים יְגֵעִים "lit. all things are tired, i.e. produce fatigue" (Ecc. 1:8), and Horace's phrase *tarda podagra*, "the slow gout, i.e. the gout that slows man"; cf. *KMW ad loc*.

34:7 The meter is 3:3. In stich a, מִי receives a full beat, in spite of its brevity; cf. *lū* in Ps. 5:6, *ki* in Ps. 27:5 and the Comm. on 32:18.
The figure in stich b is identical with that used by Eliphaz in 15:16. But while Eliphaz charges Job with lapping up iniquity like water, Elihu

accuses Job of sinful, mocking speech and of consorting with evildoers (v. 8), but not of himself perpetrating wicked deeds (D-G). This subtle but unmistakable shifting of ground is crucial for the understanding of Elihu's position — Job's massive suffering is not necessarily the result of colossal wrong-doing, as it is for the Friends. See *BGM*, chap. IX, and Special Note 30. For Elihu, suffering is primarily preventive, not punitive.

34:8 וְאֹרַח = "to journey, travel, associate with," cf. Ps. 1:1. חֶבְרָה is a fem. Qal infin.; cf. לְיִרְאָה (Deut. 8:6; II Chr. 6:33), לְאַהֲבָה (Deut. 10:15, a. e.), the guttural Heth being vocalized with a Segol. וּלְלֶכֶת which is parallel to וְאֹרַח (not with לְחֶבְרָה, D-G), is the infin. construct consec.; hence = וְהָלַךְ or וַיֵּלֶךְ; cf. לָשׂוּם (5:11) and וּלְבַקֵּשׁ (Ps. 104:21).

34:9 Elihu restates the substance of Job's contention that it does a man no good to be upright (9:22; 21:7 ff.; Mal. 3:13 f.), but the form in which he couches it is derived from Eliphaz (22:2; see the Comm.). יִסְכָּן = "be useful, profitable" is intransitive here and in 15:3; in 22:2 it is transitive. בִּרְצֹתוֹ = not "being well pleased with God" (D-G) but "being in favor with God"; cf. לִרְצֹנְכֶם "that you may find favor" (Lev. 19:5; 22:19 f.; 23:11). Stich b is crucial for the interpretation of 22:2b, which has been widely misunderstood (see the Comm. *ad loc.*).

34:10 The introductory line need not be amplified on metric grounds by an addition like חֲכָמִים הַאֲזִינוּ after לָכֵן (Dil., Bu., D-G). The adjuration is an anacrusis, outside the pattern of the 3:2 meter in this v. The construction of חָלִילָה לָאֵל מֵרֶשַׁע has its exact parallel in חָלִילָה לָּנוּ מִמֶּנּוּ (Jos. 22:29), the verb being dispensed with in the sinewy style of poetry. The force of the Lamed extends to וְשַׁדַּי in stich b.

34:11 יַמְצִאֶנּוּ the Hiphil (cf. 37:13) = "God will cause him to find, attain it, i.e. the consequences of his actions."

34:12 אַף־אָמְנָם a double asseverative: "indeed, in truth," an index of Elihu's passionate convictions.

34:13–15 A description of God's creation of the world and His giving life to His creatures, which He can withdraw at will. These facts testify that God, far from being cruel and malevolent as Job has declared, loves His creatures and is free from injustice in His dealings with them (Bu., Dil., Peake). D-G I, p. 297, doubts whether these ideas are present since they are not explicitly set forth. On the basic role of implication and allusion in biblical and oriental literature generally and in Job in particular, cf. *BGM*, chap. 14.

34:13 אָרְצָה in MT, as in 37:12, is a poetic use of the old accusative ending and is superior to the proposed revocalization אַרְצָה (D-G, Hö.). פָּקַד, the basic meaning of which is "visit, attend to," here has the nuance of "entrust,

deposit for safekeeping (and therefore returnable to the owner)." This meaning is frequent in rabbinic Heb. in the Qal נפשות פקדתם אצלי, "You deposited
souls with me" (*Pesik. Rabbati*, chap. 43), but is more frequent in the Hiphil,
המפקיד אצל חבירו "He who deposits with his neighbor" (*M. B. Metzia* 3:1).
This nuance also appears in biblical Heb. in the Hiphil (Ps. 31:6) and in the
noun פִּקָּדוֹן "deposit" (Gen. 41:36; Lev. 5:21, 23).

34:14   For the reading יָשִׂים in MT of the Occidentals, the Orientals register
a Kethib יָשִׁיב and a Qere יָשִׂים. יָשִׂים לִבּוֹ can only mean "pay heed" and the
stich interpreted"" If God pays attention to man in order to kill him" (Ibn E.),
but this negative connotation cannot be read into the idiom. The Oriental
Kethib יָשִׁיב is unquestionably to be preferred; on the meaning, see below.
The v. also contains too many nouns, the juxtaposition of רוּחוֹ וְנִשְׁמָתוֹ in one
stich being particularly unsatisfactory. לִבּוֹ, which was introduced by error,
perhaps because of the common idiom with יָשִׂים, is to be deleted. In biblical
psychology, the heart is never the seat of life, but the source of understanding
(cf. v. 34) and of desire (Nu. 14:39). Stich a now reads אִם יָשִׁיב אֵלָיו רוּחוֹ,
"If He recalls his breath (i.e. of life) to Himself"; cf. Ps. 104:29; Ecc. 12:3.
　　　The two stichs, now in excellent parallelism, constitute the protasis of
the condition completed in v. 15. If God wished to withdraw the spirit of life
from His creatures, all life would end. The implication would not be lost
upon the Hebrew reader — since God does not do this, He is obviously
beneficent toward His creatures.

34:16   אִם is not "if" but the emphatic, "indeed"; cf. Arab. *inna* and 6:13;
8:4; 14:5; 17:2, 13, 16 and the Comm. *ad loc.* בִּינָה is accented on the first
syllable, hence it is not the noun but the imperative of the verb בִּין with
cohortative He: "Therefore understand and hear this!"

34:17   Elihu argues that it is inconceivable that an enemy of justice should
rule and, therefore, Job cannot be permitted to condemn God who is righteous
as well as powerful. This argument, like the frequent appeal of the Friends
to superior age as the guarantee of superior wisdom, is far less impressive to
us than it was to the poet's contemporaries. Its force can be understood only
if the upper-class social milieu of Wisdom literature be kept in mind. Because
of their upper-class orientation, Wisdom writers regard it as self-evident that
those who rule are righteous and just (cf. Pr. 8:15, 16; 16:10–15; 20:8 f.;
22:11; 25:4 f.). Hence if God rules, He is *ipso facto* righteous. Cf. "The
Social Background of Wisdom Literature," in *PPS*, chap. 6. Obviously it
is this "self-evident" assumption that Job calls into question, scandalizing
his Friends in the process.
　　　הַאַף is an emphatic, used in questions, "indeed, really!"; cf. Gen. 18:23;
Am. 2:11. Hence "Can an enemy of justice really rule?" חבש "bind up"
(Ex. 29:9; Hos. 6:1) develops the meanings "control" and "rule"; cf. חֹבֵשׁ
(Isa. 3:7). For a similar semantic development, cf. the verb עצר "restrain,"
and יֹרֵשׁ עֶצֶר "ruler" (Jud. 18:7). In spite of the difficulties of this last passage,

the meaning of the verb is supported by the usage in the Egyptian *Tale of Sinuhe*: "My children grew up to be strong men, each man the restrainer (i.e. ruler) of his own tribe" (*ANET*, p. 162a).

צַדִּיק כַּבִּיר lit. "the righteous, powerful one"; the asyndeton is common in Arabic (Ewald). The proposal to emend the text to read וְאִם מַצְדִּיק כַּבִּיר תַּרְשִׁיעַ is not only unnecessary; it cannot mean, "Will you condemn Him who judges the mighty?" (P.), since מַצְדִּיק means not "judges" but "justifies, acquits." Elihu denies that an enemy of justice can rule; God is the righteous, powerful One. תַּרְשִׁיעַ is declarative, "Will you call wicked?"

34:18 The interrogative form הַאֲמֹר in MT, which is an anomalous combination of the interrogative particle and the infin. constr., can only be interpreted as "Is it proper to say to the king, 'you are an evildoer'?" (Ra., Ibn E., AV). As all moderns have recognized, the form is to be vocalized הָאֹמֵר "who says" (LXX, P, V), carrying on the description of God as the powerful, righteous One in v. 17. Vv. 18 and 19 describe God's justice. He castigates kings and noblemen when they are evil and shows no partiality against the poor. Stich a: "Who says even to a king 'wicked'." בְּלִיַּעַל is the all-inclusive term for "scoundrel, evildoer" (Deut. 13:14; I Sam. 30:22), one of the few compound nouns in biblical Hebrew. It is generally interpreted as בְּלִי יַעַל "without value" (cf. the root יעל meaning "be useful" in the Hiphil). Possibly it is an imprecation: "May He not ascend יַעַל (from the grave!")"; cf. the parallel with שְׁאוֹל (II Sam. 22:5 = Ps. 18:6). Stich b: " 'wicked' to a nobleman." In view of the singular רָשָׁע, נְדִיבִים is to be understood either as נָדִיב + enclitic Mem or the plural is to be construed as distributive: "to each nobleman"; cf. the Comm. on 40:29.

34:19 Stich a "He shows no partiality to princes." נִכַּר here does not carry the connotation of the verb in 21:29 (cf. the Comm. *ibid.*). It is either the Niphal "the rich is not recognized above the poor" or, better, the Piel equal to the Hiphil: "He does not recognize, etc." (Ibn E.). שׁוֹעַ "noble, opulent ‖ to נָדִיב (Isa. 32:5). כֻּלָּם = "both, i.e. the rich and the poor."

34:20 This difficult verse apparently contains a description of the instantaneous destruction of the wicked. וַחֲצוֹת לָיְלָה = "at midnight." יְגֹעֲשׁוּ עָם has been emended to יִגַּע שׁוֹעִים which is taken to mean "He smites the princes" (Bu., Kissane), or to יִגְוְעוּ שׁוֹעִים (Be., Du., D-G, Hö.), or שָׂרִים (Ehr.), "Princes die," but the proposed changes are unnecessary. עָם is here obviously used idiomatically in the connotation of "the upper classes, i.e. the People that count," cf. אָמְנָם כִּי אַתֶּם־עָם "indeed you are the People" (cf. Job 12:2 and see the Comm.) and the English use of "society" to refer to the aristocracy. Hence stich b = "the rulers are shaken up and pass away." For the verb, cf. Ps. 18:8; Jer. 25:16.

וְיָסִירוּ is a use of the third person plural as an impersonal: "The mighty is removed"; cf. 4:19; 6:2; 7:3 and see Ges.-K., sec. 144, 3, b.

לֹא בְיָד "by no human hand, but by God"; cf. Lam. 4:6; Dan. 2:34;

8:25 and see the Comm. on 20:26.

אַבִּיר = "mighty, powerful One," cf. Jud. 5:22; Jer. 46:15; Job 24:22. The change from plural to singular, especially in dealing with a class, is frequent.

The caesura. comes after לַיְלָה, as noted by the Masorah. The v. is a tristich in 4:3:3 meter, identical in pattern with v. 19.

34:23   Stich a, which Ibn E. passes over in silence, is meaningless in MT, as is clear from the proposed interpretations: (a) "He does not make false accusations against His creatures" (Ra.); or (b) "He does not still (or long) consider a man" (Dil.); (c) "He does not long attack a man," on the basis of שִׂים "set a siege" in I Ki. 20:12 (Hi.); (d) "He need not further lay it upon man," which is taken to mean that God has no need to ask man to appear in judgment, since He knows all men's thoughts (TS); (e) "For of a man He takes no further notice" (D-G). It is obvious that none of these renderings, aside from their intrinsic difficulties, are borne out by the text. Hence Reiske's brilliant emendation יָשִׂים מוֹעֵד "set a time" (cf. Ex. 9:5) has been widely accepted (Wr., Bu., Be., P.). The stich is then rendered: "For not for a man does He appoint a stated time," and explained to mean that God does not fix a time for man's judgment. However, the combination עַל אִישׁ יָשִׂים מוֹעֵד as "set a time for man" is awkward. Moreover, the idea that God does not specify the hour of judgment scarcely strengthens Elihu's position. On the contrary, this has been the complaint of Job (24:1; see the Comm.) and of the unconventional Wisdom teachers generally — that God's time of judgment remains unknown to man (cf. Ecc. 9:17 ff. and passim, and see *KMW*).

We, therefore, suggest modifying Reiske's emendation to read עַל לֹא אִישׁ שִׂים מוֹעֵד and render the verse, "It is not for man to set the time to go to God for judgment," i.e. man has no right to insist on a given time for God's judgment, as Job has done in demanding that retribution come at once and without delay; cf. 21:19a, 30. Traditional religion regarded as blasphemous the effort to "force God's hand." Thus rabbinic Judaism looked askance at efforts to compute the date of the advent of the Messiah. Cf. A. H. Silver, *Messianic Speculations in Ancient Israel* (1927).

לֹא עַל־אִישׁ is emphatic; note the word order = "not for man is it proper." For this use of עַל in the sense of "incumbent, proper" with an infinitive (שִׂים) as the subject, cf. וְעָלַי לָתֶת לְךָ "It would be incumbent upon me to give" (II Sam. 18:11); עַל הָאֶחָד לְכַלְכֵּל (I Ki. 4:7); עָלֵינוּ לַעֲשׂוֹת (Ezra 10:12; Neh. 13:13); and the famous prayer עָלֵינוּ לְשַׁבֵּחַ "It is incumbent upon us to praise the Lord." The preposition also occurs with a noun as the subject (Nu. 7:9; Ezek. 45:17; Ezra 7:11; Neh. 11:23; I Chr. 9:27, 33). In our poetic context the infinitive שִׂים is used without the Lamed although it would be easy to change the Yod of MT יָשִׂים to Lamed and read כִּי לֹא עַל אִישׁ לָשִׂים מוֹעֵד.

Stich b, "to go to God seeking judgment," employs the verb *hālakh*; cf. the similar use of *bō* (Deut. 17:9; Isa. 1:23).

34:24 יָרֹעַ from the geminate root רעע "crush, smash" (Ps. 2:9; Isa. 24:19), an Aramaism for the Hebrew רצץ. לֹא חֵקֶר does not mean "without the need of investigation" (D-G), but "without limit," the exact meaning in 5:9; 9:10; 36:26.

34:25 לָכֵן = "indeed" as in Isa. 26:14; Jer. 5:2; and perhaps in Gen. 4:15; cf. Arab. *lakinna*.

מַעְבָּדֵיהֶם an Aramaism, the noun occurring in Dan. 4:34 and common in Syriac, with a variant in Ecc. 9:1 עֲבָדֵיהֶם = "their deeds." The usual rendering "He knows their deeds" is unsatisfactory, both because of the absence of parallelism and the fact that the stich occurs in the midst of the description of the destruction of the wicked. We suggest that יַכִּיר is a defective orthography for יַעֲכֹר. The root עכר is rendered in the lexicons "disturb, trouble," but it carries the stronger connotation of "destroy" in the episode of Achan (Jos. 7:25, 26), the sacrifice of Jephthah's daughter (Jud. 11:35), the confrontation of Elijah and Ahab (I Ki. 18:17 f.), in the use of the noun נֶעְכֶּרֶת "calamity" (Pr. 15:6), as well as in Pr. 11:17, 29; 15:27. For instances of omitted Ayin, cf. Am. 8:8 נשקה Kethib, נִשְׁקָעָה Qere; יָשֵׁן = יֵעָשַׁן (Hos. 7:6), the proper name רות (= רְעוּת; cf. Pešita) and the place name בַּעֲלָה (Jos. 15:29), spelled בָּלָה (in Jos. 19:3). Hence render the v., which now exhibits excellent parallelism:

> "Indeed, He destroys their works,
> He overturns them in the night and they are crushed."

34:26 Stich a: "In the place of (or, instead of) the wicked, He strikes them down" (Ehr., Ter.) would imply that the mighty are themselves not wicked. The best procedure available is to assume a reversal of the pronominal and the nominal objects and treat the stich as equivalent to: "In their place, i.e. where they stand, He strikes down the wicked," a dubious procedure at best. Hence various emendations have been proposed, none of which commend themselves, including the best, תַּחַת חֲמָתוֹ רְשָׁעִים, which is taken to mean "His wrath shatters the wicked" (Bi., Bu.). We propose a revocalization to read תַּחַת רִשְׁעָם, "In return, i.e. in recompense, for their evil, He strikes them down." On this meaning "in return for, in recompense for" for תַּחַת, cf. לָמָּה שִׁלַּמְתֶּם רָעָה תַּחַת טוֹבָה (Gen. 44:4; also I Sam. 25:21; II Sam. 16:12; Ps. 38:21; 109:4). The noun רֶשַׁע "wickedness" occurs in vv. 8, 10, also 35:8. For its use with suffixes, cf. Deut. 9:27; Jer. 14:20; Job 35:6.

ספק generally "clap hands," in anger (Nu. 24:10), or in mockery (Lam. 2:15), here means "slap, chastise" (BDB) or "strike down."

בִּמְקוֹם רֹאִים "lit. in the place of seers, i.e. in the place where all can see, publicly."

34:27 אֲשֶׁר עַל־כֵּן = "because"; cf. כִּי עַל־כֵּן (Nu. 10:31; Ps. 45:3). הִשְׂכִּיל from its basic meaning "be prudent, wise" develops a variety of connotations including "wise in understanding God's will"; it is parallel to ידע ה' (Jer.

9:23); to בִּין (Ps. 94:8); cf. also Ps. 119:99; Dan. 9:13, 25; 11:35; 12:3. Hence here "pay heed, follow God's way."

34:28 לְהָבִיא. Like לְמַעַן, the Lamed of purpose becomes tantamount to a Lamed of result (BDB, p. 775b); cf. the Greek *hoti*, Latin *ut*, and see Jer. 7:19; Am. 2:7, etc. אֵלָיו = עָלָיו "to Him." The evildoer turns away from God (v. 27) and oppresses the poor so that their cry comes to God (v. 28).

34:29–33 These vv. are justly described by D-G (vol. 1, pp. 301 ff.) as being on the whole unintelligible or at least ambiguous. The passage has probably suffered textual damage which is unfortunately not reparable today. LXX omits the vv. Like all other efforts at interpretation which may be studied in the Commentaries, our renderings are tentative and uncertain. In view of the unconvincing and often unhebraic character of the emendations proposed, we prefer to interpret the MT, which is generally superior to the alternatives, in addition to possessing the basic advantage of being a datum and not merely a hypothesis.

34:29 Stich a: "When He grants quiet" suggests that יַרְשִׁעַ must mean "stir up, disturb." The meaning of the root probably derives from its etymology; cf. Arab. *rasaᶜa* "be loose (of limbs)." The emendations יַרְעֵשׁ (Hi., Del.) and יְשַׁע (Ehr.) are *Schlimmverbesserungen* (Bu.). The usage may be a reminiscence of Deutero-Isaiah, whose influence on Job, both in form and in content, is far-reaching. The prophet has declared הָרְשָׁעִים כַּיָּם נִגְרָשׁ כִּי הַשְׁקֵט לֹא יוּכָל "The wicked are like the raging sea that cannot rest" (Isa. 57:20). When God grants peace, man is powerless to counter His will. Stichs c and d are in antithetic parallelism to a and b, "But if God hides His face (in displeasure), who can see Him (and find favor with Him)?" God's hidden face is a calamity for man (Deut. 31:20; Isa. 8:17; 54:8; 64:6; Mic. 3:4). The idea of הסתר פנים (*Deus absconditus*) receives elaborate development in postbiblical thought, particularly in mysticism.

For stich e, which we attached to the following v., see below. This improves the rhythm of both vv. substantially.

34:30 The MT is only slightly more comprehensible than the various emendations proposed! Ra. renders vv. 30, 31: "He quiets, i.e. subdues the evildoer who rules over the poor because of the people's sins." Ibn E. adds "He causes the evildoer to rule only in order to take vengeance upon them." Both interpretations represent an unconscious or tacit emendation of מִמְּלֹךְ to מַמְלִיךְ, a reading which virtually all moderns propose. Ehr. changes יַחַד to יֶחֱזֶ (from חזה) and renders "Yet He watches over nations and tribes, that no evil man rule nor the people fall into peril."

We suggest, very tentatively, joining the last five words of v. 29 to v. 30 and reading as follows: וְעַל־גּוֹי וְעַל אָדָם יָחַד מַמְלִיךְ אָדָם חָנֵף מִמֹּקְשֵׁי עָם. The double Vav means "both . . . and" as in Arab. *wa . . . wa*; cf. Gen. 34:28; Nu. 9:14; Jos. 9:23; Ps. 76:7; Ecc. 12:2 (cf. *KMW ad loc.*); Dan 8:13; Neh. 12:29;

and see BDB, s.v. Vav 1, h, p. 253a. Render: "When over both a nation and all its people He permits a godless man to rule." אָדָם either "an individual" (cf. Lev. 1:2; 13:2) or "the constituent elements of the nation." יַחַד is a poetical synonym for כָּל "all"; cf. Ps. 33:15; 34:15; 41:8; Job 3:18; 34:16, etc.

מִמֹּקְשֵׁי עָם lit. "because of the snares set by the people, i.e. because of the offenses committed by them" (so substantially Ter.). The phrase is being construed as a subjective genitive.

V. 29 has indicated that God brings disaster upon men when He so chooses. In our view, v. 30 adds that God permits evildoers to hold sway in order to punish men and nations who have themselves been guilty of seeking to snare the innocent. That the tyrant is God's instrument for achieving justice in the world is the essence of Isaiah's doctrine of Assyria as "the rod of God's anger" (Isa. 10:5 ff.). This prophetic insight is here transferred from the nations to the life of the individual. Similarly, Deutero-Isaiah's recognition that national suffering need not necessarily be the result of national sin is transposed by the author of Job to the experience of the individual; it constitutes the essence of the response to suffering that is implicit in the Speeches of the Lord. Cf. *BGM*, pp. 132 ff., 145, 154, and see Special Note 32.

In addition, our passage contains an implied observation that the oppressed and the downtrodden are not necessarily paragons of virtue themselves — an idea intrinsically true, to be sure, but highly congenial to upperclass thinking.

For the theme of the passage, we may compare the classic utterance of Hillel: "Hillel saw a skull floating upon the waters. He said to it, 'Because you drowned others, you were drowned, and the end of those who drowned you is that they too will be drowned' " (*M. Abot* 1:6).

34:31 MT הֶאָמַר can only be rendered interrogatively: "Has he ever said (or can He ever say)?" (Ibn E., Ra., Dil., AV, RSV, Ter.). Another rendering, though appropriate to the context: "Surely it is proper to say to God," cannot be squared with MT. The verb has also been emended to the Niphal infinitive הֵאָמֵר and rendered "To God it should be said" (D-G, Ehr.). However, a direct address to Job is preferable to this oblique general formulation. Hence, read with a slight change in the word division, כִּי אֶל אֱלוֹהַּ אֱמֹר "But say instead to God, 'I have borne my punishment, I will offend no more.' " (Cf. P מטול דאלהא אמר in part; so also Be., Richter.)

נשא, which is frequent with objects like חֵטְא, עָוֹן, פֶּשַׁע, etc. (cf. BDB, p. 671a), is here used elliptically: "bear guilt, punishment." חבל "offend, act harmfully" (Neh. 1:7; cf. Job 17:1), frequent in Aram. (Dan. 4:20; חֲבוּלָה "offense against a king," Dan. 6:23). On this view, the v. links up excellently with the following v.

34:32 בִּלְעֲדֵי is a preposition in the construct, with a clause as *nomen regens*; cf. מִן (Deut. 33:11); אַחֲרֵי (Jer. 2:8); אַשְׁרֵי (Ps. 65:5, etc.). Hence stich a: "lit. apart from what I see, i.e. what I do not see, You teach me." The parallelism with stich b is excellent.

34:33 It is foolhardy in the extreme to attempt to interpret or to emend this crux! The massive problems involved are highlighted in these varied renderings:

AV: "Shall it be according to thy mind? He will recompense it, whether thou refuse or whether thou choose; not I."

RSV: "Will He then make requital to suit you — because you rejected? For you must choose and not I."

NEB: "Will He at these words condone your rejection of Him? It is for you to decide, not me."

D-G: "According to thy judgment, will he repay it? That (or because), thou hast refused it. For (or that) thou shouldst choose, not I."

Terrien: "Shall he recompense according to thy mind, and not I, just because thou refusest?"

Ehr. offers an ingenious interpretation. He treats כִּי־אַתָּה תִבְחַר וְלֹא־אָנִי as a quotation of Job's address to God, the direct object of the verb מָאַסְתָּ. In stich c, וּמָה is given the meaning "nothing" and דַּבֵּר is emended to דָּבָר. Ehr. then renders: "Shall he impose retribution according to your mind? Because you hate (to say) 'you choose, not I,' while you really know nothing."

The unsatisfactory character of all these valiant efforts to wrestle with an extraordinarily difficult v. is obvious. We suggest the following: הֲמֵעִמְּךָ "Is it from you, i.e. by your leave, with your consent?" (so Ra., Ibn E., D-G). On this meaning for מֵעִמְּךָ "originating from you or, being authorized by you," cf. the use of מֵעִם (Gen. 41:32; 1 Sam. 20:7; II Sam. 3:28; I Ki. 12:15; Isa. 8:18) and מִן (Nu. 32:22; Jer. 51:5b; Job 4:17).

יְשַׁלְּמֶנָּה "That God make recompense" (Gen. 44:4; II Sam. 3:39; Jer. 18:20; Ps. 35:12; Pr. 11:31; 13:13). The fem. suffix is neuter, referring to men's actions.

The words כִּי־מָאַסְתָּ כִּי־אַתָּה תִבְחַר containing two contrasting verbs both in the second person seem to belong together; cf. Isa. 7:15 for the use of these two verbs. It is idle to speculate whether the original text had both verbs in the same tense, as, e.g., כִּי תִמְאַס וְכִי תִבְחַר אַתָּה וְלֹא אָנִי. The words may tentatively be rendered: "Whether you reject (lit. despise) or whether you approve (lit. choose) — you not I!"

The sense of the entire passage would be as follows: By charging God with injustice, Job has in effect set himself up as the sole judge of God's actions, since he has not deigned even to invite other men like Elihu to share in the decision-making. Elihu now questions whether God should thus be dependent on Job's opinion in governing the world. This interpretation articulates well with the following verses. As against Job's unilateral assumption of authority, the consensus of wise men regards Job as both foolish (v. 35) and impious (vv. 36 f.).

וּמַה יָדַעְתָּ דַּבֵּר requires no emendation: "What you really know — speak out!"

34:34 אַנְשֵׁי לֵבָב "men of understanding." In stich b the relative is understood: "and the wise man who hears me will declare," the verb of stich a being understood here.

34:35 The closing vv. of the chapter, 35–37, constitute the citation of the words of the wise about Job addressed to Elihu.

בְּהַשְׂכֵּיל is the Hiphil of the infinitive used here as a noun; cf. Jer. 3:15 and הַמְשֵׁל (Job 25:1, and the Comm. *ad loc.*). The orthography represents the infinitive construct that is normal with a prefix; the vocalization renders the infinitive absolute used as a noun; either is satisfactory.

34:36 אָבִי manifestly not "my Father" (Ra., Ibn E.), a term never applied to God in the book. Nor is it to be emended to אִיּוֹב (Be.) or אֲבוֹי "alas," as in Pr. 23:29 (G. Hoffmann). It is best regarded as a noun derived from the root אבה "wish, desire"; cf. modern Arab. ʾabi "please" (Wetzstein, Del., Hö.) and I Sam. 24:11; II Ki. 5:13, where this meaning is preferable (P.). Hence render here: "It is my desire" (so Ibn Janah; T has a conflate: "I desire that my father in Heaven test Job"). For this meaning, cf. תְּוִי (and the Comm. on 31:35) and perhaps בִּי "please" (from בעה "request," but see BDB, p. 106a).

עַד נֶצַח is a hyperbole "for a long time"; cf. Lam. 5:20.

עַל-תְּשֻׁבֹת בְּאַנְשֵׁי אָוֶן is generally rendered "because of his responses like evil men" (D-G, Hö.). In the meaning of "answer," תְּשׁוּבָה occurs in biblical Hebrew only in Job 21:34, but it is common in postbiblical Hebrew, becoming a technical term for a rabbinic *Responsum*. If this interpretation is adopted, בְּאַנְשֵׁי must be emended to read כְּאַנְשֵׁי (D-G, Hö.).

We believe that the change is unnecessary. In a study of the semantics of the root שוב (*JBL*, vol. 52, 1933, pp. 153–62), we pointed out that the root develops the meaning of "confidence, trust, security," as for instance, בְּשׁוּבָה וָנַחַת (Isa. 30:15); מְשׁוּבַת פְּתָיִם ‖ שַׁלְוַת כְּסִילִים (Pr. 1:32). Our stich may therefore be rendered; "because of his confidence in evil men." This rendering is appropriate in the context. Job's confidence in evil men, like his consorting with them (v. 7), adds to his iniquities.

34:37 The v. exhibits a 3:3:3 meter with כִּי receiving a beat or עַל-חַטָּאתוֹ receiving two; for the principle involved, see *PPS*, p. 67. The caesura comes after חַטָּאתוֹ. In the usual division, בֵּינֵינוּ יִסְפּוֹק is rendered "among us he claps his hands, his derision" (D-G), which is jejune. The stich is then deleted as a gloss (D-G), but see Special Note 30.

With the meter suggested above, יִסְפּוֹק has פֶּשַׁע as its direct object. On the basis of the postbiblical and Aram. noun סָפֵק "doubt," the stich has been rendered "his transgressions he puts in doubt, i.e. denies" (Dh., P.). However, doubt and denial are not synonymous and no verb derived from the noun exists in rabbinic Heb. It is preferable to treat our verb as a metaplastic form of the root שפק "suffice, abound," its common significance in Aram., rabbinic Heb., and Syriac. For this meaning in biblical Heb., cf. the use in אִם־יִשְׂפֹּק עֲפַר שֹׁמְרוֹן "will the dust of Samaria be enough?" (I Ki. 20:10); וּבְיַלְדֵי נָכְרִים יַשְׂפִּיקוּ "they abound in foreign offspring" (Isa. 2:6; B. S. 15:18), and other instances. Hence render stich b: "He increases iniquity among us" and note the perfect parallelism with the verbs יֹסִיף and וְיֶרֶב in stichs a and c respectively. Here the verb is transitive, like the English verb *increase* itself. Also, see the Comm. on 36:18.

פֶּשַׁע here carries its original connotation of "rebellion against higher authority" be it human (I Ki. 12:18; II Ki. 1:1, etc.), or divine (Isa. 1:28; Hos. 14:10; Am. 4:4, etc.). Hence it virtually = "impiety."

Elihu's second speech, which has consisted of distichs virtually through-out (except vv. 19, 20; on v. 29 see the Comm.), ends in a tristich, one of the five methods available to a poet seeking to close his composition with greater power and effectiveness; cf. *PPS*, pp. 70 f.

The Third Speech (35)

Here Elihu completes his principal rejoinder to Job. Job has argued that it does man no good to live in harmony with God's will. Elihu now insists on the converse — God is so far exalted beyond man that it is ludicrous to imagine that man's actions affect Him either for good or for ill. One has only to observe the glories of nature to see evidence of the creative power of God. It is a man's fellow human beings who are affected or injured by his deeds.

Elihu then suggests another reason for the delay sometimes observed in the working of retribution in the world. All too often the sufferers cry out merely because of the pain, rather than from a genuine desire for God's presence. To be sure, such an observation is particularly congenial to a member of the upper classes, but the truth of the insight in unassailable. Elihu uses this fact to blunt the edge of the argument which he cannot totally deny, that oppression is rampant in society.

Though phrased in general terms, Elihu's contention is an oblique criticism of Job's motives in calling for God — not piety, but pain, is the driving force behind his outbursts. Nevertheless, Elihu concludes, God's justice does operate in the world and it is folly to deny it.

35 And Elihu said,

2   Do you consider this to be right,
        to say, "I am more righteous than God!"

3   or to ask, "What advantage is it for you,
        what good if I avoid sin?"

4   I will answer you,
        and your friends along with you.

5   Look up at the heavens, and see —
        behold the clouds, far above you.

6   If you sin, how do you injure Him;
        if your offenses are many, what harm is it to Him?

7   If you are righteous, what are you giving Him,
        What benefit does He receive from your hand?

8   Your wickedness affects only a man like yourself,
        and your righteousness, a fellow human being.

9   Because they are greatly oppressed, men are driven to cry out;
        they call for help because of the power of the mighty.

10   But no one says, "Where is God, my Maker,
        who sends forth songs in the night,

11   who teaches us more than the beasts of the earth
        and makes us wiser than the birds of heaven?"

12   Then men cry out — but He does not answer —
        because of the pride of evil men.

13   But it is not true that God does not hear,
        and that the Almighty does not see.

14   Although you say that you do not see Him,
        Yield before Him and trust in Him.

15   For now, if you do not, He keeps His wrath alive,
        being well aware of men's transgression.

16   Yet Job keeps mouthing empty talk,
        and multiples words without knowledge.

לה א   וַיַּעַן אֱלִיהוּ וַיֹּאמַר:

2   הֲזֹאת חָשַׁבְתָּ לְמִשְׁפָּט   אָמַרְתָּ צִדְקִי מֵאֵל:

3   כִּי־תֹאמַר מַה־יִּסְכָּן־לָךְ   מָה־אֹעִיל מֵחַטָּאתִי:

4   אֲנִי אֲשִׁיבְךָ מִלִּין   וְאֶת־רֵעֶיךָ עִמָּךְ:

ה   הַבֵּט שָׁמַיִם וּרְאֵה   וְשׁוּר שְׁחָקִים גָּבְהוּ מִמֶּךָּ:

6   אִם־חָטָאתָ מַה־תִּפְעָל־בּוֹ   וְרַבּוּ פְשָׁעֶיךָ מַה־תַּעֲשֶׂה־לּוֹ:

7   אִם־צָדַקְתָּ מַה־תִּתֶּן־לוֹ   אוֹ מַה־מִיָּדְךָ יִקָּח:

8   לְאִישׁ־כָּמוֹךָ רִשְׁעֶךָ   וּלְבֶן־אָדָם צִדְקָתֶךָ:

9   מֵרֹב עֲשׁוּקִים יַזְעִיקוּ   יְשַׁוְּעוּ מִזְּרוֹעַ רַבִּים:

י   וְלֹא־אָמַר אַיֵּה אֱלוֹהַּ עֹשָׂי   נֹתֵן זְמִרוֹת בַּלָּיְלָה:

11   מַלְּפֵנוּ מִבַּהֲמוֹת אָרֶץ   וּמֵעוֹף הַשָּׁמַיִם יְחַכְּמֵנוּ:

12   שָׁם יִצְעֲקוּ וְלֹא יַעֲנֶה   מִפְּנֵי גְּאוֹן רָעִים:

13   אַךְ־שָׁוְא לֹא־יִשְׁמַע אֵל   וְשַׁדַּי לֹא יְשׁוּרֶנָּה:

14   אַף כִּי־תֹאמַר לֹא תְשׁוּרֶנּוּ   דִּין לְפָנָיו וּתְחוֹלֵל לוֹ:

טו   וְעַתָּה כִּי־אַיִן פָּקַד אַפּוֹ   וְלֹא־יָדַע בַּפַּשׁ מְאֹד:

16   וְאִיּוֹב הֶבֶל יִפְצֶה־פִּיהוּ   בִּבְלִי־דַעַת מִלִּין יַכְבִּר:

CHAPTER 35

35:2 לְמִשְׁפָּט = "lit. to be the right, the truth," hence "right, true." Stich b: not "my righteousness is before God" but "my righteousness is greater than God's" (Del., Ew.).

35:3 מַה־יִּסְכָּן־לָךְ "What profit is it for you?" Since the passage is Elihu's restatement of Job's alleged views, לָךְ cannot refer to God, but to Job him-self. Hence stich a would be an indirect quotation and stich b a direct one. The opposite shift occurs in 19:28; 22:17 is doubtful. See the Comm. *ad loc.* Many moderns emend לָךְ to לִי (Gr., Du., Be., Bu., Hö.) and thus convert the entire v. to a direct quotation. For an instance of an indirect "virtual quotation," cf. the Comm. on 13:14.

Stich b has been rendered: (a) "What do I gain more than if I had sinned?" (Ra., D-G, P.); (b) "What would I profit from my sin?" (P.), but this can hardly be a restatement of Job's position, even by an opponent; (c) "than if I had appeased Him" (TS) on the basis of a rabbinic and Aram. use of the Hithpael התחטא, but the precise meaning and semantics of this latter verb are themselves unclear; cf. the Comm. on 41:17.

It is clear that the exigencies of meter have led to a breviloquence here. For another instance of such a contraction because of metrical needs, also involving the Mem of separation, cf.

שֶׁהֶם זָבוּ מְדֻקָּרִים מִתְּנוּבוֹת שָׂדָי

Better are those stabbed by the sword
    than (those who perish for lack of) the fruits of the field.
(Lam. 4:9, and see *CL ad loc.*)

In our v., the Mem of separation occurs without a verb, as, e.g., מֵעֵינֵי הָעֵדָה "if the thing be done away from the eyes of the community" (Nu. 15:24); מֵרִיב (Pr. 20:3). The Mem is therefore = "without," as in מִמּוּם (Job 11:1); מִפַּחַד (21:9; Pr. 1:33), מִדַּעַת "so that he has no knowledge" (Jer. 10:14; I Sam. 15:23; Isa. 7:8; 52:14; Jer. 48:45; Pr. 30:7, and see BDB, s.v. מִן, 1b, 7b). Hence "by my being removed from sin."

35:4 This v., like chap. 32, is highly significant in indicating Elihu's position which is opposed not only to Job but to that of the Friends as well. רֵעֶיךָ does not refer to "wicked men," but to Job's three Friends. It is clear that the Elihu speeches are not a mere restatement of the Friends' position. See *BGM*, chap. 9, and Special Note 28.

35:5 Since the abode of God in the heavens is so far from man, how can man's actions affect God? (Ehr.). In 22:11 ff. this distance is alleged to be the reason for Job's wrongdoing.

35:6 בּוֹ "against Him." תִּפְעָל with *Qames hatuph* goes back to תִּפְעֹל instead of the usual תִּפְעַל; cf. יִמְעַל (Pr. 16:10) as against תִּמְעַל (Lev. 5:15).

35:9 מֵרוֹב עֲשׁוּקִים: "Because of the multitude of oppressions, men cry out."
This generally accepted meaning of רוֹב = "multitude" is preferable to other
suggested views: (a) "strife, violence," the meaning assigned to רִיב in Ps.
55:10, with the *mediae Vav* being regarded as equivalent to *mediae Yod* as
in Jud. 11:25; or (b) "fear, dismay," a meaning TS finds in 4:3, 14; 26:3; 29:16.

עֲשׁוּקִים is rendered by the Vss. as the Qal participle passive, "the oppressed ones," as the subject of the verb יַזְעִיקוּ with רַבִּים in stich b adduced
as a parallel. However, עֲשׁוּקִים may also be understood as an abstract noun,
"acts of oppression" (Am. 3:9; Ecc. 4:1 first time). יַזְעִיקוּ the Hiphil equivalent
to Qal, used impersonally: "Men cry out."

In stich b, רַבִּים need not be construed as the subject of יְשַׁוֵּעוּ which is
impersonal. רַבִּים = "the mighty, powerful ones," the *nomen regens* for זְרוֹעַ;
cf. מֶלֶךְ רָב "the great king" (Ps. 48:3), בָּתִּים רַבִּים "great houses" (Am. 3:15),
a meaning which inheres also in Isa. 53:12 and Am. 5:12 (note the parallelism).

35:10 וְלֹא אָמַר the third person masc. sing. verb is impersonal, "But no
one says, etc." This is a common mode of expressing the impersonal (cf.
Gen. 11:9; 48:1, 2; Job 27:23, and often; Ges.-K., sec. 114, 3, a); hence the
change to the plural is unnecessary. עֹשָׂי with a "plural" suffix since it refers
to אֱלֹהִים (cf. Isa. 22:11; 54:5; Ps. 149:2) as against a singular suffix in Isa.
44:2; Job 4:17; 40:19. The oppressed who cry out are not moved by the
desire to know God, whose glory is manifest in the beauty of the world and
in the superior intelligence of man. This is an indirect and partial explanation of why God permits oppression to continue for awhile. Implied in this
observation is an oblique critique on Job's motives for attacking God's justice.

Stich b has been interpreted: (a) as a reference to songs of deliverance
and thanksgiving which the oppressed are able to sing in the night of oppression (D-G); (b) זְמִרוֹת rendered "strength" on the basis of the Ugaritic, *dmr*
and Ex. 15:2; Isa. 10:2; Ps. 118:14 (TS, P.), hence "who gives strength
(to the weak) in the night of affliction"; and (c) as a reference to the evildoers
who sing their obscene songs at night (Ha.).

We prefer to see in the phrase a reference to the glory of the created
world which the oppressed do not notice. Thus Isaiah (5:12) describes carousers
dissipating late into the night but not seeing "the work of God's hands,"
the heavens above, as they stagger out of their drunken revelries. The religious
spirit was particularly sensitive to God's presence at night (cf. Ps. 8:4). The
"songs" would refer to the music of the heavenly spheres familiar in ancient
Greek thought. The Hebrews also conceived of the heavenly bodies as sending
forth their voices (Ps. 19:2–5). Thus "the advent of morning and evening
You cause to sing" (Ps. 65:9; cf. Ibn E. *ad loc.*). Above all, note the magnificent
v. in Job 38:7: "When all the morning stars sang together and the sons of
God shouted for joy." T translates our v. "He does not say, this God who
made me before whom the angels on high (Greek *angeloi*) sing their praise
at night." In biblical thought angels were, of course, equated with the natural

forces and the heavenly bodies. Rabbinic thought elaborated this theme of angels singing before God in various situations; see L. Ginzberg, *Legends of the Jews*, vol. 7, index s.v. Angels.

35:11 מַלְּפֵנוּ a defectiva spelling for the Piel מְאַלְּפֵנוּ "who teaches us." It is not to be emended to מַפְלֵנוּ "who distinguishes us (Klos., D-G), as is clear from the parallelism. מִבַּהֲמוֹת "more than the beasts." On the basis of 12:7, which speaks of men learning from the animals, birds, and fish, TS renders "by means of the beasts of the earth" who proclaim God's power and goodness. The intent, however, is to highlight the creative activity of God in the creations of nature and in the unique endowment of man.

35:12 שָׁם is not "there" (Arab. *thamma*), but "then" (Arab. *thumma*). It occurs more often than D-G recognizes; in addition to Ps. 14:5; 36:13 cited, we may add Hos. 2:7, "her vineyards as of yore"; 6:7.

וְלֹא יַעֲנֶה a subordinate clause of concession which is parenthetical: "but He does not answer." Men cry out because of the pride of evil men, not because of a yearning for God's presence, and therefore they are not answered.

35:13 Stich a is generally rendered: "Surely God does not hear falsehood, or unreality, or deceit" (Ra., D-G, P.). But however imperfect the motive of the oppressed may be, their cry can hardly be described as "unreal" or "deceitful." Moreover, שָׁוְא is masc., hence the fem. suffix of יְשׁוּרֶנָּה cannot well refer to it. For both reasons, it is better to take שָׁוְא as a predicate nominative and render: "It is false that God does not hear and that the Almighty does not see it" (Ehr., TS). The suffix of יְשׁוּרֶנָּה is neuter in meaning, referring to the situation being described.

35:14 Stich a contains an indirect quotation; cf. the Comm. on 13:14 and 35:3. אַף כִּי means "how much more so" (e.g., I Sam. 23:3; II Sam. 4:10 f.; II Ki. 5:13; Ezek. 15:5; Pr. 21:27) and also "even if, even when" (Neh. 9:18), like the synonymous גַּם כִּי (Ps. 23:4).

Based upon the first meaning of אַף כִּי, the opening stich is generally rendered: "How much less (will He listen to you), when you say that you do not see Him, that the case is before Him (i.e. is pending) and that you are waiting for Him" (D-G). This interpretation depends on a view of v. 13 we have not adopted. See above.

It is preferable to regard the v. as a conditional sentence utilizing the second meaning of אַף כִּי, "Even if you say that you cannot see Him, judgment is before Him, wait for it!" (So Del., Bu., RV, margin). However, a verb would be more appropriate in stich b. Hence Perles, Du., Hö. emend דִּין to דֹּם "be still before Him," on the model of Ps. 37:7. The emendation is unnecessary. The Arab. root *daᵓna* (*mediae Ya*) means "submit, yield, obey" in a religious sense and is ideally suited to the passage (Guillaume).

וְהִתְחוֹלֵל לוֹ is generally rendered: "Wait for Him." The Qal occurs in Jud. 3:25; Mic. 1:12, the Hithpolel in Ps. 37:7, as well as here. The root

חול is a metaplastic form of יחל, a common phenomenon; cf. ינק, נוק; יטב, טוב; בוש, יבש (הוביש). However, the Polel and the Hithpolel forms may well be a denominative from תּוֹחֶלֶת "hope," carrying the nuance "trust" rather than "wait," both here and in Ps. 37:7.

35:15 This verse bristles with difficulties. Ra. renders: "Know that the visitation of God's wrath against you is like nothing, and He acts as though He does not know the great multitude of your actions," i.e. "God has punished you far less than you deserve." The difficulty involved in finding this meaning in the text is obvious. On the basis of LXX ("for He is not regarding His wrath"), stich a is revocalized as כִּי אֵין פָּקַד אַפּוֹ, which is rendered: "Because His anger punishes not" (Sieg., Bu., Be.). D-G correctly points to the fact that there is no analogy for having the subject follow the participle (cf. Ex. 33:15; Lev. 14:21), so that a further change to כִּי אֵין אַפּוֹ פָקַד would be required. We may add that "anger" as the subject of פָּקַד "punish, visit" is also strained.

In stich b, יָדַע = "know about" (Ps. 31:8); cf. וְנַפְשִׁי יֹדַעַת מְאֹד = "is well aware" (Ps. 139:14).

בַּפַּשׁ has been treated variously: (a) on the basis of Arab. *faššа*, it has been taken to mean "arrogance," but the Arab. root really means not "overflow" but "belch," and "utter calumnies." (b) from the Arab. *fasis*, "weak in mind and body, falling" (Herz, Bu., Guil.), hence "weakness." (c) It has been emended to וְלֹא יְדַעֲךָ פַּשׁ מְאֹד by TS, who translates, "that the wrath is not extinguished; it waxeth strongly," invoking the root פוש "increase" (Jer. 50:11; Nah. 3:18).

On the basis of LXX, Sym., V, "He does not notice any transgression," most modern commentators read בְּפֶשַׁע. On the elision of the Ayin in biblical orthography, see the Comm. on 34:25.

If the two stichs are taken as parallel, v. 15 must be treated as the cause and v. 16 as the effect: "Because God does not punish evil-doers and pays no attention to transgression, Job speaks folly." This is obviously impossible, since Elihu does not believe that God ignores the actions of the sinners. To avoid this difficulty, stich b is treated as the consequence of stich a: "Because God does not punish the evil-doers, *you say* that He does not notice transgressions." However, since Job's mistaken ideas have already been answered in vv. 13, 14, we would not expect at the close another citation of Job's views, particularly one left unrefuted. Du. places v. 16 before v. 10 and, omitting 36:1, places 36:2 after 35:16, but this does not really improve matters either, aside from the several assumptions that these changes require.

We believe that the Masoretic reading וְעַתָּה כִּי־אֵין פָּקַד אַפּוֹ offers a better basis for interpreting the v.: "but now, if not, i.e. if you do not submit to Him, He stores up His wrath, i.e. His anger will be visited upon you." Cf. the use of אִם אֵין in 33:33. For the idea of God's storing up punishment for the future, cf. Job's citation of the Friends' view in 21:19, 31. פָּקַד "He remembers" or "He stores up"; cf. the Comm. on 34:13.

וְלֹא is here to be understood as the interrogative-emphatic particle =

וְלֹא־יָדַע "Doesn't He know? = He surely knows." This usage, which is common in rabbinic Hebrew, is increasingly being recognized in biblical Hebrew as well. Cf. Hos. 10:8; Job 11:11; 37:24; and see the Comm. *ad loc.*, and Gordis, in *Louis Ginzberg Jubilee Volumes*, English volume, pp. 181–83. This interrogative-emphatic use of לא occurs with our verb in Lachish Letter No. 3, ll. 8–9: ולא ידעתה קרא ספר = "You surely know how to read a missive"; cf. Gordis, in *Sepher Tur Sinai*, pp. 155–57. בַּפַּשׁ is a defectiva spelling for בְּפֶשַׁע, as has already been noted. The v. now receives a clear and unforced meaning: "For now, if you do not (trust in Him), He stores up His wrath; for He is well aware of transgressions."

35:16 יִפְצֶה־פִּיהוּ carries a scornful connotation (cf. וּפֹצֶה פֶּה וּמְצַפְצֵף "who opens his mouth and chirps" (Isa. 10:14; another nuance in Ps. 22:14; Lam. 2:16; 3:46). הֶבֶל adv. acc. "lit. in emptiness"; יַכְבִּר "increases."

The Fourth Speech (36–37)

In the concluding portion of his rejoinder to Job, Elihu restates his essential ideas. God does not disregard or despise the righteous, who ultimately attain to honor. When suffering comes upon them, it is as a warning against sin. If they take the message to heart, they are restored to well-being. But if they remain obdurate, they suffer destruction, which is the inevitable consequence of sin. This is what God wishes to teach Job through the medium of his suffering.

As Elihu speaks, the signs of a gathering storm are seen in the sky, and he breaks into a paean of praise to the greatness of the Creator, whose mysterious ways are manifest in nature.

Elihu describes the autumn season which brings the miracle of rain. The downpour of rain produces food on earth, while the crashing thunder which accompanies it reveals the heavenly Judge bringing retribution upon evildoers. Then comes the winter with its own complement of wonders, the snow and the storm, when men and beasts seek shelter from the elements. Finally, the winter is past and the rains are over and gone. As the golden light of the sun cleanses the heavens of their clouds, the summer is ushered in.

These are the ways of the Almighty, who is great not only in power, but also in justice. God is therefore worthy of all reverence.

36   Elihu continued and said,
2   Bear with me a little, and I will show you
           there is something to be said for God!
3   I will marshal my knowledge from every quarter
           as I justify my Creator.
4   For, indeed, my words are not false —
           a truthful man is speaking with you.
5   Behold, God is all mighty;
           yet mighty as He is,
           He does not despise the pure of heart.
6   He does not keep the wicked alive
           but gives the afflicted their right.
7   He does not avert His eyes from the righteous;
           He seats them with kings upon the throne
           forever, and they are exalted.
8   And if He binds men in fetters
           and they are caught in the cords of affliction,
9   it is to reveal to them their deeds
           and their transgressions, when they are guilty of pride.
10   He opens their ear to discipline,
           and commands them to withdraw from iniquity.
11   If they give heed and serve Him,
           they complete their days in well-being
           and their years in pleasantness.
12   But if they do not, they pass over the river of Death
           and perish for their lack of knowledge.

13   Yet the godless in heart remain obdurate;
           they do not cry for help even when He fetters them.
14   They die in their youth,
           and their life ends in shame.
15   He redeems the afflicted through their affliction
           and uncovers their ear by the adversity they suffer.
16   He has also removed you from trouble,
           into a broad place with ample room
           and the food set on your table was rich.
17   But you did not plead the cause of the poor,
           nor the suit of the orphan.
18   Now beware, lest you be seduced by your wealth
           and your ample means for ransom lead you astray.
19   Will your possessions guard you from trouble,
           or all your exertions to achieve riches?
20   Do not long for the shelter of night
           when peoples are cut off in their place.
21   Beware, do not turn to evil —
           for you would rather sin than suffer!

22   Behold, God is exalted in His power;
           who can lay down the law like Him?
23   Who can prescribe the way for Him;
           who can say, "You have done wrong"?

24   Remember to extol His work of creation
           which men have praised in song,

לוֹ

א   וַיֹּסֶף אֱלִיהוּא וַיֹּאמַר׃

2   כַּתַּר־לִי זְעֵיר וַאֲחַוֶּךָּ   כִּי עוֹד לֶאֱלוֹהַּ מִלִּים׃

3   אֶשָּׂא דֵעִי לְמֵרָחוֹק   וּלְפֹעֲלִי אֶתֵּן־צֶדֶק׃

4   כִּי־אָמְנָם לֹא־שֶׁקֶר מִלָּי   תְּמִים דֵּעוֹת עִמָּךְ׃

5   הֶן־אֵל כַּבִּיר וְלֹא יִמְאָס   כַּבִּיר כֹּחַ לֵב׃

6   לֹא־יְחַיֶּה רָשָׁע   וּמִשְׁפַּט עֲנִיִּים יִתֵּן׃

7   לֹא־יִגְרַע מִצַּדִּיק עֵינָיו   וְאֶת־מְלָכִים לַכִּסֵּא

8   וַיֹּשִׁיבֵם לָנֶצַח וַיִּגְבָּהוּ׃   וְאִם־אֲסוּרִים בַּזִּקִּים

9   יִלָּכְדוּן בְּחַבְלֵי־עֹנִי׃   וַיַּגֵּד לָהֶם פָּעֳלָם

י   וּפִשְׁעֵיהֶם כִּי יִתְגַּבָּרוּ׃   וַיִּגֶל אָזְנָם לַמּוּסָר

11   וַיֹּאמֶר כִּי־יְשֻׁבוּן מֵאָוֶן׃   אִם־יִשְׁמְעוּ וְיַעֲבֹדוּ

      יְכַלּוּ יְמֵיהֶם בַּטּוֹב   וּשְׁנֵיהֶם בַּנְּעִימִים׃

12   וְאִם־לֹא יִשְׁמְעוּ בְּשֶׁלַח יַעֲבֹרוּ   וְיִגְוְעוּ בִּבְלִי־דָעַת׃

13   וְחַנְפֵי־לֵב יָשִׂימוּ אָף   לֹא יְשַׁוְּעוּ כִּי אֲסָרָם׃

14   תָּמֹת בַּנֹּעַר נַפְשָׁם   וְחַיָּתָם בַּקְּדֵשִׁים׃

טו   יְחַלֵּץ עָנִי בְעָנְיוֹ   וְיִגֶל בַּלַּחַץ אָזְנָם׃

16   וְאַף הֲסִיתְךָ ׀ מִפִּי־צָר   רַחַב לֹא־מוּצָק תַּחְתֶּיהָ

17   וְנַחַת שֻׁלְחָנְךָ מָלֵא דָשֶׁן׃   וְדִין־רָשָׁע מָלֵאתָ

18   דִּין וּמִשְׁפָּט יִתְמֹכוּ׃   כִּי־חֵמָה פֶּן־יְסִיתְךָ בְסָפֶק

19   וְרָב־כֹּפֶר אַל־יַטֶּךָּ׃   הֲיַעֲרֹךְ שׁוּעֲךָ לֹא בְצָר

כ   וְכֹל מַאֲמַצֵּי־כֹחַ׃   אַל־תִּשְׁאַף הַלָּיְלָה

21   לַעֲלוֹת עַמִּים תַּחְתָּם׃   הִשָּׁמֶר אַל־תֵּפֶן אֶל־אָוֶן

22   כִּי עַל־זֶה בָּחַרְתָּ מֵעֹנִי׃   הֶן־אֵל יַשְׂגִּיב בְּכֹחוֹ

23   מִי כָמֹהוּ מוֹרֶה׃   מִי־פָקַד עָלָיו דַּרְכּוֹ

24   וּמִי־אָמַר פָּעַלְתָּ עַוְלָה׃   זְכֹר כִּי־תַשְׂגִּיא פָעֳלוֹ

25 upon which all men have looked,
        though they can see it only from afar.
26 Behold, God is mighty, beyond our understanding,
        the number of His years is without end.
27 He draws up the drops of water,
        and rain is distilled from His flood,
28 which the clouds pour down
        and shower upon all men.
29 Indeed, He soars mid the spreading clouds,
        with thunderings from His pavilion.
30 Behold, He spreads His light over it
        and covers the depths of the sea.
31 For by these He nourishes nations
        and provides food in abundance.
32 The tent of Heaven He covers with lightning
        which He commands against His target.
33 His thunderclap proclaims His presence,
        and the storm, His mighty wrath.

37 At this indeed my heart trembles
        and leaps from its place.
2   Hearken well to His thundering voice,
        to the rumbling that comes from His mouth.
3   His power is heard everywhere beneath the sky
        and His lightning reaches the ends of the earth.
4   After it comes a roaring sound
        as He thunders with His majestic voice;
        nor does He restrain the lightning bolts when His voice is heard.
5   God thunders with His wondrous voice,
        doing great things we cannot grasp.
6   To the snow He says, "Fall to the earth,"
        and to the shower and the rain, "Flow down!"
7   He shuts up every man indoors,
        so that all men may know His work.
8   Then the beasts retire to their lairs
        and remain within their dens.
9   From its chamber the whirlwind comes forth
        and the cold from the scattering winds.
10 By the breath of God ice is formed
        and the wide sea is frozen fast.
11 He loads the thick cloud with moisture,
        and scatters the clouds of light.
12 They turn round and round under His guidance
        to fulfill all His commands
        on the face of the inhabited world.
13 Be it for chastisement — if they do not obey —
        or for love, He brings it all to pass.

14 Hear this, O Job,
        Stop and observe the wonders of God.
15 Do you know how God lays His command upon them,
        how He makes the lightning flash from His clouds?

כָּל־אָדָם חָזוּ־בֽוֹ		אֲשֶׁר שֹׁרְרוּ אֲנָשִֽׁים: כה
הֵן־אֵל שַׂגִּיא וְלֹא נֵדָע		אֱנוֹשׁ יַבִּיט מֵרָחֽוֹק: 26
כִּי יְגָרַע נִטְפֵי־מָיִם		מִסְפַּר שָׁנָיו וְלֹא־חֵֽקֶר: 27
אֲשֶׁר־יִזְּלוּ שְׁחָקִֽים		יָזֹקּוּ מָטָר לְאֵדֽוֹ: 28
אַף אִם־יָבִין מִפְרְשֵׂי־עָב		יִרְעֲפוּ עֲלֵי ׀ אָדָם רָֽב: 29
הֵן־פָּרַשׂ עָלָיו אוֹרֽוֹ		תְּשֻׁאוֹת סֻכָּתֽוֹ: ל
כִּי־בָם יָדִין עַמִּים		וְשָׁרְשֵׁי הַיָּם כִּסָּֽה: 31
עַל־כַּפַּיִם כִּסָּה־אֽוֹר		יִתֶּן־אֹכֶל לְמַכְבִּֽיר: 32
יַגִּיד עָלָיו רֵעֽוֹ		וַיְצַו עָלֶיהָ בְמַפְגִּֽיעַ: 33
		מִקְנֶה אַף עַל־עוֹלֶֽה:

וְיִתַּר מִמְּקוֹמֽוֹ:	אַף־לְזֹאת יֶחֱרַד לִבִּי	לז א
וְהֶגֶה מִפִּיו יֵצֵֽא:	שִׁמְעוּ שָׁמוֹעַ בְּרֹגֶז קֹלוֹ	2
וְאוֹרוֹ עַל־כַּנְפוֹת הָאָֽרֶץ:	תַּֽחַת־כָּל־הַשָּׁמַיִם יִשְׁרֵהוּ	3
יַרְעֵם בְּקוֹל גְּאוֹנֽוֹ	אַחֲרָיו ׀ יִשְׁאַג־קוֹל	4
יַרְעֵם אֵל בְּקוֹלוֹ נִפְלָאוֹת	וְלֹא יְעַקְּבֵם כִּי־יִשָּׁמַע קוֹלֽוֹ:	ה
כִּי לַשֶּׁלֶג ׀ יֹאמַר הֱוֵא אָרֶץ	עֹשֶׂה גְדֹלוֹת וְלֹא נֵדָֽע:	6
וְגֶשֶׁם מִטְרוֹת עֻזּֽוֹ:		וְגֶשֶׁם מָטָר
לָדַעַת כָּל־אַנְשֵׁי מַעֲשֵֽׂהוּ:	בְּיַד־כָּל־אָדָם יַחְתּוֹם	7
וּבִמְעוֹנֹתֶיהָ תִשְׁכֹּֽן:	וַתָּבוֹא חַיָּה בְמוֹ־אָרֶב	8
וּמִמְּזָרִים קָרָֽה:	מִן־הַחֶדֶר תָּבוֹא סוּפָה	9
וְרֹחַב מַיִם בְּמוּצָֽק:	מִנִּשְׁמַת־אֵל יִתֶּן־קָרַח	י
יָפִיץ עֲנַן אוֹרֽוֹ:	אַף־בְּרִי יַטְרִיחַ עָב	11
לְפָעֳלָם כֹּל אֲשֶׁר יְצַוֵּם	וְהוּא מְסִבּוֹת ׀ מִתְהַפֵּךְ בְּתַחְבּוּלֹתָו	12
אִם־לְשֵׁבֶט אִם־לְאַרְצֽוֹ	עַל־פְּנֵי תֵבֵל אָֽרְצָה:	13
הַאֲזִינָה זֹּאת אִיּוֹב	אִם־לְחֶסֶד יַמְצִאֵֽהוּ:	14
הֲתֵדַע בְּשׂוּם־אֱלוֹהַּ עֲלֵיהֶם	עֲמֹד וְהִתְבּוֹנֵן ׀ נִפְלְאוֹת אֵֽל:	טו

16   Do you know the outspreadings,
        the miracles wrought by the All-Knowing?

17   When your garments are hot
        and the earth is still because of the southwind,

18   can you fly with Him to the heavens
        that are hard as a molten mirror?

19   Teach us what we shall say to Him.
        We cannot draw up our case because of the all-embracing
          darkness.

20   Will He be told when I speak?
        If a man talks, will He be informed?

21   But now, after men saw no light,
        the skies grow bright —
        for a wind has passed and cleared them.

22   Out of the north comes golden splendor;
        God is clothed in awesome majesty.

23   The Almighty — whom we cannot reach —
        is great both in power and in justice;
        the man abounding in goodness He does not torment.

24   Therefore do men fear Him;
        Yes, all the wise-hearted stand in awe.

16 וְהוֹפִיעַ אוֹר עֲנָנוֹ׃　　　הֲתֵדַע עַל־מִפְלְשֵׂי־עָב

17 מִפְלְאוֹת תְּמִים דֵּעִים׃　　　אֲשֶׁר־בְּגָדֶיךָ חַמִּים

18 בְּהַשְׁקִט אֶרֶץ מִדָּרוֹם׃　　　תַּרְקִיעַ עִמּוֹ לִשְׁחָקִים

19 חֲזָקִים כִּרְאִי מוּצָק׃　　　הוֹדִיעֵנוּ מַה־נֹּאמַר לוֹ

כ לֹא־נַעֲרֹךְ מִפְּנֵי־חֹשֶׁךְ׃　　　הַיְסֻפַּר־לוֹ כִּי אֲדַבֵּר

21 אִם־אָמַר אִישׁ כִּי יְבֻלָּע׃　　　וְעַתָּה ׀ לֹא רָאוּ אוֹר

בָּהִיר הוּא בַּשְּׁחָקִים　　　וְרוּחַ עָבְרָה וַתְּטַהֲרֵם׃

22 מִצָּפוֹן זָהָב יֶאֱתֶה　　　עַל־אֱלוֹהַּ נוֹרָא הוֹד׃

23 שַׁדַּי לֹא־מְצָאנֻהוּ שַׂגִּיא־כֹחַ　　　וּמִשְׁפָּט וְרֹב־צְדָקָה לֹא יְעַנֶּה׃

24 לָכֵן יְרֵאוּהוּ אֲנָשִׁים　　　לֹא־יִרְאֶה כָּל־חַכְמֵי־לֵב׃

Chapter 36

36:1 The change in the introductory formula here does not mean that a new writer has appeared on the scene. It merely registers the fact that Elihu's long address is not yet complete; cf. the Comm. on 27:1.

36:2 The entire opening stich, with a slight change in the vocalization of the last word, could be Aram. (Ra.). כַּתַּר "wait" is an Aramaism occurring in Targumic Aramaic and is common in Syriac. זְעֵיר is an Aramaism at least as old as Isaiah (21:10, 13). חוה, which occurs in Ps. 19:3, is a favorite of our poet, both in the Dialogue (13:17; 15:17) as well as in Elihu (32:6, 10, 17).

Stich b: "For there still are words (to be spoken) on behalf of God" or "by God, through His surrogate, Elihu." Both interpretations come to the same thing.

36:3 דֵּעִי here "my knowledge (of God)" rather than "my opinion" as in 32:10; both meanings inhere in the rabbinic use of דֵּעָה.

לְמֵרָחוֹק has been rendered "to afar" as in 39:29; II Sam. 7:19; Ezra 3:13 (Del., Hö., Ehr.). It is better interpreted as "from afar" as in II Ki. 19:25 (= Isa. 37:26), a characteristic reference to Wisdom as representing the accumulated legacy of generations. On לְמִן = "from," cf. Deut. 4:32; Jud. 20:1. לְפֹעֲלִי "my Maker"; cf. the synonym used in 31:15 and 35:10. אֶתֵּן־צֶדֶק "lit. I shall ascribe righteousness, i.e. justify"; cf. נתן (1:22; Jos. 7:19), the synonymous use of יהב (Ps. 29:1, etc.).

36:4 Stich b has been rendered: "one perfect in knowledge," referring either to God as in 37:16 (Ibn E.) or to Elihu himself (D-G, P.). However, the parallelism militates against the first view. As for the second, even Elihu is not likely to claim perfect knowledge for himself, in view of his insistence that God is beyond man's comprehension (cf. 36:26). Hence it is better to render the phrase as "one perfect, wholehearted in thought, *integer*, sincere in ideas in speaking with you." TS aptly compares בֶּאֱמֶת וּבְתָמִים (Jud. 9:19).

36:5 For this, the first of many difficult vv. in the chap., a plethora of emendations has been proposed, based in part on the renderings of the Vss. LXX (= Th.) renders: "Know that God will not cast off the innocent man (*akakos*), being mighty in strength of heart." D-G assumes that stich a, therefore, read הֵן אֵל לֹא יִמְאַס תָּמִים. Actually, LXX has merely supplied an object for the verb *ad sensum* and incidentally attests to MT. T renders very periphrastically: הא אלהא רבא לא ירחק צדיקא מטול דהוא רב חילא וחכים לבא "Behold, the great God will not keep the righteous distant (reading יְרַחֵק in the Pael), because He is great in strength and wise of heart." T, therefore, regards the closing phrase as a repetition or an echo of חֲכַם לֵבָב וְאַמִּיץ כֹּחַ in 9:4, which was surely not in its text here. On the basis of T, Bu.

suggests reading stich b as: כַּבִּיר כֹּחַ וַחֲכַם לֵב. However, the phrase in 9:4 refers to man, not to God (see the Comm. *ad loc.*). Moreover, referring the amended text here to God, as does T, leaves the verb without an object, which vitiates the essential point Elihu seeks to make. Dh., followed by P., moves כֹּחַ to stich a after כַּבִּיר and changes כַּבִּיר in stich b to בְּבַר as the object of יִמְאַס, reading: הֶן אֵל כַּבִּיר כֹּחַ וְלֹא יִמְאַס בְּבַר לֵב. This gives an acceptable sense: "Behold, God is mighty in strength and He will not despise the pure of heart."

However, these transpositions and changes are not required. The presence of כַּבִּיר in both stichs suggests that the parallelism is complementary (or climactic): "a b ǁ b′ c′" as in Ps. 29:1

הָבוּ לה׳ בְּנֵי אֵלִים הָבוּ לה׳ כָּבוֹד וָעֹז

On this category, cf. *PPS*, pp. 74 f. כַּבִּיר in both stichs is the subject; it is an epithet for God as in 34:17 and in the familiar Islamic formula *ʾallahu ʾakbaru*, "God is great." It follows that the object of the verb must be contained in כֹּחַ לֵב, in which a reference to the righteous is to be sought. However, the phrase in MT cannot bear this meaning, except by a far-fetched interpretation, "strong in understanding," hence "wise, God-fearing." One need only change כֹּחַ לֵב to בַּר לֵב, which is graphically close. For "pure of heart," cf. בַּר לֵבָב (Ps. 24:4; 73:1), and then render our verse literally:

"Behold, God is mighty, but does not despise —
The mighty One (does not scorn) the pure of heart."

For another instance of complementary parallelism, in which the verb is understood in stich b, cf.

מִן־אֲרָם יַנְחֵנִי בָלָק ǁ מֶלֶךְ־מוֹאָב מֵהַרְרֵי קֶדֶם

From Aram Balak has led me,
The king of Moab, from the mountains of the East.
(Nu. 23:7)

Another instance occurs in אַפִּרְיוֹן עָשָׂה לוֹ הַמֶּלֶךְ ǁ שְׁלֹמֹה מֵעֲצֵי הַלְּבָנוֹן

"A palanquin the king has made himself,
Solomon, from the trees of Lebanon."
(Cant. 3:9)

On the structure of this verse, see *SS ad loc.*

36:6, 7 God's moral government is expressed negatively in the punishment and death of the wicked and the escape of the poor from the hands of their oppressors (v. 6). Positively, the righteous are raised to high honor — not briefly, as may happen with the wicked, but permanently (v. 7).

יִתֵּן = "grant" (30:18).

The shift from sing. to pl. is common when a given class is indicated.

36:7 Far from exercising a maddening espionage against man, as Job has bitterly complained (7:16 ff.), God manifests a loving care which is never removed from the righteous.

It is not necessary to reverse stichs b and c. The verb has been reserved for stich c for metric reasons:

> "And with kings up on the throne,
>   He seats them forever — and they are exalted."

For another instance where the poetic and the logical caesuras do not coincide, cf. the Comm. on 4:8. On the Lamed with יֹשֵׁב, cf. Isa. 3:26; Ps. 9:5.

36:8   Du., Be. and other commentators join vv. 8, 9 to v. 7 and refer the entire section to kings like Manasseh and Nebuchadnezzar, who are humbled by God and then restored to their thrones. Whether the poet referred to specific historical legends is doubtful, and the use of לָנֶצַח "forever" in v. 7 also militates against it.

The passage is better understood as referring not to kings, but to the righteous, who are often raised high by God (v. 7); if they are humbled it is part of the Divine discipline (vv. 8–11). As often in Job (see the Comm. on 8:16; 13:28), the subject is left to be understood by the reader: "If they (i.e. the righteous) are bound in fetters." The syntax is substantially improved by reading וְאָם אֲסָרָם and rendering: "If He binds them." זִקִּים "chains." חַבְלֵי־עֹנִי "cords of affliction"; cf. חֶבְלֵי־מָוֶת (Ps. 18:5).

36:9   This v. and the next constitute the apodosis of the condition introduced in v. 8, stich a: "He is telling them their (evil) deeds." The usage is identical with לְהַגִּיד לְיַעֲקֹב פִּשְׁעוֹ (Mic. 3:8). In stich b, כִּי יִתְגַּבָּרוּ is rendered: "When they behave proudly" as in 15:25. This is preferable to the rendering "grow numerous," for which Ps. 65:4 has been adduced.

36:10   Stich a: "He is thus opening their ears to instruction." וַיֹּאמֶר = "and commands (9:7) that they return from sin, i.e. repent."

36:11   וְיַעֲבֹדוּ is generally rendered "submit." TS treats the verb as an Aramaism, "if they listen and do so," from עֲבַד; cf. 34:25; Ecc. 9:1, and the classic וְשָׁמַעְנוּ וְעָשִׂינוּ (Deut. 5:24). For stich b, cf. 21:13a Qere.

בַּנְּעִימִים "in pleasantness." The use of the masc. plur. for an abstract (cf. our word in Ps. 16:5; חֲשֵׁכִים Isa. 50:10) is less common than the fem. plur.

36:12   שֶׁלַח "the river of death"; cf. 33:18. The recognition of the correct meaning of the noun renders unnecessary the complicated procedures proposed by earlier scholars. Cf. D-G II, p. 275.

בִּבְלִי דָעַת. The Beth may be equivalent to the Mem of cause: "for lack of understanding," as in 35:16, and מִבְּלִי דָעַת Isa. 5:13; Hos. 4:16. However, the context here, as well as the usage in יָמוּתוּ וְלֹא בְחָכְמָה (Job 4:21), suggests the meaning "without being aware," the reference being either to others who pay no attention to the destruction of the evil-doers or to the sinners themselves upon whom destruction comes without warning.

36:13   חַנְפֵי לֵב is generally rendered "impious in heart." It is applied in the Ugaritic epic of Aqhat to the goddess Anat as she plots to rob the youth of his bow.

יָשִׂימוּ אַף is generally rendered "store up, keep, cherish their anger against God" (Ges., Dil., D-G); cf. the use of שִׂים in Jer. 9:7; Job 22:22; and of שִׁית in Pr. 7:10. The fools, instead of recognizing that God's discipline is intended for their benefit, grow angry. It is better to interpret the phrase as "remain obdurate," for which see וַיְשֶׂם חֲזָאֵל פָּנָיו לַעֲלוֹת (II Ki. 12:18; so TS). Stich b must be understood "they do not cry out to Him when He binds them."

36:14 בַּנֹּעַר = "in youth, hence, prematurely." Stich b has been rendered "and their life among the priests of the pagan shrines" (Ter.), but the implication remains unclear. The usual rendering "among the male harlots" (Deut. 23:17; I Ki. 14:24; 15:12; 22:47; II Ki. 23:7) may possibly mean "in shame." Ehr. regards the phrase as a breviloquence: "in the age of lustful youths (who were destined for Temple harlotry), hence, when young." In view of the parallelism and in the context, the word would carry the double connotation of "shameful youth."

There is no reason for regarding the rhythm with suspicion (D-G). The entire passage contains variants of the *Qinah* meter, the basic characteristic of which is that the closing stich is shorter than the opening. Thus v. 12 is in 3:3:2 meter; v. 13 in 3:2 (or 4:3) meter; and v. 14 likewise in 3:2 meter. Cf. *PPS*, p. 68.

36:15 The Beth of בְּעָנְיוֹ and בַּלַּחַץ is not "in" but "by means of." This is Elihu's basic contribution to the discussion — the affliction and oppression coming upon the poor serve as a warning and as the instrument of their redemption. The change from sing. to plur. in referring to a class is common in Job. Hence אָזְנָם need not be emended to בְּאָזְנוֹ (ag. Bu., Du., Be.). The assonances in this v. are striking.

Intr. Note 36:16-21

This passage constitutes another extremely difficult section. Ehr. describes it as unintelligible and the Heb. offered in the proposed emendations as *haarsträubend*, "enough to make their hair stand on end." While radical changes are to be rejected, some emendations of the text are required, as will be indicated below. The general sense of the passage is apparently as follows: Job has been saved from affliction and actually been granted prosperity (v. 16). Nonetheless, he has not practiced justice for the weak against the evildoers (v. 17). Elihu warns Job against letting his wealth lead him astray (v. 18) in the mistaken belief that his possessions will safeguard him against punishment (v. 19).

36:16 הֲסִיתְךָ. Though this root has generally been polarized into a negative connotation, "entice, seduce" (I Sam. 26:19; Isa. 36:18; Job 36:18), it is also used in a neutral sense, "persuade" (Jos. 15:18 = Jud. 1:14), and is clearly used in a favorable sense, "remove from danger," in II Chr. 18:31. This latter meaning is entirely satisfactory here. The generalization in v. 14

is here applied specifically to Job: "Indeed, God has removed you from the
mouth of trouble (cf. Deut. 4:30), or of the foe." Stich b is in the accus. of
motion, "to a broad place where there is no pressure, i.e. no straitness beneath it." מוּצָק from צוּק; cf. Isa. 8:23. The noun in Job 37:10 (from יָצַק) is
not the same (ag. D-G). The fem. suffix in תַּחְתֶּיהָ refers to רַחַב. Like other
nouns originally masc., it evidently became common in gender in later Hebrew,
like צָבָא (Isa. 40:2; Dan. 8:12); מְעַט (Hag. 2:6); הָמוֹן (Ecc. 5:9; cf. *KMW
ad loc.*); פִּתְגָם (Ecc. 8:11); עָמָל (Ecc. 10:15); אוֹר (Job 36:32; see the Comm.
ad loc.). נַחַת שֻׁלְחָנְךָ = "that which is set down on your table, i.e. food."
דָשֶׁן = "full of fat."

36:17 The lit. rendering of stich a in MT: "You are filled with the judgment
of the wicked," is meaningless, quite aside from the impossibility of relating
it to stich b. TS has brilliantly suggested a different word-division, reading:
וְדִין רְשָׁעִים לֹא תָדִין וּמִשְׁפָּטַי תִּמוֹךְ which he translates: "But do not judge as
the wicked judge; hold on to My judgments." However, there are several
problems with this interpretation: (a) The sudden and unexpected injection
of God speaking in the first person; (b) This assumption necessitates treating
the entire section as a quotation of God speaking, including the emendation
of הֲסִיתָךְ in v. 16 to הֲסַתִּיךְ; (c) A rather unnatural interpretation for the words
in stich a.

P. accepts the suggested word-division in stich a, then reads: וְדִין רְשָׁעִים
לֹא תָדִין וּמִשְׁפַּט יְתֹמִים כִּזַּבְתָּ "The case of the wicked you did not judge, the
orphan's justice you falsified." The interpretation proposed for stich a is
difficult, because "judging someone's case" generally means espousing his
cause, not condemning him; cf. Isa. 1:17, "They do not judge the orphan
and the case of the widow does not come before them." So, too, in the passage
from the Ugaritic epic of King Keret which P. himself cites: "You did not
judge the cause of the widow, adjudicate the case of the wretched." The
verb can hardly have the wicked as its object. Moreover, the proposed addition in stich b of כִּזַּבְתָּ, which P. renders "you falsified," has no basis in the
text or in usage (on Job 34:6 see the Comm.); nor is it required for metric
reasons, as will be noted below.

Independently, we arrived at another solution that meets the problems
of these two proposals while preserving their advantages. We suggest a very
slight modification of MT, reading:
וְדִין רָשֵׁי עָם לֹא תָדִין וּמִשְׁפַּט יְתֹמִים
"But you did not plead the cause of the poor or the suit of the
orphan."

The negative לֹא תָדִין is to be understood in stich b.

רָשֵׁי עָם = "the poor among the people"; cf. עֲנִיֵּי־עָם (Ps. 72:4); אֶבְיוֹנֵי עַמֶּךָ
(Ex. 23:11); דַּלַּת עַם־הָאָרֶץ (II Ki. 24:14; Jer. 52:15, 16); עַם־דָּל (Pr. 28:15)
and עֲנִיִּים ‖ עַמִּי (Isa. 3:15). The homonym רָאשֵׁי עָם "heads of the people"
occurs in Job 12:25; Deut. 33:5, 21. רָשׁ "poor" is a characteristic term in
Wisdom literature (II Sam. 12:1; Ps. 34:11; Pr. 14:20; 18:28; 19:1, 7, 22,
etc.,) and is almost entirely restricted to this genre. The v. is now in *Qinah*

rhythm, which characterizes many vv. in this chap.; cf. the Comm. on 36:14 above. The slight graphic change of יִתְמְכוּ to יְתֹמִים is easily explicable in view of the similarity of Kaph and Mem. Cf. Luzzatto's justly famous emendation of בָּרוּךְ כְּבוֹד ה׳ to בְּרוּם (Ezek. 3:12); so, too, וּכְיִרְאָתְךָ is to be read וּמִי יִירָא (Ps. 90:11) and see Fr. Delitzsch, *Schreib- und Lesefehler im A.T.*, sec. 115b. On the self-evident similarity in the destiny of the poor, the widow, and the orphan see the Intr. to Job 31:16 f.

36:18 כִּי is the emphatic "indeed." חֵמָה, whether construed as a noun "wrath" (Bu.) or emended to חֹם "heat," which is taken to mean "severe misfortune" (Bi.), is syntactically impossible when followed by פֶּן, which suggests a verb to precede it. As has been widely recognized, חֵמָה is to be vocalized as חֲמֵה, the imperative of the verb חמי "see," which is common in Palestinian Aram. and in Syriac, and which in modern Syriac has the meaning of "beware" (Be., Nöldeke in *ZDMG*, vol. 54, p. 154). For the semantics, cf. the English colloquialism, "look out!"

This Aramaic root may not be a *hapax legomenon* in the Bible. We suggest that it occurs in Isa. 49:16: הֵן עַל־כַּפַּיִם חַקֹּתִיךְ חוֹמֹתַיִךְ נֶגְדִּי תָמִיד. The usual rendering is: "Behold, I have engraved thee upon My palms, thy walls are always before Me." However, the use of a verb in stich a suggests that we vocalize חֲמָתִיךְ in stich b, "I see thee before Me always," the idea of engraving being a perpetual reminder (cf. Cant. 8:6 and see Ps. 16:8, "I set the Lord always before me"). In any event, the presence of the Aram. root in our passage seems clear.

פֶּן־יְסִיתְךָ is impersonal, "lest one seduce you, i.e. lest you be seduced." For בְּשָׂפֶק the meanings "smiting of the hands," "scorning" (D-G), and "scoffing" (D-G) are not appropriate. As the parallelism makes clear, the noun is best interpreted as "amplitude, sufficiency, wealth"; cf. שֶׂפֶק (Job 20:22); יִסְפּוֹק "he increases" (Job 34:37), and the Comm. *ad loc.*

Stich b: "and let not the abundance of your money for ransom lead you astray (from the right path)."

36:19 Stich a in MT defies interpretation. The context suggests that שׁוּעֲךָ means not "cry, shout" but rather "wealth"; cf. שׁוֹעַ "nobleman, rich man" (Isa. 32:5; Job 34:19), Arab. *saʿatun* "amplitude, wealth." The *mediae Vav* root (שׁוע) is cognate to the *primae Yod* root (ישׁע).

On the basis of the first cited meaning of שׁוּעֲךָ, stich a has been rendered: "Will your cry set you outside of affliction?" (Del., Bu.), or "Can you set your cry into order without (the use of) affliction?" On the basis of the second interpretation of the noun it has been proposed to render: "Will he esteem your wealth?" (Ges.) or "Will your riches be equal to this without affliction?" Even if one overlooks the forced meanings and the necessity for supplying basic ideas lacking in the text presupposed by these and other interpretations and emendations, one major drawback remains — they are all unintelligible *per se*.

We hazard another approach. A second person object of the verb in stich a seems required, as in the entire passage (יַטֶּךָ, יְסִיתְךָ). Hence, הַיַעֲרֹךְ is to be revocalized as הַיְעִירְךָ the Hiphil of the root עור with a suffix, as TS has recognized. However, his interpretation of the v.: "Should thy wealth stir thee up, i.e. induce thee (to pervert justice)?" requires several remote additional assumptions, including the idea that our v. contains both a question and an answer! We interpret the Hiphil of the root עור as meaning "watch, guard." It occurs in יָעִיר עָלָיךְ (8:7; see the Comm. *ad loc.*), and also with a direct object in כְּנֶשֶׁר יָעִיר קִנּוֹ "like an eagle He guards His nest" (Deut. 32:11). לֹא בְצָר = "lit. a condition of no-trouble, i.e. against trouble." For this use of the neg. לֹא, like the Greek *Alpha* as a litotes, cf. Ps. 36:5; Isa. 10:7; 16:14; and see BDB s.v., sec. 2, p. 519b.

וְכֹל מַאֲמַצֵּי־כֹחַ is a *talḥin*, having both the primary meaning "strength" (cf. Am. 3:8, 14) and the secondary meaning of "wealth" (Pr. 5:10; Job 6:22). Hence our phrase conveys to the Heb. reader two senses simultaneously: "and all exertions of strength — all exertions after wealth." On this rhetorical figure, cf. the Comm. on 7:6, and see Gordis, in *Sepher M. Seidel*, pp. 255–61.

36:20 תִּשְׁאַף "pant, long for"; cf. Ecc. 1:5 and *KMW ad loc.* Hence "do not long for the night." In stich b, עַמִּים is best regarded as the subject of the infinitive לַעֲלוֹת "lit. for nations to go up, vanish in their place." On this meaning of עלה, cf. Isa. 5:24; Ps. 102:25. Elihu is apparently warning Job not to hope for the shelter of night as do other evildoers (cf., e.g., 24:13–17) because whole nations are destroyed by God overnight (cf. 34:20, 25).

36:21 בחר occurs with the preposition עַל only here, II Sam. 19:39 being different. However, the verb is used in a variety of ways, most commonly with a direct accusative, frequently with Beth and also with Lamed (I Sam. 20:30). Hence our usage is not totally ruled out as a possibility. Render: "For this, i.e. sin, you have chosen rather than suffering." Elihu accuses Job of preferring to sin rather than to suffer. Hence the emendation of עַל־זֶה to עוֹלָה (Bu., Dil., Be., St.), though not too distant graphically, is not necessary. In view of the Aram. use of בחר = "try, prove" (cf. Isa. 48:10), it has been suggested to render: "For because of this you have been tried through suffering" (Dathe, Ew., Hö., P.). This interpretation is possible, but it must be recognized that the proposed Pual reading בְּחַרְתָּ or בֹּחַרְתָּ does not occur elsewhere (in Ecc. 9:4 the Kethib in printed texts is not a Puʿal, since the vowels belong to the Qere יְחֻבַּר, a fact that has unbelievably eluded BDB, p. 104a). Guil. makes the striking suggestion that עַל־זֶה is to be read as one word, עֶלְזָה, and given the meaning "impatience" on the basis of Arab. ʿaliza. He then translates this stich: "For you have preferred impatience to resignation." Unfortunately, there is no evidence of this alleged word elsewhere in Hebrew.

36:22 יַשְׂגִּיב, elsewhere in the Qal (5:11; Deut. 2:36), here in the Hiphil, is stative, "is exalted."

In stich b, there is no real difference between (a) "who is a teacher like Him?" or (b) "who can proclaim the law like him?" On either view, it is

God's truth or God's law which is being set forth. Cf. II Chr. 15:3: "For many days for Israel there was no true (worship of) God and no priest teaching and no law" (וּלְלֹא כֹהֵן מוֹרֶה וּלְלֹא תוֹרָה). The term מוֹרֶה, "teacher," rare in the O. T. (Isa. 30:20; Pr. 5:13, "true teacher"; Isa. 9:14; Hab. 2:18, "false teacher"), becomes increasingly common in the postbiblical period, in the Qumran Scrolls (מוֹרֶה הַיַּחַד, מוֹרֶה צֶדֶק) and in medieval Hebrew.

MT is superior to LXX, which reads "ruler," based on the Aram. מָרֵא "Lord," or the reading, מוֹרָא "object of awe," for which Ehr. adduces Isa. 8:13.

For the prophets, the essence of God's law is righteousness (Isa. 28:9); for Elihu it is the teaching of suffering as a discipline.

36:23 פָּקַד "command, prescribe" or "visit to test" (Ps. 17:3; Job 7:18). God can neither be commanded nor called to account by anyone else.

36:24 In stich a, the Hiphil תַשְׂגִּיא is declarative: "Remember that you must extol (lit. declare exalted) His work."

שֹׁרְרוּ is the Polel of שׁוּר, a metaplastic form for שִׁיר, "to chant, proclaim in song," which is a favorite of Elihu; see the Comm. on 33:3, 27. This meaning is preferable to deriving it from the root שׁוּר "see" as in Nu. 24:17 (Ra., Ibn E., TS); this in spite of the verbs in the next v., as P. has properly noted.

36:25 The adverbial phrase מֵרָחוֹק "from afar" suggests the idea that man's perception of God's work is partial. Hence stich b may be given a concessive meaning, "though man can look only from afar."

36:26 The theme of man's limitations is expressed here as well. וְלֹא־חֵקֶר, "lit. beyond searching out," is "without limit."

Ter. makes the attractive suggestion that the remainder of Elihu's speech (36:26 – 37:22) is a hymn of praise to God as the Lord of Autumn (36:26 – 37:5), the Lord of Winter (37:6-13), and the Lord of Summer (37:14-24). One wishes that the references to the seasons were more explicit, and one misses the springtime in this series. Neither of these objections, however, is decisive, since allusiveness is characteristic of the poet and the possibility of a section lost cannot be ruled out.

36:27 יְגָרַע "diminish, withdraw" has a variety of nuances: (a) "reduce" (Ex. 5:8, 19; 21:10; Deut. 4:2; 13:1; Job 15:4); (b) "clip the beard" (Isa. 15:2; Jer. 48:7); (c) "withdraw the eye" (Job 36:7; probably also Ezek. 5:11); and (d) "draw off to oneself" (Wisdom) (Job 15:8). The latter meaning is appropriate here, "draw up drops of water." Elsewhere the verb is used only in the Qal and Niphal, here in the Piel.

אֵד occurs only here and in Gen. 2:6. The traditional meaning "mist" has no satisfactory etymology. Albright (*JBL*, vol. 58, 1939, pp. 102 f.) and Speiser (*BASOR*, No. 140, 1955, pp. 9-11) derive the noun from Sumerian *ID*, Akk. *edû*, the subterranean waters which are the primal source of moisture. Hence render "floodwaters."

יָזֹקּוּ from זקק "purify, distill" occurs in the Qal only here; elsewhere in the Piel (Mal. 3:3) and in the Pual (Ps. 12:7; I Chr. 28:18; 29:4). The subject of the verb cannot be "the drops" (P.), for the drops do not distill the rain. It is better to regard the third person plur. as impersonal, "They distill rain, hence rain is distilled." The Lamed may here carry the connotation "from," as C. H. Gordon has demonstrated for Ugaritic and proposed for Heb. as well.

36:28 יִזְּלוּ is intransitive in Deut. 32:2 (D-G), but is transitive here, as in Pr. 3:20; cf. Isa. 45:8.

For אָדָם רָב, rendered "abundance of men," cf. עַם־רָב (Gen. 50:20). However, רָב has been interpreted here as a by-form of רְבִיבִים "showers"; cf. Deut. 32:2 (Wr.), and more recently the Ugaritic *rb* and *rbb* have been adduced (Hö., P.). It has also been suggested that אָדָם is equivalent to אֲדָמָה "earth," on the basis of Jer. 32:2; Zech. 9:1; 13:5; Pr. 30:14b (Dahood, *CBQ*, vol. 25, 1963, pp. 123 f.). However, the evidence for this meaning of אֲדָמָה is doubtful, and the plur. verb (יִרְעֲפוּ) with a sing. noun (רָב) is difficult. Hence P. is compelled to render "they tumble on the earth in showers." The traditional rendering "they shower upon all men" is entirely satisfactory; it lacks only the virtue of novelty.

LXX, derived from Th., renders our passage "The ancient heavens shall flow and the clouds overshadow innumerable mortals." It derives שְׁחָקִים from the verb שחק "rub away" (Ex. 30:36; II Sam. 22:43 = Ps. 18:43; Job 14:19) and hence renders freely "the ancient heavens." For יִרְעֲפוּ it offers *eskiasethe nephe*, "the clouds overshadow," a conflate, both the noun and the verb being associated with, or being derived from, the noun עֲרָפֶל (Ex. 20:18; II Sam. 22:18; Isa. 60:2; and Isa. 5:30). This identification was not recognized by Schleusner in his *Lexicon*, s.v.

At this point, LXX adds an apparently free rendering of 36:33 followed by a translation of 37:1, with variations. The divergent text of LXX cannot be described as an improvement on MT. See the Comm. on v. 33 below.

36:29 The v. is usually understood as an interrogative sentence expecting a neg. answer ʾim = num: "Can anyone understand?" (cf. Jud. 5:8; Isa. 29:16); or, reading with P: אִם מִי יָבִין "Indeed, who can understand?"

מִפְרְשֵׂי־עָב = "outspreading of the clouds," which apparently occurs with a phonetic variation of Lamed instead of Reš in 37:16 מִפְלְשֵׂי עָב. תְּשֻׁאוֹת = "loud noise," used of a crowd (Isa. 22:2), the shouting of a driver (Job 39:7), and the crashing of a storm (Job 30:22 Kethib), similarly here "thunderings." סֻכָּתוֹ = "his tent of clouds, covering God"; cf. יָשֶׁת חֹשֶׁךְ סִתְרוֹ ‖ סְבִיבוֹתָיו סֻכָּתוֹ "He makes darkness His cover, all about Him is His pavilion" (Ps. 18:12).

Whether the v. is emended, transposed or retained unchanged, the subject is universally regarded as "man." However, this view breaks the continuity of the entire passage (vv. 27–33), which contains a description of God's activity in the storm. When the poet wishes to underscore man's inability to comprehend God's ways, he uses the second person in direct address; cf. 37:14–18 and 38:3 – 39:27, etc. We, therefore, suggest that יָבִין here is a denominative of בֵּין meaning "to go between." This meaning we have suggested for Deut. 32:10 יְסֹבְבֶנְהוּ יְבוֹנְנֵהוּ, where the usual rendering, "He goes around them and understands them," is totally inappropriate. The passage in Deuteronomy pictures God as hovering over Israel and protecting it like a mother-eagle with her brood, flying around them and among them in the heavens. For a similar usage in medieval Hebrew, cf. Gordis, in *Sepher Tur Sinai*, pp. 153 f. We propose the same meaning, "go among," for יָבִין in our passage.

As TS has noted, ʾim is the emphatic "indeed" (19:4; 34:12). Hence render the v.: "Indeed, He soars among the spreading of the clouds, with thunderings from His pavilion." The God of Israel is described as רֹכֵב בָּעֲרָבוֹת (Ps. 68:5), now generally rendered, "rider of the clouds" on the basis of Ugaritic; cf. also Ps. 18:11, "He rides on a cherub and flies, and soars on the wings of the wind"; Ps. 68:34, etc.

For the equivalence of the Polel and the Hiphil here proposed for יָבִין and יְבוֹנְנֵהוּ, cf. מְשִׁיבַת נָפֶשׁ (Ps. 19:8) and נַפְשִׁי יְשׁוֹבֵב (Ps. 23:3); and אֲעִידֵךְ (Lam. 2:13) and יְעוֹדֵד (Ps. 146:9).

36:30 אוֹרוֹ is usually referred to the blaze of light that surrounds God in the thundercloud (D-G), but the meaning is doubtful. Hence it is emended to אֵדוֹ "His mist" (Du., Bu., Be., Ehr.) based on Greek *ode* "song," which is taken to be an error for *edo*, a transliteration of the presumed original אֵדוֹ. T. renders אוֹר here and in 36:32 as מטרא, which may possibly represent אֵדוֹ. However, the interesting linguistic observation in the Midrash is more probably at the base of this interpretation: א״ר יוחנן כל אורה שנאמרה באליהוא אינה אלא בירידת גשמים "Rabbi Johanan said, Whenever ʾorah occurs in Elihu, it refers to the downpour of rain" (*Mid. Gen. Rabbah*, sec. 26, end).

Stich b, in spite of the familiarity of all its elements, compels an exegesis that D-G calls "incredible." The obvious rendering: "He covers Himself with the roots of the sea," is alleged to mean that God draws up the waters from the depths of the sea to cover His throne with thunderclouds! This being rightly regarded as unsatisfactory, the stich has been emended to (a) וְרָאשֵׁי הָרִים כִּסָּה "He covers the tops of the mountains" (Du., Bu., Ehr., Hö.); (b) וְשָׁרְשֵׁי הַיָּם גִּלָּה "the roots of the sea He lays bare" (Be.), which is justified by the assumption that the verb כִּסָּה intruded from v. 32a and expelled the original — an example of the long arm of coincidence, since the two verbs are diametric opposites!; and (c) reading (כִּסְאוֹ =) וְשָׁרְשֵׁי הַיָּם כִּסֹּה "the roots of the sea are His throne!" (St. John Marshall). P., who maintains that the former head of the Ugaritic pantheon dwelled at the confluence of the subterranean seas, accepts the last emendation with reservations. Actually, a verb would seem to be required by the parallelism.

We suggest either of the following approaches to our passage: As the storm grows stronger, the roots of the sea are *covered* by the downpour of rain, or on the contrary, the roots of the sea are *revealed*, since the winds drive the waters away. Cf. Ex. 14:21: "And the Lord drove the sea with a strong east wind all night and turned the sea into a dry land and the waters were split."

If this latter interpretation is adopted, it may be possible to regard the root כָּסָה as an *ʾaḍdad*, "a word of like and opposite meaning," and hence "reveal" as well as "cover." This may possibly be at the base of כֶּסֶא (Pr. 7:20); כֵּסֶה (Ps. 81:4), Aram. כסאא "full, revealed moon." The noun is generally derived from the Akk. *kuseu*, "the headdress of the Moon God, at the time of full moon" (Zimmern, in *ZA*, vol. 24, p. 317), but this etymology is far from certain.

36:31   בָּם refers to the clouds and the rain. יָדִין, generally rendered "He judges," is emended to יָזוּן, "He feeds" (Gr., Be., Bu., D-G) on the basis of the verb זון in Aram. (Dan. 4:9), which is frequent in postbiblical Heb. and occurs in the noun מָזוֹן (Gen. 45:23). However, יָדִין may be a dialectic variant for יָזוּן so that no change is required (P.).
    לְמַכְבִּיר "in abundance"; for the morphology of the noun, cf. מַשְׁחִית "destruction" (Ex. 12:13; Jer. 5:26; 51:25; Ezek. 5:16; 9:6; 21:36; 25:15), מַשְׂכִּיל, etc. (D-G). Ibn E. interprets the entire v. negatively, as describing a famine. In order to make the stichs parallel he renders לְמַכְבִּיר "expensive, rare," but there is no warrant for this rendering of the root.

36:32   The usual rendering of stich a: "He covers both palms with the light," is taken to be "a half-mythical conception of God as a lightning slinger" (D-G), but there is no warrant for this rather crass physical figure. Nor is there any improvement in the various emendations of the verb: (a) to נָסָה = נָשָׂא "He lifts" (Dh., Hö.); or (b) to נָסָה which is taken to mean "He prances" (P.).
    Another approach is far preferable, to relate כַּפַּיִם to the mishnaic Hebrew כִּפָּה "arch," which develops the special meaning of "heavenly arch, sky." Cf., e.g., הרקיע דומה לבריכה ולמעלה מן הבריכה כיפה "The firmament is like a pool and above the pool is an arch" (*Mid. Gen. Rabbah* 4, 4); העלה אותו למעלה מכיפת הרקיע "He lifted him above the arch of heaven" (*Mid. Gen. Rabbah* 25b); שלשה מלכו תחת הכיפה "Three persons ruled under the sky, i.e. over the entire world" (*B. Meg.* 11a). The dual form of כַּפַּיִם may possibly embody the idea of a double arch, since the ancients conceived of layers in the heavens; cf. the citation from the Midrash given above. Or the dual form may be used because it refers to שָׁמַיִם, an analogy for which may be adduced from Ecc. 10:18 בְּעַצְלְתַיִם = בְּעַצְלוּת יָדַיִם, cf. בְּשִׁפְלוּת יָדַיִם "lit. indolence of the hands"; cf. *KMW ad loc*. On כָּסָה with the preposition עַל, cf. Nu. 16:33; Job 21:26. Render stich a: "the tent of heaven He covers with lightning."
    In spite of 7:26, אוֹר, generally masc., is fem. here (עָלֶיהָ) and in Jer. 13:16, as is the Akk. cognate *urru* (P.). On other masc. nouns that are at times common in gender, see the Comm. on v. 16 above.
    In stich b, בְּמַפְגִּיעַ "against the target" need not be emended to בְּמִפְגָּע (Houb., Sieg., Bu., Be., D-G). On the morphology of the noun, cf. לְמַכְבִּיר "abundance," in v. 31.

36:33 רֵעַ "shouting, noise" (Ex. 32:17; Mic. 4:9) here "thunderclap," is incomprehensibly described as "dubious" by BDB. Stich a: "His thunders tell about Him, i.e., proclaim His presence."

In view of the difficulty of the v., the rendering of LXX is of interest. As was noted above at v. 28, LXX appends a potpourri of translations consisting of a very free rendering of our v.: "He has fixed a time for cattle" (testifying to יַגִּיד . . . רֵעוֹ), followed by an apparently free rendering of 37:8, "and they know the order of rest," and completed by a very loose interpretation of 37:1a, b: "Yet of all these things your understanding is not astonished, nor your heart disturbed in your body," evidently introducing the negative article *lo⁾ ad sensum*! In addition, LXX offers a more literal translation at this point: "He will declare concerning this to his friend, a portion also for unrighteousness," thus testifying to the entire consonantal text in MT.

Stich b, for which scores of interpretations have been catalogued, is a famous crux. The rendering: "The cattle tell also of His coming up, i.e. the cattle have a presentiment of the storm and announce God's approach" (Ibn E., Ew., Del.), is far-fetched. LXX interpreted מִקְנֶה as "possessions" and vocalized the last word as עַוְלָה "unrighteousness." On the other hand, T understood מִקְנֶה as derived from קָנָא "be jealous, angry" and construed אַף, similarly, as "wrath," in its various renderings: קנאתא ורוגזא "jealousy and anger" and מטנין ברוגזא "they froth in anger" (טנן is the translation in T of קָנָא at Ps. 73:3; Pr. 3:31).

On the basis of T, it has been suggested to revocalize מִקְנֶה as a Hiphil participle מַקְנֶה (Hi., Dil.) or a Piel participle מְקַנֶּה (Dil., D-G), or to emend it to מְקַנֵּא (Du., Bu., Dil.), rendering מקנה אף as "is jealous with anger" or "makes anger jealous." Perhaps the best interpretation along these lines, because it requires only a revocalization of the text, is to read מַקְנֶה אַף עַל עַוְלָה "(He tells man) what arouses anger because of iniquity" (TS). That these views leave something to be desired is painfully clear.

The difficulties may be approached, perhaps more successfully, by analyzing the grammatical form of מקנה. In biblical Heb., particularly in the later stages of the language, but not limited to them, *Lamed Aleph* verbs frequently became *Lamed Yod*, either in orthography or in vocalization or in both, as, e.g., מָצָתִי (Nu. 11:11); צָמֵתִי (Jud. 4:19); יָצָתִי (Job 1:21); וְצָמִת (Ruth 2:9). Under the influence of postbiblical Aram., from which *Lamed Aleph* verbs disappeared, the process became virtually universal in mishnaic Heb., as, e.g., מצינו, קורין, etc. It is, therefore, unnecessary to change the orthography of מקנה in order to derive it from the root קָנָא "be jealous, wrathful." In form, מִקְנֶה is a noun, originally a Qal infinitive with preformative Mem, equivalent to קִנְאָה, which is likewise originally a Qal infinitive fem. For the *Lamed Yod* form of the verb, cf. בְּקֻנֹאתוֹ (II Sam. 21:2) by the side of בְּקַנְאוֹ (Nu. 25:11). Both forms occur in Ezek. 8:4 סֵמֶל הַקִּנְאָה הַמַּקְנֶה, where the rarer *Lamed Yod* form is vocalized as a Hiphil participle. The last word is, however, a variant on הַקִּנְאָה, as is evident not only from the diffi-

culties of interpretation that the Masoretic vocalization has occasioned, but
also from the absence of the vocable in v. 5: סֵמֶל הַקִּנְאָה. The rare noun in
Ezekiel should be vocalized הַמִּקְנֶה like מִקְרָא (Nu. 10:2); מַעֲלָה (Ezra 7:9),
or as מִקְנֶה, in the meaning of "jealousy, wrath." In our passage, the noun
should be vocalized with a Ṣere, as a construct, מִקְנֶה אַף "the wrath of indignation." Similarly, the homonym מִקְנָה "purchase" (Gen. 17:12), which
is fem. in form, occurs in the masc. in מִקְנֵה הַשָּׂדֶה (Gen. 49:32).

This type of combination of synonyms is common in biblical Hebrew,
especially in Job. Cf. דֶּרֶךְ אֹרְחֹתֶיךָ (Isa. 3:12); וּמִבְצָר מִשְׂגָּב (Isa. 25:12); מָעוֹז
גֶּשֶׁם מָטָר (Pr. 8:32; Job 37:12) and מְקוֹם מִשְׁכַּן and בֵּיתֶךָ (Ps. 26:8); תֵּבֵל אַרְצוֹ
(Job 37:6). As is often the case, our phrase מִקְנֶה אַף, "the wrath of indignation," is divided for parallelistic purposes, e.g. in Deut. 29:19:

כִּי־אָז יֶעְשַׁן אַף ה׳   וְקִנְאָתוֹ בָּאִישׁ הַהוּא

It may be better to revocalize it as מִקְנֶה אַפּוֹ, though this is not absolutely
necessary; cf. יָשִׂימוּ אַף in v. 13 and such instances as the undetermined noun
חֹק, Ps. 2:7, used absolutely.

For עַל־עוֹלָה, we adopt the brilliant reading עַלְעוֹלָה "storm, whirlwind"
(Perles, Gr.) on the basis of the Aram. עַלְעוּלָא "storm" (the noun in T for
סְעָרָה, Isa. 29:6; Job 38:1; the verb in T on Job 27:21; Ben Sira 43:17
margin). The word occurs also in rabbinic Hebrew: כמה עלעולין היא מזדווגת
"How many storms a ship may encounter" (*Mid. Koh. Rabbah* 7:1; *Mid.
Cant. Rabbah* on 3:4 referring to "storms" in Isa. 21:1).

יַגִּיד "tell, proclaim," generally governs a direct object as in stich b (Ps.
9:14; 145:4, etc.), but it also occurs with the preposition עַל (Est. 6:2). Both
constructions occur with a pejorative nuance, "inform on, denounce" (Jer.
20:10; Est. 6:2); the verb is used in a favorable sense in our passage. The
verb from stich a is understood in stich b, as is frequent in biblical poetry;
cf. Ps. 114:1, 2, and see the Comm. on 36:5. With regard to the parallelism,
the structural pattern that emerges is: b (verb) c (object) a (subject) ‖
c′ (object) a′ (subject). With the longer word עלעולה serving as ballast, the
meter is 3:3.

The v. is, therefore, to be rendered:

> "His thunderclap proclaims His presence;
> His mighty wrath, the storm."

CHAPTER 37

37:1

On the metric structure of chap. 37, see Special Note 31.

אַף, emphatic, "yes, indeed," used declaratively as in Ps. 16:6, 7, 9;
Job 15:3; 19:4, and with an interrogative in Job 34:17.

וְיִתַּר, the Qal of נתר, is correctly interpreted by the Midrash as meaning
"leap": מהו ויתר יקפץ (*Mid. Lev. Rab.*, sec. 20). The root occurs in the Piel
in Lev. 11:21. TS derives the verb from the root תרר, which in Akk. means
"tremble, quake."

37:2 The emphatic use of the infinitive with the imperative of a verb is a stylistic trait of the author; cf. 13:17; 21:2, thus incidentally supporting our view of the authenticity of the Elihu chapters. The change to the sing. suffix in some of the Versions is an instance of leveling. בְּרֹגֶז may be treated adverbially, "hear His voice in trembling" (cf. Hab. 3:16), or as the object of the verb with Beth: "Hear the raging of His voice = His raging voice." וְהֶגֶה "moan, growl," a superb description of the low rumbling of the thunder in the distance. Stich b contains a subordinate clause: "The roaring that comes from His mouth."

37:3 יִשְׁרֵהוּ is generally interpreted from the root שרה, as an Aramaism meaning "loosen" (Dan. 5:16; Syriac for פָּתַח, Isa. 20:2; T for שְׁלַח, Isa. 58:6). Guil. cites Arab. *saruwa* "cast off, throw." Hence the word is rendered "He sends it forth." That the root would be a *hapax legomenon* in Heb. (Jer. 15:6 Qere is highly dubious) is not an insuperable obstacle. The parallelism, however, suggests that a noun, not a verb, is required here. The same objection applies to the emendation to יִשְׁרֵהוּ = יְשׁוּרוּהוּ "They see it" (Ehr.). We prefer to interpret יִשְׁרֵהוּ as the noun יֹשֶׁר with an attenuated vowel (*Hireq* for *Qibbuṣ*; cf. אִמְרֵי from אֹמֶר, בִּסְרוֹ from בֹּסֶר (Job 15:33); and see the Comm. on 7:3. The presence of a noun here was recognized by T, who renders תריצותיה "His rightness," and by TS, who renders: "His approval" and then explains אוֹרוֹ as "His condemnation," which is not convincing. We prefer to explain the noun as = "strength, power." This meaning inheres in סֵפֶר הַיָּשָׁר (Jos. 10:13; II Sam. 1:18; I Ki. 8:5, LXX), which means not "the Book of the Upright," but "the Book of Heroes," and in מֵישָׁרִים, which has a significance of "potency, sexual power" in Pr. 23:31; Cant. 1:4; 7:10 (see *SS ad loc.*), as well as in the rabbinic formula of approval יישר כחך "may your strength be firm" (*B. Shab.* 87a), יישר חילכם (*Mid. Gen. Rab.*, sec. 54), and יישר (*B. Ber.* 42b, 153a, a. e.).

אוֹרוֹ here "His lightning." On the parallelism of light and power in the heavens, cf. Job 25:3; Ps. 19:5, where קֻוָּם = "their power" (Arab. *kuwwatum*; cf. קַו־קָו Isa. 18:2).

37:4 The emendation of קוֹל to קוֹלוֹ (Bi., Du., Be., Bu., D-G) is unnecessary. The absolute form means "the voice par excellence"; cf. the Comm. on 36:32. וְלֹא יְעַקְּבֵם "He does not restrain them" can be derived from עָקֵב "heel" (Ibn E., Ki.) only with difficulty. It is best regarded as a metaplastic form, possibly the original, for עָכַב "hold back, restrain, delay," the form with Qoph being common in Targumic Aram. (Tar. Jonathan on Lev. 19:13, Onkelos on Gen. 19:16) and rabbinic Heb. (*B. Ber.* 7a; *Mid. Ex. Rab.*, sec. 3, and often).

The suffix has no grammatical antecedent; the reference is, however, clearly to the lightning bolts. Hence the emendations designed to supply an object, as, e.g., וְלֹא יְעַקֵּב בְּרָקָם (Bu., Be., St., D-G, Dh.) are unnecessary. The noteworthy repetition of קוֹל three times adds power to the passage and is another instance of a stylistic trait of the poet. See Special Note 4.

37:5 While D-G describes the rhythm here as 4:4 and calls it "rare" in Job (II, p. 289), Pfeiffer has called the 4:4 meter the basic pattern in Job (*IOT*, p. 687). Actually, our v. is in 4:3 *Qinah* meter; see Special Note 31. בְּקוֹלוֹ נִפְלָאוֹת = "in His wondrous voice." The suffix is added to the construct, probably because קוֹל נִפְלְאוֹתָיו would have another connotation, "the sound of His wonders."

37:6 הֱוֵא is not the Aram. form of "be, exist," which occurs five times in the O. T. (Gen. 27:29; Isa. 16:4; Ecc. 2:22, etc.) and in the Divine Name JHVH. The root means "fall," as in Arab. *haway*, a sense that may also be felt in Ecc. 11:13, which is a conflate; cf. *KMW ad loc.* The root appears also in the nouns הֹוָה (Isa. 47:11; Ezek. 7:26) and הַוָּה (Ps. 5:10; 91:3; Job 6:2, a. e., meaning "disaster." Hence: "to the snow He says, fall to the earth."

In stich b, one of the two phrases is obviously a dittography which overloads the line. The plural מְטָרוֹת occurs nowhere else. On the principle of *difficilior lectio* and the recognition of עֻזּוּ as a plural imperative verb (see below), it is preferable to regard וְגֶשֶׁם מָטָר as a dittography (Ol., Wr., Bi., Bu., D-G, Hö.). For the combination of synonyms, see the Comm. on 36:33. Render "the downpour of rains."

עֻזּוֹ as a noun, "His strength," is meaningless in the context. The parallelism requires a verb. עֻזּוֹ has therefore been emended to עֹזוּ, "be strong" (Hoff., Hö., Guil.), to תָּעֹזּוּ, "you be strong" (Du.), or to עָרְפוּ "drop down" (Be., D-G). We suggest revocalizing עֻזּוֹ as עוּזוּ from the root עוּז. This root, though probably cognate to the Arab. *ʿaʾdha* (*med waw*) "take refuge, seek protection," has undergone a slight semantic shift in Heb., as is clear from every biblical passage in which the verb occurs; it means "flee, run" commonly in the Hiphil הָעֵז אֶת מִקְנֶךָ (Ex. 9:19; cf. 9:20 הֵנִיס; הֵעִיזוּ parallel to נָדְדָה (Isa. 10:31); הָעִיזוּ אַל תַּעֲמֹדוּ (Jer. 4:6; 6:1). The construct מְטָרוֹת now needs to be revocalized as an absolute; the stich is to read וְגֶשֶׁם מְטָרוֹת עוּזוּ. On the plural ending *ōth* for masc. nouns, cf. Ges.-K., sec. 87; the tendency gains momentum in mishnaic Hebrew; cf. M. H. Segal, *Diqduq Lešōn Hamišnah*, sec. 151–64. For the waters fleeing at God's command, see Ps. 104:7.

37:7 The personal object of the verb חתם "seal, close up" may be expressed by a direct object (Isa. 8:16; Dan. 12:4) or, like other verbs of closing, such as נעל (Jud. 3:23), עצר (Gen. 20:18), סגר (I Sam. 1:6; II Ki. 4:4, 5, 33; Isa. 26:20), שׂוּךְ (Job 1:10; 3:23), גדר (Lam. 3:7), by a prepositional phrase introduced by בְּעַד, as in Job 9:7. There is, however, no need to emend בְּיַד into בְּעַד (Gr., Hi., Du., Be., D-G). *Beyad* is a divergent phonetic orthography for *beʿad* attested in the Canaanite glosses of the *Tel-el Amarna Letters* and in Job 8:4; 15:23; 27:11; Ezek. 37:19; see the Comm. *ad loc.* and Gordis, "A Note on *Yad*," in *JBL*, vol. 62, 1942, pp. 341–44.

Stich b can mean only: (a) "to know all the men that He has made," which is meaningless; or (b) "that all the men He has made may know," which lacks an object and is not relevant to the context. Obviously, מַעֲשֵׂהוּ should be the object of לָדַעַת and hence אַנְשֵׁי cannot be in the construct.

It is, therefore, emended to אֱנוֹשׁ (Bi., Hoff., Be.) or אֲנָשִׁים (Ol., Kampf., Del., Hö., P.). However, MT exhibits at times an apocopated plur. without the final Mem. This form may be due to an abbreviation by a scribe as in later Heb. mss., or may represent a phonetic elision of the final Mem, similar to the talmudic Aram. plur. without the final Nun, as, e.g., מִילִין for מִילִי. For instances of this apocopated plur., cf. שִׁירַת דּוֹדִי = שִׁירַת דּוֹדִים (Isa. 5:1); עַמִּי = עַמִּים (Ps. 144:2); רְמוֹנַי = רְמוֹנִים (Cant. 8:2; cf. *SS ad loc.*). Hence אַנְשֵׁי = אֲנָשִׁים in the meaning of "mankind," a usage characteristic of Job, particularly in the Elihu Speeches (4:13; 33:15, 16, 27; 36:24; 37:24).

During a heavy downpour, men are kept indoors and animals must seek refuge in their lairs (v. 8).

37:8   The meter is 3:3, the long word in stich b receiving two beats, exactly as in v. 9. See Special Note 31.

37:9   הַחֶדֶר and מְזָרִים are obviously astronomical terms, the precise meaning of which eludes us today. הַחֶדֶר has been interpreted as: "(a) the name of a constellation" like Arcturus (Hoff.). So LXX, which has suffered an inner Greek error; (b) a telescoped form of the phrase חַדְרֵי תֵימָן "chambers of the south" (9:9) (so Ibn E.); (c) "the regions from which the storms come"; (d) "the circular austrinus," from the root חדר "go round"; and (e) "the zodiacal circle" (G. R. Driver). Probably הַחֶדֶר refers to the chamber where the whirlwind is kept until it needs to be loosed, like the storehouses of snow and hail (38:23). The Midrash speaks of חדרי סופה וחדרי סערה (L. Ginzberg, *Ginze Schechter*, vol. 1, p. 187), which may, however, be derived from our passage.

מְזָרִים in MT need not be equated with מַזָּרוֹת (38:22) and rendered "stars" (Ibn E.), nor need the word be emended to מְזָוִים "the storehouses," Ps. 144:13 (Voigt, Bu., D-G) or זְרָמִים "the streams" (P) or זֶרֶם (D-G). The noun is the Piel participle of the verb זרה "scatter," hence "scatterers, i.e. the scattering winds," for which an excellent analogue is available in the Arab. *adhdhari*, "the scattering winds" (Quran 51:1). TS suggests the meaning "the press," a reference to the clouds from which cold water is squeezed, on the basis of the root זרר "squeeze," but his interpretation of the passage is complicated and requires too many emendations to be convincing.

37:10   יִתֶּן is impersonal; sc. הנותן, as, e.g., Gen. 31:28; 48:1, 2, and often: "ice is given, formed"; the passive in Sym., S, and T renders the sense, not the grammatical form. בְּמוּצָק has been interpreted from צוק "constrain, narrow" as "narrowness" (as in 36:16), i.e. the breadth of waters narrows, as ice forms along the edges (D-G), but this is farfetched. מוּצָק is best rendered from יצק "pour, cast" as "hardened substance," as in 38:38. In the latter passage, it refers to a mass of earth, here to ice. Note the parallelism with קֶרַח.
Stich b, "the width of waters, i.e. the wide waters of a large expanse (cf. Ps. 104:25) are turned into a frozen mass." The choice of the noun by the poet may have been influenced by the *talḥin*, where the basic meaning

"hardening" is accompanied by the secondary meaning of the homonym "narrowness" contrasted with רֹחַב "breadth." On this rhetorical figure, cf. the Comm. on 7:6.

Ehr. gives the v. a drastically opposite meaning by emending יִתֵּן to יֻתַּךְ "is poured out, melts," explaining מוּצָק by יצק "is poured out," and rendering the v.: "by the breath of God the ice is melted and the breadth of waters turns into a flow," but the emendation is uncalled for.

37:11 בְּרִי has been rendered (a) as "corn," from בָּר (S, V); (b) "chosen one," from ברר (Th., Aquila); (c) "purity" or "brightness = sunshine" (Ehr.) from the same root; or (d) "rainbow," from רְאִי (Hoff.). In rabbinic legend, *Beri* becomes the name of the angel in charge of the clouds (Ra.). The word has also been emended to בְּרָק or בָּרָד (P., D-G). It is best taken as the preposition Beth and a noun רִי "saturation" from the root רָוָה, "saturate, fill," like the nouns כִּי from כָּוָה (Isa. 3:24); עִי from עָוָה (D-G). This noun, "moisture," occurs in a variant form רְאִי in Ben Sira 31:28. On the root רוה ‖ ראה, cf. Ps. 91:16 and the Comm. on 10:15.

יַטְרִיחַ. The root, which occurs biblically only in the noun טֹרַח "trouble" (Deut. 1:12; Isa. 1:14), is common in rabbinic Heb. as a verb in the Qal and Hiphil in the abstract sense "to encumber, burden, trouble." Here the earlier concrete sense "burden, load" is clearly appropriate: "Indeed, with moisture he loads the clouds" (so most). The root has also been explained by the Arab. cognate *ṭaraḥa* "throw" (TS, Guil.).

On אַף as an asseverative, cf. the Comm. on 37:1.

In stich b, עָנָן is vocalized with a *Qameṣ* (some Heb. mss.), the absolute to serve as the subject of יָפִיץ with אוֹרוֹ as its object (LXX, V, Be., Du., D-G). However, since "God" is the subject of the verb in stich a, it is better to have the same subject in stich b and render עֲנַן אוֹרוֹ without revocalization as "the clouds of light" (*Lichtgewölk*, Hö.). As the rain-clouds grow heavy and dark with moisture, the lighter clouds are driven away and scattered.

37:12 וְהוּא "it" refers either to the lightning (Bu., Dr., Peake, D-G) or to the clouds (Dil., Du., Guil.), both of which are the agents of God's will. מְסִבּוֹת, a fem. noun, is an adverbial accusative, "in circles, roundabout"; the masc. form occurs in II Ki. 23:5; Cant. 1:12.

בְּתַחְבּוּלֹתָיו from חֶבֶל "cord, rope," hence "direction, counsel," occurs only in the plur. in Wisdom Literature (Pr. 1:5; 11:14; 20:18; 24:6). Curiously, its use in Pr. 12:5 in connection with evildoers has polarized it in modern Heb. as "evil counsel." Here: "His direction."

לְפָעֳלָם lit., "for their doing = that they may do." The plur. suffix refers to the lightning and the thunder or to the clouds. אָרְצָה, as in 34:13, is a poetic form like הַחַרְסָה (Jud. 14:18), הַמָּוְתָה (Ps. 116:15), נַחְלָה (Ps. 124:4), as well as עוֹלָתָה (Ps. 92:16); cf. Ges.-K., sec. 90, 2, note a. It need not, therefore, be understood as "earthwards" or revocalized as אַרְצֹה "His land" (P, Bu., Be., D-G). The emendation is ruled out by the absence of any national references in Job. See the Comm. on v. 13.

The v. is a tristich. In spite of the unusually long words in stich a, it is in 3:3:3 meter. See Special Note 31 for an alternative pattern. Neither the deletions (P.) nor the insertions (Dh.) proposed for the text *metri causa* are called for.

37:13 לְשֵׁבֶט = "lit. for the rod, i.e. for chastisement, punishment" contrasted with לְחֶסֶד "for mercy." The difficult intervening phrase has been variously explained or treated: (a) by the deletion of אִם, rendering the stich: "If it be punishment for His land" (Bi., Dil., Bu., Be.), but "God's land" suggests a contrast with other countries, a national reference appropriate to the Prophets and the psalmists, but not to Job and Wisdom literature. (b) to emend לְאַרְצוֹ to לִמְאֵרָה "for a curse" (Deut. 28:20; Pr. 3:33; so Du., D-G), but this creates an imbalance between two negative terms and one positive. (c) To assume the existence of a noun with prefixed Aleph from the root רצה, meaning "favor" (P.). Aside from creating a *hapax legomenon*, the same imbalance results, this time with two positive terms and one negative. (d) The emendation יְמַלֵּא רְצוֹנוֹ (Dh., Hö.), but this can hardly mean "if for punishment to do His will."

Probably the best procedure is to divide לְאַרְצוֹ into two vocables לֹא רָצוּ and render: "If they are unwilling, do not obey" (TS). Lit. the verb means "find favor, be in harmony with God," the exact meaning it possesses in בִּרְצֹתוֹ עִם אֱלֹהִים (Job 34:9; cf. also Ps. 50:18). Render stich a: "Whether it be for punishment, if they do not find favor (with God because of their disobedience)." A reminiscence of our v. apparently occurs in I Cor. 4:21, which bypasses the difficult central phrase: "Shall I come to you with a rod (*šebhet*) or in love (*ḥesed*) or in a spirit of meekness."

יַמְצִאֵהוּ is generally explained "He causes it to find its mark" (D-G, P.). But lightning can hardly be described as an instrument of God's favor. In spite of the passage from Enoch 59:1 adduced: "They give forth lightning for a blessing and a curse," lightning is always the mark of God's punishment. It is, therefore, preferable to interpret the verb as "He lets him find it, i.e. He lets man attain it, i.e. the fate appropriate to him." This is the precise nuance of the verb in 34:11 (so also TS and essentially Hö., who cites later Hebrew מְצִיאוּת "existence" and נמצא "exist"). The sense can perhaps be best rendered by the colloquial English expression, "He lets him have it."

The antecedent of the suggested plur. רָצוּ in stich a is the plur. אַנְשֵׁי in 7b; the antecedent of the sing. suffix in stich b is the sing. אדם in 7a. The chiastic structure is possible because both the sing. and plur. refer to a generic group.

37:14 עֲמֹד not "stand up" but "be silent." Cf. the Comm. on 32:16. For metric reasons the word is deleted (D-G) or transferred to stich a (Du., Be.). Neither procedure is required. The v. may be scanned as a 3:3 meter, since נִפְלְאוֹת אֵל is a single thought and requires only one beat. See Special Note 1, sec. 4 and *PPS*, pp. 67 f.

37:15 שׂוּם עַל "place a charge upon," cf. Ex. 5:8, is here used idiomatically with the object understood. To make the passage intelligible, LXX supplies an object "His works," which does not represent a variant Hebrew text (Du., D-G). The suffix refers to the natural phenomena that carry out the Divine Will.

In stich b, the Hiphil וְהוֹפִיעַ is causative: "He causes the lightning of His cloud to flash, shine forth."

37:16 The verb ידע here governs עַל which, though unattested elsewhere, is perfectly comprehensible; cf. the English "know about." מִפְלְשֵׂי עָב has been generally interpreted from the root פלס "weigh, balance" (Isa. 40:19; Pr. 16:11) and given the meaning "the balancing of the clouds laden with moisture" (Ibn E., D-G). Ra. derives the noun from rabbinic Hebrew פלש "penetrate, perforate," as, e.g., נקב מפולש "a puncture going through the skin" (*B. Suk.* 36b). Hence our phrase is explained as "clouds running along the horizon." TS utilizes the same rabbinic root and renders "the pressing of the clouds," in accordance with his view that the waters of the celestial sea were contained in water bags (cf. 38:37), which held through the summer but which became tattered and pierced and needed to be patched in the winter. See his study in *Halašon Vehasepher*, vol. 3, pp. 195–204.

However, the phrase מִפְרְשֵׂי עָב in 36:29 suggests that we have here a phonetic variant with the Lamed replacing the Res probably because of the proximity of the Lamed in מִפְלָאוֹת. As for the latter noun, it is not a mis-writing for נִפְלָאוֹת (D-G), but a variant form probably chosen because of its assonance with the Mem of מִפְלְשֵׂי (so B. Szold, Yel.). Cf. אַלְמְנוֹתָיו (Isa. 13:22; Ezek. 19:7).

תְּמִים דֵּעִים "lit. perfect in knowledge, the All-Knowing," a reference to God, different in meaning from 36:4, where the same epithet is applied by Elihu to himself. The sing. of the noun דֵּעִים occurs in 32:6.

37:17 אֲשֶׁר refers back either to the pronoun in v. 16: "You whose garments are hot" as in Hos. 14:6; Ps. 144:12; cf. BDB, s.v. 1, 3 (p. 82c), so D-G, P. and most. Or it may be equivalent to "when," hence "the time when, etc." (Jos. 4:21; I Ki. 8:31; Isa. 31:4), so Du.

דָּרוֹם is used in poetry (Deut. 33:23) or in late prose (Ezek. 13 times; Ecc. 1:6; 11:3) and often in Mishnaic Heb. Here = "the south wind." The sirocco blowing from the desert east and south is elsewhere always called קָדִים "east wind," but see Luke 12:55.

37:18 תַּרְקִיעַ is a denominative from רָקִיעַ "firmament" occurring in the Qal and the Piel (Ex. 39:3; Jer. 10:9), and meaning "beat down, stamp, flatten out" (II Sam. 22:41; Ezek. 6:11; Ps. 136:6). The verb has, therefore, been generally rendered here: "Will you beat out with Him the skies like a firma-ment?" (Ibn E., D-G, and most). On this view, the Lamed must be construed as the *nota accusativa* and עִמּוֹ rendered either "with Him" or "like Him" (9:26).

However, the entire chapter describes not the original act of creation,

but the recurrent phenomena of meteorological change. It is therefore better
to regard the Hiphil of the verb as representing a different semantic development from the original noun: "Can you soar into the heavens with Him?"
This is, incidentally, the meaning of the root in modern Hebrew. TS, on the
basis of his theory of the meteorological concepts of the ancients, renders
stich a: "Will you patch up the tattered clouds?", based on the Arabic *ruqᶜa*,
Aram. and Syriac רוקעא "patch" (Tar. Jos.), to which we may add the noun
מרקועא as in איתקליף מרקועך "your patch is peeling" (*P. Sanh.* iv, 22b).
רְאִי "mirror," like מַרְאָה (Ex. 38:8), was made of polished bronze and un-
breakable (cf. Ezek. 1:7). מוּצָק from יצק "poured out, molten hard"; cf.
I Ki. 7:23. The v. gives a superb picture of the sky giving forth no rain.
Cf. Deut. 28:23: "The skies over your head will be bronze and the earth
beneath you iron."

37:19   The shift in subject from the wonders of nature to an ironic challenge
to Job is abrupt only by our standards of literary structure. The efforts to
interpret vv. 19, 20 as referring to nature by referring the suffix to the heavens:
"Tell us what we shall say to it, i.e. the sky" (TS, Ha.) are far-fetched and
unconvincing. Nor does the transposition of these vv. after v. 21 (P.) help
matters, since v. 21 begins a description of the cleansing of the heavens after
the storm which continues in the following vv. Vv. 19 and 20 come immediately after v. 18 on the basis of the principle of association: in 18a the
question is raised whether man can soar with God to the sky. This suggests
the idea of verbal communication between God and man as well. The vv.
emphasize that God is too exalted to be impressed or disturbed by man's
puny utterances. Stich a is ironic: "You tell us what to say that will make
an impact upon Him."

הוֹדִיעֵנוּ "inform us" refers to mankind in general; cf. v. 20b.

Stich b presents the reason for the plea in stich a: "Since we cannot set
forth our arguments because of the darkness." While generally interpreted
figuratively, i.e. "ignorance" (cf. Ecc. 2:13 f.), it is better taken literally as
the darkness of the storm (Ehr.); see the Comm. on the next v.

נַעֲרֹךְ is used elliptically for נַעֲרֹךְ מִלִּים (cf. 32:14), as in Ps. 5:4; Job 33:5.
Cf. the contemporary English use of "presentation" as a "verbal statement."

הוֹדִיעֵנוּ has an Oriental Kethib הוֹדִיעֵנִי (read by LXX, P, and preferred
by Dil., Bi., Du., Be., D-G). Either reading is satisfactory, but note the
plural in the rest of the verse.

37:20   Stich a questions whether it will ever be brought to God's attention
that a man presumes to speak against Him. Stich b has been rendered: "Did
man ever say that he would be swallowed up?" which is taken to mean:
"Has any man ever spoken out against God and therefore sought his own
destruction?" (D-G) or "Does a man ask to be devoured?" (P.), but the
Heb. does not sustain this interpretation in either phrasing.

The v. structure suggests that כִּי אֲדַבֵּר and אִם־אָמַר are parallel, referring
to man's speaking out, and that, similarly, הַיְסֻפַּר לוֹ and כִּי יְבֻלָּע, both in

the third person, refer to God. כִּי is a sign of a question, like its synonym אִם, the existence of which has generally been overlooked. Cf. כִּי־הִצִּילוּ (II Ki. 18:34; in the parallel, Isa. 36:19, וְכִי); הֲכִי (Job 6:12; see the Comm.); the usage is exceedingly common in rabbinic Heb., e.g., וכי אומרים (*B. Shab.* 4a; "Do we say to a man?"); (*B. Men.* 48a; *Yoma* 7a). יְבֻלָּע is to be rendered: "be confused, confounded" (cf. Isa. 19:3, 13; 28:7; Ps. 55:10).

The v. may now be rendered: "Will He be told if I, a mere man, speak? If a man talks, will He be confounded?"

Dh., Hö., on the basis of B. Jacob (*ZATW*, 1912, p. 287), suggest another appropriate rendering, utilizing the Arab. root *balaġa* "(news) to come to one's knowledge." Stich b, which is now an excellent parallelism with stich a, may now be rendered: "If a man talks, will He be informed?" The problem with this interpretation is that it creates a *hapax legomenon*, otherwise unattested in Hebrew, when a satisfactory alternative is available.

Intr. Note 37:21–24

This passage, in spite of its familiar vocabulary, is unclear (D-G). There is, however, no reason for suspecting its authenticity on metric grounds. See Special Note 31 on the metric structure.

The efforts to reorganize the stichs in vv. 19–22 by Du. and Hö. (21a, c, 18, 20, 22a, 21b, 22b) and by P. (18, 21, 19, 20), or to emend the passage and delete part by Ehr. (v. 18) are subjective procedures that do not improve the text.

37:21 The v. is apparently a description of the bright splendor of a sunlit sky following the storm. *Veˁattāh* has been understood either consequentially or temporally. On the first view, the passage means that since men cannot see the physical light, how much less the majesty of God, but this interpretation leaves much to be inferred. Regarded temporally, *veˁattāh* introduces the change from the storm to the sunshine.

לֹא רָאוּ is impersonal. The clause has been interpreted: (a) "Men cannot see the sunlight" (Ibn E., Ew., Du., Peake), but the perfect tense militates against this view; (b) "Men do not, as a matter of experience, look upon the sunlight"; (c) "Men have not seen the light" (V, Hi., Del., D-G); (d) probably the best approach is that of Ehr., who treats stich a as a circumstantial clause: "But now, after men had not seen the light (because of the storm), it becomes bright in the sky."

In stich b, בָּהִיר "bright," the only other occurrence of the root in O. T. being in בַּהֶרֶת "bright spot, skin eruption" (Lev. 13:22 ff.). The root is an instance of ˀaḍdad, "a word of like and opposite meaning." The root means "shine, be bright" in Arabic and Ethiopic (with metathesis) and "be obscure, dark" in Syriac.

On the basis of the interpretations of stich a cited above, which treat it as the main clause, stichs b and c are subordinate circumstantial clauses: "And now men cannot gaze on the sunlight, when it is bright in the skies, and the wind has passed and cleared them." D-G objects that the sun is always too dazzling to be seen by the naked eye, but its brightness is certainly more striking after the darkness of clouds and rain. If stich a is treated as a circumstantial clause, as we prefer, stichs b and c are the main clauses: "And now, after men had seen no light, the skies brighten, for the wind has passed and cleared them."

37:22 Stich a has been interpreted: (a) lit. "gold comes from the north (Herodotus III, sec. 116; Pliny, *Historia Naturalis* 6:11; 33:7), but God's majesty is universal" (Del.). However, the two ideas are not really in contrast. (b) On the basis of Ugaritic mythological texts, the passage is explained as an allusion to the building of the palace of gold, silver and lapis lazuli on the height of Baal's mountain Zaphon (P.). However, the context does not speak of a golden palace in the north, but of gold coming from the north, and the entire context suggests a recurrent natural phenomenon, not a cosmogenic event; cf. the Comm. on v. 18 above. (c) a reference to the Aurora Borealis, the streaming rays of which appear in the northern heavens (Driver). The best view is (d) the gold refers to the bright sunlight. LXX has caught the sense superbly in its rendering: "clouds shining like gold." Rain was popularly thought to come from the north; cf. Pr. 25:23. Hence when the sun emerges, clouds will still be present in the north, but will glisten like gold in the sun's reflected rays. Guil. cites Arabic *dhihbat^un*, which the Arab lexicographers explain as "falling rain shot through by the sun's rays."

There is no need to emend to זֹהַר "brightness" (Gr., Du., Be., Bu., D-G, Hö.).

In view of Elihu's desire to extol the glory of God, the reference to the north is particularly apt. As the etymology of צָפוֹן, "the hidden," indicates, the north was the dwelling of the gods (Isa. 14:13); in Northwest Semitic myth (cf. C. H. Gordon, *UT*, p. 475, n. 2185, and Jean-Hoftitjzer, *DISDO*, p. 246). In biblical religion, Jerusalem is described as "the uttermost north" (Ps. 48:3); and Ezekiel's chariot appears "from the north" (1:4). Cf. the Comm. on 26:7. The poet utilizes this mythological background to describe the majesty of God revealed by the golden splendor of the north.

In stich b, נוֹרָא הוֹד may be rendered: "terrible in majesty" (TS), or, better, "majesty is awesome," but a verb would be preferable. Perhaps נוֹרָא is to be construed as the Niphal participle of the verb ירא = יָרָה, "shoot, throw" with Aleph, an aberrant orthography. The Lamed Aleph form occurs in the Qal, לִירוֹא בַּחִצִּים (II Chr. 26:15), in the Hiphil (II Sam. 11:24), and perhaps in the Hophal (Pr. 11:25). Hence, stich b may possibly be rendered lit. "upon God, majesty is poured forth." For the theme, cf. Ps. 93:3; 104:1.

37:23 On the metrics, see Special Note 31. The Masoretic accents treat the v. as a distich by placing the caesura after שַׂגִּיא־כֹחַ, which creates difficulties in stich b. The v. is to be scanned as a tristich with the pauses after מְצָאנֻהוּ and וּמִשְׁפָּט. Stich a contains a *casus pendens*: "The Almighty, whom we cannot fathom," or "whom we cannot reach." Stich b is to be rendered "great in power and in justice," not "judgment." Cf. Gen. 18:25; Mic. 6:8, etc.

Job has repeatedly conceded the first attribute, but denied the second; cf. 9:19. Elihu emphatically affirms both, perhaps with this assertion of Job in mind.

In stich c, וְרֹב צְדָקָה has been taken as an epithet of God, but this leaves יְעַנֶּה without an object, which must be supplied, "His creatures" (Ra.), or "those lacking in understanding if they do not fear Him" (Ibn E.). The verb has been emended to לֹא יַעֲנֶה with the object left to be inferred: "He who is abundant in righteousness does not answer those who question His rule" (Bi., Hoff., Be.) or לֹא יְעַוֵּת "He does not pervert." However, this leaves the object still unexpressed. It is far better to refer the phrase וְרֹב צְדָקָה to man and to treat it as the object of the verb: "one abounding in righteous-ness." For this use of the abstract instead of the concrete, cf. רֹב דְּבָרִים (11:2). For a similar instance where an epithet is to be referred to man rather than to God, see the Comm. on 9:4. Render stich c: "The man abounding in righteousness He does not torment."

37:24 The lit. meaning of stich b: "He sees not any that are wise of heart" (D-G) is meaningless. Hence it is taken to mean: (a) "He does not look even upon the wise of heart (who are so far beneath Him)" (Ibn E., P., and Ha.). (b) "He does not look upon those who are wise in their own conceit" (V, *qui sibi videntur sapientes*, Ra., D-G, P.). However, the phrase חֲכַם לֵב can-not have this meaning, which is expressed by the idiom חָכָם בְּעֵינָיו (Pr. 13:7; 26:5, 12, 16; 28:11). The phrase in our v. is invariably used in a favorable sense (Ex. 31:6; 35:10; 36:1, 2; Pr. 10:8; 11:29; 16:21; Job 9:4). Ehr. reads יִרְאֶה in both stichs and renders: "Only ordinary men see it; the wise in heart see it not, i.e. the greatness of God." Both the meaning attached to the terms and its appropriateness, particularly as the peroration of Elihu's speech, are dubious. This last point is generally overlooked in all the inter-pretations proposed.

We suggest revocalizing the verb in stich b as יִרְאֻהוּ = יִרְאָה and render "all those wise in heart fear Him." The repetition of the same root in both stichs is a marked characteristic of Job's style. לֹא is here used as an asservera-tive, a usage that develops from its employment in interrogative sentences expecting a negative answer (= הֲלֹא). Hence lit. "do not the wise fear Him?" = "the wise surely fear him." For this usage in biblical Heb. (e.g., Hos. 10:9; 11:5), see Gordis, in *Louis Ginzberg Jubilee Volumes* (New York, 1945), English volume, pp. 181 ff. and the Comm. on 11:11; 35:15. See now Neil Richardson, in *JBL*, vol. 90, 1971, p. 263, who so interprets the negative in II Sam. 23:5. LXX has grasped the meaning here perfectly, "the wise of heart will fear Him."

On the authenticity, integrity, and meaning of the Speeches of the Lord out of the Whirlwind (chaps. 38–42:6), and their relevance to the book, see Special Note 32.

For the meaning and metric structure of the First Speech of the Lord (chaps. 38–39), see Special Note 33.

The Lord Out of the Whirlwind

The Lord's First Speech (38–40:2)

Job, who has demanded time and again that God appear and argue with him, now has his wish granted, but on terms vastly different from those he imagined. Speaking out of a whirlwind, the Lord challenges Job to understand, let alone share, the task of creation. In powerful lines the wonders of inanimate nature are described. Heaven and earth, stars and sea, morning and night, light and darkness, are depicted. Does Job know the treasure-houses of snow and hail, the path of the flood and the lightning? Has he ever begotten the rain, the dew, the frost, or the clouds? And these reveal only part of God's creative power.

The Lord now expresses His joy in the world of living creatures. Can Job feed the lion's whelps? Does he know the miracle of birth of the mountain goat, the wild ass, or the buffalo? Has Job ever observed the swift ostrich or the fleet horse? Does he know the hawk or the falcon? They are the beloved creatures of God, who cares for and protects them all.

This basic theme — that the universe is a mystery to man — is explicitly set forth in the God speeches. There are, in addition, two other significant ideas implicit in the Lord's words. In accordance with Semitic rhetorical usage they are not spelled out, but are left to be inferred by the reader. The first is that the universe was not created exclusively for man's use, and therefore neither it nor its Creator can be judged solely by man's standards and goals. The second is even more significant. The natural world, though it is beyond man's ken, reveals to him its beauty and order. It is therefore reasonable for man to believe that the universe also exhibits a moral order with pattern and meaning, though it be beyond man's power fully to comprehend. Who, then, is Job, to reprove God and dispute with Him?

435

38 Then the Lord answered Job out of the whirlwind, saying,
2   Who is this that darkens My plan
                    by words without knowledge?
3   Gird up your loins like a man;
                    I will ask you, and you tell Me.
4   Where were you when I laid the foundations of the earth?
                    Tell Me, if you have any understanding.
5   Who marked out its measure, if you know it,
                    who stretched the plumb line upon it?
6   Upon what were the earth's pillars sunk;
                    who laid down its cornerstone,
7   when the morning stars sang together
                    and all the sons of God shouted for joy?

8   Who shut in the Sea with doors
                    when it broke forth from the womb whence it came,
9   when I made the clouds its garment
                    and dark clouds its swaddling clothes,
10   prescribing My limit for the Sea,
                    and setting for it bolts and doors,
11   saying, "Thus far shall you come, and no farther,
                    and here shall your proud waves be stayed"?

12   Have you ever commanded the morning,
                    or assigned its place to the dawn,
13   so that you might take hold of the edges of the earth
                    and the wicked be shaken from it,
14   and they be plunged into the mire,
                    and be arraigned, all put to shame,
15   for thus light is withheld from the wicked,
                    and the power of the arrogant is broken.
16   Have you trodden on the bed of the Sea
                    or walked in the recesses of the Deep?
17   Have the gates of Death been revealed to you;
                    have you seen the gates of the netherworld?
18   Have you observed the breadth of the earth?
                    Declare, if you know it all.

19   What is the way to the home of light;
                    and darkness, where is its dwelling place?
20   Can you take it to its border,
                    do you know the path to its home?
21   You surely know it, for you were born then,
                    and the number of your days is great!

22   Have you entered the storehouses of snow,
                    have you seen the storehouses of the hail,
23   which I have reserved for the time of trouble,
                    for the day of battle and war?
24   In what way are the air currents scattered
                    and is the east wind spread upon the earth?
25   Who has cleft a channel for the torrents of rain
                    and a path for the thunderbolt,

א	וַיַּעַן־יְהֹוָה אֶת־אִיּוֹב מִנ׀ הַסְּעָרָה וַיֹּאמַר:	
2	מִי זֶה׀ מַחְשִׁיךְ עֵצָה	בְּמִלִּין בְּלִי־דָעַת:
3	אֱזָר־נָא כְגֶבֶר חֲלָצֶיךָ	וְאֶשְׁאָלְךָ וְהוֹדִיעֵנִי:
4	אֵיפֹה הָיִיתָ בְּיָסְדִי־אָרֶץ	הַגֵּד אִם־יָדַעְתָּ בִינָה:
ה	מִי־שָׂם מְמַדֶּיהָ כִּי תֵדָע	אוֹ מִי־נָטָה עָלֶיהָ קָּו:
6	עַל־מָה אֲדָנֶיהָ הָטְבָּעוּ	אוֹ מִי־יָרָה אֶבֶן פִּנָּתָהּ:
7	בְּרָן־יַחַד כּוֹכְבֵי בֹקֶר	וַיָּרִיעוּ כָּל־בְּנֵי אֱלֹהִים:
8	וַיָּסֶךְ בִּדְלָתַיִם יָם	בְּגִיחוֹ מֵרֶחֶם יֵצֵא:
9	בְּשׂוּמִי עָנָן לְבֻשׁוֹ	וַעֲרָפֶל חֲתֻלָּתוֹ:
י	וָאֶשְׁבֹּר עָלָיו חֻקִּי	וָאָשִׂים בְּרִיחַ וּדְלָתָיִם:
11	וָאֹמַר עַד־פֹּה תָבוֹא וְלֹא תֹסִיף	
12	הֲמִיָּמֶיךָ צִוִּיתָ בֹּקֶר	וּפֹא־יָשִׁית בְּגָאוֹן גַּלֶּיךָ:
13	יִדַּעְתָּה שַׁחַר מְקֹמוֹ	לֶאֱחֹז בְּכַנְפוֹת הָאָרֶץ
14	וְיִנָּעֲרוּ רְשָׁעִים מִמֶּנָּה:	תִּתְהַפֵּךְ כְּחֹמֶר חוֹתָם
טו	וְיִתְיַצְּבוּ כְּמוֹ לְבוּשׁ:	וְיִמָּנַע מֵרְשָׁעִים אוֹרָם
16	וּזְרוֹעַ רָמָה תִּשָּׁבֵר:	הֲבָאתָ עַד־נִבְכֵי־יָם
17	הֲנִגְלוּ לְךָ שַׁעֲרֵי־מָוֶת	וּבְחֵקֶר תְּהוֹם הִתְהַלָּכְתָּ:
18	הִתְבֹּנַנְתָּ עַד־רַחֲבֵי־אָרֶץ	וְשַׁעֲרֵי צַלְמָוֶת תִּרְאֶה:
19	אֵי־זֶה הַדֶּרֶךְ יִשְׁכָּן־אוֹר	הַגֵּד אִם־יָדַעְתָּ כֻלָּהּ:
כ	כִּי תִקָּחֶנּוּ אֶל־גְּבוּלוֹ	וְחֹשֶׁךְ אֵי־זֶה מְקֹמוֹ:
21	יָדַעְתָּ כִּי־אָז תִּוָּלֵד	וּמִסְפַּר יָמֶיךָ רַבִּים:
22	הֲבָאתָ אֶל־אֹצְרוֹת שָׁלֶג	וְכִי תָבִין נְתִיבוֹת בֵּיתוֹ:
23	אֲשֶׁר־חָשַׂכְתִּי לְעֶת־צָר	וְאֹצְרוֹת בָּרָד תִּרְאֶה:
24	אֵי־זֶה הַדֶּרֶךְ יֵחָלֶק אוֹר	לְיוֹם קְרָב וּמִלְחָמָה:
כה	מִי־פִלַּג לַשֶּׁטֶף תְּעָלָה	יָפֵץ קָדִים עֲלֵי־אָרֶץ:

ל״ח v. 1. מִן ק׳　v. 12. יָדַעַת הַשַּׁחַר ק׳　v. 13, 15. ע׳ תלויה

26   to bring rain to a land uninhabited
        to a desert where no man lives;
27   to satisfy the desolate wasteland
        and make the dry ground bring forth grass?
28   Has the rain a father,
        and who has begotten the dew drops?
29   From whose womb did the ice come forth,
        and the frost of heaven, who has given it birth,
30   when water is congealed like stone,
        and the face of the deep is frozen over?

31   Can you bind the chains of the Pleiades
        or loose the cords of Orion?
32   Can you bring forth Mazzarot in its season
        or guide the Bear with its children?
33   Do you know the laws of the heavens;
        can you establish order on the earth?
34   Can you lift up your voice to the clouds
        that a flood of waters may cover you?
35   Can you command the lightnings to go forth;
        will they say to you, "Here we are"?
36   Who has placed wisdom in the ibis
        or given understanding to the cock?
37   Who can spread out the clouds in wisdom,
        and who can tilt the pitchers of heaven,
38   when the dust hardens into a mass
        and the clods cleave fast together?
39   Can you hunt prey for the lion
        and satisfy the young whelps' appetite
40   when they crouch in their dens
        or lie in wait in their covert?
41   Who provides for the raven its prey,
        when its young ones cry to God
        and wander about without food?

39   Do you know the time when the mountain goats are born,
        and do you watch the travail of the hinds?
2   Can you number the months they fulfill,
        and do you know the time that they give birth,
3   when they crouch, bring forth their offspring,
        and are delivered of their young?
4   Their young ones grow strong, they grow up in the open,
        they go forth, and do not return to them.

5   Who has given the wild ass his freedom?
        Who has loosed the bonds of the swift ass,
6   whose home I have made the wilderness
        and whose dwelling is the salt land?
7   He scorns the noise of the city;
        he will hear no shouts from the driver.
8   He ranges over the mountains as his pasture,
        and he searches after every green plant.

לְהַמְטִיר עַל־אֶרֶץ לֹא־אִישׁ	26	וְדֶרֶךְ לַחֲזִיז קֹלוֹת:
לְהַשְׂבִּיעַ שֹׁאָה וּמְשֹׁאָה	27	מִדְבָּר לֹא־אָדָם בּוֹ:
הֲיֵשׁ־לַמָּטָר אָב	28	וּלְהַצְמִיחַ מֹצָא דֶשֶׁא:
מִבֶּטֶן מִי יָצָא הַקָּרַח	29	אוֹ מִי־הוֹלִיד אֶגְלֵי־טָל:
כָּאֶבֶן מַיִם יִתְחַבָּאוּ	ל	וּכְפֹר שָׁמַיִם מִי יְלָדוֹ:
הַתְקַשֵּׁר מַעֲדַנּוֹת כִּימָה	31	וּפְנֵי תְהוֹם יִתְלַכָּדוּ:
הֲתֹצִיא מַזָּרוֹת בְּעִתּוֹ	32	אוֹ־מֹשְׁכוֹת כְּסִיל תְּפַתֵּחַ:
הֲיָדַעְתָּ חֻקּוֹת שָׁמָיִם	33	וְעַיִשׁ עַל־בָּנֶיהָ תַנְחֵם:
הֲתָרִים לָעָב קוֹלֶךָ	34	אִם־תָּשִׂים מִשְׁטָרוֹ בָאָרֶץ:
הֲתְשַׁלַּח בְּרָקִים וְיֵלֵכוּ	לה	וְשִׁפְעַת־מַיִם תְּכַסֶּךָּ:
מִי־שָׁת בַּטֻּחוֹת חָכְמָה	36	וְיֹאמְרוּ לְךָ הִנֵּנוּ:
מִי־יְסַפֵּר שְׁחָקִים בְּחָכְמָה	37	אוֹ מִי־נָתַן לַשֶּׂכְוִי בִינָה:
בְּצֶקֶת עָפָר לַמּוּצָק	38	וְנִבְלֵי שָׁמַיִם מִי יַשְׁכִּיב:
הֲתָצוּד לְלָבִיא טָרֶף	39	וּרְגָבִים יְדֻבָּקוּ:
כִּי־יָשֹׁחוּ בַּמְּעוֹנוֹת	מ	וְחַיַּת כְּפִירִים תְּמַלֵּא:
מִי יָכִין לָעֹרֵב צֵידוֹ	41	יֵשְׁבוּ בַסֻּכָּה לְמוֹ־אָרֶב:
יִתְעוּ לִבְלִי־אֹכֶל:		כִּי־יְלָדוֹ אֶל־אֵל יְשַׁוֵּעוּ:

חֹלֵל אַיָּלוֹת תִּשְׁמֹר:	הֲיָדַעְתָּ עֵת לֶדֶת יַעֲלֵי־סָלַע	א	לט
וְיָדַעְתָּ עֵת לִדְתָּנָה:	תִּסְפֹּר יְרָחִים תְּמַלֶּאנָה	2	
חֶבְלֵיהֶם תְּשַׁלַּחְנָה:	תִּכְרַעְנָה יַלְדֵיהֶן תְּפַלַּחְנָה	3	
יָצְאוּ וְלֹא־שָׁבוּ לָמוֹ:	יַחְלְמוּ בְנֵיהֶם יִרְבּוּ בַבָּר	4	
וּמֹסְרוֹת עָרוֹד מִי פִתֵּחַ:	מִי־שִׁלַּח פֶּרֶא חָפְשִׁי	ה	
וּמִשְׁכְּנוֹתָיו מְלֵחָה:	אֲשֶׁר־שַׂמְתִּי עֲרָבָה בֵיתוֹ	6	
תְּשֻׁאוֹת נוֹגֵשׂ לֹא יִשְׁמָע:	יִשְׂחַק לַהֲמוֹן קִרְיָה	7	
וְאַחַר כָּל־יָרוֹק יִדְרוֹשׁ:	יְתוּר הָרִים מִרְעֵהוּ	8	

ל"ח v. 41. ילדיו ק׳ ibid. אין כאן פסקא

9   Is the wild ox willing to serve you?
       Will he spend the night at your crib?
10   Can you bind him to the furrow with ropes? —
       will he harrow the valleys after you?
11   Can you trust him, since his strength is great,
       and leave your produce to him?
12   Can you rely on him to return,
       and gather in your seed and your harvest?

13   Do you know the wing of the ostrich beating joyously?
       is her pinion like that of the stork or the vulture?
14   For she leaves her eggs on the earth
       and lets them be warmed on the ground,
15   forgetting that a foot may crush them
       or a wild beast trample them.
16   Her young ones grow tough without her;
       that her labor may be in vain gives her no concern,
17   because God granted her no wisdom,
       and He gave her no share in understanding.
18   Now she soars aloft
       and laughs at the horse and his rider.

19   Do you give the horse his strength;
       Do you clothe his neck with a mighty mane?
20   Do you make him leap forward like the locust,
       while the echo of his snorting is terrible?
21   In strength and joy he paws the valley
       and bravely goes forth to face the battle.
22   He laughs at fear and is not dismayed;
       he does not draw back from the sword.
23   Past him the arrow whistles,
       the flashing spear, and the javelin.
24   Shaking with excitement he stamps the ground
       and cannot believe that the trumpet is sounding.
25   At the trumpet's faint sound he says, "Aha!"
       smelling the battle from afar,
       the shouting of the captains and the trumpet blast.

26   Is it by your wisdom that the hawk goes soaring
       and spreads his wings toward the south?
27   Is it at your command that the eagle mounts
       and makes his nest on high?
28   On the rock he makes his home,
       on the steep crag and fortress.

29   Thence he searches for food,
       his eyes ranging afar.

30   His young ones suck up blood,
       and where the slain are, there is he.

40   (Thus the Lord replied to Job, saying,)
2   Can he who argues with the Almighty instruct Him?
       Can he who reproves God answer all this?

9　הֲיֹאבֶה רֵּים עָבְדֶךָ　אִם־יָלִין עַל־אֲבוּסֶךָ׃

י　הֲתִקְשָׁר־רֵים בְּתֶלֶם עֲבֹתוֹ　אִם־יְשַׂדֵּד עֲמָקִים אַחֲרֶיךָ׃

11　הֲתִבְטַח־בּוֹ כִּי־רַב כֹּחוֹ　וְתַעֲזֹב אֵלָיו יְגִיעֶךָ׃

12　הֲתַאֲמִין בּוֹ כִּי־יָשׁוּב זַרְעֶךָ　וְגׇרְנְךָ יֶאֱסֹף׃

13　כְּנַף־רְנָנִים נֶעֱלָסָה　אִם־אֶבְרָה חֲסִידָה וְנֹצָה׃

14　כִּי־תַעֲזֹב לָאָרֶץ בֵּצֶיהָ　וְעַל־עָפָר תְּחַמֵּם׃

טו　וַתִּשְׁכַּח כִּי־רֶגֶל תְּזוּרֶהָ　וְחַיַּת הַשָּׂדֶה תְּדוּשֶׁהָ׃

16　הִקְשִׁיחַ בָּנֶיהָ לְּלֹא־לָהּ　לְרִיק יְגִיעָהּ בְּלִי־פָחַד׃

17　כִּי־הִשָּׁהּ אֱלוֹהַּ חׇכְמָה　וְלֹא־חָלַק לָהּ בַּבִּינָה׃

18　כָּעֵת בַּמָּרוֹם תַּמְרִיא　תִּשְׂחַק לַסּוּס וּלְרֹכְבוֹ׃

19　הֲתִתֵּן לַסּוּס גְּבוּרָה　הֲתַלְבִּישׁ צַוָּארוֹ רַעְמָה׃

כ　הֲתַרְעִישֶׁנּוּ כָּאַרְבֶּה　הוֹד נַחְרוֹ אֵימָה׃

21　יַחְפְּרוּ בָעֵמֶק וְיָשִׂישׂ בְּכֹחַ　יֵצֵא לִקְרַאת־נָשֶׁק׃

22　יִשְׂחַק לְפַחַד וְלֹא יֵחָת　וְלֹא־יָשׁוּב מִפְּנֵי־חָרֶב׃

23　עָלָיו תִּרְנֶה אַשְׁפָּה　לַהַב חֲנִית וְכִידוֹן׃

24　בְּרַעַשׁ וְרֹגֶז יְגַמֶּא־אָרֶץ　וְלֹא־יַאֲמִין כִּי־קוֹל שׁוֹפָר׃

כה　בְּדֵי שֹׁפָר ׀ יֹאמַר הֶאָח　וּמֵרָחוֹק יָרִיחַ מִלְחָמָה

26　רַעַם שָׂרִים וּתְרוּעָה׃　הֲמִבִּינָתְךָ יַאֲבֶר־נֵץ

27　יִפְרֹשׂ כְּנָפָו לְתֵימָן׃　אִם־עַל־פִּיךָ יַגְבִּיהַּ נָשֶׁר

28　וְכִי יָרִים קִנּוֹ׃　סֶלַע יִשְׁכֹּן וְיִתְלֹנָן

29　עַל־שֶׁן־סֶלַע וּמְצוּדָה׃　מִשָּׁם חָפַר־אֹכֶל

ל　לְמֵרָחוֹק עֵינָיו יַבִּיטוּ׃　וְאֶפְרֹחָו יְעַלְעוּ־דָם

וּבַאֲשֶׁר חֲלָלִים שָׁם הוּא׃

מ

א　וַיַּעַן יְהוָה אֶת־אִיּוֹב וַיֹּאמַר׃

2　הֲרֹב עִם־שַׁדַּי יִסּוֹר　מוֹכִיחַ אֱלוֹהַּ יַעֲנֶנָּה׃

ו. 12. ישיב ק׳　ל״ט　ו. 26. כנפיו ק׳　ו. 30. ואפרחיו ק׳

CHAPTER 38

38:1   The Divine name JHVH appears in the heading here, as well as in
40:1 and 6. Otherwise, it occurs only in the Prose Tale, but not in the Dialogue
with the Friends or in the Elihu speeches. The only exception is in 12:9, an
unconscious reminiscence of an entire phrase from Deutero-Isaiah (41:20).
In 28:28, *Adonai* appears in the common phrase "the fear of the Lord,"
which is also a locution familiar to the poet from the Hebrew literature which
served as his religio-cultural background (Isa. 33:6; Ps. 19:10; 34:12; Pr.
1:7; 2:3; 8:13 and *passim*).

The poet obviously had the Prose Tale before him. More probably, he
had reworked the traditional narrative himself, in order to use it as a framework for his Dialogue (cf. *BGM*, chap. VI, see esp. p. 73). He is, therefore,
thoroughly familiar with the Divine name. In using JHVH for the appearance
of "the Lord out of the whirlwind," he was undoubtedly influenced by the
traditional relationship of the theophany of JHVH to a storm (Ex. 19:16;
Jud. 5:6 f.; II Sam. 22:8–16 = Ps. 18:8–16; Isa. 63:19 f.; Nah. 1:3; Hab.
3:5 f.; Zech. 9:14; Ps. 50:3; 68:8 f.). The revelation of God's will to His
people at Sinai accompanied by thunder and lightning was the primal event
in the religion of Israel. So, too, this communication of God's thought to
man is enhanced by the power of the whirlwind.

The Kethib which contains the non-final *Nun* in מנהסערה (38:1) and
in מנסערה without an article (40:6) is a survival in MT from an earlier stage,
when word-divisions were not fixed, or, more probably, when final letters
had not yet been introduced. For other instances, see Neh. 2:13; I Chr.
27:12 and cf. *BTM*, pp. 98–100, and p. 173, n. 116.

38:2   עֵצָה, like בִּינָה and תְּבוּנָה, is a synonym of חָכְמָה (Jer. 49:7). It represents
the Divine plan or purpose in creation (Pr. 8:14; Job 12:13) and in governing
the world (Isa. 5:19; 46:10). It is, therefore, an attribute *in parvo* of the
practitioners and devotees of Wisdom (Isa. 11:9; Jer. 18:18; Ezek. 7:26;
Pr. 1:30; 19:20).

מַחְשִׁיךְ "hides, obscures," like the synonym in 42:3 where this passage is
quoted; cf. Ps. 139:1. The meaning is declarative: "lit. declare my plan to
be dark, obscure." The emendation to מַכְחִישׁ "denies" (TS) is unnecessary.

The v. is an instance of formal (or synthetic) parallelism like Ps. 2:6;
cf. *PPS*, pp. 75 f.

38:3   כְגֶבֶר is generally emended to כְגִבֹּר, "like a mighty hero" (P, Hoff.,
Bi., Bu., Hö., Be., TS, P.). It may be that the English phrase "like a man"
is derived from this passage, but the meaning is so clear that the change
seems to be unnecessary; the noun גֶּבֶר carries enough of the nuance of strength
and courage needed for our passage. Some scholars have interpreted the
passage in the light of the ancient ordeal of belt-wrestling (C. H. Gordon,

in *HUCA*, vol. 23, pp. 131 ff.; TS), but these erudite references seem irrelevant and indeed impossible in our passage.

38:4 The creation of the earth is pictured as the erection of a building beginning with the laying of its foundation, as in Babylonian mythology (*Enuma Elish*, IV, ll. 143 ff.).

Stich b is a response to Job's plea in 13:22.

38:5 מְמַדֶּיהָ from מֵמַד "measurement"; cf. מֵסַב I Ki. 6:29.

כִּי תֵדָע not (a) ironically, "since you know it" or (b) "do you know it?" (P.). On כִּי as a sign of an interrogative, cf. the Comm. on 36:20. However, it is somewhat awkward to have two questions in one brief stich. It is best rendered "if you know it" (Del.), parallelling v. 4b; cf. Pr. 30:4.

קָו is the plumb line used in building (Jer. 31:38; Zech. 1:16), but also for marking off for destruction (II Ki. 21:13; Isa. 34:11; Am. 7:7 f.).

38:6 אֶדֶן "foundation, pillar," used frequently of the pedestal or base of the Tabernacle in the wilderness (Ex. 26:19 et seq. and in Cant. 5:15).

יָרָה "cast, hurl," used of setting up a stone monument (Gen. 31:5); cf. the Aram. כָּרְסָן רְמִיו (Dan. 7:9), the Akk. *ramû shubtu* and *nadû uššê* "lit. throw a dwelling, i.e. settle," and the Latin *fundamenta jacere*.

38:7 The sons of God (Job 1:6, etc.; Ps. 29:2; 82:6) are the godlike beings who are members of the Divine Court serving as His messengers (cf. Greek *angeloi*) to do His bidding. Hence, they are equated with the natural forces like the wind and the fire (Ps. 104:4) and here with the heavenly bodies. The poetic imagery here may well be a reflection of older myths (e.g. Gen. 6:4), which in turn became the basis of a new astral mythology when taken literally. This magnificent verse served William Blake for one of his most impressive drawings in his "Illustrations for the Book of Job."

38:8 וַיָּסֶךְ is emended to מִי סָךְ by a long catena of scholars (Me., Wr., Bi., Bu., Be., D-G, Hö.) on the basis of V, "*quis conclusit*," but this rendering may well be an instance of leveling to the interrogative form used in v. 5. On the root סוּךְ "fence, shut in," cf. 1:10; 3:23.

בִּדְלָתַיִם is not to be emended to בְּדֶלֶת, with the two final consonants deleted as a dittography, nor is the repetition of the noun in 10b due to "poverty of language" (D-G), the use of the same root being a characteristic of the poet's style.

The sea, the primordial monster, needs to be restrained from the moment of his birth, lest he inundate and destroy the world. דְּלָתַיִם "double doors," the dual serving as an intensive; cf. the idiom in Deut. 3:5; I Sam. 23:7; Isa. 45:1; 49:31; II Chr. 8:5; Job 14:6; and see v. 10 below. The reference is to the sand that bars the overflowing of the sea (cf. Jer. 5:22; Ps. 104:9; Pr. 8:29; Job 7:12). In the Mesopotamian creation epic, Marduk places a bar to keep back the waters (*ANET*, p. 67, ll. 139 f.). The swaddling clothes in v. 9 may have been intended to restrain the violent infant at birth. Thus the monsters "Eaters and Devourers" in Ugaritic mythology are described as wrapped in swaddling clothes at birth (P.).

בְּגִיחוֹ. The choice of this root is particularly apt, since it has the connotations of (a) "bursting forth of water" as in the name of the river גִּיחוֹן (Gen. 2:13), so also in Syriac and in Ethiopic *gaḥa* "breaking forth (of light)"; (b) "rushing forth into battle" (Jud. 20:33); and (c) "breaking forth from the womb." All three nuances may be sensed in our passage, the waters at birth rushing forth to do battle, as in the Mesopotamian creation myth of the struggle between Marduk and Tiamat. The verb is transitive in Mic. 4:10 and in Ps. 22:10, גֹחִי being the participle of the *mediae Vav* or *Yod* root; cf. הַקֹּומִים (II Ki. 16:7); הַלֹּוט (Isa. 25:7); בֹּוסִים (Zech. 10:5). The verb is intransitive in Ezek. 32:2; Job 40:23, and our passage.

Stich a contains a *casus pendens* with the relative ʾ*ašer* understood: "lit. in its breaking out of the womb that it came from." The womb is the primordial abyss of water (Gen. 7:11; Ps. 36:7) "lying beneath the earth" (Gen. 48:25; Deut. 33:13) from which the sea issued at creation (Isa. 51:10).

38:9 The v. carries on the metaphor of the birth of the sea. חֲתֻלָּתֹו "swaddling clothes"; cf. Ezek. 16:4; 30:21.

38:10 וָאֶשְׁבֹּר עָלָיו חֻקִּי is explained: "I broke my boundary upon him," which is taken to mean, "I broke his strength by my law" (Ibn E.), or as an allusion to the rocks and cliffs of the shoreline (D-G). But either interpretation is too farfetched a figure. The emendations to וָאָשִׁית (Me., Wr., D-G, P.) or to a *hapax* וָאֶשְׁטֹר "I wrote" on the basis of Akk. *šatâru* (Be.) or וָאֶשְׁמֹר (Ehr.) are unconvincing and not really necessary. The basic meaning of "break" develops the connotation of "decree, decide." For the semantics, cf. the roots חרץ "sharpen" (Ex. 11:7; Jos. 10:21) and "decide, determine" (II Sam. 5:24; Job 14:3; Dan. 11:36); חצץ "divide, cut in half" (Akk. *ḥaṣâṣu* "cut in two," whence חָצָץ "gravel," Pr. 20:17; Lam. 3:16) and "decide, ordain" (Job 21:21; cf. the Comm. *ad loc.*); גזר "cut, divide" (I Ki. 3:25; II Ki. 6:4; Ps. 136:13) and "decree" (Job 22:28; Est. 2:1, and frequently in rabbinic Heb.) and the rabbinic חתך "divide, cut" (*B. Ḥul.* 48b); חותך במקום אחד "he amputates at one place" and "decide, decree," שׁם חותכין את ההלכה "for there they decide the law (*Mid. Lev. Rab.*, sec. 4) and פסק. T correctly translates פסקית עלוי גזרתי "I decreed My law upon it." חֻקִּי "my limit, boundary," the suf. being subjective, "set by Me." MT need not be emended to חק (LXX) or חֻקֹּו (Dil., Bi., Du., Be.) because of Pr. 8:20–29; our poet is not an imitator.

38:11 The omission either of תָבֹוא (Du., Be.) or of וְלֹא תֹסִיף (Bi., Studer) on metric grounds and the consequent destruction of a resonant verse is rightly stigmatized as "monstrous" by D-G, who then proceed to delete וַיֹּאמֶר. There is no genuine metric problem here. וַיֹּאמֶר may be an anacrusis, an in-

troductory word outside the meter pattern, as in Ps. 1:1; Job 39:10. Even
if the word is retained in the meter, the pattern is 4:4:

ואמֹר עד פֹּה תבֹא ולֹא תֹסיף ‖ ופֹא ישׁית בגאון גליך

The repetition of פה, with an aberrant orthography in stich b, adds
power to the decree: "to here only, etc."

Stich b in MT has been· interpreted: (a) "He will place, set down, i.e.
the decree." (b) "Go forth in battle," the verb being given a military sense
as in Ps. 3:7; Isa. 22:7. (c) rendered as an impersonal, hence passive: "Here
shall be set down the pride of your waves." Of the ancient Vss., only T תשוי
reproduces MT. P, תבתר, an inner Syriac error for תתבר "You will break,"
and V *confringes* "you will smash" suggest the reading יִשָּׁבֵר (cf. Lev. 26:19,
adopted by Ew., Wr., Baeth.). LXX *syntribesetai* "with you shall your waves
be confined," suggests the reading יִשְׁבֹּת or יָשֵׁבֶת; cf. וְהִשְׁבַּתִּי גְּאוֹן זֵדִים (Isa.
13:11; Ezek. 7:24; 30:18; 33:28). The error in MT arose through a scribal
metathesis, ישבת גאון becoming ישית בגאון. Render: "lit. here shall the pride
of your waves, i.e. your proud waves, be stayed," identical with the majestic
translation of AV.

38:12 הֲמִיָּמֶיךָ "lit. from the beginning of your days"; cf. the Comm. on
27:6 and see I Sam. 25:28; I Ki. 1:6.

In stich b, the Kethib יְדַעְתָּה שַּׁחַר differs from the Qere יִדַּעְתָּ הַשַּׁחַר in
the word division. The Kethib without the article is somewhat preferable
in a poetic passage, though there are many exceptions, e.g., Job 3:1 f.; 38:24.
The Piel of ידע, only here, may occur in Ps. 104:19; cf. the parallelism there.

38:13 The earth is compared to a coverlet or a tablecloth which is shaken
clear of all its impurities by a careful housekeeper who takes hold of the ends
of the cloth. So the evil-doers who are active in the night (cf. 25:15 f.) are
dispersed in the light of day.

לֶאֱחֹז has generally been rendered "that it, i.e. the morning, might take
hold" (D-G, JPSV). A far more vivid figure emerges if it is rendered: "so
that You might take hold of the ends of the earth," going back to the pronoun
in צִוִּיתָ (Ibn E.). On וְיִנָּעֲרוּ, "be shaken," cf. the Qal (Isa. 33:15; Neh. 5:13)
and the Niphal (Jud. 16:20; Ps. 109:23). The suspended Ayin (עין תלויה)
in this and the succeeding v., like the instance in מִיָּעַר (Ps. 80:14), is not
due to dogmatic grounds, as is the case with מְנַשֶּׁה (instead of מֹשֶׁה) in Jud.
18:30. It is the result of an accidental omission by a scribe of a letter, subsequently written in above the line by another scribe. The text was then
faithfully reproduced in all copies of the archetypal manuscript, which was
adopted by the Proto-Masoretes, who, we believe, flourished before the destruction of the Second Temple in 70 C.E. (cf. *BTM*, new edition, New York,
1972, "Prolegomenon" and chaps. 1–4).

38:14 Stich a is generally explained that at night the earth has neither
shape nor color, both of which become evident with daylight. Hence the

stich is rendered: "The earth is changed, i.e. takes on form, like the clay of a seal." It is, however, undeniable that this interpretation requires a great deal of supplementary "background" to be at all intelligible. The Vss. are not particularly helpful, except for P, which renders ונתהפך איך טינא גושמהון "their body was turned like clay"; thus vocalizing כַּחֹמֶר and interpreting the final Mem of חוֹתָם as the masc. plur. suffix. On this basis, TS proceeded to vocalize חוֹתָם as חַוָתָם, which he explains as "the body of waters contained in the clouds" on the basis of Arabic *ḥawa* "accumulate, contain." He renders the stich "their pool, i.e. (of the black clouds), was turned to clay." Not only is this interpretation far-fetched, but it creates a *hapax legomenon*.

A simpler approach may be suggested, likewise taking its point of departure from the Syriac rendering, "their body." We suggest emending חוֹתָם to חַיָּתָם "their souls, i.e. their persons." The noun חַיָּה is a favorite term of Elihu (Job 33:18, 20, 22, 28; 36:14) and occurs elsewhere only in Ezek. (7:13); and Ps. (74:19, second time; 78:50; 143:3). הפך "turn, overturn" has the connotation: (a) "change into" (Lev. 13:3, 4, 13, 20; Job 20:14; Lam. 5:2); (b) "devastate" (Jonah 3:4; Job 12:15); (c) "turn loose" (Job 30:15); cf. BDB s.v., p. 245b. The Hithpael has the meaning "to turn round and round" (Gen. 3:24; Jud. 7:13; Job 37:12). כְּחֹמֶר is to be vocalized כַּחֹמֶר = כְּבַחֹמֶר, a contraction of two prefixes into one, "as in the mire," or it is to be read בַּחֹמֶר, hence "into the mire" (Isa. 10:6; Job 27:16). For the indignity of plunging a hapless victim into filth, cf. הֹרַנִי לַחֹמֶר "he has hurled me into the mire" (Job 30:19); אָז בַּשַּׁחַת תִּטְבְּלֵנִי "You would plunge me into the pit" (9:31); וְעֹלַלְתִּי בֶעָפָר קַרְנִי "I have buried my dignity in the dust" (16:15).

In stich b, MT is explained: "They, i.e. the objects on the earth, stand up like a garment." The manifest difficulties of this interpretation have led to the emendation of וְיִתְיַצְּבוּ to וְתִצְטַבַּע "the earth is dyed like a garment"; cf. for the root, the substantives in Jud. 5:30; Jer. 12:9 (Be., Du., D-G, RSV, P.). MT may be preserved by referring the masc. plur. in 14b to the wicked (13b) and the fem. sing. in 14a to the earth (13a), so that both verses are in alternate parallelism. כְּמוֹ לְבוּשׁ is accordingly read כְּמוֹ לָבוֹשׁ "stand up as if ashamed" (Hoff., Du., Be., Hö.), but כְּמוֹ = "*as if*" is meaningless in the context.

My former student, Rabbi Gilbert Rosenthal, proposed a brilliant reading in stich b: וְיִתְיַצְּבוּ כֻּלָּם יֵבֹשׁוּ "They stand up (in judgment), all being put to shame." The emendation proposes a slight scribal metathesis, the consonants כלמבש being transcribed erroneously as כמלבש and then vocalized as כְּמוֹ לְבוּשׁ. This usage of בּוֹשׁ = "put to shame, i.e. be condemned in judgment" is very common in Deutero-Isaiah, whose influence on Job is very pronounced (הֵן יֵבשׁוּ וְיִכָּלְמוּ 41:11; 42:17; 44:9; הֵן כָּל־חֲבֵרָיו יֵבשׁוּ 44:11; 48:23; 66:5), in Jeremiah (6:15; 17:13, 18), and in Psalms (6:11; 25:3; 31:18; 35:4, 26; 40:15; 129:5, a. e.).

With these minor changes proposed for the v. (כֻּלָּם יֵבשׁוּ for חֹתָם, חַיָּתָם for חוֹתָם for כְּמוֹ לְבוּשׁ) and preferably בַּחֹמֶר for כַּחֹמֶר, the verse receives a clear and unforced meaning, entirely appropriate to the context:

"They (lit. their persons) are turned round and round in the mire,
they are arraigned (in judgment), all put to shame."

38:15 The v. is deleted (Hoff., Du., Hö.) on the ground that the evil-doers
are not destroyed each morning. A more prosaic objection can scarcely be
imagined — neither are the wicked shaken off the earth each morning! Obviously, the poet is using a hyperbole to express the thought that the light
of day deprives the evil-doers of the light they need to carry on their nefarious
plans; cf. 24:15–17, especially v. 17: "For to them all darkness is morning,
and the dawn — the terror of darkness." See the Comm. *ad loc.* זְרוֹעַ רָמָה
"lofty arm, i.e., arrogant power." G. R. Driver has rendered *rešāᶜîm* as "the
Dog-Star" and *Zerōᶜa rāmāh* as the Navigator's Line (as in NEB), the
meaning being that with dawn the stars become invisible, but this ingenious
interpretation we do not find convincing.

38:16 נִבְכֵי-יָם, from an unknown root, is explained as "the sources of the
sea" on the basis of the parallelism. It is today generally associated with
the phrase in Job 28:11 revocalized as מַבְּכֵי, on the basis of a Ugaritic parallel.
See the Comm. *ad loc.*

38:17 Note the use of the same noun in both stichs. As in v. 22 below, it
need not be emended to שֹׁעֲרֵי "gatekeepers of Sheol" on the basis of LXX,
which sought to introduce variety for Greek readers. There is, incidentally,
no reference to gatekeepers of Sheol extant in Hebrew literature.

That the depths of the sea are unknown to Job suggests the even greater
mystery of the gates of death, for the netherworld was pictured as lying
below the earth like the primordial waters, and in fact was reached by crossing
Shelaḥ, the river of death; cf. the Comm. on 33:18; 36:12.

For stich b, LXX offers a conflate periphrastic rendering: "Did the gatekeepers of Sheol, seeing you, tremble," from the two roots ראה and ירא.
Inexplicably, D-G reads רָאוּךָ or רָאִיתָ, whereas MT is incomparably superior.

38:18 The interrogative He need not be supplied on the basis of haplography,
but is understood. Cf. 37:18.

38:19 The He of הַדֶּרֶךְ is not to be deleted (Be., Bu.). It is apparently
idiomatic, occurring five times in O. T. (I Ki. 13:12; II Ki. 3:8; II Chr. 18:23
and v. 24 below).

38:20 The v. is generally treated as the conclusion of v. 19: "What is the
way that light dwells, so that you can take it back to its boundary, i.e. do
you know the dwelling place of light so that you can bring it to its appointed
place?" (D-G, P., JPSV). This interpretation can be maintained, but it
suffers from several drawbacks: (a) one must supply a phrase for 19a: "*Do
you know* the way that light dwells, etc.?"; and (b) stich b in v. 20 is not a

logical conclusion after the condition assumed for v. 19. To meet this latter difficulty, תָּבִין is explained as "teach, show" (TS, P.), which is farfetched in this context. Or it is treated as a defectiva spelling for תְּבִיאֶנּוּ which offers a more exact parallel to תקחנו. However, v. 21, the natural conclusion of the theme of light and darkness, becomes redundant if v. 20 performs the same function. Hö. cuts the Gordian knot by deleting both v. 19 and v. 20.

We believe a better approach is available. כִּי in both stichs is to be treated as the interrogative particle. For the evidence of this usage in biblical as well as postbiblical Heb., cf. the Comm. on 37:20. MT now receives a straightforward meaning that articulates perfectly with v. 21:

> "Can you take it to its border,
> Do you know the path to its home?"

38:21   יָדַעְתָּ, in the perfect tense, is an ironic expression of certainty: "You surely know." This usage is related to that of the perfect in legal transactions (Gen. 23:11; Ruth 4:3), the perfect of prophetic certitude (Isa. 3:8; 5:12, etc.), and the precative perfect (Ps. 6:10; Lam. 1:21). The existence of this latter usage has been unjustifiably denied (see Driver, *HT*, pp. 17 f., 20 f.; Gordis, *SSL*, on 1:21). The contention that Job was not present at the creation, and therefore has no right to pass judgment upon it, was already advanced by Eliphaz (15:7).

38:22   Note the use of the same noun in both stichs.

38:23   The snow and the hail are both kept stored for the day of retribution against evil-doers (Isa. 28:17; Ezek. 13:13), against crops (Ex. 9:22–26; Hag. 2:17), or in battle (Jos. 10:11). B. S. 39:29 f. may be reminiscent of our passage. The same verb is used in the identical sense in 22:30; cf. the Comm. *ad loc.* The poet is not glorifying the powers of nature *per se*; they are instruments for a moral purpose. Cf. Special Note 32.

צָר either "trouble" (Isa. 5:30; Job 15:24) or "foe" (Gen. 14:20; Deut. 32:27). If the latter meaning be preferred, עֵת can mean "doom" (Ps. 81:16; Ecc. 9:12).

38:24   The apparent reference to light in this v. after vv. 19 f. has occasioned difficulty, especially in view of the parallelism. אוֹר has, therefore, (a) been emended to רוּחַ "wind" (Ew., D-G, Hö.); (b) קְטוֹר "smoke" (Be.); (c) אֵד "mist" or "cosmic flood" (Hoff., Bi., Du.); (d) interpreted as "wind" on the basis of Akk. *Amurru*, Babylonian *awurru*, "land of the west wind" (TS).

We suggest that אוֹר here has the meaning of "air, air currents"; cf. the Greek *aer*, which, coincidentally, has all the meanings proposed for our word, "air, cloud, mist." The Greek noun originally contained a digamma *afer* and may well be a Semitic borrowing. The noun reappears in rabbinic Heb. as a borrowing from the Greek in the form אויר, e.g., האויר שממנו נעשתה הרוח

"the air, one of the elements out of which the wind was made" (*Mid. Num. Rab.*, sec. 14).

יְחָלֵק = "is divided, scattered." The Hiphil יָפֵץ need not be emended to a Qal יָפוּץ, being itself intransitive; cf. וַיָּפֶץ הָעָם (Ex. 5:12; I Sam. 13:8).

38:25 The poet declares that there is nothing haphazard even about rainfall or lightning, their paths being determined by God, whose purposes transcend man's concerns (v. 26).

תְּעָלָה "conduit" for irrigation (Ezek. 31:4), or for a reservoir (Isa. 7:3), or as a trench (I Ki. 18:32). שֶׁטֶף "rain torrent" (Ps. 32:6). For stich b, cf. 28:26.

38:26 The rain falls in order to have grass grow even in the wilderness where no man lives — an adumbration of the basic theme presented even more powerfully in the Second Speech of the Lord. See Special Notes 32 and 35.

38:27 שֹׁאָה וּמְשֹׁאָה a powerful alliterative phrase signifying total desolation; cf. Zeph. 1:15; Job 30:3. There is a striking assonance of the sibilant s in stich a, since the Sin and the Šin were pronounced very similarly if not identically, and of the Ṣade in stich b.

Stich b may be rendered lit.: "to cause to sprout the place where grass grows, i.e. the earth"; on מֹצָא in this meaning, cf. מוֹצָא מַיִם "spring of water" (II Ki. 2:21) and לַכֶּסֶף מוֹצָא "the place whence silver comes forth = mine" (Job 28:1). But this would seem to be an unnecessarily involved way of describing the earth, and, in addition, it is not parallel to stich a. It has, therefore, been suggested to read צָמֵא for מֹצָא "the thirsty land" (cf. Isa. 44:3) with a double accusative (Wr., Bu., Du., Be., D-G) or מִצִּיָּה "from the parched land" (Be., P.).

38:28 אוֹ = the conjunction ו "and." אֶגְלֵי־טָל "drops of dew" is etymologically obscure. It is hardly derived from גַּלִּים "waves" with a prosthetic Aleph (Ra., Ibn E.).

38:29 כְּפֹר "hoarfrost" (Ex. 16:14; Ps. 147:16). TS argues that קֶרַח always means "storm," not "ice," in biblical Heb.

38:30 The rendering of stich a as "like a stone (or, as with a stone) the waters are hidden" is meaningless, nor is there any basis for explaining the verb in MT as "becomes solid"; its only attested meaning is "become hidden." TS cleverly renders: "The waters are hidden as behind a stone," but it is not adequate to the passage. There are several approaches possible: (a) to emend the verb to יִתְחַבְּרוּ "would be joined together"; (b) to treat יִתְחַבָּאוּ as a dialectic variation of a verb יִתְחַמְּאוּ "hardens" from the Arab. ḥamaʾa, but this would be a *hapax*; and (c) to assume that the two verbs were accidentally transposed, so that the original read: "like a stone the

waters cohere together (יִתְלַכָּדוּ) (cf. 41:9) and the face of the deep is hidden"
(יִתְחַבָּאוּ); so Me., D-G, following Saadia, who renders the two verbs in MT
as "becomes solid" and "coheres" respectively, though the basis for his
rendering remains unclear.

38:31   The stars in their constellations are mentioned here, probably because
they were believed to exert influence on the seasons and the weather. The
heavenly bodies cannot be identified with certainty, and the ancient beliefs
regarding the stars are largely unknown, so that the specific references cannot
be spelled out. כִּימָה, generally taken as the Pleiades, has also been identified
with Canis Major, containing Sirius and Scorpion. כְּסִיל is generally identified
with Orion.

   הַתְקַשֵּׁר is not "will you adorn yourself," as in 49:18, but "will you bind
fast," as is clear from the contrasting ‖ with תְּפַתֵּחַ "will you loosen."

   מַעֲדַנּוֹת occurs in identical form in the difficult passage in I Sam. 15:32,
where it is generally vocalized מַעֲדַנִּית "stumblingly, haltingly." (But see
below.) If so treated, it is distinct in meaning from our word, as the Masorah
explicitly notes. The medieval rendering of our phrase, "the dainties of the
Pleiades," saw it as a reference to the fruits and flowers of the spring which
the constellation was believed to stimulate (Nahmanides, Gersonides); similarly, "the sweet influences of the Pleiades" (AV following the earlier English
versions). The word is best understood as a metathesis, either oral or scribal,
of מַעֲנַדּוֹת "chains, fetters." Cf. ענד 31:36a and Pr. 6:21, where it is parallel
to קשר. The meaning "bands, chains" would also be appropriate for the
Samuel passage (Driver, *Notes on Samuel*, pp. 129 f.). Guil. renders the vocable
in our passage "army, host" on the basis of an alleged Ugaritic ᵓadn.

   מוֹשְׁכוֹת need not be emended to מוֹסְרוֹת (Be.); from the root משׁך "draw,
pull" the meaning "cord" is a natural derivation, lit. "the pulling substance,"
like מוֹסְרוֹת from אסר, "binding substance."

38:32   The enigmatic מַזָּרוֹת has received a plethora of interpretations: (a) as
a phonetic variant for מַזָּלוֹת "planets"; (b) from the Arabic name for "Milky
Way"; (c) from the Akk. *maṣṣarta, mazzarta* "Guard, Keeper" (TS); (d) equal
to מַזְהָרוֹת, cf. Arabic ᵓazhara "the shining one," a name for Venus, to be
identified with *Aldebaran*, whose setting was a sign of rain (Hö.); (e) a fem.
form of the noun מְזָרִים (37:9; cf. the Comm. *ad loc.*; so Ibn E., Hoff.);
(f) = מַנְזָרוֹת "crown," hence the Corona Borealis (Mi., Ew.). We may add
the suggestion that it is equal to מַאֲזָרוֹת "girdle" with the elision of the
Aleph as in רֵים (39:9, 10) רִישׁוֹן (8:8); cf. יַפִּילוּן for יַאְפִּילוּן (Job 29:24) and the
Comm. *ad loc.* This meaning would supply an excellent basis for G. R. Driver's
interpretation of the noun as "zodiacal circle." It is difficult to make a choice
among these various views. The sing. suf. on בְּעִתּוֹ makes it preferable, though
not imperative, to regard the noun as a sing., the name of a specific star,
constellation, or planet.

   עַיִשׁ, sometimes equated with the Pleiades (so T "the Hen"), is generally
identified with the Great Bear. עַל־בָּנֶיהָ "together with her children"; on this

sense of ⁛al, cf. Gen. 32:12; I Sam. 14:32. Stich b is a *casus pendens*, lit. "the Great Bear together with her young — can you guide them?" The suggestion has been made to revocalize the verb as תְּנַחֵם (Me., Hi.) and render, "Can you console the Great Bear for her children?" On this use of ⁛al, cf. Jer. 16:7; I Chr. 19:2. On this view the v. would have reference to some mythological legend which appears in an apparent variant form in the Talmud: "Ayish went about saying, 'Give me my children,' for in the hour that the Holy One, blessed be He, sought to bring the Flood upon the earth, He took stars from Kimah and thus brought the waters upon the earth through the resulting apertures. When He wished to stop the flow of waters, He took two stars from Ayish and plugged the opening" (*B. Ber.* 58b; I Chr. 19:2).

However, the parallelism favors MT (Hö.), and, moreover, the rabbinic legend may have arisen as a homiletic expansion of this biblical passage.

38:33 הֲיָדַעְתָּ need not be emended to הַיְדַעְתָּ "inform, proclaim" or הֲיָעַדְתָּ "ordain," since parallelism never operated mechanically, as is all too often assumed. God knows the laws governing heaven and earth, because He has established them; does Job?

מִשְׁטָרוֹ. The root שטר (Akk. *šaṭâru* "write," Arab. *satara* "write or line (a book)" (Aram. שטר "document") occurs in Hebrew in the noun שֹׁטֵר "officer" (Ex. 5:14; Deut. 20:5, 8, 9, etc.), often in conjunction with judges (Deut. 16:18; Jud. 8:33; I Chr. 23:4, a. e.). However, Noeldeke (*Geschichte des Qorans*, p. 13) regards the primary meaning of the root in Arabic as "to range in order." Either meaning, "write" or "arrange," offers a satisfactory meaning for the noun מִשְׁטָר "ordinance, law." Fr. Delitzsch cites Akk. *siṭir same* "the writing of heaven," hence "the starry firmament" (*Handwörterbuch*, p. 652b). In a brilliant but involved interpretation, TS utilizes the same Akk. phrase and refers it to the mysterious message of the heavens.

The final Vav has occasioned difficulty. It has been emended to מִשְׁטָרְךָ "your authority, rule" (Ehr.) or מִשְׁטָרִי "my ordinance." On the ground that שָׁמַיִם, though grammatically a plur., is logically a sing., the noun with sing. suffix of מִשְׁטָרוֹ has been rendered "its dominion" (Ibn E., Dil., JPSV).

We would suggest that the word in MT is a scribally abbreviated plur. for מִשְׁטָרוֹת "order, lit. inscribed decrees." The omission of the final Tav of plural suffixes is a commonplace of medieval Hebrew mss. followed in printed texts, e.g. עולמו' for עולמות, שמו' for שמות, etc. This orthography is to be found in the *Damascus Scroll*, originally published by Solomon Schechter (*Fragments of a Zadokite Work*, Cambridge, 1910). Thus, at times, the manuscript omits pronominal suffixes and the plural and feminine endings of nouns: זיק for זיקות (5, 13); טמא for טמאת (4, 18); חבור for חבורת (12, 8). See Louis Ginzberg, *An Unknown Jewish Sect* (New York, 1976), p. 4. For another possible instance in the biblical text, cf. the Comm. on עֲבֹתוֹ (Job 39:10); and see שֵׁנִי = שֵׁנִית "a second time" (Est. 2:14). The corresponding masculine apocopated plural is well attested in MT; cf. חַלּוֹנֵי שְׁקֻפִים (I Ki. 6:4); רִמֹּנֵי = רִמּוֹנִים (Cant. 8:2), and cf. the Comm. on אַנְשֵׁי (Job 37:7). For the plural in *ōth*, cf. משמרות, מעמדות in rabbinic

Hebrew. There is now an excellent parallelism in our v. between "the ordinances on earth" and "the laws of the heavens," that are called the laws
of the moon and the stars in Jer. 31:34.

38:34 God has merely to raise His voice and the rain pours down. For the
vivid stich b, cf. 22:11. The emendation תְּעַנְךָ (LXX, Bu., Ehr.) is far less
vivid than MT.

38:36 This difficult v. has been interpreted along four main lines:

(A) A reference to man's spirit. טֻחוֹת refers either to the kidneys, regarded as the seat of conscience (Ra.) or the innermost part of man (Ibn E.).
The noun is explained as derived from טִיחַ "plaster"; hence "the fat covering
these body organs." To maintain the parallelism שֶׂכְוִי is explained as "the
heart" from שׂכה "look, see" (Aram. "look out, hope" as in סכותא for Heb.
מִצְפֶּה "outlook point"), apparently occurring in שְׂכִיּוֹת הַחֶמְדָּה (Isa. 2:16);
מַשְׂכִּית (Lev. 26:1, etc.). Hence שֶׂכְוִי is "the seeing organ" (Ra., Ibn E.). In
support of this view, Ps. 51:8 is cited:

הֵן אֱמֶת חָפַצְתָּ בַטֻּחוֹת   וּבְסָתֻם חָכְמָה תוֹדִיעֵנִי

"Behold, Thou desirest truth in the inmost being, therefore teach me wisdom
in my secret heart" (RSV).

(B) The v. is referred to the celestial phenomena. טֻחוֹת = "clouds"
from the basic meaning "plaster, cover" and שֶׂכְוִי "clouds" from שׂכה = סכך
"cover over" or שׂכה "see" (Dil., BDB, RSV). This view leaves unexplained
the reference to wisdom with which the objects in our v. are endowed.

(C) A reference to Egyptian gods, טֻחוֹת representing *Thot*, the Egyptian
god of wisdom, occurring in the form *dhwty* in the 18th Dynasty, and שֶׂכְוִי
being the Coptic name of the god Mercury, *souchi*. See P., p. 256, for biblio-
graphical references for this view, which he adopts.

(D) A reference to birds possessing superior wisdom (so Dh., Hö.).
טֻחוֹת is the *ibis ethiopica*, the symbol of the Egyptian god of wisdom *Thot*.
שֶׂכְוִי is the cock, a meaning vouched for by a well-attested rabbinic tradition:
"Rabbi Simon ben Lakish said, 'When I went to the district of Qan Neshraya
(i.e. *Kennesrin* on the Euphrates, or, better, the district of Gennesaret in
Palestine) היו קורין לכלה נינפי ולתרנגול שכוי they called a bride *nymphe* and
a cock *sekhwiy*'" (B. Rosh Hashanah 26a). Rabbi Levi is cited as declaring
that the word signified "cock" either in Rome (*P. Ber.* IX, 13c) or in Arabia
(*Mid. Lev. Rab.* 25, 5). On the basis of this tradition, the Jewish morning
service begins with a blessing to God הנותן לשכוי בינה להבחין בין יום ובין לילה
"who gave the cock wisdom to distinguish between day and night." This
interpretation dissociates טֻחוֹת from the passage in Ps. 51:8 — except for TS,
who interprets the latter passage as: "You desire to teach me truth by im-
parting wisdom to birds (טֻחוֹת) and to beasts" (שְׂמָמִית = סָתוּם Pr. 30:28,
which he renders "beast of prey").

Interpretation B must assume that the wisdom referred to is the wisdom
to obey God's laws, which is rather far-fetched. Interpretation A is entirely

irrelevant, not only in the specific context, but also in the Speech of the
Lord as a whole. Interpretation C is unacceptable, because in the zeal to
adduce Oriental parallels it has been overlooked that the author of Job, who
was profoundly influenced by Deutero-Isaiah, was an uncompromising mono-
theist and could not possibly describe God as giving wisdom to pagan deities
whose reality He would deny. As has already been noted, the Book of Job
contains mythology, but not myths; the poet will utilize Oriental myths as
literary embellishments, but will not accept them as literally true. Finally,
in a description of the genuine wonders of God's creation, the poet could not
possibly speak of His endowing imaginary deities with wisdom.

Interpretation D, which refers the passage to birds, has been regarded
as out of place here and as belonging with the description of living creatures,
either after 38:38 (TS) or after 39:25. The transposition is uncalled for. The
key lies in recognizing the penchant for allusion characteristic of the book.
The ibis was believed to foretell the rising of the Nile, and the cock was
popularly believed to forecast the rain (cf. J. A. Jaussen, in *Revue Biblique*,
vol. 33, 1934, pp. 574 ff.) or to announce the dawn (cf. the rabbinic citations
above). The poet has been describing meteorological phenomena with which
the ibis and the cock are familiar, but not man. The implication for man's
pretensions to wisdom is not lost on the Hebrew reader.

38:37   יְסַפֵּר, normally "counts" (cf. Isa. 40:26), would be appropriate *per se*
but does not offer a good parallelism. Ibn E. treats the verb as a denominative
from סַפִּיר "sapphire, lapis lazuli," hence "who brightens the clouds." Ehr.
interprets the verb as "disperses, scatters" by invoking the Arabic root *safara*,
as he does in 37:20 as well. The root is used of clouds in this meaning, while
the equivalence of Arabic Sin and Hebrew Samekh is somewhat problematic;
see J. Barth, *ES*, pp. 56 f. The word may represent a phonetic variance for
יְשַׁפֵּר (cf. Jud. 12:6). Stich a may then be rendered "who beautifies, i.e. clears,
the clouds in wisdom." A perhaps better interpretation is: "who spreads out
the clouds in wisdom." Cf. בְּרוּחוֹ שָׁמַיִם שִׁפְרָה (Job 26:13 and see the Comm.
ad loc.).

Stich b: "Who can tilt (lit. cause to lie down) the pitchers of heaven
(so that the rain waters pour down)?" Since the Arabic cognate *sakaba* IV
means "pour out" (Guil.), we may have here an instance of *talḥin* with both
meanings in the consciousness of the reader: (a) "pour" and (b) "lay down."
On this rhetorical device, see the Comm. on 7:6 and Gordis in *Sepher Seidel*,
Jerusalem, 5722 = 1962, pp. 255–62.

38:38   Stich a: "when the dust flows into a hard mass," both verbal forms
deriving from יָצַק "pour." For מוּצָק cf. 37:10. רְגָבִים "clods"; cf. Job 21:33.
The v. has been regarded either as a description of the parched earth before
the rain (D-G) or of the condition after the rainfall, when the dust turns
to mud (Du., Peake).

38:39   חַיָּה in late poetry "life" (cf. Ezek. 7:13; Ps. 74:19; 78:50; 143:3;
Job 33:18, 20, 22–28, and see the Comm. on 38:14). Here it has the meaning

of "appetite"; cf. the similar use of נֶפֶשׁ (Isa. 56:11; 58:10; Ps. 107:9; Pr. 27:7, and see BDB, s.v. 5, p. 660 b).

38:40 בַּסֻּכָּה = "in the covert, lair (of beasts of prey)"; cf. Jer. 25:38; Ps. 10:9; 76:3. The noun סֹךְ given in the lexicons (BDB, 697b) is nonexistent. In all the examples, the suff. is added to the stem of the fem. noun סֻכָּה, which occurs without a suff. only in our passage in the meaning "lair." On the morphology, see Special Note 9.

38:41 The young ravens address their cry to God, who provides them with food. לִבְלִי־אֹכֶל the Lamed of condition; cf. לִבְלִי־חֹק (Isa. 5:14). D-G, Hö. argue that the old and not the young animals wander about for food. Hence יִתְעוּ has been emended to (a) יִתְעֶה "the parent wanders" (Bi., Bu., D-G); (b) יִפְעוּ "they cry out," from a root used of a woman in childbirth (Isa. 42:14), in Syriac of sheep bleating and of children crying (Payne-Smith, p. 3201), and in rabbinic Hebrew of human beings crying out, e.g. שהיתה פועה ובוכה על אחיה "she cried out and wept for her brother" (*Mid. Koh. Rab.* 7:1, etc.); or (c) revocalized as יָתְעוּ from a root *ta⁣ʿta⁣ʿa* meaning "stammer" in Arabic, which, Guil. asserts, means "repeat the same thing over and over again." The latter root occurs in the Pilpel in Hebrew מְתַעְתֵּעַ (Gen. 27:12; II Chr. 36:13) in the meaning of "mock." He therefore renders "they keep repeating the same thing (i.e. the cry for food)."

Another method of meeting the difficulty is to eliminate the raven from the text by emending לָעֹרֵב to לָעֶרֶב "at evening" and therefore referring the v. to the lion's young (Wr., Bu., Be.). However, the interrogative phrase מִי יָכִין suggests a new theme, as throughout the chapter, vv. 25, 29, 36, 37.

However, the original difficulty felt here is actually nonexistent. It is refuted by Job 4:11, where the young animals are described as wandering about in search of food. Even more apposite is the widespread belief, without warrant in reality, to be sure, that the raven is cruel to its young. From this derive the German idioms *Rabenmutter* and *Rabeneltern*, "cruel mother" and "cruel parents." Folk belief is invoked in the rabbinic discussion of our passage and that of Ps. 147:9 (cf. *Mid. Lev. Rab.* 19, 1; *Mid. Tanhuma, Eqebh*, III; *Pirqe de Rabbi Eliezer*, sec. XXI). Thus Rashi comments on our v.: "The raven hates its young, so God creates gnats from their excrement that enters their mouths"; cf. Rashi on Ps. 147:9, "Our sages have explained that the ravens are cruel to their young." See TS, p. 538, for an illuminating discussion of this folk belief.

Here, too, the question of relevance has been raised illegitimately. The creatures mentioned are not arranged in logical order, or the birds of prey (39:26–30) would have come after the beasts of prey (38:39–40), not after the horse (39:19–23). The Semitic predilection for assonance is a far more likely reason for the inclusion of the raven here, עֹרֵב sounding very similar to אֶרֶב at the end of v. 40.

The principle of literary organization based on nearly identical words is the key to the structure of Mic. 4:8–5:5. Efforts by exegetes to read this section as a single unit have led to far-fetched and unconvincing interpretations. What we have here is a series of brief independent oracles juxtaposed because of the similarity of their opening words: אַתָּה (4:8; 5:1) and עַתָּה (4:9, 11, 14).

CHAPTER 39

39:1 This magnificent v. has accumulated an incredibly large number of emendations (e.g. עַשְׁתְּרוֹת יַעֲלֵי סָלַע) which is supposed to mean "the sexual lust of mountain goats" (Du.) and deletions (of עֵת, Bi., Bu., Be., Grimme, Ehr., or of לֶדֶת, Bu., Grimme), all of which are superfluous. Rhythmically, the v. is in order, being in *Qinah* meter, 4:3, with each vocable receiving one stress, as does יַעֲלֵי־סָלַע representing one thought-unit, parallel to אַיָּלוֹת; cf. מֵעַם לֹעֵז corresponding to מִמִּצְרַיִם (Ps. 114:1), also Nu. 23:7; Isa. 1:4; Mic. 6:7, and see *PPS*, p. 67, and Special Note 1, sec. 6. Substantively, the poet has chosen to focus attention on the miracle of birth in the mountain goat, so that the phrase עֵת לֶדֶת is essential to the sense.

יָעֵל occurs in the fem. יַעֲלַת־חֵן (Pr. 5:19), but the grammatically masc. form is fem. in meaning, as in the female proper name *Jael* (Jud. 4:17; 5:24). A drawing of a mountain goat has been discovered in the Tomb of Jason in Jerusalem emanating from the Maccabean era that was excavated in 1956.

חֹלֵל the Polel infin. of חוּל; cf. Isa. 51:12; Job 15:7. It is possible, but not necessary, to regard עֵת as understood in stich b; hence "do you mark the time of calving of the hinds?" (D-G). It may be rendered: "Do you watch the travail of the hinds?" אַיָּלוֹת, generally rendered "hind, deer" (Jer. 14:5; Ps. 18:34 = I Sam. 22:34; Cant. 2:7; 3:5), has been explained as "mountain goat" on the basis of the Arabic *waʾil* (Hö.) and "gazelle" (TS).

39:2 In תְּמַלֶּאנָה the imperfect tense carries the nuance "the time they must fill out." On the use of this verb to imply "complete a destined time," cf. Gen. 35:34; 29:27. The fuller fem. form לְדִתְּנָה carries an archaic flavor (Ruth 1:19), generally in pause (Gen. 21:29; 42:36; Jer. 8:7; Pr. 31:29), but not always (Ex. 35:26; Ezek. 34:23). It may have been chosen here because of the assonance with the closing syllable of stich a.

39:3 תִּכְרַעְנָה "crouch in childbirth" (I Sam. 4:19). The implication is that the process of parturition is speedy and uncomplicated. תְּפַלַּחְנָה is not to be emended to תְּפַלֵּטְנָה (Ol., Hö., D-G, TS); note the assonance with תְּשַׁלַּחְנָה. Ehr. places יַלְדֵיהֶן at the end of the v. and renders stich b "the children themselves sever the navel cord" — in which act he sees the only wonder of the mountain goat! In order to preserve MT, it is not necessary to interpret the verb causatively: "They cause their young to cleave open the womb" (D-G). פֶּלַח like בֶּקַע means "split in half," the noun פֶּלַח being used for a millstone (Jud. 9:53) or half a pomegranate (Cant. 4:7). The semantic development may be reconstructed as follows. The verb, like its synonym בָּקַע (Isa. 59:5), was originally used of hatching eggs, lit. splitting them. It then develops the general connotation "bring forth"; cf. the figurative use in English of "hatching a plot." Ha. suggests another approach. He notes that the object of splitting is described as being itself split, e.g., כִּי נִבְקְעוּ בַמִּדְבָּר מַיִם (Isa. 35:6). Hence the mother may be described as "cleaving her offspring" by giving birth to them. Whatever the semantic process, the assonance serves to validate MT.

חֶבְלֵיהֶם is not the common חֵבֶל "birth pangs" (Isa. 66:7; Hos. 13:13), "pain" (Job 21:17), which has an Aram. and Syriac cognate חַבְלָא, but a homonym meaning "foetus" and by extension "offspring" with an Arab. cognate *ḥabula* "be pregnant" (D-G, Hö., P.). The verb occurs in Ps. 7:15; Cant. 5:8, "give birth." שלח "send forth from the womb" may be the sense in 21:11. Note the rhyme here, rare in biblical poetry.

39:4 This short v. contains three Aramaisms; cf. 36:2. יַחְלְמוּ "grow strong," an Aramaism occurring also in Isa. 38:16. יִרְבּוּ "grow up"; cf. Ezek. 16:7 and Tar. Onk. for גָּדַל Gen. 21:8; 25:27 etc. בָּר an Aramaism "outside" (cf. חֵיוַת בָּרָא Dan. 2:38 = חַיַת הַשָּׂדֶה), the equivalent in T for חוּץ (II Ki. 10:24; Isa. 42:2).

The perfect tense of the verb would mean "when they have gone forth they never return"; the revocalization to יֵצְאוּ, "they go forth and do not return," is not absolutely required. לָמוֹ either "to them, i.e. to their parents" or, better, as an ethical dative, as in Job 12:11 (Hi., Dil., D-G, whose other examples are doubtful).

39:5 Ironically the poet here adopts the limited perspective of man, who normally expects these animals to be in bonds for his benefit. The wild ass is frequently referred to for his speed, his obstinacy, and his avoidance of men (Gen. 16:12; Hos. 8:9; Isa. 32:14; Job 11:10). For the noun, cf. Arabic *faraʔ* "fleet-footed." Its synonym here is the Aramaism עָרוֹד (cf. Dan. 5:21), the etymology of which is either Arab. *ᶜarada* II "flee in terror" or *gharada* "cry out (used of the wild ass)" (Müller, Noeldeke).

39:6 מְלֵחָה "salt land, non-arable wilderness" (Jer. 17:6; Ps. 107:34).

39:7 הֲמוֹן קִרְיָה "the roar of the city" (Isa. 39:7), a phrase unfortunately far truer today than when first penned. תְּשֻׁאוֹת "shouting, ranting," used of a driver here and of the roar of the heavens in 36:29; Zech. 4:7 is unclear.

39:8 יְתוּר in MT would be a noun like יְבוּל, יְקוּם; hence "the range of the mountains is his dwelling." The parallelism, however, suggests that a verb is preferable (so LXX, Ra., and virtually all moderns). Hence vocalize יָתוּר "he spies out, explores" (Nu. 13:2, 6, 7), like the Arab. *tara* IV "look intensely at" (Guil.). For the parallel verbs in this v., cf. לִדְרוֹשׁ וְלָתוּר, Ecc. 1:13 (TS). מִרְעֵהוּ = "as his pasture." Yel. points out that a Reš occurs in every word in this v. except *kol*.

39:9 The name of the animal is spelled variously in the Bible: רְאֵם (Nu. 23:22), רְאֵים (Ps. 92:11), רְמִים (Ps. 22:22), in addition to the spelling here רֵים. The רְאֵם is parallel to "ox" (Deut. 33:17), cows (Isa. 34:7), and the calf (Ps. 29:6), possessing horns that are dangerous (Ps. 22:22). Rendered "unicorn" by LXX and "rhinoceros" by V, it is generally identified with the wild ox, the wild bull, or the buffalo. It was hunted by Assyrian kings, and is depicted on the Ishtar Gate at Babylon. In a Ugaritic Baal epic (A. B. IV) the god goes hunting in the marshes of Lake Hule (*aḫ smk*), which was full of buffaloes (*mlat rumm*). אֵבוּס "crib" (Isa. 1:3).

39:10 Stich a: הֲתִקְשָׁר־רֵים בְּתֶלֶם עֲבֹתוֹ has been rendered: (a) "Can you bind the wild ox to the furrow with his cord?" (Ha.), (b) "In the furrows of his cord?" The passage has been emended to בַּעֲבוֹת תַּלְמוֹ "by the cord of his furrows" (Bu.), to בַּעֲבוֹת עָנְקוֹ "with the rope of his neck" (Hö.), or to בְּעָנְקוֹ עֲבוֹת (Be.). Simpler emendations are בְּתֶלֶם בַּעֲבֹתוֹ "to the furrow with his cord" (Bu.) and בְּתֶלֶם עֲבֹתוֹת (Sieg.). However, the last emendation, which offers the best reading, is unnecessary if we recognize Masoretic עֲבֹתוֹ as an abbreviated plur. for עֲבֹתוֹת, a type of abbreviation common in rabbinic mss. and printed texts to the present; cf. the Comm. on מִשְׁטָרוֹ (Job 38:33). Hence render "Can you bind the wild ox to the furrow by ropes?" עֲבֹתוֹ is an accusative of specification to express means; cf. רַק הַכִּסֵּא אֶגְדַּל מִמֶּךָ "only in respect to, i.e. by means of, the throne will I be greater than you" (Gen. 41:40); cf. also Gen. 7:20. The accusative is used here rather than the Beth of means, perhaps because of the desire to avoid the repetition of the letter Beth following בְּתֶלֶם. עֲבוֹת "cords, ropes" as a fetter (Jud. 15:13, 14), of animals that are sacrificed (Ps. 118:27), as a symbol of authority (Ps. 2:7), of wagon ropes (Isa. 5:18).

יְשַׂדֵּד = "harrow" (Isa. 28:24; Hos. 10:10; Akk. *sadâdu* "drag, pull"). אַחֲרֶיךָ "after you" refers to the farmer guiding his animal in plowing. It may possibly mean: "following your command."

39:11 יְגִיעַ means "the product of labor, hence produce"; cf. Deut. 28:33; Isa. 45:14; Ps. 128:2, and יָגֵעַ, Job 20:18, and the Comm. *ad loc*. For the semantic principle that a given term will express both a quality or an act and the consequence of that quality or act, cf. *KMW*, Supplementary Note D, pp. 418 ff.

39:12 The Masorah marks a Kethib יָשׁוּב and a Qere יָשִׁיב, with the accentuation following the Qere and placing the caesura after זַרְעֶךָ. Stich a would then be rendered: "Can you trust him to bring back your seed?" (JPSV). If the Kethib is read, the caesura comes immediately after יָשׁוּב. Rhythmically this produces a better meter, 3:3 rather than 4:2, and is preferred by most commentators (Me., Dil., Bu., D-G, Ehr., Hö.). Since it is no longer in pause זַרְעֶךָ needs to be revocalized as זַרְעֲךָ. If stich b is inter-

preted: "Will he gather in your seeds to the threshing floor?" (RSV, D-G),
it is necessary to emend it to read וְזַרְעֲךָ גֹּרֶן יֶאֱסֹף (P.) or וְזַרְעֲךָ גֹּרֶן יֶאֱסֹף, but
these changes are unnecessary. גֹּרֶן "threshing floor" (Deut. 15:14; Ruth 3:4)
here means "the fruit of the threshing floor, hence harvest," either as a contracted phrase for תְּבוּאַת הַגֹּרֶן (Nu. 18:30) or as an extension of the semantic
principle cited above on v. 11. Hence stich b may be rendered "Will he gather
in your seed and your harvest?" Or the two nouns may be treated as a hendiadys like עִצְּבוֹנֵךְ וְהֵרֹנֵךְ "the pain of your conception" (Gen. 3:16), rendering
it "the seed of your threshing floor." On this rhetorical usage, cf. Gordis in
Sepher Moshe Seidel, pp. 263–66.

39:13   On the problems of the section on the ostrich (39:13–18), see Special
Note 34.

   The difficulties of this passage may be gauged by the fact that many
years ago Schultens collected over 20 interpretations of this v. and the number
has grown since. An additional index of its difficulties may be found in the
fact that Ehr. emends or deletes every word in the text except כָּנָף and חֲסִידָה,
the latter of which he renders "ostrich" rather than by the universally accepted meaning of "stork."

   רְנָנִים, "lit. piercing cries," is an epithet for "ostrich," the usual term
for which is בַּת הַיַּעֲנָה "the singing bird, i.e. screeching, wailing one" (Lev.
11:16; Deut. 14:15; Mic. 1:8) from עָנָה IV "sing" Arab. *ghana*, Syriac ʿ*ani*
"chant, sing." נֶעֱלָסָה, from the root עלס (the Hithpael occurs in Pr. 7:20),
is apparently a metaplastic form of עלו, עלז, עלץ "rejoice." In Job 20:11 the
verb has another meaning; see the Comm. Hence stich a is generally rendered,
"the wing of the ostrich is joyous."

   To bring the passage into conformity with the interrogative mode employed in the First Speech of the Lord, the interrogative He is supplied to
read הַכְנַף (D-G). A more attractive suggestion is to understand here הֲיָדַעְתָּ
in v. 1 (Yel.) and render: "Do you know the joyous wing of the ostrich?"
Note אִם in stich b, introducing the second member of a double question.
The habitat of the ostrich was North Africa, southern Palestine, and Arabia
as far east as the Euphrates.

   The even more difficult stich b consists of three nouns: אֶבְרָה "wing"
(Deut. 32:11; Ps. 68:14; 91:4), which is the fem. form of אֵבֶר (Isa. 40:31;
Ps. 55:7); חֲסִידָה, which is generally not interpreted as the adj. "kindly"
but as the substantive "stork" (Lev. 11:19; Deut. 14:18; Jer. 8:7; Zech. 5:9;
Ps. 104:17); and נֹצָה "feather, plumage" (Lev. 1:16; Ezek. 17:3, 7). The
stich has been interpreted: (a) "Is it a kindly pinion and feathers?," construing
חֲסִידָה as an adj.; and (b) "Do you give wings to the ostrich and feathers to
the stork?" (Ibn E.), which cannot be read into our text without violence.
The better emendations include: (a) אִם אֶבְרַת חֲסִידָה וְנֹצָה, taken to mean
"Is it the kindly stork's pinion and feathers?" (Bu., JPSV); (b) אִם אֶבְרָה
חֲסִירָה וְנֹצָה, which is taken to mean, "Is the wing of the ostrich sluggish?"
(Hoffmann, Bu.), an emendation which P. calls "attractive," though he
renders differently, "Though her pinions lack feathers," an interpretation

which requires deleting the Vav in addition to the other changes. For a conspectus of more fanciful emendations, couched in German theological Hebrew, see D-G, II, p. 318.

The most attractive reading is אִם אֶבְרַת חֲסִידָה וְנֹצָה "Is it the wing of the stork and the falcon?" (Hö.). נֹצָה would be the fem. of נֵץ "falcon" (Lev. 11:16; Deut. 14:15; Job 39:26). Syntactically, however, the reading leaves something to be desired.

We suggest adopting the revocalization וְנֹצָה and placing a Mappiq in the He of אֶבְרָה, reading אֶבְרָה as the fem. suff. of אֵבֶר. The reading אִם אֶבְרָה חֲסִידָה וְנֹצָה is equivalent to אִם אֶבְרָה אֶבְרַת חֲסִידָה וְנֹצָה "Is her wing (i.e. the ostrich's) the wing of the stork or the falcon?"

In our view, the stich contrasts the nature of the ostrich with that of the stork and the falcon. It was popularly held that the stork was particularly affectionate and devoted to its young, hence its Hebrew name *ḥᵃsīdāh* = "the loving one." At the opposite extreme, the ostrich was popularly believed to be callous and unconcerned with the fate of its young; see the following verses and Comm. No special folk belief related to the falcon, that was regarded as manifesting the normal degree of concern for its young characteristic of birds in general. Hence the prohibition against taking the fledglings captive in the presence of their mother (Deut. 22:7). The ostrich is both callous and foolish, and, therefore, lacks both the normal instincts of the falcon or the extraordinary feelings of the stork for its offspring. Yet for all its "unnatural" behavior, the ostrich, too, is the handiwork of God, revealing the manifold character of His creation.

The contraction of phrase here assumed may be explained by the principle postulated by Ibn E. (on Ex. 13:18) מוֹשֵׁךְ עַצְמוֹ וְאַחֵר עִמּוֹ "The word pulls itself and another with it," for which he adduces עֵץ = עֵץ הַדַּעַת טוֹב וָרָע, דֶּרֶךְ הַמִּדְבָּר מִדְבָּר יַם סוּף = דֶּרֶךְ הַמִּדְבָּר יַם סוּף (Gen. 2:9), הַדַּעַת דַּעַת טוֹב וָרָע (Ex. 13:18), הָאָרוֹן אֲרוֹן הַבְּרִית = הָאָרוֹן אֲרוֹן הַבְּרִית (Jos. 3:14). The contraction may be explained even more simply as due to the exigencies of meter; cf. מְשַׁוֶּה רַגְלַי כָּאַיָּלוֹת: "He makes my feet like (the feet of) hinds" (II Sam. 22:34 = Ps. 18:34).

39:14 Scholars have been greatly exercised by the fact that the actual behavior of the ostrich does not coincide with the description given here. The ostrich does sit upon her eggs continually, though she leaves them frequently in the early period of incubation in order to go in search of food by day. She usually covers them with sand so that they are not fully exposed to the sun's rays. However, the poet is not giving a zoological description, but utilizing the folk beliefs concerning the ostrich, whose foolishness and indifference to its young (cf. the Arab. proverb "more stupid than the ostrich") were as proverbial as the alleged wisdom of the fox. For ancient beliefs regarding the ostrich abundantly cited in Oriental and classical literature, see the references in D-G, I, pp. 342–45; P., pp. 260 ff.

The verb is fem. sing. agreeing with the logical subject "ostrich," not with the grammatical plur. רְנָנִים; for this usage, cf. Lev. 2:1; 5:1, 2; I Sam. 12:21.

The v. offers a description of the alleged callous behavior of the ostrich toward its offspring, כִּי, "for," offering the proof for this trait. תְּחַמֵּם requires a suff. תְּחַמְּמֵם. The Piel is to be construed causatively, "She lets them warm up on the ground (instead of sitting on them herself)." The emendation to תַּנִּיחֵם (Be., Bu., D-G, Ehr., P.) is not necessary. TS interprets the verb in MT on the basis of the Syriac המי meaning "neglect," which would be a *hapax* in Heb., aside from the assumed correspondence of Hebrew Ḥet and Syriac He.

39:15 זוּר "squeeze, trample"; cf. Isa. 1:6; 59:5. The sing. suff. refers to the fem. plur. בֵּיצֶיהָ collectively; cf. II Ki. 3:3; Jer. 36:23; Job 6:20; and see Ges.-K., sec. 135, 5, 2.

39:16 הִקְשִׁיחַ is generally referred back to the mother ostrich and the v. interpreted, "She hardens herself against her young, making them none of hers" (D-G), or "She harshly rejects her young" (P.), on the basis of the only other use of the root in תַּקְשִׁיחַ לִבֵּנוּ "You harden our hearts" (Isa. 63:17). The masc. form of the verb is pronounced "intolerable" here (D-G); it has, therefore, been emended to תַּקְשִׁיחַ (Bi., Dil., Be., Studer), הַקְשִׁיחַ the inf. construct (Ew., Dil.), or הִקְשִׁיחָה (Hi., Sieg., Du.).

However, the passage in Isa. has an object which is lacking here. Another interpretation, that we believe substantially better, obviates the grammatical difficulty as well. The Arab. cognate *qasaḥa* means "be hard, firm, tough." We suggest this meaning for our verb, the Hiphil carrying an intransitive and inchoative meaning, "grow tough," like הִפְרִיחַ, הִזְקִין, הִרְחִיק (Job 14:8, 9). On this basic use of the Hiphil, cf. Ges.-K., sec. 57, 2. For the common use of a sing. verb before a plur. subject בָּנֶיהָ, cf. Gen. 9:23; 11:29; 21:32, and see Ges.-K., sec. 146, 2b.

Stich b is generally explained: "Her toil is in vain; there is no fear" (D-G), or "Though her labor is in vain, she is without fear" (JPSV), or "If her labor is in vain, she does not care" (Hö.). Better: "that her labor is in vain she has no fear." בְּלִי is the negative particle used in poetry = לֹא; cf. Isa. 32:10; Hos. 8:7; 9:16; Ps. 19:4; Job 41:18. The sense of the passage is clear: her young grow strong without her; she remains unconcerned that they may perish, so that her labor would be in vain.

39:17 הִשָּׁה Hiphil of נשה, like the Piel (Gen. 41:51), "caused her to forget wisdom, i.e., did not allocate wisdom to her." On 11:6, cf. the Comm.

39:18 כָּעֵת = "now," as in Nu. 23:33; Jud. 13:23; cf. כַּיּוֹם "today." תַּמְרִיא, of uncertain etymology, is usually derived from the Arab. *maraʾ, maray*, "whip, urge a horse on," hence "spur herself on by flapping wings" (Del., Du., Bu., D-G). This derivation is slightly better than that from מרה "rebel," hence, "rise above one's normal character and place" (Ra., Dh.) or the suggestion to relate the verb to the Aram. מָרֵא "master, Lord," hence "fly aloft"; to support it אַבִּיר "master, chief" is linked to אֶבֶר "wing" (TS). We suggest that the verb may be a metathesis for תַּאֲמִיר "go aloft," a denominative of אָמִיר "summit" (Isa. 17:6, 9). The Hithpael of the verb אמר "act proudly" occurs in Isa. 16:6; Ps. 94:4, and perhaps the Hiphil הֶאֱמִיר (Deut. 26:17, 18) may mean "exalt, magnify," though it is generally rendered, "declare, avow, recognize" (RSV, JPSV, NEB).

Stich b refers to the horse, who becomes the subject of the next sec. This association explains "the intrusion" of the quadrupeds among the birds. There is, therefore, no need for deleting vv. 19–25 as does Ehr. On the structure of the passage, cf. Special Note 33.

39:19 The horse, whose original habitat was the steppes of Central Asia, was brought to China, India, Mesopotamia, and Egypt about 2000 B. C. E. In the Middle East it was generally used for war, though the Sumerians used the animal for riding as well.

רַעְמָה has been generally rendered *ad sensum*, but very differently: (a) "quivering, shaking of the mane," on the basis of Ezek. 27:35; Ps. 96:11; 98:7 (Ges., Del., Dil.); (b) "terror, fear" (LXX, Saadia, Ra.), on the basis of the same passages; (c) "neighing (V); (d) "armor" (P); (e) "strength" (T); (f) "fierceness" (JPSV). Virtually all these interpretations take their point of departure from רַעַם "thunder." The most appropriate meaning is "mane," which is supported by the Arabic phrase ᵓumm riᶜm "mother of the mane," an epithet for the hyena (KB). Hö. seeks to buttress the semantics from "thunder" to "mane" by calling attention to the Greek noun *phobe*, "mane," and the verb *phobeo*, "fear."

39:20 Stich a: "Will you make him leap" or, more accurately, "Will you make him shake" (with eagerness) like the locust?" כָּאַרְבֶּה is used collectively. The simile has not generally been understood. A plague of locusts descending on crops makes the whole field appear to be shaking with their movement.

Stich b has been rendered: "the majesty of his snorting is terror." הוֹד is better understood as a phonetic variant for הֵד (Ezek. 7:7), requiring no emendation. Hence: "The echo of his snorting is awesome." On the interchange of the sounds of Ṣere and Ḥolem, cf. גֵּד = נֹאד (Ps. 33:7); מְרֵרָה (Job 16:13) = מְרֹרָה (Job 20:25; but cf. the Comm. *ad loc.*). Our exact form may exist in Isa. 30:30.

נַחְרוֹ "his snort," Jer. 8:16. אֵימָה. A noun in the predicate nominative is equivalent to an adjective (cf. Ps. 109:4; 110:3; 120:7; and Driver, *HT*, sec. 189).

39:21 The plur. verb יַחְפְּרוּ is read as the sing. by the Vss. (LXX, P, V) and emended to יַחְפֹּר by many moderns (Dr., Bi., Bu.). The verb here means "to paw"; cf. Arab. *haᵓfir* "hoof."

בָּעֵמֶק has generally been rendered: "in the valley," which is entirely satisfactory. However, the root occurs in Akk. (*emuqu*) and Ugar. ᶜmq in the meaning of "force, strength." This meaning occurs not only in Jer. 47:5 (Albright, Dahood), but also in Jer. 49:4 as well. It would also be appropriate to the context here in parallelism to בְּכֹחַ. We have here another instance of *talḥin* where the poet has chosen עֵמֶק rather than בִּקְעָה because the meaning "valley" is accompanied in the reader's consciousness by the meaning "strength." On this figure, cf. the Comm. on Job 7:6, and see Gordis, in *Sepher Moshe Seiḏel*, pp. 255–62.

נֶשֶׁק "weapons," here "battle." Cf. Ps. 140:8 and Arab. *ḥarb* "war."

39:23 The verb תִּרְנֶה need not be emended to תָּרֹנָּה (Hö.). The *Lamed He* form רנה is a variant of the geminate רנן "sing." Cf. שגה, שגג; דכה, דכך.

אַשְׁפָּה "quiver," here a metonymy for "arrow," a reference to the whining sound of the arrow going past. לַהַב "flame" is the blade of the sword (Jud. 3:22; Nah. 3:3), here "the glitter of the spear and the javelin." It can refer either to the equipment of the horse's rider or, better, to the missiles of the enemy; cf. v. 22b.

39:24 רַעַשׁ "shaking, quivering"; רֹגֶז "agitation." It has been rendered, "mid rattle and roar," which would make the phrase descriptive of the battle (P.). However, stich b and v. 25 suggest that it is the horse's eagerness for battle that is being depicted here; hence "in excitement and agitation." Render somewhat freely, "shaking in excitement, etc."

יְגַמֵּא is to be derived not from the verb in Gen. 24:17, "swallow," Aram. גמע (D-G), but from Aram. גומא "hole, pit" (so T, Ra., BDB, Yel), common in rabbinic Heb. (*M. Ḥul.* 2:9; *B. Baba Batra* 16a), hence "make holes in the ground"; cf. also גוּמָץ, Ecc. 10:8.

Stich b has been explained: (a) "He does not believe that it is the sound of the trumpet" (Ra., Ibn E., JPSV); (b) "He does not stand still" (Hö., Yel., RSV); "he cannot be held in" (NEB); (c) "He shows no firmness" (Ges., Ew.). The proposed emendations include: (a) לֹא יְמָּנַע which is taken to mean "It does not let itself be held back" (Bi.); and (b) לֹא יֵמִין וְלֹא יַשְׂמְאִיל "He does not turn to the right or to the left" (Du., Bu., Hö.), which is graphically distant from MT in addition to being "somewhat prosaic" (D-G).

However, none of these interpretations or emendations deal with the basic difficulty, the absence of a verb in the clause introduced by כִּי. Hö. assumes a lacuna in this stich, but the metric pattern (4:4 or 4:3) indicates that the line is complete. It has been suggested to read בְּקוֹל (Be., Bu.), but that can hardly mean "at the sound." The proposal to read כְּקוֹל (Bi., Bu.) is rejected by D-G because the preposition occurs in a temporal sense only with an infin. (Gen. 19:7; Isa. 10:5) or a verbal noun (Isa. 30:19; Hos. 13:6). We would suggest that קוֹל be regarded as a form of the Semitic verb appearing in Akk. *kâlu*, Arab. *ka'la* "speak," which has generally disappeared from Heb. except in the ubiquitous noun קוֹל "sound, voice." In our passage קוֹל may be the infin. so that בְּקוֹל "at the sounding" would be entirely grammatical. It is preferable to construe קוֹל as the archaic Qal participle. On the form with Ḥolem, cf. הַקּוֹמִים (II Ki. 16:7); הַלּוֹט (Isa. 25:7); בּוֹסִים (Zech. 10:5); גֹּחִי (Ps. 22:10); on הָרֹב (40:2), see the Comm. *ad loc.* and Ges.-K., sec. 32, note 1. An Arabism in Job is, of course, not strange. This approach validates the interpretation of the medievals: "He does not believe it, when the trumpet sounds."

D-G solves the problem decisively by deleting the entire stich, on the ground that it is a mere variant of בְּדֵי שֹׁפָר in v. 25a. How and why the difficult stich was added is, however, left unexplained.

39:25 בְּדֵי שֹׁפָר has been interpreted: (a) from דַי "abundance" (cf. מְדֵי, Isa. 66:23), hence "lit., in the abundance of the trumpet, i.e. as often as he hears the trumpet." Or (b) it is emended to מְדֵי (BDB). It is far better derived from the Arab. noun *dawayun* "the faint sound of a wind or a bird in flight," from the verb *daway* II "hum, rumble, rustle"; hence render "at the faint, distant sound of the trumpet" (Eitan, Yel., G. R. Driver, in *JRAS*, 1944, p. 168; Guil.). Both stichs now describe the excitement of the horse at the first intimations of battle from afar. הֶאָח "a cry of joy" (Isa. 44:16; Ezek. 25:3).

יָרִיחַ מִלְחָמָה "he scents battle." Note the assonance of Ḥeth and Reš in the entire stich. The verb, lit. "smell," expresses admirably the meaning of "senses, feels" what he cannot fully hear. On the metaphoric use of the verb which is used hyperbolically here, cf. Jud. 16:9 and see the Comm. on 14:9. P. A. H. de Boer, "Job 39:25" (in the D. W. Thomas Festschrift, *Words and Meanings*, ed. P. B. Ackroyd and B. Lindars, Cambridge, 1960, pp. 29, 38), argues that the Hiphil of the verb is intransitive and, therefore, he interprets the stich to mean that "the war horse gives out a penetrating odor, thus recalling by his smell war from afar." Not only is this rendering utterly prosaic, but it fails to reckon with the clearly transitive use of the verb in Gen. 27:27; Ex. 30:38; Lev. 26:31; Am. 5:21. So, too, in the difficult וַהֲרִיחוֹ, Isa. 11:3, which need not be taken as a noun, "his delight," but as the Hiphil 3rd pers. masc. perfect with the suffix used causatively, "lit., and he will cause him to inhale, breathe in, absorb the spirit of the Lord," the subject being either impersonal or the Lord.

Stich c is generally rendered "the thunder of captains and their shouting." The Mem of רַעַם is better taken as the enclitic, familiar in Akk. and Ugaritic, Mem + רֵעַ, and rendered "shouting," as in בְּרֵעֹה (Ex. 32:17); תָּרִיעִי רֵעַ (Mic. 4:9); רֵעוֹ (Job 36:33). תְּרוּעָה here is the "trumpet blast" (Nu. 10:5, 6). The men are urged on to battle by the shouts of their officers and the sounds of the trumpet.

39:26 יַאֲבֶר "fly, soar," a denominative from אֵבֶר, "wing" (v. 13); cf. the English verb "to wing." נֵץ "hawk, falcon," a generic term (Lev. 11:16; Deut. 14:15; cf. the Comm. on v. 13 above). Stich b may refer to either the seasonal migration southward of the birds, or the south wind (Ps. 78:26; Cant. 4:16). By association, the battle in v. 25 suggests the vulture, who is best known to man as feeding on corpses of the dead. Thus the bird in whom God exults is not merely of no use to man, but actually feeds on his body!

39:27 נֶשֶׁר is either a synonym for נֵץ or a member of the species; however, like its cognates in Arab., Akk., and Ugaritic, נֶשֶׁר is used both of the vulture and of the eagle.

Stich b has been emended to וְכִי יָכִין בֶּהָרִים קִנּוֹ (Studer, Bu., D-G) or to אִם עַל פִּיךָ יָרִים קִנּוֹ וְיִתְלֹנָן עַל שֶׁן סֶלַע (Du., Be.), a procedure which deletes "eagle" from the passage unnecessarily; see the Comm. on 6b. These emendations are also designed "to repair" the brevity of stich b (D-G), likewise without need. כִּי receives its own beat *metri causa* exactly as in כִּי יִצְפְּנֵנִי (Ps. 27:5); so, too, אִם (Mic. 6:8); לֹא (Ps. 5:6); see *PPS*, p. 67, and Special Note 1, sec. 6. Hence the meter is either 4:3 (if אִם־עַל־פִּיךָ receives two beats) or 3:3 (if the phrase receives only one), as suggested by the Masoretic Maqqeph. כִּי is the interrogative particle; cf. the Comm. on 37:20.

G. R. Driver sees in וְכִי the name of the ʾky bird, but the inclusion of two distinct creatures in one verse would be exceptional and there is no syntactic problem, in the interpretation given above, that compels the adoption of this *hapax legomenon*.

39:28 שֶׁן־סֶלַע "tooth" refers to a sharp-pointed crag.

39:29 חָפַר "dig, search"; cf. 3:21; Deut. 1:22.

39:30 יְעַלְעוּ has sustained the loss of a Lamed, being derived from the root לוע or לעע "swallow, suck." Hence read either יְלַעְלְעוּ, a quadriliteral form in the Piel, or יָלְעוּ in the Qal. On the root, cf. Ob. 1:16 and the noun לוֹע "throat" (Pr. 23:2). The theme of stich b occurs in proverbial form in Matt. 24:28; Luke 17:37: "Where the carcass is, there the eagles will be gathered together."

CHAPTER 40

40:1 This introductory formula after 38:1, like the repetition of the opening phrase in the Elihu section at the head of each chap., is designed to underscore a new theme — the folly and the arrogance involved in men's challenging God's rule. The v. is omitted by LXX and V in order to link v. 2 to the preceding.

40:2 Since a finite verb or its equivalent is required in stich a, הָרֹב has been treated in several ways: (a) it has been construed as the infinitive absolute replacing the imperfect for which וְשׁוֹב אֵלַי, "shall he return to Me?" (Jer. 3:1), is cited, but in this latter passage the infinitive is used in a consecutive context, not at the beginning. As for Jer. 7:9, also cited, here the infinitives retain their basic character and are not equivalent to finite verbs. Moreover, the parallelism between הָרֹב עִם־שַׁדַּי and מוֹכִיחַ אֱלוֹהַּ suggests that הָרֹב is best construed as a participle. (b) It has, therefore, been emended to הָרָב (Yel., D-G), but unnecessarily, since רוֹב with a Holem is the older form of the participle Qal of *mediae Vav* verbs, a form which has survived in several passages in the Bible. See the Comm. on 39:24 for examples.

יָסוֹר is generally construed as an adjective like גִּבּוֹר, שָׁכוֹר, and given the meaning "fault-finder" and the stich has been rendered: "Shall a fault-finder argue with God?" (JPSV, RSV). However, the parallelism suggests that יָסוֹר is best taken as a verb parallel to יַעֲנֶּה. The widely accepted emendation יָסוּר, to which the special meaning "yield" or "cease" is assigned (Hö., P.), has no real warrant in Heb., Isa. 11:13; Am. 6:7 being entirely different in connotation. יָסוֹר is therefore to be understood as the Qal imperfect of יסר "chastise, instruct." The Qal of יסר is rare, the only instances being Isa. 8:11; Hos. 10:10; I Chr. 15:22, which are doubtful, and the certain participle יֹסֵר, Ps. 94:10; Pr. 9:7. However, the Niphal is well attested (Lev. 26:23; Jer. 31:18; Pr. 29:19), so that the existence of the Qal may be postulated. On the other hand, יָסוֹר as a noun would be a *hapax*.

יַעֲנֶּה is best taken interrogatively parallel to stich a, not "let him answer" but "can he answer?" The fem. suff. is collective, meaning "can he answer all this, i.e. that has been set forth?" Cf. Gen. 15:6; Isa. 30:8; Am. 8:10; and see Ges.-K., sec. 135, 5, note 2. The suff. need therefore not be emended to the masc.

The v. now exhibits an excellent parallelism. In view of the wonders of the natural world, which the Lord causes to pass in review, He asks whether a man like Job, for whom they are beyond understanding, can properly instruct God or answer the implications flowing from His words. It is noteworthy that the First Speech of the Lord out of the whirlwind reaches its climax in the form of a question that is unanswerable. Similarly, God's triumphant question climaxes His rejoinder to Jonah (4:11). In both instances, complaints against God are refuted by irrefutable questions. These are two striking instances of the traditional Jewish propensity to answer a question with a question.

Job's Response (40:3–5)

Job admits that he is overwhelmed by God's power and will speak no more.

וַיַּעַן אִיּוֹב אֶת־יְהֹוָה וַיֹּאמַר׃   מ 3

הֵן קַלֹּתִי מָה אֲשִׁיבֶךָ   יָדִי שַׂמְתִּי לְמוֹ־פִי׃   4

אַחַת דִּבַּרְתִּי וְלֹא אֶעֱנֶה   וּשְׁתַּיִם וְלֹא אוֹסִיף׃   5

40 3   Job answered the Lord, saying,
　4   Behold, I am of small account; how can I answer You?
　　　　　I lay my hand to my mouth.
　5   I have spoken once, and I will not reply again;
　　　　　twice, but I will proceed no further.

40:4 Hö. moves vv. 3–5 to the beginning of Job's Second Response at 42:2. See Special Note 35 on the Second Speech of the Lord on the weighty grounds for rejecting this procedure. In this First Response, Job is not submitting to God or conceding any part of His position. In this v., he sets forth his weakness and insignificance and his determination to remain silent. In v. 5, he recalls that he has already spoken more than once and has nothing to add.

40:5 On the use of "ascending numeration" in biblical literature, particularly in Wisdom, see the Comm. on 5:19 and 33:14. The phrase "once and twice" means "more than once, several times." אֶעֱנֶה, lacking in LXX, is emended to אֶשְׁנֶה "I shall repeat it" (Hi., Ehr., D-G), but unnecessarily. The idea of repetition is frequently left unexpressed in Heb. Cf. Isa. 9:9 "Bricks have fallen, but we shall build *again* with hewn stone" (נִבְנֶה); Ps. 51:20 "May you *rebuild* the walls of Jerusalem" (תִּבְנֶה). Hence, MT = "I shall not respond again."

The Lord's Second Speech (40:6–41:26)

The Lord brushes aside Job's response, which is more evasive than submissive. Since Job had let his denial of justice in the world stand, God now addresses Himself squarely to this issue. Why does Job insist on condemning God in order that he may emerge righteous? If Job could successfully destroy all evil in the world, God would willingly pay tribute to him. The implication seems to be that there are some corners of the world where God's sway is less than total, so that a few forms of wickedness escape His punishment. But this is no reason for impugning God's justice in general.

Then follows a rhapsodic picture of two massive creatures, Behemot (40:15–24) and Leviathan (40:25–41:26). They are poetic descriptions of the hippopotamus and the crocodile, respectively, with overtones drawn from ancient Semitic mythology. It would be a foolhardy man indeed who would attempt to take these powerful beasts captive and bend them to his will. Neither of these monstrous beings can be called beautiful by man's standard. All the more vividly do they reveal the delight that God takes in the manifold forms of creation.

There are two basic implications in the poet's choice of these animals to be glorified. First, man, who is only one of God's creatures, is *not* the measure of all things and the sole test of the worth of creation. Second, man's suffering must be seen in its proper perspective within the framework of the cosmos. Evil will then seem less pervasive in the universe than Job's anguished cries have made it appear.

Thus the conventional theology of the Friends is ignored completely by God, who later denounces it as false. Instead, emphasis is placed upon the harmony and beauty of the natural world on a scale beyond man's comprehension. This suggests that there is a similar order and meaning in the moral universe, even though man cannot always grasp it. God does not deny that there is a residuum of evil in the world which remains a mystery. But man can bear the burden of this suffering more easily if he sees it against the larger background of the cosmos, if he drinks in its beauty and revels in its joy.

40 6   Then the Lord answered Job out of the whirlwind, saying;
  7   Gird up your loins like a man;
           I will ask you, and do you inform Me.
  8   Will you deny My justice,
           put Me in the wrong, so that you may be in the right?
  9   Have you an arm like God;
           can you thunder with a voice like His?
  10   Deck yourself in majesty and dignity,
           clothe yourself with glory and splendor.
  11   Scatter abroad your mighty wrath,
           and as you see each proud sinner — abase him!
  12   As you look on each arrogant one — bring him low,
           and tread down the wicked in their place.
  13   Bury them all in the dust,
           press their faces into the grave —
  14   Then I too will render you homage,
           when your right hand will have brought you victory.

  15   Behold, Behemoth, whom I fashioned along with you,
           eating grass like an ox.
  16   See, his strength is in his loins
           and his power in the muscles of his belly.
  17   He can stiffen his tail like a cedar,
           and the sinews of his thighs are knit together.
  18   His bones are tubes of bronze;
           his limbs, like bars of iron.
  19   He is the first of the works of God —
           only the well-sheathed warrior should bring a sword near!
  20   For the mountains bring him their tribute,
           and all the beasts of the field gambol there.
  21   Under the lotus plants he lies
           in the shadow of reeds, and in the marsh.
  22   The lotus trees cover him with their shadow;
           the willows of the brook surround him.
  23   Behold, he empties an entire river without haste;
           he lies at ease as he draws a Jordan into his mouth.
  24   Who can capture him with rings
           or pierce his nose with a prong?

  25   Can you seize Leviathan with a net
           or press down his tongue with a cord?
  26   Can you put a rope in his nose
           or pierce his jaw with a hook?
  27   Will he make supplication to you
           and speak to you in soft words?
  28   Will he make a covenant with you
           that you may take him as a servant forever?
  29   Can you play with him as with a bird
           or tie him up as one of your sparrows?
  30   Will traders bargain over him?
           Will they divide him up among merchants?

מ   וַיַּעַן־יְהוָה אֶת־אִיּוֹב מִן | סְעָרָה וַיֹּאמַר׃   6

אֱזָר־נָא כְגֶבֶר חֲלָצֶיךָ   אֶשְׁאָלְךָ וְהוֹדִיעֵנִי׃   7

הַאַף תָּפֵר מִשְׁפָּטִי   תַּרְשִׁיעֵנִי לְמַעַן תִּצְדָּק׃   8

וְאִם־זְרוֹעַ כָּאֵל | לָךְ   וּבְקוֹל כָּמֹהוּ תַרְעֵם׃   9

עֲדֵה־נָא גָאוֹן וָגֹבַהּ   וְהוֹד וְהָדָר תִּלְבָּשׁ׃   י

הָפֵץ עֶבְרוֹת אַפֶּךָ   וּרְאֵה כָל־גֵּאֶה וְהַשְׁפִּילֵהוּ׃   11

רְאֵה כָל־גֵּאֶה הַכְנִיעֵהוּ   וַהֲדֹךְ רְשָׁעִים תַּחְתָּם׃   12

טָמְנֵם בֶּעָפָר יָחַד   פְּנֵיהֶם חֲבֹשׁ בַּטָּמוּן׃   13

וְגַם־אֲנִי אוֹדֶךָּ   כִּי־תוֹשִׁעַ לְךָ יְמִינֶךָ׃   14

הִנֵּה־נָא בְהֵמוֹת אֲשֶׁר־עָשִׂיתִי עִמָּךְ   חָצִיר כַּבָּקָר יֹאכֵל׃   טו

הִנֵּה־נָא כֹחוֹ בְמָתְנָיו   וְאוֹנוֹ בִּשְׁרִירֵי בִטְנוֹ׃   16

יַחְפֹּץ זְנָבוֹ כְמוֹ־אָרֶז   גִּידֵי פַחֲדָו יְשֹׂרָגוּ׃   17

עֲצָמָיו אֲפִיקֵי נְחוּשָׁה   גְּרָמָיו כִּמְטִיל בַּרְזֶל׃   18

הוּא רֵאשִׁית דַּרְכֵי־אֵל   הָעֹשׂוֹ יַגֵּשׁ חַרְבּוֹ׃   19

כִּי־בוּל הָרִים יִשְׂאוּ־לוֹ   וְכָל־חַיַּת הַשָּׂדֶה יְשַׂחֲקוּ־שָׁם׃   כ

תַּחַת־צֶאֱלִים יִשְׁכָּב   בְּסֵתֶר קָנֶה וּבִצָּה׃   21

יְסֻכֻּהוּ צֶאֱלִים צִלֲלוֹ   יְסֻבּוּהוּ עַרְבֵי־נָחַל׃   22

הֵן יַעֲשֹׁק נָהָר לֹא יַחְפּוֹז   יִבְטַח | כִּי־יָגִיחַ יַרְדֵּן אֶל־פִּיהוּ׃   23

בְּעֵינָיו יִקָּחֶנּוּ   בְּמוֹקְשִׁים יִנְקָב־אָף׃   24

תִּמְשֹׁךְ לִוְיָתָן בְּחַכָּה   וּבְחֶבֶל תַּשְׁקִיעַ לְשֹׁנוֹ׃   כה

הֲתָשִׂים אַגְמֹן בְּאַפּוֹ   וּבְחוֹחַ תִּקֹּב לֶחֱיוֹ׃   26

הֲיַרְבֶּה אֵלֶיךָ תַּחֲנוּנִים   אִם־יְדַבֵּר אֵלֶיךָ רַכּוֹת׃   27

הֲיִכְרֹת בְּרִית עִמָּךְ   תִּקָּחֶנּוּ לְעֶבֶד עוֹלָם׃   28

הַתְשַׂחֶק־בּוֹ כַּצִּפּוֹר   וְתִקְשְׁרֶנּוּ לְנַעֲרוֹתֶיךָ׃   29

יִכְרוּ עָלָיו חַבָּרִים   יֶחֱצוּהוּ בֵּין כְּנַעֲנִים׃   ל

מ׳ v. 6. מִן ק׳   v. 17. פַחֲדָיו ק׳

31   Can you fill his skin with harpoons
        or his head with fishing spears?
32   If you dare lay your hand upon him,
        not long will you remember the battle!

41   Indeed, he who attacks him loses all hope,
        since at the mere sight of him, he is laid low.
2   No one is foolhardy enough to stir him up,
        for who can stand up to him in battle?
3   Who has confronted him and emerged unscathed?
        Under all the heavens — no one!

4   I will not keep silent concerning his limbs,
        or his mighty strength, or the grace of his form.
5   Who can strip off his outer garment?
        Who can penetrate his double coat of mail?
6   Who can force open the doors of his face?
        Round about his teeth is terror.
7   His back is made of layers of shields
        shut up tight as with a seal.
8   Each scale is so close to the other
        that no air can enter between them.
9   They are joined one to the other;
        they are interlocked and cannot be sundered.
10   His sneezings flash forth light;
        his eyes are like the eyelids of the dawn.
11   Out of his mouth go flaming torches—
        sparks of fire leap forth.
12   Out of his nostrils comes smoke
        as from a boiling pot or a marsh.
13   His breath kindles coals,
        and a flame comes forth from his mouth.
14   On his neck, strength abides,
        and on his face terror dances.
15   The folds of his flesh are joined together,
        firmly set upon him and immovable.
16   His breast is firm as a rock,
        firm as the lower millstone.
17   When he raises himself up, the gods are frightened
        and the mighty breakers make supplication to him.
18   If one reaches for him with the sword, it will fail —
        be it the spear, the dart, or the javelin.
19   He treats iron as straw,
        and bronze, as rotting wood.
20   The arrow cannot put him to flight;
        for him slingstones turn into stubble.
21   The club he treats as straw,
        and he laughs at the rattle of javelins.
22   His underparts are sharpest potsherds;
        he spreads out like a threshing-sledge on the mire.

וּבְצַלְצַל דָּגִים רֹאשׁוֹ:	31	הֲתְמַלֵּא בְשֻׂכּוֹת עוֹרוֹ
זֵכֶר מִלְחָמָה אַל־תּוֹסַף:	32	שִׂים־עָלָיו כַּפֶּךָ
הֲגַם אֶל־מַרְאָיו יֻטָל:	**מא** א	הֵן־תֹּחַלְתּוֹ נִכְזָבָה
וּמִי הוּא לְפָנַי יִתְיַצָּב:	2	לֹא־אַכְזָר כִּי יְעוּרֶנּוּ
תַּחַת כָּל־הַשָּׁמַיִם לִי־הוּא:	3	מִי הִקְדִּימַנִי וַאֲשַׁלֵּם
וּדְבַר־גְּבוּרוֹת וְחִין עֶרְכּוֹ:	4	לֹא־אַחֲרִישׁ בַּדָּיו
בְּכֶפֶל רִסְנוֹ מִי יָבוֹא:	ה	מִי־גִלָּה פְּנֵי לְבוּשׁוֹ
סְבִיבוֹת שִׁנָּיו אֵימָה:	6	דַּלְתֵי פָנָיו מִי פִתֵּחַ
סָגוּר חוֹתָם צָר:	7	גַּאֲוָה אֲפִיקֵי מָגִנִּים
וְרוּחַ לֹא־יָבֹא בֵינֵיהֶם:	8	אֶחָד בְּאֶחָד יִגַּשׁוּ
יִתְלַכָּדוּ וְלֹא יִתְפָּרָדוּ:	9	אִישׁ־בְּאָחִיהוּ יְדֻבָּקוּ
וְעֵינָיו כְּעַפְעַפֵּי־שָׁחַר:	י	עֲטִישֹׁתָיו תָּהֶל אוֹר
כִּידוֹדֵי אֵשׁ יִתְמַלָּטוּ:	11	מִפִּיו לַפִּידִים יַהֲלֹכוּ
כְּדוּד נָפוּחַ וְאַגְמֹן:	12	מִנְּחִירָיו יֵצֵא עָשָׁן
וְלַהַב מִפִּיו יֵצֵא:	13	נַפְשׁוֹ גֶּחָלִים תְּלַהֵט
וּלְפָנָיו תָּדוּץ דְּאָבָה:	14	בְּצַוָּארוֹ יָלִין עֹז
יָצוּק עָלָיו בַּל־יִמּוֹט:	טו	מַפְּלֵי בְשָׂרוֹ דָבֵקוּ
וְיָצוּק כְּפֶלַח תַּחְתִּית:	16	לִבּוֹ יָצוּק כְּמוֹ־אָבֶן
מִשְּׁבָרִים יִתְחַטָּאוּ:	17	מִשֵּׂתוֹ יָגוּרוּ אֵלִים
חֲנִית מַסָּע וְשִׁרְיָה:	18	מַשִּׂיגֵהוּ חֶרֶב בְּלִי תָקוּם
לְעֵץ רִקָּבוֹן נְחוּשָׁה:	19	יַחְשֹׁב לְתֶבֶן בַּרְזֶל
לְקַשׁ נֶהְפְּכוּ־לוֹ אַבְנֵי־קָלַע:	כ	לֹא־יַבְרִיחֶנּוּ בֶן־קָשֶׁת
וְיִשְׂחַק לְרַעַשׁ כִּידוֹן:	21	כְּקַשׁ נֶחְשְׁבוּ תוֹתָח
יִרְפַּד חָרוּץ עֲלֵי־טִיט:	22	תַּחְתָּיו חַדּוּדֵי חָרֶשׂ

מ׳ v. 32. אין כאן פסקא   מ״א v. 4. לו ק׳

23   He brings the deep to a boil like a pot;
                he stirs up the sea like a seething mixture.
24   He leaves behind him a shining wake —
                one would think the deep hoary-headed.
25   Nowhere on earth is there his like,
                a creature born without fear.
26   All that is lofty fears him,
                for he is king over all proud creatures.

23 יַרְתִּיחַ כַּסִּיר מְצוּלָה   יָם יָשִׂים כַּמֶּרְקָחָה:

24 אַחֲרָיו יָאִיר נָתִיב   יַחְשֹׁב תְּהוֹם לְשֵׂיבָה:

כה אֵין־עַל־עָפָר מָשְׁלוֹ   הֶעָשׂוּ לִבְלִי־חָת:

26 אֶת־כָּל־גָּבֹהַּ יִרְאֶה   הוּא מֶלֶךְ עַל־כָּל־בְּנֵי־שָׁחַץ:

CHAPTER 40:6–32

40:6, 7   On the meaning and authenticity of the Second Speech of the Lord (40:6–41:26), see Special Note 35.

Hö. deletes vv. 6, 7, but v. 6 is essential to introduce God's Second Speech and v. 7b is quoted by Job in his Second Response in 42:4b.

V. 7 is repeated here from 38:3; in both instances it is a powerful challenge at the opening of the Lord's Speech. The poet, who is not afraid to repeat the same root or word in parallel stichs, does not hesitate to repeat an entire v. when it is needed; cf. 5:9 and 9:10, and see the Comm. on the latter passage.

40:8   אַף (and הַאַף), like גַּם, is an emphatic, especially in questions, "indeed, really"; cf. Gen. 18:13, 23; Am. 2:11; Job 34:17. תָּפֵר is the Hiphil of פרר "destroy, annul, frustrate" (Job 15:4), common in the idiom הֵפֵר בְּרִית "to break or violate a covenant" (Lev. 26:44; Isa. 33:8; Jer. 11:10; Zech. 11:14). It is best taken here declaratively: "Will you declare My justice null and void, so that you may be in the right?" (so Ra.).

40:9   The poet momentarily forgets that he is speaking in the name of the Lord and refers to Him in the third person. The change is similar to, but not identical with, the fluctuation in person in prophetic discourse, where the prophet speaks at one point in the name of God and uses the first person, and then, as his human individuality comes to the fore, speaks of God in the third person.

40:10   עֲדֵה "adorn yourself" (Isa. 61:10).

40:11   For the intent of this highly important section of the Speech of the Lord, and its bearing upon the meaning of Job as a whole, see Special Note 32.

עֶבְרוֹת אַפֶּךָ "the anger of your wrath, i.e. your mighty wrath." On the use of synonyms in a construct relation, often to express a superlative, cf. וְדֶרֶךְ אֹרְחֹתֶיךָ (Isa. 3:12), מְעוֹן בֵּיתֶךָ (Ps. 26:8); and the Comm. on 36:33; 37:6. Though stich b has longer words than stich a, the meter is 3:3.

40:12   וַהֲדֹךְ. Arab. *hadaka,* "wreck a building," is here transferred to a human being; cf. the use of הרס "destroy," used both of buildings and of men (Isa. 22:19; Ps. 28:5). It need not be revocalized as הָדֵךְ, the Hiphil of דכך, "crush," which does not occur in Heb. as a verb at all, though it appears in Aram.

LXX uses different words for גֵּאֶה in 11b and 12a, to meet the taste of Greek readers. However, the use of the same root in parallel or contiguous stichs is a characteristic of Job's style, another instance of which occurs in the very next v. There is no need to replace גֵּאֶה by גָּבֹהַּ (Hö.).

40:13 חָבֹשׁ is not to be linked with the meaning of the verb "bind the head" (Ex. 29:9; Jonah 2:6), hence "bind up their faces in the hidden world" (D-G), but with the derived meaning "imprison," which is frequent in mishnaic Hebrew, as in the apothegm:

אין חבוש מתיר עצמו מבית האסורים

"A prisoner cannot free himself from the dungeon" (*M. Ber.* 8:2), and in the Arabic (*ḥabs*, "prison"). This meaning underlies חֹבֵשׁ (Isa. 3:7), which means "ruler, lit. one able to imprison." The same semantic development underlies אסר "bind, imprison" and עצר "restrain, imprison," which occurs in the difficult יוֹרֵשׁ עֶצֶר (Jud. 18:7) and in the merismus עָצוּר וְעָזוּב "the imprisoned and the free" (Deut. 32:36; I Ki. 14:10; II Ki. 14:26). פְּנֵיהֶם may be interpreted as "their presence, hence their persons"; cf. Ex. 33:15; II Sam. 17:1; Ps. 42:6, 12; 43:5; Pr. 7:15). It may, however, be taken lit.: "press their faces into the grave," an indignity added to their disaster. טָמוּן "the hidden place" may be a euphemism for "the grave."

40:14 Stich a: "I too will praise you, render you homage" (cf. Isa. 38:18; Ps. 44:9, and often). Stich b: "when your right hand will bring you victory." The verb is used not only of God saving man (Deut. 20:4; Isa. 25:8; Ps. 20:10), but also of a man triumphing over his foes through his own efforts (Jud. 7:2, "my own hand has saved me"; I Sam. 25:33; Ps. 44:4), and of God saving Himself, that is, achieving His purposes (Isa. 59:16; 63:5, "my right hand has saved Me"). The victory or salvation referred to in our passage would be Job's success in obliterating all evil and "instituting perfect justice in the world" (Kraeling). This goal, God tacitly concedes, He has not been able to achieve completely.

It is tempting to consider the possibility of an unrecorded *Tiqqun Sopherim*, "a correction of the scribes," in stich b and to suggest that the original reading was כִּי־תוֹשִׁיעַ לִי יְמִינֶךָ, "when your right hand would save, rescue Me," that is, if Job could succeed where God has not (my former student, Rabbi Sigmund Szobel). The boldness of the figure, like the one we have postulated for Hos. 4:15 (cf. Gordis, in *Louis Ginzberg Jubilee Volumes*, English volume, pp. 195–98), would explain the conscious alteration of the pronoun. For another instance of a possible *Tiqqun Sopherim* not noted in the various Masoretic lists, see the Comm. on 9:35.

On the authenticity and structure of the *Behemot* and *Leviathan* sections (40:15–24; 40:25—41:26), see Special Note 36.

On the history of the interpretation of *Behemot* and *Leviathan*, see Special Note 37.

40:15 בְּהֵמוֹת, though rendered as a plur. by the Vss. (LXX, V), is an intensive, "great beast," occurring in a sing. sense in Ps. 73:22; cf. also חָכְמוֹת (Pr. 9:1). See Special Note 37 on "The Identity of *Behemot* and *Leviathan*" for a discussion of the mythological interpretation of these creatures and the grounds for rejecting it in favor of equating *Behemot* with the hippopotamus and *Leviathan* with the crocodile. G. R. Driver denies this generally accepted identification on the ground that the hippopotamus does not have "a tail rigid as a cedar" (v. 17) or "take the cattle for its prey" (v. 20). However, the meaning he assigns to these verses is not their only possible meaning; see the Comm. *ad loc.* Moreover, in the hyperbolic description of the poet, a literal correspondence with zoological truth is not to be looked for.

 Behemot refers to the hippopotamus in Isa. 30:6. The Arabs call the creature "sea ox." The Hebrew word cannot be derived from an alleged Egyptian *p-iḥ-mw* "ox of the water," which does not exist in Egyptian!

 Today, the hippopotamus ascends the Nile no further than between the second and the third cataracts. Frescoes from ancient Egypt, however, indicate that it originally swam in lower Egypt as well, where it was captured by harpoons. The grown beast varies in length from three and a half to four feet and weighs up to 2,000 pounds.

 אֲשֶׁר עָשִׂיתִי, lacking in LXX, is omitted by Me., Bi., Sieg., Du., Be., Ehr., Hö. primarily on metric grounds. However, the introduction of a totally new and different theme after the preceding section would suggest a break in the meter pattern in order to evoke the reader's attention. Cf. אַשְׁרֵי הָאִישׁ (Ps. 1:1) and לֹא כֵן הָרְשָׁעִים (Ps. 1:6) as instances of this usage. If הִנֵּה־נָא be recognized as an anacrusis, the rest of the v. scans perfectly in 3:3 meter. While the conjunction *ʾašer* is usually omitted in poetry, it is used quite freely by the poet without receiving a beat (5:5; 6:4; 38:23; 39:6, etc.).

 עִמָּךְ either "with you, when I made you" or, better, "like you" (cf. 9:26; Ps. 106:6; Ecc. 2:16). *Behemot* is God's handiwork no less than is man.

40:16 שְׁרִירִים a *hapax* from the root שרר, "be strong," Aram. "powerful, enduring," hence "stays, supports of his belly." It is used in Modern Hebrew for "muscles," which may well be its meaning here. The muscles of the hippopotamus are peculiarly strong and thick, unlike those of the elephant (I Mac. 6:46; Josephus Ant. xii, 9, 4), which are vulnerable to attack (D-G). אֹונֹו "his strength"; see next v.

40:17 יַחְפֹּץ is generally derived from the Arabic *hafaṣa* (dotted ṣa) "lower, depress," hence "bend, arch" (P.), but the reference to the cedar makes this meaning inappropriate. Ra. renders "hardens" *ad sensum*, citing an obscure Talmudic passage חפיזא כי אופתא which he renders "hard as a tree trunk" (*B. Ḥul.* 47b). The content requires the meaning "stretch out." If our root is identical with that of the verb "desire," it would offer the only instance in Biblical Hebrew of the original, concrete meaning of the verb, which is exceedingly common in its abstract, derived sense. The etymology of the verb is uncertain, since the Arabic *hafiṭa* (dotted ṭa) "be mindful, strive hard," Aram. חפט "be zealous" are somewhat phonetically distant.

 פַּחֲדָיו "his thighs" Arabic *afḥadh* "thighs" or "his testicles" (Syriac פחדין "testicles" so V and Onkelos for אֶשֶׁךְ (Lev. 21:20). יְשֹׂרָגוּ "are knit together," cf. Lam. 1:14 and the common mishnaic verb סרג, "intertwine," as e.g., מסרגין את המיטות "one may intertwine the beds during the festival week" (*M. Moed Qatan* 1:8).

In Special Note 37, reference has been made to the medieval Catholic interpretations of *Behemot* as a symbol of sensuality. Even Aquinas, who equates *Behemot* and *Leviathan* with the elephant and the whale, explains this passage as depicting the mating of the beasts (Steinmann, p. 339). This may well be the meaning intended by the poet; note אוֹן here, which is used of sexual vigor (Gen. 49:3; Deut. 21:17; Ps. 105:36). Moreover, זָנָב is a colloquial term for the *membrum virile* in postbiblical Hebrew.

40:18 אֲפִיק "channel, river bed" (6:15), here "hollow pit, tube." גְּרָמָיו "bones," an Aramaism not necessarily late (cf. Pr. 17:22; Gen. 49:14). מְטִיל "bar"; cf. Arabic *matala*, "bend, shape iron into helmets," Aram. מטל "bar" (T for כִּידוֹן, I Sam. 17:6). Hö. suggests that the Greek *metallon*, which apparently lacks an adequate Indo-European etymology, may be a Semitic borrowing. Similarly, many years ago, Dr. Nahum Slouschz suggested a Hebrew-Phoenician origin for the Greek *techne*, from Hebrew תֹּכֶן and מְכֻנָה. The interrelations of Greek and Semitic cultures have been the subject of lively and controversial discussion in recent years, particularly in the works of C. H. Gordon and Michael Astour.

40:19 רֵאשִׁית, "first in time," carries the overtone of "the best," a nuance that would not be lost upon the Heb. reader (cf. Jer. 2:3, "Israel is holy to the Lord, the first fruit of His harvest). The hyperbole is obvious. Wisdom is described as "the first of God's ways of creation" (Pr. 8:22).

The very difficult stich b has been variously rendered: (a) "His Maker brings near his sword, i.e. God gives him powerful teeth" (D-G), but this requires an unwarranted meaning for the verb. (b) "only his Maker will bring his sword near (to attack him)" (JPSV; similarly, RSV). On the article and suff. with a participle, cf. הַמַּכֵּהוּ (Isa. 9:12); הַמְאַזְּרֵנִי (Ps. 18:33). However, the idea is strained and out of context. (c) LXX renders "made to be played with by the angels." This translation implies reading the verb as a passive participle and contains an obvious reminiscence of the midrashic interpretation of Ps. 104:26. (d) The stich has been emended to הֶעָשׂוּי יִגֹּשׁ חַרְבּוֹ (Gunkel), said to mean "which is made that he should govern the dry land," or (e) to הֶעָשׂוּי יִגֹּשׁ חֲבֵרָיו "who is made to govern his fellows" (Giesebrecht) or (f) the emendation to הֶעָשׂוּי נֹגֵשׂ חֲבֵרָיו (Du., D-G), which is taken to mean "he is made Lord of his comrades."

It may be suggested that הָעָשׂוֹ be vocalized as הֶעָשׂוּ (see 41:25), the archaic form of the Qal participle passive of *Lamed IIe* (*Vav*) verbs. It occurs several times in the Kethib where the Qere registers the later form with a Yod (cf. the Comm. on 15:22). Unlike הֶעָשׂוּ in 41:25, however, the participle here, we believe, goes back to the *Lamed Vav* root עשׂו "cover," which occurs in the proper name *Esau* and in several biblical passages; see the Comm. on 23:9. Stich b may then be rendered "only the one well-covered (with armor) may bring his sword near to attack him."

40:20 כִּי is the emphatic particle "indeed." בּוּל is either a shorter form or a haplography for יְבוּל, "produce," or, better, "tribute" (Dh., Hö.). The authenticity of the form in MT may be supported by two distinct lines of evidence, one Hebrew, the other Akkadian. The Hebrew noun יֶרַח בּוּל, "the eighth month" (I Ki. 6:38), which corresponds to the autumn month *Marḥešvan*, is connected with our noun by D. H. Müller (*Berichte der Wiener Akademie*, vol. 108, p. 977); perhaps it has the meaning of "the month of produce." The Akkadian idiom *našû bilta* means "bring tribute" and the Heb. root יבל, "bring," is also used in this sense (Isa. 18:7; Hos. 10:6; Zeph. 3:10; Ps. 68:30; 76:12). As the accentuation indicates, הָרִים is the subject of the verb. The tribute that the hills bring him is generally explained as the vegetation which serves the animal for food. Or the tribute may refer to the waterfalls and streams coming down from the mountains in which the animals disport themselves (stich b). The verb in this stich is not to be emended to יִשְׁחַק, "he will grind, destroy" (II Sam. 22:43) (Du., Hö.). Not only is the proposed verb inappropriate in the context (D-G), but the change would obliterate the emphasis in the entire sec. on the peaceful, nonpredatory character of this massive beast. Cf. vv. 21–24.

An alternative interpretation has also been proposed. TS renders בּוּל הָרִים as equivalent to the Akk. *bul seri*, "beasts of the steppe," which would be an excellent parallel to חַיַּת הַשָּׂדֶה. However, the exegesis that he develops on this passage is fanciful, as P. notes, who emends יִשָּׂאוּ to יְשַׁלָיוּ. If TS's interpretation of the phrase be accepted, no emendation is actually required. יִשָּׂאוּ would be parallel to יְשַׂחֲקוּ, "play," exactly as in 21:12, where יִשְׂאוּ is parallel to יִשְׂמָחוּ, "rejoice." The verb in both passages would be an elliptical expression for יִשְׂאוּ קוֹל, "raise the voice, sing" (so Ibn Janah), as in Isa. 42:11: יָרֹנּוּ ‖ יִשְׂאוּ; and see also Isa. 3:7; 42:2. Hence our passage might be rendered:

> "The beasts of the hills sing for him
> and the animals of the field play there."

We have retained the traditional interpretation in the Translation.

40:21 צֶאֱלִים "lotus," Arab. *ṣaʾlun*, Syriac עאלא. Depending on the habitat of Behemot preferred by the commentators, the plant is identified either with the Egyptian *nymphae lotus*, the water lily, or *zizyphus lotus*, a thorny shrub that grows in damp, hot areas from Syria to North Africa (cf. I. Löw, *Flora der Juden*, III, p. 134). קָנֶה "reed." בִּצָּה, "swamp" (Jer. 38:22; Ezek. 47:11; Job 8:11).

40:22 The v. is characterized by a marked assonance and even by rhyme. Stich a: "lit. the lotus covers him as his shadow"; צִלְלוֹ is an adverbial accusative of specification. עַרְבֵי־נָחַל "the willows of the wadi" (Lev. 23:40), identified with *populus Euphratica* growing in the wadis of Palestine (Löw, *op. cit.*, III, pp. 326 ff.).

40:23 Stich a is generally rendered: "When the Nile robs (by overflowing), he is not frightened; he is confident though the Jordan burst against his mouth" (D-G). However, עשק is everywhere else a transitive verb and the meaning assigned here is rightly pronounced "dubious" (D-G, BDB). The overflow of the Nile, which is regarded as the great blessing indispensable to the well-being of Egypt, can hardly be described as an act of robbery or wrong-doing perpetrated against the land. Hence the verb has been (a) emended to יָשֹׁק and given the meaning "dashes" (Du.) but this is highly doubtful; (b) on the basis of LXX: "If there be a flood," it has been emended to יִשָּׁפַע and rendered "overflow" (Be.), a meaning the verb possesses nowhere else; and (c) it has been emended to יִשְׁקַע "if the Nile sinks," on the basis of Am. 9:5 (Gunkel, Bu.), but the parallelism suggests an abundance of water, not its absence. Hö. interprets the verb by the Akk. *ešqu* "be strong." Hence "when the Nile is strong, i.e. high." TS renders: "when the river cheats him (of his prey) he is not concerned."

We prefer the interpretation of Ibn E., who explains the v. as depicting the hippopotamus slowly swallowing great masses of water as he lies in the shadow of the lotus plants and the reeds. This is hyperbolically expressed: "Indeed, he robs the river without haste and pours an entire Jordan into his mouth." The verb in question is used in its original basic sense. Compared to the mighty Nile, the smaller Jordan is an excellent figure for a stream of water that the hippopotamus ingests.

The unconscious use of "Jordan" virtually as a synonym for "river" is undeniable testimony of the author's Palestinian background. For a similar use of a geographical proper name ("Carmel") as a common noun, cf. Isa. 32:15.

לֹא יַחְפּוֹז is a subordinate clause of condition, "lit. he does not rush, i.e. without haste"; on the verb, cf. I Sam. 23:26; II Sam. 4:4; II Ki. 7:15, and the noun חִפָּזוֹן (Ex. 12:11; Deut. 16:3). On the syntax, cf. לֹא יַחְמוֹל "without pity" (Job 6:10). יָגִיחַ is transitive here "burst, draw forth," either as a Qal (Mic. 4:10; Ps. 22:10) or as a Hiphil, and cf. the Comm. on 38:8 and the noun *Gihon* (Gen. 2:13).

There is no need on metric grounds to delete יַרְדֵּן (D-G) or to emend it to יְאֹר (Winckler, Be.), or to delete אֶל־פִּיהוּ as a corruption of the beginning of v. 24. V. 23 may be scanned as either in 4:4 or 5:5 meter; the change to a slow rhythm is highly appropriate to the meaning of the v. The number of syllables in MT is approximately equal in both stichs, 9 or 10.

40:24 The poet declares here that man cannot capture the hippopotamus or the crocodile (vv. 25 ff.). This has been invoked as evidence that mythological creatures are being described here, since Egyptians did hunt both beasts. This is an egregious instance of the failure to reckon with poetic hyperbole. As Bu. (on 40:26) correctly pointed out, Amon-Re in his "Hymn of Victory" says of the Egyptian Pharaoh Thutmose III: "The lands of Mitanni tremble under fear of thee; I have caused them to see thy majesty as a crocodile, lord of fear in the water, unapproachable" (James H. Breasted, *Egyptian Records*, II, p. 659; *ANET*, p. 374b).

Not only does the v. in MT lack a subject, but stich a is shorter than stich b. The suggestion to add מִי הוּא to the beginning of the v. (D-G, Hö., Ehr.) is supported by the likelihood that the phrase fell out after פִּיהוּ by an aural haplography. For the phrase, cf. 17:3.

Utilizing the usual meaning of עַיִן "eye," stich a has been interpreted: (a) on the basis of LXX, "Can one take him in his sight?" which is taken to mean "when he is on guard" (D-G); (b) "Can one seize him by his eyes?" (TS); (c) It has been emended to בְּצִנִּים "with thorns, i.e. hooks?" (P.) or to בִּמְעוֹנוֹ "in his lair" (Kissane), for which there is no warrant. Dh. cites Herodotus II, 70 for a process of plastering the crocodile's eyes in order to control him. The context requires some instrument of capture. We suggest that בְּעֵינָיו means "ring," which may occur in Hos. 10:10 (Kethib בְּאָסְרָם לִשְׁתֵּי עֵינוֹתָם, "when they are caught by the double ring." In the old Heb. script the letter Ayin was a circle like the Greek Omicron, and it may have been applied to a circular trap. We today have a very imperfect knowledge of the technical vocabulary of the ancient Hebrews; note the six terms for trap in Job 18:8–10. יִקָּחֶנּוּ = "take him prisoner"; cf. Gen. 14:13; II Ki. 18:32 = Isa. 36:17.

מוֹקְשִׁים, generally "snare," has the meaning of a "lure to destruction" (Ex. 10:7; 23:7; I Sam. 18:21): Hence it would refer here to a metal tooth or trigger on which the bait was placed. Cf. וּמוֹקֵשׁ אֵין לָהּ, "Will a bird fall into the trap if there is no lure?" (Am. 3:5). Hence the noun here would mean "metal teeth, prongs." אַף may be revocalized as אַפּוֹ, as is perhaps the case above in 36:33; see the Comm. *ad loc.*

40:25 The proper chapter division is at this point, where Leviathan is introduced.

The crocodile was originally to be found near the Red Sea. Pliny mentions it in the Mediterranean north of Caesarea and refers (5:17) to a stream named *Crocodilon* generally identified with the *Nahr es Zerka*, which flows into the Mediterranean south of Carmel and north of Caesarea. The presence of the animal in this stream is also affirmed by many modern travelers; cf. G. B. Gray, "Crocodiles in Palestine," *PEQ*, October, 1920, pp. 167–76, for the literature.

The v. is interrogative, which the tone of the speaker would indicate. The verb תִּמְשֹׁךְ may contain a clever pun on the Arabic name for "crocodile," *timsaḥ*, Egyptian *pemsaḥ*, Coptic *temsaḥ* (Hö.).

40:26 אַגְמֹן "bulrush" (Isa. 9:13; 19:15; 41:12; 58:5) is here a cord made of rush fibers; for both meanings, cf. the Greek *schoinos*, "reed" and "rope." חוֹחַ "brier" (II Ki. 14:9; Pr. 26:9), then "thorn, hook" (II Chr. 33:11). In the last meaning it occurs also as חָח (Isa. 37:29; Ezek. 19:4; 29:4).

40:27 "Will the crocodile supplicate you to set him free again after he is captured?" On the use of the root in this connotation, cf. Pr. 18:23.

40:28 The covenant here is not a treaty between equals (*syntheke*), but an agreement between a sovereign and his subjugated vassal (*diatheke*). The theme of the covenant has in recent years been explored in depth; cf. G. E. Mendenhall, *The Law of the Covenant in Israel and the Ancient Near East* (Pittsburgh, 1955); D. J. McCarthy, *Treaty and Covenant* (Rome, 1963); *idem, Old Testament Covenant* (Richmond, Va., 1972).

עֶבֶד עוֹלָם, an echo of a characteristic Heb. phrase that is applied to a slave in Pentateuchal legislation (Ex. 21:6; Deut. 15:17; also I Sam. 27:13). This reminiscence of an earlier Heb. idiom and its unselfconscious application to an animal is an impressive refutation of the theory that Job is a translation from the Aramaic or the related idea that it is the work of a non-Hebrew author, Arab, Egyptian, Aramaean, or Ugaritic-Phoenician.

40:29 כַּצִּפּוֹר is a contraction of כְּבַצִּפּוֹר, "as with a bird"; cf. וְכַלַּיְלָה (5:14) and כְּאֵשׁ (Ps. 18:12). In our context, לְנַעֲרוֹתֶיךָ can refer neither to Job's daughters nor to his maidservants. There is no reason why either should be singled out from their respective male counterparts, nor is Job, in his present position, possessed of either. Finally, this interpretation is not borne out by the parallelism. Hence Gunkel inserts כַּתּוֹר, "like a pigeon," and Be. כַּיּוֹנָה, "like a dove," after וְתִקְשְׁרֶנּוּ, both for the sake of the parallelism, as well as on metric grounds. However, the two long words in stich b receive three beats; cf. Ps. 2:3a, 5b and see Special Note 1, sec. 6.

נַעֲרוֹתֶיךָ here is the Arabic *nugharun*, fem. *nugharatun*, "sparrow, swallow," as noted by D. Winton Thomas (*VT*, vol. 14, 1964, pp. 114 ff.), but there is no need to revocalize as נֹעֲרְתֶיךָ, since cognates frequently undergo vocalic change (see Gordis, in *VT*, vol. 14, 1964, pp. 492–94).

The plural is distributive, "as one of your sparrows"; cf. וַיִּקָּבֵר בְּעָרֵי הַגִּלְעָד, "he was buried in one of the cities of Gilead" (Jud. 12:7); Isa. 50:4 (כַּלִּמּוּדִים); Job 3:16 (כְּעֹלְלִים), and see Ges.-K., sec. 124, i, n. 2. On the verb with Lamed, cf. וּקְשַׁרְתָּם לְאוֹת, "You shall bind them as a sign" (Deut. 6:8). Hence stich b, "can you tie him up as one of your sparrows?" LXX read *hosper strouthion paidio*, "like a sparrow for a child," which is a conflate embodying two renderings of the noun, the common as well as the rare meaning given above, which alone is correct in the passage.

40:30 This v., like v. 25, is interrogative with the He. יִכְרוּ may be interpreted from כֵּרָה "feast" (so T), for which Fr. Del. cites Akk. *kireti iškun*, "he gave a feast." On the basis of the parallelism, it is better to explain the verb as "buy" (Deut. 2:6; but not Hos. 3:2, on which see Gordis, *PPS*, p. 251, n. 37), Arabic *kara* III "rent." Hence the verb both here and in 6:27 means "make a bargain over." See the Comm. *ad loc.*

חַבָּרִים, a *hapax* in this form, represents an occupation or activity more permanent than חֲבֵרִים, "comrade," like גַּנָּב, טַבָּח, etc. Hence it has been rendered "guildsmen, companies" either of fishermen (cf. Luke 5:7) or, preferably, of merchants. The parallelism suggests that either interpretation is possible. On the other hand, the Tyrians are described as bringing fish into Jerusalem in the period of Nehemiah (Neh. 13:16). On the basis of Ugaritic *bt ḥbr*, which is interpreted as "storeroom" (Ginsberg), or "brewery" (Albright), or "community" (Gordon), and the still unclear בֵּית חָבֶר (Pr. 21:9; 25:24), TS suggests that our noun means "keepers of the storehouses."

יֶחֱצוּהוּ = "cut in half, divide." בֵּין is not to be emended to בְּנֵי, "the nations of the Phoenicians" (LXX), but retained (Sym. V, P, T), since כְּנַעֲנִים is not a proper noun here. The noun, originally "Canaanites, Phoenicians," here means "merchants" (Isa. 23:8; Ezek. 17:4; Hos. 12:8; Zech. 11:7, 11, so read for לָכֵן עֲנִיֵּי; 14:21; Zeph. 1:11; Pr. 31:24).

40:31   שַׂכּוֹת, probably related to שִׂכִּים "thorns" (Nu. 33:55), Arab. *sakka*, IV "pierce," must have a meaning like "barbed iron" (JPSV), "pins" (TS), or, best, "harpoon" (RSV), which would be used in hunting crocodiles. צִלְצַל דָּגִים "fish spears," derived precariously from צִלְצַל "whirl, buzz" (Isa. 18:1), which is itself unclear.

40:32   The second person in this v. is impersonal, cf. the Comm. on 7:21 וְשִׁחַרְתַּנִי; the idiomatic בּוֹאֲךָ (Gen. 10:19, 30), בֹּאֲכָה (Gen. 13:10); and such passages as Pr. 19:25; 30:28. תּוֹסַף is a phonetic variant for תּוֹסֵף occurring principally in pause; cf. וָאֵלַךְ (19:10) but also elsewhere, as in תֵּלַן (17:2).

The v. is not to be broken up into three independent clauses, as "lay your hand upon him; then think of the battle; you will do so no more" (D-G). זְכֹר is best construed as a complementary inf. after תּוֹסַף (so Ra., Ibn E.): "lit. to remember the battle, you will not continue." The two imperatives in the two stichs of the v. constitute a conditional sentence: "Lay your hand . . . do not continue" is equivalent to "If you lay your hand upon him, you will not continue to remember the battle (because you will not survive)." For the idea, cf. כִּי לֹא הַרְבֵּה יִזְכֹּר אֶת־יְמֵי חַיָּיו "for not long will he remember the days of his life (because they will be brief)" (Ecc. 5:19; cf. *KMW ad lɔc.*). For this use of imperatives in conditional sentences, cf. פְּקַח עֵינֶיךָ שְׂבַע־לָחֶם "open your eyes and be sated with bread" (Pr. 20:13b); שִׁמְעוּ שָׁמוֹעַ אֵלַי וְאִכְלוּ טוֹב "Hearken to Me and enjoy the good" (Isa. 55:2; Isa. 8:10; Pr. 3:9 f.; 4:8); and see the illuminating treatment of this construction, both in Arab. and in Heb., in Driver, *HT*, pp. 188–91.

CHAPTER 41

On the text and meaning of 41:1–4, see Special Note 38.

41:1 Since תְּחַלְתּוֹ has no antecedent, it is emended to תְּחַלְתְּךָ (Hö.), which necessitates changing יֻטָּל to the second person as well. The emendation, however, is not necessary. It is characteristic of the poet's style to introduce a new subject through a pronoun without an explicit antecedent, thus creating a challenge for the reader to discover from the context who is intended. Cf. the Comm. on 8:16; 13:21; and chap. 24:3, and passim. For the psychological basis of this literary technique, cf. *BTM*, chap. XIV, "The Rhetoric of

Allusion and Analogy." Stich a "lit. indeed, his hope (i.e. of the would-be attacker) is doomed to prove false, be disappointed" (Isa. 58:11; Ps. 116:11).

Stich b, introduced by the interrogative He, is an instance of a rhetorical question expecting an affirmative answer, in which the negative *lōʾ*, which is usually inserted in questions of this type, is omitted. For instances of this usage, cf. the Comm. on 20:4; I Sam. 2:27; Jer. 31:19; and see Gordis, "A Rhetorical Use of Interrogative Sentences in Hebrew," in *AJSL*, vol. 49, 1933, pp. 212–17. Hence, הַגַם = הֲלֹא גַם "indeed, even at his mere sight, the adversary is cast down." יֻטַל from נָטַל "cast down" (Ps. 37:24).

41:2 אַכְזָר "cruel" (Job 30:21; Lam. 4:3) is here "cruel to himself, fool-hardy"; cf. B. S. 8:15.

While the Occidental Masorah reads יְעוּרֶנּוּ, with no variant, the Oriental Masorah registers a Kethib יְעִירֶנּוּ and a Qere יְעוֹרְנּוּ (*Minhat Shai*). All the variants have the suffix in the third person. The Kethib is the normal Hiphil of עוּר; the Qere may be explained as a contraction of יְעוֹרְרֶנּוּ; cf. the Comm. on וַיְכוֹנֵנּוּ (31:15).

Stich a has been rendered: "Is he not fierce when one rouses him?" (P.), or "Is he not too fierce to be stirred up?" (D-G). It is possible to treat לֹא as the emphatic interrogative = הֲלֹא "indeed"; cf. the Comm. on 37:24 and the references there cited. Hence: "Is he not foolhardy" = "He surely is foolhardy when he stirs him up." However, it may be translated "None is so fierce as to stir him up" (Ra., JPSV).

The parallelism and the context require that לְפָנַי, "before Me," be read as לְפָנָיו (so LXX, T, and some mss.).

41:3 Stich a has been rendered variously: (a) "Who has ever come before Me so that I should repay him?" and (b) "Who has given Me anything be-forehand that I should repay him?" on the basis of Deut. 23:5. However, there the nuance of giving inheres in the phrase "with bread and water" and not in our verb. (c) LXX renders: "Who will resist Me and abide, since the whole world is Mine?" Hence most scholars emend הַקְדִּימַנִי to הִקְדִּימ (Gr., Che., Du., Ehr., D-G, Hö.) and וַאֲשַׁלֵּם to וַיִּשְׁלַם and render: "Who has ever confronted him and emerged unscathed?" as in 9:4 (Me., Bi., Bu., Ehr.). קדם = "confront an antagonist" is used in the Piel (Isa. 37:33; Ps. 18:6, 9) and in the Hiphil (Am. 9:10).

Stich b in MT, when rendered literally "beneath the entire sky He is mine," is meaningless. Hence it is rendered more freely "beneath the entire sky, all is Mine." Unexceptionable as this idea is, it is irrelevant in the con-text. Hence לִי־הוּא has been emended to לֹא אֶחָד "no one" (Che.) or to מִי הוּא "who is it?" (P.) or, best, to לֹא הוּא "there is none," as in Jer. 5:12 (Gunkel, Ehr., D-G).

41:4 This v. links the theme of Leviathan's power and invincibility (דְּבַר גְּבוּרֹת) and the description of its bodily structure (חִין עֶרְכּוֹ). See Special Note 38 on the alternation of theme. Hence the emending of חִין עֶרְכּוֹ to אֵין

עֲרוֹךְ "without equal" (Ehr., Dh., Hö.), while satisfactory *per se*, eliminates an important element in the structure of the section. Virtually all commentators disregard the Qere לוֹ in favor of the Kethib לֹא "I shall not be silent about, etc."

בַּדָּיו has been rendered "his boastings, idle talk, i.e. of the man who challenges him" from the root בדה, as in 11:3 (Me., Du., JPSV). It is better interpreted as "limbs," as in 18:13; cf. the Comm. *ad loc.* דְּבַר "matter" (I Ki. 15:3; cf. also I Sam. 10:2, where LXX read sing. דְּבַר). Probably a suff. should be supplied to read גְּבוּרָתוֹ.

חִין is a *hapax*. It has been emended to חַיִל "strength" (Be.), or interpreted as a phonetic variant, as in Arab. (Guil.). TS emends to הִין a *hapax* which he interprets as "defiance" on the doubtful basis of Deut. 1:41. P. (p. 283) suggests that חִין is an accidental corruption of הִין, an epithet of the god *Koshar* occurring in some Ugaritic texts and to be read either *hayyan* or *hayyin*. P. argues that the verb וַתָּהִינוּ which occurs in Deut. 1:41 must refer to military preparations and these necessarily included incantations which the master enchanter *Hayyan-Koshar* pronounced! Hence he renders the v.: "Did I not silence his boasting by the powerful word that *Hayyin* prepared?" This presupposes reading הִין עֲרָכוֹ. An imposing superstructure indeed!

A less recondite procedure is to treat חִין as a *plene* orthography for חֵן "grace." The phonetic change from Ṣere to Ḥireq is illustrated by רִישׁ (Pr. 13:18), רִישׁוֹ (Pr. 28:19), and by forms like עִירֹה (Gen. 49:11) from עַיִר, though the morphological structure of the nouns is different. On the other hand, the spelling with Yod may simply represent a *plene* orthography of the Ṣere. Generally, such forms are vocalized with a Ṣere, e.g., הַשְׂכֵּיל, Jer. 2:15; Job 34:35; cf. also Jer. 44:4; Zech. 11:10; Ps. 142:5; Ecc. 10:10, a. e. In some instances, the *plene* spelling induces a vocalization with Ḥireq, as in תּוֹמִיךְ Ps. 16:5; cf. also Jud. 3:24; Jer. 17:18; Hos. 8:4. Examples cited in Del., *Schreib- und Lesefehler im Alten Testament*, sec. 28b, must, as always, be used with caution. עֵרֶךְ "arrangement," of bread (Ex. 40:23), of clothes (Jud. 17:10); here of bodily parts, hence = "form, structure."

41:5 גִּלָּה "revealed, stripped" (cf. Isa. 22:8; 47:2) by removing the scales that constitute his outer garment. כֶּפֶל רִסְנוֹ "his double halter" has been taken to mean "his lips" (Ra.) or "his jaws." It is better to read, with LXX, סִרְיֹנוֹ "coat of mail" (Jer. 46:4; 51:3), a scribal metathesis (Wr., D-G, Ehr.). Both stichs refer to the animal's protective scales.

41:6 "The doors of his face" is a vivid metaphor for "his lips" (Ra.) or "his jaws" (most comm.). The change to פִּיו (Bu., Ehr.) is not needed (Du., D-G).

41:7 Stich a in MT: "the channels of his shields are pride" (or "proud"). Following LXX, V, גַּאֲוָה is to be revocalized גַּוּוֹ "his back" (Houbigant, Dil., Bu., Bi., D-G, Ehr.); for the pleonastic Aleph, cf. רָאשׁ (Pr. 10:4), דָּאג (Neh.

13:6, Kethib), and the Comm. on ויאסר (Job 12:18). The "channels "are the grooves in the scales of the crocodile.

Stich b has been emended unnecessarily, צָר being changed to צֹר "flint" (Me., Du., Hoffmann), and סָגוּר to סְגֹרוֹ "his breast" (Du., Be., Hö.), on the doubtful basis of Hos. 13:8. This stich means "shut up as with a tight seal." As the next v. indicates, there is no open space between the scales where the attacker's spear could possibly penetrate.

41:8 One scale closely approaches the other. For a similar idea in an altogether different context, cf. Isa. 5:8. רוּחַ is masc. here, as in 20:3. The emendation to רֶוַח, "space," as in Gen. 32:17 (Be., Ehr., P.), is inappropriate to the verb יָבֹא, which suggests something moving like air, not stationary like space.

Both this v. and the succeeding one are omitted by LXX, a procedure followed by Bi., Du., and Hö. for v. 9. However, the omission is entirely explicable in terms of Greek taste. The explication of the idea that the body of Leviathan is impenetrable would be particularly burdensome for Greek readers, for whom Semitic parallelism in general undoubtedly posed a problem of "repetitiousness."

41:9 The v., missing in LXX, is deleted by Me., Bi., Du. as a doublet of v. 8. However, it is a poetic expansion underscoring the idea expressed in the previous v.; cf. vv. 11–13 (so also D-G).

41:10 The spray of the crocodile's sneezes glistens in the sunlight, hence "flashing forth light." עֲטִישֹׁתָיו "sneezings"; the root occurs in Arabic, Ethiopic, Aramaic, mishnaic and modern Hebrew. The noun is not to be changed to the sing. (with LXX, Sieg., Bi., Bu., Be., Hö.). For the fem. sing. subject preceding the verb, cf. Joel 1:20; Job 12:7. For the subject following the verb, cf. Pr. 20:18; Job 20:11; 27:20, and see Ges.-K., sec. 145, 4 (many of whose examples, however, like Gen. 49:22, are to be deleted, being instances of the archaic third person fem. plur.; cf. *BTM*, List 18, pp. 104 f.).

תָּהֶל Hiphil of הלל "shine"; cf. 29:3.

The eyes of Leviathan are red like the dawn. In Egyptian hieroglyphics, the eye of the crocodile was the symbol of dawn. The poet's masterful use of the phrase figuratively here is in contrast to his literal use of the figure in 3:9.

41:11 The water streaming from *Leviathan*'s mouth sparkles in the sunlight. כִּידוֹדֵי אֵשׁ, like נִיחוֹחַ from נוח, "sparks of fire," is a reduplication from כִּיד; cf. Arabic *kaᵓda* (*med. Ya.*), "a fire stick emitting sparks" (Barth, *NB*, p. 142). The same root apparently occurs also in כַּדְכֹּד, "precious stone" (Isa. 54:12; Ezek. 27:16); cf. the English colloquialism "sparkler."

MT יִתְמַלָּטוּ "escape" is superior to יִתְלַהָטוּ "are kindled" (P., V), as is clear from the parallelism.

41:12 כְּמִדּוּד = כְּדוּד "as from a cauldron." On the frequent contraction of a double preposition, cf. the Comm. on 40:29 כַּצִּפּוֹר. אַגְמֹן "swamp reed"; cf. the Comm. on 40:26. Stich b can be rendered only "as a boiling cauldron upon reeds," but the last item is, at best, superfluous. Saadia and Ra. render אַגְמֹן as "pot," a synonym for דּוּד, but there is no known evidence for this meaning. On the basis of the Arabic root ²ajama "be hot (of a day), burn up (of fire)" and the noun *ajmun* "heat (of anger)," the noun has been emended to the verb אָגֵם "boiling, steaming" (Be., Hö., Ehr., TS), but this creates a *hapax*. Instead, we suggest reading וַאֲגַם, the usual word for "swamp, troubled pool" (Ex. 7:19; 8:1; Isa. 42:15), the Nun being an instance of dittography. The stich contains two similes, "like a boiling cauldron or a marsh (from which the mist is constantly rising)." For a poet's use of two distinct similes, cf. Ps. 48:8, where, as Ehr. has brilliantly suggested, בְּרוּחַ is to be read כְּרוּחַ; the quaking of the kings is compared both to a woman in travail (v. 7b) and to a strong east wind that shatters the ships of Tarshish (see his *Kommentar zu Psalmen ad loc.*). Similarly, Ps. 23 has two metaphors for God: as a shepherd (v. 1) and as a host (v. 5). On the presence of mixed metaphors in biblical poetry and world literature, see *BGM*, pp. 202 f.

41:13 נַפְשׁוֹ, like its synonym נְשָׁמָה (4:9; 37:9), has the meaning here of "breath, breathing"; cf. Arab. *nafasa*, Hebrew בָּתֵּי הַנֶּפֶשׁ "perfume boxes" (Isa. 3:20); and הִנָּפֵשׁ "take breath, refresh oneself" (Ex. 23:12; 31:17; II Sam. 16:14).

41:14 תָּדוּץ is an Aramaism, frequently used in the general sense of "exult, rejoice" (P, T on II Sam. 1:20; Isa. 54:1, and in the traditional Jewish wedding benediction דִּיצָה וְחֶדְוָה "joy and delight"). However, its basic meaning "dance" occurs in the Syriac for Luke 1:41, 44; 6:23 and in the Hexapla of Ps. 114:4, 6, and is highly appropriate here. The reading תָּרוּץ "runs" (LXX, V, Be., TS) is far less poetic.

The root דוב, דאב may be an Aramaism for the Hebrew זוב "flow, melt." In Heb. the root דאב is used figuratively as "melt, waste away," the verb in Lev. 26:18; Jer. 31:12, 25; Ps. 88:10; and I Sam. 2:33 (וְלַאֲדִיב = וּלְהַאֲדִיב); the noun occurs only here and in Deut. 28:65 וְדַאֲבוֹן נָפֶשׁ. In our passage it has been rendered "destruction" (LXX, the same translation as for אֲבַדּוֹן in 26:6; 28:22; Ps. 88:12; Pr. 15:11; 27:30) and "despair, dismay." Hö. cites Hesiod's description of *Deimos* (terror) and *Phobos* (fear) running before the chariot of Ares, and Apuleius' describing Pallas as being accompanied by *Terror* and *Metus* (fear). The meaning in our v. remains unclear.

41:15 מַפְּלֵי בְשָׂרוֹ lit. "what falls away from his flesh," hence "the flakes or folds that fall away from the skin"; cf. מַפַּל בָּר, "refuse from the wheat" (Am. 8:6).

יָצוּק "lit. poured out, cast, firm"; cf. the vocable used as an adjective (37:18) and as a substantive (37:9).

41:16 The use of the same vocable יָצוּק in three consecutive stichs (15b, 16a, 16b) has led to suggestions for changes and deletions of the text. We have repeatedly called attention to this characteristic usage of the poet. לִבּוֹ may refer to his heart as the seat of courage (D-G) or, preferably, to his breast which is physically firm (so TS).

פֶּלַח תַּחְתִּית is the immovable lower millstone. It is surely accidental that the shorter technical term for the lower millstone שֶׁכֶב has been preserved and that only rarely in mishnaïc Heb. (*M. Baba Batra* 2:1; *Tos. Baba Batra* 1, 3), while the term for the upper millstone רֶכֶב ("riding") occurs in Deut. 24:6; Jud. 9:53; II Sam. 11:21.

41:17 מִשֵּׂתוֹ a defectiva spelling for מִשְּׂאֵתוֹ, either the noun, "before his majesty," or the inf. construct, "before his raising himself up." אֵלִים has been equated with אֵילִים "mighty ones, leaders" (Ezek. 17:13; II Ki. 24:15 Qere; see BDB, p. 18a). However, as an epithet for the waves, the meaning "gods" is preferable, *Yam* being the chief god and the waves his attendants.

Stich b is very difficult. מִשְּׁבָרִים has generally been rendered "by reason of consternation," which creates an abstract plural of שֶׁבֶר, but even this sense occurs only when it is linked with רוּחַ (Isa. 65:14; Pr. 15:4), or with מָתְנַיִם "lit. the breaking of the loins" (Ezek. 21:11), unless an ellipsis be assumed. The v. has been emended: (a) to וּמִשְּׁנָּיו גִּבּוֹרִים יִתְחַטָּאוּ taken to mean "at his teeth mighty men are dismayed" (Giesebrecht, Be., D-G); (b) to מוֹשַׁב רוֹם יִתְחַטָּאוּ "those (who dwell in) their lofty abode try to placate him" (TS; see below for the interpretation of the verb); (c) reading מִשְׁבְּרֵי יָם for מִשְׁבָּרִים and יִתְחַבָּאוּ for יִתְחַטָּאוּ, "the waves of the sea hide" (Gunkel); (d) reading מִשֶּׁבֶר מָתְנַיִם יִתְחַטָּאוּ "by reason of fear (lit. the breaking of the loins) they are prostrate" (P., who cites an Arabic root ḫṭ, "cast down," and finds in the passage an allusion to alleged Ugaritic mythological motifs, on which see Special Note 38. Besides, the Arabic root is *ḫaṭṭa*, a geminate root and not a *tertiae Aleph*).

As Ra. felt intuitively, the noun מִשְּׁבָרִים is to be rendered "waves," which requires vocalization as מִשְׁבָּרִים. The essential difficulty lies with the unique verbal form יִתְחַטָּאוּ, for which a large variety of meanings have been proposed: (a) "they are missing, lose the way," from the basic meaning of the root חטא "miss"; cf. the Comm. on 5:24 (Ra., Schultens, Ges.); (b) "they fall into confusion" (Hi., Bu., Du.); (c) "they are beside themselves (because of despair)" (JPSV); (d) "they withdraw, flee," on the basis of Ethiopic ḫt I II III "*se subducere, aufugere*" (Dh., Hö.).

The verb in the Hithpael occurs not infrequently in rabbinic literature, but unfortunately its precise meaning is not clear. Ben Jehuda, *Thesaurus*, s.v., gives three meanings: (1) "to act so as to make someone fulfill his desire or request, i.e. to importune," e.g. מה אעשה לך שאתה מתחטא לפני המקום ועושה לך רצונך כבן שמתחטא על אביו ועושה לו רצונו "What shall I do to you seeing that you importune God and He fulfills your desire as a son who importunes his father and has his wish granted" (*M. Taan.* 3:1); (2) "to act with someone affectionately," e.g. אהבתו של אברהם שהיה מתחטא לפני המלך "the love of Abraham who acted with love in the presence of the King" (*Mid. Cant. Rabba* 7:7); (3) "to appease, placate," on the basis of which TS emends and interprets, as given above.

Jastrow (*Dictionary*, pp. 448b, 449a) gives a different set of meanings to the verb: (a) "to enjoy, be gratified" נתחטא באהבה "let us indulge ourselves in love" (*B. Men.* 68b); (b) "to show oneself a nobleman," citing the same passage in *Mid. Cant. Rabba* given above, but rendering "he was generous"; (c) "to be imperious, lord it, act petulantly," citing the passage in *M. Taan.* quoted above. The nuance which Jastrow adds to the last meaning seems to us definitely implied by the text in *Taanit* and others. It may derive from the original meaning of the root, the Hithpael carrying the connotation to "act as a 'sinner,' mischievously, like an over-indulged child."

This last connotation, difficult to transmit by a single word, gives an excellent sense to our passage: "the waves importune, make supplication to Him," with the additional nuance of acting petulantly. If these connotations are correct, the passage carries the idea that just as the Sea is no longer a rebellious monster, but has been tamed and imprisoned by God (7:12; 38:8–10; see the Comm. *ad loc.*), the waves, when they rise because of Leviathan swimming through the water, do not threaten the land, but are merely acting petulantly, in sport.

MT is thoroughly satisfactory metrically, the two long words in stich b receiving three beats; cf. *PPS*, p. 66. The principle of *difficilior lectio praestat* suggests that MT is to be preferred over the various emendations and fanciful explanations proposed.

41:18 The change of the verb to the fem. תַּשִּׂיגֵהוּ is uncalled for (D-G); neither is it a *casus pendens* (P.). The v. is a conditional sentence (so Ibn E.), with the protasis expressed by a participle: "If anyone reaches for him with the sword, it (i.e. the sword) will not succeed." For instances of this usage, cf. לָכֵן כָּל הֹרֵג קַיִן שִׁבְעָתַיִם יֻקָּם "If anyone kills Cain, he (Cain) will be avenged sevenfold" (Gen. 4:15); כָּל־אִישׁ זֹבֵחַ זֶבַח וּבָא נַעַר הַכֹּהֵן "If any man offered a sacrifice, the priest's servant would come" (I Sam. 2:13); and see Gordis, "A Note on General Conditional Sentences in Hebrew," in *JBL*, vol. 49, 1930, pp. 200–203.

Stich b contains the names of three weapons: (a) חֲנִית = "spear." (b) מַסָּע = "dart?" rather than "missile stones," for which I Ki. 6:7, "foundation stones," is cited as support. The context suggests a weapon used in individual combat. Perhaps it is to be derived from the Arab. *nasagha*, "strike, hit." (c) שִׁרְיָה a *hapax*, not to be equated with שִׁרְיוֹן "armor" in I Sam. 17:5, 38 (Ra.), since an offensive weapon is indicated here. The Arab. *sirwaṭun* is "a short arrow," *siryat* "an arrowhead." Render "javelin."

41:19 עֵץ רִקָּבוֹן "rotting wood." יַבְרִיחֶנּוּ, the Hiphil, "cause him to flee, drive," a late use (Pr. 19:26; Neh. 13:28; I Chr. 8:13; 12:16).

41:20 בֶּן־קֶשֶׁת "son of the bow, arrow"; cf. בְּנֵי אַשְׁפָּתוֹ (Lam. 3:13). אַבְנֵי־קֶלַע "sling stones" (Zech. 9:15; cf. Jud. 20:16).

41:21 תּוֹתָח is rendered "javelin" or "club, mace" on the basis of Arab. *wataḥa* "beat with a club, *mitaḥatun*," or as an Akk. loanword *tartaḥu* "club, javelin" (Barth, *NB*, p. 294). נֶחְשָׁבוּ the plur. is irregular. Hö. reads נֶחְשָׁב לוֹ "is considered by him."

41:22 The poet describes the lower part of Leviathan's body as containing sharp scales, as does Aelian, *de Natura Animalium*, X, 24. Actually, the crocodile's belly is smooth. תַּחְתָּיו is here used as a substantive, "his underparts." חַדּוּדֵי חָרֶשׂ "sharp fragments of potsherds."

יִרְפַּד, "stretch out," is Qal intransitive; in the Piel it is transitive (17:13); cf. Akk. *rapâdu*, "stretch oneself out," a byform of רבד (Pr. 7:16; 31:22; LXX on I Sam. 9:25 for MT וַיְדַבֵּר). The root is distinct from its homonym רְפַּד "support, sustain" (Cant. 2:5), Arab. *rafada* "help, aid."

חָרוּץ the poetic term for "threshing sledge" (Isa. 28:17), "possessing sharp teeth" (Isa. 41:15). The prose term is מוֹרַג (II Sam. 24:22 = I Chr. 21:23; Isa. 41:15). LXX confused the word with its homonym meaning "gold."

The verb in stich b requires no revocalization as a Piel (D-G): "He is stretched out, as a threshing sledge, on the mire."

41:23 The description of Leviathan swimming through the water reaches its climax in this and the following vv., unsurpassed anywhere else in the book for esthetic power and beauty. יַרְתִּיחַ "causes to boil," a metaphor for the churning of the water. יָם "sea" is the Nile, so called in Arab. מֶרְקָחָה "perfumer's cauldron." The figure may have been chosen because of the musk-like odor of the crocodile from which the prized moschus perfume was manufactured.

41:24 A description of the water in the animal's wake. יָאִיר either transitive or intransitive (Ezek. 43:2; Ps. 139:2). Hence: "Behind him he lights up the path" or "Behind him the path lights up." יַחְשֹׁב impersonal, "one would think." לְשֵׂיבָה a superb figure for the white foam left by the passage of the animal, incidentally a perfect parallel to stich a. Hö. cites Catullus 64, 18, and Manilius, *Astronomia*, I, 706, for a comparison of the foam with the silver hair of an old man. The reading of LXX, *hosper aixmalotos*, "like a captive" (= שִׁבְיָה) and of P, rendering יַבָּשָׁה for שֵׂיבָה confirms the consonants of MT, as well as their own lack of esthetic insight. Incredibly, Gunkel accepts LXX and TS accepts P! Du. emends the verse to read: יָאִיר נְתִיב חֹשֶׁךְ אַחֲרָיו תְּהוֹם לְשָׁבִיב "He lights up the path of darkness, behind him the deep becomes a flame." None of these texts remotely approach the original in attractiveness.

41:25 עַל עָפָר "upon the dust, i.e. upon the earth"; cf. 19:25.

מָשְׁלוֹ has been derived from the root "rule," hence "there is no ruler over him" (Ra., Hi., Hoff., Dil.). Most commentators render "his likeness," perhaps an Arabism *mithluhu*. The root מָשַׁל, "be similar," is used in the Niphal (Isa. 14:10; Ps. 49:13, 21), in the Hiphil (Isa. 46:5), and in the Hithpael (Job 30:19). The form in MT here would be the Qal inf. construct, "his being similar, i.e. his likeness." There is no need to emend it to מָשְׁלוֹ (Me., Sieg., Gr., Bi., Bu., Du., Be.), even if we do not separate מָשָׁל, "proverb," from the verb "be similar," as does BDB (p. 605). הֶעָשׂוּ is not to be emended to הֶעָשׂוּי (D-G). The word is the archaic form of the Qal participle passive of a *Lamed He* verb, which occurs in the Kethib in four passages where the Qere registers the later forms (see Gordis, *BGM*, List 20, pp. 105 f.). We have postulated the older form also for וְזָהָב עָשׂוּ לַבָּעַל (Hos. 2:10) and perhaps for Job 40:19; see the Comm. *ad loc.*

לִבְלִי־חָת "without fear"; cf. Isa. 5:14; Job 38:41. The noun occurs with a suff. (Gen. 9:2), as a fem. חִתָּה in the construct (Gen. 35:5), and in the form חַתַת (Job 6:21).

41:26 MT is taken to mean "he can look down upon every high creature." However, the verb does not actually carry this connotation, and the idea as applied to the crocodile is forced. It has, therefore, been emended to אוֹתוֹ כָּל גָּבֹהַּ יִירָא, "every high creature fears him" (Gunkel, Bu., Du., Be., D-G). Ehr. regards this as rather prosaic. He therefore suggests that אֶת is a dittography from חָת in the preceding v. and reads: כָּל גָּבֹהַּ יִירָאֶהוּ, which produces the same meaning. The same confusion of roots occurs at the end of Elihu's speech. Cf. the Comm. on 37:24.

בְּנֵי שָׁחַץ. The Vss. give the phrase the limited meaning of "fish" or "creeping things." LXX: *ton en tois hydasin* "all that are in the waters." P רחשא, "creeping things." T בני כוורא "children of the pond." It is unlikely that they read בני שרץ; more probably the renderings represent an attempt to give a meaning appropriate to the habitat of the crocodile. However, this rendering is scarcely adequate for the close of God's Speech. The phrase, as in 28:8, means "proud creatures," a sense supported also by the parallelism. See the Comm. *ad loc.* for the evidence from rabbinic usage.

Job's Response (42:1-6)

The Lord's Second Speech has taught Job to recognize both the mystery and the harmony of the world. He now quotes the words of the Lord, to which he replies contritely. Job declares that his deepest wish has been granted, for his Maker has deigned to answer him. The beauty of His world constitutes an anodyne for his pain, and serves as the basis for his renewed faith in the justice of God.

This is more than submission to God — it is reconciliation and vindication for Job as well, for his contention that his suffering is no sign of guilt has not been refuted. Quite the contrary, God's admission that justice is not all-pervasive in the universe is a clear, if oblique, recognition of the truth of Job's position. Job's righteousness is explicitly set forth in the opening section of the Epilogue (42:7-10), where the Lord is angry with Eliphaz and his Friends and it is Job who must intercede for them if they are to be forgiven.

Yet, though Job is vindicated on the specific issue under discussion, he is far wiser than he was before — he now knows that the world was not created with man as its center. Since man cannot fully grasp the world, he cannot fairly judge its Creator, but the beauty of the one offers a basis for faith in the righteousness of the other.

מב א　　　וַיַּעַן אִיּוֹב אֶת־יְהֹוָה וַיֹּאמַר:

2　יָדַעְתָּ כִּי־כֹל תּוּכָל　　וְלֹא־יִבָּצֵר מִמְּךָ מְזִמָּה:

3　מִי זֶה | מַעְלִים עֵצָה בְּלִי דָעַת　　לָכֵן הִגַּדְתִּי וְלֹא אָבִין

4　נִפְלָאוֹת מִמֶּנִּי וְלֹא אֵדָע:　　שְׁמַע־נָא וְאָנֹכִי אֲדַבֵּר

5　אֶשְׁאָלְךָ וְהוֹדִיעֵנִי:　　לְשֵׁמַע־אֹזֶן שְׁמַעְתִּיךָ

6　וְעַתָּה עֵינִי רָאָתְךָ:　　עַל־כֵּן אֶמְאַס וְנִחַמְתִּי
　　עַל־עָפָר וָאֵפֶר:

42	Then Job answered the Lord,
2	I know that You can do all things
	and that no purpose of Yours can be thwarted.
3	You have said,
	"Who is this that hides My plan without knowledge?"
	Indeed, I have spoken without understanding,
	of things too wonderful for me which I did not grasp.
4	You have said,
	"Hear, and I will speak;
	I will ask you, and do you inform Me."
5	I had heard of You by hearsay,
	but now my own eyes have seen You.
6	Therefore I abase myself
	and repent in dust and ashes.

491

מ״ב v. 2. ידעתי ק׳

CHAPTER 42:1-6

Job's Second Response

42:2 On the defectiva spelling of the first person sing., preserved in the Kethib, cf. Ps. 16:2; II Ki. 18:20, both with no variants (but see the parallel in Isa. 36:5 and the Kethib in Ezek. 16:59 and Ps. 140:13, and see *BTM*, pp. 96 f.; 172, n. 207).

מְזִמָּה "purpose, plan," applied to God in Jer. 23:20. Hence the emendations proposed are gratuitous. The same theme is expressed in prose in Gen. 11:6.

42:3

On the authenticity and meaning of Job's Second Response (42:3-6), see Special Note 39.

The widely accepted view that 3a and 4 are scribal repetitions of other passages and are hence to be deleted (Hö., P.) is refuted by the verbal differences between the text here and their "sources" in Job. In our v., Job cites 38:2 with a slight verbal change (מַעֲלִים for מַחְשִׁיךְ) and responds in stich b. Cf. 21:19 for another instance of Job's citing his opponent's view and refuting it in the same v.

42:4 In stich b, Job again cites God's words, this time from the Second Speech, 40:7; cf. also 38:3. Job does not cite 40:7a because these words of challenge by God, "Gird up your loins like a man," could not be appropriately cited by Job in his response. This is particularly true, since Job wishes to emphasize the difference between merely "hearing" about God and "seeing" Him. He therefore introduces the phrase שְׁמַע־נָא וְאָנֹכִי אֲדַבֵּר into his quotation from God, in words reminiscent of Elihu (33:31b).

42:5 לְשֵׁמַע אֹזֶן "merely by the hearing of the ears, by hearsay, from afar"; cf. לְשֵׁמַע אֹזֶן יִשָּׁמְעוּ לִי "at the mere hearing of Me they obey Me" (Ps. 18:45). שְׁמַעְתִּיךָ "hear of you, receive a report about you"; cf. Ex. 18:1; II Ki. 19:11.

42:6 אֶמְאַס is not a metaplastic form for מסס "I melt" (as in Ps. 58:5; cf. the Comm. on 7:5), but "I despise my arguments" or "I abase myself"; so the Eng. Vss. and most commentators who follow LXX, which offers a conflate, "I counted myself vile and fainted." Stich b: "I repent sitting in dust and ashes."

THE EPILOGUE (Chapter 42:7–17)

The Jointure (42:7–10)

The poet now adds a few verses to serve as a link between the poetry and the conclusion of the traditional prose tale, which becomes the epilogue. Earlier, Eliphaz had grandly given Job the assurance that if he repented of his misdeeds he would be forgiven by God and even be able to intercede for other sinners. With poetic justice, the Lord now tells Eliphaz that it is he and his companions who have been guilty of untruth in their attempted defense of Him, and that they will be forgiven only if Job pleads for them. This Job proceeds to do on their behalf. His own fortunes are restored; in fact, all his possessions are doubled as a compensation for the losses he has sustained.

מב 7 וַיְהִי אַחַר דִּבֶּר יְהֹוָה אֶת־הַדְּבָרִים הָאֵלֶּה אֶל־אִיּוֹב וַיֹּאמֶר
יְהֹוָה אֶל־אֱלִיפַז הַתֵּימָנִי חָרָה אַפִּי בְךָ וּבִשְׁנֵי רֵעֶיךָ כִּי לֹא
8 דִבַּרְתֶּם אֵלַי נְכוֹנָה כְּעַבְדִּי אִיּוֹב: וְעַתָּה קְחוּ־לָכֶם שִׁבְעָה־
פָרִים וְשִׁבְעָה אֵילִים וּלְכוּ ׀ אֶל־עַבְדִּי אִיּוֹב וְהַעֲלִיתֶם עוֹלָה
בַּעַדְכֶם וְאִיּוֹב עַבְדִּי יִתְפַּלֵּל עֲלֵיכֶם כִּי אִם־פָּנָיו אֶשָּׂא
לְבִלְתִּי עֲשׂוֹת עִמָּכֶם נְבָלָה כִּי לֹא דִבַּרְתֶּם אֵלַי נְכוֹנָה
9 כְּעַבְדִּי אִיּוֹב: וַיֵּלְכוּ אֱלִיפַז הַתֵּימָנִי וּבִלְדַּד הַשּׁוּחִי צֹפַר
הַנַּעֲמָתִי וַיַּעֲשׂוּ כַּאֲשֶׁר דִּבֶּר אֲלֵיהֶם יְהֹוָה וַיִּשָּׂא יְהֹוָה אֶת־פְּנֵי
י אִיּוֹב: וַיהֹוָה שָׁב אֶת־שְׁבִית אִיּוֹב בְּהִתְפַּלְלוֹ בְּעַד רֵעֵהוּ
וַיֹּסֶף יְהֹוָה אֶת־כָּל־אֲשֶׁר לְאִיּוֹב לְמִשְׁנֶה:

42 7   After the Lord had spoken these words to Job, the Lord said to Eliphaz the Temanite, "My anger is kindled against you and against your two friends, for you have not spoken the truth about Me as has My
8   servant Job. Now then, take seven bulls and seven rams, and go to My servant Job, and offer them as a burnt offering for yourselves. My servant Job must intercede for you, for only to him will I show favor and not expose you to disgrace for not speaking the truth about Me as
9   did My servant Job." So Eliphaz the Temanite, and Bildad the Shuhite, and Zophar the Naamathite did as the Lord had told them; and the
10 Lord heeded Job's plea. Then the Lord restored the fortunes of Job, when he had interceded for his friends; and the Lord doubled all of Job's possessions.

CHAPTER 42:7–10

42:7   On the content of the jointure in the Epilogue (42:7–10) and its bearing on the unity of the Prose Tale, see Special Note 40.

Eliphaz is singled out for special censure, not only because he is the oldest and intellectually the most distinguished of the Friends, but because it is he who has presumed to "promise" Job the power of intercession for sinners if he repents (cf. the Comm. on 22:26–30). The tables are now neatly turned on Eliphaz, who is dependent on Job for God's forgiveness. The poet who is the author of this v. in the jointure thus emphasizes, obliquely but clearly, that Job's courageous and honorable challenge to God is more acceptable to Him than conventional defenses of God's justice that rest upon distortions of reality. The profundity of the v. makes it impossible to attribute it to the present folktale. On the other hand, the use of the term נְכוֹנָה, "true, correct," rather than the term נְבָלָה, "blasphemy," disproves the theory that the v. belongs to an early version, in which the Friends called upon Job to blaspheme. See Special Note 40, "The Jointure in the Epilogue."

אַחַר דִּבֵּר the use of a finite verb for introducing a clause as the *nomen regens* after a preposition occurs in אַחַר חִלֵּץ (Lev. 14:43), as well as in מִן־יְקוּמוּן (Deut. 33:11), and after a noun in תְּחִלַּת דִּבֶּר ה' (Hos. 1:2) and the moot passage in בְּרֵאשִׁית בָּרָא (Gen. 1:1). אֵלַי "about Me" = עָלַי, not "to Me" (T, Bu.). For the frequent interchange of the two prepositions, cf. I Sam. 3:12; I Ki. 6:12, the Elephantine Papyri, passim, and see BDB, 41a.

Some mss. read בְּעַבְדִּי "against my servant Job" both here and in v. 8.

In the latter passage, LXX also reads the preposition *Beth*. This reading represents an effort to "make sense" of the heinous charge against the Friends, from the standpoint of traditional religious believers, who could not comprehend the sophisticated idea that Job, and not the Friends, had spoken the truth about God. This reading is manifestly impossible from the standpoint of syntax and meaning. On נְכוֹנָה see Special Note 40.

42:8   The holocaust of seven bullocks and seven rams is identical with the seven bullocks and seven rams offered by Balaam on the seven altars (Numbers, chaps. 23 f.). The Code of Ezekiel (45:22–25) also ordains seven bullocks and seven rams as daily sacrifices. The offerings required in Leviticus, chap. 4, are substantially lower in quantity.

כִּי אִם־פָּנָיו אֶשָּׂא "lit. for only his face will I lift, i.e. only to him will I show favor." The meaning "only" is basic for the passage; cf. כִּי אִם־צְלִי־אֵשׁ "only roasted" (Ex. 12:9); כִּי אִם־אֶל־הַמָּקוֹם "only to the place" (Deut. 12:5; 16:6); כִּי אִם־חָי "only raw meat" (I Sam. 2:15), and see BDB, s.v., p. 475b. Rendering כִּי אִם as "surely" or "correcting" it to אַךְ (Du.) obliterates the ironic emphasis intended by the author.

נְבָלָה, a term for evil action of major proportions. It is applied to sexual offenses (Gen. 34:7; Deut. 22:21), blasphemy (Job 2:10), the profanation of sacred objects (Jos. 7:15), inhospitality (I Sam. 25:25). In our passage, the phrase means "to exhibit you as נְבָלִים, senseless, foolish, i.e. to expose you to disgrace."

42:9 Probably read וְצֹפֶר with the conjunction.

42:10 The idiom שׁוּב שְׁבוּת occurs with an individual only here; everywhere else it refers to a group like the nation. It occurs primarily in prophetic literature (Am. 9:14; Hos. 6:11; Jeremiah, Zephaniah, Ezekiel) and in lyric poetry (Psalms and Lamentations). It is no longer associated by scholars with the theme "bring back from captivity," but it is interpreted as using the same root for the verb and the noun; hence "lit. turn a turning, restore to the previous state." For a discussion of the idiom and its morphology, see *BTM*, pp. 122 f., and the literature there cited.

    בְּהִתְפַּלְלוֹ, "when he prayed." It has also been interpreted "because he prayed" from which the Talmud derives the ethical counsel: "Whoever seeks mercy for his friend when he himself is in need of the same blessing is answered first" (*B. Baba Kamma* 92a).

    רֵעֵהוּ is not the sing. (Du., Bu.), but equal to רֵעָיו = רֵעֵיהוּ the plur., as in I Sam. 30:26 (so LXX, P, V, T).

Job's Restoration (42:11-17)

The traditional tale of Job and his trials is now resumed in the epilogue, which together with the prologue constitutes the framework of the book. Satan does not appear, nor is God vindicated in His wager. These features of the traditional tale were probably eliminated by the poet deliberately. He must have felt, quite properly, that their reintroduction at this point would be a grave anticlimax after the profundities of the dialogue and the exalted speeches of the Lord.

Job's kinsmen and friends, who ostracized him during his suffering, come to break bread with him and comfort him, now, when he no longer needs their sympathy. Each brings a gift as a symbol of his friendship. The Lord blesses Job by giving him flocks twice the size of those he had originally owned. Since male offspring was a great blessing in the ancient Orient, he is given fourteen sons instead of the seven he had at the beginning. His daughters, however, remain three in number, though they are outstanding for their beauty, and are given an inheritance along with their brothers (an act which is striking testimony to their honored status). Job lives one hundred and forty years more, twice the normal life span, and sees four generations of his descendants.

מב 11 וַיָּבֹאוּ אֵלָיו כָּל־
אֶחָיו וְכָל־אַחְיֹתָיו וְכָל־יֹדְעָיו לְפָנִים וַיֹּאכְלוּ עִמּוֹ לֶחֶם
בְּבֵיתוֹ וַיָּנֻדוּ לוֹ וַיְנַחֲמוּ אֹתוֹ עַל כָּל־הָרָעָה אֲשֶׁר־הֵבִיא יְהוָה
עָלָיו וַיִּתְּנוּ־לוֹ אִישׁ קְשִׂיטָה אֶחָת וְאִישׁ נֶזֶם זָהָב אֶחָד: 12 וַיהוָה
בֵּרַךְ אֶת־אַחֲרִית אִיּוֹב מֵרֵאשִׁתוֹ וַיְהִי־לוֹ אַרְבָּעָה עָשָׂר אֶלֶף
צֹאן וְשֵׁשֶׁת אֲלָפִים גְּמַלִּים וְאֶלֶף־צֶמֶד בָּקָר וְאֶלֶף אֲתוֹנוֹת:
13 14 וַיְהִי־לוֹ שִׁבְעָנָה בָנִים וְשָׁלוֹשׁ בָּנוֹת: וַיִּקְרָא שֵׁם־הָאַחַת
טו יְמִימָה וְשֵׁם הַשֵּׁנִית קְצִיעָה וְשֵׁם הַשְּׁלִישִׁית קֶרֶן הַפּוּךְ: וְלֹא
נִמְצָא נָשִׁים יָפוֹת כִּבְנוֹת אִיּוֹב בְּכָל־הָאָרֶץ וַיִּתֵּן לָהֶם אֲבִיהֶם
16 נַחֲלָה בְּתוֹךְ אֲחֵיהֶם: וַיְחִי אִיּוֹב אַחֲרֵי־זֹאת מֵאָה
וְאַרְבָּעִים שָׁנָה וַיִּרְאֶ אֶת־בָּנָיו וְאֶת־בְּנֵי בָנָיו אַרְבָּעָה דֹּרוֹת:
17 וַיָּמָת אִיּוֹב זָקֵן וּשְׂבַע יָמִים:

42 11 Then there came to him all his brothers and sisters and all his former friends, and they ate food with him in his house, commiserating with him and consoling him for all the suffering that the Lord had brought upon him. Each man also gave him a piece of money and a golden ring.

12 So the Lord blessed the end of Job's life more than his beginning. He had fourteen thousand sheep, six thousand camels, a thousand yoke
13 of oxen, and a thousand she-asses. He also had fourteen sons and three
14 daughters. And he called the first, Jemimah; the second, Keziah; and the third, Keren-happuch. In all the land there were no women as
15 fair as Job's daughters. And their father gave them an inheritance among their brothers.

16 After this, Job lived a hundred and forty years and saw his sons,
17 and his sons' sons, to four generations. So Job died, an old man, satisfied with life.

v. 16. וירֹאה ק׳

42:11 On the content and spirit of the Prose Tale's conclusion (42:11–17), see Special Note 41.

By eating with Job, his kinsmen and friends give public testimony that he is no longer a pariah or a leper. LXX supplies וַיִּשְׁתּוּ, which is an addition to the original. קְשִׂיטָה "a weight of silver" (Gen. 33:19; Josh. 24:32), which is rendered, curiously, by LXX as "lamb"; this rendering may be due to an inner Greek error.

42:12 The number of sheep, camels, oxen, and asses that Job previously owned (1:3) is doubled. The implication would not be lost upon the reader that Job has been unjustly deprived of his possessions and, therefore, should be compensated by double payment, the same penalty imposed on a thief or a negligent trustee (Ex. 22:3, 6, 8).

42:13 שִׁבְעָנָה has been regarded as an error for שִׁבְעָה (D-G). However, the doubling of all of Job's possessions suggests that the word is a dual (so T). In I Chr. 25:5, Heman's prosperity is attested by his having 14 sons and 3 daughters. The form contains the diphthong *ai* spelled defectiva = שִׁבְעַיִן. On this orthography, cf. דֹּתָיְנָה and דֹּתָן (Gen. 37:7, 8), דְּבְלָתָיְמָה, דְּבְלָתָיִם (Nu. 33:46 f.; Jer. 48:22) and דבלתן (*Mesha Inscription*, line 30); עָשׁ (Job 9:9) = עָיִשׁ (38:32); and the usual spelling of ירושלם. For other instances of the biblical orthography of the diphthong, see *BTM*, p. 100. The final *He* in שִׁבְעָנָה may be the result of a conflation of שבען and שבעה (Dh.). It is more likely an archaism with the otiose suffix *āh* added for euphonic reasons; cf. such varied forms as כִּלָּנָה (Gen. 42:36; Pr. 31:29), עוּלָתָה *Qere* (Ps. 92:16) and אַרְצָה (Job 37:12), and see the Comm. *ad loc.*

In true Semitic spirit, which regarded sons as a blessing and daughters as a source of perpetual worry and concern (cf. B. S. 26:10–12; 43:9–11), the number of Job's daughters is not increased, on the theory that "enough is enough." On the other hand, though their number remains the same, they are endowed with physical attractiveness, which is no minor consolation.

42:14 יְמִימָה "dove" in Arabic (cf. Cant. 2:14; 5:2; 6:9). קְצִיעָה "cassia," a perfume (Ps. 45:8). קֶרֶן הַפּוּךְ "horn of antimony," a black powder used to beautify the eyes (II Ki. 9:30; Jer. 4:30).

42:15 Codified biblical law made no provision for daughters inheriting while the sons were alive. Only in the absence of living male heirs were the daughters permitted to receive their father's estate (Numbers, chap. 27). On the other hand, there is accumulating evidence that the status of women in customary law was higher than in the official code. Some indications are to be found in Hosea, chaps. 1–3; Pr. 31:14, 34; Ruth, chap. 4 (on which see Gordis, "Love, Marriage and Business in the Book of Ruth," in *A Light to My Path, James Myers Jubilee Volume* (Philadelphia, 1973); and in the multifarious business transactions of the woman real-estate operator, *Mibtaḥyah* documented in the *Elephantine Papyri* (cf. B. Porten in *The Archives from Elephantine*, Berkeley, Cal., 1960, pp. 235–63).

While a higher status for women may have existed in Homeric and patriarchal times, as argued by C. H. Gordon ("Homer and the Bible," in *HUCA*, vol. 26, 1955, pp. 76 ff.), we are not compelled to go back to this antique period to explain this passage, which is entirely in conformity with the customary norms of the post-Exilic era.

42:16   Both the Kethib וַיְרָא and the Qere וַיִּרְאֶה are equally satisfactory variants, with a slight edge for the Kethib. Hence the Qere is obviously not a correction of the Kethib.

LXX reads: "Job lived after the affliction 170 years and all the years he lived were 240 years" (with a variant 248). This presupposes that Job was 70 (or 78) years old at the time of his trial, a view expressed in the Midrash as well. The entire idea rests upon the erroneous conception of Job as an old man at the beginning of the narrative. Actually, Job was in the prime of life. See the Comm. on 1:6; 19:17.

On the other hand, there is no reason for giving Job a life span of only 140 years *in toto*, as does the *Jerusalem Bible* (Snaith, p. 5, n. 6). The phrase *ʾaḥărēi zōʾt* occurs only here and in Ezra 9:10 (with *kol* in II Chr. 21:18; 33:20). It is correctly understood by LXX and V as temporal, referring to the period after the events narrated in the book. Its earlier equivalent, still employed in later Hebrew, is *ʾahar haddebhārîm haʾēleh* (e.g., Gen. 15:1; 22:1; 39:7; 40:1; Est. 2:1; 3:1; Ezra 7:1).

The Hebrew text, which is undoubtedly original, disregards the earlier years which had ended in Job's misery. He is, therefore, granted 140 additional years, double the usual life span (Ps. 90:10). As against the normal experience of seeing two generations of children (Ps. 128:6), he is privileged to behold four generations of his descendants.

42:17   זָקֵן וּשְׂבַע יָמִים "old and sated with days" (Gen. 25:8; 35:29; I Chr. 29:28). The phrase carries the connotation not merely of longevity, but of a happy and contented life filled with satisfaction.

The end of the Hebrew Book of Job did not mark the conclusion of interest in him. The additions in LXX, the Apocryphal *Testament of Job*, and the vast midrashic material scattered throughout rabbinic literature all testify to the abiding fascination of the Job tradition as embodied primarily, but not exclusively, in the prose tale. The religious and philosophic issues raised by the Dialogue was a subject of profound thought by such philosophers as Maimonides and Gersonides, as well as other philosophers and theologians of the Middle Ages. In the modern period, the work of such disparate thinkers and writers as Immanuel Kant, H. G. Wells, Carl Jung, Robert Frost, and Archibald MacLeish is evidence of the powerful hold that the Book of Job continues to exercise over the minds and hearts of men.

STUDIES IN THE STYLE, STRUCTURE AND CONTENTS OF JOB.

Special Note 1 — The Principles of Biblical Prosody

In this Commentary, reference is frequently made to the principles of biblical prosody, which are set forth and, in some instances, formulated, for the first time, in *Poets, Prophets and Sages*, chapter 3 (pp. 61–94). Still important is G. B. Gray's basic work, *The Forms of Hebrew Poetry* (first published in 1915; Reprint edition, New York, 1972), which contains a valuable "Prolegomenon" by D. N. Freedman, and a useful, up-dated bibliography, to which the reader is referred for further study. It will, however, be convenient to set forth in summary form the fundamental principles to which we adhere, particularly as they apply to Job:

1. The two basic traits of biblical prosody are parallelism and meter. The efforts of some scholars like Gray to treat one feature as fundamental and the other as secondary cannot be described as successful. Generally, these two factors reenforce each other, but, at times, one will lead to a modification of the other.

2. Parallelism is the restatement of the same or a similar idea in different words, or formulation of the same truth in negative form by the presentation of the opposite idea in antithetical language.

3. Parallelism falls into five basic types: (a) synonymous; (b) antithetic; (c) complementary or climactic; (d) formal or synthetic; and (e) anadiplosis, a combination of the complementary and formal types. See *PPS, loc. cit.*

4. Biblical meter is not syllabic in character. See Special Note 3. It does not exhibit patterns of long and short syllables in alternation, as in classic Greek and Latin poetry or in medieval Arabic or Hebrew verse. Nor does it consist of patterns of stressed and unstressed syllables that characterize most Western poetry until the modern period. Biblical meter is based on a succession of thought-units, each receiving one beat. In the vast majority of instances, the thought-unit consists of one word. Generally, the meter is the result of the same number of stresses in parallel stichs, thus constituting "balanced rhythm." When the second stich is shorter than the first, an "echoing rhythm" results. On the various types of "echoing rhythm," primarily 3:2, but also 5:5, which may be broken up into 3:2 ‖ 3:2, though not always, see Section 13 below. On the 4:3 meter, see Sections 13 and 14 below.

5. The most common meter in Akkadian, as in the *Creation Myth* and the *Gilgamesh Epic*, is 2:2. In biblical poetry the basic meter is 3:3; other less frequent patterns are 2:2 and 4:4, which may often be broken up into 2:2 ‖ 2:2.

The basic meter in Job is 3:3, though the poet may vary it by adopting the 4:4 meter (as in 3:2) or using the staccato 2:2 meter (as in 3:26 or 17:1). He may also utilize different forms of the Qinah rhythm, such as 3:2 or 4:3.

Pfeiffer's statement that the basic meter of Job is 4:4 is incomprehensible, as is his insistence that every tristich is an interpolation (*ILOT*, pp. 687 ff.).

6.   The principle of one stress for each word is basic, but it may undergo modification for metric reasons. Not infrequently, several words, particularly short ones, may receive only one beat. The Masoretic *maqqēph* (hyphen) represents this characteristic in biblical accentuation. Conversely, the meter may make it necessary at times to give a stress to a short or unimportant word, like the conjunction *ki* or the negative *lōʾ*, or to assign two beats to some vocables, especially longer ones. The Masoretic *metheg* (secondary accent) is a mark of this practice. The Masoretes, however, were not consciously aware of the structure of biblical poetry. Hence the presence or absence of either device in a given Masoretic text cannot be regarded as evidence for the original mode of intoning a particular passage, which must be decided, though at times only tentatively, by a study of the poem in question.

7.   The fundamental virtue of parallelism is its power; the repetition in the second stich reenforces the truth of the idea set forth, or intensifies the depth of the emotion expressed, in the first stich. The ever-present danger of parallelism is monotony, particularly in a long composition. Hence, the poet will use every conceivable device for preserving the vigor and avoiding the monotony by modifying either the metrics or the parallelism.

Thus the poet may (a) vary the meter pattern, (b) change the number of stichs in some verses, (c) modify the word-order within the stichs, so that a, b, c will be parallelled not only by a′, b′, c′, but by a′, c′, b′, or c′, b′, a′, etc. He may change the parallelism from (a) the most frequent structure, the *consecutive*, in which a ‖ b and c ‖ d, to (b) the *alternate*, in which a ‖ c and b ‖ d, as, e.g., Hos. 5:3; Ps. 33:20 f. (This structure occurs also in prose, e.g., Ex. 29:27; Deut. 22:25–27, and is the key to Ecc. 5:17–19; see *KMW ad loc.*), or to (c) the *chiastic*, a ‖ b and d ‖ c, e.g., Hos. 2:21 f.; Pr. 23:15–16; Lam. 2:13.

8.   Chiasmus may be limited to the word-order within a verse (Job 12:16–21), or between two verses (Job 20:2–3; 27:16–17), or it may be the key to the structure of an entire passage (Job 8:12–20; see the Comm. *ad loc.*).

9.   In virtually every poem of any length, a variety of metric patterns is to be expected, either because of changing moods of the poet or out of the natural desire to avoid monotony. Though formerly disputed by many critics, this multiplicity of meters is evident in "The Song of the Sea," Exodus, chapter 15, and "The Song of Deborah" (Judges, chapter 5), as well as throughout the Book of Job. Thus "The Song of the Sea" exhibits virtually every biblical meter: 4:4 (v. 1), 3:3 (v. 2), 3:2 (v. 3), 5:5 (v. 4), 2:2 (v. 9). This variety, clearly exhibited in Akkadian and Egyptian, has been validated anew in the Ugaritic epics. See also Special Notes 6 and 7.

10.   An unbroken succession of distichs, particularly in a long composition, would become exceedingly monotonous. The poet will, therefore, not hesitate to vary his pattern by introducing tristichs at various intervals. The effort by some critics to place biblical poetry on a procrustean bed by eliminating all tristichs in favor of a uniform distich pattern (cf. the Com-

mentary on chap. 24), or, conversely, by deleting all distichs or converting them into tristichs (cf. the Commentary on chap. 34) is an all-too-common methodological error.

11. Normally, the poetic and logical caesura in a line of verse will coincide, the pause in thought being reflected by the pause in rhythm. Exceptionally, however, these two caesuras may diverge (as in 4:8), so that one stich will be longer and the other shorter than the thought expressed. This is common in all poetry.

12. Anacrusis is the presence of an introductory word or short phrase that remains outside of the meter pattern. The purpose of this technique is to attract attention for the vocative or the announcement of a special theme. This usage has not been sufficiently recognized in biblical prosody, with the result that anomalous meter patterns have been proposed for some passages. Thus, Isa. 40:3 is not an instance of 6:4 (or 2:4:4), as Gray suggests. The opening phrase *qōl qōrēʾ* is outside the meter, with the rest of the verse in 4:4 meter. Similarly, Ps. 1:1 is not an example of 2:4 meter (ag. Gray, p. 183). The first two words, *ʾašrei haʾīš*, is an anacrusis, and the rest of the verse is in 4:4:4. Note the 4:4 meter in v. 2. In Ps. 22:3, *ʾelōhai* is another instance of anacrusis with a vocative.

13. In 1882, Karl Budde published a fundamental paper, "Das hebräische Klagelied," in *ZATW*, calling attention to one important variation in biblical prosody that departs from the principle of "balanced rhythm." He noted the frequent existence of a 3:2 rhythm in elegiac poetry and, therefore, called this pattern the Qinah meter. The term, which has persisted, is not altogether fortunate, since this meter is not limited to elegies, but occurs in religious hymns, as in Psalm 27, and in love poetry, as in the Song of Songs (5:10 ff.).

Budde's concept of the Qinah rhythm as being 3:2 was criticized by Eduard Sievers, who argued that there are many instances in elegies of lines consisting of four words equally divided, particularly in Lamentations, chap. 1, and to a far lesser degree in chaps. 2–5. Budde explained these apparent exceptions as consisting of "heavy" or "long" words with more syllables followed by "light" or "short" words with fewer syllables, so that the basic echoing effect of the Qinah rhythm of a longer stich followed by a shorter is preserved. It is noteworthy that Sievers finds that fully half of the lines in Lamentations, chap. 1, possess this character, while Budde's list is far shorter (Gray, *op. cit.*, p. 118, n. 1).

We believe that Budde's contentions are justified, but that the phenomenon is to be explained differently. It has been noted in Sec. 6 that metric considerations will sometimes give to a long word two stresses or to a short word, normally unaccented, a beat of its own. Upon examination, it becomes clear that the first two words in these verses should receive 3 beats. To be sure, the recognition of this principle may be abused and all anomalies in the text may be explained away, but this is not the case in these instances. Gray's sarcastic statement, "Anyone who has sufficient ingenuity to discover an unequal division in all these sections (sc. of four words) need have little fear of being able to do so for the three succeeding chapters" (*op. cit.*, p. 119), is unjustified. If, within a long section, the meter pattern is clear and consistent, it is methodologically sound to give three beats to three words, even if two are shorter, like *ᵓein lāh menaḥēm* (Lam. 1:2c), or two beats to a longer word like *bethūlōthehā* (1:4e), and thus bring the stich into harmony with the pervading pattern of the entire poem.

Gray further contends, "It is very difficult to believe that if *rabbātī baggōyim* at the end of the second section (Lam. 1:1) is 'light,' *sārāthī bamedīnōt* at the beginning of the third is 'heavy' " (p. 118). But what must not be overlooked is that biblical poetry was not read but chanted, so that in effect we today possess little more than the libretto without the score. It is, therefore, entirely conceivable, indeed certain, that some phrases, words and syllables were repeated or given longer time and greater stress in some instances and less time and stress in others, as required by the musical chant or accompaniment.

14. Moreover, the Qinah rhythm is not limited to the 3:2 meter. This fact Budde recognized, but it has all too often been ignored by more recent critics in their treatment of poetic texts. The basic characteristic of the Qinah meter is the "echoing rhythm," which it achieves by having the second stich shorter than the first. The poet will, therefore, ring changes upon the 3:2 pattern. He may use a 5:5 meter. Above all, he may employ a 4:3 meter in order to avoid monotony and, especially, at the conclusion of a section or composition. See Sec. 21. He may use tristichs such as 3:2:2 or 4:3:3, or distichs like 4:4 ‖ 3:3, or 4:3 ‖ 3:2 (as, e.g., Isa. 49:2). In long poems particularly, he may elaborate even more complicated patterns, such as 3:2 ‖ 3:2 ‖ 3:2, the latter meter being characteristic of the Book of Lamentations.

15. Sievers, followed by Gray, regards the 4:3 pattern as an independent meter. It is better seen as a variant of the Qinah rhythm that is common in Ps. 9–10, though it is eliminated by Cheyne and Briggs by arbitrary deletions and emendations.

16. Since biblical rhythm is either "balanced" or "echoing," the second stich will not be longer than the first. Where a verse in the Masoretic text exhibits this characteristic, we believe it requires critical scrutiny. For the one well-attested exception to this rule, see Section 21. Sievers cites alleged instances of 2:3 and 3:4 rhythm (see Gray, *op. cit.*, p. 181, n. 1). Gray rightly describes these alleged meters as "rare." We are disposed to regard them as virtually nonexistent. Thus Gray's "clear-cut example" of 2:3 meter in the difficult verse Isa. 37:26 is better scanned as 4:4:3 (giving *lᵉmērāḥōq* two beats), a Qinah meter borne out by the preceding v. 25 (4:3:3) and the succeeding v. 27 (3:2 ‖ 3:2 ‖ 3:2).

On the other hand, the second half of Isa. 1:23 cited by Gray is in 3:4 meter and Jer. 2:28 is in 2:3 meter, but only because of the special principle set forth in Section 20. Lam. 3:27 is either 2:2:2 or 3:2, with a divergence between the poetic and logical caesura, a very common feature in this chapter (e.g., vv. 3, 5, 12, 19, 32). Of the passages cited, only Lam. 2:8b seems to be an authentic instance of 2:3 and Isa. 40:4a, b of 3:4 meter. Ps. 22:4, not cited in the discussion, apparently exhibits a 2:3 meter, but the exegetical difficulties suggest that the text may not be in order. The entire Psalm is in "balanced rhythm" (3:3 or 4:4) and the first two letters of *yōšĕbh* may perhaps contain the Divine name (*vᵉʾattāh qādōš JHVH,*), so that the verse would be in 3:3 meter. It is safe to regard the so-called 2:3 and 3:4 meters as generally doubtful.

17.   Rhyme does not occur in biblical poetry except accidentally, though it probably was more frequent in folk poetry than our extant sources reveal.

18.   Alliteration, which is so important in Anglo-Saxon poetry, occurs in biblical poetry as well, as in Isa. 17:2, but it is not a regular feature. It is almost nonexistent in Job, though a striking instance involving eight vocables occurs in 5:8.

19.   Much more common, but likewise not a regular feature, is assonance. An outstanding example involving the *Mem-sound* eight times occurs in 12:2. Less elaborate examples involving labials, gutturals, and liquids are frequent in Job and have often been noted, particularly by Yellin.

20.   The existence of strophes as a fundamental feature of biblical poetry cannot be demonstrated, unless the term be used so loosely as to be virtually meaningless. The only clear-cut evidence is the use of refrains in a few instances. See the discussion in Special Note 2.

21.   A poet will wish to conclude a section of a poem or speech or his composition as a whole with impressive power, not unlike the use of *fortissimo* at the close of a musical composition. The biblical poet can achieve this effect by a variety of devices to which we have called attention elsewhere: (a) increasing the number of stichs in the closing verse, e.g., Job, chaps. 10, 11, 19, 26; (b) increasing the number of syllables in the final verse, as, e.g., Job, chaps. 5, 17, 18, 21, 41; (c) lengthening the meter in the last verse, as, e.g., Mic. 6:8; Ps. 27:6 (end of section); Ps. 42–43, 48; (d) lengthening the meter in the closing stich only, as, e.g., Ps. 8, 20, 62, 66, 67, 84; (e) using two of these techniques simultaneously, as, e.g., Ps. 47. For a fuller discussion and documentation, see *PPS*, pp. 70 ff.

22.   Normally the poet will use different vocables in parallel stichs. This is so fundamental a principle that parallelism was defined by medieval Hebrew exegetes as *kephel ᶜinyān ʾeḥād bemillīm šōnōt*, "the repetition of the same idea in different words." However, even this widespread usage is not invariable, *particularly in Job*. The poet, whose mastery of the language is unmatched, did not hesitate to utilize the same verb, noun, or root in parallel stichs at will, whether for the purpose of emphasis or for subtler reasons that may escape us. On this subject, see Special Note 4.

23.   While metric considerations are important, it is methodologically unsound to emend, transpose, or delete texts solely on metric grounds. Undoubtedly, biblical poetry was not read, but chanted; cf. the verb *ᶜānāh* (Arabic *ghannay*), "chant," e.g., in Ex. 15:21; Deut. 26:5; Job 3:1, and passim). It is more than possible that when biblical poetry was chanted, some vocables, especially longer ones, received greater stress, while others were slurred.

In any event, the uncertainties still inherent in the study of biblical prosody make it highly unscientific to tamper with the text purely for metric reasons. However, when other reasons for text-critical procedures are present, metrics may legitimately be invoked as a factor. See *PPS*, p. 69, for examples.

Special Note 2 — The Theory of Biblical Strophes

In 1831, Köster first proposed the theory that strophes or stanzas exist in biblical poetry. In recent years, the position that the Job speeches are to be divided into strophes has been urged with new vigor by Kissane, Skehan, and Terrien. Obviously, a poem could — and should — be divided into sections according to the various themes treated by the author. However, if the term "strophe" is to have any significance in this context, it must mean that the poem falls into sections of equal length.

The existence of stanzas is clear in the relatively rare instances where a refrain occurs and is repeated at regular intervals, sometimes with minor changes. Such is the case in Psalms, chapters 42–43 (vv. 6–12; 43:5), chapter 49 (vv. 13, 21), and Job, chapter 28 (vv. 12, 20, where the refrain may have originally stood at the beginning of the "Hymn to Wisdom" as well). In Psalm 107 the refrain consists of two verses with a different verse inserted between them each time (vv. 6–8, 13–15, 19–21, 27–31).

On the other hand, where no such refrain is available, the theory of strophes proves abortive. Thus the effort of scholars to divide the speeches in the book of Job into strophes collides with one stubborn fact — the alleged sections are not uniform in length. In order to save the theory, some scholars have not hesitated to delete, transpose, and emend the text solely for metric reasons. Others, conscious that such procedures are methodologically unwarranted, argue that the strophes in any given speech may not be uniform in length, but may vary within some limits. Thus, Kissane proposes the following strophic pattern for the First Cycle in Job (chaps. 3–14):

> Job's First Reply to Eliphaz (chaps. 6–7): strophes of six and seven verses;
> Job's reply to Bildad's First Speech (chaps. 9–10): strophes of six verses each;
> Job's answer to Zophar's First Speech (chaps. 12–14): strophes of five or six verses each;
> Eliphaz's First Speech (chaps. 4–5): strophes of five verses each;
> Bildad's First Speech: strophes of three verses each.

This is not the entire problem with the strophe theory, even if one were to grant the legitimacy of applying the term "strophe" to sections of varying lengths. It is clear from an examination of the text that in order to arrive at this pattern of "irregular regularity," Kissane is compelled to divide the text arbitrarily, separating verses that obviously belong together and ignoring the sections into which the thought-content naturally falls.

The only conclusion that may legitimately be drawn from the extant text on Job is the one arrived at by Budde, who long ago denied the existence of strophes as an unproved and improbable theory. Similarly, Dhorme (*Le Livre de Job*, p. cl) confesses that he was compelled to give up his initial efforts to divide the speeches into strophes because the theory ran counter to the facts.

Biblical poetry has sufficient resources at its command without the necessity of introducing dubious and alien devices for which objective evidence is lacking.

The balanced treatment of the theory by G. B. Gray (*The Forms of Hebrew Poetry*, pp. 187–97) will still repay careful study. His conclusions seem to me unassailable. After allowing for cases of refrains or other equal division of the poem, he says: "For the most part, we cannot speak of greater sense-divisions in such poems at all. . . . Other poems do develop a theme in such a manner that greater sense-divisions necessarily result; in this case, it seems to me convenient in a translation to distinguish the first paragraphs resulting from these great sense-divisions by spacing between them. . . . This, however, is merely a question of translation and has nothing to do with any intention of the writer to give to the expression of his thought any further artistic form." Finally, "If we use the term 'strophe' it must mean simply a verse paragraph of indeterminate length uncontrolled by any formal artistic scheme" (*op. cit.*, pp. 190, 192).

For the literature on the "strophe," cf. F. B. Köster, "Die Strophen," in *Theologische Studien und Kritiken*, vol. IV, 1831, pp. 40–114; G. Bickell, *Das Buch Hiob nach Anleitung der Strophik und der Septuagint* (Vienna, 1894); Karl Budde, article, "Poetry," in Hastings, *Dictionary of the Bible*; G. B. Gray, *Forms of Hebrew Poetry* (London, 1915); A. Condamin, *Poèmes de la Bible* (Paris, 1933); K. Moeller, "Strophenbau in den Psalmen," in *ZATW*, 1932, pp. 56 ff.; W. A. Irwin, "Poetic Structure in the Book of Job," in *JNES*, vol. 5, 1946, pp. 26–39; E. J. Kissane, *The Book of Job* (Dublin, 1939), pp. lvi–lx; P. J. Skehan, "Strophic Patterns in the Book of Job," in *CBQ*, vol. 23, 1961, pp. 125–42; *idem*, "Job's Final Plea and the Lord's Reply," in *Biblica*, vol. 45, 1904, pp. 64 ff.; S. L. Terrien, *Job: Un commentaire* (Neuchâtel, 1963), pp. 33 f.

Special Note 3 — The Theory of Syllabic Meter

Recently a new theory of biblical metrics, which may be described as the reincarnation of the earlier approach of Edward Sievers and his school, was proposed (D. N. Freedman," Archaic Forms in Early Hebrew Poetry," in *ZATW*, vol. 72, 1960, pp. 101–107). This approach takes its point of departure from the theory of "phonetic consonantism," i.e., the orthography and pronunciation of Hebrew that is assumed to have prevailed in the 10th century B. C. E., as enunciated by W. F. Albright ("The Oracle of Balaam," in *JBL*, vol. 63, 1944, pp. 207–33) and by F. M. Cross, Jr., and D. N. Freedman (*Early Hebrew Orthography*, New Haven, 1952; "A Royal Song of Thanksgiving — II Sam. 20:2 = Ps. 18," in *JBL*, vol. 72, 1953, pp. 15–34; "The Song of Miriam," in *JNES*, vol. 14, 1955, pp. 237–50). On the basis of this assumed pronunciation, the theory then proceeds to count the syllables in each stich (or colon) in order "to reduce the meter to some arithmetic pattern" which, it is claimed, will provide "a greater degree of precision than the method of counting word stresses," which has been basic in the study of biblical poetry.

This contention notwithstanding, the facts are that no genuinely uniform pattern emerges by this procedure. Thus in a careful and balanced study of II Sam. 23:1–7 (*JBL*, 1971, vol. 90, pp. 270–76), H. Neil Richardson divides the poem into five sections: vv. 1–4, 5–8, 9–13, 14–17, 18, 19–22. These sections, which follow the poet's thought, are patently unequal in the number of stichs each contains, thus incidentally refuting the strophe-theory. As for the proposed theory of syllabic meter, the first section consists of 7, 8, 7, and 9 syllables per verse; the second of 6, 8, 7, and 7 syllables; the third section of 7, 7, 6, 5, and 10 syllables; the fourth section of 7, 7, 9, and 11 syllables; and the conclusion of 7, 6, 9, and 9 syllables. These variations are disregarded, and we are assured that the poem exhibits "remarkable balance" because the Introduction and the Conclusion each consists of 31 syllables, though it is conceded that the ancient Hebrew poet may not have counted the syllables, as do modern scholars.

There is another, perhaps even more fundamental problem with the proposed theory of syllabic meter. Obviously, the essence of meter is the presence of an identical or nearly identical pattern in the various units of the poem. However, in order to achieve a modicum of regularity in the number of syllables per unit, as in the instance cited above, proponents of the syllabic theory have been compelled to posit the length of an entire verse as the basic unit in biblical verse. They have, therefore, had to abandon the stich as the fundamental block in biblical verse and to disregard totally the presence of parallelism, which, first noted by Azariah dei Rossi and Robert Lowth, has been universally recognized as the cornerstone of biblical poetry.

When, in a correspondence on the subject with Dr. David N. Freedman, I made this point, he conceded its validity. He wrote me, "I think that Bishop Lowth did us all a disservice by over-emphasizing the word 'parallelism' and by including a great deal of material which is clearly poetic but is not parallel in structure or content" (*private communication*, November 7, 1975). However, I believe that few scholars would be prepared to accept this negative judgment on Lowth and to surrender parallelism which, together with the meter pattern, is the basic feature of biblical poetry.

One is driven to the conclusion that notwithstanding the effort and the acumen displayed by modern scholars, the theory of syllabic meter, like that of strophes, cannot be described as convincing. The only secure basis for dealing with the metrics of biblical poetry remains the theory of word-stresses. See Special Note 1.

Special Note 4 — Job's Use of Repetition in Parallelism

As has been noted in Special Note 1 (Sec. 22), an all-but-universal feature of Biblical prosody is the use of different synonyms in parallelism. There can, therefore, be no objection to Gray's judgment that "some instances at least of repetition (in the present Hebrew text) of the same term in the two parallel lines of a distich are due to scribal error" (*Forms of Hebrew Poetry*, p. 295). He goes further, however, and declares, "such repetitions as occur in the Hebrew text here do, however, appear to me now to be in themselves open to *some* suspicion, though not, of course, to be *certainly* due to textual corruption. Some may be original" (Italics his; *op. cit.*, p. 255). Beyond the general principle of variation of terms in parallelism, Gray bases his view on two principal grounds:

1.   At times, the ancient Versions, notably LXX, will utilize different synonyms to express the Hebrew text.

2.   The "clearest proof" that repetition of terms points to a corruption of the text he finds in the dittograph Ps. 18 = II Sam. 22, which exhibits four examples. In v. 7, Samuel reads *ᵓeqrāᵓ* twice, where LXX read a different verb and Ps. reads *ᵓašavvēᶜa* in the second instance. In v. 32, *mibbalᶜadei* occurs twice in Sam., but in Ps. *zūlāthī* occurs the second time. In v. 47, Sam. contains a conflate reading in stich b created by the intrusion of *ṣūr* from stich a, which is lacking in Ps. In v. 29, Sam. has JHVH twice, while Ps. reads *JHVH ᵓelōhai* the second time. A somewhat different case, as Gray concedes, occurs in v. 5.

With regard to the first argument, it is by no means implausible that LXX, writing for non-Semitic readers, to whom even normal Hebrew parallelism would be alien and appear monotonous (note the sharp contraction of the text of Job in the Greek versions), would seek to avoid the repetition of the same word by a synonym, in order to placate the taste of Greek readers.

In the Samuel-Psalm dittograph, Gray's contention may be correct and a scribal error may lie at the base of the repetition of the same term. However, the conclusion is by no means certain. It is noteworthy that in all four cases the repetition occurs in Samuel and the variation in Psalms. Aside from the widespread judgment that the Samuel version is closer to the original text from which both dittographs derive, one would have expected, if the cause were simply the accidental *lapsus calami* of a scribe, that the repetition would occur in both texts and not exclusively in one. The *possibility*, at least, exists that the repetition of terms in parallel stichs is a stylistic trait of the original poet and that a later scribe whose transcript has reached us in Psalms, actuated by the same desire to avoid "monotony" as the LXX translators, proceeded to vary the vocables in his text.

While the validity of Gray's principle in his moderate formulation may be granted, modern critics have carried it to extremes and have not hesitated to invoke the repetition of a vocable in parallel or adjacent stichs as an all-sufficient ground for emending the Hebrew text, both in Job and elsewhere. One crucial fact has been overlooked — there are 43 instances of repetition of terms in Job. Several fundamental considerations suggest that the repetition is not the result of scribal corruption, but constitutes an authentic characteristic of the poet's style:

1.   The use of the same word in parallel stichs does not run counter to the principles of Biblical parallelism. On the contrary, it is a basic feature of complementary or climactic parallelism, attested not only in Biblical poetry but in Akkadian and Ugaritic as well, as e.g. Ps. 27:1; 94:1, etc. See Special Note 1 and *PPS*, pp. 74 ff.

2.   If the presence of the same vocable in two stichs were the result of scribal error, the *distribution* of the phenomenon would be roughly equal in the various prophetic and poetic books. The fact is, however, that this phenomenon is extremely rare everywhere except in Job. The 39 poetic chapters of Job contain 43 instances, adduced below. Gray, on the other hand, cites only 3 "more or less certain" instances in the 39 chapters of Isaiah I (11:5; 16:7; 26:7, *Idem, ICC on Isaiah, ad loc.*). These latter instances may also be part of the original style of Isaiah; even if these are not, the extraordinary frequency of the usage in Job makes it clear that this is a practice of our poet, either for the sake of emphasis or for subtler reasons that we cannot generally fathom. Conscious as he was of his superb mastery of all the resources of the Hebrew tongue, the author of Job did not hesitate to use at will the same root or word in both stichs or in close proximity to one another, though in separate verses. Incidentally, synonyms were easily available in virtually every instance. Even if some examples be disputed, the remaining number is impressive.

That the Psalmist who authored II Sam. 22 = Ps. 18 may possess the same proclivity as the author of Job has already been noted. One other Hebrew poet exhibits a similar trait. Gray, who did not note the frequency of the phenomenon in *Job*, has pointed out (*op. cit.*, pp. 104 ff.) that in Lamentations, chap. 2, a word from stich a or b may be repeated in stich e or f. Actually the chapter contains 4 such instances: v. 1a and 1 f (*beʾappō* and *beyōm ʾappō*); v. 5b and 5c (*billaʿ*); 10e (*rōšām* and *rōšān*); and v. 12a and 12f (*leʾimmōtām* and *ʾimmōtām*). However, this usage in Lamentations, chap. 2, differs from Job in that there is a longer distance in the former between the repeated vocables, so that the intent is to create an echo, the effect of the Qinah rhythm generally.

These considerations based on the biblical text have been reenforced by evidence from extra-biblical literature. It is now doubly clear that the principle that repetition of the same root is ruled out in parallelism is a gratuitous assumption that had been raised to the level of an axiom. M. D. Cassuto was the first to point out that Ugaritic verse employs at times the same verb, though in different tenses or in varying voices (active or passive) (*Tarbiṣ*, vol. 14, 1942, pp. 9 ff.; *The Goddess Anath*, Jerusalem, 1953, pp. 37 ff., English trans. I. Abrahams, Jerusalem, 1971, pp. 46 ff.). In addition to Ugaritic examples, he cited some biblical instances, such as Jer. 17:14; 31:4; Ps. 69:50. Subsequently, M. Held added some Ugaritic examples such as Jer. 31:18 and Ps. 24:7 (*JBL*, vol. 84, 1965, pp. 272–82). Recently, S. Gevirtz has discussed the phenomenon and sought to adduce instances of this usage from Tel-el-Amarna, "Evidence of Conjugational Variation . . . the Amarna Letters" (*JNES*, vol. 32, 1973, pp. 99–104).

The observations of these scholars may be sharpened further. Research indicates that the repetition of the same root in parallel stichs may occur without a variation in tense or voice (e.g. Job 8:3). Moreover, it is not limited to verbs, but includes substantives as well. Finally, the practice is especially characteristic of some writers, such as the author of Job (43 examples) and the author of Lamentations, chap. 2 (4 instances).

With regard to the principle of the repetition of identical verbs enunciated by Cassuto, further analysis reveals that the practice falls into two categories, both in Ugaritic and in Hebrew:

(A) The use of the same verb in two different tenses or voices, *in two separate and parallel stichs*. Hence the meaning is identical, as it would have been if synonyms had been employed. Ugaritic examples are *UT* 51, VI, lines 34–35, 38–40; 67 I, lines 16–17; *AQHT*, lines 114–115; *ANAT*, II, lines 40–41. Biblical examples include Deut. 33:12; Isa. 60:16; Jer. 31:4; Ps. 24:7; 38:12; 69:15; Pr. 11:7.

(B) The use of the two verbs *within the same stich and in a special manner* so that they are *not* completely identical in meaning. These instances constitute a "plea-and-response" formula. The first verb is invariably in the imperative second person and the second verb is in the imperfect first person singular or plural, with a special nuance indicated below.

Thus, Jer. 17:14 *rephāʾēnī weʾērāphē . . . hōšīʿēnī weiwwāšēʿa* is to be rendered "Heal me O Lord and I shall really be healed, save me and I shall truly be saved." Other instances are Jer. 31:17e; Lam. 5:2.

(C) Similar in character to Category B is a variant that may be called the "action-and-result" formula. Here, too, the verbal root is used twice in the same stich, but in different persons. Its repetition is designed here also to give a special nuance to the second verb. Thus Jer. 31:4 *ʿōd ʾebhnēkh wenibhnēth*, "I shall yet rebuild you and you will be truly (i.e. permanently) rebuilt." So, too, Jer. 31:17 *yissartānī waʾiwwāsēr*, "You chastised me and I was really chastised, like an untrained calf, etc."

With regard to Job, it should be noted that the distribution of this usage throughout the Dialogue, the Elihu chapter, and the God Speeches supports, though it obviously cannot "demonstrate," the view of the essential unity of authorship and the integrity of the Book of Job.

The repetition of terms in Job falls into several categories:

1. As has been noted, the essential characteristic of complementary parallelism derives from the repetition of the same vocable in parallel stichs. It occurs, e.g., in 18:13; 22:30.

2. Most frequent is the repetition of the identical vocable in two parallel stichs, e.g., 8:3; 10:30; 11:7; 12:23; 22:2; 38:11, 17.

3. In some instances, MT exhibits a variant orthography of the same vocable that may have been induced by a scribe desirous of introducing "variety"; cf. 15:31 and 38:11. The motivation would seem to be similar to that of LXX in using different synonyms in translation (e.g. in 40:11b and 12a) or that of modern scholars in emending one term (e.g. Hö. *ibid.* who reads *gābhōah* for *gēʾeh*).

4. The use of different words from the same root in parallel stichs, e.g. 5:8; 20:29; 22:30; 33:21; 33:26c and 27a.

5. The use of the same vocable in adjacent verses or in close proximity, e.g. 24:7 and 10; 28:16 and 17, 19.

6. In rare cases, the repetition of the root has been obscured by the vocalization as in 37:24, or a consonantal error as in 3:8. See list below and the Comm. *ad loc.*

We append the following list of repetitions in Job:

3:8	עורר . . . . עררי־ים

(see the Comm. *ad loc.*)

5:8	אלהים . . . . אל
5:23	חית השדה . . . . אבני השדה
6:15	נחל . . . . נחלים
7:8	עיניך . . . . עין ראי
8:3	יעות . . . . יעות
9:11	עד אין . . . . עד אין

(a quotation of 5:9 and not totally identical with it; as in the case of refrains; see the Comm. *ad loc.* on 25:12.)

10:5	כימי גבר . . . . הכימי אנוש
10:30	מעט . . . . מעט
11:7	תמצא . . . . תמצא
12:23	לגוים . . . . לגוים
13:7	תדברו . . . . תדברו
13:23	וחטאתי . . . . וחטאות
15:30	ויסור . . . . לא יסור

(but see the Comm.)

15:31	בשוא . . . . בשו
17:15	ותקותי . . . . תקותי
18:5a, 6a	אור . . . . אור
18:13	בדיו . . . . בדי עור
19:20	בעור שני . . . . בעורי ובבשרי
20:29	מאל . . . . מאלהים
22:2	יסכן . . . . יסכן

(different meanings, see the Comm.)

22:30	ונמלט . . . . ימלט
24:7 and 10	ערום הלכו בלי לבוש . . . . ערום ילינו
24:17	צלמות . . . . צלמות
28:16 and 19b	בכתם טהור לא תסלה . . . . לא תסלה
28:17 and 19a	לא יערכנה . . . . לא יערכנה
29:21 and 23	ויחלו . . . . ויחלו
31:10	אחרין . . . . לאחר
32:17	אף אני . . . . אף אני

33:6	אני . . . . אני
33:21	מראי . . . . לא ראו
33:26 and 27	לאנוש . . . . לאנשים

described as a "transcriptional error" by D-G, II, p. 251.

34:28	צעקת . . . . וצעקת
35:2 and 3	אמרת . . . . כי תאמר
35:13b and 14a	לא ישורנה . . . . לא תשורנו

called "suspicious" by D-G.

37:4 (three times)	קול . . . . . . בקול . . . . . . קולו
37:24	יראהו . . . . יראה

(see the Comm.)

38:9a and 10b	בשומי . . . . ואשים
38:8a, 10b	בריח ודלתים . . . . בדלתים

ascribed by D-G to the poet's "poverty of language" (!).

38:11	עד פה . . . . ופא
38:17	שערי . . . . ושערי
38:22	אצרות . . . . ואוצרות

(note the variant orthography in MT.)

40:11b and 12a	וראה כל גאה . . . . ראה כל גאה.
40:13	טמנם . . . . בטמון
41:20b and 21a	כקש . . . . לקש
41:15b, 16a	יצוק . . . . . . יצוק . . . . . . ויצוק
(three times)	

Special Note 5 — Logic, Music, and Literary Structure

A widespread practice in commentaries and other scholarly studies on Job is the transposition of material, in order to create a more logical sequence of ideas or to avoid the treatment of the same theme at various points in a given speech. Throughout this Commentary, this procedure is stigmatized as being unsound methodology, on grounds to be discussed below.

A convenient point of departure is a major insight of W. F. Albright's most important book, *From the Stone Age to Christianity* (Baltimore, 1940). In view of his magisterial influence, it is astonishing that it has not been applied to problems of literary structure in biblical literature generally, and to Job in particular. Albright delineates three main phases in the evolution of human reasoning. The first is *proto-logical reasoning*, characteristic of primitive and ancient man, which tends to be associative rather than logically coherent and relevant. Being rooted in man's emotional nature, it finds expression in his religion, literature, music, and art. The second stage Albright calls *empirical-logical*, which characterizes reasoning based on human experience and observation. This type dominates ancient technology, commerce, law, and government. Science in the ancient world, possessing strong affinities with magic, also belongs to this empirical-logical category. The third stage Albright denominates *formal logic*, which is the contribution of the Greek thinkers of the sixth century B. C. and thereafter, introduced by Thales and continuing through Plato and Aristotle to produce medieval and modern science and philosophy.

Albright's categorization, though it is marked by a measure of over-simplification as is inevitable in any broad generalization, possesses high value. Nonetheless, it needs to be modified or supplemented in several significant respects. First, setting forth the three types of logic in chronological order tends to obscure the important fact that each stage is not surrendered with the emergence of the next, but, on the contrary, persists and coexists with its "successor." It is useful to subsume such manifestations as music, art, literature, and religion as constituting "culture," all deriving strongly, though obviously not exclusively, from man's emotional sources. On the other hand, technology, industry, commerce, law, and government, and, above all, science, are primarily rooted in man's intellectual capacities, though here emotional factors are not totally absent; these may be subsumed under the term "civilization."

Second, philosophy, which Albright places in the third category of formal logic, actually possesses strong emotive aspects in addition to its intellectual character. The various philosophic systems, none of which are logically demonstrable in spite of their intellectual claims, are basically imaginative constructs of the world belonging to man's "culture" more than to his "civilization." It follows that the "proto-logical" stage will endure, not merely as the vestigial remains of an earlier, outgrown period in man's development, but as a fundamental, active, creative factor, as long as men remain human and do not completely surrender to computers and "Big Brother."

Finally — and this is most germane to our present concern — Albright's threefold classification of logic runs the danger of offering an insufficient valuation of the mechanism of proto-logical thought, which is primarily that of association and not syllogistic coherence. Modern psychology, with its stress upon the subconscious, offers a key to the understanding of the importance of association as the most natural technique of human thought. We need only recall the importance of "free association" in psychotherapy and the role of metalogical phenomena like intuition, which is increasingly recognized as fundamental to the creative process even in science and mathematics, as Albert Einstein and other practitioners of the scientific method have attested.

Long after the full-blown emergence of the third category, works like the Talmud, which manifest on every page a great capacity for rigorous thought and even pedantic analysis, continue to be structured on the basis of association. It would, therefore, seem that the ancient Semitic mind possessed a strong affinity for associational logic, while the formal logic which emerged among the Greeks had to be consciously introduced into Semitic thought in the Middle Ages with Islamic and Jewish philosophy. The two types of reason-

ing are not so much "higher" and "lower" as different, for which Euclidean
and non-Euclidean geometry offers a partial analogy.

The importance of association for an understanding both of literary
structure and content in biblical literature, particularly in Wisdom, can
scarcely be exaggerated. We have called attention to the prime role of allusion and analogy for understanding the meaning of the entire Book of Job
in *BGM*, chap. 14, and in Special Note 32, and throughout the present work.
Very often, the association is not that of substantive similarity, but
rather of verbal identity, such as a key word or phrase linking disparate
items together. A striking case in point is afforded by Ecclesiastes 7:1 ff.,
where seven apothegms beginning with the word *ṭōbh* are brought together
in a single collection, each maxim being commented upon by the author
(see *KMW ad loc.*). In Isaiah, chap. 19, the "Burden of Egypt" (vv. 1–15)
is supplemented by a series of smaller independent oracles which are all
concerned with Egypt. The link between them lies in their opening formula,
bayyōm hahūʾ (vv. 16, 18, 19, 23, 24).
At times the association may be even more tenuous, consisting of a
similar rather than an identical key-word. In Micah 4:8—5:5, we have a
series of brief oracles introduced either by *veʾattāh* or *ʾattāh* ("you") in 4:8;
5:1, while others begin with *ʿattāh* or *veʿattāh* ("now") in 4:9, 11, 14. In all
three instances cited, the failure to recognize the associational link has led
commentators into farfetched and unsuccessful attempts to read a logically
unified theme, not borne out by the text, into the respective sections.
The principle of association is even more obvious in the structure of
talmudic literature. The entire Mishnah tractate *Eduyot* consists of reports
regarding decisions reached *bō bayyōm*, "on that day," a reference to the
Council of Jamnia in 90 C. E. Here it might be argued that the historic
session constituted a unity of theme. In Mishnah *Pesaḥim*, chap. 10, the first
pericope deals with the Passover and is germane to the subject of the treatise.
However, it is introduced by the formula *māqōm šenāhagū*, "in the place
where it is customary," etc. This serves as the link for a series of additional
pericopes dealing with matters totally unrelated to the festival. On almost
every page of the Talmud, completely unrelated subjects will be treated in
sequence merely because they bear the name of the same authority.
The Book of Job belongs both to poetry and to religion. It therefore
follows that the principle of literary organization will be associative rather
than logically relevant. The transposition of material to achieve coherence
and eliminate repetition is unjustified, both on this ground, as well as from
another perspective.
The close relationship between poetry and music suggests that the latter
can help shed more light on the former than has been generally noted. When
a given theme is treated, followed by another, and the first is then taken up
again, the phenomenon is best understood by the analogy derived from music
of a theme-with-variations rather than by the gratuitous assumption of a
dislocation in the text, with heavy-handed attempts to reconstruct the material

in an order conforming to formal Western logic. For this structure, see the Comm. on chaps. 29, 30 and the relevant Special Notes 30, 31.

The affinity of music and poetry is useful in understanding another phenomenon in Hebrew prosody previously overlooked. In Special Note 1, Section 21, and *PPS*, chap. 3, we have called attention to the widespread tendency of a poet to introduce various changes into the meter pattern in order to conclude a section or a composition on a powerful note, the equivalent of a crescendo or fortissimo.

We have suggested that the Semitic logic of association is not *per se* inferior to the Greek logic of relevance — it is merely different. But even if, as children of a scientific age, we assign a lower value to the former, one conclusion is clear — we cannot do justice to the structure of Job unless we recognize its special thought processes and the literary structure and usages to which it gives rise. For the bearing of this fundamental insight upon critical problems of structure in Job, see Special Notes 19, 20, 30, 32, and 35.

Special Note 6 — The Metrics of Chapters 1–2

The efforts by some biblical scholars like Sievers, Bruno, and others to treat the prose narratives in the Bible as verse and to impose a meter pattern upon them demonstrate that the line of demarcation between prose and verse in biblical literature is very thin. It is, therefore, no wonder that at times a single literary unit will combine ordinary prose, rhythmic prose, and metric verse. See *KMW*, pp. 110 ff., 193, 292, for a discussion of this phenomenon in Koheleth. On the principles of Hebrew metrics, including a discussion of exceptional stresses for metrical reasons, see *PPS*, chap. 3, and Special Note 1.

In the Prologue of Job the narrative is in prose, but the speeches of all the protagonists are in verse. The energy and economy of the prose-tale are heightened by the staccato effect of the two- or four-beat meter, which predominates. Whether we scan the lines as 4:4 or as 2:2 is immaterial, since the two meters are virtually identical.

The meter-pattern of the speeches in verse may be set forth as follows:

Chapter 1

v. 7	2 ‖ 2:2.		
v. 8	4:4 ‖ 2:2:2		(The words *ᵓiš tām*, being very short, receive one beat for metrical reasons.)
v. 9	4 (or 2 ‖ 2).		
v. 10	4:4 ‖ 3:3		(The first stich has a stress on *ᵓattā, sakhtā, baᶜadō,* and *bēthō*; the second stich on *ubheᶜad, kol-ᵓašer-lō* (two beats) and *missābhībh.*)
v. 11	4:4:4		(Either *ᶜal pānekhā* or *yebhārkhekā* receives two beats, because of their length and metric exigencies.)

v. 12	4:4	
v. 14	4:4	(In each stich, one of the longer words, like *ḥōrešōt* and *haʾathōnōth*, receives two beats.)
v. 15	4:4 ‖ 2:2:2	(*Vattiqqāḥēm*, *vʾeth hanneʿārīm*, and *vaʾimmāletāh*, receive two beats each.)
v. 16	4:4 ‖ 2:2:2.	
v. 17	4:4:4 ‖ 2:2:2	(Either *vayyiphšetu* or *ʿal haggemallim* receives two beats, as does *vʾeth hanneʿarim*; cf. v. 15.)
v. 18	5:4 (or 5:3).	The irregularity may be due to the prototype in v. 13. It is possible that *yayin*, which LXX omits in v. 13, is to be deleted both in verse 13 and here, thus creating a four-beat stich. In stich b, one of the words may receive two beats. In that event, the meter pattern would be 4:4. See the Comm. below.
v. 19	4:2 ‖ 4:4 ‖ 2:2:2	(In stich d, either *ʿal hanneʿārim* or *vayyāmūthū* receives two beats because of the length of the words and metric exigencies, as in v. 17. In stich e, *vaʾimmāletāh* receives two beats, as in vv. 15, 16 and 17.)
v. 21	4:3 ‖ 4:3	(The *Kinah* rhythm is obviously appropriate to the theme of the verse.)

Chapter 2

v. 2	2 ‖ 2:2.	
v. 3	4:4 ‖ 2:2:2 ‖ 4:4	(For stichs a and b, see above on 1:8. All the words of stich c, *veʿōdhenū*, *mahazīq* and *bethummāthō*, are long, and one of them receives two beats.)
v. 4	3:3:3	(This is a proverbial utterance utilizing the more basic 3:3 meter. In contradistinction to the excitement of the 2:2 pattern used by all the other protagonists, it expresses admirably Satan's relaxed attitude toward Job's misfortunes.)

Special Note 7 — The Metric Structure of Chapter 3

The metrical rules set forth above (Special Note 1, sec. 6, 9) are illustrated in the analysis of chap. 3 presented here. Thus, words linked together by the Masorah through a *maqqeph* may nevertheless receive two beats (e.g., *yehī ḥōšekh* and *ʾal yidrešēhū* in v. 4). Conversely, two vocables may receive only one accent *metri causa* (e.g., *halaylāh hahū* in v. 7; *kī lō* in v. 10; *lammāh lō* in v. 11).

The metric pattern of "Job's Lament" is as follows:

v. 3	4:4	
v. 4	4:4:4	
v. 5	3:3:3	
v. 6	4:4:4	
v. 7	4:4 or 4:3	(It is probably better not to construe *hinnēh* as an anacrusis, outside the metric scheme, but to give *halaylāh hahū* only one beat or none to *yehi*, thus scanning stich a as 4-beat meter. In stich b, *bhō* may receive no stress, so that the meter is 4:3.)
v. 8	3:3	
v. 9	3:3:3	
v. 10	3:3	
v. 11	4:3 or 3:3	
v. 12	3:3	
v. 13	3:3	
v. 14	3:3	
v. 15	3:3	
v. 16	3:3	
v. 17	4:4	
v. 18	4:4	(One of the two long words, *ʾasīrīm* or *šaʾanānū*, receives two beats.)
v. 19	4:3	
v. 20	4:3	
v. 21	3:2	
v. 22	3:3	
v. 23	4:3	
v. 24	4:3	
v. 25	3:3	
v. 26	2:2 ‖ 2:2	

Special Note 8 — On 4:12 ff. Wisdom and Revelation

TS maintains that this entire section (4:12–21) is part of a speech by Job, since Eliphaz's role is to offer consolation, while here the contention is that there is no difference in God's treatment of the just and the unjust. To be sure, the idea that God does not trust man reappears in Eliphaz's Second Speech (15:14–16) and in Bildad's Third Speech (25:4–6), but TS disposes of this difficulty by attributing 25:4–6 to Job and treating 15:14–15 as a quotation by Eliphaz of Job's words.

TS's striking interpretation is unnecessary and unconvincing. In the first instance, it requires a substantial transposition of the text for which there is no objective evidence, either internal or external. Moreover, our passage and its two companion sections actually do not declare that God is unjust to man. That point is made clearly and effectively by Job elsewhere, as in 9:22; 9:29 ff. Our passage makes no reference at all to the righteous or the sinners — its theme is only that all men are imperfect. Moreover, the contents of this speech are inappropriate for Job. If all men are imperfect, why should Job complain? Finally, throughout the Dialogue, Job demands that God appear to him, a call to which the Lord responds only in the closing section of the book (chaps. 38 ff.). In our passage here, the speaker solemnly declares that he has had a Divine revelation from on high. For all these considerations, the passage cannot emanate from Job, while it is eminently appropriate for Eliphaz.

In his First Speech, Eliphaz is presenting a comprehensive theodicy embracing all the principal elements of traditional religion. In this system an important place is occupied by the view that not even the heavenly creatures, and surely not men, are free from moral imperfection. Hence, a man has no legitimate right to complain about the troubles that come to him. For this traditional doctrine, cf. Lam. 3:34–42, and see *SSL ad loc.*; I Ki. 8:46; Ecc. 7:20; see especially Ps. 51:3–15, where it serves as the prelude to repentance and return to God. This basic doctrine is expressed in the classic formulation in rabbinic Judaism, אם רואה אדם אדם יסורין באים עליו יפשפש במעשיו "He who sees suffering coming upon him should scrutinize his actions" (*B. Ber.* 5a).

The passage has also been characterized as "one of the most uncanny in the O. T." in which "the poet toys in poetic fancy with the dread effect of contact with the Divine" (P.). Such an approach means to lose its crucial significance, both for Eliphaz's comprehensive defense of Divine justice in particular and for an understanding of Wisdom literature in general. While Wisdom teachers derived their practical authority from human experience, observation, and reason, they were keenly aware of the claims made by the priests for a Divine source for their Torah and the prophets' consciousness of a nonmediated contact with God. In an age permeated by religious consciousness, the Hakham was driven to formulate a parallel theory of Divine origin and cosmic role for Wisdom (Pr. 8:21–32; Job 28:20–27; Ben Sira 1:1–8). Eliphaz is not "toying" with the idea of Divine revelation; he is in deadly earnest.

It is noteworthy that the most graphic and circumstantial description of the process of revelation occurs not in the Prophets, but here in Wisdom literature! While the Prophets were basically concerned with the *content* rather than with the *mode* of Divine communication, Eliphaz depicts in detail the vision (vv. 12–16) that served as the medium for the message (vv. 17–21). Similarly, the book of Proverbs enshrines the classic formulation of the philosophy of history of the Torah and the Prophets: "Righteousness exalts a people, but sin is the disgrace of nations" (Pr. 14:34) and "Where there is no (prophetic) vision, the people perish, but he who keeps the Torah, happy is he" (Pr. 29:18). These points of contact are significant for the interaction of priest, legist, prophet, and sage in ancient Israel and constitute the basis for the unity out of diversity characteristic of the Hebrew Bible. See *PPS*, chap. 1, especially pp. 38 ff., for this important theme.

Special Note 9 — On 5:13. — The Inflection of the Stem of Feminine Nouns with Suffixes

It is an elementary fact in Hebrew morphology that feminine nouns when inflected have the suffix added to the Tav, e.g. בִּינָתִי, בִּינָה; כְּלִמָּתִי, כְּלִמָּה (Job 20:2). However, in a substantial number of instances, MT contains anomalous forms which have been explained either as: (a) going back to masculine nouns, e.g. סֻכֹּה from an alleged noun סֹךְ; or (b) as the result of a scribal error, e.g. כִּתְבוּנָם, a mistake for כִּתְבוּנָתָם (Hos. 13:2).

The possibility of textual corruption can, of course, not be ruled out, but the assumed existence of a whole series of masculine nouns, the absolute of which does not occur in biblical Hebrew, e.g. סֹךְ, שְׁלֵו, עֹרֶם, is highly dubious. Both assumptions, as well as the necessity for emending the text, become unnecessary, if it is recognized that while *as a rule* feminine nouns are inflected by the addition of the suffixes to the original Tav ending, *exceptionally* the suffix can be added to the absolute form, which is tantamount to its stem. Thus in Job 5:13 עָרְמָם does not presuppose a nonexistent noun עֹרֶם (so BDB), nor is it an error for עָרְמָתָם, nor does it justify the emendation to חֶרְמָם. The form is to be explained as עָרְמָם = עָרְמָה + ם. This phenomenon was recognized by some of the medievals like Ibn Ezra (cf. the Comm. on Hos. 13:2) and Kimhi, but, as has been the case elsewhere, the insight was subsequently ignored or overlooked.

The following instances of this practice, alphabetically arranged, may be cited. In the case of all the Job passages, see the Comm. *ad loc.*

1. יִתְרָם. (Job 22:20), "their wealth" = יִתְרָה + ם (Isa. 15:7; cf. Jer. 48:36); it is to be distinguished from the noun יֶתֶר (Job 4:21), "tent cord."

2. בִּלְחוּמוֹ (Job 20:23) may be = בִּלְחוּמָתוֹ "His warfare"; cf. the Comm. *ad loc.*

3. מִדָּה (Job 11:9) with *Mappiq*, "her measure" = מִדָּה + ה, hence equivalent to the more usual form מִדָּתָהּ.

Similarly מַדַּיִךְ (Jer. 13:25), not "your garment" (כְּמַדּוֹ, Ps. 109:18; מַדָּיו Jud. 3:16; 1 Sam. 4:12; 18:4; 17:38, 39), but "your measure" = מִדָּה plus a suffix which MT vocalizes as a plural because of the plene spelling = מִדָּיִךְ.

4. מְצוּדוֹ (Job 19:6), not "his trap," but "his breastworks" = מְצוּדָה + וֹ; see the Comm.

5. סֻכּוֹ (Jer. 25:38; Ps. 76:3), בְּסֻכֹּה (Ps. 10:9; 27:5); שֻׂכּוֹ (Lam. 2:6), "his tent" or "his lair" = סֻכָּה + suffix. No absolute noun סֹךְ occurs anywhere, but note the absolute סֻכָּה "lair" (Job 38:40).

6. עָרְמָם (Job 5:13), "their cunning," discussed above.

7. פִּנָּהּ (Pr. 7:8), "her corner" — פִּנָּה + ה; cf. Job 38:8.

8. צוּרָם (Ps. 49:15), "their shape" = צוּרָה + ם; cf. Ezek. 43:11, frequent in postbiblical Hebrew.

9. קִימָם (Job 22:20), "their possessions" = קִימָה plus suffix; cf. יִתְרָם above. For MT קִימוֹ see the Comm.

10. שַׁלְוִי (Ps. 30:7), "in my ease" = בְּשַׁלְוָה plus suffix.

11. תָּוִי (Job 31:35), "my desire"; תָּאוִי = תַּאֲוָה plus the first person suffix; see the Comm. *ad loc.*

Special Note 10 — On 8:12–20. The Parable of the Two Plants

That vv. 11–15 picture the short-lived prosperity of the wicked is clear and has been generally recognized. However, the succeeding passage, vv. 16–19, has usually been regarded as representing the same theme by continuing to describe the destruction of the sinner. This view of the passage is untenable on many grounds: 1) vv. 16–19 cannot be a continuation of the same metaphor, since v. 15 describes the destruction of the wicked, while v. 16 pictures the plant as still full of sap and freshness. To meet this difficulty, D-G describe vv. 16–19 as "another comparison to a plant," but they leave unexplained why a second figure of speech is needed to make the same point. 2) V. 16 is most naturally given the meaning of "freshness and vigor." The attempt to interpret it to mean: "Before the sun it is fresh, but when the sun emerges it shrivels up," is farfetched. 3) V. 17 most naturally suggests the theme of the plant's vigor. 4) V. 19, in spite of its textual difficulties, suggests the theme of the plant's growing in a new environment. The effort to explain it as "a touch of irony" (D-G) is unconvincing. 5) If the section refers to the wicked, vv. 16–19a must be understood as concessive. Moreover, this long concessive clause, which, incidentally, lacks a conjunction, does not articulate well with the brief, clear condition in v. 18a. 6) Finally, it has been overlooked that v. 20 refers to the destiny of the righteous as well as to the fate of the sinners. In this respect our passage differs fundamentally from 15:20–35 and 18:5–21, which describe only the destruction of the evildoers, as is explicitly indicated in the text at 15:34 and 18:21 respectively (ag. P.).

Our entire passage (vv. 11–15 and 16–19) belongs to the same genre as the comparison of the wicked and the righteous to two plants in Jer. 17:5–6, 7–9 and Ps. 1:3–5, the latter passage being clearly dependent on the former. The First Psalm is particularly instructive, since it exhibits a chiastic structure (v. 3 — the righteous — v. 4 — the wicked — v. 5 — the wicked — v. 6a — the righteous). Our passage likewise exhibits a clear instance of chiasmus: a — the wicked (vv. 11–15); b — the righteous (vv. 16–19); b — the righteous (v. 19a); a — the wicked (v. 19b).

In spite of the formal similarity between the parable in Jeremiah and Psalms, on the one hand, and our passage on the other, they differ significantly in content. The two former passages represent the traditional concept of Divine retribution in relatively simple terms — the righteous are like a fruitful plant, the sinner like a plant in the desert. Our passage represents a more sophisticated version of the traditional theodicy. The sinner may prosper, but only initially; the righteous may suffer adversity, but will ultimately triumph.

On the principal difficulty of this view, the apparently abrupt introduction of the new theme in v. 16, and for the textual and exegetical comments that buttress this interpretation, see the Comm. on the individual verses.

Special Note 11 — On 9:5–10. The Destructive Power of God

Job counters Eliphaz's glowing description of God's power (5:9–16) by emphasizing the negative aspects of God's might, as manifested in His overturning the mountains (v. 5), shaking the earth (v. 6), and shutting off the light of the sun and the stars (v. 7). Another sardonic parody by Job of the Friends' arguments, which has been generally misunderstood, occurs in 12:14–25.

In this section, verses 8–10 are deleted by many commentators (Be., Du., Bu.) because (a) they do not seem in keeping with the negative character of the rest of the passage, and (b) the phrases are seen as reminiscences of other biblical passages: v. 8a = Isa. 44:24d; v. 8b = Mic. 1:3b (not identical); v. 9 = Am. 5:8; v. 10 = Job 5:9.

Actually, the familiarity of Job with Deutero-Isaiah is more than linguistic, another important instance occurring in 12:9b. Moreover, the entire outlook expressed by Elihu is derived from the exilic prophet (cf. *BGM*, pp. 112–14).

With regard to v. 10, its ironic thrust, when quoted here by Job, has not hitherto been recognized. Similarly, in vv. 8a, b, and 9, the poet is citing older sources for purposes far different from those in the original contexts. Job utilizes them to underscore the violent power of God; see the Comm. on all these verses for the evidence. On this creative and original use of quotations by the unconventional Wisdom writers, often with ironic intent, see such passages as Ecc. 4:9 ff.; 5:9 f.; 8:2 ff.; 8:5 f.; and Job 12:2 ff.; 21:28 f.; and see *KMW*, pp. 103 ff.; *BGM*, pp. 169–89; *PPS*, chap. 5.

Even if the negative character of the description of God's power in vv. 8–10 is not granted, the authenticity of these vv. may be defended on another basis as well. When a poet embarks on an extended description, be it a hymn or a metaphor, it develops a life of its own without reference in each detail to the original point of departure. Cf. the *wasf* in Cant. 5:12–14, and see *SS ad loc.*

Special Note 12 — On 10:9–11. Job and the Sexual Process

The basically positive view of sex and the human body, that is characteristic of the Bible and is exemplified in the Song of Songs, expresses itself in this paean of praise to the wonders of conception and the miracle of the growth of the foetus. The embryo is fashioned out of clay, the semen being poured out like milk, solidifying like cheese, being clothed in skin and flesh, and finally being knitted together with bones and sinews. The same theme, though less explicit and detailed, is treated in Ps. 139:13–16; Ecc. 11:5; II Mac. 7:22; Wisdom of Solomon 7:2.

In postbiblical Judaism this positive attitude gave way in some measure to a growth of ascetic tendencies and a correspondingly negative attitude toward the physical elements of life (cf. *M. Abot* 3:1, where man is described as "coming from a fetid drop"). Nonetheless, normative Judaism never totally abandoned the biblical attitude. It rarely carried to extremes the position of condemnation of sex and the physical aspects of life which became a dominant strand in classical Christianity, as in the New Testament (John 1:13; I Corinthians, chap. 7), and in many of the Church Fathers like Augustine. Cf. Gordis, *Sex and the Family in Jewish Tradition* (New York, 1967), for a brief presentation of the attitudes of normative Judaism; cf. also D. M. Feldman, *Birth Control in Jewish Law* (New York, 1968). Contemporary Christian thought is seeking to recapture the biblical healthy-mindedness on sexual experience as part of its reemphasis upon its Hebraic roots; see *inter alia*, Gordis, "The Re-Judaization of Christianity," in *FM*, chap. XVIII.

Special Note 13 — On Chapter 12. The Structure and Content of Job's Third Response

Job's closing speech in the first cycle, particularly the first section (12:2–13:2), has been subjected to massive emendation, unusual even for our book, because of the difficulties of the text. The section has also been extremely contracted, almost to the point of total elimination, because of apparent irrelevancies and contradictions to Job's authentic position. Thus Siegfried omits 12:4–13:1; W. Grill (*Zur Kritik der Komposition des Buches Hiob*, Tübingen, 1890) omits 12:4–13:2. D-G delete 12:4–12 (I, p. 111). Volz leaves only five verses in Job's speech (12:2, 3, 11, 12; 13:2) and transfers the remainder (12:4–10, 13–25; 13:1) to Zophar in chap. 11 (*op. cit.*, pp. 39–40). Jastrow (*op. cit.*) omits vv. 4c, 5 in part, 6c, 10, 12, 13, 17–19, 22, 23, and 25. Ball removes vv. 4c, 6, 10 (doubtfully), and 13. Budde, on the other hand, argues forcefully against Grill and Siegfried's procedure (*Das Buch Hiob, ad loc.*; also *ThLZ*, 1891, No. 2). Dhorme places vv. 11–12 before v. 9. More recent commentators, like Hö. (who omits only v. 13) and P., are less inclined to delete passages, but they are compelled to transform the meaning of the text by interpreting declarative sentences as interrogatives, or by inserting negative particles into the text.

The key to the understanding of the passage lies in recognizing the existence of a characteristic rhetorical usage, to which we have called attention: the elaborate and varied use of quotations by Job in this, his final speech of the First Cycle. It is probably not a coincidence that in his final response in the Second Cycle (chap. 21), Job adopts the same usage on a wider scale, and that in his second and final response to "the Lord out of the Whirlwind" (42:2–6), the use of quotations is again in evidence. This observation, incidentally, buttresses the view that both the Dialogue and the God Speeches emanate from the same author. The Third Cycle has sustained radical dislocation and loss of material, so that the evidence for this usage by Job in his final response is not clear. Nevertheless, it seems to be found in 24:18–24; see *BGM*, pp. 96 f., 272, and esp. p. 329, note 6, and the Comm.

Job's rejoinder in chap. 12 is marked by pervasive irony (cf. vv. 2–4) and by the use of several categories of quotations: (a) his ironic citation of the Friends' view (vv. 7–8), which he believes is designed to deflect attention from the real argument. Note the use of the singular pronoun, which is appropriate for the Friends' addressing Job (שְׁאַל, וְתֹרֶךָ, לְךָ), but not for Job's addressing the Friends, when the plural would have been required (as, e.g., 5:21; 12:1); (b) the use of a conventional proverb to underscore Job's own view that the human mind can discriminate between sense and nonsense (v. 11); (c) the use of contrasting quotations (vv. 12–13) in order to refute the Friends' contention that wisdom is with the aged (cf. 12:12 f.; 15:9 f., 18 f.). On these and other categories of quotations in Job and in Wisdom literature generally, cf. the basic treatments in *BGM*, chap. 13, and in *PPS*, chap. 5.

TS (pp. 204 f.) recognizes the presence of quotations here and regards vv. 4–25 in toto as a citation of the Friends' position. His treatment of the passage is characteristically stimulating. We are, however, unable to accept his approach because: (a) it makes a large number of assumptions regarding lost ancient sources allegedly cited here, including myths that are no longer extant; (b) it calls for many emendations and the creation of *hapax legomena* in the text; (c) it treats vv. 11 and 12 interrogatively, but the traditional proverbial form in which they are couched and the absence of any external sign of the question militate against this interpretation; (d) it fails to note the particular slant of the passage praising God's power (vv. 14–25), which is crucial for evaluating the structure and content of the entire passage. (See our following paragraph.)

In 12:14–25, Job pays tribute to the power of God, but from his own point of view. Unlike the paeans of the Friends (4:9 ff.) which extol God's creative and beneficent activity, Job underscores the destructive and negative aspects, as he has done in 9:4 ff. (see the Comm. *ad loc.*). These he finds both in nature (12:14–15) and even more clearly in human affairs (vv. 16–25). For the poet, who is a practitioner of Wisdom, the overthrow of the established order of kings, counsellors, and priests is a disaster. This is entirely congruent with the upper-class origin of Wisdom literature generally; for the full evidence, see "The Social Background of Wisdom Literature," in *PPS*, chap. 6. This attitude is in sharp contrast to the prophetically inspired conviction that reversing the positions of the powerful and the oppressed groups in society is a mark of God's justice operating in the world (e.g., Isa. 2:12 ff.; 3:1–5; Am. 3:15) and His love for the righteous (e.g., Hannah's prayer in I Sam. 2:2–8; Ps. 113:5–7).

Read with insight and sympathy, Job's final response in the First Cycle is a powerful rebuttal of the Friends' conventional theology. For details, see the Comm.

Special Note 14 — On 17:8, 9. Virtue and Its Reward

These verses are rejected by some commentators (Peake, D-G, Hö.) as unauthentic and "impossible to integrate into the rest of Job's speech" (P.). Deleting these verses means to deprive the book of one of its most fundamental contributions to the problem of evil. The Friends have insisted that suffering is the inevitable consequence and therefore the undeniable sign of

sin, because of their conviction that without this fear of punishment, men are
certain to descend to wickedness. (Cf. Mal. 3:14):

> "You have said: It is vain to serve God
> And what profit is it that we have kept His charge,
> And that we have walked mournfully
> Because of the Lord of hosts?"

Even Koheleth has argued that the mere delay in retribution tempts
men to wrong-doing (Ecc. 8:11 f.; see *KMW ad loc.*).

Job, on the other hand, has vigorously opposed the doctrine that suffering is the inevitable consequence of sin and prosperity the guaranteed reward
for righteous living. His existential tragedy has catapulted him into a mo-
mentous insight — he cuts the link between virtue and its reward established
by utilitarian morality. The truly good man will be aghast at Job's misery,
but he will not on that account be deflected from the path of righteousness.
The good life is its own reward and justification — it does not require the
prop of a false theodicy with the cruel distortion of reality.

This theme of righteousness for its own sake is fundamental in rabbinic
ethics. Cf. *M. Abot* 4:2

מצוה גוררת מצוה ועבירה גוררת עבירה
ששכר מצוה מצוה ושכר עבירה עבירה

"One virtuous deed brings on another, and one transgression leads to another,
for the reward of a virtuous deed is a virtuous deed and the consequence of
a transgression, a transgression."

אל תהיו כעבדים המשמשים את הרב על מנת לקבל פרס אלא היו כעבדים המשמשים את
הרב שלא על מנת לקבל פרס ויהי מורא שמים עליכם.

"Do not be as servants who serve their master for the sake of reward, but
be as servants who serve their master without the desire of reward; and may
the fear of Heaven be upon you" (*M. Abot* 1:3);

אשרי איש ירא את ה' במצותיו חפץ מאד – במצותיו ולא בשכר מצותיו

"Blessed is the man who fears the Lord and delights greatly in His commandments — in His commandments, and not in the reward for His commandments." (*Mid. Psalms* 112:1).

This idea is the basis for the Rabbinic doctrine of תורה לשמה, "the study
of Torah for its own sake." A classic presentation of the doctrine of virtue
as its own reward is set forth by Maimonides in his *Commentary on the
Mishnah, Introduction to Sanhedrin*, chap. 10, now available in English in
I. Twersky, *A Maimonides Reader* (New York, 1972).

The germ of this profound insight may be found in our passage. The just
man will be deeply troubled by the injustice in the world (8a), but he will
not surrender to injustice. On the contrary, he will actively seek to combat
it (8b). He will hold fast to the practice of righteousness (9a) and, in fact,
intensify his efforts to live the good life (9b). For Job, as for biblical religion
generally, the ideal saint is not he who resigns himself to unjust suffering,
but he who actively battles against it.

Special Note 15 Arbiter — Witness — Redeemer — Job's Three Levels of Faith

The position of Job in the Dialogue is marked by a major theme and another in counterpoint, each growing stronger as the debate unfolds. On the one hand, as the argument continues, the Friends cast off any pretense to urbanity and sympathy, their onslaught on Job's rectitude becoming increasingly reckless (11:4–6; 15:4–6; 22:5 ff.). Job counters by picturing God as taking delight in the torment suffered by His creatures without cause (9:19–24; 16:7–14; 19:6–12). On the other hand, Job's growing attack upon God's violence in the present is accompanied by a new and deepening conviction of God's ultimate justice.

This faith is not easily arrived at and manifests itself in three successive stages in the Dialogue. In 9:33, Job yearns for an impartial arbiter who will hold the scales evenly between him and his cosmic opponent. In 16:19, Job is certain that there is a witness on his behalf who will speak out freely in his defense. In 19:25, Job is convinced that a vindicator, a kinsman to avenge him, will arise and act on his behalf. Thus Job's faith in the underlying rightness of the universe grows deeper as his conviction of the injustice of his suffering grows stronger.

The uncomprehending hostility of his Friends brings about important changes in the progression of Job's faith. In 9:33, Job voices a mere hope for a fair judgment, which he scarcely believes possible; in 16:19, he sees his witness as an actuality *in the present*; in 19:25, the vindicator will arise, but only *in the distant future*. This postponement of Job's vindication is, however, compensated for by a change in the mise-en-scène of the drama of salvation — while he sees his witness testifying on his behalf "in heaven" (*bašāmayim*), his avenger will arise and act for him "on earth" (*ᶜal ᶜāphār*; cf. 41:25).

Several recent commentators, notably Terrien and Pope, have insisted that Job cannot be referring to God when he speaks of a witness or a redeemer: "In this context the heavenly witness, guarantor, friend, can scarcely be God, who is already accuser, judge and executioner" (Pope, p. 118). But this division of roles, however necessary and praiseworthy in a human court, where partiality and unfairness are ever-present dangers, is superfluous in the heavenly assize, where all the functions are performed by God. This is clearly articulated in post-biblical Judaism, whose uncompromising monotheism stands firmly on biblical foundations. Cf., e.g., *M. Abot* 4:22:

הוא היוצר הוא הבורא הוא המבין הוא הדיין הוא העד הוא בעל דין הוא עתיד לדון ברוך
הוא שאין לפניו לא עולה ולא שכחה ולא משוא פנים ולא מקח שוחד שהכל שלו ודע שהכל
לפי החשבון.

"He is the fashioner, He is the creator, He is the one who understands, He is the judge, He is the witness. He is the party to the suit, He is destined to judge, blessed be He, for there is before Him neither wrong-doing nor forgetfulness nor partiality nor bribe-taking, for everything is His and know that everything is according to a just reckoning." The same theme is underscored in the solemn prayer *Unethanneh Toqeph* in the High Holy Day ritual:

אמת כי אתה הוא דיין ומוכיח ויודע ועד "It is true that You are the judge, the arbiter, the one who knows and the witness."

It may be added that neither Terrien nor Pope has ventured to explicate the identity of the being to whom Job is referring. Actually, the problem arises only because of the tendency to apply Western categories of logic to the Oriental spirit. The sharp delimitation of personality is foreign to biblical thought. In all these passages, Job is affirming his faith that behind the God of violence, so tragically manifest in the world, stands the God of righteousness and love — and they are not two but one! Thus, Job's attack upon conventional religion is actually the expression of deepest trust. Hence Job is eminently worthy of God's final encomium pronounced upon him, "You have not spoken the truth about Me, as has My servant Job" (42:10).

An effective refutation of the assumption of an unknown "third party" in Job's confrontation with God is supplied by a significant passage, the importance of which has been overlooked. At the acme of his bitterness, Job takes a vow reaffirming his integrity: "As God lives, who has robbed me of my right, and by the Almighty who has embittered my soul" (27:2). The first century sage, Rabbi Joshua ben Hananiah, who maintains that Job served God out of love, acutely notes, "A man does not swear 'by the life of the king' unless he loves him" (Rashi *ad loc.*). It is the God who has treated h:m so cruelly and embittered his existence whom Job loves and to whom he turns as the court of last appeal. No other figure appears on the horizon or is contemplated by Job.

The theme of "fleeing from God to God" is expressed in a moving passage in "The Royal Crown" by the medieval Spanish-Jewish poet, Solomon ibn Gabirol:

> Therefore though You slay me, I will trust in You.
> For if You pursue my iniquity,
> I will flee from You to Yourself,
> And I will shelter myself from Your wrath in Your shadow,
> And to the skirts of Your mercies I will lay hold
> Until You have mercy on me,
> And I will not let You go till You bless me.

(*Keter Malkhut*, sec. 38, ll. 562–66 in *Selected Religious Poems of Solomon ibn Gabirol*, ed. I. Davidson, trans. I. Zangwill, Philadelphia, 1944, p. 118.) The theme is also expressed by the medieval Italian-Hebrew poet, Immanuel of Rome, a friend of Dante:

> "When all within is dark
> And Thy just angers rise
> From Thee I turn to Thee
> And find love in Thine eyes."
> (Tr. I. Abrahams)

Rabbinic Judaism developed the two concepts of *middat haddīn*, "the quality of justice," and *middat hārahᵃmīm*, "the quality of mercy," as representing the two aspects of God. But biblical and post-biblical Judaism alike never carried these two aspects to the extreme of a genuine dualism, always holding fast to the unity of God underlying both manifestations. On these two concepts, cf. S. Schechter, *Some Aspects of Rabbinic Theology*; G. F. Moore, *Judaism in the First Centuries of the Christian Era* (3 vols., Cambridge, 1927–1930); M. Kadushin, *The Theology of Seder Eliahu* (New York, 1932); *Organic Thinking* (New York, 1938); *The Rabbinic Mind* (Chicago, 1964).

Special Note 16. On 19:23–29 — Job's Vision of His Vindicator

Many commentators have sought to rearrange these verses in a more "coherent" form, separating Job's denunciation of his Friends from his demands for a permanent memorial to vindicate him. Thus Yel. places the order as vv. 19–22, 26–29, 23–25. The proposed rearrangement on the basis of Western logic and coherence fails to do justice to the passionate and impetuous change of theme and mood characteristic of Semitic poetry in general and of Job in particular. For an instance of this sudden and radical change of mood in Semitic poetry, cf. the passage in the Babylonian poem "I Will Praise the Lord of Wisdom," cited and discussed in the Comm. *ad loc.*

The literature on vv. 25–27, perhaps the most famous and difficult passage in the book, is enormous. For a conspectus of the treatment of this passage, cf. Speer, "Zur Exegese von Hiob, 19:25–27," in *ZATW*, 1905, pp. 47–140; D-G, I, pp. 170–76; II, pp. 127–33, and all succeeding commentaries. It is impossible to summarize, let alone discuss, the vast variety of emendations and interpretations of this passage. Virtually the only element of consensus among moderns, as against older exegetes, is that the passage does *not* refer to resurrection after death, in view of Job's clear-cut rejection of the doctrine in 14:7–23.

Job begins with a bitter attack upon the hostility of his erstwhile Friends (vv. 19–20), and a pathetic plea to them, which he knows will go unheeded (vv. 21–22). With no chance of vindication in the present, he turns to the future and demands that his utterances be preserved on a monument (vv. 23–24). From the depths of despair he then rises to a vision of faith in the God of Justice, whom he sees vividly before him, acting as his kinsman and Redeemer, the avenger of the wrongs he has suffered (25:27b). But the ecstatic vision fades and with it the joy and certainty of his vindication. Job is plunged back into the intolerable present and he reverts with even greater bitterness to an attack upon his unfeeling Friends.

Rhythmically, the passage falls into two well-defined sections — the first section (vv. 20–26) is in the *qinah* rhythm (4:3) which is characterized by a longer stich followed by a shorter and is not restricted to the 3:2 meter. See Special Note 1, sec. 14, 15. In v. 24a, the longer and important word *vecōphereth* would receive two beats *metri causa* (Special Note 1, sec. 6, and Gordis, *Song of Songs-Lamentations*, New York, 1973, pp. 118–20).

The second section (vv. 27–29) is in 3 ‖ 3 meter with tristichs predominating:

v. 27   3:3:3
v. 28   3:3
v. 29   3:3:3

The change to tristichs adds greater force to the conclusion of Job's speech. On this important technique, see *PPS*, pp. 71 f. and Special Note 1, sec. 21.

Special Note 17 — On 21:17–33. The Use of Quotations in Argument

It is a noteworthy characteristic of the style of the book that at the end of each cycle Job cites the views of his opponents and reacts to them. On the First Cycle, see Special Note 13 on chap. 12; on the Second, see below. The Third Cycle has suffered drastic disarrangement and has not been completely preserved. (See Special Note 20 on chaps. 25–27.) Moreover, it ends with a soliloquy (chaps. 29–31) paralleling Job's opening complaint (chap. 3), so that there was less opportunity for a similar type of argumentation. (Cf. *BGM*, pp. 185–87.) Nevertheless, it seems probable that even here Job makes use of virtual quotations in arguing with his Friends (see Special Note 19 on chap. 24). Elihu makes frequent use of quotations, both virtual and explicit. Finally, Job's brief response to the Second God-speech (42:2–6) contains two citations (42:3a, 4; see the Comm. *ad loc.*). The use of this striking stylistic trait in all sections of the book strengthens the view of its unity of authorship. On the use of quotations in argument, cf. *PPS*, pp. 140 ff.; *BGM*, pp. 174 f., 185 ff.

As has been noted in the Introduction to the translation of this passage, vv. 17–34 are a direct rebuttal of five contentions of the Friends. The opening phrase in v. 17: "How often is the lamp of the wicked extinguished," is a quotation and rejoinder to Bildad's confident assertion: "The lamp of the wicked is extinguished" (18:6). Job then cites four additional arguments of the Friends, only one of which is introduced by a *verbum dicendi* (v. 28). The others are virtual quotations, in which the reader must recognize the source of the idea expressed. In one instance (v. 17a), the quotation is almost exact. In the others, vv. 19a, 22, 30, it is the substance of the Friends' position that Job summarizes and rebuts.

Our earlier view (in *BGM*, *PPS*) that there are four arguments of the Friends needs to be corrected accordingly. The chapter thus exhibits an instance of the pentad as an organizing literary principle. This usage was noted by Leroy Waterman in "The Book of the Covenant" (Ex. 21–24), and in the New Testament and in the rabbinic literature by G. Kittel and Saul Lieberman, respectively. (See *PPS*, p. 101, Note 1.) On the similar use of the heptad as a stylistic element in the Hebrew Bible, the New Testament and rabbinic literature, see *PPS*, chap. 4.

The failure to recognize the quotation-response structure of the passage has led many scholars to proposing many deletions and emendations, and involved far-fetched interpretations of the individual verses. See D-G, I, pp. 185 f., for an excellent summary of the exegesis. It should be added that this usage of quotations has been partially recognized by some commentators. Thus, v. 19a is taken as a quotation by Bu. and by D-G, who follow the English version and prefix, "Ye say," and apparently by Ball (*The Book of Job*, Oxford, 1922). Verse 22 is similarly treated by Hi. Yel. (*op. cit.*, p. 52) renders vv. 18, 22, and 30 as quotations, but takes v. 28 differently. On the other hand, the satiric intent of vv. 28–29 has been overlooked, and v. 30 has proved another stumbling-block in understanding Job's rejoinder. The evidence for this approach to the passage is to be found in the notes on the individual verses.

Special Note 18 — On 22:11–14. God's Distance and the Failure of Retribution

In 22:8, Eliphaz has suggested that the reason for Job's violent oppression of the poor and the weak was his conviction that the powerful rule the earth. The passage 22:11–14 offers another reason for Job's alleged wrongdoing — God is too distant and isolated from men, His dwelling being above the primordial darkness and the waters above the firmament (Gen. 1:7). V. 11 is the basis for the idea developed in vv. 12–14. Since Job cannot see through darkness or a flood of waters, he believes that God too is similarly handicapped in observing the deeds of men. The sense of the passage is: "Or since in the darkness you cannot see or when a multitude of waters covers you (you cannot see), you thought, 'God is in the heights, above the stars and therefore cannot judge men.'"

That God is far removed from men and is therefore not concerned with retribution is the contention that biblical writers frequently impute to sinners and skeptics.

Thus:

> "Woe to those who hide deep from
>   the Lord their counsel,
> whose deeds are in the dark,
> and who say, 'Who sees us?
>   Who knows us?'"   (Isa. 29:15)

> "Then he said to me, 'Son of man, have you seen what the elders
> of the house of Israel are doing in the dark, every man in his
> room of pictures? For they say, 'The Lord does not see us, the
> Lord has forsaken the land.'"   (Ezek. 8:12)

> "And they say, 'The Lord does not see;
>   the God of Jacob does not perceive.'"   (Ps. 94:7)

Koheleth invokes the physical distance between God and man to urge upon his readers the minimizing of oaths and brevity in prayer:

"Do not hasten to speak, nor let yourself be-rushed into uttering
words before God, for God is in heaven and you are on the
earth — therefore, let your words be few." (Ecc. 5:1)

While Job has complained vigorously against the traditional doctrine
that retribution comes upon the sinners ultimately, either in their own person
or in that of their children (21:19a, 30; see the Comm.), Koheleth sees in the
time-lag between sin and its retribution another motive for wrongdoing:

"Because judgment upon an evil deed is not executed speedily,
men's hearts are encouraged to do wrong, for a sinner commits
one hundred crimes and God is patient with him, though I know
the answer that 'it will be well in the end with those who revere
God because they fear Him and it will be far from well with the
sinner, who, like a shadow, will not long endure, because he
does not fear God.'" (Ecc. 8:11–13)

It is noteworthy that the medievals recognize that these verses present
Job's alleged thought. Thus Ra. so interprets v. 11, and Ibn E. v. 12 (חָשֵׁבְתָּ).

Special Note 19 — The Structure and Meaning of Chapter 24

This chapter is undoubtedly one of the most difficult in the book, with
regard to its form, its content, and its relevance to the context. As a result,
many scholars have deleted the entire chapter with the exception of the last
verse (so Du., Hö.). Others adopt a slightly less radical procedure, deleting
large sections like vv. 9–24 (Me.) or vv. 13–24, felt to be "suspicious" (D-G),
or vv. 5–8, 10–24 (Bi.).

With regard to the poetic *form*, it is argued that the chapter contains a
large number of tristichs, a meter which is at variance with the structure of
the rest of the book. Indeed, Me., Bi., Du. virtually eliminate or recast all
the distichs in the text into tristichs, before deleting all or most of the chapter.
Actually, MT contains only seven, eight, or nine tristichs in the 24 verses:
5 (?), 12, 13, 14, 15, 16, 18, (20?), 24. While this is a larger proportion than
generally obtains in Job, the argument from meter cannot be legitimately used
to declare the entire chapter inauthentic, especially since the text is very
difficult and has undoubtedly suffered corruption and the loss of material.

As concerns the *content* and *relevance*, it is clear that the first half of the
chapter (vv. 1–17) does possess a special character. After a complaint about
the failure or the delay in God's retribution in v. 1, the bulk of the chapter
contains two themes antiphonally related to one another: a description of
the depredations of the evil-doers (A, 2–4; C, 9; E, 13–17) alternating with the
description of the misery of the weak (B, 5–8; D, 10–12). Recognizing the
antiphonal structure of the chapter makes it unnecessary to "reorganize"
the material or delete it. Thus D-G, who places 8–9 after 2, deletes 10 and

11a and places 14c, 10a and b after 15. P. keeps as Job's reply vv. 1–3, 9, 21 (?), 4a, 10–15, 14c, 16, 17.

The special form of this chapter may be due to its belonging to a characteristic genre of Oriental Wisdom literature consisting of complaints on the state of the world. The Egyptian examples of this genre are, "The Protest of the Eloquent Peasant" (A. Erman, *Literature of the Ancient Egyptians*, pp. 116 ff.; *ANET*, pp. 407–409), a tale of a poor man demanding justice in the face of fraud and oppression; "The Dispute over Suicide" (*ANET*, pp. 405–407), which reflects the despair occasioned by the breakdown of society; and "The Prophecy of Nefer-Rohu" (*ANET*, pp. 444–46), which describes the social chaos of the time, but apparently ends on a note of hope in the future. Akkadian literature in this genre includes "The Pessimistic Dialogue between a Master and His Servant" (*ANET*, pp. 437 ff.), the thrust of which is enigmatic; and "The Dialogue about Human Misery," the so-called "Babylonian Koheleth" (*ANET*, pp. 438–40), which discusses piety toward the gods and the frequent absence of reward. For a more detailed discussion of this genre, see *KMW*, chap. 1; *BGM*, chap. 5.

Our entire chapter may have originally been an independent poem, belonging to this genre, or the poet may have followed pre-existing models of complaints in composing it. The author of Job represents the culmination of a long literary tradition in the ancient Middle East which he readily used, while transforming and deepening it immeasurably by the alchemy of his genius. It is abundantly clear that the poet utilized accepted patterns in literary composition, imbedding such limited compositions into his larger, all-embracing work. Thus, Eliphaz's description of the triumph of the righteous (5:19–24) follows the pattern of Psalms like 91. Bildad's description of "the two paths" in 8:12–20 has its analogues in Psalm 1 and Jer. 17:5–9, which is itself an example, like Isaiah, chap. 12, of the Prophets' use of Psalm patterns. Similarly, the Hymn to Wisdom (chap. 28) represents a self-contained literary unit which, though radically difficult in spirit, has striking affinities with Proverbs (chap. 8) and the later Ben Sira (chap. 1).

The extensive use the poet makes of quotations, to which we have repeatedly called attention, offers another illustration of the use of extant literary forms by the author for his own creative purposes.

All these considerations, based on Oriental and Hebrew Wisdom literature, help make out a case for regarding the chapter as originally an independent composition. This approach is supported strongly by the absence of the dialogic structure of confrontation that characterizes the rest of the book. Unlike chap. 28, which remains an independent poem, however, chap. 24 has been integrated quite successfully into the Dialogue of the book, as have 5:19–24 and 8:12–20.

There are no convincing grounds for excising the first part of the chapter (vv. 1–17) or denying it to Job. In its impassioned picture of human wickedness and misery, the section is entirely appropriate to Job's position, particularly as a realistic rejoinder to the Friends' constant description of the triumph of the righteous (5:19 ff.; 8:16 ff.; 11:15 ff.), and the destruction of the wicked (4:18 ff.; 8:12 ff.). In fact, in the Second Cycle (15:20 ff.; 18:5 ff.; 20:6 ff.) this contention has been virtually the only theme in the Friends' defense of God. A true picture of the tragic human condition is, therefore, entirely appropriate to Job, as a foil to the Friends' imaginary descriptions of justice triumphant. It should also be noted that the section contains an explicit complaint against God's indifference to man's agonies: "Yet God pays no heed!" (v. 12c).

The major issue of relevance arises in the second section (vv. 18–24) — which is replete with extraordinary textual and exegetical difficulties. In general, however, the basic theme of these verses, that the wicked are ultimately punished, seems to be clear. The problem is that this contention is inappropriate for Job, who has consistently argued that justice is not done. Some critics have therefore suggested that the section is part of the third speech of Bildad (Hoffmann) or Zophar (Dh., Terrien, P.). As is indicated later, we believe that part of Zophar's speech is to be found in 27:13–23. The theory that 24:18–24 belongs to Zophar would mean that part of his speech occurs before Bildad and part afterwards. In any event, assigning 24:18–24 to Zophar would mean that his speech comes before that of Bildad. Moreover, 24:25, which is clearly Job's (see the Comm.), would be a single isolated verse. However, in view of the fragmentary and dislocated character of the Third Cycle (see *BGM* and the Comm. below), these objections cannot be regarded as conclusive.

Nevertheless, we prefer another solution which avoids all these difficulties. We regard the section as Job's quotation of the Friends' ideas on the retribution imposed on the wicked. Originally, Job's presentation of the Friends' standpoint was followed by his refutation, as in chap. 21. This rebuttal was subsequently lost, like much of the material of the Third Cycle, only the closing verse, 25, surviving.

In favor of this approach, rather than assigning it to Bildad or Zophar, are the following considerations: (1) the style of 24:18–24 is of a piece with that of 24:1–17; (2) it is radically different from the style of Bildad's speech (25:2–6; 26:5–14; see the Comm.) or that of Zophar (27:14–23) and cannot easily be articulated with either; (3) it is clear that the closing verse 24:25 is appropriate in style and spirit to Job; and (4) in each Cycle of the Dialogue and after the God Speeches, Job makes use of quotations from his opponents and reacts to them (chaps. 12, 21, 40, 41:2–6).

With regard to the use of style and vocabulary for establishing date or unity of authorship, a large measure of skepticism is always in order. But we may note the use of a pronoun הֵמָּה in v. 13 (and in v. 2; see the Comm.) and probably הֵן in v. 5 as well, in order to introduce a new subject differing from the previous one. This characteristic of the poet's style has been pointed out in 8:16 (הוּא) which introduces a description of the righteous as against the wicked previously depicted, and וְהוּא (13:28) beginning a new theme, linked to the following section. Other stylistic similarities are: וַתִּשָּׁבֵר כָּעֵץ עוְלָה

(24:20) and וַיִּסַּע כָּעֵץ תִּקְוָתִי (19:10), the use of Aramaisms like קְטַל (24:14) and יְקָטְלֵנִי (13:15) and חַיִּין (v. 22), as well as a resemblance in vocabulary like תִּפְלָה (v. 12 and 1:22); יֹדְעוּ (v. 1) and לֹא־יָדַע אֵל (18:21).

These stylistic criteria, when joined to the substantive considerations advanced above, justify the view that the chapter is authentically the work of the poet and that its contents are appropriate for Job. The first section describes the oppression wreaked by powerful evil-doers upon the poor and weak, the second contains a restatement of the Friends' doctrine, that the wicked ultimately receive due retribution. The third, of which, unfortunately, only one verse has survived, originally contained Job's refutation of the conventional theology.

Section E (vv. 13–17), the final description of the evil-doers, has been rearranged by many scholars, (a) in order to bring the order of sins into conformity with the sixth, seventh, and eighth prohibitions of the Decalogue, and (b) because vv. 15 and 16 are tristichs. Thus D-G places the sequence as the murderer (14a, b), the adulterer (15), and the thief (14c and 16a). The transposition is uncalled for. Note that Hos. 4:2 has the same sequence of sins as in our text, רָצֹחַ וְגָנֹב וְנָאֹף, and there is no *a priori* reason for assuming that all the biblical writers had to follow the pattern of the Decalogue. As for the presence of tristichs, even this rearrangement leaves them undisturbed in vv. 13, 15, and 18. In point of fact, virtually the entire section (vv. 13–16) consists of tristichs. To be sure, the thief is referred to at two points (14c and 16a), which may offend our sense of logical structure, but not that of the Oriental poet. Thus he refers to the evil-doer's hatred of light and love of darkness in two distinct passages, vv. 13 and 17.

Special Note 20 — The Structure of the Third Cycle. On Chapters 25–27

That the Third Cycle has suffered great damage and cannot be meaningfully interpreted in its present form is beyond question. In our present text, Bildad is represented by a much too short speech, of only five verses (25:2-6). Job has an inordinately long speech (chaps. 26–31), in which Chapter 28 is radically distinct, both in structure and in form, from the Dialogue (see Special Note 23). In Chapter 26, vv. 5–14 describe God's power in the natural world in the same spirit and style as Chapter 25, but they are irrelevant to Job. In Chapter 27, vv. 7–11 present the faith in the ultimate discomfiture of the wicked, which is totally at variance with Job's present outlook. In the rest of the chapter (vv. 12–23), the calamity that will come upon the wicked in the ultimate prosperity of the righteous is presented in conventional terms, which are entirely congenial to the Friends but diametrically opposed to Job's standpoint.

It is therefore no wonder that virtually every scholar has attempted a restoration of the Third Cycle. A dozen such proposals are listed in Pfeiffer, *Introduction to the Old Testament*, p. 671; for additional proposals see D-G, I, p. 41; S. L. Terrien, *Job — Poet of Existence* (New York, 1957), p. 34. To these may be added the reconstruction by P. of the Third Cycle (after chap. 23) as follows: *Job's Reply:* 24:1–3, 9, 21, 4–8, 10–14b, 15, 14c, 16, 17; *Bildad:* 25:1–6; 26:5–14; *Job* 27:1; 26:1–4; 27:2–7; *Zophar:* 27:8–23; 24:18–20, 22–25.

The restoration we propose makes only one basic assumption and requires only one transposition in MT: the second section of Bildad's speech (now 26:5–14) became separated from the first section (25:1–6), and was placed after the first section of Job's response (now 26:1–4) instead of before it. It is clear that Zophar's speech has been preserved only fragmentarily in chap. 27. It is probable that other material in the Third Cycle was lost when the pages of the manuscript from which our text is descended were disarranged.

Our restoration is as follows: Following Job's response to Eliphaz in chaps. 23–24, Bildad describes the power of God (25:1–6 and 26:5–14), so that his speech is largely preserved. Of Job's response only two sections survive: (a) 26:1–4; and (b) 27:1–12, which, however, requires a new approach, on which see the Comm. Only a fragment has remained of Zophar's speech (27:13–23). Chap. 28 is an independent "Hymn to Wisdom." Chaps. 29–31 constitute Job's closing soliloquy, paralleling his original lament in chap. 3.

While our reconstruction of the Third Cycle was arrived at independently, our conclusions agree basically with those of B. A. Elzas for the Bildad speech and with those of Graetz for the Zophar speech. For a detailed discussion of the problem, see *BGM,* chap. VIII, and the Comm. The translation and the Commentary follow the proposed sequence.

Special Note 21 — On 27:7–10. Job's Former Faith

These vv. express the hope that the speaker's enemy may be in the wrong, because sinners have no hope and their pleas are not heard by God. This presentation of conventional theology obviously does not represent Job's view at this point. On the other hand, the use of the first person sing. in v. 7: "May my enemy be in the wrong," is most naturally intelligible if spoken by Job rather than by the Friends. Being, like its predecessors, in the 1st person, v. 7 links up with v. 6. Moreover, v. 8, introduced by כִּי, gives the reason for v. 7 and can hardly be the beginning of Zophar's address, as suggested by some scholars (Hö., P.). Nor can the passage be taken to mean that here Job suddenly finds his way to a new faith in God (Ew., Dil.), because his rebellious attitude is expressed again later (30:20–23; 31:35–38).

The key to the understanding of the passage lies in recognizing it as a virtual quotation, a citation of Job's previous state of mind during the time of his prosperity and well-being. On this category of "virtual quotations," which occurs also in Ps. 44:21–22; Job 31:2, 14, see *BGM,* pp. 174, 181 ff.; *PPS,* pp. 126–29. Though this rhetorical usage was not noted before, Hengstenberg and Bu. partly recognized that our passage refers to Job's previous outlook. The entire passage constitutes a unit with the preceding, with which it articulates perfectly.

Special Note 22 — Zophar's Final Speech (27:13–23)

This passage contains a description of the calamities coming upon the evil-doer and his offspring. Efforts have been made to bring this passage into harmony with Job's position. One view is that Job is here modifying his standpoint and conceding that *as a rule* disaster overtakes the wicked, but the all-important phrase we have italicized is nowhere hinted at, and the statements are entirely unqualified by any limitations. Another view is that Job is ironically telling his Friends that their unjust accusations against him make them liable to punishment (Schultens, Bu., Ehr.). There is, however, not the slightest indication that the description of the punishment of the wicked is aimed against the Friends. The passage is framed in completely' general terms. Nor is the Friends' alleged crime against Job even hinted at here. Both explanations are decidedly artificial and unconvincing (see D-G, I, p. 229).

The position of this passage after Bildad's speech (25:1–5; 26:5–14) and Job's third response (26:1–4; 27:2–12) makes it most plausible to assign this passage to Zophar, the only surviving section of his final speech.

Special Note 23 — The Hymn to Wisdom (*Chapter 28*)

On the meaning of this chapter and its independent character, see *BGM*, pp. 100–103, and the Intr. to the Translation. In addition to the larger considerations of content and style there adduced for the view that the chapter was written by the author of Job as a separate and probably earlier treatment of his basic theme, several linguistic facts point to the same conclusion. We may note some noteworthy divergences in language. The Divine epithet אֲדֹנָי in v. 28 occurs nowhere else in the book; JHVH only in 12:9 in a quotation from Isaiah (see the Comm. *ad loc.*), אֱלֹהִים (v. 23) occurs only twice elsewhere in the book (5:8; 20:29), while the Divine names אֵל and שַׁדַּי, used over 90 times in the book, do not appear here at all.

On the other hand, there is the use of בְּנֵי שַׁחַץ (28:8 and 41:26), חֲזִיז קֹלוֹת (28:27 and 38:25), and נְחוּשָׁה (28:2 and 20:24, as well as 6:12; see Comm.). Equally important are several stylistic traits characteristic of the poet elsewhere: the use of a pronoun to introduce a subject that the reader must identify (see the Comm. on 28:3) and a repetition of the same root in parallel stichs (see the Comm. on 28:19). The frequent assonances throughout the chapter (cf. Yel. *ad loc.*) are worthy of the poetic genius of the author of the book.

In sum, the style of the chapter is both similar to and different from that of the Dialogue and of the God Speeches. This is precisely the condition we would expect if it emanates from the same author in a different period of his career.

Several other "Hymns to Wisdom" as the Divine plan of creation are extant in Hebrew literature, notably Pr. 8:22–31; Ben Sira 1:1–10; 24:1–22 in the Apocrypha and Ps. 152 extant in the Qumran Scroll and in Syriac.

Hokmah is identified with the Torah, as in later rabbinic literature and the liturgy. The "Hymn to Wisdom" in the Hellenistic *Wisdom of Solomon* (10:1–21) identifies *Hokmah* with righteousness and piety.

The incapacity of man to attain to "the higher Wisdom" (*Hokmah* with the definite article) is here accepted as part of the human condition; only "the lower Wisdom," *Hokmah* (without the definite article), was revealed to man (v. 28).

This limitation on man's knowledge of ultimate truth is the source of Koheleth's deep dissatisfaction with man's estate; see *KMW*, *passim*. Ben Sira, in matter-of-fact fashion, urges his readers to accept this state of affairs and adjust to it (3:21 f.):

> Into matters too hard for you do not pry,
> and what is hidden from you do not search.
> Look at what you have been permitted,
> And have no concern with mysteries!

In our chapter, Wisdom is personified as in Pr. 8:1 ff., and frequently elsewhere (Pr. 2:1 ff.; 3:1 ff.; 5:1 ff.; 9:1 ff.). This hypostatization of Wisdom may represent a re-emergence of elements of near-Eastern mythology representing an older feminine goddess, who was described as pre-existent in the world (cf. O. S. Rankin, *Israel's Wisdom Literature*, Edinburgh, 1936; Hö. *ad loc.*). On the other hand, it is possible that biblical monotheism utilized traits borrowed from female goddesses for mythological, not mythical, purposes, that is to say, as literary embellishments and not as representations of accepted religious ideas. The two passages in Jeremiah on the worship of "the queen of heaven" (Jer. 7:18; 44:17, 18, 19, 25) obviously refer to an alien cult that infiltrated into Judah with the weakening of the state and the penetration of foreign religious and cultural influences. There is no convincing evidence that a female deity was ever part of Hebrew religion (cf. R. Patai, in *The Hebrew Goddess*, New York, 1967).

Efforts have been made both to expand and to contract the poem. Du. proposed placing the refrain of vv. 12, 20, before v. 1 in order to supply a background for the conjunction *ki* in v. 1. This is exegetically unnecessary (see the Comm. on 28:1). Actually, the presence of the refrain at the beginning of the chapter would weaken the force of the poem. By repeating the refrain at the end of each strophe except the last, the poet stresses man's technical skill and achievement. This successful activity is then contrasted with man's limitation vis-à-vis Wisdom which man cannot acquire for any price. In the following strophe Wisdom is described as known only to God.

Some scholars have deleted varying parts of vv. 14–19 that are lacking in LXX (Dil., Bi., Bu.). But since they do not follow LXX in deleting the *entire* section, they cannot logically derive support for their omissions from the absence of any particular verse in LXX. Actually, this section is indispensable on the grounds both of content and of the form. After describing men's exertions to find valuable metals and precious stones in the bowels of the earth, the poet declares that man cannot acquire Wisdom even in exchange for these precious products of his toil.

As for the form, deleting vv. 15–20, in whole or in part, disrupts the pattern of the poem in which the refrain occurs at roughly equal intervals of eleven or eight verses. Cf. the refrain in Ps. 42–43 after 5, 4, and 5 verses respectively (42:1–5, 8–11; 43:1–4) and in Ps. 107, where the refrain consists of two verses with an insert between them (vv. 6–8; 13–15; 19–21; 28–31) occurring after intervals of 5, 4, 3, and 6 verses. While the repetition of the refrain is somewhat irregular, the omission of the intervening section would destroy the strophic character of the poem completely.

The difficulties of interpretation in the first section (vv. 1–11) are due in largest measure to our lack of knowledge of the technical vocabulary of ancient mining operations. The author of Job, whom Pfeiffer calls "the most learned ancient before Plato," undoubtedly traveled outside of Palestine. He may have had in mind the operations in Lebanon, Edom, or Egypt, as well as nearer areas like the Sinai Peninsula or the Eilat region. This facet of the poet's knowledge of technology agrees well with the evidence for his familiarity with astronomy (9:7 ff.; 38:19 ff.), agriculture (14:7 ff.), and animal lore (38:38 ff.).

Special Note 24 — On 28:28. The Basic Theme of The Hymn to Wisdom

This crucial verse has frequently been deleted on grounds that (a) it is a prosaic addition (D-G, Hö., P.), and (b) that it is irrelevant, if not contradictory, to the rest of the poem. Neither contention can be sustained under analysis. וַיֹּאמֶר לָאָדָם is an anacrusis, being outside the meter pattern. The meter of the rest of the verse is probably 3:3 (if *yir'at 'adonay*, representing a single thought-unit, receives one beat, as does הִיא, being emphatic):

הֵן יִרְאַת־אֲדֹנָי הִיא חָכְמָה ‖ וְסוּר מֵרָע בִּינָה

If the phrase receives two beats, the rhythmic pattern is 4:3.

If one stress is given to סוּר מֵרָע as a single thought-unit, the verse may be scanned as in 2:2 meter, but this is less likely for the conclusion of a poem, where the tendency is to employ an extended rhythm pattern; cf. *PPS*, pp. 68–71. For anacrusis, cf. אַשְׁרֵי הָאִישׁ (Ps. 1:1); לֹא־כֵן הָרְשָׁעִים (Ps. 1:4); וְלָרָשָׁע אָמַר אֱלֹהִים (Ps. 50:16); וַיֹּרֵנִי וַיֹּאמֶר לִי (Pr. 4:4), and the introductory formulae in each section in "The Blessing of Moses" (Deut. 33:7, 8, 12; so also TS).

The Vav at the beginning of the verse is not connective, but adversative: "But to man He has said."

The Divine epithet אֲדֹנָי occurs only here in Job. The 100 mss. that read *yir'at JHVH* are levelling the text to the more usual form of the phrase (Isa. 11:33; 33:6; Pr. 10:27; 14:26, 27; II Chr. 19:9, etc.). The latter phrase may have already been pronounced *yir'at adonai* in the Second Temple period when Job was written, in view of the antiquity of the *Qere perpetuum*, אֲדֹנָי

for JHVH, which was already operative in the LXX *Kyrios* (cf. *BTM*, pp. 29 f.). Note also יִרְאַת שַׁדַּי in 6:14 and יִרְאַת אֱלֹהִים in Gen. 20:11; II Sam. 23:3; Neh. 5:15.

Basic to the meaning and relevance of the verse is the distinction between הַחָכְמָה (vv. 12, 20), which is the theme of the bulk of the poem, and חָכְמָה without the definite article in v. 28. *Hahokmah*, Wisdom par excellence, is denied to man. All that is given to man is *Hokmah*, the lower, practical Wisdom which consists of "the fear of God," i.e. religion, and "turning aside from evil," i.e. morality. D-G overlooks the presence or absence of the article and then questions whether a writer would handle the first theme so elaborately and the other so briefly (D-G, I, p. 245). It is precisely here that the poet reveals his artistry — the main theme is delivered at length and then comes the contrast, brief and overwhelming. A much older Hebrew poet reveals the same literary trait. In "The Song of Deborah" (Judges, chap. 5), the poet describes the ignominious death of Sisera (vv. 26–27). It is followed by an extended picture of his mother and her attendants anticipating his victorious, booty-laden return (11 stichs in vv. 28–30). Then comes the crashing conclusion in a single stich: "Thus perish all your enemies, O Lord!" (31a).

The idea that only religion and morality are revealed to man is quite sufficient for the conventional Wisdom teachers, who warn their charges against seeking to penetrate beyond. On the other hand, the unconventional Wisdom writers, notably Koheleth and Agur ben Yakeh (Pr. 30:1 ff.), are unable to make peace with the impassable limits placed upon man's understanding of the universe and they constantly lament man's ignorance (*KMW*, chap. 10, and *PPS*, chap. 14).

In chap. 28, the poet contents himself with setting forth the contrast between God's Wisdom and the limited wisdom available to man. This Hymn, which may originate from an earlier period in the poet's career, does not go beyond registering the fact; the implications are not drawn until later in the poet's life when he composes the God-speeches. In these final chapters that constitute the climax of the book, the author of Job parts company with Koheleth. He not only underscores man's ignorance of the Divine order, but expresses his joy at the perception of the world's beauty. This existential experience of the pattern of the natural order serves as the basis of his faith in the rationality and meaning of the moral order. This implication, derived by analogy, is not an exercise in logic; it is the unanswerable result of a deep emotional experience.

Our verse is the perfect parallel to the Prophets' proclamation of man's role in the world, as set forth in Mic. 6:8: "He has told you, O man, what is good and what the Lord God requires of you, to do justice, to love mercy and to walk humbly with your God." For the Wisdom teacher the Divine imperative is phrased differently:

> But to man He has said,
> "To be in awe of the Lord — that is wisdom,
> and to avoid evil — that is understanding."

Special Note 25 — Job's Closing Soliloquy — Part I (Chapter 29)

Chapter 29, the first in Job's closing soliloquy, falls into five sections: (1) the description of God's favor in the past = A (vv. 2–6); (2) the deference shown him by all in the city gate = B (vv. 7–10); (3) his defense of the weak against the powerful evil-doers and his aid to the needy = C (vv. 11–17); (4) his expectation that he would therefore live happily to a ripe old age = D (vv. 18–20); (5) again, the extraordinary honor shown him by all = B (vv. 21–25).

Some commentators place section E (vv. 21–25) immediately after section B (vv. 7–10), thus uniting the two passages that describe the boundless respect Job had received from his contemporaries (Bu., Be., Du., P.). TS, conscious of some of the difficulties in this procedure to be noted below, transposes vv. 7–10 after v. 20, but this creates other problems in the sequence.

Such rearrangements may satisfy our Western canons of relevance but do not reckon with the spirit of Semitic poetry, for which musical composition offers a more helpful analogy in the use of a theme and variations. The basic theme in chap. 29 is the public honor that Job received from young and old during the days of his affluence and influence. The variations are the lesser themes of God's favor and Job's high-minded ethical conduct. He returns to his basic theme (section 5), in which he compares his former position of honor to that of a king or the leader of a camel-train, which is eminently in place. It serves as a powerful antithesis to 20:1: "But now, they deride me, men younger than I, whose fathers I would have disdained to set with the dugs of my flock." The structure may be summarized as A, B, C, D, B.

The same theme-and-variations structure appears in chap. 30, which describes the misery of Job's present condition. It, too, falls into five sections: (1) a bitter description of the contempt he experiences from the dregs of society = A (vv. 1–14); (2) his picture of the pain and anguish he suffers = B (vv. 15–17); (3) the charge that God's cruelty and hatred are the root of Job's agony = C (vv. 18–23); (4) by contrast, Job declares that he has always been concerned for the poor and the unfortunate = D (vv. 24–26), a theme which becomes basic in chap. 31, the climax in his last Speech; and (5) a description of his misery = B (vv. 27–31). The pattern here, too, is A, B, C, D, B.

A similar situation of a recurrent theme prevails in Job's opening soliloquy (chap. 3). Here he expresses a desire for death, not in one consistent passage, but in two (3:10 ff. and 3:20 ff.).

Special Note 26 — Job's Closing Soliloquy — Part II (Chapter 30)

The tragedy of Job's condition is deepened by the contempt visited upon him by the most contemptible elements in society. He despises his former inferiors, both for their abject poverty (vv. 3–7) and for their low ancestry (v. 8). Thus he clearly reflects the upper-class bias of Wisdom literature in general, on which see "The Social Background of Wisdom Literature" (*PPS*, chap. 6).

As has been noted in Special Note 25 on chap. 29, the structure exhibits the use of a basic "theme and variations." The basic theme is the description of the agony and contumely which Job is now experiencing. The idea is introduced three times by *ve^cattah* (vv. 1, 9, 16). In v. 1, it clearly has the meaning "but now" standing in direct contrast to 29:25. In v. 9 it may be rendered "but now" or "and now." In v. 16 the meaning "and now" is preferable. However, the repetition of the same vocable in the Hebrew passage, though the nuances may differ, gives the passage great power and vividness. On this stylistic usage, see Special Note 27 on Chapter 31, where *^ɔim* is used similarly, and cf. the use of *māh* in Gen. 44:16 and Lam. 2:13.

The ideas that serve as variations on the principal themes are clear from a summary of the contents of the chapter. After stressing the ignoble background of his scorners (v. 1), Job describes their destitution (vv. 2–7), and then reverts to the first theme in v. 8. In vv. 9–16, Job uses various similes to picture their former respect for him. In vv. 17–23, Job depicts his misery and charges God with cruelty against him. In the extraordinarily difficult v. 24 (see the Comm.) and v. 25, Job seems to reiterate his sympathy for those in distress. He closes his reflections by describing once again the bleakness of his present condition (vv. 26–31).

The mistaken effort to apply Western canons of relevancy has led some commentators to delete the intervening section in whole or in part (vv. 1–8, Du., D-G; vv. 3–7, Bi.; vv. 2–8, Peake).

In addition, a substantive argument has been advanced in favor of the omission of the opening section (vv. 1–8) which expresses contempt for the lowly. This attitude, it is maintained, is in contrast with the noble affirmation by Job in 31:15 of the basic humanity and equality uniting him and his slaves. However, the two contradictory positions are thoroughly understandable psychologically. A master may feel sympathy and even affection for his slave and recognize that they are both equally human, and yet vigorously maintain the sense of class distinctions. Had men applied in life the ethical consequences of their faith in the fatherhood of God and the brotherhood of man, human slavery could not have persisted in Jewish, Christian and Muslim society for many centuries. Yet the record of history is tragically clear — pious believers maintained serfdom in Russia and human slavery in America for nineteen centuries after the rise of Christianity, and the institution is not yet extinct in the Muslim world even today.

It is a fact of human nature that men may honestly maintain convictions that they do not embody in their actions. A striking example of this melancholy truth is afforded by Thomas Jefferson, the famous American patriot, who was a slave-holder in Virginia all his life, though to be sure a humane and considerate master. Yet he was the author of the *Declaration of Independence*, with its ringing affirmation of the equality of all men and their inalienable right to life, liberty, and the pursuit of happiness.

Special Note 27 — Job's Code of Conduct (Chapter 31)

A. *Contents*

This Code of A Man of Honor is the noblest presentation of individual ethics in the pages of the Bible. It lists fourteen sins, from which, Job insists, he has been free:

    (1) lust (vv. 1, 2)
    (2) cheating in business (vv. 5, 6)
    (3) taking the property of others (vv. 7, 8)
    (4) adultery (vv. 9–12)
    (5) unfairness toward slaves in the courts (vv. 13–15)
    (6) callousness toward the resident poor (vv. 16–18)
    (7) lack of pity for the wayfarer (vv. 19, 20)
    (8) perversion of the just claims of the widow and the orphan (vv. 21–23)
    (9) love of gold and confidence in wealth (vv. 24–25)
   (10) the worship of the sun and the moon (vv. 26–28)
   (11) joy in the calamity of his foes (vv. 29–31)
   (12) failure to practice hospitality (v. 32)
   (13) concealing his sins because of the fear of public opinion (vv. 33, 34)
   (14) the expropriation of land of others within the letter of the law (vv. 38–40)

This catalogue of offenses is important for what it omits as well as for what it includes. Palpable crimes punishable by law like murder or theft are not even contemplated. Only adultery, which can be carried on clandestinely, is included. By and large, these are sins of the spirit committed "within the law." Generally, biblical legislation is concerned primarily with actions, which alone are subject to juridical sanctions. On the other hand, the ethics of Job, like important sections of the Holiness Code in Leviticus (19:14–18) and the Fifth and the Tenth Commandments in the Decalogue (Ex. 20:12, 17; Deut. 5:16, 18, 19), deal with inner attitudes, with sins of thought and feeling. Such are the offenses of unchastity in thought, the arrogance of wealth, joy at the discomfiture of one's enemies or the abject fear of the tyranny of mob opinion. In rabbinic thought such subtler offenses are described by several significant terms, such as דברים המסורים ללב, "matters entrusted to the heart"; פטור אבל אסור "exempt but forbidden"; פטור בדיני אדם וחייב בדיני שמים "exempt by human law but guilty by the laws of heaven." In sum, the sins listed are not the crimes of the lawbreaker; at most they are the offenses of the lawbender.

As has been noted in the Intr. to the Translation, the sins listed are all ethical, the only ritual element being the worship of heavenly bodies. Such an act is tantamount to the denial of the living God, which leads to the surrender of the ethical law emanating from Him. Similarly, the Seven

Noahide Laws which, according to rabbinic thought, are binding upon all human beings, are basically ethical. They include the prohibition of murder, of sexual immorality, of theft, of the eating of the limb of a living animal, and the positive injunction to establish a system of law and order. They also include the prohibitions of idolatry and blasphemy. (For the relationship of the Noahide Laws to the concept of natural law, see Gordis, *The Root and The Branch*, chap. 13.) The absence of ritual prohibitions here is in complete conformity with the universalistic concern of Wisdom literature in general and of the Book of Job in particular, concerned as it is with the broadly human issue of man's destiny in God's world.

B. *Structure*

There are three noteworthy literary usages in the chapter that are the key to the understanding of its contents:

I. The list of fourteen sins is not fortuitous, fourteen being a double heptad. This use of seven and its multiples — not the explicit listing of seven items, be it noted — as an organizing principle in literary compositions occurs several times in Koheleth (e.g. 7:1–14, *tobh*; 3:1–10, "the Catalogue of the Seasons," 14 distichs). It is very popular with Amos ("The Arraignment of Seven Nations," chaps. 1–2; 3:3–7; 4:6–13, etc.). Similarly, the Mishnah utilizes not only seven, but also its multiples as e.g., *Sanh.* 7:4, listing 14 categories punishable by stoning, and *M. Abot* 5:21 on "the 14 ages of man," and *Baraita de Rabbi Meir* (*Abot* 6:7), where 14 qualities induced by the study of Torah are given. On the usage in biblical, rabbinic, and New Testament literature, cf. Gordis, "The Heptad As an Element of Biblical and Rabbinic Style," in *PPS*, pp. 95–103; for Ugaritic and classical parallels, see C. H. Gordon, "Vergil and The Bible World," in *Gratz College Anniversary Volume* (Philadelphia, 1971, pp. 127 f.).

Recognition of this literary usage has important implications for the criticism of the chapter. It militates against any procedure that would destroy the double heptadic structure, such as: (a) adding other verses here, like 30:25; (b) moving passages like 31:1 f. to chap. 30 (A. Kaminka, TS); or (c) transposing verses and "unifying them" (like placing vv. 38 ff. after v. 8); or (d) interpreting lengthy sections like vv. 31–34 as referring to one offense only (TS). Some of the various proposals may be studied in D-G, I, pp. 261 f.

II. Another basic rhetorical feature of this chapter is the occurrence 20 times of the particle *ʾim*. Several times it clearly introduces a particular offense followed by a penalty. It has, therefore, been assumed by most commentators that the entire chapter is to be interpreted as a series of oaths, and that each occurrence of the conjunction *ʾim* in the chapter must introduce the oath formula, "If I did thus and so . . . may this be my punishment." This schematic approach necessitates many deletions and transpositions of material (Yel., Du., Hö. and TS, among others).

This procedure does not commend itself for several reasons: (1) it requires many extensive changes in the text; (2) the apodosis or conclusion of the alleged condition actually occurs only four or five times and is lacking ten times; (3) it is hardly likely that a long chapter containing 40 verses would follow the same unvarying formula throughout, particularly in view of the great artistic gifts of the author. D-G (*loc. cit.*) summarizes some of the various attempts to place the chapter on the procrustean bed of a preconceived theory and correctly cautions: "It would be a great mistake to reduce all this variety to the monotonous repetition of a single scheme." But the implications of this just observation have not been kept in mind.

There is no objective basis for assuming that *ᵓim* throughout the chapter must always mean "if" (15 or 16 times without and four times with the imprecatory clause). Actually, the repetition of the same word in the Hebrew gives the passage great power, while the variety in meaning avoids monotony. Cf. *māh*, which occurs three times with two different meanings in Gen. 44:16: "*What* shall we say to my lord? *What* shall we speak? Or *how* shall we clear ourselves?" (AV), and in Lam. 2:13: "*How* shall I fortify you, *what* shall I liken unto you, O daughter of Jerusalem? *What* shall I compare unto you, and comfort you, O virgin daughter of Zion?" On this latter verse, cf. Gordis, in *JThS*, XXIV (1933), 1962–63.

An even more apposite parallel occurs in "the Parable of Jotham" (Jud. 9:8–20). Here the speaker uses אם three times with great effectiveness but with different meanings. In vv. 15 and 19, אם = "if," introducing the protasis of a dual condition, both positive and negative, and with the apodosis expressed. In v. 16, which occurs between the two other instances, there is no conclusion and אם is the sign of the question: "And now, have you acted in faithfulness and integrity?"

Similarly, in this long chapter, three different uses of *ᵓim* occur: (1) "if," in the protasis of an ordinary conditional sentence (v. 19); (2) "if," in a protasis where the apodosis constitutes the penalty for the sin contemplated. In these instances "the punishment fits the crime," in accordance with the doctrine of *middah k'neged middah*, "measure for measure," which underlies the tenet of *lex talionis*, universal in ancient law (vv. 7–8, 9–10, 21–22, 38–40); (3) = *haᵓim* (Latin *num*), the sign of a question expecting a negative reply and hence without an apodosis (vv. 5, 13, 16, 19, 24, 25, 26, 33). The interrogative *ᵓim lōᵓ* is equivalent to Latin *nonne*, the sign of a question expecting an affirmative answer (vv. 20, 31).

Unfortunately, the power of the repeated particle is largely lost in translation, since it must be rendered differently in different passages. Dh. (p. 411) recognizes the use of both meanings of *ᵓim* here. He renders it as the interrogative in vv. 5, 13, 16, 24, 25, 26, 33, and as "if" in vv. 7, 9, 19, 31, 38. Similarly, Hö. renders it as the interrogative in vv. 5, 13, 16, 19, 24, 25, 26, 33, and as "if" in vv. 2, 9, 21, 38. It is this diversity in form within the overarching unity of content which prevents this chapter from becoming (*pace* Hö., p. 77!) "almost tiresome (*fast ermüdend*), making the reader impatient (*bis zur Ungeduld*)."

III. Another literary usage characteristic of this chapter which has not been recognized is the use of "virtual quotations," the device by which Job presents the belief he formerly held in the justice of God, that served as the basis of his code of moral behavior. In this case, the motivation is expressed by a question introduced by *ūmāh*, "for what" followed by an affirmation *halō* (vv. 2–4 and 14–15). The identical use of *halō* is to be found in 22:12 (see the Comm. *ad loc.*) and, together with *ʾim*, occurs interrogatively in Ps. 44:21 f.:

וַנִּפְרֹשׂ כַּפֵּינוּ לְאֵל זָר   אִם־שָׁכַחְנוּ שֵׁם אֱלֹהֵינוּ

כִּי הוּא יֹדֵעַ תַּעֲלֻמוֹת לֵב   הֲלֹא אֱלֹהִים יַחֲקָר־זֹאת

The passage is to be rendered:

> "Did we forget the name of our God,
>   or spread out our hands to a strange god?
> Surely God would have searched this out,
>   for He knows the secrets of the heart."

On this passage and the reasons why the usual rendition of *ʾim* as "if" is unsatisfactory, see *PPS*, pp. 127 ff.

The failure to reckon with this usage, to which we called attention many years ago (in *JQR*, vol. 30, 1939, pp. 123–47, and in *HUCA*, vol. 22, 1949, pp. 157–219, now in *PPS*, chap. 5, p. 153, n. 64), has led to many deletions such as vv. 2–4, 11–12, 14–15, 23, 28, etc., which leaves the chapter littl more than a torso lacking flesh and blood.

Equally unnecessary and unjustified have been the efforts of scholars to rearrange the chapters on the ground of relevance. Thus vv. 38–40 (on which see below) are placed by different scholars at six different points in chapter 31: after v. 8, v. 12, v. 15, v. 25, v. 32, or v. 34. Such procedures impose Western standards of logical coherence that are alien to the Oriental poet. Hence the section on lusting after the maiden (vv. 1 f.) does not occur in immediate proximity with the section on adultery (vv. 9 ff.). The treatment of the poor widow and the orphan (vv. 16–21) is separated from the treatment of the stranger (v. 32). The same absence of Western coherence characterizes all the biblical law codes like the Book of the Covenant (Exodus, chaps. 21–23) and the Holiness Code (Leviticus, chaps. 19–22).

The only rearrangement in the chapter called for is to place vv. 38–40b after v. 34, thus uniting the last offense with the rest of the catalogue of sins and placing the peroration (vv. 35–37) at the end of the chapter. Evidently, a scribe omitted vv. 38–40b by accident and they were added at the end of the chapter. There are other instances where the same scribal error occurred and the same procedure for rectifying it was adopted. Thus Isa. 38:21 f. belongs after v. 6, as is evident from the parallel passage in II Ki. 20:6. Once having been omitted, the verses were placed at the end of the chapter in Isaiah. In Hosea, the passage 2:1–3 in its present position clearly disturbs the context. It belongs at the end of chap. 2, but was erroneously added after chap. 1.

C. Parallels in Oriental Literature

Job's profession of integrity has analogues in other Oriental literature. In the Egyptian "Book of the Dead," which is a catalogue of mortuary texts, the deceased affirms his virtue before Osiris and forty-two judges. Before he may enter the Hall of Truth where his heart will be weighed in the scales, he must declare his freedom from sins in this "Protestation of Guiltlessness" (Wilson, in *ANET*, pp. 34 ff.). The deceased lists thirty-six offenses of which he has not been guilty, as, e.g., "I have not mistreated cattle," "I have not blasphemed the gods," "I have not killed." This text differs from Job both in form and in content: (a) It is set forth in negative declarations, not in the form of oaths or rhetorical questions; (b) it includes general affirmations of probity; (c) it lists crass offenses like murder, lacking in Job; and (d) it deals with ritual infractions very frequently (A 3, 7, 8, 17, 18, 19, 29, 30, 34, 35, 36).

In Akkadian, the "Incantation Texts" pronounced by the priest on behalf of the sufferer contain protestations of innocence (cf. Morris Jastrow, *The Religion of Babylonia and Assyria*, pp. 271–91, 307 f.). Here, too, ritual elements play a very significant role. Stylistically they are couched in question form, "Has he offended his god?", thus offering support for the view that our chapter contains bona fide questions and not merely oath-formulas.

It should not be necessary to point out that Job's personal circumstances presupposed in his "Code of Honor" differ from the situation in which he is found at the end of the narrative (chap. 2). Thus he refers to children (v. 8; see the Comm.), as he does in 19:17. He possesses fields (vv. 37 ff.). In general, the chapter gives the impression of a man enjoying power and prosperity in the present. In part, this may be due to the poet's utilizing fixed literary or legal formulae. Basically, however, the poet is not troubled with harmonizing every detail of the Dialogue with the older prose-tale that he has utilized and reworked (cf. *BGM*, chap. 6).

The fervor and moral passion of Job's confession and the richly textured literary structure in which his thoughts are couched make this chapter one of the great literary utterances in the Bible and without.

Special Note 28 — The Elihu Speeches — Their Authenticity and Content (Chapters 32–37)

These chapters have been regarded by many scholars as interpolations by a later, orthodox theologian. A detailed discussion of the critical issues involved is presented in *BGM*, chap. IX, "Elihu the Intruder," and in the Intr. to the present translation of these chapters. In essence, the objections that have been raised to the authenticity of these chapters have been based on considerations of style, content, and structure. Unfortunately, the defense of the Elihu speeches was generally presented in extreme form and, therefore, appeared unconvincing to many scholars.

A. Style

One general observation regarding the state of the text should be made.

It is undeniable that the Elihu chapters in MT contain a relatively large number of difficult, even cryptic, passages. A plausible explanation is available. There is excellent ground for postulating that the central portion of the manuscript of Job suffered major accidental damage early in its history. This injury took place after the entire book was complete, but before the Greek version (and probably the Qumran Fragment Targum) came into existence, since it reproduces our present sequence and basic text. As a result of the damage and disarray there occurred the loss of some material in the Third Cycle (see Special Notes 19, 20, 22). The same cause explains also the misplacing of a passage like 31:35–37, and the inclusion of the originally independent "Hymn to Wisdom" (chapter 28) in the book (Special Note 23). Finally, some verses became illegible or unintelligible and were consequently subjected to miscopying and changes as well, as in chap. 24 (see Special Note 19). It is clear that these accidents of transmission definitely affected the content of (the Third Cycle) chaps. 24–31; they probably extended to the Elihu speeches (chaps. 32–37) as well. This single assumption, that the text of chaps. 24–37 was damaged, would explain the presence of difficult passages in the Elihu speeches, that had become illegible and suffered errors in transmission.

Budde, who maintained the authenticity of the Elihu speeches, insisted that the style is identical with that of the rest of the book. This is overstating the case. Actually, the linguistic traits differ from the rest of the book, but only in degree, that is to say, the same phenomena occur, but in somewhat differing proportions. As will be indicated below, we believe that these stylistic variations in the Elihu speeches reflect changes in the style of the original author of the Dialogue, brought on by the passage of time. The basic facts are as follows:

With regard to the Divine names, Elihu uses *ʾEl* nineteen times, *ʾEloah* six times, *Šaddai* six times. In the rest of the book, *ʾEl* appears thirty-six times, *ʾEloah* thirty-five times, and *Šaddai* twenty-five times. For the first person singular pronoun, in the dialogue *ʾǎnî* occurs fifteen times, *ʾǎnōkhi* eleven times. In Elihu they occur respectively nine and twelve times. In the prose prologue, *ʾǎnî* occurs four times, *ʾǎnōkhi* not at all. The poetic or archaic (or archaizing) forms of the prepositions also exhibit variations. The prepositional forms with *yōdh*, *ᶜǎlei* (for *ᶜal*, "on"), *ᶜǎdei* (for *ᶜad*, "toward"), *ʾǎlei* (for *ʾel*, "to") occur only twice in Elihu, nineteen times in the poetic dialogue, thirty five times elsewhere in the Old Testament. A difference is also apparent in the enclitics. Elihu does not use the enclitics *bᵉmō*, *kᵉmō*, *lᵉmō*, or such other poetic forms as *minnî*, *bᵉlî*, *ᶜǎlēmō*. They occur eighteen times in the poetic dialogue.

However, Snaith has analyzed the pairing of Divine names in Elihu and the rest of Job and "found nothing to indicate diverse authorship" (*op. cit.*, p. 81). As he has noted, in evaluating the differences between Elihu and the rest of the book, it is important to reckon with their respective use of the *normal* forms of prepositions. His analysis demonstrates that the ratio of these special usages to the usual forms is not very different in Elihu (*op. cit.*, pp. 75 ff.; cf. esp. p. 76, n. 17).

It has been widely maintained that the Elihu chapters exhibit a much higher frequency of Aramaisms, thus demonstrating a different authorship (cf. D-G, I, pp. XLVI–XLVII). It should be noted that the list of Aramaisms in Job cited by E. Kautzsch (*Die Aramaismen im alten Testament*, Halle, 1902, p. 101) was severely criticized by Th. Noeldeke in his review in *ZDMG*, vol. LVII (1907), 412–20. A. Guillaume ("The Unity of the Book of Job," in *The Annual of the Leeds University Oriental Society*, vol. 4, 1964, p. 27), who maintains the theory of an Arabic original, holds that there is only one Aramaism in Job and none in the Elihu speeches.

We have pointed out (in *BGM*, p. 334, n. 14, and in "On Methodology in Biblical Exegesis," *JQR*, vol. 61, 1970, pp. 105–108) that it is important to recognize different categories of "Aramaisms." Thus the first type of alleged instances of Aramaisms are really words indigenous to Northwest Semitic but more common in Aramaic and usually rare or poetic in Hebrew. Snaith discusses all alleged Aramaisms (*op. cit.*, pp. 104–112) and adopts the principle that if a root is found in any other Semitic language, the word cannot legitimately be called an Aramaism. Operating with this theory, he eliminates nearly all proposed instances. This view seems to be far too sweeping. One cannot escape the distinct impression of an Aramaic coloration in Job as a whole and in Elihu in particular, as in 36:2a (see the Comm. *ad loc.* and *passim*, e.g. 16:19).

In sum, the evidence indicates that the linguistic usage of the Elihu chapters is not identical with that of the rest of the book, as Budde believed, nor is it so totally different as to demand the assumption of a different author, as most modern scholars have held.

The Elihu speeches possess one noteworthy stylistic trait which, critics were wont to declare, is to be found only in these chapters and thus constitutes an argument against their authenticity — Elihu's practice of quoting his opponents' views for the purpose of refuting them. Thus, Hö. declares that "Job and his Friends did not concern themselves overmuch with countering the statements of their predecessors" (p. 77). We have repeatedly demonstrated that the use of quotations is a basic characteristic throughout the Dialogue (see the Comm. on chaps. 12, 21, 24, 27 for major instances of this usage, as well as 13:14; 17:5). Thus, this practice of Elihu, far from negating the unity of authorship, offers impressive evidence in its favor. Elihu cites the words of Job either directly (33:11 from 13:27), or obliquely, in irony (33:7 from 9:34), or in restructured form (33:20 from 6:7; see the Comm.).

As for the injection of Job's name, Elihu is a younger man and an interloper to boot. He is worried as to whether he will gain and hold Job's attention and, therefore, addresses him by name (32:12; 33:1, 31; 34:5, 7, 35, 37; 35:16; 37:14).

It is quite likely that the poet was occupied with the composition of Job throughout his lifetime. That his style would undergo change during so extended a period is entirely to be expected and several analogies from the history of literature are available.

Goethe's *Faust* is undoubtedly the most apposite parallel, both with regard to the length of the period of composition and the consequent far-reaching changes in style and content. The *Urfaust* goes back to the poet's *Sturm und Drang* period, the third decade of his life; the first part of *Faust* did not appear until more than thirty years later, in 1808; and the second part was completed shortly before his death in 1832. In the sixty-year gestation period of the work, Goethe's conception of his theme and of the characters, as well as his poetic style and vocabulary, underwent a profound transformation. Every reader notices at once the change from the epigrammatic style of Part I to the involved, complicated mode of expression characteristic of Part II. The radical differences in subject matter are summarized by J. G. Robertson in these words: "The Second Part is far removed from the impressive realism of the *Urfaust* or even the classicism of the First Part. It is a phantasmagory; a drama, the actors in which are not creatures of flesh and blood but shadows in an unreal world of allegory. The lover of Gretchen had, as far as poetic continuity is concerned, disappeared with the close of the first part. In the second part, it is virtually a new Faust who, accompanied by a new Mephistopheles, goes out into a world that is not ours" (*Encyclopedia Britannica*, 14 ed., vol. X, p. 473b).

In fact, the two parts of Faust reveal a radical difference in conception and in style far more extensive than the stylistic variations between Elihu and the rest of Job. Not only are there relatively more obscure verses in Elihu than in the other sections of the book, but the poetry in general is more opaque and less fluid. Here, again, Goethe's *Faust* is instructive. Part I is written in clear, concrete, gnomic, almost epigrammatic style; Part II is involved, abstract and metaphysical.

Another literary parallel from an ancient work, even more germane to our thesis, is afforded by the Latin poet, Ovid. A classical scholar writes: "Ovid's *Heroides* (as they are commonly known; the original title was probably *Epistolae Heroidum*) are a corpus of 21 letters, the first fifteen being letters from mythological heroines to their lovers (e.g. Penelope to Ulysses, Medea to Jason), the last six being three pairs of letters (Paris to Helen, Helen to Paris, and two other pairs). The manuscript tradition always presents the last six as part of the same work as the first set. Since the middle of the nineteenth century it was rather common doctrine that the last six were not by Ovid. The argument rested on: (1) the character of these being different from the first set (since these are paired letters); (2) there are some metrical usages which are unusual (and without parallel in the first 15); (3) there are some peculiarities of style.

"It is now generally accepted that the last six letters are genuine. Ovid first wrote the *Heroides* as a corpus of fifteen letters, then, some years later (there are scholars who think many years later, others think just a few) he wrote the additional six and probably tacked them to a second edition of the work. Whatever metrical and stylistic differences there are may be explained by the fact that the last six were written at a later date than the first fifteen. I hasten to add that there still are reputable scholars who believe the last six spurious, though they are in a very small minority." (Private communication by Professor Howard Jacobson, University of Illinois, Urbana, Illinois, dated June 15, 1972.)

The same classical scholar points out that the old position that the letters are not Ovid's is presented by A. Palmer in his edition of the *Heroides* (Oxford, 1898), but that the Hildesheim, 1967, reprint-edition contains an introduction by L. Purser (pp. xxxi–xxxii) presenting the contrary view that the differences in style merely reflect different times of composition. The current position which regards the last six as being authentic is presented also in B. Latta, *Die Stellung der Doppelbriefe (Heroides 16–21) im Gesamtwerk Ovids* (Diss. Marburg, 1963); W. Kraus, "Die Briefpaare in Ovids Heroiden," *Wiener Studien* 65 (1950–51), 54–77. The older contrary view is maintained in E. Courtney, "Ovidian and Non-Ovidian Heroides," *Bulletin of the Institute of Classical Studies, Univ. of London* 12 (1965), 63–66.

Ovid and Goethe are by no means the only instances where writers develop far-reaching changes in theme, approach, or style with advancing years, thus setting their later works apart from their earlier writings. Shakespeare's *Tempest*, perhaps the last of his plays, differs sharply from his earlier dramas in spirit and mood. The later poems of W. B. Yeats are radically different in theme and style from his earlier lyrics. James Joyce's *Finnegan's Wake* is totally unlike his earlier novels, such as *Dubliners* or *Ulysses*.

The same phenomenon is encountered in other arts as well. In 1908, Igor Stravinsky began work on his first opera, *Le Rossignol*. "After the first act was completed, Stravinsky was interrupted by several commissions that led to the composition of *The Firebird*, *Petrouchka* and *The Rites of Spring*. Hence, when he continued work on the opera in 1913 he had undergone radical development, so that there is a stylistic break between the first act and the remaining two" (James Conlon, "Juilliard School Program Notes," May 25, 1973).

B. *Content*

With regard to the *content* of the Elihu section, the absence of any reference to the youthful interloper elsewhere in the narrative or in the poetry is entirely explicable by the fact that he is a youthful interloper whose vigorous onslaught on his elders — and betters — is both unexpected and unwelcome. Moreover, if, as we have suggested (*BGM*, chap. IX), the Elihu chapters were added later, the poet, in true Semitic fashion, would not tamper with the contents of the rest of the book merely to bring the new material into complete harmony with it.

As for the contention that Elihu adds nothing significant to the discussion, if this were true, why should a writer take the trouble to compose these chapters and interpolate them? Actually, Elihu contributes a very significant idea — that suffering often acts as a discipline, or, in biblical language, that God sends suffering as a warning in order to safeguard man against sin.

This basic idea does not exhaust Elihu's significance as a thinker. He adds a few insights, which, though admittedly subsidiary, are nonetheless important. Elihu emphasizes that it is not for man to decide when and how God's retribution is to become manifest. Two considerations militate against accusing God of injustice. Man is incapable of either injuring or benefitting his Maker (35:6–8), so that God cannot be motivated by partiality. Moreover, in creating and governing the world, God testifies to His love for His creatures (34:14 f.; 36:24 ff., 31; 37:13, 23). Hence, Divine judgment on the wicked is sure to come (34:17 ff., 27 ff.; 36:5 ff., 32 ff.).

Elihu also suggests three additional reasons for the postponement of retribution.

The punishment of tyrants may be delayed at times because the suffering they visit upon their victims may serve as God's instrument for the chastisement of evil-doers (34:29 f.; see the Comm.). In one sense, Isaiah's doctrine of the arrogant Assyrian conqueror serving as "the rod of God's anger" (Isa. 10:5–15) is here transposed to the level of the individual. On another level, the implication is clear that the submerged and suffering masses are not *ipso facto* paragons of virtue and may well be sinners in their own right. This insight is, of course, congenial to a Wisdom teacher speaking from the vantage-point of the upper classes. Nevertheless, it is a truth which, though often overlooked, is demonstrated almost daily in the individual tensions and group confrontations of contemporary life.

Nor is this all. God may hold off the punishment of the wicked rulers because he hopes for their repentance. They, too, are human and worthy of Divine compassion.

Moreover, when God does not seem to respond immediately to the cry of the oppressed, another factor may play its part. All too often those who call to Him are moved by physical pain rather than by a spiritual hunger for God (35:9–12). To use a modern phrase that is already obsolete in our age of missiles and airplane bombs, Elihu would maintain that "foxhole religion" is not enough.

Finally, Job's condemnation of God's conduct is tantamount to man's usurping God's role as Ruler and Judge of the world. Thus, in a deeper sense, Job is a rebel against his Maker (34:36 f.).

Contentions such as these are incapable of justifying "the prosperity of the wicked and the suffering of the righteous." But to the extent that they are true, they reduce the dimensions of the problem of evil.

In defending the authenticity of these chapters, Budde had again overstated the case. He had argued that Elihu's basic idea of suffering as a discipline was adumbrated nowhere else. As a matter of fact, however, the idea of suffering as a moral discipline is set forth by Eliphaz in one passage, 5:17, but very briefly, and in two verses in Pr. 3:11 f., but it was not elaborated upon by conventional Wisdom theology. Moreover, neither of these passages contemplates the possibility of suffering as a prophylactic against *future sin*.

Budde also maintained that the idea of suffering as a discipline constitutes the author's main answer to the problem of suffering. This view we find unacceptable on several grounds. The author of Job was too clear-sighted a thinker and observer of life to regard this idea as an all-sufficient explanation of the monstrous burden of evil in the world. Moreover, had this been his view, he would not have appended the God Speeches which would then appear as an anticlimax. The poet believes in the truth of Elihu's doctrine, but he does not accord it the position of primacy in his thought. Instead, he falls back upon a striking architectonic device. Since the idea of suffering as a discipline and warning contradicts the Friends' unwavering conventional theory that all suffering is the penalty for sins committed, the poet cannot attribute this insight to them. The thought also would undermine Job's insistence that he is innocent and that God is unjust, and, therefore, this new idea cannot be placed in his mouth. Hence the author creates a new character distinct from the other protagonists, whose opposition to the Friends is as vigorous as his condemnation of Job (32:2, and passim).

Elihu is the only character who bears a Hebrew name, the meaning of which is highly significant. It is identical with that of the Prophet Elijah ("Jah is my God"), who is regarded as the forerunner of God, the herald announcing His kingdom in the O. T., the N. T. and rabbinic literature. In the Book of Job, Elihu similarly precedes "the Lord speaking out of the whirlwind." Elihu's elaborate pedigree (32:5) would suggest to Hebrew readers, accustomed to etymologizing names, that as a scion of a distinguished family (Ram) he was the authentic defender of God's cause, "Elihu = JHVH is my God" who exalted Him (Barakhel) and heaped scorn (Buz) upon God's ineffective advocates (cf. *BGM*, pp. 115 f.).

The ideational background for the Elihu Speeches is to be found in Deutero-Isaiah. The great Prophet of the Exile was the first Hebrew Prophet to suggest that a people might suffer humiliation and misery, not because of its sinfulness, but because in God's plan it was a witness, a messenger, a servant of God, and a teacher of mankind (cf. Isa. 40:2; 40:27 ff., the "Songs of the Suffering Servant of the Lord," 42:1–4; 49:1–6; 50:4–9; especially 52:13–53:12, and see *BGM*, pp. 112 f., pp. 144 ff.). Through this iconoclastic idea, Deutero-Isaiah broke with the conventional Hebrew doctrine of suffering as the invariable concomitant of sin, by maintaining that suffering might be undeserved and yet not be unjust. This insight the prophet applied to the life of nations; our poet transfers it to the life of the individual. The Elihu Speeches thus occupy a special niche in the architecture of the book distinct from Job and the Friends. See the Intr. to the Translation.

C. *Structure.*

In MT, Elihu's words are divided into four speeches, three with an introductory caption, "And Elihu spoke out" (32:6–33:33; 34:2–27; 35:2–16), and the fourth, the long, final speech with the caption "and Elihu continued to speak" (36:2–37:24). Though such formulae are inserted elsewhere in the Greek (at 32:17) and in the *Hexapla* (at 34:16), the Masoretic division of Elihu's words into four speeches is sound. Thus 33:33 obviously marks the end of a speech, while 35:2 and 36:2 clearly introduce new addresses.

The material in Elihu's speeches is well-structured. After his long apology, the truculence of which does not hide his sense of embarrassment for daring to speak out at all in the presence of his elders, Elihu turns to the issue of Job's suffering. He begins by citing Job's three main contentions: (1) that he is innocent (33:8, 9); (2) that God's persecution is therefore an act of wanton power and injustice (33:10–11); and (3) that God has ignored his suffering by refusing to answer him (33:12–13).

In accordance with Semitic usage, Elihu proceeds to answer these arguments in reverse order. In chap. 33, the most important and extensive speech by Elihu, he rebuts Job's last charge that God has ignored his suffering. Elihu notes that God speaks to man in many ways, such as visions and dreams. If these fail, God may use pain and illness as His instruments. In chap. 34, Elihu rejects Job's claim that God is unjust. On the contrary, God plays no favorites, owing no obligation to any man, and He is, therefore, free to destroy the wicked. In chap. 35, Elihu obliquely attacks Job's claim to innocence by pointing out that God is too exalted to be affected by men's actions, either for good or for ill. It is men themselves who are the victims of their fellow-men's sinful actions.

Elihu's last speech recapitulates his views on suffering as a Divine warning, the possibility of restoration open to man, and the certainty of retribution for wickedness.

Actually, the climax of the book is reached in the God-Speeches, where the poet's major insight is expressed — there is a moral order, paralleling the natural order of the cosmos which is beyond man's total comprehension, yet possessing a pattern and meaning of its own. Though suffering remains in large measure a mystery to man, he may legitimately believe that it possesses a significance and function in the world, like all those aspects of nature that he has not — or not yet — fathomed.

The idea of suffering as a discipline presented by Elihu is definitely of lesser scope than this major affirmation of faith in life set forth in the God-Speeches, but it is valid nonetheless. It may well have been the distillation of the poet's personal experience, an insight at which he arrived after many years of observation of life. He, therefore, incorporates these chapters into the book without modifying the architecture of the book as a whole. Their inclusion, however, definitely enriches the treatment of the perennial issue with which men have wrestled over the centuries, and never more agonizingly than in the era of the Nazi holocaust and its aftermath.

Special Note 29 — Elihu's Apology (Chapter 32)

Critics have found the structure of this chapter unsatisfactory because of the absence of coherence and organization, and have therefore transposed or deleted various portions. Bu. deletes 11–12, 15–17, and reorders the remainder as 6–9, 13, 14, 10, 18–22. Du. omits 10 and then reads, 9, 15–17, 11a, b, 12a, 11c, 12b, c, 13, 14, 18. D-G places 11–16 after 7 and deletes 17 as a variant of 10. Hö. deletes only v. 10 and places vv. 15–17 before 11.

It is true that after describing how he had waited for the older men to speak (vv. 6, 7), Elihu concludes that age is no guarantor of wisdom (vv. 8, 9). He therefore decides to speak out (v. 10), repeats his description of his impatience at their failure to refute Job (vv. 11, 12) and their relapsing into silence (vv. 15, 16), and reiterates his determination to speak (v. 17).

Once again the poet employs the device of "theme and variations" which has been noted in chaps. 29 and 30 (see Special Notes 25 and 26). His basic theme is the irrepressible urge to speak out. In returning to this idea, Elihu adds two new motifs — he will not accept the excuse that refuting Job is beyond human capacity (vv. 13, 14), and he paints a vivid picture of his physical distress which makes it impossible for him to remain silent (vv. 17–20). Elihu concludes by serving notice that no man, neither Job nor the Friends, can expect flattery or tactful consideration at his hand.

If a contemporary reference may be forgiven, Elihu, in his love for "plain talk" vis-à-vis his elders, is a precursor of the "below thirty" generation in our day! Exactly like them, his truculence is in part a mask for his embarrassment and insecurity in the presence of his elders.

Special Note 30 — The Metric Form and Content of Chapter 34

This chapter has been regarded by many critics as an interpolation, in whole or in part. The alleged grounds are: (a) the difference in metric pattern; and (b) the inappropriateness of the contents. Upon examination, neither contention proves convincing. The presence of distichs, as well as tristichs, in the poem is no proof against the authenticity of either. The effort to place the chapter on the procrustean bed of an exclusive tristich pattern (Me., Du.) and then delete the chapter as inauthentic is arbitrary in the extreme.

Variation in meter is an important resource of the poet. Basically, MT consists of 30 distichs with six tristichs in vv. 10, 19, 20, 29, 33, 27. The elimination of the tristichs in vv. 19–20 creates more problems than it solves (cf. D-G, II, pp. 257 ff.). In v. 10, the first stich is an anacrusis, outside the meter pattern. V. 33 all but defies interpretation and cannot be legitimately utilized for any view. In v. 29, the final stich is to be attached to v. 30 and the resulting tristich in v. 30 marks the close of the section. In v. 37, the tristich brings the entire speech to a powerful and resonant conclusion. On the relevant metrical principles involved, see Special Note 1, sec. 7, 9, 10, 12 and 21.

The predominant meter in the chapter is 3:3, but the Qinah rhythm, with its variations (cf. *PPS*, p. 68), occurs: the 4:3 meter in vv. 8, 27, 28, 32, 36; 3:2 in vv. 10, 18, 26; and 4:3:3 in v. 20. The 4:4 meter probably occurs in vv. 22, 23, 29; and 2:2 in v. 31. The legitimacy of varying meter patterns in one composition has been demonstrated time and again in this work.

The methodological error of emending and deleting the text on the basis of metric theories is compounded by the argument that the contents are unsuitable, especially in a text which is, at many points, incomprehensible.

However uncertain the interpretation of this chapter is at many points, it is clear that it contributes significantly to Elihu's rebuttal of Job's insistence that God's government is unjust. Elihu points out that God's creation testifies to His love for His creatures (vv. 13–15), that He condemns and punishes the powerful evil-doers, showing no favoritism (vv. 17–19), and that He is omniscient (vv. 21–22). It is presumptuous for man to set the precise time for Divine retribution (v. 23; see the Comm.). Moreover, even the weak, who suffer oppression at the hands of the powerful, may not be free from guilt (vv. 29, 30). Hence Job should recognize his own lapses and repent (vv. 31 f.) instead of demanding the right to be the judge himself (v. 33). Since Job's accusations against God are unjustified, they add to his sins (vv. 34–39).

There are no objective grounds for deleting any part of the chapter.

Special Note 31 — The Metric Structure of Chapter 37

Various emendations and deletions have been suggested for the opening section of chap. 37 on metric grounds. These proposals stem from a failure to recognize that the entire section is in *Qinah* rhythm. It is an error to define the *Qinah* meter as being limited to a 3:2 pattern. Its basic characteristic is that the opening stich is longer than the closing one and upon this pattern many variations are rung by the poet. The Book of Lamentations is a striking demonstration of this fact. Moreover, in scanning biblical verse, the principles must be kept in mind that because of metric needs, short, unimportant words will, at times, be given a stress, and longer words may be given two beats. On these phenomena, see *PPS*, pp. 66–68, and Special Note 1, sec. 13, 14 and 15.

Chapter 37 begins with the *Qinah* rhythm in two forms, 3 ‖ 2 and 4 ‖ 3, principally the latter, and then goes over to the 3 ‖ 3 meter, which dominates biblical poetry. The structure is as follows:

v. 1   3 ‖ 2 (the meter may be 4:3, if the two words אַף־לְזֹאת in stich a and מִמְּקוֹמוֹ in stich b are each given two beats. Cf. Ps. 2:5b; 5:6.)

v. 2   4 ‖ 3 (cf. 17:14).

v. 3   4 ‖ 3. Because of the long words in stich a, containing ten syllables in the Masoretic vocalization and probably eight originally, the opening stich receives four beats, by giving one to each vocable, or none to כָּל and two to יְשָׁרֵהוּ.

v. 4   3:2 ‖ 3:2. Either וְלֹא receives its own beat, as in Ps. 5:6, or two beats are to be assigned to the long word יַעְקְבֵם.

v. 5   4:3. וְלֹא נֵדַע receives only one beat.

v. 6   4:3. הֱוֵא־אָרֶץ receives two beats, particularly since each word has a distinct idea. וְגֶשֶׁם מָטָר is to be deleted on substantive grounds. See the Comm. *ad loc.*

v. 7   3 ‖ 3. בְּיַד־כָּל־אָדָם receives two beats.

v. 8   3 ‖ 3. וּבְמְעוֹנוֹתֶיהָ receives two beats because of its length. (This v. and v. 9 can be scanned as a 3:2 meter, by giving the long word only one beat. However, the presence of a 3:3 meter in v. 7 preceding and in

vv. 10, 11 following makes it more likely that vv. 8 and 9 are in the same basic pattern.)

v. 9   3 ‖ 3. וּמִמְּזָרִים receives two beats because of its length.

v. 10   3:3.

v. 11   3:3.

v. 12   3:3:3. The verse, which is a tristich, may also be scanned as a *Qinah* meter by giving stich a four stresses and stich c three. Stich b may be given either four stresses, one on each word, because of the importance of *kol*, or three, with one stress on *kol ʾašer*; hence the meter would be either 4:4:3 or 4:3:3.

v. 13   3:3 On the reading *lōʾ rāṣū* for *lᵉarṣō*, see the Comm. Hence, stich a has three stresses (on *lᵉšebhet, lōʾ* and *rāṣū*). In stich b, the long word *yamṣiʾēhū* receives two stresses.

v. 14   3:3. The two words *niphleʾōt ʾēl* constitute a single thought and, therefore, receive only one stress. The identical pattern occurs in Isa. 1:4, where *qᵉdōš Yisrāʾēl* in stich b corresponds to JHVH in stich a and receives only one beat. Cf. Nu. 23:7; Mic. 6:7, and see *PPS*, p. 67.

v. 15   3:3.

v. 16   3:3. The phrase *ᶜal miphlesēi ᶜābh* receives two beats.

v. 17   3:3. Either *ʾašer* receives a stress or *begādekhā* receives two beats.

v. 18   3:3

v. 19   3:3. *Mah nōʾmar* receives one beat. In stich b, *lō* may receive a beat, or, more probably, *mippᵉnei ḥōšekh* would receive two beats.

v. 20   3:3. The phrase *hayesuppar lō* receives two beats.

v. 21   3:3:3. A tristich; cf. vv. 4, 12.

v. 22   3:3.

v. 23   3:3:3. A tristich; cf. vv. 4, 12, 21.

v. 24   3:3. The closing phrase *kol ḥakhmei lēbh* receives two stresses.

Special Note 32 — The Speeches of The Lord Out of the Whirlwind (38:1–41:26)

A. *Authenticity*

The Speeches of the Lord Out of the Whirlwind should logically provide the climax of the book, both because of their position and the exalted speaker to whom they are attributed. However, important problems arise with regard to the authenticity of this section as a whole and the integrity of all its contents. Both these issues ultimately depend upon a more fundamental question, the meaning and relevance of these Speeches.

First and foremost, the section is almost completely concerned with describing the glories of the natural world. There is no reference to Job's suffering or to his alleged sins or to any aspect of the Dialogue between Job and his Friends. In fact, there is no reference to mankind at all, with the exception of a short section (40:7–14) that deals with the question of the retribution of the wicked.

The apparent irrelevance of these chapters to the rest of the book has led some scholars to regard them as an independent composition, the rest of the book having been left unfinished (Vernes, Studer, Hempel, Baumgarten, Volz, Finkelstein, Kraeling, Ehrlich, in *Randglossen* VI, page 329; cf. Pfeiffer, *IOT*, p. 674, n. 3).

B. *Integrity*

Within these chapters the originality of three sections has been questioned: The description of the ostrich (39:13–18) has been deleted by some scholars, principally because it is lacking in the Septuagint, but also because it is not couched in the question form, like the rest of the First Speech (38:2–39:12). Some critics have raised questions with regard to the passages on *Behemot* (40:15–24) and *Leviathan* (40:25–41:26), on the ground that they are not interrogative in form (Ewald, Dillmann, Cheyne, Weber, Eissfeldt, and many others; cf. Pfeiffer, *op. cit.*, pp. 673–75; Rowley, "The Book of Job and Its Meaning," *Bulletin of John Rylands Library*, XLI, 1958, p. 119). Since the opening section of the Second Speech (40:7–14), as has been noted, is not a nature description, this approach is virtually tantamount to eliminating the Second Speech entirely. This has been urged on substantive grounds as well — that the Second Speech adds nothing significant to the argumentation.

The existence of two brief responses by Job (40:3–5 and 41:2–6) has also been questioned. Some scholars have deleted them in part and combined the remainder into one response after God's Speech.

C. *Meaning and Relevance*

The vast majority of scholars accept the Speeches of The Lord Out of the Whirlwind as the authentic work of the poet. There is, however, a wide disparity of views with regard to their meaning. Since they do not overtly deal with the problem of man's suffering, with which the remainder of the book is concerned, some readers see in these chapters "astonishingly poor logic that explains nothing" (Zhitlowsky). Some distinguished scholars find it so difficult to relate these chapters to the subject matter of the book as a whole that they describe the God Speeches as expressing "contempt for human beings" (Pfeiffer), marked by "unparalleled brutality and devilish scorn" (Cornill). Another critic suggests that these chapters were written ambiguously as a *double entendre*, so that the traditionalists would believe that God's power is being reaffirmed while skeptical readers would penetrate more deeply into the text and derive the correct conclusion that man's suffering is a riddle that has no solution (K. Fullerton). A more recent scholar, accurately sensing a powerful irony in these chapters, sees the key in God's finding man guilty and nevertheless acquitting him (Good, so Robert Frost).

As against these individual approaches, several other interpretations are more generally held. One view is that Job is overpowered by the description of God's vast creative might and therefore submits to Him. But this is precisely what Job has conceded time and again throughout the Dialogue (e.g.,

9:4, 19, 34, 35; 12:19, 23; 13:21–22; 23:3, 4, 6). Probably the most widely accepted interpretation of the God Speeches sees in them God's response to Job's repeated charge that He is indifferent to man's plight and, therefore, leaves all man's pleas unanswered. The Lord's response not only disproves Job's allegation, but gives him both victory and comfort, since he now experiences the nearness of God that he had passionately yearned for (Terrien). The interpretation, deeply moving as it is, is, however, not borne out either by the content or the spirit of the God Speeches. Moreover, if all that is intended by the God Speeches is to bring Job a sense of God's nearness and concern, a few lines would have sufficed instead of this long and detailed section, in which, incidentally, not a word of sympathy for Job's suffering is to be found.

For a detailed discussion of all these problems: (a) the authenticity of the God Speeches; (b) the integrity of their contents; (c) the meaning of this section; and (d) its relevance to the entire book, including an analysis of the various views proposed for meeting them and a presentation of our own approach in the interpretation of Job, the reader is referred to the *Book of God and Man*, particularly chapter X, "The Lord Out of the Whirlwind"; chapter XI, "Job and the Mystery of Suffering"; and chapter XIV, "The Rhetoric of Allusion and Analogy," as well as to the detailed exegesis of this section in the Commentary and Special Notes 33–39.

Here we shall content ourselves with a brief summary of our conclusions:

1.   Both Speeches of the Lord Out of the Whirlwind are authentic and essential to the structure and content of the book.

2.   The section on *Behemot* (40:15–24) and *Leviathan* (40:25–41:26) are integral to the argumentation. In the First Speech, the wonders of the inanimate world (38:2–38) are followed by the description of the lion (38:39–41), the mountain goat (39:1–4), the wild ass (39:5–8), the wild ox (39:9–12), the ostrich (39:13–18), the wild horse (39:19–25), the hawk and the eagle (39:26–30). All these creatures have two characteristics in common — they are all free from man's control and yet they possess a beauty that man can easily recognize. The implication is clear and unmistakable — the universe is beautiful, but man is not the measure of all things and the cosmos was not created merely for man. It follows that its Maker cannot be judged from man's limited vantage-point.

This basic theme is clearly adumbrated in two passages in the First Speech. Thus, God sends forth torrents of rain, "to bring rain to a land uninhabited, to a desert where no man lives" (38:26). A little later the poet pictures the young ravens, who are of no use to man, "crying out to God" for food, since He is their provider.

The Second Speech goes further. The hippopotamus (40:15–24) and the crocodile (40:25–41:26) are not merely not intended for man's use; they are positively repulsive by his standards. Yet God rejoices in them as well and finds them worthy expressions of His creative power. Thus, the Second Speech reenforces powerfully the contention that the universe and its Maker cannot be judged by man in anthropocentric terms.

3. Job's two independent responses (40:3–5; 42:1–6) are entirely in place. There is no justification for combining them both in a single Speech at the beginning of chapter 42. Neither is it necessary to assume that Job, in his first Speech, surrendered some elements of his position and that in his second he yielded completely, for the nature of this assumed concession in one or the other speech is nowhere spelled out. Actually, the text of the First Speech (40:3–5) contains no retreat by Job on any point. He merely reiterates that God is all-powerful and that man is weak, a point he has consistently emphasized from the beginning of the Dialogue (cf. e.g., chap. 9, especially vv. 19 ff.). Since Job has already spoken his mind more than once, he will now remain silent in the face of superior power. It is only after the Second Speech of the Lord, when the full impact of His argument has been borne in upon Him, that Job repents his error (42:1–6). His error, be it noted, resides, not in his steadfast insistence upon his innocence, which God never contravenes, but in his having presumed to challenge God and by that token to judge Him.

4. The section on the ostrich (39:13–18) is not to be deleted. It leads directly into the description of the wild horse (39:18b, 19). The change from the interrogative form employed elsewhere in the Speeches (38:2–39:12; 39:19–30) to the declarative in the case of the ostrich (39:13–18), and the hippopotamus (40:15–24), does not represent interpolations from a secondary author, but a stylistic device employed by the poet in order to avoid the monotony of a single form that would otherwise extend over 122 verses. Similarly, in "the Code of Integrity" (chap. 31), the use of the particle ʾim is varied in order to prevent monotony. An analysis of the two God Speeches reveals that each follows the pattern of interrogative-declarative-interrogative: First Speech: I, 38:2–39:12; D, 39:13–18; I, 39:19–30; Second Speech: I, 40:7–14; D, 40:15–24; I, 40:25–41:26. (The verse 40:32 is not addressed to Job, but uses the second person impersonally. See Comm. *ad loc.*)

The quest for variety in style is not exhausted by this alternation between interrogative and declarative sections. It also affects the length of the questions and their frequency.

Thus the first interrogative section (38:2–39:12) contains a barrage of short staccato questions hurled at Job in rapid succession. This section contains eighteen questions one verse in length (38:4, 5, 16, 17, 18, 24, 28, 31, 32, 33, 34, 35, 36, 41; 39:1, 10, 11, 12). There are five instances of questions running to two verses (38:2–3, 21–22, 29–30, 37–38, 39–40). There are three instances of the question running to three verses (38:19–21, 25–27; 39:2–4). There are two instances of the question running to four verses (38:12–15; 39:5–8). There is one instance of a question running to six verses (38:6–11).

In the second interrogative section, the pace is substantially more relaxed. There are only two examples of brief questions of one verse each (39:19, 26); one question extending over four verses (39:27–30); one question extending over six verses (39:20–25).

In the third interrogative section (40:25–31) there are five questions one verse in length (40:25, 26, 27, 28, 31) and two questions of two verses each

(40:29, 30), but the remainder of the Second Speech of the Lord Out of the Whirlwind becomes declarative (40:32–41:26). Thus the frequency of the questions declines in successive sections and as they become longer they take on the lineaments of descriptions, with a considerable lessening of the tension.

5. The recognition of the use of allusion and analogy is fundamental for the understanding of "the Speeches of the Lord Out of the Whirlwind." They represent the poet's ripe wisdom on man's life and the suffering that is its constant accompaniment. To be sure, man's suffering is frequently justified by the sins and shortcomings of which he is guilty, as the Friends have insisted. However, much human misery is inexplicable and hence appears unjust from man's limited perspective. That suffering may prove a discipline, as Elihu avers, is not restated here, because it represents a very partial response to the problem of evil.

The major insight of the poet, reserved for the God Speeches, is that the natural order, which was not created by God exclusively for man's use and domination, reveals a beauty and harmony that man is able to experience vividly and directly. Similarly, the moral order which emanates from the same Divine source must possess a meaning and rationality even in those aspects which are beyond man's comprehension. Acceptance of the rightness of the moral order is, therefore, not a blind act of faith; it is sustained by the visible evidence of the pattern and structure of the world about us. Faith, for the poet, is trust in things unseen on the evidence of things seen. Since the world is a unity, being the handiwork of one God, we may extrapolate from the known to the unknown and, by accepting the limitations of life, be able to face the adventure of existence.

6. The response of the Lord Out of the Whirlwind is more than an intellectual demonstration based upon analogy and the extrapolation from the visible world of nature to the invisible world of the moral order. The author is a poet, not a logician. He does not present a catalogue of the world's wonders; he sings a hymn of joy to creation. In inviting Job not merely to understand, but rather to revel in the delights of creation, God is not evading, but rather responding, to Job's cry of agony. Viewed against the background of the cosmos, man's sufferings do not disappear, but they grow smaller and more bearable as elements within the larger plan of God's world. The author of the Book of Job is both thinker and poet. The thinker calls upon Job to grasp the world and recognize man's limitations. The poet summons him to steep himself in the beauty of the world and to experience it existentially. By seizing the two staffs of understanding and emotion, man can live wisely, bravely, and joyfully in a world that is miracle as well as mystery.

7. These chapters have been hailed as among the most magnificent nature poetry ever written. Magnificent they assuredly are, but nature poetry they are not. In fact, there is, strictly speaking, no nature poetry in the Bible, only poems in praise of God, the Creator of nature. Not the world, but its Maker is extolled here and in such Psalms as 19, 23, and 104. The essence of biblical religion was the insistence, unique in the ancient world, that nature was not divine; only its Creator and Governor was worthy of

reverence, being equally the Lord of history directing the lives of men and nations.

This identification of the God of history and of nature is steadfastly maintained in the Dialogues and underpins the Speeches of the Lord Out of the Whirlwind. Neither Job nor his Friends nor Elihu, nor God Himself is able or willing to "solve" the problem of evil by making a dichotomy between nature and history, between the natural order and the moral order, between God's power and God's justice.

This unity explains the presence of two passages, one in each Speech of the Lord Out of the Whirlwind, that have seemed like irrelevant intrusions of the moral issue into nature poetry. The first passage, 38:13–15, depicts the discomfiture and punishment of evil-doers when daylight comes. It is linked to the preceding verse which deals with the coming of the dawn. By Western canons of logic, these verses seem to be irrelevant in the context. However, for the Oriental mind, the principle of psychological association is paramount in establishing the relationship of ideas. There is, therefore, no justification for the proposed deletions of 13b, 14b, and 15, or their transposition, as proposed by some scholars (Sieg., Du., Che., Be., Hö.).

The second passage, 40:7–14, comes at the beginning of the Second Speech of the Lord. In the response which immediately precedes, Job has not retreated from his position or recanted the challenge he has repeatedly hurled against God's justice. The Lord is, therefore, constrained to deal with the problem of evil in the world. Unlike the Friends, He does not deny the validity of Job's views. He makes no effort to rebut them and thus tacitly admits their truth. Job has, however, been too simplistic in his approach. The Lord ironically asks whether Job could do better than God in suppressing wickedness, rampant in the world. The question thus concedes the existence of pockets of evil not yet overcome by God.

The moral note "intrudes" into the description of nature at another point in the First Speech of the Lord. In 38:22–23, the snow and the hail are described as being stored up and reserved by the Lord for use "on the day of battle and war." For the Hebrew mind, these themes are entirely appropriate to nature poetry, since the two aspects of God as Creator and as the source of the moral law are inextricably bound up with one another.

The same union of the two themes is manifest in the Psalter. Thus, Psalm 19 begins with a description of the glories of nature (vv. 1–7), then goes over to extolling the praise of God's law (vv. 8–12), and concludes with a plea to be forgiven for sins committed (vv. 13–15). Some critics have divided the Psalm into two or even three independent units, a procedure we regard as unjustifiable. But whether the Psalm be the work of the original author or from a later editor, one fact emerges — for the ancient Hebrew the God of nature and of the moral law is one.

Another case in point is afforded by Psalm 104. The affinities of this great Psalm with Akhnaton's great "Hymn to the Aton, the Sun Disc" (*ANET*, pp. 369–71) are striking, but there is one crucial difference which must be remarked upon. The Egyptian poet does not introduce into his hymn the moral note of the destruction of the evil-doers, which is an indispensable element for the Hebrew psalmist as he contemplates the glory of God: "Let sinners be consumed from the earth and the wicked be no more. Bless the Lord, O my soul, Hallelujah" (Ps. 104:35). Here, too, many scholars have regarded the verse as an addition. But whether the line emanates from the original author or from a later editor, it is profoundly relevant and meaningful, the original author or from a later editor, it is profoundly relevant and meaningful, underscoring the unity of the two aspects of God.

In sum, genuine insight into the two "Speeches of the Lord Out of the Whirlwind" makes it clear that they are thoroughly relevant to the theme of the book and constitute its triumphant climax, a paean of praise to God that brings strength and solace to man.

D. *The Speeches of the Lord and Egyptian Onomastica*

During the past few decades, scholars have brought the Speeches of the Lord Out of the Whirlwind into relationship with Egyptian Onomastica, or "noun lists." The Babylonians also compiled "noun lists" of a similar kind which probably originated with the Sumerians. These lists represent an early pre-scientific effort at a rational classification of natural phenomena and human artifacts.

Thus the Egyptian Onomasticon of Amenemope (circa 1100 B.C.E.) carries the heading "Beginning of the Teaching about all that which Ptah has created." The list of 610 subjects which follows presents a classification of divine and human beings, animate creatures, inanimate objects, natural features, meteorological phenomena, cities, buildings, food and drink. For the literature, cf. A. H. Gardiner, *Ancient Egyptian Onomastica*, 1947; A. Alt, "Die Weisheit Salomos," *Theologische Literaturzeitung*, vol. 76, 1951, pp. 139–44; G. von Rad, "Hiob XXXVIII und die Altägyptische Weisheit," *VT Supplements* III, 1955, pp. 293–301; R. B. Y. Scott, *The Way of Wisdom* (New York, 1971), pp. 34, 36.

The list naturally recalls the first Speech of the Lord in which Job is confronted by the wonders of the creation of land and sea (38:4–11), day and night (38:20 f.), snow, wind, rain and frost (38:22–30), the constellations (38:31–33), and the rain storm (38:30), followed by the untamed beasts and birds (38:39–39:30).

The differences, however, are far more significant. As Scott has noted, these Middle Eastern "outlines of knowledge" contain no definitions or descriptions. It is, however, of the very essence of the Speeches of the Lord that the phenomena are described with enthusiastic joy. The author of Job is interested not in presenting a systematic catalogue of natural objects and human artifacts, but in evoking the sense of wonder and awe that are the root of faith. Not information but inspiration is the poet's goal. Hence the Speeches, unlike the Onomastica, are marked not by all-inclusiveness but by a high degree of selectivity. The choice of the birds and the beasts that the poet describes is neither haphazard nor motivated by "scientific considerations." Rather, the choice is governed by the author's clear purpose — emphasizing the poet's fundamental religious insight, as indicated above.

This objective is also the key to the "intrusion" of logically "irrelevant passages" in the Speech of the Lord. Such are the references to rain at three distinct points (38:25–28; 38:33 and 38:37 f.), the passage on the ibis and the cock (38:36) in the section dealing with natural phenomena, as well as the description of the raven (38:41) and the ostrich (39:13–18) in the section dealing with animals. That there are adequate literary, psychological and ideational grounds for the presence of these passages in their respective positions is indicated in this and the following Special Note and in the Commentary.

In sum, it is quite possible that the author of Job, whose range of knowledge was impressive, was familiar with catalogues of the kind extant in the Egyptian and Mesopotamian Onomastica, but as a creative thinker and poet he utilized the data they offered to serve his own literary needs and religious insights.

Special Note 33 — The First Speech of The Lord (38:1–40:2)

The first Speech falls into two sections, the first of which is itself subdivided into two parts:

A. The inanimate world (38:2–38)

    1. God's creative activity (38:4–11)
    2. God's government of the natural world (38:12–37)

B. The world of living creatures (38:39–39:30)

In rabbinic thought, these two aspects of God's sovereignty depicted by the poet in Section A are clearly differentiated; the first is called *Maˤasēh Berēšīt*, "the work of the beginning" (*M. Ḥag.* 2:1; *B. Ḥag.* 13a). The second is called *Maˤasēh Merkābhāh*, "the work of the Chariot," derived from Ezekiel, chap. 1 (*ibid.*).

Attention has already been called in Special Note 32 to the fact that the basic theme of the God-speeches — that the world is not geared merely to man's needs and desires — is already hinted in Section A in the statement that rain falls on deserts uninhabited by men (38:26).

The idea becomes clearer in Section B. The animals described in this section are all inhabitants of the wilderness of southern Palestine and the Dead Sea region. They have in common a birthright of liberty, not having been designed for man's pleasure or domesticated to his use. This basic insight is expressed with even greater vigor in the Second Speech of the Lord, in the descriptions of the hippopotamus and the crocodile (40:25 ff.).

In addition, the description of the various beasts and birds in the First Speech (38:39–39:30) serves another purpose — it reveals the boundless variety of God's creatures. Some of them, like the mountain goat and the hind, leave their mothers at birth. Others, like the ostrich, are deserted by their mothers. Moreover, the poet delights in contrasts implied or explicit. Thus, the ass and the ox were chief beasts of burden in the ancient East (Ex. 21:33; 23:4, 12; Deut. 22:10, etc.). The poet, therefore, deliberately chooses the wild ass and the wild ox for praise. The birds that are described also differ from one another. The ostrich, whether because of foolishness or hard-heartedness, is unconcerned for its young. On the other hand, the stork and the falcon, the one a peaceful creature, the other a bird of prey, are both unlike the ostrich, having one attribute in common — they are lovingly cared for by their parents (cf. Special Note 34 and the Comm. on 39:13). All this vast and varied creation is nurtured by God.

The metric pattern of this long Speech reflects the poet's skill in varying the meter and thus avoiding monotony.

The basic pattern of chap. 38 is the 3:3 meter, which runs through the entire chapter. It is possible that vv. 2 and 3 are to be scanned as 3:2, but in view of the unbroken pattern that follows and the length of their respective stichs b, it is preferable to give *bemillin belī daʿat* three stresses in v. 2 and, similarly, three stresses to the long words *veʾešalekhā vehōdīʿēnī* in 3b. The same meter is clear in vv. 4–8. In v. 9, the same meter obtains, the long word *ḥᵃtūllatō* receiving two stresses. The following verses are again in the same meter.

In chapter 39, some scholars have proposed deletions, since the opening vv. are not in the 3:3 pattern. The various deletions proposed, which gravely injure the text, are unnecessary, if it is recognized that the opening section of this chapter is in *Qinah* rhythm (3:2 or 4:3).

Chapter 39

> v. 1   4:3
> v. 2   4:3   The long word *temallᵖenāh* receives two beats.
> v. 3   3:2
> v. 4   4:3
> v. 5   4:3

The first מִי, because of its importance for the sense, receives an independent beat.

> v. 6   3:2

The poet then reverts to the basic 3:3 meter.

> v. 7   3:3
> v. 8   3:3
> v. 9   3:3   The metric requirement here gives ʿal ʾabhūsekhā two
>   beats.
> v. 10   3:3

It is noteworthy that this shift from the basic 3:3 meter (38 passim) to the *Qinah* meter (39:1–6), followed by a reversion to the 3:3 meter (39:7–30), is identical with the rhythmic pattern followed in Elihu's final speech (chaps. 36, 37), on which see Special Note 31. The use of the same metric structure in the Elihu section and in the God Speeches is not without significance for the question of the integrity and authorship of these sections of the book.

Special Note 34 — The Ostrich (39:13-18)

This passage is regarded as a secondary addition by some critics (Bi., Dil., Du., Che., Kraeling, Ter.) on several grounds: (a) it is lacking in LXX; (b) it is not couched in interrogative form; (c) the ostrich is an intrusion among the quadrupeds.

None of these arguments are conclusive. (a) The omission in LXX or even in the ms. before the translator may well be due to the difficulties of interpretation posed by the passage. Many of the omissions and the contractions in the Greek translation of Job are due to the same cause. (b) The interrogative form may well be present here, even without inserting the interrogative He before *kenāph* in v. 13, as proposed by D-G. The noun may be governed by the verb *hayāda^ctā* in 39:1. See the Comm. *ad loc.* (c) The author is a free-ranging poet led by association, not a zoologist bound by a scientific classification. The ostrich is introduced between the wild ox and the horse exactly as another bird, the raven, is included (38:41) between the lion (38:39–40) and the mountain goat (39:1–4). In our passage, the ostrich is brought in because of its speed (39:18), which is superior to that of the horse, the description of which begins in v. 19, that is linked directly to 18b.

The burden of this passage is not merely a description of another inhabitant of the wilderness. As the exegesis of v. 13 makes clear, a significant contrast is being drawn here. On the one hand, there are the cruelty and indifference to her young associated in folk-belief with the ostrich ("cruel as ostriches," Lam. 4:3). On the other hand are the affection and concern for their offspring characteristic of two otherwise quite different creatures, the "kindly" stork and the carnivorous falcon (see the Comm. on 39:13). Varied as are all three creatures, they are, nevertheless, all the handiwork of God, in which He takes delight. For a similar contrast and conclusion, in a totally different area of life, cf. Pr. 22:2: "The rich and the poor man meet; the Maker of both is the Lord."

TS offers a fascinating folktale that he "reconstructs" in order to interpret this section (*op. cit.*, pp. 544–57). Unfortunately, the involved tale does not exist in any literary source and can be found in our text only by rather forced interpretations and emendations.

Special Note 35 — The Second Speech of the Lord (40:6–41:26)

After one verse (40:2) that constitutes the conclusion of the First Speech of the Lord and is attached by the Vulgate to the preceding chapter, Job responds (42:3–5). He admits his own weakness before God and his insignificance in the face of the vast creation, and declares, very briefly, that having spoken more than once, he has nothing to add to his previous contentions. Contrary to a widely held but mistaken view, Job does not concede that he is mistaken in any of his arguments.

In view of Job's unyielding standpoint, God responds (40:7–14) in a section which, far from being an interpolation, is directly germane to the Dialogue and the theme of the book as a whole. God concedes that the world order is not perfect, that the wicked have not been completely crushed, and that the problem of evil still exists in the world. Sardonically, He challenges Job to destroy all the proud malefactors in the world and then He Himself will do Job homage (40:6–14).

The Lord now turns to His basic theme, the full implications of which are now presented. The First Speech has stressed the care and protection that God has lavished upon creatures not intended for man's use or subjugated to his will. Yet man is capable of recognizing their beauty — the graceful hind, the unchained wild ass, the untamed wild ox, the swift ostrich, the fleet horse, the swooping eagle in the sky. In the Second Speech, the Lord goes further. He proceeds to describe two creatures that are not only dangerous to man, but positively repulsive from man's perspective, the biblical *Behemot*, the hippopotamus (40:15–24), and *Leviathan*, the crocodile (40:25–41:26). Yet for God, these monstrous creatures are beautiful, for they, too, reveal the creative power of God and elicit His joy and pride.

The argument against an anthropocentric view of the universe has now been brought to its climax. What now remains for Job is not merely to yield before God, but to recognize the error implicit in his presuming to challenge a world order that transcends his limited understanding and interests.

The basic theme of the Speeches of the Lord, and, by that token, the message of the book as a whole is that men's suffering in the world cannot be explained fully by the conventional theory of sin and retribution as argued by the Friends. Nor can it be justified in terms of a moral discipline designed to guard men against wrongdoing, the idea that Elihu has contributed to the discussion. However valid these explanations may be — and the author is not disposed to deny them *in toto* — there remains a hard core of human suffering which is by no means an illusion but, on the contrary, an agonizing reality not susceptible to our understanding. Nevertheless, the existence of this evil — and it is an evil — must not be permitted to distort the true nature of the universe, which is not man-centered, or to obscure the pervasive pattern of good in the world. On the contrary, the harmony and beauty of the natural order support the faith that there is a similar pattern of meaning in the moral sphere, since both emanate from the One God. Sustained by this faith, man can bear the burden of suffering and yet find life a joyous experience, secure in the knowledge that God's world is basically good.

This truth emerges from the Two Speeches of the Lord Out of the Whirlwind. In Job's Second Response, he realizes his limitations in understanding, and humbly repents the challenge he has hurled against his Maker.

Various critical issues have been raised with regard to the authenticity and meaning of these chapters. Some scholars have rejected the Second Speech completely as a later addition. Thus Driver-Gray regard 40:7–41:30 as a variant of the original Speech of God (I, p. 348). Driver-Gray maintain that there is "no sufficient distinction of purpose from the First Speech" and that the Response of Job is not different or distinct from the First. Other scholars, like Bickell, Duhm, and Peake, have sought to combine both Speeches into one and to unite the two Responses of Job as well. It has already been pointed out that the Second Speech of the Lord and the Response of Job are each different from their earlier counterparts.

The answer to these and other issues raised depends basically on whether these chapters are relevant to the book as a whole. This question, in turn, hinges on our understanding of the meaning of the Speeches of the Lord. For an analysis of the varied views and interpretations held by scholars and for a presentation of our own approach to the theme of the book, see *BGM*, especially chaps. X, XIV, and Special Note 32 in this volume.

Distinct from these issues, and yet with a direct bearing upon them, are the questions of the nature and authenticity of the sections on *Behemot* and *Leviathan*, and whether these are creatures of the natural world, described hyperbolically by the poet, or primordial monsters who play so important a role in Oriental mythology. On this problem, see Special Notes 36 and 37.

Special Note 36 — The Authenticity and Structure of the Behemot and Leviathan Sections (40:15–24; 40:25–41:26)

That the description of these two creatures was not written by the author of the First Speech has been maintained by many critics who delete the section either as an interpolation or as a variant form of the First Speech. The grounds that have been advanced for denying the authenticity of this section are conveniently set forth in Driver-Gray, *op. cit.*, I, pp. 351 f.

They are: (1) The descriptions of the beasts are longer than in the First Speech; (2) The question form which is frequent in the First Speech is much less common in this section; (3) The constant recurrence of questions in the First Speech gives it a vividness which, it is alleged, is lacking in this section; (4) In the First Speech, the habits, actions, and temper of the animals are depicted, whereas here we have descriptions of the bodily parts of the beasts; (5) If *Behemot* and *Leviathan* are respectively the hippopotamus and the crocodile, they are predominantly Egyptian animals. If they are mythical monsters (see Special Note 37), they differ from the actual animals of Palestine described in the First Speech; (6) There are linguistic and stylistic differences between the two sections.

Basically, these objections derive from a mechanical approach to the material. They fail to reckon with the poetic talents of the poet, who would utilize every resource available to him in order to introduce variety and avoid the cardinal sin of monotony. (See Special Note 32.) It is, therefore, entirely appropriate that there be differences between the First Speech and the Second, in form and in structure and not only in content and theme, on which see Special Note 35. In the First Speech, the poet describes the motion and activity of the various animals and birds. In the case of the hippopotamus and the crocodile, these qualities do not enter into the picture; it is their physical bulk and physical repulsiveness which are the burden of the poet's theme.

He will also use the question form more sparingly, though it should be kept in mind that it is intermittent even in the First Speech (cf. 38:7–11; 39:16–18; 39:21–25), nor is it entirely absent in the Second (cf. 40:24–31; 41:3, 5). Moreover, in both Speeches the overall pattern is the same: interrogative-declarative-interrogative. (See Special Note 32.) Finally, the opinion that this section is less vivid than the First Speech is a purely subjective judgment; a different subject matter creates a different style. Driver-Gray are constrained to admit that the so-called linguistic and stylistic differences are "indecisive" and that the conclusion as to whether this section is authentic "must remain largely a matter of taste" (p. 352). We have already seen that the section marks a significant advance in the thought-pattern of the God Speeches. We, therefore, regard it as indubitably the work of the original author.

The section dealing with Leviathan (40:25–41:26) presents two basic themes: (a) praise of the invincibility of the beast, and (b) a description of his massive and powerful body. Scholars have suggested that portions of this section have been accidentally misplaced (D-G, I, p. 369). They have proposed that 41:22–24, which describes his body, belongs after v. 16, so that 41:25–26, which extols the beast's invincibility, would come immediately after vv. 17–21.

This rearrangement would organize the chapter in accordance with Western canons of logic, which cannot legitimately be used as a criterion for literary structure in an Oriental poem. Moreover, the proposed reorganization would destroy the existing pattern, which consists of a theme and counter-theme alternating with each other, a literary form which adds variety and interest.

An outline of the Leviathan section in the Masoretic text reveals this contrapuntal structure clearly:

Theme A — the difficulty in capturing the beast (40:25–41:3).
Transition — a verse linking the invincibility of the animal with the description of his bodily structure (41:4).
Theme B — a hyperbolic description of the animal's body in repose (41:5–16).
Theme A — his invincibility and power to cast terror upon all (41:17–21).
Theme B — a description of the animal in action and movement (41:22–24).
Theme A — the unique power and unconquerability of Leviathan (41:25–26).

The same technique of theme and countertheme is employed elsewhere by the poet, as in Job's initial complaint (chap. 3), and in the description of the suffering endured by the poor and the injustices inflicted upon them by the powerful, in chap. 24. On the other hand, two themes are expressed in chiastic relation in 8:11–22. See the Comm. *ad loc.*

Special Note 37 — Behemot and Leviathan — Their Identity

The interpretation of *Behemot* (40:15–24) and *Leviathan* (40:25–41:26) has oscillated through the centuries between two poles, mythical and real. In apocalyptic and rabbinic literature, *Behemot* was understood to be *šōr habbār*, the cosmic "wild ox" or "ox of the open spaces," and *Leviathan* was identified with the supernatural "great fish," both of whom would constitute the heavenly food of the righteous in the world to come. In the Middle Ages, some Christian theologians, like Albertus Magnus, conceived of *Behemot* as a symbol of sensuality and sin. Others, like Thomas Aquinas, equated *Behemot* with the elephant and *Leviathan* with the whale, for which the text of such passages as 41:5–12 offered support.

After Bochart, in his *Hierozoicon* (Book 5, chap. 15), identified *Behemot* with the hippopotamus and *Leviathan* with the crocodile, this view all but conquered the field and has remained dominant to the present. However, G. R. Driver vigorously opposes the identification of *Behemot* with the hippopotamus (*Book List, Society for O. T. Study*, 1972, p. 18). Undoubtedly under his influence, NEB renders *Behemot* by "crocodile" and *Leviathan* by "whale," placing most of the Leviathan passage (40:25–30 in the Hebrew) after 39:26–30, the description of the eagle.

As extrabiblical literature came to light, notably from Mesopotamia, the mythological interpretation was revived in modern form by T. K. Cheyne (*Job and Solomon*, p. 56, and s. v. in *Encyclopedia Biblica*), C. H. Toy (*Judaism and Christianity*, pp. 162 f.) and H. Gunkel (*Schöpfung und Chaos*, pp. 57–61), though it was vigorously criticized by Budde. The discovery of Ugaritic religious texts has recently given the mythological interpretation a new lease on life among some contemporary scholars. Thus Pope quotes from Ugaritic epics and myths extensively, in order to buttress this mythological interpretation of *Behemot* and *Leviathan*, in spite of the uncertainties that often beset the interpreter of Ugaritic material in general, and the lack of correspondence between the Ugaritic passages and the content of the Job poem. Some scholars have been so captivated by apparent parallels in Oriental literature as to lose sight of the basic exegetical test — the relevance and appropriateness of the interpretation within the context of the book of Job.

Today, it is necessary to examine anew these two rival views of *Behemot* and *Leviathan*. The older arguments in favor of the mythological theory are conveniently summarized in Driver-Gray (*op. cit.* I, pp. 351 ff.). The alleged Ugaritic parallels are assembled and discussed in Pope (*op. cit.*, pp. 268 ff., 276 ff.).

The analysis may take its departure from a study of the linguistic usage. Both terms and their synonyms or surrogates are used in the Bible on two levels: to refer to natural creatures and to mythological beings. The author of Job, like the Prophets and the Psalmists, felt free to embellish his work with mythological references to *Behemot* and *Leviathan*, as well as *Tannin* and *Rahab*.

Behemot (with *Vav*) generally refers to ordinary cattle (Joel 1:20; 2:22;

Micah 5:7; Hab. 2:17; Ps. 8:8; 49:13, 21, 51; 78:22; Job 35:11. The only exception is Deut. 32:24, where the context favors a mythological reference.

Leviathan occurs once in the meaning of a natural sea-monster (Ps. 104:26) and three times in mythological contexts (see the Comm. on 3:8 and cf. Isa. 27:1; Ps. 74:14). In Apocalyptic and Rabbinic literature, *Leviathan* is entirely restricted in use to a legendary creature in the world to come, where, together with *šōr habbār* "the ox of the open spaces," it will serve as fish in the repast of the righteous in Paradise (IV *Esdras* 6:49–52; *Apocalypse of Baruch* 24:4; *Midrash Lev. Rabba*, secs. 13 and 22). The entire corpus is surveyed in L. Ginzberg, *Legends of the Jews*, Philadelphia; see Vol. 7, Index, s. v. Leviathan. The Book of Enoch (60:7–9) speaks of *Behemot* and *Leviathan* as being separated from one another, while *Midrash Lev. Rabba*, sec. 23, refers to a cosmic battle going on between them.

Similarly, *Tannin* is used on both levels of meaning: as a sea-monster (Gen. 1:21; Ps. 148:7) or serpent (Ex. 7:9, 10, 12; Deut. 32:33; Ps. 91:13) and as a primordial dragon, the symbol of original chaos (Isa. 27:1; 51:9; Ps. 74:13; Job 7:12). On the other hand, *Rahab* is used exclusively in a mythological sense, as a sea-monster (Isa. 51:9; Ps. 89:11; Job 9:13; 26:12) symbolic of Egypt (Isa. 30:7; Ps. 87:4). The synonyms *Yam*, *Tehom* generally mean "sea, abyss, bed of the sea," as in Gen. 1:2; Isa. 11:9; Hab. 2:14). They are personified in Job 28:14, with mythological overtones, for poetical purposes, as in Ps. 42:8.

References to primordial monsters who were conquered and decapitated by the gods at creation, like Marduk in his battle with Tiamat, are both frequent and familiar in ancient Oriental literature. It is, therefore, very likely that both *Behemot* and *Leviathan* were originally mythical beasts in the Oriental cosmogony which was part of the Semitic background inherited by the Hebrews. A not inconsiderable number of Biblical passages echo this pagan background.

On the other hand, part of the luxuriant growth of post-Biblical legend may unquestionably be attributed to the existence of Biblical texts which served as a point of departure for new folk-beliefs that are now embodied in Apocryphal, Pseudepigraphical, Talmudic and post-Talmudic sources. Thus, Ps. 104:26 reads: "There go the ships, and *Leviathan* that You formed to sport in" (*lesaḥeq bō*). The final preposition (*bō*) was interpreted not spatially "in it, i.e. in the sea," but instrumentally "with it," and the verse was understood to mean that God in Heaven now engages in play with *Leviathan*. Another instance of this process may be cited from our book. In 40:31, the word *sikkot* "darts," Aramaic *sikka*, "thorn, pin, nail," was associated with the word *sukkāh* "hut, tabernacle," from which there developed the legend of סוכת עורו של לויתן "the tabernacle fashioned from the skin of *Leviathan*." (Targum and Pseudo-Rashi *ad loc.*)

In view of the dual use of both *Behemot* and *Leviathan*, the linguistic evidence cannot be regarded as decisive. Ultimately, the final arbiter, as always, is context, the appropriateness and relevance of the rival views for the understanding of the book. A careful analysis of all the arguments presented has convinced us that the mythological theory is to be rejected. That the poet is describing real creatures in the world of nature is clear on several grounds:

A. The First Speech of the Lord deals with flesh-and-blood animals and birds, from the existence of which important conclusions are drawn regarding the nature of the world and man's place in it. (See Special Note 34 on the Speeches of the Lord.) The same consideration supports the idea that *Behemot* and *Leviathan* are also natural creatures, the existence of which heightens the impact of God's argument.

B. The poetic use of hyperbole, including the possible utilization of traits from mythology, is characteristic of poetry in general and of the book of Job in particular. Hyperbole in the description of the living creatures is, therefore, to be found in the First Speech of the Lord, as well as in the Second.

C. *Behemot* is not described as horrendous and predatory, as is the creature in all creation myths. On the contrary, he is pictured as herbivorous (40:20), peacefully lying in the shadow of the rushes of the river (vv. 21–22), leisurely lapping up its waters (v. 26) and liable to capture by hunters (v. 24). *Leviathan* too may be taken captive (vv. 25 ff.) and be eaten by mortals (vv. 30, 31). The poet then underscores the paradox that these massive beasts, ordinarily peaceful, are possessed of extraordinary strength (*Behemot* 40:16–19; *Leviathan* 40:32–41:26). This paradox helps to heighten the miracle of God's creation.

D. The poet is not describing cosmic events in the past, such as are the subject matter of the Babylonian and Ugaritic epics of creation, but the appearance and habits of these creatures in the present. He must, therefore, be referring to actual beasts that fell within the poet's experience or observation.

E. The poet's purpose in glorifying the miracle of the cosmos would not be served by conjuring up mythological creatures deriving from a polytheistic background, which the poet and his contemporaries had decisively abandoned. A passing mythological reference, such as we encounter in Isa. and Ps., is conceivable, but not an extended description of primordial beasts, the reality of which the exalted monotheism of the author of Job had rejected. The point need not be labored that an uncompromising monotheism is the indispensable religious background for the book of Job and for the discussion of the issue of evil which it raises. It cannot be too strongly emphasized that Job parts company with Sumerian, Akkadian and Egyptian Wisdom precisely here — the book is not a lament on suffering, nor even a complaint to the gods, but a challenge to the one God, whose hallmark is justice and who is being charged with having violated His own standard.

We are, therefore, convinced that only a description of actual flesh-and-blood monsters, unbeautiful in man's eyes, but a source of delight to God, is relevant to the poet's purpose. Hence, *Behemot* is to be identified as the hippopotamus and *Leviathan* as the crocodile. It may be noted that Herodotus (Book II, 68–71) describes the hippopotamus immediately after the crocodile.

It remains to point out that the author's vivid description of the two beasts, whose habitat was primarily, but not exclusively, in Egypt, does not demonstrate that he was an Egyptian, as Humbert has argued. The author, whom Pfeiffer has well characterized as "the most learned ancient before Plato," was well-traveled and Egypt was surely within his itinerary. Moreover, there is impressive evidence that the hippopotamus was not limited to upper Egypt, but was originally to be found in the lower Nile. The crocodile is attested at one time in our sources for Palestine and its environs. (See the Comm. on 40:15 and 25.) Conclusive evidence of the poet's Palestinian provenance, precisely because it is unconscious, is to be found in his use of "Jordan" in 40:24 to refer to a river. See the Comm. *ad loc.*

Special Note 38 — The Text and Meaning of 41:1–4

This passage contains exegetical difficulties and textual problems, but they do not require the radical surgery that has been prescribed by many critics. The basic problem is that of the pronominal suffixes. The poet uses the first person singular to refer to God or to himself (4a). In addition, several references to the might of the crocodile or his would-be assailant were probably taken to refer to the Lord, who is the Speaker in the first person (2b, 3a), a misunderstanding perpetuated by some latter-day critics (see below). As a result, these suffixes and verbal forms were erroneously modified. These minor changes (and the reading לֹא־הוּא for לִי־הוּא in 3b) are the only ones required to give the passage relevancy and force. The radical emendations proposed, which include changing the third person to the first (Gunkel, Cheyne, Du.), and amount to a rewriting of the passage, are unnecessary, creating unhebraic texts and untenable renderings. They may be studied in DG, II, pp. 335 ff.

More recently, even more radical interpretations have been suggested. Tur Sinai proposes a characteristically ingenious mythological background for these verses, much of which, however, is hypothetical and requires radical changes in the text.

Pope has suggested that the text in vv. 1–3 has "suffered some sabotage intended to obscure gross pagan mythological allusions" (p. 281). Thus the Masoretes are charged with having tendentiously obscured the sense of 41:1b by vocalizing אֵל as אֶל and changing the v. to the plural. The resulting text reads הֲגַם אֵלִים מַרְאָיו יֻטָּלוּ, which is explained to mean "Were not the gods cast down at the sight of him?"

It is not necessary here to judge the validity or the plausibility of the elaborate mythology "reconstructed" on the basis of extant Ugaritic texts, often fragmentary and obscure, that have been confidently utilized to emend the biblical text. It is germane to our purpose, however, to make the following observations:

(a) The proposed texts that emerge are often unidiomatic Hebrew.

(b) The ancient Versions do not substantiate the claim that the text was consciously modified by the Masoretes.

(c) The biblical text contains echoes of pagan mythology far more objectionable than the alleged texts here, as, e.g., the marriage of the sons of

God with the daughters of men (Gen. 6:1 ff.). That the gods were cast down before JHVH, as emerges from Pope's reconstruction of 41:1b (highly unidiomatic, be it noted), is far less "objectionable" than the famous affirmation in the "Song of the Sea," "Who is like You among the gods, O JHVH?" (Ex. 15:11). Actually, the idea that mythological beings are cast down before God is explicitly stated in Job 9:13 and left unmodified. See the Comm. *ad loc.* for other biblical references to this motif.

(d) The entire approach rests upon the mythological interpretation of *Leviathan* that has already been dealt with and rejected in Special Note 37.

(e) Most decisively, if the Masoretes are supposed to have taken offense at v. 1, "were not the gods cast down at the sight of Him?", why do they remain unruffled by v. 17, "at His terror the gods were affrighted"?

These hypotheses have the attraction of sensational novelty, but they cannot be pronounced convincing. On the contrary, there may be more genuine creativity in a reasonable exegesis that takes its departure from MT, emending sparingly and only when the grounds are decisive.

Special Note 39 — Job's Second Response (42:3-5)

It is here, and not in his First Response, that Job recognizes his error in challenging God. God's Second Speech, which has glorified the massive *Behemot* and *Leviathan*, has powerfully driven home the truth that the world is mysterious to man and not intended for his exclusive use. Job now realizes that, failing to understand the world, he has no right to criticize its Maker. It is only now that he "abases himself and repents in dust and ashes" for challenging God.

Some scholars, overlooking the differences in content and spirit between the two Responses, combine them into one (Bi., Du., Pfeiffer). However, after 40:5 in the First Response, 42:2 ff. articulates very poorly, for after Job has declared that he will speak no more (40:5), one expects silence on his part, not a continuation of his speech (42:2 ff.). On the basic differences between the two Responses, which validate their respective positions in the book, see Special Note 35 on "The Second Speech of The Lord."

An important stylistic trait supports the view that the Second Response was written by the author of the Dialogue. As was the case at the end of the First Cycle (chap. 12), at the end of the Second Cycle (chap. 21), and near or at the end of the somewhat disorganized Third Cycle (chap. 27), Job utilizes the device of citing the words of his "opponent" (42:3a and 4b) and reacting to it. On this important literary characteristic, see *BGM*, chap. XIII, and the Comm. *ad loc.*

The obvious difference, of course, is that in the earlier instances, Job attacks his human opponents; here he submits to God's superior wisdom.

Special Note 40 — The Jointure in the Epilogue (42:7-10)

The first section of the prose narrative, 42:7-10, is not part of the original folk-tale. This is clear on several grounds:

If the two verses 42:10–11 are read consecutively, as they appear in the present text, they are redundant and anticlimactic. After Job has been restored to his previous estate and indeed been given everything in double measure (42:10 end), there is no point in his relatives' coming to comfort him and give him each a small coin to help restore his fortunes! (42:11, end). Moreover, the theme of Job's being granted double all his previous possessions in v. 10 is spelled out in detail a few verses later (vv. 12–17).

It is, therefore, clear that v. 10 belongs to the jointure written by the poet to link the Epilogue of the familiar tale to the poetic Dialogue at the end (42:7–10). It parallels the jointure which he had composed to link the Prologue to the Dialogue at the beginning (2:11–13). The purpose of these jointures is, first, to introduce the Friends for the purpose of the discussion, and, finally, to dispose of them after the Dialogue is over, since they play no role in the folk-tale.

With v. 11, the traditional narrative utilized by the poet is resumed. Obviously, the full form of the original tale must have described Job's unflinching faith and steadfast patience in the face of his calamities, and Satan's public discomfiture when his efforts to subvert Job fail. The poet has used the traditional tale as a framework, "scooping out" the center as irrelevant to his purposes. For this reason the reintroduction of Satan in the Epilogue would have diminished the majesty of God and weakened the power of the approach to suffering implicit in the Speeches of The Lord by suggesting the possibility that evil is the result of the machinations of a diabolical creature and not really under God's control.

That 42:7–10 is the poet's jointure is demonstrated by the following considerations:

(1) Only these verses (7–10) make any reference to the Friends and to the Dialogue.

(2) The fact that Job must pray for the Friends is an instance of exquisite irony. Earlier, Eliphaz had given Job a lordly assurance that if he repented he would be able to win forgiveness for sinners (22:26–30). Now Eliphaz and his Friends are compelled to turn to Job to intercede for them, because it is he who is adjudged to have spoken the truth about God.

(3) The condemnation of the Friends' position can emanate only from the poet, whose sympathies are with Job, as is clear throughout the book by the extensive Speeches given to the sufferer. However, it is clear from the very full and fair presentation of the Friends' conventional theology in the Dialogue that the poet does not regard their position as "blasphemy" (*nebhālāh*), but rather as untrue (*lōʾ . . . nᵉkhōnāh*), less than adequate for dealing with reality.

Another approach to the prose tale accepted by some scholars was proposed by Albrecht Alt. Alt, whose merit it is to have recognized that 42:7–10 is distinct from 42:11 ff., proposed the theory that the Prologue and the Epilogue are to be divided into two tales, one earlier, one later (*ZATW*, New Series, XIV, 1937, pp. 265–88). The earlier tale (chap. 1 and 42:11–17) constitutes, as it were, an outer framework; the later tale (chap. 2 and

42:7–10) an inner layer surrounding the Dialogue. On this theory, the Friends originally urged Job to blaspheme God and, therefore, were castigated by Him in the Epilogue: "For you have not spoken the truth about Me as has My servant Job" (42:8). Job, on the other hand, had remained steadfast in his faith.

This theory of two prose tales suffers from grave weaknesses upon examination:

(1)   It destroys the dramatic architecture of the five scenes alternating between earth and heaven in chaps. 1 and 2.

(2)   It leaves the first narrative hanging in the air at the end of chap. 1, which, it must be assumed, continued in a section now lost.

(3)   The new tale, which begins with chap. 2, opens abruptly, unless we make the additional assumption that it possessed an introduction which has also been lost.

(4)   In order to explain God's strong condemnation of Eliphaz and his Friends, repeated twice, "for you have not spoken the truth about Me as has My servant Job" (vv. 7, 10), the theory postulates that the Friends in the original folk-tale urged Job to blaspheme (Du., MacDonald, Kraeling). Such an assumption would make either the Friends or Job's wife superfluous in the narrative, for both of them would be urging the same course of action upon Job. It should be noted that Job's wife and the Friends appear only in chap. 2, which is assumed to be the second Job tale.

An even more conclusive argument against assigning this role to the Friends is to be found in the term employed in God's castigation of the Friends as "not speaking what is right" (42:7, 8). The word $n^e kh\bar{o}n\bar{a}h$, "right, correct, true" (Gen. 41:30; Ps. 51:12; 57:8; 78:37; 108:2; and esp. Deut. 13:15; 17:14), is a synonym of $^{\supset}emet$, "true." It could be used in the negative ($l\bar{o}^{\supset} \ldots n^e kh\bar{o}n\bar{a}h$) to describe an unsatisfactory or untrue defense of God, but is much too weak for blasphemy. For this major sin, the proper word is $n^e bh\bar{a}l\bar{a}h$, "disgrace, contumely" (Gen. 34:7; Deut. 22:21), an untranslatable term representing the nadir of moral and religious infamy. This is the root that Job has used in stigmatizing his wife's counsel when she urges him to "curse God and die." The psalmist employs the same root to describe the denial of God: "The fool ($n\bar{a}bh\bar{a}l$) says in his heart, 'There is no God'" (Ps. 14:1 = 53:1; cf. 74:22).

Special Note 41 — The Conclusion of the Prose Tale (42:11–17)

Aside from the duplication of theme between 42:10b and 42:11, which goes back to the fact that the former verse belongs to the jointure and the latter to the popular tale, the two prose sources are well articulated. D-G pass a very negative judgment upon the Epilogue, declaring that "the hand (of the author of the Prologue) has lost its cunning before it reached the Epilogue." These scholars have evidently lost sight of the characteristics of the folk-tale, which tends to fill in details in the narrative and then to preserve them jealously both in form and substance through countless retellings. The tenacity of motifs in folk-tales is a fundamental principle in the study of folklore.

The simple standpoint of the narrative is radically different from the profundity of the Dialogue. The Epilogue naively assumes that the death of the children can be compensated for by new children and that Job's suffering can be fully recompensed by living twice the normal lifespan. Since Job has been unjustly deprived of his possessions and his offspring, everything is doubled. The number of his daughters, however, remains the same, on the theory that in the case of female offspring enough is sufficient! The doubling of his possessions, his male offspring, and his lifespan is in accordance with the ancient biblical law in Ex. 22:3, 11, which ordains double payment for a theft. However, customary law evidently imposed a higher penalty than the official biblical code; note the fourfold payment mentioned in II Sam. 12:6 (where LXX reads "sevenfold") and the sevenfold penalty referred to in Pr. 6:31. With the number of his years also double the usual lifespan, Job beholds four generations of his offspring instead of the usual blessing of two.

Obviously, in the original full form of the folk-tale, utilized by the poet, Satan must surely have appeared again for a confrontation with God and for his public discomfiture in the presence of the heavenly court after Job has demonstrated his unyielding piety. On the various stages of the folk-tale that can be reconstructed, cf. *BGM*, chap. VI. In adapting the narrative for his purposes, the poet had to omit Satan. Not only would his reappearance have been anticlimactic after the Speeches of The Lord out of the Whirlwind; even more important, the entire Dialogue has been predicated on the view that the cause of Job's suffering is unknown. Satan's presence at the end would have reduced the cosmic issue of evil in God's world to the level of a wager. Job is not the hero of an Oriental folktale — he is Everyman.

Special Note 42 — The Theory of Two Job Poems and the Unity of Job

In view of the complex problems of structure and meaning posed by the book of Job, it is entirely natural that some scholars attempt to meet them by the assumption of multiple authorship as the solution to the divergences, real or alleged, to be found in the different sections of the book.

The variations between the prose tale and the poetic Dialogue have led to the theory that both parts go back to different independent authors. The inadequacies of these theories, including the Alt-MacDonald hypothesis of two independent prose tales imbedded in our present text (chaps. 1–2), are presented in *BGM*, chap. VI, which also sets forth a reconstruction of the various stages of the prose tale before it reached its final form in our book. See also Special Note 40.

In the Third Cycle (chaps. 22–32), the evidence of the loss and dislocation of material is clear. Hence virtually all scholars have attempted to restore the original sequence to the extent possible. In addition, many have assumed that chaps. 24 and 28 are of independent authorship. Our own approach to these palpable problems of the Third Cycle, which minimizes the manipulation of the text required, is presented in *BGM* (pp. 93–113, 329–31, especially p. 329, n. 6) and in this Commentary, Special Notes 19–27. As for the Elihu chapters (chaps. 32–37), their authenticity is denied by many scholars because of the problems of style, substance, and structure that they raise. These issues are discussed in depth in *BGM*, chap. IX, and in this Commentary, Special Notes 28–31.

The most crucial problem, because it bears most directly upon the meaning of the book as a whole, is the significance and relevance of the two Speeches of the Lord Out of the Whirlwind (38:1–40:2 and 40:6–41:26), each of which is followed by a brief response by Job (40:3–6 and 42:1–6). Sharply divergent views have been expressed concerning the content, tone, and relevance of these God Speeches. The authenticity of one or both has been denied by some scholars, while others have combined them into one and many have excised large sections as being inauthentic. A critical analysis of these theories and of our own solution to the questions involved is presented in *BGM*, chaps. X, XI, and XIV, and in this Commentary, Special Notes 32–39.

On the basic of the evidence presented in *BGM*, passim, and throughout this Commentary, we believe that multiple authorship is an unnecessary and, indeed, untenable hypothesis, which destroys the architecture of the book. The variety of the various sections does not reflect a plurality of sources, but rather the genius of the author in molding the disparate elements upon which he drew into a unified masterpiece.

Subsequent to the publication of *BGM* in 1965, a new theory was proposed by H. L. Ginsberg, dividing the present book of Job into two distinct and independent compositions. The bulk of his article on Job in the *Encyclopedia Judaica* (vol. 10, columns 112–23) is devoted to defending this theory which he had set forth earlier in a paper in *Conservative Judaism*, vol. 21, 1967, pp. 12–28.

According to this hypothesis, the book of Job in its present form consists of two separate, originally independent and radically different works, "Job the Patient" (JP) and "Job the Impatient" (JIP).

"Job the Patient" consists of seven sections: (a) 1:1–2:8; (b) 2:9–10; (c) 2:11–13; (d) a missing section in which the Friends are alleged to have urged Job to denounce God; (e) chaps. 27–28, in which Job refuses to repudiate God and praises "the wisdom of godliness"; and (f) a missing section in which God gives Job the assurance that He will reward his steadfastness (of which only 42:7a has survived); and (g) 42:7b–17, God's rebuke of the Friends and His rehabilitation of Job.

The second composition, "Job the Impatient," is to be found in (a) chaps. 3–26; and (b) 29:1–42:6, though with many textual changes and transpositions.

Before we turn to a brief analysis of this theory, it is important to restate same fundamental methodological principles. Because biblical studies have been carried on for millennia and a substantial body of scholarship already exists, some students are tempted to one of several courses, either to ignore the work of predecessors or to appropriate the results of their research without reference to their source. Other scholars, in a natural desire for novelty, are led to promulgate new and sensational hypotheses, which they treat as demonstrated fact not to be questioned or doubted. Unfortunately, such theories are often presented with a dogmatism and vehemence in inverse proportion to their inherent plausibility.

It, therefore, becomes necessary to recall principles that in other areas of research would be rightly regarded as self-evident to the point of banality. The first is the great gulf between a fact and a theory. The second is "Occam's Razor" — essences are not to be multiplied beyond necessity.

To apply this principle to our theme, the existence of one book of Job is a *datum*, while the theory of two books of Job is a *hypothesis*. Thus the burden of proof rests upon the proponent of the new theory. Its power to persuade depends upon the degree to which it is free from difficulties of its own. Even more important is the extent to which it offers a more coherent interpretation, or, to borrow a term from the philosophy of science, a simpler and more elegant explanation of the phenomena being investigated. The fewer the assumptions made, the greater the plausibility of the theory.

Judged by this canon of scientific method, the theory of two books of Job, we believe, cannot carry conviction. A complete analysis of the theory in detail can not be presented here. However, what we regard as its major weaknesses may be briefly indicated.

The theory of "the two Jobs" assumes that approximately four and a half chapters were "supplemented" by the addition of thirty seven chapters, that are in total contradiction to "the original." Moreover, this division of the extant book of Job is not sufficient. We are compelled to postulate a large number of subsidiary hypotheses, excisions, transpositions and changes. Thus, 4:12–19 is pronounced inappropriate for Eliphaz and transferred to Job and interpreted to mean that God "is an impossible tyrant even with the angels" (*loc. cit.*, col. 121).

The vast amount of evidence for the use of "virtual quotations" available from Sumerian, Babylonian, Egyptian, biblical, and postbiblical Hebrew literature (see *BGM*, chap. 13 as well as Special Notes 13 and 17) has now received striking confirmation in the Qumran Aramaic Targum on 22:8 (see the Comm. *ad loc.*). It becomes increasingly difficult to understand Ginsberg's statement that "*the only natural and honest* interpretation of 27:2–6" (*italics ours*) is to treat it as a fragment from a disputation completely different from the surrounding material (cols. 113, 114).

By the insistence on the unity of chaps. 27 and 28, which are then transposed to the prose tale of "Job the Patient," the theory fails to reckon with the three sections of chap. 27, which are clearly distinct in content, style, and tone. Moreover, this hypothesis ignores the special literary form of chap. 28, ("The Hymn to Wisdom"), which is vastly different from the rest of the Dialogue, being lyrical and containing a refrain, and not argumentative (See Special Notes 23 and 24). The Third Cycle, to be sure, has suffered dislocation and loss of material, but the theory of "the two Jobs" fails to utilize the resources available for restoring the Cycle in great part. (See Special Note 20) Indeed, the theory compounds the damage by its radical manipulation of the text. In addition, if "Job the Impatient" was at one time an independent work, it must be assumed that the poetic Dialogue begins with no background material being supplied to the reader, unless there was another "loss of material." Moreover, the gifted author of the work must be regarded as introducing a new and totally different character and theme into the middle of an existing work, while remaining totally unaware of the intellectual and esthetic chaos he was creating. For JP (chaps. 1–2) is followed by JIP (chaps. 3–26), again by JP (chaps. 27–28), followed again by JIP (chaps. 29–41), followed once more by JP (the bulk of chap. 42). This aside from "minor" transpositions and changes.

In sum, this dissection of the Prologue and of the Dialogue and their assignment to two distinct compositions must be pronounced subjective and arbitrary, calling for a large number of assumptions for which there is no evidence and no need, since a simpler, less complicated approach is available. See *BGM*, chap. VI and Special Notes 40–41.

Only a few other observations may be made here. It is insisted that the Friends do not "dispute Job's claim to being a good man" (col. 114) and again "of course they do not declare that Job is a scoundrel" — this in the face of 22:5–10, which begins with Eliphaz's assertion, "Indeed your evil is great and there is no end to your sins." It is maintained that "13:7–10 means only that God will punish the Friends if they paint a false picture of a just world order" *while Job is formally indicting God,* and that since Eliphaz and his two companions hold their peace until Job has finished indicting God, there is no reason for God to punish the Friends, and our passage does not resemble 42:7–8 (col. 116). The question of the anticipation of 42:7–8 aside, the assertion that the Friends remain silent until Job has finished his indictment disregards chaps. 15, 18, 20, 22, and 25, where the Friends are entirely vocal and articulate, long before Job has finished talking.

On the exegetical difficulties involved in interpreting 42:7–8 as representing God's castigation of the Friends for allegedly urging Job to blaspheme and denounce Him, see Special Notes 40–41.

In 16:19, *ᶜedhī* and *sāhadī,* "My witness," is rendered "My opponent, adversary," which contradicts the well-attested meaning of the Hebrew word *ᶜēd* in Deutero-Isaiah אַתֶּם עֵדַי (Isa. 43:10; 44:8; cf. also Isa. 44:9; Job 10:17), whose influence upon Job the article recognizes. This unusual interpretation also destroys the progression of certitude and faith that Job displays in three successive passages, moving from the hope that there might be an arbiter (*mokhiaḥ* in 9:33) to his asseveration that his witness (*ᶜēdh*) will testify in his behalf, and is now in heaven (16:19) and finally to the climax of his conviction that his Redeemer (*gōʾēl*) will rise to avenge and vindicate him, even at the end of time (19:25). See Special Notes 14 and 16.

Notwithstanding our critique of the theory, we are pleased to find ourselves in agreement on several basic positions, such as the dependency of Job on Deutero-Isaiah and consequently the date of composition of Job set in the last quarter of the fifth century B.C.E. or somewhat later. But the theory as a whole must be pronounced unconvincing and unnecessary, with no objective evidence in its favor. On the other hand, the book of Job, in the form in which it has reached us, be it remembered, is a datum and not a hypothesis. A coherent and integrated view of the book is eminently possible, given the requisite insight and the utilization of the results of research into the text, style, and cultural background of the book.

— — — — — — —

Another approach to the composition of our present book is presented by N. H. Snaith (*The Book of Job — Its Origin and Purpose*, Alec R. Allenson, Naperville, Ill., 1968). As he generously points out in the Preface (*op. cit.*, pp. VIII, 8), he has been partially anticipated in some of his conclusions by *BGM*. His theory has the merit of requiring much less atomization and manipulation of the text than those of other scholars. He believes that "the first edition of the Book of Job as it was first shaped by the author consisted of 1:1–2:10; 3 and 29–31, 38–39 and an apology by Job (41:3–5), 40:6–41:26, parts of 42:1–16, then 42:9d ('and the Lord accepted Job') and 42:10–17, but omitting the phrase 'when he prayed for his friend'." On Snaith's view, what emerges is the first draft of a typical Oriental Wisdom book of "complaint and reconciliation" like "The Babylonian Job." Snaith believes that the same author then composed a second draft by interpolating the three Friends in the Prologue and the Epilogue (2:10–13; 42:7–10), and adding the Dialogue (chaps. 4–28). Later, the author created a third edition when the Elihu speeches (chaps. 32–37) were introduced (*op. cit.*, pp. 7, 8).

While Snaith's theory avoids the assumption of multiple authorship and the radical treatment of the text, it suffers, we believe, from several drawbacks. It requires the assumption that after the first draft of the book was complete the poet decided upon a new "edition," which actually represented a totally different theme. For the second draft presents nut the trials of a just man who was rewarded for his unyielding integrity and faith in God's justice, but a vigorous onslaught hurled against the injustice of God. Further, we must believe that the poet either ignored or was unaware of the radical differences, both in the theme and in the character of the chief protagonist in the two compositions, both of which he had himself composed, in order to be able to graft the second onto the first. This alleged process of combining two radically different works cannot be compared to the revisions or rewritings by authors of earlier works, like F. J. Pailey's *Festus*, or Bulwer-Lytton's *Zacci*, which Snaith adduces to buttress his theory (*op. cit.*, p. 10). It may be added that when Goethe, in his old age, arrived at a conception of the theme and of the central characters in *Faust* that was radically different from those in Part One, he did not introduce the new material into the existing text and thus vitiate the poem. Instead, he wrote an independent work, now Part Two, of *Faust*.

In addition to these larger considerations, Snaith's theory destroys the exquisite articulation of Job's lament on the day of his birth (chap. 3) with Eliphaz's urbane opening lines (4:2–6) at the beginning of the Dialogue.

Equally significant is Job's closing soliloquy (chaps. 29–31) which begins with his melancholy reflections on his previous happy estate and present misery (29–30) and ends with his passionate avowal of integrity and his demand for a confrontation with God (31:35–37). The last chapter is extraordinarily appropriate to a challenge, but not as a preface to the reconciliation which follows in Snaith's "first edition."

Snaith also assumes that chaps. 24–28 consist of separate, independent pieces. For our reconstruction of the Third Cycle and the meaning and form of "the Hymn to Wisdom" (chap. 28), see Special Notes 20, 22, 23.

Since there is obviously no objective evidence for the existence of these assumed independent works, the principle of Occam's Razor may legitimately be applied: *essentia non sunt multiplicanda praeter necessitatem.* I believe that the view presented in these pages has the advantage of making fewer assumptions, while taking into full account all the facts and problems in the present text.

The Book of Job is the work of one poet who adopted a familiar folktale and retold it with great skill, preserving its traditional form, in order to utilize it as a framework for a discussion on the problem of man's suffering in God's world. He then creates three characters, the Friends, in order to serve as participants in the Dialogue with Job, introducing them by a brief jointure that links the Prologue to the Dialogue (2:10–17) and by another jointure at the end in order to dismiss them (42:7–10). The poetic Dialogue has two principal sections, Job confronting his human antagonists (chaps. 3–27, 29–31) and Job being confronted by the Lord out of the Whirlwind (chaps. 38–41:26).

Some time after the conclusion of his masterpiece, the poet develops another, though minor, insight into the role of suffering, distinct from the conventional affirmations of the Friends on the one hand and the vigorous negations of Job on the other. He, therefore, creates a new character, Elihu, who occupies a middle position between Job and the Friends, his words being inserted (chaps. 32–37) before the major, definitive response of the Lord. Early in the history of the transmission of the text, the middle portion of the manuscript, that contained the Third Cycle, suffered a massive dislocation in some of the speeches, as well as a loss of material. This accident occurred before the composition of the Aramaic Targum of *Job*, fragments of which have been found at Qumran, since this translation apparently follows our present order. When the remains of the Third Cycle were put together by scribes, they included an earlier poem by the author, or a member of his school, the "Hymn to Wisdom" (chap. 28) which expresses *in parvo* the basic standpoint of the Speeches of the Lord.

The book thus emerges as a superbly structured unity, the work of a single author of transcendental genius, both as a literary artist and as a religious thinker, with few peers, if any, in the history of mankind.

TABLE OF ABBREVIATIONS

The Books of the Bible

(in the order of the biblical books)

Gen. = Genesis
Ex. = Exodus
Lev. = Leviticus
Nu. = Numbers
Deut. = Deuteronomy
Jos. = Joshua
Jud. = Judges
I Sam. = I Samuel
II Sam. = II Samuel
I Ki. = I Kings
II Ki. = II Kings
Isa. = Isaiah
Jer. = Jeremiah
Ezek. = Ezekiel
Hos. = Hosea
Joel (no abbreviation)
Am. = Amos
Ob. = Obadiah
Jonah (no abbreviation)
Mic. = Micah

Nah. = Nahum
Hab. = Habakkuk
Zeph. = Zephaniah
Hag. = Haggai
Zech. = Zechariah
Mal. = Malachi
Ps. = Psalms
Pr. = Proverbs
Job (no abbreviation)
Cant. = Song of Songs
Ruth (no abbreviation)
Lam. = Lamentations
Ecc. = Ecclesiastes
Est. = Esther
Dan. = Daniel
Ezra (no abbreviation)
Neh. = Nehemiah
I Chr. = I Chronicles
II Chr. = II Chronicles

General Abbreviations

A. = Aquila
abs. = absolute
acc. = accusative
ad loc. = at that place
adv. acc. = adverbial accusative
a. e. = and elsewhere
AJSL = *American Journal of Semitic Languages*
Akk. = Akkadian
ANET = J. B. Pritchard, *Ancient Near Eastern Texts in Relation to the Old Testament* (Princeton, 1950)
Ant. = *Antiquities* (of Josephus)
Apoc. = Apocalypse
Arab. = Arabic
Aram. = Aramaic
AV = Authorized Version (of the Bible)
A. Z. = *Abodah Zarah*

B. = Babylonian Talmud

Baer = S. Baer-F. Delitzsch, *Biblia Hebraica, Job* (Leipzig, 1875)

Ball = C. J. Ball, *The Book of Job* (Oxford, 1922)

Bar. = Baruch

Barth, *ES* = J. Barth, *Etymologische Studien* (Leipzig, 1893)

Barth, *NB* = J. Barth, *Nominalbildung in den semitischen Sprachen* (Leipzig, 1889)

BASOR = *Bulletins of the American Schools of Oriental Research*

BDB = Brown-Driver-Briggs (F. Brown, S. R. Driver, and C. A. Briggs), *A Hebrew and English Lexicon of the Old Testament* (Oxford, 1907)

Be. = G. Beer, *Der Text des Buches Hiob* (Marburg, 1895)

Ber. = *Berakhot*

Ber. Rabba = *Bereshith Rabba*

BGM = Robert Gordis, *The Book of God and Man — A Study of Job* (Chicago, 1965)

Bi. = G. Bickell, *Das Buch Hiob nach Anleitung der Strophik und der Septuaginta* (Vienna, 1894)

Bik. = *Bikkurim*

B. K. = *Baba Kamma*

B. Metz. = *Baba Metzia*

Brockelmann = C. Brockelmann, *Grundriss der vergleichenden Grammatik der semitischen Sprachen*, 2 vols. (Berlin, 1908)

B. S. = Ben Sira

BTM = Robert Gordis, *The Biblical Text in the Making* (New York, 1937, 1971)

Bu. = Karl Budde, *Das Buch Hiob: Beiträge zur Kritik des Buches Hiob* (1st ed., Göttingen, 1896; 2nd ed., Göttingen, 1913)

Buhl = F. Buhl, *Canon and Text of the Old Testament* (Edinburgh, 1892)

Buttenwieser = Moses Buttenwieser, *The Book of Job* (New York, 1922)

CBQ = *Catholic Biblical Quarterly*

cf. = confer (compare)

Chajes = Z. H. Chajes

chap., chaps. = chapter, chapters

Che. = T. K. Cheyne, *Job and Solomon* (New York, 1889)

CIS = *Corpus Inscriptionum Semiticarum* (Paris, 1911), 10 vols.

col., cols. = column, columns

comm. = commentators

Comm. = the Commentary

Condamin = A. Condamin, *Poèmes de la Bible* (Paris, 1933)

conj. = conjugation

consec. = consecutive

constr. = construct

Cooke = G. A. Cooke, *North Semitic Inscriptions* (Oxford, 1903)

Cowley = A. E. Cowley, *Aramaic Papyri of the Fifth Century* (Oxford, 1921)

Cross and Freedman = F. M. Cross, Jr., and D. N. Freedman, *Early Hebrew Orthography* (New Haven, 1952)

CTL = Robert Gordis, *Commentary on the Text of Lamentations* (New York, 1968)

Da. = A. B. Davidson, *The Book of Job* (Cambridge, 1884)

Del. = Franz Delitzsch, *Das Buch Iob* (Leipzig, 1864)

Del. = Friedrich Delitzsch, *Die Schreib- und Lesefehler im Alten Testament* (Berlin-Leipzig, 1920)

D-G = S. R. Driver and G. B. Gray, *A Critical and Exegetical Commentary on the Book of Job* ("International Critical Commentary," 2 vols., New York, 1921)

Dh. = P. Dhorme, *Le Livre de Job* (Paris, 1926)

Dil. = A. Dillmann, *Hiob* (Leipzig, 1891)

dir. = direct

Dozy = R. Dozy, *Supplément aux Dictionnaires Arabes* (Leiden, 1881), 2 vols.

Driver, *HT* = S. R. Driver, *Hebrew Tenses* (Oxford, 1896)

Du. = B. Duhm, *Das Buch Hiob erklaert* (Freiburg, 1897)

Ecclus. = Ecclesiasticus

ed. = edition

Ehr. = A. B. Ehrlich, *Randglossen zur hebräischen Bibel* (Volume VI, Leipzig, 1916)

Eisenstein = J. D. Eisenstein, *Oṣar Midrašim* (New York, 1915)

Eissfeldt = O. Eissfeldt, *Der Māšāl im Alten Testament* (Giessen, 1913)

Eitan = Israel Eitan, *A Contribution to Biblical Lexicography* (New York, 1924); *idem, Studies in Hebrew Roots* (Philadelphia, 1923)

Eng. = English

Erman = A. Erman, *Literature of the Ancient Egyptians* (New York, 1927)

Erub. = *Erubin*

ES = J. Barth, *Etymologische Studien* (Leipzig, 1893)

esp. = especially

Eth. = Ethiopic

Ew. = Georg Heinrich August von Ewald, *Das Buch Hiob* (Göttingen, 1854); *idem, Die Dichter des Alten Bundes* (Göttingen, 1854, 1867)

f. = following (1 verse or page)

ff. = following (more than 1 verse or page)

fem. = feminine

Field = F. Field, *Origenis Hexaplorum quae Supersunt* (Oxford, 1875)

I Cor. = I Corinthians

I Mac. = I Maccabees

FM = Robert Gordis, *A Faith for Moderns* (New York, 1960)

Frag. = Fragment

Geiger = Abraham Geiger, *Urschrift und Uebersetzungen der Bibel* (Breslau, 1857)

Ger. = German

Gers. = Gersonides (Rabbi Levi ben Gerson), *Commentary on Job* (Translated by A. L. Lassen, New York, 1946)

Ges. = William Gesenius

Ges.-K. = W. Gesenius and E. Kautzsch, *Grammatik der Hebräischen Sprache* (28th ed.)

Ginsberg = H. L. Ginsberg, *Kithbei Ugarit* (Jerusalem, 5696 = 1936)

Ginsburg = C. D. Ginsburg, *Introduction to a Masoretico-Critical Edition of the Hebrew Bible* (New York, 1966, Reprint)

Ginzberg, *Legends* = Louis Ginzberg, *Legends of the Jews* (7 vols.) (Philadelphia, 1913–1938)

Git. = *Gittin*

Gordon = C. H. Gordon, *Ugaritic Manual* (Rome, 1955); *idem, Ugaritic Textbook* (Rome, 1965)

Gr. = Heinrich Graetz, *Emendationes in . . . . V. T. Libros* (Breslau, 1892–94)

Gray = G. B. Gray, *The Forms of Hebrew Poetry* (1st ed., 1915; Reprint Edition, New York, 1972)

Grill = W. Grill, *Zur Kritik der Komposition des Buches Hiob* (Tübingen, 1890)

Guil. = A. Guillaume, *Studies in the Book of Job* (Leiden, 1968)

Ha. = Amos Hakham, *Sepher Iyyob* (Jerusalem, 1970)

Hag. = *Hagigah*

Hastings = J. Hastings, *Dictionary of the Bible* (New York, 1902–4), 4 vols.; 1 vol. ed. (Edinburgh, 1963)

Haupt = Paul Haupt

Heb. = Hebrew

Hi. = F. Hitzig, *Das Buch Hiob uebersetzt und erklaert* (Leipzig and Heidelberg, 1874)

Hö. = G. Hölscher, *Das Buch Hiob* ("Handbuch zum Alten Testament") (Tübingen, 1937)

Hoff. = J. C. E. Hoffmann, *Hiob* (1891)

Hoffmann = W. Hoffmann

Hor. = *Horayot*

Houb. = Houbigant

HT = S. R. Driver, Hebrew Tenses

HTR = *Harvard Theological Review*

HUCA = *Hebrew Union College Annual*

Hul. = *Hullin*

Hupf. = Hermann Hupfeld

Ibn E. = Abraham Ibn Ezra, Commentary to the Bible

Ibn Janah = Abulwalid Ibn Janah, *Sepher Hariqmah* (Frankfurt-am-Main, 1855)

Ibn Masnuth = Samuel ben Nissim Masnuth, *Maᶜyan Gannim* (edited by
    Salomon Buber, Berlin, 1889)
ICC = *International Critical Commentary*
i.e. = that is
impf. = imperfect
inf. = infinitive
Intr. = Introduction
IOT = R. H. Pfeiffer, *Introduction to the Old Testament* (New York, 1941)

J. = Jerusalem (Palestinian) Talmud
JAOS = *Journal of the American Oriental Society*
Jastrow = Morris Jastrow, *The Book of Job* (Philadelphia, 1920); *idem, The
    Religion of Babylonia and Assyria* (1898)
JBL = *Journal of Biblical Literature*
Jean and Hoftijzer = Charles F. Jean and Jacob Hoftijzer, *Dictionnaire des
    Inscriptions Sémitiques de l'Ouest* (Leiden, 1965)
Jeremias = Alfred Jeremias, *Das Leben nach dem Tode* (*The Babylonian
    Conception of Heaven and Hell*) (London, 1902)
Jn. = John
JNES = *Journal of Near Eastern Studies*
JPES = *Journal of the Palestine Exploration Society*
JPSV = Jewish Publication Society Version [of the Bible]
JQR = *Jewish Quarterly Review*
JRAS = *Journal of the Royal Asiatic Society*
JSS = *Journal of Semitic Studies*
JThS = *Journal of Theological Studies* (Oxford)

K. = Kethib
Kahle = P. Kahle, *Der Masoretische Text des A. T.* (Leipzig, 1902)
KB = L. Koehler and W. Baumgartner, *Lexicon in V. T. Libros* (1st ed.,
    Leiden, 1951)
Kel. = *Kelim*
Kenn. ms. = Kennicott manuscript
Keth. = *Kethubot*
Ki. = David Kimḥi, Commentary on Job in the Rabbinic Bible (no date;
    ca. 1160–1235)
Kid. = *Kiddushin*
Kil. = *Kilayim*
Kissane = E. J. Kissane, *The Book of Job* (Dublin, 1939)
Kit., *BH* = R. Kittel, *Biblia Hebraica* (4th ed., Stuttgart, 1937)
KJV = King James Version (of the Bible)
Klos. = A. Klostermann
KMW = Robert Gordis, *Koheleth — The Man and His World* (New York,
    1951)
Kraeling = E. G. Kraeling, *The Book of the Ways of God* (New York, 1938)

Larcher = C. Larcher, *Hiob* (1957)
Lat. = Latin
Levita = E. Levita, *Masoreth Hamasoreth*, ed. C. D. Ginsburg (New York, 1967), new ed.
Levy = R. Levy, *Trésor de la Langue des Juifs Français du Moyen Age* (Austin, Texas, 1964)
Ley = Julius Ley
LGJV = Louis Ginzberg Jubilee Volumes (New York, 1941; English volume, New York, 1945)
Licht = J. Licht, *Megillat Hahodayot* (Jerusalem, 5717 = 1957)
Lieberman = S. Lieberman, *Hellenism in Jewish Palestine* (New York, 1950)
lit. = literally
Lk. = Luke
LXX = Septuagint

M. = Mishnah
Mac. = Maccabees
masc. = masculine
McKenzie = J. L. McKenzie, *The Bible in Current Catholic Thought* (New York, 1962)
Me. = Adalbert Merx, *Das Gedicht von Hiob* (Jena, 1871)
Meg. = *Megillah*
Mekh. = *Mekhilta*
Men. = *Menaḥot*
Mi. = J. H. Michaelis, *Annotationes in Hagiographa* (Halle, 1720)
Mid. = *Midrash*
Mid. Cant. Rab. = *Midrash Song of Songs Rabba*
Mid. Ex. Rab. = *Midrash Exodus Rabba*
Mid. Koh. Rab. = *Midrash Koheleth Rabba*
Mid. Lev. Rab. = *Midrash Leviticus Rabba*
Mk. = Mark
Moffat = James Moffat, *The Holy Bible* (New York, 1926)
Montgomery = J. A. Montgomery, *Arabia and the Bible* (Philadelphia, 1934)
Mowinckel = Sigmund Mowinckel, *Psalmenstudien* (Christiania, 1921–1924); *The Psalms in Israel's Worship* (New York, 1902)
ms. = manuscript
mss. = manuscripts
Mt. = Matthew
MT = Masoretic Text (of the Bible)

n. = note
NAB = New American Bible (New York, 1970)
NB = J. Barth, *Nominalbildung in den Semitischen Sprachen* (Leipzig, 1889)
NEB = New English Bible (Oxford, 1970)
neg. = negative
Nid. = *Niddah*

NSI = G. A. Cooke, *North Semitic Inscriptions*
N. T. = New Testament
NWSPJ = M. J. Dahood, "Northwest Semitic Philology and Job," in J. L. McKenzie, *The Bible in Current Catholic Thought* (1962)

obj. = object
Ohol. = *Oholot*
Ol. = Julius Olshausen, *Hiob* (Leipzig, 1852)
OLZ = *Orientalische Literaturzeitung*
opp. = opposed, opposed to
O. T. = Old Testament

p. = page
pp. = pages
P = Peshitta (Pešita)
P. = Palestinian (or Jerusalem) Talmud
P. = Marvin Pope, *Job* (Anchor Bible, New York, 1965; 3rd ed. 1973)
par. = paragraph, paragraphs
Parhon = Solomon ibn Parhon, *Mahberet Heᶜarukh* (ed. S. G. Stein, Pressburg, 1844)
part. = particle or participle
passim = throughout
Patai = R. Patai, *The Hebrew Goddess* (New York)
Peake = A. S. Peake, *Job* (Century Bible, Edinburgh and London, 1905)
Pedersen = J. Pedersen, *Israel: Its Life and Culture* (London and Copenhagen, 1926)
PEF = Palestine Exploration Fund
PEQ = *Palestine Exploration Quarterly*
Per. = F. Perles
perf. = perfect
pers. = person
Pes. = *Pesahim*
Pesik. = Pesikta
Pfeiffer = R. H. Pfeiffer, *Introduction to the Old Testament* (New York, 1941)
Pinsker = S. Pinsker, *Maboᵓ Laniqqud Haᵓašuri Vehababhli* (Vienna, 1863)
pl., plur. = plural
PPS = Robert Gordis, *Poets, Prophets and Sages* (Bloomington and London, 1971)
pred. = predicate
prep. = preposition
Pritchard = J. B. Pritchard, *Ancient Near Eastern Texts in Relation to the Old Testament* (Princeton, 1950)

Q. = Qere
q. v. = which see

Ra. = Rashi (Rabbi Solomon Yitzhaki, Commentary to the Bible)
Rankin = O. S. Rankin, *Israel's Wisdom Literature* (Edinburgh, 1936)
RB = *Revue biblique*
ref. = reference, references
Reiske = Bo Reiske
Reuss = Eduard Reuss
Rev. = Revelation
R-O = A. *Z.* Rabinowitz and A. Obronin, *Iyyob* [Commentary on Job]
    (Jaffa, 5676 = 1916)
Roberts = B. J. Roberts, *The Old Testament Text and Versions* (Cardiff, 1951)
Ros. = F. K. Rosenmüller
RSV = Revised Standard Version (of the Bible)

S = Samaritan text of the Pentateuch
Sanh. = *Sanhedrin*
sc. = scilicet
Schult. = A. Schultens, *Liber Jobi* (Leiden, 1737)
sec. = section, sections
Segal = M. H. Segal, *Diqduq Leshon Hamishnah* (Tel Aviv, 1936)
Shab. = *Shabbat*
Shev. = *Shevuoth*
Sieg. = Karl Siegfried, *The Book of Job* (Leipzig-Baltimore, 1893; English
    edition, Baltimore, 1893)
sing. = singular
SLF = Friedrich Delitzsch, *Schreib- und Lesefehler im Alten Testament* (Berlin-
    Leipzig, 1920)
Smith = Robert Payne Smith, *Thesaurus Syriacus* (Oxford, 1927)
Smith = W. Robertson Smith, *Prophets of Israel* (Edinburgh, 1882); *idem,*
    The Religion of the Semites (New York, 1969), Reprint ed.
SS = Robert Gordis, *The Songs of Songs* (New York, 1954, 1974)
Stade = B. Stade
Steuernagel = Carl Steuernagel, *Hiob* (1923)
Studer = G. L. Studer, *Das Buch Hiob* (Bremen, 1881)
subj. = subject
suf. = suffix
Suk. = *Sukkah*
Sym. = Symmachus
Syr. = Syriac

T = Targum
T. = Tosefta
Taan. = *Taanit*
Tar. = Targum
Ter. = S. L. Terrien, *Job: Un commentaire* (Neuchâtel, 1963); *idem, Job —*
    Poet of Existence (New York, 1957)

Test. Abr., XII Patr. = *Testament of Abraham, Testaments of the XII Patriarchs*

Th. = Theodotion

Thilo = Martin Thilo, *Das Buch Hiob* (Barmen, 1925)

ThLz = *Theologische Literaturzeitung*

Th. St. Kr. = *Theologische Studien und Kritiken*

Thomson = W. M. Thomson, *The Land The People* (New York, 1913 ed.)

Toh. = *Tohorot*

Trans. = Translation

TS = N. H. Tur-Sinai, *Das Buch Hiob* (Vienna-Berlin, 1920); *idem, Sefer Iyyob* (Jerusalem, 5701 = 1941); *idem, The Book of Job — A New Commentary* (Jerusalem, 1957); *idem, Lašon Vasepher* (Jerusalem, 5711 = 1950)

Twersky = I. Twersky, *A Maimonides Reader* (New York, 1972)

Umbreit = Friedrich W. C. Umbreit, *Das Buch Hiob* (Heidelberg, 1824)

UT = C. H. Gordon, *Ugaritic Textbook* (Rome, 1965)

v. = verse

V = Vulgate

van den Brock = R. van den Brock, *The Myth of the Phoenix* (Leiden, 1972)

Voight = C. Voight, *Einige Stellen des Buches Hiob* (Lauban, 1885)

vol., vols. = volume, volumes

Volz = Paul Volz, *Weisheit (Das Buch Hiob, Sprüche Jesus Sirach, Prediger),* Uebersetzt und erklaert (Göttingen, 1911)

VT = *Vetus Testamentum*

Vss. = The Versions (the Ancient Versions of the Bible)

vv. = verses

WB = R. Gordis, *The Word and the Book — Studies in Biblical Language and Literature* (New York, 1976)

Wel. = J. Wellhausen, *Prolegomenon*

Wr. = G. H. B. Wright, *The Book of Job* (London, 1883)

Yeb. = *Yebamot*

Yel. = D. Yellin, *Ḥiqre Miqra — Iyyob* (Jerusalem, 5687 = 1927)

ZA = *Zeitschrift für Assyriologie*

ZATW = *Zeitschrift fuer die Alttestamentliche Wissenschaft*

ZDMG = *Zeitschrift der Deutschen Morgenlaendischen Gesellschaft*

Zeb. = *Zebaḥim*

BIBLIOGRAPHY

A. *Texts and Versions*

The Hebrew Text

BAER, S., and F. DELITZSCH. *The Books of the Old Testament*, Leipzig, 1869–95.
GINSBURG, C. D. *Masoretic Bible.* London, 1st ed., 1894; 2d ed., 1926.
KITTEL, R. *Biblia Hebraica.* 4th ed.; Stuttgart, 1937. Edited by A. Alt and O. E. Eissfeldt (Masoretic notes by P. Kahle. Job edited by G. Beer).

The Septuagint

SWETE, H. B. *The Old Testament* in Greek. Cambridge, 1887–94.
RAHLFS, A. *Septuaginta.* 2 vols. Stuttgart, 1935.

Aquila, Symmachus, Theodotion

FIELD, F. *Origenis Hexaplorum quae Supersunt.* Oxford, 1875.

The Vulgate

STIER, R., and K. G. W. THEILE. *Polyglotten-Bibel.* 4th ed. Bielefeld-Leipzig, 1875.

The Peshita

Kethabe Kadishe. Edited by S. Lee, London, 1823.

The Targum

Qumran Targum (11Q tg Job) *Le Targum de Job de la Grotte XI de Qumran,* édité et traduit par J. P. M. van der Ploeg et A. S. van der Woude, avec collaboration de B. Jongeling, Koninklijke nederlandse Akademie van Wetenschappen. Leiden: Brill, 1972.
Mikraoth Gedoloth. Vilna, 1912, often reprinted.

Arabic

Translation by Saadiah ben Joseph Alfayyumi. ed. Joseph Qapaḥ, *Sepher Iyyob im Targum Upheruš Rabbi Saᶜadia Gaᵓon* (Jerusalem, 1970).

B. *Sources*

The Old Testament

The New Testament

The Apocrypha and Pseudepigrapha of the Old Testament. Edited by R. H. Charles. Oxford, 1913.
Works of Josephus ("Loeb Classics").
Mekilta de-Rabbi Išmael. Edited by J. Z. Lauterbach. Philadelphia, 1933.
Sifre de be Rab. Edited by M. Friedmann. Vienna, 1864.
Mišnah. Vilna edition, frequently reprinted.
Tosefta. Edited by M. S. Zuckermandl. 2d ed. Jerusalem, 1938.
The Tosefta, edited with a Brief Commentary, by Saul Lieberman, New York, 1955–   ).
Aboth de Rabbi Nathan. Edited by S. Schechter. 2d printing. New York, 1945.
Babylonian Talmud. Vilna, 1928, frequently reprinted.
Jerusalem Talmud. Krotoschin, 1866.
Midraš Rabbah on the Torah and the Megilloth. Vilna edition, frequently reprinted.
Pesikta de Rab Kahana. ed. B. Mandelbaum, New York, 1962.
Midraš Tehillim. Edited by S. Buber, Vilna, 1890.

Midraš Iyyobh. Edited by S. A. Wertheimer. Batei Midrašot. 2d ed. Edited by A. Wertheimer. Jerusalem, 5713 = 1953.

C.   *Commentaries*

This chronological list of the principal commentaries affords a survey of the history of the interpretation of Job.

SAADIAH BEN JOSEPH GAON (882–942), see under Texts and Versions
RASHI [RABBI SOLOMON ITZHAKI (1040–1105)].
SAMUEL BEN NISSIM MASNUTH. (12th cent.) *Mayan Gannim.* Edited by Salomon Buber, Berlin, 1889.
RAMBAN [RABBI MOSHE BEN NAHMAN or NAHMANIDES (1194–1270)].
RALBAG [RABBI LEVI BEN GERSHON or GERSONIDES (1288–1344)]. Translated by A. L. Lassen. New York, 1946.
MENDELSSOHN, MOSES. *Bible Commentary on Job.* Berlin, 1789.
RENAN, E. *Le Livre de Job.* 3d ed. Paris, 1864.
DELITZSCH, FRANZ. *Das Buch Job.* Leipzig, 1864.
HITZIG, F. *Das Buch Hiob uebersetzt und ausgelegt.* Leipzig and Heidelberg, 1874.
SZOLD, BENJAMIN. *Sefer Iyyob.* Baltimore, 1886.
DILLMANN, A. *Hiob.* Leipzig, 1891.
BEER, G. *Der Text des Buches Hiob.* Marburg, 1895.
BUDDE, K. *Das Buch Hiob* ("Handkommentar zum Alten Testament"). Göttingen, 1st ed., 1896; 2d ed., 1913.
DUHM, B. *Das Buch Hiob erklaert.* Freiburg, 1897.
STRASHUN, ABRAHAM DAVID, *Mᵉyaššer Nᵉbhuḥim.* Vilna, 1897.
RABINOWITZ, A. Z., and A. OBRONIN. *Iyyob.* Jaffa, 5676 = 1916.
EHRLICH, A. B. *Randglossen zur hebräischen Bibel.* Vol. VI, Leipzig, 1918.
TORCZYNER, HARRY. *Das Buch Hiob.* Vienna-Berlin, 1920.
DRIVER, S. R., and G. B. GRAY. *A Critical and Exegetical Commentary on the Book of Job* ("International Critical Commentary"). 2 vols. New York, 1921.
BALL, C. J. *Book of Job.* Oxford, 1922.
BUTTENWIESER, M. *The Book of Job.* New York, 1922.
DHORME, P. *Le Livre de Job.* Paris, 1926.
YELLIN, D. *Hiqre Miqra — Iyyob.* Jerusalem, 5687 = 1927.
KÖNIG, E. *Das Buch Hiob.* 2d ed. Gutersloh, 1929.
SZCYGIEL, P. *Das Buch Hiob.* Bonn, 1931.
HÖLSCHER, G. *Das Buch Hiob* ("Handbuch zum Alten Testament"). Tübingen, 1937.
KISSANE, E. J. *The Book of Job.* Dublin, 1939.
TORCZYNER, N. H. *Sefer Iyyob.* Jerusalem, 5701 = 1941.
SNAITH, N. H. *The Book of Job.* London, 1945.
REICHERT, V. E. *Job* ("Soncino Bible"). Hindhead, Surrey, 1946.
HERTZBERG, H. W. *Das Buch Hiob.* Stuttgart, 1949.
JUNKER, H. *Das Buch Hiob.* Würzburg, 1951.
WEISER, A. *Das Buch Hiob.* Göttingen, 1951.
STEVENSON, W. B. *Critical Notes on the Hebrew Text of the Poem of Job.* Aberdeen, 1951.
STIER, F. *Das Buch Hiob.* Munich, 1954.
TERRIEN, S. L. Exegetical Commentary in *The Interpreter's Bible.* Vol. 3. New York-Nashville, 1954.
STEINMANN, J. *Le Livre de Job.* Paris, 1955.
TUR-SINAI, N. H. *The Book of Job — A New Commentary.* Jerusalem, 1957.
FREEHOF, S. B. *The Book of Job — A Commentary.* New York, 1958.
GUILLAUME, A. *Studies in the Book of Job.* Leiden, 1960.
HORST, F. *Hiob.* Neunkirchen, 1960.
       Hiob. I. Teilband (chaps. i–xix) (Biblischer Kommentar, XVI/1), 1968.
TERRIEN, S. L. *Job* ("Commentaire de l'Ancien Testament"). Neuchâtel, 1963.

Pope, Marvin. *Job* ("Anchor Bible"). New York, 1965; 2d. ed. 1973.
Haham, A. Sepher *Iyyobh*. Jerusalem, 1970.
Neiman, D. *The Book of Job*. Jerusalem, 1972.

D. *Studies in Job and Wisdom Literature*

Bacher, W. "Das Targum zu Hiob," *MGWJ*, XX (1871).
Baumann, E. "Die Verwendbarkeit der Pesita zu Hiob für die Textkritik," *ZATW*, XVIII–XX (1898–1900).
Budde, K. *Beiträge zur Kritik des Buches Hiob*. Göttingen, 1876.
Carstensen, R. N. *Job: Defense of Honor*. Nashville, 1963.
Cheyne, T. K. *Job and Solomon*. New York, 1889.
Dahood, M. J. "Qoheleth and Recent Discoveries," *Biblica*, XXXIX (1958).
   "Northwest Semitic Philology and Job" in J. L. McKenzie, *The Bible in Current Catholic Thought*, 1962.
Dhorme, P. "Ecclesiastes ou Job?" *RB*, XXXII (1923).
Dubarle, A. M. *Les Sages d'Israël*. Paris, 1946.
Ebeling, E. "Reste Akkadischer Weisheitsliteratur," *Meissner Festschrift*, I (1928).
Eerdmans, B. D. *Studies in Job*. Leiden, 1939.
Eissfeldt, O. *Der Maschal im Alten Testament*. Giessen, 1913.
Fichtner, J. *Die altorientalische Weisheitsliteratur in ihrer israelitisch-jüdischen Ausprägung*. Giessen, 1933.
Foster, F. H. "Is the Book of Job a Translation from an Arabic Original?" *AJSL*, XLIX (1932–33).
Froude, J. A. *The Book of Job*. London, 1854.
Fullerton, K. "The Original Conclusion of Job," *ZATW*, XXIV (1924).
Gard, D. H. *The Exegetical Method of the Greek Translator of the Book of Job* ("*JBL* Monograph Series," Vol. VIII). 1952.
Gaspar, J. W. *Social Ideas in the Wisdom Literature of the Old Testament*. Washington, 1947.
Gehman, H. S. "The Theological Approach of the Greek Translator of Job 1–15," *JBL* 68 (1949).
Ginsberg, H. L. "Studies in the Book of Job," *Lešonenu*, vol. 21, 1956, 259–66.
   "Job the Patient and Job the Impatient," in *Conservative Judaism*, vol. 21, 1967, pp. 12–28.
   Art. "Job" in *Encyclopedia Judaica*.
   Koheleth (A Commentary in Hebrew), Jerusalem, 5721 = 1961.
Louis Ginzberg Jubilee Volumes (New York, 1945).
Ginzberg. Louis Ginzberg Jubilee Volumes (New York, 1945).
Gordis, R. "All Men's Book — A New Introduction to Job," *Menorah Journal*, XXXVII (1949).
   The Book of God and Man. A Study of Job (Chicago, 1965).
   "Corporate Personality in Job," *JNES*, IV (1945).
   Koheleth — The Man and His World. New York, 1951 (= KMW).
   "Qoheleth and Qumran — A Study in Style," *Biblica*, XLI (1960).
   "Quotations as a Literary Usage in Biblical, Oriental and Rabbinic Literature," *HUCA*, XXII (1949), reprinted in *PPS*.
   "The Social Background of Wisdom Literature," *HUCA*, XVIII (1943), reprinted in *PPS*.
   "The Temptation of Job — The Conflict of Tradition and Experience," *Judaism*, vol. IV, No. 3 (1955). Reprinted in *PPS*.
   The Wisdom of Ecclesiastes. New York, 1945.
Grill, W. *Zur Kritik der Komposition des Buches Hiob*. Tübingen, 1890.
Humbert, P. *Recherches sur les Sources égyptiennes de la Littérature sapientiale d'Israel*. Neuchâtel, 1929.

JASTROW, MORRIS. *The Book of Job*. Philadelphia, 1920.
 The Gentle Cynic. Philadelphia, 1919.
JUNG, C. G. *Answer to Job*. London, 1964.
KALLEN, H. M. *The Book of Job as a Greek Tragedy Restored*. New York, 1918.
KAUTZSCH, K. *Das sogenannte Volksbuch von Hiob*. Leipzig, 1900.
KEVIN, R. O. *The Wisdom of Amen-em-apt and Its Possible Dependence Upon the Hebrew Book of Proverbs*. Philadelphia, 1931.
KOHLER, KAUFMANN. "The Testament of Job," *Semitic Studies in Memory of Dr. Alexander Kohut*. Berlin, 1897.
KRAELING, E. G. *The Book of the Ways of God*. New York, 1939.
KRAMER, S. N. "Man and his God: A Sumerian Variation on the 'Job' Motif," in *Wisdom in Israel and the Ancient Orient* (Leiden, 1955).
LAMBERT, W. G. *Babylonian Wisdom Literature*. Oxford, 1960.
MACDONALD, D. B. *The Hebrew Philosophic Genius*. Princeton, 1936.
MANDL, A. *Die Peschita zu Hiob*. Leipzig, 1892.
MULLER, H. P., *Hiob und seine Freunde* (Zurich, 1970).
NOTH, M. "Noah, Daniel and Hiob in Ezekiel XIV," VT 1 (1951).
NOTH, M., and D. W. THOMAS, eds., *Wisdom in Israel and in the Ancient Near East* (Presented to H. H. Rowley on His Sixty-fifth Birthday.), VTS, iii, 1955.
OESTERLEY, W. O. E. *The Book of Proverbs*. Philadelphia, 1929.
ORLINSKY, H. M. "Studies in the Septuagint of the Book of Job," *HUCA*, XXVIII–XXXIII (1957–62).
PFEIFFER, R. H. *Le Problème du Livre de Job*. Geneva, 1915.
RAD, G. VON. *Weisheit in Israel* (Neunkirchen-Vluyn, 1970), Eng. Tr. *Wisdom in Israel* (New York, 1973).
RANKIN, O. S. *Israel's Wisdom Literature, Its Bearing on Theology and the History of Religion*. Edinburgh, 1936.
RANSTON, H. *The Old Testament Wisdom Books and Their Teachings*. London, 1930.
ROBINSON, H. WHEELER. *Suffering Human and Divine*. New York, 1939.
ROWLEY, H. H. "The Book of Job and its Meaning," *Bulletin of the John Rylands Library*, XLI (1958).
RÝLAARSDAM, J. C. *Revelation in Jewish Wisdom Literature*. Chicago, 1946.
SANDERS, J. A. *Suffering as a Divine Discipline in the Old Testament and Post-Biblical Judaism*. Rochester, N. Y., 1955.
SANDERS, PAUL. *Twentieth Century Interpretations of The Book of Job*. Englewood Cliffs, N. J., 1968.
SARNA, N. M. "Epic Substratum in the Prose of Job," *JBL* 76 (1957).
SCOTT, R. B. Y. *The Way of Wisdom* (New York, 1972).
SEGAL, M. M. *Sefer Ben Sira Hashalem*. Jerusalem, 5713 = 1953.
SHAPIRO, D. S. "The Problem of Evil and the Book of Job," *JUDAISM* 5 (1956).
SINGER, R. E. *Job's Encounter*. New York, 1963.
SKEHAN, P. W. "Strophic Patterns in the Book of Job," *CBQ* 23, 1961.
SNAITH, N. H. *The Book of Job — Its Origin and Purpose*. Napierville, Ill., 1968.
SPIEGEL, S. "Noah, Daniel and Job," *Louis Ginzberg Jubilee Volumes*. New York, 1945.
STAPLES, W. E. *The Speeches of Elihu*. Toronto, 1924.
STEVENSON, W. B. *The Poem of Job*. London, 1947.
STOCKHAMMER, M., "The Righteousness of Job," *JUDAISM* 7 (1958).
 Das Buch Hiob: Versuch einer Theodizee. Vienna, 1963.
STRAHAN, JAMES. *The Book of Job*. Edinburgh, 1913.
TERRIEN, S. L. *Job: Poet of Existence*. New York, 1957.
TSEVAT, MATTITYAHU., "The Meaning of the Book of Job," *HUCA*, vol. 37, 1966.
VOLZ, P. *Hiob und Weisheit in den Schriften des Alten Testaments*. Göttingen, 1921.
WESTERMANN, C. *Der Aufbau des Buches Hiob*. Tübingen, 1956.
WJERNIKOWSKI, A. *Das Buch Hiob nach der rabbinischen Agada*. Frankfurt, 1893.
ZHITLOWSKY, CHAIM. *Job and Faust*.

E. *General Bibliography*

ALBECK, CH. (ed.), *Sišah Sidrei Mišnah*. Jerusalem, 1954.

ALBRIGHT, W. F. *Archaeology and the Religion of Israel*. Baltimore, 1942.

BARR, J., *Semantics of Biblical Language*, Oxford, 1961.

BARTH, J., *Etymologische Studien*, Leipzig, 1893.

BARTON, G. A., *Archaeology and the Bible*. 7th ed., Philadelphia, 1937.

BEN-JEHUDA, ELIEZER. *Thesaurus* ("Millon Halašon Haivrit Hayešanah Vehaḥadašah"). 16 vols. Jerusalem, 1912–1948; reprinted 1959.

BENTZEN, A. *Introduction to the Old Testament*. 2d ed., Copenhagen, 1948.

BLANK, S. H. *Jeremiah, Man and Prophet*. Cincinnati, 1961.

　　Prophetic Faith in Isaiah. New York, 1958.

BRIGHT, JOHN. *History of Israel*. Philadelphia, 1959.

BROCKELMANN, C., *Grundriss der vergleichenden Grammatik der semitischen Sprachen*, 2 vols., Berlin, 1908.

BROWN, F., S. R. DRIVER, and C. A. BRIGGS. *A Hebrew and English Lexicon of the Old Testament*. Oxford, 1907.

BUDGE, E. A. WALLIS (ed.). *The Book of the Dead*. New York, 1956.

BUHL, F. *Canon and Text of the Old Testament*. Edinburgh, 1892.

BURCHARD, CH. *Bibliographie zu den Handschriften vom Toten Meer*. Berlin, 1957.

BURROWS, MILLAR. *Outline of Biblical Theology*. Philadelphia, 1946.

CASANOWICZ, I. M. *Paronomasia in the Old Testament*. Boston, 1894.

CHARLES, R. H. *A Critical History of the Doctrine of a Future Life*. London, 1899.

CHEYNE, T. K. *Encyclopedia Biblica*. 4 vols. New York, 1899–1903.

CHURGIN, P. *Targum Kethubim*. New York, 5705 = 1945.

COBB, W. H. *A Criticism of Systems of Hebrew Metre*. Oxford, 1905.

CORNILL, C. *Introduction to the Canonical Books of the Old Testament*. New York, 1907.

COWLEY, A. E. *Aramaic Papyri of the Fifth Century B. C.* Oxford, 1923.

DAVIDSON, ISRAEL (ed.). *Selected Religious Poems of Solomon ibn Gabirol*. Philadelphia, 1923.

DENNEFELD, L. *Introduction à l'Ancien Testament*. Paris, 1934.

DE WETTE, W. M. L. *Introduction to the Old Testament*. Vol. II. Boston, 1843.

DOZY, R. *Supplément aux Dictionnaires Arabes*. Leiden, 2d ed., 1927.

DRIVER, G. R., and J. C. MILES. *The Assyrian Laws*. Oxford, 1935.

DRIVER, S. R. *Hebrew Tenses*. Oxford, 1892.

　　Introduction to the Literature of the Old Testament. 9th ed. New York, 1913.

DUPONT-SOMMER, A. *The Essene Writings From Qumran*. Oxford, 1961.

EICHRODT, W. *Theology of the Old Testament*. Philadelphia, 1961.

EISENSTEIN, J. D. *Oṣar Midrašim*. New York, 1915.

EISSFELDT, O. *Einleitung in das Alte Testament*. Tübingen, 1934. English Translation, *The Old Testament — An Introduction*. New York, 1965.

ERMAN, A. *The Literature of the Ancient Egyptians*. Translated by A. M. Blackman. New York, 1927.

FINKELSTEIN, L. (ed.). *The Jews — Their History, Culture and Religion*. 2 vols. New York, 1960.

　　The Pharisees. 2 vols. Philadelphia, 1938.

FRANKFORT, H. *The Intellectual Adventures of Ancient Man*. Chicago, 1955.

FRAZER, J. G. *Folklore of the Old Testament*. London, 1918.

FREEDMAN, D. N., and F. M. CROSS. *Early Hebrew Orthography*. New Haven, 1952.

GASTER, T. H. *Thespis*. New York, 1950.

　　Myth, Legend and Custom in the Old Testament (New York, 1969).

GINSBERG, H. L. *Studies in Daniel*. New York, 1948.

　　Kithbei Ugarit, Jerusalem 5696 = 1936.

GINSBURG, C. D. *Introduction to a Massoretico-Critical Edition of the Hebrew Bible*, London, 1897; New York, 1966.

GINZBERG, L. *Legends of the Jews*. 7 vols. Philadelphia, 1913–38.

"The Place of Halacha in Jewish Research," in *On Jewish Law and Lore*. Philadelphia, 1955.

GLATZER, N. M. *Franz Rosenzweig — His Life and Thought*. New York, 1953.

GOETHE, J. W. *Faust*. Edited by Calvin Thomas. Boston, 1894, and often.

GOETTSBERGER, J. *Einleitung in das Alte Testament*. Freiburg-im-Breisgau, 1928.

GORDIS, ROBERT. "Al Mibneh Haširah Haivrit Haquedumah" ("On the Structure of Ancient Hebrew Poetry"), *Sefer Hašanah Liyehudei Amerikah*. New York, 5705 = 1944, reprinted in *PPS*.

"The Asseverative Kaph in Hebrew and Ugaritic," *JAOS*, vol. 63, 1943, reprinted in *WB*.

"The Bible as a Cultural Monument," in *The Jews — Their History, Culture and Religion*. Edited by Louis Finkelstein. 2d ed., New York, 1960. Reprinted in *PPS*.

The Biblical Text in the Making. Philadelphia, 1937. Augmented edition, 1971.

"The Composition and Structure of Amos," *HThR*, XXXIII (1940). Reprinted in *PPS*.

A Faith for Moderns. New York, 1960. Augmented edition, 1971.

"Hosea's Marriage and Message" in *HUCA*, vol. 27, 1954, reprinted in *PPS*.

"The Knowledge of Good and Evil in the Old Testament and the Qumran Scrolls," *JBL*, LXXVI (1957), reprinted in *PPS*.

"Lešon Miqraɔ Leɔor Lešon Ḥakhamim" in *Sefer Tur-Sinai* (Jerusalem, 5720 = 1960), reprinted in *WB*.

"Liseguloth Hameliṣah Bekhithebei Haqodeš," *Sepher Muggaš Likhebhod Doktor Mošeh Seidel*. Jerusalem, 5722 = 1962, reprinted in *WB*.

"Midrash — Its Method and Meaning," *Midstream* (Summer, 1959).

"On the Methodology of Biblical Exegesis" in *JQR*, vol. 61, 1970, reprinted in *WB*.

"A Note on Yad," *JBL*, LXII (1943), reprinted in *WB*.

Poets, Prophets and Sages. Bloomington, Indiana, 1971.

"Primitive Democracy in Ancient Israel," *Alexander Marx Jubilee Volume*. New York, 1950, reprinted in *PPS*.

"Psalm 9-10: A Textual and Exegetical Study," *JQR*, XLVIII (1957), reprinted in *WB*.

"A Rhetorical Use of Interrogative Sentences in Biblical Hebrew," *AJSL*, vol. 49, 1933, reprinted in *WB*.

The Root and the Branch: Judaism and the Free Society. Chicago, 1962.

"The Significance of the Paradise Myth," *AJSL*, LII (1936), reprinted in *WB*.

The Song of Songs and Lamentations (New York, 1973).

"Studies in the Relationship of Biblical and Rabbinic Hebrew," *Louis Ginzberg Jubilee Volumes*. New York, 1945, reprinted in *WB*.

The Word and the Book — Studies in Biblical Language and Literature (New York, 1976) = *WB*.

"Yiḥusei Hakhethibh Vehanniqqud Balašon Ha-ivrith," *Lešonenu* (5696 = 1937).

GORDON, C. H. *Before the Bible*. New York, 1963.

Ugaritic Handbook. Rome, 1947.

Ugaritic Manual. Rome, 1955.

Ugaritic Textbook. Rome, 1965.

GRAY, G. B. *The Forms of Hebrew Poetry* (Oxford, 1915, reprint edition, New York, 1972).

GRESSMANN, H. *Altorientalische Texte und Bilder zum Alten Testament*. 2 vols. Berlin-Leipzig, 1926.

GUTTMANN, MICHAEL. *Mafteaḥ HaTalmud*. Budapest, 1917.

HABERMAN, A. M. *Megillot Midbar Yehudah*. Tel Aviv, 1959.

HALLER, M., and K. GALLING. *Die Fünf Megilloth*. Tübingen, 1940.

HATCH, E. *Essays in Biblical Greek*. Oxford, 1889.

HEINISCH, P. *Theology of the Old Testament*. Collegeville, Minn., 1950.

HESCHEL, A. J. *The Prophets*. New York, 1962.

HILLER, D. R. "Delocative Verbs in Biblical Hebrew," in *JBL*, vol. 86, 1967.

HOOKE, S. H. *Middle Eastern Mythology*. Harmondsworth, Middlesex, 1963.

HORST, F. "Die Kennzeichen der Hebräischen Poesie," ThR 21, 1953.

HROZNY, F. *Code Hittite*. Paris, 1922.

ISAACS, J. *The Background of Modern Poetry*. London, 1951.

JAMES, F. *Personalities of the Old Testament*. New York and London, 1946.

JAMES, M. R. *Apocrypha Anecdota*. 2d ser., Cambridge, 1897.

KAUTZSCH, E. *Die Aramäismen im Alten Testament*. Halle an der Saale, 1902.

KING, A. R. *The Problem of Evil: Christian Concepts and the Book of Job*, 1952.

KNUDTZON, J. A. *Die El-Amarna-Tafeln*. 2 vols. Leipzig, 1915.

KOHLER, J., and F. E. PEISER. *Hamurabis Gesetz*. Leipzig, 1904.

KOHLER, K. *Jewish Theology*. Cincinnati, 1917.

KOHLER, L. *Theologie des Alten Testaments*. Tübingen, 1953.

KRAELING, E. G. *The Brooklyn Museum Aramaic Papyri*. New Haven, 1953.

KRAMER, S. N., *Sumerian Mythology*, 1961.

LEVINE, B. A. "The Netinim." *JBL*, LXXXII (1963).

LEVY, R. *Deutero-Isaiah*. Oxford, 1925.

LEWIS, C. S. *The Problem of Pain*. London, 1940.

LEWISOHN, L. *Goethe: The Story of a Man*. 2 vols. New York, 1949.

LIDDELL, H. G., and R. SCOTT. *A Greek-English Lexicon*. New York, 1883.

LOWTH, R. *Praelectiones*. Oxford, 1753.

LUZZATTO, S. D. *Oheb Ger*. Vienna, 1830.

MAIMONIDES, MOSES. *Guide to the Perplexed*. Translated by Solomon Pines (Chicago, 1963).

Introduction to Sanhedrin, *Commentary on the Mishnah* (in most editions of the Talmud).

MARGOLIS, M. L. *The Hebrew Scriptures in the Making*. Philadelphia, 1922.

MARMORSTEIN, A. *The Doctrine of Merits in the Old Rabbinical Literature*. London, 1920.

MATTHEWS, I. G. *The Religious Pilgrimage of Israel*. New York, 1947.

MEISSNER, B. *Babylonien und Assyrien*. 2 vols. Heidelberg, 1920–25.

MONTGOMERY, JAMES. *Daniel* ("International Critical Commentary"). New York, 1923.
Arabia and the Bible (Phila., 1934).

MOORE, G. F. *Judaism in the First Centuries of the Christian Era*. 3 vols. Cambridge, Mass., 1927–30.

MOWINCKEL, S. *Psalmenstudien* (Christiania, 1921–24).

MUILENBURG, J., "A Study in Hebrew Rhetoric: Repetition and Style," in *VTS*, I, 1953.

NOELDEKE, TH. *Untersuchungen zum Ahiqar-Roman*. Berlin, 1913.

NORTH, C. R. *The Suffering Servant in Deutero-Isaiah*. Oxford, 1948.

OESTERLEY, W. O. E., and T. H. ROBINSON. *Hebrew Religion: Its Origins and Development*. New York, 1930.
An Introduction to the Books of the Old Testament. New York, 1949.

OGDEN, C. K., and I. A. RICHARDS. *The Meaning of Meaning*. New York, 1930.

PEAKE, A. S. *The Problem of Suffering in the Old Testament*. London, 1904, 1947.

PEDERSEN, J. *Israel: Its Life and Culture*. London and Copenhagen, 1926.

PFEIFFER, R. H. *History of the New Testament Times*. New York, 1949.
Introduction to the Old Testament. New York, 1941.

PRITCHARD, J. B. *Ancient Near Eastern Texts Relating to the Old Testament*. Princeton, 1950.

ROBERTS, B. J. *The Old Testament Text and Versions*. Cardiff, 1951.

ROBINSON, H. WHEELER. "Basic Principles of Hebrew Poetic Form," in *Festschrift für Alfred Bertholet*, 1950.

The Cross in the Old Testament. London, 1955.

"Hebrew Poetic Form: The English Tradition," in *VTS*, I, 1953.

Inspiration and Revelation in the Old Testament. Oxford, 1946.

The Old Testament: Its Making and Meaning. Nashville, 1937.

ROBINSON, T. H. *The Poetry of the Old Testament*. London, 1947.

ROSENZWEIG, FRANZ. *Der Stern der Erlösung*. Frankfort, 1921; Eng. tr. "The Star of Redemption" by W. H. Hallo (Boston, 1972).

ROWLEY, H. H. *The Faith of Israel*. London, 1956.

The Servant of the Lord and Other Essays. London, 1952.

RYLE, H. E. *Canon of the Old Testament*, 2d ed., London, 1909.

SACHAU, E. *Aramäische Papyri und Ostraken*. Leipzig, 1911.

SEGAL, M. H. *Diqduq Lešon Hamišnah*. Tel Aviv, 5696 = 1936.

SMITH, R. PAYNE. *Thesaurus Syriacus* (Oxford, 1879–1901).

SPIEGEL, S. *Milešon Payyetanim* ("On the Language of the Medieval Poets"). New York, 1963.

"On Medieval Hebrew Poetry," *The Jews*. Edited by L. Finkelstein. New York, 1949.

STEINMÜLLER, J. E. *A Companion to Scripture Studies*. 3 vols. New York, 1941–43.

SUTCLIFFE, E. F. *The Old Testament and the Future Life*. London, 1946.

SWETE, H. B. *Introduction to the Old Testament in Greek*. Cambridge, 1914.

TAYLOR, A. *The Proverb*. Cambridge, Mass., 1931.

TCHERIKOVER, V. *Hellenistic Civilization and the Jews*. Philadelphia, 1959.

TCHERNOWITZ, CH. *Toledot Hahalakhah*. 4 vols. New York, 1934–50.

TORREY, C. C. *The Apocryphal Literature*. New Haven, 1945.

TUR-SINAI, N. H. *Halašon Vehasepher* (3 volumes). Jerusalem, 1950.

UNGNAD, A. *Aramäische Papyri aus Elephantine*. Leipzig, 1911.

VIROLLEAUD, CHARLES. *La Légende Phénicienne de Danel*. Paris, 1936.

VOLZ, P. *Jüdische Eschatologie*. Tübingen, 1903.

WEISS, I. H. *Dor Dor Vedoršav*. 5 vols. Vilna, 1871–91.

WEISS, MEIR. *Hamiqra Kidemutho* ("The Literary Form of Scripture"). Jerusalem, 1962.

WERTHEIMER, S. (ed.). *Leqet Midrašim*. Jerusalem, 1904.

WRIGHT, W. *A Grammar of the Arabic Language*. London, 1874–75.

WÜRTHWEIN, E. *Der Text des Alten Testaments*. Stuttgart, 1952.

YADIN, Y. *A Genesis Apocryphon*. Jerusalem, 1956.

YELLIN, D. *Kethabim Nibharim Letorat Hamelitzah Batanakh*. Jerusalem, 5699 = 1939.

ZEITLIN, S. "An Historical Study of the Canonization of the Hebrew Scriptures," *Proceedings of the American Academy for Jewish Research*, III (1932).

INDICES

A. *Individual Passages in the Book of Job given New or Unfamiliar Interpretations*

B. *Special Passages in Other Biblical Books Receiving New or Unfamiliar Interpretations*

Note: The first column contains the book, chapter and verse; the second column gives the verse reference in the Commentary where the interpretation is presented.